Confidence Intervals Using $s_{\overline{X}}$ $.95CI = \overline{X} \pm {}_{.975}t_{\nu}\, s_{\overline{X}}$, where $\nu = n - 1$, $(1-\alpha)CI = \overline{X} \pm {}_{1-\alpha/2}t_{\nu}\, s_{\overline{X}}$ **(11.8–11.9)**

*t*-Tests $t = \dfrac{\overline{X} - \mu}{s_{\overline{X}}}$; $t = \dfrac{(\overline{X}_1 - \overline{X}_2) - (\mu_1 - \mu_2)}{s_{\overline{X}_1 - \overline{X}_2}}$ **(11.6, 12.1)**

Variance Within Groups $s_W^2 = \dfrac{SS_W}{\nu_W} = \dfrac{\Sigma x_1^2 + \Sigma x_2^2}{\nu_1 + \nu_2} = \dfrac{\Sigma x_1^2 + \Sigma x_2^2}{(n_1 - 1) + (n_2 - 1)}$ **(12.3)**

Variance Error of the Difference in Two Independent Means $s^2_{\overline{X}_1 - \overline{X}_2} = s_W^2\left(\dfrac{1}{n_1} + \dfrac{1}{n_2}\right)$ **(12.4)**

Variance Error of the Difference in Two Paired Means $s^2_{\overline{X}_1 - \overline{X}_2} = s^2_{\overline{X}_1} + s^2_{\overline{X}_2} - 2r s_{\overline{X}_1} s_{\overline{X}_2}$ **(12.10)**

Quasi *t*-Test $t' = \dfrac{\overline{X}_1 - \overline{X}_2}{\sqrt{s^2_{\overline{X}_1} + s^2_{\overline{X}_2}}}$ **(12.8)**



Effect Size $\Delta = \dfrac{\mu_E - \mu_C}{\sigma}$, $\hat{\Delta} = \dfrac{\overline{X}_E - \overline{X}_C}{\hat{\sigma}}$ **(12.7A–B)**

Variance of a Proportion $\sigma^2 = \pi(1 - \pi)$ **(13.2)**

Standard Error of a Proportion $\sigma_p = \sqrt{\dfrac{(1-f)\pi(1-\pi)}{n}}$ **(13.7)**

Chi-square Goodness of Fit Test $\chi^2 = n_{\bullet} \sum_j \dfrac{(p_j - \pi_j)^2}{\pi_j}$ **(13.10)**

*t*-Test of *r* $t = \dfrac{r - \rho}{s_r}$, $s_r = \sqrt{\dfrac{1 - r^2}{n - 2}} = \sqrt{\dfrac{1 - r^2}{\nu}}$ **(14.1–14.2)**

Noncentrality ANOVA Parameter $\phi = \sqrt{\dfrac{\sum_j n_j \alpha_j^2}{J\sigma_\varepsilon^2}}$, $\phi = \sqrt{\dfrac{n \sum_j \alpha_j^2}{J\sigma_\varepsilon^2}}$, $\phi = \dfrac{\Delta}{2}\sqrt{n}$ **(15.22–15.24)**

Bartlett's Test of $H_0$ $\chi^2 = \nu_W \mathrm{Ln}\, s_W^2 - \sum_j \nu_j \mathrm{Ln}\, s_j^2$ **(16.11)**

The Studentized Range Statistic $q = \dfrac{\overline{X}_1 - \overline{X}_J}{s_{\overline{X}}}$, $s_{\overline{X}} = \sqrt{\dfrac{MS_{\text{error}}}{n}}$ **(17.2–17.3)**

Definition of a Contrast $\psi = \sum_j c_j \mu_j = c_1\mu_1 + c_2\mu_2 + \ldots + c_J\mu_J$ **(17.7)**

The Standard Error of a Contrast $s_{\hat{\psi}} = \sqrt{\left(\dfrac{MS_e}{n}\right)\sum_j c_j^2}$; $t = \dfrac{\hat{\psi}}{s_{\hat{\psi}}}$ **(17.8, 17.9)**

The Bonferroni Inequality $\alpha_\Sigma \leq \alpha_1 + \alpha_2 + \ldots + \alpha_C$ **(17.10)**

Spearman-Brown Formula for Reliability $\rho'_{XX} = \dfrac{L\rho_{XX}}{1 + (L-1)\rho_{XX}}$ **(20.3)**

# Statistical Methods in Education and Psychology

*Third Edition*

Gene V Glass
*Arizona State University, Tempe*

*and*
Kenneth D. Hopkins
*University of Colorado, Boulder*

**Allyn and Bacon**
Boston • London • Toronto • Sydney • Tokyo • Singapore

*To our students and friends who teach and apply statistics all over the world, for their contributions to our thinking about statistics.*

Editor-in-Chief, Education: Nancy Forsyth
Production Administrator: Joe Sweeney
Editorial-Production Service: Walsh Associates
Cover Administrator: Linda Knowles
Composition Buyer: Linda Cox
Manufacturing Buyer: Megan Cochran

**Library of Congress Cataloging-in-Publication Data**

Glass, Gene V
Statistical methods in education and psychology / Gene V Glass, Kenneth D. Hopkins.—3rd ed.
p. cm.
Includes bibliographical references (p. 651) and indexes.
ISBN 0-205-14212-5
1. Educational statistics. 2. Psychometrics. I. Hopkins, Kenneth D. II. Title.
LB2846.G55 1995
519—dc20 95-13309
CIP

Printed in the United States of America

10 9 8 7 6 5 4 3 2 1 00 99 98 97 96 95

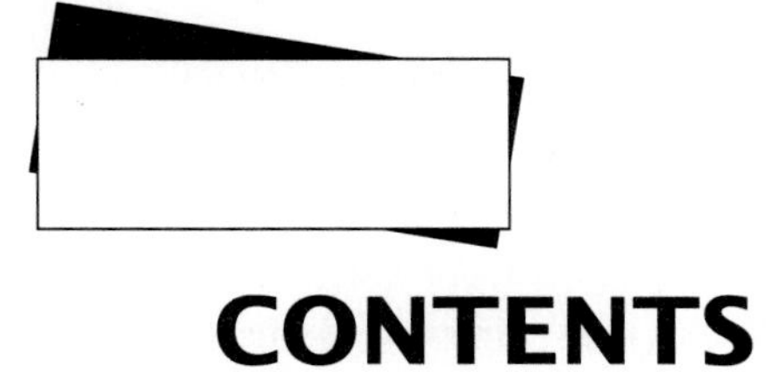

# CONTENTS

## MEASURES OF CENTRAL TENDENCY 49



5

## MEASURES OF VARIABILITY 66



6

## THE NORMAL DISTRIBUTION AND STANDARD SCORES 80



7

## CORRELATION: MEASURES OF RELATIONSHIP BETWEEN TWO VARIABLES 103

## STATISTICAL INFERENCE: SAMPLING AND INTERVAL ESTIMATION 223



11

## INTRODUCTION TO HYPOTHESIS TESTING 255

## 12

## INFERENCES ABOUT THE DIFFERENCE BETWEEN TWO MEANS 283



## 13

## STATISTICS FOR CATEGORICAL DEPENDENT VARIABLES: INFERENCES ABOUT PROPORTIONS 319



## 14

## INFERENCES ABOUT CORRELATION COEFFICIENTS 349

## ONE-FACTOR ANALYSIS OF VARIANCE 377



16

## INFERENCES ABOUT VARIANCES 422

## 17

## MULTIPLE COMPARISONS AND TREND ANALYSIS 444



## 18

## TWO- AND THREE-FACTOR ANOVA: AN INTRODUCTION TO FACTORIAL DESIGNS 482

## APPENDIX: TABLES 614



## BIBLIOGRAPHY 651

## INDEX 665

# PREFACE

This textbook is designed for a one- or two-semester course in applied statistics. The methods and concepts are applicable to empirical research in all behavioral disciplines.

The approach of this text is conceptual, not mathematical; it is not a "cookbook." A mathematical derivation of a formula does not insure real understanding, nor does the facility to insert numbers into formulas and "plug and chug." Indeed, the number of formulas used in the text is kept to a minimum; the ratio of words to mathematical symbols would rank high among statistics texts. We have stressed the understanding, application, and interpretation of concepts rather than derivation and proof or hand-computation (although footnotes attempt to provide the interested reader with ancillary mathematical notes). Unlike many texts, ours emphasizes interval estimation (and effect size) of statistical measures, not just hypothesis testing.

We have pruned away much deadwood present in some other statistics texts. Although every text claims to reflect the latest influences of computers and calculators, obsolete techniques of calculating certain statistics can still be found in some recently published texts. On the other hand, useful procedures that were excluded in previous editions because of the heavy computational labor (e.g., setting exact confidence intervals on a population proportion) are now included because of the painless functions provided by spreadsheets. Statistical power and type II errors continue to be emphasized.

We have tried to be sensitive to changes in statistical pedagogy occasioned by the widespread availability of spreadsheets (which now come with many available statistical functions, including multiple regression and analysis of variance). We strongly recommend their use for statistical computations, along with the use of the increasing number of built-in statistical functions for measures of central tendency, variability, correlation, regression, $t$-test, and the analysis of variance.

Our selection of topics has been guided by three considerations: (1) What are the most useful statistical methods? (2) Which statistical methods are the most widely used in scholarly journals in the behavioral and social sciences? (3) Which statistical methods are fundamental to further study? Most of the statistical techniques that are used in doctoral dissertations in the behavioral sciences are treated in this text.[1]

This text attempts to give a more thorough coverage of analysis of variance (ANOVA) techniques than usually found in statistics texts for social sciences, because ANOVA continues to be the most widely used statistical method in psychological and educational research. The authors propose a unique inferential strategy—the incremental universe of inference—rather than the conventional dichotomous designation of effects as being fixed or random.

The third edition of *Statistical Methods in Education and Psychology* differs from the previous editions in several respects. The third edition incorporates a unique case method approach: Data sets from three studies are used as case studies on which to apply the procedures and concepts of each chapter. The data sets were selected to have widespread understanding and appeal, regardless of major discipline. The CHAPMAN data set is based on a ten-year longitudinal study of 200 men, examining the relationship between cholesterol levels and other physiological variables with coronary events. The HSB data is from High School and Beyond study and gives data on a representative sample of 600 U.S. high school seniors, including many academic achievement measures along with several demographic and personological variables. The EXERCISE data set has data from an exercise study on forty persons. These data sets are included on the diskette in the back of the text. Suggested computer exercises are included for each chapter, although many instructors will wish to tailor their own assignments, using one or more of the data sets.[2] The files are given in various formats, some of which are readable by SPSS, SAS, BMDP, SYSTAT, MINITAB, EXCEL, LOTUS, Quattro Pro, and virtually any other statistical or spreadsheet software. It is anticipated that the case study analyses will be useful in providing the kind of experience that the typical researcher goes through in analyzing and understanding real data: frequency distributions and matters of normality and skewness, outlier identification, central tendency, variability, correlation, multiple regression, confidence intervals, hypotheses testing, and so on. It is anticipated that the continuous involvement with these data sets will help the student experience a unified "big picture" of statistical analysis, sometimes lost when there is no continuity across the various chapters. Many, if not most, students will become so interested in pursuing interesting questions of their own that they will do many analyses in addition to those included in SUGGESTED COMPUTER ACTIVITIES.

Spreadsheet software is adequate for the early chapters, but the more complex ANOVA designs found in the latter chapters will require a statistical software package. Students are encouraged to use spreadsheets for the computations, although calculators will also serve the purpose.

*SMEP* now includes a separate chapter on the use of repeated measures factors in ANOVA, correcting a shortcoming in previous editions. Trend analysis for repeated-measures factors is also included. Because many students lack special study in measurement theory, procedures for estimating reliability and the influence of measurement error receive more attention. Procedures for giving precise values for the confidence interval for population proportions are now included. Logistic regression is also included since the prediction of a dichotomous dependent variable is common and the method is now available in widely used statistical software. The most useful nonparametric alternatives techniques have also been added to the current edition.

---

[1]See Goodwin and Goodwin (1985), Brinzer and Sinatra (1982), Edgington (1974), Wick and Dirkes (1973), Michael (1970), Solso (1979), Gay, Campbell, and Gallagher (1978), and Schmidt (1972).

[2]The data files are in several formats. If you will be using a Mac rather than a PC, you will need to get the files transferred to the Mac format.

The pedagogical features continue to include diagnostic mastery tests following each chapter. Chapters have been written to be as self-contained as possible to provide more instructional options in course content and emphasis. *SMEP* has endeavored to continue to be "extraordinary in its collection of examples, exercises, and statistical tables" (Schmidt, 1972, p. 169).

In this edition, we have tried to maintain the high professional standards of the previous two editions of *SMEP*. Like its predecessors, this edition hopes to set the standard for many years to come.

In *Twenty-Five Years of Recommended Reading in Psychology, SMEP* was among the twenty-five most recommended books by graduate departments of psychology, a distinction recorded by only one other statistics book (and it was less widely used than *SMEP*). In a survey of statistics professors in graduate departments of education, it was found that *SMEP*, in comparison to the other statistics texts considered, had the highest ratings of (1) technical accuracy, (2) breadth of coverage, and (3) depth of topic coverage. *SMEP* was judged to (1) have no statistics prerequisites for comprehension, (2) have a good sequence of topics, (3) be appropriate for undergraduate and graduate work, and (4) have an orientation that is appropriate for both research consumers and producers. In a survey of the 100 top research-producing universities in education, *SMEP* was the most-used text (Brinzer & Sinatra, 1982); it continues this status today.

During the two years this text was being revised, our colleagues and students contributed in innumerable ways to our efforts. We cannot name them all here, but the following colleagues deserve special thanks for contributing recently to our education in statistical methods: Julian Stanley deserves credit for his influence as mentor and his contributions to the first edition. His modesty and heavy research commitments led to his decision not to remain as a co-author of the second edition.

Richard Jaeger, Jason Millman, and Lorrie Shepard have made several suggestions based on extensive classroom experience with *SMEP* that improved its instructional quality. Others made technical or pedagogical contributions: Maurice Tatsuoka, Edward Cureton, William Michael, James Collins, Roberta Flexer, Stuart Kahl, Victor Willson, Todd Rogers, Arlen Gullickson, Bob Hopkins, Gregory Camilli, Laura Goodwin, James Morrow, Frank Baker, and Carol Vojir. We are indebted to Bob Hopkins, Vicky Mayfield, and especially Elizabeth Burton for critically reading various chapters and providing answers to problems and exercises. We are especially grateful to Grace Vrell for her careful proofing and many excellent editorial suggestions.

# 1

# INTRODUCTION

> Statistics has become known in the twentieth century as the mathematical tool for analyzing experimental and observational data. Enshrined by public policy as the only reliable basis for judgments as to the efficacy of medical procedures or the safety of chemicals, and adopted by business for such uses as industrial quality control, it is evidently among the products of science whose influences on public and private life has been most pervasive. Statistical analysis has also come to be seen in many scientific disciplines as indispensable for drawing reliable conclusions from empirical results. . . . Not since the invention of the calculus, if ever, has a new field of mathematics found so extensive a domain of application.[1]

## 1.1 THE "IMAGE" OF STATISTICS

Popular attitudes toward statistics can be described as a mixture of awe and scientific infallibility on the one hand, and cynicism, suspicion, and contempt on the other. Freudian slips have transformed statistics into "sadistics." "Don't become a statistic" has come to mean "Don't let something evil befall you."

Statisticians have been scornfully placed in the company of liars and accused of "statisticulation"—the art of lying with statistics while maintaining an appearance of disinterested objectivity and rationality. Someone once remarked: "If all the statisticians in the world were laid end to end—it would be a good thing." A statistician has been described as a person who drowns while wading in a river having an average depth of three feet, or who sits with his head in a refrigerator and his feet in an oven and reports, "On the average, I feel fine."

Not without some justification, W. H. Auden wrote, "Thou shalt not sit among statisticians, nor commit a social science." But nonsense can be expressed as readily verbally as it can be quantitatively. Logical reasoning is a helpful safeguard against uncritical acceptance of

---

[1]T.M. Porter, *The Rise of Statistical Thinking 1820–1900* (Princeton, NJ: Princeton University Press, 1986), 3.

verbal nonsense, and knowledge of statistics can be a defense against quantitative gullibility. The study of statistical concepts and methods will reduce numerical credulity and help one to become a wise consumer of quantitative information. The first step toward correcting erroneous misconceptions of statistics is to apply oneself to the study of "statistical methods."

Some persons avoid statistics because of philosophical inclination, apprehension about its rigors, or misconceptions about the discipline. Others are content to continue to have their course charted by tradition, intuition, authoritative judgment, and common sense. Today it is recognized that there is a place for systematic, objective empirical data with which statistical methods can be immensely useful. Indeed, the use of statistical data for identifying and correcting problems (rather than opinion and impression) has been identified as a major reason for Japan's enormous industrial success (Joiner, 1985).

Knowledge of statistical methods is becoming necessary for scholarship in many, if not most, empirical disciplines. In recent decades, many graduate schools have acknowledged its importance as a research tool by replacing foreign language proficiency, which has traditionally been required for the Ph.D. degree, with course work in statistics. The substitution is apt: Statistics is an increasingly important language for communicating numerical information.

There were two quite different influences in the development of statistical methods. One stream of influence emerged from the keeping of orderly records of governmental units (state and statistics come from the same Latin root, *status*); counting, measuring, describing, tabulating, and ordering are required in the taking of censuses—all of which led to modern *descriptive statistics*. A second stream of influence resulted from the mathematics of probability, from which modern *inferential statistics* emerged. This text offers an introduction to the descriptive and inferential statistics that are most widely used in educational and behavioral research (Willson, 1980; Goodwin & Goodwin, 1985; Elmore & Woehlke, 1988). Descriptive statistics is emphasized in Chapters 2 through 8. Topics pertaining to inferential statistics move to center stage beginning with Chapter 9 (Probability) and thereafter. The issues and inferential techniques especially important in the design and analysis of experiments are given in Chapters 10–21.

## 1.2 DESCRIPTIVE STATISTICS

Descriptive statistics involves tabulating, depicting, and describing sets of data. These sets may be either *quantitative*, such as measures of height or test scores (characteristics that are continuous—differences are in degree, not kind), or the data may represent *qualitative* or categorical characteristics, such as sex, college major, or personality type. Large quantities of data generally must be organized and summarized before they are comprehensible.

With the aid of statistical techniques the human mind can more fully and accurately grasp the full import of a mass of data (e.g., How large are the scores? How variable are they? Is variable $x$ related to a second variable?). Descriptive statistics serves as a tool for describing and summarizing, and reducing to manageable form the properties of an otherwise unwieldy mass of data.

## 1.3 INFERENTIAL STATISTICS

Inferential statistics is a formalized body of methods for solving another class of problems. This general class of problems involves attempts to infer the properties of an entire set of data from inspection of only a small sample. For example, a school superintendent wishes to find the proportion of children in a large school system who come to school without breakfast (use drugs, carry the HIV virus, or whatever). Having studied statistics, the superintendent knows that it is unnecessary and inefficient to question each child; proportions for the entire district can be estimated with sufficient accuracy from a relatively small sample.

Thus the purpose of inferential statistics is to find out information for a *population* from the characteristics of a *sample* of the population. The descriptive characteristics of a sample can be generalized to the entire population, with a known margin of error, using the techniques of inferential statistics.

The design and analysis of experiments is an important branch of inferential statistical methods. These methods evaluate cause-and-effect relationships among variables. Experimental design is so important for the study of causal relationships that in some disciplines an experiment constitutes an operational definition of a causal relationship. Adults make causal inferences during all their waking moments. The frequent use of the word "because" reveals this: "The school bond failed to pass because it was not well publicized" or "He scored poorly on the intelligence test because he was too anxious." Statistical methods help researchers to describe large sets of data, to make statements about populations from information on samples, and to establish causal relationships among variables.

## 1.4 STATISTICS AND MATHEMATICS

The discipline of statistics is a branch of applied mathematics. Mastering statistical methods requires some mathematical proficiency, but less than commonly assumed. Do not think statistics is accessible only to persons with exceptional mathematical skills. In this book, intuition, logical reasoning, and simple arithmetic are also used extensively. Much of the rationale of applied statistics and many of its techniques can be learned without advanced mathematical skills.

If you have not studied mathematics, logic, or any other rigorous and deductive discipline recently, you may find studying statistics a challenge, but expect your statistical reasoning to improve with practice. In disciplines characterized by imprecise verbal discourse, a student can sustain sloppy and erroneous thinking for long periods without being aware of it. A speaker might receive an enthusiastic audience reaction to the statement, "Viable democratic and creative options are necessary to meet the individualized needs of the whole child." If the statement is scrutinized, its meaning is so ambiguous and imprecise that it is essentially meaningless. By contrast, the student of statistics is likely to be confronted abruptly and uncomfortably with the results of careless thinking. If you enjoy critical and precise thinking, this restrictive and confining mantle will soon begin to feel comfortable. The satisfying reassurance of knowing that you are mastering a logical, precise, and concise language will outweigh the work involved in learning it. Being wrong on occasion may be the price one must pay for knowing when one is correct. Not knowing if we are speaking nonsense is a luxury that we cannot afford in an age in which sense is so scarce and nonsense can be so readily broadcast.

*A word to the wise:* "Be ye doers of the word, and not hearers only, deceiving your own selves" (James 1:22). By far the greatest demand that the study of statistics exacts from the student is for careful and thorough attention to the subject. A quick reading of this book will not produce a mastery of statistics. A statistics text is not a novel. The material simply cannot be learned through casual reading. Most students will need to read each chapter more than once, at least once before, and once after, the material has been presented in class. Reading the material before hearing the related lecture will pay dividends. Chapters should be studied carefully and mastered, because the related topics and concepts are often prerequisites for subsequent chapters. The Mastery Test that follows each chapter can be a valuable learning aid, one that is rare among statistics texts. The items on these self-diagnostic tests have been designed to assess every important concept and procedure introduced in the chapter. The Mastery Tests will help you identify deficiencies in skills and understanding. Skip the Mastery Test, and you may never know where there are gaps in your understanding. Problems and Exercises following each chapter are also provided so that you can demonstrate and enhance knowledge of computational procedures and applications. The use of spreadsheet software for these statistical computations is strongly recommended.[2]

Before reading each chapter, we suggest you page through it to help you get an overview of where you are headed, and help you mentally organize the material. Scanning the Mastery Test can also help your mental preparation for the chapter.

Extensive use is made of footnotes to provide "cul-de-sacs" of interesting ancillary information without disrupting traffic on the "main highway."

## 1.5 CASE METHOD

A unique pedagogical feature of this text is the integration of working with three major studies; data that provide the student with an experience of using statistical procedures and concepts with real data as they are being learned, a vicarious practicum. Following each chapter, its concepts and procedures are applied to one of the case study data sets.

1. The CHAPMAN data set is from a cholesterol study of 200 adults who were measured on several variables and followed for ten years.
2. The HSB data set is from the High School and Beyond Study; achievement and demographic data are given for a national representative sample of 600 high school seniors.
3. The EXERCISE data set contains data on certain exercise and smoking variables for a forty-person sample.

Using the case method provides an ideal practicum for learning; it simulates the cognitive activities in the proper sequence used by researchers in understanding and interpreting variables in their data and statistical analyses. You will go through the same decision-making and interpretation activities as behavioral researchers and, hopefully, will emerge with a comprehensive overview of the role of statistics in research. You will be looking over the researcher's shoulder to experience "second-hand" how various statistical procedures give an understanding of what the data do, and do not, say. The data sets for these studies are included as data files on the diskette[3] provided with this book. Following each chapter, suggested computer activities are included that use the data from one or more of the case study data sets. The assignments are generic and can be done on virtually any package of statistical software; many can be done on spreadsheet software available in a computer

---

[2]All widely used spreadsheets include several statistical procedures that will be useful in your study of statistics.

[3]These are provided in four DOS (PC) formats; for example, the files HSB.TXT (ASCII), HSB.XLS (EXCEL), HSB.SAV (SPSS for Windows), and HSB.POR (portable format recognized by all major statistical programs) all contain the same HSB data set; one or more of these can be easily converted to Mac format.

laboratory (if not on your own computer). It is hoped that this instructional strategy will provide a simulated "hands-on" introduction to statistical measures and methods. In a real sense, the case study will provide a vicarious practicum for statistics in research.

## 1.6 OUR TARGETS

The student who works hard at the task of studying statistics can expect to gain the following fruits from this labor: a general functional literacy for information expressed quantitatively; a "consumer's knowledge" of statistics that will open doors to much of the published empirical research in a field; a command of skills in statistical methods that can contribute significantly to many research efforts; and a knowledge of statistical methods sufficient to support more advanced study.

The study of statistics not only will improve your ability to read and evaluate research literature but should help you become a more informed citizen and consumer by being better able to evaluate quantitative evidence used to support claims and conclusions. We expect with a bit of willingness and systematic effort, you will find your excursion into statistics rewarding and—well, dare we say—enjoyable!

# 2 VARIABLES, MEASUREMENT, SCALES

## 2.1 VARIABLES AND THEIR MEASUREMENT

Descriptive and inferential statistics are concerned with the study of *variables*. Variables are nonuniform characteristics (e.g., age) of observational units (e.g., persons); observational units are the entities on which measurements are obtained. The most common observational unit used in behavioral sciences and education is a person. Other units are also frequently encountered, such as states, cities, census tracts, incorporated businesses, families, school districts, schools, and classrooms. Examples of variables for persons (*personological* variables) are height, self-concept, age, reading speed, socioeconomic status (SES), sex, grade-point average, ethnicity, IQ, occupation, auditory discrimination, marital status, emotional stability, and the like. Examples of variables where the school is the observational unit might include size (number of pupils enrolled), average class size (number of students per class), number of teachers, ability (average IQ), ethnicity ratio (e.g., proportion of non-Anglo pupils), attendance (average daily attendance), and number of students receiving free lunches (as a simple measure of poverty).

Statistics are used to describe characteristics of observational units. In this book, many examples will be drawn from education and the behavioral and social sciences and will pertain to personological variables. Persons will be the most common observational units. Of course, the concepts and methods will apply equally to other units be they schools, libraries, school districts, or whatever.

## 2.2 MEASUREMENT: THE OBSERVATION OF VARIABLES

Before a variable can be treated statistically, it must be observed—that is, measured, quantified, categorized, or classified. As you come to know a person, you naturally make observations (assessments) on many variables: attractiveness, speech style, vocabulary, self-confidence, ethnicity, likability, eye color, and even political or religious persuasion. It is only when the observations are expressed in the language of numbers that they can be amenable to statistical methods. When observations are quantified or categorized and can be numbered, they can be treated statistically. A *measurement* is an observation that is expressed as a number. If these measurements differ among the units (and nearly all do), the observations represent a variable.

Measurement involves assigning numbers to things according to rules. To measure a person's height is to assign a number to the distance between the top of the head and the bottom of the feet, usually with the use of a tape measure. Measurement of a child's IQ is the assignment of a number to the sum of the correct responses that the child makes to a set of standard questions designed to assess cognitive abilities. Measurement transforms attributes like these into more familiar and tractable things—into numbers. It is not adequate for a physicist to know that iron melts at a high temperature or for a traveler that Chicago is "down the road a piece." Measurements should be as precise and as valid as possible.[1]

## 2.3 MEASUREMENT SCALES: NOMINAL MEASUREMENT

The ideas of "scales of measurement" permeate the pedagogy of research methods. The classic taxonomy of measures uses a hierarchy of four scales (or levels of measurement). There has been much discussion and controversy regarding their implications for statistical analysis since this formulation was introduced by the Harvard psychologist S. S. Stevens in 1946. We will define the four types of measurement scales and then deal with their statistical implications.

*Nominal* measurement (numerical naming) is the most rudimentary form of measurement. It is the process of grouping objects into classes or categories so that all those in a single class are equivalent (or nearly so) with respect to some attribute or property. The classes are then identified by names (technically numerals) for identification. Classification schemes in biology are examples of nominal measurement. Researchers often code the variable "gender" by assigning "0" to female and "1" to male—a specific example of nominal measurement.

When measurement is merely nominal, we use only the uniqueness property of numbers—"1" is distinct from "2" or "4," and if object $A$ is coded using a "1" and object $B$ coded "4," then $A$ and $B$ are different with respect to the attribute measured. It does *not* necessarily follow that $B$ has any more or less of the attribute than $A$. Common examples of nominal scales include college major, ethnicity, make of car, occupation, and state of residence.

The remaining scales of measurement that follow make use of three additional and common properties of numbers: Numbers can be ordered by size, they can be added, and they can be divided.

## 2.4 ORDINAL MEASUREMENT

*Ordinal* measurement is possible only when differing degrees or amounts of an attribute or variable can be discerned. Ordinal measurement is achieved when a group of things can be ranked from low to high. The numerical values of the measurements reflect differing

---

[1]The concepts and applications of behavioral measurement can be found in *Educational and Psychological Measurement and Evaluation* (7th ed.) by Hopkins, Stanley, and Hopkins (1990).

amounts of the characteristic. Athletic awards are made based on the order of finishing: first place, second place, and so on. Some interest inventories used in vocational counseling require people to order certain activities according to their preferences. A list of priorities also represents an *ordinal scale*. An ordinal scale commonly used in college admission is "percentile rank in high school class." Indeed, percentile rank on any characteristic represents a type of ordinal scale. States are frequently ranked on certain variables, since the rank order may be more easily understood than a raw measurement. To know the actual dollars spent per pupil in a given state is probably less useful to the average citizen than, for example, to know that, "our state ranks 47th out of the 50 states in what we spend per student."

## 2.5 INTERVAL MEASUREMENT

*Interval* scales represent a more highly refined measurement than ordinal scales. With interval scales, the magnitude of the differences among the observational units is defined by the numbers. The difference between 50°F and 60°F is the same as the difference between 90°F and 100°F. However, 100°F is *not* twice 50°F in terms of heat, molecular motion, or anything else. With interval measurement, the zero point on the scale is arbitrary and does not represent an absence of the characteristic measured. For example, an object at 0°C or 0°F does not indicate the total absence of heat or temperature.

At the interval level of measurement, there exists a standard unit (e.g., the Fahrenheit degree, the 24-hour day) that can be repeatedly applied to the things measured and counted.

Any interval scale can be easily converted to an ordinal scale, but ordinal scales ordinarily cannot be transformed into interval scales. If the daily high temperatures are known, the days of July can be placed in rank order from the hottest to the least hot. If only the rank order is known, one cannot transform ranks into degrees Fahrenheit or centigrade. The numbering of calendar years is an interval scale. Year one was set originally as the year of the birth of Christ.[2]

Interval measurement involves assigning numbers to objects so that equal differences in the numbers correspond to equal differences in the amounts of the attribute measured. The zero point of the interval scale can be placed arbitrarily and does not indicate an absence of the property measured.

Occasionally, ordinal measurement is more useful than interval or ratio measurement. For example, to know that a ten-year-old boy is 50 inches tall and weighs 80 lbs. is, for most purposes, less informative than to know that his percentile ranks are 5 and 95 in height and weight, respectively.

## 2.6 RATIO MEASUREMENT

*Ratio* measurement differs from interval measurement in that its zero point denotes the absence of the property measured. The measurer can perceive the absence of the property and, as with interval scales, the unit of measurement represents equal amounts of the property. Ratio scales are interval scales: An equal difference between the numbers reflects an equal difference in amount of attribute measured, regardless of where it falls on the scale—

[2]Actually, the chronologer Dionysius Exiguus (AD 500–560) was mistaken: Christ was born 6–3 BC. The incorrect zero point, however, does not affect the interval scale property by which each year is designated.

the difference between 20 and 10 is the same as the difference between 50 and 40. With ratio scales the zero point is not arbitrary, but absolute; two observations can be compared as a ratio (or percentage), for example, it is meaningful to say that *A* represents two, three, or four times as much of the variable as does *B*. Age, height, and weight are examples of ratio measurement scales. Zero height is no height at all, and a man six feet tall is twice as tall as a three-foot-tall boy. The ratio scale is so named because the ratios of its numbers are meaningful. These ratios can be interpreted as ratios of measurements of the objects' attributes. Interval scales do not allow ratio statements. For example, if June 3 had a high temperature of 90°F and March 17 had a high of 45°F, it is *not* correct to say that June 3 was twice as hot, or had twice as much heat, as March 17. One cannot make ratio-type comparisons on measures of attitude, achievement, personality, intelligence or sociometric status because at best they represent only interval scales (and some dispute the claim that they can provide interval level data). An IQ of 140 does not represent twice as much intelligence as an IQ of 70!

Most measurements in the behavioral and social sciences do not meet the conditions for a ratio scale. Figure 2.1 gives a summary of the four levels of measurement, along with examples.

## 2.7 INTERRELATIONSHIPS AMONG MEASUREMENT SCALES

Identifying the level of measurement is not always straightforward. Measurement of some variables does not fall neatly into one of the four levels of measurement. For example, when considering IQ scores from Stanford-Binet or Wechsler intelligence tests, one cannot say that an IQ of 130 represents 30% more intelligence than an IQ of 100 (a ratio interpretation). Is the difference between IQ scores of 70 and 100 the same as the difference between scores of 100 and 130 (an interval interpretation)? Probably not, but neither do IQ scores

| *Scale* | *Scale Characteristics* | *Examples* |
|---|---|---|
| RATIO | Numbers represent equal amounts from an absolute zero. Scores can be compared as ratios or percentages. | Age, dollars, time, speed, class size |
| INTERVAL | Equal differences between numbers represent equal differences in the variable or attribute being measured. | Year (A.D.), °F |
| ORDINAL | Numbers represent rank order of the variable being measured. | Any ranked variable, percentile norms, social class |
| NOMINAL | Numbers distinguish among the categories. Numbers do not represent quantity or degree. Assignment of numbers to groups is arbitrary. | Sex, ethnicity, political party, personality type |

**FIGURE 2.1** Measurement Scales: Characteristics and Examples.

represent only an ordinal scale. Indeed, if only ordinal-level measurement is achieved, only ranks (percentile ranks) should be reported. Certainly, the difference in intellectual ability between the 99th percentile rank (IQ = 137) and the 94th percentile rank (IQ = 125) is much larger than the difference between the 55th (IQ = 102) and 50th (IQ = 100) percentile ranks. The IQ scale, like many others, defies categorization as strictly ordinal or interval.

The particular scale of measurement is influenced by the interpretation to be drawn from the data. If your score on a test is 100% and my score is 50%, we can say that your score was twice as high as mine; but would you feel justified in saying that you knew twice as much about what was tested as I (a ratio interpretation)? It would be safe to conclude that you knew more than I (an ordinal interpretation). In psychophysical scaling in psychology, the physical measures of stimuli do not ordinarily show the same pattern of relationship as when the variables are scaled psychologically, for example, judgments of loudness of auditory stimuli (decibels).

In the past, many textbooks exaggerated the importance of the scale of measurement represented by the observation, claiming that the mean, variance, and many other statistical measures assume an interval scale. Since many educational and psychological variables do not represent this level of measurement, considerable emphasis was devoted to *nonparametric* statistics[3]—methods that make fewer assumptions, but are also less sensitive. It has now been shown that the disenchantment with the classical parametric methods was premature.[4] In spite of this, some current "expert systems" software designed to prescribe the "statistical methods of choice" in a given situation use Stevens' scales in the decision making.[5]

The scale represented by a measure does have important consequences for how one interprets the results. To say, for example, that a certain treatment improves IQ scores by an average of five points does not require us to establish that a gain of five points has the identical meaning for all IQ scores. Likewise, you are not committing a statistical sin if you compute your grade-point average (a mean); such a computation does not require you to assume that the difference between a grade of *C* (2.0) and *B* (3.0) has the same meaning as the difference between an *A* (4.0) and a *B* (3.0).

As we develop any statistical measure or technique, the specific assumptions and requirements for its use will be stated.

## 2.8 CONTINUOUS AND DISCRETE VARIABLES

Intuition and experience show that some variables are *continuous* (i.e., measurements of them could theoretically take on any value within a certain range), such as weight, age, or reaction time. Some variables are *discrete* (i.e., measurements of them can take on only separated values), such as number of children in a class or number of days absent. The most

---

[3]Nonparametric statistical techniques that are widely used (or that have some distinct advantage) are treated in this text. Conover (1980) is an excellent comprehensive treatment.

[4]The principal papers, studies, and arguments on this issue can be found in Townsend and Ashby (1984), Mitchell (1986), Stine (1989), Luce, Krantz, Suppes, and Tversky (1990), Velleman and Wilkinson (1993).

[5]For an excellent review and analysis of Stevens' taxonomy and its implications for statistical use, see "Nominal, Ordinal, Interval, and Ratio Typologies are Misleading," by P. F. Velleman and L. Wilkinson in *American Statistician, 47,* 65–72, 1993. They state, "Unfortunately, the use of Stevens' categories in selecting or recommending statistical analysis methods is inappropriate and can often be wrong. They do not describe the attributes of real data that are essential to good statistical analysis. Nor do they provide a classification scheme appropriate for modern data analysis methods."

familiar discrete variables are those that are measured by counting. "Number of children" gives rise to the numbers 0, 1, 2, 3, . . . and so on. It is not possible for this variable to take on intermediate values such as 1.75.

The *actual* or *exact* measurement of a continuous variable is something that can never be attained, because measurement must always stop short of the *exact value*. The *reported value* is the value that the measuring process produced. The reported and actual values of a variable do *not* coincide; reported values are approximations that yield bounds for the actual values. For example, if a person's height (to the nearest inch) is said to be 66 inches, the actual height is considered to be between 65½ inches and 66½ inches.

One sometimes wishes to establish limits around a reported value within which the exact value lies. For example, what are the lowest and highest actual heights that will result in a reported height of 58 inches if height is measured to the nearest inch? The limits for the exact value around any reported value are found by adding, and subtracting, one-half the unit of measurement from the reported value. Thus, a person with a reported height of 58 inches has an actual height between 57.5 inches (58″–½″) and 58.5 inches (58″ + ½″). The following examples clarify this point.

| *Variable* | *Unit of Measurement* | *Reported Value (example)* | *Limits of Exact Value* |
|---|---|---|---|
| Weight | pounds | 130 lbs. | 129.5-130.5 lbs. |
| Height | inches | 66″ | 65.5–66.5″ |
| Running Speed | .1 seconds | 49.5 sec. | 49.45–49.55 sec. |
| Reaction Time | .01 seconds | .53 sec. | .525–.535 sec. |
| Test Score | percentage | 78% | 77.5–78.5% |
| Grade Equivalent | .1 GE | 5.9 GE | 5.85–5.95 GE |

## 2.9 CHAPTER SUMMARY

A *variable* is a characteristic on which observational units (e.g., persons) differ—age, weight, personality type, and reading speed are examples of variables. *Measurement* is the process of assigning numbers to observational units—the numbers are measurements of a variable. These measurements or numbers have characteristics and can be classified into one of four measurement scales. *Nominal scales* represent non-ordered, categorical or qualitative variables or classifications such as gender or nationality. *Ordinal scales* represent a sequential ranking of the observational units in relation to amount or degree of the variable. An *interval scale* has equal units of measurement, but does not have an absolute zero—°C and year of birth are examples of interval scales. A *ratio scale* is an interval scale, but in addition it has an absolute zero—examples include measures of time, distance, weight, and variables measured in currency (e.g., dollars). The scale of measurement depends not only on the measurement procedure, but also on the interpretation given the numbers.

## 2.10 CASE STUDY

In the CHAPMAN data set, 200 individuals were studied for ten years to find if several variables (separately or in combination) could predict the incidence of a coronary incident (heart attack). There are seven variables [age, systolic blood pressure (SBP), diastolic blood pressure (DBP), cholesterol level, height, weight, coronary incident (0 = No, 1 = Yes)] in addition to the case number.[6] Which measurement scale is represented by each of the eight variables? Do you recognize that age, height, and weight are ratio scales? Although you may not be familiar with the measurement of blood pressure, it is expressed in millimeters of mercury—it is a linear distance, and thus represents a ratio scale. Cholesterol level is a weight measurement—milligrams per dekaliter (ten liters), and it is a ratio scale, too. Case ID # is a nominal scale—the numbers convey no quantitative information; each number is only a unique numerical name ("nominal") tag. The coronary variable is also a nominal or categorical variable.

Which of the variables are discrete? The notion of rounding makes sense only with continuous, not discrete, variables. Only ID # and the coronary incident variable are discrete; the others are continuous.

The High School and Beyond (HSB) data set includes the following variables: sex, race (Hispanic, Asian, Black, or White), SES (socioeconomic status), school type (public or private), type of high school program (general, academic, or vocational), locus of control (the extent to which one can affect one's future), self-concept (scores from low to high), motivation level, and career choice (17 categories), in addition to test scores on achievement tests in reading, writing, math, science, and civics. Identify the variables that represent nominal scales.[7] Do any of the measures represent ratio scales?[8]

The EXERCISE data set includes the variables of pulse rate, sex, age, and whether the person is a smoker. Which two of these variables represent a ratio scale?[9]

## 2.11 SUGGESTED COMPUTER ACTIVITIES

Enter the README.TXT into your word processor and become more familiar with the three data sets. Print the README.TXT for future reference. If you have spreadsheet or statistical software available to you, go through the tutorials (if you are not already familiar with the software).

## MASTERY TEST

1. Which of the following almost certainly will be variables for persons in a large statistics class?
   (a) Socioeconomic status (SES)
   (b) Speaking ability
   (c) Typing speed
   (d) Favorite food
   (e) Nationality
   (f) Musical ability
   (g) Assertiveness

---

[6] "ID #" is not usually counted as a variable, but we do so here for practice, since it is a different kind of variable.

[7] Sex, race, school type, type of high school program, and career choice are clearly nominal.

[8] No

[9] Pulse rate and age

(h) Year of birth
(i) Religious affiliation
(j) Age
(k) Political party
(l) Occupation
(m) Gender
(n) Handedness

2. Which variables in question 1 would typically be measured on nominal scales?
3. Which options in question 1 would likely be measured on an interval, but not a ratio scale?
4. Which two variables in question 1 are most likely to be measured by ratio scales?
5. As typically measured, which four variables in question 1 represent at least ordinal scales, but probably not true interval scales?
6. Can observations on an interval or ratio scale be converted to an ordinal scale (ranks)?
7. To say, "This value is 25% greater than that value," requires which type of measurement scale?
8. If one has a choice of interval, ordinal, and ratio scales for measuring a variable (e.g., height), order the scales from the least to the most desirable.
9. When persons are measured on an interval scale (e.g., date of birth), do *differences* between persons represent a ratio scale?
10. Is the measure "number of books included in a library's card catalog" a discrete variable? What measurement scale does it represent?
11. Give an example of a measure used in your major area of interest that has the properties of a ratio scale.
12. If *A*, *B*, *C*, *D*, and *F* grades are used for statistical purposes, the letters are converted to 4, 3, 2, 1, and 0. Does this represent a ratio scale? Does the measure represent at least an ordinal scale?

In Chapter 8, we will examine a study that was conducted to see how well reading success in first grade could be predicted from various kinds of information obtained in kindergarten—reading readiness, age, sex, and socioeconomic status (SES).

13. Which of the variables represents a nominal scale?
14. Which variable represents a ratio scale?
15. Would you recommend measuring age in months or in years as the unit of measurement? Why?
16. Suppose one child was 66 months of age. Is age a continuous, or a discrete variable? Give the exact lower and upper limits for this measurement.

## ANSWERS TO MASTERY TEST

1. Probably a, b, c, d, f, g, h, i, j, k, n, and (except at predominantly male or female institutions) m. Nationality (e) is a variable in many classes since not all students are citizens of the same country. Occupation (l) would be a variable except in a situation in which all persons were full-time students. In very small classes, handedness (n) and some other attributes may not vary.
2. d, e, i, k, l, m, n
3. h
4. c, j
5. a, b, f, g
6. yes
7. ratio

**8.** ordinal, interval, ratio
**9.** yes
**10.** yes; ratio
**12.** no (not a ratio scale); yes (at least an ordinal scale)
**13.** sex
**14.** age
**15.** The unit "Months" is more precise than "Years."
**16.** continuous; 65.5–66.5 months

# 3

# FREQUENCY DISTRIBUTIONS AND VISUAL DISPLAYS OF DATA

## 3.1 TABULATING DATA

Data cannot be quickly and accurately interpreted unless they are organized into a pattern and statistical summaries are provided. The Chapman case study gives data on 200 men in a ten-year longitudinal study that are presented in no particular order. If you were to visually scan these data, you would have a great deal of difficulty in making sense of these data since the numbers are not organized or presented in rank order. It would not be readily apparent whether a given score is somewhat low, somewhat high, or near the average.

The search for order, organization, and lawfulness in our experience and observations seems to be characteristically human. If a set of observations is organized, the reader is greatly aided in the task of apprehending the relevant information in the set. If the number of observations is small, only a rank-order distribution (the "scores" placed in rank-order from the highest to the lowest) may be needed to convey the important properties of the data set. Other methods of organizing and displaying data are needed when more than a few dozen scores are at issue. Table 3.1 shows the 200 cholesterol readings from the case study, arranged in order from the highest score ($X_{max}$) of 520 to the lowest score ($X_{min}$) of 135. Now one can see that a reading of 254 falls near the center of the distribution.

A rank-order distribution helps, but rarely depicts the most important characteristics of a distribution; it does not represent the magnitude of the differences among the various scores or observations. The nature of a distribution becomes more evident if the observations are grouped into homogeneous classes (intervals). The number of classes or groupings is somewhat arbitrary, but usually ten or more classes are used, depending on the purpose and the size of the group ($n$); larger numbers of observations allow more classes. The product of such a grouping arrangement is a *grouped frequency distribution*.[1]

---

[1]If the interval width is 1, the distribution is often described as an *ungrouped* frequency distribution.

**TABLE 3.1** Cholesterol[2] Data Arranged in Rank Order

| | | | | | | | |
|---|---|---|---|---|---|---|---|
| 520 | 358 | 330 | 302 | 275 | 264 | 245 | 210 |
| 474 | 357 | 328 | 298 | 274 | 261 | 244 | 208 |
| 453 | 355 | 327 | 298 | 274 | 261 | 244 | 208 |
| 428 | 353 | 322 | 296 | 274 | 260 | 243 | 206 |
| 420 | 353 | 322 | 295 | 273 | 260 | 243 | 206 |
| 420 | 352 | 320 | 294 | 273 | 259 | 243 | 203 |
| 416 | 352 | 320 | 292 | 273 | 259 | 240 | 195 |
| 403 | 348 | 320 | 290 | 273 | 259 | 239 | 193 |
| 403 | 348 | 319 | 290 | 271 | 258 | 239 | 192 |
| 394 | 346 | 317 | 286 | 271 | 257 | 238 | 190 |
| 391 | 344 | 317 | 286 | 270 | 256 | 235 | 187 |
| 390 | 343 | 315 | 285 | 269 | 254 | 235 | 187 |
| 386 | 341 | 314 | 285 | 269 | 254 | 230 | 185 |
| 386 | 341 | 314 | 284 | 269 | 253 | 229 | 178 |
| 384 | 341 | 312 | 283 | 269 | 253 | 227 | 178 |
| 383 | 341 | 312 | 283 | 268 | 253 | 225 | 178 |
| 378 | 337 | 311 | 282 | 268 | 252 | 224 | 176 |
| 370 | 337 | 311 | 282 | 267 | 252 | 222 | 173 |
| 370 | 336 | 310 | 281 | 267 | 252 | 222 | 173 |
| 369 | 336 | 307 | 280 | 266 | 251 | 219 | 172 |
| 367 | 336 | 305 | 279 | 266 | 250 | 218 | 172 |
| 365 | 334 | 304 | 279 | 266 | 248 | 218 | 166 |
| 365 | 333 | 302 | 278 | 264 | 248 | 216 | 156 |
| 363 | 333 | 302 | 277 | 264 | 246 | 214 | 156 |
| 360 | 332 | 302 | 277 | 264 | 246 | 214 | 135 |

## 3.2 GROUPED FREQUENCY DISTRIBUTIONS

To organize data into a grouped frequency distribution:

1. Find the range
2. Select the number of intervals (classes)
3. Define the score limits for the intervals
4. Tally the observations into the intervals
5. Count the tallies within each interval and express as a frequency

### Determine the Range

The range[3] is the difference between the largest observation, $X_{max}$, and the smallest observation, $X_{min}$; that is:

[2]The cholesterol measurement is the sum of the high-density lipoprotein (HDL) and low-density lipoprotein (LDL) components.

[3]Some statisticians define the range inclusively as $X_{max} - X_{min} + 1$ unit so that it extends from the upper real limit of $X_{max}$ (i.e., $X_{max}$ +.5) to the lower real limit of $X_{min}$ (i.e., $X_{min}$ –.5). The value yielded by Equation 3.1 is more common and is termed the exclusive range, which is always 1 less than the value of the inclusive range, $X_{max} - X_{min} + 1$.

$$\text{Range} = X_{max} - X_{min} \quad \textbf{(3.1)}$$

From Table 3.1: $X_{max} = 520$, and $X_{min} = 135$; hence,

$$\text{Range} = 520 - 135 = 385.$$

## Select the Number of Classes

The number of classes or intervals into which the data will be grouped is arbitrary. If the number of observations is less than 100, ten or fewer classes may be sufficient. A good guideline is to have at least ten times as many observations as classes until you have 20 or 30 intervals. If there are too many classes for the number of observations, the pattern of frequencies will appear erratic; if there are too few classes, the shape of the distribution is crudely represented. Since $n = 200$, we will target 20 intervals.

## Define the Score Limits for the Intervals

As a first approximation of the width of interval needed ($w$), divide the range by the desired *number* of intervals to be used. Thus,[4]

$$w \approx \frac{\text{Range}}{20} \quad \textbf{(3.2)}$$

$w \approx 385/20 = 19.25$, thus $w$ can be taken to be 20. The value of $w$ is rounded up or down to arrive at a convenient whole number for the class width; in this instance, $w = 20$.

Each interval of the frequency distribution should begin with a multiple of the class width; do not begin with the lowest score. Notice that for the data in Table 3.1, $X_{min}$ is 135. Using an interval width of 20 results in a lower-limit for the first (lowest) interval of 120 ($20 \times 6$); the second interval begins with 140 ($20 \times 7$), and the third with 160 ($20 \times 8$) (see column A of Table 3.2). Each interval begins with a multiple of the class width ($w$). Note that the intervals are defined so that every observation falls into one, and only one, of the *mutually exclusive classes*. Thus, the first class is 120–139 and the second 140–159 (not 120–140 and 140–160).

## Tally the Observations into the Classes

A tally is made for each observation that falls within each interval. This is illustrated in column B of Table 3.2. The traditional "picket fence" tallying scheme is fine, but the scheme suggested by Tukey (1977) is also useful. It is illustrated in Table 3.2 since it is less widely known. Tukey's method is especially useful when the number of observations in the distribution is large: The first four scores are denoted by dots at the four corners of a "square," the next four scores connect the dots to form a square; tallies "9" and "10" connect the diagonals of the square to provide a convenient counting unit of ten. For example,

[4]The symbol "$\approx$" (or "$\doteq$") means "is approximately equal to."

1 = · , 2 = : , 3 = ∴ , 4 = ∷ , 5 = ⁝∶ , 6 = ∟∶ , 7 = ⊔ , 8 = ☐ , 9 = ⧄ , 10 = ⊠ , 11 = ⊠ ·, etc. This tallying technique is illustrated in column B of Table 3.2 (also in Figure 4.1 of Section 4.2).[5]

These tallies are counted and expressed as a numeral in the "Frequency" column. If all observations have been tallied correctly, the sum of the frequencies should equal the total number of observations $n$.

**TABLE 3.2** An Illustration of the Process of Constructing a Grouped Frequency Distribution (Using data from Table 3.1)[6]

| *A* | *B* | *C* | *D* | *E* |
|---|---|---|---|---|
| *Interval* | *Tally* | *Frequency* | *Percent* | *Cumulative Percent* |
| 520–539 | · | 1 | .5 | 100.0 |
| 500–519 | | 0 | .0 | 99.5 |
| 480–499 | | 0 | .0 | 99.5 |
| 460–479 | · | 1 | .5 | 99.5 |
| 440–459 | · | 1 | .5 | 99.0 |
| 420–439 | ∴ | 3 | 1.5 | 98.5 |
| 400–419 | ∴ | 3 | 1.5 | 97.0 |
| 380–399 | ⊔ | 7 | 3.5 | 95.5 |
| 360–379 | ⧄ | 9 | 4.5 | 92.0 |
| 340–359 | ⊠ ∟∶ | 16 | 8.0 | 87.5 |
| 320–339 | ⊠ ⊔ | 17 | 8.5 | 79.5 |
| 300–319 | ⊠ ☐ | 18 | 9.0 | 71.0 |
| 280–299 | ⊠ ⧄ | 19 | 9.5 | 62.0 |
| 260–279 | ⊠ ⊠ ⊠ ⁝∶ | 35 | 17.5 | 52.5 |
| 240–259 | ⊠ ⊠ ⊔ | 27 | 13.5 | 35.0 |
| 220–239 | ⊠ : | 12 | 6.0 | 21.5 |
| 200–219 | ⊠ : | 12 | 6.0 | 15.5 |
| 180–199 | ⊔ | 7 | 3.5 | 9.5 |
| 160–179 | ⧄ | 9 | 4.5 | 6.0 |
| 140–159 | : | 2 | 1.0 | 1.5 |
| 120–139 | · | 1 | .5 | .5 |
| | | $n = 200$ | | |

[5]There are numerous instances in which you will be referred to figures, tables, and equations that are found in other chapters; the associated section number will be given to facilitate its location. Note that in addition to page numbers, section numbers also appear at the top of each page.

[6]Columns D and E will be used later in the chapter.

## 3.3 GROUPING AND LOSS OF INFORMATION

Any statistical summary fails to tell the whole story. Some information is lost when the observations are grouped into intervals. Generally, the fewer the intervals, the greater the loss of information. Figures that display statistical information involve a trade-off between useful and comprehensible summaries on the one hand, and loss of precision on the other. The question of how many classes to employ in the frequency distribution is answered by some compromise between the importance of precision and readability for the intended audience.

In the pre-computer era, textbooks in applied statistics contained many hand procedures for classifying observations into grouped frequency distributions in order to facilitate the hand computation of means, standard deviations, and other statistics. For such purposes, at least ten to twenty intervals were commonly recommended. Although forming such grouped frequency distributions speeds up hand computations, the grouping complicates the formulas with correction factors that obscure the conceptual meaning of the statistic. Fortunately, computers and hand calculators have eliminated the need for these computational considerations in the grouping decision (although some texts continue to include them, along with square root tables!). In this book, calculations will be made directly from the raw observations. Thus, simpler formulas are used and computations are more accurate (because no information is lost by grouping).

The grouping that best reveals or portrays the important features of a distribution of scores for the intended audience is now the sole consideration. A distribution of a large set of data can accommodate more intervals, but with small data sets a large number of intervals will result in a ragged appearance and defeat the purpose of a visual representation of the distribution.

## 3.4 GRAPHING A FREQUENCY DISTRIBUTION: THE HISTOGRAM

The three most common methods of graphing a distribution are (1) the histogram (bar graph), (2) the frequency (or percentage) polygon, and (3) the ogive curve. A frequency distribution is best understood from a graph. It is true, a picture *is* worth a thousand words.

The *histogram* depicts a frequency distribution where frequencies are represented by bars. The length of the bars represents the number of cases (frequency) falling within eac' interval. Figure 3.1 is a histogram showing the distribution of the cholesterol readings f 200 adults given in Table 3.1. There are numerous statistical and spreadsheet compı programs that produce histograms and other graphic displays of frequency distributi Figure 3.1, and most of the other figures in this chapter, were prepared using EXCEI of the most popular spreadsheet programs for personal computers.

Histograms can be used to represent percentages instead of, or in addition quency. Percentages are often more meaningful than simple frequencies. The "Fre (Column C) for each interval in Table 3.2 is converted to "Percent" (Column D) b the frequency by the total number of observations ($n = 200$) and multiplying th proportion by 100. Notice in the percentage histogram in Figure 3.2 that the scores within each interval is indicated by the height of the bar. When the ve expressed in percentage, rather than frequency units, the figure becomes a *per*

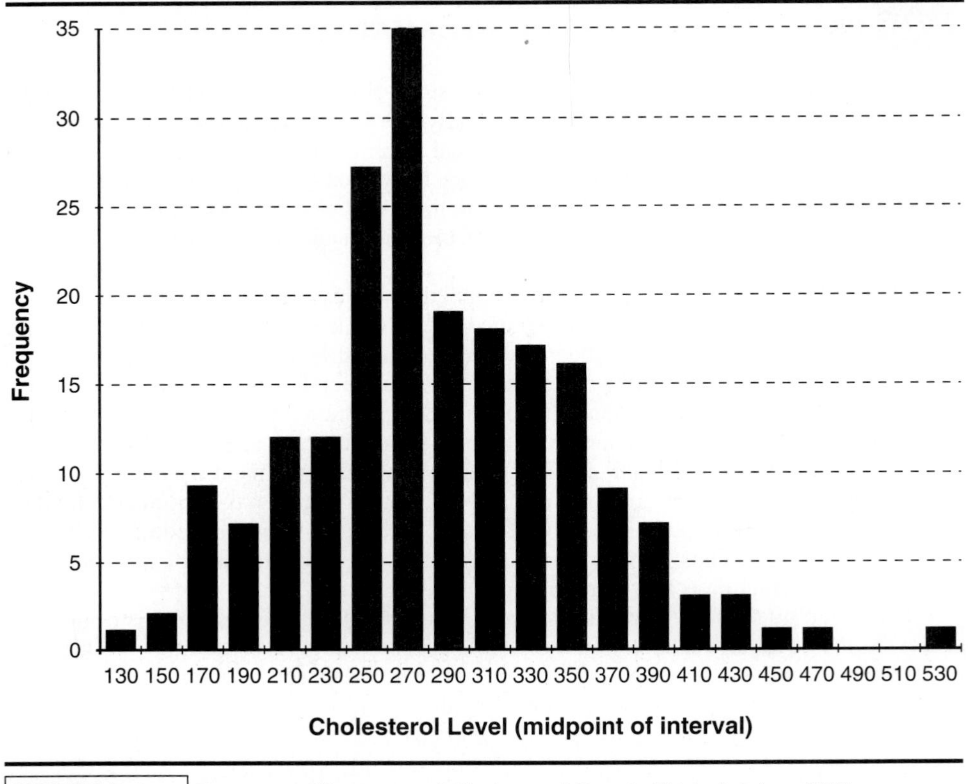


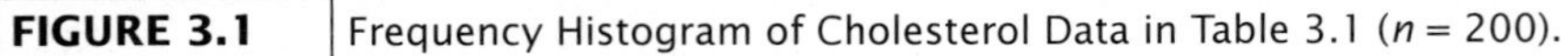

**FIGURE 3.1** Frequency Histogram of Cholesterol Data in Table 3.1 ($n = 200$).

*gram.* Percentage histograms are usually preferable to frequency histograms. Figure 3.2 illustrates a percentage histogram of the cholesterol data. Knowing that 6% of the individuals had cholesterol levels of 230±10 (Figure 3.2) is more meaningful than knowing that 12 of the sample of 200 fell within this interval (Figure 3.1), since frequencies are a function of sample size, which is arbitrary. Many computer programs allow one to "jazz up" graphs by portraying the histogram in 3D as in Figure 3.2.

## 3.5 FREQUENCY AND PERCENTAGE POLYGONS

Constructing a frequency, or percentage, polygon (a closed figure having multiple segments) is much like constructing histograms, except with polygons two additional intervals must be added so that the end points touch the baseline. An interval having zero frequency is added below the interval containing the lowest value ($X_{min}$), and a second interval with zero frequency is added above the interval containing the highest value ($X_{max}$). The top of each bar of a histogram is indicated by a horizontal line placed at the height equal to the frequency in that interval. With polygons, a point is located above the *midpoint* of each

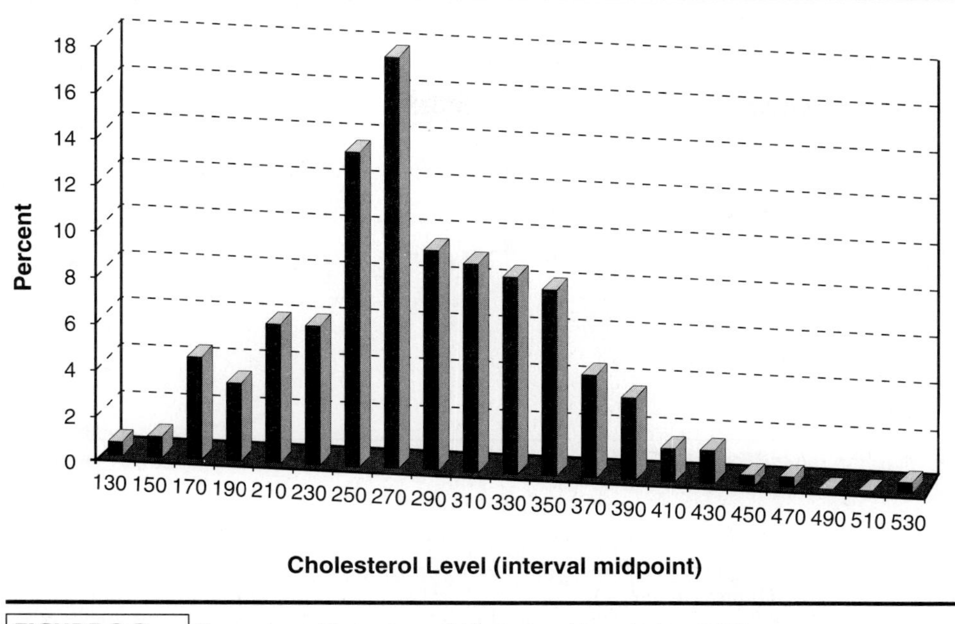

**FIGURE 3.2** Percentage Histogram of Cholesterol Levels ($n = 200$).

interval to denote the frequency (or percent) falling in each interval. These points are then connected, dot-to-dot. As with histograms, the values on the baseline ($X$-axis, horizontal axis, or abscissa) are always arranged with low values to the left and higher values to the right. If the baseline variable is a nominal/categorical variable (e.g., ethnic group, college major; see Section 2.3), a histogram should be used to display the data. Polygons are misleading in such situations since an underlying continuity is suggested that requires at least an ordinal variable.

Figure 3.3 illustrates both a frequency polygon and a percentage polygon. The vertical axis ($Y$-axis) is labeled in units of both frequency (on the left) and percent (on the right). As noted earlier, percents are more useful than frequencies when the number of observations i arbitrary, as in the number of persons in a sample. It is a simple matter to give both fr quency and percent in the same figure by labeling the vertical axis on both the right and l like Figure 3.3.

When comparing two or more distributions within the same figure, polygons are cally more effective than histograms. When the two distributions have different numb observations, percents rather than frequencies are needed to make comparison Figure 3.4 gives percentage polygons of the ages, in months, of boys and girls ir sample of entering kindergarten pupils (Shepard, Graue, and Catto, 1989). Notice are very few underaged pupils, but a substantial number of overaged children. It i that many children either enter kindergarten a year after they are eligible, or re garten. Note that this phenomenon is much more common for boys than for gir almost two overaged boys for every overaged girl.

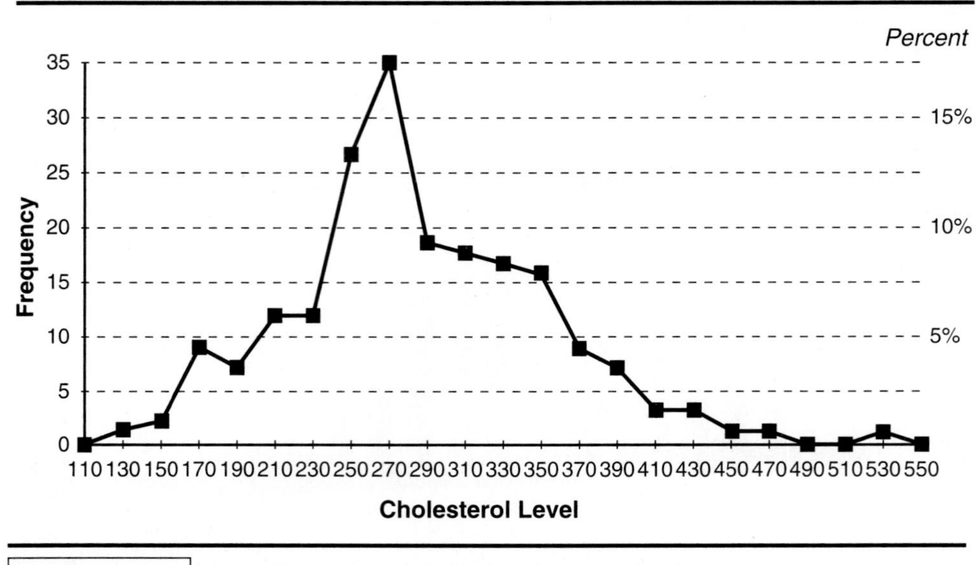


**FIGURE 3.3** Frequency (on left) and Percentage (on right) Polygon for Cholesterol Data (Table 3.1, $n = 200$).

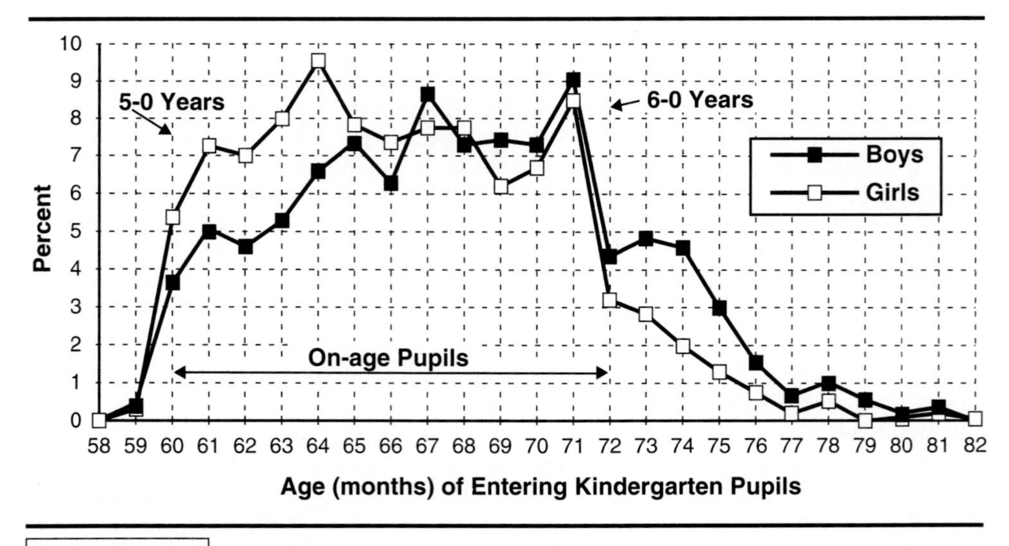


**FIGURE 3.4** Percentage Polygons of Ages (on Sept. 1) of Male ($n = 820$) and Female ($n = 737$) Kindergartners.

## 3.6 TYPES OF DISTRIBUTIONS

There is a special vocabulary for describing various types of distributions. Distribution *A* in Figure 3.5 is a *normal* distribution (or *normal* curve); it is *symmetrical* and "bell-shaped." Numerous variables, including many human characteristics, are normally distributed, or approximately so, for example, diameters of apples from the same tree, lengths of rainbow trout at one year of age, adult heights of females, percent of body fat of 6-year-old males, reaction time, running speed, and IQ scores. We will have much to say about normal distributions in Chapter 6 and thereafter.

Curve *B* in Figure 3.5 is *symmetrical* around a vertical axis, but is not normal. Distributions that have two modes (i.e., two distinctly different points around which the scores cluster) are called *bimodal*. For example, if the heights of adults were plotted, a bimodal distribution would result. The heights of females would cluster around their mode of approximately 64 inches, and the male heights would cluster around a mode of about 69 inches. Measures of certain social and political attitudes sometimes yield bimodal distributions, for example, attitude toward abortion or attitude toward Marxism. When the frequency clusters around the two modes differ substantially, the more popular value is said to be the *major mode* and the smaller hump represents the *minor mode*. A measure of hand dominance for a large group of preschool children has two distinct modes. Most children prefer the right hand for most psychomotor activities, yet five percent or so tend to prefer

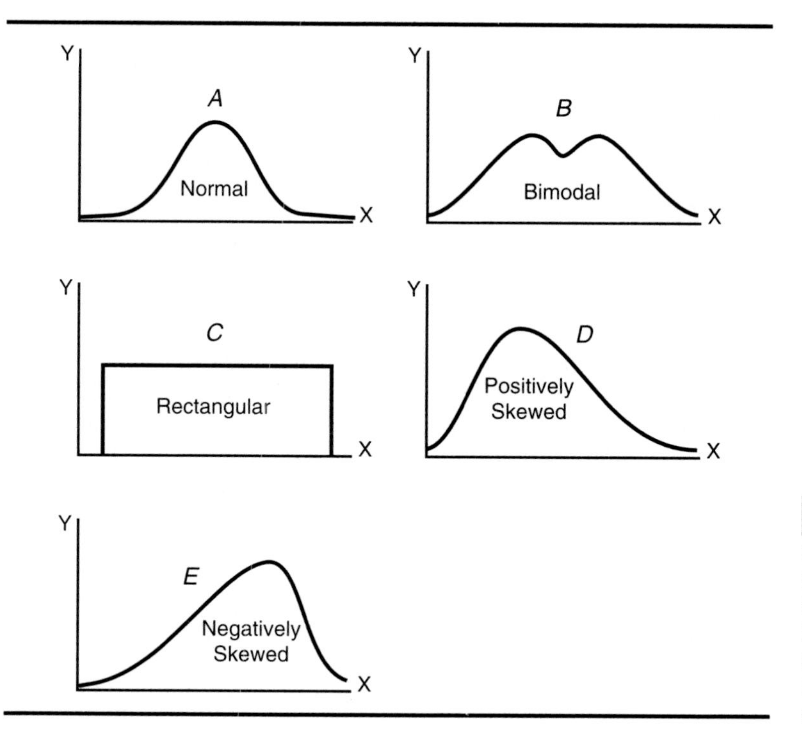


**FIGURE 3.5**

Common Types of Frequency Distributions. (The *Y*-axis represents frequency, and the *X*-axis represents the numerical value of the observations.)

the left hand. *Dichotomous* distributions, like gender, pass versus fail, and yes versus no responses, are a special type of bimodal distribution.

A *rectangular* distribution is shown as Curve $C$ in Figure 3.5. Rectangular distributions are symmetrical, the frequency is constant for all values of $X$. If a single die were tossed 10,000 times, the distribution of frequencies (1, 2, . . . , 6) would closely approximate a rectangle. A distribution of birthmonths (Jan. = 1, . . . Dec. = 12) is approximately rectangular.

*Skewed* distributions are represented in Curves $D$ and $E$. These curves are asymmetrical. The degree to which a frequency distribution is asymmetrical is described as its *skewness*. Distribution $D$ is positively skewed, that is, the scores bunch up at the low end and tail off at the high or positive end. Negative skewness is depicted in Curve $E$; the high scores are clustered together at the high end and tail off toward the left low values. In Chapter 6 (Section 6.9), we will see that the terms positive and negative result from the statistical index that describes the degree of skewness in a distribution.

If a distribution were drawn for "days absent from work during a year" for a large group of persons, it would be positively skewed. Most persons miss only a few days each year, but a few individuals miss many days because of illness. Annual family income in the United States is also skewed positively, as is the number of traffic citations received by motorists during the past ten years. Scores on an easy test will tend to be skewed negatively. Skewness can vary from mild to extreme. The statistical indices that quantify the degree of skewness in a distribution are given in Chapter 6 (Section 6.9).

It should be noted that some of these descriptive aspects of distributions are not mutually exclusive. For example, a bimodal distribution having a minor mode will be skewed in the direction of the minor mode, or a dichotomous distribution is also rectangular if each of the two categories has the same frequency. A normal distribution, however, has no skewness and is always unimodal.

## 3.7 CUMULATIVE DISTRIBUTIONS AND THE OGIVE CURVE

An *ogive* curve provides a useful and efficient method for determining *percentiles*. The *cumulative percentage* or ogive curve arranges information in such a way that the percentile rank of any observation is readily estimated. Indeed, this is the principal value of the ogive. Histograms and frequency or percentage polygons are much preferred to ogive curves for conveying the shape of the frequency distribution. Notice in Figure 3.4 that it is difficult to find out that about 17% of the kindergarten boys are overaged; this information is not readily apparent from percentage polygons or histograms. With an ogive, one can readily determine the percent of cases above or below any value; conversely, one can find the score values for the 25th, 50th, or any desired percentile.

If you know your cholesterol level, you can accurately estimate the percent of individuals that fall below or above your level.[7] Figure 3.6 is an ogive curve that displays the cholesterol data in Figure 3.3. With the ogive, the $Y$-axis represents cumulative percentages—the percent of cases below a given score. Column E of Table 3.2 gives "Cumulative Percents"—the percent of the distribution that falls within each interval *plus* the percent falling below that interval. For example, 62% of persons had cholesterol levels below 300. The computation procedures are evident from Table 3.2—the frequency within each interval is converted

---

[7]Unfortunately these data are only from males. There is some difference of opinion as to whether the distribution differs for females.

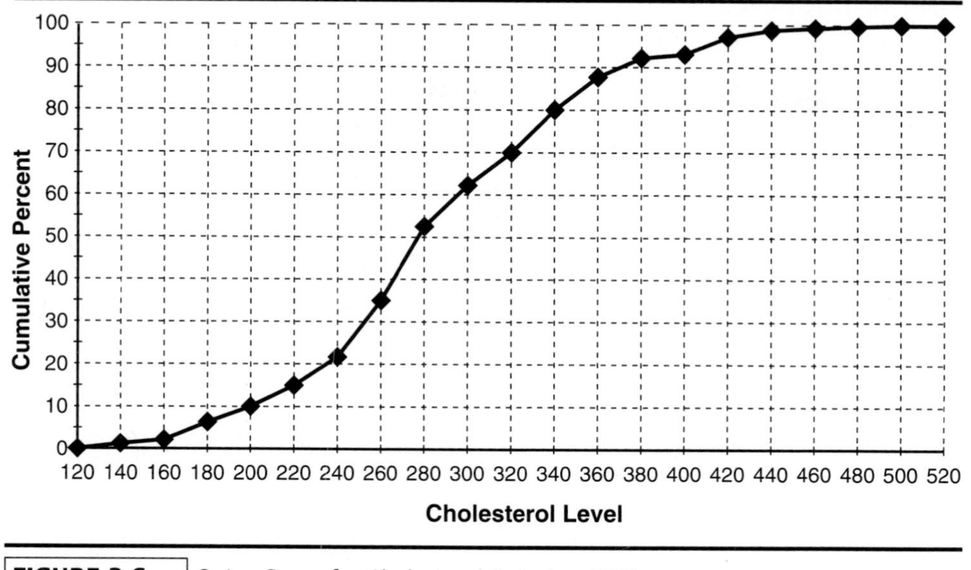


**FIGURE 3.6** Ogive Curve for Cholesterol Data ($n = 200$).

into a percent, then added to the percent falling below that interval to obtain the cumulative percent. The ogive is then graphed with "Cumulative Percent" as the vertical axis. Unlike histograms and percentage or frequency polygons, the $X$-axis gives not the midpoint, but the rounded upper limit of each interval. Note that a cholesterol value of 200 corresponds to a value of about 10 on the vertical axis, showing that approximately 10% of the persons had cholesterol levels below 200.

## 3.8 PERCENTILES

An ogive curve provides a useful and efficient method for estimating *percentiles*. Percentiles are points in a distribution below which a given percent $P$ of the cases lie. From Figure 3.6, it can be seen that 80% of the cholesterol levels were below 340; hence, 340 is said to be the 80th percentile ($P_{80}$). Similarly, 20% of the sample had cholesterol levels that exceeded 340.

What is the *median* cholesterol level? In the next chapter, we will study the median, the most widely used percentile. The median is another name for the 50th percentile ($P_{50}$). Follow an imaginary line horizontally from the cumulative percent of 50 on the $Y$-axis until it intersects the ogive curve; then read vertically down to the $X$-axis to find the cholesterol level of approximately 276—approximately half the individuals had levels below 276. Confirm from Figure 3.6 that slightly less than 10% of the individuals had cholesterol levels below 200.

Percentile norms are employed for assessing physical growth, performance on standardized tests, and many other purposes. Percentile scores also allow comparison of relative performance on two different variables—such as a child's height and weight.

### Computing Percentiles

If high precision is needed, the percentile approximations provided from an ogive may not be sufficiently accurate. The percentile or percentile rank of a score is the percent of a distribution that falls below its midpoint; one-half of the score is said to fall below its midpoint. Thus, if there are 40 scores in a distribution, and Tom's score exceeds those of 37 students, the percentile rank of his score is $(37 + .5)/40 \times 100$; the ".5" represents half of Tom's score. Expressed mathematically, when scores are ranked from low = 1 ($i = 1$) to high = $n$ ($i = n$), the percentile rank, $PR$, of the score having rank $R_i$ in the rank-ordered distribution of $n$ scores is

$$PR_i = 100\frac{(R_i - .5)}{n} \quad \textbf{(3.3)}$$

where $R_i$ is the rank of the score of interest, $X$ (ranked from the lowest to the highest).

If scores are ranked from high = 1 ($j = 1$) to low = $n$ ($j = n$), the equation becomes

$$PR_j = 100\left(1 - \frac{R_j - .5}{n}\right) \quad \textbf{(3.4)}$$

Using Equation 3.4, the percentile rank of Tom's score ($R_j = 3$) is

$$PR = 100\left(1 - \frac{3 - .5}{40}\right) = 93.75 \text{ or } 94.$$

Percentile ranks are very useful for descriptive purposes such as for interpreting an individual's performance. By way of an advance warning, percentiles have serious drawbacks when used in statistical inference. For example, if we wish to see if there is a statistically significant difference between the average performance of two groups on a standardized measure (Chapter 12), raw scores or standard scores (Chapter 6) should be used, not percentile ranks.

## 3.9 BOX-AND-WHISKER PLOTS

The *box-and-whisker* plot (or box plot, for short) is a simple and useful graph for exploring and summarizing an array of data. A box plot of the cholesterol levels is given in Figure 3.7. The "box" extends from $P_{25}$ (the first quartile, $Q_1$) to $P_{75}$ (the third quartile, $Q_3$) ($Q_1$ and $Q_3$ are termed hinges by Tukey), thus describing the middle 50% of the distribution, in this case cholesterol levels of 245 to 330. Stated differently, the *interquartile range* (the distance between $Q_3$ and $Q_1$, i.e., $Q_3 - Q_1$) defines the width of the box. The median (≈275) of the distribution is denoted by a line inside the box. The two "whiskers" extend downward from $Q_1$ to the lowest score ($X_{min}$) and upward from $Q_3$ to the highest score ($X_{max}$), unless there are extremely low or high scores (*outliers*). The maximum length of either whisker is 1.5 box lengths—observations that deviate more than 1.5 times the value of the interquartile range

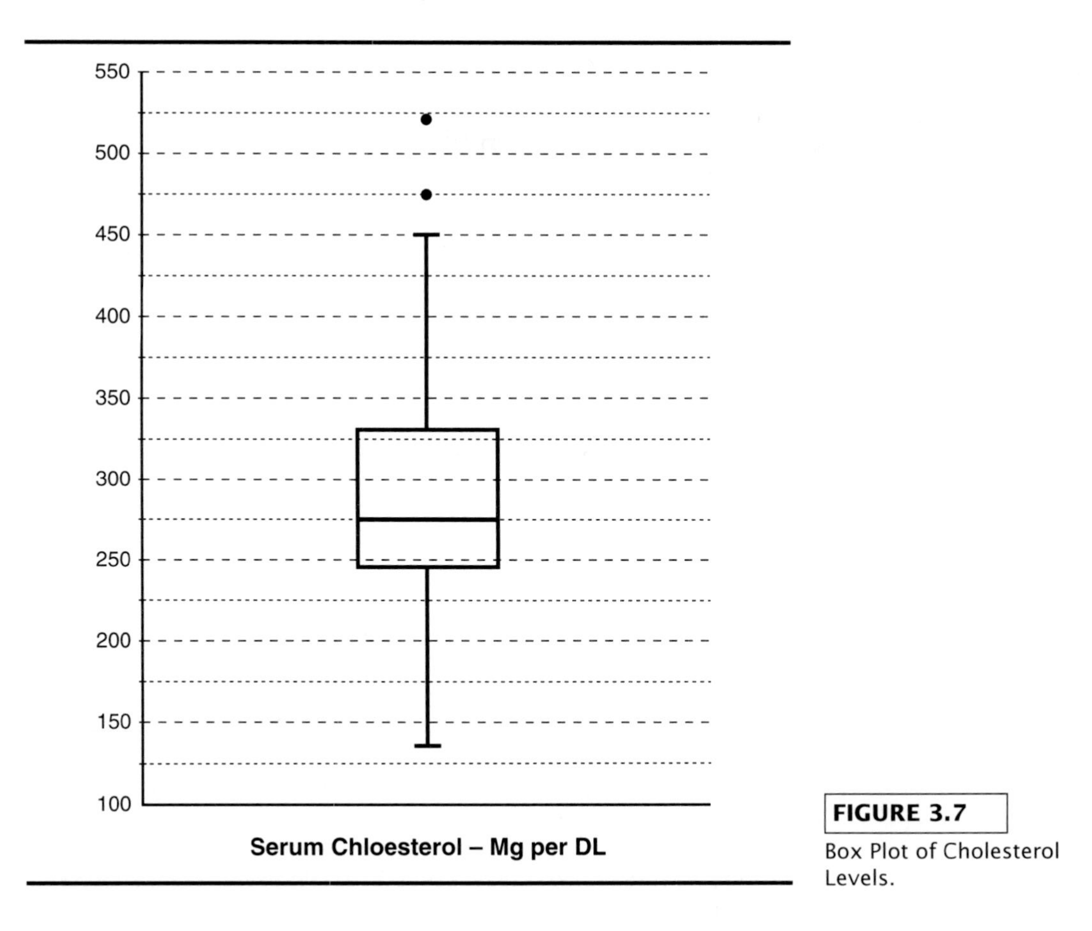


**FIGURE 3.7**
Box Plot of Cholesterol Levels.

below the point, $Q_1$, or above the point, $Q_3$, are marked as outliers.[8] Note in Figure 3.7 that two persons had cholesterol levels that were classified as outliers. Outliers should be examined for accuracy; many times they represent errors in scoring or data entry.

Box plots are especially useful for comparing two or more distributions. Figure 3.8 gives box plots from the "High School and Beyond" (HSB) case study data, which depicts the distributions of achievement scores in writing obtained by nationally representative high school seniors attending public and private schools in the United States. Study the box plots to confirm that (1) the scores tend to be higher for students in private schools, (2) the variability of scores is much greater in the public schools, (3) some public school students received scores as high as any student in private schools, and (4) the public schools have many more low scoring students. Stated differently, the achievement difference at $Q_3$ in

[8]You will learn from Chapter 6 that in a normal distribution less than 4 observations in 1,000 meet the criterion for outliers [$\geq 2.70\sigma$'s (Section 5.9) from the mean]. Note that this definition of an outlier is not adequate for large samples since 0.4% of the cases in a normal distribution meet this criterion. A further distinction as *extreme outlier* is made for observations that deviate by as much as three times the box length below $Q_1$ or above $Q_3$. In normal distributions, an extreme outlier ($\geq 4.72\sigma$'s from the mean) would be expected in only about one score in a million.

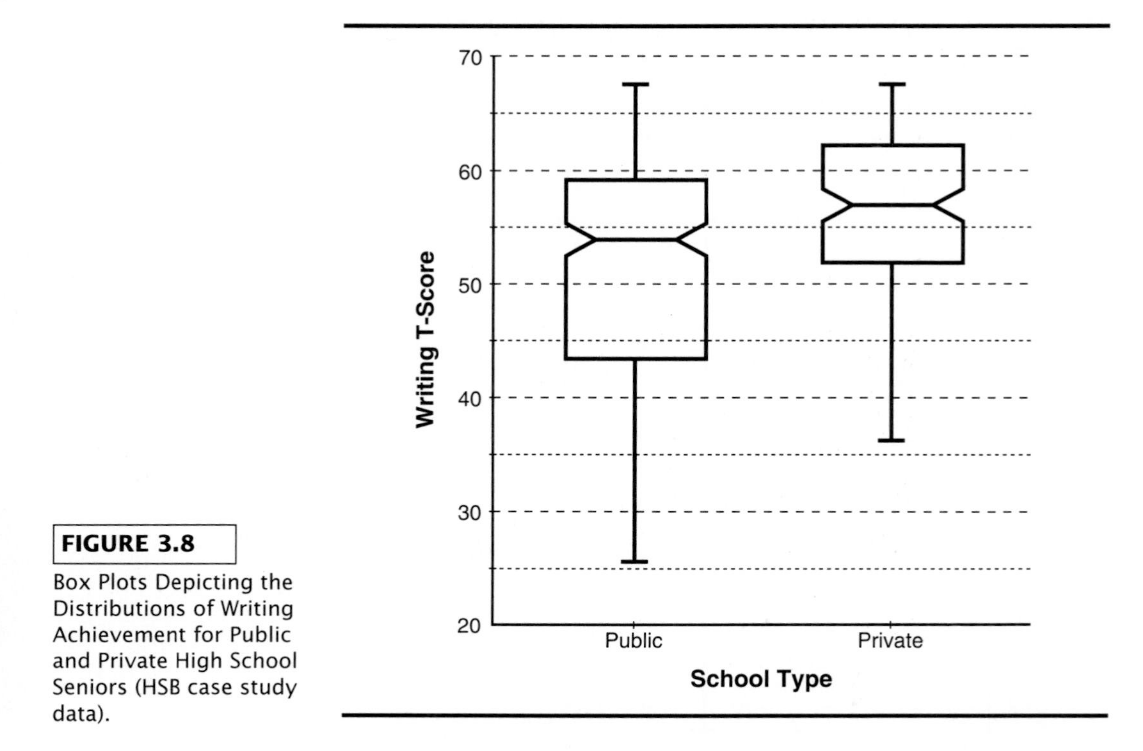


**FIGURE 3.8**

Box Plots Depicting the Distributions of Writing Achievement for Public and Private High School Seniors (HSB case study data).

favor of private school students is much smaller than it is at $Q_1$, and (5) the distribution of scores for public school students is highly negatively skewed (the distance from the median to $Q_1$ is much greater than the distance from the median to $Q_3$).

Some computer software offers "notched" box plots to emphasize the central tendency (median) of distributions. The notched box plot in Figure 3.8 illustrates output from this type of software. Figure 3.9 depicts the frequency distributions of high school seniors, males versus females, from the HSB data set in four achievement areas. Were there any outliers?[9] In which achievement area are the distributions for males and females most similar?[10] In which area do females do much better than males (describe the shape of the two distributions)?[11] In which area did the males clearly outperform the females (describe the shape of the two distributions)?[12] Compare the math distributions at $Q_1$, $Q_2$, and $Q_3$.[13]

## 3.10 STEM-AND-LEAF DISPLAYS

Another method of portraying a set of data is the *stem-and-leaf* display (Tukey, 1977), which is simply a refined grouped frequency distribution. Instead of a tally mark, the last digit of the

[9] Yes, one male in science (case #43), and one female in writing (case #107).

[10] Reading, note that both distributions appear to be normal.

[11] Writing; negatively skewed.

[12] Science; negative skewness for males, positive skewness for females.

[13] Differences are small at $Q_1$ and $Q_2$, at $Q_3$ males score higher.

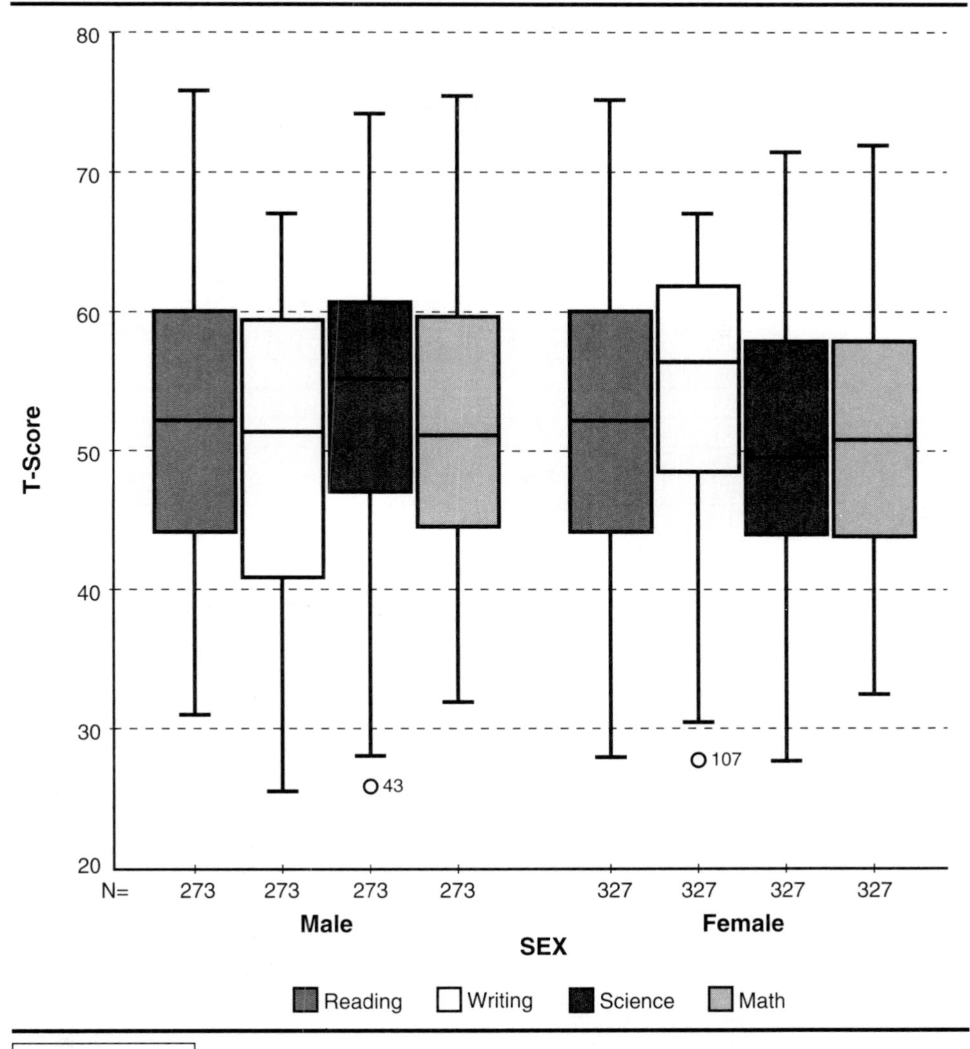

**FIGURE 3.9** Box Plots Depicting the Scores[14] of High School Seniors by Gender in Reading, Writing, Math, and Science.

observation is used to indicate an observation. A stem-and-leaf display of the data in Table 3.1 (separate distributions are given for those who did, and did not, experience a coronary incident during the decade of the study) is given in Figure 3.10. Notice this is equivalent to using an interval width of 10, rather than 20 as used in Table 3.2. The vertical line is the "stem" and the last digit of each score is a "leaf." Although less information is lost in the stem-and-leaf displays than in the conventional grouped frequency distribution (Table 3.2), the smaller interval width results in a less regular contour. Note that the distribution of persons who experienced a coronary problem tended to have relatively more persons with high cholesterol levels, although the difference may be less than you might have expected.

[14]Expressed as *T*-scores; you will become familiar with *T*-scores in Chapter 6, Section 6.7.

| | *Coronary Incident?* | |
|---|---|---|
| | *No* | *Yes* |
| *Stem* | *Leaf* | *Leaf* |
| 52 | | 0 |
| 51 | | |
| 50 | | |
| 49 | | |
| 48 | | |
| 47 | 4 | |
| 46 | | |
| 45 | 3 | |
| 44 | | |
| 43 | | |
| 42 | 0 | 08 |
| 41 | 6 | |
| 40 | 33 | |
| 39 | 04 | 1 |
| 38 | 3466 | |
| 37 | 8 | 00 |
| 36 | 03579 | 5 |
| 35 | 2233578 | |
| 34 | 11134688 | 1 |
| 33 | 023346677 | 6 |
| 32 | 00278 | 02 |
| 31 | 011244779 | 25 |
| 30 | 22247 | 25 |
| 29 | 00245688 | |
| 28 | 012234566 | 35 |
| 27 | 033344457899 | 117 |
| 26 | 0011444466677889999 | |
| 25 | 0122233344678999 | |
| 24 | 033456688 | 34 |
| 23 | 055899 | |
| 22 | 224579 | |
| 21 | 46889 | 04 |
| 20 | 36688 | |
| 19 | 0235 | |
| 18 | 577 | |
| 17 | 2233688 | 8 |
| 16 | 6 | |
| 15 | 66 | |
| 14 | | |
| 13 | 5 | |

**FIGURE 3.10**

Stem-and-Leaf Displays of Pretest Cholesterol Levels for Subjects who Did ($n = 25$), and who Did not ($n = 175$), Experience a Coronary Incident during the Ten-Year Study.

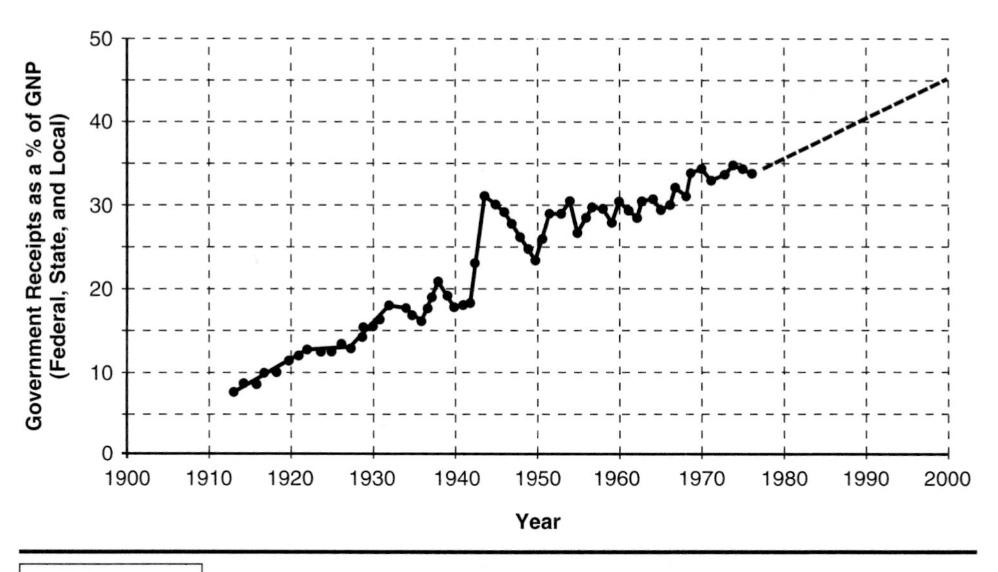


**FIGURE 3.11** An Illustration of a Time-Series Graph, "The Demise of Free Enterprise" from Augustine (1978).

## 3.11 TIME-SERIES GRAPHS

The *time-series graph*, a standard statistical figure in business and economics, is becoming common in some areas of education and psychology. It can be useful for identifying trends and changes in trends in ways that other representations of data cannot. A time-series graph is a line in which the *X*-axis, or baseline, is time and the vertical axis is a measure of the variable of interest. The time dimension can be measured in minutes, hours, days, weeks, months, or years, depending on the view that one wishes to take. Familiar examples of time-series graphs include the Dow-Jones stock price average plotted across days, the Consumer Price Index plotted across months, a patient's body temperature plotted across hours, and school enrollment plotted across years. Figure 3.11 is an illustrative time-series graph, "The Demise of Free Enterprise," provided by Augustine (1978). The extrapolated projections into the future are shown by the dashed line. Obviously, such projections into the distant future may have a large margin of error.

## 3.12 MISLEADING GRAPHS: HOW TO LIE WITH STATISTICS[15]

The ability to interpret properly, and not be misled by, information that is presented graphically is an important type of literacy for the both the layman and the professional. The general public is continually bombarded with data-based figures in newspapers and

[15]Finally, something practical that you can use!

magazines. Textbooks in all empirical disciplines are filled with graphs. Standardized achievement tests and university entrance tests are heavily weighted with graphic information that must be read critically (Tufte, 1983). Just as words can be misused to obscure the facts, so can pictures. At times, self-interest tempts one (including researchers) to use literal facts in such a way that the message is distorted. This may not be lying in a legal sense, but it accomplishes the same purpose. Graphs and charts can be organized so that they become propaganda rather than to illuminate the truth. Many, if not most, figures in the popular media are constructed to be as remarkable ("newsworthy") as possible; journalists are trained to tell an interesting story, regardless of whether words or pictures are used to tell the story. It behooves us to be on our toes so we are not credulous victims of misinformation.[16]

## Distorted Representation

A common, but not very subtle error, evident in many pictographs[17] found in the popular media is the linear-area fallacy. To get "more bang for the buck," graphic artists often repre-

**FIGURE 3.12A**
Misleading Graphs: Illustrations of Distorted Representation.[18]

[16]Several of the examples are from the excellent resource book by Tufte (1983).

[17]Histograms that use figures to represent frequencies.

[18]Sources for Figures. 3.12A: *Washington Post,* Oct. 25, 1978, p. 1; Figure 3.12B: *New York Times,* Aug. 9, 1978, p. D-2; Figure 3.12C: *Rocky Mountain News,* May 8, 1994, p. 81A.

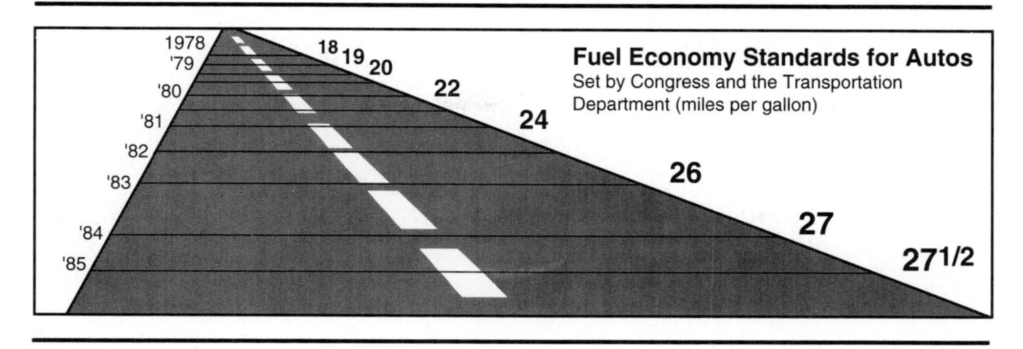


**FIGURE 3.12B** Misleading Graphs: Illustrations of Distorted Representation.

sent the frequency in a category by the height of the figure (a linear distance), yet make only one figure per category. This lack of uniform representation of a frequency conveys a distorted picture of the data. Notice in Figure 3.12A how the amount of inflation is exaggerated across the five presidencies. The data are scaled by the *length* of the dollar bill, but it is the *area* of the bills that the reader perceives. The area of the Carter dollar is less than 20% that of the Eisenhower bill, whereas the proper comparison is 100 to 44, not 100 to 20. If the bills were of the same width as the Eisenhower dollar, but were fragments with different lengths, the representation would be fair and accurate. (Isn't the result dramatic enough without fudging?) The same flaw is seen in Figure 3.12B. Figure 3.12C gives a hopelessly distorted picture of the data.[19]

## Misleading Scaling and Calibration

There is no obvious calibration in Figure 3.12C. A more common shortcoming of graphs appears in Figure 3.13, where an arbitrary beginning scale value on the vertical axis is used. Variables that represent ratio scales should begin with zero to give a proper perspective for the visual interpretation. Figure 3.13A is a common method of perceptual exaggeration; the change over time is made to appear much larger than it is. Notice how different the magnitude of the change appears in a proper figure like Figure 3.13B. Many graphs (e.g., stock prices) typically ignore the zero point and thus perceptually exaggerate the magnitude of changes.

## Combination Graphs

Combination graphs can be one of the most devious ways of giving unwarranted credibility to graphic propaganda. All three graphs in Figure 3.14 use the same data, but note that the top and middle graphs lead to opposite conclusions! This is possible by an inappropriate scaling of both variables. Combination graphs need to be scrutinized (Wainer, 1992); the actual information is usually much less convincing than the graph. *Caveat emptor!*

---

[19]Why not construct a fair histogram to get the facts straight? Use "Year" as the baseline, and MPG as the vertical axis.

**FIGURE 3.12C** Misleading Graphs: Illustrations of Distorted Representation.

The lower graph in Figure 3.14 is fair, but still equivocal. How does one properly scale the SAT? Like all cognitive and affective measures, it has no meaningful zero point because it is not a ratio scale. Since 400 is the lowest possible score and 1600 the highest possible score, perhaps these should be used to anchor the scale.

One final point about graphic displays of information must be made. Just as in written

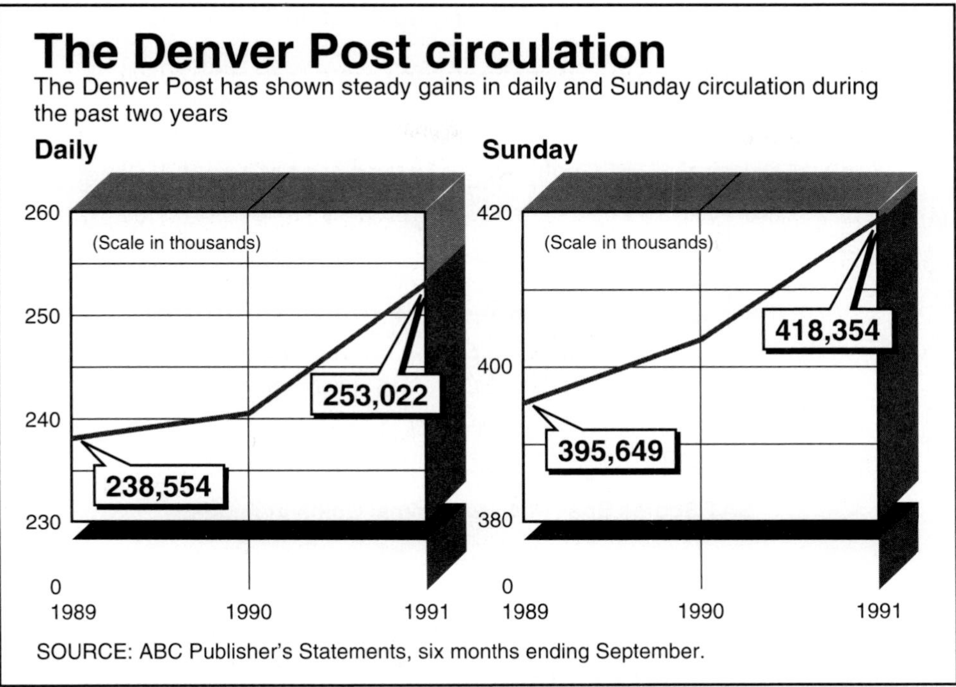


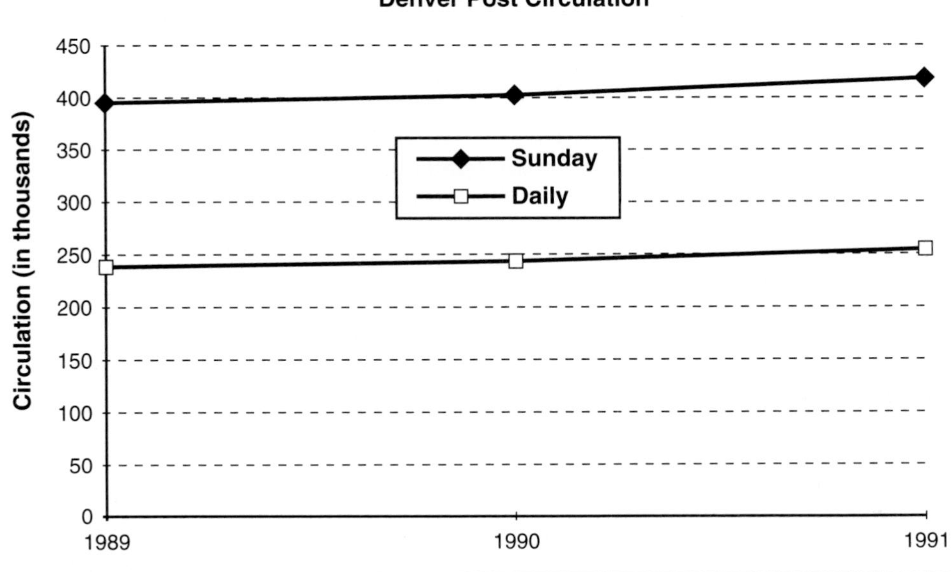


**FIGURE 3.13** An Example of Exaggerating a Trend by Ignoring the Zero Point of a Ratio Scale (top), Compared with a Fair Representation (bottom). *Denver Post*, November 3, 1991.

Public School Funding Soars; No Payoff in SAT Scores

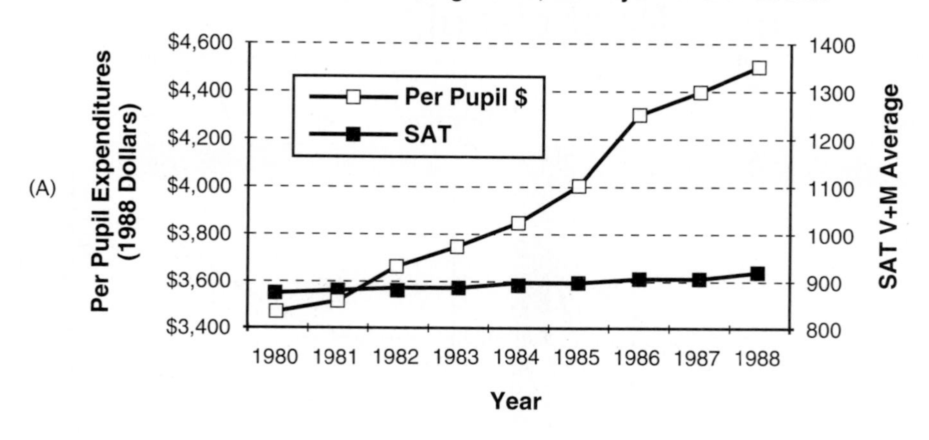


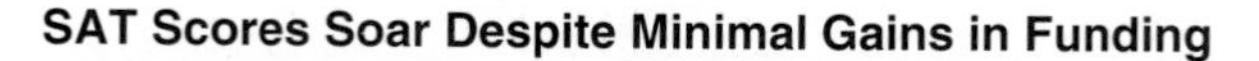


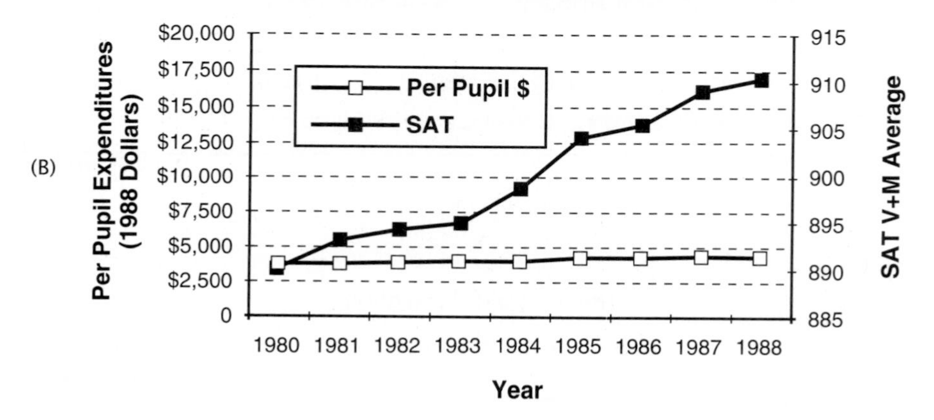

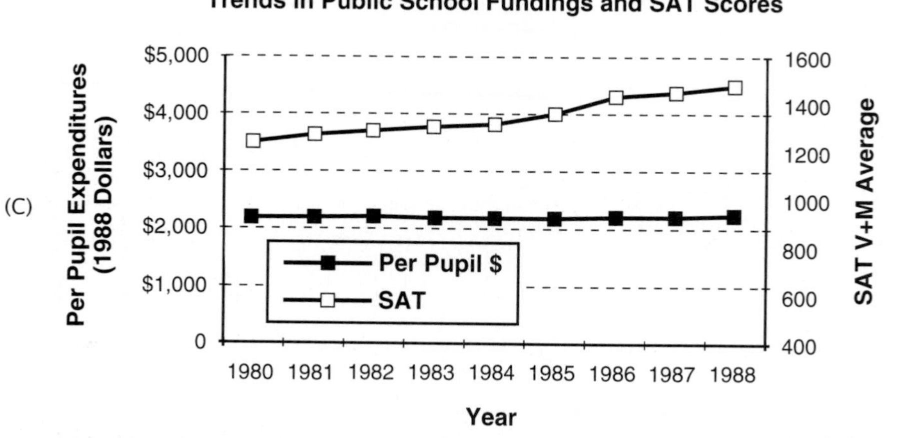


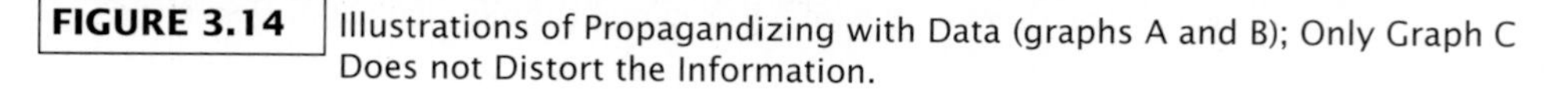
**FIGURE 3.14** Illustrations of Propagandizing with Data (graphs A and B); Only Graph C Does not Distort the Information.

communication, the intended audience has an important influence on what and how information is presented graphically. More details can be included when the graph is for an audience of professional peers than when the readers will be less interested and less sophisticated. Too much detail can be distracting and confusing to a lay audience. Figure 3.15 is an example of a graph that contains an abundance of information without becoming cluttered and confusing. The daily high and low temperatures are given with the normal temperatures as a backdrop. Note that the lines depicting the normal temperatures are regular, but not entirely smooth. These curves are based on daily averages over the past century or so; as the data base grows, these will become even less ragged. Observe that the range between the normal low and high is less during the winter than in the summer. The daily temperatures tend to increase until late July, then begin to decline until late January, although in any given year the pattern will vacillate considerably. The relative humidity did not vary greatly from month to month. On the average, New York City does not have any particularly wet or dry months.

## 3.13 CHAPTER SUMMARY

Statistical methods are tools for simplifying, organizing, and summarizing a set of observations. Statistical tables, figures, graphs, and charts can organize otherwise unwieldy quantities of data. The shape or configuration of a distribution becomes evident if the observations are grouped into intervals and displayed graphically.

Many variables in the behavioral and social sciences are normally distributed, but other kinds of distribution are also common. Skewed distributions result when observations pile up at the low or high end and drop off gradually toward the other end. A distribution is positively skewed when the tail points to the high scores; the opposite is true with negative skewness.

Frequency distributions can be expressed graphically using frequency and percentage histograms (bar graphs), polygons, box plots, and stem-and-leaf displays, among others. Histograms are appropriate when the baseline variable is categorical or nominal; frequency and percentage polygons require a quantitative baseline variable. Ogive (cumulative percentage) curves are useful for determining percentiles (the percentage of a distribution that falls below a given point), such as $Q_1$ ($P_{25}$), the median ($Q_2$ or $P_{50}$), and $Q_3$ ($P_{75}$). A box-and-whisker plot is a simple graph for conveying salient features of a distribution. A stem-and-leaf display conveys the general shape of a frequency distribution while retaining access to the values of all the original scores.

Graphs can be misused to distort data. When pictures are used to represent figures, all should be the same size. Scales having a true zero point should begin at that point to avoid exaggerating effects. Combination graphs can be particularly effective for propaganda, leading the reader to false conclusions.

## 3.14 CASE STUDY

Frequency distributions for each variable in the Chapman cholesterol study are shown in Figure 3.16. What can we learn from them? The more we know about the sample, the better we can define the population to which the findings can be generalized. We should note, for

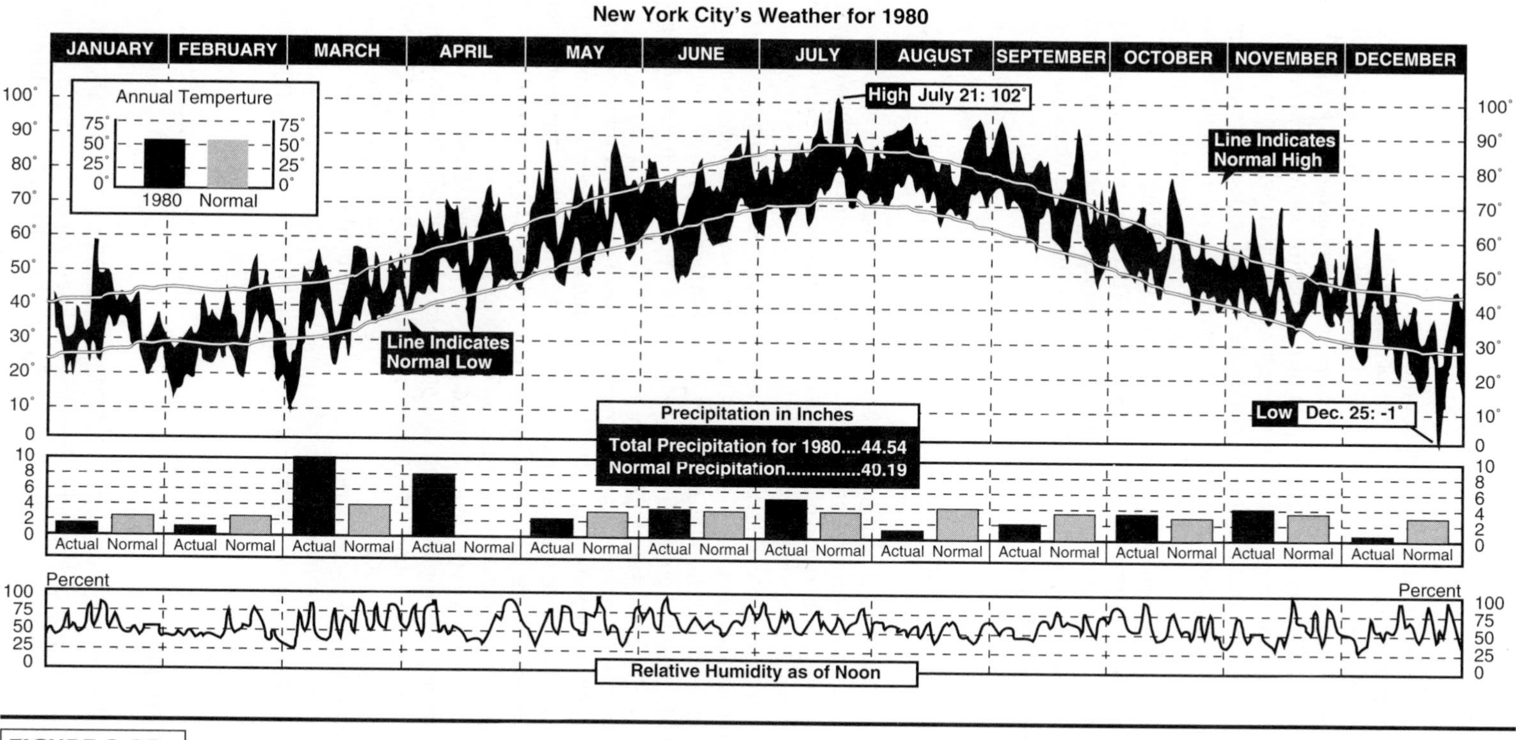

**FIGURE 3.15** An Example of Interesting Graphing: Weather for New York City.

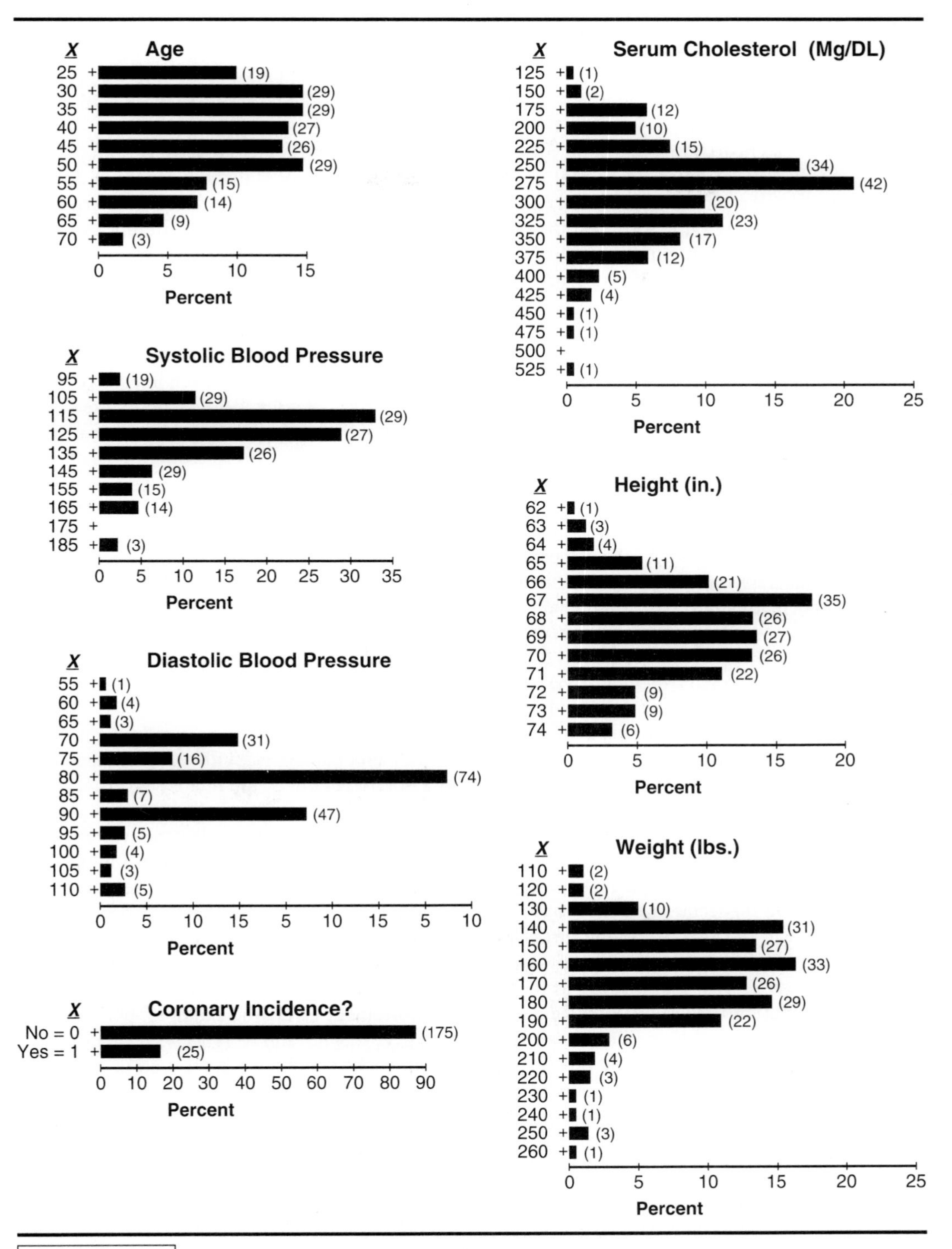


**FIGURE 3.16** Histograms of Variables in the Chapman Case Study Data.

example, that sex is not a variable in the sample, hence we cannot safely generalize any findings to females.[20]

The histograms in Figure 3.16 were produced using the FREQUENCIES program of SPSS (one of several excellent and widely used packages of statistical programs for personal and mainframe computers). The output from different software will not be organized in exactly the same form, but the product should not be fundamentally different. Note that the histograms produced by this SPSS program are drawn with horizontal bars to indicate interval frequencies. If you study Figure 3.16 after turning your book sideways, the figures will be arranged in the conventional configuration, with low scores on the lower left. Note that in addition to the percents metric, frequencies are also given in parentheses at the end of each bar; they complement each other when histograms are being interpreted.

Note that the interval size for age is 5 years; $X$ is the midpoint of each interval, thus the interval at $X = 25$ includes persons of ages 23–27 (25±2). We see that the bulk of the sample is between 30 and 50 years of age at the beginning of the study—the distribution is roughly rectangular across these intervals. There is some positive skewness as the frequencies fall off at the upper age levels.

The histogram for systolic blood pressure (SBP) is unimodal (mode = 115) and positively skewed.[21] Diastolic blood pressure (DBP) appears roughly normal, but do you notice anything peculiar? The mode is 80, yet there appear to be minor modes at 70 and 90. Is this reasonable? Perhaps some of the persons taking the measurements just rounded them to "nice whole numbers," particularly when the reading was not clinically significant. Nevertheless, this introduces a small amount of measurement error into the measurements.[22] Observe that the interval size for SBP is 10, whereas it is 5 for DBP; SBP is more variable than DBP.

The coronary incidence variable is dichotomous. The coding is arbitrary since it is a nominal variable; it is easier to interpret the numbers if "No" is coded as "0", and "Yes" as "1," as done here. Twenty-five people in the sample, or about one person in eight, had a heart problem during the decade of the study. In later chapters we will be very interested in finding which of the other variables, such as Cholesterol Level, are related to this variable, and how highly.

Figures 3.1–3.3 depicted the frequency distribution of the Cholesterol variable; the only difference here is inconsequential. An interval size of 25 was used in Figure 3.16, whereas 20 was used in Figures 3.1–3.3. The distribution appears approximately normal.

The distribution of height is roughly normal, but with fewer very tall persons than expected; chance (sampling error) will always create certain irregularities in the data on samples. Some positive skewness is apparent in weight. In this study height and weight were measured, but why go to the trouble—don't adults know their height and weight? Self-reported measures would have more measurement error; for example, perhaps very short and very thin individuals are more apt to give heights and weights with shoes on.

Can you visualize the box-and-whisker plots that could have been used to depict the distributions? Some information would have been lost, but the general patterns would have

---

[20]Although there may be a good reason for studying only males in this study (since males have a much greater incidence of coronary problems), until recent years it has been the case that medical research on females has not received comparable emphasis.

[21]Indices for quantifying the degree of skewness are given in Chapter 6.

[22]This illustrates the value of conducting a pilot study before launching into a full-scale study. Usually the pilot study will reveal unanticipated problems that can be eliminated or minimized prior to the actual study. In this case, special orientation and training appears needed for the persons taking the blood pressure measurements. Measurement error will cause the correlations between this variable and other variables to be lower (Section 7.16).

been evident. Obviously box-and-whisker plots make no sense for categorical variables like coronary.

Our case study will become even more interesting in later chapters. We will continue to analyze the results as we progress in our study of statistical methods.

## 3.15 SUGGESTED COMPUTER ACTIVITY

With reference to the High School and Beyond (HSB) case study data set found on the accompanying diskette, use computer software to obtain: (1) a frequency distribution (histogram) for at least two of the variables, and (2) a box plot, stem-and-leaf display, and an ogive curve for at least one variable.[23] Describe the distributions, and note any outliers. Using different interval widths, compare the associated frequency distributions for one of the variables.

## MASTERY TEST

1. Extremely high or low scores in a distributions are termed ____.
2. Which one of these types of distributions is best for conveying the shape of the frequency distribution of the weights of 250 students?

   (a) rank-order (b) ungrouped (c) histogram
3. If the largest observation in a set of scores is 99 and the smallest is 71, what is the range?
4. In a grouped frequency distribution, the larger the interval ($w$) the ____ (greater or less) the loss of information.
5. If the lowest score in a distribution is 51, with an interval width of 5, what should the first interval be?

   (a) 51–55 (b) 47–51 (c) 50–55 (d) 50–54
6. If the baseline variable represents a nominal variable (such as ethnicity), which method of graphic representation is preferred, histograms or frequency polygons?
7. Can a percentage polygon and a frequency polygon for one set of data be represented in the same figure?
8. Which term does not belong with the others?

   (a) $X$-axis (b) $Y$-axis (c) horizontal axis (d) abscissa
9. Percentile ranks are especially useful

   (a) for descriptive purposes (b) in statistical inference
10. Which of these graphs is best for determining percentiles?

    (a) histogram (b) percentage polygon (c) ogive curve
11. An IQ score of 90 is at $P_{25}$; what percent of IQ scores *exceed* 90?
12. Which term is *not* equivalent to the other three?

    (a) $Q_1$ (b) median (c) $P_{50}$ (d) $Q_2$

---

[23] Histograms and ogive curves can be obtained using spreadsheet programs such as EXCEL. Box plots and stem-and-leaf displays may require special statistical software such as BMDP, MINITAB, SAS, SPSS, or SYSTAT.

**13.** From Figure 3.6, ____% of the individuals had cholesterol levels of 240 or below; thus, a cholesterol level of 240 is at the ____ percentile.

**14.** Using Figure 3.6, 10% of the individuals had cholesterol levels above ____, or below ____. Could this question have been answered using only the box plot of Figure 3.7?

**15.** Compute the precise percentile rank of a cholesterol level of 240 using Eq. 3.3 and data in Table 3.1. Compare this value with the value you obtained in item 13.

**16.** If you were constructing a figure to compare the percentages of males versus females who are left-handed, which type of graph would be best?

**17.** From the box plot of Figure 3.8, which of the two distributions has the higher median? Which is more variable?

**18.** From the stem-and-leaf display in Figure 3.10, how many persons had cholesterol levels of 320?

**19.** Is the following a fair and accurate pictograph?

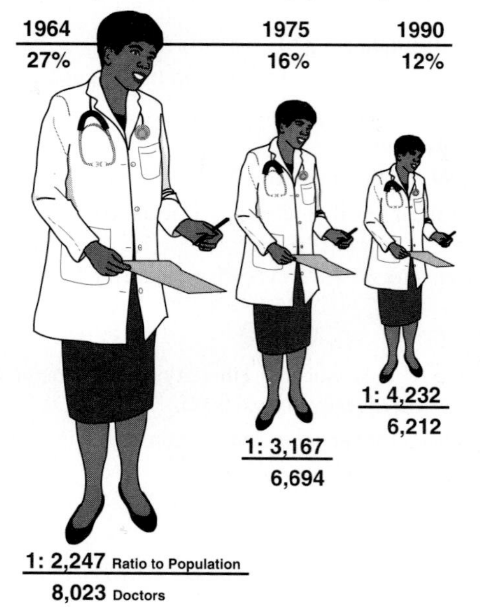


*In questions 20–24, match the verbal and graphic descriptions:*

**20.** Rectangular distribution

**21.** Bimodal distribution

**22.** Positively skewed distribution

**23.** Negatively skewed distribution

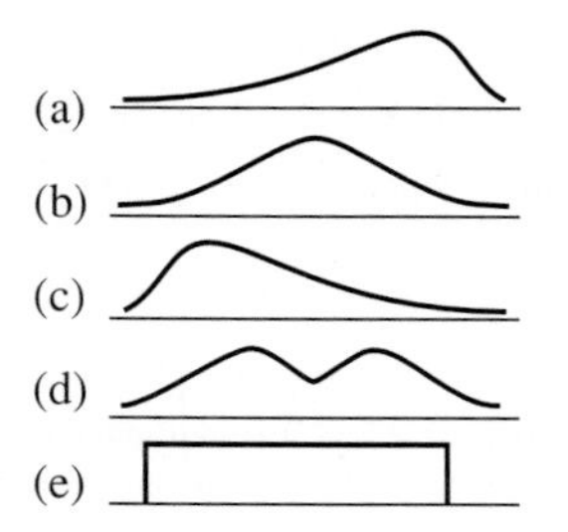

**24.** Which of the above curves (a–e) are symmetrical?

**25.** Indicate which one of the following distributions is probably negatively skewed.

(a) family income in dollars per year
(b) age at graduation from college
(c) populations of cities in the United States
(d) scores on a very easy test

**26.** In a box plot, what percent of the observations fall (a) in the box, (b) above the box, (c) below the lower whisker when there are no outliers?

**27.** In a box plot, if the whisker to $X_{min}$ is longer than the whisker to $X_{max}$, predict the shape of the distribution.

*For questions 28–30, study the two histograms below and answer the following questions.*

**28.** In the Civil War, which side (North or South) had (a) the greater number of war deaths, and (b) war deaths as a greater proportion of the population.

**29.** Besides the Civil War, which war had the greatest death rate (%)?

**30.** How does the extent of the U.S. war deaths in the Civil War compare to that of all other U. S. wars combined in terms of the number of military deaths?

**Number of War Deaths as a Percentage of the Male Population**

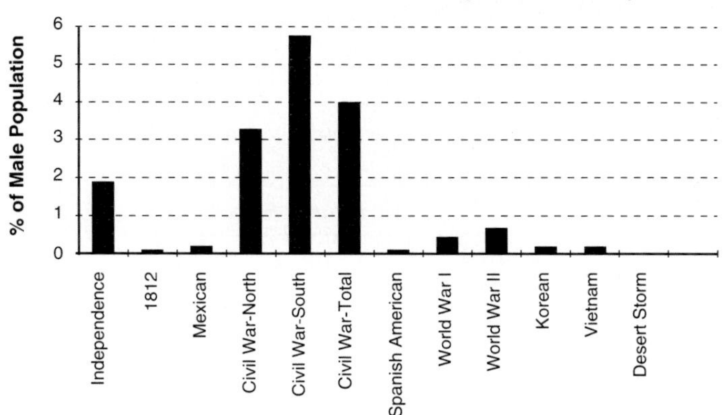

**Number of War Death in U.S. Wars**

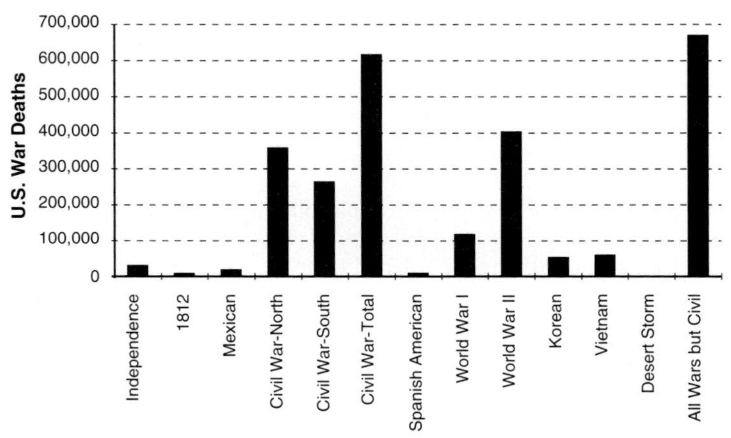

## PROBLEMS AND EXERCISES

*The following data are IQ scores for 50 persons.*

| | | | | | | | | | |
|---|---|---|---|---|---|---|---|---|---|
| 141 | 87 | 115 | 91 | 96 | 92 | 118 | 98 | 101 | 107 |
| 97 | 124 | 118 | 146 | 108 | 106 | 135 | 97 | 108 | 129 |
| 107 | 110 | 101 | 129 | 109 | 83 | 127 | 116 | 113 | 105 |
| 127 | 114 | 112 | 114 | 139 | 109 | 102 | 113 | 106 | 89 |
| 108 | 92 | 102 | 102 | 134 | 104 | 101 | 131 | 86 | 123 |

1. (a) Is the mode of the *ungrouped* data above very useful?
   (b) What is the value of the range?
   (c) Construct a frequency distribution, using an interval width of 10. (Whenever possible, select a value for $w$ that makes it easy for the reader to organize the scores.)
   (d) Using an interval width of 10, the first (lowest) interval will begin with ____.
   (e) Construct a histogram for the fifty IQ scores, using $w = 10$. Denote both frequencies and percents on the vertical axis.
   (f) Add "Cumulative Percent" to the frequency distribution, and construct an ogive curve.
   (g) From the ogive, estimate $Q_1$, the median, and $Q_3$.
   (h) Construct the box portion of a box plot for the distribution of IQ scores.
   (i) Construct a stem-and-leaf display for these data.
2. IQ scores obtained on a nationally representative sample of 2,200 children on the *Wechsler Intelligence Scale for Children (WISC)* are given below. Construct an ogive curve.

| *Interval* | *Frequency* | *Percent* | *Cumulative Percent* |
|---|---|---|---|
| 150–159 | 1 | .05 | 100.00 |
| 140–149 | 6 | .27 | 99.95 |
| 130–139 | 44 | 2.00 | 99.68 |
| 120–129 | 163 | 7.41 | 97.68 |
| 110–119 | 363 | 16.50 | 90.27 |
| 100–109 | 548 | 24.91 | 73.77 |
| 90–99 | 539 | 24.50 | 48.86 |
| 80–89 | 356 | 16.18 | 24.36 |
| 70–79 | 132 | 6.00 | 8.18 |
| 60–69 | 41 | 1.86 | 2.18 |
| 50–59 | 6 | .27 | .32 |
| 40–49 | 1 | .05 | .05 |
| | $n = 2{,}200$ | 100.00% | |

3. Plot two percentage polygons on the same graph from the following grouped frequency distributions of the grade equivalent scores in reading and math on the Cooperative Test of Basic Skills for fourth-grade students in a moderate-sized school district.

| Grade Equivalent Interval | Reading | | Math | |
|---|---|---|---|---|
| | Frequency | Percent | Frequency | Percent |
| 11.0– | 48 | 2.9 | 9 | 0.6 |
| 10.0–10.9 | 71 | 4.3 | 13 | 0.8 |
| 9.0–9.9 | 114 | 7.0 | 35 | 2.2 |
| 8.0–8.9 | 188 | 11.5 | 58 | 3.6 |
| 7.0–7.9 | 252 | 15.4 | 160 | 9.9 |
| 6.0–6.9 | 357 | 21.8 | 453 | 27.9 |
| 5.0–5.9 | 295 | 18.0 | 442 | 27.2 |
| 4.0–4.9 | 166 | 10.1 | 267 | 16.4 |
| 3.0–3.9 | 120 | 7.3 | 142 | 8.7 |
| 2.0–2.9 | 26 | 1.6 | 39 | 2.4 |
| 1.0–1.9 | 3 | .2 | 6 | .4 |
| | $n = 1{,}640$ | 100.1 | $n = 1{,}624$ | 100.1 |

(a) Which distribution has more very low scores (below 4.0)?
(b) Which distribution has more very high scores (8.0 and above)?
(c) Which distribution has the higher median?
(d) Plot these distributions as ogives on the same graph. Which distribution shows the steeper slope (more nearly vertical) between 4.0 and 7.0?
(e) Construct box-and-whisker plots. Use percentile points from the ogive curve.
(f) What accounts for the fact that the percent columns did not add up to exactly 100.0%?

**4.** The distributions of heights for boys at ages 10, 12, 14, 16, and 18 are given in the ogive curves below.[24]

(a) What is the median height for boys at age 12?
(b) How much growth in height does the median boy make between age 12 and 14?
(c) At age 16 Dean was 64 inches tall; two years later he was 72 inches tall. His percentile rank increased from about the ____ at age 16 to about the ____ at age 18.
(d) The most growth occurs for the median boy during which two-year interval?
(e) The distance between $Q_3$ and $Q_1$ is termed the *interquartile range*. Which curve has the largest interquartile range? How much taller is the boy at $P_{75}$ than the boy at $P_{25}$ at that age?

[24]Data from National Center for Health Statistics Growth Charts (1976).

**5.** Women who called for help at a suicide prevention center were classified in relation to their menstrual cycles (Mandell and Mandell, 1967). The menstrual cycle for each woman was grouped into seven periods of days beginning with the onset of the menstrual period. The incidence of eighty-seven suicide calls for each of the seven periods was 27, 7, 5, 15, 6, 9, 18. Construct a frequency and percentage polygon to portray these data graphically.

**6.** The figure below gives box plots showing the distributions of scores on a comprehensive math achievement test given to four nationally representative groups: (1) high school seniors in 1972, (2) high school seniors in 1980, (3) high school sophomores in 1980, (4) high school seniors in 1982 (Rock, Hilton, Pollack, Ekstrom, and Goertz [1985]).

(a) Is a decline in achievement evident from the box plots?

(b) The national medians for high school seniors were ____, ____, and ____ in 1972, 1980, and 1982, respectively.

(c) From the figures, is it evident that the decline exists throughout the distributions, for example, $Q_3$ fell from 19.0 in 1972 to ____ and ____ in 1980 and 1982?[25]

(d) From the data depicted by the boxes, what can be concluded regarding skewness in the distributions?

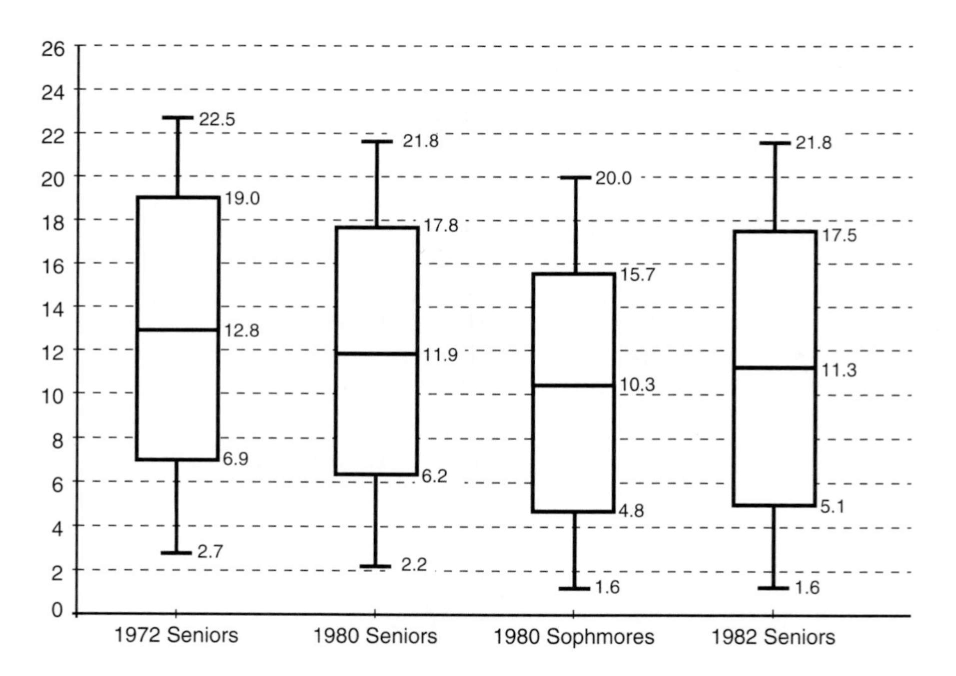


[25]Interestingly, the decline among females was less than among males. The medians for the males were 13.6, 12.8, and 11.6 for 1972, 1980, and 1982, respectively, whereas for females the medians were 12.0, 11.4, and 11.0. Note the gender difference was 1.6 points in 1972, but only .6 in 1982.

## ANSWERS TO MASTERY TEST

1. outliers
2. (c)
3. Range = $X_{max} - X_{min} = 99 - 71 = 28$
4. greater
5. (d) 50–54, because 50 is the largest multiple of the interval size ($w = 5$) that is less than the lowest score of 51.
6. histograms
7. yes
8. (b)
9. (a)
10. (c)
11. 75%
12. (a)
13. ≈ 22, 22nd
14. ≈ 370, ≈ 203, no
15. $PR = 100(44 - .5)/200 = 21.75$ or 22
16. percentage histogram
17. private; public
18. 3
19. No, the pictograph distorts the facts. A better graph would depict the number of family doctors per 10,000 persons, using a doctor figure of uniform size; thus 4.5 doctors would be depicted for 1964, 3.2 doctors for 1975, and 2.4 doctors for 1990, for example:

20. (e)
21. (d)
22. (c)
23. (a)
24. (b), (d), and (e)
25. (d)
26. 50%, 25%, 0%
27. negatively skewed
28. (a) North, (b) South
29. Independence
30. There were almost as many war deaths in the Civil War as in all other wars combined.

## ANSWERS TO PROBLEMS AND EXERCISES

1. (a) no, too few cases spread over a wide range
(b) Range = 146 – 83 = 63
(d) 80
(g) $Q_1 \approx 100$, median ≈ 108, $Q_3 \approx 118$

2. 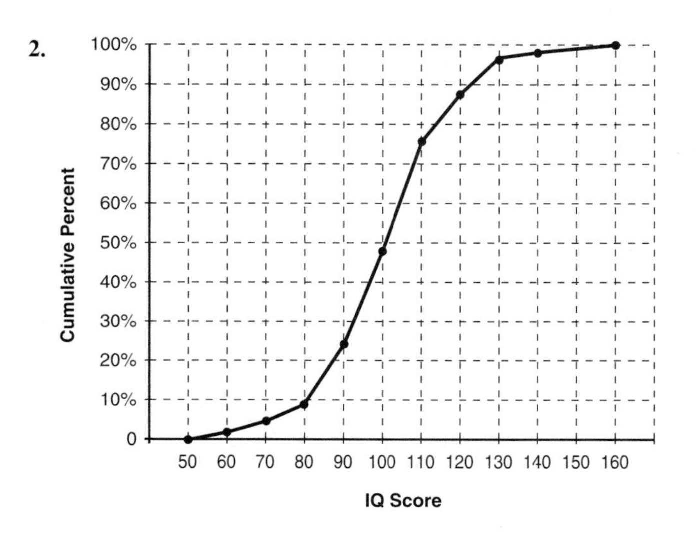

3. (a) math; (b) reading; (c) reading; (d) math; (f) rounding error
4. (a) 59″; (b) 5½″; (c) 8th, 80th; (d) 12–14; (e) age 14; $Q_3 - Q_1 = 66.5'' - 61.5'' = 5''$
6. (a) yes; (b) ≈12.8, ≈11.9, and ≈11.3; (c) ≈17.8 and ≈17.5; (d) Little or no skewness is evident.

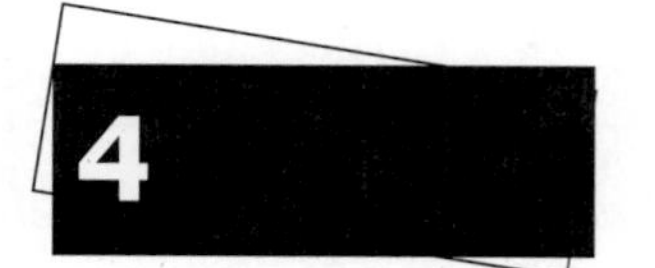

# MEASURES OF CENTRAL TENDENCY

## 4.1 INTRODUCTION

Measures of *central tendency* describe typical, average, or representative scores.[1] They convey information about the center of a distribution, but they tell only a part of the story about a set of numbers. There are several different measures of central tendency—perhaps a dozen or so. In this chapter, we will study the three widely used measures of central tendency—the mean, median, and mode. These commonly used measures are different in conception and calculation. They reflect different notions of the center of a distribution, and each of them can be the "measure of choice" for certain types of data sets. In skewed distribution, the mean, median, and mode can differ greatly. Of all statistical descriptions of data, measures of central tendency are the most widely used, not only in research, but also for quantitative information reported to the public.

## 4.2 THE MODE

The *mode* is the score or observation that occurs most frequently. In the set of scores (2, 6, 6, 8, 9, 9, 9, 10), the mode is 9 because it occurs more often than any other score. The modal letter grade given in a history course may be "B." "Smith" is the modal name in the United States. The mode can be employed even with qualitative, categorical variables—data that represent only a nominal scale of measurement. For example, there are 100 females for every 95 males in the United States; hence, the modal sex is female. Thirteen is the mode for the number of years of schooling in the United States, counting kindergarten.

When observations are grouped into classes, the midpoint of the class with the largest

[1]In education and psychology, the numbers that are analyzed are usually scores of some type. The numbers can represent variables like dollars, minutes, ratings, centimeters, and pounds; hence, the reader should view the term "scores" broadly to include any numerical measure.

| *Height* | *Tally* | *f* | *Cumulative f* | |
|---|---|---|---|---|
| 75″ | • | 1 | 192 | Mode = 68″ |
| 74″ | : | 2 | 191 | Median = 68.38″ |
| 73″ | ⁝: | 5 | 189 | Mean = 68.44″ |
| 72″ | ⊠ | 10 | 184 | Midrange = 69″ |
| 71″ | ⊠ ⧅ | 19 | 174 | Midhinge = 68.48″ |
| 70″ | ⊠ ⊠ ⁝: | 25 | 155 | Trimean = 68.43″ |
| 69″ | ⊠ ⊠ ⊠ | 30 | 130 | |
| 68″ | ⊠ ⊠ ⊠ ⁘ | 34 | 100 | |
| 67″ | ⊠ ⊠ ⊠ | 30 | 66 | |
| 66″ | ⊠ ⁘ | 14 | 36 | |
| 65″ | ⊠ : | 12 | 22 | |
| 64″ | □ | 8 | 10 | |
| 63″ | : | 2 | 2 | |

$n = 192$

**FIGURE 4.1** Frequency Distribution of the Height of 192 Adult Males.

frequency is an estimate of the mode, often termed the *crude* mode. Notice that the mode of the heights of the 192 adult males in Figure 4.1 is 68 inches because it is the midpoint of the most "popular" interval, having a frequency of 34.

Estimate the mode of the cholesterol values from the grouped frequency distribution given in Table 3.2 (Section 3.2). The midpoint of the interval with the greatest frequency is approximately 270. The crude mode can have a different value when a different interval size is used; note in Figure 3.10 (Section 3.10) that when the interval width is 10, the crude mode is estimated to be 265. As its name suggests, the crude mode is a rough estimate in many situations since it is influenced by the arbitrary value set for $w$; this is especially true if the sample size is small.

The mode is a useful *descriptive statistic* when studying nominal (categorical) variables such as race and college major, where the mean and median are not useful descriptive measures. The mode is not very useful when the number of scores $n$ is less than twice the range of scores, when scores are viewed as whole numbers.[2] As a rule of thumb, there

---

[2]If scores are decimal fractions, just ignore the decimal point when comparing the range with the number of scores.

should be at least as many scores as the value of the range (Section 3.2; Equation 3.1). In Table 3.1 (Section 3.1), the 200 cholesterol values have a range of 385, thus the range is greater than $n$. Note also that a real mode was not defined by the data; values of 269, 273, and 341 all had a frequency of four. If the sample had been twice as large, a mode near 270 would likely have resulted. Table 3.2 (Section 3.2) shows that the distribution is not bimodal. The real mode often is not clearly defined unless $n$ is at least as large as the range. The mode is not very useful in statistical inference (Section 1.3).

In the group of scores (1, 1, 1, 1, 1, 2, 2, 3, 4, 5, 5, 5, 5, 5), both 1 and 5 are modes; the frequencies illustrate a bimodal distribution. The distribution of scores is described as bimodal when the frequency distribution has two distinctly different points about which the observations tend to cluster. More specifically, the above distribution is said to be *U-shaped*; bipolar scales (e.g., attitudes toward abortion) often yield bimodal, U-shaped distributions.

A distribution is said to be bimodal even if the frequencies at the two peaks are not strictly equal (e.g., if there were only four scores of "1" in the distribution above). A distinction is made between *major* and *minor modes* in these instances. Obviously, dichotomous distributions are always bimodal. If the heights of a large sample of adults were plotted, one would expect to see a bimodal distribution, with heavy concentrations around 64 inches for females and 70 inches for males.

## 4.3 THE MEDIAN

Recall from Chapter 3 that the median is used in box-and-whisker plots. The educated layman is familiar with the median and the mean; these indices have become a part of the common core of knowledge that an educated person is assumed to have. In Chapter 3, we were reminded that the median is the 50th percentile of a distribution, the point below which half the observations fall. There will be an equal number of cases above and below the median. When the number of observations is an odd number, and the scores are arranged in rank order (such as 11, 13, 18, 19, 20), the median is the middle score (in this instance, $Md = 18$). When there is an even number of scores (such as 4, 4, 9, 11, 12, 14), the median is the point halfway between the two middle-most values [in this instance, $Md = (9 + 11)/2 = 10$]. Confirm for yourself that the median cholesterol value in Table 3.1 (Section 3.1) is 276. Note that there are 200 scores arranged in rank order, with 25 scores in each of the eight columns. Thus, the median is the point below and above which 50% (in this instance, 100) of the scores fall; that is, the median is the average of the bottom score in the fourth column (277) and the top score in the fifth column (275): $Md = (277 + 275)/2 = 276$.

If raw data are not available, but data are in a grouped frequency distribution such as in Figure 4.1, interpolating within an interval is necessary if precision is desired. For example, in Figure 4.1 there will be $n/2 = 192/2 = 96$ observations below and above the median. From the cumulative frequency column in Figure 4.1, it can be seen that 100 persons fall within or below the 68″ interval; thus, the median for this set of scores falls within the interval for 68″, the exact limits of which extend from 67.5″ to 68.5″. Since 66 of the observations fall below the lower limit of the 68″ interval, $96 - 66 = 30$ more scores are needed to reach the median. Note that there are 34 scores within the 68″ interval; these are assumed to be spread evenly throughout the interval. Thus, 30/34th of the interval is needed to reach the median; $30/34 = .88$ or 88% of the width ($w$) of the interval is added to the lower limit of the interval that contains the median. Because the intervals have a width ($w$) of 1 inch, the median ($Md$) is .88 inch above the lower limit of the interval containing the median ($L_M$), that is, $Md = 67.50'' + .88'' = 68.38$ inches.

The procedure just illustrated for calculating the median from a grouped frequency distribution containing $n$ scores is expressed mathematically in Equation 4.1.

$$Md = L_M + w\left(\frac{n/2 - f_{cum}}{f_M}\right) \tag{4.1}$$

where $L_M$ is the lower limit of the interval that contains the median, $w$ is the width of the interval, $f_M$ is its frequency, and $f_{cum}$ is number of observations falling below this interval.

We have already found the median of the distribution of cholesterol values from the raw scores. However, Equation 4.1 will be used to illustrate the process of estimating the median when individual observations are not available, but data are in a grouped frequency distribution such as in Table 3.2 (Section 3.2). Since $n = 200$, and $n/2 = 100$, the median falls within the 260–279 interval. There are 70 scores below the 260–279 interval, hence $f_{\text{cum}} = 70$, $L_{\text{M}} = 259.5$, $f_{\text{M}} = 35$, and $w = 20$. Substituting the values into Equation 4.1: $Md = 259.5 + 20(100 - 70)/35 = 259.5 + 17.14 = 276.64$

As expected, the median estimated from the grouped data (276.6) is extremely close to the actual median (276) found from the raw scores. The median determined from an ungrouped frequency distribution should be used whenever possible; but occasionally, one must use Equation 4.1 when the individual observations are not available, as in Figure 4.1. Stem-and-leaf displays allow the median to be calculated quickly and accurately.

The median can be found for any set of data when a continuum underlies the scores and they can be ranked, that is, the numbers represent either an ordinal (Section 2.4), interval (Section 2.5), or ratio scale (Section 2.6) of measurement. If members of the U. S. Senate are rated on a liberal-conservative scale, the median would fall between the 50th and 51st rating.

The median can be estimated graphically from an ogive curve, as was previously illustrated in Section 3.8, using the ogive in Figure 3.6.

## 4.4 SUMMATION NOTATION

Before expressing the formula for obtaining the mean, it is useful to be familiar with summation notation. The summation symbol, $\Sigma$, is the capital Greek letter *sigma*.[3] The symbol for the summation operator, $\Sigma$, is just a concise way of saying "the sum of." A set of $n$ scores or numbers is represented as: $X_1, X_2, \ldots, X_n$. A general way of representing any of the $n$ scores is $X_i$, read as "X sub i", where $i$ can have any value between 1 and $n$. The ordering of the subscripts is usually completely arbitrary: $X_1$ simply designates the first score, not necessarily the highest or lowest score; $X_2$ denotes the second score in the set, and so forth. If there are five numbers in the group, $n = 5$ and $X_1 + X_2 + X_3 + X_4 + X_5 = \Sigma X_i$, the sum of the $n$ scores. Using summation notation, one can denote this sum explicitly as $\Sigma_{i=1}^{n} X_i$, which is read "the sum of $X_i$ as $i$ runs from 1 to $n$". $\Sigma_{i=1}^{n} X_i = X_1 + X_2 + \ldots + X_n$.

In almost all instances in this book, the summation includes all $n$ values of $X_i$. Hence, the lowest value of $i = 1$ and the highest value of $n$ are implicit and will be eliminated from

[3]In the next chapter, we will become familiar with the lower case sigma, $\sigma$, which denotes the standard deviation of a population.

the summation sign, unless they are needed to avoid ambiguity, that is, $\Sigma_{i=1}^{n} X_i = \Sigma_i X_i = \Sigma X_i$, or even $\Sigma X$ if there is no ambiguity. Thus,[4]

$$\sum_i X_i = X_1 + X_2 + \ldots + X_n \qquad \textbf{(4.2)}$$

## 4.5 THE MEAN

You probably learned to compute the *average* or *mean* of a set of numbers while you were in elementary school. The mean, or more explicitly the arithmetic mean,[5] of a set of observations is simply their sum, $\Sigma X_i$, divided by the number of observations, $n$.

$$\overline{X} = \frac{\sum_i X_i}{n} \qquad \textbf{(4.3)}$$

Unfortunately, in nontechnical communication the word "average" is sometimes used when referring to the median. To avoid ambiguity, use the term "mean" rather than "average." The common symbol for the mean of a sample of scores is $\overline{X}$. The bar above $X$ denotes the mean of the sample. For example, if $X_1 = 40$, $X_2 = 45$, and $X_3 = 65$, then the sum of the $n = 3$ scores is: $\Sigma_i X_i = 40 + 45 + 65 = 150$; using Equation 4.3, $\overline{X} = 150/3 = 50$. The sum of the $n = 192$ $X_i$'s in Figure 4.1 is 13,141, thus $\overline{X} = 13{,}141/192 = 68.44$.

It is apparent that the concepts of mean and median are usually meaningless with categorical variables (nominal scales) such as college major or nationality. The question "What is the mean or median occupation in the United States?" makes no sense. As previously noted, the mode has meaning even with categorical variables (see Section 2.3).

## 4.6 MORE SUMMATION NOTATION

Before certain properties of the mean are discussed, it will be helpful to illustrate certain properties of expressions involving summation. At times, we need to do something to a set of numbers before they are summed. Suppose each of $n$ numbers is multiplied by 2 and then these $n$ products are summed. The desired sum will be $2X_1 + 2X_2 + \ldots + 2X_n$. This sum is the same as $2(X_1 + X_2 + \ldots + X_n)$. Using summation notation, $(X_1 + X_2 + \ldots + X_n)$ can be replaced by $\Sigma X_i$ (see Equation 4.2). The result can be summarized as follows:

$$2X_i + 2X_2 + \ldots + 2X_n = \sum_i 2X_i = 2\sum_i X_i$$

This result did not come about because of any special property of the number 2; if $c$ stands for any constant number (i.e., a number that does not change regardless of $i$), then:

[4] It is conventional to locate the lower and upper limits for the summation just below and above the summation sign respectively. However, when the limits occur in the text, they will be positioned to the immediate right of the summation sign to improve legibility.

[5] Since the term *mean*, without a modifier, always denotes the arithmetic mean, when the term "mean" is used, "arithmetic mean" is implicit. It should be noted, however, that there are other means that have occasional uses in applied statistics, for example, the harmonic mean $[HM = n/(\Sigma_i 1/X_i)]$, and the geometric mean $[GM = n/\sqrt{(X_1)(X_2)\ldots(X_n)}]$. Because these have limited application, they are not included in this textbook.

$$cX_1 + cX_2 + \ldots + cX_n = \sum_i cX_i = c\sum_i X_i \qquad \textbf{(Rule 1) (4.4)}$$

If the constant $c$ is to be added to each of $n$ numbers, one writes $X_1 + c, X_2 + c, \ldots, X_n + c$. The sum of these $n$ new numbers is:

$$(X_1 + c) + (X_2 + c) + \ldots + (X_n + c) = \sum_i (X_i + c)$$

The order in which numbers are added is inconsequential; hence, numbers can always be regrouped in any order for adding:

$$\sum_i (X_i + c) = (X_1 + X_2 + \ldots + X_n) + (c + c + \ldots + c)$$

The first sum in parentheses on the right-hand side above is $\Sigma X_i$. The second sum equals $nc$, consequently:

$$\sum_i (X_i + c) = \sum_i X_i + \sum_i c = \sum_i X_i + nc \qquad \textbf{(Rule 2) (4.5)}$$

Observe from Equation 4.3 that:

$$\overline{X} = \frac{1}{n}(X_1 + X_2 + \ldots + X_n) = \frac{1}{n}\sum_i X_i$$

## 4.7 ADDING OR SUBTRACTING A CONSTANT

What would happen to the value of the mean if a constant were added to each of the $n$ scores? What would happen to the mean of the distribution: 60, 64, 70, 75, 76, if we give a bonus of 5 points to each of the five scores? The scores in the augmented distribution become: 65, 69, 75, 80, 81, and the new mean is 370/5 = 74.0. It is no coincidence that the new mean is 5 points greater than the original mean of 69.

If a constant $c$ is added to each score in a distribution that has a mean of $\overline{X}$, the mean of the revised scores will have a mean[6] of $\overline{X} + c$. Obviously, the pattern holds if a constant $c$ is subtracted from each of the $n$ scores; the mean of the augmented distribution is $\overline{X} - c$.

## 4.8 MULTIPLYING OR DIVIDING BY A CONSTANT

If each score in a distribution having a mean of $\overline{X}$ is multiplied by a constant, $c$, $(cX_1 + cX_2 + \ldots + cX_n)$, the mean of the set of augmented scores is $c\overline{X}$:

[6]Proof: $\frac{1}{n}\sum_i (X_i + c) = \frac{1}{n}\sum_i X_i + \frac{1}{n}\sum_i c = \overline{X} + \frac{1}{n}nc = \overline{X} + c$

$$\frac{\sum_i cX_i}{n} = \frac{c\sum_i X_i}{n} = c\overline{X}$$

Recall that dividing by $c$ is equivalent to multiplying by $1/c$. Thus, if every observation in a distribution is divided by $c$, the mean of the augmented distribution is $(1/c)(\overline{X}) = \overline{X}/c$.

## 4.9 SUM OF DEVIATIONS

If $\overline{X}$ is subtracted from the score $(X_i - \overline{X})$, the resulting difference $(x_i)$ is a *deviation* or *deviation score*:

$$x_i = X_i - \overline{X} \quad \textbf{(4.6)}$$

Obviously, the value of $x_i$ is positive for scores that are larger than the mean, and negative for $X_i$'s below $\overline{X}$. If one were to find the deviation for each of the $n$ scores in the set, the sum of the $n$ deviation scores would be exactly zero.[7] This will be illustrated using the distribution of five scores (60, 64, 70, 75, 76) given in Section 4.7. The mean is 69; the deviations are $x_1 = 60 - 69 = -9$, $x_2 = -5$, $x_3 = 1$, $x_4 = 6$, $x_5 = 7$; the sum of the deviations equals $\Sigma_i x_i = (-9) + (-5) + 1 + 6 + 7 = 0$.

## 4.10 SUM OF SQUARED DEVIATIONS

A fourth property of the mean concerns the $n$ deviation scores. The *sum of the squared deviations* of scores from their mean is less than the sum of the squared deviations from any other point. For example, if one found the difference between each score and the median, squared these differences, then summed them, the value of the sum would be larger than if deviations defined by Equation 4.6 were used. For example, if we squared the five $x_i$'s given in Section 4.9, we obtain $(-9)^2 + (-5)^2 + (1)^2 + (6)^2 + (7)^2 = 81 + 25 + 1 + 36 + 49 = 192$. Contrast this with the squared deviations of each of the five scores from the median (70) which equal $(-10)^2 + (-6)^2 + (0)^2 + (5)^2 + (6)^2 = 100 + 36 + 0 + 25 + 36 = 197$; $197 > 192$. This property of the mean (that the sum of the squared deviations are less from the mean than from any other point) illustrates the *least squares criterion*, a criterion that is widely used in the derivation of many important statistical techniques.

It is interesting to note that although the sum of the deviations from the mean is 0, and the sum of the squared deviations is least from the mean, the sum of the *absolute* deviations[8] is least from the median. Note that for our five scores the sum of the absolute values of the deviations from the median is $10 + 6 + 0 + 5 + 6 = 27$, which is less than if the scores are deviated from the mean $(9 + 5 + 1 + 6 + 7 = 28)$.

---

[7] Proof that the sum of the deviation scores, $\Sigma_i x_i$, is zero:

$$\sum_i x_i = \sum_i (X_i - \overline{X}) = \sum_i X_i - \sum_i \overline{X} = \sum_i X_i - n\overline{X} = \sum_i X_i - n\frac{\sum_i X_i}{n} = \sum_i X_i - \sum_i X_i = 0$$

[8] Recall that the absolute value of any number is positive (the sign is disregarded); thus, the absolute value of –9, written as |–9| is 9.

## 4.11 THE MEAN OF THE SUM OF TWO OR MORE SCORES

Later chapters use a composite variable created by adding two or more variables for each of the $n$ subjects. Suppose $K$ scores are obtained for each of the $n$ persons in a sample, and the $K$ scores are summed to form a composite, or total score. The *mean of a sum* is simply the sum of the $K$ means, as defined in Equation 4.7:

$$\overline{X}_{1+2+\ldots+K} = \overline{X}_1 + \overline{X}_2 + \cdots + \overline{X}_K = \Sigma_k \overline{X}_k \quad \textbf{(4.7)}$$

If the means of two midterm examinations are $\overline{X}_1 = 40$ and $\overline{X}_2 = 45$, and the mean of the final examination is $\overline{X}_3 = 65$, what is the mean of the total scores, $\overline{X}_{1+2+3}$? From Equation 4.7:

$$\overline{X}_{1+2+3} = \overline{X}_1 + \overline{X}_2 + \overline{X}_3 = 40 + 45 + 65 = 150$$

## 4.12 THE MEAN OF A DIFFERENCE

Suppose a gain score (i.e., the difference between two scores) is found for each of the $n$ persons in a sample by subtracting one score from the other. For example, if $X_1$ is a pretest and $X_2$ is a posttest, the gain can be found by subtracting the pretest from the posttest for each of the $n$ pairs of scores. What is the mean gain, $\overline{X}_{2-1}$? Your intuition is correct, the mean gain is simply the difference in the two means, $\overline{X}_2 - \overline{X}_1$, as denoted in Equation 4.8:

$$\overline{X}_{2-1} = \overline{X}_2 - \overline{X}_1 \quad \textbf{(4.8)}$$

If the mean IQ score on the pretest is 97 and the mean of the posttest is 104, the mean difference, $\overline{X}_{2-1}$, is 7 points.

## 4.13 MEAN, MEDIAN, AND MODE OF TWO OR MORE GROUPS COMBINED

Suppose the means, medians, and modes of scores from two or more different samples are known and one wishes to find the mean, median, and mode for the aggregated data.[9] This is a simple matter in the case of the mean; but for the median and mode, it is necessary to construct a combined distribution, aggregating the data from the $J$ groups. The ease with

[9]Note that the mean of the aggregate of two or more samples (Section 4.13) is different from the mean of the sum of two scores on the same group of persons ($\overline{X}_{1+2} = \overline{X}_1 + \overline{X}_2$ in Section 4.11). In Section 4.11, a composite score for each of the $n$ subjects is formed. In Section 4.13, $n_2$ additional subjects are added to the $n_1$ subjects in the distribution to form a distribution of $n_{\bullet} = n_1 + n_2$ subjects.

which the mean of the combined groups is found reveals an advantage of summary statistics defined in terms of simple algebraic operations, such as adding and dividing, and having every score in a group included in the calculation of the statistic. The median and mode are found by the operations of counting and ranking. The means and $n$'s for $J = 3$ sixth-grade classes on a standardized reading test were:

$$\text{Class 1: } \bar{X}_1 = 6.91 \quad n_1 = 24$$

$$\text{Class 2: } \bar{X}_2 = 7.72 \quad n_2 = 33$$

$$\text{Class 3: } \bar{X}_3 = 6.75 \quad n_3 = 27$$

The total number of scores from all three groups combined ($n_{\bullet}$) is equal to $n_1 + n_2 + n_3 = 24 + 33 + 27 = 84$ (i.e., $n_{\bullet} = \Sigma_j n_j = n_1 + n_2 + \ldots + n_J$). The *grand mean* of the combined groups ($\bar{X}_{\bullet}$) is simply the sum of the 84 scores divided by 84 ($n_{\bullet}$). The combined group mean is *not* the average of the three group means (unless $n_1 = n_2 = n_3$). Rearranging Equation 4.3 shows that the sum of the scores in a group is simply $\Sigma_i X_i = n\bar{X}$. For example, the sum of the scores in class 1 is (24)(6.91) = 165.84. Similarly, for classes 2 and 3, the sums are (33)(7.72) = 254.76 and (27)(6.75) = 182.25, respectively. The sum of all scores for all three groups, $\Sigma_j \Sigma_i X_{ij}$, is: 165.84 + 254.76 + 182.25 = 602.85. Thus, the grand mean, $\bar{X}_{\bullet}$, of the three classes is 602.85/84 = 7.18.

The general equation for the grand mean that results from aggregating the data from the $J$ groups is expressed in Equation 4.9:

$$\bar{X}_{\bullet} = \frac{(n_1\bar{X}_1 + n_2\bar{X}_2 + \ldots + n_J\bar{X}_J)}{n_{\bullet}} = \frac{\sum_i n_j\bar{X}_j}{n_{\bullet}} \qquad \textbf{(4.9)}$$

Hence, if there are four groups ($J = 4$) to be combined, Equation 4.9 becomes:

$$\bar{X}_{\bullet} = \frac{n_1\bar{X}_1 + n_2\bar{X}_2 + n_3\bar{X}_3 + n_4\bar{X}_4}{n_{\bullet}}$$

If each of the $J$ groups has the same number of scores ($n_1 = n_2 = n_3 = n_4 = n$), the denominator becomes $4n$; the $n$ in the numerator and denominator cancel, and Equation 4.9 becomes:

$$\bar{X}_{\bullet} = \frac{\not{n}(\bar{X}_1 + \bar{X}_2 + \bar{X}_3 + \bar{X}_4)}{4\not{n}} = \frac{(\bar{X}_1 + \bar{X}_2 + \bar{X}_3 + \bar{X}_4)}{4}$$

This confirms the intuitive notion that if the $J$ groups are the same size, the mean of the aggregate, $X_1 + X_2 + X_3 + X_4$, is the same as the unweighted average of the four means, $\bar{X}_1 + \bar{X}_2 + \bar{X}_3 + \bar{X}_4$.

Finding the median or the mode of the *combined distribution* formed by aggregating $J$ groups is less straightforward. For both the mode and median, the original data must be available before these measures of central tendency on the aggregate can be found.

## 4.14 INTERPRETATION OF MODE, MEDIAN, AND MEAN

Each measure of central tendency is best in certain circumstances. The sense in which the mode is the most representative score is straightforward. More persons score at the mode than at any other score. The median divides the entire set into halves; $n/2$ observations are below the median, and $n/2$ observations are above the median. Suppose that the scores 1, 3, 6, 7, and 8 are placed along a number line (i.e., marked on a ruler):

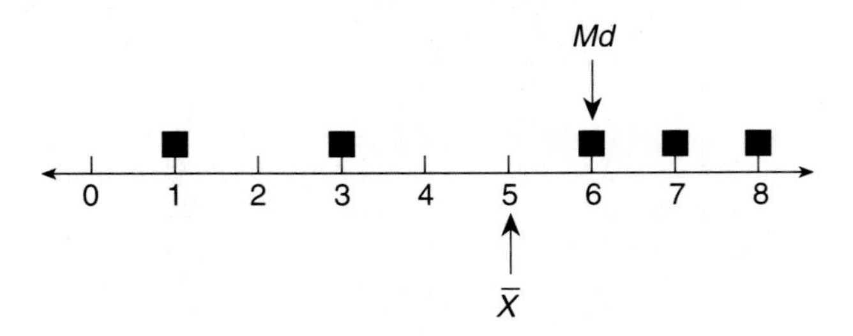


The median of the set of scores is 6. The *median of a group of scores* is that point on the number line such that the sum of the distances of all scores in the group to that point is smaller than the sum of distances to any other point. If the median is substituted for every score in the group, less average error results than if the mean, mode, or any other value is used as the reference point, where *error* is defined as the absolute distance of each score from the reference point.

The mean is the center of gravity of a distribution. If the frequencies are viewed as uniform boxes and the number line as a seesaw, the mean is that point at which the seesaw would be balanced. The *mean of a group of scores* is that point on the number line such that the sum of the squared distances of all scores to that point is smaller than the sum of the squared distances to any other point. If the mean is used to represent every score in the distribution, the sum of the squared errors that result is at a minimum. This is termed the *least-squares criterion* in statistics: The sum of squared deviations of scores from a point is least about the mean than about any other point (see Section 4.10). The mean can be described as the least-squares measure of central tendency.[10]

## 4.15 CENTRAL TENDENCY AND SKEWNESS

In *unimodal, symmetric distributions*, such as the normal curve in Figure 4.2A, the *mean* ($\bar{X}$), *median* (*Md*), and *mode* (and the other measures of central tendency mentioned in this chapter) *will be equal*. For example, the mean IQ is 100, the median IQ is 100, and the mode IQ score is 100. In symmetric distributions, such as in Figures 4.2B and 4.2C, the mean and

[10]Certain other *midsummary* measures of central tendency are occasionally used, especially for exploratory data analyses (Tukey, 1977): *Midrange* = $(X_{max} + X_{min})/2$, *Midhinge* = $(Q_1 + Q_3)/2$, and *Trimean* = $(Q_1 + 2Md + Q_3)/4$. The midhinge is the middle of the box in box-and-whisker plots (Section 3.9). In distributions that are approximately symmetrical, the values of the various measures of central tendency will have quite similar values.

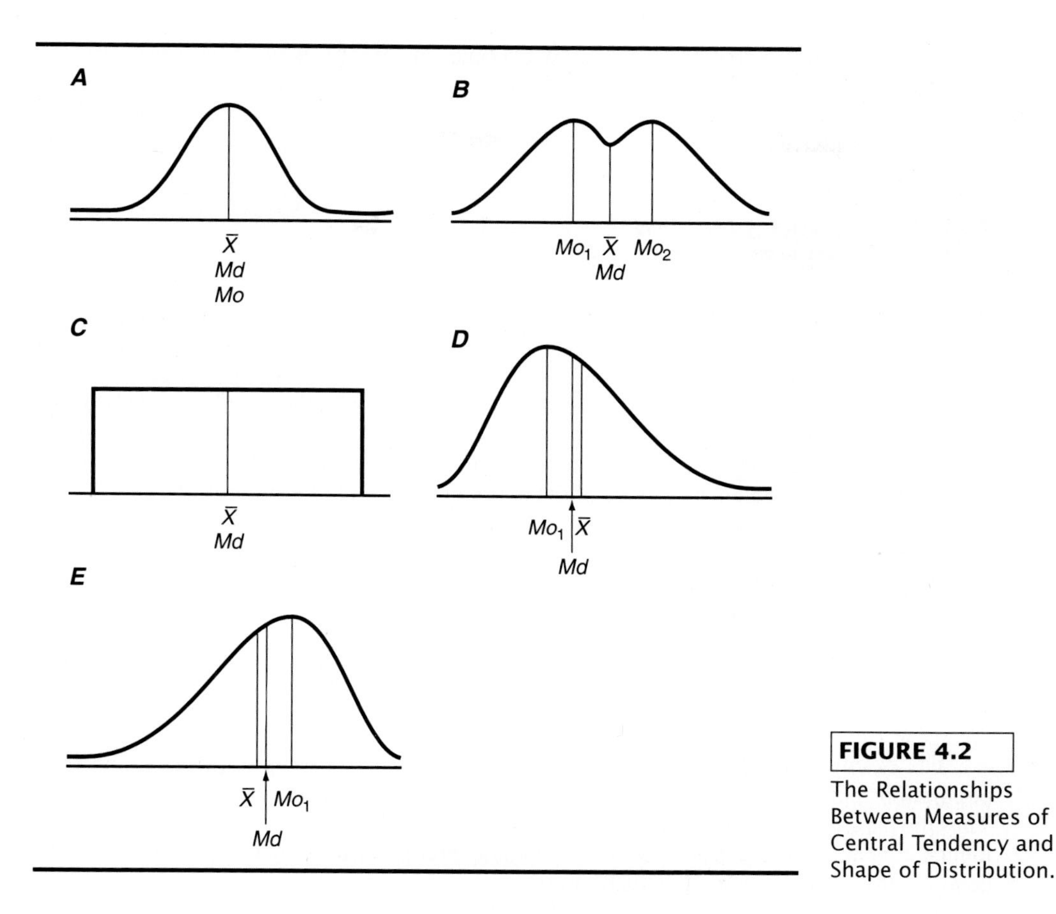


**FIGURE 4.2**
The Relationships Between Measures of Central Tendency and Shape of Distribution.

median will be the same. Note that a true rectangular distribution, such as Figure 4.2C, has no mode; Figure 4.2B, however, has two modes; it is a *bimodal* distribution.

In skewed distributions like Figures 4.2D and 4.2E, the mean is *pulled* toward the *tail*. Consequently, in a positively skewed distribution, the mean has a larger value than either the median or the mode. The mean is less than the median or the mode in a distribution that is negatively skewed. In skewed distributions, the median falls between the mean and mode—usually closer to the mean than to the mode. With unimodal curves of moderate asymmetry, the distance from the median to the mode is approximately twice that of the distance between the median and the mean. The following equation can be used to obtain an estimate of the mode, median, or mean when the other two measures are known.

$$Mode \approx 3(Median) - 2(Mean) \quad \textbf{(4.10)}$$

Using Equation 4.10, if the median is 104 and the mean is 106, confirm that the mode would be estimated to be 100; 3(104) – 2(106) = 100.

Notice the notion that 50% are below average (the mean), is *not* necessarily true. In distributions that are severely positively skewed, there can be 70%, or even more,[11] of the scores below average! Of course, with negatively skewed distributions more than half the scores will be above average.

## 4.16 MEASURES OF CENTRAL TENDENCY AS INFERENTIAL STATISTICS

When the data represent a sample of observations from the population to which one wishes to generalize, the data for the sample are inferential statistics (Section 1.3). When used inferentially, the measures of central tendency based on a random sample of observations are estimates of the corresponding values, called *parameters*, in the population. If 100 faculty members were randomly sampled from the entire population of 1,000 at State University, would the mean, median, and mode age of the 100 faculty members be precisely the same as the mean, median, and mode of the entire population? The symbol, $\overline{X}$, denotes the mean of a sample; $\overline{X}$ is used to estimate the mean of the population, $\mu$ (the lower case Greek letter, "mū"). Intuitively, one realizes that the value for the sample would rarely precisely equal that for the population. The difference between a statistic and the parameter being estimated by that statistic is *sampling error.*

$$\text{Sampling error} = \text{Statistic} - \text{Parameter} \quad \textbf{(4.11)}$$

For example, sampling error is the difference between a sample mean, $\overline{X}$, and the population mean, $\mu$. In inferential statistics, lower case Greek letters denote parameters. Thus the parameter, $\mu$, is estimated by the inferential statistic, $\overline{X}$. Sampling error is a fundamental concept in inferential statistics; an understanding of sampling is crucial for comprehending any application of statistical inference.

Why is the mean used so much more frequently in behavioral research than the median, or the mode, even though the median is usually a better descriptive measure of central tendency, especially if distributions are skewed? The principal reason for the dominance of the mean is that sampling error tends to be smaller for the sample mean than for the sample median; the mode tends to have more sampling error than either the mean or the median. In other words, the difference between the statistic, $\overline{X}$, and the parameter, $\mu$, is usually less than that for the sample median and the population median, which is less than the sampling error for the mode. Stated differently, as an inferential statistic, the mean has greater precision than the median, which is more precise than the mode. To obtain the same degree of precision for the median that $\overline{X}$ possesses for estimating $\mu$ with a sample of $n$ observations, the sample size would need to be increased by more than 50%.[12]

In practice, the issue of precision has carried too much weight in the choice of statisti-

---

[11]Actually, it is mathematically possible for every score except one to be below, or above, average. For example, if the variable being measured is days-spent-in-jail, and only one of your classmates has had this experience, then all classmates except one would fall below the average!

[12]In Chapter 10, we shall see that when the distribution is normal and $n$ is large, the sample median requires a sample size of $1.57n$ or 57% larger in order to have the same sampling error as that associated with $\overline{X}$ for a sample size of $n$.

cal measures. The measure that is the most useful for the intended purpose should be used. Medians are rarely compared in inferential statistics. Almost always, only means are compared because of the inertia of precedent, rather than a thoughtful examination of what information is useful.

## 4.17 WHICH MEASURE IS BEST?

It is apparent that there is no single answer to the question of which measure is best. If the variable under consideration represents only a nominal scale (e.g., political affiliation, college major, medical diagnosis, or occupation), there is no choice; only the mode is appropriate.

The mean lends itself more readily to further statistical treatment than the other two measures of central tendency, but it lies far from the bulk of scores in extremely skewed distributions. Perhaps 60% of American families have an annual income less than the nationwide average when the average is defined as the mean. Hence, the median is usually the preferred descriptive measure with skewed distributions.

## 4.18 CHAPTER SUMMARY

There are three common measures of central tendency. The mean is the most widely used, the most precise for inferential purposes, and is the foundation for statistical concepts that will be introduced in subsequent chapters. The mean is the ratio of the sum of the observations to the number of observations. The value of the mean is influenced by the value of every score in a distribution. Consequently, in skewed distributions the mean is "drawn" toward the elongated tail more than is the median or mode. For estimating $\mu$, the mean of the sample, $\overline{X}$, is more precise (has less sampling error) than the sample median.

The median is the 50th percentile of a distribution. It is the point in a distribution from which the sum of the absolute differences of all $n$ scores is at a minimum. If these differences were squared, however, the sum would be least about the mean, not the median. Hence, the mean is said to be the measure of central tendency that satisfies the least-squares criterion. In perfectly symmetrical distributions, the median and mean have the same value. When the mean and median differ greatly, the median is usually the most meaningful measure of central tendency for descriptive purposes. The mode, unlike the mean and median, has descriptive meaning even with nominal scales. The mode is the most frequently occurring observation. When the median is applicable, the mode is the least useful measure of central tendency, especially for inferential purposes. In symmetric unimodal distributions, the mode, median, and mean have the same value.

## 4.19 CASE STUDY

Measures of central tendency for the cholesterol study are given in Table 4.1.[13] (ID #, a perfectly rectangular distribution, is included as a variable just for practice.) Note for

[13] SPSS output from FREQUENCIES procedure.

**TABLE 4.1** Descriptive Information for Case Study Variables ($n = 200$)

| *Variable* | *Mean* | *Median* | *Mode* | $X_{min}$ | $Q_1$ | $Q_3$ | $X_{max}$ | *Range* |
|---|---|---|---|---|---|---|---|---|
| Age | 42.6 | 42 | 40 | 23 | 33 | 52 | 70 | 53 |
| Systolic B.P. (SBP) | 121.6 | 120 | 110 | 90 | 110 | 130 | 190 | 100 |
| Diastolic B.P. (DBP) | 81.6 | 80 | 80 | 55 | 75 | 90 | 112 | 57 |
| Cholesterol Level | 285.1 | 276 | 264 | 135 | 245 | 332 | 520 | 385 |
| Height (in.) | 68.6 | 68 | 67 | 62 | 67 | 70 | 74 | 12 |
| Weight (lbs.) | 165.2 | 163 | 141 | 109 | 147 | 180 | 262 | 153 |
| Coronary? (0 = N, 1 = Y) | .125 | 0 | 0 | 0 | 0 | 0 | 1 | 1 |
| ID # | 100.5 | 100.5 | — | 1 | 50.5 | 150.5 | 200 | 199 |

certain variables (especially Age, DBP, and Height) that the means, medians, and modes differ by only a small amount; this suggests that these variables are not highly skewed. For certain other variables (SBP, Cholesterol Level, and Weight) the modes differ substantially from the means and medians. These modes were determined by the computer and are based on an ungrouped frequency distribution (i.e., $w = 1$); modes are not very stable when the range of scores is large. Unless the number of scores ($n$) is at least twice as large as the range ($X_{max} - X_{min}$), the mode is so unstable as to have little value. The modes for the Age, Height, and Coronary variables are meaningful because $n$/range > 2 for these variables. The mode found using Equation 4.10 (or crude mode [Section 4.2]) is a better estimate of the population mode.

The coarse rounding discussed in Section 3.3 robbed the SBP mode of meaning: Mode = $Q_1$ = 110! Could you use Equation 4.10 to estimate the mode for SBP if it had been measured more precisely? Note from Equation 4.10 that the difference "median – mode" tends to be twice the value of "mean – median." Since the mean (121.6) is 1.6 units greater than the median (120), the mode is predicted to be 2(1.6) = 3.2 less than the median, or approximately 116.8. Likewise, the mode weight of the population is closer to 158.6 lbs. than to the value of 141 lbs. found in Table 4.1. If the number of observations in a distribution is not at least twice the value of the range, it is probably best not to report a value for the mode.

Some degree of positive skewness ($\overline{X} > Mdn$) is suggested in Table 4.1 for all variables except ID, although the skewness is very slight with Age, DBP, and Height. This is confirmed by noting that the distance between $Q_1$ and $Mdn$ is less than the distance between $Mdn$ and $Q_3$. Note that the mean of a dichotomous variable coded 0 and 1 is the proportion of the sample that is in category 1; note also that quartiles have little value with dichotomous variables.

Research published in the behavioral sciences has tended to provide the reader with inadequate information about the distributions of the variables under study; typically, the only measure of central tendency reported is the mean, with no information on skewness (Hopkins & Weeks, 1990). There has been improvement in recent years, due primarily to the widespread availability of personal computers that produce graphs of good quality (like Figure 3.16).

## 4.20 SUGGESTED COMPUTER EXERCISE

Use spreadsheet or statistical software to find the mean, median, and mode of all continuous variables in the HSB data set.

## MASTERY TEST

*Questions 1 to 4 refer to the following distribution of observations of the variable X:*

1, 3, 6, 8, 9, 9, 10, 10, 10

1. What is the value of the mode?
2. What is the value of $n$? What is the median? (Do not use Equation 4.1.)
3. What is the value of $\Sigma_i X_i$? What is the value of the mean?
4. Describe the shape of the distribution.

*Questions 5 to 18 pertain to the three common measures of central tendency.*

5. Which requires only a nominal scale?
6. Which is the middle-most score?
7. Which is the point below and above which half the observations fall?
8. Which is influenced by the value of every observation?
9. Which two must be equal in a symmetrical distribution?
10. Will all three be equal in a normal distribution?
11. Which will have the largest value in a positively skewed distribution?
12. Which will have the largest value in a negatively skewed distribution?
13. Which of the three is neither the largest nor the smallest in skewed distributions?
14. Which lends itself best to other arithmetic operations?
15. Which is used most widely in inferential statistics?
16. Which can be estimated accurately from ogive curves?
17. Which is easily estimated from histograms or frequency polygons?
18. Which is equal to $P_{50}$ and $Q_2$?
19. Think of a distribution of scores for which the mean is 65.5, the median is 64, and the mode is 60. Suppose you later learn that one of the scores is in error. Instead of 70, the score should have been 90. Which measure of central tendency will certainly change?
20. If there were forty observations in the distribution in question 19, what would be the value for the mean after changing the score of 70 to 90?
21. If the mean salary for the ten female faculty members in a department is $45,000 and for the forty male faculty members is $50,000, what is the mean salary for all fifty faculty members?
22. If most students in your statistics class had read this chapter so carefully that they knew the answers to almost all questions on this Mastery Test, the scores would be expected to be

    (a) normally distributed.
    (b) skewed negatively.
    (c) skewed positively.
    (d) bimodal.
    (e) rectangular.

*For questions 23 and 24, assume the mean of Test 1 is 40 and the mean of Test 2 is 50, and n = 93.*

**23.** What is the mean of the sum of the two tests, $\overline{X}_{1+2}$?

**24.** What is the mean difference between the two tests, $\overline{X}_{2-1}$?

## PROBLEMS AND EXERCISES

**1.** Find the mean, median, and mode of the following set of scores:
1.2, 1.5, 1.7, 2.1, 2.4, 2.4, 2.7, 2.8, 3.0, 3.0, 3.0, 3.0, 3.1, 3.1, 3.4

**2.** Suppose the number 1.0 is added to each of the fifteen scores in the preceding problem. What will be the value of the mean and median of these fifteen augmented scores?

**3.** Suppose that each of the fifteen scores in the distribution in problem 1 is multiplied by 3. What would be the value of the mean and median of the resulting scores?

**4.** Find the median and estimate the mode of the 100 scores in the following grouped frequency distribution:

| *Interval* | *Frequency* |
|---|---|
| 45–49 | 8 |
| 40–44 | 12 |
| 35–39 | 40 |
| 30–34 | 26 |
| 25–29 | 10 |
| 20–24 | 4 |
| | $n = 100$ |

**5.** If the midpoint of each score interval in problem 4 is multiplied by its frequency, and these products are summed and divided by 100, a value of 35.50 results. Name this statistic.

**6.** Group A contains ten scores, the mean and median of which are 14.5 and 13, respectively. Group B contains twenty scores, the mean and median of which are 12.7 and 10, respectively. What is the mean of the thirty scores obtained from combining Groups A and B? Can the median of the combined groups be determined from the information given here?

**7.** During a recent decade, the mean income in the South increased 74% for whites and 113% for nonwhites. What was the mean increase for both groups combined? Among every 100 workers, 82 were white.

**8.** The seven members of the Sunday Afternoon Picnic Society live along a straight stretch of Highway 101. Their homes are positioned along the highway as shown below:

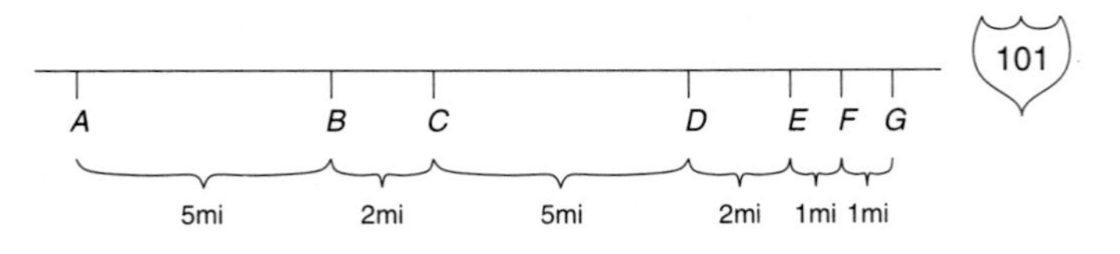


Since any point along Highway 101 is a fine place for a picnic, at which point along the road should the members hold their picnic so that the minimum amount of gasoline is used? The point represents which measure of central tendency?

## ANSWERS TO MASTERY TEST

1. 10
2. $n = 9$, $Md = 9$
3. $\Sigma_i X_i = 66$, $\overline{X} = 7.33$
4. skewed negatively
5. mode
6. median
7. median
8. mean
9. mean and median
10. yes
11. mean
12. mode
13. median
14. mean
15. mean
16. median
17. mode
18. median
19. mean
20. 66.0
21. $\overline{X}_{\bullet} = \$49{,}000$
22. (b)
23. 90
24. 10

## ANSWERS TO PROBLEMS AND EXERCISES

1. $\overline{X} = 2.56$; Median = 2.8; Mode = 3.0
2. $\overline{X} = 3.56$; Median = 3.8
3. $\overline{X} = 7.68$; Median = 8.4
4. Median = 35.75; Mode = 37
5. The mean
6. Mean = 13.3. No; combined median cannot be determined knowing only the group medians and $n$'s.
7. $\overline{X}_{.} = 81.02$ or 81%
8. Point D, the median

# 5

# MEASURES OF VARIABILITY

## 5.1 INTRODUCTION

The two most important statistical characteristics of any distribution of observations are its central tendency (Chapter 4) and its variability or heterogeneity (Chapter 5). Most empirical research in the social and behavioral sciences provides information on at least one measure of central tendency and at least one measure of variability or dispersion. Since measures of central tendency do not describe the extent of the differences among the $n$ scores, other statistical measures are needed to describe the degree of variation in the distribution of scores. In this chapter, the descriptive and inferential values of commonly used measures of variability are discussed—the range, the semi-interquartile range, the variance, and the standard deviation. The important distinctions between populations and samples and between parameters and statistics are also considered.

## 5.2 THE RANGE

The range is the difference between the largest ($X_{max}$) and the smallest ($X_{min}$) scores in a distribution. For example, in the distribution (10, 12, 13, 13, 15, 18), $X_{max}$ is 18 and $X_{min}$ is 10; hence, the range is $18 - 10 = 8$. The set of scores (–0.2, 0.4, 0.8, 1.6) has a range of $1.6 - (-0.2) = 1.8$.

Although the descriptive meaning of the range as a measure of variability is clear, it has certain drawbacks. Because the range is fixed by the values of just two scores, the differences among the remaining $n - 2$ scores are ignored. One aberrant score or *outlier* can greatly increase the range. Notice that each of the five distributions in Figure 3.5 (Section 3.6) has approximately the same range, yet the degree of dispersion within the five groups differs considerably. The range in a sample of scores has little value as an inferential statistic (i.e., as an estimate of the range in the population), as will become clear later in this chapter.

## 5.3 H-SPREAD AND THE INTERQUARTILE RANGE

In Section 3.9, the quartiles of a distribution of scores were discussed: The first quartile, $Q_1$, is the point on the scale below which 25% of the scores lie; it is the 25th percentile. $Q_2$ is the median or 50th percentile. The point below which 75% of the scores lie defines $Q_3$. The distance (range) between the first and third quartiles of a group of scores, that is, $Q_3 - Q_1$, is the *interquartile range*. A synonym for $Q_3 - Q_1$ is *H-spread* (Tukey, 1977), the distance between the lower hinge $Q_1$ and the upper hinge $Q_3$. The *semi-interquartile range, Q,* is half the distance between the third and first quartiles, that is,

$$Q = \frac{Q_3 - Q_1}{2} \qquad \textbf{(5.1)}$$

$Q$ can be a useful descriptive measure of variability. If two groups of scores have the same value of $Q$, they are likely to possess similar patterns of heterogeneity. In distributions that are not severely skewed, $Md \pm Q$ can be used to reconstruct the approximate score limits within which the center half of the scores fall.[1]

On most IQ tests, $Md \approx 100$ and $Q \approx 10$. Therefore, approximately 50% of persons have IQ scores that lie between $Md - Q = 100 - 10 = 90$ and $Md + Q = 100 + 10 = 110$. Obviously, if instead of the median, the *midhinge* $(Q_1 + Q_3)/2$ (Section 4.14) is used as the point of reference, then midhinge $\pm\ Q$ will reproduce the H-spread and will always contain the middle 50% of the $n$ scores. Like the range, the interquartile range and $Q$ have limited value as inferential statistics.

## 5.4 DEVIATION SCORES

Note that the range, the H-spread, and the semi-interquartile range do not involve every individual score in a group of scores. Most other measures of variability are influenced by the value of every score. Deviation scores, $x_i = X_i - \overline{X}$, obviously reflect something about the degree of variation in a set of scores. A set of scores with great heterogeneity will tend to have large deviation scores. Conversely, what would the deviation scores be if there was no variation in a distribution of scores, for example, 9, 9, 9, 9, ···, 9? The mean is 9; hence, every score would have a deviation of $9 - 9 = 0$.

## 5.5 SUM OF SQUARES

In any distribution, the sum of the deviation scores (Section 4.9) is always exactly zero: $\Sigma_i x_i = \Sigma_i(X_i - \overline{X}) = 0$. Thus, it cannot serve as a measure of variability, but the absolute values of the deviations can be summed and their mean (the average deviation $= \Sigma_i |x_i|/n$) can be determined. The average deviation is rarely used as a measure of variability because the process of taking absolute values often leads to intractable mathematics and limits its use for inferential purposes. Instead of working with the absolute values of deviation

---

[1] In Chapter 6, we will see that in a normal distribution $Q = .674\sigma$, or $\sigma \approx 1.5Q$. In other words, when a distribution is approximately normal, one can estimate $\sigma$ from $Q$, or vice versa.

scores, it is preferable to square each deviation (Section 4.10) and then sum the squared deviations to obtain the quantity *sum of squares*, $\Sigma_i x_i^2$. For a set of $n$ scores, the sum of squares[2] is:

$$\sum_i x_i^2 = \sum_i (X_i - \overline{X})^2 = (X_1 - \overline{X})^2 + (X_2 - \overline{X})^2 + \ldots + (X_n - \overline{X})^2 = x_i^2 + x_2^2 + \ldots + x_n^2 \quad \textbf{(5.2)}$$

## 5.6 MORE ABOUT THE SUMMATION OPERATOR, Σ

If the summation operation, $\Sigma$, is applied to a term that is raised to a power (e.g., $\Sigma_i x_i^2$), the summation follows the operation implicit in the exponent. If $x_1 = 3$, $x_2 = -1$, and $x_3 = -2$, then $\Sigma_i x_i^2 = (3)^2 + (-1)^2 + (-2)^2 = 14$. Note that $\Sigma_i x_i^2 \neq (\Sigma_i x_i)^2$; the quantity $(\Sigma_i x_i)^2$ equals 0.

A common expression in statistical analysis is:[3]

$$\sum_i (X_i + c)^2 = (X_1 + c)^2 + (X_2 + c)^2 + \ldots + (X_n + c)^2$$

Now $(X_i + c)^2 = (X_i + c)(X_i + c)$, which equals $(X_i^2 + 2cX_i + c^2)$. The expression within the parentheses may be written $n$ times as follows:

$$X_1^2 + 2cX_1 + c^2$$

$$X_2^2 + 2cX_2 + c^2$$

$$\vdots \quad \vdots$$

$$X_n^2 + 2cX_n + c^2$$

What is the sum of the first column? It is $X_1^2 + X_2^2 + \ldots + X_n^2 = \Sigma_i X_i^2$. And the second column sums to $2cX_1 + 2cX_2 + \ldots + 2cX_n = 2c(X_1 + X_2 + \ldots + X_n)$, which may be written concisely as $2c\Sigma_i X_i$. The sum of the third column is $c^2 + c^2 + \ldots + c^2 = nc^2$. Putting together these three column sums gives:

$$\sum_i (X_i + c)^2 = \sum_i X_i^2 + 2c \sum_i X_i + nc^2 \quad \textbf{(5.3)}$$

---

[2]There are several alternative formulas for computing sum of squares. Before the wide availability of hand calculators, certain formulas facilitated the computation of sum of squares by hand. The sum of squares is easy to calculate when the mean is a whole number. Without a hand calculator, however, the computation of $\Sigma_i x_i^2$ using Equation 5.2 is tedious. A formula for sum of squares that uses raw scores ($X_i$) instead of deviations ($x_i$) is useful if hand computation is necessary (See Glass & Hopkins, 1984, pp. 50–51 for derivation.): $\Sigma_i x_i^2 = \Sigma_i (X_i - \overline{X})^2 = \Sigma_i X_i^2 - 2n\overline{X}^2 + n\overline{X}^2 = \Sigma_i X_i^2 - n\overline{X}^2$.

[3]If your algebra is rusty, you may have difficulty following the algebraic progression; if so, trust us that the mathematics is correct. We would not mislead you.

Though it is correct to proceed in this way, by writing each individual expression and summing columns, it is not necessary. Instead, one can "distribute the summation sign" before each term, as follows, and secure the same result more directly:

$$\begin{aligned}\sum_i (X_i + c)^2 &= \sum_i (X_i^2 + 2cX_i + c^2)\\ &= \sum_i X_i^2 + \sum_i 2cX_i + \sum_i c^2\\ &= \sum_i X_i^2 + 2c\sum_i X_i + nc^2\end{aligned}$$

Note carefully that the summation sign was placed in front of each of the three terms *after* squaring.

## 5.7 THE VARIANCE OF A POPULATION

When a distribution contains all $N$ observations in the population, the variance $\sigma^2$ (the lower case Greek letter sigma) of that set of observations is the mean of the squared deviation scores as defined by Equation 5.4. (Indeed, *mean square* is a synonym for variance.)

$$\sigma^2 = \frac{\sum_i x_i^2}{N} = \frac{\sum_i (X_i - \mu)^2}{N} \qquad \textbf{(5.4)}$$

In other words, Equation 5.4 shows that the variance in a population of observations is equal to the sum of the squared deviations from the population mean (see Section 4.16) divided by $N$, the total number of observations in the population.

## 5.8 THE VARIANCE ESTIMATED FROM A SAMPLE

An observed set of scores rarely contains all the $N$ observations in the population. Equation 5.4 should not be used when one is working with a sample of $n$ observations, but only when using the entire population of $N$ observations. If one has IQ scores from a random sample of 100 persons, the symbol for the mean of the 100 observations is the statistic, $\overline{X}$, and not the parameter, $\mu$. Obviously, there will be some sampling error in the random process of selecting the sample of 100 persons that would cause the sample mean, $\overline{X}$, to differ somewhat from the parameter, $\mu$. One would not be surprised if $\overline{X}$ were not precisely 100.00 even though $\mu$ is 100.00.

The numerical value of the sum of squares will differ somewhat, depending on whether $\overline{X}$ or $\mu$ is used as the point of reference for deviation scores. In Chapter 4, you learned that the sum of the squared deviations is less from the mean than from any other point. Hence, in a sample of scores, the value of $\Sigma_i(X_i - \overline{X})^2$ will be less than the value of $\Sigma_i(X_i - \mu)^2$, (except in the rare event when $\overline{X}$ exactly equals $\mu$).

Ideally, an estimate of the population *variance* would be based on $\Sigma_i(X_i - \mu)^2$, but cannot be done because $\mu$ is not known. Using $\overline{X}$ to estimate the unknown parameter, $\mu$, causes the sum of squares to be less than it would if the $n$ deviations were from $\mu$. One can correct for this bias by dividing by a number somewhat less than $n$, but precisely how much less? Interestingly, the bias in estimating the variance in the population that accrues from deviating the $n$ $X_i$'s from the statistic $\overline{X}$ (rather than from the parameter $\mu$) is exactly compensated for by dividing the sum of squares, $\Sigma_i(X_i - \overline{X})^2$, by $n - 1$. (Compare Equation 5.4 with Equation 5.5.) The expression $n - 1$ is the *degrees of freedom* associated with the variance estimate. Throughout this book, the value of the degrees of freedom will be denoted by $\nu$ (the lowercase Greek letter nu, pronounced "new"). The estimate of the variance in the population, $s_X^2$ (or simply $s^2$ if there is no ambiguity), yielded by Equation 5.5 is an *unbiased* estimate of the parameter, $\sigma^2$. It is the ratio of the sum of squares in the sample data, $\Sigma_i(X_i - \overline{X})^2$, divided by the degrees of freedom, $\nu$:

$$s^2 = \frac{\sum_i (X_i - \overline{X})^2}{(n-1)} = \frac{\sum_i x_i^2}{\nu} \quad (5.5)$$

Although the variance has limited usefulness as a descriptive statistic, it has a very important place in inferential statistics.

### Calculating $s^2$

The calculation of the estimated population variance, $s^2$, will be illustrated using a sample of six scores selected randomly from the population.

| $X_i$ | $x_i = X_i - \overline{X}$ | $x_i^2$ | |
|---|---|---|---|
| 1 | $1 - 3 = -2$ | 4 | |
| 3 | $3 - 3 = 0$ | 0 | $\overline{X} = \frac{\sum_i X_i}{n} = \frac{18}{6} = 3.0$ |
| 3 | $3 - 3 = 0$ | 0 | |
| 0 | $0 - 3 = -3$ | 9 | $s^2 = \frac{\sum_i x_i^2}{\nu} = \frac{\sum_i x_i^2}{n-1} = \frac{30}{5} = 6.0$ |
| 4 | $4 - 3 = 1$ | 1 | |
| 7 | $7 - 3 = 4$ | 16 | |
| $\Sigma_i X_i = 18$ | | $\Sigma_i x_i^2 = 30$ | |

## 5.9 THE STANDARD DEVIATION

Notice that the metric (unit of measurement) for the variance is different from that of the original observations; if we are measuring standing height in inches, the unit of measurement (metric) for the variance is square inches. Consequently, it is not very useful as a descriptive measure, which sets the stage for a close relative of the variance, the standard deviation. The standard deviation, denoted as $\sigma$ to represent the parameter and $s$ for the sample estimate, is defined as the square root of the variance $\sigma^2$ (or $s^2$). If the variance estimate $s^2$ is 16, then $s = \sqrt{16} = 4$.

In the next chapter the standard deviation will be used extensively. Its meaning and interpretation are more fully developed there.[4]

## 5.10 THE EFFECT OF ADDING OR SUBTRACTING A CONSTANT ON MEASURES OF VARIABILITY

Recall from Section 4.7 that if a constant $c$ is added to each score in a distribution, then the mean of the augmented distribution is the mean of the original distribution $\overline{X}$, plus the constant $c$: $\overline{X} + c$. The deviation of the $i$th observation, $X_i$, in the augmented distribution then is:

$$(X_i + c) - (\overline{X} + c) = X_i + c - \overline{X} - c = X_i - \overline{X}$$

Thus, adding or subtracting a constant has no effect on the value of the deviation, $x_i$, for any score and hence does not change the value of the range, $Q$, the sum of squares, the variance, the standard deviation, or any other widely used measure of variability. Thus, the variability of the distribution (15, 18, 19) is the same as the variability of the distribution in which the constant 10 has been added to each score (25, 28, 29); or the same as that of the distribution that results when 5 is subtracted from each score (10, 13, 14). Recall that subtracting a constant is mathematically equivalent to adding a constant, $c$, where $c$ is a negative number.

## 5.11 THE EFFECT OF MULTIPLYING OR DIVIDING BY A CONSTANT ON MEASURES OF VARIABILITY

If each score in a distribution is multiplied by a constant, $c$, the mean of the transformed distribution is $c\overline{X}$ (see Section 4.8). The sum of squares of the new distribution, $cX_1$, $cX_2$, ..., $cX_n$, is $\Sigma_i(cX_i - c\overline{X})^2$. The constant $c$ can be factored out of the expression within the parentheses as follows:

$$\sum_i(cX_i - c\overline{X})^2 = \sum_i\left[c(X_i - \overline{X})\right]^2 = \sum_i c^2(X_i - \overline{X})^2 = c^2\sum_i(X_i - \overline{X})^2 = c^2\sum_i x_i^2$$

---

[4]The coefficient of variation ($CV$) is another measure of variability that can be useful if the observations represent a ratio scale (see Section 2.6). The $CV$ is the ratio of the standard deviation to the mean, expressed as a percent: $CV = 100\sigma/\mu$, estimated by $100s/\overline{X}$. Suppose we wish to compare the relative variability in the weights of females at one versus three years of age. At 12 months of age, $\sigma_1 \approx 2.23$ lbs. and $\mu_1 \approx 21.2$ lbs. [$CV_1 = 100(2.23)/21.2 = 10.5$], and at 36 months of age, $\sigma_2 \approx 3.19$ lbs. and $\mu_2 \approx 30.7$ lbs. [$CV_2 = 100(3.19)/30.7 = 10.4$]; the relative variability in weight is essentially the same at ages one and three. One could use coefficients of variation to determine whether humans are more variable in weight than they are in height since both measures represent ratio scales. (For an additional description, see Snedecor and Cochran, 1980, p. 37.)

Thus, the variance of the transformed distribution is the original variance, $s^2$, times the square of the constant, $c^2$. The variance of the distribution after the original scores have each been multiplied by $c$ is:

$$s_{cX}^2 = \frac{\text{(Sum of Squares)}}{\nu} = \frac{c^2 \sum_i x_i^2}{\nu} = c^2 s^2 \qquad \textbf{(5.6)}$$

For example, if $s = 4$ for a given distribution and if each score in that distribution is multiplied by $c = 3$, the variance of the augmented distribution (using Equation 5.6) is: $(3)^2(4)^2 = (9)(16) = 144$.

Since the standard deviation is the square root of the variance, the standard deviation of the transformed distribution in which each score has been multiplied by a constant is:

$$s_{cX} = \sqrt{c^2 s^2} = |c|\, s \qquad \textbf{(5.7)}$$

The vertical lines around $c$ in Equation 5.7 denote the absolute value of $c$. Consequently, the standard deviation of a distribution after it has been multiplied by $c$ is the same as when it is multiplied by $-c$; a distribution cannot have a negative standard deviation.

If each score in the distribution $X_1, X_2, \ldots, X_n$, is multiplied by $c = 1/s$, what is the standard deviation of the transformed distribution, $X_1/s,\ X_2/s, \ldots, X_n/s$? Since $c = 1/s$, then from Equation 5.7:

$$\sqrt{c^2 s^2} = \sqrt{\left(\frac{1}{s}\right)^2 s^2} = 1$$

These transformations (i.e., subtracting $\overline{X}$ and multiplying by $1/s$) will be used in the next chapter (Section 6.3). Recall that dividing by a constant, $c$, is equivalent to multiplying by the reciprocal of the constant, $1/c$ (see Section 4.8).

## 5.12 VARIANCE OF A COMBINED DISTRIBUTION[5]

In Chapter 4, the mean of a set of scores formed by combining scores from two separate samples was found to be a simple weighted average of the means of the two groups (see Equation 4.9). The computation of the variance for a combined distribution is more complicated. It will be seen that the variance of the entire set of scores formed by aggregating scores from groups 1 and 2 depends on the variances and means of the two groups. Notice that if the scores in group 1 are (3, 3, 3), and the scores in group 2 are (5, 5, 5), then the variance of the combined distribution (3, 3, 3, 5, 5, 5) is not zero even though $s_1^2 = 0$ and $s_2^2 = 0$.

The formula for obtaining the variance of a distribution that results from aggregating

---

[5]See Section 7.19 for equations for the variance of a sum; for the variance of a difference, see Section 7.20.

the data from $J$ samples is given by Equation 5.8. The combined distribution contains $n_{\bullet} = n_1 + n_2 + \ldots + n_J = \Sigma_j n_j$ scores.

$$s^2 = \frac{\sum_j v_j s_j^2 + \sum_j n_j(\overline{X}_j - \overline{X}_{\bullet})^2}{(n_{\bullet} - 1)} \tag{5.8}$$

The mean of the combined distribution, the grand mean, $\overline{X}_{\bullet}$, is given by Equation 4.9: $\overline{X}_{\bullet} = \Sigma_j n_j \overline{X}_j / n_{\bullet}$

Suppose that scores for a sample of ten females and a sample of twenty males are to be combined into a single distribution:

$$\overline{X}_1 = 50,\ s_1^2 = 36,\ n_1 = 10,\ v_1 = n_1 - 1 = 9$$

$$\overline{X}_2 = 41,\ s_2^2 = 30,\ n_2 = 20,\ v_2 = 19$$

Using Equation 5.8, the variance of the distribution after aggregating the data for the two samples is:

$$s^2 = \frac{v_1 s_1^2 + v_2 s_2^2 + n_1(\overline{X}_1 - \overline{X}_{\bullet})^2 + n_2(\overline{X}_2 - \overline{X}_{\bullet})^2}{n_{\bullet} - 1}$$

In the example:

$$n_{\bullet} = n_1 + n_2 = 10 + 20 = 30, \text{ and } \overline{X}_{\bullet} = \frac{(10)(50) + (20)(41)}{30} = 44$$

Substituting values into the equation:

$$s^2 = \frac{9(36) + (19)(30) + 10(50 - 44)^2 + 20(41 - 44)^2}{30 - 1} = 49.45$$

## 5.13 INFERENTIAL PROPERTIES OF THE RANGE, $s^2$, AND $s$

For each measure of variability (and for all other statistical measures as well), sampling error[6] decreases as the size of the sample, $n$, increases. This property is known as *consistency*. All widely used sample statistics have this property.

### Expected Values and Unbiasedness

The sample variance, $s^2$, is a measure of variability that has the very desirable statistical property of *unbiasedness*. Its value for a random sample of observations from the popula-

[6]Recall from Equation 4.11 that: Sampling error = statistic − parameter.

tion is an unbiased estimate of the variance of all observations in the population. In other words, the statistic, $s^2$, is an unbiased estimator of the parameter $\sigma^2$. An unbiased estimator is one for which the mean sampling error is 0, that is, overestimates and underestimates tend to balance out in the long run. An unbiased statistic tends to be neither larger nor smaller, on the average, than the parameter it estimates.

Statisticians say that if a statistic is unbiased, the *expected value* of the statistic is equal to the parameter it estimates. The expected value of a sample statistic is its long-run mean value across all possible samples from the population. For example, as shown by Equation 5.9, the expected value of the sample variance, $E(s^2)$, is equal to the variance in the population, $\sigma^2$; $s^2$ is said to be an unbiased estimator of $\sigma^2$.

$$E(s^2) = \sigma^2 \qquad \textbf{(5.9)}$$

Thus, the average of the sample variance over all possible samples of size $n$ from the population is exactly equal to the population variance, $\sigma^2$. This would not have been true if the sample variance had been defined in Equation 5.5 with $n$ instead of $\nu = n - 1$ in the denominator.

Recall from Chapter 4 that the mean possesses desirable inferential properties. The sample mean, $\overline{X}$, is an unbiased estimator of the population mean, $\mu$: $E(\overline{X}) = \mu$. Other things being equal, unbiased statistics are preferred in statistical inference.

Our intuition would tell us that if $E(s^2) = \sigma^2$, then $s$ should also be an unbiased estimator of $\sigma$. Surprisingly, square roots of unbiased statistics are not unbiased estimates of the square root of the related parameters, that is $E(s) \neq \sigma$. Fortunately, the bias in using $s$ as an estimator of $\sigma$ is negligible unless $n$ is very small. On the average, $s$ tends to underestimate $\sigma$, but the bias is very small—only 5% when $n = 6$, that is, $E(s) = .95\sigma$ when $n = 6$. The bias is only 1% when $n = 20$, that is, $E(s) = .99\sigma$. Since published research usually involves $n$'s larger than 20, the degree to which $s$ underestimates $\sigma$ is inconsequential, and the amount of bias can be disregarded for practical purposes.[7]

A serious shortcoming of the range as a measure of variability in the population is that its value is greatly influenced by the sample size. Since the range is determined by only the largest and smallest observations, other things being equal, the larger the sample, the larger the range. This is not true with unbiased statistics like $s^2$. The expression $E(s^2) = \sigma^2$ does not depend on $n$; the statement is true whatever the size of the sample. Note we are *not* saying that the estimate of the population variance is just as good from a small sample as from a large sample. There will be more sampling error when $n$ is small, but the mean sampling error for repeated random samples will be 0 whether $n$ is large or small.

Table 5.1 shows the influence of sample size on the expected value of the range, $s^2$, and $s$ in the sample. The comparison of the range with the expected value of $s^2$ and $s$ for the sample are given using $\sigma = 10$ as an example. Table 5.1 gives the range, $s^2$, and $s$ that would be expected in a random sample from the population where $\sigma = 10$ for sample sizes ranging from 2 to 1,000.

---

[7]The degree of bias for any sample size, $n$, can be found using the formula: The expected value of $\{1 + 1/[4(n - 1)]\}s = \sigma$ if $X$ is normally distributed. The formula can be used to obtain an unbiased estimate of $\sigma$ for $s$ if $n$ is known. A graphic representation of the degree of bias with respect to $n$ is given by Hopkins, Glass, and Hopkins (1987, p. 42).

**TABLE 5.1** The Expected Values of the Range, $s^2$, and $s$ as a Function of Sample Size of $n$ Observations from a Random Sample from a Normal Distribution in which $\sigma = 10$

| *If* $\sigma = 10$ $n$ | *Expected Value of the Range* | *Expected Value of* $s^2$ | *Expected Value of* $s$ | *Expected Value of Range/*$s$ |
|---|---|---|---|---|
| 2 | 11 | 100 | 8.0 | 1.4 |
| 5 | 23 | 100 | 9.4 | 2.4 |
| 10 | 31 | 100 | 9.73 | 3.2 |
| 20 | 37 | 100 | 9.87 | 3.7 |
| 50 | 45 | 100 | 9.95 | 4.5 |
| 100 | 50 | 100 | 9.97 | 5.0 |
| 200 | 55 | 100 | 9.987 | 5.5 |
| 500 | 61 | 100 | 9.993 | 6.1 |
| 1,000 | 65 | 100 | 9.997 | 6.5 |

Table 5.1 shows that the expected size of the range varies markedly with the sample size, while the expected variance remains unchanged regardless of the value of $n$. The expected value of the standard deviation changes little, and gradually approaches the parameter, $\sigma = 10$, as $n$ increases. As a consequence, the range has very limited value as an inferential statistic. The range, however, is frequently useful for descriptive purposes, and helps identify obvious errors in scoring or recording. The range should be considered a complement to, and not a substitute for, $s^2$ or $s$.

## 5.14 CHAPTER SUMMARY

If a distribution contains all the observations in the population, the measures of central tendency and variability are parameters, not inferential statistics. The variance and standard deviation in the population are denoted by the symbols $\sigma^2$ and $\sigma$, respectively.

If the distribution contains only a random sample of $n$ observations from the population, the measures of central tendency and variability are sample statistics. Estimates of the population variance and standard deviation are denoted by the symbols $s^2$ and $s$, respectively. The variance ($s^2$), standard deviation ($s$), and range are widely used measures of variability. Each has the statistical property of consistency, but only $s^2$ provides an unbiased estimate of the corresponding parameter, $\sigma^2$. The sample standard deviation, $s$, underestimates the related parameter $\sigma$, although the degree of bias is negligible unless $n$ is very small. The range is an unstable measure and is greatly influenced by $n$.

If a constant is added to each score in a distribution, the values of variance and other measures of variability are unchanged. If each score in a distribution is multiplied by a constant, $c$, the standard deviation of the transformed distribution is $|c|s$, where $s$ is the original standard deviation. The variance in the augmented distribution is $c^2s^2$.

**TABLE 5.2** Descriptive Information for Cholesterol Case Study Variables ($n = 200$)

| *Variable* | $\overline{X}$ | *Md* | *s* | $Q_1$ | $Q_3$ | *Q* | *Q/s* | $X_{min}$ | $X_{max}$ | *Range* | *Range/s* |
|---|---|---|---|---|---|---|---|---|---|---|---|
| Age | 42.6 | 42 | 11.6 | 33 | 52 | 9.5 | 1.22 | 23 | 70 | 53 | 4.7 |
| Systolic B.P. (SBP) | 121.6 | 120 | 16.7 | 110 | 130 | 10 | 1.67 | 90 | 190 | 100 | 6.0 |
| Diastolic B.P. (DBP) | 81.6 | 80 | 10.0 | 75 | 90 | 7.5 | 1.33 | 55 | 112 | 57 | 5.7 |
| Cholesterol Level* | 285.1 | 276 | 65.0 | 245 | 332 | 43.5 | 1.49 | 135 | 520 | 385 | 5.9 |
| Height (in.) | 68.6 | 68 | 2.5 | 67 | 70 | 1.5 | 1.67 | 62 | 74 | 12 | 4.8 |
| Weight (lbs.) | 165.2 | 163 | 24.9 | 147 | 180 | 16.5 | 1.51 | 109 | 262 | 153 | 6.1 |
| Coronary? (0=N, 1=Y) | .125 | 0 | .33 | 0 | 0 | 0 | — | 0 | 1 | 1 | 3.0 |
| ID # | 100.5 | 100.5 | 57.9 | 50.5 | 150.5 | 50 | 1.15 | 1 | 200 | 199 | 3.5 |

*Cholesterol level is the composite of HDL and LDL levels.

## 5.15 CASE STUDY

Most published research does not provide frequency distributions of the important variables; only the mean and standard deviation are given in many studies. Additional information (see Section 6.9) is needed to inform the reader as to whether there is skewness in a distribution. Variability and other information for the variables in the cholesterol study are given in Table 5.2. Since SBP and DBP are measured in the same units (metric), their variabilities can be compared—SBP is much more variable than DBP. Hence, an elevation of 20 units is much more common with SBP than with DBP. $X_{\text{min}}$ and $X_{\text{max}}$ are particularly useful in identifying data entry errors—values that are not possible or reasonable.[8] One of the most common mistakes made in statistical analyses is to assume that there are no errors in the data. One should look for unlikely or unreasonable values and double check before launching into other statistical analyses. Many, if not most, theses and research studies are well along in the statistical analyses, only to find that there are errors in the data.

For height, the interquartile range extended from 67″ to 70″. Twenty-five percent of the sample had cholesterol levels above 332, whereas a reading of 245 placed one at $P_{25}$. When a variable is dichotomous, $s$ and $Q$ are not useful descriptive statistics.

Observe that the standard deviation is roughly 50% greater than $Q$ ($s/Q \approx 1.5$) for several of the variables. When the variable is normally distributed and $n$ is large, $\sigma/Q$ equals 1.48. In other words, the value of $Q$ will be about two-thirds of a standard deviation when the variable is approximately normally distributed. The $s/Q$ ratio is less than 1.5 for rectangular distributions (note Age and ID #).

In Table 5.1, note that the expected value for the range is 5.5 times larger than the expected value of $s$ when the distribution is normal and $n = 200$. In Table 5.2, the ratio of the range to $s$ is given in the right-most column. Note that, except for the dichotomous and rectangularly distributed variables, the values of Range/$s$ do not differ greatly from 5.5. A rule of thumb worth remembering is that when the distribution is approximately normal, and the sample size is 100, one can expect the range to be about five times the value of $s$.

---

[8]Inspecting frequency distributions (such as those found in Tables 3.1 and 3.2, Sections 3.1 and 3.2) is even better, but frequency distributions are not always available.

## 5.16 SUGGESTED COMPUTER EXERCISE

Using the data from the HSB data set, obtain the range, variance, and standard deviation of all continuous (non-categorical) variables using the speadsheet and statistical software available to you.

## MASTERY TEST

*Consider this sample of three scores, 40, 45, 50:*

1. What is the value of the range?
2. $\overline{X} = ?$
3. The sum of squares, $\Sigma_i x_i^2 = ?$
4. For computing $s^2$, how many degrees of freedom, $\nu$, are there?
5. What is the value of $s^2$?
6. What is the value of $s$?
7. If each score is increased by 10 points, will the values of $s^2$ and $s$ be affected?
8. If each score is multiplied by 10, what are the new values of $s^2$ and $s$?
9. What is the value of $\Sigma_i x_i^2$? Is $\Sigma_i x_i^2 = (\Sigma_i x_i)^2$?
10. Complete the analogy: $s^2$ is to a sample as $\sigma^2$ is to ____.

*Questions 11–17 pertain to three measures of variability for data obtained from a random sample of n observations—range, standard deviation (s), and variance ($s^2$).*

11. Which is unbiased even when $n$ is very small?
12. Which has a value that, on the average, is much greater when $n = 100$ than when $n = 20$?
13. Which is technically biased, but for practical purposes is essentially unbiased, if $n$ is 20 or more?
14. Which is simplest to calculate?
15. Which has the same expected value regardless of sample size?
16. Do all have the property of consistency?
17. Which is *not* expressed in the same units as the original observations?
18. If all scores in a distribution are not equal, will the range always be larger than the standard deviations?
19. To compute $s$ or $s^2$, is the sum of squares divided by the sample size, $n$, or by $n - 1$?
20. What is the symbol and name for $n - 1$?
21. What symbol represents the population standard deviation?
22. What symbol represents the size of a sample?
23. What symbol represents the mean of a population?
24. If the variance of IQ scores is found to be 225, what is the value of the standard deviation?
25. Using Table 5.1, and assuming that a sample of $n = 100$ is randomly drawn from a population with standard deviation 15, estimate the range in the set of 100 scores.

26. The heights of American women are approximately normally distributed with $\mu \approx 64.5''$ and $Q \approx 1.5''$. The middle 50% of heights fall between ____ and ____.
27. Which one of these has a value that is one-half the other two: $Q$, H-spread, interquartile range?
28. When does $Md \pm Q$ precisely equal the points, $Q_1$ and $Q_3$?
29. The scores in group 1 are (7, 8, 12); their variance, $s_1^2$, is equal to 7.0. The scores in group 2 are (15, 16, 20); *by inspection,* what is $s_2^2$?
30. The variance of the combined distribution, $s_{\bullet}^2$, formed by combining groups 1 and 2 in item 29 will be: (a) < 7 (b) 7 (c) > 7

## PROBLEMS AND EXERCISES

1. Calculate the (a) range, (b) interquartile range, (c) $Q$, (d) $s^2$, and (e) $s$ for the following set of scores. (*Hint:* To simplify calculations, you can first subtract 100 from all scores. This will not change the value of any of the measures of variability.)

| | | | | | |
|---|---|---|---|---|---|
| 125 | 116 | 114 | 111 | 122 | 115 |
| 113 | 106 | 118 | 114 | 112 | 102 |

   (f) Are the relative sizes of the obtained values of the range and $s$ reasonable (see Table 5.1)?
2. Calculate the standard deviation of the combined distribution in Mastery Test question 29.
3. In a perfectly normal distribution, $Q = .674\sigma$. Rearrange this equation such that $\sigma = ?$. Use this equation and the information in Mastery Test question 26 to estimate the standard deviation of the heights of American women.
4. Using the information from the preceding question and Table 5.1, what is the range between the tallest and shortest woman that would be expected in a random sample of size $n$, when: (a) $n = 5$, (b) $n = 10$, (c) $n = 50$, (d) $n = 100$, and (e) $n = 1{,}000$?
5. Why do basketball teams from large high schools tend to be taller than teams from small high schools? (see Table 5.1)

## ANSWERS TO MASTERY TEST

1. 10
2. 45
3. 50
4. 2
5. 25
6. 5
7. no
8. $s^2 = (10)^2(25) = 2{,}500$; $s = 10(5) = 50$
9. $\Sigma_i x_i^2 = (-5)^2 + (0)^2 + (5)^2 = 50$; no [note that $(\Sigma_i x_i)^2 = 0$]
10. population
11. variance
12. range (see Table 5.1)
13. standard deviation
14. range
15. variance
16. yes
17. variance
18. yes
19. $n - 1$
20. $\nu$, degrees of freedom
21. $\sigma$
22. $n$
23. $\mu$
24. 15
25. 5(15) = 75
26. 63″ and 66″
27. $Q$
28. when the distribution is perfectly symmetrical
29. 7.0
30. (c)

## ANSWERS TO PROBLEMS AND EXERCISES

1. (a) 23; (b) $Q_3 - Q_1 = 117 - 111.5 = 5.5$; (c) 2.75; (d) 38.91; (e) 6.24; (f) yes
2. $s_{\bullet} = 4.98$
3. (a) $\sigma = Q/.674 = 1.5/.674 = 2.23''$
4. (a) 5.4″; (b) 7.1″; (c) 10″; (d) 11.2″; (e) 14.5″
5. The range for larger samples is greater than for smaller samples.

# 6

# THE NORMAL DISTRIBUTION AND STANDARD SCORES

## 6.1 THE IMPORTANCE OF THE NORMAL DISTRIBUTION

The *normal distribution,* also known as the Gaussian curve or the normal probability curve, is the most fundamentally important distribution in statistics. The normal curve is used extensively in all subsequent chapters. Its use in this chapter will be illustrated by describing the performance of an individual or group using standard scores. Other more important applications of the normal distribution will be evident in the following chapters. Measures of *skewness* and *kurtosis*, which describe and quantify the extent to which a distribution deviates from a true normal distribution, will also be considered.

### Historical Background

The study of the normal distribution dates from at least the seventeenth century. It was noticed, for example, that if an object were weighed repeatedly, the observed weights were not identical; there was some variation among the measurements. If enough measurements were taken, the distribution of the observations displayed a regular pattern, a pattern now recognized to be the normal distribution. Errors of observation of many kinds were found to follow this same pattern. In fact, the distribution was initially called the "normal curve of errors."

## 6.2 GOD LOVES THE NORMAL CURVE

It was soon discovered that observations other than measurement error resulted in normal, or approximately normal, curves. If ten fair coins were tossed, the number of heads recorded in the toss, and the procedure repeated many times (actually an infinite number), the distribution in Figure 6.1 would result. Note that the *expected value* (Section 5.13) for the number of heads is 5, which is the mean, $\mu$, of the theoretical distribution shown in Figure

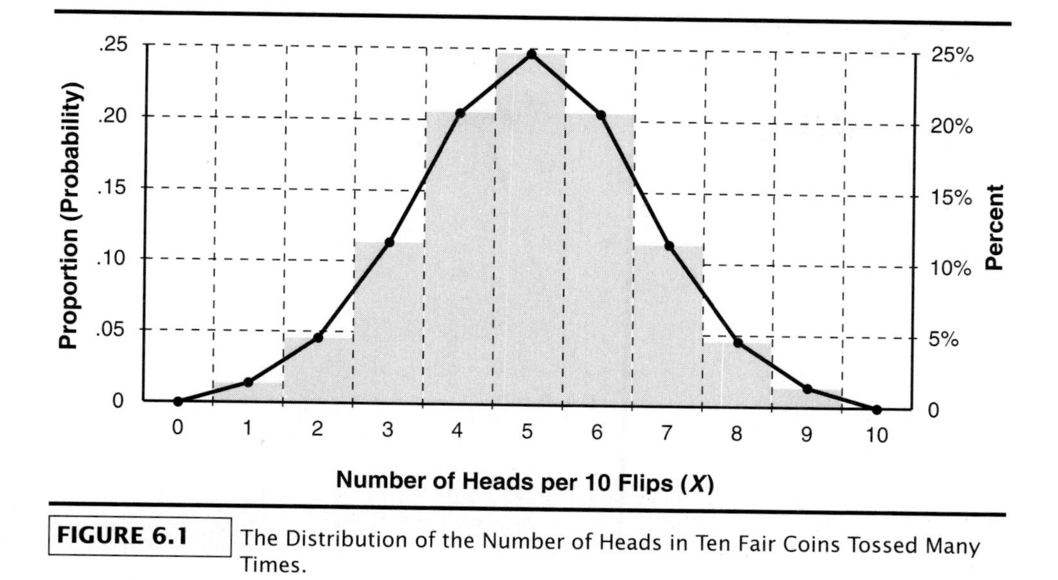


**FIGURE 6.1** The Distribution of the Number of Heads in Ten Fair Coins Tossed Many Times.

6.1. In normal distributions the mean is also the mode—the value of $\mu$ occurs more frequently than any other score. Figure 6.1 shows that almost 25% of the sets of ten tosses results in five heads; but for 75% of the sets of ten flips, the number of heads is not five, but varies symmetrically about five; four and six heads were each observed in more than 20% of the sets. The distribution is symmetrical and approximately normal, but note that it does not result from errors of measurement, but from the laws of chance. No collection of empirical observations would look exactly like a perfect normal distribution because the latter is a mathematical abstraction. For example, the distribution of number of heads in Figure 6.1 is *discrete* (i.e., has gaps), not *continuous*; there are no points between 4 and 5, or between 5 and 6, for instance. The true normal distribution is continuous; there are no gaps. Variables like time, distance, and weight are continuous and can be measured so there are virtually no gaps. If the number of coins flipped were increased to 100, and the number of heads recorded in many repeated tosses, then the distribution of the number of heads would approach the mathematical normal distribution much more closely. Of course, the approximation would be even better if 1,000 fair coins were tossed.

Late in the nineteenth century Francis Galton, an Englishman, took systematic measurements of many physical, psychological, and psychomotor characteristics on large samples of persons and found that the distributions of the measurements were very close approximations to the normal distribution. Figure 6.2 illustrates his findings using the heights of 8,585 adult men born in Great Britain during the nineteenth century. Note how closely the distribution approximates a normal curve.

It is fortunate that the measurements of many variables in all disciplines have distributions that are good approximations of the normal distribution, for example, reaction times for children at ten years of age, size of wings of a given species of butterfly, heights for a given variety of plant, daily high temperature on January 15 for the past century. Refined measures of most cognitive, psychomotor, and many affective and other human

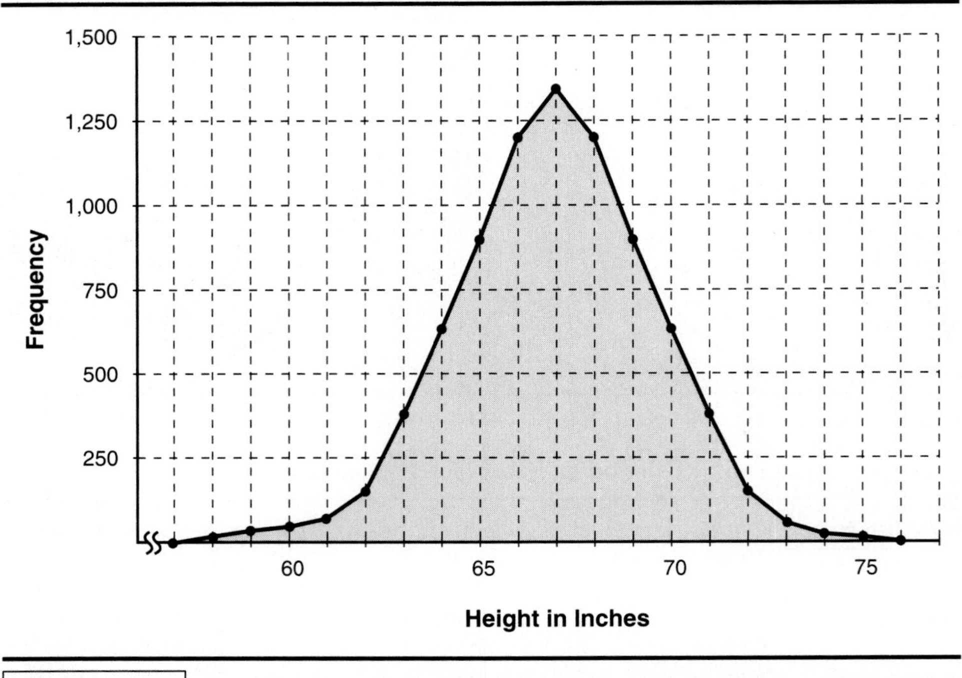


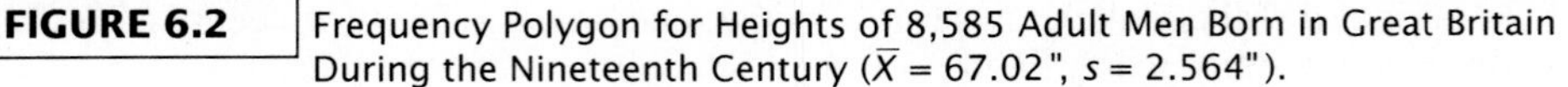

**FIGURE 6.2** Frequency Polygon for Heights of 8,585 Adult Men Born in Great Britain During the Nineteenth Century ($\bar{X}$ = 67.02", $s$ = 2.564").

characteristics have empirical distributions that are approximately normal. Indeed, God loves the normal curve.

No set of empirical observations is ever perfectly described by the normal distribution. Even if a variable were perfectly normally distributed, the observed distribution would never be perfectly normal. There is sampling error inherent in any finite set of data that will result in some departure from the mathematical curve, but the shape is often extremely close to the theoretical normal curve. The discrepancy is frequently so small that it can be disregarded for practical purposes.

Building on the work of Pascal (1623–1662), de Fermat (1601–1665), and Bernoulli (1654–1705), Abraham DeMoivre (1667–1754) was able to show that the mathematical curve that approximates the curve that connects the tops of the lines in Figures 6.1 and 6.2 is described by the following equation:

$$u = \frac{1}{\sigma\sqrt{2\pi}} e^{-\frac{1}{2}[(X-\mu)/\sigma]^2} \quad \textbf{(6.1)}$$

where $u$ is the height of the curve above any given value of the variable, $X$;
$\pi$ is the ratio of the circumference of a circle to its diameter; $\pi = 3.14159\ \ldots$;
$e$ is the base of the system of natural logarithms, $e = 2.71828\ \ldots$; and
$\mu$ and $\sigma$ are the mean and the standard deviation of the variable, $X$.

Equation 6.1 is the equation for the *normal distribution*. We shall have little to do directly with Equation 6.1 as such, although it was used to generate the normal curve table, Table A in the Appendix.

The empirical distribution of IQ scores is almost perfectly normal between 70 and 130. Although the commonly observed empirical bell-shaped curves of errors, height, IQ, and other variables have piqued the curiosity of scientists of many different stripes, *the prominence of the normal distribution in inferential statistics is primarily due to its mathematical properties.* No other distribution has such desirable properties with which the mathematical statistician can do magic. Many technical problems in statistics have been solved only by assuming the observations in the population are normally distributed. Specific instances will appear in later chapters.

The ubiquity of the normal curve sometimes leads to the mistaken notion that there is a necessary link between it and almost any good set of data, but many variables are definitely *not* normally distributed. For example, many sociological variables, such as social class, socioeconomic status, income, level of education, and family size, are skewed. Certain social and political attitudes, such as attitude toward abortion, have bimodal distributions. Such variables as age, ethnicity, religion, and college major obviously are not normally distributed.

The graph of Equation 6.1 yields the familiar, symmetric, bell-shaped curve known as the *normal curve*. One speaks of a normal curve, because Equation 6.1 imparts a characteristic shape to the graph. All normal curves have the following properties: unimodal, symmetry, points of inflection[1] at $\mu \pm \sigma$, tails that approach (but never quite touch) the horizontal axis[2] as they deviate from $\mu$. Not all curves with these characteristics are normal (as you will see in Section 6.9). The normal curve has a smooth, altogether handsome countenance—a thing of beauty.

## 6.3 THE STANDARD NORMAL DISTRIBUTION AS A STANDARD REFERENCE DISTRIBUTION: *z*-SCORES

A raw score of 42 on a test means little, but to know that this score is 1½ standard deviations ($1.5\sigma$) above the mean tells us that it is quite high relative to the other scores in the distribution. If the mean and standard deviation are known, the individual scores can be pictured relative to the entire set of scores in the distribution. Observations expressed in standard deviation units from the mean are termed *z-scores*. For IQ scores where $\mu$ is 100 and $\sigma$ is 15, an IQ score of 130 can be transformed to a *z-score* of 2. It is two standard deviations above the mean. A *z*-score of –2 is two standard deviations *below* the mean, or equivalent to an IQ score of 70. Equation 6.2 defines a *z*-score:

$$z_i = \frac{X_i - \mu}{\sigma} = \frac{x_i}{\sigma} \quad \textbf{(6.2)}$$

[1]A point of inflection is the precise point at which a smooth curve changes from concave (down-sloping) to convex (up-sloping). It is found using calculus; it is the point at which the second derivative of the equation equals zero.

[2]The mathematician would say that "the curve approaches the *X*-axis *asymptotically*" or "the *X*-axis is the asymptote of the curve."

In other words, a $z$-score tells us how many standard deviations the given scores is above or below the mean. It is very informative when scores are expressed in terms of standard deviations from the mean $\mu$, that is, $z$-scores. For almost any application of the normal curve, one wants to know how many standard deviations a score lies above or below the mean. Knowing this, questions about the area between points or scores, $X_1$ and $X_2$ (or heights of the curve above any point), can be answered by reference to the standard normal curve (see Table A in the Appendix). The *shape* of a curve does not change when a *constant* is added or subtracted from each score or when each score is multiplied or divided by a *constant*. Thus, when $\mu$ is subtracted from each score and these differences are divided by $\sigma$ (see Equation 6.2), the shape of the distribution is not changed.

Any set of scores with mean $\mu$ and standard deviation $\sigma$ can be transformed into a different set of scores with a mean of 0, and a standard deviation of 1; the transformed score, $z$, describes how many standard deviations the score falls above or below the mean of the distribution. These points are summarized in the following statement: If $X$ is normally distributed with mean $\mu$ and standard deviation $\sigma$, then $z_i = (X_i - \mu)/\sigma$ has a normal distribution with a mean of 0, and standard deviation of 1. By making use of the definition of a $z$-score in Equation 6.2, Equation 6.1 can be simplified (Heffernan, 1988):

$$u = \frac{1}{\sqrt{2\pi}} e^{-\left(\frac{z^2}{2}\right)} \qquad \textbf{(6.3)}$$

The normal curve in Equation 6.3 and Figure 6.3 is a special one because it has been chosen as a standard. It is known variously as the *unit normal curve* or the standard (or standardized) normal distribution.

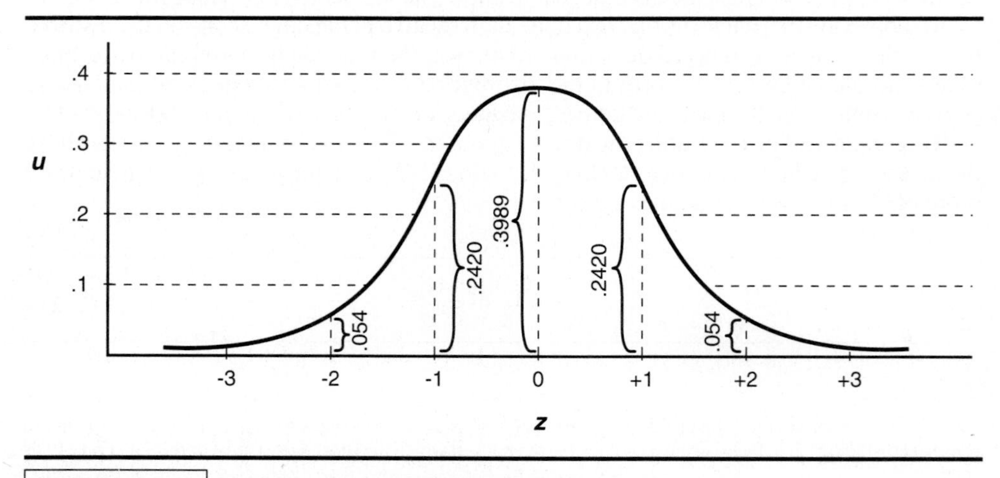


**FIGURE 6.3** The Standard Normal Distribution, $\mu = 0$ and $\sigma = 1$.

## 6.4 ORDINATES OF THE NORMAL DISTRIBUTION

In rare circumstances, it is necessary to find the ordinate $u$, the height of the curve, at a given value of $z$. Solving Equation 6.3 for $u$ when $z$ is given is far too inconvenient (unless one is proficient with a scientific hand calculator that has a variable exponent function). Table A in the Appendix gives the ordinate $u$ for values of $z$ in the standard normal curve. The highest point on the curve is above the point $z = 0$ (see Figure 6.3 and Table A); when $z = 0$ is inserted in Equation 6.3, the height (ordinate) $u$ is .3989. Notice in Figure 6.3 that the ordinate $u$ equals .2420 at $z \pm 1.0$, and that $u = .0540$ at $z \pm 2.0$. For practice, locate these values in Table A.

## 6.5 AREAS UNDER THE NORMAL CURVE

In many applications of statistics, it is necessary to know the area of the normal curve (i.e., the proportion of the distribution) that falls below a particular value of $z$. To find the proportion of scores that falls below any particular score in a normal distribution, the score is converted to a $z$-score. The proportion is then read from the normal curve table, Table A. For example, in Figure 6.2, what proportion of the men were shorter than 70 inches? Stated differently, what is the percentile rank of 70 inches?[3] Assuming a normal distribution with a mean of 67.02″ and a standard deviation of 2.56″, $X_1 = 70''$ expressed as a $z$-score, using Equation 6.2, is:

$$z_1 = \frac{70 - 67.02}{2.56} = \frac{2.98}{2.56} = 1.16$$

One then finds $z = 1.16$ in Table A and in the adjacent column reads $p$, the proportion of the curve that falls below $z_1 = 1.16$. For $z_1 = 1.16$, $p_1 = .8770$; thus, 87.7% of the area (or observations) in a normal distribution falls below a $z$-score of 1.16 (see Figure 6.4). Or, stated differently, only 1 −.8770 = .1230 (12.3%) of the men were taller than 70″.

What proportion of the heights in Figure 6.2 falls between 66″ and 70″? If the proportion of heights below $X_2 = 66''$ is subtracted from the proportion below 70″, the difference is the proportion between 66″ and 70″. A height of 66″ corresponds to a $z$-score of −.40 [$z_2 = (66 - 67.02)/2.56 = -.398$, which rounds to −.40]. From Table A, the area below $z_2 = -.40$ is found to be .3446 (see Figure 6.4). Of the .8770 of the heights below 70″, .3446 are below 66″; therefore, .8770 − .3446 = .5324 (or 53.24%) of the cases fall between 66″ and 70″.[4]

The steps just illustrated can be summarized as follows: The area between $X_1$ and $X_2$

---

[3]The heights in Figure 6.2 are not representative of the United States population, for which $\mu = 69.7''$ and $\sigma = 2.6''$ in 1976.

[4]Chebyshev's inequality proves that the proportion of the area of any distribution that is beyond the points $\pm z$ is less than $1/z^2$. Thus there is never more than $1/2^2 = .25$ of the distribution that is more than two standard deviations ($z = 2$) from the mean. For symmetric unimodal distributions, the maximum area beyond $\pm z$ is $4/(9z^2)$ (Dixon and Massey, 1983). Thus, there can be no more than $4/[9(2)^2] = 1/9$ or 11.1% of the area falling in the tails beyond the points $z = -2$ and $z = +2$ in symmetric unimodal distributions.

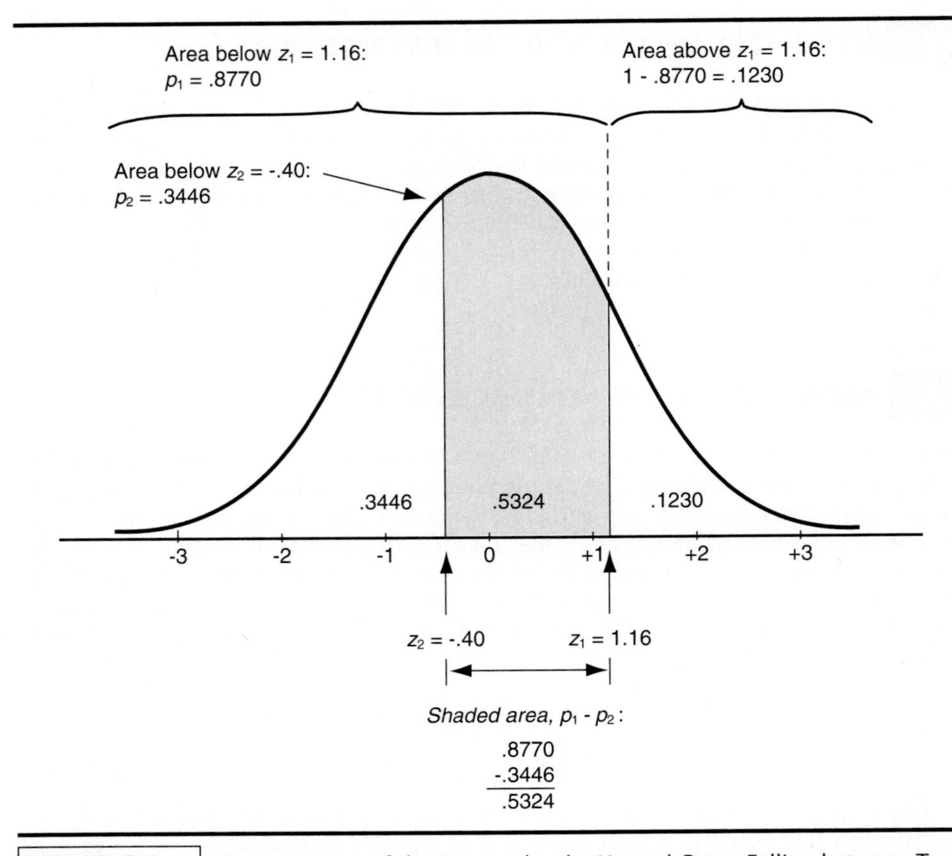


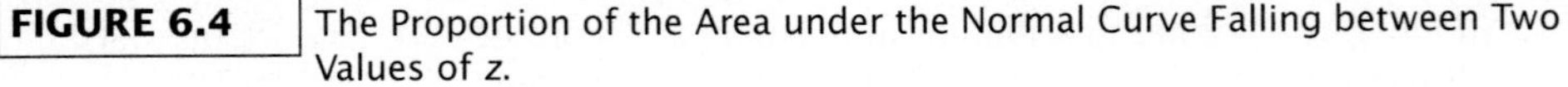
**FIGURE 6.4** The Proportion of the Area under the Normal Curve Falling between Two Values of *z*.

in the normal distribution with mean $\mu$ and standard deviation $\sigma$ is the area between $z_1 = (X_1 - \mu)/\sigma$ and $z_2 = (X_2 - \mu)/\sigma$ in the standard normal distribution.

## 6.6 OTHER STANDARD SCORES

It is easier to interpret observations when they are expressed as standard scores rather than as raw scores. With *standard scores*, the mean and standard deviation always have the *same fixed values*. To know that an IQ score on the Wechsler Intelligence Scale is 120 means little unless one knows also that $\mu = 100$; in addition, to know that $\sigma = 15$ enables the score of 120 to be interpreted much more meaningfully.

The *z*-score scale ($\mu = 0$, $\sigma = 1$) is the most widely used standard score scale in statistics, but any observation expressed in standard deviation units from the mean is a *standard score*. Most standardized tests of intelligence, achievement, interest, and personality report performance in standard scores. Such measures rarely use *z*-scores because other standard-score scales that do not involve negative numbers or decimals are preferred.

A $z$-score can be converted to any other standard score ($S$) using the general formula in Eq. 6.4:

$$S_i = \mu_S + (\sigma_S)z_i \quad (6.4)$$

where $S_i$ is the new standard score equivalent to $z_i$;
$\mu_S$ is the mean of the new standard-score scale;
$\sigma_S$ is the standard deviation of the new standard-score scale; and
$z_i$ is the $z$-score for the $i$th observation.

## 6.7 *T*-SCORES

*T*-scores[5] are widely used to report performance on standardized tests and inventories. *T*-scores are standard scores with a mean ($\mu_T$) of 50 and a standard deviation ($\sigma_T$) of 10. To convert $z$-scores to *T*-scores, Equation 6.4 becomes

$$T_i = 50 + 10z_i \quad (6.5)$$

An example will illustrate certain advantages of standard scores. Suppose a ten-year-old boy is 46″ tall and weighs 76 pounds. Are his height and weight commensurate? Who knows without norms? However, expressed as *T*-scores (30 and 70, respectively) his weight problem becomes readily apparent—he is at the 2nd percentile in height, but the 98th percentile in weight!

If a student in grade 5.1 (first month of grade 5) obtained an IQ score of 130 and grade-equivalent scores of 6.4 and 6.1 on the standardized reading and arithmetic tests, respectively, how does her achievement compare with her measured scholastic aptitude (IQ)? The corresponding *T*-scores of 70, 60, and 60 show that the student's relative superiority above the mean on the intelligence test was twice as great as her degree of exceeding the mean on the reading and arithmetic tests.[6]

Figure 6.5 shows the relation of $z$-scores, *T*-scores, and several other standard-score scales. Observe that converting raw scores to standard scores does not alter the shape of the distribution or change the percentile ranks of any observation. Standard scores have the advantage of having a common mean and standard deviation that facilitates interpretation.

Notice that the frequently mentioned Wechsler IQ scale is a standard-score scale with $\mu = 100$ and $\sigma = 15$. The scale employed by the historic Stanford-Binet Intelligence Scale (form L-M) differs little ($\mu = 100$, $\sigma = 16$).[7] An IQ score of 145 on the Wechsler has the same $z$-score and percentile rank as a Stanford-Binet score of 148.

---

[5]The *T*-scale (named in honor of the early educational psychologist, Edward Lee Thorndike) was originally proposed as a *normalized* standard score (Section 6.11); in most current applications *T*-scores are not normalized, but are simply a linear transformation (Section 7.9) of raw scores.

[6]If more explanation and practice using the normal distribution and standard scores are desired, you may find the programmed instruction in Chapters 2 and 3 of Hopkins, Stanley, and Hopkins (1990) helpful.

[7]Prior to the 1960 revision of the Stanford-Binet, performance was expressed as a ratio IQ: IQ = 100(Mental Age/Chronological Age). The standard deviation of IQ scores fluctuated from one age to another, consequently the associated percentile rank for a given IQ score varied considerably from age to age. Now, virtually all cognitive aptitude tests use standard scores.

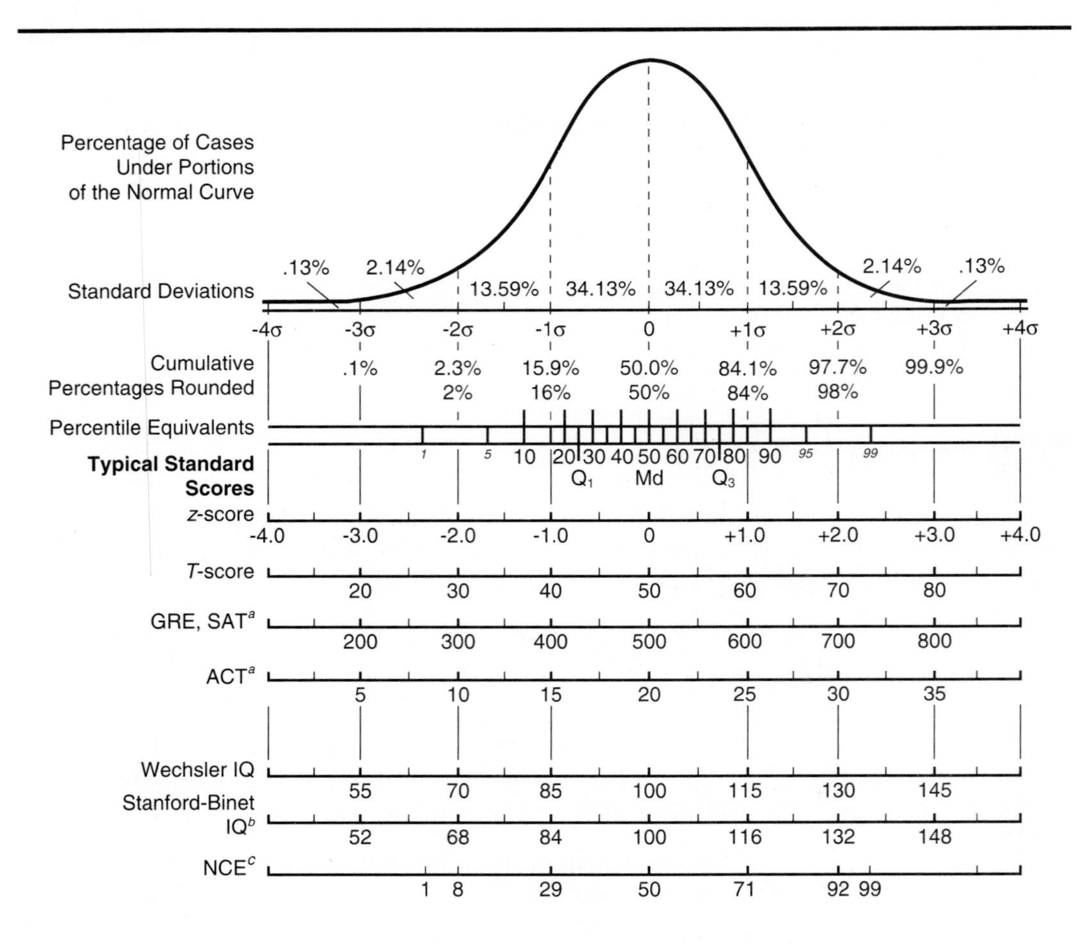


Distribution of scores of many standardized educational and psychological tests approximate the form of the normal curve shown at the top of this chart. Below it are shown other standard scores that are used by certain tests.

The zero (0) at the center of the baseline shows the location of the mean (average) raw score on a test, and the symbol $\sigma$ (sigma) marks off the scale of raw scores in standard deviation units.

Most systems are based on the standard deviation unit. Among these standard score scales, the *z*-score and the *T*-score are general systems that have been applied to a variety of tests. The others are special variations used with College Entrance Examination Board tests, the Graduate Records Examination, and other intelligence and ability scales.

Tables of norms, whether in percentile or standard score form, have meaning only with reference to a specified test applied to a specified reference population. The chart does not permit one to conclude, for instance, that a percentile rank of 84 on one test necessarily is equivalent to a *z*-score of +1.0 on another; this is true only when each test yields essentially a normal distribution of scores and when both scales are based on identical or very similar groups of people.

[a]Score points (norms pertain to university students and not the general population). (GRE = Graduate Record Examination, SAT = Scholastic Aptitude Test of the College Entrance Examination Board, ACT = American College Testing Assessment.) Certain of these tests are not rescaled to better allow comparisons over time. Consequently, current means are lower than means given above.

[b]Standard-score IQ's with $\sigma = 16$ are also used on certain other intelligence tests.

[c]The NCE ("Normal Curve Equivalent") scale is an ill-conceived normalized scale used in the evaluation of certain federally funded educational programs. The NCE scale has $\mu = 50$ and $\sigma = 21$; and the NCE unit is 1/98 of the distance between the 1st and 99th percentiles, expressed in *z*-score units. The NCE scale invites the confusion of NCE standard scores with percentiles.

**FIGURE 6.5** Illustrations of Various Standard Score Scales. (Adapted from Test Service Bulletin No. 48, The Psychological Corporation, New York, by permission of The Psychological Corporation.)

One may wonder why statisticians bothered to invent standard scores; why not just provide percentiles, which are easier to interpret? For all the clarity and simplicity of percentile scores, they are unsatisfactory for many statistical operations such as averaging and correlation (Chapter 7). The difference between the heights of two women at the 50th and 55th percentiles is much smaller than the height difference between two women at the 90th and 95th percentiles. Compare the *z*-scores in the normal distribution at the 50th and 55th versus the 90th and 95th percentiles: $P_{50}$ corresponds to a $z$ of 0 and $P_{55}$ to a $z$ of .126, a difference of .126$\sigma$; whereas, $P_{90}$ corresponds to a $z$ of 1.282 and $P_{95}$ to a $z$ of 1.645, a difference .363$\sigma$; and the difference between $P_{90}$ and $P_{95}$ is almost three (2.88) times greater than the difference between $P_{50}$ and $P_{55}$! In terms of the heights in Figure 6.2, the difference between $P_{50}$ and $P_{55}$ is only .33 inches, whereas the difference between $P_{90}$ and $P_{95}$ is .93 inches. Stated differently, in IQ units, $P_{50}$ and $P_{55}$ differ by less than two (1.89) IQ points, whereas $P_{90}$ and $P_{95}$ differ by more than five (5.45) points. Standard scores avoid this distortion and lend themselves readily to meaningful summary statistical calculations.

## 6.8 AREAS UNDER THE NORMAL CURVE IN SAMPLES

This chapter has assumed that the population mean ($\mu$) and standard deviation ($\sigma$) of a normal distribution are known. If the mean and standard deviation are estimated from a sample (i.e., $\overline{X}$ and $s$ are used since $\mu$ and $\sigma$ are not known) and inferences are made to the population, the proportion found in Table A is not precise, but only an approximation; the accuracy of the approximation is determined by how accurately $\overline{X}$ and $s$ estimate $\mu$ and $\sigma$. When the random sample contains 100 or more scores, the $z_i$-value for an observation ($X_i$) using $\overline{X}$ and $s$ will differ from the true $z$-value (i.e., the $z$-value using $\mu$ and $\sigma$) by .1 or less in most situations.[8] This degree of precision is adequate for most purposes. One should be wary of using Table A for inferential purposes if $\overline{X}$ and $s$ are based on very small samples and when the frequency distribution is not normal.

## 6.9 SKEWNESS

A complete description of a distribution should include not only its central tendency and variability, but also the degree of asymmetry or skewness. The nature and extent of skewness is visually apparent from well-constructed frequency polygons and histograms, but these are rarely available in published research. Besides, mere observation of a distribution is imprecise and cannot be communicated accurately in words or numbers. There are two common measures of skewness. Recall (Section 4.15) that skewness influences the mean, median, and mode in a predictable way. In positively skewed distributions, the mean will have the largest value, and the mode the lowest; the relationship is reversed with negatively skewed distributions.

Figure 6.6 was constructed to illustrate various degrees of skewness. All the curves were converted to standard scores so they all have the same mean and standard deviation, but differ in skewness. Of course, the differences among the mean, median, and mode in-

[8]Technically only $(X_i - \mu)/\sigma$ is a $z$-ratio; $(X_i - \overline{X})/s$ is termed a $t$-ratio. If $n$ is large, there will be little difference between the $z$ and the $t$ associated with an observation. The $t$-distribution is widely used in statistics and will be used extensively beginning in Chapter 11.

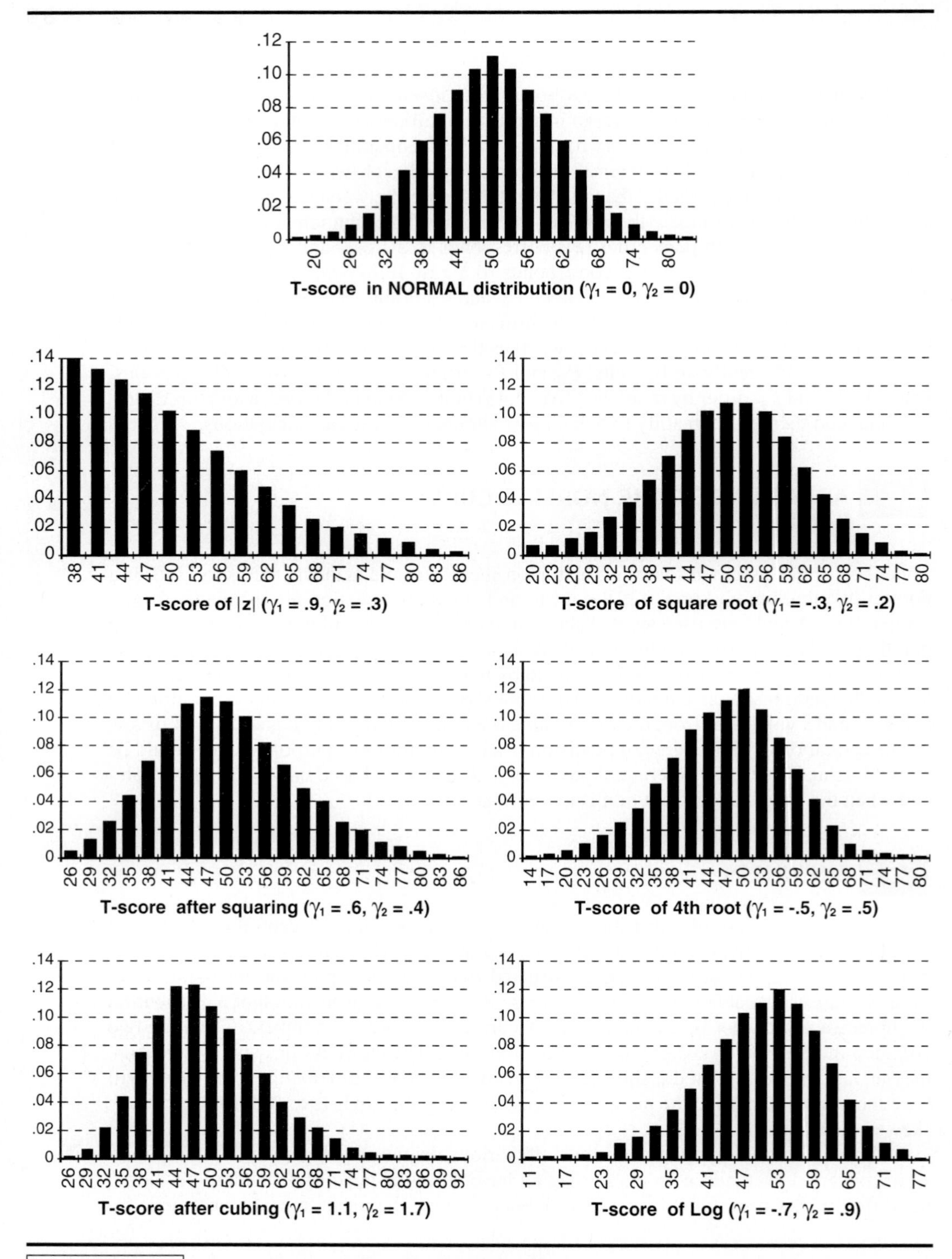

**FIGURE 6.6** Distributions Illustrating Various Degrees of Positive and Negative Skewness.

crease as the magnitude of the skewness increases. Indeed, Karl Pearson suggested Equation 6.6 as a useful and an easily interpreted measure of skewness in the population:

$$\Omega = \frac{\mu - \text{Mode}}{\sigma} \quad \textbf{(6.6)}$$

Notice that the skewness index, $\Omega$, describes the distance from the mean to the mode parameters in standard deviation units; it is the $z$-score of the mode with a change in sign. If $\Omega = .5$, the mean is $.5\sigma$ above the mode.

When used inferentially, the formula is usually revised so that the median can replace the mode because the sample median has much less sampling error than the mode of a sample. Recall that the distance between the mean and mode is approximately three times the distance between the mean and the median for regular unimodal distributions (see Equation 4.10, Section 4.15). Equation 6.7 provides a useful alternative for estimating $\Omega$ from the sample mean and median:

$$sk = \frac{3(\overline{X} - Md)}{s} \quad \textbf{(6.7)}$$

Pearson proposed a second measure of skewness, $\gamma_1$, which is preferred for inferential use.[9] If each of the $N$ scores in a frequency distribution is transformed to a $z$-score and then cubed $[(z_i)(z_i)(z_i) = z_i^3]$, the mean of the $z_i^3$ scores is $\gamma_1$:

$$\gamma_1 = \frac{\Sigma_i z_i^3}{N} \quad \textbf{(6.8)}$$

Note that $\gamma_1$ is a parameter; when $s$ is used rather than $\sigma$ in the computation of the $z$-scores, $\gamma_1$ is estimated by the statistic $\hat{\gamma}_1$.[10] The various curves in Figure 6.6 illustrate several degrees of positive and negative skewness. The curves were obtained by performing mathematical transformations (Section 6.11) on the normally distributed $T$-scores in the top curve. The six curves with various degrees of skewness provide some frame of reference for interpreting the $\gamma_1$ skewness index;[11] the curves on the left illustrate various degrees of positive skewness ($\gamma_1 > 0$) and the curves on the right are negatively skewed. $\Omega$ is more informative than $\gamma_1$ for visualizing the degree of skewness and reconstructing the frequency distribution; $\gamma_1$ is superior for inferential purposes (Snedecor and Cochran, 1980, pp. 78–79). Note that $\Omega$ can be estimated for the curves in Figure 6.6.[12]

---

[9] This is the measure used by BMD, SPSS, SAS and virtually all other computer programs.

[10] The circumflex, "^" above a Greek letter denotes not the parameter, but an estimate of the parameter, for example, $s = \hat{\sigma}$ (say, "sigma hat").

[11] The curves were created by applying a mathematical transformation to scores from a normal distribution. For example, if scores from a normal distribution are squared, the $\gamma_1$ changes from 0 to .6.

[12] Since all distributions are expressed using $T$-scores ($\mu = 50$, $\sigma = 10$), and the mode is the value with the greatest frequency, $\Omega = (\text{Mode} - 50)/10$.

Although it is not yet common practice, researchers should routinely report the degree of skewness to describe the shape of the distributions of interest (Hopkins & Weeks, 1990). This information is also useful for the interpretation of certain measures (e.g., correlation coefficients) and statistical tests (e.g., homogeneity of variance, Section 12.10) that can be affected by skewness.

## 6.10 KURTOSIS

Up to this point, three properties or features of groups of scores have been described: central tendency, variability, and symmetry. A fourth property, *kurtosis*, completes the set of characteristics of distributions of scores that are of interest in analyzing data. One may wish to know whether there are more or fewer extreme scores[13] than expected in a normal distribution. The customary measure of kurtosis, $\gamma_2$, is the mean of the distribution of $z_i^4$ scores (i.e., $z$'s raised to the fourth power) minus the constant 3 (which is the mean $z_i^4$ value for the normal curve).[14]

$$\gamma_2 = \frac{\Sigma_i z_i^4}{N} - 3 \quad (6.9)$$

Figure 6.7 gives three distributions (on the left) that have the same means and standard deviations (i.e., expressed in $T$-scores), but have negative kurtosis. They are termed *platykurtic* distributions. (The prefix "platy" means flat or broad.) These curves have fewer extreme scores than found in a normal distribution. Note that $\gamma_2$ for a symmetrical dichotomous distribution is –2 and –1.2 for a rectangular (uniform) distribution. When the kurtosis is based on a sample of $n$ observations, the kurtosis index is a statistic and denoted by $\hat{\gamma}_2$.

The three curves on the right are from the $t$-distribution family with 5, 10, and 25 degrees of freedom; this distribution will be used extensively beginning in Chapter 11. The $t$-distributions have more extremely high or low scores than does the normal distribution, which gives $\gamma_2$ a positive value. In the normal distribution, the value of $\gamma_2$ is 0; it is said to be *mesokurtic* ("meso" means intermediate). Distributions in which the kurtosis index is positive are described as *leptokurtic* ("lepto" means slender or narrow). Highly skewed distributions tend to be leptokurtic because they have more scores that are far from the mean than does the normal distribution.

Ordinarily, there is far less interest in the kurtosis of a distribution as a descriptive statistic than in its central tendency, variability, and skewness. Kurtosis is important for evaluating the accuracy of certain statistical tests (e.g., see Section 13.8).

---

[13]Shiffler (1988) has shown that the largest possible $z$-score for any observation is limited by sample size $n$: $z_{max} = (n-1)/\sqrt{n}$. For example, if $n = 4$, $z_{max} = 1.5$; if $n = 100$, $z_{max} = 9.9$.

[14]In some sources –3 is absent from the formula for kurtosis; without the –3 in Equation 6.9, the normal distribution would have a kurtosis index of 3.

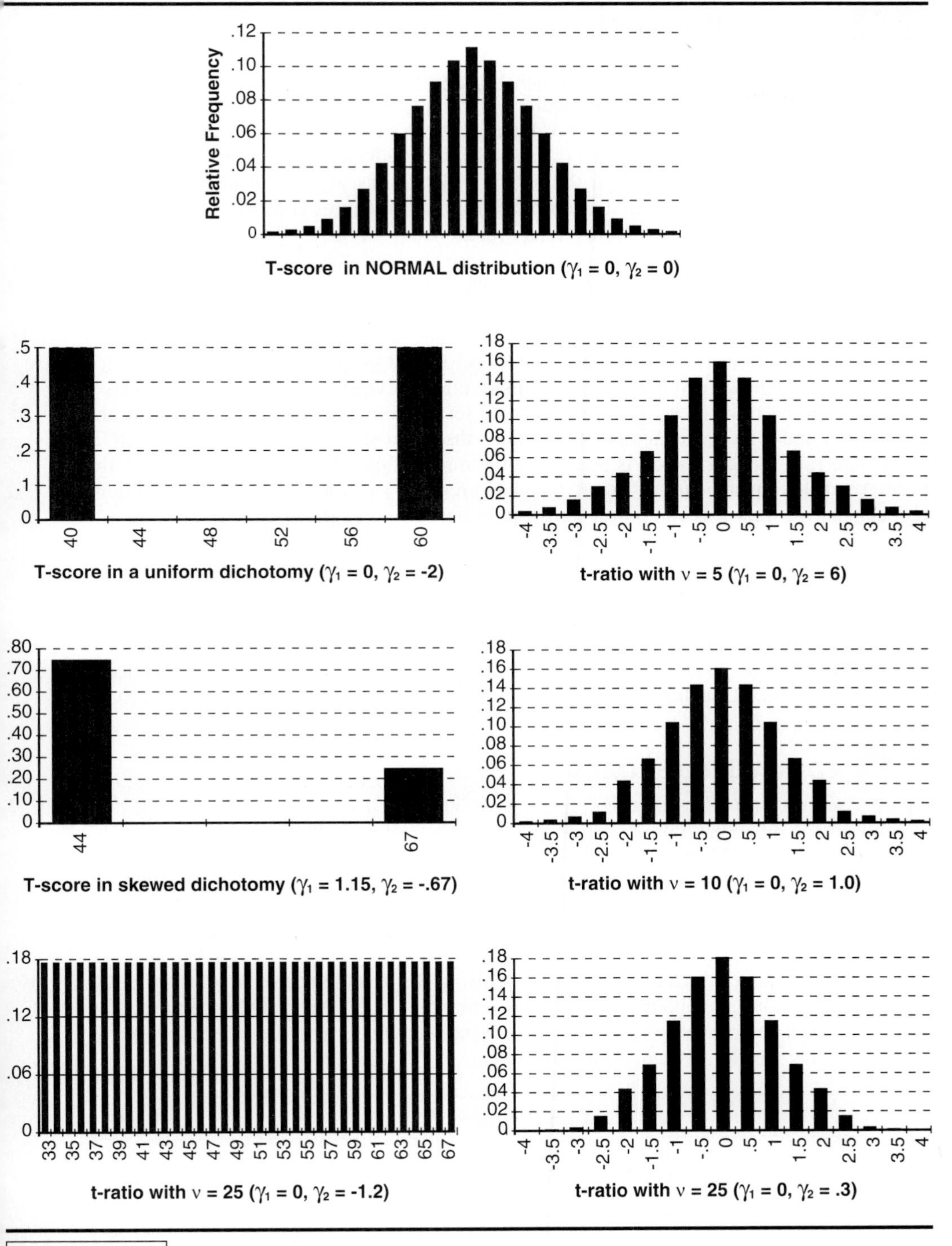

**FIGURE 6.7** Symmetric Curves Differing in Kurtosis.

## 6.11 TRANSFORMATIONS[15]

Many statistical methods assume a normal distribution in the populations being studied. Although many of these methods work quite well even when the assumption is not satisfied, it is sometimes desirable to convert the original scores to another metric in which the distribution is more nearly normal. It often happens that a certain change of scale, such as using the square root, reciprocal, or logarithm of the observations, will result in less skewness than in the original observation. Transformations can sometimes convert non-linear relationships between two variables into a linear relationship (Section 8.28).

Figure 6.6 illustrates how the shape of a normal distribution is altered by six mathematical transformations. Notice that if the mathematical process is reversed, the normal distribution would be reproduced (except for the distribution of absolute values, $|z|$). For example, if we started with a distribution that has slight negative skewness like the $T$-scores of the square root transformation (immediately below and to the right of the normal distribution), and square its members, a normal distribution will result. In other words, negative skewness can be reduced by raising the scores to a power greater than 1. Likewise, the square root and log transformations will reduce the positive skewness in a distribution. If the square root transformation is applied to the distribution "$T$-score after squaring," the normal distribution at the top of Figure 6.6 would result. Thus, root and log transformations reduce positive skewness and power transformations reduce negative skewness.

Transformations are not an end in themselves; but certain other statistical procedures may require that a variable be normally distributed, or have a linear relationship with another variable, and that may require a transformation. The best transformation is often difficult to find, and success in finding a good transformation is frequently a matter of trial and error. Additional guidelines can be found in Kirk (1982, pp. 81–84); Winer, Brown, and Michels (1991); Lee (1975, pp. 288–291); Dixon and Massey (1983, Chapter 16); Snedecor and Cochran (1980, Chapter 15); and Tukey (1977, Chapter 3).

## 6.12 NORMALIZED SCORES

When it can be assumed that the variable being measured is normally distributed, but the observations are not normally distributed because of faulty measurement, the observed distribution is sometimes *normalized*, that is, the distribution is forced to approximate the normal distribution as closely as possible. This transformation is monotonic (the rank order of $X_i$'s is maintained), but is non-linear (the relative distances between scores are not maintained, see Section 7.12).

Usually normalized scores are expressed using the $T$-score scale ($\mu = 50$, $\sigma = 10$). Normalized $T$-scores are obtained by first converting the original scores to percentiles, then converting each percentile to the $T$-score corresponding to that percentile in a normal distribution. In other words, this sequence is followed:

$$X_i \rightarrow P_i \rightarrow z_i \rightarrow T_i \quad \textbf{(6.10)}$$

For example, suppose a raw score of 37 is at the 10th percentile in the original distri-

[15]More explicitly, this should read non-linear transformations (i.e., transformations that change the shape of a distribution). The $z$-scale and $T$-scale (Equations 6.2 and 6.5) are linear transformations of $X$ (Section 7.9).

bution. From Table A in the Appendix, one can see that the $z$-score that is associated with the 10th percentile in the normal distribution is –1.282. The $T$-score that corresponds to $z = -1.282$ (Equation 6.5) is $T = 50 + 10(-1.282) = 37.18$ or 37 ($T$-scores are usually rounded to the nearest whole number.) Unless the observed distribution deviates substantially from the normal distribution in skewness or kurtosis, normalized $T$-scores will differ little from non-normalized $T$-scores.[16]

## 6.13 CHAPTER SUMMARY

The measurements of many variables in the social and behavioral sciences have distributions that are closely approximated by the normal distribution. In addition, many distributions used in inferential statistics are normally distributed.

The normal distribution is symmetrical, unimodal, and bell-shaped. There is a known proportion of the curve below any $z$-score in a normal distribution. These proportions can be found from Table A by expressing the observation as a $z$-score, the number of standard deviations that the observation falls above or below the mean [$z_i = (X_i - \mu)/\sigma$].

Besides $z$-scores, there are other widely used standard-score scales. The most popular is the $T$-scale that sets $\mu = 50$ and $\sigma = 10$.

Skewness and kurtosis indices describe two ways in which a distribution differs from the normal distribution. Non-normal distributions can often be made to be more nearly normal by using certain mathematical transformations on the scores.

## 6.14 CASE STUDY

In previous chapters, we have studied the variables in the case study with respect to central tendency and variability. We did observe skewness in certain of the variables. In this chapter, we quantify the degree of skewness, $\gamma_1$, and kurtosis, $\gamma_2$.

The skewness index, $\hat{\gamma}_1$, is a measure of asymmetry; ID # has a skewness index of .00 because the distribution is perfectly rectangular and symmetrical. The distribution of height is only slightly asymmetrical. Notice that all the other distributions are skewed positively; the degree of the skewness is substantial for the SBP, weight, and coronary variables. Note that a dichotomous variable like coronary will be skewed to the extent that the frequencies in the two categories are unequal; they are very unequal here, hence, the large value for $\hat{\gamma}_1$.

Table 6.1 gives $\hat{\gamma}_1$ and $\hat{\gamma}_2$ indices when the scores on each variable are converted to $T$-scores. Although for all variables the mean $T$-score is 50 and the standard deviation is 10, the shape of the distribution has not changed; thus, the skewness and kurtosis indices are

---

[16]On rare occasions, one may need to know the mean and standard deviation within a segment of the normal distribution. The mean $z$-score for a given section of the normal distribution between the points $z_a$ and $z_b$ (where $z_b > z_a$) is the difference in the corresponding ordinates $u_a$ and $u_b$ at $z_a$ and $z_b$ divided by $p$, the proportion of cases falling within the segment. Thus, $\mu_z = (u_a - u_b)/p$. To find the mean of scores falling between the median and $Q_3$ expressed as a $z$-score, do the following: From Table A, read that the ordinates corresponding to $z_a$ and $z_b$ are $u_a = .3989$ and $u_b = .3178$. Hence, $\mu_z = (.3989 - .3178)/.25 = .3244$. The same procedure can be used to find the mean of the scores in the tail of the normal distribution (Kelley, 1939). The mean $z$-score in the top quarter of normally distributed scores is $\mu_z = (.3178 - 0)/.25 = 1.27$; conversely, the mean of scores below $Q_1$ is $\mu_z = (0 - .3178)/.25 = -1.27$.

The variance of $z$-scores within a section of the normal distribution is $\sigma_z^2 = [p(z_a u_a - z_b u_b) - (u_a - u_b)^2]/p^2$. The variance of $z$-scores between the median and $Q_3$ is $\sigma_z^2 = \{.25[(0)(.3989) - (.674)(.3178)] - (.3989 - .3178)^2\}/(.25)^2 = .0380$, and $\sigma_z = .195$. For the top or bottom quarter of the normal distribution, $\sigma_z = .490$.

**TABLE 6.1** Descriptive Information for Chapman Case Study Variables ($n$ = 200)

| | | | *T-scores* | | $\sqrt{T}$ | | $LOG_{10}T$ | |
|---|---|---|---|---|---|---|---|---|
| *Variable* | $\hat{\gamma}_1$ | $\hat{\gamma}_2$ | $\hat{\gamma}_1$ | $\hat{\gamma}_2$ | $\hat{\gamma}_1$ | $\hat{\gamma}_2$ | $\hat{\gamma}_1$ | $\hat{\gamma}_2$ |
| Age | .28 | –.80 | .28 | –.80 | .07 | –.96 | –.15 | –.97 |
| Systolic B.P. (SBP) | 1.51 | 3.50 | 1.51 | 3.50 | 1.23 | 2.47 | .96 | 1.70 |
| Diastolic B.P. (DBP) | .45 | .76 | .45 | .76 | .22 | .58 | –.01 | .55 |
| Cholesterol Level | .41 | .42 | .41 | .42 | .05 | .09 | –.31 | .16 |
| Height (in.) | .10 | –.35 | .10 | –.35 | .05 | –.34 | .01 | –.33 |
| Weight (lbs.) | .84 | 1.54 | .84 | 1.54 | .55 | .91 | .28 | .52 |
| Coronary? (0=N, 1=Y) | 2.29 | 3.25 | 2.29 | 3.25 | 2.29 | 3.25 | NA | NA |
| ID # | .00 | –1.2 | .00 | –1.2 | –.56 | –.63 | –.56 | –.625 |

identical to those for the raw score distributions. This type of conversion from one scale to a different scale that does not change the configuration of the frequency distribution is termed a *linear transformation*.[17]

The positive skewness in SBP could be reduced if certain *non-linear* transformations are employed, for example, if the actual blood pressure values are replaced by their square roots or logs.[18] We will illustrate the effect of two transformations—square root and logarithms.[19] In Table 6.1, skewness and kurtosis indices are given for the distributions of the square root (SQRT) transformation, $\sqrt{X}$. Note that the SQRT transformation reduces positive skewness, for example, for age the skewness was reduced from .28 to .07. The SQRT transformation will introduce negative skewness for symmetrical distributions like ID #. Since skewed distributions are leptokurtic ($\hat{\gamma}_2 > 0$), the SQRT transformation also reduces the leptokurtosis (i.e., $\hat{\gamma}_2$ is decreased) in the distributions. The transformations have no effect on a dichotomous distribution, but they will change its mean and variance.

The effect of the square root transformation on the shape of the distribution of cholesterol level is illustrated in Figure 6.8. The printout is from the computer program SPSS FREQUENCIES, which will superimpose a normal distribution backdrop if requested. (This program also produces a variety of statistical information including measures of central tendency, variability, skewness, and kurtosis.) Although the differences between the two distributions are not striking, a study of both distributions will reveal that the outlier ($X$ = 520) that contributes greatly to the positive skewness and kurtosis, becomes less extreme after the square root transformation.[20]

Table 6.1 gives $\hat{\gamma}_1$ and $\hat{\gamma}_2$ indices after a second non-linear transformation has been applied to the raw scores, that is, when each $X_i$ is replaced by $\log_{10}X_i$. This LOG transformation reduces positive skewness, or increases negative skewness, even more than the SQRT

[17]The topic of linear transformations is treated more extensively in Chapter 7, Section 7.12.

[18]Note in Figure 6.6 how the shape of the distribution changes depending on the particular transformation that is applied.

[19]It is unlikely that transformations would be used in the actual study, especially based on what we know about the variables at this point; they are included primarily for illustrative purposes.

[20]Confirm that in the raw score distribution, the outlier 520 in the distribution with a mean of 285.11 and a standard deviation of 65.04 is 3.61 (= $z$) standard deviations above the mean. After the square root transformation, the mean and standard deviation were 16.775 and 1.927, respectively, and $\sqrt{520}$ = 22.804, which is 3.13 (= $z$) standard deviations from the mean.

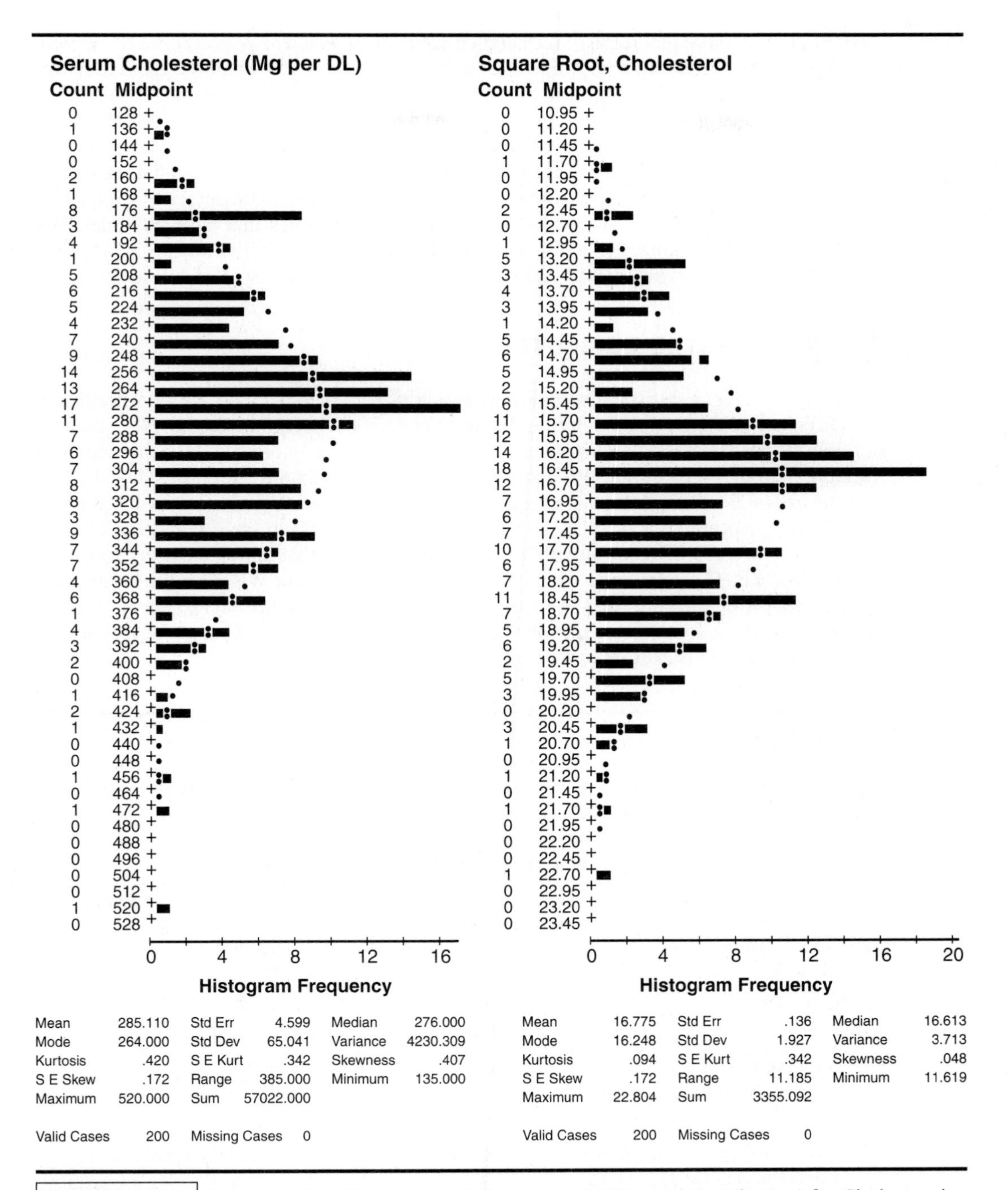


**FIGURE 6.8** Frequency Distributions (with Superimposed Normal Distribution) for Cholesterol and Square Root Transformation of Cholesterol Variables.

transformation. Note that for age, the original value of $\hat{\gamma}_1$ was .28; $\hat{\gamma}_1$ decreased to .07 with the SQRT transformation, and $\hat{\gamma}_1$ became slightly negative (–.15) when the LOG transformation was applied. If our goal was to coerce the distributions into approximate normality as closely as possible, we would apply neither transformation to coronary nor ID #. We would choose the SQRT over the LOG transformation for age and cholesterol level, and the LOG transformation for all others. Based on our current analyses, we would not use transformations; other considerations pertaining to transformations will be considered in Chapter 7.

We could remove most of the skewness in all the variables that have an underlying continuum if we normalized (Section 6.12) the distributions, but normalizing is appropriate only when there is a problem with the measurement scale, which is not the case here.

## 6.15 SUGGESTED COMPUTER EXERCISE

Using speadsheet or statistical software, compute skewness indices for all the variables in the HSB case study data set including ID, but not career (CAR) and RACE. Note that the variable ID has a rectangular distribution, thus has no skewness. Note that the dichotomous variable School Type (SCTYP) is highly skewed, but SEX is only slightly skewed. Note that the use of $T$-scores does not necessarily indicate that a variable is normally distributed, for example, writing (WRTG). Use a transformation on WRTG to see if you can reduce its skewness (since WRTG is negatively skewed, create another variable that is the square or cube of the WRTG scores). See what happens to the skewness of WRTG if the square root or log transformations are used. Recompute the skewness to see how the skewness is affected by the transformations. Obtain histograms and examine the change in appearance before and after the transformations.

## MASTERY TEST

*Information on certain standardized intelligence and achievement tests is given. Answer questions 1 to 10 assuming the scores are normally distributed.*

***Iowa Test of Basic Skills Grade-Equivalent Scores***

| | | *Reading* | | | *Arithmetic* |
|---|---|---|---|---|---|
| | *Wechsler IQ* | *Grade 3* | *Grade 5* | *Grade 8* | *Grade 5* |
| $\mu$ | 100 | 3.0 | 5.0 | 8.0 | 5.0 |
| $\sigma$ | 15 | 1.0 | 1.4 | 1.9 | 1.1 |

1. An IQ score above 115 is obtained by what percent of the population?
2. If a fifth-grade student obtains a percentile rank of 84 in reading, what is the grade-equivalent score?
3. What is the grade-equivalent score for the same relative performance as in question 2 ($P_{84}$) in arithmetic at grade 5?
4. Jack was reading at 6.1 when he entered grade 8. If his Wechsler IQ is equivalent to the same percentile rank, what is it?
5. If Jack's score in question 4 is valid, he reads better than about what percentage of children in his grade?

6. Upon entering grade 3, approximately what percent of third-grade children:
   (a) obtains a reading grade-equivalent score of 3.0 or better?
   (b) obtains a score of 4.0 or better?
   (c) obtains a score of 5.0 or better?
7. On the reading test, what percent of beginning third-grade students (3.0) score no higher than the average beginning second-grade students (2.0)?
8. At grade 5, is a grade-equivalent score of 6.0 relatively better (i.e., does it have a higher percentile equivalent) in arithmetic than in reading?
9. In reading, what percentages of third-grade students score below grade-equivalent scores of 2.0, 3.0, 4.0, and 5.0, respectively?
10. How much reading gain in grade-equivalent units is required during the five years between grades 3.0 and 8.0 to:
    (a) maintain a percentile equivalent of 50?
    (b) maintain a percentile rank of 84?
11. If $X_3 = 176$ with $\mu = 163$ and $\sigma = 26$, express $X_3$ as:
    (a) a $z$-score. (b) a $T$-score. (c) a percentile equivalent.
12. If IQ's were perfectly normally distributed, how many persons in the United States would have IQ's exceeding 175? (Assume $\mu = 100$, $\sigma = 15$, and $N = 250{,}000{,}000$.)
13. What percentage of IQ scores would fall between:
    (a) 90 and 110? (b) 80 and 120? (c) 75 and 125?
14. If men's heights are distributed normally, approximately how many men in 10,000 will be 6′6″ or taller? (Use $\mu = 69.7''$, $\sigma = 2.6''$)
15. Which of these is not a characteristic of a normal distribution?
    (a) symmetrical (b) unimodal (c) skewed (d) mesokurtic
16. Which of these reflects the poorest performance on a test? Assume a normal distribution.
    (a) $P_{10}$ (b) $z = -1.5$ (c) $T = 30$
17. With a sample of 1,000 representative observations, which of these is probably least accurately characterized by the normal distribution?
    (a) scores on a musical aptitude test
    (b) number of baby teeth lost by age eight
    (c) size of reading vocabulary of twelve-year-old children
    (d) number of times attended a religious service in the past year
    (e) scores on an inventory measuring interest in politics
18. If raw scores are changed to $z$-scores, would the shape of the distribution be changed?
19. If $z$-scores are multiplied by 10, the standard deviation increases from ____ to ____.
20. What is the variance in a distribution expressed as (a) $z$-scores? (b) $T$-scores?
21. Small changes in $z$-scores near the mean (e.g., from 0 to .5) correspond to large or small changes in percentile equivalents. Large $z$-score changes near the extremes (e.g., 2.0 to 2.5) correspond to large or small changes in percentile equivalents.
22. If for a class of gifted children $\mu = 140$, $\sigma = 10$, and skewness $sk = .6$ (Equation 6.7), estimate the mode and median of the distribution of scores.
23. What is the skewness index, $sk$, for the distribution of cholesterol levels in the Chapman study? (Use Equation 6.7 and Table 5.2.)
24. The square root and log transformations will reduce ____ (positive or negative) skewness in a distribution. (See Figure 6.6)

## PROBLEMS AND EXERCISES

1. Find the area under the normal curve which lies:

   (a) above $z = 1.00$
   (b) below $z = 2.00$
   (c) above $z = 1.64$
   (d) below $z = -1.96$
   (e) between $z_1 = 0$ and $z_2 = 3.00$
   (f) above $z = -.50$
   (g) between $z_1 = -1.50$ and $z_2 = 1.50$

2. Find the ordinates of these $z$-scores in the normal distribution:

   (a) $z = 2.25$ (b) $z = -.15$

3. Find the $z$-scores that are exceeded by the following proportions of the area under the normal distribution:

   (a) .50 (b) .16 (c) .84 (d) .05 (e) .005 (f) .995 (g) .10

4. If in the general population of children, Stanford-Binet IQ's have a nearly normal distribution with mean 100 and standard deviation 16 (see Figure 6.5), find the percentile equivalent of each of the following IQ's:

   (a) 100 (b) 120 (c) 75 (d) 95 (e) 140

5. Suppose Mary obtained the following percentiles on five subtests on the *McCarthy Scales of Children's Abilities*:

| *Subtest* | *Percentile* |
|---|---|
| Verbal | 98 |
| Perceptual | 99.9 |
| Quantitative | 50 |
| Memory | 84 |
| Motor | 16 |

*Use Figure 6.5 to answer the exercises below.*

   (a) If Mary's Motor performance improved by $1\sigma$, the percentile equivalent would increase from 16 to ____, or ____ percentile units.
   (b) If the Verbal score improved by $1\sigma$, the percentile equivalent on the Verbal tests would increase from 98 to ____, or ____ percentile units.
   (c) In standard deviation units, is the size of the difference between Mary's performance on the Verbal and Perceptual tests the same as the difference between her Motor and Quantitative scores?
   (d) If expressed in $T$-scores, would the change from $P_{16}$ to $P_{50}$ in exercise (a) be equal to the change from $P_{98}$ to $P_{99.9}$ in exercise (b)?

6. The manual for the *Metropolitan Achievement Tests* (MAT) contains no report of standard deviations for the grade equivalent (GE) scales but does give percentile ranks as indicated:

| *Percentile for Fall of Grade 5* | *Grade Equivalents* | |
|---|---|---|
| | *Reading* | *Math* |
| 84 | 9.0 | 6.8 |
| 50 | 5.0 | 5.0 |
| 16 | 3.0 | 3.4 |

   (a) Estimate the GE standard deviation for the reading and math tests. [$\sigma \approx (P_{84} - P_{16})/2$]

(b) Which distribution is more sev.

(c) Would the mean GE be greater st? Explain.

(d) Using the estimated standard deviation on the math test, approximately what percent of beginning fifth-grade students obtain GE scores above 6.0 on the MAT? Assuming normal distributions, compare this figure with the corresponding figure for the ITBS Arithmetic Test (see data preceding question 1 on the Mastery Test).

**7.** "Grading on the normal curve" was popular in some circles a few decades ago. The most common method used the following conversion. Using this system, what percent of A's, B's, C's, D's, and F's are expected with a normal distribution of scores?

| *Grade* | *z-score* |
|---|---|
| A | above 1.5 |
| B | .5 to 1.5 |
| C | –.5 to .5 |
| D | –1.5 to –.5 |
| F | below –1.5 |

**8.** If many naive examinees guess randomly on each of the 100 items on a true-false test, the mean would be expected to be $50 = \mu$, with $\sigma = 5$. What percent of examinees would be expected to earn scores of 65 or more?

**9.** Each of eleven students in a class was asked to respond to a sociometric measure in which they identified the three persons who had showed the most leadership ability. The scores (number of nominations) for each student are given below. View the group as a population, not as a sample.

| $X_i$ | $x_i$ | $z_i$ | $z_i^2$ | $z_i^3$ | $z_i^4$ |
|---|---|---|---|---|---|
| 9 | 6 | 2.4 | 5.76 | 13.824 | 33.1776 |
| 5 | 2 | .8 | .64 | .512 | .4096 |
| 5 | 2 | — | — | — | — |
| 4 | 1 | .4 | — | — | — |
| 3 | 0 | .0 | .00 | .000 | .0000 |
| 2 | –1 | –.4 | .16 | — | — |
| 2 | –1 | –.4 | .16 | –.064 | .0256 |
| 1 | –2 | –.8 | .64 | –.512 | .4096 |
| 1 | –2 | –.8 | .64 | –.512 | .4096 |
| 1 | –2 | –.8 | .64 | –.512 | .4096 |
| 0 | –3 | | 1.44 | –1.728 | 2.0736 |
| $\Sigma X_i =$ ___ | $\Sigma x_i =$ ___ | $\Sigma z_i =$ ___ | $\Sigma z_i^2 =$ ___ | $\Sigma z_i^3 =$ ___ | $\Sigma z_i^4 =$ ___ |

(a) What are the mean, median, and mode of the distribution?

(b) Supply the missing *z*-score ($\sigma = 2.5$).

(c) Supply the missing values in the $z_i^2$, $z_i^3$, and $z_i^4$ columns, and find the sums of each column.

(d) Compute the skewness ($\gamma_1$) and kurtosis ($\gamma_2$) indices of the distribution.

**10.** Suppose a student can qualify for $100 in additional state aid designated for special remedial reading by scoring 2.0 or more grade equivalents below his current grade level status. For a typical, representative school district with approximately 4,000 students per grade level, how much more state aid would the district receive for its fifth graders given that the Metropolitan (MAT) was given rather than the Iowa (ITBS)? The standard deviations are 3.0 and 1.4 for the

MAT and ITBS, respectively; use 5.0 for both means. Assume normality and round $z$-scores to the second decimal place.

**11.** Knowing $\sigma = 15$ on the Wechsler IQ scale, estimate $Q$.

**12.** Some academic departments use the *Miller Analogies Test* for selecting graduate students. Although only raw scores are reported, for students applying for graduate study the mean and standard deviation are approximately 48 and 17, respectively. If applicants at a certain prestigious university are expected to be in the upper 10%, what is the minimum raw score expected on the Miller?

**13.** Prove that $\Sigma_i z_i^2 = N$.

## ANSWERS TO MASTERY TEST

**1.** 16%
**2.** 6.4
**3.** 6.1
**4.** 85
**5.** 16%
**6.** (a) 50%, (b) 16%, (c) 2%
**7.** 16%
**8.** yes
**9.** 16%, 50%, 84%, and 98%
**10.** (a) 5.0 (b) 5.9
**11.** (a) $z = (176 - 163)/26 = .50$
(b) $T = 50 + 10(.50) = 55$
(c) $P_{69}$
**12.** $z = (175 - 100)/15 = 5.0$;
$(.0000002867)(250{,}000{,}000) \approx 80$
**13.** (a) .7486 – .2514 =.4972 or about 50%
(b) .9082 – .0918 = .8164 or 82%
(c) .9525 – .0475 = .9050 or 91%
**14.** $z = (78 - 69.7)/2.6 = 3.19$;
$(.00071)(10{,}000) = 7.1$ or about 7
**15.** (c)
**16.** (c)
**17.** (d)
**18.** no
**19.** 1.0 to 10
**20.** (a) $(1)^2 = 1$; (b) $(10)^2 = 100$
**21.** large, small
**22.** Mode ≈ 134, Md ≈ 138 (See Equation 4.10)
**23.** –.42
**24.** positive

## ANSWERS TO PROBLEMS AND EXERCISES

**1.** (a) .1587 (b) .9772 (c) .0505 (d) .025 (e).4987 (f) .6915 (g) .8664
**2.** (a) .0317 (b) .3945
**3.** (a) 0.00 (b) +1.00 (c) –1.00 (d) +1.645 (e) +2.58 (f) –2.58 (g) +1.28
**4.** (a) 50 (b) 89 (c) 6 (d) 38 (e) 99
**5.** (a) 50, 34 (b) 99.9, 1.9 (c) yes, $1\sigma$ in each instance (d) yes, $T$-score increase of 10 in each instance
**6.** (a) $\sigma_R \approx 3.0$, $\sigma_M \approx 1.7$ (b) reading (c) reading; greater positive skewness (d) MAT: $z = .59$, 28% above 6.0; ITBS: $z = .91$, 18% above 6.0
**7.** A: 7%, B: 24%, C: 38%, D: 24%, F: 7%
**8.** .0013 or .13%, or roughly one student in 1,000
**9.** (a) mean = 3.0, median = 2, mode = 1; (b) .8, –1.2 (c); (c) $\Sigma X = 33$, $\Sigma x = 0$, $\Sigma z = 0$, $\Sigma z^2 = 10.88$, $\Sigma z^3 = 11.52$, $\Sigma z^4 = 37.3760$; (d) $\gamma_1 = 11.52/11 = 1.05$, $\gamma_2 = 37.376/11 - 3 = .40$
**10.** MAT: $z = -.67$, $(.2514)(4{,}000)(100) =$ \$100,560; ITBS: $z = -1.43$, $(.0764)(4{,}000)(100) =$ \$30,560, or \$70,000 more using MAT
**11.** From Table A, $Q = .674\sigma$, $Q = 10$
**12.** 70
**13.** $\Sigma_i z_i^2 = \Sigma_i (X_i - \mu)^2/\sigma^2 = (1/\sigma^2)\Sigma_i (X_i - \mu)^2 = (1/\sigma^2)(N\sigma^2) = N$

# 7

# CORRELATION: MEASURES OF RELATIONSHIP BETWEEN TWO VARIABLES

## 7.1 INTRODUCTION

Measures of correlation are used to describe the relationship between two variables. In addition, correlation is an important part of many other statistical techniques. In this chapter, we will present the meaning, use, and computation of common measures of relationship.

Behavioral research frequently assesses the degree of association between two variables. The variables may be on many different kinds of observational units: persons, classes, schools, sites, cities, or the like. For example: Is absenteeism related to socioeconomic status (SES) for high school students? Is class size related to achievement growth for first grade classes? Do competitive cultures have a greater incidence of peptic ulcers? Can GPA be better predicted from SES than from IQ? To answer questions such as these, measures of relationship (correlation coefficients) are needed.

Most persons have a general understanding of correlation. Two variables are correlated if high scores on one variable tend to "go together" with high scores on the second variable. Likewise, if low scores on variable $X$ tend to be accompanied by low scores on variable $Y$, then the variables $X$ and $Y$ are correlated. The degree of correlation between variables can be described by such terms as strong, low, positive, or moderate, but these terms are not very precise. If a coefficient of correlation is computed between the two sets of scores, the relationship is described more precisely. A coefficient of correlation is a statistical summary of the degree and direction of relationship or association between two variables.

## 7.2 THE CONCEPT OF CORRELATION

There is a substantial, but by no means perfect, positive correlation between annual income and the taxes paid to IRS. Husbands and wives tend to be alike in age, amount of education, and many other ways. The sons of tall fathers tend to be taller than average, and the sons of short fathers tend to be shorter than average. Children resemble their siblings in intelligence more closely than they resemble their cousins. In fact, some degree of positive correlation between members of families is usually found for almost any characteristic, such as personality, attitude, interest, ability, and health variables.

Statistical measures have been devised to quantify the relationships among variables. Karl Pearson (1857–1936) derived a measure of relationship called the *product-moment coefficient of correlation*, signified by $r$ in a sample and by $\rho$ (the Greek letter rho) for the population parameter. The correlation coefficient has been employed extensively in almost all social sciences since the beginning of the century. It is widely used in virtually all behavioral and social sciences.

## 7.3 SCATTERPLOTS

An intuitive understanding of the meaning of correlation coefficients (such as those given in Table 7.1) is enhanced by studying some illustrative scatterplots. In a scatterplot of dots or tallies, each mark represents the intersection of two scores (one pair of observations) such as heights of fathers ($X$) and sons ($Y$), or age ($X$) paired with blood pressure ($Y$). In a sample of cities, the two variables, number of policemen per 10,000 persons ($X$) and the number of crimes per 10,000 persons ($Y$) can be correlated. *The chief purpose of the scatterplot is for the study of the nature of the relationship between two variables.* The scatterplot also enables one to see whether a computed $r$ will accurately summarize the relationship between the two variables; $r$ is appropriate only for *linear* relationships. The relationship between two variables is linear if a straight line, a regression line, more closely

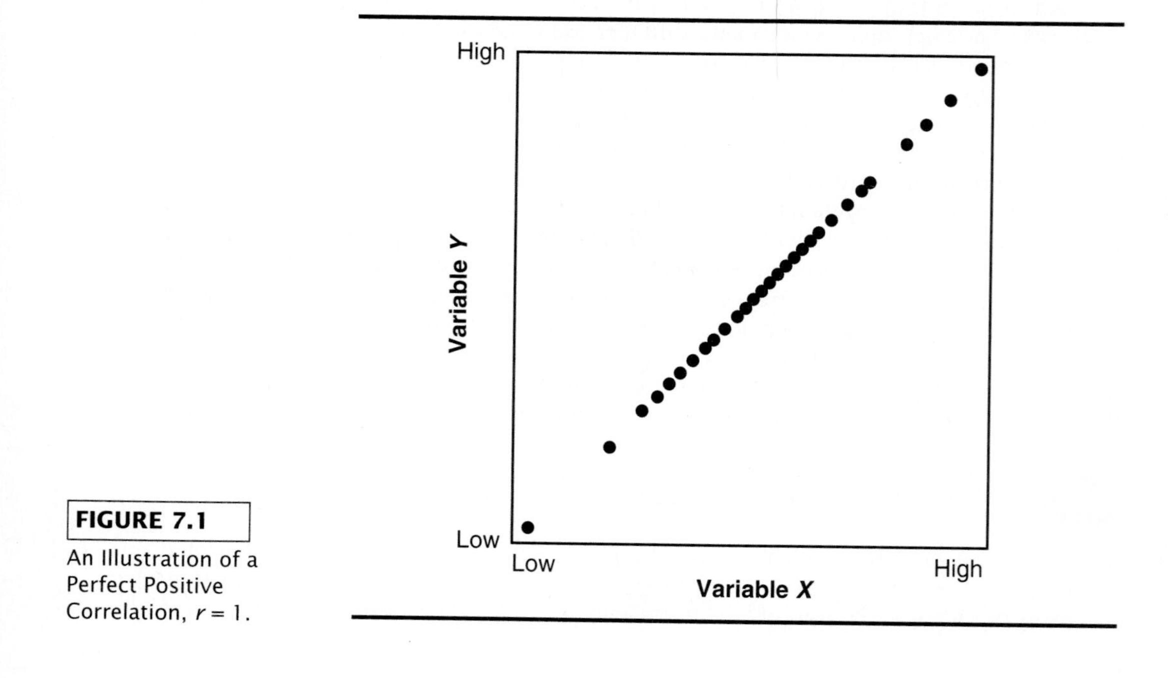


**FIGURE 7.1**

An Illustration of a Perfect Positive Correlation, $r = 1$.

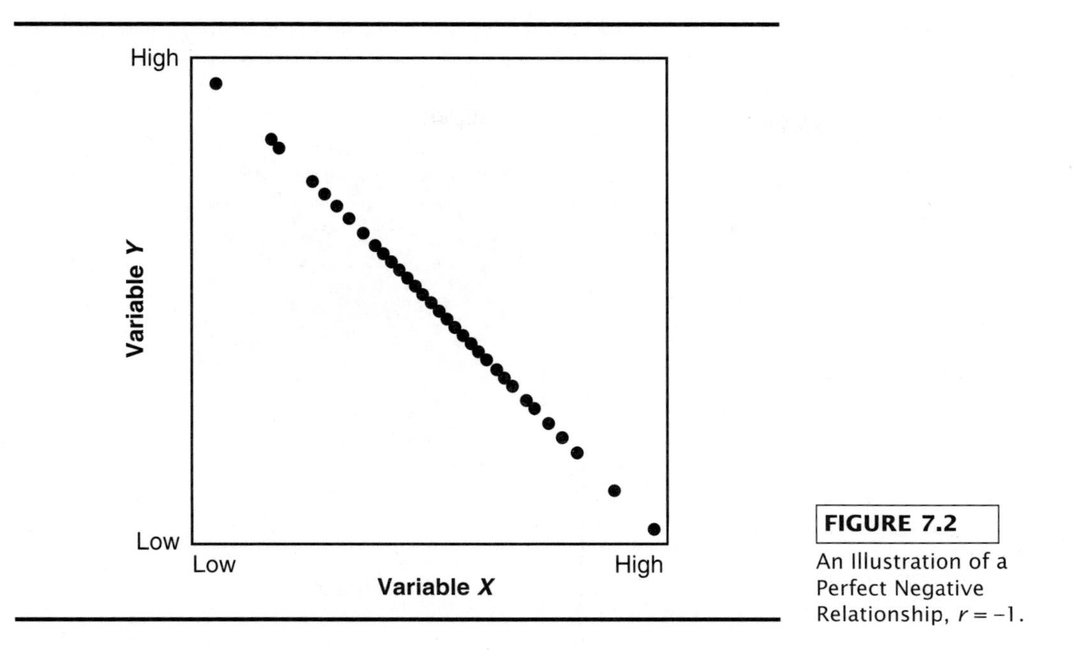


FIGURE 7.2
An Illustration of a Perfect Negative Relationship, $r = -1$.

fits the dots of the scatterplot than does a smooth curve. Stated differently, if the base variable, *X*, is viewed as vertical slices or class intervals, the mean of *Y* for each slice is found, and these slice means are connected, the resulting line would be more or less straight if the relationship is linear.[1]

A perfect positive linear relationship ($r = 1.00$) is shown in Figure 7.1—the dots fall in a rising straight line. For example, centigrade and Fahrenheit temperatures correlate +1.0, as would weights expressed in pounds versus kilograms; if one is known, the other can be predicted perfectly.

A perfect negative relationship ($r = -1.0$) is illustrated in Figure 7.2. The time required to travel one mile correlates –1.0, perfectly and negatively, with running speed. If everyone attempts all items on an objective test, the number of right answers will correlate –1.0 with the number of wrong answers. In practice, *r*'s of +1.0 or –1.0 are rare; nevertheless, these values set the limits for observed correlation coefficients. The meaning of various values of *r* becomes clearer with experience.

In Figure 7.3, the scatterplot depicts no relationship between variables *X* and *Y* ($r = 0.00$). A high score on *Y* is just as likely to occur with a low score on *X* as with a high score on *X*. If for a sample of graduate students, cholesterol level is correlated with GRE score, the scatterplot would be similar to Figure 7.3.

---

[1]If the two variables are linearly related, as the sample size increases, the means of the slices will fall closer and closer to a straight line. Curvilinear relationships will be illustrated in Section 7.7.

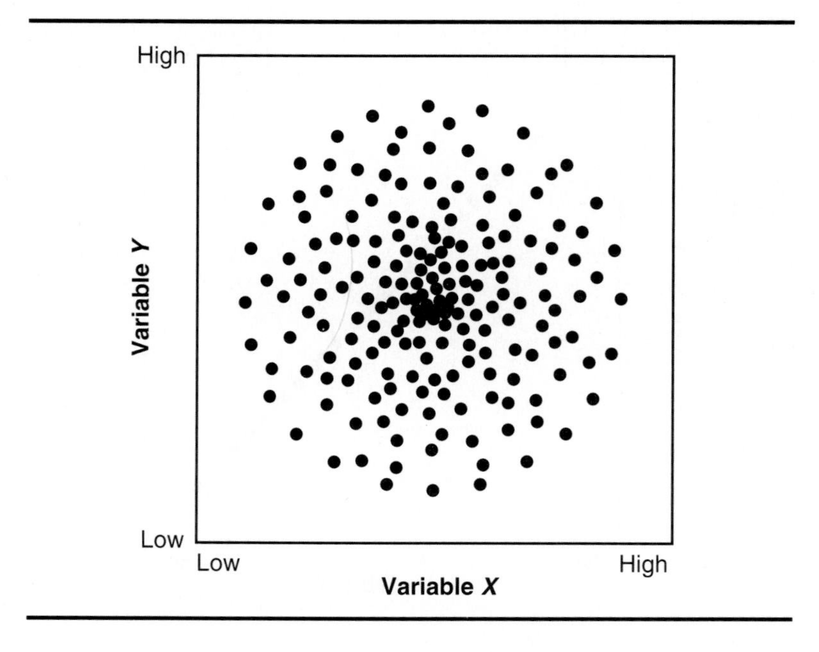


**FIGURE 7.3**

An Illustration of No Correlation, $r = 0$.

## 7.4 THE MEASUREMENT OF CORRELATION

The Pearson correlation coefficient quantifies the *magnitude* and *direction* of the linear relationship between two variables, such as height and weight of individuals, or between the same variable on pairs of observations, like the height of fathers and sons. The variables to be correlated can be any measure except those representing nominal scales (see Section 2.3) that are not dichotomies, for example, reading grades ($X$) and math grades ($Y$), age ($X$) and speed of running the 100-meter dash ($Y$), or amount of education ($X$) and political conservatism ($Y$). The value of $r$ can range from –1.0 for a perfect inverse or negative relationship (see Figure 7.2), through 0 for no correlation (as in Figure 7.3), and up to +1.0 for perfect direct or positive relationship (see Figure 7.1).

As shown in Figures 7.1 and 7.2, the sign (+ or –) of the correlation coefficient indicates the direction of the relationship. When low scores on $X$ are accompanied by low scores on $Y$ and high scores on $X$ by high scores on $Y$, the correlation between $X$ and $Y$ is positive. If high scores on $X$ are associated with low scores on $Y$ and vice versa, the correlation is negative.

Correlation coefficients allow us to compare the strength and direction of association between different pairs of variables. For example, by comparing the respective correlation coefficients, one can say that siblings are more similar in grade point average ($\rho \approx .7$) than they are in IQ scores ($\rho \approx .5$). Also, the correlation coefficient could be used to establish that the relationship between cognitive and psychomotor abilities ($\rho \approx .2$) is less than the relationship between verbal and mathematical abilities ($\rho \approx .6$). For a third example, the IQ scores of adopted children are more highly related to the IQ scores of their biological parents ($\rho \approx .4$) than to the IQ scores of their adopting parents ($\rho \approx .25$) (see Munsinger, 1975).

In Table 7.3, GRE Quantitative test scores are given for 121 students along with $T$-scores these students earned on the final examination in a course in applied statistics.

Peruse the numbers to confirm that there is some relationship between the two variables; students with higher GRE scores tend to have higher final exam scores than students with lower GRE scores. However, notice in the scatterplot (Figure 7.6) that the relationship is not high ($r \approx .41$).

## 7.5 THE USE OF CORRELATION COEFFICIENTS

How highly are the variables of age, undergraduate grade point average, sex, and the Graduate Record Examination scores related to performance in applied statistics? Table 7.1 gives the correlations with two outcome measures: course grade and *T*-score within the statistics class. Note, not surprisingly, these two criteria are highly correlated ($r \approx .89$).[2] The pattern of correlations is similar for both criteria.

Younger students did slightly better than older students (note the negative *r*'s).

GPA had almost no relationship to either criterion.

Females, however, had somewhat higher GPAs ($r = .11$).

In spite of a sizable difference in GRE Quantitative scores favoring the males ($r \approx -.33$), there was virtually no difference between the males and females (as a group, the males did negligibly better than the females on the *T*-score criterion measure[3]).

GRE Analytic and Quantitative scores were moderately related to the criteria (*r*'s of .38 to .42); the *r*'s for GRE Verbal scores were somewhat lower.

Note also that the GRE Analytic measure correlated somewhat more highly with GRE Quantitative ($r = .66$) than with the GRE Verbal measure ($r = .56$).

A second exercise in using correlation coefficients is found in Table 7.2 where correlation coefficients are used to address the classic nature-nurture studies of measures of intelligence. Table 7.2 gives correlation coefficients between performance on cognitive ability (IQ) tests for persons with varying degrees of genetic and environmental similarity. Data on academic achievement, height, and weight are also given in Table 7.2. Notice that environment has a much greater relationship with scholastic achievement than it does with IQ. For example, in Table 7.2 the correlation between the scholastic achievement of pairs of unrelated children reared together is .52; but the correlation between their IQ scores is only .23. Notice also that although height is less influenced by environment than weight, a strong hereditary factor is evident in weight (e.g., $r = .88$ for identical twins reared apart).

## 7.6 INTERPRETING *r* AS A PERCENT

The correlation coefficient cannot be interpreted directly as a percentage. However, it can be interpreted as a percent in one important sense—when we work in standard deviation or standard-score units. The correlation coefficient is the ratio of how far from the mean of *Y* (the predicted variable) individuals tend to be relative to how far they are from the mean of

---

[2]The correlation would be even higher if all of the instructors used the same grading standards.

[3]The negative *r*'s with sex show that the high numbers on one variable tend to go with low numbers on the other variable. Since, for these data, 1 = M and 2 = F, negative *r*'s indicate that females had lower scores. Obviously, if the coding were reversed, the *r*'s would have the same absolute value, but the opposite sign. Unlike continuous variables, one must know the coding for dichotomous variables before a correlation coefficient can be interpreted.

**TABLE 7.1** The Correlation Coefficients among Several Variables[4] and Performance in a Course in Applied Statistics ($n = 121$)

| | AGE | GRE-A | GRE-Q | GRE-V | SEX | GPA | GRADE | *T* |
|---|---|---|---|---|---|---|---|---|
| AGE | 1.00 | –.23 | –.19 | +.01 | +.13 | –.17 | –.08 | –.04 |
| GRE-A | –.23 | 1.00 | +.66 | +.56 | –.03 | +.24 | +.42 | +.38 |
| GRE-Q | –.19 | +.66 | 1.00 | +.35 | –.33 | +.00 | +.40 | +.41 |
| GRE-V | +.01 | +.56 | +.35 | 1.00 | +.07 | +.21 | +.32 | +.19 |
| SEX | +.13 | –.03 | –.33 | +.07 | 1.00 | +.11 | .00 | –.03 |
| GPA | +.17 | +.24 | +.00 | +.21 | +.11 | 1.00 | +.06 | +.04 |
| GRADE | –.08 | +.42 | +.40 | +.32 | –.00 | +.06 | 1.00 | +.89 |
| *T* | –.04 | +.38 | +.41 | +.19 | –.04 | +.04 | +.89 | 1.00 |

*X* (the predictor) when the differences are expressed in standard deviation units. If $r = .60$, then persons tend to be only 60% as far from the mean of *Y* as they are from the mean of *X* in standard deviation units. For example, using the findings in Table 7.2, assume a person named Jane with an IQ score of 130, and predict the IQ score of other persons who vary from this person in genetic and environmental similarity. Jane is 30 points above the mean; her identical twin Jan is predicted to have an IQ score that is 91% ($r = .91$) as far from the mean as is Jane's: $.91 \times 30 = 27$. Jan's predicted IQ is 127. If Jane has siblings, on the average their IQ's would be expected to be only 50% ($r = .50$) as far from the mean as is Jane's; the mean of Jane's siblings is predicted to be $.50 \times 30 = 15$ points above the mean, or 115. If Jane has an adopted sister, Mary, she is predicted to have an IQ that is 23% as far from the mean as Jane, or her predicted IQ is $100 + .23 \times 30 = 107$. These examples illustrate the sense in which *r* can be interpreted as a percentage.

Jim is very short; he is at the second percentile ($P_2$). From Table 7.2, we see that the heights of siblings correlate .50. Can you predict the percentile rank of Jim's siblings? Jim is 2 standard deviations below the mean ($z_X = -2.0$); $r = .50$ means that his siblings will tend to be only 50% as far from the mean of the height of their gender group as is Jim; their predicted *z*-score in height is $.50 \times (-2.0) = -1.0$. On the average, his siblings are predicted to be at the 16th percentile ($P_{16}$). In Chapter 8, the principal use for *r* is prediction: The *z*-score on the predicted variable *Y* is *r* times the *z*-score on the variable from which the prediction is made.

Viewed differently, $1 - r$ describes the amount or regression toward the mean that is expected when variable *Y* is predicted from variable *X*. Statistically, it matters not which

[4]GRE = Graduate Record Examination: A = Analytic, V = Verbal, Q = Quantitative; GPA = undergraduate grade-point average; GRADE = course grade (A = 4, B = 3, etc.); and *T* = within class *T*-score based on students' composite scores for the course. Sex is coded: 1 = M, 2 = F.

**TABLE 7.2** The Relationships among Measures of Intelligence, Academic Achievement, Height, and Weight for Persons of Varying Genetic Similarity, Reared Together and Apart*

| | *Identical Twins Reared* | | *Fraternal Twins Reared* | *Siblings Reared* | | *Unrelated Children Reared* | |
|---|---|---|---|---|---|---|---|
| | *Together* | *Apart* | *Together* | *Together* | *Apart* | *Together* | *Apart* |
| Intelligence (IQ) | .91 | .67 | .64 | .50 | .40 | .23 | .00 |
| Achievement | .96 | .51 | .88 | .81 | .53 | .52 | .00 |
| Height | .96 | .94 | .50 | .50 | .50 | .00 | .00 |
| Weight | .93 | .88 | .59 | .57 | .43 | .24 | .00 |

*Data from Newman, Freeman, and Holzinger (1937), Erlenmeyer-Kimlinger and Jarvik (1963), and Sternberg (1982). The values in the table are not based on the controversial research of Sir Cyril Burt.

variable is $X$ and which is $Y$. Unrelated children reared apart have weights that correlate .00; thus, regardless of whether the first child is light or heavy, the best prediction of the weight of the second child is $P_{50}$; there is regression all the way to the mean. On the other hand, siblings reared in different homes have weights that are moderately related ($r = .43$). Jim's weight is 10 pounds under the average of his sex and age; this shows that his genetic brother who was reared in a different household, is expected to be $.43 \times 10 = 4.3$ pounds below average when he is Jim's age.

## 7.7 LINEAR AND CURVILINEAR RELATIONSHIPS

Only the degree of linear relationship is described by $r$ or $\rho$; the value of $r$ is a measure of the linear relationship between $X$ and $Y$. If $X$ and $Y$ are perfectly linearly related (i.e., $r = 1.0$ or $r = -1.0$), the points in the scatterplot will fall on a straight line, as illustrated in Figures 7.1 and 7.2. If the points in a scatterplot cluster around a straight line that could be drawn through the points, some degree of linear relationship exists between $X$ and $Y$. If the points in a scatterplot appear to follow a curved line rather than a straight line, the relationship between $X$ and $Y$ is said to be *curvilinear*. Since $r$ measures only the linear relationship between $X$ and $Y$, if the actual relationship is curvilinear, the value of $r$ will underestimate the degree of the relationship. This illustrates the importance of examining scatterplots when studying the relationship between variables. It is unlikely, although possible, for a strong curvilinear relationship to exist, and yet the computed value of $r$ be zero! If $X$ and $Y$ are linearly related, the meaning of $r$ is unequivocal. However, if $X$ and $Y$ have some sort of curvilinear relationship, a different measure of relationship should be used (Section 8.27).

Compare Figures 7.3 and 7.4; the value of $r$ is approximately zero in each figure, even though there is obviously a definite relationship between $X$ and $Y$ in Figure 7.4, but no systematic relationship is apparent in Figure 7.3. Figure 7.4 illustrates that one should not conclude that two variables are unrelated merely because $r$ is zero.

A major purpose of scatterplots is to insure that the relationship is linear, at least approximately, before viewing $r$ as an accurate indication of the degree of relationship between $X$ and $Y$. If there is a substantial nonlinear relationship between the two variables, it

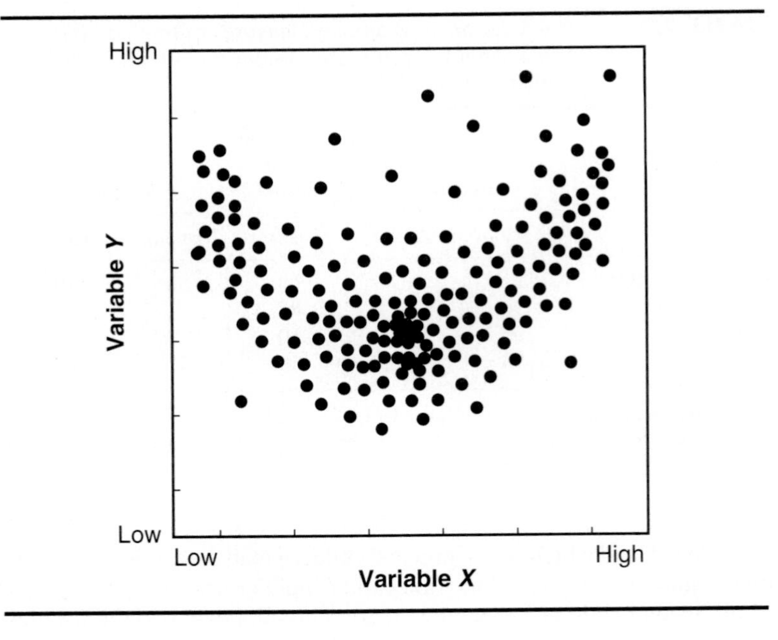


**FIGURE 7.4**

An Illustration of a Substantial Curvilinear Relationship that Yields $r \approx 0$.

will be apparent from a study of the scatterplot unless $n$ is small (e.g., see Figure 8.9 in Section 8.27).[5]

Fortunately, the relationship between most variables in the behavioral sciences and education is essentially linear. More than 95% of all correlation coefficients reported in research literature in the behavioral and social sciences are Pearson $r$'s. Curvilinear relationships do exit between age and many psychomotor skills that involve coordination for adults. Curvilinear relationships are rare between cognitive and psychomotor skills, although spurious curvilinearity can result from poorly developed measures. For example, educational and psychological test scores sometimes have an inadequate "ceiling" or "cellar" for a given group of persons; that is, the test may be too easy or too difficult, with the result that many persons obtain very high or very low scores. In Figure 7.5A, scores for Test $X$ are skewed positively because the test is too difficult for these examinees; scores on Test $Y$ are negatively skewed because of inadequate test "ceiling"; the curvilinearity is an artifact of inappropriate measures in this instance.

The curvilinearity between the variables in Figure 7.5B is real and not due to faulty measures. If $r$ were computed in Figure 7.5B, it would seriously underestimate the degree of the relationship between the two variables. Note how the scatterplot is indispensable in interpreting this relationship: Life expectancy is strongly related to income when the income is less than $2,000, but has no relationship above this point.

The value of $r$ for the data in Figure 7.5A is not large; it is probably only about .30. If more difficult items of the same content area were added to Test $Y$ and more easy items added to Test $X$, the value of $r_{XY}$ would increase substantially. The scatterplot of the test

---

[5]A statistical procedure for testing for nonlinearity is given in Section 14.21.

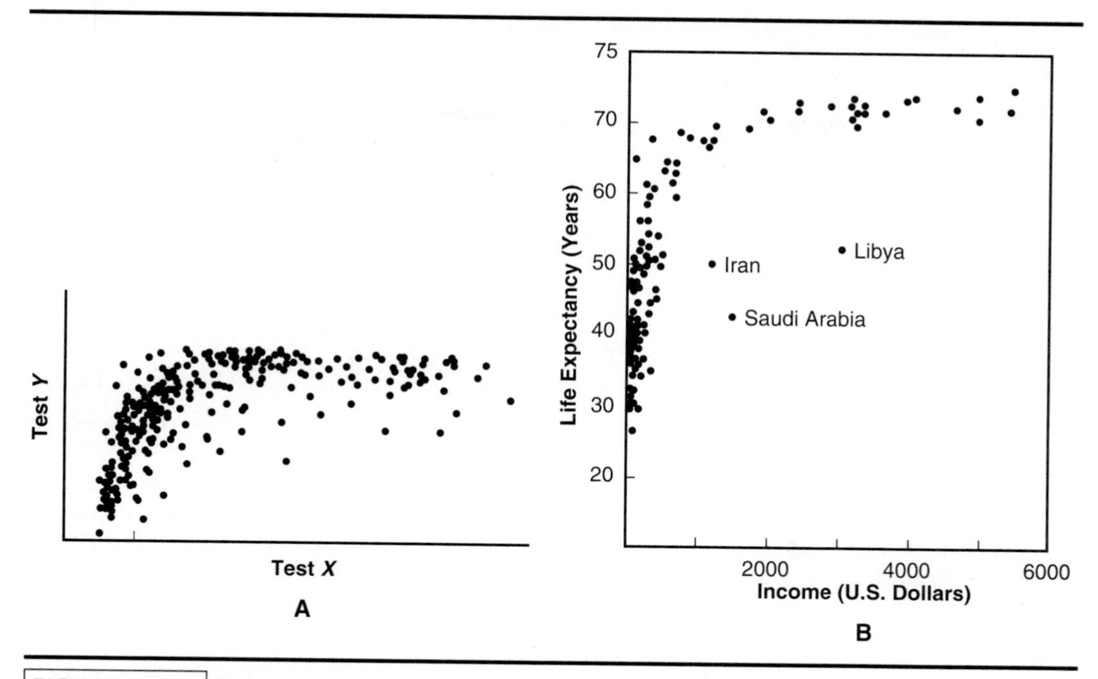


**FIGURE 7.5** Scatterplots Depicting Nonlinear Relationships.

scores for the modified tests would probably show substantial linear relationship. Note, however, that $r$ gives a conservative, minimum estimate of the relationship between two variables; a curvilinear correlation coefficient will never be less than $r$ for any set of data. The value of $r$ would be expected to increase somewhat if the scores in the two distributions were transformed to distributions that were more nearly normal (see Section 6.11), but these correlations would remain considerably less than if the measures were more adequate. In the next chapter (Section 8.27), a correlation coefficient, $\eta$ (the Greek letter eta) is introduced that does not require the relationship between $X$ and $Y$ to be linear.

## 7.8 CALCULATING THE PEARSON PRODUCT-MOMENT CORRELATION COEFFICIENT, *r*

The Pearson correlation coefficient can be obtained if the standard deviations of two variables, $s_X$ and $s_Y$, and their *covariance*, $s_{XY}$, are known. The covariance is a perfectly good measure of association in many problems in the physical sciences and engineering. The covariance is not a good measure if the units of measurement of the variables are arbitrary. Most ratio scales (Section 2.6) have nonarbitrary units of measurement, such as inches, seconds, dollars, and pounds. Most variables in the social and behavioral sciences, however, are measured on an arbitrary scale; hence, correlation coefficients are preferred to covariances as measures of relationship. Recall that variance, $s^2$, was defined in Equation 5.5 as (since two variances are involved, subscripts are needed to distinguish $s_X{}^2$ from $s_Y{}^2$):

$$s_X^2 = \frac{\sum_i x_i^2}{n-1} = \frac{\sum_i (X_i - \overline{X})^2}{n-1} \quad \text{or} \quad \frac{\sum_i (X_i - \overline{X})(X_i - \overline{X})}{n-1}$$

The covariance of variables $X$ and $Y$, denoted by $s_{XY}$ is defined similarly, as shown in Equation 7.1:

$$s_{XY} = \frac{\sum_i x_i y_i}{n-1} = \frac{\sum_i (X_i - \overline{X})(Y_i - \overline{Y})}{n-1} \tag{7.1}$$

where $X$ and $Y$ are raw scores and $\overline{X}\ \overline{Y}$ are the means for variables $X$ and $Y$. If there is no association between $X$ and $Y$, the covariance will be zero; but unlike the correlation coefficient, it has no numerical upper or lower limits. The Pearson product-moment[6] correlation is obtained when the covariance $s_{XY}$ is divided by each standard deviation, $s_X$ and $s_Y$, (or equivalently, by the product of the two standard deviations) as shown in Equation 7.2:[7]

$$r = \frac{s_{XY}}{s_X s_Y} \quad \text{or, in terms of parameters,} \quad \rho = \frac{\sigma_{XY}}{\sigma_X \sigma_Y} \tag{7.2}$$

## 7.9 A COMPUTATIONAL ILLUSTRATION OF *r*

Unless $n$ is very small, procedures for calculating $r$ are very time consuming even if a hand calculator is available. Fortunately, most calculations where $n$ is large are now performed using computers that compute $r$ automatically. However, we recommend that several $r$'s be computed by hand to remove some of the mystery about how correlation coefficients are

[6]The term "product-moment" results from the fact that the products of the first moments of $X$ and $Y$ are used in defining $r$. The term "moment" in physics refers to the distance of an object from its center of gravity, which is the mean of a frequency distribution. Hence, $x_i = X_i - \overline{X}$ and $y_i = Y_i - \overline{Y}$ are moments and $x_i y_i$ is a product of the moments. Unless otherwise indicated, the terms correlation and correlation coefficient are short for "Pearson product-moment correlation coefficient."

[7]Equivalent alternative expressions include:

$$r = \frac{\sum_i x_i y_i}{\sqrt{\left(\sum_i x_i^2\right)\left(\sum_i y_i^2\right)}} = \frac{\sum_i X_i Y_i - n\overline{X}\overline{Y}}{\sqrt{\left(\sum_i X_i^2 - n\overline{X}^2\right)\left(\sum_i Y_i^2 - n\overline{Y}^2\right)}}$$

obtained.[8] Since we usually want to know $\overline{X}$, $\overline{Y}$, $s_X$, and $s_Y$, as well as $r$, Equation 7.2 is particularly useful in the event hand computation is required.

The variances of $X$ and $Y$, the square roots of which give the standard deviations for Formula 7.2, can be obtained conveniently using Equation 5.5. Equation 7.3 gives a simple computational formula for the *covariance* between $X$ and $Y$:

$$s_{XY} = \frac{\sum_i X_i Y_i - n\overline{X}\overline{Y}}{n-1} \qquad \textbf{(7.3)}$$

Some actual data will be used to illustrate the computation of $r$. GRE-$Q$ scores and statistics $T$-scores for 121 students in an applied statistics course are given in Table 7.3. The steps for computing $r$ [(1) compute $s_X$, (2) compute $s_Y$, (3) compute $s_{XY}$, and (4) insert the results into Equation 7.2] are also illustrated in Table 7.3.[9]

## 7.10 SCATTERPLOTS

The $X$ and $Y$ values in Table 7.3 are represented in the scatterplot in Figure 7.6. The figure allows a visual check that no computation error has been made, as well as providing a rough indication that the relationship is linear. From Figure 7.6, it is apparent that the relationship is moderate, linear, and positive; hence, the computed value of .41 for $r$ appears reasonable. The $X$-variable is always plotted on the horizontal axis with values increasing from left to right; the $Y$-variable is plotted on the vertical axis with lower values toward the baseline.

It is good practice to study the scatterplot for any important relationship to insure that outliers are not present. The value of $r$ can be greatly distorted by even one or two outliers, since either $X$ or $Y$ is extremely low or high. Often, an outlier is an aberrant score, resulting from a data entry error.[10] Sometimes an outlier is *not* from the same population as remaining observations. For example, in Figure 7.6, one of the very low GRE Quantitative scores was from a student who was a recent immigrant from a non-English speaking country; the low score was probably depressed by his or her limited proficiency in English. Note that if scores below 400 in Figure 7.6 were eliminated from the data set, the value of $r$ would increase.[11] Outliers should *not* be excluded just because they represent exceptions to a general trend. Note the three outliers in Fig. 7.5B; they should remain a part of the data set unless there is reason to question the accuracy of the data.

---

[8] Anyway, if we had to do it by hand in the old days, why should you be spared?

[9] In practice, all of the standard spreadsheets have built-in, straightforward procedures for computing the correlation coefficient that do not require the "x", "y", and "xy" columns shown in Table 7.3. These are included to illustrate the steps and make you appreciate your spreadsheet's capabilities.

[10] It is virtually impossible to avoid some errors in data entry. For example, Table 7.1 is based on eight variables for 121 persons, or approximately 25,000 keystrokes. Even with 99.99% accuracy in data entry, at least a couple of errors will result. The importance of checking for errors in data entry can hardly be overemphasized. It is all too often done cursorily; hence, serious errors can be missed.

[11] For additional reading on outliers see Tukey (1977), Snedecor and Cochran (1980), and Winer, Brown, and Michels (1991).

**TABLE 7.3** An illustration of the Computation of *r*: GRE-*Q* Scores with *T*-Scores in Statistics ($n = 121$).

| | GRE-Q | T | | | | | GRE-Q | T | | | | | GRE-Q | T | | | |
|---|---|---|---|---|---|---|---|---|---|---|---|---|---|---|---|---|---|
| ID# | X | Y | x | y | xy | ID# | X | Y | x | y | xy | ID# | X | Y | x | y | xy |
| 1 | 500 | 55 | –60 | 5 | –300 | 42 | 490 | 58 | –70 | 8 | –560 | 83 | 660 | 56 | 100 | 6 | 600 |
| 2 | 500 | 49 | –60 | –1 | 60 | 43 | 720 | 60 | 160 | 10 | 1600 | 84 | 580 | 49 | 20 | –1 | –20 |
| 3 | 430 | 28 | –130 | –22 | 2860 | 44 | 770 | 65 | 210 | 15 | 3150 | 85 | 500 | 50 | –60 | 0 | 0 |
| 4 | 510 | 35 | –50 | –15 | 750 | 45 | 540 | 58 | –20 | 8 | –160 | 86 | 780 | 66 | 220 | 16 | 3520 |
| 5 | 320 | 55 | –240 | 5 | –1200 | 46 | 450 | 38 | –110 | –12 | 1320 | 87 | 510 | 53 | –50 | 3 | –150 |
| 6 | 510 | 51 | –50 | 1 | –50 | 47 | 580 | 61 | 20 | 11 | 220 | 88 | 510 | 50 | –50 | 0 | 0 |
| 7 | 500 | 58 | –60 | 8 | –480 | 48 | 460 | 23 | –100 | –27 | 2700 | 89 | 560 | 56 | 0 | 6 | 0 |
| 8 | 480 | 57 | –80 | 7 | –560 | 49 | 650 | 50 | 90 | 0 | 0 | 90 | 400 | 46 | –160 | –4 | 640 |
| 9 | 580 | 51 | 20 | 1 | 20 | 50 | 530 | 49 | –30 | –1 | 30 | 91 | 440 | 46 | –120 | –4 | 480 |
| 10 | 570 | 60 | 10 | 10 | 100 | 51 | 480 | 43 | –80 | –7 | 560 | 92 | 620 | 39 | 60 | –11 | –660 |
| 11 | 480 | 50 | –80 | 0 | 0 | 52 | 650 | 37 | 90 | –13 | –1170 | 93 | 430 | 49 | –130 | –1 | 130 |
| 12 | 520 | 53 | –40 | 3 | –120 | 53 | 670 | 33 | 110 | –17 | –1870 | 94 | 490 | 48 | –70 | –2 | 140 |
| 13 | 720 | 65 | 160 | 15 | 2400 | 54 | 550 | 52 | –10 | 2 | –20 | 95 | 440 | 46 | –120 | –4 | 480 |
| 14 | 540 | 45 | –20 | –5 | 100 | 55 | 410 | 40 | –150 | –10 | 1500 | 96 | 500 | 52 | –60 | 2 | –120 |
| 15 | 420 | 36 | –140 | –14 | 1960 | 56 | 700 | 64 | 140 | 14 | 1960 | 97 | 570 | 55 | 10 | 5 | 50 |
| 16 | 580 | 54 | 20 | 4 | 80 | 57 | 660 | 66 | 100 | 16 | 1600 | 98 | 400 | 52 | –160 | 2 | –320 |
| 17 | 550 | 50 | –10 | 0 | 0 | 58 | 490 | 34 | –70 | –16 | 1120 | 99 | 430 | 49 | –130 | –1 | 130 |
| 18 | 400 | 47 | –160 | –3 | 40 | 59 | 590 | 63 | 30 | 13 | 390 | 100 | 700 | 63 | 140 | 13 | 1820 |
| 19 | 500 | 30 | –60 | –20 | 1200 | 60 | 540 | 32 | –20 | –18 | 360 | 101 | 470 | 43 | –90 | –7 | 630 |
| 20 | 490 | 47 | –70 | –3 | 210 | 61 | 760 | 51 | 200 | 1 | 200 | 102 | 700 | 46 | 140 | –4 | –560 |
| 21 | 520 | 57 | –40 | 7 | –280 | 62 | 730 | 66 | 170 | 16 | 2720 | 103 | 500 | 27 | –60 | –23 | 1380 |
| 22 | 580 | 56 | 20 | 6 | 120 | 63 | 710 | 56 | 150 | 6 | 900 | 104 | 670 | 53 | 110 | 3 | 330 |
| 23 | 510 | 50 | –50 | 0 | 0 | 64 | 670 | 50 | 110 | 0 | 0 | 105 | 660 | 35 | 100 | –15 | –1500 |

| | | | | | | | | | | | | | | | | | |
|---|---|---|---|---|---|---|---|---|---|---|---|---|---|---|---|---|---|
| 24 | 540 | 53 | –20 | 3 | –60 | 65 | 370 | 52 | –190 | 2 | –380 | 106 | 800 | 56 | 240 | 6 | 1440 |
| 25 | 430 | 31 | –130 | –19 | 2470 | 66 | 500 | 57 | –60 | 7 | –420 | 107 | 720 | 58 | 160 | 8 | 1280 |
| 26 | 780 | 59 | 220 | 9 | 1980 | 67 | 400 | 40 | –160 | –10 | 1600 | 108 | 630 | 57 | 70 | 7 | 490 |
| 27 | 530 | 43 | –30 | –7 | 210 | 68 | 730 | 48 | 170 | –2 | –340 | 109 | 630 | 65 | 70 | 15 | 1050 |
| 28 | 620 | 55 | 60 | 5 | 300 | 69 | 670 | 61 | 110 | 11 | 1210 | 110 | 750 | 56 | 190 | 6 | 1140 |
| 29 | 660 | 39 | 100 | –11 | –1100 | 70 | 640 | 53 | 80 | 3 | 240 | 111 | 580 | 55 | 20 | 5 | 100 |
| 30 | 460 | 42 | –100 | –8 | 800 | 71 | 580 | 60 | 20 | 10 | 200 | 112 | 570 | 39 | 10 | –11 | –110 |
| 31 | 770 | 59 | 210 | 9 | 1890 | 72 | 720 | 65 | 160 | 15 | 2400 | 113 | 500 | 46 | –60 | –4 | 240 |
| 32 | 250 | 54 | –310 | 4 | –1240 | 73 | 430 | 47 | –130 | –3 | 390 | 114 | 590 | 21 | 30 | –29 | –870 |
| 33 | 700 | 69 | 140 | 19 | 2660 | 74 | 620 | 56 | 60 | 6 | 360 | 115 | 510 | 57 | –50 | 7 | –350 |
| 34 | 410 | 52 | –150 | 2 | –300 | 75 | 490 | 45 | –70 | –5 | 350 | 116 | 740 | 46 | 180 | –4 | –720 |
| 35 | 560 | 56 | 0 | 6 | 0 | 76 | 550 | 63 | –10 | 13 | –130 | 117 | 530 | 54 | –30 | 4 | –120 |
| 36 | 520 | 48 | –40 | –2 | 80 | 77 | 540 | 51 | –20 | 1 | –20 | 118 | 440 | 42 | –120 | –8 | 960 |
| 37 | 500 | 45 | –60 | –5 | 300 | 78 | 450 | 29 | –110 | –21 | 2310 | 119 | 540 | 51 | –20 | 1 | –20 |
| 38 | 570 | 48 | 10 | –2 | –20 | 79 | 720 | 53 | 160 | 3 | 480 | 120 | 710 | 62 | 150 | 12 | 1800 |
| 39 | 480 | 58 | –80 | 8 | –640 | 80 | 510 | 52 | –50 | 2 | –100 | 121 | 680 | 57 | 120 | 7 | 840 |
| 40 | 460 | 56 | –100 | 6 | –600 | 81 | 480 | 36 | –80 | –14 | 1120 | $\overline{X} = 559.6$ | | $50 = \overline{Y}$ | | $\Sigma xy = 54{,}050$ | |
| 41 | 560 | 33 | 0 | –17 | 0 | 82 | 560 | 40 | 0 | –10 | 0 | $s_X = 111.0$ | | $10 = s_Y$ | | | |

$$s_{XY} = \frac{\Sigma xy}{n-1} = \frac{54{,}050}{120} = 450.42$$

$$r = \frac{s_{XY}}{s_X s_Y} = \frac{450.4}{(111)(10)}$$

$r = .4053$

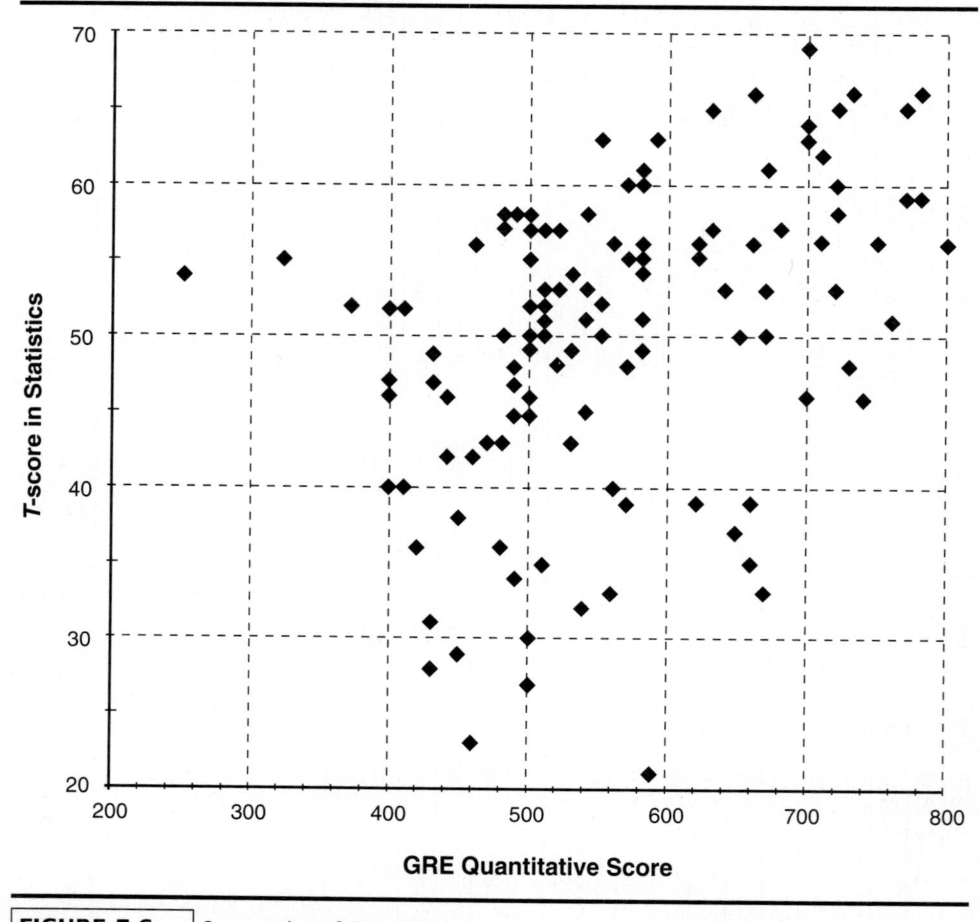


**FIGURE 7.6** Scatterplot of GRE-*Q* Scores and *T*-scores in Statistics ($r = .41$).

## 7.11 CORRELATION EXPRESSED IN TERMS OF *z*-SCORES

For conceptual purposes, it is useful to derive the formula for the correlation coefficient when both variables are expressed in *z*-scores. Since by definition the standard deviation of any distribution expressed in *z*-scores is exactly 1, when *X* and *Y* are expressed in the *z*-score metric:

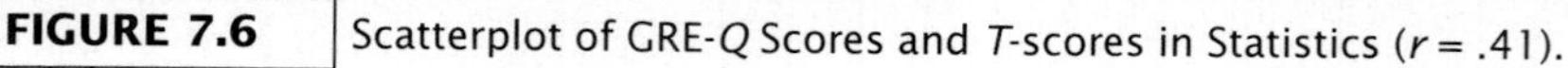

$$r = \frac{s_{XY}}{s_X s_Y} = s_{XY}, \text{ and } \rho = \frac{\sigma_{XY}}{\sigma_X \sigma_Y} = \sigma_{XY} \quad \textbf{(7.4)}$$

**TABLE 7.4** Illustrations of the Fact that Linear Transformations of Variables Affect Means and Standard Deviations, but Not the Correlation between $X$ and $Y$

| *Variable X* | | | *Variable Y* | | | |
|---|---|---|---|---|---|---|
| *Scores* | *Mean* | *Standard Deviation* | *Scores* | *Mean* | *Standard Deviation* | $r_{XY}$ |
| a. $X_i$ | $\bar{X}$ | $s_X$ | $Y_i$ | $\bar{Y}$ | $s_Y$ | .50 |
| b. $(X_i + 50)$ | $(\bar{X} + 50)$ | $s_X$ | $Y_i$ | $\bar{Y}$ | $s_Y$ | .50 |
| c. $(X_i - 100)$ | $(\bar{X} - 100)$ | $s_X$ | $10Y_i$ | $10\bar{Y}$ | $10s_Y$ | .50 |
| d. $\dfrac{(X_i - \bar{X})}{s_X}$ | 0 | 1 | $\dfrac{10(Y_i - \bar{Y})}{s_Y} + 50$ | 50 | 10 | .50 |

Equation 7.4 shows when both $X$ and $Y$ are expressed as $z$-scores the value of $r$ and the covariance are one and the same:

$$\rho = \sigma_{XY} = \frac{\sum_i z_{X_i} z_{Y_i}}{N} \tag{7.5}$$

Note that when $\rho = 1$, $\Sigma_i z_{X_i} z_{Y_i} = N$; $\rho$ will equal 1 only when the two $z$-scores are identical for all $N$ persons.[12]

## 7.12 LINEAR TRANSFORMATIONS AND CORRELATION

Any transformation of $X$ or $Y$ that does not change the corresponding $z$-scores does not affect the correlation coefficient. A special class of transformations called linear (namely, $X' = aX + b$, when $a$ is positive) results in identical $z$-scores for the original and the transformed scores; hence, $r_{XX'} = 1.0$, or $r_{YX} = r_{YX'}$. Thus, the correlation between $X$ and $Y$ will be identical if computed between raw scores, $z$-scores, $T$-scores, or other linear transformations of $X$ or $Y$. This fact is illustrated in Table 7.4. Notice that the addition of a constant to all $X$-values (or $Y$-values) does not affect $r$. This is also true for subtracting, multiplying, or dividing by non-zero constants; these all result in linear transformations of the original scores.

Figure 7.7 is a scatterplot for 200 adult males: $X$ is height in inches and $Y$ is weight in pounds, and the value of $r$ is .41 . What is $r$ if height were expressed in centimeters and weight in kilograms? These transformations are linear; thus, the correlation will be unaffected by the unit used for variable $X$ or $Y$.[13]

[12] If the $z$-scores in Equation 7.5 are estimated (i.e., based on sample means and standard deviations rather than population parameters), "$n - 1$" replaces "$N$" in the equation.

[13] Can you visualize the slight positive skewness in the weights?

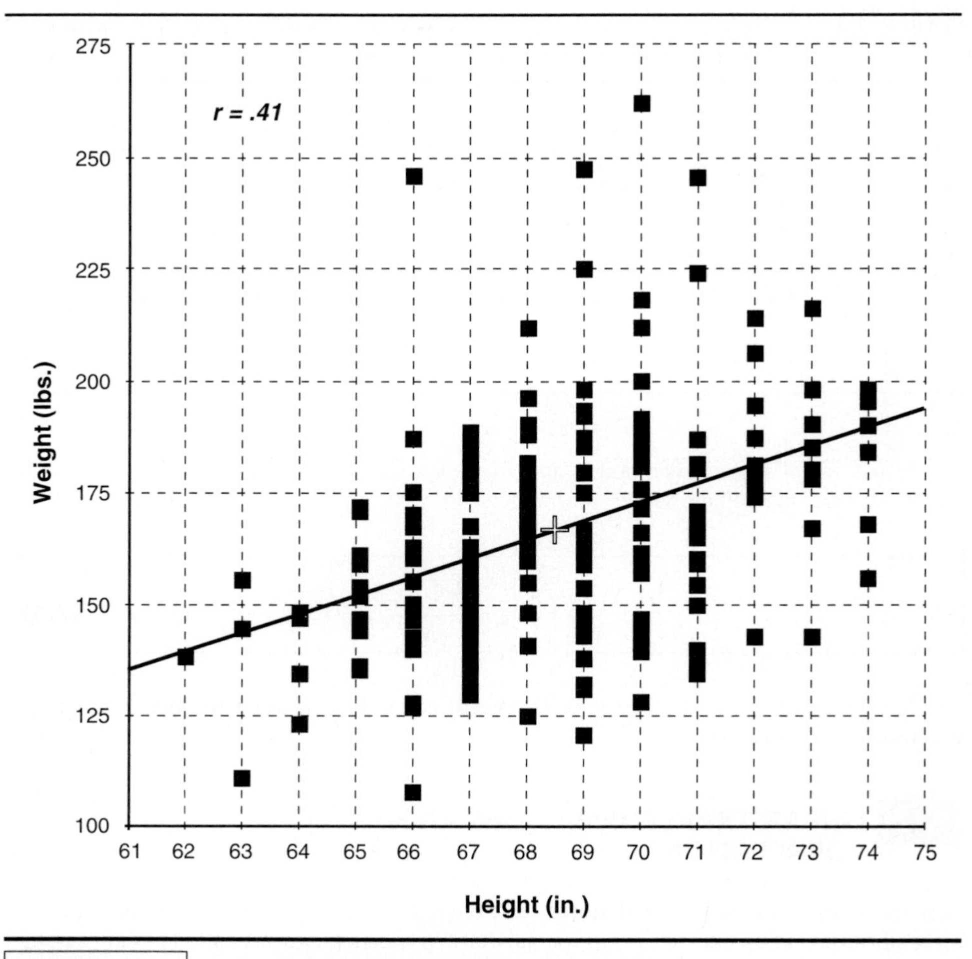


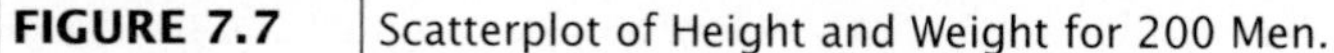
**FIGURE 7.7** Scatterplot of Height and Weight for 200 Men.

## 7.13 THE BIVARIATE NORMAL DISTRIBUTION

The interpretation of correlation has close ties with the normal distribution and the bivariate normal distribution. Correlation describes the way in which scores on a variable $X$ are related with scores on a second variable $Y$, a bivariate relationship.

If a large group of persons is measured in two ways—for example, each person's IQ score ($X$) and school attitude score ($Y$)—the data can be represented in a bivariate frequency distribution. For each person, there is a pair of scores, a score on $X$ and a score on $Y$. A bivariate frequency distribution depicts three dimensions: $X$ and $Y$ and frequency. It displays the frequency with which each different pair of $X$ and $Y$ scores occurs in a group of persons. Figure 7.8 is a bivariate frequency distribution for a large group of persons measured on IQ ($X$) and school attitude ($Y$). The frequency for each unique combination of $X$ and $Y$ is represented by the height of the "spikes." To read Figure 7.8, note, for example, that approxi-

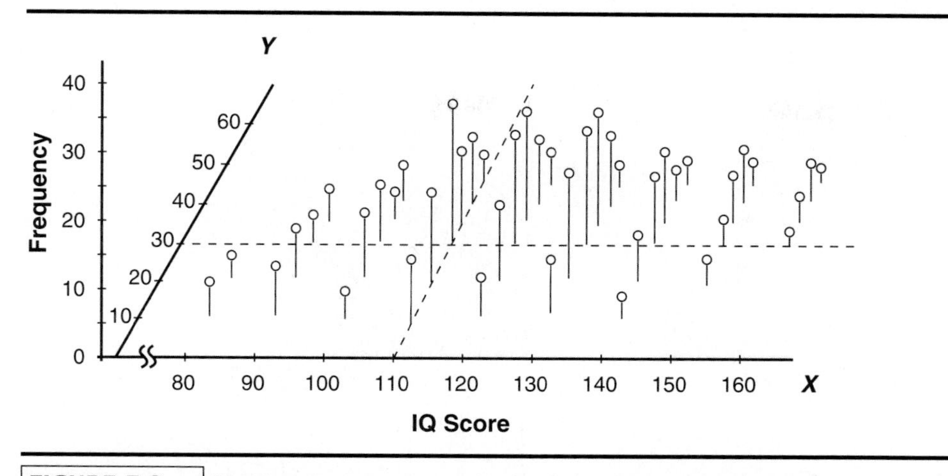


**FIGURE 7.8** Bivariate Frequency Distribution for a Large Group of Persons Measured on IQ (*X*) and School Attitude (*Y*).

mately twenty persons had IQ scores of 110 (variable *X*) and scores of 30 on the attitude variable *Y*. The height of the line at the intersection of 110 and 30 must be measured against the vertical scale of frequencies.

Many bivariate frequency distributions built from data gathered in educational and psychological settings have the characteristic, bivariate normal shape. The geometric figure that represents the frequencies in a bivariate frequency distribution resembles a flat bell. This smooth, continuous, bell-shaped surface provides a mathematically convenient and satisfactory representation of numerous bivariate frequency distributions.

The *bivariate normal distribution* is actually a family of three-dimensional surfaces; as the correlation between *X* and *Y* increases, the bell will be increasingly elongated. One member of this family appears in Figure 7.9.[14]

All bivariate normal distributions have the following characteristics:

1. For each value of *X*, the distribution of the associated *Y*-values is a normal distribution, and vice versa.
2. The *Y*-means for various values of *X* fall on a straight line; the relationship is linear. The same is true for *X*-means for various values of *Y*.
3. The scatterplots possess homoscedasticity; the variance in the *Y*-values is uniform across all values of *X*. Conversely, the variance in *X*-values is constant for all values of *Y*.

Distributions using actual data are never as beautiful as the perfect, mathematical distributions like that represented in Fig. 7.9, but the empirical distributions approach the theoretical distributions as the sample size increases. In other words, sampling error decreases as *n* increases. Figure 7.10 illustrates an empirical bivariate normal distribution. The height of the slices represents frequency. Note that the distribution of *Y* for any value of *X* is approximately normal in form. The raggedness results from sampling error; if *n* were larger, the figure would become smoother like Figure 7.9.

[14]Note that if a cloth were draped over the points in Figure 7.8, it would resemble Figure 7.9.

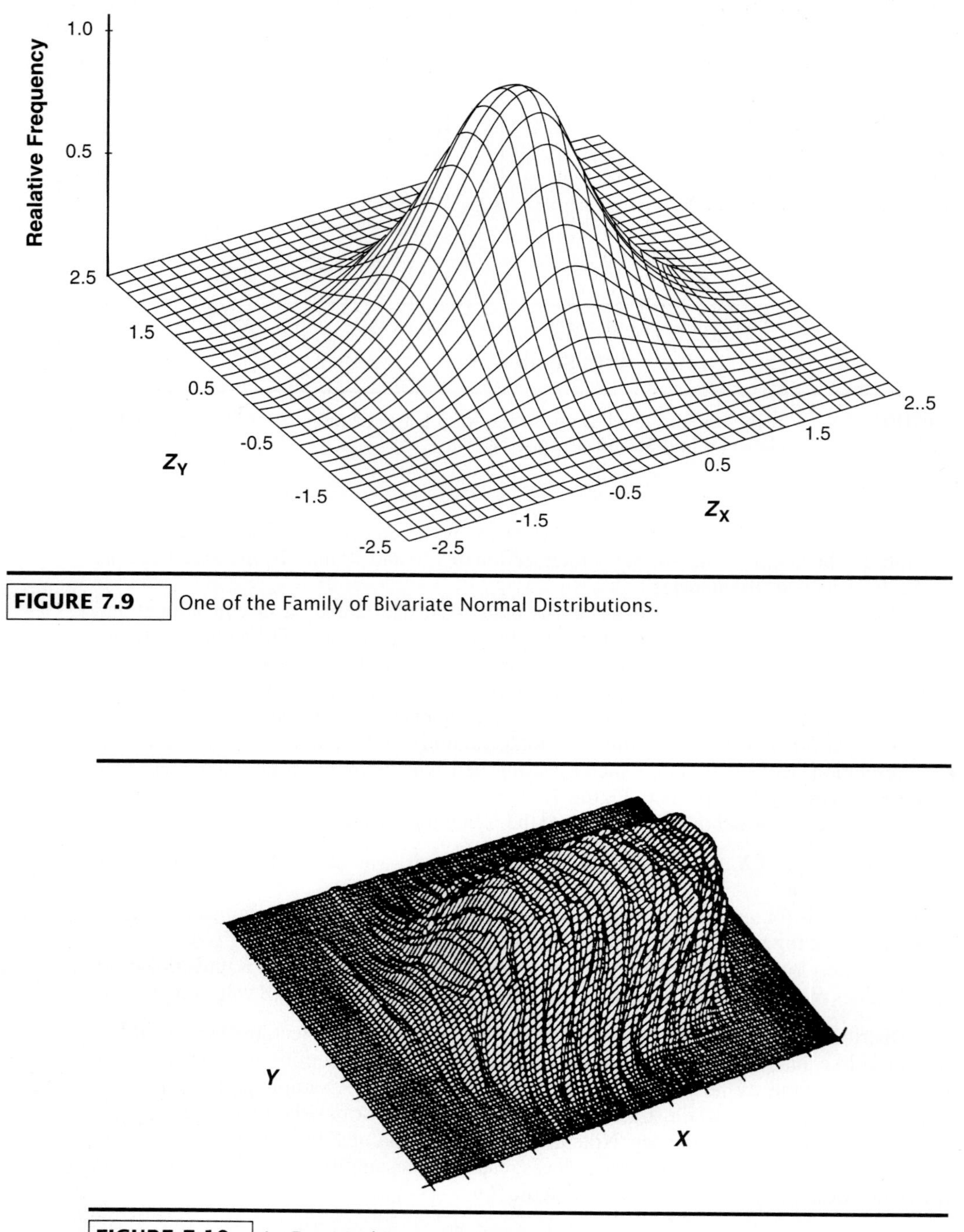


FIGURE 7.9 One of the Family of Bivariate Normal Distributions.

FIGURE 7.10 An Empirical Bivariate Normal Distribution.

## 7.14 EFFECTS OF VARIABILITY ON CORRELATION

Although correlation coefficients are ubiquitous in the social, behavioral, and natural sciences, a surprising number of researchers are unaware of two influences that can have a substantial effect on the numerical value of $r$: the variability of the sample (Section 7.14) and measurement error (Section 7.16). The heterogeneity of the sample has an important influence on $r$. Other things being equal, the greater the variability among the observations, the greater the value of $r$. For example, in a school having students with relatively homogeneous socioeconomic status (SES) backgrounds, the correlation between SES and achievement, or between SES and any other variable, will be much less than in a school that is very heterogeneous in SES.

If one uses a test (e.g., GRE) to select students for admission or employment, the heterogeneity of the selected sample (often termed *range restriction*) is less than the heterogeneity for the entire group of applicants. If the GRE scores for the admitted students are then correlated with some criterion (e.g., GPA), the value of $r$ will be much less than if data were available on the entire group of applicants. Figure 7.11 illustrates this common range restriction phenomenon and its consequences on correlation coefficients. Note that there is

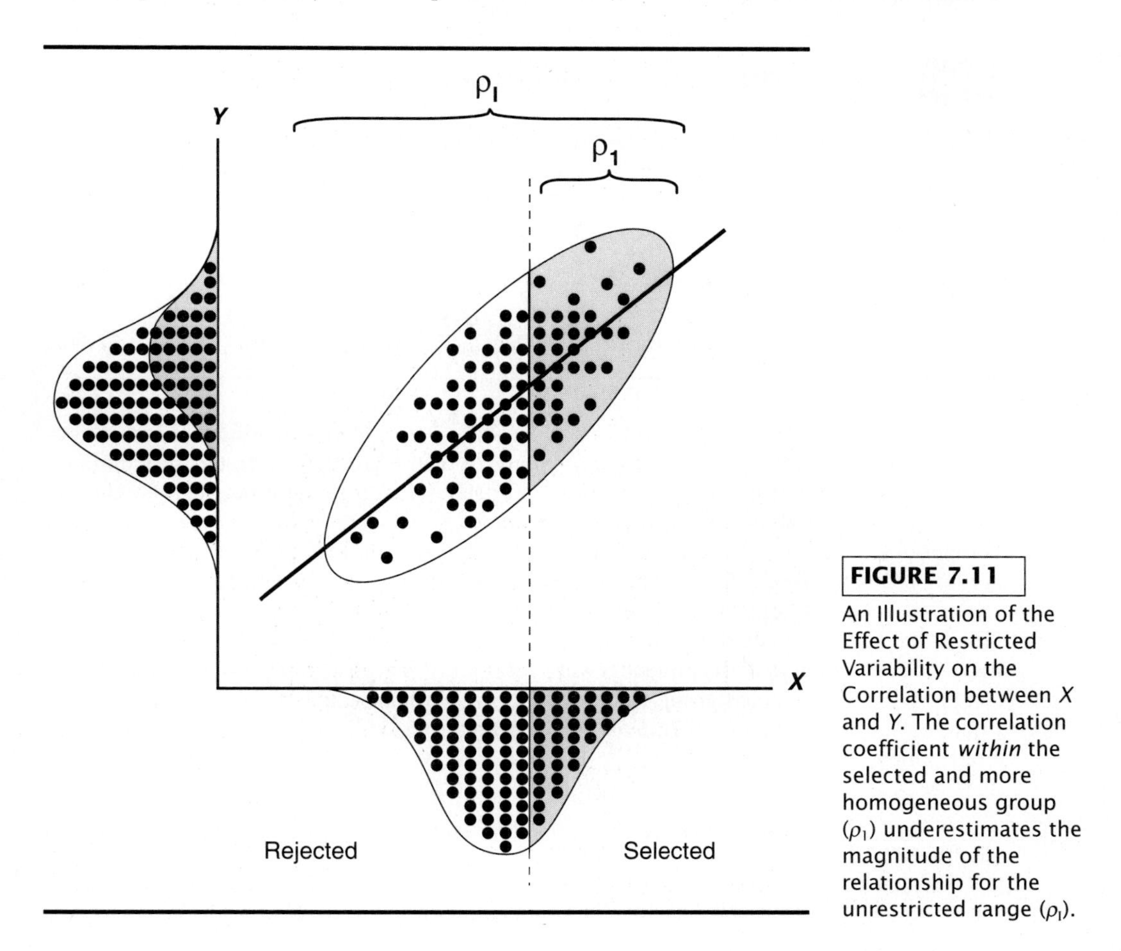


**FIGURE 7.11**

An Illustration of the Effect of Restricted Variability on the Correlation between $X$ and $Y$. The correlation coefficient *within* the selected and more homogeneous group ($\rho_1$) underestimates the magnitude of the relationship for the unrestricted range ($\rho_I$).

only a moderate correlation remaining between the two variables within the selected group (shaded area), yet a substantial correlation exists for the entire group (the ellipse). Much misinterpretation of correlation has resulted from the lack of understanding of this concept.[15] The correlation between achievement and IQ will be much less for students in a gifted program than for a representative group of students. For example, a correlation between test performance and job performance of .64 for a total group ($n = 1{,}031$; Thorndike, 1949) of aspiring pilots dropped to a correlation of only .18 for those ($n = 136$) who eventually qualified (i.e., as defined by Equation 7.6, $r_I$ was .64, whereas $r_1$ was only .18). The correlation between GPAs in high school and GPAs in college will be much greater in less selective colleges than in colleges that require outstanding academic performance in high school for admission. The correlation between height and weight for students in grade one will be much less than the correlation obtained on all students in grades 1–6. Both correlations are correct, but much misinterpretation of research findings has resulted from ignoring this phenomenon.

In the case study, the correlation between height and weight for the sample of 200 men was .41 (Figure 7.7); if the correlation is computed only on men who are taller than the median ($\geq 69''$, $n = 99$), $r$ falls to .18. Can you see the parallel in this finding to the scatterplot in Figure 7.11?

## 7.15 CORRECTING FOR RESTRICTED VARIABILITY

If one knows the correlation for one group ($\rho_1$) and the standard deviations of $X$ for this group ($\sigma_1$) and the new group ($\sigma_I$), the correlation for the new group ($\rho_I$) can be obtained from Equation 7.6, assuming a linear relationship and homoscedasticity. When the ratio $\sigma_I/\sigma_1 > 1$, then $\rho_I > \rho_1$; when $\sigma_I/\sigma_1 < 1$, then $\rho_I < \rho_1$:

$$\rho_I^2 = \frac{\rho_1^2(\sigma_I/\sigma_1)^2}{1 + \rho_1^2(\sigma_I/\sigma_1)^2 - \rho_1^2} \tag{7.6}$$

The principal value of Equation 7.6 is *not* for the purpose of estimating $\rho_I$. More importantly, Equation 7.6 illuminates the consequence of restricted or exaggerated variability on the value of $r$ so that it can be interpreted properly. The correlation between height and weight would be perhaps .9 if all students in grades K–12 were included in the sample, but perhaps .4 if students in a single grade level were studied. Suppose all applicants for college A with a College Board SAT verbal score of below 600 were rejected, and all those with scores of 600 or higher were accepted (a simplistic, yet statistically "clean" example). Given that for the selected applicants, the correlation between SAT and GPA was .5, estimate the correlation $\hat{\rho}_I$ if all applicants were accepted.[16] Suppose that the standard deviation of the SAT in the selected group is 50 and 100 in the unrestricted group. Therefore, using Equation 7.6, a correlation of .76 would be expected if the college had an open door admissions policy:

[15] Inexplicably, most applied statistics texts fail to treat this topic or the effect of measurement error on $r$ (Section 7.16).

[16] In statistics, a circumflex ("^" or "hat") above a symbol for a parameter, denotes an *estimate* of the parameter—it is a *statistic* that estimates the parameter; thus, $\bar{X} = \hat{\mu}$, $s = \hat{\sigma}$, $r = \hat{\rho}$, et cetera.

$$\hat{\rho}_I^2 = \frac{(.5)^2(100/50)^2}{1+(.5)^2(2)^2-(.5)^2} = \frac{(.25)(2)^2}{1+(.25)(4)-.25} = \frac{1.00}{1.75} = .5714$$

$$\hat{\rho}_I = \sqrt{.5714} = .7559 \text{ or } .76$$

The validity of Equation 7.6 rests on the assumptions of a linear relationship between *X* and *Y* and homoscedasticity (bivariate normality, Section 7.13). The assumptions appear to be met in Figure 7.11. In many instances, however, these assumptions are suspect. In other instances where linearity is known from previous research, Equation 7.6 has been shown to be quite accurate. The fact that the observed correlation between two variables is influenced markedly by the heterogeneity of the sample is true, even when the assumptions underlying Equation 7.6 are suspect. Equation 7.6 will yield accurate estimates only when samples are large, and therefore there is little sampling error in the estimates of $\sigma$ and $\rho$, and where the conditions of linearity and homoscedasticity are met.[17]

Selecting a restricted sample on variable *X* is not the only way in which the heterogeneity of a sample and $r_{XY}$ is reduced. In a sample of adults who are high school graduates, the correlation between IQ and reading ability will be less than for a random sample of adults. Since the sample of high school graduates will have fewer persons who are poor readers and who have very low IQ scores, the sample will be more homogeneous on both of these variables, and the reduced variability will cause the value of *r* to be less than its value in the unrestricted sample.[18]

## 7.16 EFFECT OF MEASUREMENT ERROR ON *r* AND THE CORRECTION FOR ATTENUATION

The presence of measurement error has an important influence on the value of *r*. Measurement error in the observations of *X* or *Y* reduces the numerical value of *r*. The degree to which a set of scores is confounded by measurement error is represented in the *reliability coefficient* of that measure. The reliability coefficient is the correlation between two parallel measures of the variable of interest. We could estimate the reliability of a bathroom scale by weighing a group of individuals, reweighing them, then finding *r* between the two sets of weights—when *r* describes the relationship between two parallel measures, it is a reliability coefficient.[19]

---

[17]See Gullickson and Hopkins (1976) for detailed information on the accuracy of Equation 7.6.

[18]When persons are restricted on variable 3, and variable 3 is correlated with variable 1 or variable 2, $r_{12}$ is less than if there was no selectivity on variable 3. This type of selectivity is sometimes termed *incidental* selection. The correlation in a more, or less, homogeneous sample can be estimated using a complex formula that can be found in Lord and Novick (1968). It assumes that there are linear relationships and homoscedasticity among all pairs of the variables. The formula is rarely needed, but the concept is needed to interpret correlation coefficients properly.

[19]It is outside the scope of this book to develop a fuller rationale for reliability coefficients. Procedures for estimating reliability when only one test is administered can be found in Hopkins, Stanley, and Hopkins (1990) and Linn (1987). The most common method used in such situations is Cronbach's alpha: $r_{XX} = [\text{I}/(\text{I}-1)](1-\Sigma\sigma_i^2/\sigma^2)$, where I is the number of items or parts, $\Sigma\sigma_i^2$ is the sum of the variances of the I items or parts, and $\sigma^2$ is the variance in the total scores. If a measure cannot be divided into parts, some type of test-retest method must be employed. Suppose students were asked three questions in which they described their attitude toward mathematics on a 1–5 rating scale; the variance in the inventory scores for the groups of students was 10.0, and the variances for each of the three questions were 2.2, 1.8, and 1.4. Cronbach's alpha estimates the reliability coefficient for the three-item inventory to be: $3/2(1-5.4/10.0) = .69$. The .69 is an estimate of the correlation between the observed scores and a hypothetical set of scores that would have resulted if the students were given a second parallel inventory. Procedures for estimating reliability using analysis of variance are given in Chapter 20.

The reliability coefficient of a measure can be viewed as that proportion of its variance that is *not* error; if variable $X$ has a reliability coefficient of .90, this means that 10% of its variance, $s_X^2$, is due to measurement error.[20] Stated differently, suppose we measure the variable $X$ a second time in an independent and parallel way—the correlation between the two parallel measurements of the same variable is the reliability coefficient, $r_{XX}$, of the measure. Note that if measures of a variable $Y$ do not correlate with parallel measures of the same variable (i.e., $r_{YY}$ is 0), it cannot be predicted by any other variable. If a variable does not correlate with itself, how can it correlate with any other variable? If the variable, Teaching Ability, cannot be assessed reliably, no other variable can predict it very well. The variables Weight and Height are substantially related, but we can imagine ways of measuring each of these variables (e.g., by "eyeball" guesses) that contain much measurement error that would decrease the correlation between the weight and height measures. The well established correlation of .5 between the heights of fathers and sons is only .35 when the sons are 12 months of age (Wingerd, 1970); without doubt the decrease is influenced by the difficulty (i.e., measurement error) of obtaining accurate measures of height for less than fully cooperative subjects!

Other things being equal, the greater the measurement error in $X$ or $Y$, the lower $r_{XY}$ will be. Stated differently, as two variables are measured more accurately, the value of $r$ between them will increase, unless $r = 0$. For example, intelligence and achievement standardized test scores tend to correlate approximately .6, but if the tests were shortened (e.g., to ten-item tests), the observed $r$ would fall to perhaps .3. If we eliminate some of the measurement error in either or both, the obtained correlation will increase accordingly. To illustrate: The upper portion of Figure 7.12 is a scatterplot of scores on two short tests for a group of applied statistics students; note that $r = .38$. Actually, Tests 1 and 2 in the upper scatterplot were a subset of items from each of two longer tests. The only difference between the upper and lower scatterplots is that the tests in the lower scatterplot are longer; other things being equal, longer tests are more reliable (i.e., have less measurement error) than shorter tests. The correlation in the lower scatterplot is .66; both tests contained items of the same type and difficulty, but fewer items were used to construct the upper scatterplot. In interpreting any correlation coefficient, we must keep in mind how $X$ and $Y$ were measured, and preferably know the values of the reliability coefficients, $r_{XX}$ and $r_{YY}$.

Suppose 100 adults are asked to write down their heights and weights—height and weight are measured by self-report. Then the correlation between height and weight was found. Next, the same 100 adults are weighed and measured with a tape measure and a scale, and the correlation between height and weight found—each method yields a value of $r$ between height and weight. How would the two values of $r$ compare? The second value would be expected to be higher because the measurements will contain less measurement error.[21]

One can interpret a correlation coefficient more meaningfully if the reliability coefficients of the two variables are known. It was noted above that in the simplest case, the reliability coefficient for a measure of $X$ is the correlation coefficient between two independent, parallel measures of $X$. For example, if each individual in the sample were weighed on one scale, then weighed again on the same (or another) scale, the correlation between the two sets of weights is the reliability coefficient of this measure of weight. The value of $r_{XX}$

[20] An excellent overview of the meaning of reliability is given by Traub and Rowley (1991).

[21] Examples of measurement error: Short persons may tend to round their heights up, heavy persons may tend to underreport their weights, self-reports may be with or without clothing, shoes, et cetera.

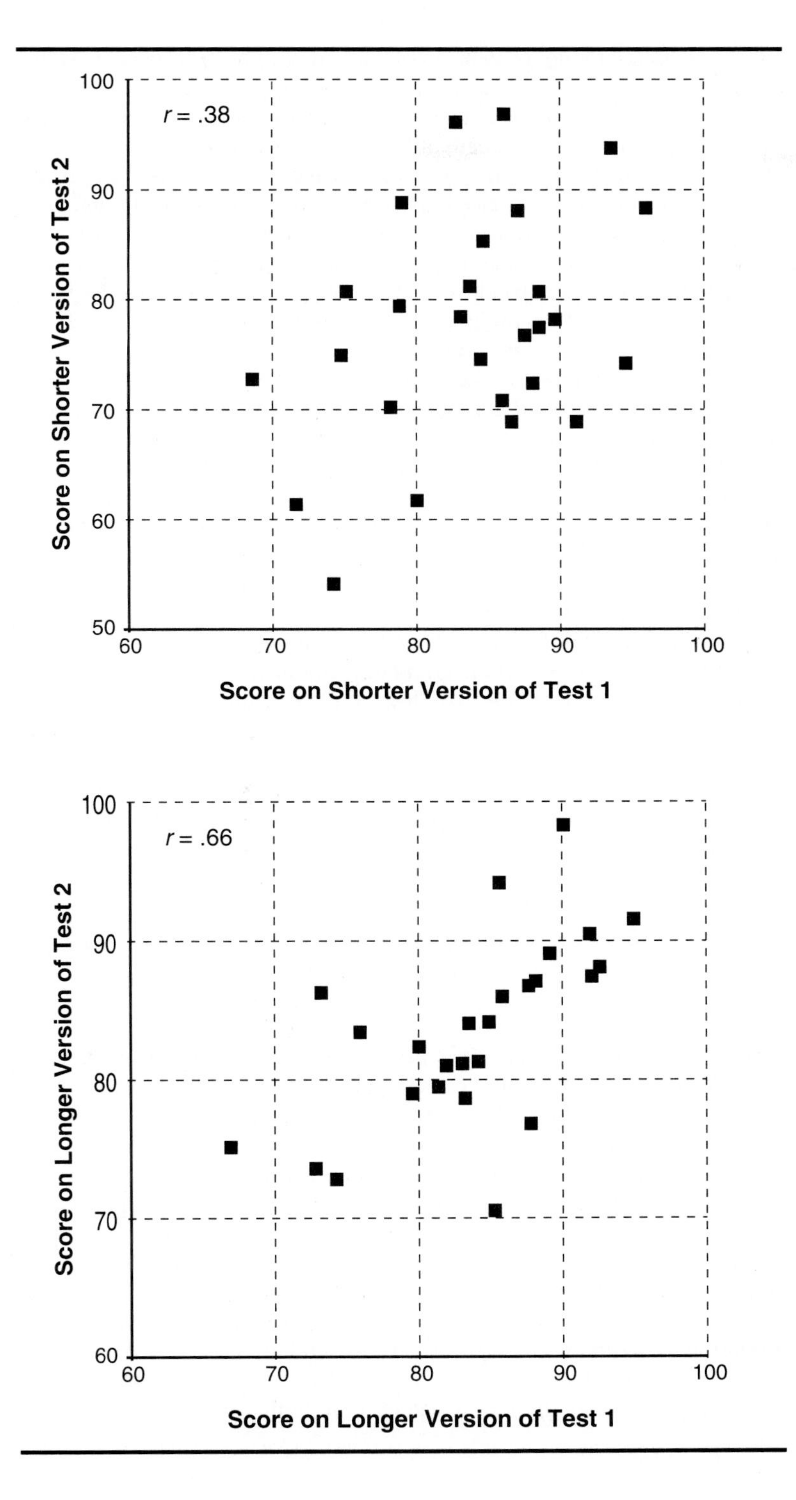

**FIGURE 7.12**

Two Scatterplots Illustrating the Effect of Measurement Error on *r*.

will not be 1.00—at least a small amount of measurement error will be present (e.g., standing position on the scale, leaning, angle of reading, etc.). Likewise, on the height measurements, there will be some measurement error resulting from body stretch, tape measure, method of judging top of head, and so on. Indeed, the reliability of length measurements of infants (some of which are less than cooperative with this measurement "nonsense") is less than .75 (Stember, Lewis, Hester, Clark, & Hopkins, 1995)! The more uniform and standardized the measurement procedures, the less the measurement error, and the higher the reliability coefficients of the measures. Researchers should assess and report the reliability of their measures whenever possible. A correlation coefficient of .50 between two variables that have relability coefficients of, for example, only .60 means something quite different from $r = .50$ where the reliability coefficients equal .90.

In the 1960s, there was much interest in the measurement of creativity in psychology and education. Because early studies found that the correlation between IQ scores and performance on creativity tests was only about .5, many concluded that creativity tests were measuring different abilities from conventional intelligence tests. When the smoke cleared, it was found that the low correlation was due primarily to the fact that the creativity tests had very low reliability coefficients. If two creativity tests do not correlate highly, neither test will correlate highly with any other measure.

Surprisingly, there is a way to estimate the correlation between two variables that would be observed if both of the variables are measured without any measurement error; we can correct $r_{YX}$ for the *attenuation* resulting from measurement error. This correction for attenuation requires that the correlation coefficient and the reliability coefficients for $X$ and $Y$ be obtained (Hopkins, Stanley, & Hopkins, 1990, p. 359). Equation 7.7 estimates the correlation between variables $X$ and $Y$ that would result if all measurement error were removed from both measures ($r_{X_\infty Y_\infty}$); this is sometimes described as the correlation between *true* scores on the two variables. Note that $r_{X_\infty Y_\infty}$ is an extrapolated value and should be interpreted accordingly (Rogers, 1976; Hakstian, Schroeder, and Rogers, 1988). Note also that if the reliability coefficients are underestimated, then $r_{X_\infty Y_\infty}$ will be overestimated.

$$r_{X_\infty Y_\infty} = \frac{r_{XY}}{\sqrt{r_{XX} r_{YY}}} \quad \textbf{(7.7)}$$

It is widely assumed that essay and objective achievement tests are measuring different variables because they do not correlate highly, but essay tests, as typically scored, do not have high reliability. One study (Bracht & Hopkins, 1970) found that essay and objective achievement tests over the same content in a college course did not correlate highly: $r_{XY} = .38$. However, both measures were quite short, and hence were not very reliable ($r_{XX} = .50$; $r_{YY} = .39$). Using Equation 7.7, the correlation between the two sets of scores, assuming both measures were made perfectly reliable is: $r_{X_\infty Y_\infty} = r_{XY}/\sqrt{r_{XX} r_{YY}} = .38/\sqrt{(.50)(.39)} = .86$. Advanced placement essay and multiple-choice tests in history only correlated .50; the reliability coefficient of the multiple-choice test was .91, but only .44 for the essay test (Bridgeman & Lewis, 1994). Equation 7.7 estimates that the low reliability of the essay test accounts for much of the low correlation between the two test formats; a correlation of .79 between them would be expected if the measurement error were removed from both test formats. The principal reason the two types of tests did not correlate more highly appears to be due to measurement error.

## 7.17 THE PEARSON *r* AND MARGINAL DISTRIBUTIONS

The maximum value[22] of the correlation coefficient is 1.0 and can be attained only when the marginal distributions of $X$ and $Y$ have exactly the same shape. The *marginal distribution* of $X$ is simply the frequency distribution of the $X$-values; the marginal distribution of $Y$ is the frequency distribution of the $Y$-values. Figure 3.16 gives the frequency distribution for all variables in the case study. The coronary variable is dichotomous, the others are unimodal and continuous; the maximum value for $r$ between a dichotomous variable and normally distributed variables is well below 1.0. If $X$ is normally distributed and $Y$ is skewed, the maximum value of $r$ is somewhat less than 1. How much less? The less similar the shapes, the lower the maximum value for $r$ (Carroll, 1961). With a little practice, one can visualize the shape of the marginal frequency distributions from data in the scatterplot. Is it apparent that both $X$ and $Y$ appear to be normally distributed in Figures 7.1, 7.2, 7.3, and 7.11 (when all cases are used)? Is it evident that $X$ is skewed positively in Figures 7.5A and 7.5B? When scores on one or both variables are subjected to a nonlinear transformation to make the two distributions more similar in shape, slight increases in the value of $r$ could result. Typically, transformations have little effect on $r$ unless they profoundly change the shape of the frequency distribution, that is, if the correlation between the $X$ values and the transformed $X$ values ($X'$), $r_{XX'}$, is very high, then $r_{YX} \approx r_{YX'}$.

## 7.18 THE EFFECT OF THE UNIT OF ANALYSIS ON CORRELATION: ECOLOGICAL CORRELATIONS

Care is needed to define the unit of analysis when describing a relationship, and to make inferences that are consistent with that definition. The correlations among observational units that are the *aggregates* of other units (e.g., schools, census tracks, cities, states, etc.) are sometimes described as *ecological correlations*. The unit of analysis usually has dramatic effects on the value of the correlation coefficient between two variables. For example, in a comprehensive meta-analysis of 489 findings about the correlation between socioeconomic status (SES) and achievement, the median value of $r$ was only .221 when pupils were the observational unit (White, 1982). When the unit of analysis was some aggregate such as school, school district, and the like (e.g., $X$ = school mean on the SES measure, $Y$ = school mean on the standard achievement test), the median value of $r$ was much greater—.730.[23] The standard deviation of individual scores on standardized achievement tests is typically about three times greater than for school averages (Hopkins, Stanley, & Hopkins, 1990, pp. 396–397). However, of the variation that does exist among school means, a substantial proportion of it can be accounted for by SES—not the case for individuals. If a different observational unit (e.g., city, school district, or state) is used, the value of the correlation coefficient can be expected to differ accordingly. The meaning and interpretation of $r$ is necessarily limited to the observational units that were used. The correlation

---

[22]To prove that the value of $r_{XY}$ cannot exceed +1, expand $\Sigma(z_X - z_Y)^2$, which is always $\geq 0$, and use the fact that $\Sigma z_X^2 = \Sigma z_Y^2 = N$, and $\rho_{XY} = \Sigma z_X z_Y / N$. To prove that $\rho_{XY}$ cannot be less than −1, work with $\Sigma(z_X + z_Y)^2$.

[23]For example, in the HSB data set of 600 students, $r_{\text{READING,SES}} = .29$, but when school means for a school district of 83 schools were used, $r_{\text{READING,SES}} = .86$.

between two variables can differ markedly depending on which observational unit is employed.[24] The correlation between the verbal and math test of the SAT is approximately .5 for students, but approximately .9 when state averages are used.

## 7.19 THE VARIANCE OF A SUM[25]

The variance of a sum of two or more scores is needed frequently in statistics. The standard deviation on each of the Verbal (*X*) and Quantitative (*Y*) sections of the Graduate Record Examination (GRE) is approximately 100. If a combined $X + Y$ score is obtained for each examinee, what is its variance or standard deviation? The variance of a sum of two scores is the following (see Glass and Stanley, 1970, pp. 127–129, for proof):

$$s_{X+Y}^2 = s_X^2 + s_Y^2 + 2r_{XY}s_Xs_Y \quad \textbf{(7.8)}$$

where $s_X^2$ is the variance of variable *X*, $s_Y^2$ is the variance of variable *Y*, and $r_{XY}$ is the correlation between variables *X* and *Y*. From Equation 7.2 it can be seen that the expression $r_{XY}s_Xs_Y$ equals the covariance between variables *X* and *Y*. Notice that if the two variables are *independent* (i.e., $r_{XY} = 0$), the variance of the sum equals the sum of the variances:

$$s_{X+Y}^2 = s_X^2 + s_Y^2 \quad \textbf{(7.9)}$$

Given that $r = .543$, the variance of the sum, GRE $V + Q$, from Equation 7.8 is $s_{V+Q}^2 = (100)^2 + (100)^2 + 2(.543)(100)(100) = 30{,}860$, and $s_{V+Q} = 175.67$ or 176.

Suppose that both of Lola's GRE scores are 600. She is one standard deviation above the mean, $P_{84}$, of each test. Is her composite score, $V + Q$, also precisely one standard deviation above the mean? Because the mean of the composite scores, $V + Q$, is 1,000 (Section 4.11) and the standard deviation of the aggregate score, $s_{V+Q}$, is 176, Lola's composite score of 1200 is $200/176 = 1.14$ standard deviations above the mean composite score. Although she is at the 84th percentile on each of the two tests, Table A of the Appendix shows she is at the 87th percentile for the composite.

If a variable is formed from the sum of three scores, its variance can be found from Equation 7.10; the logic underlying Equation 7.8 is extended to three addends in Equation 7.10:

$$s_{X+Y+Z}^2 = s_X^2 + s_Y^2 + s_Z^2 + 2r_{XY}s_Xs_Y + 2r_{XZ}s_Xs_Z + 2r_{YZ}s_Ys_Z \quad \textbf{(7.10)}$$

---

[24]For example, sociological and anthropological research typically uses aggregated observational units such as group means for neighborhoods, cities, et cetera, and finds high correlations between SES and achievement. These high values of *r* have often been interpreted as if SES can account for much, if not most, of the achievement differences among students, whereas it actually accounts for less than 10% of the variance among students within an ethnic group (White, 1982). Accounting for whatever variance there is among schools or other units of analysis is a very different question than accounting for the differences among students.

[25]Sections 7.19 and 7.20 are a belated completion of Chapter 5; since the concept of correlation is used in the equations, the delay was necessary. Note that in Section 7.19 two observations are summed for each of the *n* subjects, whereas in Section 5.12 additional subjects are being added to a distribution.

Notice that if the variables are uncorrelated, the variance of the sum is the sum of the variances, just as in Equation 7.9. The logic on which Equation 7.10 is based is easily extended to any number of variables, and is widely used in statistical derivations.

## 7.20 THE VARIANCE OF A DIFFERENCE

In later chapters, use is made of the difference between two scores $X$ and $Y$ (i.e., $X - Y$), and the variance of the distribution of difference scores, $s^2_{X-Y}$, which can be determined from Eq. 7.11:

$$s^2_{X-Y} = s_X^2 + s_Y^2 - 2r_{XY}s_Xs_Y \quad \textbf{(7.11)}$$

As expected, Equation 7.11 shows that as the value of $r_{XY}$ increases, the variance of the difference scores decreases. The variance of the difference between GRE-$V$ and $Q$ scores ($V - Q$), given that, $s_V = s_Q = 100$, and $r_{VQ} = .543$ from Equation 7.11 is $s^2_{V-Q} = (100)^2 + (100)^2 - 2(.543)(100)(100) = 9{,}140$, and $s_{V-Q} = 95.6$, that is, the standard deviation of the difference, $s_{V-Q}$, is 95.6.

Suppose your GRE-$V$ exceeds your GRE-$Q$ score by 100 points, is this unusual? Find the $z$-score for a value of 100 in a distribution with $\mu = 0$ and $\sigma = 95.6$: $z = (100 - 0)/95.6 = 1.05$. From Table A, we find that almost 14.69% of examinees will have a GRE-$V$ score that is at least 100 points greater than the corresponding GRE-$Q$ score. In other words, about one person in seven will have such a difference; it is not very unusual.

In the sections to follow, situations will be considered in which one or both of the variables are in the form of ranks or dichotomies.

## 7.21 ADDITIONAL MEASURES OF RELATIONSHIP: THE SPEARMAN RANK CORRELATION, $r_{\text{ranks}}$

Raw data may be in the form of ranks, or raw scores can be converted to ranks. "Rank in graduating class" is an example of the conversion of scores to ranks: Grade-point averages are computed for each of 500 students; a rank of 1 is assigned the highest GPA, 2 to the next highest, . . . , 500 to the lowest. "Judges' rankings of excellence of a recitation" is an example in which the original data are expressed as ranks: Ten students recite a passage, and a judge assigns the rank 1 to the best recitation, 2 to the second best recitation, . . . , and 10 to the worst. Data are often gathered in this form when more refined measurements are not convenient or possible. No matter how the ranks 1, 2, . . . , $n - 1$, $n$ are generated, the correlation, $r_{\text{ranks}}$, between the two sets of ranks for the same $n$ persons can be computed.

The Spearman[26] rank correlation, $r_{\text{ranks}}$, is only a shortcut version of product-moment Equations 7.2, 7.4, or 7.5, tailor-made to fit situations in which both variables are expressed as ranks.[27]

---

[26]Attributed to the British psychologist Charles Spearman (1863–1945).

[27]Another measure of relationship between two sets of ranks is Kendall's tau (see Glass and Stanley, 1970, pp. 176–179). Due to its infrequent use, it is not discussed here.

The Spearman rank correlation between highway speed limits and traffic fatalities is computed in Table 7.5. Note that $r$ could not be computed unless West Germany was excluded or unless a numerical value was supplied as the speed limit; both of these options are undesirable. These difficulties can be avoided by using rank correlation. In addition, the outlier (the extremely high fatality figure for Turkey—it is 4.2 standard deviations above the mean!) will have much less influence on $r_{\text{ranks}}$ than on $r$.

When $X$ and $Y$ are ranks and there are no ties, both distributions have the same mean and the same variance,[28] the values of which are governed solely by $n$, the number of pairs. Equation 7.2 can be simplified, and becomes Equation 7.12:[29]

$$r_{\text{ranks}} = 1 - \frac{6\sum_i D_i^2}{n(n^2 - 1)} \qquad \textbf{(7.12)}$$

where $n$ is the number of pairs and $D_i$ is the difference between the two ranks for the $i$th case.

Note that $r_{\text{ranks}}$ is a special case of $r$; $r$ (Equation 7.2) and $r_{\text{ranks}}$ (Equation 7.12) will be identical when $X$ and $Y$ are ranks and when there are no tied ranks.[30] When tied ranks occur, Equation 7.12 for $r_{\text{ranks}}$ and Equation 7.2 for $r$ will be very close in value, but not identical. Even though the mean of the numbers 1, 2, ..., $n$ does not change when ties in the ranks occur, the variance of the ranks is slightly less than for the rectangular distribution (i.e., each rank has a frequency of 1) assumed in Equation 7.12. Consequently, the variance simplifications in the formula for $r$ that led to Equation 7.12 are not exact. Fortunately, even when there are ties, $r$ and $r_{\text{ranks}}$ will differ trivially. For example, although there are many ties on $X$ in Table 7.5, the value of $r$ between the two sets of ranks is .27, which differs only slightly from $r_{\text{ranks}} = .29$.[31]

## 7.22 THE PHI COEFFICIENT: BOTH *X* AND *Y* ARE DICHOTOMIES

When both $X$ and $Y$ are dichotomous variables, the data can be thought of as arranged in two columns of 0's and 1's where each row gives the two scores for one person. For example,

---

[28]For $n$ ranks, the mean rank is $(n + 1)/2$, and the variance is $(n^2 - 1)/12$.

[29]See Glass and Stanley (1970, pp. 173–175) for derivation.

[30]There are three possible ways to proceed in the calculation of $r_{\text{ranks}}$ when tied ranks occur: (1) Use the computational formula for $r$ (Equation 7.2) on the data; this will always give $r_{\text{ranks}}$ whether any ranks are tied or not; (2) Compute an approximation via Equation 7.12; (3) Use a formula (see Kendall, 1962) that incorporates corrections of the two variances for the ties in the ranks. With the current availability of calculators and computers, when extreme precision is needed use method (1) and compute the $r$ between the ranks using Equation 7.2 or 7.4, assigning ranks to tied measurements by the averaging method described.

[31]When it can be assumed that the underlying variable that is expressed in ranks is normally distributed, ranks are sometimes transformed to normalized $T$-scores (Section 6.12). If both $X$ and $Y$ are ranks and both have underlying normal distributions, the $r$ between their normalized scores will tend to be slightly greater than the correlation between ranks. On the other hand, if both underlying variables were distributed rectangularly, $r$ would be slightly less than $r_{\text{ranks}}$. To normalize ranks or scores, the percentile ($P_i$) associated with each of the $n$ ranks ($R_i$) is determined using the equation: $P_i = 1 - (R_i - .5)/n$. Using Table A, each percentile, ($P_i$) is transformed to a $z$-score, which is converted to a $T$-score using Equation 6.5 in Section 6.7.

**TABLE 7.5** An Illustration of the Computation of the Spearman Rank Correlation between Highway Speed Limits (X) and Traffic Fatalities/100,000,000 Driver Miles (Y) for Fifteen Countries

| | | | *Ranks* | | *Difference in Ranks* | |
|---|---|---|---|---|---|---|
| *Country* | *Speed Limit* | *Fatalities* | *X* | *Y* | *D* | $D^2$ |
| West Germany | none | 7.9 | 1 | 8 | –7 | 49 |
| Italy | 87 mph | 6.4 | 2 | 9 | –7 | 49 |
| France | 81 | 8.0 | 3 | 7 | –4 | 16 |
| Hungary | 75[a] | 14.5 | 5[a] | 3 | 2 | 4 |
| Belgium | 75 | 10.5 | 5 | 6 | –1 | 1 |
| Portugal | 75 | 22.5 | 5 | 2 | 3 | 9 |
| Britain | 70 | 4.0 | 7 | 14 | –7 | 49 |
| Spain | 62 | 12.4 | 10 | 5 | 5 | 25 |
| Denmark | 62 | 4.8 | 10 | 11 | –1 | 1 |
| Netherlands | 62 | 6.0 | 10 | 10 | 0 | 0 |
| Greece | 62 | 12.9 | 10 | 4 | 6 | 36 |
| Japan | 62 | 4.7 | 10 | 12 | –2 | 4 |
| Norway | 56 | 4.2 | 13.5 | 13 | .5 | .25 |
| Turkey | 56 | 32.2 | 13.5 | 1 | 12.5 | 156.25 |
| United States | 55 | 3.3 | 15 | 15 | 0 | 0 |

$\Sigma D^2 = 399.5$

$$r_{ranks} = 1 - \frac{6\sum_i D_i^2}{n(n^2-1)}$$

$$= 1 - \frac{6(399.5)}{15(225-1)}$$

$$= 1 - \frac{2,397}{3,360}$$

$$= 1 - .7134$$

$$= .2866 \text{ or } .29$$

[a]When ties occur on X or Y, assign the average of the ranks involved to each score, for example, $(4 + 5 + 6)/3 = 5$ for $X = 75$.

ten students in academic trouble in their sophomore year of college might be observed on the variables Marital Status and Dropped-Out-of-College (see Table 7.6). Arbitrarily, we define 1 = Married and 0 = Not-Married for variable $X$, and on variable $Y$, 1 = Dropped-Out and 0 = Did-Not-Drop-Out. The Pearson correlation coefficient, $r$, is a measure of the relationship between $X$ and $Y$. The Pearson product-moment coefficient calculated on dichotomous data is called the *phi coefficient* and is denoted by $r_\phi$ or $\phi$.[32] The value of $r_\phi$ for the data

[32]Although $\phi$ is frequently used to denote the correlation coefficient, we will use $r_\phi$ to be consistent with the use of Greek letters to represent parameters.

**TABLE 7.6** Illustration of the Calculation of the Phi Coefficient $r_\phi$

| *Student No.* | *X* *Marital Status* *(Married = 1; Not Married = 0)* | *Y* *Attrition* *(Dropped Out = 1; Remained = 0)* | *Calculations* |
|---|---|---|---|
| 1 | 0 | 0 | $p_x = \frac{4}{10} = .4 \quad q_x = \frac{6}{10} = .6$ |
| 2 | 1 | 1 | |
| 3 | 0 | 1 | |
| 4 | 0 | 0 | $p_y = \frac{5}{10} = .5 \quad q_y = .5$ |
| 5 | 1 | 1 | |
| 6 | 1 | 0 | |
| 7 | 0 | 0 | $p_{xy} = \frac{3}{10} = .3$ |
| 8 | 1 | 1 | |
| 9 | 0 | 0 | |
| 10 | 0 | 1 | $r_\phi = \frac{p_{xy} - p_x p_y}{\sqrt{p_x q_x p_y q_y}}$ |
| | $\Sigma X = 4$ | $\Sigma Y = 5$ | |
| | | | $r_\phi = \frac{.3-(.4)(.5)}{\sqrt{(.4)(.6)(.5)(.5)}} = .408$ |

in Table 7.6 is .408. Equation 7.2 for $r$ can be replaced with a still simpler, but algebraically identical formula, when the data on $X$ and $Y$ are dichotomous.

Let $p_x$ be the proportion of people scoring 1 on $X$; $q_x$, the proportion scoring 0 on $X$, will be equal to $1 - p_x$. The proportion scoring 1 on $Y$ is denoted by $p_y$, and $q_y = 1 - p_y$. Finally, let $p_{xy}$ denote the proportion of persons scoring 1 on both $X$ and $Y$. With these definitions, the equation for $r$ can be simplified algebraically[33] to Equation 7.13:

$$r_\phi = \frac{p_{xy} - p_x p_y}{\sqrt{p_x q_x p_y q_y}} \quad \textbf{(7.13)}$$

Note the simple calculations for $r_\phi$ in Table 7.6 when Equation 7.13 is used.

When one has no particular interest in the proportions $p_x$ and $p_y$ and finds it more convenient to tabulate dichotomous bivariate data in a contingency table (a table showing the joint occurrences of pairs of scores on two variables in a group), $r_\phi$ can be calculated more directly using a different formula. Students in an applied statistics class were asked whether they regularly ate breakfast. The results, broken down separately for males and females, are given in Table 7.7. Is there a relationship between gender and breakfast eating?

For each cell of a contingency table like Table 7.7, let the letters $a$, $b$, $c$, and $d$ be substituted for the actual frequencies so that we can give a general method for the computation of $r_\phi$ directly from the cell frequencies. Note from Table 7.7 that the number of persons

[33]See Glass and Hopkins (1984, pp. 98–99) for derivation of Equation 7.13.

**TABLE 7.7** Contingency Table Depicting the Relationship between Gender and Breakfast for Twenty-Seven Students in Applied Statistic

| | | $X$: Gender | | |
|---|---|---|---|---|
| | | Female (0) | Male (1) | Totals |
| $Y$ | Yes (1) | $8 = a$ | $6 = b$ | $14 = a + b$ |
| | No (0) | $9 = c$ | $4 = d$ | $13 = c + d$ |
| | Totals | $17 = a + c$ | $10 = b + d$ | $27 = n$ |

scoring 0 on $X$ and 1 on $Y$ is denoted by the letter $a$. The total number of persons scoring 0 on $X$ is $a + c$. The total number of persons represented in the table is $n$.

It can be shown by substituting such equivalences as $p_x = (b + d)/n$, $p_y = (a + b)/n$, and $p_{xy} = b/n$ into Equation 7.13 that the phi coefficient for the data arranged in a contingency table like Table 7.7 is yielded by Equation 7.14:

$$r_\phi = \frac{bc - ad}{\sqrt{(a+c)(b+d)(a+b)(c+d)}} \tag{7.14}$$

To illustrate the calculation of $r_\phi$ using Equation 7.14, the data in Table 7.7 will be used:

$$r_\phi = \frac{(6)(9)-(8)(4)}{\sqrt{(17)(10)(14)(13)}} = \frac{22}{\sqrt{30,940}} = \frac{22}{175.9} = .125$$

The positive value of $r_\phi$ shows that persons with 1's on $X$ are more likely to have 1's on $Y$. Thus, males had a slightly greater tendency to eat breakfast regularly—60% of the males eat regular breakfasts, while 47% of the females eat breakfast regularly.

Recall that $r$ can never attain the value of +1 or –1 unless the marginal distributions of $X$ and $Y$ are identical in shape (Section 7.17). Likewise, $r_\phi$ can have a theoretical maximum absolute value of 1 only if $p_x = p_y$. If $p_x$ differs greatly from $p_y$, the maximum value of the phi coefficient, $r_\phi$, can be much below 1; for example, if 10 of 100 males have a given characteristic and none of the 100 females have the characteristic, $r_\phi$ is only .33, the maximum value possible.

## 7.23 THE POINT-BISERIAL COEFFICIENT

When one dichotomous variable [e.g., sex, high school graduate (yes or no)] is correlated with a continuous measure, the formula for the product-moment correlation coefficient can be simplified. Pearson derived the formula in 1901 and called it the *point-biserial correlation coefficient*, denoted by $r_{pb}$. (The term biserial refers to the fact that there are two series

**TABLE 7.8** Calculation of the Point-Biserial Correlation Coefficient.

Females: $n_0 = 17,\ \overline{Y}_0 = 64.35$ in.

$s_Y = 3.75$ in. $n_{\bullet} = 17 + 10 = 27$

Males: $n_1 = 10,\ \overline{Y}_1 = 69.90$ in.

$$r_{pb} = \frac{\overline{Y}_1 - \overline{Y}_0}{s_Y}\sqrt{\frac{n_1 n_0}{n_{\bullet}(n_{\bullet} - 1)}} = \frac{69.90 - 64.35}{3.75}\sqrt{\frac{(10)(17)}{(27)(27-1)}} = (1.48)\sqrt{.2422} = .728$$

of persons being observed on $Y$: those who scored 0 and those who scored 1 on the dichotomous measure, $X$.) Equation 7.15 is a simplified formula for $r_{pb}$:

$$r_{pb} = \frac{\overline{Y}_1 - \overline{Y}_0}{s_Y}\sqrt{\frac{n_1 n_0}{n_{\bullet}(n_{\bullet} - 1)}} \quad \textbf{(7.15)}$$

where $\overline{Y}_1$ is the mean of $Y$ for those with scores of 1 on $X$; $\overline{Y}_0$ is the mean of $Y$ for those who scored 0 on $X$; $s_Y$ is the standard deviation of all $n$ scores on $Y$; $n_1$ is the number of persons scoring 1 on $X$; $n_0$ is the number of persons scoring 0 on $X$; and $n_{\bullet} = n_1 + n_0$.

Equation 7.15 represents an algebraic simplification of the Pearson product-moment correlation coefficient formula when $X$ is a dichotomous variable. Notice that the first half of Equation 7.15 is simply the difference in means of the two groups expressed in standard deviation units. The calculation of $r_{pb}$, describing the degree of relationship between gender and height for twenty-seven adults, is illustrated in Table 7.8.

Notice that the two means differ by 1.48 standard deviations, which is approximately twice the value of $r_{pb}$. When $n_1$ and $n_0$ are approximately equal, $\overline{Y}_1$ and $\overline{Y}_0$ will differ by approximately $2r_{pb}$ standard deviations[34] ($s_Y$), that is, when $n_1 \approx n_0$:

$$\frac{\overline{Y}_1 - \overline{Y}_0}{s_Y} \approx 2r_{pb} \quad \textbf{(7.16)}$$

Of course, the maximum value of $r_{pb}$ is always less than 1.0 because the two marginal distributions can never be the same shape (unless $Y$ is also a dichotomy, in which case $r_{\phi}$ is the proper coefficient, not $r_{pb}$).

## 7.24 THE BISERIAL CORRELATION[35]

Suppose that a variable $X$ is measured dichotomously, but a more extensive or refined assessment would produce a normal distribution of scores on $X$; so the dichotomous vari-

[34] This is a close relative of the effect size measure (Section 12.8).

[35] The biserial and tetrachoric measures of association are less widely used than the other measures of correlation included in this chapter; Sections 7.24–7.26 are included primarily for reference purposes, and can be skipped without serious consequences.

able has an underlying normal distribution. The dichotomy is not a true dichotomy, such as gender, but is an artifact of crude measurement (e.g., pass-or-fail grading). The next two coefficients to be studied, the biserial and tetrachoric correlations (Section 7.26), are *approximations* to what the Pearson product-moment coefficients would be if the two crude categories were replaced by a refined measure that yields scores that are normally distributed.

The *biserial correlation coefficient* is an estimate of the product-moment correlation between the continuous variable, $Y$, and the hypothetical normally distributed scores on $X$ that are assumed to underlie the dichotomy, 0 or 1. For example, the $Y$ scores might be scores on the Scholastic Aptitude Test, and the $X$ scores might be 0's and 1's on a test item measuring cognitive flexibility. With more elaborate tests of cognitive flexibility, it might be possible to produce a wide range of cognitive flexibility scores that would be nearly normally distributed. Then the $r$ between these two arrays of scores on $X$ and $Y$ could be computed. What do the $Y$ scores and the dichotomous scores on $X$ tell about the value of $r$? The biserial correlation coefficient $r_{bis}$ offers an answer to this question. It is important to emphasize that $r_{bis}$ is an approximation to $r$; it does *not* describe the relationship between the *observed* $X$ and $Y$ values; that is done by $r_{pb}$.

Suppose one wishes to study the relationship between IQ scores and the amount of time students need to complete a test. Suppose that the allotted testing time has expired and twelve of the forty students still have not finished. If one uses the data on the twenty-eight students who finished the test, the range of testing time, variable $X$, will be restricted and the resulting $r$ will underestimate the true relationship (see Section 7.14). Variable $X$ could be reduced to two categories, "completed" and "not completed," and $r_{pb}$ could be computed. This $r_{pb}$ would underestimate the degree of relationship since the individual differences among persons within the two categories are ignored. The best alternative is to obtain an extrapolated estimate of $r$; that is, to compute $r_{bis}$. The computation of $r_{bis}$ using Equation 7.17 is illustrated in Table 7.9:

$$r_{bis} = \frac{\bar{Y}_1 - \bar{Y}_0}{s_Y}\left(\frac{n_1 n_0}{u n_{\bullet}^2}\right) \tag{7.17}$$

where $u$ is the ordinate or probability density of the unit normal distribution at $p_1$, found using Table A; $p_1$ is the proportion of cases in group 1 (i.e., $p_1 = n_1/n_{\bullet}$); other symbols were defined previously in Equation 7.15.

**TABLE 7.9** A Computational Illustration of the Biserial Correlation Coefficient between Test-taking Time and Test Scores

Did not finish: $n_0 = 12$, $\bar{Y}_0 = 105.1$

Finished: $n_1 = 28$, $\bar{Y}_1 = 113.3$

$s_Y = 16.0$, $n_{\bullet} = 40$

$u = .3477$ (To find $u$ from Table A, enter $p = n_0/n_{\bullet}$ in the column "Proportion of Area Above (or Below) $z$," and read $u$ in the adjacent column.)

$$r_{bis} = \frac{\bar{Y}_1 - \bar{Y}_0}{s_Y}\left(\frac{n_1 n_0}{u n_{\bullet}^2}\right) = \frac{113.3 - 105.1}{16.0}\left(\frac{(28)(12)}{(.3477)(40)^2}\right) = (.5125)(.6040) = .310$$

A word or two about the range of possible values for $r_{bis}$ is in order. Unlike almost any other commonly used correlation coefficient, $r_{bis}$ can sometimes take on values below $-1$ and above $+1$. The only significance of these extreme values of $r_{bis}$ is that they reflect either incorrectness of the assumption that the $Y$-scores are normally distributed, or sampling error, when $n$ is small, that produces a markedly platykurtic distribution (Section 6.10) of $Y$-values in the sample. The unpleasant fact remains that values of $r_{bis}$ exceeding 1.0 are occasionally obtained, especially with small samples. When $n$ is small, $r_{bis}$ is a very crude approximation of $r$; indeed, it is probably best not to use $r_{bis}$ when $n$ is small, especially when $p_1$ differs considerably from .5.

Another caution pertaining to $r_{bis}$ results from the fact that if the variable underlying $X$ is not normally distributed, or the relationship is not linear, $r_{bis}$ and $r$ can differ by as much as .2 (Nunnally & Bernstein, 1994, p. 127). For these reasons, $r_{bis}$ should not be viewed as an adequate substitute for $r$ but only as a crude approximation, unless the underlying assumptions are known to be met and $n$ is large, at least 100.

## 7.25 BISERIAL VERSUS POINT-BISERIAL CORRELATION COEFFICIENTS

For any set of data, $r_{pb}$ can be transformed to $r_{bis}$ by Equation 7.18:

$$r_{bis} = r_{pb}\sqrt{\frac{n_1 n_0 (n_{\bullet} - 1)}{u^2 n_{\bullet}^3}} \qquad \textbf{(7.18)}$$

In comparing the values of $r_{bis}$ and $r_{pb}$, it is useful to know that the minimum value of the factor under the radical ($\sqrt{\ }$) in Equation 7.18 is approximately 1.25 (i.e., when $n_1 = n_0$ and $n_{\bullet}$ is large). Consequently, $r_{bis} \geq 1.25 r_{pb}$. As the proportion, $p$, of the observations in the larger or smaller group deviates from .5, the value of $r_{bis}$ will be more than 25% larger than $r_{pb}$; for $p$ = .6, .7, .8, .9, and .95, $r_{bis}/r_{pb}$ increases to 1.27, 1.32, 1.43, 1.71, and 2.11, respectively.

## 7.26 THE TETRACHORIC COEFFICIENT

When *both* $X$ and $Y$ are artificial dichotomies with underlying normal distributions, the *tetrachoric correlation coefficient*, $r_{tet}$, provides an extrapolated estimate of $r$. Before computers, the computation of $r_{tet}$ was commonly used to circumvent the huge computational burden required when many $r$'s were needed. If twenty-five variables are being studied and the $r$ between each pair is desired, 300 $r$'s would have to be calculated! The use of $r_{tet}$ declined dramatically as computers became accessible. Nevertheless, situations arise in which $r$ cannot be computed directly, but an estimate is desired of what $r$ would be if variables $X$ and $Y$ are characterized by bivariate normality. For example, suppose two yes-no questions on an attitude survey were

$X$: Do you favor the legalization of marijuana?

$Y$: Do you approve of the legalization of abortion?

It is reasonable to assume there are gradations in attitudes on both $X$ and $Y$. If more refined scales were developed for detecting the shades of gray in both attitudes, the value of $r$ can

**TABLE 7.10** Calculation of the Tetrachoric Correlation Coefficient

| | | Question $X$ No | Yes | Totals | Proportions |
|---|---|---|---|---|---|
| Question $Y$ | Yes | 90 ($a$) | 110 ($b$) | 200 | .50($p_y$) |
| | No | 190 ($c$) | 10 ($d$) | 200 | .50($q_y$) |
| | Totals | 280 | 120 | 400 ($n_\bullet$) | |
| | Proportions | .70 ($q_x$) | .30 ($p_x$) | | |

$u_x = .3477$
$u_y = .3989$
[To find $u_x$ (and $u_y$) from Table A, enter $p_x$ (and $p_y$) in the "Proportion . . ." column and read $u_x$ (and $u_y$) in the adjacent column.]

$$r_{tet} = \frac{bc - ad}{u_x u_y n_\bullet^2} = \frac{(110)(190) - (90)(10)}{(.3477)(.3989)(400)^2}$$

$$r_{tet} = .901$$

be estimated by $r_{\text{tet}}$. Using the data from Table 7.10, Equation 7.19 for $r_{\text{tet}}$ can be used to approximate $r$:

$$r_{\text{tet}} = \frac{bc - ad}{u_x u_y n_\bullet^2} \quad \textbf{(7.19)}$$

where $a$, $b$, $c$, and $d$ are cell frequencies as defined in the table and $u_x$ and $u_y$ are ordinates of the unit normal distribution at $p_x$ and $p_y$, where $p_x$ and $p_y$ are the proportions responding "1" (i.e., Yes = 1) on measures $X$ and $Y$, respectively, and $n_\bullet$ is the total number of cases. The computation of $r_{\text{tet}}$ is illustrated in Table 7.10.

The interpretation of $r_{\text{tet}}$ is similar to $r_{\text{bis}}$ in that it is an estimate of what the observed $r$ would be if both variables were measured more accurately and, therefore, would yield normal distributions and be linearly related. Even when these conditions are met, $n$ must be quite large (400 or more) before the estimates of $r$ provided by $r_{\text{tet}}$ are reasonably accurate.

How do $r_{\text{tet}}$ and $r_\phi$ compare for the data in Table 7.10? From Equation 7.14, $r_\phi$ is found to be .546—much less than the $r_{\text{tet}}$ of .901. The observed relationship between the two dichotomies is described by $r_\phi$, whereas $r_{\text{tet}}$ is an extrapolated estimate of the relationship when the measures of $X$ and $Y$ are characterized by bivariate normality.

## 7.27 CAUSATION AND CORRELATION

Figure 7.13 shows the extremely high relationship ($r$ =.95) between the number of storks observed and the population of Oldenburg, Germany, for each of seven years.[36] Was your childhood hypothesis correct after all?

[36]These data, along with the primary sources, can be found in Box, Hunter, and Hunter (1978).

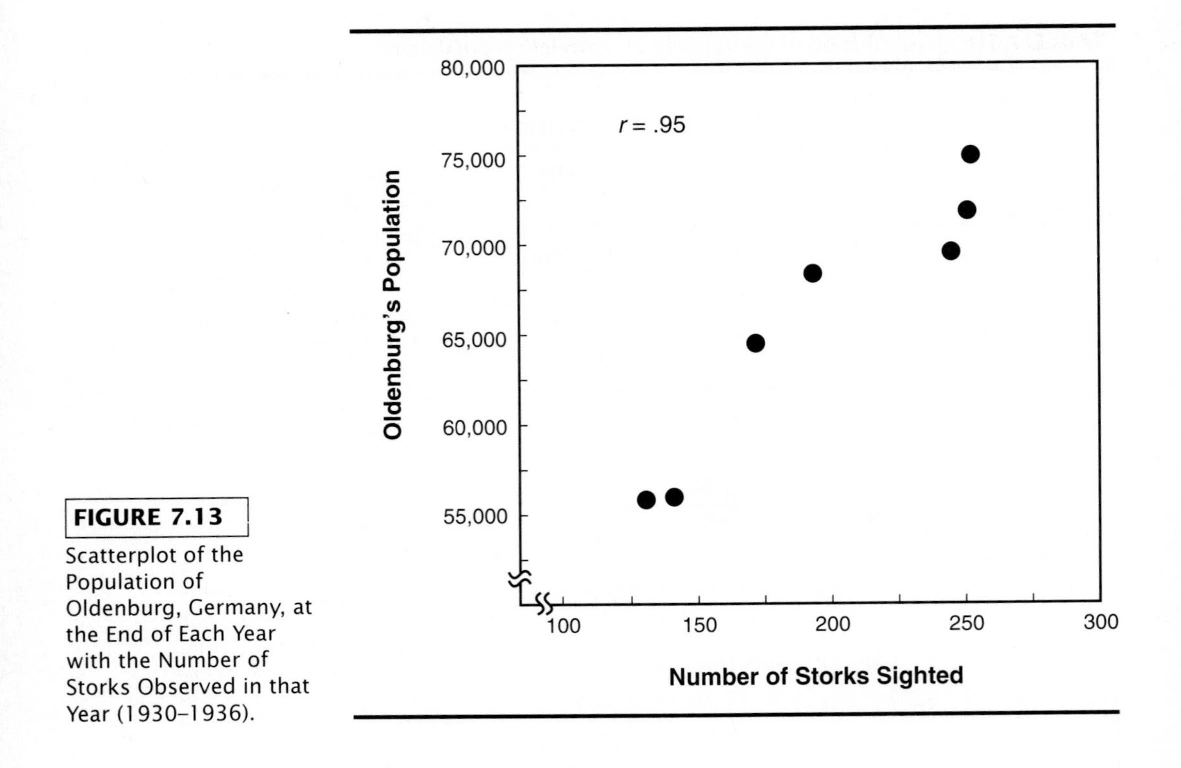


**FIGURE 7.13**

Scatterplot of the Population of Oldenburg, Germany, at the End of Each Year with the Number of Storks Observed in that Year (1930–1936).

The presence of a correlation between two variables does not necessarily mean there exists a causal link between them. Although correlation can be useful in identifying causal relationships when coupled with other methodological approaches, it is a dangerous and potentially misleading test for causation when used alone. First, even when one can presume that a causal relationship does exist between the two variables being correlated, $r_{XY}$ does not tell whether $X$ causes $Y$ or $Y$ causes $X$. Second, often variables other than the two under consideration could be responsible for the observed association. Third, the relationships that exist among variables in behavioral and social sciences are almost always too complex to be explained in terms of a single cause. Juvenile delinquency, to take one of many possible examples, is the result of many influences, besides being a complex concept itself that cannot be described adequately by any single measurement.

Some examples of the problems that arise in attempts to unearth causal relationships with correlation techniques will help illustrate these points. For example, it is probably true that in the United States there is a positive correlation between the average salary of teachers in high schools and the percentage of the schools' graduates who enter college. Does this imply that well paid teaching staffs cause better trained high school graduates? Would the percentage of high school graduates entering college rise if the pay of teachers were increased? Certainly affirmative answers to these questions are not justified by the association alone. The relationship between the two factors is not simple. One prominent variable not yet mentioned is the SES level of the community that influences its ability to pay both teachers' salaries and college tuitions.

It has been found that the percentage of dropouts in each of a number of high schools is negatively correlated with the number of books per pupil in the libraries of those schools. However, common sense tells us that piling more books into the library will no more affect the dropout rate than hiring a better truant officer will bring about a magical increase in the holdings of the school library.

Some researchers do not stop with one fallacious conclusion—that is, that correlation is prima facie evidence for causation—but draw a second one as well. They assume a certain direction for the causal relationship. This is only natural, since our minds are often made up as to the nature of a causal relationship between two phenomena before we gather data and compute $r_{XY}$. Let us investigate a plausible example more closely. Many studies have reported correlation coefficients of –.2 or so between test anxiety ($X$) and performance on ability tests ($Y$). Does this imply that high anxiety has caused the pupils to perform poorly on the test and that low anxiety pupils, not being handicapped by fear, were more able to perform to the limits of their ability? This conclusion has successfully tempted many researchers. Why is it not equally plausible that ability differences cause anxiety? Might not less clever pupils become more anxious when their ability is tested, while bright students find the experience less anxiety producing? What is involved here is the question of whether $X$ can be said to cause $Y$ or $Y$ to cause $X$. A simple correlation coefficient between $X$ and $Y$ cannot by itself prove either claim. Suffice it to say that studies of association alone, without experimental substantiation, are often difficult to interpret causally. Experimental approaches to this problem that involve making one group of students anxious and comparing their scores on the ability test with those of a control group have not established a cause-and-effect relationship (Allison, 1970; French, 1962; Chambers, Hopkins, and Hopkins, 1972).

Failure to recognize that correlation may not mean causation is a widespread logical error. Attending religious services is generally believed to be valuable in many ways; the positive relationship between the rate of service attendance and honesty, for example, does not necessarily prove that children are more honest because they attend services. Underlying and causing both attendance and honesty may be, for example, training in the home.

If one correlated $X$, the number of police officers per 1,000 residents in large cities in the United States with the amount of crime, it is likely that we would find a positive correlation; the cities with the greatest densities of policemen have the most crime. Of course, it is absurd to conclude that if a city reduced the number of policemen that its crime would go down. It is plausible that there is a negative causal relationship between these variables; if more policemen were employed, the amount of crime would decrease. Correlation means only that one variable can be predicted from knowledge of another variable.

## Zero Correlation and Causation

Just as a positive correlation cannot be said to represent causation, so a zero correlation does not necessarily prove the absence of a causal relationship. For example, some studies with college students have found no correlation between hours of study for an examination and test performance. Does this mean that the amount of study by a student had no effect on his test score? Of course not. Some bright students study little and still achieve average scores, whereas, some of their less gifted classmates study diligently but achieve only an average performance. A controlled experimental study would almost certainly show some causal relationship.

### Negative Correlation and Causation

Even a negative correlation does not rule out the possibility of a positive, direct causative relationship. For example, suppose the weights of 1,000 persons are obtained and they are asked the question: Of your last ten soft drinks, how many were diet drinks? It is quite likely that $r_{XY}$ is positive, but does choosing diet, rather than high calorie soft drinks increase weight?! Although the correlation is positive, choosing diet drinks probably decreases the person's calorie intake. In this case, the correlation is positive, but the causative relationship is negative.

From the preceding discussion, it should be clear that one must be very careful not to infer causation from correlation coefficients. Likewise, one cannot prove that there is no causal relationship between $X$ and $Y$ from zero or negative correlation coefficients. Nonzero correlation coefficients do show that $Y$ can be predicted better if $X$ is known than if it is unknown, or, equivalently, knowledge of $Y$ improves the predictability of $X$. Prediction does not necessarily require any information or assumptions about causation. Stay off this slippery slope!

## 7.28 CHAPTER SUMMARY

The scientific study of relationships between variables requires an objective and precise measure to describe the degree of relationship between two variables. The Pearson product-moment correlation $r$, or $\rho$ for the parameter, is the most common measure of the degree of relationship between two variables. The degree of relationship can vary from $-1.0$, through 0, to $+1.0$. The magnitude of the relationship is indicated by the absolute value of the correlation coefficient. The sign (+ or –) of a coefficient only shows the direction of the relationship. A coefficient of zero indicates no correlation between two variables. A positive correlation shows that "high numbers on $X$ are associated with high numbers on $Y$" and that "low numbers on $Y$ are associated with low numbers on $X$."

Correlation coefficients considered in Chapter 7 describe the degree of linear relationship between $X$ and $Y$; the true association is underestimated if a curvilinear relationship exists between $X$ and $Y$. A scatterplot allows a visual check of linearity (statistical tests for curvilinearity are given in subsequent chapters).

The size of the correlation $r$ between two variables is unaffected by linear transformations of the variables (adding or subtracting a constant, or multiplying or dividing by a positive number). This type of transformation of $X$ or $Y$ does not alter the shape of the distribution, the percentile rank of any observation, the $z$-score for any observation, or the correlation of $X$ with any other variable. Transforming raw scores to standard scores is the most common type of linear transformation.

The value of the correlation coefficient is greatly influenced by the heterogeneity of the sample; the less the variability, the lower the value of $r$ and vice versa. The presence of measurement error in either variable will cause the observed correlation to be attenuated. One can estimate what the correlation coefficient would be if measurement error were removed from both variables using the correction for attenuation.

The general formula for the Pearson $r$ is applicable when either or both $X$ and $Y$ are ranks or dichotomous, but the resulting coefficients are denoted by special names. The product-moment formula can also be simplified for hand computation. When both $X$ and $Y$ are expressed as ranks, the Spearman rank correlation is obtained. When one variable is a dichotomy, the correlation is termed a point-biserial coefficient; if both variables are dichotomies, the correlation is a phi coefficient. When a dichotomous variable is not a true

**TABLE 7.11** Correlation Matrix for Case Study Variables

| | AGE | SBP | DBP | CHOL | HT | WT | CORON |
|---|---|---|---|---|---|---|---|
| AGE | 1.00 | .44 | .39 | .41 | –.25 | .06 | .27 |
| SBP | .44 | 1.00 | .80 | .23 | –.15 | .19 | .19 |
| DBP | .39 | .80 | 1.00 | .23 | –.12 | .31 | .17 |
| CHOL | .41 | .23 | .23 | 1.00 | –.13 | .04 | .18 |
| HT | –.25 | –.15 | –.12 | –.13 | 1.00 | .41 | –.07 |
| WT | .06 | .19 | .31 | .04 | .41 | 1.00 | .14 |
| CORON | .27 | .19 | .17 | .18 | –.07 | .14 | 1.00 |

dichotomy, but can be assumed to have an underlying normal distribution and a linear relationship with the other variable, extrapolated estimates of $r$ are provided by the biserial coefficient. If both variables are viewed as artificial dichotomies, the tetrachoric coefficient estimates the $r$ that would be obtained if both variables are linearly related and were measured precisely.

Correlation must be carefully distinguished from causation. There can be correlation without causation and vice versa.

## 7.29 CASE STUDY

The Pearson correlation coefficients among the seven variables included in the case study are given in Table 7.11. Cholesterol level is a principal variable of interest in this study; consider the array of $r$'s in the column, CHOL.

The story told by the $r$'s is this: None of the correlations is high, but the variable most highly correlated with cholesterol level is age. Older persons tended to have higher levels (see scatterplot in Figure 7.14). There was a tendency for persons with higher blood pressure, both SBP and DBP, to have slightly higher cholesterol levels. Weight had almost no relationship with cholesterol level, $r = .04$. The negative correlation (–.13) with height is very low in magnitude (see scatterplot in Figure 7.14), but shows that taller persons tended to have slightly lower cholesterol levels.[37]

The highest relationship in Table 7.11 is between SBP and DBP, $r = .80$; this very high relationship shows that persons who have low SBP tend to have low DBP as well (see scatterplot in Figure 7.14). It does not mean that there is little difference between $X$ and $Y$, but that one's relative standing on $X$ and $Y$ would not differ greatly. Stated differently, the standard scores or percentile ranks on the two variables would be similar for most persons.

[37]Whether these correlations are statistically significant (i.e., represent something other than a chance relationship) is considered in Chapter 14.

Height and weight correlated .41; what would the value of $r$ be if both were converted to $T$-scores, then correlated? Since the change to $T$-scores or $z$-scores is a linear transformation, the value of $r$ would remain .41. If we found each person's percentile ranks on height and weight, then found $r$ between the percentile ranks, would $r$ remain precisely .41? No, because the conversion to percentile ranks is not a linear transformation—the distribution of percentile ranks is a rectangular distribution. When normally distributed variables are expressed as percentile ranks, we would expect the correlation to be slightly less than the correlation between the original measurements.

Recall that the coronary variable is dichotomous; hence, correlations with CORON are point-biserial $r$'s. Note that all of the correlations are low. Age correlates with a coronary incident more highly than any other variable. Note that there is only a small relationship between cholesterol level and coronary; SBP and DBP are as highly related to coronary as is cholesterol level, with weight not far behind. Were you expecting the correlation between cholesterol level and coronary to be higher? In Chapter 8, the emphasis is on using $r$'s to predict $Y$ from $X$.

For the same data set, $r_{bis}$'s will always be larger in absolute value than $r_{pb}$'s; would it be appropriate to convert the $r_{pb}$'s to $r_{bis}$'s? Since the coronary variable is a true dichotomy, biserial $r$'s would be inappropriate and misleading.

For illustrative purposes, suppose we did not know the actual heights, but only whether each person was taller (1) or shorter (0) than 68 inches. The correlation between weight and the artificial dichotomy drops from .4057[38] to .3310. The biserial $r$'s could provide an estimate of what the correlations between height and the other variables would be if indeed height had been measured along the full scale. The mean weight for 99 of the 200 men with heights greater than 68 inches is 173.5 pounds; the mean weight for the 101 men below 68 inches is 157.0 pounds, and $s_Y = 24.9$. In addition, $p = 99/200 = .495$, and the ordinate $u$ is .3989. Substituting these values in Equation 7.17, $r_{bis} = .4152$; $r_{bis}$ is almost identical with $r$ because the relationship between the two variables is linear.

Recall from Sec. 7.25 that the biserial correlation, $r_{bis}$ is approximately 25% larger than $r_{pb}$ when the proportions in each dichotomy are approximately .5. Thus, using the simple rule of thumb, our estimate of $r$ would be very accurate: 1.25(.3310) or .4138! Note, however, that $r_{bis}$ answers a "what if" question; if we did not have actual heights, we could not observe the .41 correlation or use it to predict for individual cases (like we will be doing in Chapter 8). Naturally we prefer $r$ to $r_{bis}$ whenever possible.

Note that age is correlated with SBP (see scatterplot in Figure 7.14), DBP, and cholesterol level. Does cholesterol level correlate with coronary incident if age is held constant, that is, for persons of the same age, is cholesterol level correlated with coronary incident? In Chapter 8, we will learn how to give a statistical answer to this question using partial correlation. We will also learn how to use the variables in combination to predict cholesterol level or coronary incident with maximal accuracy.

Illustrative scatterplots for the case study are given in Figure 7.14. There is no obvious nonlinearity in any of the scatterplots.

The scatterplot in the upper left-hand portion of Figure 7.14 depicts the relationship between age and cholesterol level. Notice that there is greater spread in the cholesterol levels at the older ages; the scatterplot lacks homoscedasticity.[39] The scatterplot in the lower left-hand portion depicts the high relationship between DBP and SBP. Note there is room

---

[38]Obviously, the correlations in Table 7.11 were rounded to two places.

[39]Chapter 8 will give more information concerning homoscedasticity; in particular, see Section 8.25.

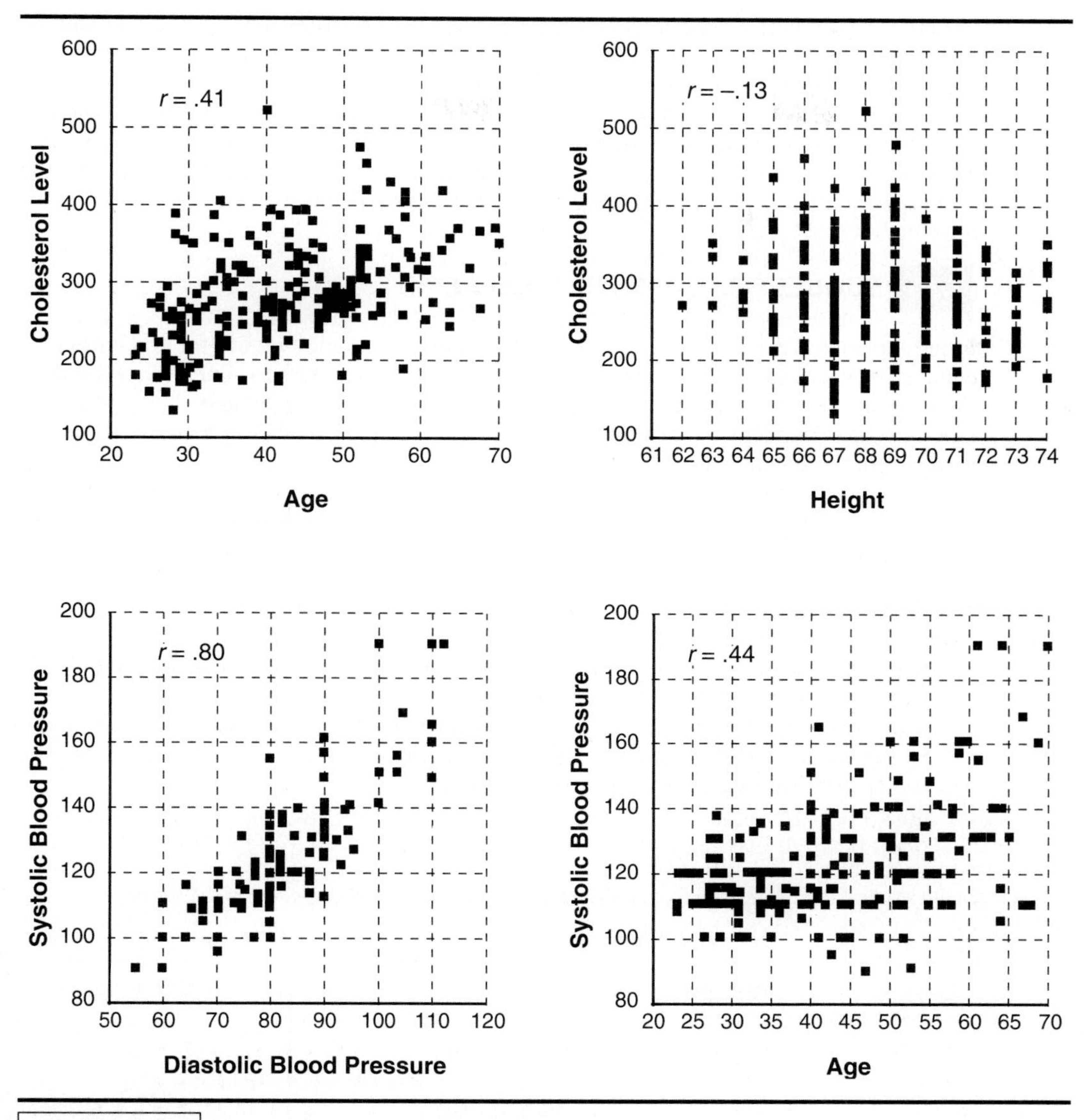


**FIGURE 7.14** Illustrative Scatterplots from Case Study.

for individual exceptions even with $r = .80$—four persons with DBP of 100 had SBP ranging from 140 to 190.

The scatterplot in the upper right-hand portion of Figure 7.14 shows the slight negative correlation between height and cholesterol level; taller persons tended to have slightly lower cholesterol levels. Why are all of the points in straight lines? Height was recorded only to the nearest inch; if height had been measured more accurately, how would the correlations of height with the other variables have changed? Rounding to the nearest inch introduces a small amount of measurement error; the correlations would have been fractionally higher with more refined measurement of height.

The scatterplot in the lower right-hand portion of Figure 7.14 shows that the relationship lacks homoscedasticity. SBP can be predicted more accurately at the younger ages; SBP is much more variable for persons over 60 than for persons 20–40. Notice how the scatterplots enhance an understanding of the relationship described by the $r$'s.

## 7.30 SUGGESTED COMPUTER EXERCISE

Using the High School and Beyond data set, obtain a correlation matrix for all continuous and dichotomous variables. Examine selected scatterplots for outliers, linearity, and homoscedasticity. Select only students whose RDG score is greater than 50 and obtain the correlation ($r_2$) between RDG and WRTG and compare with the correlation between these two variables based on all students ($r_1$); why is $r_1 > r_2$?[40]

## MASTERY TEST

1. Which of these correlation coefficients indicates the strongest relationship?
   (a) .55 (b) .09 (c) −.77 (d) .1
2. With which of the coefficients given as options to question 1 do the $X$-observations below $\overline{X}$ tend to be associated with $Y$-observations above $\overline{Y}$?
3. Suppose a measure of political conservatism is administered to representative samples of persons of ages 15, 20, 30, 45, and 60 and that the respective means were 60, 85, 80, 70, and 65. The correlation between age and political conservatism is
   (a) 1.0 (c) linear
   (b) −1.0 (d) curvilinear

*In questions 4 to 8, select the scatter diagram that best matches the relationship described.*

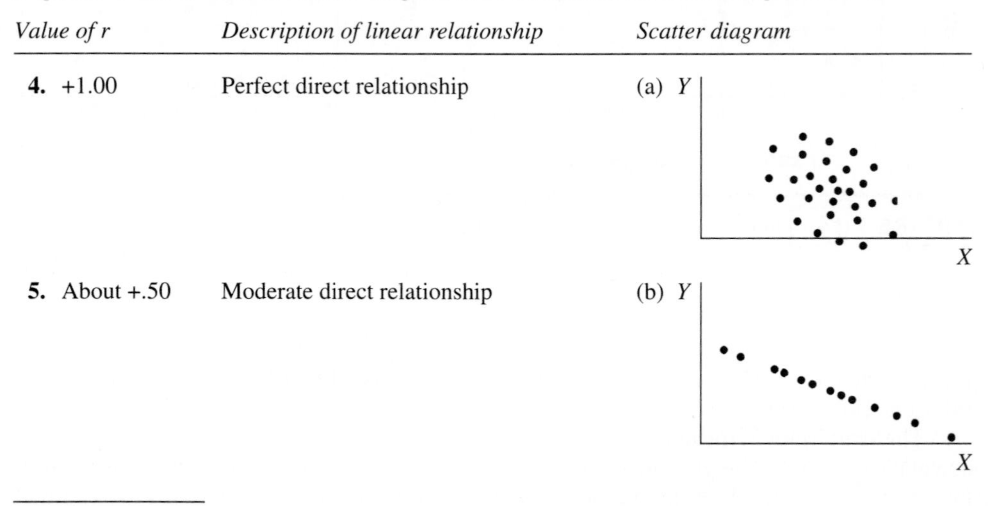

| *Value of r* | *Description of linear relationship* | *Scatter diagram* |
|---|---|---|
| **4.** +1.00 | Perfect direct relationship | (a) |
| **5.** About +.50 | Moderate direct relationship | (b) |



[40]Hint: Compare the standard deviations and see Section 7.14.

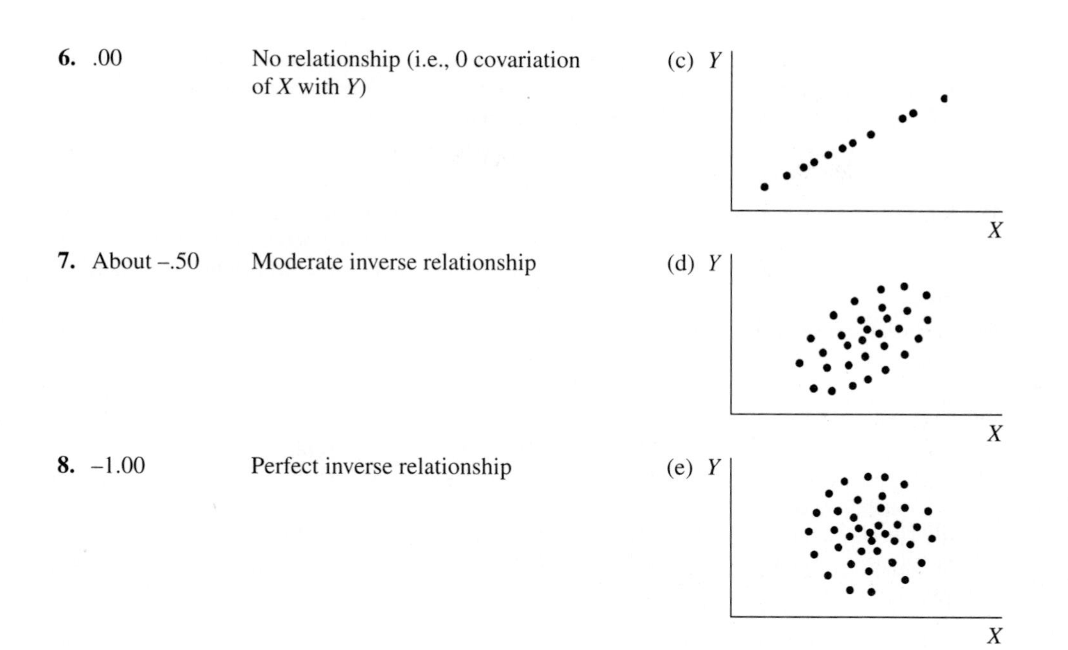


**9.** Indicate whether the expected correlation between the two designated variables would be positive, negative, or zero. (Assume the population for the following items "a" to "i" is all persons in grade 10 in the nation.)

(a) *X*, height in inches; *Y*, weight in pounds
(b) *X*, age in months; *Y*, time in seconds required to run fifty yards
(c) *X*, reading achievement in grade-placement units; *Y*, arithmetic achievement in grade-placement units
(d) *X*, shoe size; *Y*, citizenship rating of student on a 10-point scale by his or her teacher
(e) *X*, arithmetic achievement in *T*-score units; *Y*, number of days absent from school during the year
(f) *X*, social security numbers; *Y*, IQ's
(g) *X*, interest in sports; *Y*, interest in politics
(h) *X*, total miles traveled by a car; *Y*, year in which the car was manufactured
(i) *X*, maximum daily temperature; *Y*, amount of water used by residents

**10.** If $r_{XY} = -.8$ in part (h) of question 9, what would the value of $r_{XY}$ be if *Y* were changed from "year in which the car was manufactured" to "age of vehicle"?

**11.** The correlation of *X* with *Y* is .60; the correlation of *X* with *W* is –.80. Is *X* more closely linearly related to *Y* or to *W*?

**12.** If the correlation between *X* and *Y* is .5, what will the value of *r* be if the *X*-values are linearly transformed to *T*-scores and then correlated with *Y*?

**13.** If $r = 1$ and $z_X = -.5$, what is $z_Y$?

**14.** If $r = -1$ and $z_Y = .8$, what is $z_X$?

**15.** The IQ's using Test A are consistently 10 points higher than the IQ's using Test B. What is the largest possible value for *r*?

**16.** Brown calculated the covariance of height (*X*) in feet (e.g., 67 in. becomes 5.58 ft.) and running speed in seconds (*Y*). He obtained a covariance of 2.30 on a sample of fifty students. From the same original data that Brown collected, Smith calculated the covariance of height in inches ($X$) and running speed in minutes ($Y$) (e.g., 69 sec. becomes 1.15 min.). Smith obtained a value of .46. Compare the correlations between $X$ and $Y$ obtained by Brown and Smith.

**17.** For a particular set of data, $s_X = 15$ and $s_Y = 3$. What is the largest that $s_{XY}$ could possibly be? (Hint: $r$ cannot be larger than +1; $r = s_{XY}/s_Xs_Y$.)

**18.** Suppose by observation alone you estimated the heights ($X$) and weights ($Y$) of each of your classmates and that you calculated the correlation coefficient ($r_1$) between these observations. How would this coefficient $r_1$ compare with the coefficient $r_2$ using data from a scale and tape measure to determine $X$ and $Y$? Why?

**19.** One study on heart attacks reported that persons who attend church regularly had a lower risk of heart attacks than nonchurchgoers. Which one of the following statements is correct?

(a) If you start attending church more regularly, your chances of a heart attack are certain to be reduced.
(b) There is definitely no causal relationship between the two variables.
(c) If you are a regular churchgoer, you are less likely to have a heart attack than if you are a nonchurchgoer.
(d) The correlation provides definitive information pertaining to causation.

**20.** In which college would you expect the correlation between IQ and grade-point average to be greatest?

| | *College* | | |
|---|---|---|---|
| *IQ* | *A* | *B* | *C* |
| $\mu$ | 108 | 112 | 120 |
| $\sigma$ | 10 | 12 | 8 |

**21.** Which college in question 20 would you expect to have the lowest value for $r$?

**22.** One study reported the correlation between IQ and creativity as being quite low ($r = .2$). The standard deviation of the IQ scores of the sample was approximately 5. What would be the effect on $r$ if the sample did not have restricted variability in IQ?

**23.** A study of 280 teacher trainees reported almost no correlation ($r = .1$) between GPA and teaching performance (supervisor's ratings). It was also reported that a correlation of only .21 was found between the independent ratings given by two supervisors on the 280 prospective teachers. How does the latter information affect the interpretation of the $r = .1$?

**24.** One study found that mothers' self-reported pre-pregnancy weights correlated .87 with actual weights. What explains the lack of agreement that exists?

(a) measurement error
(b) non-normal distributions
(c) ecological correlation
(d) restricted variability
(e) nonlinear transformations

**25.** In the case study, the correlation between systolic blood pressure (SBP) and diastolic blood pressure (DBP) was .80. Assuming both measures had a reliability coefficient of .95, estimate the correlation between SBP and DBP if both were measured without measurement error. If the blood pressure measures had been obtained carelessly by a novice, the expected correlation between SBP and DBP would have been ____ (<, =, >) .80.

*For items 26–31, match the type of correlation coefficient on the right that is appropriate for measuring the relationship between X and Y as described on the left.*

**26.** $X$: Handedness (R or L); $Y$: Reading Comprehension Score — (a) $r$

**27.** $X$: Gender; $Y$: Pass (1) or Fail (0) — (b) $r_{pb}$

**28.** $X$: Writing $T$-score; $Y$: Spelling Percent Correct Score — (c) $r_{bis}$

**29.** $X$: Attractiveness (ranks); $Y$: Popularity (ranks) — (d) $r_{\phi}$

**30.** $X$: IQ; $Y$: GPA — (e) $r_{tet}$

**31.** $X$: IQ (above or below 100); $Y$: GPA (above or below 2.5) — (f) $r_{ranks}$

**32.** From the relationship in Figure 7.5B, note that when the annual per person income reaches approximately ____ or more that life expectancy reaches a plateau at about ____ years.

## PROBLEMS AND EXERCISES

1. (a) Compute the Pearson correlation coefficient $r$ between the following ten pairs of arithmetic and IQ scores:

| *Pupil* | *IQ* | *Arithmetic* | *Pupil* | *IQ* | *Arithmetic* |
|---|---|---|---|---|---|
| A | 105 | 15 | F | 96 | 10 |
| B | 120 | 23 | G | 107 | 4 |
| C | 83 | 11 | H | 117 | 30 |
| D | 137 | 22 | I | 108 | 18 |
| E | 114 | 17 | J | 130 | 14 |

(b) Plot a scatter diagram for the ranks in problem 1. Scale the plot so that the horizontal and vertical spans for $X$ and $Y$ are approximately equal. Does the relationship appear to be curvilinear? Does the value of $r$ seem reasonable?

(c) On the IQ variable, how do the mean and standard deviation of the sample in problem 1 compare with corresponding national parameters ($\mu = 100$, $\sigma = 15$)?

**2.** One study reported the importance of eight morale factors for employees and employers as indicated:

| | *Rank* | |
|---|---|---|
| *Factor* | *Employers* | *Employees* |
| A. Credit for work done | 1 | 7 |
| B. Interesting work | 2 | 3 |
| C. Fair pay | 3 | 1 |
| D. Understanding and appreciation | 4 | 5 |
| E. Counseling on personal problems | 5 | 8 |
| F. Promotion based on merit | 6 | 4 |
| G. Good working conditions | 7 | 6 |
| H. Job security | 8 | 2 |

(a) Compute $r_{ranks}$.

(b) Compute Pearson $r$ using the ranks for the $X$ and $Y$ values.

(c) Which two factors contributed most to the negative correlation?

3. The data given in the table below show the relationship between verbal and nonverbal IQ's from the Lorge-Thorndike Intelligence Test (LT) and reading and arithmetic achievement as measured by the Iowa Test of Basic Skills (ITBS). At each grade level, each correlation is based on approximately 2,500 nationally representative pupils.

| | *Verbal IQ* | | | *Nonverbal IQ* | | |
|---|---|---|---|---|---|---|
| | *Grade* | | | *Grade* | | |
| | *3* | *5* | *7* | *3* | *5* | *7* |
| Reading | .68 | .76 | .81 | .53 | .65 | .67 |
| Arithmetic | .66 | .72 | .74 | .61 | .68 | .71 |

On the basis of this information, are the following statements true or false?

(a) The correlation between the intelligence and achievement measures appears to increase with grade level.
(b) The nonverbal IQ's correlate as highly with achievement as verbal IQ's.
(c) Verbal and nonverbal IQ's tend to correlate slightly higher with reading than with arithmetic.
(d) The correlation between both measures of achievement and both measures of intelligence is substantial at each of the three grade levels.

4. A researcher demonstrated a correlation of –.52 between average teacher's salary ($X$) and the proportion of students who drop out of school before graduating ($Y$) across 120 high schools in her state. She concluded that increasing teachers' salaries would reduce the dropout rate. Comment on her conclusion.

5. A researcher correlated the MTAI scores of a group of 100 experienced secondary school teachers with the number of students each teacher failed in a year. He obtained an $r$ of –.39. He concluded that teachers tend to fail students because they do not have "accepting" attitudes toward students. Comment on the researcher's methods and conclusions.

6. (a) When heights of girls or boys at ages three and twenty are expressed as $T$-scores, the covariance is approximately 70. What is the correlation coefficient between height at the two ages?
(b) What is the covariance if the two variables are expressed as $z$-scores?
(c) If it were learned that at age three height was expressed in inches, but at age eighteen it was expressed in centimeters, would the value of $r$ be affected?
(d) If it were learned that shoes were removed before taking measurement at age three but not at age twenty, would the inconsistency have a consequential effect on $r$?
(e) If the subjects were measured with and without shoes on both occasions, which correlation would be slightly larger?

7. In question 22 of the Mastery Test, assume the statistics are parameters, assume a linear and homoscedastic relationship between IQ and creativity, and estimate the correlation in the population ($\rho_l$) using $\sigma_l = 15$ and Equation 7.6.

8. A correlation ($\rho_l$) is .8 in the unrestricted population in which the standard deviation equals 10. Use Equation 7.6 to estimate the correlation ($\rho_1$) in a group in which the standard deviation is 5.

9. Examine the scatterplot at the beginning of the Problems and Exercises section in Chapter 8. The scatterplot shows the relationship between IQ scores at grades five and seven for 354 students on the California Test of Mental Maturity.

(a) Does the relationship appear to be linear?
(b) Does the scatterplot appear to have the property of homoscedasticity?
(c) Does the reported $r$ of .83 appear to be reasonable in view of the degree of scatter in the scatterplot?

**10.** Measures of spelling ability and spatial ability were given to 10,000 representative high school seniors, half of which were girls (Bennett, Seashore, and Wesman, 1974). The means and standard deviations for each sex were

| | *Spelling* | | *Spatial* | |
|---|---|---|---|---|
| | *Mean* | *s* | *Mean* | *s* |
| Boys (1) | 71.8 | 17.3 | 34.3 | 13.0 |
| Girls (0) | 80.2 | 14.5 | 30.9 | 11.9 |

The standard deviation for the distribution combining boys and girls into one distribution was found to be 16.5 and 12.6 for spelling ability and spatial ability, respectively. Compare the two point-biserial correlation coefficients (Equation 7.15) to determine which ability is more highly related to sex.

**11.** One study found that of the twenty-seven beginning first grade children scoring below 40 on the Metropolitan Readiness Test, only one received a letter grade of B or better in reading at the end of first grade (Hopkins and Stanley, 1981, p. 100). For the 125 pupils scoring 40 or better, sixty-eight received a grade of B or better. Assuming there is a normal distribution underlying each of these variables and that they are linearly related (Section 7.26), estimate the value of $r$ had refined, continuous measures been obtained for both variables.

**12.** Artificial dichotomies were created for height ($0 \leq 68''$, $1 = >68''$) and weight ($0 \leq 163$ lbs., $1 > 163$ lbs.) in the case study. The resulting contingency table is given below:

| | | *Height (X)* 0 | 1 | *Row Totals* | *Proportion* |
|---|---|---|---|---|---|
| Weight ($Y$) | 1 | (a) 36 | (b) 62 | 98 | .490 ($p_y$) |
| | 0 | (c) 65 | (d) 37 | 102 | |
| Column Totals | | 101 | 99 | 200 ($n_\bullet$) | |
| Column Proportion | | | .495 ($p_x$) | | |

Use Equation 7.14 to compute the Pearson correlation (phi coefficient, $r_\phi$) between the two dichotomies. Use Equation 7.19 to compute $r_{\text{tet}}$ to estimate $r$, the correlation that would exist if both variables were measured? (Obviously we know the answer in the case study; this item will illustrate the accuracy of the $r_{\text{tet}}$ extrapolation.) Is $r_{\text{tet}}$ a good approximation of $r$ in this situation?

**13.** Table 7.11 and Figure 7.14 reveal that in the case study, age and cholesterol level correlated $.41 = r_1$. Table 5.2 shows that the standard deviation of age was $s_1 = 11.6$ years. What if the study had limited the age range to 40–50 (rather than to 20–70), how would the value of the correlation be affected? For the restricted age range, the value of the standard deviation would have been about $2.9 = s_1$ assuming a rectangular distribution of age. Estimate $r_1$ (Equation 7.6). Examine Figure 7.14 to confirm that this dramatically different value for $r$ is reasonable.

**14.** A 90-minute multiple choice test in biology had a reliability coefficient of .93, and scores on this exam correlated .73 with scores on a three-question 75-minute biology essay test, which had a reliability coefficient of .66 (Bridgeman & Lewis, 1994). When allowance is made for measurement error, is there much uniqueness associated with the two test formats? Estimate the relationship if both measures were made perfectly reliable.

## ANSWERS TO MASTERY TEST

1. (c)
2. (c)
3. (d)
4. (c)
5. (d)
6. (e)
7. (a)
8. (b)
9. (a) positive (b) zero
   (c) positive (d) zero
   (e) negative (f) zero
   (g) zero (h) negative
   (i) positive
10. .8
11. $W$
12. .5
13. $z_Y = -.5$
14. $z_X = -.8$
15. 1.0
16. Since the relative standings (ranks and corresponding standard scores) of the $X$'s and $Y$'s are unaffected, $r$ is unaffected by the metric employed. In other words, feet to inches and seconds to minutes are both examples of linear transformations which do not affect the correlation between the two variables.
17. Maximum covariance is $s_X s_Y = (3)(15) = 45$.
18. $r_2$ would be higher since it would contain less measurement error.
19. (c)
20. College $B$, because $\sigma$ is greatest
21. College $C$
22. The $r$ would increase considerably.
23. The reliability of the criterion measure appears to be extremely low, hence the true correlation between GPA and performance would be expected to be much higher.
24. (a)
25. $$r_{X_\infty Y_\infty} = \frac{r_{XY}}{\sqrt{r_{XX} r_{YY}}} = \frac{.80}{\sqrt{.95(.95)}} = \frac{.80}{.95} = .84; < .80$$
26. (b)
27. (d)
28. (a)
29. (f)
30. (a)
31. (e)
32. $2,000; 70

## ANSWERS TO PROBLEMS AND EXERCISES

1. (a) $r = .517$
   (b) No; yes
   (c) $\bar{X} = 111.7$ (considerably above $\mu = 100$); $s = 15.7$ (very similar to $\sigma = 15$)
2. (a) $r_{\text{ranks}} = -.095$
   (b) $r = -.095$
   (c) A and H
3. (a) true
   (b) false
   (c) false (with verbal IQ, true; with nonverbal IQ, false)
   (d) true
4. The researcher is inferring a causal relationship solely from correlational evidence. She has no justification for doing so. It may well be the case, and probably is, that teachers' salaries and the dropout rate are *both* functions of the social and economic status of the community and that increasing teachers' salaries in a given school would not bring about a decrease in the dropout rate.
5. The researcher mistakenly assumed correlation equals causation.
6. (a) $.7 = [70/(10 \times 10)]$
   (b) .7
   (c) no
   (d) no, since roughly a constant was added to height at age 20
   (e) without shoes, because heel thickness would introduce a small amount of uncontrolled and irrelevant variation (measurement error)
7. $\hat{\rho}_I^2 = .273$, $\hat{\rho}_I = .52$

**8.** $\hat{\rho}_1 = .55$

**9.** (a) yes
(b) yes
(c) yes

**10.** Spelling: $r_{pb} = -.25$; Spatial: $r_{pb} = .13$

**11.** $r_{tet} = .71$

**12.** $$r_\phi = \frac{(62)(65)-(36)(37)}{\sqrt{(101)(99)(98)(102)}} = .270;$$

$$r_{tet} = \frac{(62)(65)-(36)(37)}{(.3989)(.3989)(200)^2} = .424.$$

yes (.424 versus .405)

**13.** $s_I/s_1 = .25$; $r_I = [(.41)^2(.25)^2]/[1+(.41)^2(.25)^2-(.41)^2] = .012$

**14.** no; $r_{X_\infty Y_\infty} = \dfrac{r_{XY}}{\sqrt{r_{XX} r_{YY}}}$ (Equation 7.7). $r_{X_\infty Y_\infty}$
$$= \frac{.73}{\sqrt{(.93)(.66)}} = .93.$$

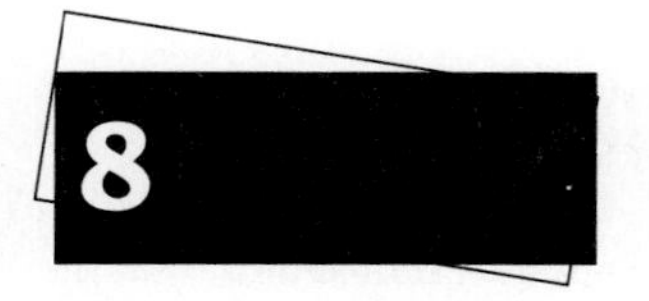

# REGRESSION AND PREDICTION

How are observations on one variable used to predict those on another variable? What is the margin of error in these predictions? Prediction and correlation are opposite sides of the same coin. Chapter 7 focused on correlation, the degree of relationship between two variables. In Chapter 8, the primary interest is in using correlation to predict a criterion measure. Most criteria are like GPA, job performance ratings, and reading scores, in that the values can be ordered along a continuum. Regression is usually the statistical method of choice when the predicted variable is an ordinal, interval, or ratio scale.

## 8.1 PURPOSES OF REGRESSION ANALYSIS

One major use of statistical methods is to forecast or predict future events. Insurance companies set premiums based on statistical predictions. The cost of automobile insurance for minors is greater than that for adults because age often correlates with—that is, predicts—accident frequencies and payout costs. Colleges often admit or reject applicants primarily based on predictions about their probable future scholastic performance made from scholastic aptitude tests and academic performance in high school. Delinquency and dropout prevention programs frequently use early indicators or predictors in identifying persons who appear likely to become delinquents or dropouts. In vocational counseling and personnel selection, implicit or explicit predictions of various job related criteria are made from variables such as age, interests, aptitudes, sex, and experience. These examples involve prediction. The degree of reliance on statistical considerations in making these predictions varies greatly from one application to another. Insurance companies rely heavily on statistical or actuarial predictions, whereas rarely is the selection of employees and students made on purely statistical considerations.

Multiple regression has been the principal statistical methodology in pay discrimination lawsuits (Roberts, 1980). Relevant antecedent variables (e.g., seniority, education, beginning salary, job classification) are used to predict salary for employees in a workplace. If race or sex correlates with salary when the other relevant variables are held constant, the courts have ruled that there is prima facie evidence of race or sex discrimination.

By using statistical methods, the accuracy of predictions of a *dependent* variable (a criterion or outcome variable) from one or more *independent* predictor variables can be maximized. In statistical parlance, the dependent variable $Y$ is said to be a function of one or more independent variables ($X_1, X_2, X_3, \ldots, X_m$).[1] No *causal* association is required or assumed. Indeed, causation is beside the point in forecasting. The higher the correlation, the better is the prediction; the lower the correlation, the greater is the margin of error in the predictions. We will begin with linear regression, the simplest situation—predicting a continuous dependent variable ($Y$) from a single independent variable ($X$), where $X$ and $Y$ are linearly related measures that are both normally distributed.

The underlying rationale for simple regression extends easily to more complex applications such as multiple regression in which there are two or more independent variables.

## 8.2 THE REGRESSION EFFECT

Unless $r = 1.0$ or $-1.0$, all predictions of $Y$ from $X$ *regress* toward the mean; the percentile of the predicted $Y$ will be closer to 50 than the percentile of $X$. Francis Galton (1822–1911) first documented this *regression effect* when studying the relationship between the characteristics of parents and their children. The classic illustration of the regression effect is given in Figure 8.1, where the heights of 192 father-son combinations are tallied. In addition to the bivariate distribution (i.e., the scatterplot), the marginal distributions of $X$ (father's height) and $Y$ (son's height) are given in Figure 8.1 at the top and to the right, respectively. The tallying method used in these two marginal distributions is that of Tukey (1977) (Section 3.2). Notice that $\overline{X}$ and $s_X$ are approximately equal to $\overline{Y}$ and $s_Y$, respectively, and that both variables appear to be normally distributed when allowance is made for sampling error.

If all sons had exactly the same height as their fathers, all tallies in Figure 8.1 would fall in the shaded boxes and $r$ would be 1.0. Study Figure 8.1 and observe, as Galton did, that the sons of tall fathers tend to be taller than average, but shorter than their fathers; that is, the sons regressed toward the mean. Similarly, there is a trend for the sons of short fathers to be taller than their fathers, but shorter than average; they also regressed toward the mean.[2]

The mean height of the sons of fathers of a given height is plotted within each column of Figure 8.1. The sons' column means have been connected by a broken line. For example, for fathers who were 63 inches tall, the mean height of the sons was 66.5 inches; fathers who were 73 inches tall had sons whose mean height was 72 inches.

Notice that the more the fathers' height ($X$) deviates from its mean ($\overline{X}$), the greater the difference in the sons' mean height (the dashed line) from that of their fathers (the straight line drawn through the shaded area). This is always true whenever the absolute value of $r$ is less than 1.0; the more $X$ deviates from $\overline{X}$, the greater will be the amount of regression. Note that in Figure 8.1 the distributions of $X$ and $Y$ have means and standard deviations that are essentially equal; the distributions of $X$ and $Y$ are equally heterogeneous even with the

---

[1]Plus any portion of the dependent variable that is not predictable (error) from this set of independent variables.

[2]Apparently, Galton did not initially recognize the ubiquity of this phenomenon and termed it "the law of filial regression." Actually, there is a regression effect when any two variables are not perfectly correlated.

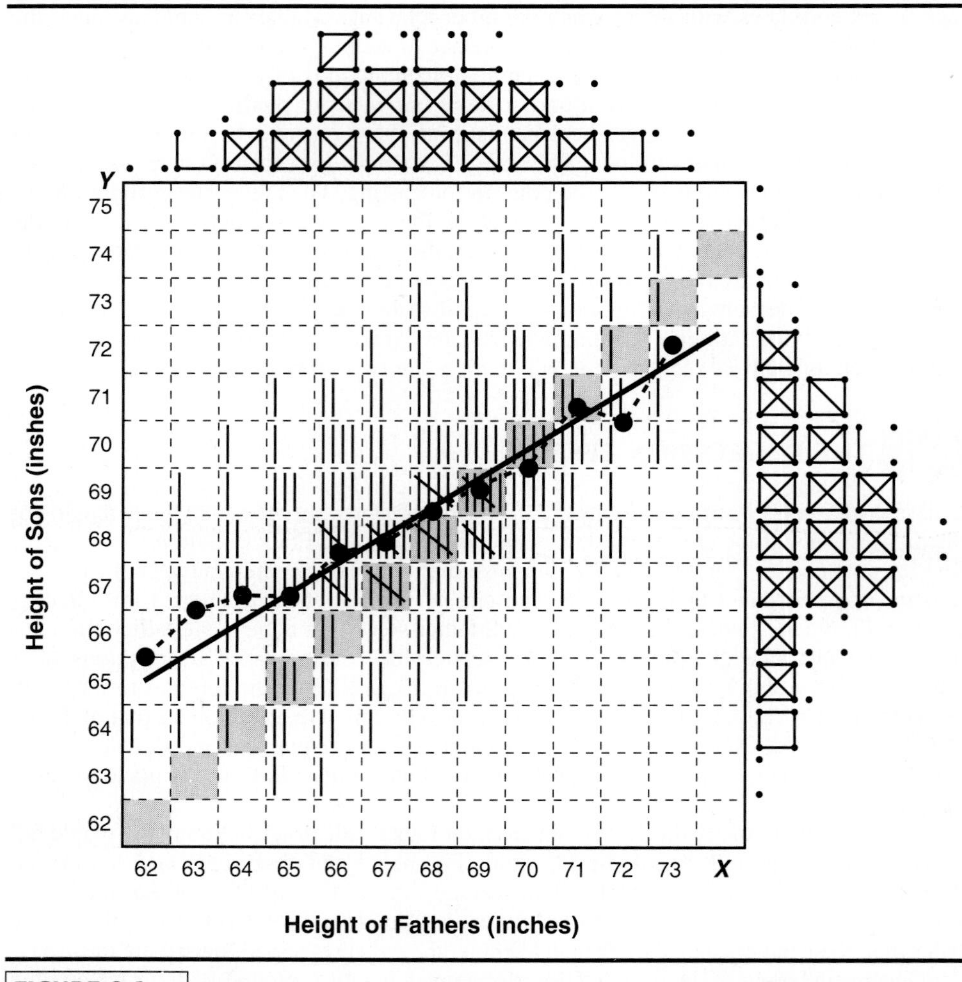


**FIGURE 8.1** An Illustration of the Regression Effect ($r = .56$) for 192 Fathers and Sons (data from McNemar, 1962). The marginal distributions are approximately normal, as shown at the top (fathers: $\bar{X} = 67.68''$, $s_X = 2.50''$) and to the right (sons: $\bar{Y} = 66.44''$, $s_Y = 2.33''$).

regression effect. The sons were not more homogeneous in height than were their fathers, yet as a general rule the percentile ranks of sons, given a certain percentile rank for fathers, tend to be closer to 50 than that of the fathers.

## 8.3 THE REGRESSION EQUATION EXPRESSED IN STANDARD *z*-SCORES

The most conceptually illuminating way of statistically expressing the regression phenomenon (or, equivalently, the prediction of *Y* from *X*) occurs when *X* and *Y* are expressed as $z$-scores. Equation 8.1 is the simplest form of the regression equation; it shows that for person $i$, the predicted $z$-score[3] on the dependent variable, $\hat{z}_{Y_i}$, is the product of the $z$-score on $X$ ($z_{X_i}$) and the correlation coefficient ($r_{XY}$ or simply $r$ where there is no ambiguity) between $X$ and $Y$:

$$\hat{z}_{Y_i} = r\, z_{X_i} \qquad \textbf{(8.1)}$$

For example, if $r = .60$ and $z_{X_i} = 1.0$, then $\hat{z}_{Y_i} = .6$; or if $r = .60$ and $z_{X_i} = -2.0$, then $\hat{z}_{Y_i} = -1.2$. Notice, *except when the correlation is perfect,* the absolute value of $\hat{z}_Y$ is always less than $z_X$; that is, the $\hat{z}_Y$ value regresses toward the mean $z$-score (0). How much less is $\hat{z}_Y$ than $z_X$? If Equation 8.1 is rearranged, it is apparent that $r$ is the ratio of $\hat{z}_Y$ to $z_X$ (i.e., $r = \hat{z}_Y / z_X$) and $r$ can be seen as the "rate of change" in $\hat{z}_Y$ per unit of change in $z_X$. The correlation coefficient between $X$ and $Y$ in Figure 8.1 is approximately .5. Hence, from Equation 8.1, it is evident that, on the average, a son tends to be only half (.5) as many standard deviations from the mean ($\bar{Y}$) of sons as the fathers are from their mean ($\bar{X}$). For example, for fathers who are two standard deviations below the mean ($z_X = -2.0$), the sons' average is only one standard deviation below the mean ($\hat{z}_Y = -1.0$); thus, fathers who were at the 98th percentile had sons who were at the 84th percentile, on the average (see Figure 8.1).

Since $r = \hat{z}_Y / z_X$, one can see the sense in which the correlation coefficient can be directly interpreted as a proportion or a percentage. If $r = .8$ and if $X$ and $Y$ are expressed as standard $z$-scores, for any given score on the independent variable the expected $z$-score on the dependent variable ($\hat{z}_Y$) is only .8 (or 80%) as far from its mean as $z_X$ is from its mean. For example, if $r = .8$ and $z_X = 1.0$, then $\hat{z}_Y = .8$, which is 80% as far from the mean of the dependent variable as $z_X$ is from the mean of the independent variable. In other words, $(1 - r) \times 100\%$ gives the percentage of regression involved in the predictions.

Understanding what is denoted by Equation 8.1 enhances the interpretation of correlation coefficients, especially when the standard deviations of $X$ and $Y$ are the same, as in Figure 8.1, or when standard scores are used. The IQ scale is a standard score with $\mu = 100$ and $\sigma = 15$. Many studies have found that the IQ scores of parents correlate about .5 with the IQ scores of their children ($\rho \approx .5$). This means that on the average, the child's IQ score deviates from 100 only half as much as the parent's does. For example, mothers with IQ scores of 130 have children who average 115; stated differently, mothers at the 98th percentile have children whose average is at $P_{84}$. Or, the children of fathers with IQ scores of 80 have an average IQ score of 90.[4]

## 8.4 USE OF REGRESSION EQUATIONS

It may seem peculiar to talk about predicting $Y$ from $X$, because, as in the example, one must have both $X$ and $Y$ to compute the $r$, which is required in the regression equation (Equation 8.1). Obviously, if the scores on the criterion (the $Y$'s) are known, it would make no sense to use Equation 8.1 to predict them. However, not only does the correlation coefficient between

[3]Recall that the "hat" above a symbol denotes a *prediction* of the value of the quantity symbolized.

[4]Do not make the common mistake of assuming that this means that the children are more homogeneous in IQ scores than the parents; recall that $\sigma_X = \sigma_Y = 15$. Redefine the parents' IQ scores as $Y$ and the children's scores as $X$, and the numbers remain unchanged. Some truths are counterintuitive.

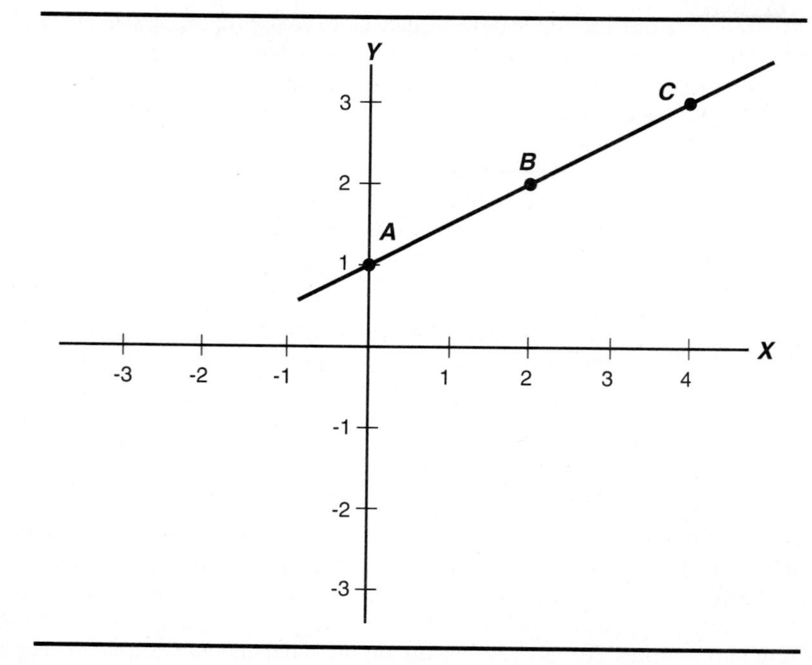


**FIGURE 8.2**

Two-Dimensional ($X$ and $Y$) Cartesian Coordinate System.

$X$ and $Y$ describe the degree of association between $X$ and $Y$, but this correlation will also facilitate the prediction of criterion scores ($Y$'s) from the independent variables ($X$'s) for persons that were not represented in the data in Table 8.1. The purpose of a regression equation is to make predictions for a new sample based on the findings of a previous sample.

For intuitive and conceptual purposes, regression and prediction have been discussed in terms of $z$-scores. The underlying concepts are best understood without the distractions resulting from unequal means and unequal variances of $X$ and $Y$. In actual practical application, however, it is more convenient to use regression equations that predict raw scores, $\hat{Y}$'s (not $\hat{z}_Y$'s), from observations on $X$ (not $z_X$). Before proceeding further with the discussion of this topic, some geometry should be reviewed.

## 8.5 CARTESIAN[5] COORDINATES

A *Cartesian* coordinate system is depicted in Figure 8.2. The axes of the coordinate system—the perpendicular $X$ and $Y$ lines—divide the plane. This coordinate system is a means of marking off the plane so that every point can be identified by a pair of numbers, $(X, Y)$. The point (0, 0) is called the *origin* of the system and lies at the point where the two axes intersect. The first number of any pair is the distance one must travel *horizontally* from the origin (the $X$ distance) to reach the point, and the second number is the distance the point lies *vertically* from the origin. The point $A$ in Figure 8.2 corresponds to the pair of numbers (0, 1). The first number is called the $X$ coordinate; the second number is called the $Y$-coordi-

[5]Named after the French philosopher-mathematician René Descartes. If you have been away from algebra I for awhile, hopefully this will bring back pleasant memories.

nate. The point *B* corresponds to the pair of numbers (2, 2); it lies two units to the right of the origin and two units above the origin.

Eventually, a method of predicting a set of scores will be detailed that uses a straight line in a plane to describe the set of predicted scores. It will be useful to know the manner in which any straight line in a plane can be completely described by a simple equation.

In Figure 8.2, the straight line *L* crosses the *Y-axis* at point *A* (0, 1). For each unit of increase in *X*, the line rises one-half unit on *Y*. The following points lie on line *L*: (0, 1), (1, 1.5), (2, 2), (3, 2.5), (4, 3), et cetera. For the line *L* in Figure 8.2, the *Y* value of any point on the line equals one-half the *X* value plus 1, that is, $Y = .5X + 1$. The equation $Y = .5X + 1$ is the equation for the straight line in Figure 8.2. The *Y-intercept* of line *L* is 1 because it is the value of *Y* where line *L* intersects the *Y*-axis. The number, .5, is the *slope* of the straight line *L*. The slope is the number of units the line rises for each unit of movement to the right on the *X*-axis, here 1:2.

The equation $Y = bX + c$ is the general form for the equation of a straight line. It says simply that the pairs of points (*X*, *Y*) that lie on any straight line are related so that for any *X* value the *Y* value paired with it can be found by multiplying *X* by some number *b*, and adding a second number *c* to this product. This is a linear transformation of *X* to find *Y*.

## 8.6 ESTIMATING *Y* FROM *X*: THE RAW-SCORE REGRESSION EQUATION

Given an individual's score on variable *X*, what prediction can be made about his score on variable *Y*? For example, how accurately can test scores in statistics be predicted from the GRE Quantitative Test score (GRE-Q)?

To find the equation for predicting the score of a person on the dependent variable *Y* from scores on the independent variable *X*, one must know the correlation between *X* and *Y*, in addition to the means and standard deviations for both variables. Data must be gathered on some number *n* of students who have taken the GRE and who subsequently take the statistics course. Next a regression equation must be established that predicts the score on *Y* for any *X*, using the least squares criterion (see Section 8.9). This equation then can be used to predict scores on *Y* from scores on *X*. Equation 8.2 is the regression equation for predicting raw scores on *Y* from raw scores on *X*. The predicted criterion score for individual *i*, $\hat{Y}_i$, is the product of the *regression coefficient*[6] *b* and the raw score on $X_i$ plus a constant *c*, the *intercept*.

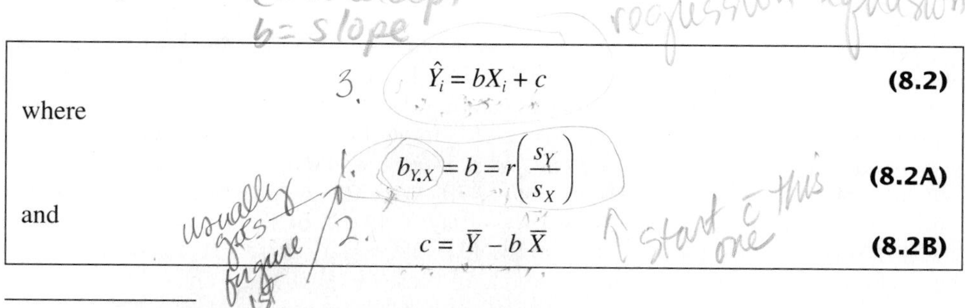

$$\hat{Y}_i = bX_i + c \qquad \textbf{(8.2)}$$

where

$$b_{Y.X} = b = r\left(\frac{s_Y}{s_X}\right) \qquad \textbf{(8.2A)}$$

and

$$c = \overline{Y} - b\overline{X} \qquad \textbf{(8.2B)}$$

[6]We have consistently tried to use subscripts for variables only when ambiguity would otherwise result. Thus we use *s* if only one variable is involved, but $s_X$ and $s_Y$ if we are dealing with two variables. Likewise, the "XY" subscript for $r_{XY}$ is unnecessary and *r* suffices if only two variables are involved. Since we are predicting *Y* (i.e., $\hat{Y}$) in Equation 8.2, it follows that the regression coefficient required is $b_{Y.X}$; hence, the subscript "$_{Y.X}$" is unnecessary.

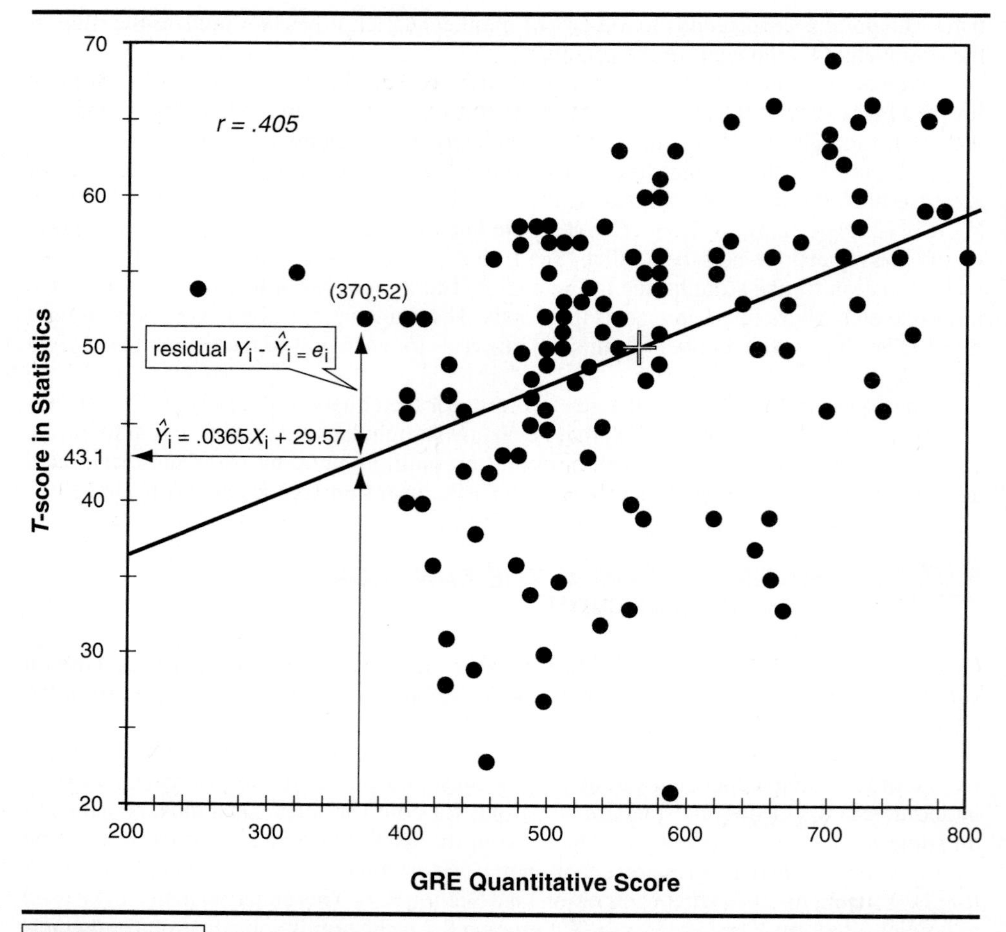


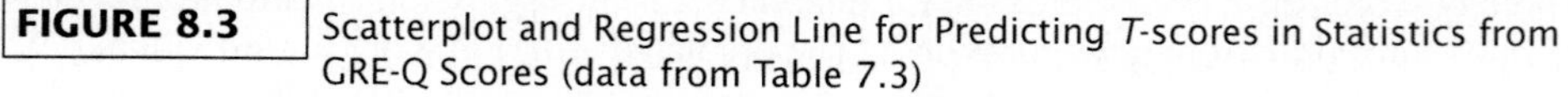

**FIGURE 8.3** Scatterplot and Regression Line for Predicting *T*-scores in Statistics from GRE-Q Scores (data from Table 7.3)

GRE-Q scores and subsequent performance in an applied statistics course (expressed in *T*-scores) were given in Table 7.3 (Section 7.9). For these data, $\overline{X} = 559.6$, $s_X = 111.0$, $\overline{Y} = 50$, $s_Y = 10$, and $r = .4053$. Using Equation 8.2A, $b = .4053(10/111) = .0365$. From Equation 8.2B: $c = 50 - (.0365)(559.6) = 29.57$. Using Equation 8.2, the regression equation for these data is $\hat{Y}_i = .0365X_i + 29.57$. What *T*-score would be predicted for student #65 ($Y_{65}$) in Table 7.3 who had a GRE-Q score of 370 ($X_{65}$)? The predicted score on the examination, for student #65 is $\hat{Y}_i = (.0365)(370) + 29.57 = 43.075$ or 43.1.

If $\hat{Y}_i$ were obtained for each value of the 121 values of $X_i$, these 121 $\hat{Y}_i$'s would fall on a straight line—the regression line or the line of "best fit." Figure 8.3 gives the associated scatterplot for these data. Note the intersection of $\overline{X}$ and $\overline{Y}$ (denoted by "+") falls on the regression line; the regression line for any group of data points goes through the point $(\overline{X}, \overline{Y})$ regardless of the value of *r*.

**TABLE 8.1** An Illustration of How the Total Variance in the Criterion ($s_Y^2$) Is Equal to the Variance in the Predicted Scores ($s_{\hat{Y}}^2$) plus the Variance in the Residuals ($s_e^2$), Using the Regression Equation: $\hat{Y}_i = .0365X_i + 29.57$

| *ID#* | $X_i$ | $Y_i$ | $\hat{Y}_i$ | $e_i = Y_i - \hat{Y}_i$ |
|---|---|---|---|---|
| 1 | 500 | 55 | 47.8 | 7.2 |
| 2 | 500 | 49 | 47.8 | 1.2 |
| 3 | 430 | 28 | 45.3 | −17.3 |
| 4 | 510 | 35 | 48.2 | −13.2 |
| 5 | 320 | 55 | 41.3 | 13.7 |
| ... | ... | ... | ... | ... |
| ... | ... | ... | ... | ... |
| 65 | 370 | 52 | 43.1 | 8.9 |
| ... | ... | ... | ... | ... |
| ... | ... | ... | ... | ... |
| 118 | 440 | 42 | 45.6 | −3.6 |
| 119 | 540 | 51 | 49.3 | 1.7 |
| 120 | 710 | 62 | 55.5 | 6.5 |
| 121 | 680 | 57 | 54.4 | 2.6 |
| Mean | | 50 | 50 | 0 |
| Sum of Squares | | 12,000 | 1,971 | 10,029 |
| Variance | | 100 | 16.4 | 83.6 |

Find $X_{65} = 370$, move vertically until you intersect the regression line, then move horizontally until you intersect the $Y$-axis ( $\hat{Y}_{65} = 43.1$).

## 8.7 ERROR OF ESTIMATE

The predicted value on the criterion, $\hat{Y}_i$, will rarely exactly equal the score that is actually observed, $Y_i$. There is some error in estimating $Y$ from $X$, even when we are doing the best job possible. The difference, $Y_i - \hat{Y}_i$, is the *residual* for student $i$. In other words, $\hat{Y}_i$ + residual$_i = Y_i$; the residual is the error ($e_i$) in estimating $Y$ from $X$ for the $i$th person:

$$residual = e_i = Y_i - \hat{Y}_i = Y_i - (bX_i + c) \quad \textbf{(8.3)}$$

The residual for student #65 is illustrated in Figure 8.3. The actual GRE-Q score is 370 = $X_{65}$, and the observed value on the criterion is 52 = $Y_{65}$. Earlier we found, from the regression equation, that the predicted $T$-score for student #65 is: $\hat{Y}_1$ = (.0365)(370) + 29.57 = 43.1. For $X_{65}$ the residual (or error of estimate) is: $e_{65} = Y_{65} - \hat{Y}_{65} = 52 - 43.1 = 8.9$ (See Table 8.1). The positive value for the residual shows that the observed score was greater than the predicted score. All scores below the regression line in Figure 8.3 have negative residuals; all scores above the regression line have positive residuals.

## 8.8 PROPORTION OF PREDICTABLE VARIANCE, $r^2$

Suppose a table were constructed for the 121 students in Table 7.3 giving observed scores ($\hat{Y}_i$'s), predicted scores ($Y_i$'s), and residuals ($e_i$'s). The purpose of this table is only to illustrate how $r^2$ can be interpreted as the proportion of variance in $Y$ that is predictable from $X$. Table 8.1 gives a portion of such a table.

The means of the $Y$ and $\hat{Y}$ distributions are equal, and the mean of the residuals is 0; this will always be the case. The sum of squares[7] in the $\hat{Y}$'s $[SS_{\hat{Y}} = \Sigma_i(\hat{Y}_i - \bar{Y})^2]$ plus the sum of squares in the residuals $[SS_{\text{residuals}} = \Sigma_i(e_i - 0)^2 = \Sigma_i e_i^2]$ will equal the total sum of squares in the observed scores ($\Sigma y^2$ or $SS_Y$):

$$SS_Y = SS_{\hat{Y}} + SS_{\text{residuals}} \quad \textbf{(8.4)}$$

$SS_{\hat{Y}}$ is said to be the sum of squares due to the regression, that is, the sum of squares in the *predicted* values of the dependent variable ($\hat{Y}_i$'s). $SS_{\text{residuals}} = SS_e$ is the sum of the squared residuals. The ratio of $SS_{\hat{Y}}$ to $SS_Y$ gives the proportion of the sum of squares that is predictable from use of the regression equation, and will equal $r^2 = SS_{\hat{Y}}/SS_Y$.[8]

The pattern is the same when variances are compared:

$$s_Y^2 = s_{\hat{Y}}^2 + s_e^2 \quad \textbf{(8.5)}$$

The proportion of the total variance in $Y$ that is predictable from the regression equation is the ratio of $s_{\hat{Y}}^2$ to $s_Y^2$, which equals $r^2$:

$$r^2 = \frac{\text{(Predictable Variance)}}{\text{(Total Variance)}} = \frac{s_{\hat{Y}}^2}{s_Y^2} \quad \textbf{(8.6)}$$

In our example, $r^2 = (.4053)^2 = .1643$. The proportion of variance in $Y$ that is *unpredictable* is $1 - r^2 = s_e^2/s_Y^2 = 1 - (.4053)^2 = 1 - .1643 = .836$. Expressed differently:

$$r^2 = 1 - \frac{s_e^2}{s_Y^2} \quad \textbf{(8.7)}$$

---

[7] "SS" denotes "sum of squares" (the sum of the squared deviations from the mean of the variable); thus, $SS_Y = \Sigma(Y_i - \bar{Y})^2 = \Sigma y_i^2$, and $SS_{\hat{Y}} = \Sigma(\hat{Y}_i - \bar{Y})^2 = \Sigma \hat{y}_i^2$. The "SS" notation is simpler and will ordinarily be used in subsequent chapters.

[8] $r^2$ is sometimes called the coefficient of determination, an unfortunate choice of terms since it encourages the misconception that correlation means causation.

## 8.9 LEAST-SQUARES CRITERION

The statistical criterion used to arrive at the values for $b$ and $c$ is the *least-squares criterion*.[9] The equations yield values for $b$ and $c$ such that the sum of the squared residuals is as small as possible; that is, $\Sigma_i e_i^2 = e_1^2 + e_2^2 + e_3^2 + \ldots + e_n^2$ assumes its minimal value.

The use of the least-squares criterion is convenient and is generally preferred in inferential statistics. However, other criteria are possible and can have advantages in certain situations. For example, $b$ and $c$ could be chosen so that the sum of the absolute values of the residuals is at a minimum, that is, to minimize the quantity $\Sigma_i |e_i| = |e_1| + |e_2| + |e_3| + \ldots + |e_n|$. This criterion would place the regression line through the column medians, rather than the column means. (You will recall from Section 4.14 that the median of a group of scores is the point around which the sum of the absolute deviations of the scores from that point is least, whereas the mean is the least-squares measure of central tendency.) Although the median regression line could easily be calculated, it would have more sampling error than does the least-squares regression line.[10]

Why would the mean of these $n$ residuals or errors of estimate not be a suitable measure of how well $Y$ is predicted from $X$? The average value of the residuals is *always* zero when it is calculated on the same $n$ pairs of scores that produced $b$ and $c$. Remember that the sample mean had the property that $\Sigma(X_i - \overline{X}) = 0$. The principle of estimation that makes the least-squares regression line a minimum-variance estimator of $Y$ scores is the same principle that makes $\overline{X}$ a least-squares measure of central tendency. If a single score had to be used to estimate every score in a group, the sample mean ($\overline{X}$) would do so with the smallest sum of squared residuals.

No knowledge of the shapes of the frequency distributions of $X$ and $Y$ is needed to derive the least-squares regression coefficients $b$ and $c$. The values of $b$ and $c$ in Equation 8.2 produce the straight line that minimizes the sum of squared residuals, regardless of the nature of the scatterplot of the $X$ and $Y$ scores.

Nothing has been assumed about whether the dependent and independent variables are normally distributed. However, we will learn that inferential advantages accrue if we can assume that $X$ and $Y$ have a bivariate normal distribution (Section 7.13).

## 8.10 HOMOSCEDASTICITY AND THE STANDARD ERROR OF ESTIMATE

In a bivariate normal distribution (Section 7.13), the variance of scores on $Y$ will be the same for all values of $X$. This condition of equal variance of $Y$ scores for each value of $X$ is known as *homoscedasticity* (the roots of this word mean *equal spread*). The scatterplot in Figure 8.1 appears to have homoscedasticity—regardless of the father's height, the variance of the sons is about the same. If it appears that there is greater variance for sons whose fathers are near the mean height—think again: The range in the sons' heights is greater because there

---

[9]See Glass and Stanley (1970, Appendix C) for mathematical proof.

[10]The use of the criterion of least squares for establishing a prediction line is over 150 years old. Karl Gauss (1777–1855), German mathematician, physicist, and astronomer, is generally credited with having developed the criterion of least squares. In one form or another, it underlies a large portion of theoretical and applied statistical work.

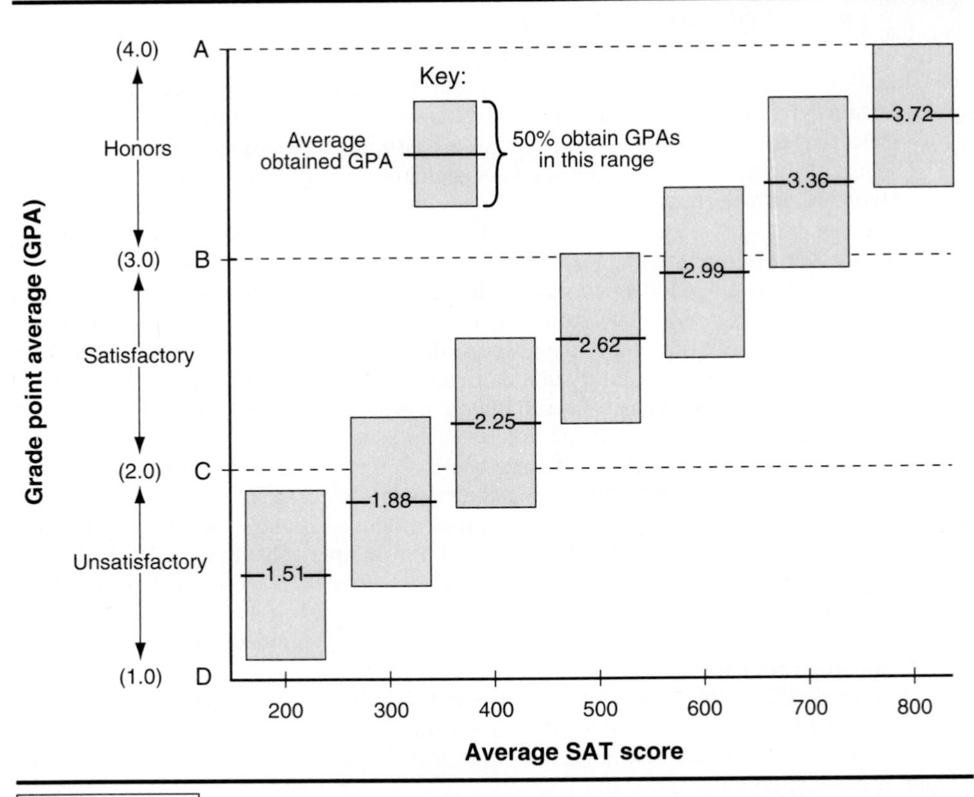


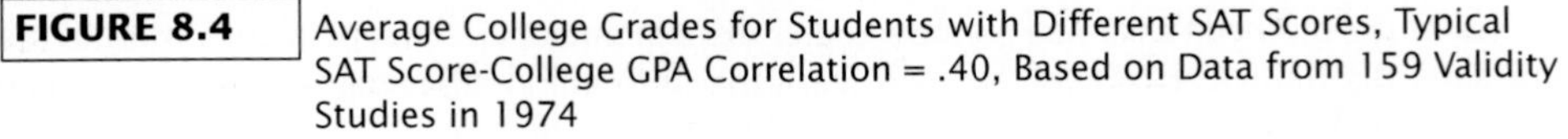
**FIGURE 8.4** Average College Grades for Students with Different SAT Scores, Typical SAT Score-College GPA Correlation = .40, Based on Data from 159 Validity Studies in 1974

are more of them. Recall from Table 5.1 that as the number of scores increases, the range will increase even when $\sigma^2$ is constant.

It is important to note that pure homoscedasticity is a property of populations of bivariate data. One should not expect precise equality of variances of $Y$ scores for any two values of $X$ when the $n$'s are small. The variances of the scores in the twelve columns in Figure 8.1 are not equal, but they are reasonably close—as close as expected when allowance is made for chance fluctuations (sampling error).[11]

Figure 8.4 gives information about predicting GPA's in college from SAT scores, based on 159 different studies at colleges and universities in the United States. The mean GPA and the box portion of box plots is given for the distribution of GPA's for SAT scores of 200, 300, …, and 800. If Maria has an average SAT score of 500 (the average of the SAT Verbal and Math tests), what is her predicted GPA in college? Persons like Maria have an average GPA of 2.62 so the best prediction is a B– average. The figure labels as "Honors" a GPA of 3.0; what is the likelihood that Maria will perform at the honors level? The upper end of the

[11]Statistical tests for homoscedasticity are given in Chapter 13.

box (3.0) corresponds to $Q_3$ for persons with SAT = 500, thus approximately 25% achieve a GPA of 3.0 or higher and fall in the honors category.

Can you visualize the regression line in Figure 8.4? Draw a line using a straight edge. If you connect the decimal points in the seven boxes, you will approximate the regression line. You will also confirm that the relationship is linear; when the column means are connected, the resulting line does not deviate significantly from a straight line. Note that the spread within the boxes is almost identical; this illustrates homoscedasticity.

One measure of the accuracy of predicting $Y$ from $X$ is the variance of the residuals. The variance of the population of $N$ residuals $e_i = Y_i - \hat{Y}_i$ is called the *variance error of estimate* or the variance of the residuals and is denoted by $\sigma_{Y.X}^2$. In other words, $\sigma_{Y.X}^2$ is the variance of the $Y$-scores for individuals who have the same $X$-score. Note that when homoscedasticity is present, $\sigma_{Y.X}^2$ is the variance in $Y$'s, when $X$ is held constant at any point. If Equation 8.7 is expressed in terms of parameters, and we substitute $\sigma_{Y.X}^2$ for its alias, $\sigma_e^2$, Equation 8.8 is obtained:

$$\sigma_{Y.X}^2 = \sigma_Y^2(1 - \rho^2) \qquad \textbf{(8.8)}$$

The positive square root of the variance error of estimate is called the *standard error of estimate*:

$$\sigma_{Y.X} = \sigma_Y\sqrt{(1-\rho^2)} \qquad \textbf{(8.9)}$$

Or, expressed in terms of statistics rather than parameters:

$$s_{Y.X}^2 = s_Y^2(1 - r^2) \qquad \textbf{(8.10)}$$

Study Figure 8.5 to see how the standard error of estimate can be used to set an interval around a predicted score $\hat{Y}_i$, within which a known proportion of the actual scores will fall. If a bivariate normal distribution can be assumed, then $\hat{Y}_i$ can be viewed as the mean of the $Y_i$'s for persons with scores of $X_i$ on the independent variable. The $e_i$'s will be normally distributed and have a standard deviation that is estimated by $s_{Y.X} = s_Y\sqrt{(1-r^2)}$ (see Equation 8.10).[12]

If the prediction equation is applied to a large group of persons, the procedures used to find areas under the normal curve (Section 6.5) can be applied:

1. Approximately 68% will have actual scores that lie within one $s_{Y.X}$ of their predicted score, $\hat{Y}_i$.
2. Approximately 95% will have actual scores that lie within two $s_{Y.X}$'s of their $\hat{Y}_i$.

These statements are valid when the bivariate normality assumption is met; the distribution of actual $Y$ scores is normal around a mean of $\hat{Y}_i = bX + c$, with a standard deviation

[12]Note in Figure 8.4 that $Q \approx .40$; recall that $\sigma \approx 1.5Q$, thus, we can estimate the standard deviation of the residuals for any SAT value. The regression line (connecting the midpoints of the boxes) gives the mean; using Table A, we can learn the probability of any GPA for any SAT.

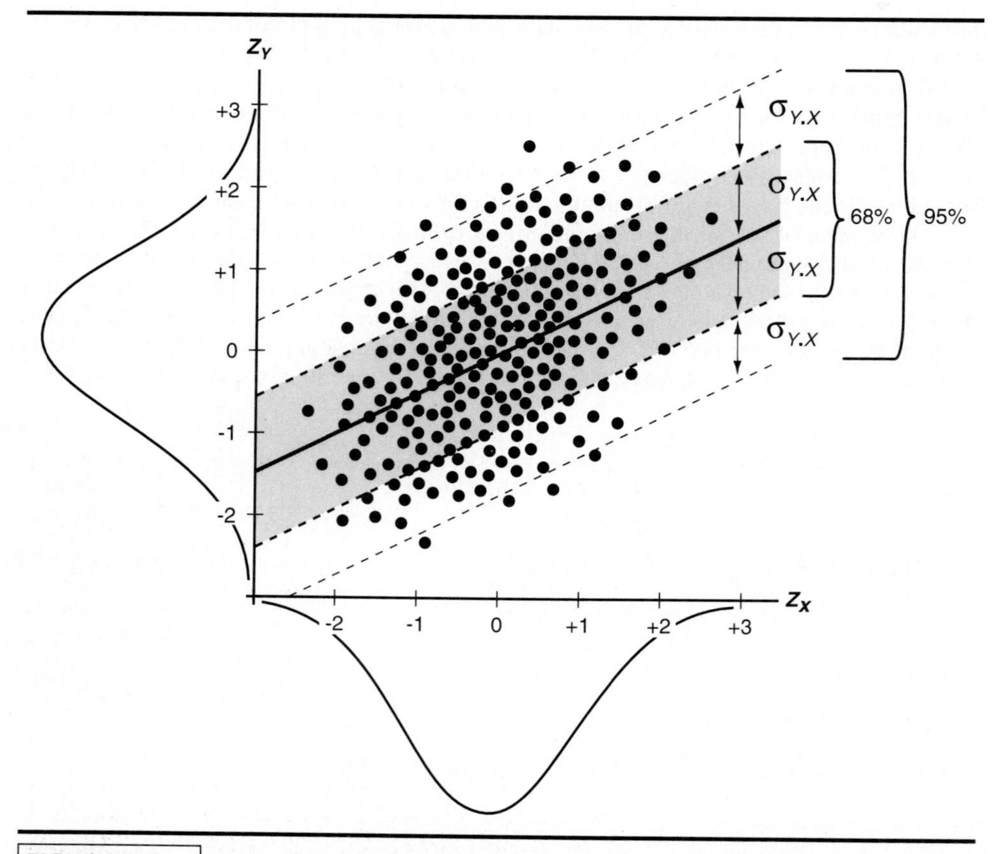


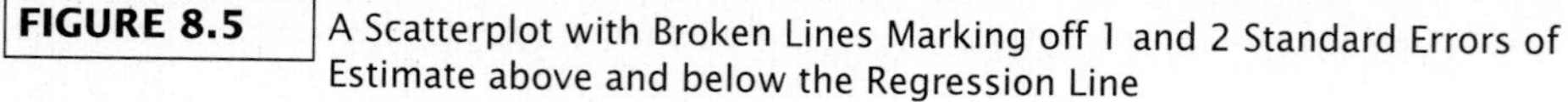

**FIGURE 8.5** A Scatterplot with Broken Lines Marking off 1 and 2 Standard Errors of Estimate above and below the Regression Line

of $s_{Y.X}$ for all values of $X$.[13] Notice in Figure 8.5 that although the mean of the normal distribution of the $Y$ scores differs for every unique value of $X$, the standard deviation $s_{Y.X}$ does not depend on the value of $X_i$.

## 8.11 REGRESSION AND PRETEST-POSTTEST GAINS

One of the most subtle and perplexing sources of invalidity in behavioral research results from the phenomenon of regression, the regression effect. Even seasoned researchers have

[13]For the exact estimation procedures that remove the "approximately" from statements 1 and 2 see Dixon and Massey (1983, pp. 217–218). The statements are precise only when $X_i = \overline{X}$. The actual percentages will be somewhat less than the percentages in statements 1 and 2 as $X_i$ deviates from $\overline{X}$, especially if $n$ is small and $X_i$ deviates two or more standard deviations from $\overline{X}$. The boundary lines in Figure 8.5 are straight only when the entire population is represented; when the scatterplot is based on a sample, the boundary lines for 68% and 95% are hyperbolas.

frequently failed to account for its influence. The regression effect has spoiled many otherwise good research efforts. Studies of atypical and extreme groups are especially vulnerable to the regression phenomenon. A simple statistical truism is that when subjects are selected because they deviate from the mean on some variable, regression will occur on other variables, unless the correlation is 1.0.

Many studies on academic remediation and treatment of the handicapped and other deviant groups follow this pattern. Those in greatest *need* are selected on a *pretest*, a treatment is administered, and a reassessment on a *posttest* then follows. For example, suppose that a large representative sample of two-year-old children are given an intelligence test. Children with IQ scores below 80 are given a special treatment (e.g., cognitive enrichment) for one year and then retested. Assume that the time interval between the pretest and posttest was such that there was absolutely no practice effect.[14] If the treatment had absolutely no effect, how would the experimental group fare on the posttest? Common sense says that, on the average, the scores would remain the same. Unfortunately, our intuition is often wrong when the regression phenomenon is lurking behind the scene.

For purposes of illustration, assume that the correlation ($\rho$) between the pretest IQ scores at age two with posttest IQ scores at age three is .6, a reasonable estimate for two-year-olds (Sternberg, 1982). Figure 8.6 depicts the illustrative situation: The population means on the pretest and posttest are 100; the pretest and posttest variances are identical (i.e., the treatment has no effect). Note in Figure 8.6 that there is a definite and pronounced tendency for subjects to regress toward the mean to the extent that, on the average, subjects tend to be only .6 as far from the posttest mean as they were from the pretest mean. That is, on the average, examinees tend to deviate only 60% as much from the posttest mean as they did from the pretest mean. Those examinees with pretest IQ scores of 80 would, on the average, be only 60% as far below the posttest mean; they would be expected to have an average posttest score of 88, a spurious gain of 8 points. Those with even lower pretest scores would have scores that would increase by more than 8 points, for example, those initially having IQ scores of 70 (30 points below the mean) would appear to have gained 12 points with a posttest mean of about 82 ( $\hat{Y} = 82$, or 18 points below the posttest mean).

The standard error of estimate $\left(\sigma_{Y.X} = \sigma_Y\sqrt{1-\rho^2} = 15\sqrt{1-.6^2} = 12\right)$ gives the standard deviation of posttest scores of persons having the same pretest scores. Using the standard error of estimate($\sigma_{Y.X}$), one can accurately predict the proportion of those with a given pretest score who will fall above or below any other IQ score on the posttest, provided the common assumptions of linearity and homoscedasticity between the two variables are met. Those scoring 70 on the first test will have a mean of 82 on the second test, with a standard deviation of 12 IQ points. Using a normal curve table, it is readily apparent that about 84% of those with pretest IQ scores of 70 will regress and therefore receive higher IQ scores on the posttest. One-half will gain 12 or more IQ points; one-sixth will have IQ's that increased by 24 or more points (i.e., obtain IQ scores of 94 or more). Further, of those with an initial IQ of 70, about 7% will obtain an IQ score of 100 or more on the second test, even in the absence of any treatment or practice effect. Obviously, what may appear to a naive investigator to be striking improvements can result solely from the regression effect. The following example will also serve to illustrate the problems.

One study treated infants born to mentally retarded mothers with an extensive regimen of sensory stimulation. The offspring were found to have much higher IQ scores than their

[14]On cognitive ability tests, there is little residual practice effect after an interval of three months (Hopkins, Stanley, & Hopkins, 1990, pp. 145–146).

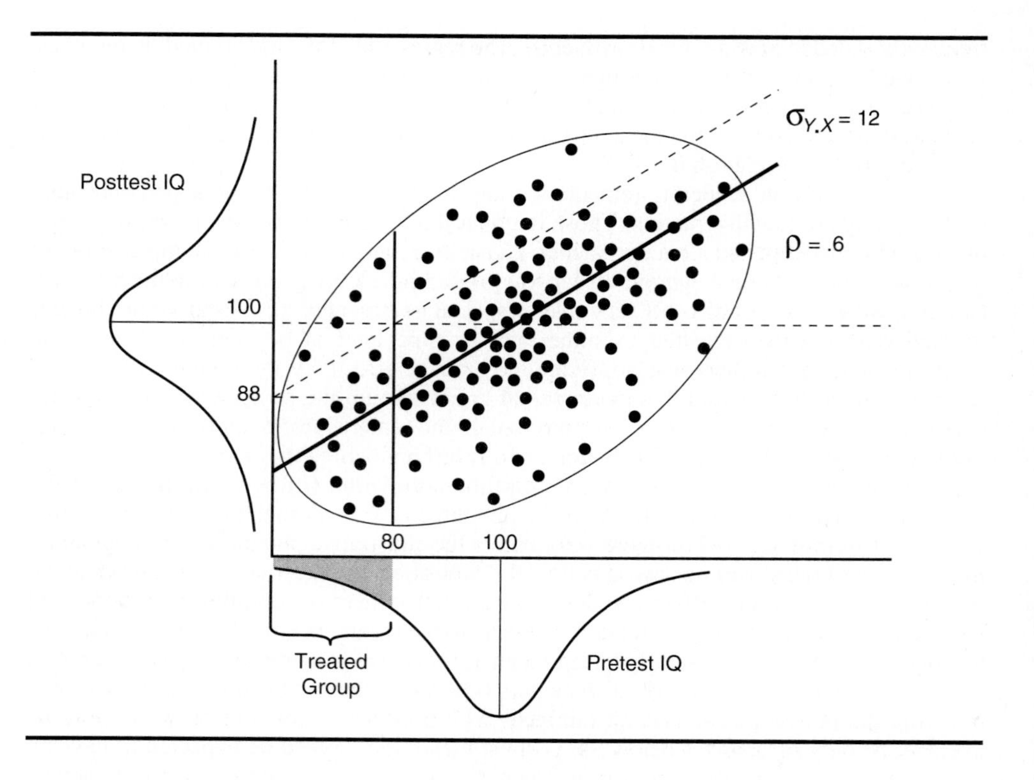


**FIGURE 8.6** Hypothetical Situation in Which a Deviant Group is Selected and Administered an Inefficacious Treatment.

mothers, and the authors uncritically attributed the increase to the sensory stimulation experiences. From the regression effect alone, what would the difference in mean IQ scores have been? Since the parent-child correlation of IQ's is approximately .5, for mothers with an IQ score of 70, the children would be expected to have a mean of 85 even without the sensory stimulation! On the average, a child's IQ tends to be only half as far from 100 as is the mother's or father's. There are many other examples in which ignorance of the regression effect has resulted in its being interpreted as a treatment effect.

Studies using "matched pairs" also usually suffer from a lack of control over the regression effect (see Hopkins, 1969; Shepard & Hopkins, 1977). Matched pair designs use matching because the two populations being compared have different means, and matching is used to try to control for this difference. The individual members of the pairs each regress toward the means of their respective population, and thus are not really equivalent on the variable on which they are matched.[15] Beware of studies that select individuals who deviate

[15]If the matched pair design is used, the matching should be done on predicted true scores, not on observed scores. An individual's predicted true score deviates from the mean by $\rho_{XX}$ times the observed deviation. Thus, the predicted true IQ score for a person scoring 130 on a test with a reliability coefficient of .90 is 127 [i.e., 100 + .90(30) = 127].

from the population mean, then compare their original scores with subsequent scores, and studies that use a matched pair design.

## 8.12 PART CORRELATION

Concepts from regression and correlation are combined in part correlation and partial correlation. These concepts are of interest themselves; but, more importantly, they are building blocks for understanding the subsequent topics of multiple regression and multiple correlation (Section 8.15). Partial correlation is a logical extension of part correlation; it is treated in Section 8.13.

A researcher wishes to find the correlation between a measure of scholastic aptitude $X_1$ (IQ scores) and achievement gains during an instructional unit, but important decisions about how to measure achievement gains must be faced. Posttest scores $X_2$ on a valid achievement test are not what this researcher means by achievement gains. A high correlation of IQ with the achievement test score would be expected even though no learning took place during instruction.

Administering parallel forms of the achievement test before ($X_3$) and after ($X_2$) instruction, then subtracting the pretest score from the posttest score ($X_2 - X_3$) for each student produces a measure that is far closer to the researcher's notion of a measure of achievement gain. One difficulty remains: Such a posttest-minus-pretest measure, $X_2 - X_3$, is contaminated by the regression effect; the gain scores, $X_2 - X_3$, usually correlate negatively[16] with pretest scores, $X_3$.

Usually gain scores will have a negative correlation with the pretest scores, that is, $r_{3,2-3} < 0$; this is a problem with the use of gain scores.

A better method to measure gain or change is to predict posttest scores ($\hat{X}_2$) from pretest scores ($X_3$) and use the deviation, $X_2 - \hat{X}_2$, as a measure of the gain, above and beyond what is predictable from the pretest alone. Note that this deviation is the residual by which the posttest, $X_2$ is predicted from the pretest, $X_3$. This deviation, termed *residual gain*, is illustrated in Figure 8.7. The residual gain score is denoted by $e_{2.3}$ because it is precisely the same as the error made in predicting $X_2$ from $X_3$ using the least squares regression line. The correlation of $e_{2.3}$ with $X_3$ is always zero. As a measure of learning, $e_{2.3}$ has the property that the measure of how much has been learned is unrelated ($r = 0$) to initial performance.

The correlation of $X_1$ with $e_{2.3}$ is a *part correlation*, $r_{1(2.3)}$. It is the correlation of $X_1$ (IQ) with $X_2$ (achievement posttest) after the portion of the posttest, $\hat{X}_2$, that can be predicted from the pretest, $X_3$, has been removed from $X_2$. It is the correlation of IQ scores with the residual gain beyond what is predicted from the achievement pretest, $X_3$.[17] For example, in Table 8.1 the residuals are given on a statistics test that has been predicted from the GRE. If these residuals are correlated with gender, the resulting correlation is a part correlation—the correlation of gender with that part of the statistics test scores that are not related to the GRE. If females do no better than males with identical GRE scores, the part correlation will be 0. The computational labor of computing this correlation directly is unnecessary, but it can be obtained from Equation 8.11. The part (or semi-partial)

[16]The gain score will correlate negatively with pretest scores if the variance is the same on both the pretest and the posttest. If the variance on the posttest is greater than on the pretest, gain scores can correlate positively with pretest scores.

[17]Part correlation and semi-partial correlation are synonymous.

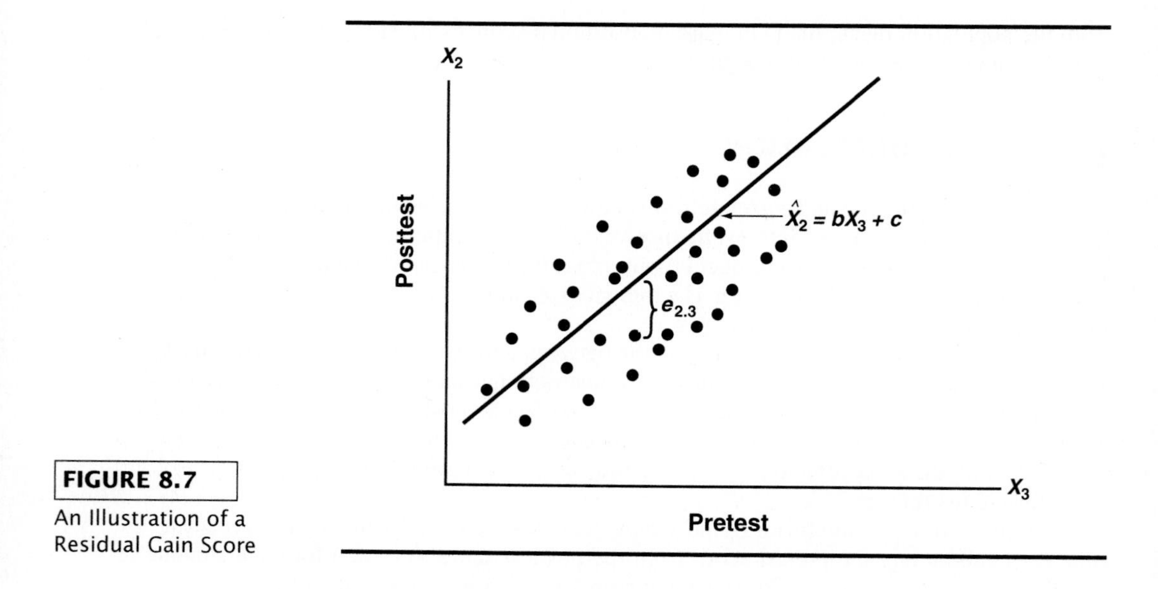


**FIGURE 8.7**

An Illustration of a Residual Gain Score

correlation of variable 1 with the residuals on variable 2 having been predicted by variable 3 is:

$$r_{1(2.3)} = \frac{r_{12} - r_{13}r_{23}}{\sqrt{1 - r_{23}^2}} \quad \textbf{(8.11)}$$

## 8.13 PARTIAL CORRELATION

Partial correlation is a simple extension of part correlation. The correlation of $X_1$ and $X_2$ with $X_3$ "held constant," removed, or partialed out is a partial correlation. Partial correlation is simply the correlation of the residuals $e_{1.3}$ and $e_{2.3}$. The partial correlation of $X_1$ and $X_2$ with $X_3$ partialed out is symbolized by $r_{12.3}$.

As with part correlation, the actual calculation of the residuals is not necessary to obtain $r_{12.3}$. The *partial correlation* coefficient can be calculated directly from $r_{12}$, $r_{13}$, and $r_{23}$ by using Equation 8.12:

$$r_{12.3} = \frac{r_{12} - r_{13}r_{23}}{\sqrt{(1 - r_{13}^2)(1 - r_{23}^2)}} \quad \textbf{(8.12)}$$

What interpretation can be given to $r_{12.3}$? Suppose in a large sample of children, ranging from six to sixteen years of age, a correlation of reading ability with visual perceptual ability (eye coordination, scanning speed, etc.) of .64 is found. The conclusion that some children read better than others because of greater visual perceptual abilities is tempting, but the cautious researcher will avoid jumping to this conclusion.

It is obvious that as children grow older they develop greater eye coordination and other perceptual abilities as a part of maturation. Moreover, the same children receive instruction in school that makes them better readers year after year, up to a point. Could it be that measures of both reading, $X_1$, and visual perceptual ability, $X_2$, increase or improve with age, in the one case because of increased exposure to instruction, and in the other because of physical maturation? If the correlation of reading ability and visual perceptual ability were near zero at each age (instead of over the range from six years to sixteen years), the $r_{12}$ of .64 for the entire group of children would have far different implications than if the correlation were .64 with age held constant. How can one estimate the value of $r_{12}$ for any single age? If the relationship is linear and is characterized by homoscedasticity, this correlation equals the partial correlation of variable 1 (reading ability) and variable 2 (visual perceptual ability) with variable 3 (age) held constant: $r_{12.3}$.

When the assumptions are met, then $r_{12.3}$ equals the value of $r_{12}$ obtained by correlating $X_1$ and $X_2$ for a group of individuals of the same age. For example, in the preceding illustration, suppose that $r_{12} = .64$, $r_{13} = .70$, and $r_{23} = .80$. The value of $r_{12.3}$ from Equation 8.12 is:

$$r_{12.3} = \frac{.64 - (.70)(.80)}{\sqrt{\left[1-(.70)^2\right]\left[1-(.80)^2\right]}} = .19$$

Thus, one would estimate the value of $r_{12}$ for children of the same chronological age to be only .19. If enough children of the same chronological age were available, $r$ could be calculated for them alone to check the previous result. The partial correlation coefficient serves the purpose of estimating $r_{12}$ for a single level of chronological age even when there are not enough persons at any single chronological age to obtain a reasonable estimate by direct calculation. Notice that the illustrative situation is closely related to the effect of heterogeneity on $r$ (Section 7.14).

In the case study (Table 7.11), the correlation between cholesterol level ($X_1$) and coronary ($X_2$) was found to be $.18 = r_{12}$. However, age ($X_3$) correlated with both of these variables: $r_{13} = .411$, and $r_{23} = .267$. Estimate the correlation between cholesterol level and coronary for persons of the same age (i.e., remove the confounding of the relationship with age). Using Equation 8.12, confirm that $r_{12.3} = .08$—the relationship is very low when age is eliminated from the relationship.

## 8.14 SECOND-ORDER PARTIAL CORRELATION

$r_{12.3}$ is called a *first-order* partial-correlation coefficient because the influence of one variable $X_3$ is partialed out. Partial correlation also can be used to remove the influence of two or more variables. A second-order partial correlation coefficient extends the rationale for controlling the effects of two variables. The partial correlation between $X_1$ and $X_2$ with the influence of both $X_3$ and $X_4$ removed is:

$$r_{12.34} = \frac{r_{12.3} - r_{14.3}r_{24.3}}{\sqrt{(1-r_{14.3}^2)(1-r_{24.3}^2)}} \quad \textbf{(8.13)}$$

The *second-order partial correlation* coefficient is the correlation between the residuals for $X_1$ with residuals for $X_2$ after each has been predicted via multiple regression (Section 8.15) using the two variables $X_3$ and $X_4$ as predictors. In the case study, one could find the correlation between cholesterol level with coronary holding both age and height constant using Equation 8.15.

## 8.15 MULTIPLE REGRESSION AND MULTIPLE CORRELATION

The prediction of a dependent variable from a single independent variable was considered in Section 8.6. In many, if not most, statistical predictions, more than one variable is used in making the prediction. *Multiple regression* is the statistical method most commonly employed for predicting $Y$ from two or more independent variables. For example, most colleges use at least two variables (high school rank-in-class and SAT or ACT scores) to predict college GPA. The purpose of multiple regression is to predict variable $Y$ (the dependent variable), with maximal accuracy, from a linear combination of $m$ independent variables $X_1, X_2, \ldots, X_m$. It is a linear regression equation because the independent variables (the $X$'s) have exponents of 1.[18]

In Section 8.9, one independent variable ($X$) is used to predict the best (least-squares) estimate of the dependent variable ($Y$). The regression equation, $\hat{Y}_i = bX_i + c$, yields the best estimate of $Y_i$ (the score of the $i$th person on the dependent variable). Using the criterion of least squares, the values for $b$ and $c$ are selected such that the sum of the squared residuals (errors), $\Sigma e^2_{Y \cdot X}$, is as small as possible. This type of estimation is sometimes termed simple or univariate regression because there is only a single independent variable. A multivariate prediction of the $Y$ variable given scores on $m$ independent variables is expressed in Equation 8.14:

$$\hat{Y}_i = b_1 X_{1_i} + b_2 X_{2_i} + \ldots + b_m X_{m_i} + c \qquad \textbf{(8.14)}$$

Equation 8.14 defines the raw-score multiple regression equation. The least squares criterion is employed to find the values of the regression coefficients ($b_1, b_2, \ldots, b_m$) and the intercept $c$. Their values are such that the sum of squared residuals ($\Sigma_i e_i^2$) is minimized for the set of values of $Y$ and $X_1, X_2, \ldots, X_m$:

$$\sum_i e_i^2 = \sum_i (Y_i - \hat{Y}_i)^2 = \sum_i \left[ Y_i - \left( b_1 X_{1_i} + b_2 X_{2_i} + \cdots + b_m X_{m_i} + c \right) \right]^2 \qquad \textbf{(8.15)}$$

A second sense in which the $b$'s and $c$ are "best" is that they weight the $m$ predictors so that the correlation between predicted $\hat{Y}$'s and the observed $Y$'s is maximal. The Pearson product-moment correlation between $Y$ and $\hat{Y}_i$ is a measure of how well the best weighting of the $m$ independent variables predicts or correlates with the dependent variable, $Y$. This

[18]Nonlinear or polynomial regression models are available in most statistical software packages, but have not been widely used in behavioral research.

special case of Pearson's $r$ is called the *multiple correlation* and is denoted as $R_{Y.12\ldots m}$. The regression coefficients and intercept in Equation 8.14 not only provide $\hat{Y}_i$ (the least-squares estimates of the $Y_i$'s), but also yield the highest possible correlation between $\hat{Y}$ and $Y$. The $b$'s weight the $m$ independent variables optimally so that they are combined in a way that $Y$ is predicted as accurately as possible.

## 8.16 THE STANDARDIZED REGRESSION EQUATION

The raw-score regression equation (Equation 8.14) can be simplified when all variables are expressed as standard $z$-scores. In the standardized regression equation, all variables are linearly transformed to standard scores having a mean of 0 and a standard deviation of 1.

Equation 8.1, $\hat{z}_Y = rz_X$, is a standardized regression equation when there is a single independent variable. Similarly, with $m$ predictors, each expressed in standard $z$-score form, the standardized regression equation is

$$\hat{z}_{Y_i} = \hat{\beta}_1 z_{1_i} + \hat{\beta}_2 z_{2_i} + \ldots + \hat{\beta}_m z_{m_i} \qquad \textbf{(8.16)}$$

The regression coefficients $\hat{\beta}_1$, $\hat{\beta}_2$, ..., $\hat{\beta}_m$ are sometimes termed "beta weights,"[19] standardized regression coefficients, or, more explicitly, standard partial regression coefficients—standard to denote $z$-scale, and partial because the effects of the other variables are held constant. In other words, $\hat{\beta}_1$ is short for $\hat{\beta}_{Y1.23\ldots m}$.

### An Illustration with Two Independent Variables

How well can reading performance (scores on an end-of-year standardized reading test, $Y$) be predicted prior to grade one using reading readiness (RR) test scores ($X_1$) and IQ scores ($X_2$)? What is the optimal weighting of RR and IQ scores that will give the best prediction of the criterion $Y$? Table 8.2 gives the correlation matrix for the three variables ($X_1$, $X_2$, and $Y$) for 157 pupils.

**TABLE 8.2** Correlations among Reading Readiness (RR) Scores, IQ Scores, and Reading Performance for 157 First Grade Pupils

| | $X_1$ | $X_2$ | $Y$ | $\bar{X}$ | $s$ |
|---|---|---|---|---|---|
| RR Score, $X_1$ | 1.00 | .466 | .612 | 49.0 | 10.3 |
| IQ Score, $X_2$ | | 1.00 | .541 | 102.8 | 14.7 |
| Reading Score, $Y$ | | | 1.00 | 26.0 | 8.10 |

In this application ($m = 2$), Equation 8.16 becomes:

$$\hat{z}_{Y_i} = \hat{\beta}_1 z_{1_i} + \hat{\beta}_2 z_{2_i}$$

[19]The use of the Greek lower case letter beta, $\beta$, is unfortunate since it is not a parameter, and its use is inconsistent with the conventional use of Greek letters to represent parameters.

The least-squares estimates of the beta weights when $m = 2$ are close relatives of part and partial correlation coefficients:

$$\hat{\beta}_1 = \frac{r_{Y1} - r_{Y2}r_{12}}{1 - r_{12}^2} \qquad \hat{\beta}_2 = \frac{r_{Y2} - r_{Y1}r_{12}}{1 - r_{12}^2} \qquad \textbf{(8.17)}$$

The correlation between all pairs of variables is needed to arrive at a regression equation. The matrix of correlations for the sample problem is given in Table 8.2. Table 8.2 shows that both RR and IQ correlated substantially with the criterion (.612 and .541). How can the information on $X_1$ and $X_2$ be weighted optimally to maximize the accuracy in the predictions of $Y$? The beta weights are found from Equation 8.17, using the $r$'s in Table 8.2:

$$\hat{\beta}_1 = \frac{(.612) - (.541)(.466)}{1 - (.466)^2} = \frac{.3599}{.7828} = .460$$

$$\hat{\beta}_2 = \frac{.541 - (.612)(.466)}{(1 - (.466)^2)} = .327$$

Thus, the standardized regression equation is:

$$\hat{z}_Y = .460z_1 + .327z_2$$

To illustrate the use of this equation, predict $Y$ for students who are one standard deviation above the mean on both $X_1$ and $X_2$, that is, $z_1 = 1$ and $z_2 = 1$. When $z_1 = 1$ and $z_2 = 1$ are substituted into the standardized regression equation, the predicted $z$-score on $Y$ (that is, $\hat{z}_Y$) is obtained: $\hat{z}_Y = .460(1) + .327(1) = .787$. Students who are one standard deviation above the mean both on variable 1 and variable 2 have scores that average .787 standard deviations above $\bar{Y}$, that is, $\hat{z}_Y = .787$. From Table 8.2, $\bar{Y} = 26.0$ and $s_Y = 8.1$; thus, $\hat{Y} = 26.0 + .787(8.1) = 32.4$. From the norm tables for the reading test, a raw score of 32.4 is found to correspond to a grade-equivalent score of 2.6 (the average score at the sixth month of grade two). It is inconvenient to convert $X_1, X_2, \ldots, X_m$ to $z$-scores, and to convert $\hat{z}_Y$ to $Y$. The raw-score regression equation is more expedient for making predictions. What then is the use of beta coefficients? Differences in raw score regression coefficients are greatly influenced by the standard deviations of the independent variables, and cannot be compared; beta coefficients do not have this problem. Holding IQ constant, reading increases .46 standard deviations when RR is increased by one standard deviation; holding RR constant, reading increases .327 standard deviations when IQ is increased by one standard deviation.

## 8.17 THE RAW-SCORE REGRESSION EQUATION

What is the predicted average reading grade for students having an RR score of 55 and an IQ score of 120? These scores could be converted to $z$-scores ($z_1 = .583$ and $z_2 = 1.17$) and $\hat{z}_Y$ could be obtained using the standardized regression equation given in Section 8.16 ($\hat{z}_Y = .460(.583) + .327(1.17) = .651$). $\hat{z}_Y$ could then be converted to $\hat{Y}$ ($\hat{Y} = \bar{Y} + \hat{z}_Y s_Y = 26.0 + .651(8.10) = 31.27$). However, the raw-score regression equation (Equation 8.14) makes the conversions to and from $z$-scores unnecessary:

$$\hat{Y}_i = b_1 X_{1_i} + b_2 X_{2_i} + c.$$

The regression coefficients ($b_m$'s), can be obtained from the beta weights:

$$b_m = \hat{\beta}_m \left( \frac{s_Y}{s_m} \right) \qquad \textbf{(8.18A)}$$

and the intercept ($c$) is

$$c = \bar{Y} - b_1 \bar{X}_1 - b_2 \bar{X}_2 - \ldots - b_m \bar{X}_m \qquad \textbf{(8.18B)}$$

Notice in Equation 8.18A that raw-score regression coefficients and the beta weights will be equal when the standard deviations, $s_Y$ and $s_m$, are equal. Using Equation 8.18A, the $b_1$ and $b_2$ can be obtained from $\hat{\beta}_1$ and $\hat{\beta}_2$ (together with the standard deviations found in Table 8.2):

$$b_1 = \frac{(.460)(8.10)}{10.3} = .362 \text{ and } b_2 = \frac{(.327)(8.10)}{14.7} = .180$$

And, from Equation 8.18B, the intercept $c$ is:

$$c = 26.0 - (.362)(49.0) - (.180)(102.8) = -10.24$$

The raw-score form of the regression equation, therefore, is:

$$\hat{Y}_i = .362 X_{1_i} + .180 X_{2_i} - 10.24$$

For students with $X_1 = 55$ and $X_2 = 120$, the predicted reading score is:

$$\hat{Y} = .362(55) + .180(120) - 10.24 = 31.27$$

Compared to the standardized regression equation, notice how much more convenient the raw-score regression equation is to use. Beta weights, however, are more useful for evaluating the relative contributions of the independent variables because all variables are standardized.

## 8.18 MULTIPLE CORRELATION

The correlation between $Y$ and $\hat{Y}$ when the prediction is based on two or more independent variables is termed *multiple correlation.* When there are two predictors, as in the reading example, the multiple correlation coefficient, $R_{Y.12}$, can be obtained from Equation 8.19. This equation yields the square of the multiple correlation, $R^2_{Y.12}$, which describes the proportion of variance in the criterion ($Y$) that is predicted by the multiple regression equation:

$$R^2_{Y.12} = \frac{r^2_{Y1} + r^2_{Y2} - 2r_{Y1}r_{Y2}r_{12}}{1 - r^2_{12}} \qquad \textbf{(8.19)}$$

Supplying the $r$'s from Table 8.2 into Equation 8.19:

$$R^2_{Y.12} = \frac{(.612)^2 + (.541)^2 - 2(.612)(.541)(.466)}{1 - (.466)^2} = .458$$

and $R_{Y.12} = .677$. Notice that the correlation between $Y$ and $\hat{Y}$ increased to .677 when both IQ and RR scores are combined to predict $Y$, whereas the correlation was .612 when the better of the two predictors, RR, was used singly. Stated differently, the proportion of the variance in $Y$ that was predictable increased from $(.612)^2 = .375$ to .458.

Notice that the multiple correlation would have been much higher if the two independent variables were not correlated; if $r_{12} = 0$, then $R^2_{Y.12} = r^2_{Y1} + r^2_{Y2}$. Notice that $r_{12}$ is a measure of redundancy between the two independent variables. If $r_{12} = 1.0$, there is no unique information in the second variable, hence the ability to predict any criterion is not improved by using both $X_1$ and $X_2$. To the extent that $r_{12}$ approaches 0, $X_1$ and $X_2$ contain unique, non-redundant information.

The concepts of unique and redundant variance are illustrated in Figure 8.8; the variance of each variable is depicted as a square.

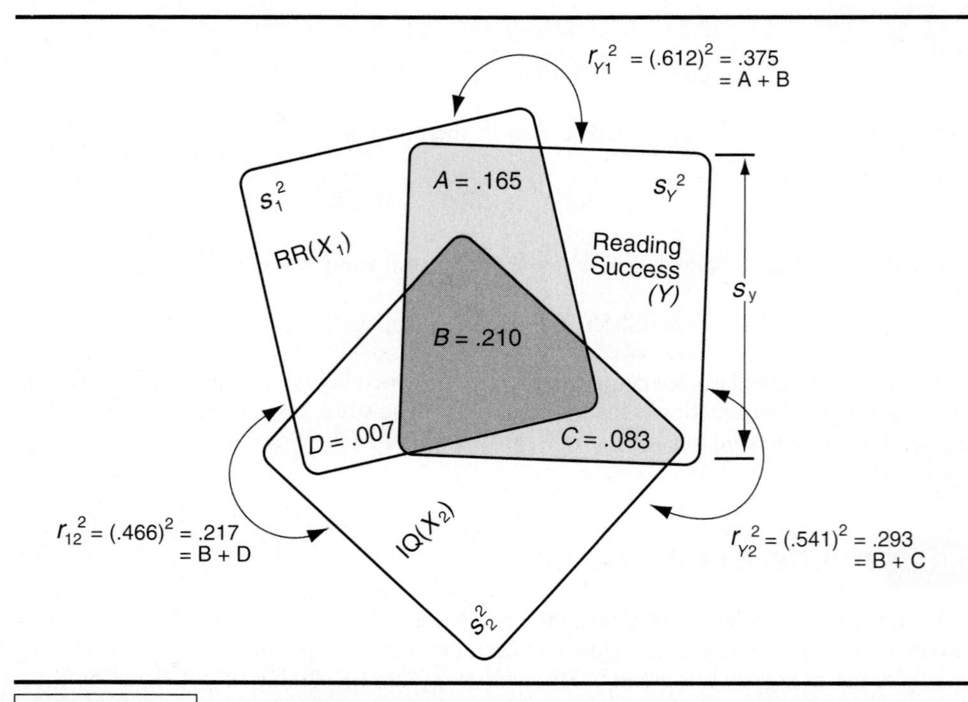


**FIGURE 8.8** Redundant and Unique Variance among Two Independent Variables and a Dependent Variable, Based on Data in Table 8.2.

Areas $A$ and $B$ represent the variance in $Y$ that is predictable from $X_1$: $A + B = r_{Y1}^2 = (.612)^2 = .375$ or 37.5% of the variance in $Y$ that is predictable from $X_1$. The proportion of variance in $Y$ that is predictable from $X_2$, $r_{y2}^2 = (.541)^2 = .293$, is depicted by areas $B$ and $C$. Likewise, areas $B + D$ represent the common variance between $X_1$ and $X_2$, $r_{12}^2 = (.466)^2 = .217$ or 21.7%. Thus, the relevant and unique variance in $X_2$ for predicting $Y$ is shown as area $C$. Since $R_{Y.12}^2 = .458$, and area $A + B = .375$, area $C = .458 - .375 = .083$. Area $B$ represents relevant variance in $X_2$ for predicting $Y$, but redundant variance is already accounted for by $X_1$. Since $B + C = .293$, and $C = .083$, $B = .210$.

The total variance in $Y$ that is predictable from $X_1$ and $X_2$ is represented by areas $A + B + C = .458$. How does this figure compare to the figure that would result if $X_1$ and $X_2$ contained no redundant information? If $r_{12} = 0$, then $R_{Y.12}^2 = r_{Y1}^2 + r_{Y2}^2 = .375 + .293 = .668$; hence, $R_{Y.12} = .817$. It is apparent that in multiple regression it is desirable to have independent variables that correlate highly with the dependent variable, but have low intercorrelations with each other.

It should be noted that multiple correlation coefficients (unlike simple Pearson $r$'s) can never be negative. The regression coefficients are always calculated in such a way that $R$ will be zero or positive.

In rare instances, predictors that do not correlate with the criterion can increase the multiple correlation by suppressing irrelevant variance in other independent variables. For example, if $r_{Y1} = .5$, $r_{Y2} = 0$, and $r_{12} = .4$, then (from Equation 8.19) $R_{Y.12} = .55$; thus, variable 2 increased the predictable variance in $Y$ (even though $r_{Y2} = 0$) by suppressing irrelevant variance in variable 1. Variable 2 is termed a *suppressor variable*.

## 8.19 MULTIPLE REGRESSION EQUATIONS WITH THREE OR MORE INDEPENDENT VARIABLES

The computations of regression coefficients ($\hat{\beta}$'s or $b$'s) for three or more independent variables, although not theoretically complex, are very tedious and time consuming when done by hand. Fortunately, the actual computations of regression coefficients are usually done using standard computer programs available at all university computer facilities. In Sections 8.16 and 8.17 standardized and raw-score multiple regression equations were employed for the case in which two independent variables, $X_1$ and $X_2$, are used to predict $Y$. The underlying rationale and application extend logically to situations in which there are three or more independent variables. The independent variables can include any combination of demographic, cognitive, psychomotor, and affective variables, and variables such as age, IQ, GPA, height, sex, socioeconomic status, reaction time, interests, and ethnicity.

## 8.20 STEPWISE MULTIPLE REGRESSION

In Section 8.18 we demonstrated that an *additional predictor* is effective to the extent that it contributes relevant and unique variance, with respect to the set of predictor variables. If $r_{Y1} = .5$, $r_{Y2} = .5$, and $r_{Y3} = .4$, will $R_{Y.12}$ necessarily be larger than $R_{Y.13}$? Certainly not; if $r_{12} = 1$, then $X_2$ is totally redundant and will not increase the accuracy in predicting $Y$, compared to using $X_1$ alone; whereas if $r_{13} = 0$, $R_{Y.13} = .64$.

Much, if not most, behavioral research to find a multiple regression equation uses *stepwise multiple regression* computer programs. In stepwise multiple regression, the best predictor is selected in step 1, and a one-predictor regression equation is produced along with the multiple correlation and various other statistics such as the standard error of estimate. In step 2, the independent variable that would contribute the greatest amount of unique relevant variance is selected and a two-predictor regression equation is produced and $R_{Y.12}$ is determined. The variable selected in step 2 is the variable that has the highest correlation with $Y$ when the previously entered independent variable is partialed out. Each successive step progresses in like manner: The next predictor variable is entered into the regression equation that has the greatest partial correlation with the criterion when all variables already included in the previous regression equation have been partialed out.

## 8.21 ILLUSTRATION OF STEPWISE MULTIPLE REGRESSION

The independent variables in Table 8.2 are only two of five predictors that were studied in order to forecast reading success in grade one. The larger study asked, "How accurately can end-of-year first-grade reading performance be predicted from a pupil's age (CA), sex, socioeconomic status (SES), reading readiness (RR), and IQ scores?" Table 8.3 gives the correlations, means, and standard deviations for the variables of the study. Notice that all five independent variables correlated positively with the criterion, although the correlations for CA, SES, and sex are quite low: .050, .209, and .197, respectively.

The stepwise multiple regression is summarized in Table 8.4. The regression equation after step 2 is the same equation found in Section 8.17. Notice in step 3 that the variable sex was selected because it complements the first two predictors ($X_1$ and $X_2$) more than the variable SES. Even though SES had a slightly higher correlation with the dependent variable $Y$, the variable sex added more relevant unique information than did SES. Stated differently, the second-order partial correlation, $r_{Y5.12} = .201$, was greater than either $r_{Y4.12} = .069$ or $r_{Y3.12} = -.038$; thus, variable 5 (sex) added more relevant unique information to RR and IQ than did variable 4 (SES) or variable 3 (CA).

Use the regression equation after step 5 in Table 8.4 to predict the reading test score for Carmen, 77 months of age, with a SES score of 32, with RR = 50 and IQ = 120: $\hat{Y}_1 = .360(50) + .165(120) + 2.44(2) + .023(32) - .026(77) - 10.95 = 30.46$. In other words, Carmen is predicted to be about .5 standard deviations above the mean ($\bar{Y} = 26.0$ and $s_Y = 8.1$; $\hat{z}_Y = (30.36 - 26.0)/8.1 = .53$), having an approximate percentile rank of 70.

**TABLE 8.3** Correlations among Variables Used in Predicting Grade One Reading Performance ($n = 157$)

| | *(IQ)* $X_2$ | *(CA)* $X_3$ | *(SES)* $X_4$ | *(Sex)* $X_5$ | $Y$ | *Mean* | $s$ | *Measure* |
|---|---|---|---|---|---|---|---|---|
| RR: $X_1$ | .466 | .252 | .160 | .055 | .612 | 49.0 | 10.3 | Lee-Clark RR Test |
| IQ: $X_2$ | | −.119 | .265 | .072 | .541 | 102.8 | 14.7 | CTMM IQ Test |
| CA: $X_3$ | | | −.053 | −.081 | .050 | 76.8 | 4.11 | Age in Months |
| SES: $X_4$ | | | | −.040 | .209 | 32.3 | 21.6 | Duncan Scale |
| Sex: $X_5$ | | | | | .197 | 1.48 | .501 | (Male = 1, Female = 2) |
| $Y$ | | | | | | 26.0 | 8.10 | Lee-Clark Reading Test |

**TABLE 8.4** Stepwise Multiple Regression for Variables in Table 8.3

| | | | | | Partial r's | | | | |
|---|---|---|---|---|---|---|---|---|---|
| *Step* | $R_{Y.1...m}$ | $SS_{res}$ | $s_{Y.1...m}$ | *Variable Entered* | *RR* $X_1$ | *IQ* $X_2$ | *CA* $X_3$ | *SES* $X_4$ | *Sex* (M = 1, F = 2) $X_5$ |
| 0 | ... | 10237.0 | 8.1007 | ... | .612 | .541 | .050 | .209 | .197 |
| 1 | .612 | 6405.4 | 6.428 | $X_1$(RR) | | .366 | −.135 | .142 | .206 |
| $(\hat{Y}_i = .481X_{1_i} + 2.41)$ | | | | | | | | | |
| 2 | .677 | 5549.6 | 6.003 | $X_2$(IQ) | | | −.038 | .069 | .201 |
| $(\hat{Y}_i = .362X_{1_i} + .180X_{2_i} - 10.24)$ | | | | | | | | | |
| 3 | .693 | 5325.3 | 5.900 | $X_5$(Sex) | | | −.021 | .083 | |
| $(\hat{Y}_i = .358X_{1_i} + .175X_{2_i} + 2.40X_{5_i} - 13.16)$ | | | | | | | | | |
| 4 | .69526 | 5288.5 | 5.899 | $X_4$(SES) | | | −.017 | | |
| $(\hat{Y}_i = .356X_{1_i} + .167X_{2_i} + 2.46X_{5_i} + .023X_{4_i} - 13.01)$ | | | | | | | | | |
| 5 | .69537 | 5286.95 | 5.917 | $X_3$(CA) | | | | | |
| $(\hat{Y}_i = .360X_{1_i} + .165X_{2_i} + 2.44X_{5_i} + .023X_{4_i} - .026X_{3_i} - 10.95)$ | | | | | | | | | |

How does the prediction for Carmen compare with that of Sean who has the same values on all independent variables except sex? Sean's predicted reading score would be 2.44 points lower, or 28.02.

## 8.22 DICHOTOMOUS AND CATEGORICAL VARIABLES AS PREDICTORS

Dichotomous variables such as sex can be used as independent variables if they are numerically coded, as in the previous example: M = 1, F = 2. Obviously, this code must be known before the point-biserial *r*'s can be properly interpreted. Notice in Table 8.3 that sex correlated .197 with *Y*, reading test scores. The positive value for *r* shows that the gender given the higher numerical code (females in this case) had higher reading test scores. If the code M = 2, F = 1 had been used, $r_{Y5}$ would have been −.197; the sign of *r* would have been reversed, but its absolute value would be unchanged.

Categorical variables having $J = 3$ or more categories must be broken into $J - 1$ dichotomies (sometimes called dummy or indicator variables) in order to be used for prediction. For example, if there are three ethnic groups, two independent variables are required: $X_1$ is "Do you belong to ethnic group A?" with responses coded: No = 1, Yes = 2. The $X_2$ variable follows the identical pattern: "Do you belong to ethnic group B?" What about the individuals in the third ethnic group? They are defined indirectly by having 1's (No's) for both $X_1$ and $X_2$.

## 8.23 THE STANDARD ERROR OF ESTIMATE IN MULTIPLE REGRESSION

Does the use of CA complement the other predictors (see step 5 in Table 8.4)? Not really. The multiple correlation was increased by only .0001 after CA was added as a predictor. Moreover, the standard error of estimate $s_{Y.12345} = 5.917$ is actually larger than the value for the previous step, $s_{Y.1245} = 5.899$. How can this be since the multiple correlation increased and the sum of the squared residuals is less in step 5 than in step 4? Note that Equation 8.10 is only an approximation. More precisely:

$$s^2_{Y.12...m} = \frac{SS_{\text{residuals}}}{n-m-1} = \frac{SS_{\text{residuals}}}{\nu} \qquad \textbf{(8.20)}$$

The denominator, $n - m - 1$, defines the degrees of freedom ($\nu$). Recall from Section 5.8 that the sum of squares ($SS$) divided by its degrees of freedom ($\nu$) is a variance—in this case the variance of the residuals. From step 4 to step 5, the decrease in the numerator of Equation 8.20 was proportionately less than the decrease in the denominator. Thus, the ratio (i.e., $s^2_{Y.12345}$) in step 5 is greater than the ratio in step 4 (i.e., $s^2_{Y.1245}$).

Notice in Table 8.4 that steps 4 and 5 provided virtually no increase in the multiple correlation; this is not unusual. In most prediction studies in the behavioral sciences, there is little increase in the multiple correlation after the best three or four predictors have been included in the multiple regression equation.

## 8.24 THE MULTIPLE CORRELATION AS AN INFERENTIAL STATISTIC: CORRECTION FOR BIAS

The regression coefficients are determined in such a way as to yield the highest possible correlation between $Y$ and $\hat{Y}$, which is the multiple correlation $R_{Y.123...m}$. In the process of optimizing the weighting of the predictors, there is a certain amount of capitalizing on chance (fitting error). To the extent that there is sampling error (Equation 4.11) in the $r$'s and in the standard deviations of the dependent and independent variables, the optimizing procedures involved in obtaining the multiple regression equation cause the multiple correlation $R_{Y.123...m}$ to be systematically higher than the corresponding parameter, $\rho_{Y.123...m}$ (where the $\hat{Y}$'s are from a regression equation using $\rho$'s and $\sigma$'s, rather than $r$'s and $s$'s).

Several "shrinkage" formulas[20] have been proposed to remove the "error fitting" from the multiple correlation $R_{Y.123...m}$. Equation 8.21 is the most widely used:[21]

$$\text{adj } R^2_{Y.12\cdots m} = R^2_{Y.12\cdots m} - \left(1 - R^2_{Y.12\cdots m}\right)\left(\frac{m}{n-m-1}\right) \qquad \textbf{(8.21)}$$

---

[20]Olkin and Pratt (1958) derived a formula for the unbiased estimate of $\rho_{Y.123...m}$. Much simpler formulas have been developed that yield adjusted multiple $R$'s that are only trivially different (Lord & Novick, 1968, p. 286; Carter, 1979).

[21]This is the correction employed in SPSS, SAS, and BMDP computer packages. Equation 8.21 yields results that are essentially equal to those resulting from the Olkin-Pratt and Wherry formulas (the methods offered in the previous edition of this book).

where ${}_{adj}R^2_{Y.12...m}$ is an estimate of $\rho^2_{Y\hat{Y}}$ and $R^2_{Y.12...m}$ is the square of the multiple correlation from the regression equation based on $n$ cases and $m$ predictor variables. In the sample problem with $R^2_{Y.12345} = (.69537)^2 = .48354$, $n = 157$, and $m = 5$, the adjusted multiple correlation, estimated from Equation 8.21 is:

$$_{\text{adj}}R^2_{Y.12345} = .48354 - (1 - .48354)\left(\frac{5}{157-5-1}\right) = .48354 - (.51646)\left(\frac{5}{151}\right) = .46644$$

$$_{\text{adj}}R_{Y.12345} = .6830$$

The adjusted multiple $R$ is just slightly less than the value reported in Table 8.4 of .69537.[22] The correction would have been much greater if $n$ had been much smaller or if $m$ had been much larger. For example, if $n = 25$, other things remaining constant, the corrected $R$ would have been .59; Or if $m = 25$, other things remaining constant, the corrected $R$ would have become .62. As the ratio $m/n$ increases, the amount of error fitting (*bias*) increases. Apply Equation 8.21 to the situation in which $m = 25$, $n = 50$, and $R_{Y.123...25} = .80$, and confirm that the corrected multiple ${}_{adj}R$ shrinks to .51 (${}_{adj}R^2 = .265$). In one study, the authors obtained a multiple $R$ of .6 based on twenty-one variables and sixty persons. The ${}_{adj}R$ of .08 illustrates that almost all the relationship was due to error fitting!

The rationale underlying Equation 8.21 is to estimate the square of the multiple correlation, not as the proportion of sum of squares in the criterion that is predictable, but using unbiased estimators of unpredictable and total variance:

$$_{\text{adj}}R^2_{Y.12\cdots m} = 1 - \frac{s^2_{Y.12\cdots m}}{s^2_Y} \qquad \textbf{(8.22)}$$

where $s^2_{Y.12...m}$ is obtained from Equation 8.20. Thus, in the sample problem in Table 8.4:

$$_{\text{adj}}R^2_{Y.12345} = 1 - \frac{(5.917)^2}{(8.1007)^2} = .4665$$

$$_{\text{adj}}R_{Y.12345} = .6830$$

which agrees with the value for ${}_{adj}R_{Y.12345}$ found using Equation 8.21. In other words, Equation 8.22 estimates the parameter for the multiple correlation by using unbiased estimates of the parameters $\sigma^2_{Y.12...m}$ and $\sigma_Y^2$. If Equation 8.20 is used to find the value of the standard error of estimate, then the corrected multiple correlation can be estimated directly from Equation 8.22, and Equation 8.21 is unnecessary.

It is important to note that shrinkage formulas like Equation 8.21 make an adjustment for error fitting assuming there were only $m$ independent variables. If stepwise multiple regression is employed and a regression equation is developed using only a subset of the available predictors, there will remain a bias (inflation) in the multiple correlation. Equation 8.21 should be applied to $R$ after all available predictors have been used. The best solution to the problem of spuriously high multiple correlations is to have 50 or 100 cases for every predictor, in which case the degree of inflation will be minimal.

---

[22]Using the Olkin-Pratt procedure, the corrected multiple correlation was .6854.

## 8.25 ASSUMPTIONS[23]

The regression procedures that have been discussed and illustrated make the following assumptions:

1. The $Y$ scores are *independent* and *normally distributed* at all points along the regression line; that is, the residuals are normally distributed. (There is no assumption that the independent variables are normally distributed. The independence assumption is not required for descriptive statistics, but only in the context of statistical inference.)
2. If $\hat{Y}$ values are plotted on the $X$-axis and $Y$ values on the vertical axis, there is a *linear relationship* between the $Y$'s and $\hat{Y}$'s—at all points along the straight regression line, the residuals have a mean of zero.
3. The variance of the residuals is uniform for all values of $\hat{Y}$. This characteristic is known as *homoscedasticity*.

## 8.26 CURVILINEAR REGRESSION AND CORRELATION

Most cognitive and psychomotor variables that are measured on refined instruments have linear relationships. However, if two variables to be used in a multiple regression have a nonlinear relationship, one should try various transformations (Section 8.28) to see if the relationship can be transformed into a linear relationship. If these procedures are unsuccessful, more complex regression equations can be used—equations that allow the independent variables to be raised to powers other than one, polynomial regression equations. Fortunately, most computer program packages have programs for determining polynomial regression equations as well as multiple regression equations.

## 8.27 MEASURING NONLINEAR RELATIONSHIPS BETWEEN TWO VARIABLES: $\eta$

It has been emphasized repeatedly that the Pearson product-moment $r$ describes only the degree of *linear* relationship between $X$ and $Y$. How does one describe the degree of relationship between $X$ and $Y$ that does not require the relationship to be linear? As an example of a non linear relationship, consider the hypothetical data in Figure 8.9 relating age, $X$, to psychomotor performance, $Y$. Although the Pearson $r_{XY} = -.077$, a visual inspection of the scatterplot suggests that the relationship is nonlinear; therefore, $r$ is an inappropriate measure of the degree of relationship between $X$ and $Y$. Although in the example there are an equal number of persons in each of the $J = 7$ age groups, the procedures are identical when the numbers per group are not equal. It is obvious from Figure 8.9 that the scores on this

---

[23]In most regression models, an additional assumption is listed, namely, that the independent variables are fixed, not random (Section 19.2). Fixed variables have values that are selected by the investigator and are not the result of random sampling. Sex and Chronological Age in the sample multiple regression problem (Section 8.21) are examples of fixed independent variables: Both sexes in the population are represented and over-aged and under-aged pupils were excluded. The other three independent variables, IQ, RR, and SES are random variables—not all the particular values within the population to which the regression equation might be applied are represented in the sample. Fortunately, the regression methods that interest us yield identical results whether the independent variables are fixed or random (Snedecor and Cochran, 1989).

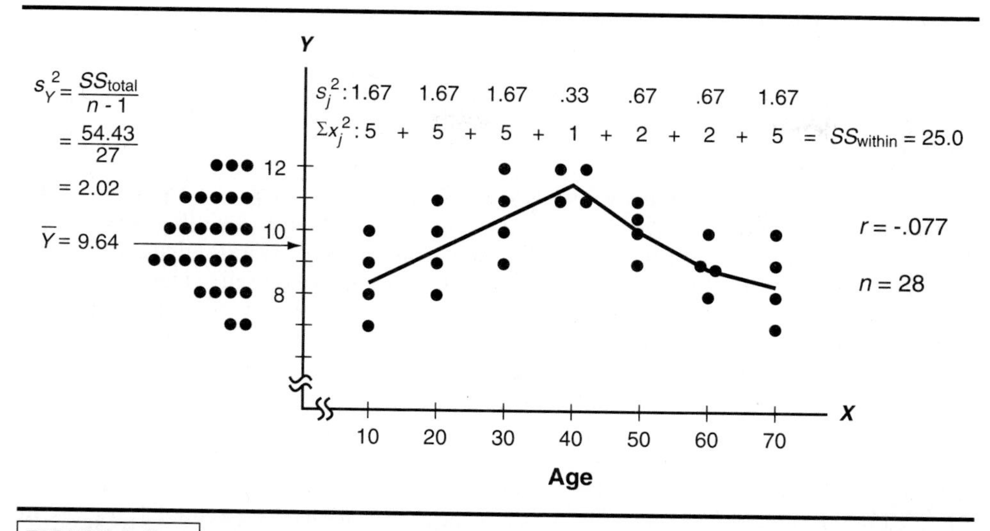

**FIGURE 8.9** An Illustration of a Nonlinear Relationship between Age and Psychomotor Performance

subtest rise in straight line fashion from age ten to a peak at age forty and then decline rather rapidly. The data depicted in Figure 8.9 are tabulated in Table 8.5. Equation 8.23 defines a measure of the relationship (linear or nonlinear) between $X$ and $Y$, and is denoted $\eta$ (the Greek letter eta) for the parameter and $\hat{\eta}$ for an estimate. ($\eta^2$ is also termed the "correlation ratio.") Note from Equation 8.23 that, unlike $r$, $\eta$ is always positive:

$$\hat{\eta}^2_{Y.X} = 1 - \frac{SS_{within}}{SS_{total}} \quad \textbf{(8.23)}$$

where $SS_{total} = \Sigma_j \Sigma_i (Y_{ij} - \overline{Y}_{\bullet})^2$, that is, the sum of the squared deviations for all $n_{\bullet}$ scores from the mean of all $n_{\bullet}$ scores, $\overline{Y}_{\bullet}$.

**TABLE 8.5** Psychomotor Performance of 28 Persons in Seven Age Groups

| | *Age* | | | | | | | |
|---|---|---|---|---|---|---|---|---|
| | *10* | *20* | *30* | *40* | *50* | *60* | *70* | |
| *j*: | *1* | *2* | *3* | *4* | *5* | *6* | *7 = J* | |
| | 7 | 8 | 9 | 11 | 9 | 8 | 7 | |
| | 8 | 9 | 10 | 11 | 10 | 9 | 8 | |
| | 9 | 10 | 11 | 12 | 10 | 9 | 9 | |
| | 10 | 11 | 12 | 12 | 11 | 10 | 10 | |
| Means: | 8.5 | 9.5 | 10.5 | 11.5 | 10.0 | 9.0 | 8.5 | $\overline{Y}_{\bullet} = 9.64$ |
| $SS_j$: | 5.0 | 5.0 | 5.0 | 1.0 | 2.0 | 2.0 | 5.0 | |

$\Sigma_j SS_j = SS_{within} = 25.00$

$SS_{\text{within}}$ is obtained in the following manner: For each of the $J = 7$ different $X_j$'s, the corresponding $Y$-scores are deviated from their own mean, $\overline{Y}_j$, and the sum of squares for each of the $J$ groups is calculated, and aggregated to form $SS_{\text{within}}$. For example, in Table 8.5 the sum of squares for group $j = 1$ (age ten) is $(7 - 8.5)^2 + (8 - 8.5)^2 + (9 - 8.5)^2 + (10 - 8.5)^2 = 5.0$. This process is repeated for each of the $J$ groups. Finally, the $J = 7$ sums of squared deviations are combined; the result is $SS_{\text{within}}$.

For the data in Table 8.5, the value of $SS_{\text{total}}$ is 54.43 and the value of $SS_{\text{within}}$ is 25.00. Hence, the value of $\hat{\eta}_{Y.X}$ is $\sqrt{.541} = .736$, since $\eta^2_{Y.X} = 1 - 25.00/54.43 = 1 - .459 = .541$.

The following considerations bear on the interpretation of $\eta_{Y.X}$. Notice that subscript "$Y$" precedes the "dot," followed by the subscript, "$X$". $\eta_{Y.X}$ is a measure of the extent to which $Y$ is predictable from $X$ by a "best-fitting" line, a line that may be either straight or curved. It is important to note that $\eta_{Y.X}$ and $\eta_{X.Y}$ will generally have different values. This is contrary to our experience with $r$, for which it is always true that $r_{XY} = r_{YX}$. We can illustrate the fact that $\eta_{Y.X}$ and $\eta_{X.Y}$ may not be equal using Figure 8.9. If a person's age is 20, $Y$ can be predicted to be near 9. However, if a person's $Y$ score is 9, the associated age $X$ cannot be accurately predicted; the person might either be around age 20 or age 60. Hence, $Y$ can be predicted from $X$ reasonably well, but $X$ cannot be predicted well from $Y$. These facts are reflected in the values of $\hat{\eta}_{Y.X} = .736$; whereas $\hat{\eta}_{X.Y}$ (which was not calculated) is close to zero, $\hat{\eta}_{X.Y} = .126$.

The difference in the value of $\hat{\eta}_{Y.X}$ and the value of $r_{YX}$ represents nonlinearity in the data set. The value $\hat{\eta}_{Y.X}$ will always be somewhat larger than $r_{YX}$ in a sample. Use of this fact is made to test for nonlinearity (Chapter 17). The curvilinear prediction line for predicting $Y$ from $X$ appears in Figure 8.9.

## 8.28 TRANSFORMING NONLINEAR RELATIONSHIPS INTO LINEAR RELATIONSHIPS

A nonlinear relationship can sometimes be converted into a more nearly linear relationship by a mathematical transformation of $X$ or $Y$ (or both). Growth curves of infants have a curvilinear relationship with age; however, it has been shown that this relationship becomes essentially normal if $X$ is not age, but a logarithmic transformation of age (Pomerance and Krall, 1981). The strong nonlinear relationship in Figure 7.4 (Section 7.7) would become somewhat more nearly linear if the abscissa were not $X$, but log $X$, $\sqrt{X}$, $\sqrt[3]{X}$, et cetera, and/or the ordinate were not $Y$ but $Y^2$ or $Y^3$. Transformation can also reduce the skewness evident in both $X$ and $Y$ (Section 6.11).[24]

## 8.29 DICHOTOMOUS DEPENDENT VARIABLES: LOGISTIC REGRESSION

Multiple regression is the method of choice when the intent is to predict performance on a criterion for which the numbers fall on a continuum. The assumption of bivariate normality cannot be met when the criterion is a dichotomy or a categorical variable. The prediction of dichotomous (0 versus 1) criterion variables is common, such as predicting who will and

[24] Additional considerations of various kinds of nonlinear relationships are found in Chapter 17 (Trend Analysis—Section 17.19).

who will not (a) drop out of school, (b) contract a certain disease, (c) be alive at age 80, (d) complete a doctoral program, (e) default on a loan, or (f) be a repeat offender if a felon. The underlying rationale for *logistic*[25] *regression* is very similar to that for multiple regression, even though the mathematical criterion of maximum likelihood rather than least squares is employed; the independent variables should be correlated with the dichotomous criterion and contribute non-redundant information. Logistic regression does *not* assume that the dependent variable (probability of being in the group coded 1) is a linear function of the independent variables.

The probability of an event (e.g., falling in group 1) can be expressed as:

$$\text{probability of event "1"} = \frac{1}{1+e^{-z}} \tag{8.24}$$

where $e$ is the base of the natural logarithms (≈2.718), and $z$ is found from the use of an equation that weights the predictors optimally. Obviously, the probability of being in category 1 will be greater than 0, but less than 1:

$$z = B_1X_1 + B_2X_2 + \cdots B_mX_m + C \tag{8.25}$$

where the coefficients, $B_1, B_2, \ldots, B_m$, and the constant, $C$, are determined mathematically to maximize the likelihood that the prediction is correct. Like multiple regression, the computations are too complex to be done by hand.

Logistic regression is an alternative statistical method. It makes fewer restrictive assumptions than multiple regression.[26] The conceptual and statistical rationale for logistic regression is conceptually similar to multiple regression—combine information from a set of independent variables to predict with maximal accuracy the probability of falling into category 1 or 0 of the dichotomous dependent variable. Most comprehensive computer program packages have procedures for discriminant analysis and several also include logistic regression. If one understands the rationale and procedures for multiple regression, the extension to discriminant analysis or logistic regression is a logical progression.

From the Chapman data set, with the criterion variable being: 1 = coronary incident, and 0 = non-coronary incident (during the decade of the study), Equation 8.25 is:

$$z = .057(\text{Age}) + .005(\text{CHOLES}) - .010(\text{DIABP}) + .007(\text{SYSBP}) + .019(\text{WT}) - .079(\text{HT}) - 3.980$$

where the values for the independent variables were obtained at the beginning of the study.[27] Use this equation to estimate the probability that a fifty-year-old man with a choles-

[25]The term "logistic" is related to the fact that the logarithm of the odds is sometimes called the "logit."

[26]Discriminant analysis (Section 8.30) is an alternative statistical procedure for predicting a criterion that represents a nominal scale. Unlike discriminant analysis, logistic regression does not assume that the independent variables are normally distributed and have homogeneous variance-covariance matrices for all groups being contrasted (Stevens, 1986). Logistic regression uses maximum likelihood, rather than the least-squares statistical criterion to obtain coefficients.

[27]Recall that the data are based on men.

terol level of 300, diastolic blood pressure of 90, systolic blood pressure of 130, weight of 200 pounds, and a height of 70 inches will have a coronary during the next ten years:

$$z = .057(50) + .005(300) - .010(90) + .007(130) + .019(200) - .079(70) - 3.980 = -1.350$$

and, from Equation 8.24, the probability[28] of a coronary equals:

$$\frac{1}{1+e^{-(-1.35)}} = \frac{1}{1+e^{1.35}} = \frac{1}{1+3.857} = \frac{1}{4.857} = .206$$

that is, the chances are approximately one in five that this man, and his statistical twins, will experience a coronary incident sometime during the next ten years.

## 8.30 CATEGORICAL DEPENDENT VARIABLES WITH MORE THAN TWO CATEGORIES: DISCRIMINANT ANALYSIS

Far less common is the situation in which the variable to be predicted is a nominal scale with more than two categories, such as predicting college major, occupation, or diagnosis. *Discriminant analysis* is the most widely used statistical method for predicting a categorical outcome variable in which there are two or more groups. In discriminant analysis, a new variable (called the discriminant or discriminant variable) is constructed from the independent variables that are weighted in such a way that the mean score on the discriminant variable for one group differs maximally from the mean discriminant score of the other group(s).[29] Based on the discriminant score, the probability of falling into each category can be calculated for each case. Unlike multiple regression, discriminant analysis allows one to specify the proportions that would fall into each category. These proportions can be calculated for each case. Unlike multiple regression, discriminant analysis allows one to specify the proportions that would fall within each category when no information is available; these "prior probabilities" affect the probabilities yielded by discriminant analysis.[30]

## 8.31 CHAPTER SUMMARY

Correlation and regression are opposite sides of the same coin. If $r = 1.0$, there is no regression toward the mean; if $r = .5$, scores tend to regress half the distance to the mean in standard score units. Stated differently, scores tend to regress by an amount, $1 - r$, in standard deviation units.

The expression $\hat{z}_Y = rz_X$ is the simplest form of the regression equation; equivalently, $r = \hat{z}_Y/z_X$ shows $r$ to be an expected rate of change in $z_Y$ per unit change in $z_X$. The correlation of the criterion scores with the predicted criterion scores is $r$; $\hat{z}_Y$ is simply a linear transformation of $z_X$, that is, $\hat{z}_Y = rz_X$. The variance in $\hat{z}_Y$-values is $r^2$ and is the proportion of

[28]To obtain the value of $e^{1.35}$, enter 1.35 on your calculator, then hit the $e^x$ key to obtain $(2.718)^{1.35} = 3.857$.

[29]In analysis of variance (Chapter 15) terminology, the coefficients in discriminant analysis are selected so that the ratio "between-groups sum of squares/within-groups sum of squares" is a maximum.

[30]Related to Bayes's theorem (Section 9.7)

variance in the criterion that is predictable from the independent variable ("coefficient of determination" is an unfortunate alias of $r^2$).

The differences between observed $Y_i$'s from predicted $\hat{Y}_i$'s are termed "residuals" or "errors of estimate." The standard deviation of residuals is termed the "standard error of estimate" ($s_{Y.X}$); $s_{Y.X}$, together with $\hat{Y}$ can estimate the proportion of observed $Y_i$-values that are expected to fall above or below any $Y$-value, assuming bivariate normality. Bivariate normal distributions are three-dimensional bell-shaped "hats," with varying degrees of elongation. Linearity and homoscedasticity are characteristics of all bivariate normal distributions.

The regression line (the $\hat{Y}_i$'s) is defined by the least-squares criterion—no other straight line can be drawn that will have so small a sum of the squared residuals. In multiple regression, two or more predictors are used to predict a dependent variable. The resulting correlation between $Y$ and $\hat{Y}$, values based on the optimally weighted predictors, is maximal; this is termed the "multiple correlation coefficient." The multiple $R$'s from a sample overestimate the corresponding parameter because they capitalize on sampling error ("fits error"). The degree of bias increases as the number of predictors ($m$) increases and the sample size ($n$) decreases. Ideally, for every independent variable to be used in obtaining a prediction equation, one should have fifty or more cases so that the amount of sampling error in the regression weights and the multiple correlation will be minimized. Multiple $R$'s can never be negative.

Partial correlation can be useful to estimate the correlation between two variables with the effects of one or more other variables statistically held constant. Partial correlations are correlations between residuals after both variables have been predicted by one or more ancillary variables.

Standardized regression coefficients ("beta weights") are regression coefficients when all variables are expressed as $z$-scores. Since all independent variables have a variance of 1, beta weights can be compared more directly than regression coefficients for raw scores of $X_1, X_2, X_3, \ldots, X_m$.

In stepwise multiple regression, the variable that correlates most highly with the criterion is selected first. The second variable that enters the regression equation is the variable that adds the greatest amount of unique, relevant variance, that is, the variable that has the highest partial correlation with the dependent variable.

Although the degree of variability greatly influences the correlation coefficient, it does not affect the predicted values on the dependent variable or the standard error of estimate. When a relationship between two variables is nonlinear, it often can be converted into a linear relationship by employing various mathematical transformations. The magnitude of a nonlinear relationship can be described by $\eta$; $\eta^2$ describes the proportion of variance in the criterion that is predictable, allowing the regression line to be a smooth curve.

When the dependent variable is not continuous, but dichotomous, discriminant analysis or logistic regression is preferable to multiple regression. If there are more than two categories of a nominal variable, discriminant analysis is the statistical method of choice.

## 8.32 CASE STUDY

Although no curvilinearity between cholesterol level with age is apparent in the scatterplot in Figure 7.14, we will estimate $\eta$ and study the matter further. We will form five age groups: 1: 21–30, 2: 31–40, 3: 41–50, 4: 51–60, and 5: 61–70. The means, standard deviations and other descriptive information are given in Table 8.6.

**TABLE 8.6** Descriptive Information on Cholesterol Levels for Five Age Groups

| *Age Group (J)* | $n$ | $\overline{Y}$ | $s_Y$ | $SS_{Within}$[31] | |
|---|---|---|---|---|---|
| 1 | 39 | 234.8 | 58.32 | 129,246 | |
| 2 | 53 | 283.8 | 63.70 | 211,000 | |
| 3 | 51 | 288.0 | 50.94 | 129,744 | |
| 4 | 41 | 318.2 | 64.37 | 165,740 | |
| 5 | 16 | 317.8 | 54.74 | 44,947 | $680{,}677 = SS_{within}$ |
| Total Group | 200 | 285.11 | 65.04 | $841{,}810 = SS_{total}$ | |

[31]That is, sum of squares within each of the five age groups

Equation 8.23 defines $\hat{\eta}^2$: $\hat{\eta}^2 = 1 - SS_{within}/SS_{total}$. Note above that for the cholesterol level for the total group: $\overline{Y} = 285.1$ and $s_Y = 65.0$; thus $s_Y^2 = (65.04)^2 = 4230.2 = SS_{total}/(n-1)$; therefore $SS_{total} = 4230.2(199) = 841{,}810$. The value of $SS_{within}$ found in Table 8.6 is 680,677; thus $\hat{\eta}^2 = 1 - 680{,}677/841{,}810 = 1 - 0.809 = .191$; hence, $\hat{\eta} = .437$, which is not significantly greater than $r = .41$. Consequently, we can use the standard linear regression equation to predict the mean of the cholesterol level for any age group. Table 5.2 gave the needed data for age: $\overline{X} = 42.6$, $s_X = 11.6$. Construct the regression equation, $Y_i = bX_i + c$, for predicting cholesterol level from age (Equations 8.2–8.2B):

$$b = r\frac{s_Y}{s_X} = .41\frac{65.0}{11.6} = 2.30$$

$$c = \overline{Y} - b\overline{X} = 285.11 - 2.30(42.6) = 187.1$$

Consequently the regression equation becomes: $\hat{Y}_i = 2.3X_i + 187.1$.

Predict the mean and standard deviation of cholesterol level at 35 years of age. At $X = 35$, the average cholesterol level is estimated to be: $\hat{Y}_i = 2.3(35) + 187.1 = 267.6$. Since the scatterplot appears to evidence homoscedasticity,[32] Equation 8.10 can be used to estimate the standard deviation of cholesterol levels at age 35: $s_{Y.X}^2 = s_Y^2(1 - r^2) = (65.0)^2(1 - .41^2) = (4225)(.832) = 3514.8$, or $s_{Y.X} = 59.3$. If you are a male of age 35 and your cholesterol level is 208, how do you compare with your age peers?[33]

## Multiple Regression

A multiple regression equation was developed[34] for predicting cholesterol level ($Y$) from age ($X_1$), systolic blood pressure ($X_2$), diastolic blood pressure ($X_3$), height ($X_4$), and weight ($X_5$):

$$\hat{Y}_i = 2.08X_{1_i} - .01X_{2_i} + .08X_{3_i} - .67X_{4_i} + .01X_{5_i} + 196.85$$

[32]Statistical tests for homoscedasticity are treated in Chapter 16.

[33] A cholesterol level of 208 is 59.6 points, or approximately one standard error of estimate ($s_{Y.X}$) below the mean of 267.6; thus, your cholesterol level is below that of about 84% of your age peers.

[34]This can be obtained from any statistical software package or spreadsheet.

To illustrate the use of the regression equation, predict the cholesterol level for Lee: Age = 60, SBP = 130, DBP = 75, height = 73″, and weight = 190 lbs.:

$$\hat{Y}_i = 2.08(60) - .01(130) + .08(75) - .67(73) + .01(190) + 196.85$$

$$\hat{Y}_i = 279.3$$

Notice how the regression coefficients can be used to predict a difference in the dependent variable from a change in any of the five independent variables. The regression coefficient for age ($b_1$) equals 2.08, thus the predicted increase in $Y$ (cholesterol level) is about 2 units per year. If the person above were 10 years younger, predict the cholesterol level: It would be 2.08(10) or 20.8 units less or 258.5.

The standard error of estimate is 59.3. Can you estimate the proportion of persons who statistically look like Lee but will have cholesterol levels below 200? The distribution of residuals will have a mean of 0, and a standard deviation ($s_{Y.12345}$) of 59.3, thus $z = (200 - 279.3)/59.3 = -1.34$. We remember from Chapter 6 that in a normal distribution 16% of the observations will fall beyond a point that is one standard deviation below the mean, (e.g., $z = -1$); thus, less than 16% of Lee's statistical twins would have cholesterol levels below 200. Finding $z = -1.34$ in Table A, we see that .901 or about 9% of the cases would be expected to fall below 200. What percent of Lee's statistical twins would have cholesterol levels above 300? Since 300 is $(300 - 279.3)/59.3 \approx .35 = z$, we find from Table A that about 36% would be expected to have cholesterol levels above 300.

## Standardized Regression Equation

The corresponding standardized regression equation is

$$\hat{z}_{Y_i} = .372\hat{\beta}_{1_i} + (-.002)\hat{\beta}_{2_i} + .084\hat{\beta}_{3_i} + (-.026)\hat{\beta}_{4_i} + .004\hat{\beta}_{5_i}, \text{ or,}$$

$$\hat{z}_{Y_i} = .372\hat{\beta}_{1_i} - .002\hat{\beta}_{2_i} + .084\hat{\beta}_{3_i} - .026\hat{\beta}_{4_i} + .004\hat{\beta}_{5_i}.$$

Note that the standardized regression coefficients differ greatly from the raw score regression coefficients. The beta coefficients illuminate the fact that the lion's share of the prediction is carried by the age variable.

Note that although SBP and DBP both correlated equally ($r = .23$ with the dependent variable, see Table 7.7), their respective regression coefficients are not only unequal, but they differ in sign (–.002 versus .084)! This illustrates an important caution, and a frequent error in interpreting multiple regression analyses: *Regression coefficients* should *not* be interpreted causally; furthermore, the interpretation of regression coefficients to assess the importance or influence of a variable is risky business (Darlington, 1968). Variables that correlate equally with the criterion may have very different regression coefficients.

## Normality of Residuals

A distribution of the residuals should be approximately normal if probabilities based on the normal curve are applied to the residuals. Most multiple regression programs offer options for plotting residuals. Figure 8.10 is a plot of the *standardized residuals* provided by the computer. If each residual is divided by the standard error of estimate, it becomes a type of

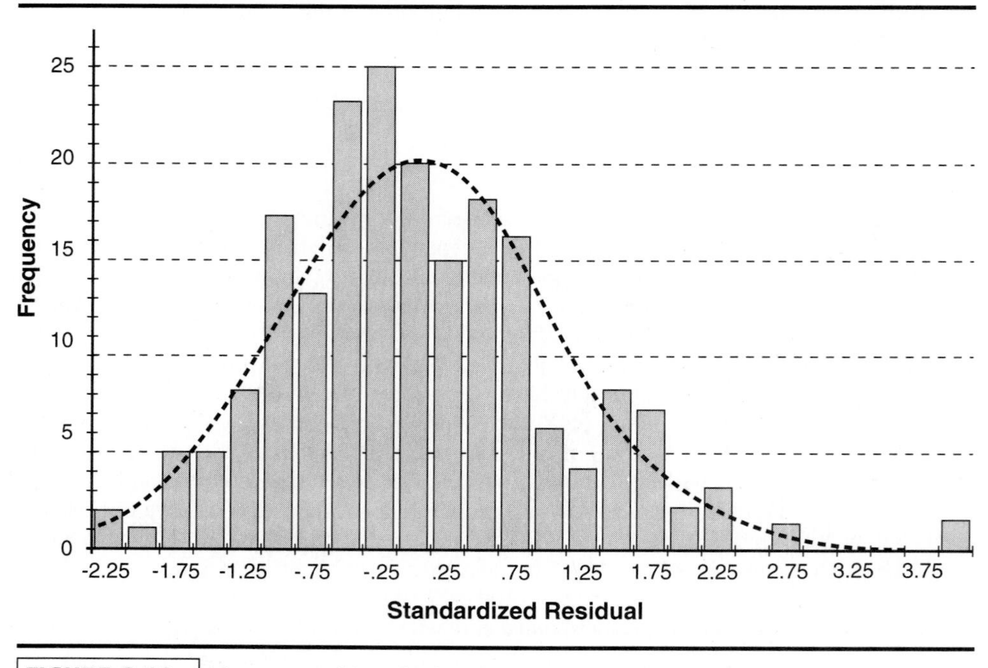


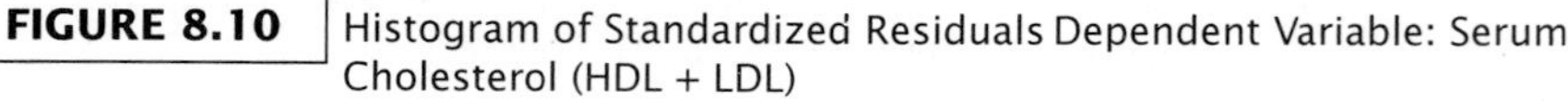

**FIGURE 8.10** Histogram of Standardized Residuals Dependent Variable: Serum Cholesterol (HDL + LDL)

$z$-score.[35] A visual check suggests that the normality assumption of the residuals is not unreasonable.[36] There were two outliers ($z \geq 2.70$), but no extreme outliers (i.e., no standardized residuals is greater than 4.72; see Section 3.9).

An orthodox multiple regression makes assumptions that can be evaluated by studying the residuals. If the relationship is linear, there should be no correlation between the absolute values of the residuals and $\hat{Y}$ (predicted values on the criterion). A visual check of the scatterplot is usually sufficient to detect a substantial nonlinear relationship. Figure 8.11 is a multiple regression computer output that plots residuals on the vertical axis in relation to predicted $z$-scores on $Y$ ($\hat{z}_Y$). No obvious relationship is apparent from the scatterplot; thus, there is nothing to suggest a nonlinear relationship. The correlation between the absolute values of the residuals with $\hat{z}_Y$ was actually .002. If the relationship is linear with homoscedasticity, the correlation of $\hat{Y}$ and the absolute values of the residuals will not differ significantly from 0.

## 8.33 SUGGESTED COMPUTER ACTIVITY

Using the High School and Beyond data set, use multiple regression to predict writing scores using as independent variables: sex, school type, SES, self-concept, and motivation measures. Determine which of the set of predictors are superfluous.

[35] $z_i = (Y_i - \hat{Y}_i)/s_{Y.12\ldots m}$

[36] Procedures for testing the assumption of normality are considered in Chapter 14.

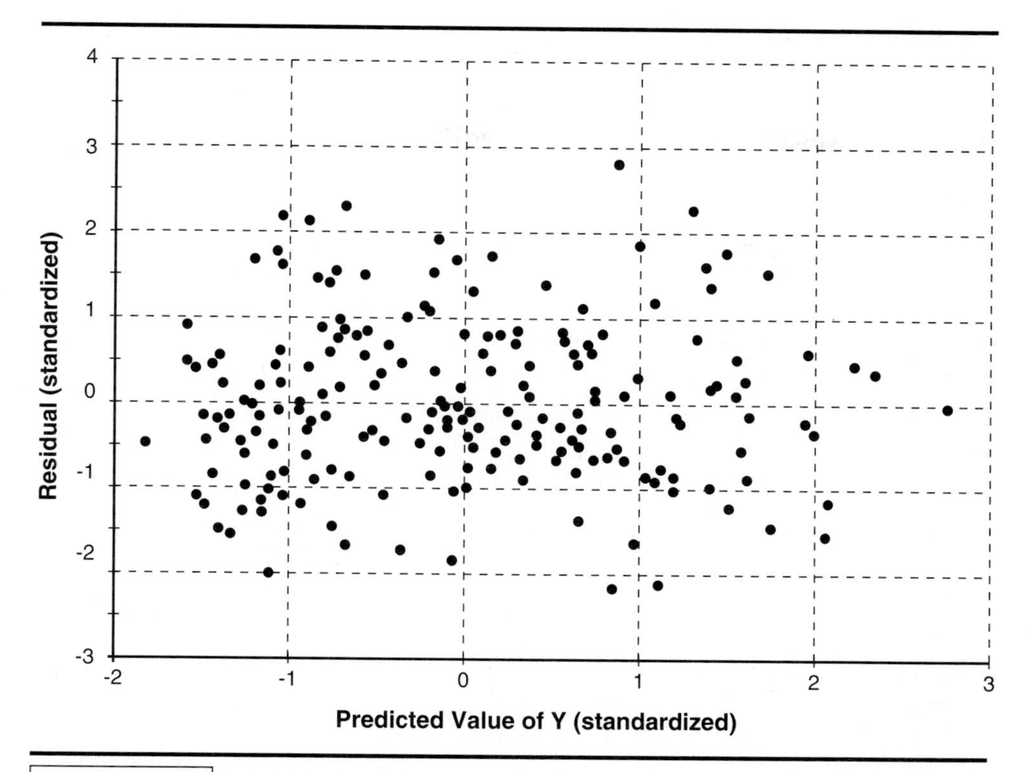


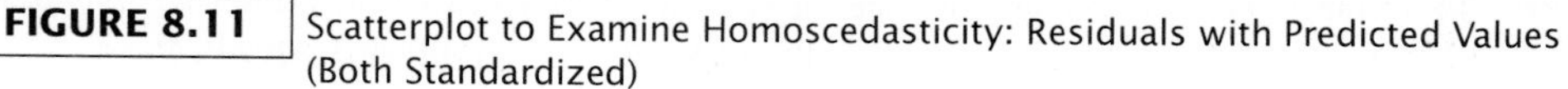
**FIGURE 8.11** Scatterplot to Examine Homoscedasticity: Residuals with Predicted Values (Both Standardized)

## MASTERY TEST

**1.** Which term least belongs with the other three?

(a) independent variable (b) predictor variable
(c) X-variable (d) criterion variable

**2.** Which term least belongs with the other three?

(a) dependent variable (b) independent variable
(c) predicted variable (d) criterion variable

**3.** Which term least belongs with the other three?

(a) percentile (b) correlation (c) regression (d) prediction

**4.** If $r = .5$ and $z_X = 2.0$, what is $\hat{z}_Y$?

**5.** The $\hat{z}_Y$ from item 4 would be expected to correspond to what percentile in the entire distribution of $Y$? Assume a normal distribution.

(a) $P_{50}$ (b) $P_{75}$ (c) $P_{84}$ (d) $P_{98}$

**6.** If $r = .5$, for persons at $P_2$ on $X$, what is their average percentile on $Y$?

(a) $P_{50}$ (b) $P_{75}$ (c) $P_{16}$ (d) $P_2$

7. If $r = -.6$ and $z_X = -1.5$, what is $\hat{z}_Y$?
8. If $r = 1.0$, are scores on $X$ and $Y$ certainly identical for all pairs of observations?
9. If $r$ is greater than 0, is the variance in predicted $z$-scores on $Y$ (the $\hat{z}_Y$'s) less than 1.0?
10. If $r = .8$, do persons below the mean on $X$ tend to have higher $z$-scores on $Y$ than on $X$?
11. If for $z_X = 1.0$, and $\hat{z}_Y = .75$, is $r = .75$?
12. Other things being equal, as the value of $r$ increases, does the standard error of estimate increase?
13. When predicting $Y$ from $X$, if $s_X = s_Y = 15$, does the correlation coefficient ($r$) equal the regression coefficient ($b$)?
14. In a bivariate normal distribution, is the regression of $Y$ on $X$ always linear?
15. In $z$-score units, will $s_{Y.X}$ always equal $s_{X.Y}$?
16. If $s_Y = 10$ and $r = .6$, what is the value of $s_{Y.X}$? $\left(s_{Y.X} = s_Y\sqrt{1-r^2}\right)$
17. Assume bivariate normality.
    (a) If $s_{Y.X} = 8$, what percentage of the actual $Y$-scores will be within 8 points of the predicted values?
    (b) What percentage of the observations on $Y$ will be more than 8 points higher than predicted?
    (c) Will the percentage under-predicted by more than 8 points be expected to be the same as in (b) above?
18. The correlation between a parent's IQ score and the IQ score of an offspring is about .5; moreover, we know that $\mu_X = \mu_Y = 100$ and that $\sigma_X = \sigma_Y = 15$.
    (a) Estimate the average IQ of children of mothers with IQ = 130.
    (b) Estimate the average IQ of children of fathers with IQ = 90.
    (c) Estimate the average IQ of children of mothers with IQ = 100.
19. The average IQ of both parents correlates approximately .6 with their offspring's IQ ($Y$). From the information given, what is the value of the standard error of estimate for predicting $Y$?
20. If $s_{Y.X} = 12$, the observed IQ scores will be within 12 points of the predicted IQ's for what percentage of the children?
21. For high multiple correlations, one wants independent variables that correlate (high or low?) with the dependent variable and correlate (high or low?) with each other.
22. To estimate the correlation between variables $X$ and $Y$ with the effects of variable $Z$ removed from both $X$ and $Y$, one would use
    (a) partial correlation (b) part correlation
    (c) multiple correlation (d) point-biserial correlation
23. Match the term in the left-hand column with its definition in the right-hand column.

| | |
|---|---|
| A. $r_{XY.Z}$ | (a) regression coefficient |
| B. $b_{Y.X}$ | (b) simple correlation |
| C. $r$ | (c) standard error of estimate |
| D. $s_{Y.X}$ | (d) multiple correlation |
| E. $R_{Y.XZ}$ | (e) second-order partial correlation |
| F. $\hat{Y}$ | (f) predicted $z$-score on $Y$ |
| G. $\hat{z}_Y$ | (g) predicted score on $Y$ |
| H. $r_{X(Y.Z)}$ | (h) beta weight |
| I. $\beta_1$ | (i) correlation ratio (eta squared) |
| J. $\hat{Y}_i - Y_i$ | (j) residual |
| K. $r_{12.34}$ | (k) part correlation |
| L. $\eta^2_{Y.X}$ | (l) first-order partial correlation |

**24.** If variable $Y$ is predicted from variable $X$ and the resulting residuals are correlated with variable $Z$, this correlation is a

(a) part correlation
(b) partial correlation
(c) multiple correlation
(d) stepwise multiple correlation
(e) beta weight

**25.** The correlation in the previous question would be denoted as

(a) $r_{ZY.X}$
(b) $r_{Z(Y.X)}$
(c) $R_{Z.YX}$
(d) $\beta_{Z.YX}$

**26.** When all variables are standardized using the $z$-scale, the regression coeffficients for the $m$ predictor variables are

(a) equal
(b) beta weights
(c) equal to raw-score regression coefficients
(d) parameters

**27.** If $r_{Y1} = 0$, $\hat{\beta}_1$

(a) may be positive
(b) may be negative
(c) may be zero
(d) two of the above
(e) all of the above

**28.** If $r_{Y1} = r_{Y2} = r_{12} = .5$, what is the value of the multiple correlation, $R_{Y.12}$? (See Equation 8.19).

**29.** If $r_{YA} = .4$, $r_{YB} = .5$, $r_{YC} = .4$, $r_{AB} = .5$, $r_{AC} = 0$, and $r_{BC} = 0$, which of the predictor variables, $A$, $B$, or $C$, will be selected in Step 1, a stepwise multiple regression?

**30.** Which independent variable will be entered in Step 2?

**31.** Using the related multiple regression equation in Table 8.4 (Step 3), predict the reading test score for a girl having an IQ score of 130 and a RR score of 60. What is the predicted score for a boy with the same scores?

**32.** In a multiple regression involving five predictors and 206 persons, the sum of the squared residuals is 800. What is the value of the standard error of estimate $s_{Y.12345}$? (Use Equation 8.20.)

**33.** In the previous question, estimate ${}_{\text{adj}}R_{Y.12345}$ if $s_Y^2 = 8$ (see Equation 8.22).

**34.** When viewed as an inferential statistic, the observed multiple correlation $R_{Y.12...m}$

(a) is unbiased
(b) tends to overestimate the value of the parameter
(c) tends to underestimate the value of the parameter

**35.** The degree of bias in $R_{Y.12...m}$ will be least in which of these situations?

(a) $n$ is large and $m$ is large
(b) $n$ is small and $m$ is large
(c) $n$ is large and $m$ is small
(d) $n$ is small and $m$ is small

**36.** Which one of these is not assumed in multiple regression?

(a) Variable $Y$, the dependent variable, is normally distributed
(b) All independent variables are normally distributed

(c) The scatterplot possesses homoscedasticity
(d) The relationship between the $Y$'s and $\hat{Y}$'s is linear

**37.** Eta, $\hat{\eta}$, will exceed $r$ except when
(a) $SS_{\text{within}} = SS_{\text{residuals}}$
(b) $SS_{\text{within}} < SS_{\text{total}}$
(c) $SS_{\text{total}} = SS_{\text{residuals}}$
(d) $r = 0$

**38.** Does $r_{YX} = r_{XY}$? Does $\hat{\eta}_{Y.X}$ usually have exactly the same value as $\hat{\eta}_{X.Y}$?

**39.** Is the use of regression coefficients recommended to determine the causal influence of the various independent variables?

**40.** If the magnitude of the residuals increases as $\hat{Y}$ increases, homoscedasticity is confirmed. (true or false)

*Based on the information given for predicting performance on the criterion variables specified in items 41–44, which one of the following procedures is the method of choice?*

Multiple Regression (MR)
Logistic Regression (LR)

**41.** To predict GPA from a sibling's GPA and IQ score.

**42.** To predict whether a child will, or will not, drop out of school.

**43.** To predict a child's adult height from the child's sex, height at age two, and the height of the child's mother and father.

**44.** To predict the probability that a graduate school applicant will attain a Ph.D. degree from undergraduate GPA, GRE scores, age, sex, letters of recommendation (converted to a five-point numerical scale).

**45.** To predict college major from age, sex, SES, high school grade point average, and SAT scores, and other personological variables, which statistical procedure is recommended?

## PROBLEMS AND EXERCISES

**1.** The figure on page 193 is a computer produced scatterplot of IQ scores obtained by 354 children tested at grade five ($X$) and two years later in grade seven ($Y$). Before finding the regression equation $Y_i = bX_i + c$ for predicting $Y$ from $X$, study the scatterplot and answer the following questions.
(a) What were the lowest and highest IQ scores obtained at grade five?
(b) What were the lowest and highest IQ scores obtained at grade seven?
(c) Does the regression appear linear?
(d) Does the scatterplot appear to possess homoscedasticity?
(e) Does the scatterplot appear to be approximately bivariate normal?
(f) Compute $b_{Y.X} = r(s_Y/s_X) = b$.
(g) Compute $c = \bar{Y} - b\bar{X}$.
(h) Express the regression equation using $b$ and $c$.
(i) Bob obtained a CTMM IQ score of 140 at grade five. Predict his IQ score on the same test at grade seven.
(j) Sam's IQ score at grade five was 70. Predict his grade seven IQ score.

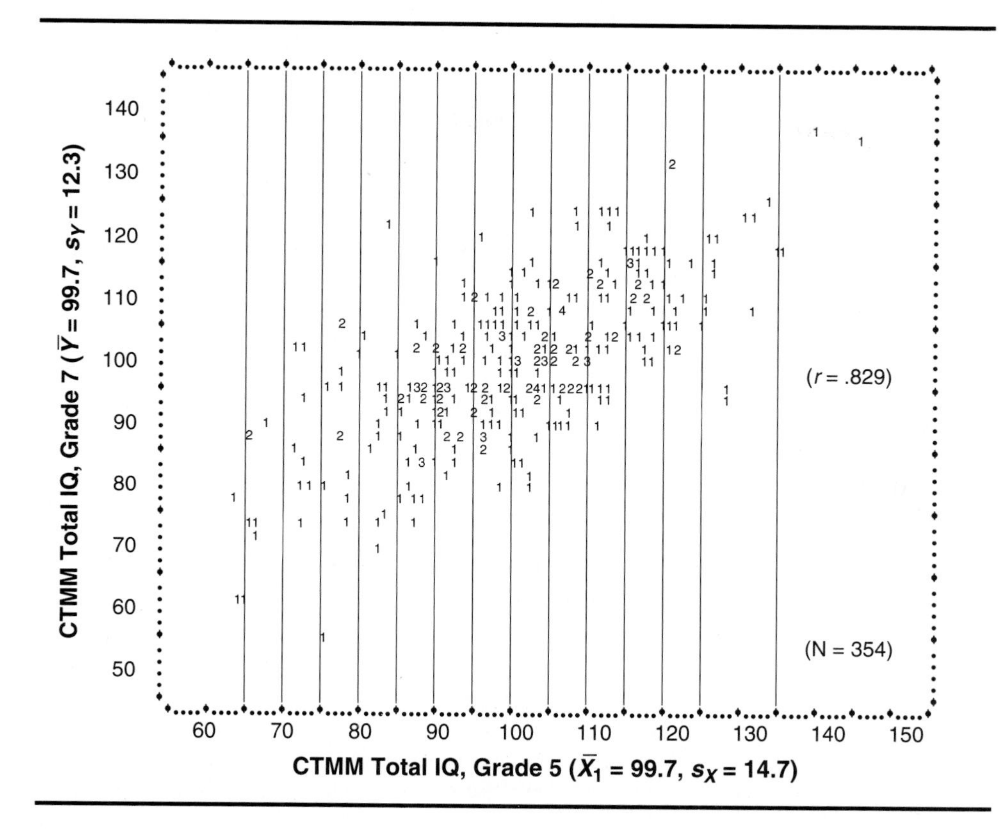


(k) Draw in the regression line in the figure (use $X$'s and $Y$'s from exercises "i" and "j").
(l) Compute the standard error of estimate, $s_{Y.X}$.
(m) What percentage of the grade seven predictions will be within seven points of the observed values?
(n) Draw in dotted lines one $s_{Y.X}$ above and one $s_{Y.X}$ below the regression line.
(o) Chances are about 2 in 3 that Bob's IQ score at grade seven will be between ____ and ____, and that Sam's IQ score will be between ____ and ____.
(p) Assuming bivariate normality, what percentage of those who score 140 at grade five will score as high or higher at grade seven?
(q) Assuming bivariate normality, for every 1,000 persons scoring 70 at grade five, how many would be expected to receive average scores of 100 or better at grade seven?
(r) In the same study, grade three IQ scores ($X_2$) correlated .755 and .651 with IQ scores at grades five ($X_1$) and seven ($Y$), respectively. What is $R_{Y.12}$?
(s) How much of the grade seven IQ variance is predictable using both $X_1$ and $X_2$ as predictors? Compare with $r_{12}^2$. Does variable $X_2$ add substantial relevant variance to that found in variable $X_1$?
(t) Determine the standardized multiple regression equation:

$$\hat{z}_Y = \hat{\beta}_1 X_i + \hat{\beta}_2 X_2$$

(u) Persons who exceeded the means of $X_1$ and $X_2$ each by one standard deviation, tended to exceed $Y$ by ____ standard deviation.

(v) Determine the raw-score multiple regression equation:

$$\hat{Y}_i = b_1 X_{1_i} + b_2 X_{2_i} + c$$

(w) Predict the grade seven IQ score for a student having an IQ score of 140 at both grade three and grade five. Compare with item "i".

(x) Correct $R_{Y.12}$ for bias, and estimate the parameter, $\rho_{Y.12}$. Why does ${}_{\text{adj}}R_{Y.12}$ differ so little from $R_{Y.12}$?

(y) What is the correlation between IQ scores at grades five and seven for persons who had the same IQ score at grade three (i.e., hold grade three IQ scores constant)?

(z) By inspecting the scatterplot, how would the value of $\hat{\eta}_{Y.X}$ compare with $r_{YX}$?

**2.** In the national standardization of the Lorge-Thorndike Intelligence Test and the Iowa Test of Basic Skills, nonverbal IQ scores correlated .82 with reading grade-equivalent scores at grade eight:

| | *IQ* | *Reading* |
|---|---|---|
| $\mu$ | 100 | 8.0 |
| $\sigma$ | 15 | 2.0 |
| | $\rho = .82$ | |

(a) Determine the regression equation to predict grade-equivalent scores in reading from the nonverbal IQ scores. Assume bivariate normality.

(b) What is the average reading score for persons with IQ scores of 100 at grade 8.0?

(c) Persons with IQ scores of 90 have what average reading score at grade 8.0?

(d) Compare the percentile equivalents in exercise 2(c) for $X$ and $\hat{Y}$.

(e) What percentage of the entering eighth-grade pupils with IQ = 90 read above grade level (8.0)? What is the value of $s_{Y.X}$?

(f) What percentage of students at grade 8.0 with IQ = 90, score 9.1 or higher on the reading test?

(g) What is the average reading score for beginning eighth graders at $P_{98}$ on the intelligence test?

(h) What is the reading score in percentile units? (See 2g.)

(i) What percentage of students at grade 8.0 with IQ scores of 130, obtain reading scores below grade level (8.0)?

**3.** One large remedial reading study selected seventh grade students who were reading 2.0 grades or more below grade level (7.0) on a standardized reading test. These students were given special reading treatment and tested one year later with the standardized reading test. The mean scores of the treated groups increased 1.4 grade equivalents from 4.5 to 5.9 during the year interval between the pretest and posttest. Answer the remaining exercises using the following information given from the test manual; assume these "norms" were based on a large representative sample that was tested at the beginning of grade seven (7.0), and again one year later (8.0).

| *Grade 7* | *Grade 8* |
|---|---|
| $\bar{X} = 7.0$ | $\bar{Y} = 8.0$ |
| $s_X = 1.8$ | $s_Y = 1.9$ |
| $r = .8$ | |

(a) What is the regression coefficient $b$?
(b) What is the intercept $c$?
(c) What is the predicted score on the posttest corresponding to the mean pretest score for the treated group?
(d) How does the actual gain compare with the predicted gain?

**4.** The correlation of the mother's height is about .5 with the height of her sons or daughters. The correlation of the father's height with his offspring is the same. The correlation of heights of husbands and wives has been found to be approximately .3.

(a) How accurately can children's height be predicted—that is, what is the multiple correlation—using the height of both parents as predictors?
(b) Other things being equal, what would be the multiple correlation if, instead of .3, the husband-wife correlation were 0.0?
(c) Other things being equal, what would be the effect on $R$ if the husband-wife correlation were greater than .3?
(d) Estimate the correlation between height of mother ($M$) and of daughter ($D$) with no variation in father's height ($F$). For example, for 1,000 daughters whose fathers are 5 ft 8 in., what is the correlation between the daughters' height with their mothers' heights?
(e) Why is $r_{DM.F}$ less than $r_{DM}$ in exercise 4d?

**5.** Commercial speed-reading clinics often quote research showing the correlation of reading speed ($S$) with reading comprehension ($C$), suggesting that if speed is improved, comprehension will also be enhanced. The partial correlation between speed and comprehension drops to nearly zero when intelligence is partialed out. Explain.

**6.** If teaching success could be predicted in advance, the information could be used for selection purposes. The predictability of teaching ability of graduate teaching assistants was studied using various predictors including Graduate Record Examination verbal ($V$) and quantitative ($Q$) scores and undergraduate GPA ($G$) (Vecchio & Costin, 1977). Student satisfaction ratings on a five-point scale were used as the criterion ($Y$). The results are given:

| | $Q$ | $G$ | $Y$ | $s$ | *Mean* |
|---|---|---|---|---|---|
| $V$ | .53 | .32 | .34 | 75 | 623 |
| $Q$ | | .16 | .17 | 87 | 637 |
| $G$ | | | .00 | .30 | 4.56 |
| $Y$ | | | | .41 | 3.67 |

(a) Determine step 1 of the stepwise multiple regression equation $\hat{Y}_i = bX_i + c$.
(b) From the partial correlations $r_{YQ \cdot V}$ and $r_{YG \cdot V}$ determine which predictor variable will be added in step 2.
(c) Determine the standardized multiple regression equation at step 2.
(d) What is the $\hat{z}_Y$ for a person who is $+1s$ above the mean of both predictor variables?
(e) Determine the multiple regression equation at step 2 in raw-score form.
(f) What is the predicted criterion score for a person with $V = 700$ and $G = 3.2$?
(g) What is the multiple correlation $R_{Y \cdot VG}$ associated with Step 2?
(h) How much of the variance in the criterion is predictable using $V$ and $G$?
(i) If step 3 were carried out, would $R_{Y \cdot VGQ}$ be negligibly increased over $R_{Y \cdot VG}$? If the proportion of variance in $Y$ that is predictable from $V$, $G$, and $Q$ is .1225, what is $R_{Y \cdot VGQ}$?

**7.** Figure 8.1 gives a scatterplot of heights of fathers and sons. The mean heights of the sons grouped by the height of the fathers is given below. Compute eta ($\hat{\eta}_{Y \cdot X}$) and compare with $r_{XY} = .56$.

| *Father's Height* | $n$ | $\bar{Y}$ | $s_Y$ | $SS_{Within}$ |
|---|---|---|---|---|
| 73″ | 5 | 72.0 | 2.1 | 4.5 |
| 72″ | 8 | 70.3 | 1.9 | 23.5 |
| 71″ | 15 | 70.6 | 2.3 | 73.6 |
| 70″ | 20 | 69.5 | 1.6 | 49.0 |
| 69″ | 26 | 69.1 | 1.9 | 88.7 |
| 68″ | 26 | 68.6 | 2.0 | 96.3 |
| 67″ | 25 | 67.8 | 2.0 | 95.4 |
| 66″ | 29 | 67.6 | 2.1 | 122.8 |
| 65″ | 19 | 66.8 | 2.2 | 86.5 |
| 64″ | 12 | 66.8 | 1.7 | 33.7 |
| 63″ | 6 | 66.5 | 1.9 | 17.5 |
| 62″ | 2 | 65.5 | 2.1 | 4.5 701.4 = $SS_{\text{within}}$ |
| Total Group | 193 | 68.4 | 2.33 | 1041.6 = $SS_{\text{total}}$ |

## ANSWERS TO MASTERY TEST

1. (d)
2. (b)
3. (a)
4. $\hat{z}_Y = 1.00$
5. (c)
6. (c)
7. +.9
8. Not necessarily, but each pair would have identical $z_X$ and $z_Y$ scores.
9. yes
10. yes, $\hat{z}_Y = .8z_X$
11. yes
12. no, it decreases.
13. yes, $b_{Y.X} = r\left(\frac{s_Y}{s_X}\right) = r\left(\frac{15}{15}\right) = r$
14. yes
15. yes (but not in raw-score units)
16. $s_{Y.X} = 10\sqrt{1 - .36} = 8$
17. (a) 68%
    (b) 16%
    (c) yes
18. (a) 115
    (b) 95
    (c) 100
19. 15(.8) =12
20. 68%
21. high; low
22. (a)
23. A–(l)
    B–(a)
    C–(b)
    D–(c)
    E–(d)
    F–(g)
    G–(f)
    H–(k)
    I–(h)
    J–(j)
    K–(e)
    L–(i)
24. (a)
25. (b)
26. (b)
27. (e)
28. .577
29. B
30. C
31. 35.9, 33.5
32. 2.0
33. $\sqrt{.5} = .707$
34. (b)
35. (c)
36. (b)
37. (a)
38. yes, no
39. no
40. false
41. MR

42. LR
43. MR
44. LR
45. discriminant analysis

## ANSWERS TO PROBLEMS AND EXERCISES

1. (a) 64 and 146
   (b) 55 and 138
   (c) yes
   (d) yes
   (e) yes
   (f) $b_{Y.X} = \frac{.829(12.3)}{14.7} = .694$
   (g) $c = 99.7 - (.694)(99.7) = 30.5$
   (h) $\hat{Y} = .694X + 30.5$
   (i) $\hat{Y} = .694(140) + 30.5 = 128$
   (j) $\hat{Y} = .694(70) + 30.5 = 79$
   (l) $s_{Y.X} = 12.3\sqrt{1-(.829)^2} = 12.3(.559) =$ 6.88 or approximately seven points
   (m) approximately 68%
   (o) 121, 135(128 ± 7); 72, 86(79 ± 7)
   (p) $\frac{Y-\hat{Y}}{s_{Y.X}} = \frac{140-128}{6.88} = 1.74$; from Appendix Table A; only 4%
   (q) $\frac{Y-\hat{Y}}{s_{Y.X}} = \frac{100-79}{6.88} = 3.05$; from Appendix Table A; only about one person per 1,000
   (r) .830
   (s) .6887 is negligibly greater than .6872
   (t) $\hat{z}_{Y_i} = .785z_{1_i} + .058z_{2_i}$
   (u) .84
   (v) $\hat{Y}_i = .657X_{1_i} + .046X_{2_i} + 29.4$
   (w) $\hat{Y} = 127.8$ or 128
   (x) $\hat{R}_{Y.12} = .829$ because $n$ is large and $m$ is only 2.
   (y) $R_{Y1.2} = .678$
   (z) Eta would be negligibly larger than $r$ because the relationship is linear.
2. (a) $b = \frac{(.82)(2.0)}{15} = .11$;

   $c = 8.0 - (.11)(100)$

   $= -3;\ \hat{Y} = bX + c$

   $= .11X - 3$
   (b) 8.0
   (c) $\hat{Y} = .11(90) - 3 = 9.9 - 3 = 6.9$
   (d) An IQ of 90 is equivalent to $z = \frac{90-100}{15} = -.67$, and from Appendix Table A, $P_{25}$; a reading score of 6.9 is equivalent to $\frac{6.9-8.0}{2.0} = -.55$,
   (e) $\hat{Y} = 6.9$;

   $s_{Y.X} = 2.0\sqrt{1-(.82)^2}$

   $= 2.0(.572) = 1.1$; hence,

   $z = \frac{8.0-6.9}{1.1} = 1.0$;

   hence, only 16%
   (f) $z = \frac{9.1-6.9}{1.1} = 2.0$; hence, about 2%
   (g) $P_{98}$ = IQ of 130, $\hat{Y}$ - .11(130) – 3 = 11.3
   (h) $z = \frac{11.3-8.0}{2.0} = \frac{3.3}{2.0}$

   $= 1.65$ or $P_{95}$
   (i) $z = \frac{8.0-11.3}{1.1} = -3$ or .13%
3. (a) $b = r\left(\frac{s_Y}{s_X}\right) = .8\left(\frac{1.9}{1.8}\right) = .84$
   (b) $c = \bar{Y} - b\bar{X} = 8.0 - (.84)(7.0) = 2.1$
   (c) $\bar{Y} = (.84)(4.5) + 2.1 = 5.9$
   (d) They are equal: 1.4 grade equivalents.
4. (a) $R^2 = .385$; $R = .62$
   (b) $R^2 = .5$; $R = .71$
   (c) $R$ would decrease.
   (d) $r_{DM.F} = .42$
   (e) Since $R_{MF}$ is greater than zero, if we hold the father's height constant, we restrict the variance in the mother's height, and, other things being equal, the less the variance in $X$, the lower the correlation $r_{YX}$. (See Figure 7.11.)
5. The correlation between speed and comprehension appears to result from the cor-

relation of each with IQ. For persons of the same IQ, there is little correlation between speed and comprehension. Hence, since an increase in reading speed will not increase IQ, it would be expected to have little effect on comprehension.

**6.** (a) $\overline{Y}_i = .00186V_i + 2.51$
(b) $r_{YQ \cdot V} = -.013$, $r_{YG \cdot V} = -.122$; $G$ will be selected since its absolute value is greatest
(c) $\hat{z}_{Y_i} = .379z_{V_i} - .121z_{G_i}$
(d) .258
(e) $\overline{Y}_i = .00207V_i - .165G_i + 3.133$
(f) 4.06
(g) .34
(h) .12 or 12%
(i) yes, .35

**7.** $\hat{\eta}^2 = 1 - 701.4/1{,}041.6 = .3266$; hence, $\hat{\eta} \approx \sqrt{.3266} \approx .57 \approx r$

# 9

# PROBABILITY

## 9.1 INTRODUCTION

Researchers often attempt to generalize from their observations. They make a tacit assumption that the set of data has some generalizability—if they gathered more data tomorrow, it would reflect the same general trend. Inferences differ in their likelihood of being correct all the way from "extremely unlikely" to "almost certain." From the standpoint of logic, all inferences contain uncertainty. Statisticians have developed methods that assign probabilities to inferences. Inferential reasoning is a principal method of science. The language of everyday life—"extremely unlikely" or "almost certain"—lacks precision.

Statisticians do not completely agree as to how to assign probabilities to statements or how to choose to which statements to assign probabilities. Nonetheless, their preference for objectivity and quantification springs from values regarding the nature and methods of science.

The remaining chapters deal with assigning a probability value to an inference. The methods that statisticians have developed allow one to state, for example, "There is a positive relationship between IQ and grade-point average, and the probability of obtaining such a large $r$ by chance is very small—only .01 if there really is no correlation in the population." Only certain basics of probability theory can be addressed in a single chapter; probability theory is a large and complex body of knowledge. The finer points in probability theory are not needed for using and interpreting the probability statements used in statistical inference. An intuitive understanding of probability is, however, necessary to interpret the statistics of hypothesis testing and interval estimation.

## 9.2 PROBABILITY AS A MATHEMATICAL SYSTEM

Probability can be viewed as a system of definitions and operations pertaining to a sample space. The idea of a *sample space* is basic. Every probability statement is related to a sample space of some sort; indeed, statements of probability are statements about sample spaces.[1]

A sample space can be defined as a set of points. These points can represent persons, businesses, cities, schools, et cetera. An *event* is an observable happening like the appearance of heads when a coin is flipped, or that a person is watching television. There are usually many points in the sample space, each of which is an example of an event. For instance, the sample space may be a set of six white and three black balls in an urn. This sample space has nine points. An event might be "A ball is white." This event has six sample-space points. How many points in the sample space does the event "A ball is black" have? The event "A ball in this urn is red" has no sample points. "A ball in this urn is either white or black" is also an example of an event. Notice that many different events can be defined on the same sample space.

A statement of probability is made about the relative frequency of an event that is associated with a sample space. A capital letter, $A$, $B$, $C$, ..., will stand for an event; the "probability of the event $A$" will be denoted by $P(A)$.

**Definition:** The probability of the event $A$, $P(A)$, is the ratio of the number of sample points that are examples of $A$ to the total finite number of sample points in the sample space, assuming all sample points are equally likely.

Let $A$ be the event "a 3 face of a die," where the sample space is the set of the six faces of a die. How many sample points are examples of the event $A$? Obviously, only one. The total number of sample points is six. Hence, the probability of the event $A$ (3) is:

$$P(A) = \frac{\text{Number of Examples of } A}{\text{Total Number of Sample Points}} \qquad \textbf{(9.1)}$$

$$P(A) = \frac{1}{6}$$

If $B$ is the event "an even numeral" in this die-tossing example, find $P(B)$. $B$ can be restated as "a 2 or 4 or 6." Since $B$ consists of three points in the sample space of six points, $P(B) = 3/6 = 1/2$. What is $P(C)$ if $C$ is the event 7? $P(C)$ is $0/7 = 0$, because 7 is not in the sample space of this problem. If $D$ is the event "an even or odd numeral," what is $P(D)$? The answer is $6/6 = 1$.

Suppose there is an urn that has four white balls in it and a finite, but unspecified, number of black balls. The probability of an event cannot be determined. A probability statement can be made only when the sample space is defined completely.

The definition of the probability of an event can be expressed using an alternative approach. Consider a sample space composed of a specified number of sample points. Denote each of the sample points by "$a_i$": $a_1$, $a_2$, ..., $a_n$. Every event that is defined within the sample space is composed of a related set of sample points.

---

[1]The notion of a sample space is actually a relatively recent development in probability theory, dating back only to the 1920s.

**Definition:** A probability function is a rule of correspondence that associates with each event $A$ in the sample space, a number $P(A)$ such that:

1. For any event $A$, $1 \geq P(A) \geq 0$.
2. The sum of the probabilities for all distinct events is 1.
3. If $A$ and $B$ are mutually exclusive events, that is, have no sample points in common, the $P(A \text{ or } B) = P(A) + P(B)$.

If it is assumed that the probability of every elementary event $a_i$ is $1/N$, where $N$ is the total number of sample points, then the probability of the event $A$ that is composed of $r$ sample points[2] is:

$$P(A) = \frac{1}{N} + \frac{1}{N} + \ldots + \frac{1}{N} = \frac{r}{N} \quad \textbf{(9.2)}$$

The probability of event $A$, $P(A)$, is the ratio of the number, $r$, of sample points that are examples of $A$ to the total number of sample points, $N$, that is, $r/N$.

Both routes bring us to the same definition for $P(A)$. While the second definition might be the preference of the mathematician, the first definition of $P(A)$ is more intuitive.

### Combining Probabilities

Suppose an urn contains five red, three white, and two black balls. Three events might be of interest: (1) $A$, a ball is red, (2) $B$, a ball is white, or (3) $C$, a ball is black. These three events are mutually exclusive; each sample point is an example of one and only one event.

The question arises, "What is the probability that a ball is red or white?" This event, the *union* of $A$ and $B$, shall be denoted by the symbol $A \cup B$ and its probability by $P(A \cup B)$.

## 9.3 FIRST ADDITION RULE OF PROBABILITIES

When the events $A$ and $B$ are mutually exclusive, the probability of either $A$ or $B$, $P(A \cup B)$, is:

$$P(A \cup B) = P(A) + P(B) \quad \textbf{(9.3)}$$

From the example above, we have:

$$P(A \cup B) = P(A) + P(B) = \frac{5}{10} + \frac{3}{10} = \frac{8}{10} \text{ or } .8$$

[2]The symbol conventionally used in probability theory for this purpose is $r$, not to be confused with the correlation coefficient.

Find $P(A \cup C)$. Since events $A$ and $C$ are mutually exclusive:

$$P(A \cup C) = P(A) + P(C) = .5 + .2 = .7.$$

Similarly, the value of $P(B \cup C) = P(B) + P(C) = .3 + .2 = .5$.

### Non-mutually Exclusive Events

In some sample spaces, two events are not mutually exclusive; a single sample point may be an example of both events $A$ and $B$. A playing card can be both an ace and a diamond. Consider the possible outcomes (heads or tails) of flipping a fair coin three times in a row, or three fair coins once. The eight possible outcomes make up the sample space:

1. HHH
2. HHT
3. HTH
4. HTT
5. THH
6. THT
7. TTH
8. TTT

Each of the eight outcomes is equally likely, that is, each has probability 1/8. What is the probability of heads on the first flip? The answer is 4/8 or 1/2. What is the probability of heads on flips 1 and 2? The answer is 2/8 or 1/4.

Now define two events, $A$ and $B$, using the sample space just defined:

$A$: Heads on flips 1 and 2
$B$: Heads on flips 2 and 3

The sample points that are examples of event $A$ are the first two events (HHH and HHT) in the sample space. The first and fifth outcomes (HHH and THH) are the sample points corresponding to event $B$. The symbol $A \cap B$ shall denote the new event, the *intersection* of $A$ and $B$. (Note the symbols $\cup$ and $\cap$ are analogous to the words *or* and *and*.) In the example, $A \cap B$ is the event "heads on flips 1 and 2 and heads on flips 2 and 3". Since all the sample points are equally likely, the probability of the event $A \cap B$ is:

$$P(A \cap B) = \frac{\text{Number of Sample Points that Are Examples of } A \cap B}{\text{Total Number of Sample Points}} \quad \textbf{(9.4)}$$

The total number of sample points is 8. Only one sample point, HHH, is an example of the event $A$ "heads on flips 1 and 2"; and also an example of event $B$ "heads on flips 2 and 3". So the probability of the event $A \cap B$ is 1/8.

Look back at the first addition rule of probabilities and notice the condition that the two events $A$ and $B$ are mutually exclusive. In the example just discussed, $A$ and $B$ were *not* mutually exclusive. The outcome HHH was an example of both events $A$ and $B$. But what is the probability of $A$ or $B$, $P(A \cup B)$, when $A$ and $B$ are not mutually exclusive? The "Second Addition Rule of Probabilities" is needed to answer this question.

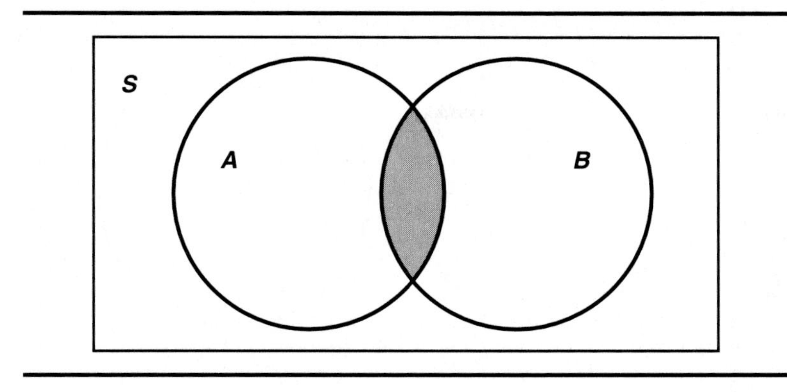

**FIGURE 9.1**

Venn diagram of the intersecting events *A* and *B* in the sample space *S*.

## 9.4 SECOND ADDITION RULE OF PROBABILITIES

The probability of either event $A$, or event $B$, or both is expressed as:

$$P(A \cup B) = P(A) + P(B) - P(A \cap B).$$

The Venn diagram in Figure 9.1 is a graphic portrayal of this situation, and should help clarify the meaning of the term $P(A \cap B)$. The events $A$ and $B$ are not mutually exclusive, that is, they have some sample points in common in the sample space $S$. The probability of event $A$ is represented by the area of circle $A$; the probability of event $B$ is represented by the area of circle $B$. The probability of $A$ or $B$, or *both*, is that area of $S$ that is inside the boundaries of both $A$ and $B$. The shaded portion in Figure 9.1 is that set of sample points in both events $A$ and $B$, that is, those points in the *intersection* $A \cap B$.

How does one find the entire area covered by $A$ and $B$? First, find the area of $A$ that is not shared by $B$. Add to it the area of $B$ not shared by $A$, and then add the area common to both—the intersection of $A$ and $B$:

$$P(A \cup B) = [P(A) - P(A \cap B)] + [P(B) - P(A \cap B)] + P(A \cap B)]$$

The first two terms following the equal sign, $P(A) - P(A \cap B)$, give the area of $A$ minus the area in common with $B$. $P(B) - P(A \cap B)$ gives the area of $B$ minus its area in common with $A$. The desired area is found by adding in the area common to $A$ and $B$, $P(A \cap B)$. The previous equation simplifies to

$$P(A \cup B) = P(A) + P(B) - P(A \cap B) \qquad \textbf{(9.5)}$$

Equation 9.5 establishes the *second addition rule of probabilities*. Notice that if one had simply added $P(A)$ and $P(B)$ to find $P(A \cup B)$, the portion in common to $A$ and $B$, $P(A \cap B)$, would contribute twice to the sum, because $A$ and $B$ are not mutually exclusive areas. The intersection must be included only once; consequently it must be subtracted once as shown in Equation 9.5.

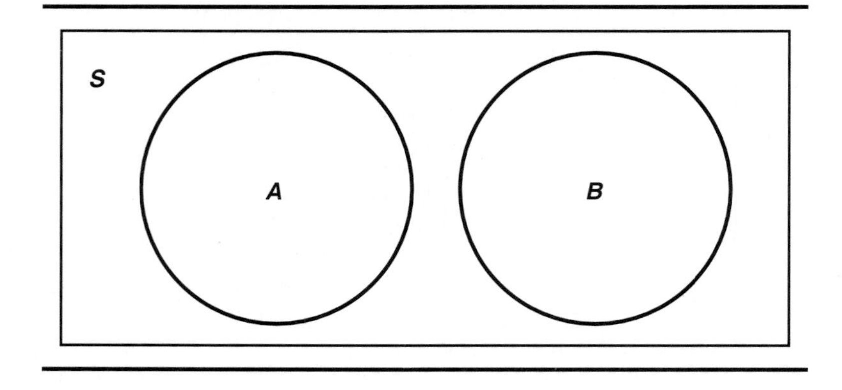


**FIGURE 9.2**

Venn diagram of the mutually exclusive events $A$ and $B$ in the sample space $S$.

Notice the first addition rule of probabilities (Equation 9.3) is just a special case of the second rule (Equation 9.5), that is, in the case when $P(A \cap B) = 0$. If $A$ and $B$ are mutually exclusive events in $S$, then they do not overlap. See Figure 9.2, where there is no area in common to $A$ and $B$; hence $P(A \cap B) = 0$. More generally, $P(A \cup B) = P(A) + P(B) - P(A \cap B)$. If $A$ and $B$ are mutually exclusive, then $P(A \cap B) = 0$. Therefore, if $A$ and $B$ are mutually exclusive:

$$P(A \cup B) = P(A) + P(B) - 0 = P(A) + P(B)$$

In much the same manner as the mathematical systems of geometry and algebra, probability theory can be developed from a small set of axioms and definitions. Also in the same manner, probability theory can serve as a model for what is going on in a certain class of events in the world around us. James Bernoulli (1654–1705) was the first to relate probability statements to physical events.[3] An example of the application of a formal probability statement to an actual set of actions will illustrate the relationship between theory and application.

Suppose an urn contains four white and six black balls. The balls are identical in size, shape, and weight and thoroughly mixed so that if one were to reach in and pull one out, it is equally likely that any one of the ten balls would be selected; each ball has one chance in ten of being chosen. A ball is taken out and its color is recorded. The ball is returned to the urn, the balls in the urn are stirred thoroughly, and the act is repeated under the same conditions. This act is performed many times, say, 10,000. After the 10,000th drawing of a ball, suppose a count is taken of the number of times a white ball was drawn. Intuition says that the ratio of the number of times a white ball is drawn to 10,000 will be very close to 4/10 = .4. It is unlikely the ratio is exactly 4/10 but it will be very close.

If the ten balls are regarded as a sample space, and if $A$ is the event "a ball is white," then $P(A)$ is exactly .4. The question arises, "Will the formal probability of an event as calculated from theory correspond closely to the relative frequency of the occurrence of the

[3]The "Bernoulli distribution" is another name for the binomial distribution that you may have long forgotten from high school algebra. This distribution has only two classes of independent events in the sample space, for example, heads or tails, hit or miss, event $A$ or not-event $A$.

event?" The answer to this question is the key to the relationship of probability theory and its application. The answer is yes when the underlying assumptions are met. Suppose an event $A$ either does, or does not, occur on every trial of an act. The probability that $A$ will occur, $P(A)$, is the same for all trials of the act. For example, the act may be flipping a fair coin, $A$ may be the event "heads," and it is assumed that the probability of heads (1/2) is the same from one flip to the next. It is also assumed that every trial is independent of, in no way affected by, every other trial. Now after $N$ trials of the act, the proportion of times $A$ has occurred is $p$. It can be proved that $p$ gets closer and closer to $P(A)$ as $N$ becomes larger and larger. The proportion of times $A$ occurs can be made closer and closer to $P(A)$ (the probability calculated from the sample space) by performing the act an increasing number of times. So $P(A)$ tells what will happen *in the long run* if the actions are actually performed under the conditions laid down previously.

The preceding paragraph is a statement of the *law of large numbers*. The law of large numbers is important for the application of probability, of which statistical inference is one such application. The law of large numbers is closely related to the statistical property of consistency, encountered previously in Chapter 5.

## 9.5 MULTIPLICATION RULE OF PROBABILITIES

There exists a multiplication rule for probabilities that is important for statistical inference. Suppose a coin is flipped five times in a row. Assume that the probability of heads is ½ on each flip and that the flips are independent (the outcomes are uncorrelated and have no influence on one another). The multiplicative rule for probabilities states that the probability of getting five straight heads is (1/2)(1/2)(1/2)(1/2)(1/2) = 1/32. A general statement of the rule follows:

**Multiplication Rule of Probabilities:** The probability that $A$, which has probability $P(A)$, will occur $r$ times in $r$ independent trials is:

$$P(A) \cdot P(A) \cdot \ldots \cdot P(A) = P(A)^r \qquad \textbf{(9.6)}$$

### Illustrations

Assume that the probability that your next child will be a girl is[4] 1/2 or .5 = $P(G)$. Since the sex of one child has no effect on the sex of any subsequent child, the probabilities are independent. Thus, the probability of five consecutive girls (or boys) from Equation 9.6 is:

$$P(G)^5 = \left(\frac{1}{2}\right)^5 = \frac{1}{32} = .03125 \approx .03$$

In other words, of every 32 families that have five children, one (or about three of 100) would be expected to have all girls. Suppose a sixth child is now expected, what are the odds that it is girl? The odds are 1 in 2; past events that are independent have no influence on future events. To believe otherwise is to believe in the "Gambler's Fallacy" (Section 9.12), and be in jeopardy of wasting a great deal of your money.

[4]Actually the probability is slightly less than .49, but we will keep the numbers simple and use .5.

**TABLE 9.1** Sample Space of Outcomes of Tossing a Pair of Dice (One Red, One Green)

| *R,G* | *R,G* | *R,G* | *R,G* | *R,G* | *R,G* |
|---|---|---|---|---|---|
| 1,1 | 2,1 | 3,1 | 4,1 | 5,1 | 6,1 |
| 1,2 | 2,2 | 3,2 | 4,2 | 5,2 | 6,2 |
| 1,3 | 2,3 | 3,3 | 4,3 | 5,3 | 6,3 |
| 1,4 | 2,4 | 3,4 | 4,4 | 5,4 | 6,4 |
| 1,5 | 2,5 | 3,5 | 4,5 | 5,5 | 6,5 |
| 1,6 | 2,6 | 3,6 | 4,6 | 5,6 | 6,6 |

Suppose a toddler is attracted to your computer and pecks keys randomly on the keyboard. What is the probability that the result of the first six characters are M-O-T-H-E-R? For simplicity, assume that there are 100 keys on your keyboard; the probability of a correct peck is, therefore, .01. Since there are six independent events, the probability that the first six random pecks will result in "mother" is $(.01)^6 = .000000000001$ or only one chance in a trillion[5] (1/1,000,000,000,000)!

The following examples illustrate the probability rules developed so far. Consider a roll of a pair of dice; one die is red and the other is green. The sample space of possible outcomes has 36 points, as shown in Table 9.1. Suppose event $A$ is "a 1 on the red die" and event $B$ is "a 1 on the green die." $P(A \cap B)$ is found by dividing the number of sample points that are examples of $A \cap B$ (both $A$ and $B$) by the total number of sample points (36). Verify that the probability that both $A$ and $B$ occur is equal to $P(A) \cdot P(B)$, $(1/6)(1/6) = 1/36$.

Find $P(A \cup B)$, the probability of event $A$ or event $B$, remembering that $P(A \cup B) = P(A) + P(B) - P(A \cap B)$. $P(A \cap B)$ is 1/36 because only the point "1,1" is common to $A$ and $B$; thus, $P(A \cup B) = 6/36 + 6/36 - 1/36 = 11/36$.

Two events are *independent* if and only if $P(A \cap B) = P(A) \cdot P(B)$. Independence is an important concept in statistics and probability, and statistical independence is a much used concept in subsequent chapters.

## 9.6 CONDITIONAL PROBABILITY

If $P(A)$ and $P(B)$ are known, the *conditional* probability of $B$ given $A$, denoted as $P(B|A)$, is:

$$P(B \mid A) = \frac{P(A \cap B)}{P(A)} \tag{9.7}$$

[5]In scientific notation this is $1.00 \times 10^{-12}$. A 17-key sequence, such as I- -L-O-V-E- -S-T-A-T-I-S-T-I-C-S, has a probability of only $(.01)^{17}$ or 1 in $10^{34}$; if one entered a random 17-key sequence once every second, this particular sequence would be expected only once every 317,000,000,000,000,000,000,000,000 (or $3.17 \times 10^{26}$) years! Scientists have estimated the age of the earth at about 5 billion ($5 \times 10^9$) years; thus, the probability that this 17-key sequence would have occurred even once since the beginning of the earth is $(5 \times 10^9)/(3.17 \times 10^{26}) = 6.34 \times 10^{17}$ (less than 1 chance in 100,000,000,000,000,000; $p < .00000000000000001$)! If one billion individuals were each striking 17 keys randomly each second, the probability remains infinitesimal (1 in 100,000,000). Contrast the probability of the simple I- -L-O-V-E- -S-T-A-T-I-S-T-I-C-S to the incredibly greater complexity of a DNA molecule!

In Figure 9.1, note that the conditional probability $P(B|A)$ (read "the probability of $B$ given $A$") is represented by the ratio of the area $A \cap B$ to the area $A$. In the example in Section 9.5: $P(A) = 1/6$ and $P(A \cap B) = 1/36$; thus using Equation 9.7, the probability of $B$ given $A$ is $1/36 \div 1/6 = 1/6$. Given $A$ (1 on the red die), the probability of $B$ (1 on the green die) is 1/6.

Suppose that the sample space is American adults and $B$ is "a woman" and $A$ is "a college graduate." Given that a college graduate is selected ($|A$), what is the probability that it is a woman, that is, what is $P(B|A)$? Currently, the probability of selecting a college graduate is approximately $.26 = P(A)$, and the probability of selecting a woman college graduate is $.115 = P(A \cap B)$. Given $A$, that a college graduate is selected, the probability of $B$, a woman, is

$$P(B \mid A) = \frac{.115}{.26} = .44$$

Notice that $P(B|A)$ is not equal to $P(A|B)$. In this example, given $B$, a woman, $P(B) = .5$, the probability of $A$, a college graduate, is:

$$P(A \mid B) = \frac{P(A \cap B)}{P(B)} = \frac{.115}{.5} = .23$$

## 9.7 BAYES'S THEOREM

Equation 9.7 is the simplest version of Bayes's theorem,[6] a theorem that describes the relationship among various conditional probabilities. Equation 9.7 may be expressed alternatively as:

$$P(A \mid B) = \frac{P(A \mid B)P(B)}{P(A \mid B)P(B) + P(A \mid \overline{B})P(\overline{B})} \qquad \textbf{(9.8)}$$

where $\overline{B}$ is read "not $B$."

Let event $B$ be "an automobile accident during the next year" and event $A$ be "a course in driver education." What is the probability of event $B$ (an accident in the next year), given $A$ (driver education), that is, what is $P(B|A)$? Assume that $P(B) = .1$; thus $P(\overline{B}) = 1 - P(B) = .9$. Also, assume that $P(A|B)$, the probability of having driver education given that a person has had an accident, is .50; and that $P(A|\overline{B})$, the probability of having driver education given that a person has *not* had an accident, is .7. From Equation 9.8, the probability of an accident ($B$), given driver education ($A$) is:

$$P(B \mid A) = \frac{(.5)(.1)}{(.5)(.1) + (.7)(.9)} = .0735$$

Thus, the probability of an accident has been reduced by 26.5%, from .10 to .0735, given the person had driver education.

---

[6]The theorem is named for its originator, the English clergyman and mathematician Thomas Bayes (1702–1761), who first used probability inductively and established a mathematical basis for probabilistic inference.

**TABLE 9.2** Permutations of Three Letters: *A*, *B*, and *C*

| *1st letter* | *2nd letter* | *3rd letter* | *Permutation* |
|---|---|---|---|
| A | B | C | 1. ABC |
| | C | B | 2. ACB |
| B | A | C | 3. BAC |
| | C | A | 4. BCA |
| C | A | B | 5. CAB |
| | B | A | 6. CBA |

Bayes's theorem provides exact results, providing the prior probabilities, the probabilities entered into Equation 9.8, are accurate. Obviously, the practical difficulty in the application of the theorem lies in knowing the prior probabilities. These probabilities have often been viewed as degrees of belief, or personal probabilities. The topic has occasioned much controversy among statisticians who favor a strict relative-frequency interpretation of probability and those who would allow for a more subjective interpretation. Discriminant analysis (Section 8.30) makes use of prior probabilities and Bayes's theorem in determining probabilities that a given case falls in a given category, given a prior probability of being in that category.

## 9.8 PERMUTATIONS

Two additional concepts that crop up repeatedly in probability illustrations are permutations and combinations (Section 9.9).

A *permutation* of a set of objects (the letters *A*, *B*, and *C*, for example) is an arrangement of them in which order is considered. A different ordering of the objects is a different permutation. How many different permutations or orderings are there of the letters *A*, *B*, and *C*? To find out, one can set about the task of writing them down and counting them, as shown in Table 9.2.

The first letter can be either A, B, or C. Suppose it is A, the top third of Table 9.2. If the first letter is A, the second letter can be either B or C. If the second letter is B, then the third letter must be C. So ABC is one possible permutation. There are three possible letters for the first position. After one letter is assigned to the first position, there are two possible letters for the second position. Hence, the number of possible permutations of the three letters A, B, and C is $(3)(2)(1) = 6$.

If there are $N$ distinct objects, one can make $N(N-1)(N-2)\ldots(2)(1)$ different permutations of them. This product can be denoted simply by $N!$ (read "$N$ factorial"). $N!$ is the product of the numbers from 1 through $N$ and equals the number of permutations of $N$ distinct objects.[7] ($0!$ is defined mathematically to equal 1.)

The value of $N!$ increases dramatically as $N$ increases. Would you work a year for 12! pennies? (12! pennies = 479,001,600¢ = \$4,790,016). To illustrate the incredible size of 12!, imagine that you have one dozen eggs in a carton and that you want to form every

[7]Many calculators have a factorial (!) key that provides almost instant answers to $N!$ questions.

possible permutation, or arrangement, of them in the egg carton. Assume you can make a new arrangement in ten seconds, which you do continuously during your eight hour working day. If you keep at this job five days a week fifty-two weeks a year, you would require approximately 640 years to make every possible arrangement! If you and each successive generation of your descendants donate 50 years to this task, it would be finished by your great, great, great, great, great, great, great, great, great, great, great grandchild. We suggest you take our word for it.

On the Wechsler intelligence tests, an examinee must put five cartoon pictures in the correct chronological order. What is the probability that an examinee will arrive at the correct order by chance? Since $5! = 120$, the probability of a "lucky guess" is only $1/120$.

## 9.9 COMBINATIONS

The concept of combinations arises when one is selecting some number of objects $r$ from a set of $N$ objects. A *combination* of objects is a distinct set of objects in which order is not considered. When $r = N$, that is, $N$ objects are selected from $N$ objects, all the objects are selected and there is only one combination (although there are $N!$ permutations). If $r = 1$, one object is selected from $N$ objects, and there are $N$ combinations. The problem is to find a general expression for the number of combinations that exist when $r$ things are selected from $N$ things.

Consider four objects, A, B, C, and D. How many different combinations can be made by selecting two letters at a time from these four? The answer is six: AB, AC, AD, BC, BD, CD. Notice that for combinations, order is not considered; AB is one combination, and BA is the same combination. (See the first two columns of Table 9.2, where the six permutations form three combinations.)

Suppose $r$ objects are being selected from $N$ objects. How many different combinations are there? For the time being, regard order as important, and then later combine all the sets that are different only because of order. If $r$ objects are being selected from $N$, then there are $N$ choices for the first object, $(N-1)$ choices for the second, $(N-2)$ for third, $(N-3)$ for the fourth, and so on until there are $(N-r+1)$ choices for the $r$th object. So, the *total of different permutations* of $r$ objects from $N$ objects, where order is considered, is equal to:

$$N(N-1)(N-2)\ldots(N-r+1) \quad \textbf{(9.9)}$$

How many permutations are there for $N = 4$ objects, taking $r = 3$ at a time? Using Equation 9.9, the answer is found to be $(4)(3)(2) = 24$ permutations. There are $r$ terms in this product corresponding to the $r$ objects selected. However, for each unique combination of $r$ objects, there are $r!$ permutations; in the example, $r = 3$ and $r! = 3! = 6$. Hence, the number of combinations of $r$ objects selected from $N$ objects, ignoring the order among the $r$ objects, is the number of permutations of the $r$ objects selected from $N$ objects (Equation 9.9) divided by the number of permutations within a combination.

$$\binom{N}{r} = \frac{N(N-1)(N-2)\ldots(N-r+1)}{r!} \quad \textbf{(9.10)}$$

The expression to the left of the equal sign in Equation 9.10 is read "the number of combinations of $r$ things taken from $N$ things."

It can be shown[8] that the number of permutations of $r$ objects taken from $N$ objects is:

$$N(N-1)(N-2)\ldots(N-r+1)=\frac{N!}{(N-r)!} \tag{9.11}$$

When this substitution is made in Equation 9.10, the number of combinations of $N$ things taken $r$ at a time is given by:

$$\binom{N}{r}=\frac{N!}{r!(N-r)} \tag{9.12}$$

## Examples

How many different combinations are there of $r = 3$ things taken from $N = 5$ things?

$$\binom{5}{3}=\frac{5!}{3!(5-3)!}=\frac{5!}{3!2!}=\frac{5\cdot 4\cdot \not{3}\cdot 2\cdot 1}{(\not{3}\cdot 2\cdot 1)(2\cdot 1)}=\frac{5\cdot 4}{2\cdot 1}=\frac{20}{2}=10$$

Note from Equation 9.9 that there are (5)(4)(3) permutations of five things taken three at a time. Each combination has $r! = 3! = 6$ permutations; thus, the sixty permutations represent 60/6 combinations. Each of the ten combinations of five things taken three at a time has $(3)(2)(1) = 6$ permutations.

Ten persons are eligible to serve on a committee. The committee must be composed of only five persons. How many different five member ($r = 5$) committees could be formed from the ten available persons ($N = 10$)? From Equation 9.12:

$$\binom{10}{5}=\frac{10!}{5!(10-5)!}=\frac{10!}{5!5!}=\frac{10\cdot 9\cdot 8\cdot 7\cdot 6\cdot \not{5}\cdot \not{4}\cdot \not{3}\cdot \not{2}\cdot \not{1}}{(5\cdot 4\cdot 3\cdot 2\cdot 1)(\not{5}\cdot \not{4}\cdot \not{3}\cdot \not{2}\cdot \not{1})}=\frac{30{,}240}{120}=252$$

## 9.10 BINOMIAL PROBABILITIES

When we have a Bernoulli-type (two classes of independent events) sample space and the probability of each event class is known, we can find the probability of any outcome. Let $A$ (success) denote one class of events; let $B$ (failure) denote the other class. Further, let $p$ represent the probability of event $A$ (i.e., the proportion of the sample space occupied by $A$

---

[8]Note that $N! = N(N-1)(N-2)\ldots[(N-r)+1](N-r)[(N-r)-1]\ldots(1)$. Write out $N!$ in the numerator and $(N-r)!$ in the denominator and cancel the terms common to both numerator and denominator and express $(N-r)[(N-r)-1]\ldots(1)$ as $(N-r)!$ to obtain Equation 9.11.

events);[9] $q = 1 - p$ denotes the probability of event $B$. The probability of a particular permutation, for example, four $A$'s (successes) followed by a $B$ (failure), then another $A$ (success), $(A, A, A, A, B, A)$, is $p \cdot p \cdot p \cdot p \cdot q \cdot p = p^5q$.

Notice that the result, $p^5q$, is the same no matter where in the sequence the outcome $B$ falls. Thus, the *probability of any sequence of N independent Bernoulli events* depends only on the probability of event $A$ on any trial ($p$), and the number of $A$'s in the sequence ($r$). In other words, the probability of a given sequence of $r$ successes in $N$ events, where $p$ is the probability of outcome $A$ on any of the $N$ independent trials and $q = 1 - p$ is the probability of outcome $B$ (a non-$A$ event on any trial), is:

$$p^r q^{N-r} \tag{9.13}$$

When tossing a pair of fair die, what is the probability of (7, 7, 7, not-seven, 7) in five tosses? In Table 9.1, we see that in the sample space, the proportion of 7's is $6/36 = 1/6 = p$. The probability of a non-seven then is $q = 1 - p = 1 - 1/6 = 5/6$. Thus, from Equation 9.13, the probability of this sequence is:

$$p^4q^{5-4} = p^4q = (1/6)^4(5/6) = 5/7{,}776 = .000643$$

or roughly 6 chances in 10,000.

Rarely would our interest be in a particular sequence or permutation; we would usually be more interested in the probability of obtaining four 7's in five tosses, for example. Note that there are five different permutations, each with the same independent probability (.000643), that would result in the same combination; consequently, the probability of one of the five occurring is 5(.000643) = .003215, or about 3 chances in 1,000.

More generally, from Equation 9.12, note that there are $N!/[r!(N - r)!]$ sequences that result in $r$ successes in $N$ trials. If $N = 5$, and $r = 4$, there are five sequences that result in this combination.

$$\frac{N!}{r!(N-r)!} = \frac{(5 \cdot 4 \cdot 3 \cdot 2 \cdot 1)}{(4 \cdot 3 \cdot 2 \cdot 1)(1)} = 5$$

Generalizing the above rationale, we come to the following conclusion. Where the probability of the result $A$ is $p$ and the probability of a non-$A$ result is $1 - p = q$, the probability of observing result $A$ in $r$ of $N$ independent occasions is:

$$\frac{N!}{r!(N-r)!}(p^r q^{N-r}) \tag{9.14}$$

Keep in mind that $p^rq^{N-r}$ is the probability of any one of the $N!/[r!(N - r)!]$ sequences that result in $r$ successes in $N$ trials. Suppose there is a ten-item multiple choice test, with each item containing four options. What is the probability of obtaining a score of 80% from

[9] To be completely consistent in notation, since a parameter is denoted, $\pi$ rather than $p$ should be used. We shall compromise in this application, however, and use the conventional symbols, $p$ and $q$.

random guessing? In this situation, $N = 10$, $r = 8$, and the probability of a success on any item is $p = \frac{1}{4}$. The probability of guessing correctly on 8 (not 8 or more) of the 10 items is:

$$\frac{10!}{8!(10-8)!}\left(\frac{1}{4}\right)^8\left(\frac{3}{4}\right)^2 = 45\left(\frac{1}{65,536}\right)\left(\frac{9}{16}\right) = \left(\frac{405}{1,048,576}\right) = .000386$$

or less than 4 chances in 10,000.

What is the probability of answering 8 or more of the 10 items correctly? We need to find the probability of answering 9 items correctly, and the probability of answering all 10 questions correctly, and sum the three probabilities. The probability of 9 from Equation 9.14 is $(10!/9!)[(1/4)^9(3/4)] = 10(1/262,144)(3/4) = 30/1,048,576$; the probability of answering all ten correctly is $(1/4)^{10} = 1/1,048,576$. Thus the probability of answering 8 or more of the 10 four-option questions correctly merely by guessing is only $(405 + 30 + 1)/1,048,576 = 436/1,048,576 = .0004158$.[10]

The *binomial expansion* is an application of the binomial theorem you were probably introduced to in high school algebra. It is a general expression that gives the probabilities for any number of outcomes of an event $A$ in $N$ independent Bernoulli trials, where $p$ is the probability of event $A$ on any one trial. The number of $A$'s is the exponent for $p$ in any of the $N + 1$ terms of the expansion:

$$(p+q)^N = p^N + \frac{N!}{(N-1)!1!}p^{N-1}q + \frac{N!}{(N-2)!2!}p^{N-2}q^2 + \cdots + \frac{N!}{1!(N-1)!}pq^{N-1} + q^N \quad \textbf{(9.15)}$$

The binomial expansion or distribution can be used to compare any dichotomous set of observations with a theoretical distribution to answer such questions as,

"In the distribution of male offsprings to mothers who carry the gene for hemophilia, what is expected if hemophilia is a Mendelian recessive trait?"

"Are more babies male than female?"

"Do husbands score higher on need-for-achievement measures than do their wives?"

"In a mental telepathy experiment, is the number of 'hits' greater than chance?"

"Can you toss more than 50% heads in a series of coin tosses?

"Can a naive examinee beat the odds and obtain a score that is greater than can be expected from chance alone?"

"When faced with true-false questions, are examinees more likely to guess T than F?"

"Is the proportion of dropouts who are male greater than the proportion who are female?"

## 9.11 THE BINOMIAL AND SIGN TEST

The *sign* test is a special "non-parametric"[11] application of the binomial distribution in which there are $N$ paired observations, such as matched pairs in an experiment ($E$ vs. $C$). If

---

[10] Or $4.16 \times 10^{-4}$ in scientific notation (often appearing as 4.16E-4 in computer output).

[11] "Non-parametric" is an unfortunate term applied to statistical methods that apply to data that represent nominal or ordinal scales of measurement, or to a data set where normality and other assumptions are not made about parameters of the distribution of observations in the parent population (Conover, 1980, p. 92). "Distribution-free" is a synonym of "non-parametric."

the treatment has no effect, we should expect the $E$ pair-member to surpass the $C$ pair-member in one-half ($p = .5$) of the $N$ comparisons. Suppose only 5 matched pairs are available. We randomly assign one pair-member to get the $E$ treatment, the other pair-member serving as the control. On the posttest, we find that in 4 of the 5 comparisons $E$ outperformed $C$. How probable is it that we would observe that $E$ outperformed $C$ in 4 or more of the comparisons by chance? Based on Equation 9.15, the probability of exactly 4 "hits" is $5(1/2)^4(1/2) = 5(1/2)^5 = 5/32$; the probability of 5 "hits" is $(1/2)^5 = 1/32$; thus, the probability of 4 or more "hits" in 5 comparisons is $5/32 + 1/32 = 6/32 = .1875$, or roughly 1 chance in 5. Our expectation that $E$ is effective lacks strong evidence. However, if we continue to add cases with the same success ratio, our case will become much stronger.[12]

In the sign test, and many other applications of the *binomial test*, when $p = q = .5$, the product of each of the $N + 1$ "$pq$" terms equals $p^N$, which greatly simplifies the computation. If a basketball player makes 50% of his free throws, and if he takes 12 free throws in a game, how likely is it that he will make 10 or more? Since $p^N = (1/2)^{12} = 1/4{,}096$; the probability of making all 12 is 1/4,094; the probability of making 11 is 12/4,096; the probability of making 10 is $[(12)(11)/2]/4{,}094 = 66/4{,}096$. Thus, the probability of making 10 or more of the 12 free throws is $(1+12+66)/4{,}096 = 79/4{,}096 \approx .02$ (not very likely). Note, however, the probability of missing 10 or more of the 12 has the same probability.[13]

Table O in the Appendix gives the probability for observing $r$ $A$'s in $N$ events when $p = .5$. Suppose we want to investigate whether this generation is taller than the previous generation, as we have been led to believe. We ask the twenty-five members of the statistics class to compare their heights with that of their parents of the same sex at the same age. If this generation is no taller than the previous generation, we would expect $.5 = 50\%$ of the students to be taller than their parents. We collect data and find that twenty of the twenty-five are taller than their same-sex parent. How probable is it that we would observe 20 $A$'s out of $25 = N$ Bernoulli trials? In Table O, find the row for $N = 25$ and the column for $N - 5 = 25 - 5 = 20$ $A$'s (or for 5 $B$'s). The intersection contains the value .00204, which is the probability that twenty *or more* $A$'s would be observed in twenty-five independent events when $p = .5$. Since our result is so unlikely if this generation is no taller than the previous generation, we conclude that this generation is taller.[14]

## 9.12 INTUITION AND PROBABILITY

The study of probability can be interesting and entertaining. Historically, the concepts of probability evolved in connection with games of chance. Those who make use of probability theory are generally awed by the intricacy and excitement of the system and the way in which it produces results that are often quite in disagreement with intuition (unless one's intuition has been developed by experience with calculated probabilities). A few examples of surprising results will illustrate the untrustworthiness of intuition.

First, the classic "birthday problem": What is the probability that at least two people in

---

[12] Can you confirm that the probability of 8 success in 10 trials is $(45 + 10 + 1)/1{,}024 = 56/1{,}024 = .055$?

[13] This problem makes the dubious assumption that the probabilities are independent. If there is any validity to the notion that on a given occasion a player may get "hot," the model does not hold. Whether there are nonrandom sequences such as hitting streaks or slumps in baseball (or whether they are just unusual sequences that are expected infrequently) can be tested by the "runs" test (Dixon & Massey, 1983).

[14] In Chapter 11, you will see that we have just rejected the statistical hypothesis that the parameter $\pi$ is .5.

a group of twenty-three have the same birthday anniversary? Assume that the people are drawn randomly from a population of persons in which all 365 birthdays (not counting 29 February) are equally likely. One often obtains intuitive guesses that the probability is .10 or .001 or even smaller. Surprisingly, it is more likely than not that the probability that at least two people out of twenty-three have the same birthday is .507! Naturally the probability is even higher as the size of the group increases; it is practically certain that in a group of 150 persons at least two people will have the same birthday (Feller, 1957, pp. 31–32.).

A certain TV show has three "windows." Behind one there is an expensive prize; there is nothing of real value behind the other two. The contestant keeps what is behind the window chosen. Suppose that, after the contestant selects a window, the host always raises one of the two other windows—behind which there is nothing of value, then gives the contestant the choice to remain with the initial choice or to change to the other unopened window. What is the wiser choice? You may feel that the odds started out even, and remain even, so that there is no advantage or disadvantage to remaining with the original choice. If your intuition is that your odds of winning are increased by changing, you are right. The odds of winning change from 1/3 to 2/3 when the contestant leaves the initial choice.

What is the probability that a student will obtain a score of 75 on a 100 item true-false test by guessing randomly on each question, given that the average[15] chance score, $\mu$, is 50 and the standard deviation, $\sigma$, is 5? The score of 75 is $z = 5$ standard deviations above the chance mean. From Table A in the Appendix, the probability can be read as less than one chance in 1,000,000! What is the probability of a score above 60%? Since 60% is two standard deviations above the mean, only one randomly guessing student out of fifty will obtain a score greater than 60.

The "gambler's fallacy" represents another example in which intuitive notions of probability often lead to erroneous conclusions. If the football captain has won the coin flip by calling heads for the first three games, should he change to tails on the next flip? If a craps shooter failed to throw a 7 on ten straight throws of a pair of dice, is he more likely to throw a 7 on the next throw than if he has thrown three 7's in a row? If the first four children in a family are boys, are the chances that the next child will be a girl different from what they would be if the four previous children had been two boys and two girls or all girls? If you think so, shame on you—you are guilty of the "gambler's fallacy." If the probabilities of the event in question are independent, as they are in the examples above, the probability of a future event is unaffected by any pattern of past results. Whatever the number of heads, prior to a given toss, the probability of heads on the next toss of a fair coin is .5. This is confirmed by the conditional probability equation (Equation 9.7). In the sample space of four tosses of a coin there are sixteen events or permutations: *HHHH*, *HHHT*, *HHTH*, *HHTT*, ... *TTTH*, *TTTT*. If $A$ is *HHH* for the first three tosses, then $P(A) = 2/16 = 1/8$; and if $B$ is $H$ for the fourth toss, then $P(A \cap B) = 1/16$, the probability of head ($B$) given three previous heads ($A$), that is:

$$P(B \mid A) = \frac{P(A \cap B)}{P(A)} = \frac{1/16}{1/8} = .5$$

[15] $\mu = k/a$, where $k$ is the number of items on the test and $a$ is the number of response options per item. The standard deviation of the chance score is $\sigma = \sqrt{k\pi(1-\pi)}$, where $\pi = 1/a$ (see Hopkins, Stanley, & Hopkins, 1990). For large $k$, the distribution will be approximately normal.

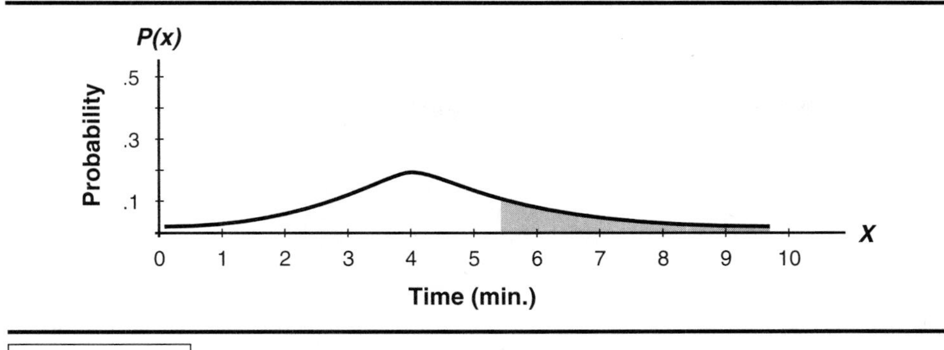


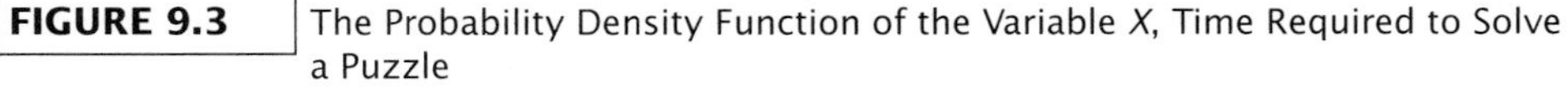

**FIGURE 9.3** The Probability Density Function of the Variable *X*, Time Required to Solve a Puzzle

## 9.13 PROBABILITY AS AN AREA

The probabilities of observing values of continuous variables, for example, height, are conveniently represented by mathematical curves known as probability distributions. Suppose a continuous random variable *X* takes on values from 0 to 10. For example, *X* could be the time required for students to solve a certain puzzle. A student may solve it almost immediately, or she may take as long as ten minutes. Presumably, the length of time required to solve the problem is known for a large number of different subjects. Figure 9.3 represents a graph drawn in which the "time to solution" is graphed against the "proportion of subjects requiring that time."

The proportion of subjects requiring between two and four minutes to solve the puzzle can be regarded as the probability that a subject selected at random from the population will require that amount of time to solve the puzzle. The entire area under the curve in Figure 9.3 is set to 1, so the area under the curve between any two points $X_1$ and $X_2$ is the probability that a randomly selected subject will require between $X_1$ and $X_2$ minutes to solve the puzzle. The probability that a randomly selected subject will take more than 5.3 minutes is equal to the shaded area in Figure 9.3. What area corresponds to the probability that a randomly selected subject will take less than 1 minute? (The small area between 0 and 1.)[16] If the proportion of the area under the curve in Figure 9.3 between 6 and 10 were .17, then in a group of 100 randomly chosen subjects we would expect about seventeen persons to take between six and ten minutes to solve the puzzle.

The statistician frequently plots the values a continuous random variable can assume so that the area between any two values of the variable equals the probability that the variable will assume a value between those two values. The resulting graph is called a probability density function. The graph can often be expressed as a mathematical function so that the ordinate $P(X)$ can be found by substituting any value of the random variable $X$. For ex-

[16]Theoretically, the probability that a person will take *exactly* one minute (or any other *precise* value), for example, 1.000 ... minutes, is zero; in such situations, the height of the curve is the "probability density" of the value.

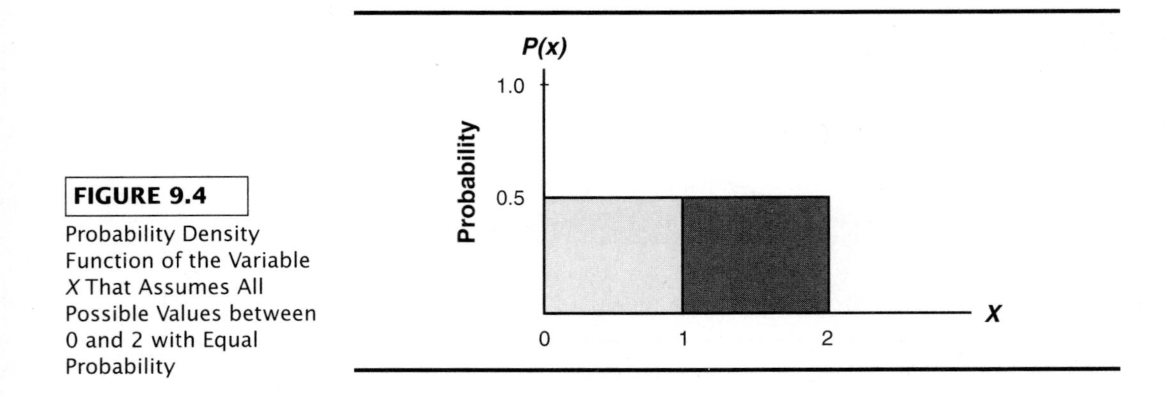


**FIGURE 9.4**

Probability Density Function of the Variable *X* That Assumes All Possible Values between 0 and 2 with Equal Probability

ample, assume $X$ is a random variable that can take on any value between 0 and 2 with equal probability. If $P(X) = 1/2$ for all $X$, then the resulting graph (Figure 9.4) will be the probability density function of $X$. For example, the area under the curve of the rectangle in Figure 9.4 is exactly 1 (i.e., $0.5 \times 2.0$). The lightly shaded area is the probability that $X$ takes on a value between 0 and 1; the probability equals .5.

## 9.14 COMBINING PROBABILITIES

Suppose we perform a sign test to investigate our research hypothesis that husbands express a higher level of need-for-achievement than do their wives, and suppose the study was replicated by two other researchers. Suppose all three studies found a slight difference in favor of the husbands with probability levels of .09, .06, and .11. None of these studies separately would give convincing evidence of the research hypothesis, but does your intuition suggest that a combination of the three studies would lead to a different conclusion?

There are several methods for addressing this situation, but the "most serviceable under the largest range of conditions is the method of adding $z$'s" (Rosenthal, 1978). The "method of adding $z$'s," also known as the Stouffer method, is quite simple and direct: First, convert each of the $p$-values to its corresponding $z$-score from Table A. Second, sum the $z$'s and divide by the square root of the number of probabilities being combined, and third, find the $p$-value of the obtained $z$-value from Table A.

For our three $p$-values of 09, .06, and .11, the corresponding $z$-scores are 1.341, 1.555, and approximately[17] 1.225; their sum is 4.121, which, divided by the square root of three (1.732), is 2.379. Note from Table A, the proportion of the area above $z = 2.38$ in a normal distribution is .0087; thus, the probability of obtaining three independent $p$-values of .06, .09, and .11 is less than .01. Hence, taken as a composite set of information, the conclusion is warranted than husbands do indeed have a higher level of need-for-achievement than do wives. Note however, the $p$'s must be independent; the procedure cannot be used within a single study having multiple measures.

[17]This is best done using a spreadsheet (e.g., using the NORMDIST function in EXCEL), although the results from Appendix Table A are quite acceptable.

## 9.15 EXPECTATIONS AND MOMENTS

Moments are characteristics of distributions defined in terms of expectations. The definition of the expectation of a random variable will be considered first.

**Definition:** If $X$ is a discrete random variable that takes on the values $X_1, X_2, \ldots, X_n$ with probabilities $p_1, p_2, \ldots, p_N$, then the *expectation* of $X$ denoted by $E(X)$ is defined as:

$$E(X) = p_1X_1 + p_2X_2 + \ldots + p_NX_N = \sum_{j}^{N} p_jX_j \qquad \textbf{(9.16)}$$

where $p_1 + p_2 + \ldots + p_N = 1 = \Sigma_j p_j$.

Another symbol denoting the expectation of $X$ is $\mu$, the Greek lowercase letter mu. $E(X) = \mu$, the mean of the population of $X$'s.

The names "expectation" and "expected value" are synonymous. Some examples of expectations are as follows:

1. Suppose $X$ is the random variable that has six possible values, 1, 2, ..., 6. The events of the sample space could be the six sides of a die. Assume that a probability of 1/6 is associated with each value of $X$. What is the value of $E(X)$? From Equation 9.16:

$$E(X) = \sum_{j}^{6} p_jX_j = \frac{1}{6}(1) + \frac{1}{6}(2) + \frac{1}{6}(3) + \frac{1}{6}(4) + \frac{1}{6}(5) + \frac{1}{6}(6) = \frac{1}{6}(1 + 2 + \ldots + 6)$$
$$= \frac{21}{6} = 3.5$$

   In this example, $E(X) = \mu = 21/6 = 3.5$. In repeatedly rolling the die, one can expect to average 3.5 points.

2. A particular slot machine has payoffs of \$0.00, \$0.50, \$1, \$2, and \$25. The probabilities associated with each of these occurrences are .80, .15, .04, .01, and .001, respectively. Define a random variable $X$ that takes on the four values 0, 50, 100, 200, and 2500 cents with probabilities .80, .15, .04, .01, and .001. What is the value of $E(X)$?

$$\mu = E(X) = .80(0) + .15(50) + .04(100) + .01(200) + .001(2500)$$
$$= 0 + 7.5 + 4.0 + 2.0 + 2.5 = 16$$

   If it costs 25 cents for each trial on this slot machine, would you like to play? If you feed \$25 into the machine, how much can you expect to lose? (\$9)

3. Let $X$ be the four random values that correspond to the number of heads in four flips of a fair coin. $X$ can take on the values 0, 1, 2, 3, and 4. Find $E(X)$. If you write out the sixteen equally probable events in the sample space, that is, *HHHH*, *HHHT*, ..., *TTTT*, you will find the probabilities associated with 0, 1, 2, 3, 4 are 1/16, 1/4, 3/8, 1/4, and 1/16, respectively. Thus:

$$E(X) = \sum_{j}^{4} p_jX_j = \frac{1}{16}(0) + \frac{1}{4}(1) + \frac{3}{8}(2) + \frac{1}{4}(3) + \frac{1}{16}(4) = 2$$

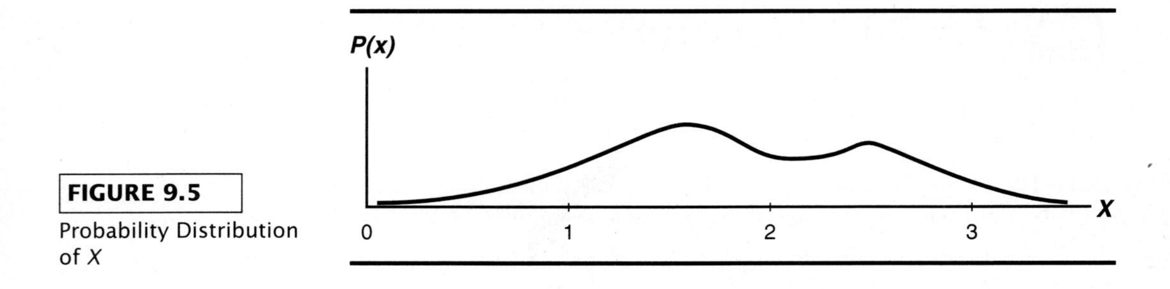


**FIGURE 9.5**
Probability Distribution of $X$

"In the long run," one can expect to average two heads in four random tosses of a fair coin.

If $X$ is a continuous variable instead of a discrete one, then an algebraic function describes the form of its probability distribution. If $X$ is continuous, one cannot assign a probability to a single value of $X$. Instead, statements about the probability that $X$ lies in an interval are made. For these reasons, the definition given for $E(X)$ in Equation 9.16 cannot be applied to a continuous random variable. Unfortunately for those without recourse to knowledge of integral calculus, it is difficult to define the expectation of a continuous variable.

Suppose $X$ is a continuous random variable and the probability distribution of $X$ looks like the one in Figure 9.5. There is an algebraic rule that gives the height of the curve in Figure 9.5 for every value of $X$. The area under the curve is 1 unit. The probability that $X$ will assume a value between, for example, 2 and 3 is equal to the area under the curve between those two points.

**Definition:** The *expectation* of the continuous random variable $X$ is the sum of the products formed by multiplying each value that $X$ can assume by the height of the probability function curve above that value of $X$.

Since $X$ can take on infinitely many values with continuous random variables, you might wonder how you could multiply each of the separate values of $X$ by the height of the curve at $X$ to find its expectation. This is the problem that recourse to the integral calculus solves. If you are not familiar with calculus, take it on faith that it can be done, in a precise but somewhat indirect way, by "integration."

The expectation of a continuous random variable $X$ is denoted by $E(X)$ or $\mu$, as is the expectation of a discrete variable.

## 9.16 CHAPTER SUMMARY

The probability of event $A$ can be viewed as the ratio of the number of points of $A$ to the total number in the sample space. Often intuitive notions regarding probability are quite inaccurate.

If events $A$ and $B$ are mutually exclusive, the probability of either $A$ or $B$, $P(A \cup B)$, is $P(A) + P(B)$. If events $A$ and $B$ are not mutually exclusive, $P(A \cup B) = P(A) + P(B) - P(A \cap B)$, where the last term is the probability of both $A$ and $B$.

If event $A$ has probability $P(A)$, the probability that $A$ will occur $n$ times in $n$ independent trials is $P(A)^n$.

The probability of event $B$, given event $A$, is conditional probability, $P(B|A)$, and equals $P(A \cap B)/P(A)$.

Each unique ordering or arrangement of $n$ objects is a permutation. There are $n!$ permutations of $n$ objects. The set of objects irrespective of order is a combination. The number of combinations of $n$ things taken $r$ at a time is $n!/[r!(n-r)!]$.

## 9.17 SUGGESTED COMPUTER ACTIVITY

From spreadsheet or statistical software, select a random sample of 25 numbers between 1 and 1,000.

## MASTERY TEST

1. What is the probability of tossing a "6," $P(6)$, with one toss of a die?
2. How many sample points are there in the sample space in question 1?
3. Are the sample points mutually exclusive?
4. What is the probability of not tossing "6," $P(\bar{6})$?
5. What is the probability of tossing "6's" in two tosses of a die?
6. Given that one "6" has been tossed, what is the conditional probability that the second toss will also be a "6"?
7. On a five-option multiple choice test, what is the probability of selecting the correct answer from a random guess?
8. What is the probability of correctly guessing the right answer on all ten items of a five-option multiple choice test?
9. Although 651412 and 214165 are different permutations, they represent a single ____.
10. What is the probability of correctly guessing ten of ten true-false questions?
11. How many permutations are there in the previous question? (For example, T, T, F, T, T, F, F, F, T, T, is one permutation.)
12. How many different doubles teams in tennis are possible with a class of twenty members?
13. The probability of throwing two consecutive "snake eyes" with the toss of a pair of dice is $(1/36)^2 = 1/1{,}296$. If you have just tossed "snake eyes," what is the probability the next toss will be "snake eyes"?
14. Which of these random variables are discrete and which are continuous:
    (a) number of students enrolled in a statistics class
    (b) running speed of ten-year-olds
    (c) result from the toss of a pair of dice
    (d) height of adult males
15. What is the expected number of girls in two-child families if the probabilities associated with 0, 1, and 2 girls are 1/4, 1/2, and 1/4, respectively?
16. Probability density pertains to
    (a) continuous random variable
    (b) discrete random variable
17. If 25% of the area in a probability distribution falls between 90 and 100, what is the probability that a case selected at random will fall between 90 and 100?

18. If event $A$ influences the probability of event $B$, events $A$ and $B$ are not ____.
19. What is the probability of drawing four aces without replacement from a deck of fifty-two cards? (Hint: probability of ace on first card is 4/52; on second, 3/51; etc.)

## PROBLEMS AND EXERCISES

1. Let a pack of fifty-two playing cards be the sample space $S$ of interest. Determine the probabilities of each of the following events:
   (a) $A$ is "a card is the ace of spades." Find $P(A)$.
   (b) $B$ is "a card is an ace." Find $P(B)$.
   (c) $C$ is the event that "a card is a spade." Find $P(C)$.
   (d) $D$ is "a card is a diamond," and $C$ is "a card is a spade." Find $P(D \cap C)$.
   (e) $C$ is "a card is a spade" and $B$ is "a card is an ace." Find $P(C \cup B)$.
2. Suppose that in a certain locale 3% of the children of kindergarten age have severe perceptual problems and 6% of the children of the same age have emotional problems. Also, 1.5% of the same group of children have both perceptual and emotional problems. Children suffering from either problem or both must receive teaching apart from normal pupils. What is the probability that a child entering kindergarten will require special teaching, that is, will have either perceptual or emotional problems or both?
3. (a) Find 15!/13!
   (b) Find 6!/[3!(6-3)!]
   (c) What is the value of $N$ if $(N + 1)!$ is exactly ten times larger than $N!$?
4. An experimenter wishes to have subjects learn a list of paired associations in all possible orders of the six pairs. Each subject can learn the list only once. How many subjects would be required if a different subject is required for every possible ordering of the six pairs?
5. (a) How many combinations are there of six things taken four at a time—find $\binom{6}{4}$.
   (b) Find $\binom{5}{1}$, $\binom{5}{2}$, $\binom{5}{3}$, $\binom{5}{4}$, and $\binom{5}{5}$.
6. The varsity basketball team has twelve members. How many possible "starting fives"—the five players who start the game—could the coach form from his team of twelve players?
7. (a) Verify that $\binom{4}{0} + \binom{4}{1} + \binom{4}{2} + \binom{4}{3} + \binom{4}{4}$ is equal to $2^4$. (In general, $\Sigma_i^N \binom{N}{i} = 2^N$
   (b) How many different combinations are there of six things, in groups of size 0 to 6 inclusively, that is, what is $\Sigma_{i=0}^{6} \binom{6}{i}$?
8. How many five-item tests can be formed by ten items split into two tests of five items each?
9. A student takes a ten-item true-false test but does not know the answers to five of the items. If he guesses randomly between true and false on each of the five items,
   (a) What is the probability that he will earn a perfect score of 10?
   (b) What is the probability that he will guess incorrectly on all five questions?
   (c) What is the probability that his score will be 6, 7, 8, or 9? (Hint: Subtract probabilities for scores of 5 and 10 from 1.00.)
10. In a fictitious experiment, convicts volunteered for study of the causal relationship between smoking and lung cancer. The convicts were matched into five matched pairs so that both pair mates were of the same age. Within each pair of convicts, a coin was flipped to determine which convict would continue smoking two packs of cigarettes a day and which one would not be allowed cigarettes for the duration of the experiment. At the end of the ten-year experimental period, the five smokers in each pair had lung cancer; none of the nonsmokers had lung cancer. Suppose that at the outset of the experiment, a convict in each pair had undiagnosed lung cancer.

(a) What is the probability that the five initially cancerous convicts would be randomly assigned to be the five experimental smokers?
(b) If there had been ten pairs, rather than five, what is the probability that the cancerous convict in each of the ten pairs would have been assigned to the smoking group?

**11.** In the general population, Stanford-Binet IQ's are nearly normally distributed with a mean of 100 and a standard deviation of 16. By referring to Table A in the Appendix, determine the following probabilities:

(a) A randomly sampled person will have an IQ between 80 and 120.
(b) A randomly sampled person will have an IQ above 140.
(c) Three independently randomly sampled persons will all have IQ's above 92.

**12.** The variable $X$ takes on the values 0, 1, 2, 3, and 4 with probabilities 0, 2/5, 1/5, 1/5, and 1/5, respectively. What is the value of $E(X)$, the expected value of $X$?

**13.** The sample space for tossing a pair of dice is given in Table 9.1.

(a) Determine the probability for each value of $X$, for 2, 3, 4, …, 12.
(b) What is the expected value of $X$, $E(X)$?
(c) What is probability that $X \neq 7$?
(d) What is the probability of "7" on three consecutive throws?
(e) Given the consecutive "7's," what is the probability of "7" on the next toss?
(f) What is the probability of "7's" on four of five tosses?
(g) What is the probability of "7's" on four or more of five tosses?

**14.** In an experiment comparing a new product with the standard product, the new product was preferred by 23 of the 30 subjects in the taste test. Is the new product better, or can this be explained by chance? Use Table O to learn the probability of 23 $A$'s out of 30 Bernoulli events.

## ANSWERS TO MASTERY TEST

**1.** 1/6
**2.** 6
**3.** yes
**4.** 5/6
**5.** $(1/6)^2 = 1/36$
**6.** $P(B|A) = (1/36)/(1/6) = 1/6$
**7.** 1/5
**8.** $(1/5)^{10} \approx .0000001$
**9.** combination
**10.** $(1/2)^{10} = 1/1{,}024$
**11.** 1,024
**12.** $\binom{20}{2} = \frac{20!}{2!(20-2)!} = 190$
**13.** 1/36
**14.** (*a*) and (*c*) are discrete, (*b*) and (*d*) are continuous.
**15.** $E(X) = 1/4(0) + 1/2(1) + 1/4(2) = 1$
**16.** (a)
**17.** .25
**18.** independent
**19.** $(4/52)(3/51)(2/50)(1/49) = 24/6{,}497{,}400 \approx .0000037$

## ANSWERS TO PROBLEMS AND EXERCISES

**1.** (a) $P(A) = 1/52$
(b) $P(B) = 4/52 = 1/13$
(c) $P(C) = 13/52 = 1/4$
(d) $P(D \cap C) = 0/52 = 0$
(e) $P(C \cup B) = 13/52 + 4/52 - 1/52 = 16/52 = 4/13$

**2.** $A$: a child has perceptual problems.
$B$: a child has emotional problems.
$A \cap B$: a child has both perceptual and emotional problems.
$P(A) = .03$, $P(B) = .06$, $P(A \cap B) = .015$.
$P(A \cup B) = .03 + .06 - .015 = .075$

**3.** (a) 210
(b) 20
(c) If $N = 9$, then $(n + 1)! = 10! = 10(9!)$.

**4.** $6! = 720$

**5.** (a) 15
(b) 5, 10, 10, 5, and 1

**6.** $\binom{12}{5} = 792$

**7.** (a) $1 + 4 + 6 + 4 + 1 = 16$; $2^4 = 16$
(b) $2^6 = 64$

**8.** $\binom{10}{5} = 252$

**9.** (a) $P(A)^n = (1/2)^5 = 1/32$ or .03125
(b) 1/32 or .03125
(c) $1 - 1/32 - 1/32 = 30/32 = 15/16$ or .9375

**10.** (a) $(1/2)^5 = 1/32$
(b) $(1/2)^{10} = 1/1{,}024$

**11.** (a) .7888
(b) .0062
(c) $(.6915)^3 = .3307$

**12.** $E(X) = 2\frac{1}{5}$

**13.** (a) 1/36, 1/18, 1/12, 1/9, 5/36, 1/6, 5/36, 1/9, 1/12, 1/18, 1/36
(b) $E(X) = \Sigma_j p_j X_j = 7$
(c) 5/6
(d) $(1/6)^3 = 1/216$
(e) 1/6
(f) $\frac{N!}{(N-1)!1!} p^{N-1} q, \left(\frac{5!}{4!}\right) = 5$, hence

$$5\left(\frac{1}{6}\right)^4 \left(\frac{5}{6}\right) = \frac{25}{7{,}776} = .0032150$$

(g) $p^N = (1/6)^5 = 1/7{,}776$; thus, $26/7{,}776 = .0033436$

**14.** The probability of observing 23 or more $A$'s when $N = 30$ is only .00261, good news for the marketing department.

# 10

# STATISTICAL INFERENCE: SAMPLING AND INTERVAL ESTIMATION

## 10.1 OVERVIEW

In the preceding chapters, statistical inference has been of incidental concern—only a minor theme. Beginning with this chapter, we will focus on estimating parameters using inferential statistical methods. One of the primary purposes of statistical methods is to allow generalizations about populations using data from samples. This chapter introduces ideas that are of fundamental importance in all succeeding chapters.

Nearly all public opinion polls and surveys, such as the Gallup and Harris polls, involve selecting a sample, obtaining data on that sample, and then making inferences about the entire population. Rarely are all members of the population observed; usually only a small fraction of the elements in the population is sampled. The Nielsen ratings of the popularity of television programs are based on the viewing habits of a sample of less than one home in 10,000 (.01%) in the population. The computerized projections of winners in political elections are nothing more than sophisticated applications of the concepts of this chapter. Before considering the theory underlying statistical inference, some fundamental definitions and concepts must be reviewed.

## 10.2 POPULATIONS AND SAMPLES: PARAMETERS AND STATISTICS

The principal use of statistical inference in empirical research is to obtain knowledge about a large class of persons, or other statistical units, from a relatively small number of persons. Inferential statistical methods employ *inductive reasoning*—reasoning from the particular to the general and from the observed to the unobserved. Inferential statistical reasoning addresses such questions as: "What can I say about the age at which the average child in the United States (the population) first utters a sentence, given that the average was 202 weeks for a sample of twenty-five children?" Any exhaustive (finite or infinite ) set or collection of things (units) that we wish to study, or about which we wish to make inferences, is called a *population*. A sample of $n$ persons, or other statistical units, is a part, or subset, of a population of $N$ persons. A sample is of little inferential value if it is not representative. Many samples reported by the popular media (e.g., volunteer "call in" samples) are essentially useless because they are almost certainly not representative. A sample should be selected in a deliberate fashion from the population so that the characteristics of the population can be estimated with a known margin of error.

Measurements taken on members of a population can be described in the ways that have been discussed in the preceding chapters. Means, medians, variances, and percentiles can be computed on the data from a sample of a population. The correlation between height and weight for sixteen-year-old females in the United States could be of interest. Recall that the values of various descriptive measures computed for populations are called *parameters*; for samples, these same descriptive measures are called *statistics*. As we have seen in previous chapters, the parameter describes a population in the way a statistic describes a sample. It is customary to denote statistics by Roman letters and parameters by Greek letters. The symbol $\overline{X}$ stands for the sample mean, and the Greek letter $\mu$ stands for the population mean. The sample variance is denoted by $s^2$ and the population variance by $\sigma^2$. The statistic $r$ is an estimate of the parameter $\rho$.

A statistic computed on a sample is an estimate of the parameter in the population. An *estimator* is some function of the scores in a sample that produces a value, called the *estimate*. The estimate gives some information about a parameter. For example, the sample mean $\overline{X}$ is an estimate of the mean or average score in the population. A random sample of 100 eight-year-olds might yield 104.65 for a sample mean on the Stanford-Binet Intelligence Scale. This value, 104.65, would be an estimate of the mean test score in the population sampled.

## 10.3 INFINITE VERSUS FINITE POPULATIONS

For most research purposes, populations are assumed to be infinite, not finite, in size. However, the truly infinite populations that come easily to mind are somewhat artificial or imaginary, for example, the collection of all positive numbers, the collection of all possible measurements of a person's weight, the collection of tosses of two dice that could be made throughout eternity, or all six-year-olds who will ever exist. Almost any interesting population of physical items (as opposed to conceptual possibilities) is finite in size, for example, all living persons in the Western Hemisphere, all possible orderings of twenty stimuli (20!), all public high schools in California, or all social workers in New York City. A finite population may be extremely large—the proverbial "grains of sand on earth," the number of census tracts in the United States, or all first-grade children in California. If it is conceivable that the process of counting the elements of the population could be completed, then the population is technically finite. Fortunately, it is generally not necessary to worry about the distinction between finite and infinite populations. As discussed later, unless the fraction of the elements sampled (i.e., the sampling fraction, $n/N$) is .05 (i.e., 5%) or greater, the techniques for making inferences to finite populations and those for infinite populations give essentially the same results. Even if the sampling fraction is as much as 10%, the results from using the simpler methods, which assume that $N$ is infinitely large, are only slightly less precise than the results from using procedures that take the sampling fraction into account.

In short, most applied statistical techniques are based on the assumption that an infinite population is being sampled. If the population is quite large and the sample from the population constitutes only a small proportion of the population (i.e., $n/N < .05$), the fact that the population is not actually infinite is of little concern. It is common to speak of a population as being "virtually infinite," that is, the population although finite, is very large, and statistical techniques that assume an infinite population will be used. In most illustrations and procedures of this chapter, the populations are assumed to be virtually infinite in size.

## 10.4 RANDOMNESS AND RANDOM SAMPLING

The concept of random sampling is closely tied to probability (Chapter 9). The validity of a statistical inference depends on how representative the sample is of the population. To evaluate the preferences of all voters in the United States, common sense tells us not to interview people on a street corner.

The method used to select the sample is of utmost importance in judging the validity of the inferences made from the sample to the population. The novice is often more concerned with the size of a sample than with its representativeness. A representative sample of 100 may be preferable to a nonrepresentative sample of 1,000,000.

A classic illustration of how *not* to sample occurred in 1936 in the Presidential preference poll conducted by the now-defunct periodical *Literary Digest*. Postcards were sent to a nonrepresentative sample of 12,000,000! The sample was selected from automobile owners and telephone directories. Although the response rate was poor (21%), the 2,500,000 who returned the postcards are one of the largest samples on record. Although 57% of the respondents indicated a preference for the Republican candidate Alf Landon, Franklin Roosevelt was elected by the greatest majority in history up to that time, carrying all states except Maine and Vermont.

What went wrong? How can George Gallup's projections be presumed to be accurate with his sample of less the 2,000 persons when the *Literary Digest* was misled by a sample that was more than 1,000 times larger? The size of a sample can never compensate for a lack of representativeness (bias). Automobile owners and families with telephones were not a representative sample of voters in 1936. In addition, the 21% who returned the questionnaire probably were not even a representative sample of the 12,000,000 who received the postcards. (The possible self-selection bias among those who return questionnaires continues to this day to be the greatest threat to the validity of mail surveys.)

The *Literary Digest* survey, apart from the biased sampling plan, utilized an extremely inefficient strategy. To anyone with a modicum of statistical understanding, it would have been evident that a sample only one-thousandth (.1%) as large as that used by the *Literary Digest*, if representative, would be exceedingly precise. Even in the era of the penny postcard, the postage for 12 million postcards would have been $120,000! Statisticians worth their salt would have known that $120 ($n = 12,000$) would have served as well.[1]

---

[1]Another common misinterpretation of surveys, especially political polls, is evidenced when the findings are generalized over a period of time, for example, to predict the result in an upcoming election. During the course of a campaign, voter preferences usually vacillate considerably as issues and positions are clarified or changed. In forecasting an election, it is the population of actual voters, those who will in fact vote (not the registered voters, not even those who say that they intend to vote, or those who say they voted in the last election of the same type), that is the relevant population. The population of actual voters is never a truly representative sample of the population of registered voters, which in turn, is never a representative sample of those eligible to be registered voters. In interpreting any poll, one must bear in mind the pollsters' definition of the population as well as the fact that the generalizability (or lack of it) of the results over time is not addressed by the statistics per se.

### Types of Samples

Samples, and the estimates calculated from them (statistics), serve to give information about the characteristics of the population sampled. There are several legitimate and illegitimate ways in which samples can be selected from a population. Simple random sampling is the most widely used and acceptable way to sample, though there are other appropriate methods.

## 10.5 ACCIDENTAL OR CONVENIENCE SAMPLES

Accidental or convenience sampling is a very common, but inappropriate, method of obtaining a sample. Convenient, but haphazard, collections of observations are usually of little value in estimating parameters. Results from street corner polls, polls of the audience of a particular television or radio program, or readers of a particular magazine cannot be generalized beyond such groups without great risks. Commercial advertisements often report data on their products obtained on samples of unknown representativeness. One should be wary of conclusions based on accidental samples.

## 10.6 RANDOM SAMPLES

In random sampling, every unit in the population has an equal and independent chance of being selected for the sample. That is, not only must the probability of selecting any individual (or unit) in the population as a participant be the same as for selecting any other individual in the population, but also, the probability of selecting any given person must not be affected by (that is, must be independent of) whether any other person is selected.

As in all texts on statistical methods, the greatest emphasis in this and subsequent chapters is given to simple random sampling.[2] Before a sample will adequately serve as a basis for making estimates of population parameters, it must be representative of the population.

This criterion of representativeness presents a problem. How would one know for certain whether a sample is representative of a population unless the characteristics of the entire population are known? And if the characteristics of the entire population are known, why does one need a sample with which to estimate them? This quandary is resolved when one realizes that *random sampling* of a population will produce samples that, in the long run, are representative of the population and, in the short run, have known probabilities of the accuracy with which the population is represented. If a sample is randomly drawn, it is likely to be representative of the population in all respects, that is, the statistic differs from the parameter only by chance on any variable, real or illusory, measured or not measured. Through the "magic" of statistical theory, the degree of this difference can be estimated. The method of random selection of samples will ensure, within a certain margin of error, representativeness of the samples and, hence, will permit establishing limits within which the parameters fall with a particular probability.

The ability to estimate the *degree of error* due to chance (sampling error) is an impor-

[2]More sophisticated sampling plans, such as stratified sampling, cluster sampling, and two-stage sampling, are dealt with in textbooks devoted exclusively to sampling, such as the classics, William Cochran's *Sampling Techniques* (1977) or Leslie Kish's *Survey Sampling* (1965), or Richard Jaeger's *Sampling in Education and the Social Sciences* (1984).

tant feature of a random sample. It is not possible to estimate the error with accidental sampling and many other sampling methods because they contain unknown types and degrees of bias in addition to sampling error. For example, if one were to choose 100 households listed on a given page in the telephone directory one would not have a random sample of the population of households in a city. This sample of 100 is not representative of the population, and it is nonrepresentative in unknown ways and to an unknown extent. The initial letter used in surnames varies in frequency among ethnic groups. It is possible that the 100 households listed on a given page have a common ethnic identification (e.g., Anderson). Perhaps ethnicity is related to voter preference, brand preference, income, attitude toward public schools, or whatever is being surveyed. Obviously, the results of such a sample cannot be said to be representative of the population.

However, if 100 households were randomly sampled from the population, it would be possible to answer such questions as "How likely is it that a randomly drawn sample of 100 households will have a mean income that differs by less than $500 from the mean income of all households in the directory?"[3] From the data for a random sample we can generalize the results to the population with a known margin of error.[4]

The process of inferential statistical reasoning involves finding an estimate of a parameter from a sample and then determining the expected amount of sampling error in estimating the parameter. It is not surprising, then, that inferential statistics is based on the assumption that the sample was obtained randomly from populations.

The following is an example of random sampling using a table of random digits. From the 3,000 students at Fairview High School, Principal Howe wishes to estimate the percent of students currently using drugs. It is impractical and unnecessary to try to have all students respond to an anonymous questionnaire. By methods that will be introduced later, Howe finds that the percent using drugs in a random sample of 100 probably will not differ by more than 5% from the corresponding percent in the population of 3,000.

It can be said that the sampling error will almost certainly be less than 10%. Howe instructs her secretary to assign a four-digit number from 0001 to 3000, starting at the beginning of the alphabetical file of the student roster. She then goes to her table of random numbers (such as Table B in the Appendix) to make the selection.[5] The first task is to find a point of entry into the table. With the book open to the first page, she lays the point of her pencil on the page of random digits with her eyes closed. Suppose the two digits closest to her pencil point are 5 and 3. She then moves to the intersection of row 5 and column 3 of the table to begin making selections. Moving along row 5 and starting with column 3, Howe sees the digits 0947. By grouping digits into groups of four and reading down, the numbers 1572, 2993, 4477, 8488, 2169, ... are obtained. Her secretary will now compile the names of those persons who have identification numbers 1572, 2993, 2169, and so on. But what about 4477, 8488, and other numbers greater than the number in the population (3,000)? There are only 3,000 persons in Howe's population, so no one has these identification numbers. These numbers are simply disregarded. What happens if the same number comes up a

---

[3]Of course, the households in the city and the households listed in the telephone directory are not always the same. A few households have no telephone; others (an increasing proportion) have unlisted numbers.

[4]What is the probability that random sampling will result in a sample of only one particular ethnic group? Even if ethnic group A represents 90% of the population, from Chapter 9 (Section 9.5), we know that the probability is exactly calculable: $(.9)^{100} = .000027$. This is one simple example of how random sampling will permit an exact probability calculation.

[5]Most personal computers and some hand calculators have a built-in function for generating random numbers.

second time? If it does, it is disregarded the second time it comes up. The sampling continues as though nothing had happened. In this manner Principal Howe can be assured of the randomness of her sample. Each member of the population has an equal and independent chance of being chosen in the sample.

Why should Howe have gone to this trouble to obtain a random sample? Why did she not just go through the files and choose 100 persons she thought would be representative of all 3,000? Would this judgment not give a more representative sample than leaving the process to mindless chance? No, the random sample will probably be better than a judgmental sample. Many factors can operate on the principal's judgment to make her judgmental sample unrepresentative. If the principal were more likely to select those she knew by name, her judgmental sample would be biased in several possible ways. It might have a greater proportion of student leaders, scholars, or troublemakers than in the population. If she selects her sample randomly, these biases cannot affect the selection. Random selection prevents any systematic biases, plus, unlike judgmental selection, it allows the margin of error to be estimated.

## 10.7 INDEPENDENCE

In Chapter 9, two events were said to be independent if they had nothing to do with each other, if they were uncorrelated. If the coin that is tossed before a football game has come up heads for the last five tosses, this in no way affects the probability of heads in game six. Similarly in selecting a random sample, the chance of selecting one person is unrelated (independent) to the probability for any other persons. In true random sampling, each element in the population has the same probability (equiprobability) of being selected for the sample, and the fact that element 143 was selected in no way affects the probability that element 144 or any other element will be selected.

An example of sampling in which the observations are not independent will illustrate what will be avoided when random sampling is used. Suppose a researcher wants to assess the attitudes of school administrators in California about some issue (e.g., the voucher plan). The researcher plans to interview fifty administrators. To minimize costs (logistic as well as dollar), the researcher decides to select five districts randomly, then select ten administrators randomly within each of these districts. Will the researcher have a true random sample of the population? No, once the districts are selected, all administrators not in these districts have no probability of being included in the sample. The researcher has a random sample of districts (albeit an extremely small sample), but cannot use $n = 50$ for the statistical computations.[6]

Non-independence of the observations in a sample that is presumed to be a random sample is a prevalent fault in all types of behavioral and social research. Many studies are analyzed incorrectly because the researcher is not aware of what is and what is not a random sample. Countless theses and many other published studies stumble on this basic problem.

A flaw common in field studies in education is to select schools or classes randomly and then analyze the data as if students had been selected randomly. Suppose there are 50 elementary schools in a large school district that is considering lengthening the school day by one hour. Suppose five schools are selected randomly to be in the experimental ($E$) group (e.g., longer school day), and the other schools serve as control ($C$) schools. The probability is .10 that any child will be in the $E$ group; the condition of equiprobability obtains, but the

[6]This is an example of cluster sampling.

selection of each student has *not* been independent. If Sue and George are both in Lincoln School, one of the schools in group $E$, then Sue and George must both receive method $E$. There is no chance for Sue to receive treatment $E$ and George to receive treatment $C$. Any analysis that treats the students in the $E$ and $C$ groups as though they are a random sample of $n$ separate observations is not legitimate because the sampling units were schools, not individual students. The proper method of statistical analysis in such circumstances (cluster sampling) often manages to elude even seasoned researchers.[7]

Except in surveys, it is almost impossible to select a true random sample from the population because of logistic barriers. Nevertheless this is the goal, and researchers should strive to get as close to the goal as they possibly can. Generalizations made from research should acknowledge discrepancies between the sample actually used and a true random sample.

This section on random sampling is concluded with an alternative statement of the definition of simple random sampling. This statement on simple random sampling is equivalent to the one given earlier in Section 10.6:

> If the sampling of $n$ observations from a population of $N$ observations is random, then regardless of what the first $m$ choices were, the probability of any particular observation $X_i$ being chosen on the $(m + 1)$st selection is $1/(N - m)$.

## 10.8 SYSTEMATIC SAMPLING

To draw a sample of the 100 students from the 3,000 students at Fairview High School (a sampling fraction of $n/N = 1/30$), Principal Howe selected a number randomly between one and thirty from the table of random numbers and then picked the student corresponding to that number and every thirtieth student thereafter from the student roster. For example, if the random number selected were thirteen, the 13th, 43rd, 73rd, 103rd, ..., 2,983rd students from the list would comprise the sample. A sample of this kind is known as a *systematic sample*. Likewise, selecting every hundredth word in a dictionary would yield a 1% systematic sample of words.

A practical advantage of systematic samples is that they are often easier to obtain, or to explain to another person who must select the sample, than random samples. Systematic samples of persons are usually representative samples. Indeed, the results from systematic samples tend to be slightly more accurate than results from simple random samples, but inconsequentially so. The orderly systematic sampling process allows less opportunity for sampling error to occur. The chief disadvantage of systematic sampling is that there is no satisfactory way to determine precisely how accurate the estimates are in the long run. What is usually done is to behave as if the sample were drawn randomly. The findings from a systematic sample of persons will almost always differ trivially from a random sample. Unlike accidental sampling, systematic sampling is an acceptable scientific sampling technique for most research purposes. Properly employed, findings on random and systematic samples are said to be generalizable, that is, one can be confident that the findings on the sample are not biased and that they are generalizable within a known margin of sampling error to the parent or target population.[8]

---

[7]See Section 19.22 for the proper method of analysis.

[8]Systematic sampling is hazardous only if the data are cyclic (as they often are in time sampling) and the sampling fractions happen to coincide with the cycle. For example, if boys and girls were required to sit in alternate seats and a systematic sample of every second desk (e.g., desks 2, 4, 6, etc.) was selected, the sample would result in a disproportionate number of one sex.

## 10.9 POINT AND INTERVAL ESTIMATES

In previous chapters, all examples of statistical inference involved *point estimates*, that is, a single point or value was used to estimate a parameter. The expression $E(\overline{X}) = \mu$ denotes that the statistic, $\overline{X}$, is an unbiased point estimate of the parameter, $\mu$. An *interval estimate* builds on the concept of the point estimate, but in addition conveys the degree of accuracy of the estimate. Interval estimation is a valuable, but much underused, inferential statistical method in behavioral and social research.

As the term suggests, an *interval estimate* is a range or band within which the parameter is presumed to lie, with a certain degree of confidence. For example, the mean reading vocabulary of university students has been estimated at 156,000 words. The point estimate of the parameter is 156,000; but if the sample of students on which this statistic was obtained is small, the interval estimate could be large, for example, from 112,000 to 200,000. If we know only the point estimate, we do not know how good the estimate is. The interval estimate gives a lower and an upper limit for the parameter; we can be quite confident that the true average vocabulary size is probably somewhere within the interval indicated. On the other hand, if the interval estimate were 152,000 to 160,000, then the parameter, $\mu$, would be estimated rather precisely.

The understanding of the underlying rationale for interval estimates demands a grasp of *the most fundamentally important concept of inferential statistics, the concept of the sampling distribution*. Subsequent chapters cannot be adequately comprehended without understanding the concept of a sampling distribution. Mastering the concept presents a challenge, but the fruit is well worth the effort.

## 10.10 SAMPLING DISTRIBUTIONS

The concept of a sampling distribution is absolutely critical in inferential statistics. In this chapter, the concept of the sampling distribution of the mean is illustrated. Once the concept of the sampling distribution of the mean is mastered, the concept is easily extended to other statistical measures such as proportions, variances, or correlation coefficients.

The statistician determines the degree of precision to be expected from statistics on random samples from knowledge of the corresponding sampling distributions. A statistic or estimator calculated on a sample has a certain sampling distribution. You can imagine the process of choosing a random sample of size $n$ from a certain population, calculating $\overline{X}$, and repeating the process many, many times. If this process of randomly drawing a sample from the population were repeated thousands of times, it would be possible to construct a frequency distribution of the thousands of sample statistics (e.g., means) that were obtained. *The frequency distribution of the statistics, $\overline{X}$'s, is the sampling distribution of the mean*. The term "sampling distribution" indicates that the frequency distribution is not of individual observations ($X$'s), but of statistics (such as $\overline{X}$'s) from an infinite number of random samples of size $n$.

Suppose we wished to know the average number of books that students in a given school district checked out from the public library in that city during a particular year. From a roster listing all students, I select a random sample of, for example, $n = 25$ students and find the number of books each has checked out, and calculate the mean for my sample ($\overline{X}_1$); you do likewise, and find the mean of your sample ($\overline{X}_2$). Do we expect our sample means to be exactly equal? No, we know intuitively that there will be some difference between $\overline{X}_1$

and $\bar{X}_2$ due to chance (sampling error). If everyone else also replicates the study and finds the mean for a random sample of $n = 25$ persons, the distribution of all these means (actually an infinite number) is the sampling distribution of the mean when $n$ is 25. The mean of this sampling distribution of $\bar{X}$'s is the parameter, $\mu$. This is succinctly stated in the expression, $E(\bar{X}) = \mu$. This also shows that the sample mean, $\bar{X}$, is an unbiased point estimate of the parameter, $\mu$. The standard deviation of this distribution is considered in the next section.

## 10.11 THE STANDARD ERROR OF THE MEAN

For simplicity, we will first consider the situation in which the variable of interest in the parent population, $X$, is normally distributed, and in which $\mu$ and $\sigma$ are known. Bear in mind that the purpose at this point is pedagogical and conceptual; by specifying these conditions, important characteristics about sampling distributions can be illustrated without distracting qualifying statements. In Chapter 11, the more typical situation in which $\mu$ and $\sigma$ are not known will be considered.

On many intelligence scales, the distribution of IQ scores is normal with parameters, $\mu = 100$, and $\sigma = 15$. If $n = 25$ observations are randomly drawn from the populations of normally distributed $X$'s, how much will the mean of the twenty-five observations ($\bar{X}$) differ from the parameter ($\mu$), that is, how great is the sampling error ($\bar{X} - \mu$)?

Equation 10.1 gives the standard deviation of the sampling distribution of the sample means ($\bar{X}$'s), called *the standard error of the mean* and denoted by $\sigma_{\bar{X}}$. The standard error of the mean is the standard deviation of the sampling error in $\bar{X}$'s when a random sample of size $n$ is employed:[9]

$$\sigma_{\bar{X}} = \frac{\sigma}{\sqrt{n}} \qquad \textbf{(10.1)}$$

In the example with $\sigma = 15$ and $n = 25$, the parameter $\sigma_{\bar{X}}$ is found to have a value of 3.0 (Equation 10.1):

$$\sigma_{\bar{X}} = \frac{15}{\sqrt{25}} = \frac{15}{5} = 3.0$$

The $\sigma_{\bar{X}}$ value of 3.0 indicates the following: If a random sample of twenty-five observations were drawn from the parent population, the mean ($\bar{X}$) of these twenty-five $X_i$'s was computed, and this process was repeated, again finding the mean ($\bar{X}$) of the second set of twenty-five random observations, and this process was repeated an infinite number of times, the standard deviation of this sampling distribution, $\sigma_{\bar{X}}$, would be 3.0. In other words, the standard deviation of the distribution of sampling error in the $\bar{X}$'s, (i.e., $\bar{X} - \mu$),

[9]Equation 10.1 assumes that the number of observations in the population ($N$) is infinitely large. Occasionally in survey research, the sample of $n$ observations represents a non-negligible proportion of $N$. In this case, the variance in the sampling distribution is precisely described by the equation $\sigma_{\bar{X}}^2 = (1 - n/N)\sigma^2/n$. However, unless the sampling fraction $n/N$ is .10 or more (i.e., the sample represents 10% or more of the population), the precise value of $\sigma_{\bar{X}}$ is at most 5% smaller than the value yielded by Equation 10.1 (see Section 10.3).

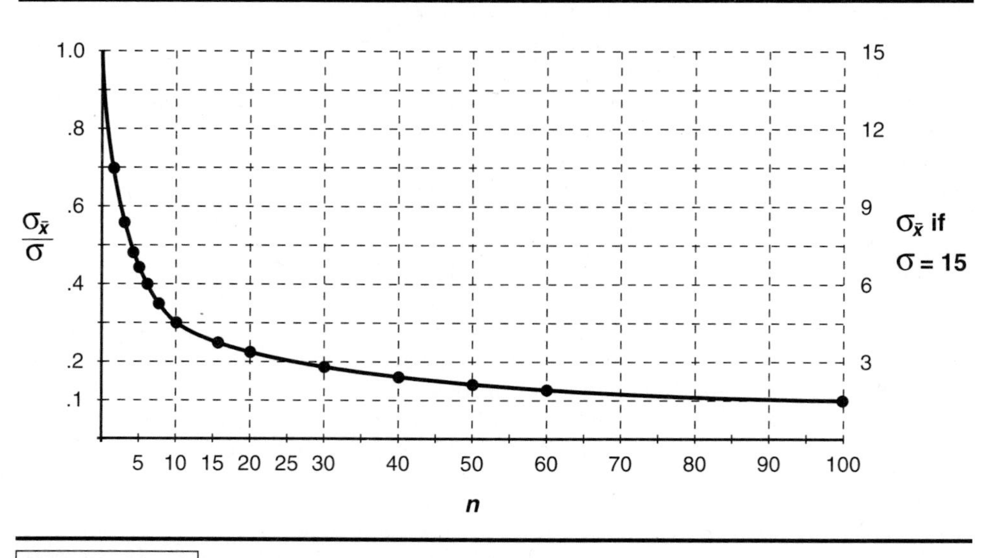


**FIGURE 10.1** The Relationship of $n$ and $\sigma_{\bar{X}}$

is 3.0. Sampling error is the difference between the statistic (in this case, $\bar{X}$) and the corresponding parameter (in this case $\mu$).

## 10.12 RELATIONSHIP OF $\sigma_{\bar{X}}$ TO $n$

As the sample size $n$ increases, the magnitude of sampling error decreases, as shown in Equation 10.1. For example, with $\sigma = 15$ and $n = 25$, $\sigma_{\bar{X}} = 3$; but if $n = 100$, $\sigma_{\bar{X}} = 1.5$; and if $n = 225$, $\sigma_{\bar{X}} = 1$. This is illustrated in Figure 10.1. Note that the value of $\sigma_{\bar{X}}$ is halved when $n$ is quadrupled.

Regardless of $n$, the values of $\bar{X}$ are normally distributed and have a mean of $\mu$ and a variance of $\sigma_{\bar{X}}^2 = \sigma^2/n$. The expression $E(\bar{X}) = \mu$ is just another way of saying that the mean of the sampling distribution of $\bar{X}$'s equals $\mu$—it says that the expected value of a sample mean is equal to the parameter. In our IQ illustration, the expression $E(\bar{X}) = \mu = 100$ succinctly and explicitly denotes that the mean of the sampling distribution of sample means is 100. *The expected value of any statistic is the mean of its sampling distribution.*

Likewise, $E(s_{\bar{X}}^2) = \sigma_{\bar{X}}^2 = \sigma^2/n$ shows that the variability of the sampling error $(\bar{X} - \mu)$ is inversely related to sample size, $n$.

## 10.13 CONFIDENCE INTERVALS

In the hypothetical illustration of IQ scores, the mean of the parent population ($\mu$) is known. Consequently, there is no need to use $\bar{X}$ to estimate $\mu$. Imagine for the moment the unlikely situation in which $\sigma$ was known, but $\mu$ was not known. How could $\bar{X}$ be used to estimate $\mu$? For any value of $n$, it is true that $E(\bar{X}) = \mu$, but this does not tell how much sampling error is to be expected in the $\bar{X}$-value. If $n = 225$, then $\sigma_{\bar{X}} = \sigma/\sqrt{n} = 1.0$; hence, 68% of the means in the sampling distribution would differ 1.0 point or less from $\mu$. For example, suppose many different random samples with $n = 225$ were selected, and $\bar{X}$ was computed for each sample. If we placed a band of $\sigma_{\bar{X}} = 1.0$ point above and below (±) each of the $\bar{X}$-values, the value of $\mu$ would lie within 68% of the intervals around the sample means. In other words, the .68 confidence interval is $\bar{X} \pm \sigma_{\bar{X}}$, as shown in Equation 10.2. The lower limit of the .68 confidence interval (*CI*) is $\bar{X} - \sigma_{\bar{X}}$; the upper limit of the interval is $\bar{X} + \sigma_{\bar{X}}$. The ".68" refers to the confidence coefficient of the confidence interval. 68% of the confidence intervals would contain the parameter, $\mu$:

$$.68CI = \bar{X} \pm \sigma_{\bar{X}} \tag{10.2}$$

Equation 10.2 shows that if the value of $\sigma_{\bar{X}}$ is added to and subtracted from each $\bar{X}$-value, the parameter $\mu$ would lie within 68% of such intervals (in the example, from 1.0 IQ score point below each $\bar{X}$ to 1.0 above each $\bar{X}$).

In practice, the researcher ordinarily has only one mean, $\bar{X}$, the mean of the sample of $n$ observations. There is no way of knowing whether the particular mean ($\bar{X}$) is one of the 68% that falls within one standard error ($\sigma_{\bar{X}}$) of $\mu$. We usually want to be more than ".68 confident" that our confidence interval contains the parameter, $\mu$. Consequently, a wider confidence interval is more common. The .90 *CI* is defined as:

$$.90CI = \bar{X} \pm 1.645\sigma_{\bar{X}} \tag{10.3}$$

In the long run, the parameter $\mu$ will be contained within 95% (nineteen out of twenty) of .95 confidence intervals. The .95 *CI* is the most commonly used confidence interval:

$$.95CI = \bar{X} \pm 1.96\sigma_{\bar{X}} \tag{10.4}$$

Or, equivalently:

$$\text{probability}(\bar{X} - 1.96\sigma_{\bar{X}} < \mu < \bar{X} + 1.96\sigma_{\bar{X}}) = .95$$

Or, for any confidence coefficient, $1 - \alpha$:

$$(1 - \alpha)CI = \bar{X} \pm {}_{1-\alpha/2}z\sigma_{\bar{X}} \tag{10.5}$$

Recall from the normal curve table (Table A) that a $z$-score of $-1.96$ corresponds to $P_{2.5}$, the 2.5th percentile, and that $z = 1.96$ corresponds to $P_{97.5}$. Equation 10.4 shows that if $1.96\sigma_{\bar{X}}$ is added to, and subtracted from, the sample mean ($\bar{X}$), one can be "95% confident" that the parameter $\mu$ lies somewhere within this interval ($\bar{X} \pm 1.96\sigma_{\bar{X}}$). To be even more confident, one can use the .99 confidence interval (${}_{.995}z = 2.576$):

$$.99CI = \bar{X} \pm 2.576\sigma_{\bar{X}} \quad \textbf{(10.6)}$$

## 10.14 CONFIDENCE INTERVALS WHEN $\sigma$ IS KNOWN: AN EXAMPLE

An example will now be presented of how a confidence interval estimate is used. The example will be developed in considerable detail to illustrate the rationale of the underlying theory.

Consider a researcher who has set out to find the average IQ of the approximately 500,000 adopted children in the United States as measured by the Wechsler Intelligence Scale for Children (WISC). The WISC is an individual verbal and performance intelligence test that must be administered by trained examiners and therefore is quite expensive compared to group intelligence tests. The available funds for this study will cover 100 test administrations, but no more. The researcher has good reason to believe that the adopted children are no more homogeneous or heterogeneous than the population of children used in the norming of the WISC, but there is reason to believe that their average score might differ from the norm (100). Hence, assume that the standard deviation of WISC IQ's in this population is 15, the same as in the norm group.[10]

A random sample of 100 WISC IQ scores will be taken from the population of 500,000 adopted children in which $\sigma = 15$. The researcher will calculate $\bar{X}$ as a point estimate of the unknown $\mu$, but the confidence interval around $\bar{X}$ should also be established. To be "95% confident," Equation 10.4 will be used. With $n = 100$, one can be confident that the sampling distribution of $\bar{X}$-values is normal with a mean, $\mu$, and with a standard deviation, $\sigma_{\bar{X}}$, or $\sigma/\sqrt{n} = 15/\sqrt{100} = 1.5$. We have already seen from Equation 10.4 (or Table A) that 95% of the area under the normal curve lies within 1.96 standard deviations of the mean ($\pm 1.96\sigma$). The sampling distribution of $\bar{X}$ for samples of 100 from a normal population with $\sigma = 15$ appears in Figure 10.2, $\sigma_{\bar{X}} = 1.5$. Thus, 95% of the area under this curve lies within $\mu \pm 2.94$ because $1.96(1.5) = 2.94$.

Suppose the researcher found the mean of the 100 IQ scores was $105.0 = \bar{X}$. The .95 confidence interval for $\mu$ then is $105.0 \pm 2.94$, or from 102.06 to 107.94, conventionally expressed as (102.06, 107.94). In other words, the value of $\mu$ for the population of adopted children is probably at least 102.06 and perhaps as high as 107.94. If more precision is desired, that is, a narrower confidence interval, the sample size must be increased. From Equation 10.1, one sees that if $n = 225$, then $\sigma_{\bar{X}} = 1.0$; if $n = 400$, then $\sigma_{\bar{X}} = .75$; if $n = 900$, then $\sigma_{\bar{X}} = .5$.

Confusion will result unless the distinction between $\mu \pm 1.96\sigma_{\bar{X}}$ and $\bar{X} \pm 1.96\sigma_{\bar{X}}$ is clear. Although 95% of $\bar{X}$'s fall within $\mu \pm 1.96\sigma_{\bar{X}}$, $\mu$ is a fixed value and does not vary. On the other hand the $\bar{X}$'s vary considerably, thus the associated confidence intervals will also vary. They will all be of the same width, but the anchor points (the $\bar{X}$'s) will vary. $\mu$ will lie within the interval, $\bar{X} \pm 1.96\sigma_{\bar{X}}$, for 95% of the $\bar{X}$'s.

---

[10]The argument that $\sigma$ is known and $\mu$ is not known is extremely unlikely. In almost all instances, $\mu$ and $\sigma$ are either both known or both unknown. We assumed here that $\sigma$ is known and $\mu$ is unknown in order to keep the problem of interval estimation simpler than it would be if both $\sigma$ and $\mu$ had to be estimated from the same sample. This latter case, in which both $\sigma$ and $\mu$ are unknown, is by far the more common and realistic situation. The solution to the problem of interval estimation of $\mu$ when $\sigma$ is unknown was the first step in the development of modern inferential statistical methods; this solution was not presented until early in this century. It is due to W. S. Gossett, who wrote under the pseudonym of "Student".

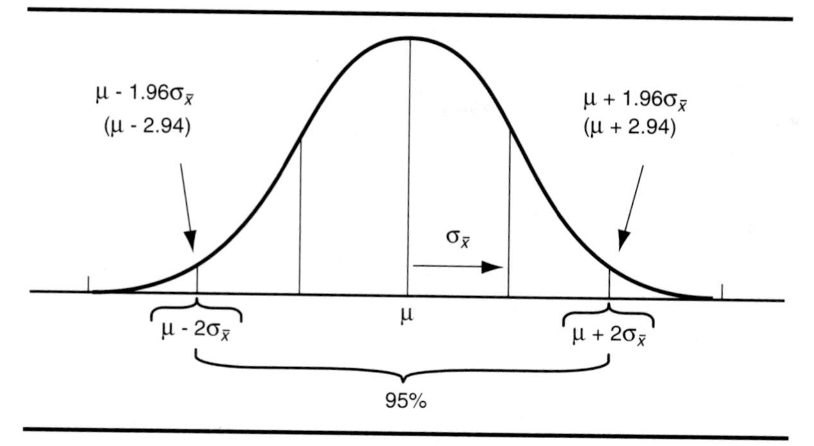


**FIGURE 10.2**
Sampling Distribution of $\bar{X}$ for Random Samples of Size 100 from a Parent Population with $s = 15$, Hence $s_{\bar{X}} = 1.5$

## 10.15 CENTRAL LIMIT THEOREM: A DEMONSTRATION

The central limit theorem states that the sampling distribution of means ( $\bar{X}$'s) from random samples of $n$ observations approaches a normal distribution regardless of the shape of the parent population. The validity of the central limit theorem allows statistical inferences to a much broader range of applications than would otherwise be possible.[11] Since the central limit theorem is vital for a proper understanding of statistical methods, it will be illustrated extensively with actual empirical sampling distributions of $\bar{X}$'s with sample sizes, $n$, varying from 1 to 25. A primary purpose of all the distributions to follow in Figure 10.3 is to demonstrate the validity of the central limit theorem. Many (actually 10,000 in Figure 10.3) random samples of $n$ observations were drawn from three different types of parent populations—normal, rectangular, and skewed. The effect of sample size $n$ and non-normality in the parent populations on the sampling distribution of means is illustrated by using sample sizes, $n$'s, of 1, 2, 5, 10, and 25. As Figure 10.3 is perused, the basis for the following two generalizations should become apparent:

1. Even for non-normal parent populations, the shape of the sampling distributions rapidly approaches normality as $n$ increases.
2. As $n$ increases, the variability of the sampling distribution of $\bar{X}$ decreases; the decrease is accurately described by Equation 10.1 ($\sigma_{\bar{X}} = \sigma/\sqrt{n}$ ) even if the parent population is non-normal.

Three parent populations are defined such that all have equal means ($\mu_1 = \mu_2 = \mu_3 = 100$) and equal standard deviations ($\sigma_1 = \sigma_2 = \sigma_3 = 15$). However, the populations differ markedly in shape—one is normal, another is rectangular (kurtosis, $\gamma_2 = -1.2$), and the third is highly skewed ($\Omega = .7$). These three parent populations are shown in Panel A of Figure 10.3.

Each bar in the percentage histograms gives the percentage of observations for each IQ score. For example, in the parent populations the percentage of IQ scores of 100

[11]It is the reason the $t$-test (Chapters 11–12) and ANOVA (Chapters 15–20) can be accurately used with variables that are not normally distributed.

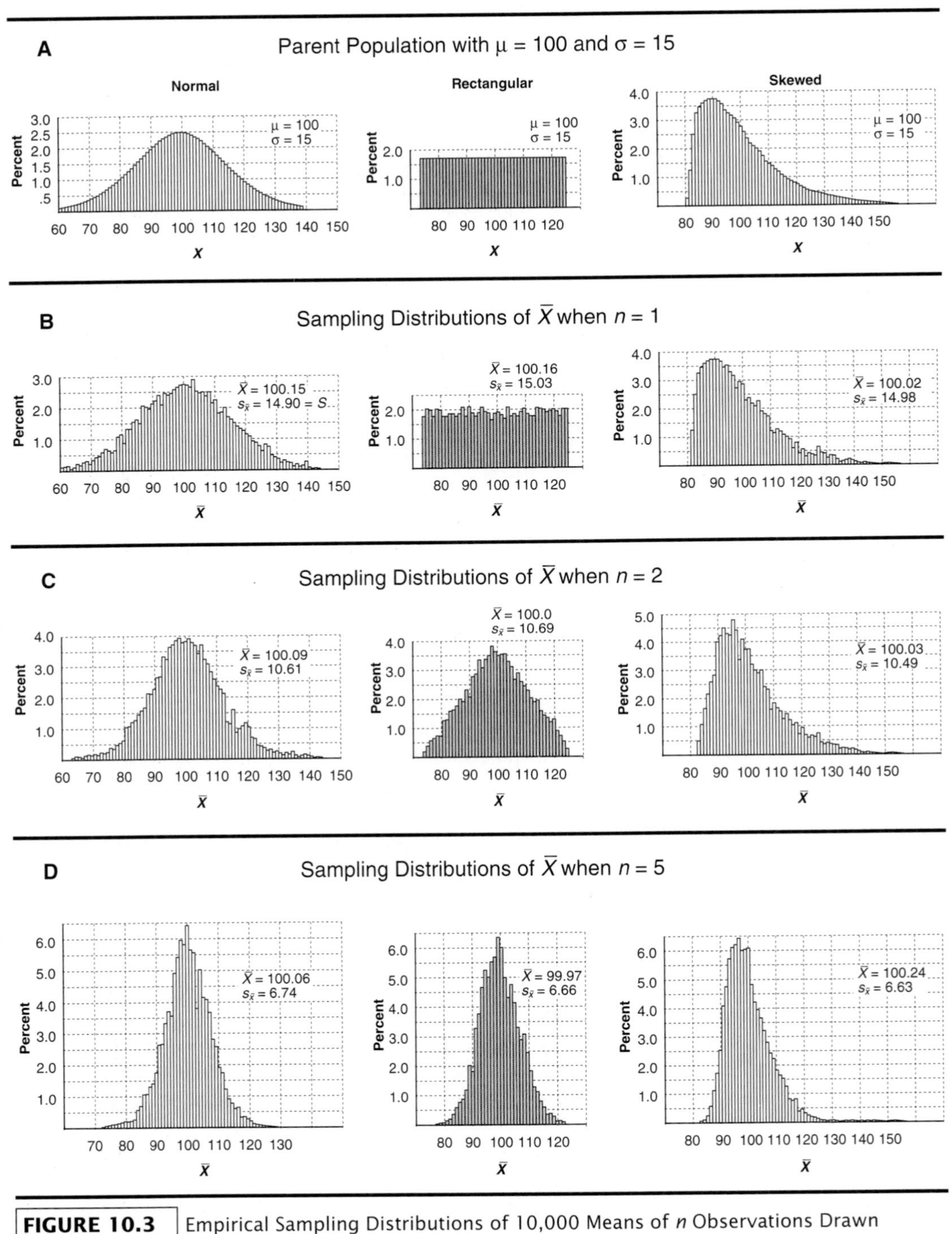


**FIGURE 10.3** Empirical Sampling Distributions of 10,000 Means of $n$ Observations Drawn Randomly from Normal (left), Rectangular (center), and Skewed (right) Parent Distributions in which $\mu = 100$ and $\sigma = 15$. Sample size ($n$) is 1, 2, and 5 in Panels B, C, and D, respectively. Panels E and F give sampling distributions for $n = 10$ and $n = 25$.

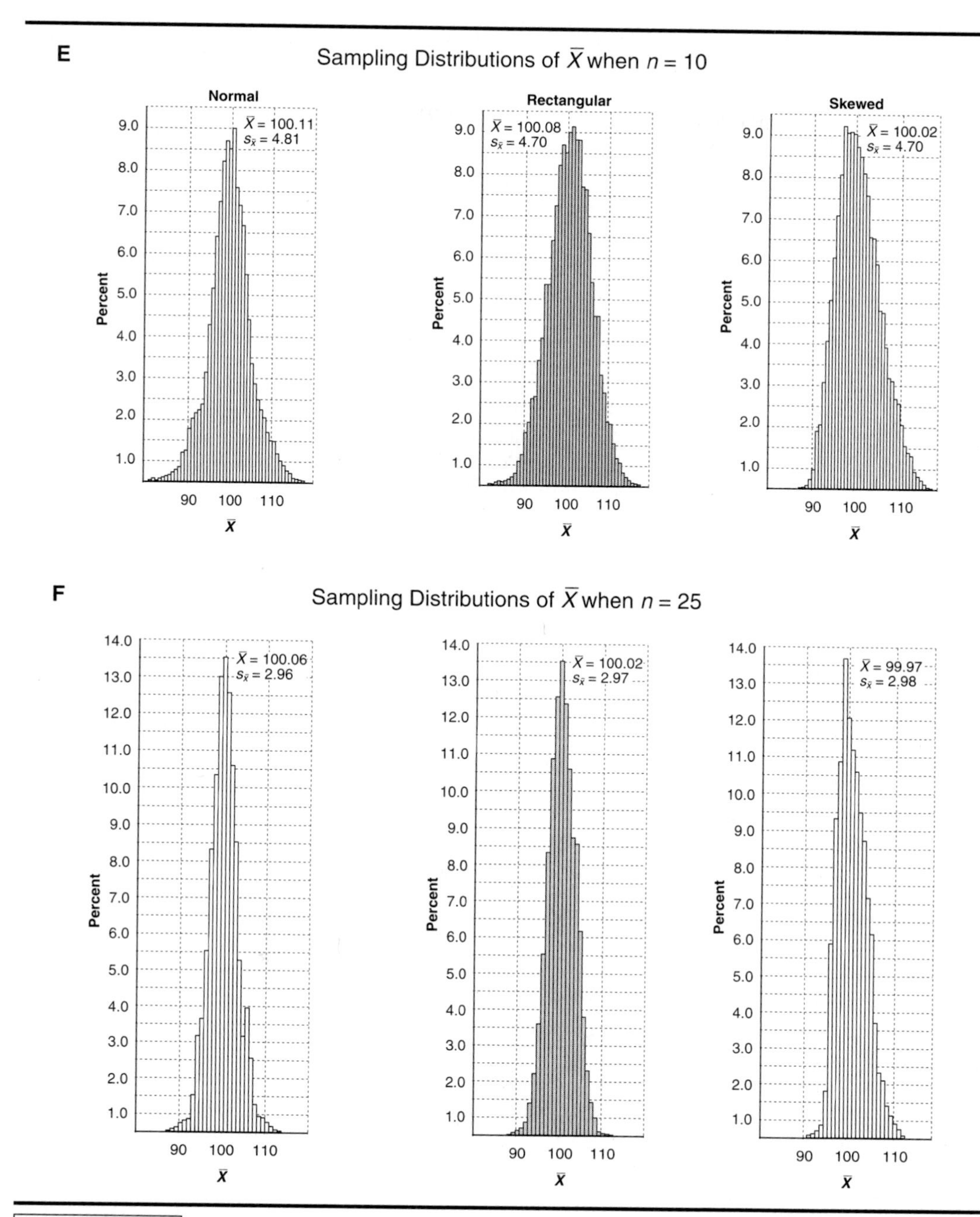

FIGURE 10.3 *(Continued)*

**TABLE 10.1** A Comparison of Observed Values of $s_{\bar{X}}$ (Based on 10,000 $\bar{X}$'s) and Theoretical Values of $\sigma_{\bar{X}}$ for Various Sample Sizes When the Three Parent Populations (Normal, Rectangular and Skewed) Sampled Have Equal Means and Standard Deviations ($\mu = 100$ and $\sigma = 15$)

| | $s_{\bar{X}}$ | | | | | |
|---|---|---|---|---|---|---|
| *Parent Population* | $n = 1$ | $n = 2$ | $n = 5$ | $n = 10$ | $n = 25$ | $n = 100$ |
| Normal | 14.90 | 10.61 | 6.74 | 4.81 | 2.96 | 1.498 |
| Rectangular | 15.03 | 10.69 | 6.66 | 4.70 | 2.97 | 1.487 |
| Skewed | 14.98 | 10.49 | 6.63 | 4.70 | 2.98 | 1.479 |
| $\sigma_{\bar{X}} = \sigma/\sqrt{n}$ | 15 | 10.61 | 6.71 | 4.74 | 3.00 | 1.500 |

(where $\mu = 100$ and $\sigma = 15$) is 2.66% for the normal distribution (see left-most figure in Panel A), 1.89% for the rectangular distribution (see middle figure in Panel A), and 2.58% for the skewed distribution (see right-most figure in Panel A) shown in Figure 10.3.

Note that Panels B, C, and D of Figure 10.3 are empirical sampling distributions in which $n = 1$, 2, and 5, respectively. For example, for Panel D, a sample of five observations was selected randomly from the normal parent population, the mean of these five observations was computed, and this process was repeated 10,000 times. The left-most figure in Panel D is the frequency distribution of these 10,000 means[12]—that is, this figure is an empirical sampling distribution of the mean when $\mu = 100$, $\sigma = 15$, and $n = 5$. If the process had been repeated, not 10,000 but 1,000,000 times, the empirical sampling distribution would have become almost perfectly symmetrical and normal. The small amount of irregularity evident in the sampling distributions from the normal population would virtually disappear and the empirical sampling distribution would coincide with the theoretical sampling distribution.

Observe that the mean of all of the sampling distributions, the mean of the $\bar{X}$'s, is approximately $100 = \mu$ in each figure. Indeed, the expression $E(\bar{X}) = \mu$ is another way of saying that the mean of the sampling distribution of an infinite number of samples (not just 10,000 as in Figure 10.3) is the parameter $\mu$. In Panels B to E of Figure 10.3, the sample sizes are small (1, 2, 5, and 10); some degree of non-normality in the parent population continues to be evident in the sampling distributions, but progressively less so as $n$ increases. Panel F gives the three corresponding empirical sampling distributions when $n$ was increased to 25. Notice that the sampling distributions for the normal, rectangular, and skewed populations are very similar, yet $n$ is only 25. To the untrained eye, the distributions in Panel F may not appear to be normal, but this is only because the vertical (Percent) axis has been scaled uniformly in Panels A to F so that the decrease in the variability of the sampling distribution would be evident. The sampling distributions in Figure 10.3 demonstrate that even in non-normal distributions the standard deviation of the $\bar{X}$'s—that is, the standard error of the mean—equals the standard deviation of the parent population divided by the square root of the sample size: $\sigma_{\bar{X}} = \sigma/\sqrt{n}$.

In Table 10.1, the standard errors, $s_{\bar{X}}$ (each based on 10,000 means for the various sampling distributions), are reported along with the theoretical value, $\sigma_{\bar{X}} = \sigma/\sqrt{n}$. For

[12]The authors are indebted to George Kretke for this computer simulation demonstration. It is estimated that this demonstration done by hand using a table of random numbers and a hand calculator would have required approximately 2,500 hours—approximately one full working year!

example, when samples of $n = 25$ were drawn from a skewed parent population, the resulting 10,000 sample means had a standard deviation of 2.98, which agrees almost perfectly with the theoretical standard error of the mean, $\sigma/\sqrt{n} = 15/\sqrt{25} = 3$. In other words, *even when the parent population is not normal, the formula $\sigma_{\bar{X}} = \sigma/\sqrt{n}$ accurately depicts the degree of variability in the sampling distribution.*

## 10.16 THE USE OF SAMPLING DISTRIBUTIONS

The notion of a sampling distribution is used by the mathematical statistician to derive the techniques of inferential statistics. Researchers do not create their own sampling distribution by repeatedly drawing samples from a population. That would be not be feasible and is unnecessary. In practice, only one sample of $n$ cases is drawn; then the theory underlying the sampling distribution is used to establish a confidence interval. For example, an investigator might draw a sample of $n = 200$ cases and establish a single confidence interval, say, the .95 confidence interval, around $\bar{X}$. Many samples are not drawn to construct an actual sampling distribution of $\bar{X}$. Instead, one has a single interval, extending perhaps from 46.5 to 51.5. Is $\mu$ in this interval? It is not possible to know for certain. Is it rational to act as though $\mu$ is in this interval? Indeed it is, since in the long run $\mu$ would be missing from only 5% of the .95*CI*'s. The technique of interval estimation is based on the theoretical concept of the sampling distribution with its notion of infinitely many samples drawn and their means distributed in some known fashion.

## 10.17 PROOF[13] THAT $\sigma_{\bar{X}}^2 = \sigma^2/n$

The proof is straightforward that whatever the shape of the parent population, the sampling distribution of $\bar{X}$ has a mean of $\mu$ and variance of $\sigma^2/n$, where $\mu$ and $\sigma^2$ are the mean and variance of the population sampled and $n$ is the sample size. $X$ is the variable being measured on the population; its mean is $\mu$ and its variance is $\sigma^2$. A random sample of size $n$ has a first observation $X_1$, a second observation $X_2$, …, and an $n$th observation $X_n$; $X_1$ is merely the *first* score chosen in each sample, not the smallest score. Therefore, the collection of all possible $X_1$'s, that is, all first scores chosen in all possible random samples from the population, forms a population with mean $\mu$ and variance $\sigma$. Thus, $X_1, X_2, \ldots, X_n$ are each random variables from a population with a mean of $\mu$ and a variance of $\sigma^2$.

The sample mean equals $(X_1 + X_2 + \ldots + X_n)/n$. The mean of the sampling distribution of means equals the *expected value* of $\bar{X}$:

$$E(\bar{X}) = E\left[\frac{(X_1 + X_2 + \ldots + X_n)}{n}\right]$$

$$= \left(\frac{1}{n}\right)E(X_1 + X_2 + \ldots + X_n)$$

$$= \left(\frac{1}{n}\right)[E(X_1) + E(X_2) + \ldots + E(X_n)]$$

[13]This section is a more mathematical presentation of the concepts presented intuitively in Sections 10.11 and 10.12. Although not essential for a conceptual understanding, it is provided for students who desire a closer look at the related mathematics.

Now $X_1$ has the same distribution over samples as does $X_2$ or any other $X_i$. Its population mean and variance are $\mu$ and $\sigma$; hence, the last term in the equation above equals:

$$E(\overline{X}) = (\tfrac{1}{n})(\mu + \mu + \ldots + \mu) = (\tfrac{1}{n})(n\mu) = \mu$$

Stated in words, regardless of the shape of the parent population, the expected value of $\overline{X}$ is the mean $\mu$ of the sampling distribution of the sample means, which is also the mean of the population being sampled. How much will $\overline{X}$ vary from sample to sample? If each sample contains more than one observation, the variance of the sample means will be smaller than the variance of the parent population. Notice that if $n = 1$, the sampling distribution of the mean would be the same as the frequency distribution of the parent population, as shown in Panel B of Figure 10.3. If samples with $n = 1$ were repeatedly drawn and a sampling distribution of these "sample means" were constructed, the variance of the original population, $\sigma^2$, and the variance of the sampling distribution of the "means" of samples of size 1 would be the same; $\sigma^2/n = \sigma^2/1 = \sigma^2$:

$$E(s_{\overline{X}}^2) = \sigma_{\overline{X}}^2$$

What is the variance of the means of samples of size $n = 2$ from a population? Let the population variance be $\sigma^2$. For each sample, $\overline{X} = (X_1 + X_2)/2$ is calculated. $X_1$ and $X_2$ are arbitrary designations for the first and second observations randomly drawn and are not related to the size of the scores. Consequently, over all random samples, $X_1$ has variance $\sigma^2$ and so does $X_2$. Because the samples are randomly drawn, there is no relationship ($\rho = 0$) between the values of the first and second observations in any sample. Since $X_1$ and $X_2$ are uncorrelated, the correlation, and the covariance, is zero between the first and second observations in a sample over infinitely many random samples from a population.

Now the variance over random samples of $\overline{X} = (X_1 + X_2)/2$ is denoted as follows:

$$\sigma_{\overline{X}}^2 = \sigma_{(X_1+X_2)/2}^2$$

When a variable is multiplied by a constant (in this instance, ½), the variance of the resulting variable is the original variance multiplied by the square of the constant (Section 5.11). Therefore,

$$\sigma_{(X_1+X_2)(1/2)}^2 = (\tfrac{1}{2})^2 \sigma_{(X_1+X_2)}^2$$

If two variables are uncorrelated, then the variance of the sum of the two variables is the sum of their variances (Equation 7.8). We argued that $X_1$ and $X_2$ are uncorrelated:

$$(\tfrac{1}{2})^2 \sigma_{X_1+X_2}^2 = \tfrac{1}{4}(\sigma_{X_1}^2 + \sigma_{X_2}^2 + 2\rho_{X_1X_2}\sigma_{X_1}\sigma_{X_2}) = \tfrac{1}{4}(\sigma_{X_1}^2 + \sigma_{X_2}^2)$$

The variance of $X_1$ over repeated random samples is $\sigma^2$, and so is the variance of $X_2 : \sigma_{X_1}^2 = \sigma_{X_2}^2 = \sigma^2$. Therefore, the equation can be written as follows:

$$\left(\tfrac{1}{4}\right)(\sigma_{X_1}^2 + \sigma_{X_2}^2) = \left(\tfrac{1}{4}\right)(2\sigma^2) = \sigma^2/2$$

The equation expresses the conclusion of the argument: The variance of the mean of samples of size 2 from a population with variance $\sigma^2$ is equal to $\sigma^2/2$. In this instance, $n = 2$ and $\sigma_{\bar{X}}^2 = \sigma^2/2$. This is no coincidence. It is true in general that for random samples of size $n$, $\sigma_{\bar{X}}^2 = \sigma^2/n$.

If random samples of size $n$ are taken from a population with variance $\sigma^2$, then the variance of the mean, $\bar{X} = (X_1 + X_2 + \ldots + X_n)/n$, over $n$ samples is given by:

$$\sigma_{\bar{X}}^2 = \sigma_{(X_1+X_2+\ldots+X_n)/n}^2$$

The right-hand side of the previous equation shows $\sigma_{\bar{X}}^2$ to be the variance of $(1/n)$ times the variance of the sum of the $n$ *uncorrelated* variables $X_1, X_2, \ldots X_n$. Therefore:

$$\sigma_{\bar{X}}^2 = \left(\tfrac{1}{n}\right)^2 \sigma_{(X_1+X_2+\ldots+X_n)}^2$$

Each variable $X_i (i = 1, 2, \ldots, n)$ has a variance of $\sigma^2$ and is uncorrelated with the other $n - 1$ variables. Therefore, the variance of the sum of the $n$ uncorrelated variables is the sum of the variances of the variables, because each of the $n(n - 1)/2$ covariance is 0. Thus:

$$\left(\tfrac{1}{n}\right)^2 \sigma_{(X_1+X_2+\ldots+X_n)}^2 = \left(\tfrac{1}{n}\right)^2 (\sigma_{X_1}^2 + \sigma_{X_2}^2 + \ldots + \sigma_{X_n}^2)$$

Because each variable has the same variance $\sigma^2$, the previous equation can be written as:

$$\left(\tfrac{1}{n}\right)^2 (\sigma^2 + \sigma^2 + \ldots + \sigma^2) = \left(\tfrac{1}{n}\right)^2 (n\sigma^2) = \frac{\sigma^2}{n} \quad \textbf{(10.7)}$$

A fundamental relationship is expressed in Equation 10.7. *The variance of the means of random samples of size* n *from a population with variance* $\sigma^2$ *is equal to* $\sigma^2/n = \sigma_{\bar{X}}^2$. The expression $\sigma_{\bar{X}}^2$ has traditionally been called the *variance error of the mean*. Its positive square root (Equation 10.8), is the *standard error of the mean:*

$$\sigma_{\bar{X}} = \frac{\sigma}{\sqrt{n}} \quad \textbf{(10.8)}$$

The standard error of the mean, $\sigma_{\bar{X}}$, is the standard deviation of the sampling distribution of the means of an infinite number of samples, each of size $n$, from a population with variance $\sigma^2$. Notice that in Table 10.1 and Figure 10.3 that the population from which samples were drawn had a standard deviation of 15, and the standard deviation of the sampling distribution of means of random samples of various sizes is in agreement with Equation 10.8. For example, when $n = 10$: $\sigma_{\bar{X}} = \sigma/\sqrt{n} = 15/\sqrt{10} = 4.74$; whereas in Table 10.1, the values of $s_{\overline{X}}$ were 4.81, 4.70, and 4.70 for the normal, rectangular, and skewed distributions, respectively.

## 10.18 PROPERTIES OF ESTIMATORS

An estimate is a value of a sample statistic that equals the value of a population parameter plus some amount of error. For example, the sample mean $\overline{X}$ is an estimator of the population mean $\mu$. There is a close analogy between the way in which a sample mean is calculated and the way in which one might calculate a population mean. It is logical to think of $\overline{X}$ as estimating $\mu$. However, there are other ways of treating sample data to arrive at a value that estimates $\mu$. Why not use the sample median or the sample mode as an estimate of $\mu$? It is certainly possible to do this; however, by the criteria used in assessing the properties of an estimator, $\overline{X}$ turns out to be a better estimator of $\mu$ than either the sample median or the sample mode (Section 4.16).

In the following three sections, the properties of estimators of parameters will be examined. What are the different ways in which parameters can be estimated? Is one estimator to be preferred over all others for estimating a certain parameter, and why? The properties of unbiasedness, consistency, and efficiency will be considered.

## 10.19 UNBIASEDNESS

As discussed in Section 5.13, an estimator, $\hat{\theta}$, is said to be unbiased for estimating a parameter, $\theta$, if the mean of the sampling distribution of the sample estimates equals the value of the parameter being estimated. Equivalently, an estimator, $\hat{\theta}$, is unbiased if its expected value, $E(\hat{\theta})$, is equal to the parameter, $\theta$, being estimated.

Whatever the nature of the population being sampled, the sample mean, $\overline{X}$, is an unbiased estimator of the population mean, $\mu$. Notice in Figure 10.3 that the value of the population mean, $\mu$, is 100 and that the mean of any of the empirical sampling distributions of $\overline{X}$ is approximately 100. This illustrates the unbiasedness of $\overline{X}$ as an estimator of $\mu$. If samples are drawn randomly from a normal distribution or some other symmetric distribution, then the sample median is also an unbiased estimator of the population mean, $\mu$. In other words, the average of the medians on an infinite number of random samples from a normal distribution equals $\mu$, the mean of the normal distribution (which is, of course, also its median).

There are many examples of biased estimators. Suppose one wishes to estimate $\rho$, the correlation between two variables in the population. Imagine that for a particular population $\rho = .75$. The mean of the sampling distribution of the sample correlation coefficient, $r$, will be slightly less than .75 for any finite sample size. Thus, $r$ is a negatively biased estimator of $\rho$.[14] When the expected value of a statistic is less than the parameter being estimated, it is said to be *negatively biased*. Conversely, if $E(\hat{\theta}) > \theta$, $\hat{\theta}$ is said to be *positively biased*. In Equation 5.5, the variance in a sample is defined as $s^2 = \Sigma(X_i - \overline{X})^2/(n-1)$. It might have been more natural to measure variability by simply taking the average of the $n$ squared

[14]The extent of the bias is exceedingly small—less than 1% if $n > 25$ (Olkin, 1967, p. 111).

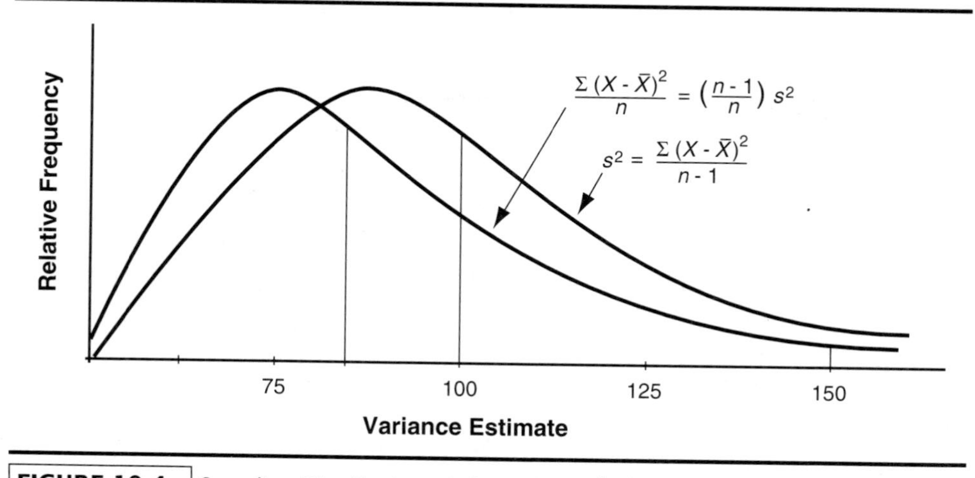


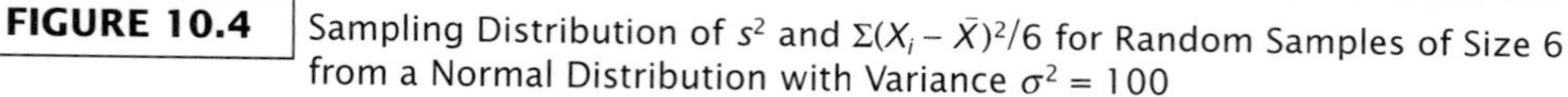
**FIGURE 10.4** Sampling Distribution of $s^2$ and $\Sigma(X_i - \bar{X})^2/6$ for Random Samples of Size 6 from a Normal Distribution with Variance $\sigma^2 = 100$

deviations around the sample mean. Instead, it was decided to place $(n - 1)$ in the denominator of $s^2$ because the quantity $s^2$ is an unbiased estimator of the population variance $\sigma^2$; whereas, $\Sigma(X_i - \bar{X})^2/n$ is negatively biased as an estimator of $\sigma^2$. That is:

$$E\left[\frac{\sum_i (X_i - \bar{X})^2}{n}\right] < \sigma^2$$

Suppose that we took *many* random samples from any population with variance $\sigma^2$ and calculated $s^2$ each time. The average of these sample variances would equal $\sigma^2$. Hence, $s^2$ is an unbiased estimator of $\sigma^2$. If instead, $\Sigma(X_i - \bar{X})^2/n$ had been calculated on each sample, the average of these quantities would have been smaller than $\sigma^2$, namely $[(n - 1)/n]\sigma^2$. Of course, if $n$ were quite large—100 or more for example—the difference between $s^2$ and $\Sigma(X_i - \bar{X})^2/n$ would be very small, because the value of $(n - 1)/n$ (the ratio of the degrees of freedom to sample size) would approach 1, and the estimator would contain only a small bias as an estimator of $\sigma^2$.

Suppose that one has a normal distribution with mean $\mu = 0$ and variance $\sigma^2 = 100$. If an infinite number of random samples of size $n = 6$ were drawn from the population and both $s^2$ and $\Sigma(X_i - \bar{X})^2/6$ were calculated for each sample, the two sampling distributions in Figure 10.4 would be obtained.

Notice that the mean of the sampling distribution of $s^2$ is 100 the value of $\sigma^2$. This illustrates the unbiasedness of $s^2$ in this instance, that is, $E(s^2) = \sigma^2$. The mean of the sampling distribution of $\Sigma(X_i - \bar{X})^2/6$ is equal to 83.33. In this instance, the bias introduced into the estimation of $\sigma^2$ by using $n$ in place of $n - 1$ in the denominator of the sample variance is sizable, that is, $(n - 1)/n = 5/6$ here.

How was it decided that the denominator of the sample variance should be $n - 1$ (i.e., the degrees of freedom, $\nu$) in order for $E(s^2) = \sigma^2$? It was not determined empirically or by trial-and-error that $n - 1$ gives the unbiased estimator. It can be proved mathematically[15] that $s^2$ is an unbiased estimator of $\sigma^2$.

The quantity $s^2$ is an unbiased estimator of $\sigma^2$. Your intuition might lead you to conclude that since $s^2$ is an unbiased estimator of $\sigma^2$, that the sample standard deviation, $s$, is consequently an unbiased estimator of $\sigma$, the population standard deviation, but it would mislead you (Section 5.13). A nonlinear transformation (Section 7.12, e.g., $\sqrt{X}$) of an unbiased estimator, $\bar{X}$, does not produce an unbiased estimator.

The sample standard deviation is a negatively biased estimator of the population standard deviation. The amount of bias depends on $n$ and the shape of the population being sampled. If the population is normal, the mean of the sampling distribution of $s$, $\mu_s$, is slightly less than $\sigma$. Specifically:

$$E(s) = \mu_s = \left(\frac{4n-4}{4n-3}\right)\sigma \qquad \textbf{(10.9)}$$

Equation 10.9 can be rearranged to provide an unbiased estimate of $\sigma$:

$$E\left\{\left[1 + \frac{1}{4(n-1)}\right]s\right\} = \sigma \qquad \textbf{(10.10)}$$

It is obvious from Equation 10.10 that the amount of bias, the difference between $\mu_s$ and $\sigma$, is $s/[4(n-1)]$.[16] The bias in $s$ is small unless $n$ is extremely small. For example, if $n$ is 26, $s$ will underestimate $\sigma$ by only 1%, on the average.

Table 10.2 presents some parameters, their estimators, and statements that the estimator is biased or unbiased. As you study Table 10.2, notice that the sample median and sample mode can be used to estimate the parameter $\mu$. Note that for certain statistics, whether the estimator is biased or unbiased depends upon the shape of the distribution of the population from which samples are drawn.

## 10.20 CONSISTENCY

A second property of estimators is *consistency*. A consistent estimator, even if biased, tends to get closer and closer to the value of the parameter as the sample size becomes larger. All commonly used estimators, such as those in Table 10.2, whether biased or unbiased, are consistent. For example, the sample standard deviation is not unbiased, but it is a consistent estimator of $\sigma$. By taking an ever larger sample, the mean $s$ in the sampling distribution will come closer to $\sigma$ in value. The larger the sample becomes, the less $s$ and $\sigma$ tend to differ. This can be seen algebraically when $n$ approaches infinity in Equation 10.10.

---

[15]The algebraic proof is cumbersome and will not be presented here; it can be found in Edwards (1964, pp. 29–36).

[16]If $n$ is very small, a negligible degree of bias remains in Equation 10.10. For example, if $n = 2$, 3, and 4, Equation 10.10 yields $1.25s$, $1.125s$, and $1.083s$, respectively; whereas, the precise values for perfectly unbiased estimates are trivially larger: $1.253s$, $1.128s$, and $1.085s$, respectively (Dixon & Massey, 1983).

**TABLE 10.2** Biasedness or Unbiasedness of Various Estimators (Statistics) of Parameters of Various Populations

| *Parameter* | *Type of Population* | *Estimator* | *Bias in Estimator* |
|---|---|---|---|
| *Range* | Any population | *Range* | Negatively biased |
| $\mu$ | Any population | $\overline{X}$ | Unbiased |
| $\mu$ | Symmetric | *Md* | Unbiased |
| $\mu$ | Symmetric and unimodal | *Mode* | Unbiased |
| $\mu$ | Skewed | *Md* | Biased |
| $\mu$ | Skewed | *Mode* | Biased |
| $\sigma^2$ | Any population | $s^2$ | Unbiased |
| $\sigma$ | Normal | $s$ | Negatively biased |
| $\rho$ | Bivariate normal | $r$ | Negatively biased |

## 10.21 RELATIVE EFFICIENCY

The third property of estimators is *efficiency*. Efficiency refers to the *relative precision* with which an estimator estimates a parameter. Efficiency also refers to the relative degree of sampling error associated with the estimator. Efficiency is more important in the application of statistics than either unbiasedness or consistency. The variance error of the sample mean, $\sigma^2/n$, is a measure of efficiency of $\overline{X}$ as an estimator of $\mu$. The variance, or standard, error of an estimator is one of its most important properties. The *variance error* of any statistic is the variance of the sampling distribution of the statistic.

Suppose the value of the population mean of a particular normal distribution is to be estimated. One way of estimating $\mu$ is to find the mean, $\overline{X}$, of a sample of size $n$. However, in symmetric populations, the sample median and $\overline{X}$ are unbiased estimators of $\mu$, so which is better? This question can be answered by considering the relative efficiencies of the two estimators. Which estimator of $\mu$, the sample mean or the sample median, varies less from sample to sample; which has a smaller variance error?

If the variance $\sigma^2$ of the normal population sampled is 225 and the sample size $n$ is 9, then the variance of the sampling distribution of $\overline{X}$'s is (Equation 10.7) $\sigma_{\overline{X}}^2 = \sigma^2/n = 225/9 = 25$, or $\sigma_{\overline{X}} = 5$. How does this compare to the variance error of the sample median, $\sigma_{Md}^2$? If an infinite number of random samples, each of large size $n$, are drawn from a normal population with mean $\mu$ and variance $\sigma^2$, and the median *Md* is calculated for each sample, the frequency distribution of these sample medians (i.e., the sampling distribution of *Md*) will be normally distributed with mean $\mu$ and its variance is given in Equation 10.11:

$$\sigma_{Md}^2 \approx \frac{1.57\sigma^2}{n} \approx 1.57\sigma_{\overline{X}}^2 \quad \textbf{(10.11)}$$

Expressed in terms of standard errors, rather than variance errors, Equation 10.11 becomes:

$$\sigma_{Md} \approx \frac{1.25\sigma}{\sqrt{n}} \approx 1.25\sigma_{\overline{X}} \quad \textbf{(10.12)}$$

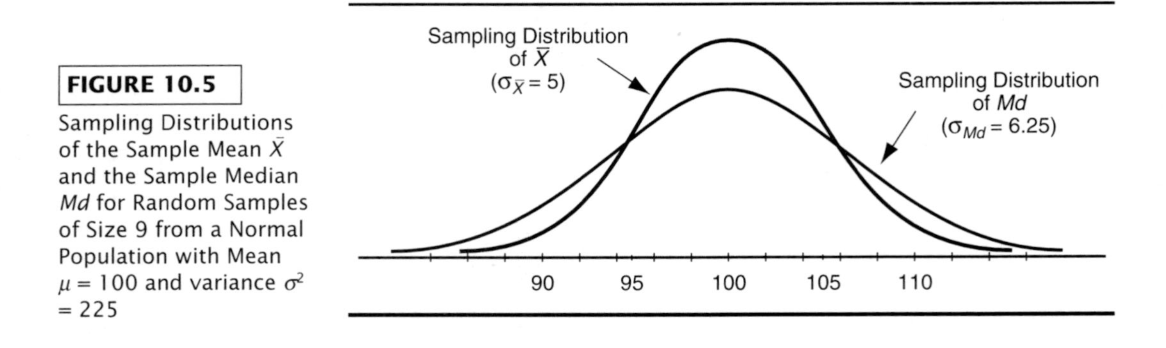


**FIGURE 10.5**

Sampling Distributions of the Sample Mean $\overline{X}$ and the Sample Median *Md* for Random Samples of Size 9 from a Normal Population with Mean $\mu = 100$ and variance $\sigma^2 = 225$

Note that the standard error of the sample median, $\sigma_{Md}$, is $(1.25)\sigma_{\overline{X}}$. Figure 10.5 depicts the sampling distributions of $\overline{X}$ and *Md* for samples of size 9 from a normal distribution with $\sigma = 15$.

The standard error of the sample median in Figure 10.5 is equal to $(1.25)\sigma/n = (1.25)(5)$, or $\sigma_{Md} = 6.25$; or 25% larger than $\sigma_{\overline{X}} = 5.0$. Figure 10.5 reveals that the sample median will vary more than the sample mean over repeated samples. Note that only 16% of the sample means will be larger than 105 ($z = 1$)while about 21% of the sample medians will be larger than 105 ($z = .80$, Table A). Thus, $\overline{X}$ is a more efficient estimator of $\mu$ than *Md*; relative efficiency is the ratio of the variance of the more efficient estimator to the variance of the less efficient estimator. The *efficiency of Md relative to* $\overline{X}$ is defined as the ratio of their variance errors. When $n$ is large:

$$\text{Re}\textit{lative efficiency of Md} \approx \frac{\sigma_{\overline{X}}^2}{\sigma_{Md}^2} \approx \frac{\sigma^2 / n}{(1.57)\sigma^2 / n} \approx \frac{1}{1.57} \approx .637 \approx 63.7\%$$

meaning that for normally distributed measures the median is less than two-thirds as efficient as the arithmetic mean.

One interpretation of relative efficiency is that if the median of a sample of 100 observations is used to estimate $\mu$, the same degree of precision of estimation could be attained by drawing a sample of sixty-four observations and computing $\overline{X}$. More precisely, the relative efficiency of $\overline{X}$ versus *Md* is influenced by $n$. Figure 10.6 shows that the relative efficiency of $\overline{X}$ and *Md* in normal populations are equal when $n = 2$, but that *Md* rapidly approaches its asymptote of .637 as $n$ increases. For another comparison of relative efficiency, Figure 10.6 also shows that the efficiency of the midrange, $(X_{max} + X_{min})/2$, (Section 4.5) is greater than that of the *Md* for $n \leq 6$, but continues to decline progressively as $n$ increases.

Statisticians have generally used both the criteria of unbiasedness and efficiency when making their choice of a "best" estimator of a parameter. Because all commonly used estimators have the property of consistency, and all have little or no bias when $n$ is large, the *criterion of efficiency becomes the major criterion for applied use of inferential statistics.* The greater efficiency of the mean is the principal reason it is used much more than the median in statistical inference, in spite of the fact that the median often has superior descriptive and interpretive properties (Section 4.17).

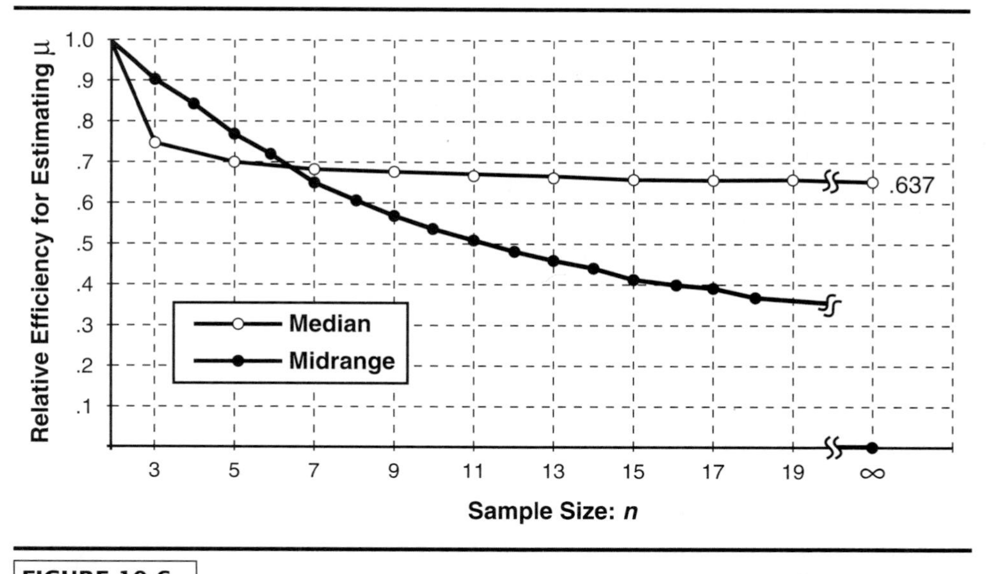


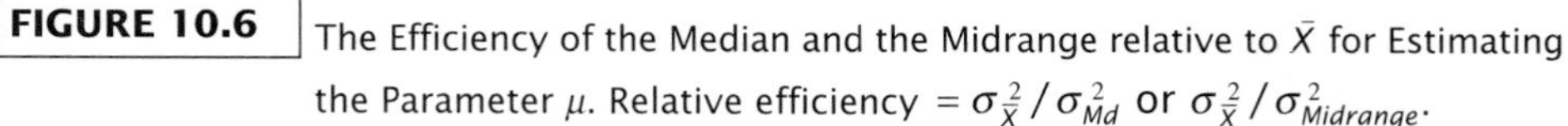
**FIGURE 10.6** The Efficiency of the Median and the Midrange relative to $\bar{X}$ for Estimating the Parameter $\mu$. Relative efficiency $= \sigma^2_{\bar{X}} / \sigma^2_{Md}$ or $\sigma^2_{\bar{X}} / \sigma^2_{Midrange}$.

## 10.22 CHAPTER SUMMARY

Many applications of inferential statistics actually involve parent or target populations of finite size, not infinite populations. The ratio of the sample size $n$ to the size of the population is known as the sampling fraction, $n/N$. Unless the sampling fraction is 1/20 or more, there are negligible differences in using the simpler inferential techniques that assume $N$ is infinite.

The most important characteristic of a sample is representativeness. The representativeness of samples that are selected randomly can be calculated probabilistically. In random sampling, each unit (person, school, city, etc.) has an equal and independent chance of being selected for the sample. Random samples are often obtained using a list of random numbers. Most well designed systematic samples and random samples differ inconsequentially. Accidental samples should not be used for inferential purposes.

Point and interval estimation are both useful. If $\bar{X} = 56.0$, 56.0 is a point estimate of $\mu$. If the .95 confidence interval is 54–58, (54, 58) is an interval estimate for the value of $\mu$. Properly employed, 95% of the .95*CI*'s for any statistic will "capture" the corresponding parameter being estimated.

A sampling distribution is a frequency distribution of statistics, such as $\bar{X}$, *Md*, $s^2$, $r$, and so on. In this chapter, the sampling distribution of the mean was examined extensively.

The central limit theorem states that even if the parent population is not normal, the sampling distribution of $\bar{X}$ will be approximately normal as $n$ increases. If $n > 25$, the sampling distribution of $\bar{X}$ is essentially normal and confidence intervals for $\mu$ can be assumed to be accurate even for non-normal populations.

A major purpose of this chapter has been to present the theory and a portion of the practice of interval estimation. This has been done in considerable detail because the comprehension of the rationale of this highly useful inferential statistical technique is critical. In subsequent chapters, numerous examples of the construction of confidence intervals will be met. In each instance, some of the particulars of the calculation of the confidence interval will be different from those presented in this chapter.

In this chapter, for instructional purposes, $\sigma$ was assumed to be known even though in practice this is rarely the case. This allowed us to avoid many distracting qualifying statements. In Chapter 11, we will face the more typical situation in which $\sigma$ is not known. The second major branch of inferential statistics, hypothesis testing, will also be introduced in Chapter 11.

## 10.23 CASE STUDY

From a normally distributed population with $\mu$ = 100 and $\sigma$ = 15, 450 IQ scores were randomly sampled.[17] If viewed by rows, they can be considered as 50 random samples with $n = 9$. Notice the fifty means in the $\overline{X}$ column; these can be viewed as a sampling distribution. In this population, the mean of the sampling distribution is ____. The mean of the 50 means in Table 10.3 is ____; the difference is due to ____ ____. Indeed, the sampling error in each of the 50 $\overline{X}$'s could be found by subtracting ____ from each of the 50 $\overline{X}$'s.[18]

From theory, the standard deviation of the 50 $\overline{X}$'s, is $\sigma_{\overline{X}} = \sigma / \sqrt{n}$ (Equation 10.1), or, in this example, with $n = 9$, $\sigma_{\overline{X}}$ = ____. Compare this value with the standard deviation of the 50 $\overline{X}$'s.[19]

If one takes each of the 50 sample means and creates an interval, $\overline{X}_j \pm \sigma_{\overline{X}} = \overline{X}_j \pm 5$, the value of the parameter, $\mu$, would be expected to fall within ____% of the intervals. In other words, in Table 10.3, we would expect $\mu = 100$ to fall within 5 points of the sample mean in approximately ____ of the intervals. Count the actual number of the fifty .68 intervals that "captured" the parameter (either the upper limit of the interval is below 100, or the lower limit of the interval is above 100)—does the theory seem to work?[20]

Now, consider the means of the nine columns as nine samples with $n = 50$. Does there tend to be less sampling error with $n = 50$ than when $n = 9$? The standard error of the mean, $\sigma_{\overline{X}}$, when $n = 50$, is ____, less than half the value as when $n = 9$. Consequently, the width of the .68*CI*'s would be ____ (wider or narrower).[21]

## 10.24 SUGGESTED COMPUTER ACTIVITY

If you have access to software that will generate random numbers (such as Microsoft EXCEL[22]), have the computer draw a random sample of $n$ = 10 scores from a normal population ($\mu$ = 100, $\sigma$ = 15). Have the computer find $\overline{X}$ and $s$ for the sample, and set the .68

---

[17]Using EXCEL's random number generator.

[18]100; 100.53, sampling error; 100

[19]5; It is very close: 5 vs. 4.77.

[20]68%; .68 × 50 or 34; 33 of the .68*CI*'s captured $\mu$; Yes!

[21]yes; 2.12; narrower

[22]In EXCEL, there is a random number generator that allows you to specify the shape of the parent population, in addition to $\mu$ and $\sigma$.

**TABLE 10.3** 450 Randomly Drawn IQ Scores from a Normal Distribution ($\mu = 100$, $\sigma = 15$).

| | A | B | C | D | E | F | G | H | I | $\overline{X}$ | $s$ |
|---|---|---|---|---|---|---|---|---|---|---|---|
| **1** | 83 | 108 | 104 | 119 | 110 | 104 | 112 | 127 | 115 | **109.1** | **12.3** |
| **2** | 70 | 116 | 102 | 69 | 99 | 111 | 104 | 74 | 117 | **95.9** | **19.3** |
| **3** | 104 | 114 | 78 | 77 | 87 | 106 | 107 | 115 | 112 | **100.0** | **15.0** |
| **4** | 92 | 70 | 80 | 103 | 86 | 101 | 102 | 94 | 91 | **90.9** | **11.1** |
| **5** | 98 | 134 | 93 | 98 | 106 | 95 | 108 | 114 | 79 | **102.8** | **15.5** |
| **6** | 76 | 102 | 120 | 99 | 78 | 114 | 104 | 96 | 112 | **100.2** | **15.1** |
| **7** | 140 | 98 | 85 | 110 | 107 | 80 | 101 | 98 | 102 | **102.5** | **17.2** |
| **8** | 110 | 78 | 115 | 114 | 92 | 95 | 106 | 111 | 129 | **105.5** | **15.0** |
| **9** | 107 | 103 | 85 | 105 | 117 | 111 | 115 | 89 | 83 | **101.9** | **12.9** |
| **10** | 92 | 102 | 101 | 127 | 104 | 66 | 110 | 126 | 139 | **107.5** | **21.7** |
| **11** | 77 | 98 | 102 | 131 | 105 | 116 | 94 | 112 | 80 | **101.6** | **17.0** |
| **12** | 117 | 91 | 100 | 95 | 100 | 95 | 106 | 99 | 91 | **99.3** | **8.0** |
| **13** | 109 | 117 | 117 | 92 | 87 | 97 | 111 | 79 | 114 | **102.6** | **14.2** |
| **14** | 117 | 102 | 109 | 98 | 105 | 106 | 101 | 104 | 117 | **106.7** | **6.8** |
| **15** | 105 | 109 | 100 | 116 | 111 | 87 | 81 | 104 | 110 | **102.5** | **11.6** |
| **16** | 84 | 137 | 105 | 76 | 92 | 89 | 90 | 139 | 112 | **102.7** | **22.7** |
| **17** | 89 | 91 | 92 | 115 | 131 | 133 | 98 | 108 | 75 | **103.5** | **19.8** |
| **18** | 108 | 96 | 93 | 97 | 96 | 131 | 104 | 111 | 107 | **104.9** | **11.8** |
| **19** | 110 | 83 | 94 | 108 | 83 | 95 | 108 | 97 | 133 | **101.3** | **15.6** |
| **20** | 91 | 84 | 76 | 99 | 104 | 96 | 106 | 84 | 113 | **94.8** | **11.9** |
| **21** | 112 | 95 | 96 | 101 | 88 | 107 | 118 | 102 | 81 | **99.9** | **11.6** |
| **22** | 124 | 113 | 109 | 107 | 68 | 107 | 105 | 112 | 122 | **107.5** | **16.2** |
| **23** | 97 | 80 | 120 | 87 | 105 | 89 | 69 | 101 | 111 | **95.4** | **15.9** |
| **24** | 100 | 101 | 105 | 76 | 73 | 98 | 109 | 76 | 98 | **93.0** | **13.7** |
| **25** | 112 | 68 | 99 | 87 | 87 | 87 | 101 | 88 | 104 | **92.5** | **12.9** |
| **26** | 115 | 88 | 109 | 117 | 101 | 95 | 128 | 134 | 93 | **109.0** | **16.1** |
| **27** | 111 | 134 | 110 | 120 | 100 | 108 | 107 | 102 | 97 | **109.9** | **11.5** |
| **28** | 96 | 91 | 95 | 82 | 80 | 114 | 101 | 98 | 66 | **91.4** | **14.0** |
| **29** | 143 | 112 | 90 | 78 | 109 | 98 | 124 | 87 | 88 | **103.2** | **20.7** |
| **30** | 122 | 97 | 94 | 102 | 92 | 134 | 97 | 66 | 112 | **101.8** | **19.7** |
| **31** | 94 | 116 | 94 | 99 | 108 | 68 | 113 | 111 | 105 | **100.9** | **14.5** |
| **32** | 90 | 99 | 85 | 115 | 112 | 101 | 100 | 116 | 101 | **102.2** | **10.6** |
| **33** | 93 | 100 | 81 | 108 | 90 | 106 | 100 | 110 | 113 | **100.0** | **10.3** |
| **34** | 110 | 100 | 97 | 109 | 68 | 74 | 116 | 105 | 96 | **97.2** | **16.2** |
| **35** | 120 | 104 | 97 | 105 | 91 | 104 | 106 | 78 | 89 | **99.4** | **12.0** |
| **36** | 89 | 82 | 100 | 85 | 114 | 117 | 104 | 125 | 73 | **98.7** | **17.8** |
| **37** | 97 | 70 | 109 | 101 | 95 | 124 | 87 | 129 | 107 | **102.1** | **18.2** |
| **38** | 96 | 102 | 82 | 97 | 94 | 88 | 109 | 104 | 109 | **97.9** | **9.2** |
| **39** | 93 | 72 | 103 | 78 | 108 | 82 | 108 | 114 | 86 | **93.7** | **15.1** |
| **40** | 101 | 112 | 75 | 121 | 106 | 93 | 97 | 90 | 98 | **99.1** | **13.3** |
| **41** | 99 | 101 | 102 | 71 | 106 | 128 | 99 | 91 | 114 | **101.3** | **15.6** |
| **42** | 100 | 69 | 87 | 84 | 107 | 101 | 89 | 102 | 88 | **91.9** | **11.7** |
| **43** | 106 | 85 | 105 | 93 | 105 | 96 | 115 | 105 | 95 | **100.5** | **9.1** |
| **44** | 124 | 90 | 112 | 90 | 81 | 92 | 77 | 110 | 92 | **96.2** | **15.6** |
| **45** | 87 | 87 | 76 | 105 | 80 | 88 | 100 | 128 | 116 | **96.2** | **17.1** |
| **46** | 80 | 99 | 85 | 104 | 91 | 118 | 95 | 102 | 78 | **94.7** | **12.9** |
| **47** | 107 | 109 | 95 | 122 | 112 | 98 | 123 | 81 | 86 | **103.7** | **14.8** |
| **48** | 123 | 94 | 124 | 111 | 92 | 75 | 114 | 121 | 97 | **105.6** | **17.1** |
| **49** | 100 | 92 | 97 | 105 | 88 | 96 | 103 | 105 | 120 | **100.6** | **9.4** |
| **50** | 107 | 73 | 109 | 112 | 93 | 113 | 111 | 121 | 108 | **105.1** | **14.3** |
| $\overline{X}$ | **102.6** | **97.4** | **97.9** | **100.5** | **96.9** | **100.5** | **103.8** | **103.8** | **101.5** | *100.53* | **14.4** |
| $s$ | **15.2** | **16.5** | **12.2** | **15.0** | **13.0** | **15.7** | **11.2** | **16.3** | **16.1** | *4.77* | |

confidence interval (Equation 10.2) for $\mu$. Repeat this process 25 times, and count the number of the .68*CI*'s that captured $\mu$ (it should not vary significantly from $.68 \times 25 = 17$). Find the standard deviation of the 25 $\bar{X}$'s ($s_{\bar{X}}$) and compare to $\sigma_{\bar{X}}$. Make a frequency distribution of the 25 means to see if it is roughly normal. Find the mean of the 250 randomly selected observations, and set the .95*CI* for $\mu$.

Repeat the activity, randomly sampling from a rectangular (or uniform) distribution. Observe the central limit theorem working before your very eyes.

## MASTERY TEST

*The selection of a random sample requires which of the following? (Answer T or F.)*

1. The observations must be normally distributed.
2. Each observation must have an equal chance of being chosen for the sample.
3. The selection of any one observation must be independent of that for all other observations.

*In a mail survey, of the randomly sampled 400 social workers who were sent questionnaires, 240 returned them.*

4. Can the 240 be considered a random sample of the population of social workers?
5. Can the 240 be considered a representative sample of the 400?
6. Can the 60% of the sample who responded be considered to represent approximately 60% of the population—the 60% who would have responded had they been sent questionnaires?
7. A sample of 100 families was randomly selected for a structured interview survey. Interviews with eighteen of the families were not conducted because of the unwillingness to cooperate, incorrect addresses, "vicious dogs," or "nobody home." Can the eighty-two be viewed as a random sample of the original population sampled?
8. A psychologist followed up a group of chronic alcoholics who had undergone two weeks of intensive therapy at a state hospital by a treatment team composed of psychiatrists, clinical psychologists, social workers, and vocational counselors. Only about thirty-six of 108 could be located eight weeks after treatment. Twenty-five of the thirty-six were coping satisfactorily. Can it be concluded that about two-thirds (i.e., $25/36 = .69$) of those treated appear to be getting along adequately? Why?

*A sample of twelfth-grade students at Lincoln High School is to be tested. Will the following procedures result in a random sample of 100 students from the population of seniors at the school?*

9. Test twenty twelfth-grade students in each of five randomly selected classes.
10. Select the first 100 seniors who arrive at school on a given day.
11. Use a table of random numbers and select 100 seniors from those who volunteered to participate.
12. Randomly select 100 seniors from those present on a given day.
13. Randomly draw 100 seniors from an alphabetical listing of all students.
14. If every tenth name on the roster were selected after randomly selecting the initial name, what kind of a sample would result? Would this be a representative sample?

*On the Wechsler Intelligence Scales, IQ's are normally distributed with $\mu = 100$, $\sigma = 15$. Suppose a random sample of nine persons was tested, the mean computed, and this process repeated 1,000 times.*

15. Estimate the value of the standard deviation of the 1,000 means.
16. About what percentage of the sample means with $n = 9$ would exceed 105? 110?
17. About what percentage of the means would fall between 95 and 105? Between 90 and 110?
18. Would the $\bar{X}$'s be normally distributed?

**19.** What is the variance of this distribution of $\overline{X}$'s?

**20.** If $n = 225$ (not 9), what would be the value of $\sigma_{\overline{X}}$?

**21.** If $n = 225$, what percentage of $\overline{X}$'s would deviate by less than 1 point from 100—that is, would be expected to fall within the interval 99.0–101.0?

**22.** If the observations in a frequency distribution are not normally distributed and $n$ is small, will the sampling distribution of sample means be *precisely* normally distributed?

**23.** Will the sampling distribution of means be approximately normal if $n$ is 25 or so, even if the frequency distribution of $X$-values is not normal?

**24.** What is the mathematical theorem that indicates that the sampling distribution of $\overline{X}$ approaches normality as $n$ increases, regardless of the shape of the distribution in the parent population?

**25.** Suppose that instead of selecting a truly random sample, for convenience, the last name on each page of a telephone directory was selected. Would this sample probably be quite representative of the population of listings in the telephone directory?

**26.** Assuming that $\sigma$ is known for a normal distribution of observations, is it true that $\overline{X} \pm 1.96\,\sigma_{\overline{X}}$ yields a .95 confidence interval for any value of $n$?

**27.** When the distribution is normal and $\sigma$ is known, if two samples of 100 observations are drawn randomly from the same parent populations, will the two resulting .68 confidence intervals be identical?

*Are the following pairs of terms synonymous and equivalent?*

**28.** (1) The standard error of $\overline{X}$ and (2) the standard deviation of the sampling distribution of $\overline{X}$.

**29.** (1) $\sigma^2/n$ and (2) the standard error of $\overline{X}$.

**30.** (1) $\sigma_{\overline{X}}{}^2$ and (2) the variance of the sampling distribution of $\overline{X}$.

**31.** (1) The population variance $\sigma^2$ and (2) $n$ times the $\sigma^2_{\overline{X}}$.

**32.** (1) The mean of the sampling distribution of $\overline{X}$ and (2) $\sigma^2_{\overline{X}}$.

**33.** (1) $E(\overline{X})$ and (2) $\mu$.

**34.** (1) $\mu$ and (2) $(\Sigma X)/n$.

**35.** (1) $\overline{X}$ and (2) $(\Sigma x)/n$.

**36.** (1) $s^2$ and (2) $\Sigma x^2/(n-1)$.

**37.** If you conducted many studies on many different topics, in the long run, what percentage of your .95 confidence intervals would be expected to contain the parameter you were estimating?

**38.** Where would an increase in $n$ of 20 have the greatest effect on reducing the size of the confidence intervals?

(a) increasing $n$ from 5 to 25
(b) increasing $n$ from 10 to 30
(c) increasing $n$ from 40 to 60

**39.** Which type of estimate, point or interval, more properly conveys the degree of accuracy in the estimate?

**40.** In a normal distribution is $E(Md) = E(\overline{X}) = \mu$?

**41.** The statistical property denoted in the previous question is
(a) consistency (b) efficiency (c) unbiasedness

**42.** Using the options in the previous question, which property is primarily responsible for the greater use of the mean instead of the median or mode in inferential statistics?

**43.** Using Figure 10.6, the same degree of precision using $Md$ to estimate $\mu$ with $n = 100$ can be obtained using $\overline{X}$ with a sample size of ____.

## PROBLEMS AND EXERCISES

**1.** By using the table of random digits (Table B in the Appendix), draw a random sample of five students from the following set of sixteen:

| | | | |
|---|---|---|---|
| Juan | Win | Kyle | Anthony |
| Jacob | Mansoor | Susan | Saul |
| Alice | Maurice | Martha | Taji |
| Roberta | Kato | Parvin | Mohsahn |

**2.** Enter the table of random numbers (Table B) and select two random digits. Determine the mean of these two numbers and repeat the process until you have twenty-five means. Tally the twenty-five means into a sampling distribution.

(a) What is the shape of the frequency distribution of the individual random digits (not means)?
(b) Does the distribution of the twenty-five $\overline{X}$'s appear to be bell-shaped?
(c) Compute the mean of these twenty-five means. What parameter is being estimated? What is the numerical value of $\mu$?
(d) Compare the mean of your means (part c) with $\mu$.
(e) If you continued finding means for pairs of random numbers until you had 100 means, would the sampling distribution be expected to be unimodal? Would the sampling distribution be expected to appear more nearly normal? Would the range of the distribution of $\overline{X}$'s be expected to increase?
(f) If, instead of finding the mean for two numbers, you determined the mean of eight random numbers, and repeated the process twenty-five times, would the value of $\mu$ be altered?
(g) In part f would the value of $\sigma_{\overline{X}}$ decrease?
(h) In part f would the sampling distribution be more nearly normal?
(i) What mathematical principle accounts for the approximate normality of the sampling distribution as $n$ becomes larger?
(j) If you computed the standard deviation of the set of twenty-five means, what is the appropriate symbol?
(k) What is the parameter being estimated in part j?

**3.** A sample of size $n$ is to be drawn randomly from a population with mean $\mu$ and variance $\sigma^2$. The sample size is sufficiently large that the sampling distribution of $\overline{X}$ can be assumed to be normal. Determine the probabilities that $\overline{X}$ will be between the following pairs of points:

(a) $\mu + \sigma_{\overline{X}}$ and $\mu - \sigma_{\overline{X}}$
(b) $\mu + 1.96\ \sigma_{\overline{X}}$ and $\mu - 1.96\ \sigma_{\overline{X}}$
(c) $\mu + 2.58\ \sigma / \sqrt{n}$ and $\mu - 2.58\ \sigma / \sqrt{n}$
(d) $\mu + .675\ \sigma_{\overline{X}}$ and $\mu - .675\ \sigma_{\overline{X}}$

**4.** A sample of size $n$ is to be drawn from a population of normally distributed $T$-scores with mean 50 and variance 100. Complete the following table by calculating the variance error and standard error of $\overline{X}$ for various sample sizes.

| | $n$ | $\sigma^2_{\overline{X}}$ | $\sigma_{\overline{X}}$ |
|---|---|---|---|
| (a) | 1 | — | — |
| (b) | 2 | — | — |
| (c) | 4 | — | — |
| (d) | 8 | — | — |
| (e) | 16 | — | — |
| (f) | 100 | — | — |
| (g) | 200 | — | — |
| (h) | 400 | — | — |
| (i) | 1,000 | — | — |

(j) As $n$ is doubled, how was $\sigma^2_{\overline{X}}$ affected?

(k) As $n$ is quadrupled, how was $\sigma_{\overline{X}}$ affected?

(l) If $n = 1$, is the sampling distribution of $\overline{X}$ identical to the frequency distribution, and does $\sigma = \sigma_{\overline{X}}$ when $n = 1$?

**5.** In 1976 the mean height of women in the United States was found to be $\mu \approx 64.5$ in. with a standard deviation of $\sigma \approx 2.3$ in.

(a) Estimate the standard deviation of the sampling distribution if $n = 100$.

(b) If $n = 100$, find the width of the .95 confidence interval for $\sigma = 2.3$ in. (assume that $\mu$ was unknown).

(c) How large a sample is required in order for $\sigma_{\overline{X}}$ to equal .10?

6. When $n$ is small, the sampling distribution of $s^2$ is positively skewed with a mean of $\sigma^2$ (see Figure 10.4). Recall the relationship between the mean and median in a positively skewed distribution. Is the probability of obtaining a value of $s^2$ that exceeds $\sigma^2$ greater than, equal to, or less than .50?

## ANSWERS TO MASTERY TEST

**1.** F
**2.** T
**3.** T
**4.** no
**5.** no
**6.** yes
**7.** no
**8.** No—the thirty-six are probably not a representative sample of the 108
**9.** no
**10.** no
**11.** no
**12.** no
**13.** yes
**14.** a systematic sample; yes
**15.** $\sigma_{\overline{X}} = 15/\sqrt{9} = 5$
**16.** $z = \dfrac{105-100}{5} = 1.0$, 16%; $z = 2.0$, 2.3%
**17.** 68%; 95%
**18.** yes, approximately
**19.** $\sigma_{\overline{X}}^2 = (5)^2 = 25$
**20.** $\sigma_{\overline{X}} = 15/\sqrt{225} = 1.0$
**21.** 68%
**22.** No, but the difference will be negligible unless $n$ is very small.
**23.** yes
**24.** the central limit theorem
**25.** yes, but probably not the population of homes with telephones because of unlisted numbers
**26.** yes, but the value of $\sigma_{\overline{X}}$ will differ for each value of $n$
**27.** no, .68 $CI = \overline{X} \pm \sigma_{\overline{X}}$, but the value of $\overline{X}$ will vary from sample to sample
**28.** yes
**29.** no, $\sigma^2/n$ equals $\sigma_{\overline{X}}^2$, not $\sigma_{\overline{X}}$
**30.** yes
**31.** yes—square both sides of the equation $\sigma_{\overline{X}} = \sigma/\sqrt{n}$; $\sigma_{\overline{X}}^2 = \sigma^2/n$, and rearrange to obtain $\sigma^2 = n\sigma_{\overline{X}}^2$
**32.** no: $\mu \neq \sigma_{\overline{X}}^2$
**33.** yes
**34.** no: rarely is $\overline{X}$ precisely equal to $\mu$
**35.** no: $\overline{X} = (\Sigma X)/n$, not $(\Sigma x)/n$; $\Sigma x = 0$
**36.** yes
**37.** 95%
**38.** (a)
**39.** interval estimates
**40.** yes
**41.** (c)
**42.** (b)
**43.** 64

## ANSWERS TO PROBLEMS AND EXERCISES

**2.** (a) rectangular
(b) It should.
(c) $\mu$, the mean of the population of single random digits: $\mu = (0 + 1 + \ldots + 9)/10 = 4.5$
(d) They should be fairly close.
(e) yes, yes, yes (see Table 5.1)
(f) no
(g) Yes: $\sigma_{\overline{X}} = \sigma/\sqrt{n}$; if $n = 8$, $\sigma_{\overline{X}}$ is only one-half the value of $\sigma_{\overline{X}}$ for $n = 2$.
(h) yes
(i) the central limit theorem
(j) $s_{\overline{X}}$
(k) $\sigma_{\overline{X}}$

**3.** (a) .68
(b) .95
(c) .99
(d) .50

**4.**

| | $\sigma_{\overline{X}}^2$ | $\sigma_{\overline{X}}$ |
|---|---|---|
| (a) | 100 | 10 |
| (b) | 50 | 7.07 |
| (c) | 25 | 5 |
| (d) | 12.5 | 3.54 |
| (e) | 6.25 | 2.5 |
| (f) | 1 | 1 |
| (g) | .5 | .707 |
| (h) | .25 | .5 |
| (i) | .1 | .316 |

(j) $\sigma_{\overline{X}}^2$ for $2n$ is one-half $\sigma_{\overline{X}}^2$ for $n$
(k) $\sigma_{\overline{X}}^2$ for $4n$ is one-fourth $\sigma_{\overline{X}}^2$ for $n$; hence, $\sigma_{\overline{X}}$ for $4n$ is one-half $\sigma_{\overline{X}}$ for $n$
(l) yes

**5.** (a) $\sigma_{\overline{X}} = 2.3/\sqrt{100} = .23$ in.
(b) $\pm1.96\sigma_{\overline{X}} = \pm1.96(.23 \text{ in.}) = \pm.45$ in.; width = .90 in.
(c) $n = 529$

**6.** less than .50

# 11

# INTRODUCTION TO HYPOTHESIS TESTING

## 11.1 INTRODUCTION

In Chapter 10, one of the most useful techniques of statistical inference was developed, the inferential technique known as interval estimation. In this chapter, another important inferential technique, *hypothesis testing*, is introduced.

Statistical hypothesis testing has become a ubiquitous feature of research in the social and behavioral sciences. Many professional journals can be only partially comprehended if the reader is not aware of the theory and techniques of hypothesis testing. Most empirical research in the behavioral sciences uses hypothesis testing or interval estimation.

The ideas of hypothesis testing in this chapter make the discussion to follow a challenge, and mastery of these concepts for most students will require several careful readings. Fortunately, most concepts used in interval estimation also play central roles in hypothesis testing.[1] An understanding of random sampling, sampling distributions, and probabilities that are associated with confidence intervals are essential to an understanding of hypothesis testing. Hypothesis testing and interval estimation are carried out with different languages, but we shall see that they usually produce equivalent results, or results that are easily converted from one to the other. The basic question addressed by both procedures is: "How do we make inferences regarding the population from a sample of observations?"

## 11.2 STATISTICAL HYPOTHESES AND EXPLANATIONS

The history of testing statistical hypotheses began in the early eighteenth century. Perhaps the earliest example of a formal statistical hypothesis test appears in a publication dated 1710 and written by John Arbuthnot (1667–1735): *An Argument for Divine Provi-*

---

[1]The process of building a conceptual superstructure is relentless in statistics; no sooner has one concept been introduced, and it is being used as the foundation for yet another concept.

*dence, Taken from the Constant Regularity Observed in the Births of Both Sexes.* Noting that for eighty-two consecutive years the statistical records showed that more males were born than females, Arbuthnot argued that the hypothesis that male and female births are equally likely (each with a probability of .5) was refuted by these data, for if the probability of a male birth were precisely .5, then the probability of eighty-two consecutive years in which more males than females were born would be infinitesimally small: $(1/2)^{82}$ or approximately 0.000,000,000,000,000,000,000,0002. Arbuthnot concluded that the greater portion of male births to female births was an act of divine providence; the sacred institution of monogamous marriage was being maintained since males were more likely to be killed in war or work before reaching adulthood.

Arbuthnot's study illustrates a critically important point in empirical research that employs statistics. Statistics allow one to find the probability of some event, given certain conditions and assumptions; but statistics per se *never* supply the explanation or interpretation for a phenomenon. If you toss a coin ten times and get ten heads, the probability of this result given a fair coin is very small: $(1/2)^{10} = 1/1{,}024 \approx .001$. You will conclude that there is an explanation other than chance, but statistics do not tell you whether the coin was biased, the tossing was unfair, whether psychokinesis was operating, whether you are a "winner" (lucky), whether you are hallucinating, or whether God ordained it.

Arbuthnot's statistics are unimpeachable, but you may or may not agree with his explanation. Your world view may offer another theory to explain the phenomenon (such as the sperm carrying the Y-chromosome has slightly less mass to propel, hence wins the race to the ovum more than 50% of the time). Like Arbuthnot, the modern researcher is much concerned with the probabilistic consideration of various hypotheses.

## 11.3 STATISTICAL VERSUS SCIENTIFIC HYPOTHESES

The statistical decision that a researcher makes is a decision about the tenability of a statistical hypothesis. There are two types of hypotheses that should be distinguished: scientific hypotheses and statistical hypotheses. A *scientific hypothesis* is an anticipated and predicted outcome based, at least loosely, on theoretical considerations. A scientific hypothesis is an informed guess, stated as a testable proposition. The formulation of a good scientific hypothesis is often the result of a creative insight.

The strategy of hypothesis testing involves a decision regarding a statistical hypothesis, $H_0$—a decision about whether $H_0$ is false. *A statistical hypothesis is simply a statement about the numerical value of an unknown parameter.* In Table 11.1, illustrative statistical hypotheses are given. The statistical hypothesis can involve a statement about a single parameter (as in hypotheses *A*, *B*, *C*, *F*, *I* or *J*), or the hypothesis can pertain to a difference between two or more parameters (as in hypotheses *D*, *E*, *G*, *H*, or *K*). Note that the eleven hypotheses in Table 11.1 are statements about parameters. Each $H_0$ specifies a numerical value for some parameter (or a difference between parameters, which is itself a parameter). For example, hypothesis *A* ($H_0$: $\mu = 100$) is a statistical hypothesis; it is a statement that the numerical value of the mean of a population is 100. This could be the hypothesis of interest if, for example, we are estimating the average IQ in the population of left-handed persons.

Hypothesis *B* shows that if all observations in the population were included, that is, if $n = N$, the value of the parameter for the mean would be 0. In this chapter, we will be particularly concerned with testing statistical hypotheses like *A* and *B*.

**TABLE 11.1** Illustrative Statistical Hypotheses

| | |
|---|---|
| *A*. $H_0$: $\mu = 100$ | The population mean is 100. |
| *B*. $H_0$: $\mu = 0$ | The population mean is 0. |
| *C*. $H_0$: $\sigma = 15$ | The standard deviation in the population is 15. |
| *D*. $H_0$: $\mu_1 - \mu_2 = 0$ (or $\mu_1 = \mu_2$) | The means of populations 1 and 2 are equal—there is no difference in the parameters $\mu_1$ and $\mu_2$. |
| *E*. $H_0$: $\sigma_1^2 - \sigma_2^2 = 0$ (or $\sigma_1^2 = \sigma_2^2$) | The variance in population 1 is equal to the variance in population 2. |
| *F*. $H_0$: $\rho_{XY} = 0$ | The correlation coefficient between variables *X* and *Y* in the population is 0. |
| *G*. $H_0$: $\rho_1 - \rho_2 = 0$ (or $\rho_1 = \rho_2$) | The difference between the correlation coefficient in population 1 and in population 2 is 0. |
| *H*. $H_0$: $\mu_1 = \mu_2 = \mu_3$ | The means in the three populations: 1, 2, and 3, are equal. |
| *I*. $H_0$: $\rho_{Y.123} = 0$ | The multiple correlation, $\rho_{Y.123}$, in the population is 0. |
| *J*. $H_0$: $\pi = .5$ | The proportion in the population ($\pi$) is .5. |
| *K*. $H_0$: $\pi_1 - \pi_2 = 0$ (or $\pi_1 = \pi_2$) | The proportion in population 1 equals the proportion in population 2. |

Hypothesis *C* in Table 11.1 states that a particular population has a standard deviation of 15. The hypothesis, $H_0$: $\sigma^2 = 225$, is of course equivalent to hypothesis *C*. Hypothesis *D* states that there is no difference in the means of two populations. Hypothesis *D* is an example of a two-sample test of means in contrast to hypotheses *A* and *B*, which are one-sample tests of means. Procedures for testing hypotheses like *C* through *K* are treated in subsequent chapters. Fortunately, once the procedures and concepts are understood for testing hypotheses regarding the mean, it is a straightforward matter to apply the concepts to the testing of other statistical hypotheses like *C* through *K* in Table 11.1.

It is important to distinguish scientific and statistical hypotheses. It is quite possible to test statistical hypotheses about very trivial matters that possess limited generality and not a glimmer of importance. We could have a jar of peas and ask samples of females and males to guess how many peas are in the jar. We could test hypothesis *D* to see if the male and female means of their guesses were significantly different. Not all scientific hypotheses need to be tested statistically; and by no means are all statistical hypotheses of practical or scientific interest.

## 11.4 TESTING STATISTICAL HYPOTHESES ABOUT $\mu$

A statistical hypothesis is assumed to be either true or false. By using inferential statistical methods, the researcher makes a decision within a certain margin of error as to whether the statistical hypothesis, for example, $H_0$: $\mu = 100$, is tenable or whether it must be rejected as false. To reject $H_0$ is to reject the statement that $\mu = 100$; to reject $H_0$: $\mu = 100$ is to conclude that $\mu \neq 100$. The four steps required for the testing of any statistical hypothesis are given in Table 11.2.

**TABLE 11.2** The Four Steps in Testing Statistical Hypotheses Regarding $\mu$

| | |
|---|---|
| Step 1. | State the *statistical hypothesis* $H_0$ to be tested (e.g., $H_0$: $\mu = 100$). |
| Step 2. | Specify the *degree of risk of a type-I error*, that is, the risk of *incorrectly* concluding that $H_0$ is false when it is true. This risk, stated as a probability, is denoted by $\alpha$ (alpha) and is the probability of a type-I error. In most applications, $\alpha = .05$. |
| Step 3. | Assuming $H_0$ to be correct, *find the probability* ($p$) of obtaining a sample mean ($\overline{X}$) that differs from $\mu$ by an amount as large or larger than what was observed (e.g., if $\mu = 100$, and $\overline{X} = 108$, calculate the probability of observing a difference between $\overline{X}$ and $\mu$ of 8 or more points). |
| Step 4. | *Make a decision regarding* $H_0$—whether to reject the hypothesis (e.g., if the probability $p$, from Step 3 is less than $\alpha$, $H_0$ is rejected and we conclude that $\mu \neq 100$). |

The purpose of hypothesis testing is to make a decision about whether a statistical hypothesis is tenable. When the probability ($p$) of the difference observed in the sample is small if $H_0$ were indeed true (i.e., smaller than the maximum acceptable risk, $\alpha$), the researcher concludes that the statistical hypothesis $H_0$ is false. The statistical hypothesis will be rejected at the $\alpha$-level of significance.

Suppose you are observing a game of craps in which a stranger wins consistently. The thought crosses your mind that the dice may be loaded toward 7's. The statistical hypothesis that you entertain is that the dice are fair, not wanting to accuse someone falsely. You observe the stranger roll the dice and note that "7" appeared in five of the eight tosses (i.e., data are gathered). The probability of this happening if the dice are true is very small.[2] Intuition tells you that something is operating in the system other than chance, even though you may not be able to determine the probability mathematically. You make a mental note to avoid the stranger (i.e., you reject the statistical hypothesis). You are a wise and unprejudiced soul with a good intuitive sense of probability, and a hypothesis tester of sorts.

## 11.5 TESTING $H_0$: $\mu = K$, A ONE-SAMPLE $z$-TEST

To illustrate the four steps in testing hypotheses about $\mu$ (Table 11.2), suppose we want to learn whether the mean IQ of adopted children differs from the mean for the general population of children ($\mu = 100$).

1. The statistical hypothesis is $H_0$: $\mu = 100$.
2. Set $\alpha = .05$ (.05 is the most commonly chosen value for $\alpha$).
3. In a random sample of $n = 25$ adopted children, a mean ($\overline{X}$) of 96.0 is obtained. The probability, $p$, is determined that one would obtain a sample mean, $\overline{X}$, for twenty-five observations that differs from $\mu = 100$ by four or more points, if indeed $H_0$: $\mu = 100$ is true.
4. If the probability ($p$) is smaller than $\alpha$ (.05), the statistical hypothesis ($H_0$: $\mu = 100$) will be rejected at the .05 level of significance. If $p > \alpha$, $H_0$ is not rejected; hence, $H_0$ continues to be tenable.

[2]From Sections 9.10–9.11, we find that the probabilities of five, six, seven, and eight 7's are 7,000/1,679,616, 700/1,679,616, 40/1,679,616 and 1/1,679,616, respectively. Thus, the probability of obtaining five or more 7's in eight tosses is 7,741/1,679,616 = .0046.

The decision one makes regarding $H_0$ is either to reject $H_0$ (hence conclude $\mu \neq 100$) or accept $H_0$ (that is, conclude that $\mu = 100$ is tenable). The decision is based on the probability that one would observe a difference (i.e., sampling error) between $\overline{X}$ (96.0) and $\mu$ (100) $\geq 4$ (the observed difference) if, indeed, $H_0$ were true. With a sample mean of 96.0 for a random sample of twenty-five adopted children, is $H_0$ tenable, or must it be rejected?

If $\mu = 100$ and $n = 25$, how frequently would a sample mean ($\overline{X}$) of 96 or less be observed? How frequently would a sample mean differ by four or more points from the population mean? From the national test norms, it is known that $\sigma = 15$. Hence, the standard deviation of the sampling distribution of means (i.e., standard error of the mean, $\sigma_{\overline{X}}$) when $n = 25$ is shown by Equation 10.1 to be $15/\sqrt{25} = 3.0$.

Recall from Chapter 6 that to find the area in a normal distribution beyond any point, $X$, the deviation of $X$ from the mean of the distribution, that is, $x = X - \mu$, is divided by the standard deviation of the distribution, $\sigma$, to obtain the $z$-ratio (Equation 6.2):

$$z = \frac{X - \mu}{\sigma}$$

Since we are dealing with a sampling distribution, the observations in the normal distribution are sample means ($\overline{X}$'s) and the standard deviation is the standard error of the mean ($\sigma_{\overline{X}}$); hence, the $z$-ratio or $z$-test becomes

$$z = \frac{\overline{X} - \mu}{\sigma_{\overline{X}}} \qquad \textbf{(11.1)}$$

By entering the $z$-value in the normal curve table (Appendix Table A), the probability of obtaining a sample mean of 96.0 or less, if indeed $H_0$ is true, can be determined. In the example with $\overline{X} = 96.0$:

$$z = \frac{\overline{X} - \mu}{\sigma_{\overline{X}}} = \frac{96.0 - 100}{3.0} = -1.33$$

From Table A, the proportion of the normal curve falling below the point $z = -1.33$ is found to .0918. Hence, when $\mu = 100$, we would observe $\overline{X}$'s that are below 96.0 in .0918 (9.18%) of samples when $n = 25$. Similarly, we would expect $\overline{X}$'s to be 104.0 or greater in 9.18% of the samples of twenty-five cases. Thus, the probability of observing a $\overline{X} - \mu$ difference as large 4 points is $p = 2(.0918) = .1836$; since $p$ is greater than $\alpha = .05$, $H_0$ is not rejected.

## 11.6 TWO TYPES OF ERRORS IN HYPOTHESIS TESTING

If $\mu = 100$ and $n = 25$, the probability of the mean of a sample, $\overline{X}$, differing from 100 by four or more points is 2(.0918) =.1836. If $H_0$: $\mu = 100$ is true, yet were to be consistently rejected whenever the sample mean is below 96 or above 104, the risk of error in the decision is approximately 18% ($\alpha = .1836$). When $H_0$ is true, but it is rejected, a type-I error is made. In practice, $H_0$ is rejected when the probability, $p$, that the sample mean deviates from the hypothesized value of $\mu$ by the amount of the observed difference is less than the prespecified $\alpha$. $H_0$ continues to be tenable if $p$ is greater than $\alpha$,[3] that is, $H_0$ is not rejected if $p > \alpha$. In our example we would not reject $H_0$, since $p = .18 > \alpha = .05$. Notice however, that *we have not proven $H_0$ to be true*; we have only concluded that it is tenable. The probability is only .18 that we would observe a value of $\bar{X}$ that differs by four or more points from 100 if $H_0$ is true. However, the probability of .18 does exceed the maximum risk of a type-I error that we have decided to take, that is, $p > \alpha = .05$. To accept $H_0$ simply indicates that we will continue to entertain the possibility that $H_0$ is true, that is, the possibility that $H_0$ is true is not unreasonable, but notice that $H_0$ has not been proven to be correct. Likewise, the decision to reject $H_0$ is a decision also attended by a risk of error; to reject $H_0$ does not prove that $H_0$ is false. The failure to make such distinctions as the difference in meaning between "not rejecting $H_0$" and "proving $H_0$ to be correct" has led to the misinterpretation of much research (Hopkins, 1973).

Statistical inferential techniques using only the data from a sample can never establish the truth of a hypothesis with certainty—no statistical hypothesis can be accepted or rejected with 100% confidence. Rejecting $H_0$ when it is true is termed a type-I error. Conversely, when $H_0$ is accepted, $H_0$ is not proven to be true—just that the evidence against the proposition is not sufficiently strong to reject it. Failure to reject $H_0$ when it is false is termed a type-II error. The probability of a type-I error is symbolized by $\alpha$; the probability of a type-II error is denoted by $\beta$. Of course, no errors are involved when a true $H_0$ is accepted or a false $H_0$ is rejected.

## An Example in Which $H_0$ is Rejected

Suppose that, instead of 96, the random sample of twenty-five adopted children had a mean IQ score of 108. The $z$-ratio would then be $z = (\bar{X} - \mu)/\sigma = (108 - 100)/3 = 2.67$. From the normal curve in Appendix Table A, it is found that only .0038 of the area in a normal curve falls above a point 2.67 standard deviations above the mean. Note the black portion of the curve in Figure 11.1. The black portion of each tail represents .0038 of the area under the curve. Hence, when $\mu = 100$, the probability of observing a value for $\mu$ that differs from $\mu = 100$ by eight or more points is $p = 2(.0038) = .0076$, that is, 76 chances in 10,000.[4] In other words, there is less than one chance in 100 that the sampling error $(\bar{X} - \mu)$ would be as large as eight points when $H_0$: $\mu = 100$ is true. What then is the decision regarding the truth of $H_0$: $\mu = 100$ when $\bar{X} = 108$ is observed? $H_0$ would be rejected at the .05 level (indeed, even at the .01 level) of statistical significance—there is a statistically significant difference between $\bar{X} = 108$ and $\mu = 100$. The probability of making a type-I error in such situations, when the absolute value of $z$ is 2.67, is less than .01. Although we were willing to take a 5% risk of a type-I error, the risk is less than 1%. Obviously, the .01 level gives us greater assurance than the .05 level that indeed $H_0$ is false.

---

[3]For no good reason other than convenience and simplicity, a 5% risk of a type-I error ($\alpha = .05$) has become conventional. As you progress in your understanding of statistical inference, you will be able to make intelligent decisions regarding the type-I error risk that is appropriate in a given situation, rather than adhering slavishly to $\alpha = .05$. In certain situations, it is appropriate to set $\alpha = .1$ or even higher; in other instances, $\alpha$ should be set at .01 or even .001.

[4]The probability of a type-I error is generally not reported as .0076, as it might appear from Figure 11.1. The extreme of precision implicit in the .0076 value is precisely accurate only if all statistical assumptions are perfectly achieved. Hence, researchers usually report statistical significance at the .05, .02, .01, or .001 level, rather than a value that may be less precise than the numbers suggest, such as .0064 or .0122.

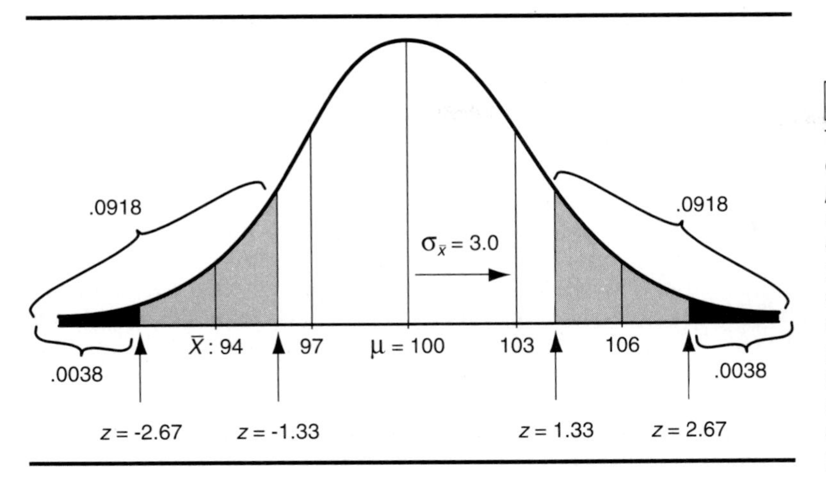


**FIGURE 11.1**

The sampling distribution of $\bar{X}$ when $\mu = 100$ and $\sigma = 15$, and $n = 25$. The probability of obtaining a sample mean that deviates by 4 or more points from $\mu$ is darkened. The black portions reflect the probability of obtaining a sample mean that deviates by 8 or more points from $\mu = 100$.

In summary, the steps in testing hypotheses of the type, $H_0$: $\mu = K$ are the following: (1) state the statistical hypothesis; (2) specify $\alpha$; (3) determine the probability, $p$, of observing an event that deviates by at least as much as what was observed, entertaining for the moment that $H_0$ is true; (4) if $p$ is less than $\alpha$, reject $H_0$ and conclude that the parameter being estimated has a value different from that stated by $H_0$. If $p > \alpha$, $H_0$ is not rejected, and $H_0$ continues to be tenable.

Notice that when $H_0$ is not rejected, we did not say that it has been proven to be true, or even that $H_0$ is probably true. What we have found is that the evidence against the defendant, $H_0$, is not sufficient to convict him or her—a reasonable doubt remains.

## 11.7 HYPOTHESIS TESTING AND CONFIDENCE INTERVALS[5]

Confidence intervals are probably the most useful of all types of inferential statistical procedures (Tukey, 1960, p. 429). In making interval estimates, we attempt to reach conclusions that are reasonable by presenting a range of possible values, so defined that there can be high confidence that the "true" value, the parameter, lies within this range. Interval estimates depict the degree of precision in our parameter estimates.

If a confidence interval is set about $\mu$, one can see the logical unity between hypothesis testing and interval estimation. If $\bar{X} = 108$, $\sigma = 15$, and $n = 25$, the .99 confidence interval on $\mu$ is: $\bar{X} \pm 2.576\sigma_{\bar{X}} = 108 \pm 2.576(3.00) = 108 \pm 7.73 = (100.27, 115.73)$

In other words, the .99 confidence interval extends from 100.27, its lower limit, to 115.73, its upper limit. Notice that the .99 confidence interval does *not* contain the hypothesized value of 100 for $\mu$. *When the .99 confidence interval does not include the value of the parameter specified by the statistical hypothesis, this is tantamount to stating that the statistical hypothesis is rejected at the .01 level of significance.* Likewise, if one rejects $H_0$: $\mu =$

[5]The procedures we employ are eclectic, being drawn from both Neyman-Pearson and Fisher, and are not an orthodox example of either.

$K$ at the .05 level, the .95 confidence interval will not include the hypothesized value $K$ for the parameter.

On the other hand, when $H_0$ is *not* rejected at the .05 level, as in the initial example with $\overline{X} = 96$ (Section 11.6), we can be reasonably sure that the value for the parameter being estimated lies within the .95 confidence interval. With $\overline{X} = 96$, the .95 confidence interval is $\overline{X} \pm 1.96\sigma_{\overline{X}} = 96 \pm 1.96(3.00) = 96 \pm 5.88$, or between 90.12 and 101.88. This is often denoted as: $.95CI = (90.12, 101.88)$. Note that the value of 100 specified in the statistical hypothesis for $\mu$ lies within the .95 confidence interval; hence, $H_0$ is *not* rejected at the .05 level.

These examples serve to illustrate how the inferential techniques of interval estimation and hypothesis testing are two sides of the same coin. From a confidence interval, one can easily determine the outcome of testing a hypothesis about $\mu$; $H_0$ is tenable ($p > \alpha$) for all values contained within the $1 - \alpha$ confidence interval. Conversely, from the knowledge that $H_0$: $\mu = 100$ was rejected at the $\alpha = .05$ level, one knows that the .95 confidence interval for $\mu$ does not contain the value of 100. A bit of computation is required to define the limits for the .95 confidence interval.

To see the preceding argument in its mathematical form, consider Equation 11.1:

$$z = \frac{\overline{X} - \mu}{\sigma_{\overline{X}}} \sim N(0,1)$$

where "$\sim N(0, 1)$" means "is distributed normally, with population mean 0 and population variance 1." Therefore, the probability ($p$) that the observed $z$ will be less than $|1.96|$ is .95:

$$p\left(-1.96 < \frac{\overline{X} - \mu}{\sigma_{\overline{X}}} < 1.96\right) = .95 \qquad \textbf{(11.2)}$$

Multiplying the inequality in parentheses by $\sigma_{\overline{X}}$ gives the following expression:

$$p(-1.96\sigma_{\overline{X}} < \overline{X} - \mu < 1.96\sigma_{\overline{X}}) = .95$$

Thus, in the example in which $n = 25$ and $\sigma = 15$, $\sigma_{\overline{X}} = 3$; the probability, $p$, that $(-5.88 < \overline{X} - \mu < 5.88) = .95$. Or equivalently, if $\overline{X}$ differs by 5.88 from the hypothesized value of $\mu$, $H_0$ can be rejected at the .05 level of significance.

## 11.8 TYPE-II ERROR, $\beta$, AND POWER

Quite literally, so far in this chapter only half the story of statistical hypothesis testing has been told. In this section, the other side of the story will be presented. The standard technique for testing an hypothesis, such as $H_0$: $\mu = 100$ using the $z$-test, is to select a level of significance $\alpha$, find the critical values of $z$ (Table A), draw a sample and compute $\overline{X}$ and then, depending on the value of $z$, accept or reject $H_0$. In the previous section, we showed how to determine the probability of a given value at least as large as $\overline{X}$ when $H_0$ was in fact true.

It was acknowledged that the decision "$H_0$ is false" could be incorrect and that, in the long run, this probability is $\alpha$. Now we acknowledge that the decision to accept $H_0$, that is, to conclude that "$H_0$ is tenable" can also be incorrect. In other words, we can accept $H_0$ when it is false, for example, conclude that $\mu = 100$ remains tenable when in fact $\mu \neq 100$. The error of *accepting a false* $H_0$ is termed an error of the second kind or a *type-II error*. The probability of a type-II error will be calculated.

To test $H_0$, the investigator establishes critical regions of $\overline{X}$ that lead to the rejection of $H_0$ (as was done in Figure 11.1). Since $\alpha = .05$, a $|z|$-ratio of 1.96 is required to reject $H_0$. Note from Table A that .025 of the area falls below $z = -1.96$ in a normal distribution; another .025 of the area falls above $z = 1.96$: $.025 + .025 = .05 = \alpha$. If $\mu$ is actually 100, there is one chance in twenty ($\alpha = .05$) that the investigator will reject $H_0$: $\mu = 100$, even though it is true, that is, there is a 5% chance that the investigator will make a type-I error.

## 11.9 POWER

What if $\mu$ really equals 110? In this case where $H_0$: $\mu = 100$, we want to reject it in favor of the conclusion that $\mu \neq 100$. What is the probability that $H_0$ will be rejected? *This probability of rejecting an* H$_0$ *when it is false is the power of a statistical test.* Assume that $\mu = 110$; in Figure 11.2, the power of the $z$-test is depicted by the area under the right-hand curve that falls above the critical value of $z$. The critical region for $\mu$ is at a $z$-value $\geq 1.96$, or $\overline{X}$ values above 105.88: $\overline{X} + 1.96\sigma_{\overline{X}} = 100 + (1.96)(3.00) = 105.88$. Hence, the power of the $z$-test to reject $H_0$ when $\mu$ equals 110 is the area above $\overline{X} = 105.88$ under the right-hand curve—the curve that depicts the sampling distribution of $\overline{X}$ when $\mu = 110$ and $n = 25$. This area is approximately 91% of the total area under the right-hand curve in Figure 11.2. Thus, the power in this instance is .91.

How was the value of .91 obtained? The standard error of the mean, $\sigma_{\overline{X}}$, is not affected by the value of $\mu$, thus $\sigma_{\overline{X}} = 3.00$ for both curves in Figure 11.2. The value of 105.88 corresponds to a $z$-ratio of $(105.88 - 110)/3.00 = -1.37$ in the right-hand distribution. In Table A, we find that $\beta = .0853 \approx .09$ (i.e., $p = .09$) of the area falls below the critical value needed to reject $H_0$.[6]

The area under the curve on the right in Figure 11.2 (the sampling distribution of $\overline{X}$ when $\mu = 110$ and $n = 25$) below 105.88 is a measure of the probability that $\overline{X}$ will fail to exceed the critical value even though $H_0$ is false; this area represents $\beta$, the probability of a type-II error. The area in question is about 9% of the total area under the curve. Hence, $\beta$ is approximately .09. Since $\mu$ is actually 110, the probability of *not* committing a type-II error, that is, the power of the statistical test, is given by $1 - \beta = .91$. Now, try to convince yourself that if $\mu$ were equal to 90, the same hypothesis-testing procedure would run the same risk of a type-II error and have the same power (.91) as when $\mu = 110$.

## 11.10 EFFECT OF $\alpha$ ON POWER

Suppose one had chosen to test $H_0$: $\mu = 100$ against $H_1$: $\mu \neq 100$, but with $\alpha = .10$. If $\mu = 110$, study Figure 11.2 to confirm that the power of the statistical test is greater than with $\alpha = .05$. From Table A, the critical $z$-value for $\alpha = .10$ is $|1.645|$; .05 of the critical area is found in each tail. The minimum value of $\overline{X}$ for which $H_0$ will be rejected is $1.645\sigma_{\overline{X}} = 1.645(3.00)$

---

[6]Actually, there also exists an infinitesimal chance ($p = .0000003$) that $H_0$ will be rejected in favor of the alternative hypothesis $H_1$ when $\mu = 110$ and $\overline{X}$ is below 94.12 (or $z = -1.96$). This bit of esoteria is sometimes termed a type-III error—when $H_0$ is rejected, but the direction of the difference is incorrect.

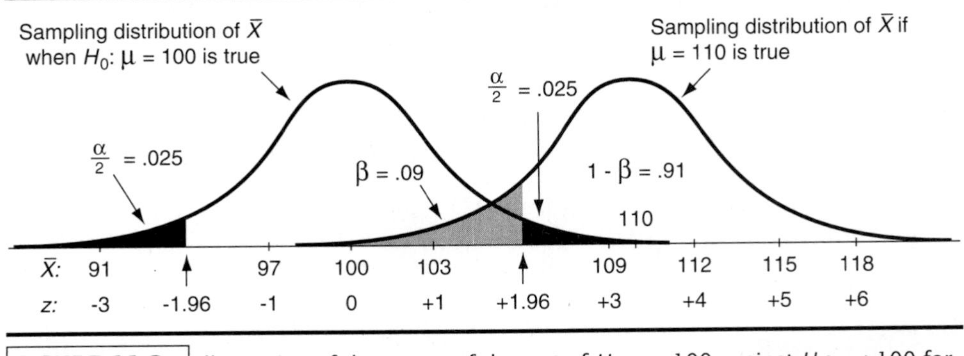


**FIGURE 11.2** Illustration of the power of the test of $H_0$: $\mu = 100$ against $H_1$: $\mu \neq 100$ for the case in which $\mu = 110$, $\sigma_{\bar{X}} = 3$, and $\alpha = .05$.

= 4.94 points from the value for the parameter that is stated in the statistical hypothesis (100). Power at $\alpha = .10$ is then the proportion of the right-hand curve in Figure 11.2 that falls above 104.94. The value of 104.94 corresponds to a $z$-ratio of $-1.687 = (104.94 - 110)/3.00$ in the right-hand distribution, thus $\beta = .046$ and power $(1 - \beta)$ for $\mu = 110$ and $\alpha = .10$ is .954.

## 11.11 POWER AND THE VALUE HYPOTHESIZED IN THE ALTERNATIVE HYPOTHESIS

It will further increase our grasp of the concepts being developed if the power of the test of $H_0$: $\mu = 100$ (with $\alpha = .05$ and $\sigma_{\bar{X}} = 3$) is determined when $\mu = 105$ instead of 110. The critical regions of the test remain the same as in Figure 11.2 ($\leq 94.12$ and $\geq 105.88$). The sampling distribution of $\bar{X}$ for samples of size 25 is unchanged from Figure 11.2 when $H_0$: $\mu = 100$ is true. It appears in Figure 11.3 along with the sampling distribution of $\bar{X}$ for $n = 25$ and $\sigma = 15$ when $\mu = 105$.

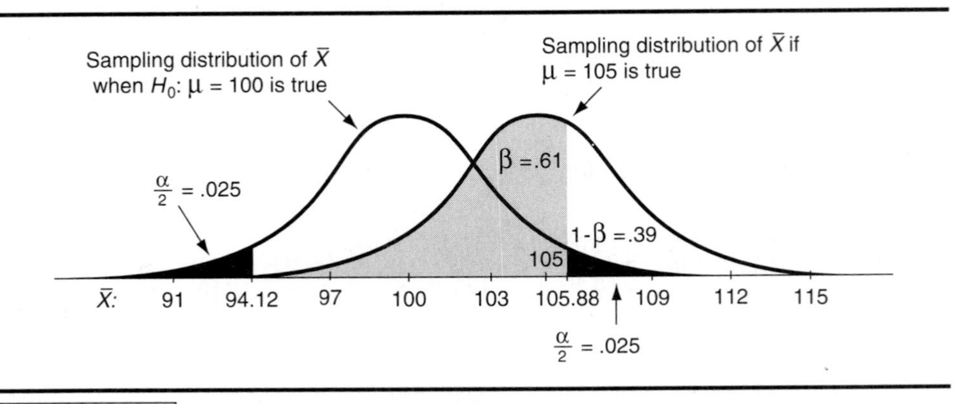


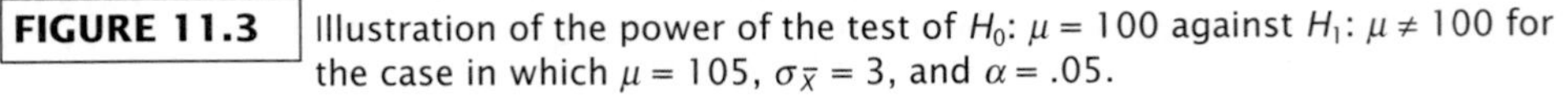
**FIGURE 11.3** Illustration of the power of the test of $H_0$: $\mu = 100$ against $H_1$: $\mu \neq 100$ for the case in which $\mu = 105$, $\sigma_{\bar{X}} = 3$, and $\alpha = .05$.

The area under the curve on the right in Figure 11.3 (with $\mu = 105$) that falls above the critical value of 105.88 can be found from Table A: $z = (105.88 - 105)/3.00 = .29$; thus the power of the test of $H_0$: $\mu = 100$ is only .39. Of course, it then follows that $\beta = .61$.

It is almost never the case in behavioral research that the power of a hypothesis test for just one alternative value of the parameter is sufficient for designing research. Generally, we want to find the power of the test for a few different values of the parameter. Often the power is determined for (1) the largest value of the parameter that is reasonable, (2) the smallest value of the parameter that would be of practical interest, and (3) an intermediate value that represents the most reasonable expectation or "best guess." If additional values for the parameter are taken, a power curve like Figure 11.4 can be constructed.

The values of the power are plotted against the various values of the parameter ($\mu$ in this case) and then the points are connected by a smooth line. The resulting power curve, the power of the test against all alternative values of the parameter, is determined. The power curve for the test of $H_0$: $\mu = 100$ against $H_1$: $\mu \neq 100$ for $\sigma_{\bar{X}} = 3.00$ and $\alpha = .05$ appears as Figure 11.4.

Note in Figure 11.4 that the values of the power for $\mu = 110$ and $\mu = 105$ are .91 and .39, respectively, just as they were calculated to be in Figures 11.2 and 11.3. Notice also that when $\mu = 100$ (that is, if $H_0$ is true) there is a probability equal to $\alpha = .05$ of making a type-I error—of rejecting $H_0$ when it is true.

It is apparent in Figure 11.4 that the power of the test increases and approaches 1.00 as

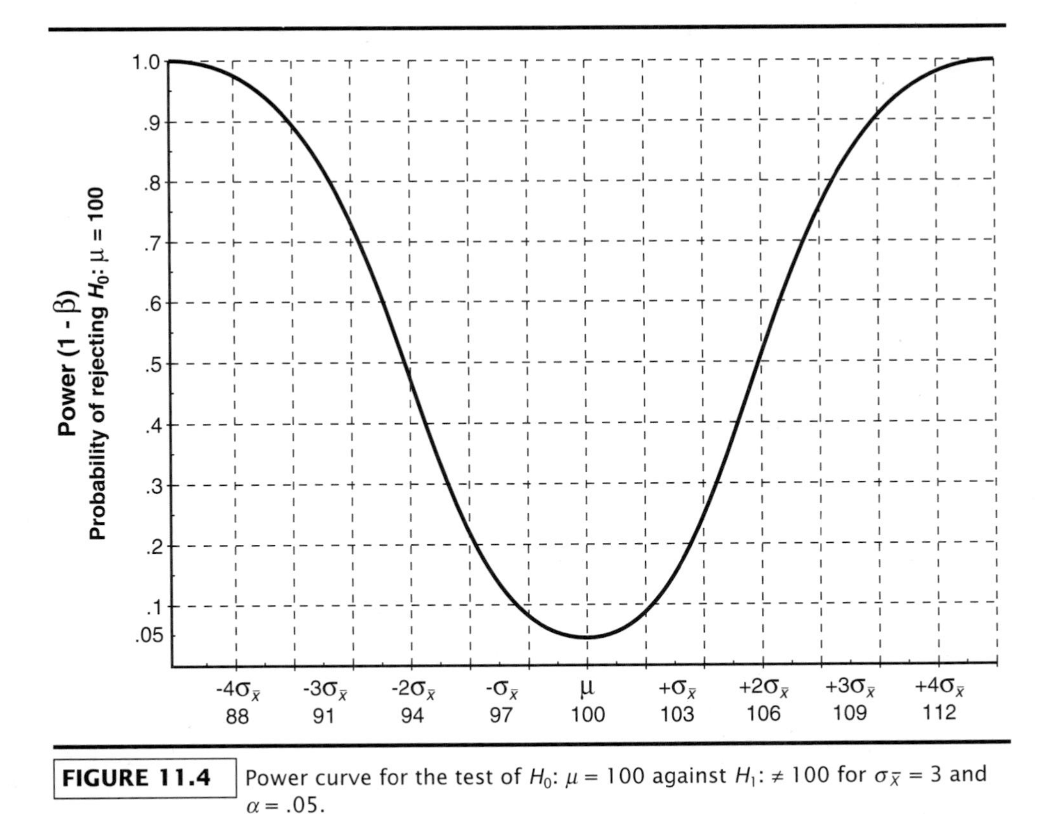


**FIGURE 11.4** Power curve for the test of $H_0$: $\mu = 100$ against $H_1$: $\neq 100$ for $\sigma_{\bar{X}} = 3$ and $\alpha = .05$.

the difference between the true value of $\mu$ and the hypothesized value of $\mu$ (100 in this case) increases. This is comforting to know, but it is a contingency not under the control of researchers as they do not "set" the true value of $\mu$, indeed it is what they are trying to find out. However, the sample size $n$ and the level of significance $\alpha$ are under the researchers' control. For any value of $\mu$ (other than the hypothesized value of 100), the power of the test of $H_1$: $\mu \neq 100$ increases as $n$ is increased.

Observe that if $n$ is increased from 25 to 100, $\sigma_{\overline{X}} = \sigma/\sqrt{n}$ is reduced from 3.00 to $15/\sqrt{100} = 1.50$ (Equation 10.1); $H_0$: $\mu = 100$ will be rejected if $\overline{X} \geq (1.96)(1.50) + 100 = 102.94$. When $\mu = 105$, 91% of the actual (right-hand) sampling distribution falls above 102.94 (i.e., $z = (102.94 - 105)/1.5 = -1.37$); hence, the power is .91. The correspondence of this result with that from $\mu = 110$ and $n = 25$ is not accidental: When $n$ is quadrupled ($n_2 = 4n_1$), the power remains constant for a difference that is half that which was associated with $n_1$.

Ordinarily, one is well advised to take the largest sample that is practical and then determine if this sample size has adequate power for detecting a difference large enough to be of interest. If a sample is so large that the power of the test of $H_0$ is extremely high (e.g., .99) even if the true value of the parameter is only slightly different from the value specified in $H_0$, then it is unnecessary to use such a large sample. It may well be true that the power would drop to only .97 if a sample only half as large is taken. If so, the size of the sample can be reduced with trivial loss in power. Nevertheless, the confidence intervals will be even smaller with the very large sample.

Researchers often strive for power $\geq .90$ with $\alpha = .05$. More often, however, one finds that power is low even for detecting differences large enough to be of practical importance. For example, using a "two-tailed" (Section 11.13) test, the power for detecting a five-point difference in the mean IQ in Figure 11.3 was only .39 with $n = 25$ and $\alpha = .05$. The power increases to .91 if $n = 100$.

## 11.12 METHODS OF INCREASING POWER

The following can be said about hypothesis-testing procedures:

1. For a given value of the parameter being tested, the power of the test of $H_0$ increases as the sample size, $n$, increases.
2. For a given value of the parameter being tested, the power of the test of $H_0$ increases as $\alpha$ (the probability of rejecting a true null hypothesis) is increased, for example, from .05 to .10.
3. Other things being equal, the power of the test of $H_0$ increases as the true value of the parameter being tested deviates further from the value hypothesized for it in $H_0$. For example, in the situation depicted in Figure 11.4, the power when testing $H_0$: $\mu = 100$ is much greater when $\mu$ equals 110 or 90 than when $\mu$ equals 105 or 95.

The first two relationships are quite important since $\alpha$ and $n$ can be controlled to some extent by the investigator. It is advisable in some circumstances to run a risk of a type-I error as large as .10, that is, $\alpha = .10$, to insure a reasonable power for a test. The third factor mentioned above is rarely under the control of the investigator.[7]

---

[7]Power is also effected by the reliability of the criterion measure (Hopkins & Hopkins, 1979; Rogers & Hopkins, 1988a, 1988b).

The popular notion among novice researchers is that the statistician is the person who tells them "how large a sample to take." Presumably, the statistician derives this decision about sample size from studying cost per observation, costs of committing type-I and type-II errors, and the power of the test for different sample sizes and particular alternative values of the parameter about which a hypothesis is to be tested. The theory is very accommodating in areas such as business when these costs and specific alternative values of the parameter can be specified (Cleary & Linn, 1969; Kraemer & Thiemann, 1987; Lipsey, 1990). However, in research in education and the social sciences, it is rare that the various kinds of costs can be specified with any confidence.

## 11.13 NONDIRECTIONAL AND DIRECTIONAL ALTERNATIVES: TWO-TAILED VERSUS ONE-TAILED TESTS

An alternative hypothesis, $H_1$, can be designated as either nondirectional ("two-tailed") or directional ("one-tailed"). The alternative $H_1$: $\mu \neq 0$ is nondirectional in that it states only that $\mu$ is not equal to 0 and does not specify in which direction, above or below, $\mu$ deviates from 0. Consider the pair of hypotheses $H_0$: $\mu = 100$ and $H_1$: $\mu > 100$. In this instance, the alternative hypothesis is directional; it is presumed that either $\mu$ equals 100 or it is greater than 100. The investigator believes that $\mu$ could not possibly be less than 100. Evidence will be gathered that will either support the hypothesis that $\mu$ is above 100 or that will allow $H_0$: $\mu = 100$ to remain tenable.

One consequence of stating the directional alternative $H_1$: $\mu > 100$ is that now all the critical region for rejection of $H_0$ in favor of $H_1$ is in one tail of the sampling distribution of $\bar{X}$. In other words, only $\bar{X}$-values above 100 will lead one to decide in favor of $H_1$ over $H_0$; hence, all of the critical region for rejection of $H_0$ is in the right-hand tail of the sampling distribution of $\bar{X}$, as shown in Figure 11.5. A value of $\bar{X}$ below 100 certainly does not favor the hypothesis that $\mu > 100$ over the hypothesis that $\mu = 100$. Since only the two conditions $\mu = 100$ or $\mu > 100$ are covered by the hypotheses, an $\bar{X}$ of less than 100 would imply the tenability of $H_0$, no matter how small $\bar{X}$ is.

If $\alpha_1 = .05$, it is found from Table A that 5% of the area in a normal distribution exceeds the $z$-ratio of 1.645. One-tailed tests shall be distinguished from two-tailed by the subscripts of $\alpha$: $\alpha_1$ and $\alpha_2$; if no subscript is given, a nondirectional hypothesis is implied. If $\alpha_1 = .05$, the critical region, as shown in Figure 11.5, includes all points above $\mu + 1.645\sigma_{\bar{X}}$; if $\sigma_{\bar{X}} = 3$, all values of $\bar{X}$ above $100 + (1.645)(3) = 104.94$ will allow $H_0$ to be rejected with $\alpha_1 = .05$.

It should be apparent from comparing Figures 11.5 and 11.3 that the directional hypothesis will have greater power for rejecting $H_0$ when $\mu > 100$. Note in Figure 11.3 that the power with $\alpha_2 = .05$ was approximately .39, whereas the power at $H_1$: $\mu > 100$ and $\alpha_1 = .05$ is considerably higher—approximately .51.

The fact that the critical region lies in one tail of the sampling distribution of the statistic, as illustrated in Figure 11.5, has made popular the phrase "one-tailed test" for a signifi-

[8]Whether a test statistic has grown out of the history of statistics in such a manner that one or two tails of a sampling distribution lie beyond the critical values of a statistic is quite arbitrary. We shall see in Chapter 16, for example, that a nondirectional hypothesis about a set of population means is tested by referring a test statistic to one tail of the F-distribution.

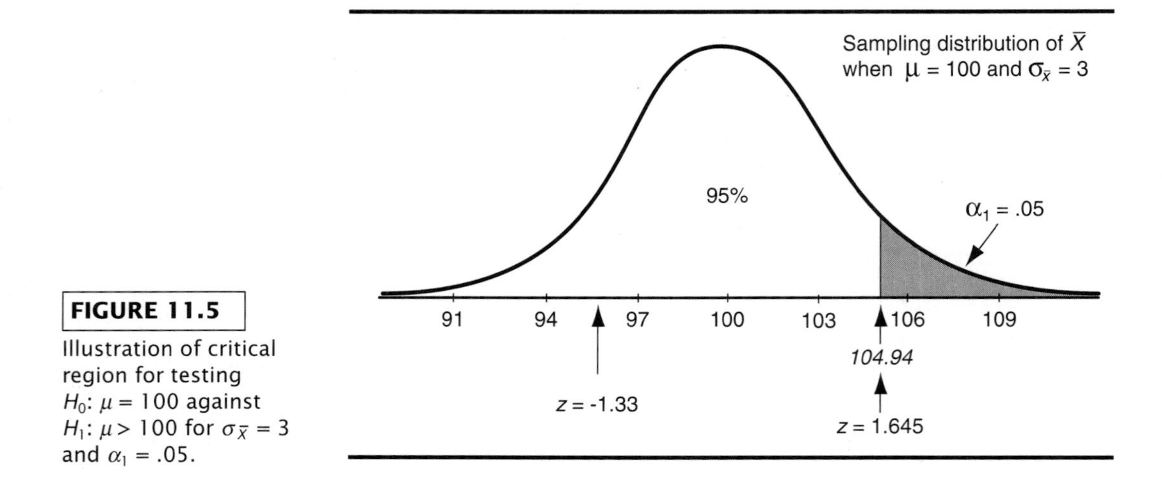


**FIGURE 11.5**

Illustration of critical region for testing $H_0$: $\mu$ = 100 against $H_1$: $\mu$ > 100 for $\sigma_{\overline{X}}$ = 3 and $\alpha_1$ = .05.

cance test of a directional hypothesis. This usage is sometimes ambiguous, however. The important distinction is between nondirectional and directional alternative hypotheses.[8]

Directional tests can be used where they do not fit the situation. There are always persons who do not play by the rules, and others who fail to understand where one-tailed tests are, and are not, safe. For example, one who hypothesizes that $\mu$ = 100 against $\mu$ > 100 must look the other way and conclude that $H_0$ is tenable even if $\overline{X}$ is 80. The rules do not allow you to change to a two-tailed test just because you were unwise to use a one-tailed test in the first place.

It is imperative that the researcher specify the directional alternative hypothesis before conducting the study. One must commit oneself to a directional test prior to collecting any data or obtaining any empirical clue as to how the results are turning out. If a researcher claims to have made a directional test with $\alpha_1$ = .05 after seeing the data—that is, if he or she hypothesizes $\mu$ > 100 because he senses that $\overline{X}$ is going to be larger than 100—he or she is deluding himself or herself, and probably others. The actual probability of a type-I error in this instance is $\sigma_2$ = .10, not $\alpha_1$ = .05. If one has not definitely opted for a directional hypothesis before inspecting the data, the temptation to make a one-tailed test later on must be resisted—it is a statistical sin to not play fair when estimating the probability of a type-I error. Otherwise, the stated probability of a type-I error is spurious. The following are some illustrations in which a directional hypothesis might be justified:

1. Does early cognitive enrichment increase IQ scores?
2. Do ten-year-olds make greater progress in learning to play the piano than eight-year-olds?
3. Does stature increase between ages eighteen and twenty?
4. Are students who have not had a statistics course able to obtain scores higher than a chance score on a statistics examination?
5. Is life expectancy less for smokers than for nonsmokers?
6. Do children receiving balanced diets have better school attendance than children whose diets are nutritionally inadequate?

---

[8]Whether a test statistic has grown out of the history of statistics in such a manner that one or two tails of a sampling distribution lie beyond the critical values of a statistic is quite arbitrary. We shall see in Chapter 16, for example, that a nondirectional hypothesis about a set of population means is tested by referring a test statistic to one tail of the *F*-distribution.

## 11.14 STATISTICAL SIGNIFICANCE VERSUS PRACTICAL SIGNIFICANCE

When $n$ is very large, even a trivial difference may be large enough to be highly statistically significant. For example, if $n = 2{,}000$ and $\overline{X} = 101$, one would reject $H_0$: $\mu = 100$ at the .01 level of statistical significance. Obviously, a one-point IQ difference has little or no practical significance even though it may be highly significant in a statistical sense.[9] "Statistically significant" simply means that the difference was greater than would be expected by chance (sampling error); it does not mean that the difference is large or important. It is unfortunate that the term "significant" was ever chosen to denote the untenability of $H_0$. Perhaps the term "reliable" would have been a better term for describing sample results and would less often be confused with practical significance or importance.

Significance testing has been relied upon excessively. Often where significance statements have been made, it would have been better to provide a confidence interval within which the value of the parameter would be expected to lie (Box et al., 1978, p. 109).

The use of confidence intervals can reduce the likelihood that the failure to reject $H_0$ will be misinterpreted as proving $H_0$ to be true since the confidence interval forces one to acknowledge reasonable boundaries for the parameter. As previously stated, rejecting $H_0$ at a given value for $\alpha$ only indicates that the symmetrical $1 - \alpha$ confidence interval does *not* include the value for the parameter that was specified by $H_0$. For example, in the illustration in which $\overline{X} = 101$, $\sigma = 15$, and $n = 2{,}000$, the .99 confidence interval for $\mu$ extends from 100.13 to 101.87. Thus the *CI* reduces the opportunity of confusing a highly statistically significant IQ difference with a *practically* significant IQ difference.

## 11.15 CONFIDENCE LIMITS FOR THE POPULATION MEDIAN

A confidence interval for the population median can be determined from a random sample of $n$ observations of a continuous (i.e., ordinal, interval, or ratio) variable from any normal or non-normal population. If in a rank-order distribution of $n$ observations the subscripts denote the low-to-high ordinal rank (thus $X_1$ and $X_n$ represent the lowest and highest scores, respectively), the $(1 - \alpha)CI$ for the population median falls between $X_L$ and $X_U$, where $U$ is determined from Equation 11.3 (Snedecor & Cochran, 1980):

$$U \geq \frac{(n+1)}{2} + \frac{{}_{1-\alpha/2}z\sqrt{n}}{2} \quad {}_{1-\alpha/2}z\sqrt{n} \qquad \textbf{(11.3)}$$

and

[9] Unhappily, Kruskal and Majors (1989) found that one-fifth of a sample of research papers used statistical significance to measure the relative importance of variables. For an entertaining illustration of the inordinate influence of statistical significance in medical research, see Salsburg (1985).

$$L = n - U + 1 \tag{11.4}$$

Thus for .95 *CI*, ${}_{.975}z = 1.96$; hence:

$$U \geq \frac{(n+1)}{2} + \frac{(1.96\sqrt{n})}{2} \tag{11.3A}$$

$$U \geq \frac{(n+1)}{2} + .98\sqrt{n}$$

For example, if $n = 25$, $U \geq (25+1)/2 + .98\sqrt{25} = 13 + 4.9$; hence, $U = 13 + 5 = 18$ (fractional values must be rounded upward), and $L = 25 - 18 + 1 = 8$. Therefore, the lower limit for the .95*CI* about the population median is $X_8$ and the upper limit is $X_{18}$. Confirm in Table 3.1 that the .95*CI* for the population median extends from 269 ($X_{86}$) to 286 ($X_{115}$), since $n = 200$.

## 11.16 INFERENCES REGARDING $\mu$ WHEN $\sigma$ IS NOT KNOWN: *t* VERSUS *z*

For pedagogical purposes,[10] the concepts and procedures of hypothesis testing have been illustrated with the *z*-test (Equation 11.1)—the ratio of (1) the difference between the a statistic and the hypothesized value of its parameter to (2) its standard error parameter, or in this instance:

$$z = \frac{\overline{X} - \mu}{\sigma_{\overline{X}}}$$

$$\text{where, } \sigma_{\overline{X}} = \frac{\sigma}{\sqrt{n}}.$$

The examples used are not typical of actual research; rarely is the value of the parameter $\sigma$ known. If the parameter $\sigma$ is unknown, the value of $\sigma_{\overline{X}}$ cannot be determined, but it can be estimated. The statistic $s$ is used to estimate $\sigma$, but estimates always introduce some sampling error (i.e., $s - \sigma$) into the system. When $\sigma$ is not known, the standard error of the mean is estimated by Equation 11.5:

$$s_{\overline{X}} = \frac{s}{\sqrt{n}} \tag{11.5}$$

When the parameter $\sigma_{\overline{X}}$ is not known and the estimate $s_{\overline{X}}$ is used, the ratio in Equation 11.6 is termed a *t*-ratio (not a *z*-ratio, see Equation 11.1):

[10]Otherwise, we would have to face the distracting complexity of non-normal sampling distributions before the concept of sampling distributions was understood.

$$t = \frac{\overline{X} - \mu}{s_{\overline{X}}} \qquad (11.6)$$

When $n$ is large, $s$ and $s_{\overline{X}}$ become very accurate estimates of $\sigma$ and $\sigma_{\overline{X}}$, respectively. Hence, $t$ and $z$ differ negligibly for large $n$; but when $n$ is small, $t$ and $z$ may differ considerably. The use of $s_{\overline{X}}$ rather than $\sigma_{\overline{X}}$ results in sampling distributions that, although symmetrical, are not perfectly normal. These distributions are known as *Student's*[11] t*-distributions.*

Unlike the normal distribution, there is not just one $t$-distribution; there exists a *family* of $t$-distributions. There is a different $t$-distribution for every value of $\nu$, where $\nu$ is the number of degrees of freedom[12] associated with the estimate of the parameter in the denominator of the $t$-test. In Equation 11.6, $\nu = n - 1$ (see Equation 5.5). *When* $H_0$ *is true, the* t*-distribution is known as the central* t*-distribution.*

## 11.17 THE t-DISTRIBUTION

All the central $t$-distributions are described by symmetric ($\gamma_1 = 0$), unimodal curves with a mean of 0. Whereas the variance of the $z$-distribution is 1, the variance of the *t-distribution* with $\nu$ degrees of freedom is greater than 1; the variance of the $t$-distribution is $\nu/(\nu - 2)$. When $\nu$ is small, $t$-distributions are leptokurtic (see Section 6.10). Leptokurtic distributions have thicker tails than the normal distribution; Thus, for $\alpha_2 = .05$, the corresponding critical $t$-value is larger than 1.96 because the area of the $t$-distribution beyond $|t| = 1.96$ is greater than .05. As the degrees of freedom increase, the $t$-distribution becomes approximately normal (see Figure 11.6). For example, when $\nu = 5$, the kurtosis[13] (Section 6.10) $\gamma_2 = 6$, but when $\nu = 25$, $\gamma_2 = .3$.

When $\nu$ is infinitely large, the $t$-distribution is the same as the normal distribution. The $t$-distributions with degrees of freedom 1, 5, and 25 appear along with the normal distribution in Figure 11.6. Try to visualize the $t$-distribution with $\nu = 100$ in Figure 11.6; it would be visually indistinguishable from the normal distribution.

Figure 11.7 graphically depicts the relationship between the critical $t$-ratios and degrees of freedom for common values of $\alpha$. Notice that the critical $t$-values rather quickly approach the corresponding critical values for $z$ (i.e., when $\nu = \infty$) as $\nu$ increases. Figures 11.6 and 11.7 illustrate that as $\nu$ increases, the value of $t$ associated with the $p$th percentile, ${}_pt$, approaches the $z$-value associated with that same percentile, ${}_pz$.[14]

In subsequent discussions of statistical inference, selected percentile points in a $t$-distribution (e.g., critical values of $t$) must be found. The $p$th percentile in the $t$-distribution with $\nu$ degrees of freedom will be denoted by ${}_pt_\nu$. Commonly used percentiles in the $t$-

---

[11]The solution to the problem of hypothesis testing when $\sigma$ is unknown might well be taken as the dawn of modern inferential statistical methods. It was found in 1908 by William S. Gosset who published it under the pseudonym "Student," hence the term "Student's" $t$-distribution.

[12]The expression "degrees of freedom" ($\nu$) will be encountered many times in subsequent chapters. It is a statistical concept that has to do with "what is left over" after allowance is made for the number of mathematical restrictions imposed (number of parameters that must be estimated) on a set of data. Do not expect a flash of insight that will give this complex statistical concept rich intuitive meaning.

[13]The kurtosis of a $t$-distribution is: $\gamma_2 = 6/(\nu - 4)$, where $\nu \neq 4$.

[14]This is expressed mathematically as $\lim_{\nu \to \infty} {}_pt_\nu = {}_pz$.

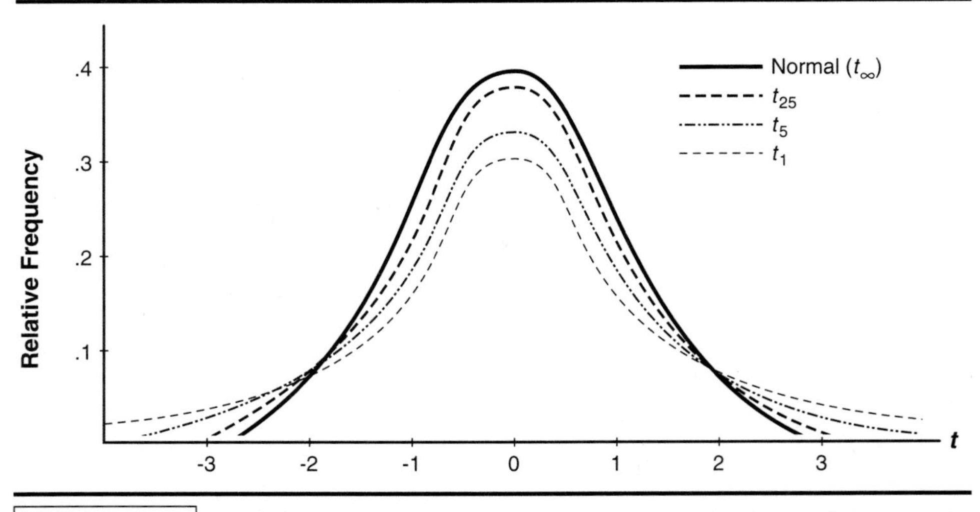


**FIGURE 11.6** The $t$-distributions with 1, 5, and 25 degrees of freedom and the normal distribution.

distributions appear in Table C in the Appendix. Find there, for example, that the 95th percentile in the $t$-distribution with ten degrees of freedom, that is, ${}_{.95}t_{10}$, is equal to 1.812.

Only the upper percentile points in the $t$-distributions appear in Table C. Because $t$-distributions are symmetrical, it is unnecessary to tabulate both upper and lower percentile points. The symmetry of all $t$-distributions establishes that:

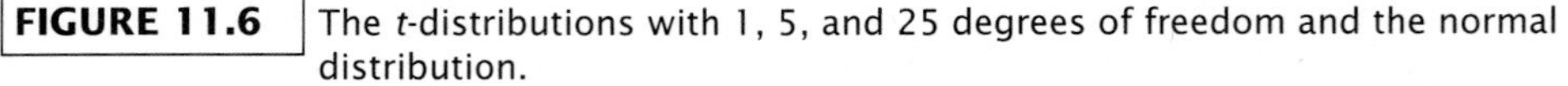

$$-{}_{p}t_{\nu} = {}_{1-p}t_{\nu} \text{ or } \left|{}_{p}t_{\nu}\right| = \left|{}_{1-p}t\right| \tag{11.7}$$

That is, the negative of the $p$th percentile in the $t$-distribution with $\nu$ degrees of freedom equals the $(1 - p)$th percentile in the same distribution. For example, ${}_{.95}t_{10} = 1.81$, therefore ${}_{.05}t_{10} = -1.81$. The critical $t$-values with $\alpha_2 = .10$ and $\nu = 10$ are $\pm 1.81$, that is, $|t| = 1.81$.

## An Illustration

Suppose ten overweight persons went on a particular diet for one month and lost an average of 3.11 lbs., ($\overline{X} = 3.11$, $s = 5.62$). Can the statistical hypothesis that the true mean weight has not changed, $H_0$: $\mu = 0$, be rejected with $\alpha_2 = .10$? Using Equation 11.5, the standard error of the mean is found, $s_{\overline{X}} = s/\sqrt{n} = 5.62/\sqrt{10} = 1.78$.

The statistical (or null) hypothesis can be tested using the $t$-test given in Equation 11.6:

$$t = \frac{\overline{X} - \mu}{s_{\overline{X}}} = \frac{3.11 - 0}{1.78} = 1.75$$

To obtain the critical $t$-value, ${}_{.95}t_9$, enter Table C at $\nu = n - 1 = 9$, and $\alpha_2 = .10$; find the critical value of $t$ to be $1.83 = {}_{.95}t_9$. Thus, an observed $t$-value greater than $|1.83|$ is

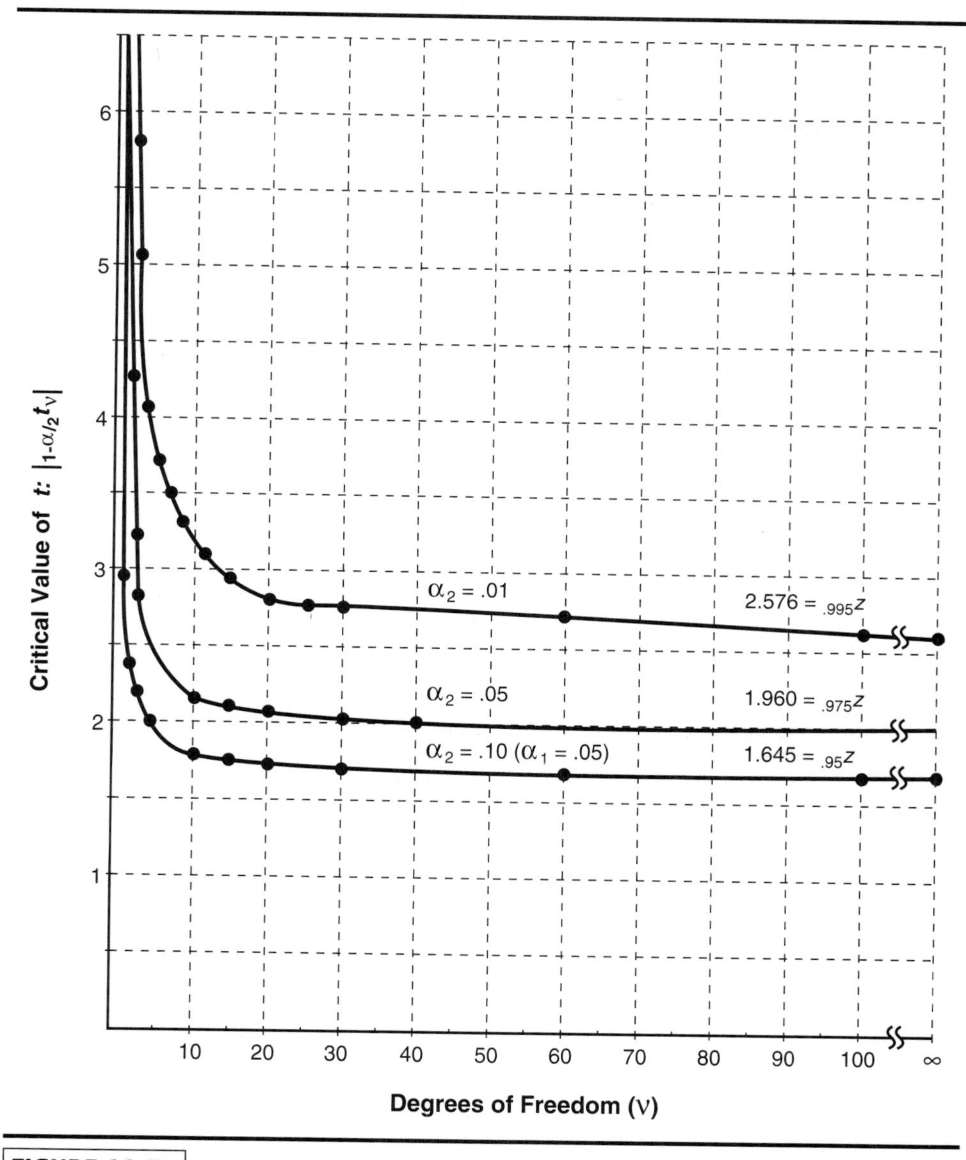


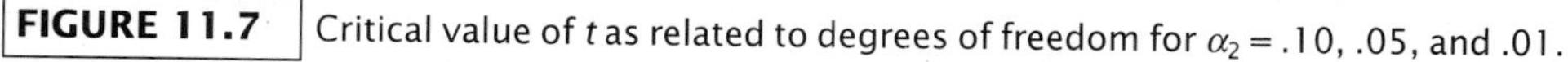

**FIGURE 11.7** Critical value of *t* as related to degrees of freedom for $\alpha_2 = .10$, .05, and .01.

required to reject $H_0$ with $\alpha_2 = .10$. Consequently, from our data, we cannot reject the hypothesis that the mean weight change in the population ($\mu$) is 0 because to do so would be taking a risk greater than .10. By studying Table C, we can see that $.20 > p > .10$; that is, the absolute value of the observed *t*-ratio (1.75) is greater than the critical *t*-value at $\alpha_2 = .20$ ($_{.90}t_9 = 1.38$).

What if "Lady Luck" has played a trick on us: What if $\mu \neq 0$? Suppose that the entire population of overweight persons like those in our illustration went on the diet for one month and we measured the weight loss (pretest – posttest) and found that $\mu > 0$. If this is the case, in our illustration we made a type-II error—we failed to reject $H_0$, yet it was untrue. Indeed, with such a small $n$ (10), type-II errors are very common.

## 11.18 CONFIDENCE INTERVALS USING THE *t*-DISTRIBUTION

Somewhat wider confidence intervals result when $s_{\overline{X}}$ is used than if $\sigma_{\overline{X}}$ were known. For example, regardless of $n$, the .95 confidence interval is $\overline{X} \pm 1.96\sigma_{\overline{X}}$ when $\sigma$ (and hence, $\sigma_{\overline{X}}$) is known. However, when $\sigma$ is unknown and is estimated from the sample as $s_{\overline{X}}$, the .95 confidence interval for $\mu$ is:

$$.95CI = \overline{X} \pm {}_{.975}t_{\nu}\, s_{\overline{X}}, \text{ where } \nu = n - 1 \qquad \textbf{(11.8)}$$

More generally:

$$(1 - \alpha)CI = \overline{X} \pm {}_{1\text{-}\alpha/2}t_{\nu}\, s_{\overline{X}} \qquad \textbf{(11.9)}$$

Table C gives the critical value of $t$—the number of standard errors of the mean, $s_{\overline{X}}$, that must be added to and subtracted from $\overline{X}$ for the .90, .95, and .99 and other $1 - \alpha$ confidence intervals for various values of $\nu$. For example, when $\nu = n - 1 = 9$, the $.90CI$ is $\overline{X} \pm 1.83s_{\overline{X}}$. In this example, $.90CI = 3.11 \pm 1.83(1.78) = 3.11 \pm 3.26$ or (–.15, 6.37). The parameter, $\mu$, the true weight change in the population, may be anywhere from a loss of 6.37 lbs. to a gain of .15 lbs. We make this statement with 90% confidence; 90% confidence means that if we replicated the study many times, only 10% of the .90*CI*'s will fail to encompass the parameter.

Would a one-tailed test be appropriate in this example? Probably not, since it is not unthinkable that the post-weights will be greater than the pre-weights.

In summary, to find the confidence interval for $\mu$ when $\sigma$ is unknown, which is virtually always:

1. Compute $\overline{X}$ and $s_{\overline{X}}$ ($s_{\overline{X}} = s/\sqrt{n}$) using the random sample of $n$ observations from the parent population.
2. Find the critical value of $t$ required with $\nu = n - 1$ using the desired confidence coefficient (${}_{1-\alpha/2}t_{\nu}$) in Appendix Table C.
3. Use these values in Equation 11.9: $\overline{X} \pm {}_{1-\alpha/2}t_{\nu}s_{\overline{X}}$.

## 11.19 ACCURACY OF CONFIDENCE INTERVALS WHEN SAMPLING NON-NORMAL DISTRIBUTIONS

The data in Figure 10.3 (Section 10.15) demonstrate empirically the validity of the probabilities associated with confidence intervals. Table 11.3 gives the observed percentage of 10,000 sample means that actually included $\mu$ in their .68 confidence intervals (using Equa-

**TABLE 11.3** Proportion of .68 Confidence Intervals That Included the Value of $\mu$ in 10,000 Random Samples from Normal, Rectangular, and Skewed Parent Populations

| *Sample Size* | *Parent Population* | *Proportion of .68 Confidence Intervals that Captured* $\mu$ |
|---|---|---|
| $n = 1$ | Normal | .682 |
| | Rectangular | .574 |
| | Skewed | .752 |
| $n = 2$ | Normal | .682 |
| | Rectangular | .667 |
| | Skewed | .714 |
| $n = 5$ | Normal | .686 |
| | Rectangular | .679 |
| | Skewed | .695 |
| $n = 10$ | Normal | .674 |
| | Rectangular | .681 |
| | Skewed | .689 |
| $n = 25$ | Normal | .682 |
| | Rectangular | .678 |
| | Skewed | .704 |
| $n = 100$ | Normal | .679 |
| | Rectangular | .687 |
| | Skewed | .690 |

tion 11.9) when the samples were randomly drawn from three different kinds of parent populations: normal, rectangular, and skewed. It is evident from Table 11.3 that the *confidence intervals are quite accurate even for non-normal distributions* with samples as small as $n = 5$.

## 11.20 CHAPTER SUMMARY

Hypothesis testing is the most widely employed technique of statistical inference in educational and behavioral research. This chapter illustrated the hypothesis testing procedure using statistical hypotheses of the type $H_0$: $\mu = K$ (i.e., testing whether $\mu$ is equal to some specified number). In hypothesis testing, one finds the probability ($p$) of observing a difference as large or larger than ($\bar{X} - \mu$) if $H_0$ is true. If $p$ is smaller than the pre-specified risk of a type-I error, $\alpha$ (usually .05), $H_0$ is rejected (and $H_1$: $\mu \neq K$ is accepted) at the $\alpha$-level of statistical significance. If one rejects $H_0$ at $\alpha = .05$, in the long run type-I errors (rejecting $H_0$ when it is true) will be made in about one such decision in twenty (5%). If $H_0$ is rejected at the .01 level, a type-I error will be made in less than one such decision in 100. If $H_0$ is not rejected, a type-I error cannot be made, but a type-II error is a possibility. A type-II error is the failure to reject $H_0$ when it is untrue.

The smaller the risk of a type-I error (rejecting a true $H_0$), $\alpha$, the greater the risk of a type-II error (failing to reject a false $H_0$), $\beta$. Conversely, one has greater power (i.e., less likelihood of making a type-II error) when $\alpha = .10$ than when $\alpha = .05$ or $\alpha = .01$. The probability of *not* making a type-II error is termed power, and equals $1 - \beta$. Statistical power can be increased by using a large sample size, $n$, "relaxing" $\alpha$ (e.g., from .05 to .10), or making a directional alternative hypothesis when it can be justified.

When $\sigma$ is known (and hence $\sigma_{\bar{X}}$ can be determined), the $z$-ratio, $z = (\bar{X} - K)/\sigma_{\bar{X}}$, is the proper test statistic to test $H_0$: $\mu = K$. The critical values of $z$ are fixed and do not vary with $n$. If $\sigma$ is unknown, the $t$-ratio $t = (\bar{X} - K)/s_{\bar{X}}$, is employed. Sampling error appears in both the numerator and denominator of the $t$-test.

Whereas there is only one normal distribution, there are an infinite number of central $t$-distributions, one for each degree of freedom associated with the $s_{\bar{X}}$ estimate. With few degrees of freedom, the $t$-distribution is highly leptokurtic (large tail area and very peaked near the center), but quickly approaches a normal distribution as the number of degrees of freedom ($\nu$) increase. In the limit ($\nu = \infty$), the $t$-distribution becomes a normal distribution. The critical values of $t$ depend on the number of degrees of freedom ($\nu$) associated with the denominator of the $t$-ratio (e.g., $\nu = n - 1$ in this chapter). The critical values of $t$ approach the critical values for $z$ as $n$ increases.

Hypothesis testing and interval estimation are two photographs of the same hypothesis shot from two different vantage points. To say that $H_0$ is rejected at $\alpha_2 = .05$ is equivalent to saying that the .95 confidence interval around $\bar{X}$ does not contain the hypothesized value of $\mu$. If .99*CI* is (60, 66), any statistical hypothesis for $\mu$ having a value less than 60 or greater than 66 would be rejected at the .01 level of significance. Statistical significance (even at the .001 level) does not necessarily imply a large difference or practical significance. However, without establishing that one has statistical significance, one has not established significance of any type.

## 11.21 CASE STUDY

Table 5.2 gives means and standard deviations for the variables used in the case study. Use this information to set the .95*CI* for the cholesterol variable. (Why will you use Equation 11.8 and *not* Equation 10.4: $\bar{X} \pm 1.96\sigma_{\bar{X}}$?)[15] Compare the .95*CI* with the .99*CI*. (How large a sample would be needed to reduce the width of the *CI*'s by half?)[16]

Compare .95*CI*'s for SBP and DBP. (Why is the interval for SBP so much larger?)[17] Recall from Table 6.1 that SBP is skewed positively ($\gamma_1 = 1.51$); will this seriously influence the accuracy of its .95*CI*?[18]

Suppose the 74 persons with Cholesterol Levels of 300 or more were put on a special cholesterol-free diet for three months, then retested, and the difference ($X_{pre} - X_{post}$) calculated for each of the 74 persons. The mean change in Cholesterol Level was 10.0, and the standard deviation of the distribution of change scores was 40. State $H_0$, set $\alpha_2 = .05$, and test $H_0$; can $H_0$ be rejected at the .01 level? Will the .95*CI* include the value of 0? If we had planned it before we saw the data, could a one-tailed test have been justified?[19]

---

[15]Because $\sigma$ is not known.

[16] $s_{\bar{X}} = s/\sqrt{n} = 65/\sqrt{200} = 4.60$; ${}_{.975}t_{199} \approx 1.972$; $.95CI = 285.1 \pm 1.972(4.60) = 285.1 \pm 9.07 = (276.0,\ 294.2)$; ${}_{.995}t_{199} \approx 2.601$. The .99*CI* is 2.601/1.972 = 1.32 times wider: (273.1, 297.1). If the sample size were quadruped, the *CI*'s would be only about 50% as wide (see Equation 11.5).

[17]For SBP: $.95CI = 121.6 \pm 2.33$; for DBP: $.95CI = 81.6 \pm 1.39$; because $s$ is so much larger for SBP than for DBP.

[18]No, see Table 11.3.

[19] $H_0$: $\mu = 0$; $s_{\bar{X}} = 40/\sqrt{74} = 4.65$; $t = 10.0/4.65 = 2.15$; reject $H_0$ at the .05 level since $p < .05 = \alpha$; No, 2.15 < 2.48, therefore $.01 < p < .05$. No, the .95*CI* for $\mu$ is 10.0 ± 1.994(4.65) or (.73, 19.27). Probably, since it is unreasonable to expect that a cholesterol-free diet would cause an increase in cholesterol level.

## MASTERY TEST

1. $z$ is to $\sigma_{\overline{X}}$ as $t$ is to ____.
   (a) $\sigma$ (b) $\sigma^2$ (c) $s$ (d) $s_{\overline{X}}$
2. Which of these can be properly regarded as statistical hypotheses?
   (a) $\overline{X} = 63.0$ (c) $\sigma = 10$ (e) $s = 10.00$
   (b) $\mu = 1.2$ (d) $\rho = .50$ (f) $r = 0$
3. Do statistical hypotheses pertain to parameters or statistics?
4. When are $\sigma_{\overline{X}}$ and $\sigma$ equal?
5. How large must $n$ be for the standard deviation of the sampling distribution of the mean $\sigma_{\overline{X}}$ to be only 10% as large as the standard deviation of the frequency distribution $\sigma$?
6. If $z = 2.0$, we can reject $H_0$
   (a) at the .01 level of significance
   (b) at the .05 level of significance, but not at the .01 level
   (c) at neither the .01 nor the .05 levels
7. Which one of the following is least likely to have occurred by chance, that is, the result of sampling error?
   (a) $z = -3.1$ (b) $z = .00$ (c) $z = 2.0$ (d) $z = 2.58$
8. When $H_0$ is true, is the probability of observing a $z$-value greater than 1.31 the same as the probability of observing a $z$-value less than $-1.31$?
9. What is the symbol that denotes the risk of a type-I error that one is willing to tolerate?
10. Assuming $H_0$ is true, the probability of observing a sample mean which deviates as far from $\mu$ as the $\overline{X}$ obtained is denoted by the letter ____.
11. If $p < \alpha$, would $H_0$ be rejected?
12. If $p > \alpha$, does $H_0$ continue to be tenable?
13. If a particular .95 confidence interval for $\mu$ extends from 47.2 to 63.4, which two of the following statistical hypotheses would be rejected at the .05 level of significance?
    (a) $\mu = 45$ (b) $\mu = 50$ (c) $\mu = 55$ (d) $\mu = 60$ (e) $\mu = 65$
14. Assume $H_0$: $\mu = 100$ was rejected with $\alpha = .01$.
    (a) Would the value of 100 fall within the .99 confidence interval?
    (b) Would the value of 100 fall within the .95 confidence interval?
15. To reject $H_0$, which one of the following significance levels requires the largest difference between $\overline{X}$ and the hypothesized value of $\mu$?
    (a) the .01 level (b) the .05 level (c) the .10 level
16. The $t$-statistic is used to test $H_0$: $\mu = K$ when ____ is not known.
    (a) $n$ (b) $\overline{X}$ (c) $\sigma$ (d) $\alpha$
17. When $n = 20$, are the critical values slightly larger for $t$ than for $z$?
18. In which one of the following cases do the critical values of $z$ and $t$ differ most?
    (a) $n = 5$ (b) $n = 10$ (c) $n = 100$ (d) $n = \infty$
19. In testing $H_0$: $\mu = K$, where $K$ is some numerical constant, which is more commonly employed as a test statistic, $z$ or $t$? Why?
20. Is the $t$-distribution a true, normal distribution?
21. For the following values of $n$, what are the associated degrees of freedom in testing $H_0$: $\mu = K$?
    (a) 11 (b) 60 (c) 101

**22.** If $H_0$ is true but has been rejected, what type of error has been made?

(a) type-I error (b) type-II error (c) no error

**23.** If $H_0$ is true and has not been rejected, has a type-II error been made?

**24.** When $H_0$ is true, what is the probability $H_0$ will be rejected at the .05 level, that is, the probability of a type-I error?

**25.** If $\alpha = .05$ and $H_0$ is not rejected, do we know the probability of a type-II error?

**26.** If $\alpha = .05$, yet $p < .01$, can $H_0$ be rejected at the .01 level of significance?

**27.** At the same $\alpha$-level, the absolute value of the critical $t$-ratio is greater for tests of

(a) nondirectional hypotheses (b) directional hypotheses

**28.** If the critical $t$-values are 2.1 and –2.1, and the .05 level is selected,

(a) a one-tailed test is being employed (b) a two-tailed test is being employed

**29.** If $\alpha = .05$ and $\nu = 20$, what are the critical $t$-values for making the following?

(a) a two-tailed $t$-test (b) a one-tailed $t$-test

**30.** In Question 29, what is the probability of a type-I error for the following?

(a) a nondirectional hypothesis (b) a directional hypothesis

**31.** If a directional hypothesis is appropriate and $\alpha = .05$, which will have greater power?

(a) a one-tailed test (b) a two-tailed test

**32.** If $H_0$ is false and we fail to reject it, we have made

(a) a type-I error
(b) a type-II error
(c) a type-I error and a type-II error
(d) no error

**33.** ____ is to $\alpha$ as type-II error is to ____.

*Use the following information to answer questions 34 through 37: if $H_0$: $\mu = 100$, $\alpha_2 = .05$, $\sigma = 15$, and $n = 25$, but $\mu$ is actually 105*

**34.** What is $\beta$? (Use Figure 11.3.)

**35.** What is the probability of rejecting $H_0$?

**36.** Are the answers to questions 34 and 35 consistent with those obtained using Figure 11.4?

**37.** If $n$ is increased from 25 to 100, the value of the standard error of the mean, $\sigma_{\bar{X}}$, will be reduced from 3 to ____.

**38.** Using Table A, determine the critical value for $z$ for $\alpha_2 = .10$. Is it identical with that for $\alpha_1 = .05$?

**39.** If $H_0$ is false and $\alpha$ is increased (relaxed) from .01 to .05, other things remaining constant, power will

(a) decrease (b) remain constant (c) increase

**40.** If the parent population is skewed, the proportion of .68 *CI*'s that captured $\mu$ in Table 11.3 was $\geq .68$

(a) only when $n$ was large
(b) only when $n$ was $\geq 25$
(c) only when $n \leq 25$
(d) when $n \geq 1$

## PROBLEMS AND EXERCISES

**1.** Give definitions of each of the following:

(a) null hypothesis, $H_0$
(b) alternative hypothesis, $H_1$
(c) type-I error
(d) type-II error
(e) level of significance, $\alpha$
(f) power of a test, $1 - \beta$
(g) critical region

**2.** The mean height ($\mu$) of the population of adult males in the United States is 69.5 in. and the standard deviation ($\sigma$) is 3 in. Suppose the mean height $\overline{X}$ of a sample of twenty-five mentally retarded males was found to be 67.5 in. Does $\overline{X}$ differ significantly from the $\mu$ of 69.5 in.? Using this information answer the following questions (Assume $\sigma = 3$ for the mentally retarded male population.):

(a) State $H_0$ numerically.
(b) From the information provided, would you employ $z$ or $t$ as the test statistic?
(c) Is it appropriate to specify $H_1$: $\mu < 69.5$ *after* finding that $\overline{X} = 67.5$?
(d) What is the value of $\sigma_{\overline{X}}$?
(e) What is the value of $z$?
(f) Will $H_0$ be rejected with $\alpha_2 = .01$?
(g) Would the critical values for $z$ remain the same if $n$ were increased to 100?
(h) Would $\sigma_{\overline{X}}$ remain the same if $n$ were increased to 100?

**3.** In each of the following instances, indicate whether a type-I error, type-II error, or no error was committed by the researcher:

| $H_0$ | $H_1$ | *True value of* $\mu$ | *Researcher's decision based on* $\overline{X}$ |
|---|---|---|---|
| a. $\mu = 0$ | $\mu \neq 0$ | 0 | Reject $H_0$ |
| b. $\mu = 0$ | $\mu \neq 0$ | 5 | Reject $H_0$ |
| c. $\mu = 0$ | $\mu \neq 0$ | 0 | Do not reject $H_0$ |
| d. $\mu = 0$ | $\mu \neq 0$ | −3 | Do not reject $H_0$ |

**4.** The hypotheses $H_0$: $\mu = 0$ and $H_1$: $\mu \neq 0$ were tested with a sample of $n = 50$ $\alpha_2 = .05$. The sample $\overline{X}$ was sufficiently large that $H_0$ was rejected. What is the probability that a type-II error was committed? (Hint: Can one commit a type-II error when one rejects $H_0$?)

**5.** A researcher draws a sample of $n = 100$ observations from a normal distribution for which $\sigma = 10$. He reasons correctly that if $\mu = 50$, the sampling distribution of $\overline{X}$ will be normally distributed with a mean of 50 and a standard deviation of 1. Further, he decides to reject $H_0$: $\mu = 50$ if $\overline{X}$ is above 52 or below 48. What is the probability that he will reject the null hypothesis? (Hint: Approximately what proportion of the sampling distribution falls below 48 or above 52? What is the approximate value of $\alpha$? Which symbol is appropriate, $\alpha_1$ or $\alpha_2$?)

**6.** In each of the following instances, indicate whether the critical region for rejection of $H_0$ lies in the upper (right) tail, lower (left) tail, or is divided between both tails of the sampling distribution of $\overline{X}$. If $\alpha = .05$ and, $\mu = 0$, in each instance given the proportion of the critical area that will fall in the upper tail.

(a) $H_0$: $\mu = 0$, $H_1$: $\mu \neq 0$
(b) $H_0$: $\mu = 0$, $H_1$: $\mu > 0$
(c) $H_0$: $\mu = 0$, $H_1$: $\mu < 0$

**7.** Jack is testing $H_0$: $\mu = 10$ at the $\alpha_2 = .05$ level with a sample size of $n = 25$. Jill is testing $H_0$: $\mu = 10$ at the $\alpha_2 = .05$ level with a sample of $n = 100$,

(a) Does Jack or Jill have the larger probability of committing a type-I error, or is this probability the same for both?
(b) If $\mu$ is actually 12, does Jack or Jill have the larger probability, $\beta$, of committing a type-II error? Who will have greater power?
(c) If $\sigma = 10$ and $\mu = 12$, approximately how much power will Jack have? How much power will Jill have? (Try to answer without using Figure 11.4.)

**8.** From Figure 11.4, estimate the power of the test of $H_0$: $\mu = 100$ against $H_1$: $\mu \neq 100$, for $n = 25$, $\sigma_{\bar{X}} = 3$, and $\alpha_2 = .05$ when:

(a) $\mu = 96$ (c) $\mu = 106$ (e) $\mu = 110$ (g) $\mu = 114$
(b) $\mu = 104$ (d) $\mu = 108$ (f) $\mu = 112$ (h) $\mu = 100$

**9.** If $\mu = 0$ and $\sigma_{\bar{X}} = 2$, how large ($\pm$) must $\bar{X}$ be to allow $H_0$ to be rejected? (If $H_1$ is directional, assume $H_1$: $\mu > 0$.)

(a) $\alpha_1 = .10$
(b) $\alpha_2 = .10$
(c) $\alpha_1 = .05$
(d) $\alpha_2 = .05$
(e) $\alpha_1 = .01$
(f) $\alpha_2 = .01$
(g) What is $\alpha_2$ if the critical $z$-value is 3.29?
(h) In order to reduce the values in $\sigma_{\bar{X}}$ by one-half, the sample size $n$ would need to be increased to ____.
(i) If the sample size were increased to $16n$, the value of $\sigma_{\bar{X}}$ would equal ____.

**10.** Suppose a standardized reading test was given to a *sample* of sixteen sixth-grade students enrolled in a special reading enrichment program. In the eighth month of the school year, their mean grade-equivalent score was 8.00. Suppose that the value of $\sigma$ is unknown, but $s$ for the sixteen pupils was 1.80. The investigator is curious about whether he can conclude that the *population* of pupils in the enrichment program have a mean which differs from 6.8, which represents the mean of all pupils in the nation in the eighth month of the sixth grade.

(a) What is $H_0$?
(b) Should $z$ or $t$ be used?
(c) What is the value for the denominator of the $t$-ratio?
(d) Calculate $t$.
(e) What are the critical values for $t$ at $\alpha_2 = .05$ and $\alpha_2 = .01$?
(f) Can $H_0$ be rejected at .05? at .01?
(g) Construct the .95 and .99 *CI* for $\mu$; are the results consistent with those in part f?
(h) Can we be certain that the significantly higher mean is the result of the special enrichment program?

**11.** The sixteen GE scores in question 10 are given: 4.6, 5.2, 5.5, 6.4, 7.2, 8.1, 8.4, 8.5, 8.7, 8.9, 9.2, 9.6, 9.8, 9.9, 10.0, 10.0

(a) Construct the .95 *CI* for the population using median Equations 11.3A and 11.4.
(b) Is $H_0$: population median = 6.8 tenable with $\alpha_2 = .05$?
(c) Construct the .68 *CI* using Equations 11.3 and 11.4.

## ANSWERS TO MASTERY TEST

1. (d)
2. (b), (c), and (d)
3. parameters
4. When $n = 1$, $(\sigma_{\overline{X}} = \sigma / \sqrt{n})$
5. $n = 100$; hence, $\sigma_{\overline{X}} = \sigma / \sqrt{100} = .1\sigma$.
6. (b)
7. (a)
8. yes
9. $\alpha$
10. $p$
11. yes
12. yes
13. (a) and (e)
14. (a) no (b) no
15. (a)
16. (c)
17. yes, with $\alpha_2 = .05$, critical value of 1.96 is required for $z$ ($_{.975}z = 1.96$), but 2.093 for $t$ ($_{.975}t_{19} = 2.093$)
18. (a)
19. $t$, because $\sigma$ is usually not known
20. no, although the $t$-distribution rapidly approximates a normal distribution as $n$ increases.
21. (a) $\nu = 10$
    (b) $\nu = 59$
    (c) $\nu = 100$
22. (a)
23. no: a type-II error results when $H_0$ is false and yet has not been rejected.
24. .05
25. no
26. yes: $\alpha$ represents the maximum risk that we are willing to take.
27. (a)
28. (b)
29. (a) $|_{.975}t_{20}| = 2.09$
    (b) $_{.95}t_{20} = 1.72$
30. .05 in both ($\alpha_1 = .05$, $\alpha_2 = .05$)
31. (a)
32. (b)
33. type-I error, $\beta$
34. .61
35. .39
36. yes
37. 1.5
38. 1.645, yes
39. (c)
40. (d)

## ANSWERS TO PROBLEMS AND EXERCISES

1. (a) The null hypothesis $H_0$ is a hypothesis about a parameter or parameters of a distribution that may or may not be "nullified" (rejected) on the basis of evidence provided by a sample from the distribution.
   (b) The alternative hypothesis $H_1$ is a hypothesis about a parameter of a distribution that specifies values of the parameter other than that specified in $H_0$. If $H_0$ is rejected, $H_1$ is accepted, and vice versa.
   (c) A type-I error is the rejection of $H_0$ when it is true.
   (d) A type-II error is the acceptance of $H_0$ when it is false.
   (e) The level of significance $\alpha$ is the maximal allowable probability of committing a type-I error.
   (f) The power of a test $1 - \beta$ is the probability of rejecting $H_0$ when it is false.
   (g) The critical region is all those values of a sample statistic for which the investigator will reject $H_0$ if his sample yields one such value.
2. (a) $H_0$: $\mu = 69.5$
   (b) $z$ (since $\sigma$ is known)
   (c) no
   (d) $\sigma_{\overline{X}} = \sigma / \sqrt{n} = 3 / \sqrt{25} = .6$
   (e) $z = (\overline{X} - \mu)/\sigma_{\overline{X}} = (67.5 - 69.5)/.6 = -3.33$
   (f) yes: $|z| = 3.33 > 2.576$.
   (g) yes
   (h) no; $\sigma_{\overline{X}}$ would equal $\sigma / \sqrt{n} = 3 / \sqrt{100} = .3$
3. (a) type-I error
   (b) no error

(c) no error
(d) type-II error

4. A type-II error cannot be committed if $H_0$ were rejected since the definition of a type-II error is that it is the failure to reject a false $H_0$.
5. $1 = \sigma_{\overline{X}}$; $2(.0228) = .0456 = p$; $\alpha_2$
6. (a) Critical region is split between both tails, .025.
(b) upper tail, .05
(c) lower tail, 0
7. (a) The probability of a type-I error is the same for both researchers; $\alpha = .05$.
(b) Jack has a larger probability of committing a type-II error when $\mu = 12$; Jill has more power.
(c) Jack: power $\approx .16$;
Jill: power $\approx .50$
8. (a) $\approx .27$
(b) $\approx .27$
(c) $\approx .52$
(d) $\approx .76$
(e) $\approx .91$
(f) $\approx .98$
(g) $\approx .99$
(h) 0. One cannot fail to reject a false $H_0$ (and commit a type-II error) when indeed $H_0$ is true. The probability of rejecting $H_0$ is .05, but since $\mu = 100$, $.05 = \alpha$, which is the probability of making a type-I error.
9. (a) $2(1.282) = 2.564$
(b) $2(1.645) = 3.290$
(c) $2(1.645) = 3.290$
(d) $2(1.96) = 3.92$
(e) $2(2.326) = 4.652$
(f) $2(2.576) = 5.152$
(g) $\alpha_2 = .001$
(h) $4n$
(i) .5
10. (a) $H_0$: $\mu = 6.8$
(b) $t$
(c) $s_{\overline{X}} = s/\sqrt{n} = 1.8/\sqrt{16} = .45$
(d) $t = (\overline{X} - \mu)/s_{\overline{X}} = 8.0 - 6.8/.45 = 2.67$
(e) Since $\nu = \nu - 1 = 15$, critical $t$-values are 2.131 and 2.947 for $\alpha_2 = .05$ and $\alpha_2 = .01$, respectively.
(f) yes at .05, no at .01
(g) yes: .95 $CI = \overline{X} \pm 2.13\, s_{\overline{X}} = 8.0 \pm 2.13(.45) = 8.0 \pm .96$, or (7.04, 8.96); 99 $CI = 8.0 \pm 2.95(.45) = 8.0 \pm 1.33$, or (6.67, 9.33). The value of 6.8 falls within the .99 *CI* but not within the .95 *CI*.
(h) No, perhaps they were bright students who performed excellently in spite of a poor enrichment program. Causal statements like this require the use of control groups.
11. (a) $U = (16+1)/2 + .98\sqrt{16} = 8.5 + 3.92 = 12.42$ or 13 (fractional values are rounded upwards). $X_{13} = 9.8$; $L = 16 - 13 + 1 = 4$, .95 $CI = (X_4, X_{13}) = 6.4$ to 9.8.
(b) yes, since .95 *CI* "captures" 6.8.
(c) $U = 8.5 + 1.00\sqrt{16}/2 = 10.5$ or 11; $L = 16 - 11 + 1 = 6$, .68 $CI = (X_6, X_{11})$ or (8.1, 9.2).

# INFERENCES ABOUT THE DIFFERENCE BETWEEN TWO MEANS

## 12.1 INTRODUCTION

In this chapter, the inferential techniques used in examining the difference between two means will be explained and illustrated. In most cases, the techniques for testing the significance of a statistic and for constructing a confidence interval for the parameter will be given. The discussion of the inferential techniques will take the following form:

1. **Statement of the null hypothesis,** $H_0$, and the alternative hypothesis, $H_1$, the alternative hypothesis will always be "nondirectional" unless stated otherwise;
2. **Statement of the assumptions** made in making the test;
3. **Identification of the test statistic** employed in testing $H_0$;
4. **Definition of the sampling distribution** of the test statistic under both $H_0$ and $H_1$;
5. **Determination of critical values** of the test;
6. **Construction of a confidence interval** around the sample statistic;
7. **An illustration;** and
8. **Special considerations** (if any).

## 12.2 TESTING STATISTICAL HYPOTHESES INVOLVING TWO MEANS

In Chapter 11, hypotheses of the type $H_0$: $\mu = K$ were tested. Methods for deciding whether $\overline{X}$ differed significantly from the numerical value, $K$, that was hypothesized for the parameter $\mu$ were developed. Far more often, however, our interest is in the *difference* between two means: Is there a difference in the means of populations 1 and 2? For example, for each of the following questions, the statistical hypothesis is $H_0$: $\mu_1 = \mu_2$. Is the treatment effective? Do girls read better than boys? Does drug $X$ reduce hyperactivity more than a placebo? Does anxiety level influence test performance? Is there a difference between the number of dollars per student spent for children of middle versus lower socioeconomic status?

## 12.3 THE NULL HYPOTHESIS, $H_0$: $\mu_1 - \mu_2 = 0$

In each of the preceding questions the statistical hypothesis is $H_0$: $\mu_1 = \mu_2$, or equivalently, $H_0$: $\mu_1 - \mu_2 = 0$; that is, the means in populations 1 and 2 are equal—there is no difference in the parameters, $\mu_1$ and $\mu_2$. This type of statistical hypothesis is known as the null hypothesis, the hypothesis that the researcher hopes to *nullify*. The hypotheses $\mu = 0$, $\rho = 0$, and $\mu_1 - \mu_2 = 0$ are all examples of null hypotheses.

When two sample means are compared (e.g., the mean of a treatment group, $\overline{X}_E$, versus the mean of a control group, $\overline{X}_C$), the research interest is in whether the treatment had any effect, that is, whether $\mu_E = \mu_C$ is implausible. If the treatment had no effect, the difference in the two sample means, $\overline{X}_E - \overline{X}_C$, is due to chance (sampling error); hence, $\mu_E$ equals $\mu_C$ and $\mu_E - \mu_C = 0$, as stated in the null hypothesis.

When two means are compared, the value that is hypothesized for the difference between $\mu_1$ and $\mu_2$ is 0;[1] that is, $H_0$: $\mu_1 - \mu_2 = 0$.

## 12.4 THE *t*-TEST FOR COMPARING TWO INDEPENDENT MEANS[2]

If a random sample of persons receives a special treatment and a second independent sample does not, the two resulting means, $\overline{X}_1$ and $\overline{X}_2$, are said to be independent. However, if a sample is pretested, then receives the treatment, and then is posttested, pretest scores ($X_{1_i}$'s) and posttest scores ($X_{2_i}$'s) will be paired or correlated, and thus, not independent. (The *t*-test for paired or correlated observations is treated in Section 12.13.)

**Statistical Hypothesis.** The hypothesis to be tested is that the difference between the two population means ($\mu_1$ and $\mu_2$) is equal to zero; the alternative hypothesis is $\mu_1 \neq \mu_2$; $H_0$: $\mu_1 - \mu_2 = 0$, and $H_1$: $\mu_1 - \mu_2 \neq 0$.

**Assumptions.** It is assumed that $X_1$ is normally distributed in the population with mean $\mu_1$ and variance $\sigma^2$; it is also assumed that $X_2$, is normally distributed in the population with mean $\mu_2$ and variance $\sigma^2$ (i.e., $\sigma_1^2 = \sigma_2^2 = \sigma^2$). The assumption that the variances in the two populations are equal is known as the assumption of homogeneity of variance.[3] Furthermore, it is assumed that a sample of $n_1$ is randomly drawn from population 1 and that an *independent*[4] sample of size $n_2$ is drawn randomly from population 2.[5]

---

[1]Any other value for $\mu_1 - \mu_2$ (e.g., 10) can be the statistical hypothesis; however, this is rarely the research question.

[2]The *t*-test for means is mathematically equivalent to the analysis of variance (Chapter 15) when the number of groups equals 2. The *t*-test is widely used to test many hypotheses, not just those involving means. It is frequently encountered in published research in many disciplines.

[3]If $\sigma_1^2 \neq \sigma_2^2$ *and* $n_1 \neq n_2$, use procedures described in Section 12.10.

[4]The independence assumption would be violated if, for example, sample 1 were girls and sample 2 were their brothers; the two means of brother-sister pairs would correlate on almost any variable.

[5]The major consequence of this assumption of independent samples is that the two sample means, $\overline{X}_1$ and $\overline{X}_2$, will be uncorrelated across repeated random samples from the two populations.

**Test Statistic.** $H_0$: $\mu_1 - \mu_2 = 0$ is tested by employing the test statistic, $t$. A general expression for the $t$-test ($t$-statistic) is:

$$t = \frac{\hat{\psi} - \psi}{s_{\hat{\psi}}} = \frac{\textit{Statistic} - \textit{Parameter}}{s_{\textit{Statistic}}}$$

Since the parameter is a constant, the standard deviation of the difference between the statistic ($\hat{\psi}$) and the parameter ($\psi$) is the same as the standard deviation of the statistic (Section 5.10); thus, the denominator in the expression above is expressed as $s_{\textit{Statistic}}$, and $t$ = (observed difference in $\hat{\psi}$ and $\psi$)/$s_{\hat{\psi}}$.

Note that, unlike the $z$-ratio or $z$-test (Equation 11.1), the denominator with the $t$-ratio (Equation 11.6) is not a parameter, but a statistic. With the $z$-ratio, only the numerator contains sampling error; whereas, sampling error influences both the numerator and denominator in the $t$-ratio.[6] The sampling error (the difference between $\sigma_{\bar{X}_1-\bar{X}_2}$ and $s_{\bar{X}_1-\bar{X}_2}$) in the denominator causes the distribution of $t$-ratios to deviate from perfect normality, even if the original observations (the $X_i$'s) are normally distributed as assumed in the mathematical derivation.

For testing the difference between two independent means, the $t$-test becomes:

$$t = \frac{(\bar{X}_1 - \bar{X}_2) - (\mu_1 - \mu_2)}{s_{\bar{X}_1-\bar{X}_2}} \quad \textbf{(12.1)}$$

In the typical application in which $H_0$: $\mu_1 - \mu_2 = 0$, Equation 12.1 simplifies to:

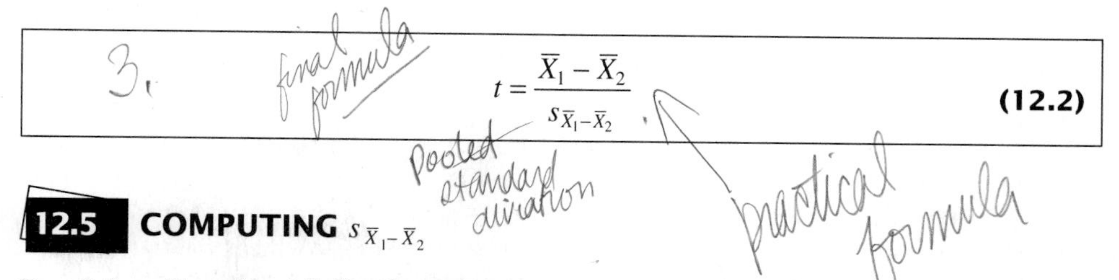


$$t = \frac{\bar{X}_1 - \bar{X}_2}{s_{\bar{X}_1-\bar{X}_2}} \quad \textbf{(12.2)}$$

## 12.5 COMPUTING $s_{\bar{X}_1-\bar{X}_2}$

Recall from Equation 5.5 (Section 5.8) that a variance estimate, $s^2$, is the ratio of the sum of squares, $\Sigma x^2$, to degrees of freedom, $\nu$:

$$s^2 = \frac{\textit{Sum of Squares}}{\textit{Degrees of Freedom}} = \frac{\Sigma x^2}{\nu}$$

Notice that when there are two samples, there are two separate estimates of $\sigma^2$: $s_1^2$ and $s_2^2$, where $s_1^2 = \Sigma x_1^2/(n_1 - 1)$, and $s_2^2 = \Sigma x_2^2/(n_2 - 1)$.

[6]If $\sigma_1^2$ and $\sigma_2^2$ are known, the $z$-test is used to test the null hypothesis, and the assumption of homogeneity of variance ($\sigma_1^2 = \sigma_2^2$) is not made. The critical value for $|z|$ is 1.96 regardless of $n_1$ and $n_2$. However, $\sigma_1^2$ and $\sigma_2^2$ are rarely known when testing means.

Regardless of the sample size, both $s_1^2$ and $s_2^2$ are unbiased estimates of $\sigma_1^2$ and $\sigma_2^2$, respectively (Section 5.13). If $\sigma_1^2 = \sigma_2^2$ as indicated in the assumptions in Section 12.4, then both $s_1^2$ and $s_2^2$ are independent estimates of the same parameter; that is, $\sigma_1^2 = \sigma_2^2 = \sigma^2$. It would be inefficient to use either $s_1^2$ or $s_2^2$ to estimate $\sigma^2$. Hence, the data from both samples are aggregated or "pooled" to obtain the best, most efficient estimate of $\sigma^2$—that is, the pooled sums of squares from within groups, $SS_W$, is divided by the pooled within-groups degrees of freedom, $\nu_W$, to obtain the within-groups estimate of variance, $s_W^2$.

$$s_W^2 = \frac{SS_W}{\nu_W} = \frac{\Sigma x_1^2 + \Sigma x_2^2}{\nu_1 + \nu_2} = \frac{\Sigma x_1^2 + \Sigma x_2^2}{(n_1 - 1) + (n_2 - 1)} \quad \textbf{(12.3)}$$

The pooled within-groups variance estimate, $s_W^2$, is based on the pooled degrees of freedom, $\nu_1 = (n_1 - 1)$ and $\nu_2 = (n_2 - 1)$; that is, $\nu_W = \nu_1 + \nu_2$ (or $n_1 + n_2 - 2$). The pooled estimate of the population variance is more precise than an estimate based on only $n_1 - 1$ or $n_2 - 1$ degrees of freedom. It can be expected to have less sampling error (Section 10.20) than either $s_1^2$ or $s_2^2$.

Once the unbiased estimate of the population variance, $s_W^2$, is obtained from the two samples, Equation 12.4 makes it a simple matter to estimate the variance in the sampling distribution of differences in sample means, $s_{\overline{X}_1-\overline{X}_2}^2$, and its square root, $s_{\overline{X}_1-\overline{X}_2}$, the standard error of the differences in means:

$$s_{\overline{X}_1-\overline{X}_2}^2 = s_W^2\left(\frac{1}{n_1} + \frac{1}{n_2}\right) \text{ or } s_{\overline{X}_1-\overline{X}_2} = s_W\sqrt{\frac{1}{n_1} + \frac{1}{n_2}} \quad \textbf{(12.4)}$$

**Sampling Distribution.** When $H_0$ is true, the sampling distribution of $t$ (Equation 12.1) over sets of samples is that of Student's $t$ with $\nu_W = \nu_1 + \nu_2 = n_1 + n_2 - 2$ degrees of freedom.

When $H_1$ is true and hence $\mu_1 \neq \mu_2$, the distribution of the $t$ ratios (Equation 12.1) from many replicated studies does *not* have a mean of 0, but instead has a mean of $(\mu_1 - \mu_2)$. It is termed a *non-central* $t$-distribution (non-central denoting that $H_0$ is not true).

**Critical Values.** For testing $H_0$ against $H_1$ at the $\alpha$-level of significance, the critical values from the central $t$-distribution are compared against the observed $t$-ratio from Equation 12.1. The critical value of $|t|$ is ${}_{1-\alpha/2}t_\nu$,[7] where $\nu = \nu_1 + \nu_2 = n_1 + n_2 - 2$.) For a one-tailed $t$-test, the critical value is ${}_{1-\alpha}t_\nu$).[8]

**Confidence Interval.** The $1 - \alpha$ confidence interval for $(\mu_1 - \mu_2)$ is constructed around $\overline{X}_1 - \overline{X}_2$ as follows:

---

[7] $|{}_{\alpha/2}t_\nu| = {}_{1-\alpha/2}t_\nu$

[8] For the $t$-ratio using a one-tailed test, the mean of the group *predicted* to have the smaller mean must be subtracted from the mean of the group predicted to have the larger mean. For a two-tailed test, it is inconsequential whether the numerator is $(\overline{X}_1 - \overline{X}_2)$ or $(\overline{X}_2 - \overline{X}_1)$, since the absolute value of $t$ will not be affected.

$$(1-\alpha)CI = (\overline{X}_1 - \overline{X}_2) \pm {}_{1-\alpha/2}t_v s_{\overline{X}_1-\overline{X}_2} \quad \textbf{(12.5)}$$

## 12.6 AN ILLUSTRATION

Suppose a researcher wished to ascertain whether an intensive treatment of environmental stimulation would increase the intelligence of infants. The eighteen infants in an experimental group were randomly assigned from the thirty-six available, the remaining eighteen infants served as the control group. After two years of the treatment, an intelligence test was administered to all thirty-six children. Hypothetical results for each group are given in Table 12.1. The $t$-test procedures outlined in Sections 12.4 and 12.5 are illustrated in Table 12.1, with $\alpha_2 = .05$.

**TABLE 12.1** An Illustration of the $t$-Test Comparing Means for Independent Groups

| *Experimental Group* | *Control Group* |
|---|---|
| $\overline{X}_1 = 108.10$ | $\overline{X}_2 = 98.40$ |
| $n_1 = 18$ | $n_2 = 18$ |
| $s_1^2 = 289.00$ | $s_2^2 = 196.00$ |
| $\Sigma x_1^2 = 4{,}913^a$ | $\Sigma x_2^2 = 3{,}332$ |

$$t = \frac{\overline{X}_1 - \overline{X}_2}{s_{\overline{X}_1-\overline{X}_2}} \quad \text{where} \quad s^2_{\overline{X}_1-\overline{X}_2} = s_W^2\left(\frac{1}{n_1}+\frac{1}{n_2}\right);$$

and

$$s_W^2 = \frac{\Sigma x_1^2 + \Sigma x_2^2}{v_1 + v_2} = \frac{4{,}913 + 3{,}332}{17+17} = \frac{8{,}245}{34} = 242.50$$

Hence

$$s^2_{\overline{X}_1-\overline{X}_2} = 242.50\left(\frac{1}{18}+\frac{1}{18}\right) = 26.944, \text{ thus } s_{\overline{X}_1-\overline{X}_2} = 5.19$$

Therefore,

$$t = \frac{108.10 - 98.40}{5.19} = \frac{9.70}{5.19} = 1.87; \quad {}_{.975}t_{34} \approx 2.04$$

$|t| < 2.04$, thus, $p > .05$, hence $H_0$ is tenable with $\alpha = .05$.

[a]If necessary, the sum of squares $\Sigma x^2$ can easily be determined from $n$ and $s^2$: since $s^2 = \Sigma x^2/(n-1)$, then $\Sigma x^2 = s^2(n-1)$. $\Sigma x^2$ is also equal to $\Sigma x^2 = \Sigma X^2 - n\overline{X}^2$ (see footnote in Section 5.5).

Note in the example that $H_0$ cannot be rejected. The critical value of $t$ with 30 degrees of freedom for $\alpha_2 = .05$, that is ${}_{.975}t_{30}$, is 2.04.[9] Since the obtained $t$-ratio of 1.87 is less than the critical $t$ of 2.04, $H_0$ cannot be rejected. The evidence is not strong enough to reject chance (sampling error) as the explanation for the difference between $\bar{X}_1$ and $\bar{X}_2$—at least it is not strong enough if one must maintain $\alpha_2 = .05$ protection against a type-I error. It is worth noting, however, that had $\alpha_2$ been set = .10, the difference would have been significant.

Note that the value of the pooled variance estimate $s_W^2$ (242.5) is the mean of the two sample values, $s_1^2$ and $s_2^2$. This will be true when the $n$'s are equal, that is, $s_W^2 = (s_1^2 + s_2^2)/2$ when $n_1 = n_2$.

Note also that the value of the denominator of the $t$-test is greatly influenced by sample size. Other things being equal, the larger the value of $n$, the smaller the value of $s_{\bar{X}_1 - \bar{X}_2}$. For a fixed mean difference, the smaller denominator results in a larger $t$-ratio. This illustrates why one is less likely to make type-II errors with large $n$'s: If the $n$'s are large, even small mean differences can result in large $t$-ratios.

The central $t$-distribution with 30 degrees of freedom is graphed in Figure 12.1. The associated $t$-values at percentiles .5, 2.5, 5, 95, 97.5, and 99.5 are indicated. For example, when $H_0$ is true and $\nu = 30$, a $t$-ratio of $-1.70$ or less would be observed in 5% of the $t$-tests. One also observes $t$-values of +1.70 or higher 5% of the time. In other words, when $\alpha_2 = .10$, the critical value for $t$ is $|t| = 1.70$; $H_0$ is rejected at $\alpha = .10$. Five percent of the area under the curve in Figure 12.1 falls to the left of the point $t = -1.70$, another 5% to the right of $t = 1.70$. In the example, $\alpha_2$ was set at .05; hence, $H_0$ would be rejected only if the observed $t$ is below $-2.04$ or greater than 2.04. When $H_0$ is true, 95% of the obtained $t$'s would fall within the range $\pm 2.04$.

If $\mu_1 \neq \mu_2$, the observed $|t|$ = values will tend to be larger than when $\mu_1 = \mu_2$ because the expected value of $\bar{X}_1 - \bar{X}_2$ is $\mu_1 - \mu_2$, not 0. $E(\bar{X}_1 - \bar{X}_2) = 0$ only when $\mu_1 = \mu_2$. Hence, a false $H_0$ will be rejected in more than 5% of the $t$-tests when $\alpha = .05$. If the observed $t$-ratio exceeds, in absolute value, the critical $t$-value, we will reject $H_0$ and be correct in the decision when $\mu_1 \neq \mu_2$. However, if $|t| <$ critical $t$, a type-II error will be made if $\mu_1 \neq \mu_2$. Observe in Figure 12.1 that the smaller the probability of a type-I error ($\alpha$), the larger the associated critical $t$-values. Recall (Section 11.12) that there is a greater risk of a type-II error ($\beta$) with $\alpha = .01$ than with $\alpha = .05$. If $\alpha$ had been set equal to .10 in Table 12.1, $H_0$ would have been rejected at the .10 level of statistical significance, since $1.87 > 1.70$.

Notice again the tradeoff: the greater the risk of making a type-I error ($\alpha$), the smaller the risk of making a type-II error ($\beta$). Accordingly, power is decreased as $\alpha$ is "tightened" from .05 to .01, or from .10 to .05.

It is good practice to report probability values ($p$) as precisely as possible; $p$ is the proportion of the central $t$-distribution beyond the absolute value of the observed $t$. Rather than report $p > .05$, it is more informative to report $.10 > p > .05$. It is always good practice to give the most *stringent* level at which $H_0$ can be rejected. Even if one sets $\alpha = .05$, $H_0$ can be rejected at the .01 level if the obtained $t$-ratio exceeds the critical $t$ for $\alpha = .01$. As a reader of research, one is not obligated to operate at the same value for $\alpha$ used by the researcher. One may decide that the 10% risk of a type-I error is more than offset by increased power—the decreased chance of a type-II error.

---

[9] Since $\nu = 34$ is not given in Table C, the closest smaller value for $\nu$ is used. The difference between ${}_{.975}t_{30}$ and ${}_{.975}t_{34}$ is negligible: $2.042 = {}_{.975}t_{30} > {}_{.975}t_{34} > {}_{.975}t_{35} = 2.030$. If extreme precision is needed, one can obtain critical values from EXCEL and certain other spreadsheets. One can also interpolate (i.e., ${}_{.975}t_{34} = {}_{.975}t_{35} + ({}_{.975}t_{30} - {}_{.975}t_{35})/5 = 2.030 + (.012)/5 \approx 2.032$. Most computer programs give actual $p$'s when significance tests are performed.

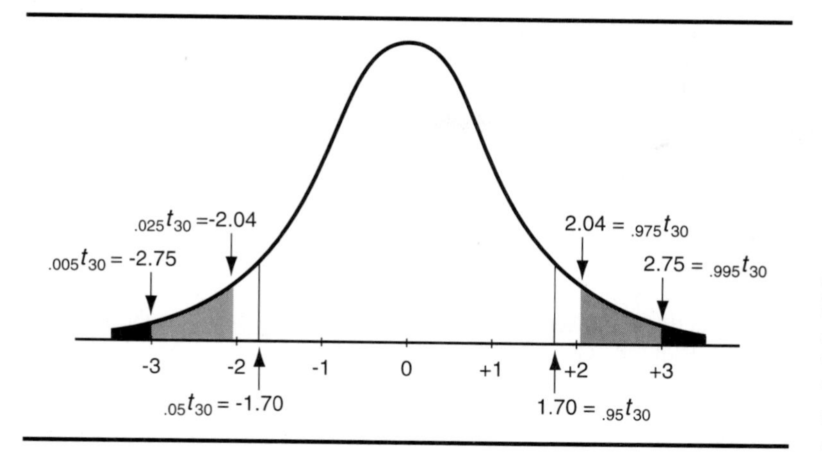

A central $t$-distribution with 30 degrees of freedom. Critical areas are shown for $\alpha_2 = .10$, $\alpha_2 = .05$, and $\alpha_2 = .01$.

## 12.7 CONFIDENCE INTERVALS ABOUT MEAN DIFFERENCES

Recall from Chapter 11 (Sec. 11.18) that the .95 confidence interval for $\mu$ is:

$$.95CI = \overline{X} \pm ({}_{.975}t_{\nu})s_{\overline{X}}, \text{ where } s_{\overline{X}} = \frac{s}{\sqrt{n}}$$

Similarly, using Equation 12.6, one can, and should, set a $CI$ for a difference in means irrespective of whether $H_0$: $\mu_1 = \mu_2$ is rejected. Equation 12.6 gives the .95 confidence interval around mean differences:

$$.95CI = (\overline{X}_1 - \overline{X}_2) \pm ({}_{.975}t_{\nu})s_{\overline{X}_1-\overline{X}_2} \quad \textbf{(12.6)}$$

For the data given in Table 12.1, the observed mean difference ($\overline{X}_1 - \overline{X}_2$) was 9.70, with $s_{\overline{X}_1-\overline{X}_2} = 5.19$ and $\nu = 34$. Thus, by using Equation 12.6, we can be 95% confident that the true value of $\mu_1 - \mu_2$ falls within the $.95CI$:

$$.95CI = 9.70 \pm (2.04)(5.19) = 9.70 \pm 10.59, \text{ or between } -.89 \text{ and } 20.29$$

Expressed succinctly, $.95CI = (-.89, 20.29)$. In other words, the true treatment effect ($\mu_1 - \mu_2$) probably lies between $-.89$ and 20.29. The fact that the .95 confidence interval includes the value of 0, tells us that $H_0$: $\mu_1 - \mu_2 = 0$ is not rejected at $\alpha_2 = .05$.

## 12.8 EFFECT SIZE

When the dependent variable is expressed in a metric that is well understood (e.g., inches, pounds, dollars, minutes), the meaning of the confidence interval can be easily interpreted.

Measures of IQ, GPA, and grade equivalents also allow the reader to attach some non-arbitrary meaning to the magnitude of differences.

However, differences in means expressed in raw-score units on tests of arbitrary length are often difficult to interpret. A difference in means of five points on a twenty-five-item test would be expected to become a difference of twenty points if a 100-item test were used. Using percentage scores rather than raw scores on cognitive and psychomotor measures is a step in the right direction, but percentage scores are not very useful on attitude and many other kinds of scales where right-wrong scoring usually makes no sense.

In situations in which the metric of the dependent variable is arbitrary, the use of effect size to convey the magnitude of a difference can be helpful (Glass, McGaw, & Smith, 1981). Most often the effect size is used to describe the difference between the mean of experimental ($\overline{X}_E$) and control ($\overline{X}_C$) groups.

The effect size (*ES* or $\Delta$) is simply the *z*-score (Equation 6.2) of the mean of the experimental group ($\overline{X}_E$) referenced in the frequency distribution of the control group, that is, $\overline{X}_E - \overline{X}_C$ is expressed in standard deviation units. In terms of parameters, the effect size is:

$$\Delta = \frac{\mu_E - \mu_C}{\sigma} \quad \textbf{(12.7A)}$$

$\Delta$ is estimated by:

$$\hat{\Delta} = \frac{\overline{X}_E - \overline{X}_C}{\hat{\sigma}} \quad \textbf{(12.7B)}$$

In most instances, $s_C$ is used as an estimate of $\sigma$. Thus, for the data in Table 12.1, where $ES = \hat{\Delta} = (108.10 - 98.40)/\sqrt{196} = 9.70/14.0 = .69$, hence the difference in the two means is estimated to be .69 standard deviations.[10]

## 12.9 *t*-TEST ASSUMPTIONS AND ROBUSTNESS

The three assumptions (Section 12.4) made in the mathematical derivation of the central *t*-distribution (i.e., the sampling distribution of *t*-ratios when $H_0$ is true) are as follows: (1) the $X_i$'s within each of the two populations are normally distributed; (2) the two population variances, $\sigma_1^2$ and $\sigma_2^2$, are equal; and (3) the individual observations, $X_i$'s, are independent.

### Normality

The statistician makes the assumption of normality *not* primarily because the normal curve is approximated by the distributions of many variables, but because of an important math-

[10] $\sigma$ can also be estimated by $s_W$, but $s_C$ is preferred since in certain instances the treatment can affect the heterogeneity as well as the mean of the treatment group. The statistical properties of $\Delta$ have been examined by Hedges (1981) and Hedges and Olkin (1985).

ematical property of normal distributions. The mean and variance of samples from a normal distribution are statistically independent[11] (the values of $\overline{X}$'s and $s^2$'s over repeated samples from the same normal population would correlate to zero). In the past, researchers have gone to great lengths to insure that the observations are normally distributed (Section 6.11). For example, if the dependent variable were positively skewed, instead of analyzing the actual scores, their square roots or logs might be analyzed (if $X$ is positively skewed, the distribution of $\sqrt{X}$ or $logX$ will be less skewed—see Figure 6.6).

Fortunately, much research has revealed (see Glass, Peckham, & Sanders, 1972; Sawilowsky & Blair, 1992) that violation of the assumption of normality has almost no practical consequences in using the two-tailed *t*-test. When the normality assumption is violated in many different ways, Figure 12.2 illustrates the proportion of *t*-tests in which the null hypothesis is rejected when it was true (i.e., the proportion of type-I errors) when the nominal $\alpha_2$ is set at .05 or .01—that is, when the critical *t*-values based on $\nu$ and $\alpha_2$ (Table C) are used. The dark areas denote the proportion of type-I errors when $\alpha_2 = .01$; the gray areas, when $\alpha_2 = .05$. The shapes of the population distributions are abbreviated along the baseline, for example, the "R/R" in the left-hand portion of the horizontal axis indicates that the two populations were rectangular in shape (platykurtic). The number in the upper portion of the bars gives the sample size, $n$ (if only one value is given, then $n_1 = n_2$). Note in the first two bars, that the actual proportions of type-I errors differed little from the nominal values of .01 and .05. The third column of Figure 12.2 shows that when $n_1 = 5$ and $n_2 = 5$ and both population distributions are skewed, $H_0$ will be rejected in approximately 3% of the tests with the nominal $\alpha$-value ($\alpha_2$) = .05. The fourth column reveals that $H_0$ will be rejected at $\alpha_2 = .05$ in about 4% of the tests when the sample size is increased to $n_1 = n_2 = 15$. The bars for "N/S" (one population is normal and the other is skewed) reveal that with $n$'s of 5 somewhat more type-I errors will occur than $\alpha_2$ stipulates (.07 vs. .05, and .018 vs. .01); yet when the $n$'s are increased to 15, there is no practical difference between the nominal and actual alphas. For larger sample sizes, the probability statements are even more accurate.

Beginning with the bar "L/ L" (both distributions are leptokurtic), the two sample sizes are different: $n_1 = 5$ and $n_2 = 15$, yet the actual and nominal proportions of type-I errors differ little. Note that when the $n$'s were 15 or more, the actual proportion of type-I errors was within 1% of the nominal value for alpha for both the .05 and .01 levels, a negligible discrepancy for practical purposes.[12] Observe that even when the dependent variable was a dichotomy (i.e., $\pi = .5$, .6, and .75), the nominal $\alpha$ was negligibly different from the actual $\alpha$. Of course, it is the central limit theorem working behind the scene, producing sampling distributions that are approximately normal, that results in the robustness to non-normality, because it is from the sampling distributions that probability statements are derived.

The probability of a type-II error (power) is virtually unaffected by marked non-normality (Boneau, 1960; Sawilowsky & Blair, 1992). Consequently, the condition of normality can be largely disregarded as a prerequisite for using the two-tailed *t*-test. The *t*-test is robust with respect to failure to meet the normality assumption. For one-tailed tests, accurate probability statements require a sample size of at least 20 in the smaller group (Sawilowsky & Blair, 1992).

---

[11]For proving that $\overline{X}$ and $s^2$ are independent, see Zehna (1991).

[12]In one bizarre, and nonrepresentative distribution (a gap between an outlier group of $2\sigma$), a sample size of 30 was required before the probability statements were accurate (Sawilowsky & Blair, 1992). Extremely small $p$-values (for example, .001) are not very precise when assumptions are violated (Wilcox, 1995).

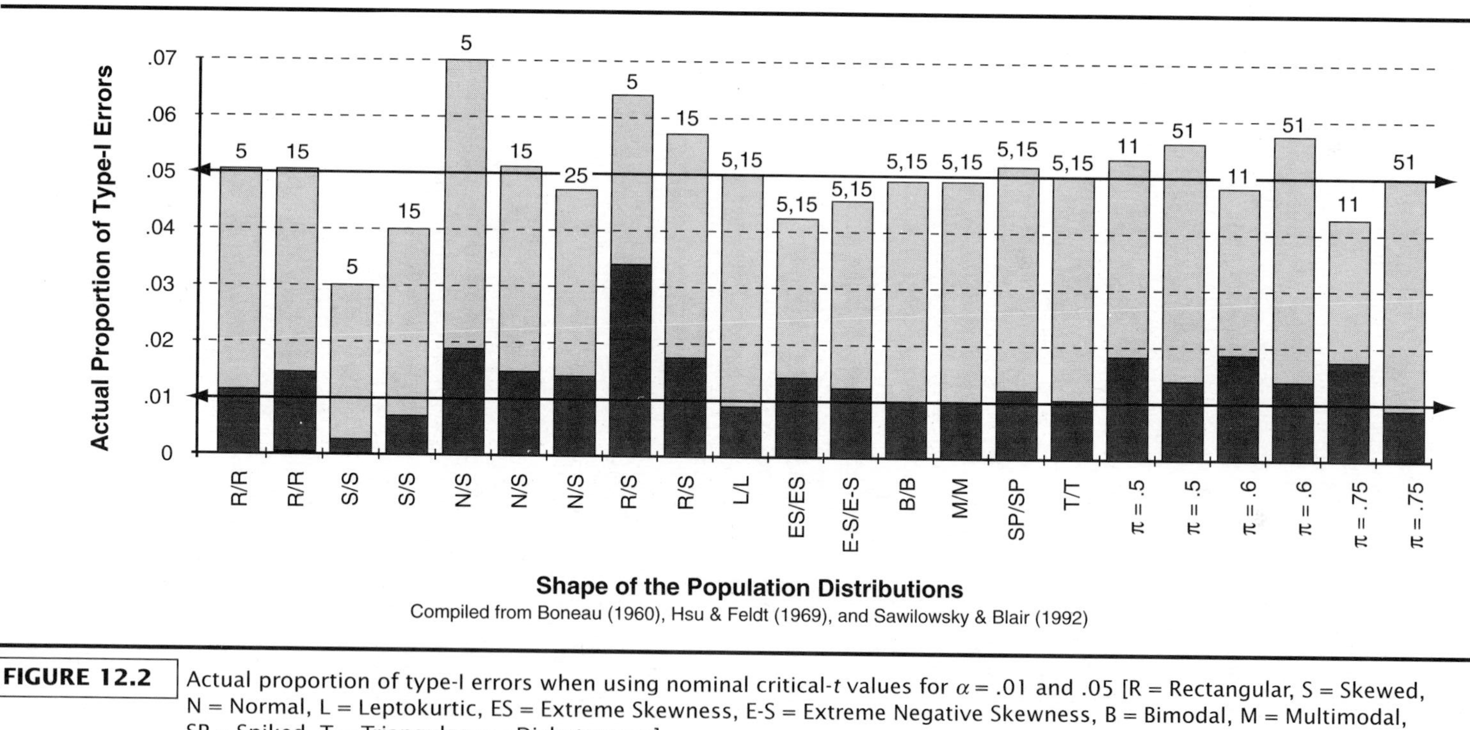


**FIGURE 12.2** Actual proportion of type-I errors when using nominal critical-$t$ values for $\alpha = .01$ and .05 [R = Rectangular, S = Skewed, N = Normal, L = Leptokurtic, ES = Extreme Skewness, E-S = Extreme Negative Skewness, B = Bimodal, M = Multimodal, SP = Spiked, T = Triangular, $\pi$ = Dichotomous]

## 12.10 HOMOGENEITY OF VARIANCE

The homogeneity-of-variance assumption[13] legitimizes the use of a single variance estimate from the aggregate of the sum of squares from both groups ($SS_W$) and the associated pooled degrees of freedom ($\nu_W$). If $\sigma_1^2 = \sigma_2^2$ then the expected value of both $s_1^2$ and $s_2^2$ is the parameter $\sigma^2$; that is, $E(s_1^2) = E(s_2^2) = \sigma^2$. If both $s_1^2$ and $s_2^2$ are unbiased estimates of a common parameter ($\sigma^2$), it would be inefficient not to combine (pool) the information from both samples to achieve a better, more accurate estimate of the parameter $\sigma^2$.

### Consequences of Heterogeneous Variances

Several researchers have studied the empirical consequences of violating the assumption of homogeneity of variance. This research has been extensively reviewed by Glass, Peckham, and Sanders (1972). It has been shown that the $t$-test is robust with respect to violation of the homogeneity-of-variance assumption when $n_1 = n_2$. Indeed, for practical purposes one need not even test the assumption of homogeneity of variance when the $n$'s are equal. Figure 12.3 illustrates the effects of heterogeneous variance when the $n$'s are equal and when they are not. The relative size of $\sigma_1^2$ and $\sigma_2^2$ is given along the baseline; for example, if $\sigma_1^2/\sigma_2^2 = 2$, $\sigma_2^2$ is one-half as large as $\sigma_1^2$. The relative size of the $n$'s is given to the right of the curves.

Note that when the larger sample is from the population with the larger variance—that is, when $n_1/n_2 > 1$ and $\sigma_1^2/\sigma_2^2 > 1$—the $t$-test is conservative with respect to committing type-I errors. The three lower curves indicate that when the critical $t$-values from Table C are used and "$\alpha_2$" is set at .05 the probability of rejecting a true null hypothesis is less than .05. For example, if $n_1$ is twice as large as $n_2$ ($n_1/n_2 = 2$) and $\sigma_1^2$ is five times larger than $\sigma_2^2$ ($\sigma_1^2/\sigma_2^2 = 5$), then the null hypothesis will be rejected in less than 2% of such situations when it is true. Hence, when $n_1 > n_2$ and $\sigma_1^2 > \sigma_2^2$ an even smaller risk of a type-I error is taken when $H_0$ is rejected than is claimed.[14] If $H_0$ is rejected at the .05 level when $\sigma_1^2 > \sigma_2^2$ and $n_1 > n_2$, we need have no concern about violating the homogeneity-of-variance assumption. In Figure 12.3, we can see that the true probability of a type-I error is always less than the nominal probability when the larger $n$ and larger variance are paired.

The three upper curves give the true $\alpha$ when $n_2 > n_1$ and $\sigma_1^2 > \sigma_2^2$. When the larger sample has the smaller variance, the true $\alpha$ is greater than the nominal (apparent) probability of a type-I error, "$\alpha$." How much greater? In Figure 12.3, note that if $\sigma_1^2/\sigma_2^2 = 5$, $n_1/n_2 = 1/5$, and the critical $t$-value for $\alpha_2 = .05$ from Table C is used, the probability of a type-I error is not .05 but .22! If $n_1/n_2 = 1/8$ or less, the true $\alpha$ would be even higher. Of course, $\sigma_1^2/\sigma_2^2 = 5$ are extremely heterogeneous variances that would rarely be encountered in practice; but situations in which $n_1/n_2 = 1/10$ or less are not rare. When a larger sample has the smaller variance, the true $\alpha$ will exceed "$\alpha$," the apparent probability of a type-I error. If $\sigma_1^2 > \sigma_2^2$, $n_2 > n_1$, and $H_0$ is not rejected, why does one need not be concerned about violating the homogeneity-of-variance assumption? If $H_0$ is not rejected when the true $\alpha$ is greater than .05, $H_0$ would not be rejected if the true $\alpha$ is .05. For example, if $p = .06$ or .11, it is superfluous to inquire whether $p < .05$. When testing $H_0$: $\sigma_1^2 = \sigma_2^2$, $\alpha$ should be relaxed to at least .10 to avoid using the conventional $t$-test when it will yield probabilities ($p$) that are too high or too low.

---

[13]No doubt the principal reason Gosset ("Student") assumed homogeneity of variance was to simplify the mathematics.

[14]Before you celebrate this added protection, the down side is that it also results in a less powerful test for rejecting a false $H_0$.

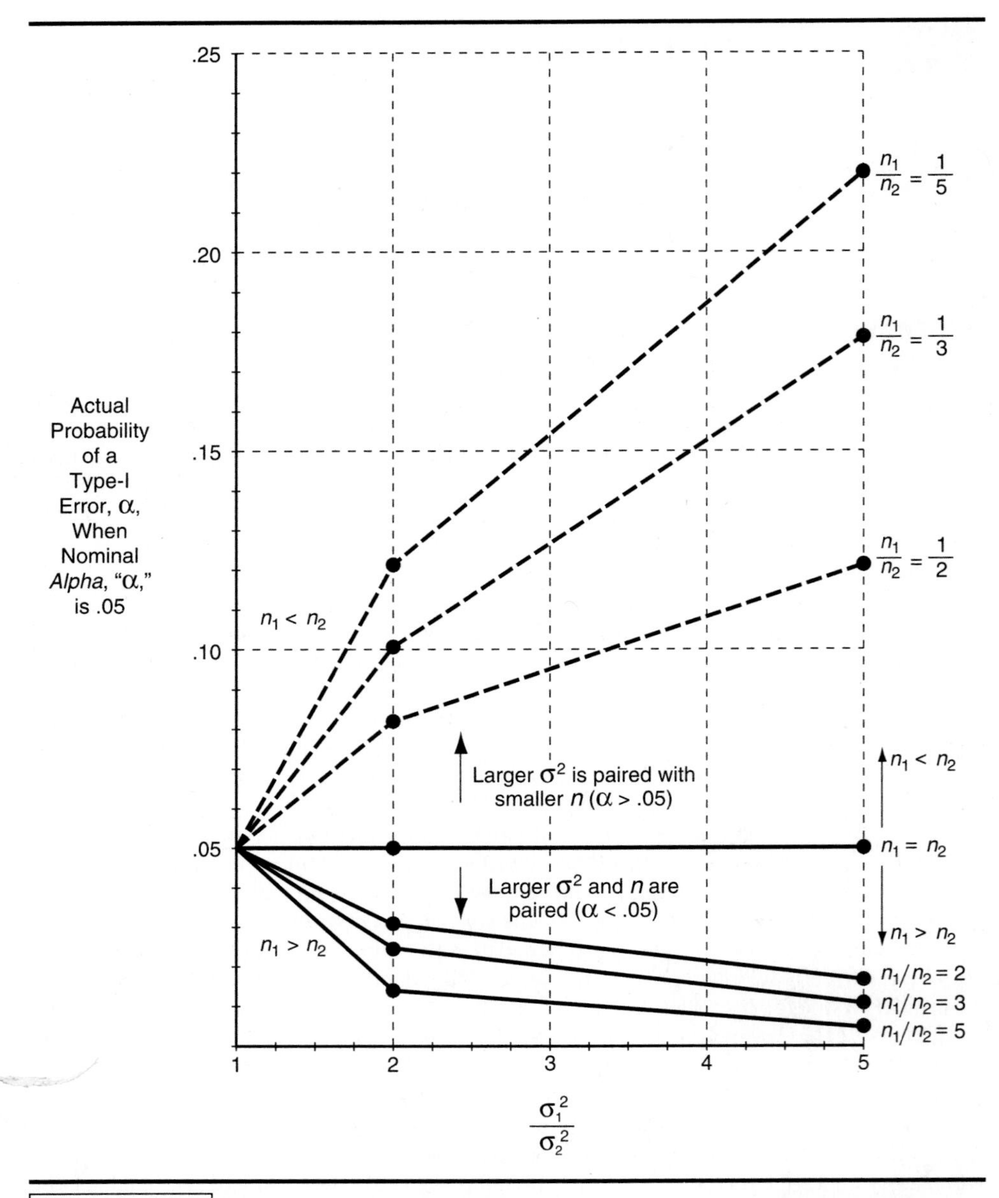


**FIGURE 12.3** The effect of heterogeneity of variance on alpha ($\alpha$), the probability of a type-I error, for various ratios of $\sigma_1^2/\sigma_2^2$ and $n_1/n_2$, using the two-tailed *t*-test when the nominal significance, "$\alpha$," is .05. (Data from Scheffé [1959] and Hsu [1938].)

## 12.11 WHAT IF SAMPLE SIZES ARE UNEQUAL AND VARIANCES ARE HETEROGENEOUS[15]: THE WELCH *t'* TEST?

If $n_1 \neq n_2$ and $\sigma_1^2 \neq \sigma_2^2$, the hypothesis $H_0$: $\mu_1 = \mu_2$ can be evaluated using the Welch $t'$-test:

$$t' = \frac{\bar{X}_1 - \bar{X}_2}{\sqrt{s_{\bar{X}_1}^2 + s_{\bar{X}_2}^2}} \qquad \textbf{(12.8)}$$

The $t'$-distribution closely approximates a $t$-distribution when the degrees of freedom are adjusted by differentially weighting $n$'s and variances. The degrees of freedom for the $t'$ statistic ($\nu'$) are obtained using the Welch formula:

$$\nu' = \frac{A}{B}, \qquad \textbf{(12.9)}$$

$$\text{where } A = \left(s_{\bar{X}_1}^2 + s_{\bar{X}_2}^2\right)^2$$

$$\text{and } B = \frac{\left(s_{\bar{X}_1}^2\right)^2}{\nu_1} + \frac{\left(s_{\bar{X}_2}^2\right)^2}{\nu_2}$$

Thus, if $s_{\bar{X}_1}^2 = s_1^2/n_1 = 12$, $s_{\bar{X}_1}^2 = 3$, $\nu_1 = n_1 - 1 = 6 - 1 = 5$, and $\nu_2 = n_2 - 1 = 21 - 1 = 20$, then $A = (12 + 3)^2 = 225$, and $B = (12)^2/5 + (3)^2/20 = 29.25$. Thus, $\nu' = 225/29.25 = 7.69$ or 8 (round to the nearest whole number). The critical value for $t'$ is read from the conventional $t$-table (Table C); with 8 degrees of freedom, $_{.975}t_8 = 2.306$. Note that the critical value for $t$ is greater than if the homogeneity of variance assumption were tenable: $\nu = n_1 + n_2 - 2 = 28$, and $_{.975}t_{28} = 2.048$. The larger critical value for $t'$ shows that $t'$ is slightly less powerful than $t$ when the homogeneity of variance assumption is met.[16] Since one can never know if the population variances are equal (because of type II errors), a compelling case can be made that $t'$ (not $t$) be the standard test of $H_0$: $\mu_1 = \mu_2$, in spite of the fact that current practice is to the contrary.

## 12.12 INDEPENDENCE OF OBSERVATIONS

The independence condition simply means that the observations within or between the two groups are not paired, dependent, correlated, or associated in any way. If the two sets of

[15]Methods for testing $H_0$: $\sigma_1^2 = \sigma_2^2$ are given in Chapter 15.

[16]There are other methods that accommodate heterogeneous variance (Wilcox, 1989). The quasi-$t'$ test is the best in most circumstances (Tomarken & Serlin, 1986). Equations 12.8 and 12.9 illustrate the method used by many computer programs for the "Unequal Variances $t$-test" that is included in the output along with the conventional $t$-test (so that the user can have these results at hand in case the conventional $t$-test is not appropriate).

scores are paired in some way, the *t*-test for paired observations should be used. If John copies some of his answers from Mary, $X_{John}$ and $X_{Mary}$ obviously are not independent. If variable $X$ is a pretest and variable $Y$ is a posttest, the two sets of observations would not be independent, but correlated. In certain situations, it is difficult to ascertain whether the condition of independence is met (Section 19.22). If an individual is represented by more than one score, the scores would not be independent. Suppose an immediate posttest ($X$) is given to persons in the $E$ and $C$ groups, and a delayed posttest ($Y$) is given some time later; a *t*-test could be applied to $X$ and/or $Y$, but both $X$ and $Y$ could not be combined into one set of $2n$ observations because there would be two nonindependent scores for each individual. However, a *t*-test could be performed on the *average* of the two scores, or on the *difference* between the two posttest scores; they would be a single observation for each individual.

The condition of independence of observations is important. Without it, probability statements pertaining to type-I or type-II errors will not be accurate. With proper experimental control, dependency among the observations can usually be prevented, or taken into account in the analysis. More will be said regarding independence in subsequent chapters. The special case of nonindependence in which two sets of observations are paired will now be considered.

## 12.13 TESTING $H_0$: $\mu_1 = \mu_2$ WITH PAIRED OBSERVATIONS

When each observation in group 1 can be linked to or paired with an observation in group 2, the two sets of observations are dependent or correlated.[17] The procedures for testing paired observations differ in only two respects from those for independent observations: procedures for finding (1) the standard error of the difference in means, $s_{\bar{X}_1 - \bar{X}_2}$, and (2) degrees of freedom.

**Statistical Hypothesis.** Population 1 has mean $\mu_1$ and population 2 has mean $\mu_2$. The null hypothesis to be tested is the same as in Section 12.3:

$$H_0: \mu_1 - \mu_2 = 0$$

$$H_1: \mu_1 - \mu_2 \neq 0$$

**Assumptions.** It is assumed that the sample of paired observations is randomly drawn; both sets of observations are normally distributed in the population with the same variance $\sigma^2$. In this instance, the samples are not independent, that is, a correlation between $\bar{X}_1$ and $\bar{X}_2$ over repeated pairs of samples is expected. The following are examples of dependent samples: Sample 1 is a sample of one-year-old infants and sample 2 consists of the same children one year later; sample 1 is a group of boys and sample 2 is the group of their sisters; sample 1 is husbands and sample 2 is their wives; sample 1 is the collection of scores on a reaction-time test made by a group of persons before administration of a drug and sample 2 is the collection of scores made by the same persons after taking the drug. Of course, when

[17]The rare exception to this statement would occur if the variable on which the observations were paired did not correlate with the variable on which the two groups are to be compared. Obviously, it would be pointless to pair observations in such situations.

there are two, or more, scores on the same group (e.g., pretest and posttest scores), the scores are dependent, and the $t$-test for paired observations is required. Since $n_1 = n_2 = n$ for the $t$-test for paired observations, the test is robust with respect to the assumptions of homogeneity of variance.

**Test Statistic.** It will always be possible to "pair off" observations from two sets of correlated observations. The pairs may be defined by "brother–sister," "before–after," "twin 1–twin 2," "matched partner 1–matched partner 2," et cetera. Hence, data gathered from dependent samples will be in the form of $n$ pairs of observations $\overline{X}_{1_i}$ and $\overline{X}_{2_i}$ for $i = 1, \ldots, n$. This pairing of the data from dependent samples will be used to test the hypothesis that $\mu_1 - \mu_2 = 0$. The hypothesis that $\overline{X}_1$ and $\overline{X}_2$ have the same mean, that is, that $\mu_1 = \mu_2$ is equivalent to the hypothesis that $\mu_1 - \mu_2$ has a mean of 0 in the population. The $n$ differences, $\overline{X}_{1_i} - \overline{X}_{2_i}$, are also assumed to be normally distributed.

When observations are paired, Equation 12.10 (and not Equation 12.4) should be used to find $s_{\overline{X}_1 - \overline{X}_2}$, the denominator of the $t$-test.[18] The degrees of freedom for the $t$-test for paired observations is $\nu = n - 1$, where $n$ is the number of pairs (not the number of scores):

$$s^2_{\overline{X}_1 - \overline{X}_2} = s^2_{\overline{X}_1} + s^2_{\overline{X}_2} - 2rs_{\overline{X}_1}s_{\overline{X}_2} \qquad \textbf{(12.10)}$$

where $s^2_{\overline{X}_1} = \dfrac{s_1^2}{n}$ and $s^2_{\overline{X}_2} = \dfrac{s_2^2}{n}$, and $\nu = n - 1$ degrees of freedom.

Notice that the correlation between the two sets of observations reduces the denominator of the $t$-test (compare Equation 12.10 with Equation 12.8). Consequently with the same sample size, the paired $t$-test is usually more powerful than the independent groups $t$-test.

**Sampling Distribution.** If $H_0$: $\mu_1 - \mu_2 = 0$ is true, then the distribution of $t$ in Equations 12.1 and 12.2 will be the central $t$-distribution with $\nu = n - 1$. If $H_1$: $\mu_1 - \mu_2 \neq 0$, then $t$ in Equations 12.1 and 12.2 will have a distribution identical in *shape* to the Student's $t$-distribution with $\nu = n - 1$, but the mean $t$ will be different from zero in a direction and by an amount depending on the size of $\mu_1 - \mu_2$.

**Critical Value.** The critical $t$-value for testing $H_0$ against $H_1$ at the $\alpha$-level of significance by means of the $t$-statistic in Equations 12.1 and 12.2 is ${}_{1-\alpha/2}t_\nu$.

**CI.** The $1 - \alpha$ confidence interval for $\mu_1 - \mu_2$ is set around the observed difference in means, $\overline{X}_1 - \overline{X}_2$, using Equation 12.5:

$$(1-\alpha)CI = (\overline{X}_1 - \overline{X}_2) \pm {}_{1-\alpha/2}t_\nu s_{\overline{X}_1 - \overline{X}_2}$$

where $\nu = n - 1$.

[18]Note that Equation 12.10 is an application of Equation 7.11. The $r$ in Equation 12.10 is the correlation between $\overline{X}_1$'s and $\overline{X}_2$'s over repeated samples. For example, suppose the study was replicated by all your $n$ classmates, each classmate has a value for $\overline{X}_1$ and another value for $\overline{X}_2$; the correlation between these two sets of $\overline{X}$'s is $r_{\overline{X}_1\overline{X}_2}$. Fortunately, when observations are randomly selected, the correlation between the observations $r_{12}$ also estimates the correlation between the two sets of means.

**TABLE 12.2** An Illustration of the *t*-Test for Correlated Observa
($n = 50$) Using Data from Wechsler (1967)

| *Retest*[a] | *1st Test* | |
|---|---|---|
| $\bar{X}_1 = 109.2$ | $\bar{X}_2 = 105.6$ | $s_{\bar{X}_1} = \frac{s_1}{\sqrt{n_1}} = \frac{(13.3)}{\sqrt{50}} = 1.88$ |
| $s_1 = 13.3$ | $s_2 = 14.8$ | |
| | $r = .91$ | $s_{\bar{X}_2} = \frac{s_2}{\sqrt{n_2}} = \frac{(14.8)}{\sqrt{50}} = 2.09$ |

$$s^2_{\bar{X}_1-\bar{X}_2} = s^2_{\bar{X}_1} + s^2_{\bar{X}_2} - 2rs_{\bar{X}_1}s_{\bar{X}_2}$$

$$= (1.88)^2 + (2.09)^2 - 2(.91)(1.88)(2.09)$$

$$s^2_{\bar{X}_1-\bar{X}_2} = 7.90 - 7.15 = .75$$

$$s_{\bar{X}_1-\bar{X}_2} = .866$$

$$t = \frac{\bar{X}_1 - \bar{X}_2}{s_{\bar{X}_1-\bar{X}_2}} = \frac{109.2 - 105.6}{.866} = \frac{3.6}{.866} = 4.16; \ {}_{.9995}t_{49} \approx 3.50$$

Reject $H_0$ at .001 level ($p < .001$)

$$.95\ CI = \bar{X}_1 - \bar{X}_2 \pm {}_{.975}t_{49}s_{\bar{X}_1-\bar{X}_2}$$

$$= 3.6 \pm (2.01)(.866) = 3.6 \pm 1.74 \text{ or } (1.86,\ 5.34)$$

Effect size[b], $\hat{\Delta}$, (Equation 12.7): $109.2 - 105.6)/15 = .24\sigma$

[a]We selected the group having the larger mean as group 1. This designation is arbitrary when testing nondirectional hypotheses.

[b]Since from the test norms $\sigma = 15$, this value can be used in Equation 12.7. If one uses $\hat{\sigma} = s = \sqrt{(s_1^2 + s_2^2)/2} = 14.0$, $\hat{\Delta} = .26\hat{\sigma}$.

**Illustration.** To estimate the "practice effect" on the Wechsler Preschool and Primary Scale of Intelligence (WPPSI), 50 five-year-old children were tested, then retested two to four months later (Wechsler, 1967). Obviously, there would be some correlation between the two sets of scores. Note that if there is no correlation between variables 1 and 2, since $n_1 = n_2$, Equation 12.10 is mathematically equivalent to Equation 12.4, which gives $s_{\bar{X}_1-\bar{X}_2}$ for independent observations. Notice in Equation 12.10 that as $r$ increases, the value of $s_{\bar{X}_1-\bar{X}_2}$ decreases. The *t*-test for dependent observations is illustrated in Table 12.2 using Wechsler's data.

The practice effect was highly significant—$H_0$ is rejected at the .001 level of statistical significance.[19] Note that a highly *statistically significant* difference (e.g., $p < .001$) does *not*

[19]Actually a directional or one-tailed hypothesis could have been justified in this situation, since the possibility that the retest $\mu_2$ is less than $\mu_1$ is essentially nil. Obviously the additional power was not needed in this case.

necessarily indicate a *large difference* in means. If $n$ is large (or $r$ is very high), even a small difference in means can result in a large $t$-ratio, and yield a highly significant difference. *Level* of statistical significance should never be used to convey the *magnitude* of a difference. Instead, the effect size (Section 12.8) and a *CI* for the difference in the population means should be used for this purpose. As computed in Table 12.2, the effect size ($\Delta$) is estimated to be $.24\sigma$. The .95*CI* for the mean practice effect (i.e., the difference in population means, $\mu_2 - \mu_1$) is estimated to fall between 1.86 to 5.34 IQ points. The *CI* limits can also be expressed in standard deviation units, that is, the .95 *CI* for $\Delta$ extends from 1.86/15 = $.12\sigma$ to 5.34/15 = $.36\sigma$. If $H_0$ is true, there is less than one chance in 1,000 of obtaining a mean difference at least as large as that observed (3.6 points) for $n = 50$, that is, it is extremely improbable that the practice effect is zero. The estimates of $\Delta$ and the .95*CI* give a better metric for judging the magnitude of the practice effect.

## 12.14 DIRECT-DIFFERENCE METHOD FOR THE *t*-TEST WITH PAIRED OBSERVATIONS

Suppose the ability test scores were used to form pairs of students—the two members of each pair have the same score. If we randomly assigned one member of each pair to the method $E$ group and the other member to the method $C$ group, the observations on the outcome (dependent) variable between the pairs would be correlated. Within both groups, the students with higher ability scores will probably tend to score higher on the posttest. The degree of correlation between the paired observations needs to be taken into account in the analysis. This type of research design[20] is generally more powerful than a simple random assignment of persons to method without equating pairs of students ("stratifying") on IQ (see Section 12.15), that is, we are more likely to find a treatment effect if it is there (but no more likely to make a type-I error). The values of the $\bar{X}$'s, $s$'s and $r$ could be computed, and Equation 12.10 could be used to obtain $s_{\bar{X}_1-\bar{X}_2}$.

There is a more direct computational procedure that avoids the necessity of computing $r$.[21] A $t$-test formula for dependent samples that is mathematically equivalent to the procedure used in Table 12.2 is as follows:

$$t = \frac{\bar{X}_1 - \bar{X}_2}{s_{\bar{X}_1-\bar{X}_2}} = \frac{\bar{X}_d}{s_{\bar{X}_d}} \quad \textbf{(12.11)}$$

where $\bar{X}_d$ is the mean difference, $(\bar{X}_1 - \bar{X}_2)$, and $s_{\bar{X}_d}$ is the standard error of the mean difference ($s_{\bar{X}_d} = s_{\bar{X}_1-\bar{X}_2}$):

$$s_{\bar{X}_d} = \frac{s_{X_d}}{\sqrt{n}} \quad \textbf{(12.12)}$$

[20]It is known as the randomized blocks design.

[21]With the wide availability of computers, this is no longer an important advantage. The procedure has some practical utility, however, even when computers are used. When running some other procedure that does not test means, it is sometimes expedient to have the computer create a new variable, $d_i = Y_i - X_i$. A $t$-test can easily be made by dividing the mean of this variable by its standard error (Equation 12.11).

(Notice that Equation 12.11 is simply an application of Equation 11.6 in which $\mu = 0$.)

## Computational Steps

The scores of ten neurologically impaired children on two different Wechsler intelligence subtests (Verbal and Performance) are given in Table 12.3. Note the simple steps in computing $t$ for correlated samples using the direct-difference method.

**TABLE 12.3** An Illustration of the Direct-Difference Method of the t-test for Paired Observations: Verbal vs. Performance IQ Scores for Ten Neurologically Impaired Children.

| *Person* | *Verbal (1)* | *Performance (2)* | *Difference:* $X_{d_i} = X_{1_i} - X_{2_i}$ |
|---|---|---|---|
| 1 | 80 | 70 | +10 |
| 2 | 100 | 80 | +20 |
| 3 | 110 | 90 | +20 |
| 4 | 120 | 90 | +30 |
| 5 | 70 | 70 | 00 |
| 6 | 100 | 110 | −10 |
| 7 | 110 | 80 | +30 |
| 8 | 120 | 120 | 00 |
| 9 | 110 | 80 | +30 |
| 10 | 90 | 70 | +20 |
| | $\overline{X}_1 = 101.0$ | $\overline{X}_2 = 86.0$ | $\Sigma X_d = 150$ |
| | $(s_1 = 16.6)$ | $(s_2 = 17.1)$ | $\overline{X}_d = 15.0$ |

A. *Direct-Difference Method* (Equation 12.12)

$$\overline{X}_d = \frac{\Sigma X_d}{n} = \frac{150}{10} = 15.0$$

$$s^2_{X_d} = \frac{\Sigma x_d^2}{n-1}$$

$$\Sigma x_d^2 = \Sigma X_d^2 - n\overline{X}_d^2 = (10)^2 + (20)^2 + \ldots + (20)^2 - 10(15.0)^2$$

$$\Sigma x_d^2 = 4100 - 2250 = 1850$$

$$s^2_{X_d} = \frac{\Sigma x_d^2}{n-1} = \frac{1850}{9} = 205.6$$

$$s^2_{\overline{X}_d} = \frac{s^2_{X_d}}{n} = \frac{205.6}{10} = 20.56, \ s_{\overline{X}_d} = 4.53$$

$$t = \frac{\overline{X}_d}{s_{\overline{X}_d}} = \frac{15.0}{4.53} = 3.31, \ {}_{.995}t_9 = 3.25$$

Reject $H_0$ at .01 level $(p < .01)$

$$.95CI = \overline{X}_d \pm {}_{1-\alpha/2}t_v s_{\overline{X}_d}$$

$$= 15.0 \pm (2.26)(4.53) = 15.0 \pm 10.2 \text{ or } (4.8,\ 25.2)$$

**TABLE 12.3** *Continued*

B. (Equation 12.10) ($r_{12} = .64$)

$$s^2_{\bar{X}_1-\bar{X}_2} = s^2_{\bar{X}_1} + s^2_{\bar{X}_2} - 2rs_{\bar{X}_1}s_{\bar{X}_2};\ s^2_{\bar{X}_1} = \frac{s_1^2}{n} = \frac{(16.6)^2}{10} = 27.6$$

$$s^2_{\bar{X}_2} = \frac{(17.1)^2}{10} = 29.2$$

$$= 27.6 + 29.2 - 2(.64)\left(\sqrt{27.6}\right)\left(\sqrt{29.2}\right)$$

$$= 20.5$$

$$s_{\bar{X}_1-\bar{X}_2} = 4.53$$

$$t = \frac{\bar{X}_1 - \bar{X}_2}{s_{\bar{X}_1-\bar{X}_2}} = \frac{101.0 - 86.0}{4.52} = 3.31$$

1. Take the difference ($X_d$) between the paired observations for each of the $n$ pairs and find the mean difference ($\bar{X}_d$).
2. Find the variance ($s^2_{X_d}$) of the difference scores.
3. Find the standard error of the mean difference using Equation 12.12:

$$s_{\bar{X}_d} = \frac{s_{X_d}}{\sqrt{n}}$$

4. The ratio of $\bar{X}_d$ to $s_{\bar{X}_d}$ is $t$; compare $t$ with the critical $t$-value (i.e., the appropriate percentile in the central $t$-distribution with $\nu = n - 1$ degrees of freedom, where $n$ is the number of pairs, not the total number of observations).

In the example in Table 12.3, the obtained $t$ of 3.31 was greater than the critical $t$ of 3.25 for $\alpha_2 = .01$; hence, $H_0$ is rejected at the .01 level. Panel B shows that if the correlation between the Verbal and Performance tests had been used ($r$ =.64) and the standard error of the difference in means determined using Equation 12.10, the value of $s_{\bar{X}_1-\bar{X}_2}$ would also have been precisely .453—the two procedures are alternate routes to the same destination.

The effect size (Section 12.8) of the mean difference is $\hat{\Delta} = (101.0 - 86.0)/15 = .10$.

## 12.15 CAUTIONS REGARDING THE MATCHED-PAIR DESIGNS IN RESEARCH

When properly used, a research design that results in correlated observations can be more powerful than a design in which the subjects are randomly assigned to two independent treatment groups. As stated previously, if subjects are grouped into homogeneous pairs on a variable (such as IQ) that correlates with the criterion (such as reading performance), and then one member of each pair is randomly assigned to each of the two treatment groups, the resulting $t$-test (for paired observations) will have greater power than a design in which the same subjects are randomly assigned to treatment groups without pairing. This type of research design *should not be confused* with the conventional matched-pair design in which there is no random assignment following the pairing.

Matched-pair designs have been widely used and misused in behavioral research. Their purpose is to match or pair each person in group A (e.g., delinquents) with a person in group B (e.g., non-delinquents) on some variable (e.g., IQ), then compare the two groups on a dependent variable (e.g., reading ability). Researchers are mistaken if they believe that they have fully equated the groups in intelligence. One may conclude erroneously that a significant difference on some dependent variable such as reading proficiency, is due, not to intelligence differences, but to the delinquency factor. The fallacy of the matched-pair design is the assumption that matching equates the groups on the matching variable. If the groups have different means on that variable (and if not, why match?), the matching does not fully equate the groups on that variable. The pair members will each regress toward the means of their respective populations when they are retested. In other words, if immediately after we have obtained our matched pairs, we retest our delinquents and non-delinquents on another intelligence test, the non-delinquents would regress toward their mean ($\approx 100$) and the delinquents would regress toward their mean ($\approx 90$). It is beyond the scope of this book to develop fully the underlying rationale for this subtlety;[22] the matching fallacy results primarily from measurement error and the regression effect (Section 8.11). The practical consequence of the use of matched-pair designs is that the groups are rarely truly equated on the variable on which they are matched.

## 12.16 POWER WHEN COMPARING MEANS

In Chapter 11, the concept of statistical power, and its practical importance in research was developed. Current practice in all empirical disciplines gives insufficient attention to power in the planning stages of research. As a consequence, many studies are conducted that have little chance of finding a significant difference between means, even when there is a substantial difference between $\mu_1$ and $\mu_2$. The research in many fields has been reviewed to assess the power of published studies for detecting small ($.2\sigma$), medium ($.5\sigma$), and large ($.8\sigma$) effect sizes[23] (Section 12.8); these were summarized by Lipsey (1990), and are given in Table 12.4. To help quantify the magnitude of these effect sizes, in IQ scores, small, medium, and large effect sizes correspond to a treatment that increased IQ scores by an average of 3, 7.5, and 12 points. In grade equivalents, $.5\sigma$ is more than half a school year (e.g., see Mastery Test for Chapter 6). Notice that less than half the studies in social psychology, education, and several other disciplines had less than .50 power for detecting an effect size of $.5\sigma$! Power should be estimated in the planning stage of a study to see if the probability for finding an existing effect if it exists is great enough to make the study promising. Procedures for estimating power when comparing means are given in Chapter 15, along with tables to provide quick estimates. Power can be increased (Hopkins, 1973; Hopkins & Chappell, 1994) by:

1. Increasing the potency of the treatment (e.g., allowing the treatment to run for a longer period)
2. Increasing sample sizes

---

[22]See Thorndike (1963), Hopkins (1969), and Shepard and Hopkins (1977) for a more complete treatment of the matched-groups fallacy.

[23]These estimated values for small, medium, and large effects sizes follow Cohen (1988).

**TABLE 12.4** Statistical Power of Research Studies in Various Disciplines[25]

| | *Power for Effect Size* | | |
|---|---|---|---|
| *Discipline* | *Small (.2σ)* | *Medium (.5σ)* | *Large (.8σ)* |
| Applied Psychology | .25 | .67 | .86 |
| Social Psychology | .18 | .48 | .83 |
| Education | .13 | .47 | .73 |
| Mathematical Education | .24 | .62 | .83 |
| Evaluation Research | .28 | .63 | .81 |
| Speech Pathology | .16 | .44 | .73 |
| Marketing | .24 | .69 | .87 |
| Management | .31 | .77 | .91 |
| Medicine | .14 | .39 | .61 |
| Communication | .18 | .52 | .79 |
| Occupational Therapy | .37 | .88 | .93 |
| Sociology | .55 | .84 | .94 |
| Gerontology | .37 | .88 | .96 |

3. Making one-tailed tests when they can be justified
4. Relaxing $\alpha$ (e.g., from .05 to .10)
5. Using the most efficient statistical tests (e.g., using a parametric test such as the *t*-test rather than the non-parametric median test (Section 13.14), or using an analysis of covariance rather than an analysis of variance design)
6. Increasing the reliability of the dependent variable[24]

## 12.17 NON-PARAMETRIC ALTERNATIVES: THE MANN-WHITNEY TEST AND THE WILCOXON SIGNED RANK TEST

The Mann-Whitney test evaluates the hypothesis that two *independent* groups have been drawn from the same population. In its derivation, no assumptions are made about the shape of the parent populations; there is no normality assumption. Scores from both samples are placed into a composite distribution, then ranked from the highest to the lowest scores to see if the ranks tend to be higher for one group. Most computer packages include a group of non-parametric programs which will include the Mann-Whitney. Special tables are required for hand-computation.[26] A generation ago, the Mann-Whitney was widely recommended as an alternative to the independent groups *t*-test when distributions were not normally distributed or when the two variances were not homogeneous.[27] Studies that dem-

[24]See Cleary and Linn, 1969; Hopkins and Hopkins, 1979; Rogers and Hopkins, 1988; Williams and Zimmerman, 1989; Humphreys and Drasgow, 1989.

[25]Adapted from Lipsey (1990, p. 23).

[26]See Conover (1980), Hollander and Wolfe (1971), and Siegel and Castellan (1988) for computational procedures and special tables.

[27]Contrary to a misconception popularized by Siegel's (1956) influential book, heterogeneous population variances distort the accuracy of its probability statements when the ratio of $n$'s differs substantially from 1 just as it does (see Figure 12.3) for the *t*-test (Zimmerman, 1987, 1992; Gibbons & Chakraborti, 1991).

onstrated the robustness of the $t$-test to violations of normality and homogeneity of variance (when $n_1 = n_2$) have contributed to the reduced use of the Mann-Whitney because it is somewhat less powerful. The Welch $t'$ performs well in situations for which the $t$-test and Mann-Whitney test are inappropriate (unequal $n$'s and unequal variances). In instances where there are extreme outliers (which have an inordinate influence on the accuracy of the $t$-test when samples are small), the Mann-Whitney is not the best procedure; the scores should be converted to ranks (as if the Mann-Whitney test were to be used), then (as suggested by Conover & Iman, 1981) employ the Welch $t'$ test.[28]

The Wilcoxon signed rank test is a close relative of the Mann-Whitney, and is designed for paired observations. The difference between each pair of observations is ranked to see if one group tends to have higher scores. Most computer packages include a group of nonparametric programs which will include the Wilcoxon test. Special tables are required for hand computation.[29] The principal utility of the Wilcoxon test is in instances where there are extreme outliers. The Wilcoxon test is then generally preferred to the $t$-test; although if the $t$-test is performed on ranks (as defined in the previous paragraph), the results will be very similar (Conover & Iman, 1981), except when $n$ is very small.

## 12.18 CHAPTER SUMMARY

The statistical hypothesis specifies a numerical value for some parameter; another name for this hypothesis is the null hypothesis—the hypothesis that the researcher intends to nullify. The typical null hypothesis holds that the value of some parameter is 0. The null hypothesis states that any difference in the two means is attributable to chance (sampling error). If the probability of observing a difference in means as large as that which was observed by chance is very small, that is, if $p < \alpha$, the $H_0$ is rejected and we conclude either that $\mu_1 > \mu_2$, if $\overline{X}_1 > \overline{X}_2$, or that $\mu_2 > \mu_1$, if $\overline{X}_2 > \overline{X}_1$.

The $t$-test is usually used to test the statistical hypothesis $H_0$: $\mu_1 - \mu_2 = 0$. The $t$-test allows one to determine the probability of observing a difference in means as large or larger than that which was observed when indeed the null hypothesis is true. There are three assumptions underlying the $t$-test: The observations in the two populations are characterized by normality, homogeneity of variance, and independence.

The $t$-test is robust to violating the assumption of normality. It is also robust to violating the assumption of homogeneity of variance when $n$'s are equal. If $n_1 > n_2$ and $\sigma_1^2 > \sigma_2^2$, the true $\alpha$ is less than the nominal alpha, "$\alpha$"; but if $n_2 > n_1$ and $\sigma_1^2 > \sigma_2^2$, the true $\alpha$ is greater than "$\alpha$." The independence assumption is important; violating this assumption can result in serious errors in the estimation of probabilities of type-I and type-II errors. Unfortunately, there is no simple way of evaluating whether the independence assumption is met. One type of nonindependence can be handled by the $t$-test for paired observations.

If the observations are matched or paired in some manner, the $t$-test for dependent observations should be used. Any positive correlation between the pairs of observations

---

[28]Another option that could be considered when there is a rational basis for assuming that the underlying variable (not necessarily the measures) is normally distributed, is to convert the ranks to normalized (Section 6.12) $T$-scores.

[29]See Conover (1980), Hollander and Wolfe (1971), and Siegel and Castellan (1988) for computational procedures and special tables.

reduces the value of the standard error of the difference in means, $s_{\overline{X}_1-\overline{X}_2}$. When the samples are independent, $\nu = n_1 + n_2 - 2$, but when the observations are in the form of $n$ pairs, $\nu = n - 1$. Care must be exercised in the interpretation of matched-pair studies since rarely are the groups truly equated on the matching variable. When the dependent variable is expressed in a metric that is arbitrary or lacks clear and precise meaning, the use of the effect size can be useful for conveying the magnitude of the difference in means. The effect size is the mean difference expressed in standard deviation units.

The Mann-Whitney and Wilcoxon signed rank tests are less powerful than the $t$ and Welch $t'$ tests, but can be useful if the distribution contains extreme outliers. Alternatively, if the scores are converted to ranks, the difference in the mean ranks can be assessed using parametric statistical methods such as the $t$-test or Welch $t'$ test.

## 12.19 CASE STUDY

The sample of 200 persons was divided into groups: those who had a coronary incident (coded "1") and those who did not have any coronary problem (coded "0") during the decade of the study. To offer some practice in the interpretation of $t$-tests, the two groups were compared on the seven variables that are available to us: age, SBP, DBP, cholesterol level, height, weight, and ratio of weight/height (each expressed as a $T$-score). The SPSS T-TEST procedure yielded the computer output below for the dependent variable, age. For the first dependent variable, the statistical notation and explanatory notes have been added using italics.

$t$-tests for independent samples of
CORON Coronary Incidence? 1 = YES, 0 = NO ←*Independent Variable*

| *Variable* | *Number of Cases (n)* | *Mean ($\overline{X}$)* | *SD (s)* | *SE of Mean ($s_{\overline{X}}$)* |
|---|---|---|---|---|
| AGE Age (yrs. at beginning) ←*Dependent Variable* | | | | |
| CORON = 1 | 25 | 50.7600 | 9.984 | 1.997 |
| CORON = 0 | 175 | 41.3886 | 11.420 | .863 |

$(\overline{X}_1 - \overline{X}_2)$→ Mean Difference = 9.3714

Levene's Test for Equality of Variances: $F = 1.256$, $p = .264$

[Levene's test evaluates the homogeneity of variance assumption:[30] $H_0$: $\sigma_1^2 = \sigma_1^2$; since $p > .10$, $\sigma_1^2 = \sigma_1^2$ is tenable. Hence, it is legitimate to use the conventional $t$ ("Equal") to test $H_0$: $\mu_1 = \mu_2$ and set the confidence interval. If $\sigma_1^2 = \sigma_1^2$ is not tenable ($p < .10 = \alpha$), the quasi (Welch) $t'$ test ("Unequal") must be used.]

[30]For testing the homogeneity of variance assumption, $H_0$: $\sigma_1^2 = \sigma_1^2$, $\alpha$ should be set at .10 or .20 to prevent the use of the conventional $t$-test when it will be too liberal or too conservative. Note that $t'$ will be more powerful (and give a smaller $p$-value) than $t$ when the larger $n$ and larger variance are paired, as occurs later for the dependent variable, *HT*. We prefer the $t'$ in all situations.

*t*-test for Equality of Means

| *Variances* | *t-value* | *df(ν)* | *2-Tail Sig(p)* | $s_{\bar{X}_1-\bar{X}_2}$ *SE of Diff* | *95% CI for* $\mu_1-\mu_0$ |
|---|---|---|---|---|---|
| Equal<br>↑*Conventional t-test* | 3.89 | 198 | .000 | 2.407 | (4.62, 14.12) |
| Unequal<br>↑*quasi t' test* | 4.31 | 33.65 | .000 | 2.176 | (4.95, 13.79) |

The Levene[31] test showed the homogeneity of variance assumption to be tenable ($p = .446$), therefore the conventional *t*-test ("Equal" = "equal variances") can be used. Notice the null hypothesis for age is rejected ($p < .001$)[32]; the mean age of those having a coronary incident was considerably higher than for those with no coronary difficulty (50.8 vs. 41.4). Since group 1 (coronary incident) is older than group 0, age will need to be controlled[33] to insure that the difference on any other variance is not due to the age difference.

The *t*-tests for the other six dependent variables follow:

| *Variable* | *Number of Cases* | *Mean* | *SD* | *SE of Mean* |
|---|---|---|---|---|
| SYSBP SYSTOLIC BP | | | | |
| CORON 1 | 25 | 130.1200 | 20.833 | 4.167 |
| CORON 0 | 175 | 120.4229 | 15.727 | 1.189 |

Mean Difference = 9.6971
Levene's Test for Equality of Variances: $F = 3.282$, $p = .042$

*t*-test for Equality of Means

| *Variances* | *t-value* | *df* | *2-Tail Sig* | *SE of Diff* | *95% CI for Diff* |
|---|---|---|---|---|---|
| Equal | 2.76 | 198 | .006 | 3.513 | (2.77, 16.63) |
| Unequal | 2.24 | 28.04 | .033 | 4.333 | (.82, 18.58) |

Because the homogeneity of variance[34] assumption was not tenable for SBP ($p = .042 < \alpha = .05$), the *t*'-test ("Unequal") must be used to test $H_0$: $\mu_1 = \mu_2$ and to set the confidence interval for $\mu_1 - \mu_2$. $H_0$: $\mu_1 = \mu_2$ is rejected at the .05 level ($p = .033$). The mean SBP of the "Coronary Incident" group (group 1) was significantly higher than the mean of the "nor-

---

[31]In spite of the f[illegible] that the Levene is the default test for homogeneity of variance on many statistical programs, it is not the b[illegible]t choice, as you will see in Chapter 16.

[32]Never report $p = .000$ (the ".000" on the output only means that $p < .0005$); since in any statistical test $p$ is never 0; use $p < .001$ for ".000" or $p < .0001$ if output shows ".0000".

[33]For example, using partial correlation (Section 8.13) or the analysis of covariance (ANCOVA, see Chapter 21).

[34]Previous versions of SPSS use different (and usually better) tests of homogeneity of variance; both are considered in Chapter 16.

mal" group—the mean difference (.95*CI*) being at least .82, and perhaps as much as 18.58 greater. What is the effect size?[35]

| *Variable* | *Number of Cases* | *Mean* | *SD* | *SE of Mean* |
|---|---|---|---|---|
| DIABP DIASTOLIC BP | | | | |
| CORON 1 | 25 | 86.1200 | 11.865 | 2.373 |
| CORON 0 | 175 | 80.9429 | 9.563 | .723 |

Mean Difference = 5.1771
Levene's Test for Equality of Variances: $F = 3.399$, $p = .067$

*t*-test for Equality of Means

| *Variances* | *t-value* | *df* | *2-Tail Sig* | *SE of Diff* | *95% CI for Diff* |
|---|---|---|---|---|---|
| Equal | 2.45 | 198 | .015 | 2.110 | (1.02, 9.34) |
| Unequal | 2.09 | 28.63 | .046 | 2.481 | (.10, 10.25) |

The "normal" group (group 0) also had a significantly lower ($p = .046$) DBP average than did the "coronary incident" group. The effect size for DBP, 86.12 – 80.94)/9.56 = 0.54, was similar to that found for the SBP variable, .54 vs. .62 "sigmas".

| *Variable* | *Number of Cases* | *Mean* | *SD* | *SE of Mean* |
|---|---|---|---|---|
| CHOLES Serum Cholesterol—Mg per DL | | | | |
| CORON 1 | 25 | 315.7200 | 76.120 | 15.224 |
| CORON 0 | 175 | 280.7371 | 62.330 | 4.712 |

Mean Difference = 34.9829
Levene's Test for Equality of Variances: $F = .819$, $p = .366$

*t*-test for Equality of Means

| *Variances* | *t-value* | *df* | *2-Tail Sig* | *SE of Diff* | *95% CI for Diff* |
|---|---|---|---|---|---|
| Equal | 2.55 | 198 | .012 | 13.718 | (7.93, 62.04) |
| Unequal | 2.20 | 28.78 | .036 | 15.936 | (2.38, 67.58) |

The mean cholesterol level of the "normal" group was significantly lower than for the "coronary incident" group. The effect size, 315.72 – 280.74)/62.33 = 0.56, is similar in magnitude to that for SBP and DBP. Of course, since the groups also differed considerably in age, at this point, we are not certain whether there remains any cholesterol level differ-

[35] $\hat{\Delta} = (130.12 - 120.42)/15.73 = 0.62$ standard deviations; use $s_1$, the standard deviation of the "normal" group, as $s_C$.

ence that cannot be explained by the age difference.[36] Set the .90 confidence interval for $\mu_1$ and for $\mu_2$, and the .95*CI* for $(\mu_1 - \mu_2)$. Note that $s_{\overline{X}_1}$ and $s_{\overline{X}_2}$ are included in the output.[37]

The two groups did not differ significantly in height ($p = .331$). The "normal" group did, however, weigh significantly less ($p = .044$; $\overline{X}_1 = 174$ lbs. vs. $\overline{X}_2 = 164$ lbs.

Notice that the seventh *t*-test uses the ratio of weight to height (using *T*-scores) as the dependent variable; in other words, it is a better measure of obesity than weight alone because it controls for stature. Notice that the null hypothesis can be rejected at the .01 level ($p = .008$) for this variable; whereas for weight alone, the findings were less significant ($p = .044$). The *T*-scores in weight for the CHD group averaged about 14% ($\overline{X} = 1.137$) higher than their *T*-scores in height, whereas the *T*-scores for the normals had almost identical averages ($\overline{X} = 1.009$).

| *Variable* | *Number of Cases* | *Mean* | *SD* | *SE of Mean* |
|---|---|---|---|---|
| HT Stature—inches | | | | |
| CORON 1 | 25 | 68.1200 | 1.922 | .384 |
| CORON 0 | 175 | 68.6400 | 2.567 | .194 |

Mean Difference = –.5200
Levene's Test for Equality of Variances: $F = 4.082$, $p = .045$

*t*-test for Equality of Means

| *Variances* | *t-value* | *df* | *2-Tail Sig* | *SE of Diff* | *95% CI for Diff* |
|---|---|---|---|---|---|
| Equal | –.97 | 198 | .331 | .534 | (–.53, 1.57) |
| Unequal | –1.21 | 37.45 | .235 | .431 | (–.35, 1.39) |

| *Variable* | *Number of Cases* | *Mean* | *SD* | *SE of Mean* |
|---|---|---|---|---|
| WT Body Weight—LBS | | | | |
| CORON 1 | 25 | 174.5600 | 25.295 | 5.059 |
| CORON 0 | 175 | 163.8514 | 24.666 | 1.865 |

[36]One factor ANCOVA is mathematically equivalent to partial correlation—they will yield identical *p*-values. The significant difference between the CORON groups found in the above *t*-test disappears when ANCOVA (covarying on age) is used (*p* drops from .012 to .273). Viewed from the perspective of correlation (Chapter 14), the significance of the point-biserial correlation of CORON (C) and Y (Cholesterol level), ($r_{YC} = .1783$, $p = .012$), drops to .0781 ($p = .273$) when age is partialed out ($r_{YC.A} = .0781$). Note also that the significance of the point biserial ($p = .012$) is identical to the significance of the *t*-test for the difference between the two means. In Chapter 21 ("Problems and Exercises"), we will use the same data and compare the two groups after they have been statistically equated (using ANCOVA) on age.

[37]For the "normal" group (Table C), ${}_{.95}t_{194} \approx 1.654$; hence, .90*CI* for $\mu_1 = 280.74 \pm (1.654)(4.712) = 280.74 \pm 7.79$ or (273.0, 288.5). For the "coronary incident" group, ${}_{.95}t_{24} = 1.711$, and .90*CI* for $\mu_2 = 315.72 \pm (1.711)(15.22) = 315.72 \pm 26.04$ or (289.7, 341.8). Based on the sample data, estimate how much $\mu_2$ exceeds $\mu_1$. The .95*CI* for $(\mu_2 - \mu_1)$ is $(\overline{X}_2 - \overline{X}_1) \pm {}_{.975}t_{198}s_{\overline{X}_1 - \overline{X}_2}$. Since $|t| = |\overline{X}_1 - \overline{X}_2|/s_{\overline{X}_1 - \overline{X}_2}$, thus $s_{\overline{X}_1 - \overline{X}_2} = |\overline{X}_1 - \overline{X}_2|/|t| = 34.98/2.55 = 13.72$. Therefore, $.95CI = 34.98 \pm (1.653)(13.73) = 34.94 \pm 22.70$ or (12.2, 57.6); the population mean of the "coronary incident" group is probably at least 12.2 units higher than $\mu_1$, and perhaps as much as 57.6—we can make this statement with 95% confidence.

Mean Difference = 10.7086
Levene's Test for Equality of Variances: $F = .060$, $p = .807$

*t*-test for Equality of Means

| *Variances* | *t-value* | *df* | *2-Tail Sig* | *SE of Diff* | *95% CI for Diff* |
|---|---|---|---|---|---|
| Equal | 2.02 | 198 | .044 | 5.290 | (.27, 21.14) |
| Unequal | 1.99 | 30.88 | .056 | 5.392 | (.29, 21.72) |

| *Variable* | *Number of Cases* | *Mean* | *SD* | *SE of Mean* |
|---|---|---|---|---|
| WTT_HTT Ratio: T(wt.)/T(ht.) | | | | |
| CORON 1 | 25 | 1.1374 | .239 | .048 |
| CORON 0 | 175 | 1.0094 | .222 | .017 |

Mean Difference = .1280
Levene's Test for Equality of Variances: $F = 1.056$, $p = .305$

*t*-test for Equality of Means

| *Variances* | *t-value* | *df* | *2-Tail Sig* | *SE of Diff* | *95% CI for Diff* |
|---|---|---|---|---|---|
| Equal | 2.67 | 198 | .008 | .048 | (.034, .22) |
| Unequal | 2.52 | 30.17 | .017 | .051 | (.024, .23) |

There is only one pair of variables, SBP and DBP, in which the paired *t*-test can be applied. Even though the results of the test are obvious beforehand (calling for a one-tailed test),[38] we will run the test just for fun. The SPSS output follows:

*t*-tests for paired samples

| *Variable* | *Number of pairs* | *2-tail Corr* | *Sig* | *Mean* | *SD* | *SE of Mean* |
|---|---|---|---|---|---|---|
| SYSBP SYSTOLIC BP | | | | 121.635 | 16.702 | 1.181 |
| | 200 | .802 | .000 ←*This tests H: $\rho = 0$ (Chapter 14).* | | | |
| DIABP DIASTOLIC BP | | | | 81.590 | 9.994 | .707 |

Paired Differences

| *Mean* | *SD* | *SE of Mean* | *t-value* | *df* | *2-tail Sig* |
|---|---|---|---|---|---|
| 40.045 | 10.533 | .745 | 53.77 | 199 | .000 |
| 95% *CI* (38.58, 41.51) | | | | | |

[38]A one-tailed test could also have been justified on the blood pressure and weight variables because it is implausible that the CHD population would have lower means on these variables.

The mean SBP (121.6) was significantly higher than the mean DBP (81.6)—note the extremely high value of $t$ (53.77); the critical value of $t$ at $\alpha_1 = .0005$ is 3.340, we are virtually certain that the observed difference is not the result of sampling error. As anticipated, the two variables were highly correlated ($r = .802$). The .95*CI* for the difference in the diastolic and systolic means is very close to 40, (38.6, 41.5).

## 12.20 SUGGESTED COMPUTER ACTIVITY

Using the HSB data set, compare the means for the private and public school students on all achievement areas and affective variables. Compare the results for $t$ and $t'$ tests. When is the use of the $t'$ essential for credibility of the findings?[39]

Using the EXERCISE data set compare the means of the males vs. females on pre-exercise pulse rate (PULSE_1). Also compare the smokers and non-smokers on PULSE_1. Why does the $t$ and $t'$ question not arise in these comparisons?[40] Create a new variable, PUL_GAIN, which is the difference in the post-exercise and pre-exercise pulse rates, and compare the smokers and non smokers on this variable. Compare the males and females on PUL_GAIN.

## MASTERY TEST

1. Which of the options are statistical hypotheses associated with testing for a *difference* in means?
   (a) $H_0$: $\mu = 100$ (b) $H_0$: $\mu_1 - \mu_2 = 0$ (c) $H_0$: $\bar{X}_1 - \bar{X}_2 = 0$
2. Are the two expressions $\mu_1 - \mu_2 = 0$ and $\mu_1 = \mu_2$ identical in meaning?
3. Can hypothesis (b) in question 1 be appropriately termed a null hypothesis?
4. If the pretest mean weight of 100 adults in a weight-loss program was compared to the posttest mean for the same 100 persons, would the two means be independent?
5. Which of these is *not* assumed for purposes of performing the $t$-test of differences between means of independent samples?
   (a) $X$'s normally distributed within both populations
   (b) $\sigma_1^2 = \sigma_2^2$
   (c) $n$ very large
6. When testing $H_0$: $\mu_1 = \mu_2$ and $n_1$ and $n_2$ are very small, the shape of the $t$-distribution is
   (a) normal (c) bimodal
   (b) rectangular (d) leptokurtic
7. If all assumptions are met, in which of these situations will the central $t$-distribution differ least from a normal distribution?
   (a) $n_1 = 10$, $n_2 = 10$
   (b) $n_1 = 50$, $n_2 = 20$
   (c) $n_1 = 20$, $n_2 = 20$
8. Is the central $t$-distribution for any value of degrees of freedom symmetric around 0?

[39] Since the $n$'s differ greatly in this situation, $t'$ *must* be used when $\sigma_1^2 = \sigma_2^2$ is not tenable.

[40] Because the $n$'s are equal, the $t$-test is accurate (robust) even with heterogeneous variance.

9. Which of these denotes an *estimate* of the standard error of the difference between two means?
   (a) $s_{\bar{X}_1-\bar{X}_2}$ (c) $s_{\bar{X}_1-\bar{X}_2}$
   (b) $s_{\bar{X}}$ (d) $s_{\bar{X}_1-\bar{X}_2}^2$
10. Does ${}_{.10}t_{60} = -{}_{.90}t_{60}$?
11. If $\nu = 60$, what is the critical value for $t$, with $\alpha_2 = .10$, $\alpha_2 = .05$, and $\alpha_2 = .01$? (Use Table C.)
12. The probability of a type-I error is least for which one of the following?
    (a) $\alpha_2 = .10$
    (b) $\alpha_2 = .05$
    (c) $\alpha_2 = .001$
    (d) $\alpha_2 = .01$
13. Other things being equal, the probability of a type-II error is least for which one of the following?
    (a) $\alpha_2 = .10$
    (b) $\alpha_2 = .05$
    (c) $\alpha_2 = .001$
14. With $\alpha = .05$, will the critical $t$-values decrease as $n$ increases?
15. With $\nu = 60$, $\alpha_2 = .05$, and $s_{\bar{X}_1-\bar{X}_2} = 2.0$, how large must $\bar{X}_1 - \bar{X}_2$ be before $H_0$ would be rejected?
16. If $s_1^2 = 50$ and $s_2^2 = 100$, when will the pooled variance estimate $s^2$ equal 75.0?
17. If $s_1^2 = 60$ and $s_2^2 = 40$, will the within groups variance estimate, $s_W^2$, equal 50 if $n_1 = n_2$?
18. Square the expression: $s\sqrt{\dfrac{1}{n_1} + \dfrac{1}{n_2}}$
19. If the observed $t$-ratio with $n_1 = 11$ and $n_2 = 11$ is 2.0, which of these are correct if $\alpha_2 = .05$?
    (a) pooled $\nu = 20 = \nu_1 + \nu_2$
    (b) critical $t$-value at $\alpha_2$ of $.05 = 2.09$
    (c) $p > .05$
    (d) $.10 > p > .05$
    (e) $p < .05$
    (f) $p < .10$
20. Does an increase in sample size decrease the probability of a type-I error?
21. For a fixed value of $\alpha$, does an increase in sample size decrease the probability of a type-II error?
22. Which of these are correct?
    (a) $E(s) < \sigma$
    (b) $E(s^2) = \sigma^2$
    (c) $E(s^2_{\bar{X}_1-\bar{X}_2}) = \sigma^2_{\bar{X}_1-\bar{X}_2}$
23. If $s = 8$ and $n = 10$, what is $\Sigma x^2$?
24. If $s^2_{\bar{X}_1-\bar{X}_2} = 1.0$ and $n_1 = n_2 = 10$, what is $s_W^2$?
25. If $n_1 = n_2 = n$, show that $s_{\bar{X}_1-\bar{X}_2} = \sqrt{2}\, s_{\bar{X}}$.
26. In question 25, how much more variable is the sampling distribution of mean *differences* ($\bar{X}_1 - \bar{X}_2$) than the sampling distribution of means? (Compare $s_{\bar{X}_1-\bar{X}_2}$ with $s_{\bar{X}}$.)
27. Which one of these is *not* a mathematical assumption underlying the $t$-test for independent means?
    (a) The $X$'s are normally distributed within each group.
    (b) $\sigma_1^2 = \sigma_2^2$
    (c) Each observation is independent of the other observations.
    (d) $n_1 = n_2$

**28.** If the null hypothesis is true, is it possible to make a type-II error?

**29.** If the null hypothesis is true, what is the most probable or expected value of $t$?

(a) $E(t) = 0$
(b) $E(t) = 1$

**30.** Suppose population variances are heterogeneous: $\sigma_1^2 = 300$, $\sigma_2^2 = 100$. In which of the following situations will the heterogeneous variance affect the researcher's conclusion regarding the null hypothesis? That is, in which situation must the investigator be concerned about the assumption that $\sigma_1^2 = \sigma_2^2$? ($H_0$: $\mu_1 = \mu_2$)

(a) $n_1 = n_2$ and $H_0$ is rejected
(b) $n_1 = n_2$ and $H_0$ is tenable
(c) $n_1 = 50$, $n_2 = 20$, and $H_0$ is rejected
(d) $n_1 = 50$, $n_2 = 20$, and $H_0$ is tenable
(e) $n_1 = 20$, $n_2 = 50$, and $H_0$ is rejected
(f) $n_1 = 20$, $n_2 = 50$, and $H_0$ is tenable

**31.** The assumptions of normality must be tested before interpreting the $t$-test in which of the situations below?

(a) $n_1 = 5$, $n_2 = 5$
(b) $n_1 = 10$, $n_2 = 50$

**32.** For testing $H_0$: $\mu_1 = \mu_2$, in which of these situations can the assumption of homogeneity of variance be safely ignored?

(a) $n_1 = n_2 = 10$
(b) $n_1 = 100$, $n_2 = 200$
(c) $n_1 = 5$, $n_2 = 15$
(d) $n_1 = 50$, $n_2 = 50$

**33.** Which of these statements have been demonstrated empirically for the $t$-test?

(a) It is robust with respect to the normality assumption.
(b) It is robust with respect to the homogeneity-of-variance assumption when $n$'s are equal.
(c) It is robust with respect to the independence assumption.

**34.** In Figure 12.2 with $n_1 = n_2 = 15$, both populations I and II were skewed. What was the correct probability of a type-I error (i.e., what was the actual $\alpha$) when "$\alpha$" = .05?

**35.** Using Figure 12.3, if $\sigma_1^2 = 10$, $\sigma_2^2 = 5$, $n_1 = 10$, and $n_2 = 50$, estimate the correct probability of a type-I error if "$\alpha$" = .05.

**36.** In which of these situations are the observations correlated?

(a) Strength is measured at ages ten and twelve for the same twenty-one children.
(b) At age five, the reading scores of fifty boys and fifty girls are compared.
(c) Pretest and posttest IQ scores are compared for the treated group.
(d) Forty students taking general psychology are randomly assigned to either treatment $A$ or $B$ and $H_0$: $\mu_A = \mu_B$ is tested.
(e) Delayed posttest achievement scores were compared with immediate posttest scores for all participants.
(f) Grade-equivalent scores in reading were compared with those in math for 100 bilingual students.

**37.** Suppose a researcher failed to recognize that the observations were positively correlated in example (a) of item 36, and the $t$-test for independent observations was used. How would the results differ with the results from the appropriate $t$-test for correlated observations? Answer true or false for the following.

(a) The value of $\overline{X}_1 - \overline{X}_2$ would differ.
(b) The researcher's value for $s_{\overline{X}_1 - \overline{X}_2}$ would be too large.
(c) The researcher's value for the $t$-ratio would be too small.

**38.** For $\alpha_2 = .05$, the researcher in question 37 probably uses a critical $t$-value of ____, whereas the appropriate critical $t$-value is ____.

**39.** Even though the correct analysis has a larger critical $t$-value, will the correct analysis have more power for rejecting $H_0$: $\mu_{10} = \mu_{12}$?

**40.** To answer which of the following questions does a one-tailed test appear justified. (More than one answer may be correct.)

(a) Does going to college result in a change in measured intelligence (IQ)?
(b) Do bright college students (high scores on college board exams) study more or less than not-so-bright college students?
(c) Do math majors score higher than English majors on the Quantitative Aptitude Test of the Graduate Record Examination?
(d) Does the reaction time at age seventy differ from reaction time at age forty?

**41.** Table 12.3 illustrates the direct-difference method of testing for differences between correlated means; hence, $r$ was not computed. Suppose you wish to know the value of $r$. Rearrange Equation 12.10 below so that only $r$ is to the left of the equals sign.

$$s^2_{\bar{X}_1-\bar{X}_2} = s^2_{\bar{X}_1} + s^2_{\bar{X}_2} - 2rs_{\bar{X}_1}s_{\bar{X}_2}$$

Hence, $r = ?$

**42.** If on the WAIS ($\sigma = 15$) $\bar{X}_E = 109$ and $\bar{X}_C = 100$, express the mean difference as an effect size.

## PROBLEMS AND EXERCISES

**1.** An experiment was conducted on the effects of "advance organizers" (introductory material that mentally organizes the material to be learned) on achievement in abstract mathematics. Fifty college students were randomly assigned to two groups: Twenty-five subjects in group 1 studied a 1,000-word essay on topology after having been exposed to an advance organizer on the subject; twenty-five subjects in group 2 read the same essay on topology after having read a 1,000-word historical sketch of Euler and Riemann, two famous mathematicians. At the end of the experimental period, each group was given an objective test on the topological concepts. The dependent variable $X$ was "number of correct answers." The following results were obtained:

| *Group 1 (Advance Organizer)* | *Group 2 (Historical Sketch)* |
|---|---|
| $n_1 = 25$ | $n_2 = 25$ |
| $\bar{X}_1 = 7.65$ | $\bar{X}_2 = 6.00$ |
| $s_1^2 = 6.50$ | $s_2^2 = 5.90$ |

(a) State $H_0$.
(b) What is the value of $s_W^2$, the pooled within groups variance estimate?
(c) Compute $s_{\bar{X}_1-\bar{X}_2}$.
(d) Compute $t$.
(e) What is the critical $t$-value if $\alpha_2 = .05$?
(f) Is $H_0$ rejected?
(g) Conclusion:
(h) Give the .90 CI for $\mu_1 - \mu_2$.
(i) Express the mean difference as an effect size (use $s_W$ from part b for the standard deviation).

**2.** In a test of reading achievement in a statewide assessment program, fourteen reading items were included that had been previously administered to a national sample of students. The state and national percentages of students who correctly answered each of the fourteen items are given. Use the direct-difference $t$-test for correlated observations to determine whether $H_0$: $\mu_S = \mu_N$ is tenable with $\alpha_2 = .05$.

*Percentage Correct*

| *Item* | *State* $X_S$ | *Nation* $X_N$ | $X_S - X_N = X_d$ |
|---|---|---|---|
| 1 | 83 % | 83 % | 0 |
| 2 | 81 | 76 | 5 |
| 3 | 75 | 76 | –1 |
| 4 | 76 | 82 | –6 |
| 5 | 40 | 35 | 5 |
| 6 | 76 | 74 | 2 |
| 7 | 78 | 68 | 10 |
| 8 | 27 | 27 | 0 |
| 9 | 60 | 66 | –6 |
| 10 | 67 | 67 | 0 |
| 11 | 66 | 64 | 2 |
| 12 | 67 | 62 | 5 |
| 13 | 92 | 91 | 1 |
| 14 | 73 | 63 | 10 |
| | $\Sigma X_S = 961$ | $\Sigma X_N = 934$ | $\Sigma X_d = 27$ |
| | $\bar{X}_S = 68.64\%$ | $\bar{X}_N = 66.71\%$ | $\bar{X}_d = 1.93\%$ |

(a) $s^2_{X_d} = ?$ (c) $t = ?$

(b) $s^2_{\bar{X}_d} = ?$ (d) Is $H_0$ rejected?

(e) .95 $CI$ for $\mu_d = ?$

(f) Is the statistical unit persons or items?

(g) Which of these interpretations of the .95 confidence interval is correct in this example?

(i) If these fourteen items had been administered to *all students* in both populations, we have .95 confidence that the value of $\mu_d$ falls between –.86% and +4.72%.

(ii) If a huge number of reading *items* like these fourteen were administered to these same samples, we have .95 confidence that the state average $\mu_S$ would be not less than –.86% below the national average $\mu_N$ nor more than 4.72% above $\mu_N$.

**3.** Suppose we wish to know whether a certain method of diet control has long-term efficacy for reducing weight. Ten adults were weighed ("pretested") prior to receiving a prescribed treatment and then were reweighed ("posttested") one year later.

The pretest weight was subtracted from the posttest weight to obtain a "change" score ($X_i = X_{Pre_i} - X_{Post_i}$) for each person. The mean and standard deviation of this distribution of change scores were: $\bar{X}_d = 3.11$ and $s_{X_d} = 5.62$.

(a) Is $H_0$: $\mu = 0$ tenable at $\alpha_2 = .10$?

(b) Give the .90 $CI$ for $\mu$.

**4.** In a remedial reading study, the 125 students who scored more than 2.0 grade equivalents below their current grade level participated in a remedial reading program. The pupils were retested after eight months in the program. The results are given.

| *Pretest* | | *Posttest* |
|---|---|---|
| $\overline{X}_{Pre} = 4.5$ | | $\overline{X}_{Post} = 5.9$ |
| $s_{Pre} = 1.8$ | | $s_{Post} = 1.9$ |
| $s_{\overline{X}_{Pre}} = .16$ | | $s_{\overline{X}_{Post}} = .17$ |
| | $r = .8$ | |

(a) Is a one-tailed test justified? What is the critical $t$ for $\alpha_1 = .01$?
(b) Did the mean increase significantly?
(c) Could $H_0$: $\mu_{Pre} = \mu_{Post}$ be rejected with $\alpha_1 = .001$?
(d) Was the gain in means greater than .8 grade equivalents—that is, can $H_0$: $\mu_{Post} - \mu_{Pre} = .8$ be rejected at $\alpha_1 = .0005$?
(e) Do these results prove the remedial reading program was very effective?

**5.** The effect of an all-day ($E$) versus the conventional ($C$) half-day kindergarten on subsequent reading performance was evaluated by comparing mean scores of the forty-one $E$ students and the thirty-five $C$ students on a standardized reading test administered at the end of grade two (De Rosia, 1980). The results are given:

| | $E$ | $C$ |
|---|---|---|
| $\overline{X}_j$ | 64.53 | 63.56 |
| $s_j$ | 11.1 | 10.4 |
| $n_j$ | 41 | 35 |

(a) Perform a $t$-test to evaluate $H_0$: $\mu_E = \mu_C$ at $\alpha_2 = .10$.
(b) Set .90 *CI* for $\mu_E - \mu_C$.
(c) Estimate the effect size $\hat{\Delta}$.
(d) Does the study prove there was absolutely no differential efficacy?

**6.** The authors surveyed an introductory statistics course and asked students to rate (anonymously) how well they liked statistics. The results for the twelve males were: $\overline{X}_M = 5.25$ and $s_M^2 = 6.57$; for the thirty-one females: $\overline{X}_F = 4.37$ and $s_F^2 = 7.55$.

(a) Is there a statistically significant ($\alpha_2 = .10$) difference in means?
(b) Set a .90 *CI* about *each mean* (not about the difference in means).
(c) Express the difference in means as an effect size $\hat{\Delta}$, (use $s_W$ for the denominator).
(d) If $s_M^2$, $s_F^2$, $\overline{X}_M$, and $\overline{X}_F$ remained constant but the sample was quadrupled, would $H_0$ have remained tenable? Compare this $t$ with that in part (a).

**7.** In a study of the effects of special curricular study of Mexican culture on students' stereotypes of Mexican Americans, two-thirds of the students were randomly assigned to the experimental ($E$) and one-third to the control ($C$) group (Schon, Hopkins, & Vojir, 1982). All students responded anonymously to a posttest attitude inventory.

(a) For the following posttest scores, test $H_0$: $\mu_E = \mu_C$ at $\alpha_2 = .10$.

| | $E$ | $C$ |
|---|---|---|
| $\overline{X}_j$ | 53.25 | 54.42 |
| $s_i^2$ | 129.0 | 70.0 |
| $n_j$ | 59 | 31 |

(b) Contrast the posttest mean of the Mexican American ($M$) students with that of the Anglo ($A$) students. Using $\alpha_2 = .05$, and give the .95 *CI* for $\mu_M - \mu_A$.

| | $M$ | $A$ |
|---|---|---|
| $\overline{X}_j$ | 59.19 | 51.22 |
| $s_j^2$ | 53.2 | 112.4 |
| $n_j$ | 27 | 63 |

(c) A change score was obtained for each student by subtracting the posttest score from a pretest score. Statistics for these change scores are given. (i) Did the $E$ group change significantly? (ii) With $\alpha_2 = .05$, did the $E$ group change significantly more (or less) than the $C$ group? (Note that the change scores are independent.)

*Change Scores*

| | $E$ | $C$ |
|---|---|---|
| $\overline{X}_j$ | 1.73 | 1.93 |
| $s_j$ | 8.10 | 5.44 |
| $n_j$ | 59 | 31 |

8. Show that when $n_1 = n_2$, the standard error of the difference between two independent means $s_{\overline{X}_1-\overline{X}_2}$ (Equation 12.4) is equivalent to $\sqrt{s^2_{\overline{X}_1} + s^2_{\overline{X}_2}}$.
9. In Figure 8.1 (Section 8.2), the heights of 192 pairs of fathers ($X_1$) and sons ($X_2$) are given. Are people getting taller—is the difference in the means of the two generations greater than would be expected from sampling error—is the null hypothesis tenable?
   $\overline{X}_1 = 67.68$, $s_1 = 2.50$, $\overline{X}_2 = 68.44$, $s_2 = 2.33$, and $r = .56$.
   Compare the value of $s_{\overline{X}_1-\overline{X}_1}$ with what its value would have been if the two samples had been independent, and state the resulting consequences on power.

## ANSWERS TO MASTERY TEST

1. (b)
2. yes
3. yes
4. no
5. (c)
6. (d)
7. (b) ($\nu = 68$)
8. yes
9. (a)
10. yes
11. 1.67, 2.00, 2.66
12. (c)
13. (a)
14. yes
15. If $|\overline{X}_1 - \overline{X}_2| \geq 4.0$, $|t| \geq 2.00$, and $H_0$ is rejected.
16. When $n_1 = n_2$
17. yes
18. $s^2\left(\frac{1}{n_1} + \frac{1}{n_2}\right)$
19. (a), (b), (c), (d), (f)
20. no
21. yes
22. All are correct (see Section 5.13).
23. Since $s^2 = (8)^2 = 64$, $\Sigma x^2 = 9(64) = 576$.
24. $s^2_{\overline{X}_1-\overline{X}_2} = s^2_W\left(\frac{1}{n_1} + \frac{1}{n_2}\right)$;

    $$s^2_W = \frac{s^2_{\overline{X}_1-\overline{X}_2}}{\frac{1}{n_1} + \frac{1}{n_2}} = \frac{1.0}{\frac{1}{10} + \frac{1}{10}} = \frac{1.0}{.2} = 5.0$$
25. $$s_{\overline{X}_1-\overline{X}_2} = s\sqrt{\frac{1}{n} + \frac{1}{n}} = s\sqrt{\frac{2}{n}} = s\frac{\sqrt{2}}{\sqrt{n}}$$
    $$= \frac{\sqrt{2}s}{\sqrt{n}} = \sqrt{2}s_{\overline{X}}$$

**26.** Since $s_{\overline{X}_1-\overline{X}_2} = 1.414 s_{\overline{X}}$, $s_{\overline{X}_1-\overline{X}_2}$ is 41% larger than $s_{\overline{X}}$.
**27.** (d)
**28.** no
**29.** (a)
**30.** (d) and (e)
**31.** Neither (a) nor (b)
**32.** (a) and (d)
**33.** (a) and (b)
**34.** Actual $\alpha = .04$.
**35.** Actual $\alpha = .12$.
**36.** (a), (c), (e), (f)
**37.** (a) false
(b) true
(c) true
**38.** $_{.975}t_{40} = 2.02$, whereas $_{.975}t_{20} = 2.09$.
**39.** Yes, some positive correlation between the measurements at ages ten and twelve will reduce the value of $s_{\overline{X}_{10}-\overline{X}_{12}}$, and hence will yield a larger $t$-ratio for the same difference in means.
**40.** (a), (c), (d)
**41.** Add: $2rs_{\overline{X}_1}s_{\overline{X}_2}$ to both sides:

$$s^2_{\overline{X}_1-\overline{X}_2} + 2rs_{\overline{X}_1}s_{\overline{X}_2} = s^2_{\overline{X}_1} + s^2_{\overline{X}_2}.$$

Subtract $s^2_{\overline{X}_1-\overline{X}_2}$ from both sides:

$$2rs_{\overline{X}_1}s_{\overline{X}_2} = s^2_{\overline{X}_1} + s^2_{\overline{X}_2} - s^2_{\overline{X}_1-\overline{X}_2}.$$

Divide by $2s_{\overline{X}_1}s_{\overline{X}_2}$:

$$r = \frac{s^2_{\overline{X}_1} + s^2_{\overline{X}_2} - s^2_{\overline{X}_1-\overline{X}_2}}{2s_{\overline{X}_1}s_{\overline{X}_2}}$$

**42.** $\hat{\Delta} = \dfrac{(\overline{X}_E - \overline{X}_C)}{\sigma} = \dfrac{9}{15} = .6$, or $.6\sigma$.

## ANSWERS TO PROBLEMS AND EXERCISES

**1.** (a) $H_0\colon \mu_1 - \mu_2 = 0$
(b) $s_W{}^2 = 6.20$;
(c) $s_{\overline{X}_1-\overline{X}_2} = 2.49\sqrt{\dfrac{1}{25}+\dfrac{1}{25}}$
$= 2.49(.283) = .704$
(d) $t = \dfrac{7.65-6.00}{.704} = 2.34$
(e) $\nu = n_1 + n_2 - 2 = 48$; $_{.975}t_{40} = 2.021$. (The precise critical $t$-value would fall between $_{.975}t_{40} = 2.021$ and $_{.975}t_{50} = 2.008$: we use the closest, but smaller, $\nu$-value.)
(f) yes
(g) $\mu_1 > \mu_2$; the advance organizer appears to have facilitated achievement.
(h) $.90\ CI = 1.65 \pm 1.68(.704)$
$= 1.65 \pm 1.18$
or (.47, 2.83)
(i) $\hat{\Delta} = 1.65/2.49 = .66$

**2.** (a) $s^2_{X_d} = \dfrac{\Sigma x_d^2}{n-1}$;

$$\Sigma x_d^2 = \Sigma X_d^2 - n\overline{X}_d^2$$
$$= 304.9$$
$$s^2_{X_d} = \frac{\Sigma x_d^2}{n-1} = \frac{304.9}{13} = 23.5$$

(b) $s^2_{\overline{X}_d} = \dfrac{s^2_{X_d}}{n} = \dfrac{23.5}{14} = 1.68$,
$s_{\overline{X}_d} = 1.29$
(c) $t = \dfrac{\overline{X}_d}{s_{\overline{X}_d}} = \dfrac{1.93}{1.29} = 1.50$
(d) no: $t = 1.50 < 2.16 = {}_{.975}t_{13}$
(e) $.95\ CI = \overline{X}_d \pm ({}_{.975}t_{13})(s_{\overline{X}_d}) =$
$1.93 \pm (2.16)(1.29) = 1.93 \pm 2.79$ or $-.86\%$ to $4.72\%$
(f) items
(g) ii

**3.** (a) $s_{\overline{X}} = 5.62/\sqrt{10} = 1.78$;
$t = 3.11/1.78 = 1.75$;
$H_0$ is tenable.
(b) $3.11 \pm 1.83(1.78)$
$3.11 \pm 3.26$
$(-.15, 6.37)$

**4.** (a) yes: $_{.99}t_{124} \approx 2.36$.
(b) yes,

$$t = \frac{5.9-4.5}{\sqrt{(.16)^2 + (.17)^2 - 2(.8)(.16)(.17)}}$$
$$= \frac{1.4}{.105} = 13.3,\ p < .0005.$$

(c) yes

(d) $t = \dfrac{(\overline{X}_{\text{Post}} - \overline{X}_{\text{Pre}}) - (\mu_{\text{Post}} - \mu_{\text{Pre}})}{s_{\overline{X}_{\text{Post}} - \overline{X}_{\text{Pre}}}}$

$= \dfrac{(1.4) - (.8)}{.105} = \dfrac{.6}{.105} = 5.71$

Yes: $H_0$ rejected at .0005 level; the increase in scores is significantly greater than .8 grade equivalent.

(e) No, the posttest scores are influenced by the regression effect. The fact that $H_0$ can be confidently rejected only indicates that something more than *chance* is influencing the scores. In other words, a significance test never *explicates* the *cause* for the difference, but only indicates that the difference is greater than can be reasonably attributed to chance (sampling error). It is the design of the study that allows the researcher to specify causes. (This same example was used in Chapter 8's Problems and Exercises question 3 in which the significant increase in posttest scores was attributable to regression.)

**5.** (a) $s_W^2 = 116.3$, $s_W = 10.78$

$s_{\overline{X}_E - \overline{X}_C} = 10.78\sqrt{\left(\dfrac{1}{41} + \dfrac{1}{35}\right)} = 2.48$

$t = .97/2.48 = .39$, $H_0$ is tenable.

(b) .90 $CI = .97 \pm (1.67)(2.48) =$ (–3,17, 5.11)

(c) $\hat{\Delta} = .09$

(d) No, failure to reject $H_0$ does not prove $H_0$ to be true.

**6.** (a) $t = .96$ (or –.96), $H_0$ is tenable.

(b) .90 CI for $\mu_M$:
$5.25 \pm (1.80)(.740) = (3.92, 6.58)$
.90 CI for $\mu_F$:
$4.37 \pm (1.70)(.494) = (3.53, 5.21)$

(c) $.88/2.70 = .33$

(d) $t = 1.93$, ${}_{.90}t_{174} = 1.65$; reject $H_0$ at .10; $t$ is doubled.

**7.** (a) $s_W = 10.44$, $s_{\overline{X}_E - \overline{X}_C} =$

$10.44\sqrt{\dfrac{1}{59} + \dfrac{1}{31}} = 2.31$; $t = -.51$,

$H_0$ is tenable.

(b) $s_W = 9.74$, $s_{\overline{X}_M - \overline{X}_A} = 2.24$; $t = 3.56$, reject $H_0$ at .001; .95 $CI$: (3.52, 12.42)

(c) No, $t = 1.73/1.05 = 1.64$, $p > .05$; no, $t = -.12$.

**8.** When $n_1 = n_2 = n$,

$$s_{\overline{X}_1 - \overline{X}_2} = \sqrt{\frac{\Sigma x_1^2 + \Sigma x_2^2}{2(n-1)}\left(\frac{2}{n}\right)}$$

$$= \sqrt{\left(\frac{\Sigma x_1^2}{n-1} + \frac{\Sigma x_2^2}{n-1}\right)\left(\frac{1}{n}\right)}$$

$$= \sqrt{\frac{s_1^2}{n} + \frac{s_2^2}{n}}$$

$$= \sqrt{s_{\overline{X}_1}^2 + s_{\overline{X}_2}^2}$$

**9.** Yes: $t = -4.65$, $H_0$ is rejected, $p < .001$. If the two samples were independently drawn from their respective populations, other things being equal, the value of $s_{\overline{X}_1 - \overline{X}_2}$ would not have been .164 (as it actually is), but .247. Thus, the value of $s_{\overline{X}_1 - \overline{X}_2}$ would have been 50.6% greater, which would have reduced the observed $t$-ratio to 3.08. This illustrates the fact that the paired $t$-test usually has greater statistical power than the independent $t$-test.

# 13

# STATISTICS FOR CATEGORICAL DEPENDENT VARIABLES
## Inferences about Proportions

## 13.1 OVERVIEW

Many research questions in education and the social sciences deal with proportions or percentages. For example, do the proportions of psychotic disorders, suicides, peptic ulcers, illiterates, unemployed, and so on differ among cultures? In previous chapters, hypotheses about means were considered. Now attention is focused on methods of inference for testing hypotheses about proportions. Proportions are especially common when groups are compared on a categorical or nominal (Section 2.3) variable. Notice that each of the following questions implies a hypothesis regarding a categorical variable.

On true-false tests, is the proportion of correct answers that are keyed "true" equal to .5? Does the suicide rate differ among social classes? Is drug use associated with religious beliefs? Does the school dropout rate differ among various ethnic groups?

## 13.2 THE PROPORTION AS A MEAN

Within the sample of $n$ observed units, designate the number who possess the characteristic in question as $n_i$. The sample proportion $p$ is the ratio of $n_i$ to $n$:

$$p = \frac{n_i}{n}$$

The statistic $p$ is an estimator of the parameter $\pi$.[1] In fact, if one thinks of a dichotomous variable $X$ that equals "1" when the characteristic of interest is present, and "0" when

---

[1]We will use the symbol $\pi$ (the Greek lowercase letter, "pi") to denote the proportion in the population that falls in a given category. The parameter $\pi$ is estimated by the corresponding proportion $p$ in the sample. The symbol $\pi$ should not be confused with its use in geometry where it is the ratio of the circumference to the diameter of a circle and has the value of about 3.14. Use of the $\pi$ and $p$ symbols is consistent with the use of Greek letters for parameters and Roman letters for sample estimates.

it is not present, then $p$ is to $\pi$ as $\overline{X}$ is to $\mu$. For example, suppose that "male gender" is the characteristic being measured. A person's "score," is denoted by $X_i$, and set $X_i = 1$ if the person is male and 0 if female. If in a sample of $n$ persons there are $n_i$ males (persons coded as 1's), then the frequency of males is:

$$\sum_i X_i = X_1 + X_2 + \ldots + X_n, \text{ and}$$

$$\overline{X} = \frac{\sum_i X_i}{n} = \frac{n_i}{n} = p \quad \textbf{(13.1)}$$

The population mean of the variable is $\pi$. Thus, $p$ is a mean of the dichotomous variable in the sample, and has all of the properties of a sample mean ($\overline{X}$), i.e., $E(p) = \pi$, in the same way that $E(\overline{X}) = \mu$. It can be said that the sampling distribution of $p$ will become normal as $n$ increases, as described by the central limit theorem (Section 10.15).

## 13.3 THE VARIANCE OF A PROPORTION

$$\sigma^2 = \sum_i \frac{(X_i - \mu)^2}{N} = \sum_i \frac{(X_i - \pi)^2}{N}$$

which is mathematically equal[2] to:

$$\sigma^2 = \pi(1 - \pi) \quad \textbf{(13.2)}$$

where $\pi$ is the proportion in the population in the category scored as "1." Thus, the standard deviation of a dichotomous variable is:

$$\sigma = \sqrt{\pi(1 - \pi)} \quad \textbf{(13.3)}$$

Since the frequency distribution of a dichotomous variable is in sharp contrast to the normal distribution (every observation is at one extreme or the other), the standard deviation cannot be used descriptively like it can when the distribution is normal. It is, however, a stepping stone on the way to finding the standard deviation of the sampling distribution of $p$—the standard error of $p$.

---

[2]*Proof:* If in the population of observations, $X_1, X_2, \ldots, X_N$, the proportion of 1's is $\pi$ and the proportion of 0's is $1 - \pi$:

$$\sigma^2 = \frac{1}{N}\sum_{i=1}^{N}(X_i - \pi)^2 = \frac{1}{N}\left[N\pi(1-\pi)^2 + N(1-\pi)(-\pi)^2\right]$$
$$= \pi(1-\pi)^2 + (1-\pi)(-\pi)^2 = \pi(1-\pi)$$

## 13.4 THE SAMPLING DISTRIBUTION OF A PROPORTION: THE STANDARD ERROR OF *p*

The central limit theorem states that whatever the shape of the frequency distribution—even if it is bimodal, dichotomous, or some other configuration—the sampling distribution of the mean (in this case, $p$) will approach the normal distribution as $n$ increases (as illustrated in Figure 10.3).

Suppose you randomly selected a sample of 100 persons from a defined population (e.g., a large university) and found the proportion $p$ who carried a certain gene (or the HIV virus, or some other characteristic). Now suppose you replicate the study many, many times, each time selecting a new random sample of 100 persons. The distribution of these many values of $p$ will be essentially normal, with a mean[3] $\approx \pi$. The standard deviation of this sampling distribution is termed the *standard error of the proportion.*

How much would the sample proportions, $p_i$'s, in the many random samples of $n = 100$ persons differ from the parameter, $\pi$ (the proportion in the entire population of $N$ persons)? The variance error of a proportion (i.e., the variance of the $p_i$-values) is given in Equation 13.4:[4]

$$\sigma_p^2 = \frac{\sigma^2}{n} = \frac{\pi(1-\pi)}{n} \tag{13.4A}$$

$$\hat{\sigma}_p^2 = \frac{\hat{\sigma}^2}{n} = \frac{p(1-p)}{n} \tag{13.4B}$$

The standard error of the proportion (i.e., the standard deviation of the $p_i$-values) is given by Equation 13.5.

$$\sigma_p = \frac{\sigma}{\sqrt{n}} = \sqrt{\frac{\pi(1-\pi)}{n}} \tag{13.5A}$$

$$\hat{\sigma}_p = \sqrt{\frac{p(1-p)}{n}} \tag{13.5B}$$

Suppose that in this population $\pi = .50$. The students' $p$-values will be approximately normal, with a mean of .50, and a standard deviation (from Equation 13.5A) of $\sqrt{(.50)(.50)/100} = .05$. In other words, when $n = 100$, about two-thirds (68%) of the $p$'s

[3]If we had an infinite number of students replicating the study, the mean of the $p$'s would precisely equal $\pi$.

[4]More precisely, $\sigma_p^2 = (1 - n/N)\,\pi(1 - \pi)/n$; but in most statistical applications $N$ is viewed as infinitely large, such that $(1 - n/N) \approx 1$ and drops out, leaving Equation 13.4. Occasionally in survey research, however, $N$ is a known finite value and the sampling fraction, $n/N$, can be used to gain some precision. If $n/N$ is small (e.g., .05 or less), the inclusion of the sampling fraction factor in the formula has only a trivial effect on the standard error. See Section 10.3 for additional discussion of finite population models.

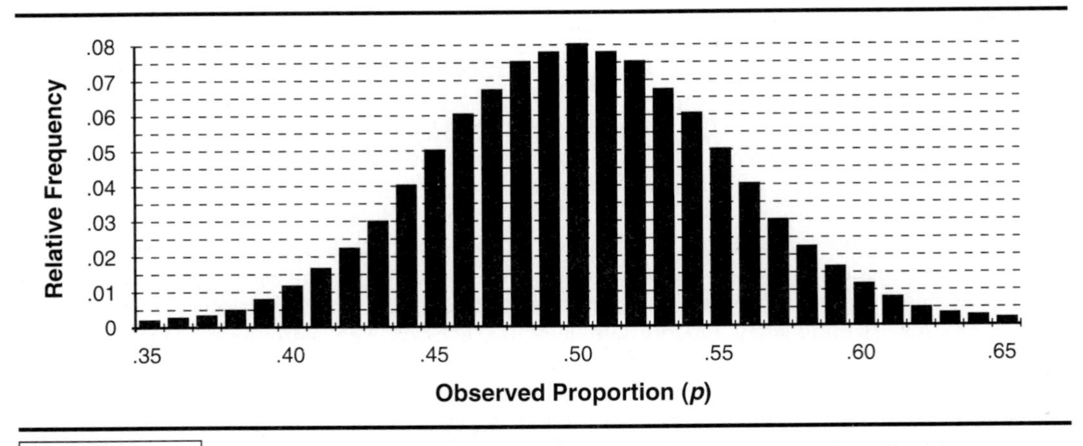


**FIGURE 13.1** Sampling Distribution of the Proportion ($p$) in Random Samples when the Proportion in the Population ($\pi$) is .50 ($n = 100$).

from random samples differ from $\pi = .50$ by .05 or less ($\pi \pm \sigma_p = .50 \pm .05$, or between .45 and .55); about 95% of the $p$'s would fall between .40 and .60 ($\pi \pm 2\sigma_p$).[5] The sampling distribution of $p$ when $\pi = .50$ and $n = 100$ appears in Figure 13.1.

Of course, in the real world of research, there will not be many studies estimating $\pi$, but only one. That study will yield a single value for $p$—the value from the random sample of 100 persons. This $p$-value is just one of the infinite number of observations in the sampling distribution. What is the probability that the value $p$ will be in error by .10 or more when $\pi = .5$? Less than 5% of $p$'s differ from $\pi$ by as much as .10. In other words, if a band of width $\pm 2\sigma_p$ were placed about each value of $p$ in the sampling distribution, approximately 95% of such intervals would include the parameter $\pi$ (which, in this example, is .50). Stated differently, approximately 95% of the .95 confidence intervals will achieve their objective and "capture" the parameter $\pi$.

## 13.5 THE INFLUENCE OF $n$ ON $\sigma_p$

What if $n = 400$ instead of 100? The standard error of $p$ (Equation 13.5A) is then $\sigma_p = \sqrt{(.50)(.50)/400} = .025$. In other words, when the sampling distribution is approximately normal (see Figure 13.4), about 68% of the sample $p$'s will be within .025 ($\pm\sigma_p$) of the parameter $\pi$, and the $.95CI \approx p \pm 2\sigma_p$. How large a sample size is needed to reduce the value of $\sigma_p$ to .0125? By studying Equation 13.5A and Figure 13.2, it should be evident that a fourfold increase in $n$ will reduce the value of $\sigma_p$ by one-half; thus, if $\pi = .50$, and $n = 1600$,

[5]These proportions assume that the sampling distribution is continuous, which is true if $n$ is large. As shown in Figure 13.1, when $n = 100$, the sampling distribution of $p$ is not continuous, but discrete—the distribution changes are not perfectly smooth, but are in discrete units. Nevertheless, the error in the probability statements is of little practical consequence unless $n$ is small. If the exact sampling distribution of a proportion is desired, the binomial distribution (Section 9.10) can be used for any combination of $\pi$ and $n$.

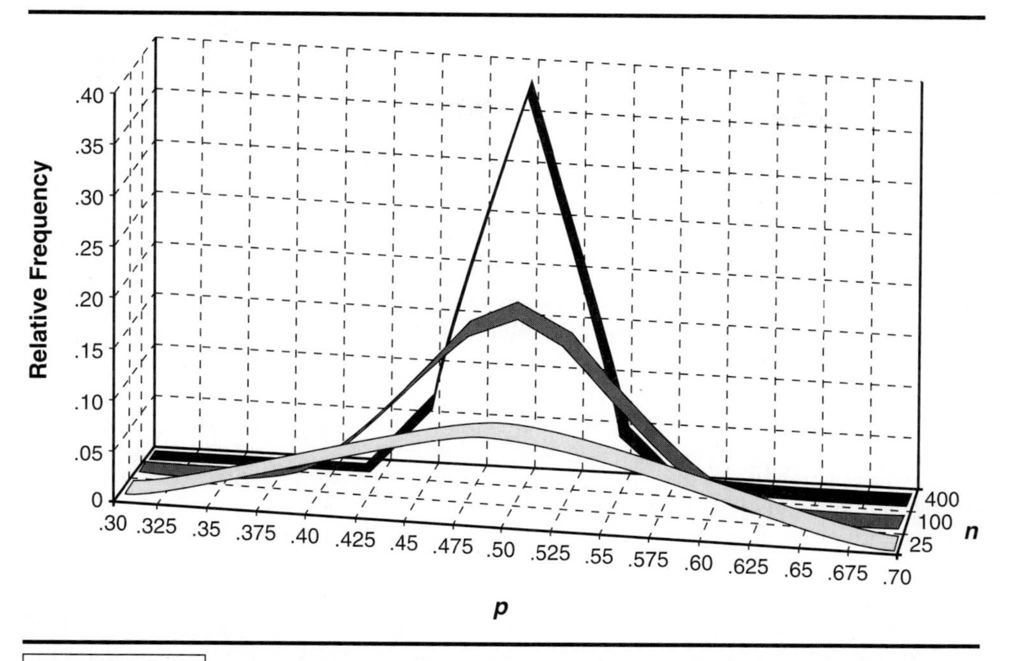


**FIGURE 13.2** Sampling Distributions of $p$ for Sample Sizes ($n$) of 25, 100, and 400 when the Population Proportion ($\pi$) is .50; Standard Errors are .10, .05, and .025, respectively.

$\sigma_p \approx .0125$. Figure 13.2 gives the sampling distributions of $p$ with $n = 25$, 100, and 400 with $\pi = .50$; the standard deviations ($\sigma_p$) of these three distributions are .10, .05, and .025, respectively.

Note that when $\pi = .50$, one $p$ in six will be .40 or less with $n = 25$; but with $n = 100$, only 2% of the random samples will yield a $p$-value $\leq .40$. With a sample size of 400, .40 is four standard errors below the mean and only one $p$ in more than 30,000 would be less than .40 (from Table A, .000032 for $z = -4.00$).

## 13.6 INFLUENCE OF THE SAMPLING FRACTION ON $\sigma_P$

How is the value of $\sigma_p$ influenced by the sampling fraction (Equation 13.6)—the proportion of the population that is sampled?

$$f = \frac{n}{N} \quad \textbf{(13.6)}$$

Equations 13.4A–B and 13.5A–B assume that there is an infinite population, thus $f = 0$. Equation 13.7 gives the standard error of the proportion when $f > 0$:

$$\sigma_p = \sqrt{\frac{(1-f)\pi(1-\pi)}{n}} \quad \textbf{(13.7)}$$

Notice that the value of $\sigma_p$ when $f > 0$ is $\sqrt{(1-f)}$ times the value yielded by Equation 13.5A. If $f = .01$, the value of $\sigma_p$ yielded by Equation 13.7 is $\sqrt{.99} = .995$ or 99.5% of the value yielded assuming $f = 0$ (Equation 13.5A). If 5% of the population is sampled, $\sigma_p$ from Equation 13.7 is 97.5% as large as when the sampling fraction is 0. It seems paradoxical, but it is true, that the accuracy of a sample estimate primarily depends on the size of the sample and almost not at all on the proportion of the population that is sampled. One thousand cases, drawn randomly, gives an estimate of 50 million voters' preferences that is almost as accurate as 1,000 cases drawn randomly from a city of 100,000 voters.[6] Television ratings and voter preferences can be estimated quite accurately for the nation from an infinitesimally small proportion of the population of viewers or voters, if the sample is selected randomly.[7] Intuitively, it might seem that if the size of the population is extremely large, then the sample required to achieve a specified degree of accuracy would need to be larger than if the population is not as large. However, differences in the sampling fraction, $n/N$, have little practical consequence unless the sample is composed of 5% or more of the population. In practice, $N$ is almost always assumed to be infinitely large. In survey research, however, there are some situations in which the sampling fraction is large enough that it should be taken into account to provide narrower and more precise confidence intervals. For example, if a random sample of 25% of the school superintendents in a given state is selected and they are interviewed and asked if they favor some proposal (e.g., the voucher plan, merit pay, etc.), and if the researcher uses Equation 13.5A rather than Equation 13.7, the confidence interval for $\pi$ will be conservative, and more than 15% too wide ($1/\sqrt{.75} = 1.155$).

## 13.7 THE INFLUENCE OF $\pi$ ON $\sigma_p$

How is the value of $\sigma_p$ influenced by the value of $\pi$? Note from Equations 13.5A and 13.7 that the value of $\pi(1 - \pi)$ is at a maximum when $\pi = .50$. Thus for any value of $\pi$, $\sigma_p \leq \sqrt{(.50)(.50)/n} = .5/\sqrt{n}$—Equation 13.5A provides the *maximum* value of the standard error when $\pi$ is set at .5. Notice that the sample proportion $p$ based on $n = 400$ observations is rarely in error by more than .05 from the parameter $\pi$. If $n = 1{,}600$, $p$ will rarely deviate more than .025 from $\pi$; this illustrates the precision of modern methods of opinion polling and survey research.

The sampling distribution of $p$ is perfectly symmetrical only when $\pi = .50$; if $n$ is small, as $\pi$ deviates from .50, the sampling distribution becomes increasingly skewed. Note that if $\pi = .90$, that $p$ can exceed $\pi$ by only .10 or less, yet can theoretically underestimate $\pi$ by .90. When the sample size is small, the sampling distribution of $p$ is positively skewed if $\pi$ has a very small value (e.g., .10); as shown in Figure 13.3, the sampling distribution of $p$ is negatively skewed if $\pi$ is much greater than .50. Figure 13.3 gives the sampling distributions of $p$ for $\pi = .9, .8, \ldots, .2$ and .1, when a very small sample size ($n = 10$) is used.

[6]For example, if $\pi = .50$, and $n/N = 1{,}000/50{,}000{,}000$, $\sigma_p = .01581$; if $n/N = 1{,}000/100{,}000$, $\sigma_p = .01573$ (see previous footnote 4). For the special problems in political polling, see footnote 1 in Chapter 10.

[7]In actual practice, true random samples are not common.

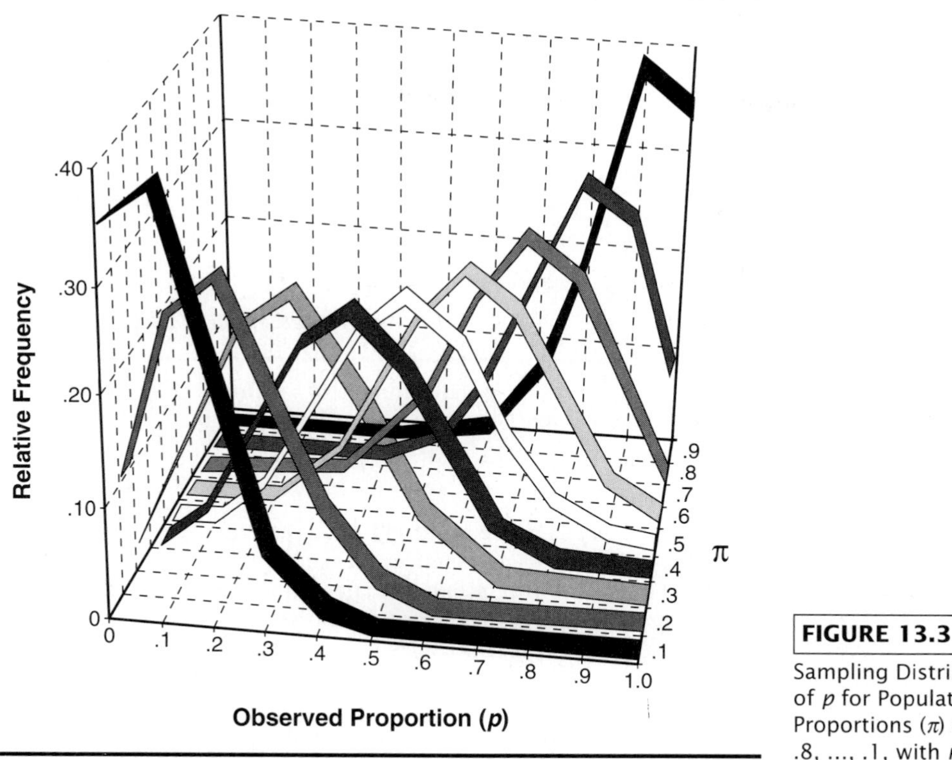


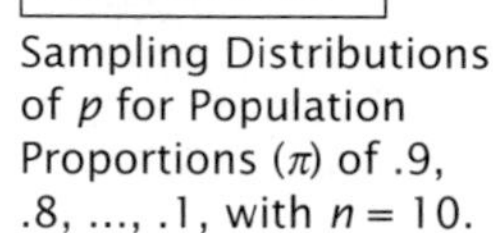
FIGURE 13.3

Sampling Distributions of $p$ for Population Proportions ($\pi$) of .9, .8, ..., .1, with $n = 10$.

## 13.8 CONFIDENCE INTERVALS FOR $\pi$

The central limit theorem (Section 10.15) holds that the sampling distribution of the mean of any distribution will approach a normal distribution as $n$ increases. Consequently, since $p$ can be viewed as a mean (Section 13.2), the shape of the sampling distribution of $p$ becomes normal as $n$ increases. But how large does $n$ need to be before it is safe to assume normality—when is it safe to use Equation 13.5B and estimate the $95CI$ for $\pi$ using $p \pm 1.96\hat{\sigma}_p$? Although several sources have offered guidelines regarding the sample size needed,[8] the use of these rules is too crude to give the needed accuracy (Cochran, 1977, p. 57; Jaeger, 1984, p. 58). As can be inferred from Figure 13.3, the sample size that is necessary to give accurate .95 confidence intervals for $\pi$ using $p \pm 1.96\hat{\sigma}_p$ is influenced greatly by the value of $\pi$. Figure 13.4 gives the sample size required for the sampling distribution of $p$ to be approximately normal (Cochran, 1977, p. 58)—the approximation being close enough that the .95 confidence intervals using $p \pm 1.96\hat{\sigma}_p$ will be no more than 1% in error.

---

[8]Such as $n > 100$ (Hays, 1988) and $n\pi$ [or $n(1 - \pi)$, whichever is smaller] $> 10$ (Moore & McCabe, 1989). In the previous edition, we, too, were guilty of promulgating a crude procedure, for which we must now apologize. Computers have rendered these inaccurate guidelines obsolete.

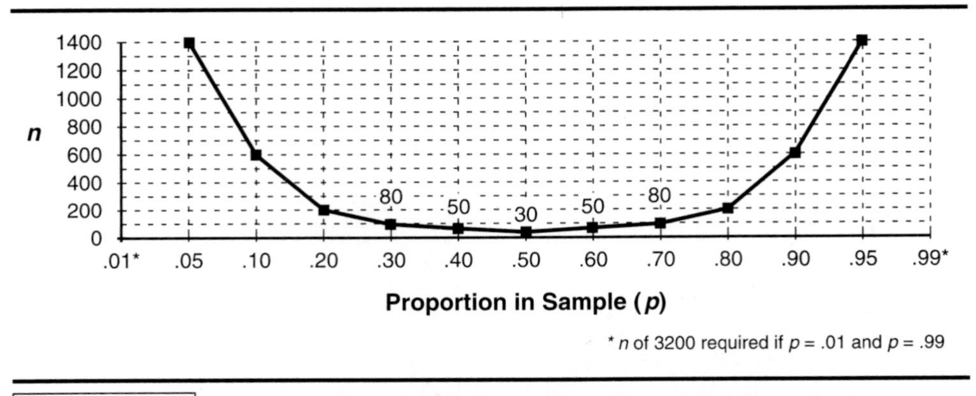

**FIGURE 13.4** Minimum Sample Size ($n$) Needed for Use of the Normal Approximation When Setting Confidence Intervals for the Proportion ($\pi$) in the Population.

Note in Figure 13.4 that when $p$ is between .40 and .60, a sample size of 50 or less may suffice, but when $p$ is $\leq .20$ or $\geq .80$, very large samples are required. For example, if $p = .90$, $n$ needs to be at least 600 before $p \pm 1.96\hat{\sigma}_p$ accurately approximates the $.95CI$. Obviously, there are many situations for which the normal approximation is insufficient.

Several methods proposed for setting confidence intervals for $\pi$ based, not on the normal distribution, but on the binomial distribution (Hald, 1952; Sachs, 1982; Burstein, 1971; Hays, 1988, including the widely reproduced graphs from Pearson & Hartley, 1966). Recently, however, it has been demonstrated that these methods yield confidence intervals that tend to be too wide, but that the method proposed by Ghosh (1979)(Equations 13.8A–D) is very accurate and is now the method of choice for all values of $p$ and $n$.

For the Ghosh method the lower limit of the $1 - \alpha\ CI$ for $\pi$, $\pi_L$, for a given sample size, $n$, and sample proportion, $p = f/n$, is given by Equation 13.8A, where $q = 1 - p$, and $z$ is the critical value $_{1-\sigma/2}z$.

$$\pi_L = \frac{n}{n+z^2}\left[p + \frac{z^2}{2n} - z\sqrt{\frac{pq}{n} + \frac{z^2}{4n^2}}\right] \qquad \textbf{(13.8A)}$$

The upper limit of the $1 - \alpha CI$ for $\pi$, $\pi_U$, is given by Equation 13.8B:

$$\pi_U = \frac{n}{n+z^2}\left[p + \frac{z^2}{2n} + z\sqrt{\frac{pq}{n} + \frac{z^2}{4n^2}}\right] \qquad \textbf{(13.8B)}$$

If $\alpha = .05$, the critical $z$-value, $_{.975}z$, is 1.960, and the lower and upper limits for the $.95CI$ for $\pi$ are simplified in Equations 13.8C and 13.8D:

$$\pi_L = \frac{n}{n+3.84}\left[p + \frac{1.92}{n} - 1.96\sqrt{\frac{pq}{n} + \frac{.96}{n^2}}\right] \quad \textbf{(13.8C)}$$

$$\pi_U = \frac{n}{n+3.84}\left[p + \frac{1.92}{n} + 1.96\sqrt{\frac{pq}{n} + \frac{.96}{n^2}}\right] \quad \textbf{(13.8D)}$$

*Example.* Suppose in a random sample of 20 persons, 3 are found to carry a certain recessive gene ($p = .15$). Estimate the proportion $\pi$ in the population that carry this gene. Using the $.95CI$ when $n = 20$, $f = 3$, and thus $p = 3/20 = .15$, the lower limit for $\pi$ from Equation 13.8C is found to be:

$$\pi_L = \frac{20}{20+3.84}\left[.15 + \frac{1.92}{20} - 1.96\sqrt{\frac{(.15)(.85)}{20} + \frac{.96}{(20)^2}}\right]$$

$$= .8389[.15 + .096 - 1.96\sqrt{.006375 + .0024}]$$

$$= .8389[.246 - .1836] = .8389(.0624) = .052$$

Similarly, from Equation 13.8D:

$$\pi_U = .8389[.246 + .1836] = .8389(.4296) = .360$$

Thus, the $.95CI$ for $\pi$ is (.052, .360).

## 13.9 QUICK CONFIDENCE INTERVALS FOR $\pi$

Approximate confidence intervals can be obtained quickly using Figure 13.5.[9] One study of stuttering (Howie, 1981) found ten stutterers who were identical twins. In nine of these twin pairs, both stuttered ($p = .9$—90% concordance). The .95 confidence interval for $\pi$ (the proportion of the entire population of stutterers who are identical twins whose twin also stutters) is found by locating $p$ (the sample proportion) on the baseline axis, then reading upward to find the two points where $p$ intersects with $n$, the curved lines that correspond to the sample size. From these two points, read across to the vertical axis to find the upper and lower limits of the confidence interval. For example, with $p = .9$ and $n = 10$, the lower limit of the .95 confidence interval is found to be .58; the upper limit is .98. In other words, one can be 95% confident that, had the entire stuttering population of identical twins been surveyed, the concordance would be somewhere between 58% and 98% of the pairs. Notice

[9]Figure 13.5 was constructed based on the Ghosh (1979) method, which has been shown to be more accurate than the widely used Pearson-Hartley graph based on the binomial. For certain values of $n$ ($n = 5$ and $n = 10$), the $CI$ values have been refined.

that the skewness in the sampling distribution is evident in the two "arms" of the confidence interval—the lower limit is .32 (.90 – .58) units below $p = .90$, but the upper limit is only .08 units above the observe proportion, $p$.

In the same study, thirty stutterers were found who were frateral twins. In only two of the thirty pairs did both stutter. In the population of fraternal twins who stutter, using Figure 13.5, estimate the concordance rate.[10]

With care, the *CI*'s from Figure 13.5 can be more accurate than those obtained using $p \pm 1.96\hat{\sigma}_p$ if the sampling distribution of $p$ is skewed (see Figure 13.4). When reading research that fails to provide the reader with confidence intervals for $\pi$ (unfortunately, all too common), Figure 13.5 can be useful. For general research reporting of proportions or percentages, Equations 13.8A–B should be used.

## 13.10 TESTING $H_0$: $\pi = K$

1. The statistical *hypothesis* to be tested is that in the population, the proportion $\pi$ which possesses a particular characteristic is equal to a value $K$ (where $1 > K > 0$): $H_0$: $\pi = K$. Similarly, the alternative hypothesis is $H_1$: $\pi \neq K$.
2. For purposes of testing $H_0$ against $H_1$, we need only to *assume* that a *random* sample of size $n$ is drawn from the population and that the sampling distribution of $p$ is approximately normal (see Figure 13.4).
3. $H_0$ can be *tested* by means of the $z$-test. If $H_0$ is true then $z$ (Equation 13.9) has a mean equal to 0 and a standard deviation equal to 1.

$$z = \frac{p - \pi}{\sigma_p} = \frac{p - \pi}{\sqrt{\pi(1 - \pi)/n}} \qquad \textbf{(13.9)}$$

4. To *test* $H_0$ *against* $H_1$ at the $\alpha_2$-level of significance, the value of $z$ in Equation 13.9 is compared with its critical value. For a one-tailed test, the critical value of $z$ is ${}_{1-\alpha}z$ in the unit-normal distribution (Table A). Thus if $\alpha_1 = .05$, the critical value for $z$ is ${}_{.95}z = 1.645$. For a nondirectional test, the critical values of $z$ are $|{}_{1-a/2}z|$ For example, if $\alpha_2 = .05$, $H_0$ is rejected at the .05 level if $|z| \geq 1.960 = {}_{.975}z$.

   If the combination of $n$ and $p$ is insufficient to produce a sampling distribution of $p$ that is approximately normal (Figure 13.4), the null hypothesis can be tested using the chi-square goodness-of-fit test. This topic is treated later in this chapter (Section 13.11).[11]
5. Equations 13.8A–B give accurate *confidence intervals* for $\pi$, for any sample size and any value of $p$. Figure 13.5 provides quick and approximate confidence intervals. If the sample size is large enough for a given value of $p$ to produce normality in the sampling

---

[10] $p = 2/30 \approx .07$; the approximate .95*CI* for $\pi$ is (.02, .21). If Equations 13.8C–D are used: (.018, .213), illustrating that the graphic approximations are not seriously in error. Notice that the .95*CI*'s for the identical and fraternal twins do not overlap, (.02, .21) vs. (.58, .98); when two *CI*'s do not overlap, $H_0$: $\pi_1 = \pi_2$ can always be rejected. A more powerful and precise test of this hypothesis is given in Section 13.12.

[11] The binomial test (Section 9.11) can also be used; it gives precise probability statements, regardless of $n$. Another alternative is to set a confidence interval for $\pi$; if $K$ is not contained within the $1 - \alpha$ *CI*, the statistical hypothesis can be rejected at the $\alpha$-level.

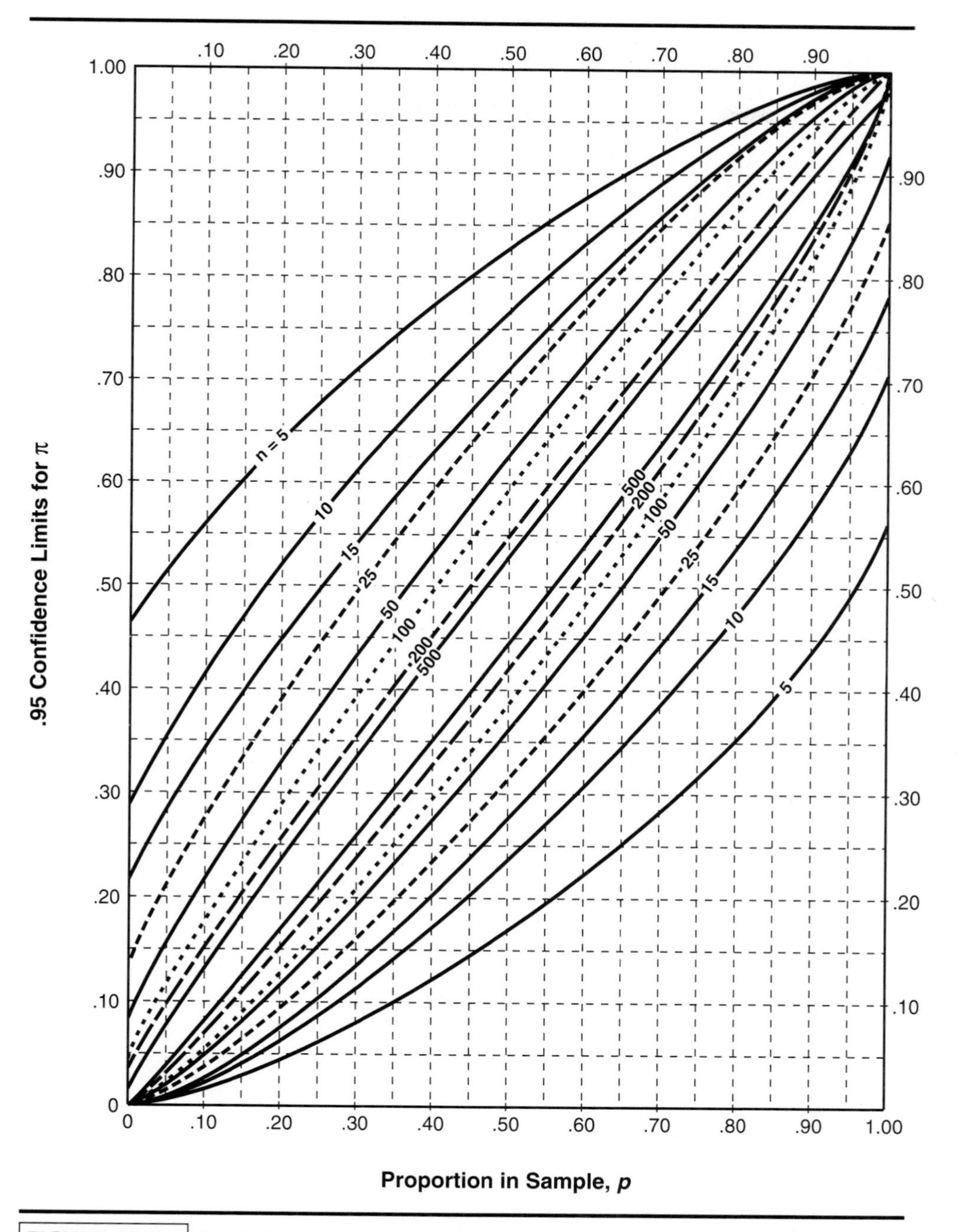


**FIGURE 13.5** Graph for .95 Confidence Limits for the Parameter, $\pi$, from $p$ and $n$.

distribution (Figure 13.4), approximate .95 confidence intervals for $\pi$ can be obtained from: $p \pm 1.96\hat{\sigma}_p$.

6. *Example.* The superintendent of a school district wishes to take a poll one month before a city election to determine the chances of the proposed school bond receiving a majority of the votes. The hypothesis to be tested at the $\alpha_2 = .01$ level of significance is that $\pi$ (the proportion of the 25,000 registered voters who favor the school bond), is .50; the alternative hypothesis is that $\pi \neq .50$. A random sample of $n = 100$ registered voters is drawn; when questioned, $f = 65$ voters indicated that they favored the school bond. The value of $p$ is $f/n = .65$. The value of $z$ (Equation 13.9) is:

$$z = \frac{p-\pi}{\sigma_p} = \frac{p-\pi}{\sqrt{\pi(1-\pi)/n}} = \frac{.65-.50}{\sqrt{.50(.50)/100}} = \frac{.15}{.05} = 3.00$$

The $z$ value of 3.00 is compared with the absolute value of the critical $z$-value of 2.576. Since $3.00 > 2.576$, it can be concluded that $p = .65$ is significantly greater than .50 at the .01 level.

The .95 confidence interval for $\pi$ can be estimated quickly from Figure 13.5; it extends from approximately .55 to .73. More precise values are found using Equations 13.8A–B, for example, the $.99CI$ for $\pi$: (.550, .731).

## 13.11 TESTING EMPIRICAL VERSUS THEORETICAL DISTRIBUTIONS: THE CHI-SQUARE GOODNESS-OF-FIT TEST

The chi-square ($\chi^2$) test statistic can be used to find whether the observed proportions in two or more categories differ significantly from a priori or theoretically expected proportions. For example, several hereditary traits are determined by Mendel's dominance-recessive law—a recessive trait is manifest only if a recessive gene is paired with another identical recessive gene. The chi-square goodness-of-fit statistic has played a prominent part in establishing the genetic cause for several animal and human traits and conditions. Let us step back in history a couple of decades and ask the research question: "Is cystic fibrosis (or albinism, sickle cell anemia, phenylketonuria, etc.) a recessive trait, that is, a condition that is evidenced only when two recessive genes are paired?" Suppose we study the children of normal fathers and normal mothers who are known to be "carriers" (persons having one parent who had cystic fibrosis). If, indeed, the genetics of cystic fibrosis follow the dominance-recessive Mendelian theory, one-fourth of the offspring should have cystic fibrosis, the other three-fourths should be normal. In other words, theory predicts 25% of the children should have the malady and 75% should not, or $\pi_1 = .25$ and $\pi_2 = .75$. Of 200 children born to parents who are both carriers, we find that 42 of them have cystic fibrosis. Is the Mendelian hypothesis tenable as an explanation for the condition? $H_0$: $\pi_1 = .25$ (or equivalently, $\pi_2 = .75$). Does the proportion $p_1$ of $42/200 = .21$ differ significantly from the proportion that is hypothesized? Does $p_1 = .21$ differ significantly from $\pi_1 = .25$? This null hypothesis can be tested using the chi-square goodness-of-fit test. In other words, do $p_1 = .21$ and $p_2 = .79$ differ significantly from the hypothesized values for the parameters: $\pi_1 = .25$, and $\pi_2 = .75$? The chi-square statistic $\chi^2$ represents the extent to which the $J$ observed proportions, $p_j$'s, differ from the hypothesized or expected proportions, $\pi_j$'s. The chi-square statistic is defined in Equation 13.10:

$$\chi^2 = n_{\bullet} \sum_j \frac{(p_j - \pi_j)^2}{\pi_j} \quad \textbf{(13.10)}$$

In words, in Equation 13.10, the difference in the observed and expected proportion for each of the $J$ categories is squared, then divided by the expected proportion for that category.[12] $\chi^2$ is the sum of these quotients for all $J$ categories multiplied by $n_{\bullet}$. In the cystic fibrosis example, there are two categories; the two observed proportions are $p_1 = .21$ and $p_2 = .79$; the associated expected proportions are $\pi_1 = .25$ and $\pi_2 = .75$. Substituting these values into Equation 13.10, we find:

$$\chi^2 = n_{\bullet} \sum_j \frac{(p_j - \pi_j)^2}{\pi_j} = n_{\bullet}\left[\frac{(p_1 - \pi_1)^2}{\pi_1} + \frac{(p_2 - \pi_2)^2}{\pi_2}\right]$$

$$= 200\left[\frac{(.21 - .25)^2}{.25} + \frac{(.79 - .75)^2}{.75}\right] = 200\left[\frac{(.04)^2}{.25} + \frac{(.04)^2}{.75}\right]$$

$$= 200(.00640 + .00213) = 200(0.00853) = 1.706$$

Is a chi-square of 1.71 significant at the .05 level? Table D in the Appendix gives the critical values for $\chi^2$ for various degrees of freedom. *When using the $\chi^2$ goodness-of-fit test, the number of degrees of freedom ($\nu$) is 1 less than the number of categories ($\nu = J - 1$).* In our example, $\nu = 2 - 1 = 1$. In Table D, the critical value of $\chi^2$ with $\alpha = .05$ and $\nu = 1$ is 3.84 (i.e., ${}_{.95}\chi_1^2 = 3.84$). Our $\chi^2$-value of 1.71 is less than the critical $\chi^2$-value; hence, $p > .05$, and the statistical hypothesis ($H_0$: $\pi_1 = .25$) is tenable; the data are congruent with the Mendelian explanation. The .95*CI* for $\pi_1$ using Equations 13.8C–D is (.16, .27), which is consistent with the prediction from theory.

For hand computation, percentages are often easier to use than proportions. Equation 13.10 expressed in the percentage metric $P_j$ rather than proportions $p_j$ is:

$$\chi^2 = \frac{n_{\bullet}}{100} \sum_j \frac{\left(P_j - 100\pi_j\right)^2}{100\pi_j} \quad \textbf{(13.11)}$$

*Example.* If stress is a factor in precipitating heart attacks, perhaps attacks are more common on certain days than on others (e.g., weekends vs. work days). Day of week on which heart attacks occurred was tallied for 89 workers of a large company. The null

[12]The formula for $\chi^2$ is given in most other textbooks as $\chi^2 = \Sigma[(f_o - f_e)^2/f_e]$, where $f_o$ and $f_e$, respectively, denote observed and expected frequencies in each category. This formula is mathematically equivalent to Equation 13.10, which, we feel, is more conceptual and intuitive. With the conventional formula, the values of observed and expected frequencies must be converted to percentages or proportions to be interpretable since they are greatly influenced by $n$, whereas the proportions $p$ and $\pi$ are not. Equation 13.10 was derived (Hopkins, 1971) by substituting in the above formula $np$ for $f_o$ and $n\pi$ for $f_e$ and factoring out $n$. Notice that frequencies and proportions differ only by a constant factor of $n_{\bullet}$; testing the departure of observed from expected frequencies is equivalent to testing the departure of observed from expected proportions since $p_j = f_j/n$ (or $f_j = np_j$). Notice that $\pi_1 + \pi_2 + \ldots + \pi_J$ will always equal 1.

**TABLE 13.1** Is Coronary Attack Associated with Day-of-Week? A Computational Illustration of the Chi-Square Goodness-of-Fit Test.

| | *Observed* | | *Expected %* | | | |
|---|---|---|---|---|---|---|
| | $f_j$ | $P_j$ | $100\pi_j$ | $P_j - 100\pi_j$ | $(P_j - 100\pi_j)^2$ | $\frac{(P_j - 100\pi)^2}{100\pi j}$ |
| Sunday | 16 | 17.98 | 14.29 | 3.69 | 13.6161 | .953 |
| Monday | 11 | 12.36 | 14.29 | –1.93 | 3.7249 | .261 |
| Tuesday | 12 | 13.48 | 14.29 | –0.81 | 0.6561 | .046 |
| Wednesday | 14 | 15.73 | 14.29 | 1.44 | 2.0736 | .145 |
| Thursday | 12 | 13.48 | 14.29 | –0.81 | 0.6561 | .046 |
| Friday | 10 | 11.24 | 14.29 | –3.05 | 9.3025 | .651 |
| Saturday | 14 | 15.73 | 14.29 | 1.44 | 2.0736 | .145 |
| Total | 89 | | | | | $\chi^2 = 2.247$ |

hypothesis is that, in the population, the distribution is rectangular (each day is equal in frequency): $H_0$: $\pi_1 = \pi_2 = \pi_3 = \pi_4 = \pi_5 = \pi_6 = \pi_7 = 1/7$ (1/7 = .1429 or 14.29%). The computations are given in Table 13.1: (1) the observed frequencies are converted to percentages, (2) the expected percentage for each category is determined, (3) the difference between the observed percentage and the expected percentage is obtained for each of the seven categories, (4) this difference is squared, then divided by the expected frequency, (5) the value of $\chi^2$ is the sum of these seven values, (6) the observed $\chi^2$ value is compared to the critical chi-square value, ${}_{1-\alpha}\chi^2_v$ (where $v = J - 1$). $H_0$ is rejected if the observed value for $\chi^2$ is greater than the critical $\chi^2$-value; $H_0$ is *not rejected*, but is tenable, if the critical value is greater than the observed value of $\chi^2$. In Table 13.1, the observed value for $\chi^2$ (2.247) is less than the critical value, ${}_{.95}\chi^2_6 = 12.59$; Thus, the null hypothesis is tenable ($p > .05$)[13]—the data do not suggest that heart attacks are more common on certain days of the week.

When the chi-square statistic is used to determine whether observed proportions are significantly different from theoretically expected proportions, it is usually termed the $\chi^2$ *goodness-of-fit test*; $\chi^2$ reflects the degree to which the *empirical* observations "fit" the *theoretical* expectations. In a true-false test, the expected proportion $\pi = .5$ is determined from theory—one-half of the choices should be true if the choices were made randomly. The $\chi^2$ goodness-of-fit test can assess whether any observed distribution differs from any theoretical distribution.

The chi-square goodness-of-fit test can be used to test whether a pair of dice is unbiased, whether a sample of questionnaires returned is geographically representative, whether the number of automobile fatalities differs by month or day of week, whether the percent-

[13]Indeed, from Table D note that $p > .80$. It is good practice to inform the reader as to the probability of obtaining a value as large or larger than the value of the test statistic ($\chi^2$ in this instance) if the null hypothesis is true. To know that $p > .80$ allows us to be more confident that a type-II error has not been made than knowing only that $p > .05$. Most computer programs will print out the actual probability (in this instance, $p = .896$); when available, the actual probability should be reported rather than a less precise statement such as $p > .80$. Many spreadsheets (e.g., the CHIDIST paste function in EXCEL) give the precise probability when the observed $\chi^2$-value and are entered as arguments. Rounding errors can cause the observed value of $\chi^2$ and $p$ from hand computation to differ slightly from those supplied by a computer program.

age of extroverts varies by astrological sign, whether a set of observations are normally distributed,[14] and so forth.

### *z*-test versus $\chi^2$

Recall from Section 13.10 that when the $z$-test was used to test the hypothesis $H_0$: $\pi = .5$, the $z$-ratio of 3.00 was obtained. If the value of $z$ is squared, 9.00 is obtained, exactly the value that we would obtain if the $\chi^2$ goodness-of-fit test were applied. When there is only one degree of freedom, $\chi^2 = z^2$ (see Section 16.2.).

## 13.12 TESTING DIFFERENCES AMONG PROPORTIONS: THE CHI-SQUARE TEST OF ASSOCIATION[15]

In one of the early investigations regarding the effects of smoking, the relationship between smoking and coronary heart disease (CHD) was examined. A sample of 120 men employed by Western Electric who had developed CHD were matched on age with 120 employees who did not have CHD. Is there a predictable relationship between smoking and CHD? All of the men in both groups were classified into one of four smoking categories: (1) non-smoker, (2) less than one pack per day, (3) one pack per day, and (4) more than one pack per day. Table 13.2 gives the contingency table (the cross-tabulation of the frequencies for the combinations of categories of two variables is known as a contingency table). If a table has $R$ rows and $C$ columns, it is described as an $R$-by-$C$ contingency table, where $R$ and $C$ can take any value of 2 or more. For example, Table 13.2 would be described as a "2-by-4" contingency table.

The frequencies ($n_{rc}$) in each column in Table 13.2 have been divided by the number of observations in that column ($n_{\bullet c}$) and multiplied by 100 to find the percentage ($P_{rc}$) of the observations in each column that fall into each row. For example, in Table 13.2, $100n_{11}/n_{\bullet 1} = (100)(42)/103 = 40.8\%$ ($= P_{11}$) of the non smokers had CHD. Likewise, the observed percentage of nonsmokers without CHD is 59.2% ($= P_{21}$). The observed percentage of the persons in each smoking category that falls into each cell is shown in Table 13.2. Notice also that the row totals $n_{r\bullet}$ have been converted into percentages to give the percent of the observations that falls into each row.[16]

[14]See Glass and Hopkins (1984, p. 285) for a worked example. It is no longer included because there are more powerful tests of normality such as the Shapiro and Wilk's test and the Lilliefors (Kolmogorov-Smirnov) test (Conover, 1980). In previous decades, a test of normality was needed to legitimize the $t$-test (Chapters 11–12) and the analysis of variance (Chapters 15–19) because their derivations are based on the statistical assumption of normality. Since robustness studies have found that violations of this assumption have inconsequential effects on the accuracy of the probability statements, it is rarely used for that purpose today. Its principal use now is to address the inferential question of normality per se, not as a preliminary test for other analyses.

[15]A distinction is sometimes made between a chi-square test of independence and a chi-square test of homogeneity. The latter fixes the number of observations sampled within a category; the former classifies observations into categories after a sample has been drawn. The computation and practical interpretation of both procedures are identical. We use the "$\chi^2$ test of association" to subsume both types and will not distinguish between them.

[16]The value of $\chi^2$ will be the same regardless of which factor is designated as the column (or row) variable. However, interpretation is facilitated if categories of persons appear as columns; for example, it is usually more meaningful to ask, "what percentage of nonsmokers have CHD," than "of persons with CHD, what percentage are smokers?"

If there is no association between smoking and CHD, the cell percentages within each row should not differ greatly. For example, if the null hypothesis is true, the percentages in the cells of the first row (40.8%, 45.2%, 60.9%, and 64.5%) differ only by chance from the expected proportion for the entire first row, 50.0% = $100\hat{\pi}_{1.}$. In other words, is the null hypothesis tenable? $H_0$ states that the population percentages in the first row are all equal (and, hence, do not differ significantly from each other). Stated differently, can all differences among the $p$'s within each row be attributable to sampling error? If the entire population were queried, would the proportions with CHD be equal—is $H_0$: $\pi_{11} = \pi_{12} = \pi_{13} = \pi_{14}$ tenable? With the chi-square test of association (unlike the chi-square goodness-of-fit test), the parameter of any expected proportion, $\pi$, is unknown, and cannot be estimated a priori; the expected proportion must be estimated from the data. If the null hypothesis is true, the best estimate of the parameter, $\pi_1$ (the proportion in the population having CHD), is obtained by finding the proportion of the $n_{\bullet\bullet}$ observations that falls into the first row: $n_{1\bullet}/n_{\bullet\bullet} = .50$ in the example. With the $\chi^2$ test of association, the symbol $\hat{\pi}$ is used rather than $\pi$, since the precise value of the parameter $\pi$ is unknown; the "^" denotes that the value is an estimate.[17] The double summation signs give the formula (Equation 13.12) for the $\chi^2$ test of association for an $R \times C$ contingency table an unfriendly look, but it is really not that bad: (1) For any cell find the difference in the cell percentage and the expected percentage (percent of the total observations that fall in that row), and square this difference; (2) divide this value by the expected percentage for the cell, then multiply it by $n_{\bullet c}/100$; (3) the value of $\chi^2$ for the $R \times$ C contingency table is the sum of these values across all cells.[18] In the lower portion of Table 13.2, the chi-square statistic is computed using Equation 13.12:

$$\chi^2 = \sum_{r=1}^{R}\sum_{c=1}^{C} \frac{n_{\bullet c}}{100} \frac{(P_{rc} - 100\hat{\pi}_{r\bullet})^2}{100\hat{\pi}_{r\bullet}} \qquad \textbf{(13.12)}$$

In the chi-square test of association, the chi-square statistic has degrees of freedom equal to $(R - 1)(C - 1)$, where $R$ is the number of rows and $C$ is the number of columns. In the example, $R = 2$ and $C = 4$; hence, $\nu = (2 - 1)(4 - 1) = 3$. In Table D, the critical $\chi^2$-value at $\alpha = .05$ is found to be 7.82, that is, ${}_{.95}\chi_3^2 = 7.82$. Since the observed $\chi^2$ is larger than 7.82, $H_0$ is rejected at the .05 level. If $H_0$ is true, discrepancies in $p$'s and associated $\hat{\pi}$'s as large as those that were observed would occur in less than five in every 100 replicated studies. Therefore, the null hypothesis is rejected at .05 level, and it is concluded that there is some association between the two variables—the chances of one having coronary heart disease are associated with the smoking group to which one belongs. The $\chi^2$ test of association evaluates whether or not the two factors in the contingency are correlated. If the percentage of the non smokers and the three categories of smokers with CHD had been exactly the same, the value of $\chi^2$ would have been zero. The value of $\chi^2$ increases as the observed proportions within a given row differ among the groups being contrasted. Does the significant chi-square indicate that each of the four groups differs significantly from the other

---

[17]Recall that the caret ("hat") above a symbol for a parameter denotes an estimate of the parameter beneath. Thus, $\hat{\mu}$ and $\hat{\sigma}$ are aliases for $\bar{X}$ and $s$. In the chi-square goodness-of-fit test, theory supplies the value of the parameter $\pi$; in the chi-square test of association, estimates of the parameter must be used.

[18]Equation 13.12, using proportions instead of percentages is:

$$\chi^2 = \sum_{r=1}^{R}\sum_{c=1}^{C} n_{\bullet c} \frac{(p_{rc} - \hat{\pi}_{r\bullet})^2}{\hat{\pi}_{r\bullet}}$$

**TABLE 13.2** Illustration of Computation of the Chi-Square Test of Association from Percentages.

| | *Smoking Category* | | | | |
|---|---|---|---|---|---|
| *Coronory Heart Disease* | *Nonsmoking* | *Less than One Pack* | *One Pack* | *More than One Pack* | *Row Totals* |
| Yes | $42 = n_{11}$<br>$40.8\% = P_{11}$ | $19 = n_{12}$<br>$45.2\% = P_{12}$ | $39 = n_{13}$<br>$60.9\% = P_{13}$ | $20 = n_{14}$<br>$64.5\% = P_{14}$ | $120 = n_{1\bullet}$<br>$50.0\% = 100\pi_{1\bullet}$ |
| No | $61 = n_{21}$<br>$59.2\% = P_{21}$ | $23 = n_{22}$<br>$54.8\% = P_{22}$ | $25 = n_{23}$<br>$39.1\% = P_{23}$ | $11 = n_{24}$<br>$35.5\% = P_{24}$ | $120 = n_{2\bullet}$<br>$50.0\% = 100\pi_{2\bullet}$ |
| Column Totals | $103 = n_{\bullet 1}$ | $42 = n_{\bullet 2}$ | $64 = n_{\bullet 3}$ | $31 = n_{\bullet 4}$ | $240 = n_{\bullet\bullet}$ |

$$\chi^2 = \frac{103}{100}\frac{(40.8-50.0)^2}{50} + \frac{103}{100}\frac{(59.2-50.0)^2}{50} + \frac{42}{100}\frac{(45.2-50.0)^2}{50} + \frac{42}{100}\frac{(54.8-50.0)^2}{50}$$

$$\frac{64}{100}\frac{(60.9-50.0)^2}{50} + \frac{64}{100}\frac{(39.1-50)^2}{50} + \frac{31}{100}\frac{(64.5-50.0)^2}{50} + \frac{31}{100}\frac{(35.5-50.0)^2}{50}$$

$\chi^2 = 9.56$; ${}_{.95}\chi^2_3 = 7.82$, $p < .05$ (actual $p$ from computer: $p = .023$)

three groups? Not necessarily, although in Table 13.2 the trend appears plausible. However, suppose in a 3 × 2 contingency table in which parents, teachers, and principals are compared on attitudes toward school choice (favor or do not favor); parents may differ significantly from both teachers and principals, but teachers and principals may not differ. Separate 2 × 2 contingency tables can be formed to help isolate which groups differ from which other groups.[19]

## 13.13 OTHER FORMULAS FOR THE CHI-SQUARE TEST OF ASSOCIATION[20]

When computing $\chi^2$ by hand and the data in a contingency table are given in frequencies, the $\chi^2$-statistic can be computed directly and more expediently (although less intuitively)

[19]Sophisticated procedures for making comparisons or finding trends among three or more groups when the null hypothesis is rejected are given in Chapter 17. When the outcome variable is a dichotomy, as in Table 13.2, the $p$-value yielded by chi-square ($p = .023$) will differ trivially from the $p$-value ($p = .022$) from a one-factor ANOVA (Hopkins, Vojir, & Hester, 1996). Similarly, in Table 13.3 the $p$-values are .42 for $\chi^2$, vs .43 for the $t$-test.

[20]Some sources and computer programs state that chi-square should not be used unless the minimum expected frequencies are five or more in each cell. Roscoe and Byars (1971, 1979), Conover (1974), and Camilli and Hopkins (1978, 1979) have shown that the chi-square statistic works well even when the average expected frequency is as low as 2. (Note that average expected frequency is less restrictive than minimum expected frequency.) In addition, the Yates "correction for continuity" that is usually recommended for 2 × 2 contingency tables is not only unnecessary, but causes the already conservative values for $\alpha$ to be even more conservative (Camilli & Hopkins, 1978). Fisher's exact probability test for 2 × 2 contingency tables with very small expected frequencies is often recommended, but is unnecessary since the $\chi^2$-test of association gives accurate probability statements even with very small $n$'s.

**TABLE 13.3** Computation Illustration of the $\chi^2$ Median Test.

| | *Males* | *Females* | *Row Totals* |
|---|---|---|---|
| Above median | $n_{11} = 4$ | $n_{12} = 15$ | $n_{1\bullet} = 19$ |
| Below median | $n_{21} = 8$ | $n_{22} = 17$ | $n_{2\bullet} = 25$ |
| Column totals | $n_{\bullet 1} = 12$ | $n_{\bullet 2} = 32$ | $n_{\bullet\bullet} = 44$ |

Equation 13.13: $$\chi^2 = n_{\bullet\bullet}\left[\sum_{r=1}^{2}\sum_{c=1}^{2}\frac{n_{rc}^2}{n_{r\bullet}n_{\bullet c}} - 1\right]$$

$$\chi^2 = 44\left[\frac{4^2}{19(12)} + \frac{15^2}{19(32)} + \frac{8^2}{25(12)} + \frac{17^2}{25(32)} - 1\right]$$

$$= 44(.070175 + .370066 + .213333 + .361250 - 1)$$

$$= 44(1.014825 - 1)$$

$$\chi^2 = .652; \ _{.90}x^2 = 2.71, \ p > .10$$

Equation 13.14: $$\chi^2 = \frac{n_{\bullet\bullet}(n_{11}n_{22} - n_{12}n_{21})^2}{n_{1\bullet}\, n_{2\bullet}\, n_{\bullet 1}\, n_{\bullet 2}}$$

$$= \frac{44[4(17) - 15(8)]^2}{(19)(25)(12)(32)}$$

$\chi^2 = .652$; $.30 > p > .50$ (actual $p = .42$)

from cell, row, and column frequencies ($n$'s) as described in Equation 13.13:

$$\chi^2 = n_{\bullet\bullet}\left[\sum_{r=1}^{R}\sum_{c=1}^{C}\frac{n_{rc}^2}{n_{r\bullet}n_{\bullet c}} - 1\right] \qquad \textbf{(13.13)}$$

where $n_{rc}$ is the number of observations in the $rc$th cell of the contingency table; $n_{r\bullet}$ is the number of observations in the $r$th row of the table; $n_{\bullet c}$ is the number of observations in the $c$th column of the table; and $n_{\bullet\bullet}$ = the total number of observations. When $R = C = 2$, Equation 13.13 simplifies to:

$$\chi^2 = \frac{n_{\bullet\bullet}(n_{11}n_{22} - n_{12}n_{21})^2}{n_{1\bullet}\, n_{2\bullet}\, n_{\bullet 1} n_{\bullet 2}} \qquad \textbf{(13.14)}$$

Equations 13.13 and 13.14 will be illustrated in Table 13.3.[21]

## 13.14 THE $\chi^2$ MEDIAN TEST

Students in a beginning statistics course were asked to rate themselves anonymously on a 0 to 9 point scale to the degree that they considered themselves to be happy. The median for the forty-four students was 7.3. The numbers of males and females that rated themselves above or below the median are given in Table 13.3. The $\chi^2$ computation is illustrated using Equations 13.13 and 13.14. (Since the ratings are in discrete units, there will not be precisely 50% above and below the median of 7.3—ratings 8 and 9 are above the median, ratings 0–7 are below the median.)

Notice that each student appears only once in the contingency table; the student is either male or female, and is either above or below the median. The observations are *independent* (see Section 13.16) and the $\chi^2$ test is a valid test of whether males or females report higher or lower happiness ratings. This application of the $\chi^2$ test of association is known as the median test since it tests whether the medians of the groups are different. The obtained $\chi^2$ of .652 is less than the critical $\chi^2$-value with $(R - 1)(C - 1) = 1$ degree of freedom (${}_{.90}\chi_1^2 = 2.71$); hence, the null hypothesis that the two median parameters are equal cannot be rejected at the .10 level of significance. Although only 33% of the males were above the median compared to 47% of the females, the difference does not approach significance because of the small sample size.

Of course, the $t$-test could have been used to compare attitude scale means; indeed, the $t$-test is considerably more powerful (i.e., more likely to detect differences in the parameters) than the $\chi^2$ median test. The median test can be used to compare two *or more* groups, whereas the $t$-test is limited to only two groups. In this way, it is like the analysis of variance (Chapter 15) in that any number of groups can be compared simultaneously, that is, $H_0$: $\pi_1 = \pi_2 \ldots = \pi_J$ can be evaluated with a single omnibus test.[22]

## 13.15 CHI-SQUARE AND THE PHI COEFFICIENT

The value of $\chi^2$ is greatly influenced by $\nu$ and $n$, hence its numerical value is essentially useless as a measure of the degree of association between the two variables of a contin-

---

[21] An alternative and mathematically equivalent test of equal proportions in two independent samples in 2 × 2 contingency tables is the $z$-test:

$$z \approx \frac{p_{11} - p_{12}}{\sqrt{\hat{\pi}_{1\bullet}(1-\hat{\pi}_{1\bullet})\left(\dfrac{1}{n_{\bullet 1}} + \dfrac{1}{n_{\bullet 2}}\right)}}$$

where $p_{11} = n_{11}/n_{\bullet 1}$, $p_{12} = n_{12}/n_{\bullet 2}$, and $\hat{\pi}_{1\bullet} = (n_{11} + n_{12})/n_{\bullet\bullet}$. When the $z$-test is used, $z^2 = \chi^2$ (where $\chi^2$ is obtained from Equation 13.13 or 13.14). Notice the similarity of the $z$-test to the $t$-test for independent means (Equations 12.2 and 12.4).

[22] Contrary to popular opinion, when one of the variables in a contingency table is dichotomous, the $p$-value yielded by $\chi^2$ is virtually identical to that from a one-factor analysis of variance (Chapter 15), where the dichotomous variable (1 or 0) is the dependent variable. A one-factor analysis of variance using the data in Table 13.2 yields $p = .022$ (vs. .023 for $\chi^2$). For the data in Table 13.3, the $p$-values are .419 and .431 for $\chi^2$ and analysis of variance (or the $t$-test), respectively.

gency table. But in a $2 \times 2$ contingency table, the chi-square test statistic for a test of association can be easily converted to its close relative, the phi coefficient, $r_\phi$ (see Section 7.22), as given in Equation 13.15:

$$r_\phi = \sqrt{\frac{\chi_1^2}{n}} \quad \textbf{(13.15)}$$

where $n$ is the total number of observations in the $2 \times 2$ contingency table. For example, if in the contingency in Table 13.3, $\chi^2 = .652$, then $r_\phi = \sqrt{.652/44} = \sqrt{.0148} = .1217$.

Notice how easily Equation 13.15 is converted into a test of significance for $r_\phi$, that is a test of $H_0$: $\rho_\phi = 0$.

$$\chi^2 = nr_\phi^2 \quad \textbf{(13.16)}$$

Thus in Table 7.7 (Section 7.22), in which $r_\phi = .125$, $n = 27$, the computed value of chi-square from Equation 13.16 is $(27)(.125)^2 = .422$. At the .05 level of significance, the critical value of chi-square for one degree of freedom is 3.84 (Table D); therefore, the computed chi-square value is not statistically significant. The null hypothesis that gender is unrelated to breakfast eating behavior remains tenable.

As another example, consider the data in Table 7.9 (Section 7.26), in which $r_\phi = .546$ with $n = 400$; from Equation 13.16, $\chi^2 = 400(.546)^2 = 119.25$. The critical value at $\alpha = .001$ from Table D, is ${}_{.999}\chi_1^2 = 10.83$; therefore, $H_0$: $\rho_\phi = 0$ can be rejected at the .001 level, that is, there is a positive relationship between attitudes toward the legalization of marijuana and the legalization of abortion.[23]

## 13.16 INDEPENDENCE OF OBSERVATIONS

The $\chi^2$-statistic can be used with any contingency table in which each observation is *independent* from the other observations. Independence in this context means that each observation qualifies for one and only one cell—that is, the categories are mutually exclusive—there is only one entry per observation unit. The most common observational unit in educational and psychological research is a person. Suppose students in several classes were queried regarding some question, if some students were in more than one of the classes, the observations would not be completely independent. To be entirely independent, all observations must be on different persons (or other observational units).

Suppose a questionnaire of ten items on attitude toward school was administered to a sample of fifty urban and fifty rural school students. Each student responded with a positive or negative response to each of the ten questions. One could legitimately tally the responses separately for each question and apply the chi-square test of independence to see if there

[23]Although rarely used, the degree of association between two measures, each with two or more levels, can be described by another close relative of the chi-square statistic, the coefficient of contingency, $C = \sqrt{\chi^2/(n+\chi^2)}$.

was a difference in the responses for elementary versus secondary school students. However, the ten contingency tables could not be aggregated into a composite table of 1,000 "cases" since each person would be represented ten times—the observations would not be independent. The dependence would seriously affect the probability of a type-I error. One could, though, compare the urban and rural students by obtaining each student's score on the set of ten questions, and then employing the median test (Section 13.14), or better, the *t*-test (Section 12.2).

## 13.17 INFERENCES ABOUT $H_0$: $\pi_1 = \pi_2$ WHEN OBSERVATIONS ARE PAIRED: McNemar's Test for Correlated Proportions

Suppose a group of voters indicates whether they intend to vote for or against a certain candidate, and after hearing a debate, the same group responds again to the same question. The research question of interest here is whether there has been a significant change in the proportion of voters who favor the candidate. The $\chi^2$ test of association for the $2 \times 2$ contingency table that we studied in Section 13.12 would evaluate a different question; that is, whether there is a relationship between voter preferences before and after the debate. In this research design calling for paired observations, we want to know if there been a significant shift toward or away from the candidate. Table 13.4 presents some illustrative data for McNemar's chi-square test for paired observations.

The hypotheses to be tested are identical to the hypotheses in Section 13.12, namely, $H_0$: $\pi_1 = \pi_2$ against $H_1$: $\pi_1 \neq \pi_2$. As with all techniques involving dependent samples, it is necessary to link each observation before the debate with its paired observation after the debate. As is the case with the present example, the most frequent application of McNemar's test for correlated proportions is to research designs in which the two sets of observations are from the same group of persons observed at two different points in time. The proportion of persons favoring the candidate ("for") on the initial dichotomous measure, is $p_1$. Likewise on the second measure, the proportion favoring the candidate is $p_2$. McNemar's test (Equation 13.17) is used to test the null hypothesis, $H_0$: $\pi_1 = \pi_2$.

**TABLE 13.4** McNemar's Test for Correlated Proportions in a 2 × 2 Contingency Table.

| | | *Before Debate* | |
|---|---|---|---|
| | | *"Against"* | *"For"* |
| *After Debate* | *"For"* | $n_{11} = 13$ | $n_{12} = 20$ |
| | *"Against"* | $n_{21} = 23$ | $n_{22} = 4$ |

$$\chi^2 = \frac{(n_{22} - n_{11})^2}{n_{22} + n_{11}} = \frac{(4-13)^2}{4+13} = \frac{(-9)^2}{17} = 4.76$$

**TABLE 13.5** McNemar's Test for Correlated Proportions in a 2 × 2 Contingency Table.

| | | *Before Film* | |
|---|---|---|---|
| | | *"Against"* | *"For"* |
| *After Film* | *"For"* | $n_{11} = 35$ | $n_{12} = 20$ |
| | *"Against"* | $n_{21} = 20$ | $n_{22} = 25$ |

$$\chi^2 = \frac{(n_{22} - n_{11})^2}{n_{22} + n_{11}} = \frac{(25-35)^2}{25+35} = \frac{(-10)^2}{60} = 1.67,\ p^{24} \approx .20$$

$$\chi^2 = \frac{(n_{22} - n_{11})^2}{n_{22} + n_{11}} - \quad \textbf{(13.17)}$$

Note in Table 13.4, that $n_{22}$ is the number who changed from "For" to "Against" the candidate, and $n_{11}$ is the number who changed from "Against" to "For." The critical value for the 2 × 2 contingency table in testing $H_0$ at the .05 level of significance is ${}_{.95}\chi_1^2 = 3.84$. Since the computed $\chi^2$ of 4.76 exceeds the critical value of 3.84, $H_0$ is rejected at the .05 level. From Table 13.4 it is apparent that there was a significant increase in the proportion of persons favoring the candidate since the proportion of voters favoring the candidate increased from .40 ($p_1 = 24/60$) to .55 ($p_2 = 33/60$).

As a second example, suppose a sample of $n = 100$ persons is asked to indicate whether they approve of capital punishment both before and after viewing a film dealing with that issue. Illustrative data for this research design are tabulated in Table 13.5.

Notice that prior to the film, the proportion of the sample who approved of capital punishment was .45 ($p_1 = 45/100$), whereas the proportion increased to $p_2 = 55/100 = .55$ after the film. Are the two proportions significantly different—do they differ only due to sampling error? Is the change statistically significant or does $H_0$: $\pi_1 = \pi_2$ remain tenable? In the lower portion of Figure 13.5, the observed value of $\chi^2$ was 1.67 (Equation 13.17). Since the observed chi-square value of 1.67 is smaller than the associated critical value of 3.84 (Table D), the null hypothesis is retained as tenable at the .05 level; these data fail to give convincing evidence that the file impacts viewers attitudes toward capital punishment.

## 13.18 CHAPTER SUMMARY

Categorical dependent variables are very common in behavioral research. The proportion $p$ of the sample that falls in a given category is an estimate of the proportion of the population

[24]The precise probability statement yielded by McNemar's test ($p = .197$) will differ trivially from the $p$-value ($p = .198$) yielded by the $t$-test for paired observations (or repeated-measures ANOVA, Chapter 20) for the dichotomous dependent variable: 0 = "against" and 1 = "for." This illustrates the robustness of the $t$-test (and ANOVA to non-normality.

in this category, $\pi$. Since $p$ is a mean, $E(p) = \pi$. The sampling distribution of sample proportions, $p$, is influenced by both the value of $\pi$ and sample size, $n$. As $\pi$ deviates from .50, the sampling distribution becomes increasingly skewed. The central limit theorem is at work, which causes the sampling distributions to become less skewed and more nearly normal as $n$ increases. The size of the sample required for the sampling distribution to be approximately normal varies greatly depending on the value of $\pi$. If the sampling distribution is approximately normal, the standard error of $p$, $\sigma_p$, can be used to establish approximate confidence intervals for the parameter $\pi$. Approximate confidence intervals about a proportion can also be estimated easily using the chart in Figure 13.5 even when samples are small and the sampling distribution is severely skewed. More accurate confidence limits can be obtained by using equations (Equations 13.8A–B) that do not assume that the sampling distribution is normal.

The $z$-test can be used to test whether a sample proportion differs significantly from the hypothesized value of the parameter $\pi$. The chi-square test is used to determine whether observed proportions or percentages differ from expected proportions or percentages. When the expected proportions are determined a priori based on theory, the $\chi^2$ test is a "goodness-of-fit" test (does the distribution of the empirical observation "fit" the theoretical distribution?). The chi-square goodness-of-fit test can determine whether the shape of a distribution differs from any theoretical distribution.

When the expected frequencies (proportions) are estimated from the data to be analyzed, the $\chi^2$ test is termed a test of association. It answers the question, "Are the two factors independent, or is there some degree of association or correlation between the two factors?" In such applications, the degrees of freedom for the $\chi^2$ test are the product $(R - 1)(C - 1)$, where the number of rows and columns in a contingency table are $R$ and $C$, respectively. The median test is a special application of the $\chi^2$ test of association. The magnitude of the association in $2 \times 2$ tables can be described by the phi coefficient, $r_\phi$. The McNemar test can be used to test $H_0$: $\pi_1 = \pi_2$ when the proportions are not independent but are from paired observations.

## 13.19 CASE STUDY

In the clinical trials to study the efficacy of AZT, persons with AIDS were randomly assigned to receive AZT or a placebo. Neither the subjects nor their physicians knew whether they were receiving AZT or the placebo (commonly referred to as a "double-blind" study). As evident in the contingency table below, after four months on the drug, one of the 137 subjects in the $E$ (AZT) group had died, whereas 19 of the 145 persons in the $C$ (placebo) group had died. Notice that the frequencies are converted to percentages to facilitate interpretation. Notice also that the expected percentages were 92.9% for the top row and 7.1% for the bottom row. The computer output for the chi-square test of association is given below.[25] Since AZT could conceivably be either helpful or harmful, a nondirectional $\chi^2$ test was used. A $\chi^2$-value of 16.37 was obtained for the $2 \times 2$ contingency table, which for $(2 - 1)(2 - 1) = 1$ degree of freedom yields $p = .00005$. In other words, if the null hypothesis were true, an association as great as that which was observed with the experimental data would be observed by chance only 5 times in 100,000;[26] hence, $H_0$ was rejected and it was con-

[25]Computed using SPSS for Windows.

[26]A $t$-test yields a $p$-value that is essentially equivalent: $p = .00004$.

cluded that AZT extends the life expectancy of persons with AIDS. Confidence intervals could be set for any of the cell proportions using Equations 13.8A–13.8B. The .95*CI*'s for the mortality proportions were (.00, .04) and (.08, .20) for the *E* and *C* groups, respectively.

| *Outcome* | *AZT Experimental Group 1* | *Control Group 2* | *Row Total* |
|---|---|---|---|
| *Alive* | 136<br>99.3% | 126<br>86.9% | 262<br>92.9% |
| *Dead* | 1<br>.7% | 19<br>13.1% | 20<br>7.1% |
| *Column Total* | 137<br>48.6% | 145<br>51.4% | 282<br>100.0% |

$\chi^2 = 16.37, p = .00005$

## 13.20 SUGGESTED COMPUTER ACTIVITY

Using the HSB data set, answer the following question using the chi-square test of association. Does the ratio of females to males (the students are seniors) differ among the four racial groups? Is race related to SES, school type (SCTYP), or type of high school program (HSP)?

## MASTERY TEST

1. If $n$ is 100, the *largest* value for $\sigma_p$ will result when $\pi =$ ____. ($\sigma_p = \sqrt{\pi(1-\pi)/n}$; find the answer by trial and error.)
2. If $n$ is 100 and $\pi = .5$, what is the value of $\sigma_p$?
3. If one repeatedly draws random samples with $n = 100$ from a population in which 50% ($\pi = .50$) favored candidate $A$, how often would a sample in which at least 60% ($p = .60$) favored candidate $A$ be obtained?
4. In question 3, what percentage of repeated samples would show between .45 and .55 of the respondents favoring candidate $A$?
5. If 80% of the population of voters favor a bond issue, what is the value of $\sigma_p$ for the following values of $n$?

   (a) $n_1 = 25$ (b) $n_2 = 100$ (c) $n_3 = 400$
6. What generalization regarding the precise relationship between $n$ and $\sigma_p$ is suggested in question 5? (Note: $n_2 = 4n_1$, $n_3 = 4n_2 = 16n_1$.)
7. Suppose $\sigma_p = .05$ with $n = 100$. If $n$ is reduced to 25, what will be the value of $\sigma_p$?
8. In a sample of $n = 100$ teachers, fifty preferred merit pay. Set a .95 confidence interval around the sample proportion of .50. Use $p \pm 2\hat{\sigma}_p$.

9. Use Figure 13.5 to determine the .95 confidence interval in question 8. Compare the results with that for question 8.
10. Use Figure 13.5 to establish the $.95CI$ for $\pi$ if:
    (a) $p = .2, n = 50$ (c) $p = .6, n = 50$
    (b) $p = .4, n = 50$ (d) $p = .6, n = 100$
11. Other things being equal, which of the confidence intervals will span the largest range of values?
    (a) $.90CI$ (b) $.95CI$ (c) $.99CI$
12. Which one of these symbols denotes the critical value for chi-square when $\alpha = .05$ with 2 degrees of freedom?
    (a) ${}_{.90}\chi_2^2$ (b) ${}_{.95}\chi_2^2$ (c) ${}_{.95}\chi^2$
13. Which is largest?
    (a) ${}_{.90}\chi_1^2$ (b) ${}_{.95}\chi_1^2$ (c) ${}_{.99}\chi_1^2$
14. Which is largest?
    (a) ${}_{.95}\chi_1^2$ (b) ${}_{.95}\chi_2^2$ (c) ${}_{.95}\chi_3^2$
15. In the $\chi^2$ goodness-of-fit test, are the expected proportions known prior to the collection of data?
16. In a $2 \times 5$ $\chi^2$ test of association, the critical value with $\alpha = .01$ is symbolized by which of the following?
    (a) ${}_{.99}\chi_1^2$ (b) ${}_{.99}\chi_4^2$ (c) ${}_{.99}\chi_5^2$ (d) ${}_{.01}\chi_4^2$
17. In Table D in the Appendix, study the pattern of ${}_{.50}\chi^2$-values for various degrees of freedom. What do you observe?
18. If the $\chi^2$ goodness-of-fit test is used to test data that are grouped into eight classes, what is the critical value with $\alpha = .05$?
19. If the data from a $3 \times 3$ contingency table yield a chi-square value of 9, is the relationship between the two variables statistically significant with $\alpha = .05$?
20. Which $\chi^2$ test should be used to see if the proportion of left-handedness was significantly different for 116 boys from that for 78 girls?
    (a) goodness-of-fit (b) test of association
21. In which of the following applications, can the $\chi^2$-statistic be used?
    (a) to compare proportions, $H_0$: $\pi_1 = \pi_2$
    (b) to determine if two categorical variables are associated
    (c) to compare medians in two groups
    (d) to compare medians in three or more groups
22. In a $3 \times 4$ contingency table, if $H_0$ were rejected using $\chi^2$, is it possible that $p = \hat{\pi}$ in some cells?
23. If the $\chi^2$ computation involves only one variable or factor (i.e., does not involve a contingency table), we can be sure that it is which of the following?
    (a) a goodness-of-fit $\chi^2$ test (b) a $\chi^2$ test of association
24. If $r_\phi = .20$ and $n = 100$,
    (a) Can $H_0$: $\rho_\phi = 0$ be rejected at the .05 level?
    (b) Can $H_0$: $\rho_\phi = 0$ be rejected at the .01 level?

*Suppose the 120 students who want to take Algebra I during period 3 have a choice of instructors. Four different instructors are available. Suppose a $\chi^2$ is used to determine if the proportion desiring (or avoiding) certain teachers differs significantly from chance.*

25. What is the expected proportion, $\pi$, for each instructor?

26. What is the critical value for $\chi^2$ with $\alpha = .05$?
27. If the computed $\chi^2$ is 15.4, could $H_0$ be rejected at the .05 level? at the .01 level? at the .001 level?
28. For what values of $\pi$ is it safe to assume that the sampling distribution of $p$ (the proportion in a sample of size 100) is approximately normally distributed?

## PROBLEMS AND EXERCISES

1. On true-false exams, is "True" the correct answer on half the questions? Examinations from several disciplines were studied. The results below for 90 items is typical.

*Ninety Items Classified by Correct Answer*

| *"True"* | *"False"* |
|---|---|
| 55 | 35 |

(a) What is the expected proportion for each of the two categories if the keying of the items is random?
(b) Is $H_0$: $\pi_1 = \pi_2 = .5$?
(c) What is the value of $\chi^2$?
(d) What is the critical value of $\chi^2$ at $\alpha = .05$?
(e) Is $H_0$ rejected at $\alpha = .05$?
(f) Is $H_0$ rejected at $\alpha = .01$?
(g) Set a $.95CI$ for $\pi_1$ (proportion "true") using Figure 13.5.

2. Is the correct answer on a multiple-choice test more likely to be in one response position than another? The following table gives the position of the correct answer for 100 items on one standardized cognitive test.

*Item Classified by Position of Correct Option*

| Position | 1 | 2 | 3 | 4 | 5 | Total |
|---|---|---|---|---|---|---|
| Frequency | 16 | 24 | 25 | 21 | 14 | 100 |

(a) Convert the observed frequencies to observed percentages.
(b) What are the expected percentages ($100\pi_j$) for all five cells? (Or, $H_0$: $100\pi_j = ?$)
(c) Compute $\chi^2$ using percents.
(d) What are the degrees of freedom of this chi-square test?
(e) What is the critical value for $\chi^2$ at $\alpha = .05$?
(f) Is $H_0$ tenable?

3. In problem 5, in answer to the question, "How happy has your home life been?" 92 of 1,405 high school students answered "Unhappy." Use Equations 13.8A and 13.8B to set the .95 confidence interval for the proportion, $\pi$, in this population who would give the same answer to this question, assuming this sample is representative. Why is the confidence interval so narrow?

4. A recent study examined genetic correlates of homosexuality in males. The male siblings of three groups were compared: (1) the identical twins of homosexuals, (2) the male fraternal twins of homosexuals, and (3) the foster brothers of homosexuals. Since all three groups were reared in the same homes, it was hypothesized that the concordance rates would be the same for all three

groups if homosexuality is due solely to environmental factors. The contingency table below gives the concordance data for the three groups of siblings (based on self-report).

| | *Identical Twins* | *Fraternal Twins* | *Foster Siblings* | *Row Totals* |
|---|---|---|---|---|
| *Yes* | $P_{11} = 51.79\%$<br>29 | $P_{12} = 22.22\%$<br>12 | $P_{13} = 10.53\%$<br>6 | $28.14\% = P_{1\bullet}$<br>47 |
| *No* | $P_{21} = 48.21\%$<br>27 | $P_{22} = 77.78\%$<br>42 | $P_{23} = 89.47\%$<br>51 | $71.86\% = P_{2\bullet}$<br>120 |
| *Column Totals* | 56 | 54 | 57 | 167 |

(a) Use Equation 13.13, and compute $\chi^2$.
(b) Can $H_0$ be rejected with $\alpha = .01$? . . . with $\alpha = .001$?
(c) Use Figure 13.5 to set .95*CI*'s for the concordance proportions ($\pi_{11}$, $\pi_{12}$, and $\pi_{13}$) for each of the three populations.
(d) Precise values for the *CI*'s require Equations 13.8A and 13.8B. Apply these equations for estimating $\pi_{13}$ (concordance proportion for foster siblings).

**5.** In a study of 1,405 high school and college students, a study found the following relationships between religious participation and the question, "How happy has your home life been?" Observed frequencies and percentages are given for each cell.

| | | *Participation in Religious Activities* | | | | |
|---|---|---|---|---|---|---|
| | | *Not at all* | *Very little* | *Somewhat* | *Very much* | *Row Totals* |
| *Answer to "How happy has your home life been?"* | Very happy | 105 (50%) | 257 (59%) | 368 (68%) | 151 (70%) | 881 (63%) |
| | Fairly happy | 78 (38%) | 149 (34%) | 153 (28%) | 52 (24%) | 432 (31%) |
| | Unhappy | 25 (12%) | 30 (7%) | 24 (4%) | 13 (6%) | 92 (7%) |
| | Column Totals | 28 | 436 | 545 | 216 | $1405 = n_{\bullet\bullet}$ |

(a) What is the critical $\chi^2$-value at $\alpha = .001$?
(b) Can $H_0$ be rejected with $\alpha = .001$?
(c) Conclusion?

**6.** A large group of men who smoked twenty or more cigarettes daily were compared with an equal number of similar men who had never smoked regularly (Hammond, 1964). The number of deaths during the following three-year period was more than twice as great among the smokers. Use Equation 13.14 and test the null hypothesis using the following data.

| | *Smokers* | *Nonsmokers* | *Row Totals* |
|---|---|---|---|
| Deaths | 1,385 | 662 | 2,047 |
| Living | 35,590 | 36,313 | 71,903 |
| Column Totals | 36,975 | 36,975 | 73,950 |

**7.** Based on 1,000 men within each group, the numbers of deaths within various age groups are given. Does the proportion of deaths differ among the four age groups? Use Equation 13.13.

| | *40's* | *50's* | *60's* | *70's* | *Row Totals* |
|---|---|---|---|---|---|
| Smokers | 30 | 75 | 157 | 337 | 599 |
| Nonsmokers | 10 | 34 | 85 | 199 | 328 |
| Column Totals | 40 | 109 | 242 | 536 | 927 |

**8.** Using the data in problem 5 following Chapter 3, determine whether the incidence of the eighty-seven suicide calls was significantly related to menstrual cycle. Use Equation 13.11.

**9.** A sample of 69 teachers (29 White and 40 Black) were asked whether they perceived "poor children" to be generally responsible or irresponsible. A phi coefficient of correlation was calculated between the race of the teacher, X, and the teacher's perception of "poor children," *Y*. A value of $r_\phi = .24$ seemed to indicate a weak relationship between the variables. White teachers tended to perceive "poor children" as irresponsible more than did Black teachers. Using the techniques of Section 13.15, test the hypothesis at the .05 level of significance that in the population of teachers sampled "teacher's race" and "perception of 'poor children' as irresponsible" are uncorrelated.

**10.** In one study, the relationship between student behavior and barometric pressure under conditions of high relative humidity was investigated. Four hundred thirteen classrooms were divided among three different barometric pressures (high, medium, low) and the teachers classified the behavior of the class as either normal, "squirmy," lethargic, or hyperactive.

| | | *Barometric Pressure* | | | |
|---|---|---|---|---|---|
| | | *Low* | *Medium* | *High* | *Totals* |
| *Class behavior* | Hyperactive | 30 | 34 | 5 | 69 |
| | "Squirmy" | 79 | 39 | 16 | 134 |
| | Normal | 60 | 97 | 23 | 180 |
| | Lethargic | 13 | 15 | 2 | 30 |
| | Totals | 182 | 185 | 46 | 413 |

Use the chi-square test (Equation 13.12) to test the null hypothesis at the .05 level of significance that barometric pressure and class behavior are independent in the population of classrooms sampled.

**11.** The relationship between pupils' self-concepts (above average versus below average) and whether they were members of a homogeneous or heterogeneous (with respect to classroom) group has been studied. The following data were obtained from a sample $n = 568$ seventh-grade pupils:

| | *Homogeneous* | *Heterogeneous* | *Totals* |
|---|---|---|---|
| Above | 137 | 159 | 296 |
| Below | 108 | 164 | 272 |
| Totals | 245 | 323 | 568 |

Use the $\chi^2$ median test to test the null hypothesis of independence of self-concept and classroom grouping in the population sampled at both the .10 and .05 levels of significance.

12. Use Equation 7.14 to determine the correlation $r_\phi$ between the attitudes, before and after the film, in the $2 \times 2$ contingency table of Table 13.4 in Section 13.17. Is $H_0$: $\rho_\phi = 0$ tenable at the .05 level?
13. If two of a random sample of 25 adolescents indicate that they have seriously contemplated suicide, estimate the proportion $\pi$ in the population that is represented by giving the .90 confidence interval.

## ANSWERS TO MASTERY TEST

1. For any value of $n$, the largest value of $\sigma_p$ occurs at $\pi = .5$.
2. $\sigma_p = \sqrt{\frac{(.5)(.5)}{100}} = .05$
3. $p = \pi + 2\sigma_p = .50 + 2(.05) = .60$ or $z = 2$, hence, in approximately 2% of the samples, the observed $p$ would equal or exceed .60.
4. approximately 68%, $(\pi \pm \sigma_p)$
5. $\hat{\sigma}_p \sqrt{\frac{(.8)(.2)}{n}} = \frac{.4}{\sqrt{n}}$
   (a) $\sigma_p = \frac{.4}{5} = .08$
   (b) $\sigma_p = \frac{.4}{10} = .04$
   (c) $\sigma_p = \frac{.4}{20} = .02$
6. If $n$ is quadrupled, $\sigma_p$ is reduced by half.
7. $\sigma_p = .10$
8. $.95CI = .5 \pm 2(.05) = .4$ to $.6$
9. $.95CI = .4$ to $.6$ (same result as in question 8)
10. (a) approximately .11 to .33
    (b) approximately .27 to .54
    (c) approximately .46 to .73
    (d) approximately .50 to .69
11. (c)
12. (b)
13. (c)
14. (c)
15. yes
16. (b)
17. The value of ${}_{.50}\chi^2$ (the median in the $\chi^2$-distribution) is approximately equal to the corresponding $\nu$-value, especially as $\nu$ increases.
18. ${}_{.95}\chi_7^2 = 14.07$
19. No, $p > .05$; ${}_{.95}\chi_4^2 = 9.49$
20. (b)
21. in all four (a–d)
22. yes
23. (a)
24. (a) yes, $\chi^2 = 100(.2)^2 = 4.0 > 3.84 = {}_{.95}\chi_1^2$
    (b) no, ${}_{.99}\chi_1^2 = 6.64$
25. $\pi = \frac{30}{120} = .25$
26. ${}_{.95}\chi_3^2 = 7.82$
27. Yes, $15.4 > 7.82$; yes, $15.4 > 11.34$; no, $15.4 < 16.27 = {}_{.999}\chi_3^2$; $.01 > p > .001$
28. $.28 < \pi < .72$ (See Figure 13.4.)

## ANSWERS TO PROBLEMS AND EXERCISES

1. (a) $\pi_1 = \pi_2 = .5$
   (b) yes
   (c) $\chi^2 = n_{\bullet}\Sigma\frac{(p_j - \pi)^2}{\pi}$

$$= 90\left[\frac{(.611 - .50)^2}{.50} + \frac{(.389 - .50)^2}{.50}\right]$$

$$= 90\left[\frac{(.111)^2}{.50} + \frac{(.111)^2}{.50}\right] = 90(.0493) = 4.44$$

(d) ${}_{.95}\chi_1^2 = 3.84$
(e) yes, since $4.44 > 3.84$, $p < .05$
(f) no: ${}_{.99}\chi_1^2 = 6.64$; $.05 > p > .01$;
(g) (.51, .71)

2. (a) Since $n_{\bullet} = 100$, the observed frequencies are also the observed percentages.
(b) $H_0$: $100\,\pi = 20$
(c)
$$\chi^2 = \frac{n_{\bullet}}{100}\Sigma\frac{(P-100\pi)^2}{100\pi}$$
$$= \frac{\not{1}\not{0}\not{0}}{\not{1}\not{0}\not{0}} \times \left[\frac{(16-20)^2}{20} + \frac{(24-20)^2}{20} + \frac{(25-20)^2}{20} + \frac{(21-20)^2}{20} + \frac{(14-20)^2}{20}\right]$$
$$= \left[\frac{(4)^2 + (4)^2 + (5)^2 + (1)^2 + (6)^2}{20}\right]$$
$$= \frac{16+16+25+1+36}{20} = \frac{94}{20}$$
$$= 4.70$$
(d) $\nu = J - 1 = 5 - 1 = 4$
(e) ${}_{.95}\chi_4^2 = 9.49$
(f) yes: $p > .05$

3. (.054, .080); because $n$ is quite large.

4. (a) $\chi^2 = 167(1.1507 - 1) = 25.16$;
(b) yes, yes;
(c) ≈ (.38, .65), (.12, .35), and (.04, .22);
(d) (.049, .211)

5. (a) ${}_{.999}\chi_6^2 = 22.46$
(b) $\chi^2 = 34.83 > 22.46$, $p < .001$
(c) There was a positive relationship between amount of participation in religious activities and self-rated happiness of home life.

6. $\chi^2 = 262.6$, $p < .001$; $H_0$ is rejected at the .001 level.

7. no, $\chi^2 = 3.44$, $p > .10$, ${}_{.90}\chi_3^2 = 6.25$

8. $\chi^2 = 31.17$; $p < .001$, ${}_{.999}\chi_6^2 = 22.46$

9. $\chi^2 = 69(.24^2) = 3.97$, ${}_{.95}\chi_1^2 = 3.84$; reject $H_0$ at .05 level.

10. The obtained value of $\chi^2$ is 24.6. The 95th percentile in the $\chi^2$ distribution with six degrees of freedom is 12.59. Hence, reject the null hypothesis of "no association" between the two factors of classification at the .05 level. Indeed, reject $H_0$ at the .001 level since ${}_{.999}\chi_6^2 = 22.46$.

11. The obtained value of $\chi^2$ is approximately 2.50. The 90th and 95th percentiles in the $\chi^2$ distribution with one degree of freedom are 2.71 and 3.84, respectively; hence the obtained $\chi^2$ is nonsignificant at the .10 (and .05) level.

12. No, $r_\phi = .465$, $\chi^2 = 12.97$, $p < .001$.

13. $\pi_L = .9023(.08 + .0541 - .1044) = .027$
$\pi_U = 3(2.31)/[23 + 3(2.31)] = .23$; $.9023(.08 + .0541 + .1044) = .215$
$.90CI = (.027, .215)$

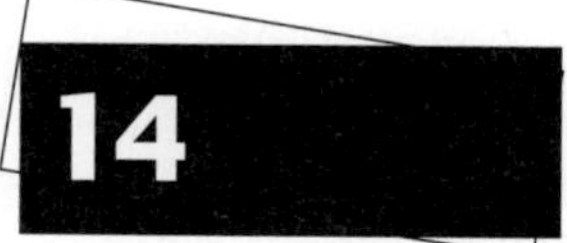

# INFERENCES ABOUT CORRELATION COEFFICIENTS

## 14.1 TESTING STATISTICAL HYPOTHESES REGARDING $\rho$

How does one decide whether a correlation coefficient, $r$, obtained on a sample is statistically significant (greater than zero in the population); how is $H_0$: $\rho = 0$ tested? A representative sample of new mothers is selected and the relationship between two variables is examined: weight-gain during pregnancy, $X$, and birthweight of the baby, $Y$. Both measures are approximately normally distributed; it is reasonable to believe that the relationship between the two variables is bivariate normal (Section 7.13). Interest centers on $\rho$, the Pearson product-moment correlation, $r$, between $X$ (mother's weight-gain) and $Y$ (baby's birthweight) in the population.

We will reason inductively from the sample, $r$, to the population, $\rho$. A decision will be made about a statistical hypothesis that specifies that $\rho$ is a particular number. Partly out of habit, partly because of tradition, and partly because it is a sensible choice,[1] the hypothesis that in the population the correlation between $X$ and $Y$ is zero ($H_0$: $\rho = 0$) will be tested. On the basis of the observed $r$ from the sample, we will decide either to reject this hypothesis or accept it as tenable.

What constitutes a sensible test of the hypothesis $H_0$: $\rho = 0$ in this situation? Should one compute $r$ for the sample, then decide that $H_0$ is true if $r$ is zero, or that $H_0$ is false if $r$ is not zero? Obviously not; we know that any statistic based on samples contains sampling error. It is quite possible for $\rho$ to equal 0 in the population and for $r$ to be substantially different from 0 in a sample. In fact, if $\rho = 0$, an $r$ of .5, .6, or even larger is possible! Such $r$'s are very improbable when $\rho = 0$ unless $n$ is very small, but they are possible (in the same way that it is possible to toss a coin ten times and obtain 10 "heads"). This presents a perplexing

[1]The good sense in hypothesizing that $\rho = 0$ is at least twofold: $\rho = 0$ is the midpoint between positive and negative correlations; and zero correlations between variables are particularly important—they indicate that the two variables are independent.

problem: Even if in the population, $\rho = 0$, any value of $r$ from –1 to +1 is a theoretical "possibility" (i.e., has a probability greater than zero) in a random sample of observations. Consequently, regardless of the value of $r$ for the sample, one cannot with absolute certainty conclude that $\rho$ is, or is not, zero. This important principle underlies all tests of statistical hypotheses: In testing any statistical hypothesis, the researcher's decision that the hypothesis is tenable, or that it is false, is never made with absolute certainty; a *risk* of making an incorrect decision is *always present*. The purpose of statistical hypothesis testing is to enable one to control and assess that risk.

In the *Infant Growth Study* (Stember, Lewis, Hester, Clark, & Hopkins, 1995), measures of mother's weight-gain and birthweight, $X$ and $Y$, were obtained for a representative sample of 658 newborn infants. The correlation between $X$ and $Y$ was computed and found to be .212.

There is uncertainty in the decision about whether the observed value of $r$ is due to chance—does $r$ differ from 0 only because of sampling error? An $r$ of .212 does not differ greatly from 0; on the other hand, the sample size is quite large. This brings us to a familiar problem; how does one estimate the value of a parameter from a statistic that contains some degree of sampling error? As in previous chapters, the inferential problems of hypothesis testing are addressed through the concept of a sampling distribution; the basic theory is the same as in Chapters 10 and 11, but we now apply it to correlation coefficients.

## 14.2 TESTING $H_0$: $\rho = 0$ USING THE *t*-TEST[2]

When $\rho = 0$, the ratio defined in Equation 14.1 has a $t$-distribution with $\nu = n - 2$ degrees of freedom, where $n$ is the number of *pairs* of scores:

$$t = \frac{r - \rho}{s_r} \qquad \textbf{(14.1)}$$

where $s_r$ is an estimate of the standard error of $r$:

$$s_r = \sqrt{\frac{1 - r^2}{n - 2}} = \sqrt{\frac{1 - r^2}{\nu}} \qquad \textbf{(14.2)}$$

In most applications, $H_0$: $\rho = 0$; when this is the case, Equation 14.1 simplifies to Equation 14.1A:

$$t = \frac{r}{s_r} \qquad \textbf{(14.1A)}$$

[2]The $t$-test for testing $H_0$: $\rho = 0$ is slightly more powerful than either the $z$-test, where $z = r/\sigma_r$ and $\sigma_r = 1/\sqrt{n-1}$, or the $z$-test using the Fisher Z-transformation of $r$ (Equations 14.4 and 14.5): $z = Z/(1/\sqrt{n-3})$. For practical purposes, the differences among the $z$-tests and the $t$-test are negligible; the decision regarding $H_0$ would almost always be the same for all.

In the study of mothers' weight-gains and infants' birthweights, $r = .212$ and $n = 658$. Does the $r$ represent a genuine relationship or is it only a chance finding—is $H_0$: $\rho = 0$ tenable? Using Equation 14.2, we find that the standard error of the correlation coefficient is:

$$s_r = \sqrt{\frac{1-r^2}{n-2}} = \sqrt{\frac{1-(.212)^2}{658-2}} = \sqrt{.0014559}$$

$$s_r = .0382$$

From Equation 14.1A, we find the $t$-ratio:

$$t = \frac{r}{s_r} = \frac{.212}{.0382} = 5.55$$

The critical value for $t$ is found from Table C in the Appendix; 5.55 is considerably larger than the critical value[3] for $t$ even at $\alpha_2 = .001$: ${}_{.9995}t_{656} \approx 3.310$. Although the correlation coefficient is quite small, the $r$ is significantly greater than 0 at the .001 level. Because $n$ is quite large, even such a small value of $r$ as .212 is extremely improbable if indeed, $\rho = 0$; thus, we reject $H_0$ ($p < .001$).

Equation 14.1A can be rearranged to yield the *minimum* value for which $H_0$: $\rho = 0$ can be rejected. In other words, the *critical value* of $r$ can be found by supplying the degrees of freedom ($\nu = n - 2$) and the critical value of $t$:

$$r_{\text{critical}} = \frac{t}{\sqrt{t^2 + \nu}} \qquad \textbf{(14.3)}$$

More explicitly:

$${}_{1-\alpha/2}r_\nu = \frac{{}_{1-\alpha/2}t_\nu}{\sqrt{{}_{1-\alpha/2}t_\nu^2 + \nu}}$$

where $t$ is the critical value of $t$ (i.e., ${}_{1-\alpha/2}t_\nu$). The critical $t$ for Equation 14.3 can be read from Table C. When the value of $\nu = n - 2$ and the associated critical $t$-value for $n - 2$ degrees of freedom are substituted into Equation 14.3, the result is the minimum $r$ necessary to reject $H_0$: $\rho = 0$. For example, how large must $r$ be to reject the null hypothesis at $\alpha_2 = .05$, if $n = 25$? From Table C, ${}_{.975}t_{23} = 2.07$; hence, from Equation 14.3:

$$r_{\text{critical}} = \frac{2.07}{\sqrt{(2.07)^2 + 23}} = \frac{2.07}{\sqrt{27.285}} = .396$$

---

[3]Recall that when the precise value for $\nu$ is not tabled, the closest, but lower value of $\nu$ is used to be conservative. The exact value of the critical $t$ can be found by supplying $\alpha$ and $\nu$ to certain software and spreadsheets. The precise critical $t$ is 3.305 which differs trivially from 3.310. The exact probability is reported in most statistical software and spreadsheets. The probability (from EXCEL TDIST) of observing an $r$ of .212 with $n = 658$ is incredibly small: $p = .00000004$! It is probably best to report $p$ only to three of four decimal places, for example, $p < .001$ or $p < .0001$, since the probabilities are exact only when all assumptions are perfectly met.

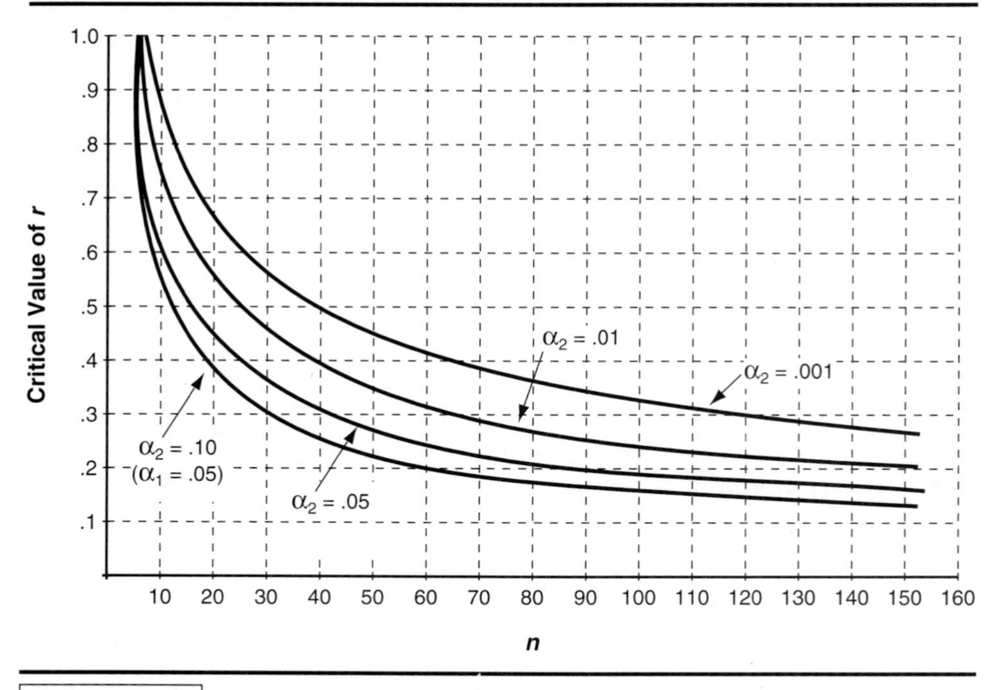


**FIGURE 14.1** Critical values of Pearson's $r$ for rejecting $H_0$: $\rho = 0$ with $\alpha_2 = .001$, $\alpha_2 = .01$, $\alpha_2 = .05$, and $\alpha_2 = .10$ ($\alpha_1 = .05$) for various sample sizes.

Hence, if $n = 25$, one does not need to compute $t$ (Equation 14.1) since the critical value for $r$ is .396; if $|r| < .396$, $H_0$ is tenable; if $|r| \geq .396$, $H_0$ is rejected at $\alpha_2 = .05$. The critical values of $r$ (for various $n$'s and $\alpha$-values) are graphed in Figure 14.1 . Notice in Figure 14.1 how the critical value of $r$ decreases as $n$ increases, especially when $n$ is small. Note also that larger values of $r$ are required for smaller values of $\alpha$. If $n$ is large, very small values of $r$ lead to rejection of $H_0$: $\rho = 0$. If $r = .3$ and $n = 50$, $H_0$: $\rho = 0$ would not be rejected at $\alpha_2 = .01$ because $r = .3$ is less than .37, the critical $r$ for $n = 50$ with $\alpha_2 = .01$, but if $n = 150$ and $r = .30$, $H_0$ can be rejected at the .001 level.

Figure 14.1 can also be used to determine the sample size $n$ associated with a particular critical value for $r$. For example, how large a sample is required to reject $H_0$: $\rho = 0$ if the observed value of $r$ is .4? The null hypothesis will be rejected at $\alpha_2 = .10$, $\alpha_2 = .05$, $\alpha_2 = .01$, and $\alpha_2 = .001$ if the $n$'s are 18, 25, 40, and 65, respectively.

Table J in the Appendix gives the precise critical values of $r$ for one- and two-tailed tests at various values of $\alpha$ and $n$. For example, if $n$ = 1,000, even a very small value of $r$ ($|r| \geq .104$) will allow the null hypothesis ($\rho = 0$) to be rejected at $\alpha_2 = .001$. If $n$ = 10,000, even $r = .04$ would be statistically significant at the .001 level! Statistical significance obviously does not mean that the relationship between the two variables is high; it only means that we can be confident that it is *not* zero.

For our example with $r = .212$ and $n = 658$, from Table J, we find that if $n = 500$ (the closest conservative value), $H_0$: $\rho = 0$ will be rejected at $\alpha_2 = .001$ if $r \geq .147$. The $r$ of .212 exceeds the critical $r$ of .147; thus, $H_0$ is rejected at the .001 level.

## 14.3 DIRECTIONAL ALTERNATIVES: "TWO-TAILED" VS. "ONE-TAILED" TESTS

Just as when testing means, a statistical test for $H_0$: $\rho = 0$ can be designated as either nondirectional or directional. A nondirectional test leads to the conclusion that either $\rho > 0$ or $\rho < 0$ when $H_0$: $\rho = 0$ is rejected. If logic allows the investigator to conclude that either $\rho < 0$ or $\rho > 0$ is unreasonable, there are advantages to using a one-tailed test. If it can be safely assumed that if $\rho$ does not equal zero then $\rho$ is greater than zero (i.e., that $\rho \geq 0$), a directional test is in order. If a value of $\rho$ less than 0 is unreasonable, the evidence will show that either $\rho$ is positive or that it is tenable to continue to hold that $\rho$ is zero. For example, if we wish to see if hand size and foot size are correlated, a one-tailed test should be used because a negative correlation is unreasonable—if there is a relationship, it will be positive. Likewise, if we wish to study the relationship between spelling ability and math ability, logic suggests that if there is a correlation, it will be positive. Note that we do not have to foresee a relationship between $X$ and $Y$; we only need to be able to conclude that if there is a relationship it will not be negative (or positive).

One consequence of making a directional test is that the critical region for rejection of $H_0$ falls in one tail of the sampling distribution of $r$ for $\rho = 0$. The fact that the critical region "lies in one tail" of the sampling distribution of the statistic under the null hypothesis has made the term "one-tailed test" popular for a significance test of a directional hypothesis. Likewise "two-tailed" and "nondirectional" tests are synonymous. Notice in Figure 14.1 that if $n = 30$, $H_0$: $\rho = 0$ will be rejected with a nondirectional hypothesis ($\alpha_2 = .05$) only if $r$ is at least .36; whereas, with a directional hypothesis ($\alpha_1 = .05$) $H_0$ can be rejected with a smaller correlation coefficient ($r \geq .31$).

One should not employ directional tests thoughtlessly (Section 11.13). To be perfectly legitimate, for example, if $H_0$ is $\rho = 0$ and $H_1$ is $\rho > 0$, one must look the other way and refuse to budge from the conclusion that $\rho$ is zero even if a sample of 1,000 yields an $r$ of $-.9$! Once committed to a one-tailed test, one should not reverse position and perform a nondirectional test. However, when properly guided by sound logic, theory, or previous research, one-tailed tests are appropriate and more powerful than two-tailed tests. In other words, if $X$ and $Y$ are really correlated, we have a greater chance of arriving at the correct conclusion (i.e., of rejecting $H_0$) by using a one-tailed test when it can be justified.

Directional tests might be justified in testing the correlations for the following pairs of variables, where reason suggests that each pair of variables is positively correlated: reading vocabulary and speaking vocabulary, age and strength for pupils in grades one through twelve, spelling ability and IQ, musical aptitude and IQ, and socioeconomic status and grade-point average. Reason also suggested that a one-tailed test could be justified if we hypothesize that achievement in algebra I is negatively correlated with absenteeism, where a positive correlation is unreasonable.

A directional test for $H_1$: $\rho > 0$ does *not* require knowledge that indeed $\rho > 0$; it only requires that negative values for $\rho$ can be safely regarded as unreasonable (or vice versa). One-tailed tests should not be employed when there is a reasonable possibility that the parameter $\rho$ can be either positive or negative. Unless otherwise specified, it is conventional to assume that statistical tests are nondirectional. Directional tests, however, are much more common when testing hypotheses regarding correlations than when comparing means or proportions.[4]

---

[4]Indeed, the default option in SPSS and certain other statistical software employs one-tailed tests. Of course, if a two-tailed test is being used, it is a simple matter to double the $p$-value yield by the one-tailed test.

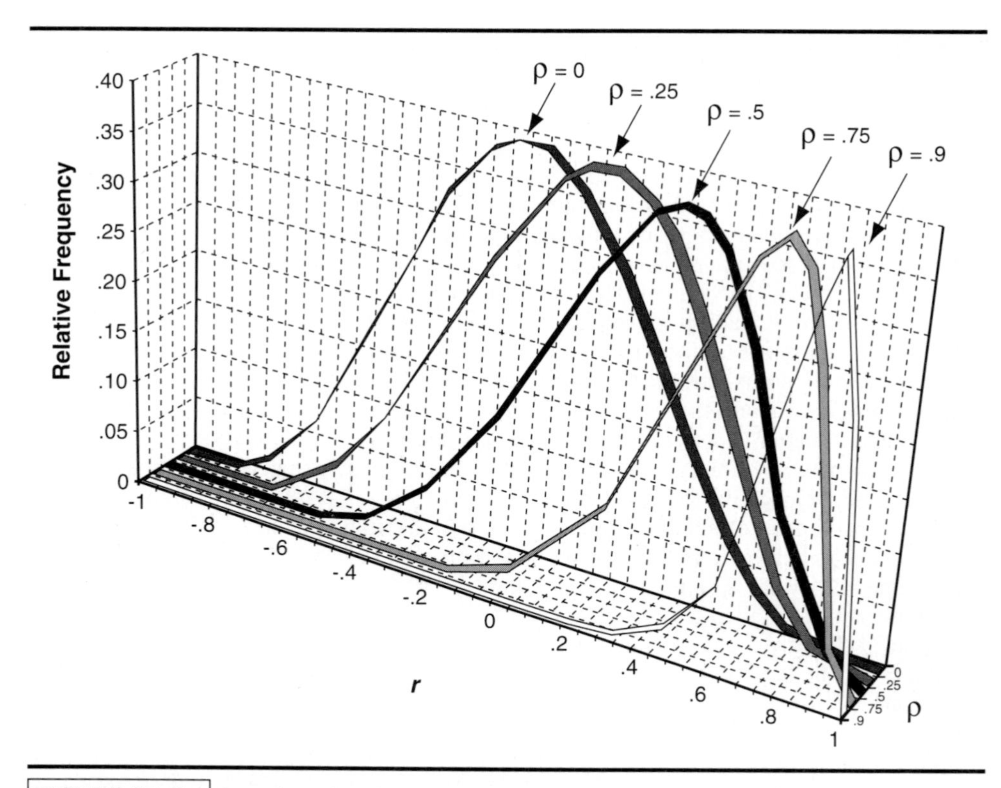


**FIGURE 14.2** Sampling distributions of $r$ for $\rho = .9, .75, .5, .25$, and 0 with $n = 10$.

## 14.4 SAMPLING DISTRIBUTION OF *r*

The sampling distribution of $r$ for all values of $\rho$ other than 0 is not normal, but skewed to some degree. The correlation between the heights of identical twins is ≈ .95 (from Table 7.1). If one only has a sample of five pair of twins on which to estimate this parameter, what could happen? If $n = 5$, one could possibly find a value of .99+, or one might find $r = .50$—note the largest possible positive value for sampling error $(r - \rho)$ is .05 (because the highest possible value of $r$ is 1)—there is more room to vary on the lower side of $\rho$ than on the higher side. The sampling distribution is neither normal nor symmetrical.[5]

Figure 14.2 depicts the sampling distributions of $r$ with $n = 10$ for five populations: when the parameter $\rho$ is = .9, .75, .50, .25, and 0. Note that the distribution is symmetrical only when $\rho = 0$, and that the skewness increases as $\rho$ deviates from 0. Note from Figure 14.2 that with a random sample of $n = 10$ observations from a population with $\rho = .75$, an $r$ of 0 or less will be observed occasionally ($\rho$ will be underestimated by .75 or more units)! Can $r$ be overestimated by .75 units? Since the maximum value for $r$ is 1.0, $r$ can exceed the

[5]Obviously, this $n$ is ridiculously small for such a purpose; the illustration serves to illuminate the skewness in the sampling distribution.

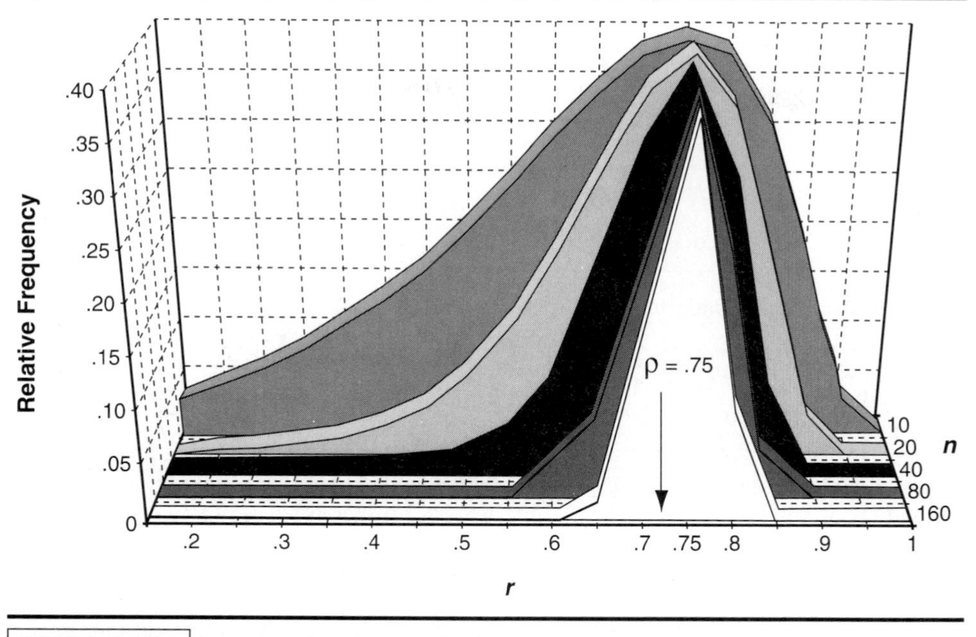


**FIGURE 14.3** Sampling distributions for $\rho = .75$ for $n = 10, 20, 40, 80$, and 160.*

*Figures 14.2 and 14.3 were produced using spreadsheet software: $r$'s were transformed to Fisher $Z$s. The ordinates for the $z$-ratios for various values of $Z$ (for specified values of $r$) were obtained using Equation 6.3.

parameter $\rho$ at most by .25; consequently, the sampling distribution of $r$ is skewed. The more that $\rho$ differs from zero, the greater the skewness.

When $\rho$ is greater than zero, the sampling distribution is negatively skewed, as in Figure 14.2. When $\rho$ is negative, the situation is just the reverse, and the sampling distribution will be positively skewed.[6] Obviously, if the sampling distribution is skewed, the common procedure for setting confidence intervals (adding and subtracting a constant value to the sample statistic) will not yield accurate limits. As $n$ increases, the sampling distribution of $r$ becomes more nearly normal (and less variable), as shown in Figure 14.3. Figure 14.3 gives the sampling distributions of $r$ for $\rho = .75$ when the sample sizes varies from 10 to 160. Note that as $n$ increases, the skewness decreases, but some skewness is still evident in the sampling distribution even when $n = 160$.

## 14.5 THE FISHER Z-TRANSFORMATION

R. A. Fisher devised a mathematical transformation, $Z$, of $r$ that has an approximately normal sampling distribution irrespective of $\rho$ or $n$. This transformation, known as

[6]The skewness in sampling distributions is similar to that for sample proportions (see Figure 14.2).

Fisher's Z-transformation,[7] is a trigonometric function of $r$:[8]

$$Z = \tanh^{-1} r \qquad \textbf{(14.4A)}$$

Equivalently, but expressed in natural logarithms:[9]

$$|Z| = .5 \ \mathrm{Ln}\left(\frac{1+|r|}{1-|r|}\right) \qquad \textbf{(14.4B)}$$

Or, expressed in common logarithms:

$$|Z| = 1.1513 \ \mathrm{Log}\left(\frac{1+|r|}{1-|r|}\right) \qquad \textbf{(14.4C)}$$

If you do not have access to a calculator or spreadsheet with the trigonometric function or the natural or common log function, Table E in the Appendix gives the values for $Z$ for values of $r$ from 0 to 1.00 in steps of .005. The sign of $Z$ is always the same as that of $r$. Verify from your calculator or spreadsheet or Table E that for $r = .395$, $Z$ is .418, and that for $r = -.775$, $Z$ is $= -1.033$.

Fisher showed that, unlike the sampling distribution of $r$, the sampling distribution of $Z$ for samples from a bivariate normal distribution approaches normality rapidly. The variance of $Z$ (unlike that of $r$) is independent of the value of the parameter $\rho$ even if samples are not large. Figure 14.2 depicted the sampling distributions of $r$ when the sample size is small ($n = 10$) and the values of the parameter, $\rho$, are 0, .25, .5, .75, and .90. Note the increase in the skewness of the sampling distributions as $\rho$ deviates from 0. If, instead of building sampling distributions of the $r$'s, the sampling distributions of the corresponding $Z$'s were built, the sampling distributions of the $Z$'s would be nearly normal, with the mean equal to the parameter $Z$ that corresponds to $\rho$, that is, $Z_\rho$. The sampling distributions of the $Z$'s for $\rho = 0$, .25, .5, .75, and .9 with $n = 10$ are given in Figure 14.4. The standard error of Fisher $Z$ (i.e., the standard deviation of the sampling distribution) is determined only by $n$; note in Figure 14.4 that the variability of the five curves is equal. The standard error of Fisher $Z$, $\sigma_Z$, is given by Equation 14.5. It is needed to set confidence intervals for $\rho$:

$$\sigma_Z = \frac{1}{\sqrt{n-3}} \qquad \textbf{(14.5)}$$

---

[7]Not to be confused with $z$ of the $z$-ratio or $z$-test. We will use the capital letter $Z$ when speaking of Fisher's $Z$; we will continue to use the lowercase $z$ for the $z$-test or $z$-score.

[8]$Z$ is the hyperbolic arctangent of $r$, that is, $Z = \tanh^{-1} r$. On many calculators with trigonometric functions, $Z$ may be obtained by entering the value of $r$ (e.g., .4), pressing the "inverse" key, **INV**, then pressing the **tanh** key. If for $r = .4$, you get $Z = .42365$, your procedures are correct. To convert $Z$ back to $r$, enter $Z$, then press the **tanh** key. On some calculators, one must use the **hyp** (for hyperbolic) and **tan⁻¹** keys to obtain $Z$ from $r$, and **hyp** **tan** to go from $Z$ to $r$. On the EXCEL spreadsheet, the paste function "FISHER( )" returns the Fisher $Z$ transformation when the value of $r$ is supplied in the parentheses.

[9]A brief explanation of natural and common logarithms ("logs") can be found in Section 16.9.

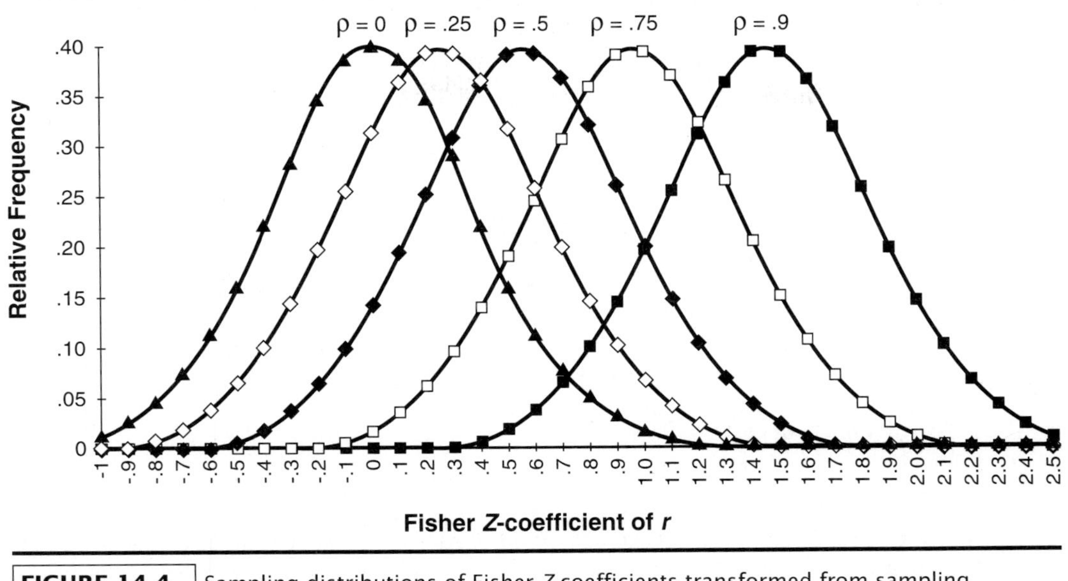


FIGURE 14.4 Sampling distributions of Fisher Z-coefficients transformed from sampling distributions for $\rho = 0, .25, .5, .75$, and .9 ($n = 10$).

## 14.6 SETTING CONFIDENCE INTERVALS FOR $\rho$

Fisher's Z-transformation provides what is needed for a solution to the problem of placing confidence intervals around $r$. In Equation 14.5, the standard deviation of $Z$ over repeated random samples is $1/\sqrt{n-3}$, regardless of the value of $\rho$. Hence, 95% of the $Z$'s obtained in repeated random samples will lie within 1.96 standard deviations (a distance of $1.96\sigma_Z$) of $Z_\rho$; and 99% of the $Z$'s will lie within a distance of $2.576\sigma_Z$ of $Z_\rho$. The distribution of $Z$ is approximately normal regardless of the size of $n$. Consequently, if $1.96\sigma_Z$ is added to $Z_r$, and subtracted from $Z_r$, we can be 95% confident that the parameter $Z_\rho$ falls within this interval. The procedure for forming .95 confidence intervals is illustrated in Figure 14.5.

To illustrate the steps outlined in Figure 14.5, one study reported an $r$ of .83 between the IQ's of thirty pairs of identical twins reared apart. Obviously, with $n = 30$, $r$ is not a

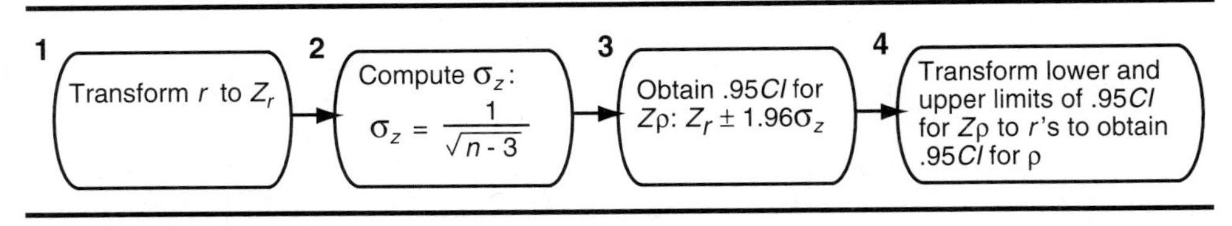


FIGURE 14.5 Flowchart for setting .95 confidence interval for $\rho$.

precise estimate of $\rho$. Suppose a confidence interval with confidence coefficient .95 is desired:

1. $r$ is transformed into $Z_r$:[10] for $r = .83$, $Z_r = 1.188$.
2. The standard error of $Z$ is found using Equation 14.5:

$$\sigma_Z = \frac{1}{\sqrt{n-3}} = \frac{1}{\sqrt{30-3}} = .1925$$

3. The 95% confidence interval on $Z_\rho$ is found:

$$Z_r \pm 1.96\sigma_Z = 1.188 \pm (1.96)(.1925) = 1.188 \pm .377, \text{ or } (.811, 1.565)$$

4. The lower and upper limits of the confidence interval for $Z_\rho$ are transformed back into the corresponding values of $r$. What are the values of $r$ which correspond to $Z$'s of .811 and 1.565? A Fisher $Z$ of .811 corresponds to an $r$ of .670, and a $Z$ of 1.565 corresponds to an $r$ of .916. Therefore, the 95% confidence interval for extends from .670 to .916, often expressed as (.670, .916).

One may feel quite confident that the value of $\rho$, the population correlation coefficient, is between .670 and .916. Notice that the limits of the .95 confidence interval, .670 and .916, are not equidistant from the observed $r$ of .83. This result is expected because this sampling distribution of $r$ is negatively skewed (see Figure 14.2).

How does the interval (.67, .92) compare with that for identical twins reared together? One study reported a correlation of .93 between IQ scores of eighty-three pairs of identical twins reared together. An $r$ of .93 corresponds to a $Z$ of 1.658. With $n = 83$, the standard error of $Z$, $\sigma_Z$, is .112; the .95 confidence interval therefore is $1.658 \pm 1.96(.112) = 1.658 \pm .220$, or (1.438, 1.878). The transformation of the lower and upper $Z$-limits of the .95 confidence interval back to correlation coefficients yields limits on $\rho$ of .893 and .954. Notice the width of this confidence interval is much narrower than the previous interval for identical twins reared apart; this results because of the larger $n$ in this instance (83 vs. 30).[11]

## 14.7 DETERMINING CONFIDENCE INTERVALS GRAPHICALLY

A quick and reasonably accurate .95 confidence interval for $\rho$ can be read directly from Figure 14.6. For example, if $r = .20$ with $n = 25$, enter the figure along the base axis at +.20 and read upward until the curved line for $n = 25$ is met; then read the value of that point on the vertical axis (–.21, for $r = .2$ and $n = 25$). The lower limit of the .95 confidence interval is then –.21. To find the upper limit, continue going upward until the other curved line for $n = 25$ is met; and again read the value on the vertical axis (+.55). The .95 confidence interval for $\rho$ with $r = .20$ and $n = 25$ extends, then, from approximately –.21 to +.55. Note that Figure 14.6 cannot be used to accurately approximate the confidence interval in our example with $r = .212$ and $n = 658$.

---

[10]Use your calculator (or a spreadsheet) if it has the hyperbolic arctangent trigonometric function (see footnote 8 earlier in this chapter.) Table E will also give results that are satisfactory.

[11]Practice by setting the .95*CI* for $\rho$ using the example where $r = .212$ and $n = 658$? Your answer agrees with ours if you found (.138, .284); the value for the parameter, $\rho$, is probably at least .138, and perhaps as high as .284.

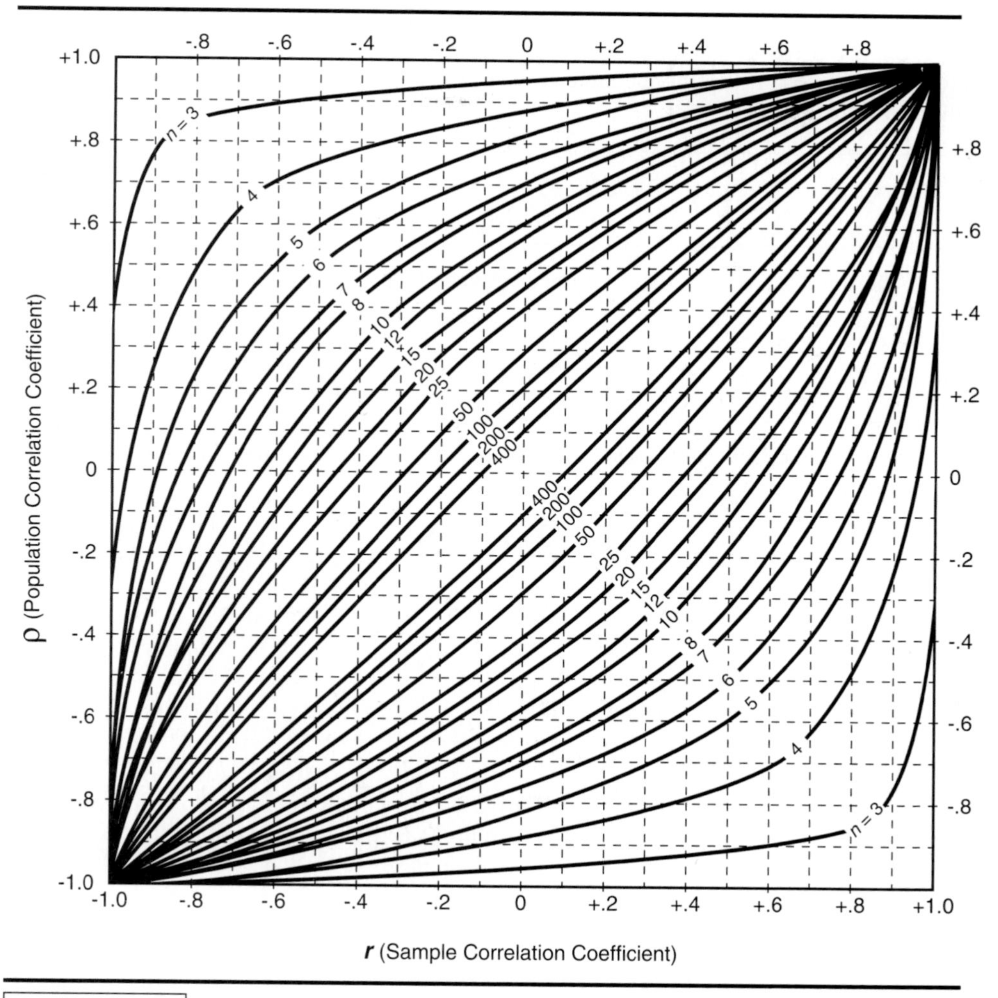


**FIGURE 14.6** .95 confidence intervals around $r$ for $\rho$ for $n = 3, 4, \ldots, 400$. Enter $r$ on base axis and read $\rho$'s where $r$- and $n$-values intersect. For example, the .95 confidence interval for $\rho$ if $r = +.6$ and $n = 50$ is .4 to .76. (Reprinted with E. S. Pearson and H. O. Hartley, eds., *Biometrika Tables for Statisticians*, 2nd ed. [Cambridge: Cambridge University Press, 1962], by permission of the *Biometrika* Trustees and Cambridge University Press.)

## 14.8 TESTING THE DIFFERENCE BETWEEN INDEPENDENT CORRELATION COEFFICIENTS: $H_0$: $\rho_1 = \rho_2$

Earlier, the .95 confidence intervals for $\rho$ were determined for identical twins reared apart and reared together. Do the two $r$'s differ significantly? Can the null hypothesis $H_0$: $\rho_1 = \rho_2$ be rejected? At such times, one is interested in hypotheses regarding *differences* in $\rho$'s. Are the IQ's of identical twins reared together correlated more highly than the IQ's of identical twins reared apart? If intellectual performance is determined solely by heredity, the $\rho$'s would be expected to be equal. To test the hypothesis, $H_0$: $\rho_1 = \rho_2$, the $z$-test will be employed. The $z$-test for testing the significance of the difference between independent $r$'s is given in Equation 14.6:

$$z = \frac{Z_1 - Z_2}{\sigma_{Z_1 - Z_2}} \tag{14.6}$$

where the standard error of the difference between Fisher $Z$'s is:

$$\sigma_{Z_1 - Z_2} = \sqrt{\sigma_{Z_1}^2 + \sigma_{Z_2}^2} = \sqrt{\frac{1}{n_1 - 3} + \frac{1}{n_2 - 3}} \tag{14.7}$$

The $r$'s for the IQ scores of identical twins reared apart and together were given in the preceding section:

***Identical Twins***

| *Reared Together* | *Reared Apart* |
|---|---|
| $r_1 = .93$ | $r_2 = .83$ |
| $n_1 = 83$ | $n_2 = 30$ |
| $Z_1 = 1.658$ | $Z_2 = 1.188$ |
| $\sigma_{Z_1}^2 = 1/(83 - 3) = .0125$ | $\sigma_{Z_1}^2 = 1/(30 - 3) = .0370$ |

The $r$'s have been transformed to Fisher $Z$'s; the variances of the $Z$'s have been computed and the standard error of the difference in $Z$'s is determined from Equation 14.7.

$$\sigma_{Z_1 - Z_2} = \sqrt{\sigma_{Z_1}^2 + \sigma_{Z_2}^2} = \sqrt{.0125 + .037} = .2225$$

The $z$-ratio for testing $H_0$: $\rho_1 = \rho_2$ using Equation 14.6 is:

$$z = \frac{Z_1 - Z_2}{\sigma_{Z_1 - Z_2}} = \frac{1.658 - 1.188}{.2225} = \frac{.470}{.2236} = 2.11$$

The observed $z$-ratio 2.11 is compared with the critical $z$-value, which is always 1.96 with $\alpha_2 = .05$. Since 2.10 > 1.96, $H_0$: $\rho_1 = \rho_2$ can be rejected at the .05 level.[12] With these data the correlation of IQ's of identical twins reared together is significantly higher than the correlation of IQ's of identical twins reared apart.[13]

[12]The .95*CI* for the *difference* between Fisher $Z$-coefficient parameters is $Z_1 - Z_2 \pm 1.96\sigma_{Z_1 - Z_2}$.

[13]Could a directional hypothesis have been justified in this situation? Since it is not plausible that the IQ's of twins reared apart would correlate more highly than the IQ's of twins reared together, a directional hypothesis could have been justified if it had been decided upon before the data were inspected. Even if a "one-tailed" test had been used, the null hypothesis would not have been rejected at the .01 level; for $\alpha_1 = .01$, the critical value of $z$ is 2.326 (from Table A).

## 14.9 TESTING DIFFERENCES AMONG SEVERAL INDEPENDENT CORRELATION COEFFICIENTS: $H_0$: $\rho_1 = \rho_2 = \ldots = \rho_J$

The procedure in Section 14.8 works well when there are only two correlation coefficients to be compared. But what if there are three or more $r$'s? In the HSB data set, the correlation[14] between gender (1 = F, 2 = M) and scores on the math test was computed for each of the four ethnic groups. Are the differences among the four $r$'s large enough to allow $H_0$: $\rho_1 = \rho_2 = \rho_3 = \rho_4$ to be rejected? In other words, is the gender difference on the math test greater in certain ethnic groups than in others? The hypothesis, that all differences in the $r$'s are due to sampling error, can be tested using Equation 14.8[15]:

$$\chi^2 = \sum_j w_j Z_j^2 - w_{\bullet}\bar{Z}_W^2 \quad \textbf{(14.8)}$$

where, $w_j = n_j - 3$, $w_{\bullet} = \Sigma w_j$, $\nu = J - 1$, and the weighted average $Z$ within the $J$ groups, $\bar{Z}_W$, is

$$\bar{Z}_W = \frac{\sum_j w_j Z_j}{w_{\bullet}} \quad \textbf{(14.9)}$$

The procedure is illustrated in Table 14.1. Each of the $J = 4$ values of $r$ (column 4) is converted to the corresponding Fisher $Z$ (column 5); each $Z$ is then multiplied by its weight, $w_j = n_j - 3$ (column 3) to obtain $w_j Z_j$ (column 6). Column 7 is the product of Columns 5 and 6; it is summed, and the weighted average $Z$, $\bar{Z}$, is computed using Equation 14.9. Equation 14.8 is used to obtain the value of $\chi^2$. If the $J$ values of $Z$ are all estimates of the same parameter, then the value yielded by Equation 14.8 will have a chi-square distribution with $\nu = J - 1$ degrees of freedom; if the computed $\chi^2$ exceeds the critical value, ${}_{1-\alpha}\chi^2_{\nu}$, $H_0$: $\rho_1 = \rho_2 = \ldots = \rho_J$ is rejected ($p < \alpha$).

It is evident in Table 14.1 that the null hypothesis cannot be rejected even at the .10 level, since $\chi^2 = 2.85 < 6.25 = {}_{.90}\chi_3^2$. The gender differences among the four ethnic groups can be viewed as resulting from sampling error; hence, the null hypothesis is tenable. Although it might appear that the gender difference was greater among Hispanics than for certain other ethnic groups,[16] these differences are not statistically reliable (generalizable).

---

[14] These are point-biserial correlation coefficients (Section 7.23). Larger $r$'s indicate a larger difference between the means of males and females. Since males have the higher code on the gender variable, positive $r$'s indicate that the mean of the males was greater than the mean of the females. When the proportions in each of the two categories are approximately equal (as in this case), the value of the $2r \approx \hat{\Delta}$, in other words, $r$ is approximately half the value of the effect size (Section 12.8).

[15] Equation 14.8 is due to Hedges and Olkin (1985). It differs trivially, but is computationally simpler from the method included in the previous edition of this book, and is superior to certain alternative methods (Alexander, Scozzaro, & Borodkin, 1990).

[16] Procedures for testing which of the $J$ values of $r$ differ significantly from which other $r$'s are given in Section 17.23.

**TABLE 14.1** A Test of $H_0$: $\rho_1 = \rho_2 = \ldots = \rho_J$, Where the $J$ $\rho$'s Are Independent.

| (1) *Ethnicity* | (2) $n_j$ | (3) $w_j = n_j - 3$ | (4) $r_j$ | (5)a $Z_j$ | (6) $w_jZ_j$ | (7) $w_jZ_j^2$ |
|---|---|---|---|---|---|---|
| Hispanic | 71 | 68 | .2541 | .2598 | 17.6658 | 4.5894 |
| Asian | 34 | 31 | .1136 | .1141 | 3.5369 | .4035 |
| Black | 58 | 55 | .1544 | .1556 | 8.5605 | 1.3324 |
| White | 437 | 434 | .0516 | .0516 | 22.4143 | 1.1576 |
| | | $w. = 588$ | | | $\Sigma_j w_j Z_j = 52.1774$ | $7.4829 = \Sigma_j w_j Z_j^2$ |

Equation 14.9:

$$\bar{Z}_W = \frac{\sum_j w_j Z_j}{w.} = \frac{52.1774}{588} = .0887 \ (\bar{r} = .089)$$

Equation 14.8:

$$X^2 = \sum_j w_j Z_j^2 - w.\bar{Z}_W^2 = 7.4829 - 588(.0887)^2 = 2.8529 > {}_{.90}\chi^2_3 = 6.25, \ p > .10$$

[a]These figures result from transforming $r$'s to $Z$'s via the FISHER "paste function" on the EXCEL spreadsheet. If you use Table E or retain fewer decimal places, your results will differ slightly due to rounding error. It is best not to round until the computations are completed.

## 14.10 AVERAGING *r*'S

In certain situations one needs to be able to average two or more $r$'s. For example, one study investigated the degree of relationship between forty-two teachers' ratings of students' achievement levels with the students' scores on standardized achievement tests. To eliminate difference among the teachers in rating leniency, a correlation was computed for each of the forty-two teachers. To obtain the best estimate of this relationship the $r$'s need to be averaged. However, the skewness in the sampling distributions of $r$ (Figure 14.2) would cause the correlation to be underestimated. The recommended procedure for averaging homogeneous $r$'s is to use Fisher $Z$'s. From Equation 14.9, find the weighted average $Z_W$-value, then transform $Z_W$ to the corresponding value of $r$.[17] Note in Table 14.1 that the average[18] of the four values of $r$ is: $Z_W$ (transformed via Table E) = $r$ = .089.[19]

## 14.11 TESTING DIFFERENCES BETWEEN TWO DEPENDENT CORRELATION COEFFICIENTS: $H_0$: $\rho_{31} = \rho_{32}$

Two correlation coefficients cannot be assumed to be independent if they are based on the same sample. The situation would arise if one wished to compare the validity of the SAT

[17]The average value for the teachers was .74 (Hopkins, George, & Williams, 1985).

[18]Fisher noted that there is a slight bias in each $Z_j$-value, which accumulates to make $r$ slightly too large. The correction is to reduce each $Z_j$ by $r/(2(n_j - 1))$. This correction can usually be ignored since its effects are trivial except when sample sizes are very small or $J$ is very large.

[19]See Olkin (1967) for additional technical information on averaging $r$'s.

(variable 1) with the ACT (variable 2) for predicting GPA (the criterion) in college, and the two correlation coefficients, $r_{C1}$ and $r_{C2}$, were computed on the same students. Or as a further example, if we wish to see if mothers' IQ scores correlate ($r_{C1}$) more highly with their children's IQ scores than do fathers' IQ scores ($r_{C2}$), Equation 14.6 is not appropriate. Recent research indicates that Equation 14.10 can be used[20] for testing $H_0$: $\rho_{C1} = \rho_{C2}$. The three variables (1, 2, and $C$) are "trios"—the three measures are obtained on each observational unit (often persons), and $r_{12}$ is the correlation between variables 1 and 2:

$$t = (r_{31} - r_{32})\sqrt{\frac{(n-3)(1+r_{12})}{2\left(1 - r_{31}^2 - r_{32}^2 - r_{12}^2 + 2r_{31}r_{32}r_{12}\right)}} \quad \textbf{(14.10)}$$

with degrees of freedom: $\nu = n - 3$. Equation 14.10 assumes that the criterion is normally distributed and the relationships between the criterion and each predictor are linear and evidence homoscedasticity.

In Table 8.4, the validities of pre-grade-one reading readiness (1) and IQ (2) scores for predicting subsequent reading success ($C$) were $r_{C1} = .612$ and $r_{C2} = .541$ respectively, with $r_{12} = .466$ and $n = 157$. Is $H_0$: $\rho_{C1} = \rho_{C2}$ tenable at $\alpha_2 = .10$? Using Equation 14.10:

$$t = (.612 - .541)\sqrt{\frac{(157-3)(1+.466)}{2[1-(.612)^2-(.541)^2-(.466)^2+2(.612)(.541)(.466)]}}$$

$$= (.071)\sqrt{\frac{225.76}{.8484}} = 1.158$$

which is below the critical value of 1.66, for $\alpha_2 = .10$ and $\nu_2 = 154$. Thus, $H_0$ remains tenable, that is, one cannot conclude in this study that the IQ scores correlate less highly with later reading performance than do reading readiness scores.

## 14.12 INFERENCES ABOUT OTHER CORRELATION COEFFICIENTS[21]

The remaining sections of this chapter consider significance testing procedures for the correlation coefficients presented in Chapters 7 and 8. The presentation of inferential techniques will be greatly simplified since space does not permit detailed treatments such as those in the previous sections of this chapter. Procedures will be presented with which the null hypothesis of no correlation between variables $X$ and $Y$ can be tested against a nondirectional alternative hypothesis. Where possible, a test statistic will be defined that

---

[20]Meng, Rosenthal and Rubin (1992) give an equation that is slightly more accurate than the Hotelling $t$ (Equation 14.10). The difference is inconsequential, however, and Equation 14.10 is much simpler computationally. (See also Hendrickson & Collins, 1970.)

[21]For testing for heterogeneity among a set of $J > 2$ nonindependent correlations, see Olkin and Finn (1990) and Meng, Rosenthal, and Rubin (1992). Olkin (1967) devised a procedure for testing $H_0$: $\rho_{12} = \rho_{34}$ when $r_{12}$ and $r_{34}$ are obtained on the *same* subjects. For example, in a longitudinal study to see if height and weight at birth correlate differently than height and weight at age one, use Olkin's $z$-test: $z = \sqrt{n}\,(r_{12} - r_{34})/\hat{\sigma}_{r_{12}-r_{34}}$, where $\hat{\sigma}^2_{r_{12}-r_{34}} = (1 - r_{12}^2)^2 + (1 - r_{34}^2)^2 + r_{12}r_{34}(r_{13}^2 + r_{14}^2 + r_{23}^2 + r_{24}^2) + 2(r_{13}r_{24} + r_{14}r_{23}) - 2(r_{12}r_{13}r_{14} + r_{12}r_{23}r_{24} + r_{13}r_{23}r_{34} + r_{14}r_{24}r_{34})$.

has a known sampling distribution when the two variables being correlated are unrelated—whether they are measured dichotomously, with ranks, or otherwise—that is, have a coefficient of zero in the population. In each instance, the significance testing procedure will be illustrated.[22]

## 14.13 THE POINT-BISERIAL CORRELATION COEFFICIENT $r_{pb}$

By inspection of the formula for $r_{pb}$ (Section 7.23), it can be seen that $r_{pb}$ is equal to zero if and only if $\overline{Y}_1 = \overline{Y}_0$:

$$r_{pb} = \frac{\overline{Y}_1 - \overline{Y}_0}{s_Y}\sqrt{\frac{n_1 n_0}{n_{\bullet}(n_{\bullet} - 1)}} \quad \textbf{(14.11)}$$

Equation 14.1A can be used to test $H_0$: $\rho_{pb} = 0$ by replacing $r$ with $r_{pb}$:

$$t = \frac{r_{pb}}{\sqrt{\dfrac{1 - r_{pb}^2}{n_{\bullet} - 2}}} \quad \textbf{(14.12)}$$

is approximately distributed as Student's $t$-distribution with $\nu = n_{\bullet} - 2$ when $\rho_{pb} = 0$. In a sample of size $n_{\bullet} = 27$, an $r_{pb}$ of .728 was found between sex and height (Table 7.8). The $t$-test (Equation 14.12) of $H_0$: $\rho_{pb} = 0$ is:

$$t = \frac{.728}{\sqrt{\dfrac{1 - (.728)^2}{27 - 2}}} = \frac{.728}{\sqrt{\dfrac{.4700}{25}}} = 5.31$$

The $t$-ratio of 5.31 exceeds the critical $t$ of 3.73 for $\alpha_2 = .001$ and $\nu = 25$ (Table C). Hence, it is extremely unlikely that $\rho_{pb}$ is zero for the population sampled; thus, $H_0$ is rejected at the .001 level.

Table J in the Appendix can also be used to test $H_0$: $\rho_{pb} = 0$; note that the $r_{pb}$ of .728 exceeds the critical $r$ of .597 for $\alpha_2 = .001$, found in Table J for $\nu = 25$.

Testing the null hypothesis that a population value of the point-biserial correlation coefficient is zero is mathematically equivalent to testing the hypothesis that in the population those persons coded 1 on the dichotomous variable have a mean equal to the population mean of the persons coded 0 on the dichotomy, that is, $H_0$: $\mu_1 = \mu_0$. For example, the $r_{pb}$ of .728 was based on a sample of ten males whose mean height was 69.90 in. and seventeen females whose mean height was 64.35 in. If Equations 12.2 and 12.4 (Sections 12.4 and 12.5) are used to test $H_0$: $\mu_1 = \mu_0$:

---

[22]Procedures for testing the significance of phi coefficients were treated in Section 13.15.

$$t = \frac{\overline{X}_1 - \overline{X}_0}{s_W\sqrt{\frac{1}{n_1} + \frac{1}{n_0}}} = \frac{69.90 - 64.35}{2.623\sqrt{\frac{1}{10} + \frac{1}{17}}} = 5.31$$

which is identical to the $t$ from Equation 14.12.

## 14.14 SPEARMAN'S RANK CORRELATION: $H_0$: $\rho_{\text{ranks}} = 0$

The sampling distribution of $r_{\text{ranks}}$ given zero correlation between two sets of ranks $X$ and $Y$ in the population cannot be characterized in terms of any well-known statistical distribution for $n$ less than approximately 10. For $n > 10$, the sampling distribution when the population Spearman rank-correlation coefficient is zero is approximated by Student's $t$-distribution. In fact, for $n > 30$, Equation 14.1A may be used, substituting $r_{\text{ranks}}$ for $r$:

$$t = \frac{r_{\text{ranks}}}{\sqrt{\frac{1 - r_{\text{ranks}}^2}{n - 2}}} \quad \textbf{(14.13)}$$

is approximately distributed as Student's $t$-distribution with $\nu = n - 2$ when the population value $\rho_{\text{ranks}}$ is zero.

The exact sampling distribution of $r_{\text{ranks}}$ when $n$ is less than 30 has been determined and is used in testing the null hypothesis of no relationship between the two ranked variables (see Kendall, 1962). Selected percentiles in the sampling distributions of $r_{\text{ranks}}$ for various values of $n$ have been determined and appear in Table K in the Appendix. As an example of how Table K is read, a value of $r_{\text{ranks}}$ greater than .794 or less than –.794 is required for significance at the $\alpha_2 = .01$ level when $n = 11$. By comparing Tables J and K, it is evident that larger critical values are required for $r_{\text{ranks}}$ than for $r$, although the difference becomes negligible as $n$ increases.

## 14.15 PARTIAL CORRELATION, $H_0$: $\rho_{12.3} = 0$

Equation 14.14 can be used to test the null hypothesis that the first-order partial correlation (Section 8.13) in the population is 0 (Equation 14.14 is similar to Equation 14.1 for "zero-order" partial correlations, i.e., $r_{12}$):

$$t = \frac{r_{12.3}}{\sqrt{\frac{1 - r_{12.3}^2}{n - 3}}} \quad \textbf{(14.14)}$$

Express more generally for any partial correlation coefficient:

$$t = \frac{r_{12.3\ldots p}}{\sqrt{\dfrac{1 - r_{12.3\ldots p}^2}{\nu}}} \qquad (14.15)$$

where $\nu = n - p$, and $p$ is the number of variables in the set. For first-order partial correlations ($r_{12\cdot3}$), $p = 3$; for second-order correlations ($r_{12\cdot34}$), $p = 4$, and so on. Table J may also be used to test $H_0$: $\rho_{12\cdot3\ldots p}$ by entering $\nu$ (not $n$). Thus, if $n = 30$, $r_{12\cdot34}$ must be at least .374 to allow rejection of $H_0$ at $\alpha_2 = .05$ ($\nu = 26$).

## 14.16 SIGNIFICANCE OF A MULTIPLE CORRELATION COEFFICIENT

The null hypothesis that the multiple correlation in the population is zero can be tested using the $F$-test in Equation 14.16.[23]

$$F = \frac{R_{Y\cdot12\ldots m}^2}{(1 - R_{Y\cdot12\ldots m}^2)}\left(\frac{n - m - 1}{m}\right) \qquad (14.16)$$

where $m$ is the number of predictor (independent) variables. When the null hypothesis is true, the distribution of the $F$-statistic is described by the central $F$-distribution with $\nu_1 = m$ degrees of freedom in the numerator and $\nu_2 = n - m - 1$ in the denominator. In Table 8.4 (Section 8.21), $R_{Y\cdot12345} = .69537$ with $n = 157$. Is $H_0$ tenable? Using Equation 14.16:

$$F = \frac{(.69537)^2}{[1 - (.69537)^2]}\left(\frac{157 - 5 - 1}{5}\right) = (.9363)(30.2) = 28.27$$

which exceeds the critical value, ${}_{.999}F_{5,151} = 4.42$; hence, the multiple correlation coefficient is highly significant and the null hypothesis is rejected.

Equation 14.16 is equivalent to Equation 14.17, which is also widely used, where $\nu_1 = m$, and $\nu_2 = n - m - 1$.

$$F = \frac{\text{Sum of squares due to regression}/\nu_1}{\text{Residual sum of squares}/\nu_2} = \frac{SS_{\hat{Y}}/\nu_1}{SS_e/\nu_2} \qquad (14.17)$$

From Equation 8.20, it can be seen that the denominator of Equation 14.17 is the variance error of estimate, $s_{Y\cdot12\ldots m}^2$. Recall from Section 8.8 that $R^2$ gives the proportion of the total sum of squares (or variance) that is predictable from the $m$ predictors; hence, $1 - R^2$ is the proportion of unpredictable (residual) variance. Thus, if both the numerator and de-

[23]Note that for $m = 1$, Equation 14.16 is the square of Equation 14.1; see Section 16.12 and note that when the numerator of the $F$-ratio has $\nu = 1$, then $F = t^2$.

nominator of Equation 14.16 are multiplied by $SS_{total}$, Equation 14.17 results. Most computer printouts use Equation 14.17 to test the null hypothesis that the multiple correlation in the population is zero.

## 14.17 STATISTICAL SIGNIFICANCE IN STEPWISE MULTIPLE REGRESSION

As previously discussed in Section 8.20, the researcher often has access to many more predictor variables than are needed. Typically after the best three or four predictors are selected, the multiple correlation is essentially unaffected by the use of additional independent variables. Note in Table 8.4 (Section 8.21) that the multiple correlation coefficients were .612, .677, .693, .69526, and .69537 when five independent variables were used in a stepwise multiple regression. Are all the increases statistically significant—does the addition of the "next best" predictor increase the multiple correlation enough so that the null hypotheses $H_{01}$: $\rho_{Y\bullet 1} = \rho_{Y\bullet 12}$, $H_{02}$: $\rho_{Y\bullet 12} = \rho_{Y\bullet 123}$ $H_{03}$: $\rho_{Y\bullet 123} = \rho_{Y\bullet 1234}$, and so on, can be rejected? Often the decision is made to use only the number of predictors that continue to significantly increase the multiple correlation. Equation 14.18 can be used to test $H_0$: $\rho_{Y\bullet 12\ldots m2} = \rho_{Y\bullet 12\ldots m1}$, where $m_2$ and $m_1$ are the number of predictors, and $m_2 - m_1 = q \geq 1$:

$$F = \frac{\dfrac{R^2_{Y.12\ldots m_2} - R^2_{Y.12\ldots m_1}}{q}}{\dfrac{1 - R^2_{Y.12\ldots m_2}}{n - m_2 - q}} \tag{14.18}$$

where the degrees of freedom for the critical value of $F$ has $\nu_1 = m_2 - m_1$ and $\nu_2 = n - m_2 - q$.

For example, let us test whether the increase from $R_{Y\bullet 1} = .612$ to $R_{Y\bullet 12} = .677$ was statistically significant when $n = 157$. Since $q = m_2 - m_1 = 2 - 1 = 1$, Equation 14.18 becomes:

$$F = \frac{\dfrac{R^2_{Y.12} - R^2_{Y.1}}{1}}{\dfrac{1 - R^2_{Y.12}}{n - 2 - 1}} = \frac{(.677)^2 - (.612)^2}{\dfrac{1 - .4583}{157 - 3}} = 23.82$$

The observed $F$-ratio is much larger than the critical value, $_{.999}F_{1,154} \approx 11.4$; hence, $H_0$ is rejected at the .001 level.[24]

Is the increase from $R_{Y\bullet 12} = .677$ to $R_{Y\bullet 123} = .693$ also significant? Using Equation 14.18:

$$F = \frac{(.693)^2 - (.677)^2}{\dfrac{1 - .4802}{157 - 4}} = 6.45$$

[24]This test is mathematically equivalent to testing $r_{Y2.1}$ for significance using Equation 14.15; for example, from Table 8.4, $r_{Y2.1} = .366$, which, using Equation 14.15, yields $t = 4.88$. Hence, $t^2 = 23.82 = F$ as yielded by Equation 14.18. Other steps are similarly equivalent.

which, from Table F in the Appendix, is found to be significant at the .025 level. Thus, the use of the third independent variable significantly improved the accuracy of prediction.

Does step 4 increase the multiple correlation coefficient in the population—is $H_0$: $\rho_{Y\cdot1234} = \rho_{Y\cdot123}$ tenable? The use of Equation 14.18 yields $F = .92$, which does not approach significance. Thus for practical purposes, one can do as well with the three predictors in steps 1, 2, and 3 as with the addition of predictors 4 and 5. Predictors 4 and 5 add no significant, unique, or relevant information.

## 14.18 SIGNIFICANCE OF THE BISERIAL CORRELATION COEFFICIENT $r_{\text{bis}}$

Although the exact sampling distribution of $r_{\text{bis}}$ (Section 7.24) is not known, if $n$ is large and the population biserial correlation coefficient is zero, the sampling distribution of $r_{\text{bis}}$ should be approximately normal with a mean of 0 and a standard deviation of:

$$\hat{\sigma}_{r_{\text{bis}}} = \frac{\sqrt{n_0 n_1}}{u n_\bullet \sqrt{n_\bullet}} \qquad \textbf{(14.19)}$$

where $n_\bullet$ is the sample size, $n_1$ and $n_0$ are the number of persons "scoring" 1 and 0, respectively, on the dichotomous variable ($n_\bullet = n_1 + n_0$), and $u$ is the ordinate of the unit-normal curve at the point above which the $n_1/n_\bullet$ proportion of the area under the curve lies. The value of $u$ can be found from Equation 6.3 or Table A.

When the population biserial correlation coefficient departs from zero, the value of $\sigma_{r_{\text{bis}}}$ is diminished by $1/\sqrt{n_\bullet}$ times the square of the population value of $r_{\text{bis}}$. When the population value, $\rho_{\text{bis}}$, is different from zero, the sampling distribution of $r_{\text{bis}}$ becomes non-normal and is skewed toward zero.

Empirical sampling studies by Lord (1963) and Baker (1965) have shown that the large-sample estimate of the standard error of $r_{\text{bis}}$ is nearly exact even for samples as small as 15.

Suppose that for a sample of size 36 in which $n_1 = 16$ and $n_0 = 20$, the value of $r_{\text{bis}}$ is $-.145$. The value of $\sigma_{r_{\text{bis}}}$ when the population biserial coefficient is zero is estimated by:

$$\hat{\sigma}_{r_{\text{bis}}} = \frac{\sqrt{(16)(20)}}{(.3951)(36)\sqrt{36}} = .210$$

If the population value $\rho_{\text{bis}}$ is zero, $r_{\text{bis}}/\hat{\sigma}_{r_{\text{bis}}}$ will be approximately normally distributed with mean of 0 and a standard deviation of 1 (over repeated random samples of size $n$).

$$z = \frac{r_{\text{bis}}}{\hat{\sigma}_{r_{\text{bis}}}} = \frac{-.145}{.210} = -.69$$

A $z$-value of $-.69$ is not unusual when sampling from a unit-normal distribution; the probability of obtaining by chance a $z$-value greater than $|.69|$ is .2451. Hence, evidence does not exist to allow rejection of the null hypothesis that the population biserial correlation coefficient is zero.

## 14.19 SIGNIFICANCE OF THE TETRACHORIC CORRELATION COEFFICIENT $r_{\text{tet}}$

When the null hypothesis of no relationship between $X$ and $Y$ (two normally distributed variables measured as dichotomies) is true, the sampling distribution of the sample tetrachoric correlation coefficient $r_{\text{tet}}$ is approximately normal for $n > 20$ with a mean of 0 and a standard deviation, $\sigma_{r_{\text{tet}}}$, which is estimated by:

$$\hat{\sigma}_{r_{\text{tet}}} \approx \frac{1}{u_x u_y}\sqrt{\frac{p_x p_y q_x q_y}{n_{\bullet}}} \tag{14.20}$$

where $n_{\bullet}$ is the sample size, $u_x$ (found from Table A) is the ordinate for the $z$-score in the unit-normal curve above which the $p_x$ proportion of the area lies ($p_x = n_x/n_{\bullet}$ = the proportion of persons "scoring" 1 on variable $X$), $u_y$ is the ordinate for the $z$-score in the unit-normal curve above which the $p_y$ proportion of the area lies ($p_y = n_y/n_{\bullet}$ = the proportion of persons "scoring" 1 on variable $Y$).

Thus, when $n$ is moderately large and $\rho_{\text{tet}} = 0$:

$$z = \frac{r_{\text{tet}}}{\hat{\sigma}_{r_{\text{tet}}}}$$

has a mean of 0 and a standard deviation equal to 1. The hypothesis that the population tetrachoric correlation coefficient is zero is rejected at $\alpha_2 = .05$ if $|z| > 1.96$.

The data in Table 7.10 (Section 7.26) were gathered to study the relationship between two variables $X$ and $Y$ that are believed to be normally distributed, but can only be measured dichotomously. The value of $r_{\text{tet}}$ was found to be .90 and $n$ was 400. Using Equation 14.20 and the data in Table 7.10, the standard error of $r_{\text{tet}}$ is estimated to be .0826; thus, the value of the $z$-ratio is $z = .90/.0826 = 10.90$, which far exceeds the critical value of $z$ of 3.29 with $\alpha_2 = .001$ (Table A ). The hypothesis that the tetrachoric correlation in the population is zero is rejected.

## 14.20 SIGNIFICANCE OF THE CORRELATION RATIO, $\eta^2$

Recall that $\eta$, eta, is a measure of association that describes the degree of relationship (linear or nonlinear) between two variables $X$ and $Y$ (Section 8.27). The $F$-statistic[25] (Equation 14.21) can be used to test the null hypothesis that in the population, the correlation ratio (or coefficient eta) is zero, that is, $H_0$: $\eta_{Y \bullet X} = 0$:

[25]This may also be expressed in the terminology of analysis of variance (Chapter 15): $F = (SS_B/\nu_B)/(SS_W/\nu_W) = MS_B/MS_W$, where $SS$ = sum of squares, $MS$ = mean square, and the subscripts "B" and "W" denote "between" and "within," respectively.

$$F = \frac{\dfrac{\hat{\eta}^2_{Y.X}}{J-1}}{\dfrac{1-\hat{\eta}^2_{Y.X}}{n-J}} \tag{14.21}$$

where $J$ is the number of levels or categories of the $X$-variable into which the $n$ observations are grouped.

The value for the correlation ratio, $\eta^2$ between age and scores on a test in Section 8.27 was found to be .541, based on $n = 28$ persons who were classified into $J = 7$ age groups. Is this value significantly greater than 0? The $F$-ratio found using Equation 14.21 is:

$$F = \frac{\dfrac{.541}{7-1}}{\dfrac{1-.541}{28-7}} = 4.12$$

The critical $F$ is ${}_{1-\alpha}F_{(J-1)(n-J)}$, or in this case ${}_{.99}F_{6,21} = 3.87$. Consequently, the null hypothesis can be rejected at the .01 level.

## 14.21 TESTING FOR NONLINEARITY OF REGRESSION

The $F$-test in Equation 14.21 does not presume that there is a nonlinear relationship between $X$ and $Y$. Recall from Section 8.27 that if the regression is perfectly linear, $\eta^2$ and $\rho^2$ will be equal in value. If the relationship is nonlinear, $\eta^2$ will be larger than $\rho^2$; thus, the difference in $\eta^2$ and $r^2$ is a measure of nonlinearity. The $F$-test[26] for nonlinearity where the $n$ observations are grouped into $J$ levels of groups is:

$$F = \frac{\dfrac{\hat{\eta}^2_{Y.X} - r^2}{J-2}}{\dfrac{1-\hat{\eta}^2_{Y.X}}{n-J}} \tag{14.22}$$

(Note that the denominator is identical to that in Equation 14.21.) For the illustration in Section 8.27 where $r = -.077$ ($r^2 = .0059$) and $\eta^2 = .541$:

$$F = \frac{\dfrac{.541-.0059}{7-2}}{\dfrac{1-.541}{28-7}} = 4.89$$

[26]This may be expressed in analysis of variance terms (Section 17.21):

$$F = \frac{SS_{\text{nonlinear}}/(J-2)}{SS_{\text{within}}/(n-J)}, \text{ where } SS_{\text{nonlinear}} = (1-r^2)SS_{\text{total}} - SS_{\text{within}}$$

which exceeds the critical ${}_{.99}F_{5,21} = 4.10$; thus, there is a significant nonlinear relationship between $X$ and $Y$. The statistical hypothesis that the relationship in the population is linear can be rejected at the .01 level.

## 14.22 CHAPTER SUMMARY

The most direct method for testing the statistical hypothesis $H_0$: $\rho = 0$ is to enter Table J or Figure 14.1, which gives the critical value of $r$ needed to reject the null hypothesis. These critical values depend only on $n$ and $\alpha$. The critical values of $r$ increase as $n$ decreases and as $\alpha$ decreases (e.g., from .05 to .01).

The sampling distribution of $r$ is normal when $\rho = 0$. It is skewed to the extent that $\rho$ deviates from 0. The skewness becomes progressively less and the sampling distribution becomes more nearly normal as $n$ increases.

The Fisher $Z$-transformation has a distribution that is approximately normal irrespective of $n$ and $\rho$. It is used to set confidence intervals for $\rho$, although Figure 14.6 can be used for this purpose if high precision is not needed. Fisher $Z$-coefficients are also used in the $z$-test for independent $r$'s and in the $\chi^2$ test for $J$ independent $r$'s. If $r$'s are obtained on different subjects, they are independent; two $r$'s obtained on the same group of persons are not independent, and formulas that take the type and degree of dependency into account should be employed.

The $t$-tests for assessing the significance of point-biserial, Spearman rank, and partial correlation coefficients are very similar to testing $H_0$: $\rho = 0$. The critical values for $r_{\text{ranks}}$ are slightly larger than for $r$, but the differences become negligible as $n$ increases. The critical value for $r_{12.3\ldots p}$ is identical to that for $r$ except that it has $p$ fewer degrees of freedom for the same value of $n$. All procedures utilizing Pearson product-moment correlation coefficients assume that the joint distribution of $X$ and $Y$ has bivariate normality (Section 7.13). The significance tests of biserial and tetrachoric correlations use the $z$-test and require large $n$'s to be precise.

The significance of (1) multiple correlation coefficients, (2) additional predictor variables in stepwise multiple correlation, (3) the correlation ratio, and (4) nonlinearity of regression are tested using the $F$-statistic.

## 14.23 CASE STUDY

In Table 7.11, a correlation matrix is given for all variables in the case study. Since $n = 200$, how large must $r$ be in order to reject $H_0$: $\rho = 0$ with $\alpha_1 = .01$?[27] Which of the variables correlated significantly with cholesterol level (CHOL)?[28] If Equation 8.12 is used to estimate the correlation between CHOL and CORON for persons of the same age (i.e., the partial correlation, holding age constant): $r_{12.3} = .079$. Can $H_0$: $\rho_{12.3}$ be rejected with $\alpha_1 = .05$?[29]

---

[27] From Table $J$, $H_0$ is rejected if $r \geq .164$ for $\alpha_1 = .01$.

[28] Age, SBP, DBP, CORON.

[29] No, $t = .079 / \sqrt{.005044} = 1.11 < 1.65$, therefore $H_0$ cannot be rejected.

## 14.24 SUGGESTED COMPUTER ACTIVITY

Obtain the correlation matrix between all dichotomous and continuous variables in the HSB data set. Compare the two-tailed significance levels ($p$'s) for the point-biserial correlations between SCTYP and the achievement variables with those when the $t$-test were used (Section 12.20).[30] Obtain the $.95CI$ for $\rho$ for the correlation between SES and RDG.[31] In this instance, why is Figure 14.6 not useful?[32] Select each gender separately and obtain the matrix of $r$'s. Is the relationship between RDG and SCI different for males versus females (Section 14.8)?

## MASTERY TEST

1. Other things being equal, and $\rho \neq 0$, is the probability of a type-II error, $\beta$, greater with $\alpha_2 = .01$ or with $\alpha_2 = .05$?
2. Using Figure 14.1, determine how large a sample is needed to allow rejection of $H_0$: $\rho = 0$ with an $r$-value of .3 under the following circumstances.
   (a) when $\alpha_2 = .001$ (d) when $\alpha_1 = .05$
   (b) when $\alpha_2 = .01$ (e) when $\alpha_2 = .10$
   (c) when $\alpha_2 = .05$
3. Assume $H_0$: $\rho = 0$ is true.
   (a) Will the probability that it will be rejected increase as $n$ increases?
   (b) Will the critical value of $r$ decrease as $n$ increases?
   (c) Will the critical value of $r$ be larger at $\alpha = .05$ than at $\alpha = .01$?
4. Which one of these statements *best* describes the reason the Fisher $Z$-transformation is needed?
   (a) The sampling distribution of $r$ is skewed when $\rho \neq 0$.
   (b) The $t$-test and $z$-test for $H_0$: $\rho = 0$ are not powerful for small $n$'s.
   (c) The sampling distribution of $r$ is not normal when $\rho = 0$.
5. If $r = .5$, which of the following .90 confidence intervals for $\rho$ are plausible?
   (a) –.1 to .51 (c) .42 to .57
   (b) –.2 to .84 (d) .48 to .55
6. Knowledge of which concepts were required in answering question 5?
   (a) The sampling distribution of $r$ is approximately normal with large $n$'s.
   (b) The sampling distribution of $r$ is positively skewed when $\rho > 0$, unless $n$ is large.
   (c) The sampling distribution of $r$ is negatively skewed when $\rho > 0$, unless $n$ is large.
7. Other things being equal, which of these will span the greatest distance (range of values)?
   (a) the $.68CI$ (b) the $.95CI$ (c) the $.99CI$
8. Which of these determine the value of $\sigma_Z$?
   (a) $r$ (b) $n$ (c) $\rho$
9. Using Figure 14.6, determine the .95 confidence interval if $r = +.20$ and $n = 50$.

---

[30]The corresponding $p$-values should be identical.

[31]Most software does not have this option; you many need to compute it using your calculator or spreadsheet.

[32]$n > 400$

10. Given $n = 100$:
    (a) Which one of the following $r$'s will have the confidence interval with the greatest numerical span? $r = -.5$, $r = .00$, $r = .5$, $r = .8$
    (b) Which $r$ in part a will have the smallest range of values?
    (c) Will the $CI$'s for $r = -.5$ and $r = .5$ have the same width?
11. If $n = 30$, what is the critical value for each of the following to reject $H_0$ with $\alpha_2 = .01$?
    (a) $r$ (b) $r_{pb}$ (c) $r_{ranks}$ (d) $r_{12.345}$
12. In which of these situations would a directional alternative hypothesis about $\rho$ be reasonable?
    (a) age and height among middle-school students
    (b) male-female and popularity among high-school students
    (c) neurotic traits and GPA in college
    (d) SES and school achievement
    (e) IQ and number of languages spoken
13. When used appropriately, directional tests of $H_0$: $\rho = 0$ are more powerful than nondirectional tests. (T or F)
14. In which of these situations are the correlation coefficients independent?
    (a) $r_{\text{height, Weight}}$ for boys compared to that for girls
    (b) $r_{\text{IQ, achievement}}$ for this year's fourth graders with that for this year's fifth graders
    (c) $r_{\text{IQ, achievement}}$ at grade four with that for the same students in grade five
    (d) $r_{\text{IQ, reading}}$ with $r_{\text{IQ, math}}$ for this year's fourth graders
    (e) $r_{\text{IQ, achievement}}$ for Anglos vs. Hispanics
    (f) $r_{\text{GPA, IQ}}$ for this year's tenth graders, with those for this year's eleventh and twelfth graders
15. Which equation should be used in situations a, b, d, e, and f above?
16. The $t$-test for testing $H_0$: $\rho_{pb} = 0$ is identical to the $t$-test for testing $H_0$: ____.
17. If $R_{Y.123} = .30$ and $n = 104$, which equation should be used to determine if the null hypothesis is tenable at $\alpha_2 = .05$?
18. If, with the addition of a fourth independent variable in a multiple regression, the value of $R_{Y.1234}$ increased to .40, which equation would be used to see if the increase in the multiple correlation from .30 to .40 is statistically significant?
19. What is the central assumption underlying most of the inferential tests on correlation coefficients?
20. Which two of these equations are "large sample" methods, that is, they use a $Z$-test and assume that $n$ is so large that there is virtually no sampling error in estimating the standard error of the test statistic—14.12, 14.13, 14.14, 14.15, 14.16, 14.19, 14.20?

## PROBLEMS AND EXERCISES

1. Using Table J, determine the minimum value of $r$ at which $H_0$: $\rho = 0$ will be rejected for $\alpha_1 = .05$, $\alpha_2 = .10$, $\alpha_2 = .05$, $\alpha_2 = .01$, and $\alpha_2 = .01$:
    (a) with $n = 25$
    (b) with $n = 100$
    (c) If it is predicted that $\rho > 0$, with $n = 25$ and $r = .35$, would $H_0$ be rejected at the .05 level? At the .01 level?
2. Use Table J (a) to determine the critical value for $r$ if $n = 1{,}000$ at $\alpha_2 = .01$.
    (b) If $r = .10$ and $n = 1{,}000$, would $H_0$: $\rho = 0$ be rejected at the .01 level?
    (c) If $r = -.10$ and $n = 1{,}000$, would $H_0$: $\rho = 0$ be rejected at the .01 level?

**3.** If $r = .80$, compute the .68 confidence interval for $\rho$ (to two-decimal-place accuracy):

(a) if $n = 12$ (c) if $n = 103$
(b) if $n = 28$ (d) if $n = 403$

**4.** A correlation of .50 was observed on 236 students between verbal IQ's from group intelligence tests at grade one and IQ's ten years later (Hopkins & Bracht, 1975). The corresponding correlation for nonverbal IQ's was only .29.

(a) Can both null hypotheses ($H_0$: $\rho = 0$) be rejected at $\alpha_1 = .01$? (Use Table J.)
(b) Use Figure 14.6 to establish .95 confidence intervals for the two corresponding parameters.
(c) Are these two correlations independent—could Equation 14.6 be used to test $H_0$: $\rho_1 = \rho_2$?

**5.** By studying the results from problem 3, describe the effects of $n$ on the shape and variability of the sampling distribution of $r$.

**6.** On a group intelligence test, IQ scores of 150 girls at grade three correlated .75 with IQ scores four years later. The corresponding $r$ for 154 boys was .71 (Hopkins & Bibelheimer, 1971). Is $H_0$: $\rho_1 = \rho_2$ tenable at $\alpha_2 = .05$?

**7.** The correlation between numerical ability test scores and course grades in Spanish I was found to be .56 for a sample of 204 students. A correlation of .40 was reported between verbal reasoning test scores and grades in Spanish I for a different sample of 186 students (Bennett et al., 1974).

(a) Set .68 confidence intervals about each $r$ (to two-decimal-place accuracy) using Fisher's $Z$-transformation.
(b) In the population to which these two samples belong, do grades in Spanish I correlate more highly with numerical than with verbal ability scores with $\alpha_2 = .05$?

**8.** Earlier in this chapter, it was found that the correlation of the IQ's of identical twins reared apart was significantly lower than the correlation for identical twins reared together. Compare the $r$'s (i.e., $H_0$: $\rho_1 = \rho_2$) for identical twins reared apart with those of fraternal twins reared together with $\alpha_2 = .01$.

| *Identical Twins Reared Apart* | *Fraternal Twins Reared Together* |
|---|---|
| $r_1 = .83$ | $r_2 = .54$ |
| $n_1 = 30$ | $n_2 = 172$ |

**9.** A correlation of .73 was observed between instructor's interest and enthusiasm and the general excellence of the instructor with $n = 247$ (Houston, Crosswhite, & King, 1974). Establish the .95 confidence interval using Figure 14.6 and compare with the .95 confidence interval obtained using Fisher $Z$-coefficients. Is there a practical difference between the two .95 confidence intervals?

**10.** One study intercorrelated intelligence ($X$), reading rate ($Y$), and reading comprehension ($Z$) in a sample of $n = 80$ college students. The following correlation coefficients were obtained: $r_{XY} = -.034$, $r_{XZ} = .422$, $r_{YZ} = -.385$. Test the null hypothesis at the .10 level of significance that $\rho_{XY} = \rho_{XZ}$, that is, that intelligence is correlated with both reading rate and reading comprehension to the same degree. Can $H_0$ be rejected at the .01 level?

**11.** Estimate the partial correlation between reading rate and reading comprehension, holding IQ score constant (see Equation 8.12). Use Table J to see if $H_0$: $\rho_{ZY.X} = 0$ can be rejected at the .001 level of significance. The number of degree of freedom, $\nu = ?$ (See item 10.)

**12.** The correlation between high-school rank-in-class and college GPA was .50 for 200 students. When the college admissions test was used as a second predictor, the multiple correlation $R_{Y.12}$ became .55. Was the increase statistically significant? At what level?

13. The correlation of teachers' ratings and their students' reading ability was .80 for 103 primary students. On a separate group of 103 upper-elementary students the correlation was .70. On a group of 103 middle-school students the correlation was .60. Are these $r$'s significantly different at the .05 level? At the .01 level? What is the average correlation, $\bar{r}$?

14. Assume that the correlation ration $\hat{\eta}^2_{Y.X}$ between age and height for 55 boys (five *at each age* 6, 7, ..., and 16) was found to be .70.

    (a) Is the relationship statistically significant?
    (b) If $r = .6$ is there a significant nonlinear relationship?

15. For the relationship between the heights of 192 pairs of fathers and sons (Figure 8.1, $r = .56$), it was found that $\eta = .57$, with $J = 12$. The null hypothesis is that the relationship is linear—that the difference between the values of $r$ and $\hat{\eta}_{Y.X}$ can be attributed to sampling error. Test this hypothesis using Equation 14.22 (Section 14.21).

## ANSWERS TO MASTERY TEST

1. $\beta$ is greater with $\alpha_2 = .01$.
2. (a) approximately 120
   (b) approximately 72
   (c) approximately 45
   (d) approximately 31
   (e) approximately 31
3. (a) No; but if $\rho \neq 0$, the probability of rejecting $H_0$ will increase.
   (b) yes
   (c) No; critical values of $r$ are greater at $\alpha = .01$ than $\alpha = .05$.
4. (a)
5. (a) no (c) yes
   (b) yes (d) no
6. (a) and (c)
7. (c)
8. (b); $\sigma_Z = \dfrac{1}{\sqrt{n-3}}$
9. approximately −.08 to +.46
10. (a) .00 (b) .8 (c) yes
11. (a) .463 (c) .478
    (b) .463 (d) .487
12. (a) and (d)
13. T
14. (a), (b), (e), (f)
15. (a) 14.6 (e) 14.6
    (b) 14.6 (f) 14.6
    (d) 14.10
16. $H_0$: $\mu_1 = \mu_0$
17. 14.16
18. 14.18
19. bivariate normality
20. 14.19, 14.20

## ANSWERS TO PROBLEMS AND EXERCISES

1. (a) .337, .337, .396, .462 .505
   (b) .165, .165, .196, .232, .256
   (c) $H_0$ is rejected at the .05 level but not at the .01 level. With $n = 25$, critical $r$-values at $\alpha_1 = .05$ and $\alpha_1 = .01$ are .337 and .462, respectively.
2. (a) .081
   (b) Yes, $p < .01$.
   (c) Yes; $\alpha_2 = .01$ indicates a nondirectional test; $|r| > .081$.
3. (a) .64 to .89 (1.099 ± .333)
   (b) .72 to .86 (1.099 ± .200)
   (c) .76 to .83 (1.099 ± .100)
   (d) .78 to .82 (1.099 ± .05)
4. (a) Yes, both $r$'s (.50 and .29) exceed the critical value of $r$ (.164) for $n = 200$ and $\alpha_1 = .01$, indeed $p < .0005$.
   (b) .95*CI* with $r = 50$; .4 to .6; .95*CI* with $r = .29$; .16 to .42.
   (c) No, the $r$'s are not independent since they were both obtained on the same 236 persons.

**5.** As $n$ increases, variance in sampling distribution decreases. As $n$ increases, sampling distribution becomes less skewed.

**6.** Yes, $z = \frac{.973 - .887}{.116} = .741 < 1.96$; therefore, $H_0$ is tenable,

**7.** (a) for $r = .56$: .51 to .61 ($.633 \pm .071$)
for $r = .40$: .34 to .46 ($.424 \pm .074$)

(b) Yes; $z = \frac{.633 - .424}{\sqrt{(.071)^2 + (.074)^2}}$

$$= \frac{.209}{\sqrt{.01052}} = 2.04,\ p < .05$$

**8.** $Z_1 = 1.188,\ Z_2 = .604,$

$\sigma^2_{Z_1} = .0370,$

$\sigma^2_{Z_2} = .0059;$

$$z = \frac{1.188 - .604}{\sqrt{.0370 + .0059}} = \frac{.584}{.207} = 2.82;$$

reject $H_0$ at $\alpha_2 = .01$.

**9.** $.95CI = .66$ to $.77$; $\sigma_Z = .064$, $Z \pm 1.96\sigma_Z = .929 \pm .125 = .804$ to $1.054$, or .67 to .78; no, the difference is inconsequential.

**10.** $t = 2.68$ (Equation 14.10), $H_0$ rejected at the .05 and .01 levels.

**11.** $r_{YZ.X} = -.409$, yes, $\nu = 77$.

**12.** $F = 14.83$, ${}_{.999}F_{1,197} \approx 11.2$, $p < .001$

**13.** $\chi^2 = 8.30$, yes, no ($.05 > p > .01$); $\bar{r} = .71$.

**14.** (a) Yes, $F = [(.70)/(11 - 1)]/[(1 - .70)/(55 - 11)] = .070/.00682 = 10.27$ ${}_{.999}F_{10,44} \approx 3.87$, $p < .001$

(b) Yes, $F = [(.70 - .36)/(11 - 2)]/.00682 = 5.54$; ${}_{.999}F_{9,44} \approx 4.02$, $p < .001$

**15.** $F = \frac{(.57)^2 - (.56)^2/(12-2)}{[1-(.57)^2]/(192-12)}$

$$= \frac{(.3249 - .3136)/10}{(.6751)/(180)} = \frac{.00113}{.00375} = .30$$

${}_{.75}F_{10,154} \approx 1.28$, therefore $H_0$ is tenable; sampling error can easily account for the difference in $r$ and $\eta_{Y.X}$.

# ONE-FACTOR ANALYSIS OF VARIANCE

## 15.1 INTRODUCTION

In Chapter 12 statistical procedures for comparing two means were considered. But what if there are three or more means? The statistical technique known as the analysis of variance (ANOVA)[1] is used to determine whether the differences among the $J$ ($J \geq 2$) means are greater than would be expected from sampling error alone. Of all the inferential statistical techniques in education and the behavioral sciences, ANOVA is the most widely used (Edgington, 1974; Wick & Dirkes, 1973; Willson, 1980). In this chapter, one-factor ("one-way") ANOVA will be considered. Two-factor and three-factor ANOVA, which allow the effects of two and three independent variables to be examined simultaneously, are treated in Chapter 18.

## 15.2 WHY NOT SEVERAL *t*-TESTS?

If the means of three groups are to be compared, why not make $t$-tests between each pair of means, that is, why not test the three null hypotheses separately: $\mu_1 = \mu_2$, $\mu_1 = \mu_3$, and $\mu_2 = \mu_3$? Suppose the grades (A = 4, B = 3, etc.) given to the public schools by five groups (parents, students, teachers, administrators, and school board members) were to be compared. How many different $t$-tests would be required to compare each group with every other group? If there are $J$ groups, the number of separate $t$-tests (i.e., pairwise comparisons) will be $J(J - 1)/2$. Since, in this example, $J$ is 5, the number of comparisons is 5(4)/2 or 10.

If $J$ is 5, what is the probability of a type-I error among the ten pairwise comparisons of the five means—what is the probability of rejecting a true null hypothesis within the set? When we make only one $t$-test with $\alpha = .05$, then $\alpha$ is indeed .05. However, whenever more

[1]For an interesting historical account of the analysis of variance, see Kruskal (1980).

than one $t$-test is made, the probability of one or more type-I errors within the set is greater than .05. Since ten $t$-tests would be required to make all possible pairwise comparisons when $J = 5$, and since in each of the ten there is a 5% chance of making a type-I error, the probability of incorrectly rejecting at least one null hypothesis is far greater than .05. Indeed, if all $t$-tests were independent, the probability of at least one type-I error would be .40.[2]

The dependency among the $t$-tests makes things even more complex; it is impossible to determine the actual value of $\alpha$ for several different, non-independent $t$-tests.[3] Nevertheless, it is evident that a major problem with multiple $t$-tests is that the probability of one or more type-I errors becomes quite large as the number of groups ($J$) increases.

The statistical technique known as the analysis of variance (ANOVA) was developed by the English statistician, Sir Ronald Fisher, and introduced in his classic, *Statistical Methods for Research Workers* (1925).[4] ANOVA permits the control of $\alpha$ at a predetermined value when simultaneously testing the equality of any number ($J$) of means. In ANOVA, all differences for all pairs of $J$ means are examined simultaneously to see if one or more of the means deviates significantly from one or more of the other means. In other words, the ANOVA answers the question, "Does at least one of the $J$ means differ from at least one of the other $J$ means by more than would be expected from sampling error?" Stated differently, "Is the variance among the $J$ means (an aggregated measure of all mean differences) greater than would be expected if the null hypothesis is true?" Notice that, in ANOVA, the null hypothesis is an omnibus hypothesis:

$$H_0\text{: } \mu_1 = \mu_2 = \mu_3 = \ldots = \mu_J$$

If the omnibus null hypothesis is tenable (i.e., if evidence is insufficient to reject it), one ordinarily does not proceed with further statistical comparisons of means.[5] The analysis of variance is a method of statistical inference that evaluates whether there is any systematic (i.e., nonrandom) difference among the set of $J$ means. Thus, ANOVA has three definite advantages over separate $t$-tests when $J > 2$: (1) It yields an accurate and known type-I error probability, whereas the actual $\alpha$ for the set of several separate $t$-tests is high yet undetermined; (2) It is more powerful (when $\alpha$ is held constant)—that is, if the null hypothesis is false, it is more likely to be rejected; (3) It can assess the effects of two or more independent variables simultaneously (Chapters 18–19). For these reasons, ANOVA has become the "workhorse" for comparative studies in education and the behavioral sciences.

## 15.3 ANOVA NOMENCLATURE

As an example of a one-factor ANOVA, assume that we want to know if anxiety affects test performance. Subjects will be randomly assigned to low, moderate, or high anxiety test-taking

[2] $p = 1 - (1 - \alpha)^K$, if the $K$ comparisons are independent; for $\alpha = .05$; $p = 1 - (.95)^K$. If $K = 10$, $p = 1 - (.95)^{10}$ or $1 - .60 = .40$. Stated differently, the probability of at least one type-I error in the set of $K$ independent comparisons is $\alpha_\Sigma = 1 - (1 - \alpha)^K$.

[3] It is known that the probability of a type-I error for the set of $K$ $t$-tests is never greater than $K\alpha$, where $\alpha$ is the value for each of the $K$ comparisons (see Chapter 17).

[4] This classic has gone through fourteen editions, and has been published in French, German, Italian, Japanese, Spanish, and Russian.

[5] There are exceptions to this generalization, namely when certain select hypotheses are specified in advance, such as with planned orthogonal contrasts. These techniques are treated in Chapter 17.

| Treatment | | |
|---|---|---|
| *1* | *2* | *3* |
| $X_{11}$ | $X_{12}$ | $X_{13}$ |
| $X_{21}$ | $X_{22}$ | $X_{23}$ |
| $X_{31}$ | $X_{32}$ | $X_{33}$ |
| $X_{41}$ | $X_{42}$ | $X_{43}$ |
| $X_{51}$ | $X_{52}$ | $X_{53}$ |
| $X_{61}$ | $X_{62}$ | $X_{63}$ |
| $X_{71}$ | $X_{72}$ | $X_{73}$ |
| $X_{81}$ | $X_{82}$ | $X_{83}$ |
| $X_{91}$ | $X_{92}$ | $X_{93}$ |
| $\overline{X}_1$ | $\overline{X}_2$ | $\overline{X}_3$ |
| $s_1^2$ | $s_2^2$ | $s_3^2$ |

**FIGURE 15.1**

Layout of data from an experiment comparing $J$ = three levels ($j$ = 1, 2, 3) of the treatment factor and nine ($i$ = 1, 2, ..., 9 = $n$) replicates.

conditions. The factor (or independent variable) in this study is anxiety condition or treatment, of which there are three; the three categories of the *treatment factor* are termed *levels*. Suppose twenty-seven students will be randomly assigned to one of the three levels; thus, there will be nine students taking a test under high anxiety conditions, nine different students will be taking the test under moderate (normal) anxiety conditions, and nine other students will take the test under low anxiety conditions. Each student is said to be a *replicate*; thus, there are nine replicates ($n$ = 9) for each of the three levels ($J$ = 3) of the treatment.

The purpose of the study is to see if test performance is influenced by the treatment (anxiety conditions). Thus, the treatment is said to be the independent variable (cause) and scores on the test would be the dependent variable (effect). The purpose of ANOVA is to evaluate if the differences in the $J$ means are larger than would be expected from sampling error (chance).

In the present example, the researcher wants to know if the different treatments (anxiety conditions) produce differences in test performance. The twenty-seven test scores, the $X_{ij}$'s, can be tabulated as represented in Figure 15.1. The $j$ subscript defines the level of the treatment group (1, 2, or 3); the $i$ subscript denotes the replicate or observation (1, 2, ..., 9 = $n$).

When there are the *same* number of observations (replicates) for every one of the $J$ levels of the factor, the design is said to be *balanced*, that is, $n_1 = n_2 = \ldots = n_J = n$ (subscripts for $n$ are superfluous in balanced designs, but are needed unless all $n$'s are equal).

## 15.4 ANOVA COMPUTATION

### TOTAL SUM OF SQUARES, $SS_{total}$

Recall from Chapter 5 that $s^2 = \Sigma x_i^2/\nu = SS/\nu$, where "$SS$" is short for "sum of squares." Actually, it is the sum of the squared deviations, $x_i^2 = (X_i - \overline{X})^2$. In ANOVA, extensive use is made of *sums of squares* (*SS*) in testing the null hypothesis: $H_0$: $\mu_1 = \mu_2 = \ldots = \mu_J$. The total sum of squares ($SS_{\text{total}}$) in any set of data is a composite that reflects all sources of variation: treatment effects and sampling error. $SS_{\text{total}}$ is defined as the sum of the squared deviations of every score from the grand mean, $\bar{X}_{\bullet}$ (the mean of the $n_{\bullet}$ observations, where $n_{\bullet} = n_1 + n_2 + \ldots + n_J = \Sigma n_j$; for a "balanced" design, $n_{\bullet} = Jn$):

$$SS_{\text{total}} = \sum_j \sum_i x_{ij}^2 = \sum_j \sum_i (X_{ij} - \bar{X}_{\bullet})^2 \qquad \textbf{(15.1)}$$

In one-factor ANOVA, the total sum of squares ($SS_{\text{total}}$) is decomposed into two independent and unique parts ("sources of variation").[6] One portion of the sum of squares is due to differences *between*[7] group means; the second portion is the result of differences among the observations *within* the groups:

$$SS_{\text{total}} = SS_{\text{Between}} + SS_{\text{Within}} \qquad \textbf{(15.2)}$$

## 15.5 SUM OF SQUARES BETWEEN, $SS_B$

The sum of squares *between* ($SS_B$) results from the differences among group means, as defined in Equation 15.3. In other words, $\alpha_j$ is the difference between the mean of group *j* ($\mu_j$) and the grand mean ($\mu$), that is, $\alpha_j$ is said to be the *effect* of treatment *j*: $\alpha_j = \mu_j - \mu$; it[8] is estimated by:

$$\hat{\alpha}_j = \bar{X}_j - \bar{X}_{\bullet} \qquad \textbf{(15.3)}$$

The sum of squares resulting from differences between group means ($SS_B$) is given by Equation 15.4, where $n_j$ is the number of observations in group *j*, and $\alpha_j$ is the effect of treatment *j*:

$$SS_B = \sum_j n_j \hat{\alpha}_j^2 = \sum_j n_j (\bar{X}_j - \bar{X}_{\bullet})^2 \qquad \textbf{(15.4)}$$

If the ANOVA design is balanced (i.e., the *n*'s are equal), Equation 15.4 simplifies to:[9]

$$SS_B = n \sum_j \hat{\alpha}_j^2 = n \sum_j (\bar{X}_j - \bar{X}_{\bullet})^2 \qquad \textbf{(15.5)}$$

---

[6] In Chapter 18, ANOVAs with two or more factors are treated, in which case $SS_{\text{total}}$ is broken down into additional effects.

[7] "Among" is proper grammatically, but "between" is standard terminology.

[8] This alpha is not related to the probability of a type-I error. Sorry for the possible confusion, but this is the standard notation. The context will rarely result in any confusion.

[9] The classical formula for hand-calculating $SS_B$ was given in the previous editions of this book, but Equations 15.4 and 15.5 are computationally simpler and more conceptually related to the hypothesis being tested. With the availability of calculators and computer spreadsheets for computation, Equations 15.4 and 15.5 are preferable.

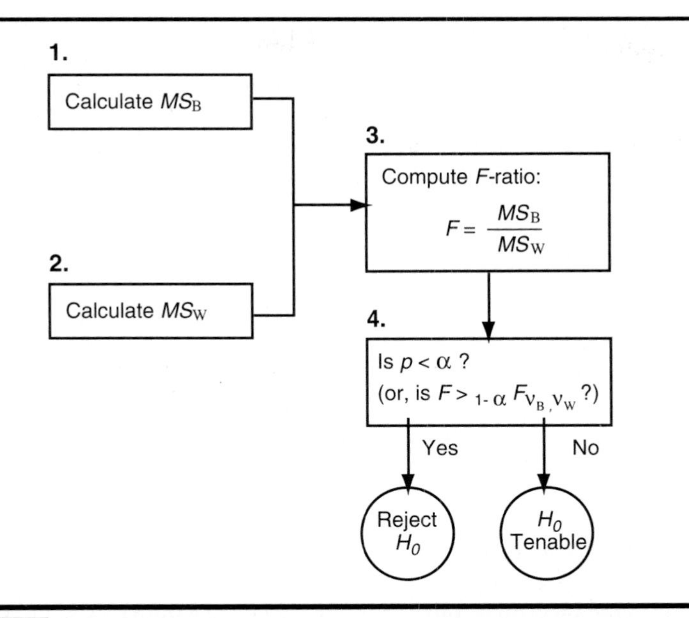


**FIGURE 15.2** Computational procedures for one-factor ANOVA involving $J$ means and $n_{\bullet}$ total observations.

## 15.6 SUM OF SQUARES WITHIN, $SS_W$

The sum of squares within group 1 is $\Sigma_i x_{i1}^2 = SS_1$. The sum of squares within all $J$ groups is shown by Equation 15.6:

$$SS_W = \sum_j \sum_i (X_{ij} - \overline{X}_j)^2 = SS_1 + SS_2 + \ldots + SS_J \quad \textbf{(15.6)}$$

Typically the mean, $\overline{X}$, and variance, $s^2$, are computed for each of the $J$ groups; the sum of squares for group $j$ is easily obtained by rearranging Equation 5.5: $SS_j = \nu_j s_j^2 = (n_j - 1)s_j^2$. $SS_W$ can also be obtained indirectly by rearranging Equation 15.2:

$$SS_W = SS_{\text{total}} - SS_B \quad \textbf{(15.7)}$$

In Chapter 5, we divided a sum of squares by its degrees of freedom to obtain a variance estimate (Equation 5.5). ANOVA employs the $F$-test, which is the ratio of two independent variance estimates. The computational procedures for a one-factor ANOVA are outlined in Figure 15.2.

When $SS_B$ and $SS_W$ are computed and are divided by their respective degrees of freedom, $\nu_B$ and $\nu_W$ (steps 1 and 2), two independent estimates of variance (called "mean squares")[10] are obtained. When the null hypothesis is true, both variance estimates are estimating the same parameter, $\sigma^2$, the variance among the observations in the population. The ratio $MS_B/MS_W$ is the $F$-ratio (step 3); the expected value of this ratio, $F$, is approximately 1.0.[11] However, when $H_0$ is false (i.e., when the $J$ population means are not equal), the expected value of the numerator is larger than the expected value of the denominator. Hence, when $H_0$ is false, the expected value of the $F$-ratio is greater than 1.0. When the observed $F$-ratio is greater than the critical $F$-ratio, $H_0$ is rejected (step 4).

The critical values for $F$ for various combinations of degrees of freedom and $\alpha$-levels are found in Table F of the Appendix. These are the values of the $F$-ratio needed in order to reject $H_0$.

## 15.7 ANOVA COMPUTATIONAL ILLUSTRATION

In the *Infant Growth Study* (Stember et al., 1995), the weights at one month of age were compared for (1) breast-fed, (2) bottle-fed, and (3) both (breast-fed and bottle-fed) infants. The means and variances for the three groups are given in Table 15.1, along with the calculations for obtaining $SS_B$, $SS_W$, $MS_B$, and $MS_W$. If the null hypothesis is true, the expected values of $MS_B$ and $MS_W$ are equal: $E(MS_B) = E(MS_W) = \sigma^2$.

The null hypothesis $H_0$: $\mu_1 = \mu_2 = \mu_3$ is tested by comparing the obtained $F$-ratio ($F = MS_B/MS_W$) with the critical value: ${}_{1-\alpha}F_{\nu_B,\nu_W}$ obtained from Table F, or better, by computer. The critical value is the 1-$\alpha$th percentile in the *central* $F$-distribution—the sampling distribution of the $F$-ratio when $H_0$ is true. If we are employing the conventional risk of a type-I error, $\alpha = .05$, the null hypothesis is rejected when the observed $F$-ratio is larger that the 95th percentile point of the $F$-distribution with 2 and 60 degrees of freedom. If the critical $F$ is greater than the observed $F = MS_B/MS_W$, $H_0$ remains tenable.

The value of the $F$-ratio for the data in Table 15.1 is $F = 4.65$. In Table F, we find the following percentile points in the central $F$-distribution: ${}_{.75}F_{2,60} = 1.42$, ${}_{.90}F_{2,60} = 2.39$, ${}_{.95}F_{2,60} = 3.15$, ${}_{.975}F_{2,60} = 3.93$, and ${}_{.99}F_{2,60} = 4.98$. The central $F_{2,60}$-distribution is the distribution of $F$-ratios that would result if $H_0$: $\mu_1 = \mu_2 = \mu_3$ is true, and the study was replicated many, many times, and a frequency distribution of the resulting $F$-values from the ANOVA's were graphed.

The obtained value of $F = 4.65$ from the ANOVA for the data in Table 15.1 falls above the 97.5th percentile in the $F$-distribution with 2 and 60 degrees of freedom (${}_{.975}F_{2,60} = 3.93$). If $H_0$: $\mu_1 = \mu_2 = \mu_3$ were true, an $F$-ratio as large or larger than 3.93 would occur with a probability less than .025. Hence, $H_0$ is rejected ($p < .025$, or better, from computer, $p = .013$).

## 15.8 ANOVA THEORY

The better one understands the underlying rationale for a statistical procedure, the greater the likelihood that it will be properly used and interpreted.

Suppose that the null hypothesis $H_0$: $\mu_1 = \ldots = \mu_J$ is true. That is, the $J$ population means about which one wishes to make an inference all have exactly the same numerical value. According to ANOVA theory, there are $J$ populations, all of which are assumed to be

---

[10]Notice that $\sigma^2 = \Sigma x^2/N$ or $\sigma^2$ = Sum of Squares$/N$, hence $\sigma^2$ can be viewed as a *mean* square.

[11]More precisely, $E(F) = \nu_e/(\nu_e - 2)$; in the one-factor ANOVA, $\nu_e = \nu_W$. A more thorough discussion of the theory related to the $F$-test appears later in this chapter.

**TABLE 15.1** Infant Weights at One Month for Three Modes of Feedings: Computational Illustration for One-Factor ANOVA with Unequal *n*'s.

| | *Groups* | | | |
|---|---|---|---|---|
| | *1* *Breast* | *2* *Bottle* | *3* *Both* | *Composite* |
| $n_j$ | 23 | 32 | 8 | $63 = n_{\bullet}$ |
| $\overline{X}_j$ | 9.8264 | 8.9672 | 8.8707 | $9.2594 = \overline{X}_{\bullet}$ |
| $\hat{\alpha}_j$ | 0.5670 | –0.2922 | –0.3887 | $[\hat{\alpha}_j = \overline{X}_j - \overline{X}_{\bullet}]$ |
| $s_j^2$ | 0.6936 | 1.6078 | 1.1520 | |
| $SS_j$ | 15.2582 | 49.8418 | 8.0639 | $[SS_j = \nu_j s_j^2]$ |

Step 1, Compute $SS_B$ [Equation 15.4].

$$SS_B = \Sigma_j n_j \hat{\alpha}_j^2 = 23(.5670)^2 + 32(-.2922)^2 + 8(-.3887)^2 = 11.3351$$

Step 2, Compute $SS_W$ [Equation 15.6].

$$SS_W = SS_1 + SS_2 + SS_3 = 15.2582 + 49.8418 + 8.0639 = 73.1639$$

Step 3, Compute $MS_B$.

$$MS_B = SS_B/\nu_B = 11.3351/2 = 5.6676 \; [\nu_B = J - 1]$$

Step 4, Compute $MS_W$.

$$MS_W = SS_W/\nu_W = 73.1639/60 = 1.2194 \; [\nu_W = \Sigma\nu_j = \nu_1 + \nu_2 + \nu_3]$$

Step 5, Compute $F$-ratio:

$$F = MS_B/MS_W = 5.6676/1.2194 = 4.65$$

Step 6, Compare $F$-ratio with Critical-$F$ and act on $H_0$:

$${}_{1-\alpha}F_{\nu_B,\nu_W} = {}_{.95}F_{2,60} = 3.15;\; F = 4.65 > 3.15,\; H_0 \text{ is rejected at } \alpha = .05.$$[12]

***ANOVA Summary Table***

| *Source* | $\nu$ | *MS* | *F* | *p* |
|---|---|---|---|---|
| *Between* | 2 | 5.6676 | 4.65 | <.025 |
| *Within* | 60 | 1.2194 | | |

normally distributed and have identical means, $\mu$, and equal variances, $\sigma^2$ (See Figure 15.3, panels A and B). In essence, if the null hypothesis is true, there are not $J$ different statistical populations—there is only one. Thus, when drawing $J$ samples, one is actually drawing $J$ independent samples from a single normal distribution that has a mean of $\mu$ and a variance of $\sigma^2$.

[12]Indeed, since $F = 4.65 > 3.93$, $H_0$ can be rejected at $\alpha = .025$. Most computer programs (or computer spreadsheets such as EXCEL) print the exact probabilities. The probability of observing an $F_{2,60} \geq 4.65$ when the null hypothesis is true and all ANOVA assumptions are met is .013.

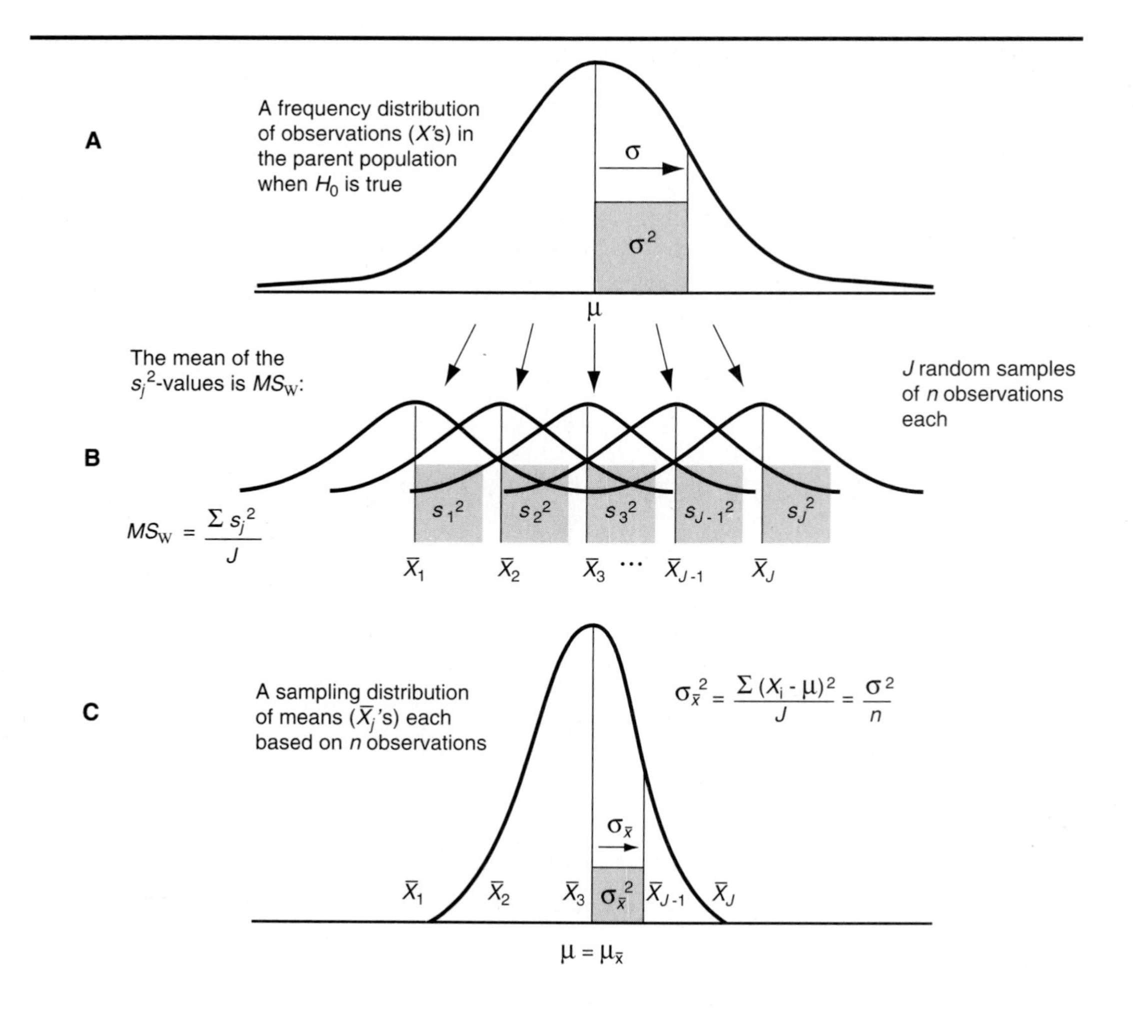


1. Since $s_{\bar{X}}^2 = \frac{s^2}{n}$, $ns_{\bar{X}}^2 = s^2$. Hence, $E(ns_{\bar{X}}^2) = \sigma^2$; $ns_{\bar{X}}^2$ is called the mean square between, or $MS_B$.

2. $\frac{\Sigma s_j^2}{J} = \frac{(s_i^2 + \ldots + s_J^2)}{J} = s_W^2$ ; $E(s_W^2) = \sigma^2$; $s_W^2$ is called the mean square within, or $MS_W$

3. Therefore, the expected value $F = \frac{MS_B}{MS_W} \approx 1$ when the null hypothesis is true.

**FIGURE 15.3** Theoretical basis of the ANOVA. The variance error of the mean, $s_{\bar{X}}^2$, when multiplied by $n$, gives an unbiased estimate of the variance among the observations in the frequency distribution of the parent population when the null hypothesis is true.

## 15.9 MEAN SQUARE BETWEEN GROUPS, $MS_B$

In Chapter 10, it was demonstrated that, when $J$ random samples of size $n$ are drawn from a distribution, the expected value of the mean of the $J$ sample means is $\mu$ and the expected value of the variance for the two sample means will be $\sigma_{\bar{X}}^2 = \sigma^2/n$ (Equation 10.1 squared). If $J$ samples are drawn from a single population (i.e., $H_0$ is true), the variance of these $J$ sample means has an expected value of $\sigma^2/n = \sigma_{\bar{X}}^2$. If this equation is rearranged, we see that when $H_0$ is true $n$ times the variance of the $J$ sample means ($ns_{\bar{X}}^2$) yields an estimate of the population variance, $\sigma^2$ (See Figure 15.3, panel C). Hence, $E(ns_{\bar{X}}^2) = \sigma^2$. This estimate of the variance in the population is the *mean square between*. Study the various terms in Equation 15.8A:

$$ns_{\bar{X}}^2 = n\sum_j \frac{(\bar{X}_j - \bar{X}_{\bullet})^2}{J-1} = \frac{n\sum_j \hat{\alpha}_j^2}{J-1} = MS_B \qquad \textbf{(15.8A)}$$

Equation 15.8A gives the numerical value of $MS_B$ in ANOVA. Note that $MS_B$ is defined in just such a way that the differences among the $J$ sample means yield an unbiased estimate of $\sigma^2$, the variance of the population sampled, when the null hypothesis regarding population means is true. If $H_0: \mu_1 = \mu_2 = \ldots = \mu_J$ is true, $ns_{\bar{X}}^2 = MS_B$ will differ from $\sigma^2$ only because of sampling error, which in the long run will average zero; if $H_0$ is false, $E(MS_B) > \sigma^2$.

When $n$'s are unequal, each of the $J$ effects, $\hat{\alpha}_j = \bar{X}_j - \bar{X}_{\bullet}$, are weighted by $n_j$ before they are summed, as denoted in Equation 15.8B:

$$MS_B = \frac{\sum_j n_j(\bar{X}_j - \bar{X}_{\bullet})^2}{J-1} = \frac{\sum_j n_j(\hat{\alpha}_j)^2}{J-1} \qquad \textbf{(15.8B)}$$

## 15.10 MEAN SQUARE WITHIN GROUPS, $MS_W$

Each of the $J$ samples (Figure 15.3, panel B), has a variance, $s_j^2$, which is an unbiased estimate of the population variance, $\sigma^2$. Obviously, if these $J$ variance estimates are averaged, an even better estimate of $\sigma^2$ is obtained: $E[(s_1^2 + s_2^2 + \ldots + s_J^2)/J] = \sigma^2$. In a balanced design, the mean of the $J$ sample variances is the *mean square within*, $MS_W$.[13]

$$\sum_j \frac{s_j^2}{J} = \frac{s_1^2 + \ldots + s_J^2}{J} = MS_W \qquad \textbf{(15.9)}$$

Notice that, when the null hypothesis is true, both $MS_W$ and $MS_B$ yield an unbiased estimate of the population variance, $\sigma^2$; but an important fact about $MS_W$ is that, unlike

[13]If $n$'s are not equal, $MS_W$ is the weighted mean of the $J$ variances: $MS_W = \Sigma \nu_j s_j^2 / \nu_W$.

$MS_B$, it is an unbiased estimate of $\sigma^2$ whether or not the null hypothesis is true. Thus, if $H_0$ is false, we expect $MS_B$ to be larger than $MS_W$.

## 15.11 THE *F*-TEST

In Sections 15.7–15.8 we saw that if the null hypothesis ($H_0$: $\mu_1 = \mu_2 \ldots = \mu_J$) is true, then $MS_B$ and $MS_W$ both estimate the same parameter, $\sigma^2$, $MS_B$ and $MS_W$ are *independent* estimates of $\sigma^2$ (when the ANOVA assumptions are met). If one compares $MS_B$ and $MS_W$, for example, by taking their ratio, $F = MS_B/MS_W$, one obtains evidence of whether they are estimating the same parameter $\sigma^2$. If the ratio $F = MS_B/MS_W$ is not much greater than 1, then it is reasonable to assume that they are both estimating $\sigma^2$, that is, the evidence against the null hypothesis is not strong enough to reject it. But how much larger than 1 must the ratio $MS_B/MS_W$ be in order to reject the null hypothesis? This is determined by referring the observed value of $F$ to the central $F$-distribution (Table F); this distribution describes the distribution of $F$-ratios when $H_0$ is true.

If $H_0$: $\mu_1 = \mu_2 \ldots = \mu_J$ is false, then the variance estimate from the $J$ sample means ($MS_B$) will be larger than it is when $H_0$ is true and, hence, larger than $MS_W$. In other words, $MS_B$ estimates a number larger than $\sigma^2$ when $H_0$ is false. $MS_W$, however, is expected to estimate the same parameter $\sigma^2$ (the average variance within the $J$ groups) whether or not $H_0$: $\mu_1 = \mu_2 \ldots = \mu_J$ is true, because it is based on variances *within* the $J$ samples and is unaffected by any difference among the $J$ sample means. Consequently, a false null hypothesis is expected to yield a ratio, $F = MS_B/MS_W$, that is greater than 1.

Such are the reasons for forming $F = MS_B/MS_W$, and referring it to the $F$-distribution. If the observed $F$-ratio is not larger than 95% of the $F$-ratios that would result when $H_0$ is true, $H_0$ is regarded as tenable—the evidence is not strong enough to reject it without taking a risk of a type-I error greater than .05. Stated differently, if the ratio $MS_B/MS_W$ is less than the critical-$F$, ${}_{1-\alpha}F_{J-1,n_\bullet-J}$, $H_0$ is tenable; if $F = MS_B/MS_W$ is larger than the critical-$F$, $H_0$ is rejected—the probability of such a result solely from chance (sampling error) is less than $\alpha$.

If $H_0$: $\mu_1 = \mu_2 = \mu_3 = \ldots = \mu_J$ is rejected, does it necessarily follow that $\mu_1 \neq \mu_2 \neq \mu_3 \neq \ldots \neq \mu_J$? Certainly not; perhaps $\mu_1 > \mu_2 = \mu_3 = \ldots = \mu_J$, or $\mu_1 = \mu_2 > \mu_3 = \ldots = \mu_J$, or any one of several patterns of results is possible. How, then, does one decide which means differ significantly from which other means? The answer to this question is the focus of Chapter 17, "multiple comparisons."

## 15.12 ANOVA WITH EQUAL *n*'S

The ANOVA hand computations for a balanced design (Equations 15.8A and 15.9) are more straightforward than when the $n$'s are unequal and the effects must be weighted accordingly. Consider the following example:

A study addressed the question of scoring bias on essay tests. An essay examination (with an attached photograph) was graded by a large group of graders who were randomly assigned to one of three groups that differed in only one respect. The "student" in the attached photograph was either (1) low, (2) medium, or (3) high in attractiveness. There were $n = 96$ persons within each of the three groups of graders. The only nonrandom difference among the three groups was the physical attractiveness of the "student" who wrote the essay. The dependent variable was the score assigned to the essay. The means and variances for each of the three groups are given in Table 15.2.

**TABLE 15.2** Computational Illustration for a One-Factor ANOVA with Equal n's.

| | *Groups* | | | |
|---|---|---|---|---|
| | *1* *Low* | *2* *Medium* | *3* *High* | *Composite* |
| $n$ | 96 | 96 | 96 | $288 = n_{\bullet}$ |
| $\overline{X}_j$ | 22.98 | 25.78 | 26.56 | $25.11 = \overline{X}_{\bullet}$ |
| $s_j^2$ | 77.33 | 82.45 | 72.24 | |

Step 1. Compute $MS_B$[14] (Equation 15.8A).

$MS_B = ns_{\overline{X}}^2;\ s_{\overline{X}}^2 = 3.544$

$MS_B = 96(3.544) = 340.24$

Step 2. Compute $MS_W$ (Equation 15.9).

$MS_W = (s_1^2 + s_2^2 + s_3^2)/3 = 77.34$

Step 3. Compute $F$-ratio: $F = MS_B/MS_W$.

$F = 340.24/77.34 = 4.40$

Step 4. Compare $F$-ratio with critical-$F$ and act on $H_0$: $\mu_1 = \mu_2 = \mu_3$.

${}_{1-\alpha}F_{\nu_B,\nu_W} = {}_{.95}F_{2,285} \approx {}_{.95}F_{2,200} = 3.04$

$F = 4.40 > 3.04$; $H_0$ is rejected at $\alpha = .05$

(Indeed, since $F = 4.40 > 3.76$, $H_0$ can be rejected at $\alpha = .025$.)[15]

***ANOVA Summary Table***

| *Source* | $\nu$ | *MS* | *F* | *p* |
|---|---|---|---|---|
| *Between* | 2 | 340.24 | 4.40 | <.012 |
| *Within* | 285 | 77.34 | | |

The $(1 - \alpha)CI$ for each of the $J$ means (see also Equation 11.9) can be obtained using the expression below:

$$(1-\alpha)CI = \overline{X}_j \pm \sqrt{{}_{1-\alpha}F_{1,\nu_W}(MS_W / n_j)}$$

For the $.95CI$ for the means in Table 15.2:

$$.95CI = \overline{X}_j \pm \sqrt{{}_{.95}F_{1,285}(77.34/96)}$$

[14]This can be obtained most easily by entering the three means into a calculator (or spreadsheet) that has a built-in variance ($s^2$) function.

[15]Most computer programs (or spreadsheets such as EXCEL) print the exact probabilities. The probability of observing $F_{2,285} = 4.45$ when the null hypothesis is true and all ANOVA assumptions are met is .012.

Using ${}_{.95}F_{1,285} \approx 3.89$:

$$.95CI = \bar{X}_j \pm \sqrt{3.89(77.34/96)} = \bar{X}_j \pm 1.77$$

The $.95CI$'s for groups 1, 2, and 3 are (21.21, 24.75), (24.01, 27.55), and (24.79, 28.33), respectively.

## 15.13 A STATISTICAL MODEL FOR THE DATA

In this and following sections,[16] one-factor ANOVA will be viewed in more mathematical terms. In ANOVA, it is assumed that any score can be represented by a linear model. The term "linear" applies because the components are not squared, cubed, and so on—none of the terms are raised to powers other than 1.

Consider the following linear model for the $X_{ij}$'s:

$$X_{ij} = \mu + \alpha_j + \varepsilon_{ij} \quad \textbf{(15.10)}$$

$X_{ij}$ is the score for person $i$ in group $j$; it is viewed as having three components:

$\mu$ is the population mean; $\mu$ is a constant, and reflects the overall "elevation" of the scores.

$\alpha_j$ is the effect of treatment $j$; it is a constant for all scores in group $j$. $\alpha_j$ reflects the increase or decrease in these scores that is associated with treatment $j$, (i.e., $\alpha_j = \mu_j - \mu$)].

$\varepsilon_{ij}$ is the "error" for the score $X_{ij}$. It is the *residual* of the score $X_{ij}$ when predicted from $\mu$ and $\alpha_j$ (i.e., rearrange Equation 15.10: $\varepsilon_{ij} = X_{ij} - \mu - \alpha_j$).

Remember that $\mu$, $\alpha_j$, and $\varepsilon_{ij}$ are numbers. If $\mu$ is 12, $\alpha_2$ is +2, and $X_{12}$ is 13, then $\varepsilon_{12}$ is $13 - 12 - 2 = -1$. The main interest of the researcher concerns the effects, $\alpha_j$'s: $\alpha_j$ reflects the effect treatment $j$ has on the scores. The grand mean $\mu$ is ordinarily of little interest (unless $X$ represents a gain score such as posttest minus pretest). The original research question, "Do the effects of these three treatments differ; do the three sample means differ by more than would be expected solely from sampling error?", can now be stated more precisely: "Is it true that $\alpha_1 = \alpha_2 = \alpha_3 = 0$, that is, is $H_0$ true?" Is the conclusion that the three population means have the same value tenable? This null hypothesis can be tested by ANOVA.

A method for testing the hypothesis $H_0$: $\alpha_1 = \alpha_2 = \alpha_3$ is needed because each $\alpha_j$ does not equal 0. If there were no sampling error in the linear model, we could simply look at the means of the scores in the three groups, and reject the null hypothesis if differences were observed. However, sampling error is present when we deal with samples. How does sampling error arise? It comes about in various ways. First, the results of the experiment run at any one time will undoubtedly be different from the results when it is replicated on a new

[16]Sections 15.13 to 15.21 give a mathematical basis for ANOVA. Sections 15.1 to 15.12 should be thoroughly mastered before proceeding with Sections 15.13 to 15.21. Correct applications of ANOVA do not necessarily require a mastery of Sections 15.13 to 15.21.

random sample of subjects. Second, persons (or other observational units) are inherently different even when they are treated alike (thus, the $\varepsilon$'s within a group will vary). Third, errors of measurement arise when an attempt is made to measure the subjects. These errors are due to measurement error (unreliability) of the measuring instrument such as a test or questionnaire. The greater the reliability of the measure, the less the influence of measurement error (Section 7.16). Fourth, errors can arise from uncontrolled events during the experiment (e.g., weather, time of day, illness, etc.). Additional error can arise if the postulated linear model is not correct. All these sources of error combine to make the results of the experiment today different from what would have been obtained yesterday or tomorrow if the experiment were replicated on different random groups of subjects.

## 15.14 ESTIMATES OF THE TERMS IN THE MODEL

What one actually observes in the experiment are the $n$ observations on the dependent variable for each of the $J$ groups, $X_{ij}$'s. The parameters $\mu$, $\alpha_j$, and $\varepsilon_{ij}$ are unknown. Fortunately, statisticians have found a way to estimate the parameters in the linear model. Estimates of $\mu$, $\alpha_j$, and $\varepsilon_{ij}$ can be obtained by employing the *least-squares criterion*. These least-squares estimates are denoted by $\hat{\mu}$, $\hat{\alpha}_j$, and $\hat{\varepsilon}_{ij}$. In the process of obtaining the estimates, the parameters of greatest interest, $\alpha_1, \alpha_2, \ldots, \alpha_J$, are assumed to sum to zero: $\alpha_1 + \alpha_2 + \ldots + \alpha_J = 0$. This is a reasonable restriction since the $\alpha_j$'s are thought of as elevators or depressors above or below a general level that is embodied in the parameter $\mu$. By placing this restriction on the $\alpha_j$'s, the statistician determines that the $\alpha_j$'s will have the properties of deviations from a mean, $\mu$, since in any distribution the sum of deviations around its mean is zero (Section 4.9). The statistician has found that:

$$\hat{\mu} = \overline{X}_{\bullet}$$
$$\hat{\alpha}_j = \overline{X}_j - \overline{X}_{\bullet}$$
$$\hat{\varepsilon}_{ij} = X_{ij} - \overline{X}_j, \text{ denoted by } e_{ij}$$

The model estimates (Equation 15.10) are made to fit the observed data such that:

$$X_{ij} = \hat{\mu} + \hat{\alpha}_j + e_{ij}$$

Notice that:

$$X_{ij} = \overline{X}_{\bullet} + (\overline{X}_j - \overline{X}_{\bullet}) + (X_{ij} - \overline{X}_j) \quad \textbf{(15.11)}$$

The first term on the right is $\mu$, the second term is $\alpha_j$, and the last term is $e_{ij}$.

## 15.15 SUMS OF SQUARES

In ANOVA, it is assumed that the numerator and denominator of the $F$-test are two *independent* estimates of the variance parameter, $\sigma^2$, when $H_0$ is true. In this section, we will demonstrate that the total sum of squares ($SS_{\text{total}}$) is composed of two *independent* (uncorrelated or orthogonal) components: (1) the sum of squares between groups ($SS_B$), and (2) the sum of squares within groups ($SS_W$). First, subtract the grand mean $\overline{X}_{\bullet}$ from each side of Equation 15.11:

$$X_{ij} - \overline{X}_{\bullet} + (\overline{X}_j - \overline{X}_{\bullet}) + (X_{ij} - \overline{X}_j) = \hat{\alpha}_j + e_{ij}$$

Next, square each side of the above equation and sum both sides over $j$ and $i$:

$$\sum_j \sum_i (X_{ij} - \overline{X}_{\bullet})^2 = \sum_j \sum_i (\hat{\alpha}_j + e_{ij})^2$$

The quantity on the left in the above equation is the *total sum of squares*, $SS_{\text{total}}$. For the *entire* set of numbers obtained in a study the sum of the squared deviation of each number from the grand mean is the *total sum of squares*.

Now consider the right side of the above equation. Notice that if we let $a$ represent $\hat{\alpha}_j$ and $b$ stand for $e_{ij}$, then the right side involves the quantity $(a + b)^2 = a^2 + 2ab + b^2$. So that:

$$SS_{\text{total}} = \sum_j \sum_i (\hat{\alpha}_j^2 + 2\hat{\alpha}_j e_{ij} + e_{ij}^2) = \sum_j \sum_i \hat{\alpha}_j^2 + 2\sum_j \sum_i \hat{\alpha}_j e_{ij} + \sum_j \sum_i e_{ij}^2 \qquad \textbf{(15.12)}$$

Within each of the $J$ groups, $\hat{\alpha}_j$ is a constant for all $n$ scores; hence:

$$\sum_j \sum_i \hat{\alpha}_j^2 = \sum_j n\hat{\alpha}_j^2 = n\sum_j \hat{\alpha}_j^2$$

Recall that the sum of the deviations from the mean is zero. Since the $e_{ij}$'s within each group are these deviations (Equation 15.12), the $e_{ij}$'s sum to zero. If each score in a distribution of scores that sum to zero is multiplied by a constant (in this case $\hat{\alpha}_j$), the sum of the products within each of the $J$ groups is also zero (Equation 4.4):

$$\sum_i \hat{\alpha}_j e_{ij} = \hat{\alpha}_j \sum_i e_{ij} = 0$$

Thus, the middle term in Equation 15.12 is equal to zero, and Equation 15.12 becomes

$$SS_{\text{total}} = \sum_j n\hat{\alpha}_j^2 + \sum_j \sum_i e_{ij}^2 = SS_B + SS_W \qquad \textbf{(15.13)}$$

The total sum of squares ($SS_{\text{total}}$) has been partitioned (divided) into two additive components: (1) the sum of squares between groups ($SS_B$), and (2) the sum of squares within groups ($SS_W$). $SS_{\text{total}}$ reflects all the variation in the set of $Jn$ scores; thus, the name "analysis of variance," abbreviated to ANOVA, has evolved. This analysis will be used to test the null hypothesis, $H_0$: $\alpha_1 = \alpha_2 = \ldots = \alpha_J = 0$.

## 15.16 RESTATEMENT OF THE NULL HYPOTHESIS IN TERMS OF POPULATION MEANS

The null hypothesis $H_0$: $\alpha_1 = \alpha_2 = \ldots = \alpha_j = 0$ can be restated in an equivalent but slightly different form. Since $\alpha_1 = \overline{X}_1 - \overline{X}_{\bullet}$ is an unbiased estimator of $\alpha_1$, $E(\hat{\alpha}_1) = \alpha_1$:

$$E(\hat{\alpha}_1) == E(\overline{X}_1 - \overline{X}_{\bullet}) = E(\overline{X}_1) - E(\overline{X}_{\bullet}) = \mu_1 - \mu = \alpha_1$$

Similarly, $\alpha_2 = \mu_2 - \mu$ and $\alpha_j = \mu_J - \mu$.

The null hypothesis can be expressed as $(\mu_1 - \mu) = (\mu_2 - \mu) = \ldots = (\mu_J - \mu)$. Add $\mu$ to each of these three terms and the null hypothesis becomes: $\mu_1 = \mu_2 = \ldots = \mu_J$. Hence, in the linear model, $X_{ij} = \mu + \alpha_j + e_{ij}$, the null hypothesis that $\alpha_1 = \alpha_2 = \ldots = \alpha_J = 0$ is the same as the hypothesis that the means of the populations from which the samples are drawn are all equal, that is, $H_0$: $\mu_1 = \mu_2 = \ldots = \mu_J$.

## 15.17 DEGREES OF FREEDOM

Associated with each sum of squares value ($SS_{\text{total}}$, $SS_B$, and $SS_W$) is an integer, $\nu$, called the "degrees of freedom." Degrees of freedom is a name borrowed from the physical sciences where it denotes a characteristic of the movement of an object. If an object is free to move in a straight line only, it has one degree of freedom; an object that is free to move through any point in a plane, such as a bowling ball rolling down an alley, has two degrees of freedom; a ball in a handball court has three degrees of freedom: It can go from back to front, side to side, and floor to ceiling. Degrees of freedom enter into analysis of variance (ANOVA) by way of its geometric interpretation.

### Degrees of Freedom Between Groups, $\nu_B$

Consider first the degrees of freedom associated with $SS_B$; the definition of $SS_B$ (Equation 15.4) is:

$$SS_B = \sum_j n_j \hat{\alpha}_j^2 = \sum_j n_j (\overline{X}_j - \overline{X}_{\bullet})^2$$

If the design is balanced, Equation 15.4 can be simplified:

$$SS_B = n \sum_j \hat{\alpha}_j^2$$

and the group means (i.e., $\overline{X}_1$, $\overline{X}_2$, ..., $\overline{X}_J$) are related to the grand mean $\overline{X}_{\bullet}$ as defined by the equation:

$$\frac{\sum_j \overline{X}_j}{J} = \frac{\overline{X}_1 + \overline{X}_2 + \ldots + \overline{X}_J}{J} = \overline{X}_{\bullet} \qquad (15.14)$$

If $J = 3$, $\overline{X}_{\bullet} = 6$, $\overline{X}_1 = 3$, and $\overline{X}_2 = 7$, what must $\overline{X}_3$ be? $\overline{X}_3$ must be 8. If $\overline{X}_{\bullet} = 4$, $\overline{X}_2 = 3$, and $\overline{X}_3 = 4$, then $\overline{X}_1$ must be 5. If $\overline{X}_{\bullet}$ is a certain number, after values are assigned to $J - 1$ means, the last mean is already determined—it must have the specific value that satisfies the equation. The degrees of freedom for $SS_B$ are one less than the number of groups:

$$\nu_B = J - 1 \tag{15.15}$$

## Degrees of Freedom Within Groups, $\nu_W$

From Equation 15.6, the sum of squares within is:

$$SS_W = \sum_j \sum_i (X_{ij} - \overline{X}_j)^2$$

For group 1, the computation of $SS_W$ is:

$$(X_{11} - \overline{X}_1)^2 + (X_{21} - \overline{X}_1)^2 + \ldots + (X_{n1} - \overline{X}_1)^2$$

By definition, $X_{11}, X_{21}, \ldots, X_{n1}$ and $\overline{X}_1$ are related:

$$\frac{X_{11} + X_{21} + \ldots + X_{n1}}{n} = \overline{X}_1$$

If $\overline{X}_1$ were equal to 12.40, to how many of the $n$ quantities $X_{11}$ through $X_{n1}$ could one assign any number and still retain the value of 12.40 for $\overline{X}_1$? The answer is $n - 1$; thus, the degrees of freedom for group 1, $\nu_1$, are $n_1 - 1$. Similarly, the degrees of freedom within group 2 are $\nu_2 = n_2 - 1$. Hence, the degrees of freedom within all $J$ groups, $\nu_W$, are $(n_1 - 1) + (n_2 - 1) + \ldots + (n_J - 1)$, or:

$$\nu_W = \nu_1 + \nu_2 \ldots + \nu_J = \sum_j \nu_j \tag{15.16}$$

Since $(n_1 - 1) + (n_2 - 1) + \ldots + (n_J - 1) = n_{\bullet} - J$, the degrees of freedom within groups can be expressed as:

$$\nu_W = n_{\bullet} - J \tag{15.16A}$$

For balanced designs, the degrees of freedom within groups equation simplifies to:

$$\nu_W = J(n - 1) \tag{15.16B}$$

### Total Degrees of Freedom, $\nu_{total}$

From Equation 15.1:

$$SS_{total} = \sum_j \sum_i x_{ij}^2 = \sum_j \sum_i (X_{ij} - \bar{X}_{\bullet})^2 = (X_{11} - \bar{X}_{\bullet})^2 + (X_{21} - \bar{X}_{\bullet})^2 + \ldots + (X_{nJ} - \bar{X}_{\bullet})^2$$

The terms involved are related as follows:

$$\frac{X_{11} + X_{21} + \ldots + X_{nJ}}{n_{\bullet}} = \bar{X}_{\bullet}$$

Of the $n_{\bullet}$ observations on the left of the equation, all but one ($n_{\bullet} - 1$) of them can take any value without restriction. The final ($n_{\bullet}$th) number is fixed, however, to satisfy the value of $\bar{X}_{\bullet}$ in the equation above. The degrees of freedom for $SS_{total}$ equal $n_{\bullet} - 1$, one less than the total number of observations, that is:

$$\nu_{total} = n_{\bullet} - 1 \qquad \textbf{(15.17)}$$

When $n$'s are equal:

$$\nu_{total} = Jn - 1 \qquad \textbf{(15.17A)}$$

## 15.18 MEAN SQUARES: THE EXPECTED VALUE OF $MS_W$

A sum of squares ($SS$) divided by its degrees of freedom ($\nu$) is called a mean square ($MS$) or a variance estimate. In one-factor ANOVA, only two mean squares will be of interest: the mean square between ($MS_B = SS_B/\nu_B$), and the mean square within ($MS_W = SS_W/\nu_W$).

The expected value of a statistic is the *mean* of its sampling distribution. If an experiment were repeated an infinitely large number of times, then the average of this population of $MS_W$ values would be $E(MS_W)$. The expected value of $MS_W$ is denoted by $E(MS_W)$.

$E(MS_W)$ can be written in terms of a characteristic of the normal populations from which the scores obtained in the experiment are a random sample. First view $MS_W$ in a slightly different way. Here is a balanced ANOVA design:

$$MS_W = \frac{SS_W}{\nu_W} = \frac{\sum_j \sum_i (X_{ij} - \bar{X}_j)^2}{J(n-1)}$$

$$= \frac{1}{J}\left[\frac{\sum_i (X_{i1} - \bar{X}_1)^2}{n-1} + \frac{\sum_i (X_{i2} - \bar{X}_2)^2}{n-1} + \ldots + \frac{\sum_i (X_{iJ} - \bar{X}_J)^2}{n-1}\right]$$

Notice that $\Sigma_i(X_{i1} - \bar{X}_1)^2/(n - 1)$ is the sample variance of group 1; it is denoted by $s_1^2$. The sample variance of group 2 is $s_2^2$, and so on. Therefore, since the $n$'s are equal, $MS_W = (s_1^2 + s_2^2 + \ldots + s_J^2)/J$, that is, $MS_W$ is the *mean* of the sample variances of the $J$ groups.

Recall that $E(s_j^2) = \sigma_j^2$ (the variance of the population from which the scores in group $j$ were randomly sampled). If each of the $J$ populations had the same variance, $\sigma^2$, Equation 15.18 shows that the expected value of $MS_W$ is $\sigma^2$:

$$E(MS_W) = \frac{1}{J}E(s_1^2 + \ldots + s_J^2) = \frac{1}{J}[E(x_1^2) + \ldots + E(s_J^2)] \quad \textbf{(15.18)}$$
$$= \frac{1}{J}(\sigma^2 + \sigma^2 + \ldots + \sigma^2) = \frac{J\sigma^2}{J} = \sigma^2$$

The size of $MS_W$ does *not* depend on the means of the $J$ populations in the experiment. $MS_W$ is "mean-free," reflecting only the variability among the measures within groups. Such variability is around each of the $J$ group means, rather than around the grand mean of all the groups. Whether all of the groups are samples from the same normal population or all the populations have different means, $E(MS_W)$ will have the same expected value, $\sigma^2$, when the ANOVA assumptions are met.

## 15.19 THE EXPECTED VALUE OF $MS_B$

Unlike, $MS_W$, the expected value of the mean square between, $E(MS_B)$, depends on the values of the population means. If all the population means are equal, then the null hypothesis, $H_0$: $\mu_1 = \mu_2 = \ldots = \mu_J$ is true. If $H_0$: $\mu_1 = \mu_2 = \ldots = \mu_J$ is true, that is, if all the populations from which the samples in the experiment are randomly selected have the same mean, then $E(MS_B)$ is $\sigma^2$. If, however, any of the population means is different from any other, then $E(MS_B)$ will be larger than $\sigma^2$. If one or more population means are different from the others, then the null hypothesis $H_0$ is false. The expected value of $MS_B$ is:

$$E(MS_B) = \sigma^2 + \frac{n\sum_j \alpha_j^2}{J-1} \quad \textbf{(15.19)}$$

where $\sigma^2$ is the variance in each population, $n$ is the number of subjects in each group, $J$ is the number of groups, and $\alpha_j$ is the difference in the mean of the $j$th population and the grand mean (i.e., $\alpha_j = \mu_j - \mu$). For simplicity, $\Sigma_j\alpha_j/(J-1)$ is often denoted $\sigma_\alpha^2$; hence, Equation 15.19 can be expressed more simply as:[17]

$$E(MS_B) = \sigma^2 + n\sigma_\alpha^2 \quad \textbf{(15.19A)}$$

To summarize:

1. If $H_0$ is true, then:

$$E(MS_W) = E(MS_B) = \sigma^2$$

2. If $H_0$ is false, then:

[17]Technically, $\sigma_\alpha^2$ is not a variance unless the factor represents a random variable. Nevertheless, the simpler notation is common (e.g., Winer et al., 1991).

$$E(MS_W) = \sigma^2, \text{ and}$$

$$E(MS_B) = \sigma^2 + n\sigma_\alpha^2$$

Note that if $H_0$ is false, $E(MS_B) > E(MS_W) = \sigma^2$.

In any experiment, $MS_B$ and $MS_W$ are calculated. By comparing $MS_B$ to $MS_W$, one can assess whether $H_0$ is plausible. If $MS_B$ is much larger than $MS_W$, their ratio, $MS_B/MS_W = F > 1$, and it becomes more likely that $H_0$ is false. The $F$-ratio is the ratio of two independent variance estimates; $MS_B$ and $MS_W$ are independent (Section 15.15) when the $n$ observations are randomly drawn from normally distributed parent populations.

Suppose for the moment that three samples of $n$ scores are drawn at random from a normal population. This is a case of $H_0$ being true. The scores sampled could be placed in a table, such as Table 15.1, and the $MS_B$ and $MS_W$ could be computed. Would you be surprised if $MS_B$ and $MS_W$ did not have the same numerical value? Of course not; although their expected values would be equal, sampling error will cause the observed values of $MS_W$ and $MS_B$ to vary from one sampling to the next. The sample values of $MS_W$ and $MS_B$ will fluctuate independently from one sampling of $n_{\bullet}$ scores to the next (the experiment that was actually run is considered to be one case of sampling $n_{\bullet}$ scores).

When $MS_B$ is large relative to $MS_W$, can we regard such an occurrence as evidence that $H_0$ is false? How can we be sure that a large value of $MS_B$ relative to $MS_W$ did not occur simply by random fluctuation in scores? In a later section (Section 15.25) we will see how to control the proportion of times that we reject $H_0$ incorrectly, that is, the probability of a type-I error.

## 15.20 SOME DISTRIBUTION THEORY

In Chapter 16, it will be seen that a chi-square variable (Section 16.2) with one degree of freedom has the form:[18]

$$\frac{(X-\mu)^2}{\sigma^2} = z^2 \sim \chi_1^2$$

that is, the squared normal-deviate, $z^2$, is distributed as (~) chi square with 1 degree of freedom when $X$ is a normally distributed variable with population mean of $\mu$ and variance, $\sigma^2$. This statement can be denoted concisely as: $X \sim NID\,(\mu, \sigma^2)$, which specifies that the $X_{ij}$'s are independent, normally distributed, and have a mean of $\mu$ and a variance of $\sigma^2$.[19]

Suppose $n$ scores are randomly drawn from a normal distribution with mean and variance of $\mu$ and $\sigma^2$. Since independent chi-square variables have the additive property (Section 16.2), the quantity:

$$\frac{(X_1-\mu)^2}{\sigma^2} + \frac{(X_2-\mu)^2}{\sigma^2} + \ldots + \frac{(X_n-\mu)^2}{\sigma^2} \sim \chi_n^2$$

[18]The symbol "~" is short for "is distributed as."

[19]Some sources use the expression $N(0, \sigma^2)$ rather than $NID(0, \sigma^2)$.

The sum of $n$ squared $z$-scores has a chi-square distribution with $n$ degrees of freedom, that is, this sum computed on many repeated samples of $n$ scores has a known frequency distribution, $\chi_n^2$, where $\nu = n$.

If $X_1, \ldots, X_n$ are $n$ independent observations from a normal population with variance $\sigma^2$, then (see Wilks, 1962):

$$\frac{(X_1 - \overline{X})^2}{\sigma^2} + \frac{(X_2 - \overline{X})^2}{\sigma^2} + \ldots + \frac{(X_n - \overline{X})^2}{\sigma^2} \sim \chi_{n-1}^2$$

Therefore,

$$\frac{\sum_i (X_i - \overline{X})^2}{\sigma^2} \sim \chi_{n-1}^2$$

Also,

$$\frac{\sum_i (X_{ij} - \overline{X}_j)^2}{\sigma^2} \sim \chi_{n-1}^2$$

Notice that $\overline{X}$ (the sample mean of the $n$ observations) has replaced $\mu$ (the mean of the population from which the observations were selected). Note also, the chi-square variable has $n - 1$ (not $n$) degrees of freedom.

For the experiment given in Problems and Exercises 5 at the end of this chapter, $J = 3$ and $n = 10$:

$$SS_W = \sum_i (X_{i1} - \overline{X}_1)^2 + \sum_i (X_{i2} - \overline{X}_2)^2 + \sum_i (X_{i3} - \overline{X}_3)^2$$

If the first quantity on the right of this equation is divided by $\sigma^2$, it would have the distribution $\chi_9^2$ (chi-square with 9 degrees of freedom). This is so because the scores in group 1 were randomly drawn from a normal population with variance $\sigma^2$. The same can be said for the other two quantities on the right of the equation. Since all three quantities are distributed as $\chi_9^2$, then their sum divided by $\sigma^2$ is distributed as $\chi_{9+9+9}^2$ or $\chi_{27}^2$ (chi-square with 27 degrees of freedom). Hence, for the example:

$$\frac{SS_W}{\sigma^2} \sim \chi_{27}^2$$

$SS_W$ divided by $\nu_W = 27$ is $MS_W$; then:

$$\frac{SS_W / \nu_W}{\sigma^2} \sim \frac{\chi_{\nu_W}^2}{\nu_W} \text{ or } \frac{MS_W}{\sigma^2} \sim \frac{\chi_{27}^2}{27}$$

This fact will be saved for future use.

In general, how is the mean $\overline{X}$ of a group distributed? That is, what frequency distribution would result if $n$ scores were repeatedly sampled at random from a population and the mean computed for each sample? If each of the means, $\bar{X}$'s, is based on $n$ scores randomly drawn from a normal population, the means will (1) be normally distributed, (2) have mean $\mu$, and (3) have variance $\sigma^2/n$. In other words, $\bar{X} \sim NID(\mu, \sigma^2/n)$.

Using these facts, we can see that the distribution of $(\bar{X} - \mu)/\sqrt{\sigma^2/n}$ has a mean of zero and a variance of 1; hence, it is a $z$-ratio. Consequently:

$$\frac{(\bar{X}-\mu)^2}{\sigma^2/n} = \frac{n(\bar{X}-\mu)^2}{\sigma^2} \sim \chi_1^2$$

If the null hypothesis is *true*, then:

$$\frac{\sum_j n(\bar{X}_j - \bar{X}_{\bullet})^2}{\sigma^2} \sim \chi_{J-1}^2$$

because under that condition $E(\bar{X}_1) = E(\bar{X}_2) = E(\bar{X}_3) = E(\bar{X}_J) = \mu$. That is, each of the three $\bar{X}_j$'s is an independent random sample from a normally distributed, infinite population of $\bar{X}_j$'s having a mean of $\mu$. The original assumption that the three populations sampled in the experiment had the same variance $\sigma^2$ permits this conclusion. In the example, $J = 3$ and $n = 10$; hence, if each side of the equation is divided by $J - 1 = 2$, then

$$\frac{\sum_j 10(\bar{X}_j - \bar{X}_{\bullet})^2}{2\sigma^2} = \frac{MS_B}{\sigma^2} \sim \frac{\chi_2^2}{2}$$

provided the null hypothesis is true.

From Equation 16.6 (Section 16.5), the ratio of two independent chi-square variables, each of which is divided by its degrees of freedom, has an $F$-distribution:

$$\frac{\dfrac{\sum_j 10(\bar{X}_j - \bar{X}_{\bullet})^2}{2\sigma^2}}{\dfrac{\sum_j \sum_i (X_{ij} - \bar{X}_j)^2}{27\sigma^2}} = \frac{\dfrac{\sum_j 10(\bar{X}_j - \bar{X}_{\bullet})^2}{2}}{\dfrac{\sum_j \sum_i (X_{ij} - \bar{X}_j)^2}{27}} \sim F_{2,27}$$

Notice that since $\sigma^2$ appears in both numerator and denominator it can be canceled out.

The numerator of the previous equation is $MS_B$ and the denominator is $MS_W$. To summarize then, if the null hypothesis, $H_0$: $\mu_1 = \mu_2 = \ldots = \mu_J$, is true then:

$$\frac{\dfrac{SS_B}{\nu_B}}{\dfrac{SS_W}{\nu_W}} \sim F_{\nu_B,\nu_W} \quad \text{or} \quad \frac{MS_B}{MS_W} \sim F_{\nu_B,\nu_W}$$

In the example, if $H_0$: $\mu_1 = \mu_2 = \mu_3$ is true, the ratio of the mean square between, $MS_B$, to the mean square within, $MS_W$, has an $F$-distribution with degrees of freedom: $\nu_B = 2$ and

$\nu_W = 27$. The $F$-ratio ($MS_B/MS_W$) is the *test statistic* that is used to test $H_0$. When $H_0$ is true, the $F$-distribution is described as the *central* $F$-distribution.

## 15.21 THE *F*-TEST OF THE NULL HYPOTHESIS: RATIONALE AND PROCEDURE

To illustrate the distribution theory for ANOVA, suppose three groups of ten scores were randomly sampled from each of three normally distributed populations having the same mean and variance, and the value of $F = MS_B/MS_W$ calculated each time. If this process is repeated an infinite number of times, the plot of the obtained $F$-ratios will be the central $F$-distribution, $F_{2,27}$, given in Figure 15.4. Note in Figure 15.4 that the $F$-ratios are all greater than zero, and a few are quite large; indeed, five percent of the computed $F$-ratios exceed 3.36, i.e., $_{.95}F_{2,27} = 3.36$ is the critical value of $F$ with $\alpha = .05$.

In contrast to the situation described above, now suppose three samples of ten scores were randomly selected from three different normally distributed populations and equal variations, but with *unequal* means: $\mu_1 \neq \mu_2 \neq \mu_3$. Under these conditions, $MS_B$ is expected to be larger than if $H_0$ were true, whereas $MS_W$ continues to have an unexpected value of $\sigma^2$. Hence, the sampling distribution of $F = MS_B/MS_W$ is not a *central* $F$-distribution, but a *noncentral* $F$-distribution. Fortunately, the effect on the distribution of the $F$-ratios when the null hypothesis is false can be determined. It is important to remember that the expected value of the $F$-ratio is larger [$E(F) > 1$] when the null hypothesis is false than when it is true [$E(F) \approx 1$].[20] The sampling distribution of the $F$-ratios obtained is depicted in the "noncentral" $F$-distribution, $F_\phi$,[21] in Figure 15.4.

Notice that the distribution of $F$-ratios in the noncentral distribution shifts to the right more (i.e., the ratios tend to be larger) when the null hypothesis is false than when it is true. Even so, some of the values in the central $F$-distribution, $F_{2,27}$, are larger than some of the values in the noncentral $F$-distribution, $F_\phi$. Is an $F$-ratio greater than 3.37 more likely to occur if one is sampling under conditions of a true or false null hypothesis? Compare the areas under the two curves to the right of the point 3.37 and see which area is larger (i.e., which shows a greater probability of yielding a value of $F > 3.37$).

Any percentile points of the curve of the central $F$-distribution, $F_{2,27}$, can be determined; Table F in the Appendix gives the critical values of $F$ such that only 5% or 1% of the values in the curve will exceed these points when $H_0$ is true. Using Table F, it can be found that the 95th percentile in the curve $F_{2,27} \approx 3.37$ (i.e., with 2 degrees of freedom in the numerator and 27 degrees freedom in the denominator); the 99th percentile $\approx 5.45$. Table F reports the 75th, 90th, 95th, 97.5th, 99th, and 99.9th percentiles for various central $F$-distributions. The $F$-distribution depends on two values: the degrees of freedom for the numerator and the degrees of freedom for the denominator of the $F$-ratio. To find the $1$-$\alpha$th

---

[20] In other words, when the null hypothesis is false, $E(F) > 1$, but when $H_0$ is true, $E(F) = \nu_W/(\nu - 2) \approx 1$, see Section 16.6.

[21] Sampling distributions of test statistics (e.g., $t$ and $F$) are described as "central" when the null hypothesis is true. The symbol "$\phi$" denotes a "noncentrality" parameter, not to be confused with the phi coefficient (Section 7.22). $\phi$ is a composite measure of the differences among the $J$ means and sample size. We will be computing $\phi$ in Section 15.26 in order to estimate power.

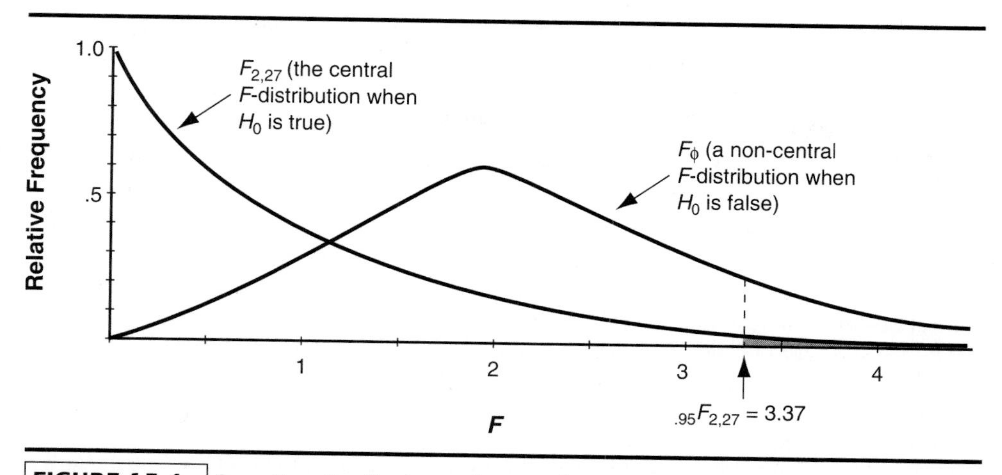


**FIGURE 15.4** Sampling distributions of $F = MS_B/MS_W$ when $H_0$ is true (curve $F_{2,27}$) and when $H_0$ is false (curve $F_\phi$).

percentile in the curve $F_{2,27}$, find the intersection of column 2 and row[22] 26 and find the *F*-ratio associated with $\alpha$. For example, confirm that the value of ${}_{.95}F_{2,26} = 3.37$.

What if the experiment were run and an *F*-ratio of 6.51 were obtained? The 95th percentile of the curve, ${}_{.95}F_{2,27} \approx 3.37$. When the null hypothesis is true, the *F*-ratios form the curve $F_{2,27}$. If the null hypothesis were true, an *F*-ratio of 6.51 would be a rare event indeed. Less than five times in 100, a value as large or larger than 3.37 would be obtained if the null hypothesis were true; an *F*-ratio of 5.53 ($\approx {}_{.99}F_{2,27}$) or larger would occur only one time in 100, on the average. If the null hypothesis is false, large values of *F* are much more probable.

The researcher reasons accordingly: If the value of the *F*-ratio obtained would occur less than five times in 100 when the null hypothesis is true (i.e., if it is greater than the critical value, ${}_{1-\alpha}F_{\nu_B \nu_W}$), then I shall conclude that the null hypothesis is false. It seems likely that such a value indicates a false null hypothesis since large values are more likely if the null hypothesis is false.

Choosing the 95th percentile of the curve $F_{2,27}$ as the point on which the decision about $H_0$ hinges is rather arbitrary. One could have chosen the 90th, 99th, or 99.9th percentile. What if the 50th percentile had been chosen? That is, what if one had agreed to reject the null hypothesis if the *F*-ratio were greater than ${}_{.50}F_{2,27}$? If the null hypothesis were true, one would have a probability of .50 of rejecting $H_0$ (calling it false). If researchers agreed on the 50th percentile point to make their decisions, half of them would be concluding that one method is better than another when the methods were actually no different. Researchers want to guard against these mistakes (type-I errors); so they agree to conclude that the null hypothesis is false when values equal to or greater than the value of *F* obtained have a small

---

[22]When the desired $\nu_W$ is not tabled, use the closest, but lesser, value. In computer analyses, the precise *p*-value will be printed. Exact critical values and *p*-values can be found from spreadsheets (such as EXCEL) that have the "FINV" function: ${}_{.95}F_{2,27} = 3.354$, and ${}_{.99}F_{2,27} = 5.488$. We will use critical values for $\nu_W = 26$ as approximations for $\nu_W = 27$ since they are given in Table F, for example, ${}_{.95}F_{2,26} = 3.37 \approx {}_{.95}F_{2,27}$.

probability of occurring when the null hypothesis is true. A "small probability" means .10, .05, or .01. These values correspond to using the 90th, 95th, and 99th percentiles, respectively, in the central $F$-distribution.

## 15.22 TYPE-I VERSUS TYPE-II ERRORS: $\alpha$ AND $\beta$

Even if the $F$-ratio from a study is large, we cannot be absolutely certain that the null hypothesis is false. Such absolute assertions are not possible in hypothesis testing. In making a conclusion such as "$H_0$ is rejected" or "$H_0$ is tenable," we are never absolutely certain of the truth of the conclusion. The conclusion to reject $H_0$ will be incorrect a certain percent (10%, 5%, 1%, etc.) of the time they are made when $H_0$ is true. (In Section 15.26 we will learn how to determine the probability of arriving at the correct conclusion when $H_0$ is false.)

Suppose the three treatment conditions have absolutely no effect on test scores. Suppose the experiment were replicated by each student in a large statistics class; each student computes an $F$-ratio and draws a conclusion regarding $H_0$. Although unknown to the researcher, $H_0$ is true. The distribution $F_{2,27}$ that the obtained $F$-ratios will follow is the central $F$-distribution with 2 and 27 degrees of freedom. Five percent of the area under the $F_{2,27}$ curve lies to right of the point, $3.37 \approx {}_{.95}F_{2,27}$. With $\alpha = .05$, $H_0$ will be rejected only when the obtained $F$-value exceeds 3.37. Since $H_0$ is true (in this illustration), the mistake of rejecting $H_0$ when it is true will be made by 5% of the students, that is, $\alpha = .05$.

Notice the $\alpha$-value that was selected is an arbitrary decision. If $\alpha = .01$ had been chosen, the critical $F$-ratio would be the 99th percentile in the $F_{2,27}$ distribution; if $H_0$ is true, then on the average only one student in 100 would obtain an $F$-ratio $\geq 5.53$ ($= {}_{.99}F_{2,26} \approx {}_{.99}F_{2,27}$); in these instances, the student would conclude, incorrectly, that $H_0$ is false. The size of $\alpha$ is under the researcher's control; it can be made as large or small as he or she wishes. There are two states that can exist as discussed in Sections 11.6 and 11.8: $H_0$ can be true or it can be false. A researcher agrees to make one of two conclusions after inspecting the data. Either $H_0$ will be rejected as the explanation, or $H_0$ will be accepted (i.e., viewed as a tenable explanation). The four possible outcomes of an experiment are shown in Figure 15.5.

If $H_0$ is true and is not rejected (lower left-hand cell), the decision is correct. If $H_0$ is false and is rejected (upper right-hand cell), the conclusion is also correct. However, if $H_0$ is rejected when it is true, a type-I error has been committed. If $H_0$ is false and is not rejected, a type-II error (Section 11.8) is the result. The probability of committing a type-I error is denoted as $\alpha$. The size of $\alpha$ can be controlled, thus making the chances of incorrectly rejecting $H_0$ very large ($\alpha = .20$ or .30) or very small ($\alpha = .01$ or .001). It is customary to set $\alpha$ at .05, although the value should depend on the particular circumstances of a given analysis. If the number of subjects in a study is very small, $\alpha$ might be set at .10 or higher.

The size of $\alpha$ influences the probability of making a type-II error, $\beta$. The probability of failing to reject a false null hypothesis is also under the control of the researcher to some extent. The value of $\beta$ depends on the number of subjects in the experiment and the value of $\alpha$ chosen, among other things. The probability of correctly rejecting $H_0$ when it is false is denoted by $1 - \beta$; thus the probability of a type-II error is $\beta$. The value of $1 - \beta$ is described as the *power* of a statistical test—the probability of rejecting $H_0$ when it is false. Other things being equal, smaller values of $\alpha$ (e.g., .01 vs. .05) are associated with lower power, $1 - \beta$. The value of $1 - \beta$ is of immense importance in planning research studies. All too often power considerations are neglected, even by otherwise competent researchers. Time and money can be invested in an investigation in which the probability of discovering a true

| | $H_0$ is true | $H_0$ is false |
|---|---|---|
| Reject $H_0$ | Type I error ($\alpha$) | No error is made ($1-\beta$) |
| Do not reject $H_0$ | No error is made ($1-\alpha$) | Type II error ($\beta$) |

**FIGURE 15.5** Four possible outcomes of a test of a statistical hypothesis.

difference among treatments (i.e., power) is small, even if the treatment effects are as great as anticipated (Hopkins, 1973). That is, even if $H_0$ is false, the researcher has little chance of discovering it—there is a high probability, $\beta$, that $H_0$ will not be rejected even though it is false.

It may happen if $\alpha$ is set at .05 that the corresponding value of $1-\beta$ might be .20; but if $\alpha$ were .10, $1-\beta$ could be .50. Ordinarily, it is prudent to take a slightly greater risk of a type-I error, $\alpha$, for a substantial increase in the probability, $1-\beta$, of finding a real difference between the treatments. Just how large $\alpha$ and $\beta$ should be, or how $\alpha$ should be changed to compensate for a large $\beta$ are questions often requiring a thoughtful compromise. Which is worse: to conclude that a treatment is effective when it is not (type-I error), or to say that it is not effective when, in fact, it is (a type-II error)? It depends on the circumstances. The questions are basically about the losses that ensue from errors and the benefits of being correct. These are not questions to which statisticians necessarily give more enlightened answers than other knowledgeable observers. In applied research, type-II errors are typically more serious (to fail to identify a treatment that is effective is worse than to claim one treatment is better than another, when both are equally effective).

The definitions of $\alpha$ and $\beta$ and their relationship are depicted in Figure 15.6. Note that power would be decreased if $\alpha$ were changed from .05 to .01.

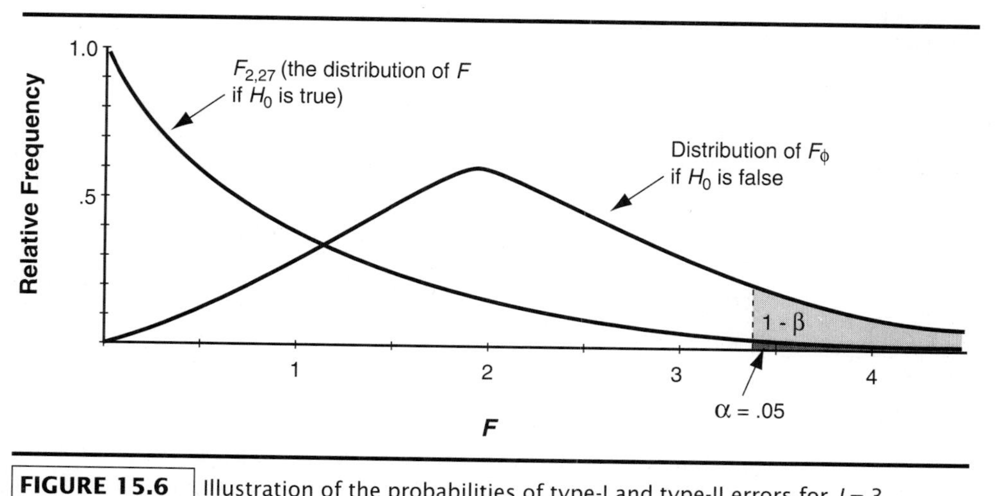


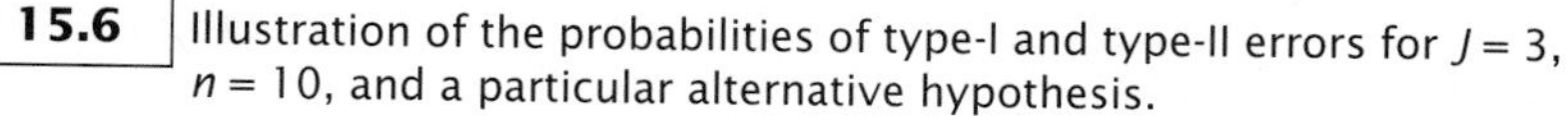
**FIGURE 15.6** Illustration of the probabilities of type-I and type-II errors for $J = 3$, $n = 10$, and a particular alternative hypothesis.

The calculation of the power of the $F$-test of $H_0$ will be illustrated in Sections 15.26–15.29.

## 15.23 A SUMMARY OF PROCEDURES FOR ONE-FACTOR ANOVA

A comparison of $J$ means is desired. Within each of the $J$ groups, there are $n$ independent observations (replicates). The sequence for the ANOVA will be illustrated using the steps for testing a hypothesis employed in Chapter 13. A linear model is postulated to explain the data: $X_{ij} = \mu + \alpha_j + \varepsilon_{ij}$, where $\alpha_j = \mu_j - \mu$, $\varepsilon_{ij} = X_{ij} - \mu_J$, and $\Sigma_j n_j \alpha_j = 0$ (or, when the $n$'s are equal, $\Sigma_j \alpha_j = 0$).

1. **Hypotheses.**

   $H_0$: $\mu_1 = \mu_2 = \ldots = \mu_J$ ($H_0$: $\alpha_1 = \alpha_2 = \ldots = \alpha_J$)
   $H_1$: $\Sigma_j \alpha_j^2 \neq 0$ (i.e., not all $\mu_j$'s are equal)

2. **Assumptions.**

   $\varepsilon_{ij} \sim NID(0, \sigma_\varepsilon^2)$

3. **Test Statistic.**

   $F = MS_B/MS_W$

4. **Sampling Distribution.**

   If $H_0$ is true, the $F$-ratio has a central $F$-distribution with $\nu_B$ and $\nu_W$ degrees of freedom, $F_{\nu_B, \nu_W}$.

5. **Critical Value:** ${}_{1-\alpha}F_{\nu_B, \nu_W}$.

   If $F > {}_{1-\alpha}F_{\nu_B, \nu_W}$, then $H_0$ is rejected at the $\alpha$ level of significance ($p < \alpha$).

## 15.24 CONSEQUENCES OF FAILURE TO MEET THE ANOVA ASSUMPTIONS: THE "ROBUSTNESS" OF ANOVA

Recall that in the derivation of the one-factor fixed-effects[23] model ANOVA it is assumed that $\varepsilon_{ij} \sim NID(0, \sigma_\varepsilon^2)$. Within each of the $J$ groups, the observations[24] are independent and normally distributed[25] about their mean $\mu_j$ with variance $\sigma_\varepsilon^2$.

The model implies that an observation can be thought of as the simple sum of three components: one that reflects the general elevation of the measurements, $\mu$; a second, $\alpha_j$, reflecting the increment or decrement on the dependent variable resulting from the effect of

[23]The distinction between fixed-effects vs. random ANOVA models is developed in Chapter 19.

[24]Since for each of the $J$ groups, $\varepsilon_{ij} = X_{ij} - \mu - \alpha_j$, and for each group $\mu$ and $\alpha_j$ are constants, $\varepsilon_{ij}$ is a linear transformation (Section 7.12) of the raw observations, $X_{ij}$'s; thus, the ANOVA assumptions regarding the distributions of $\varepsilon_{ij}$ and $X_{ij}$ are synonymous. Note that $\sigma_X^2 = \sigma_\varepsilon^2 = \sigma_W^2$, which is often designated simply as $\sigma^2$.

[25]Normality can be tested via several different tests, including the $\chi^2$ goodness-of-fit test (Section 13.11); homogeneity of variance is treated in Sections 16.7–16.11.

treatment $j$; and a component, $\varepsilon_{ij}$, that comprises things usually referred to in the behavioral sciences as "individual differences" and "measurement error," among others. This linear model ($X_{ij} = \mu + \alpha_j + \varepsilon_{ij}$) can fail accurately to describe the true events. For example, the effect of treatment $j$ may not be the same for all persons exposed to treatment $j$. For example, some students may benefit more from a particular treatment than others. Research suggests that the magnitude of the practice effect on mental ability tests is greater for brighter students than for duller ones. If this is plausible, a two-factor ANOVA should be employed (see Chapter 18) so that possible differential effects by ability level can be examined statistically.

The assumptions, $NID(0, \sigma_\varepsilon^2)$, state that the $\varepsilon_{ij}$'s within each of the $J$ populations are independent, and have a normal distribution with a population mean (expectation) of 0 and variance of $\sigma^2$. Three distinct violations of this assumption can be considered: (1) non-normality, (2) heterogeneity of variance among groups, and (3) nonindependence. When these assumptions are met, the distribution of scores within each of the $J$ groups will differ from the normal distribution because of sampling error. Any difference among the $J$ sample variances ($s_j^2$'s) is also the result of sampling error. Furthermore, since the $n$ observations within each of the $J$ populations were randomly drawn, they are independent.[26]

What if certain ANOVA assumptions are not met? There have been many studies done to assess the consequences of violating statistical assumptions (i.e., assumptions made in the derivation of the procedure). Such studies are described as "robustness" studies because they evaluate whether the procedure remains "hearty" (gives accurate results) when the assumptions are violated. We now turn our attention to the effects of violations of the ANOVA assumptions of normality and homogeneity of variance on the accuracy of the probability statements (i.e., $p$'s) and power. This line of research follows the steps outlined below.

1. Given a true null hypothesis, find the critical value of $F$ (${}_{1-\alpha}F_{\nu_B,\nu_W}$). This percentile will be the value that is exceeded by $\alpha$ of the $F$-ratios obtained in an ANOVA when the null hypothesis is true and the ANOVA assumptions are met.
2. By empirical or mathematical means, the actual percentage of $F$-ratios exceeding ${}_{1-\alpha}F_{\nu_B,\nu_W}$ is found when the null hypothesis is true and the variances are heterogeneous or the populations are non-normal or both.
3. The "nominal" significance level, $\alpha$, and the actual significance level (the percentage of $F$'s exceeding ${}_{1-\alpha}F_{\nu_B,\nu_W}$) are compared. If these percentages differ negligibly, the procedure is said to be robust.

Fortunately, robustness studies have confirmed that the $t$-test findings associated with the normality and homogeneity of variance assumptions generalize to ANOVA (see Figures 12.2 and 12.3; Sections 12.9–12.11). The studies on the empirical consequences of failure to meet ANOVA assumptions have been reviewed (Glass, Peckham, & Sanders, 1972); the principal conclusions are:

1. Non-normality has negligible consequences on type-I and type-II error probabilities unless the populations are highly skewed, the $n$'s are very small, or "one-tailed" tests[27] are employed (see Figure 12.2).

---

[26]Failure to satisfy the independence assumption can be serious. The correlated or dependent groups $t$-test is an appropriate statistical technique (if only two treatments are being compared) when the nonindependence of the $\varepsilon_{ij}$'s is due to pairing observations, such as when comparing pretest and posttest scores. (If $J > 2$, see Chapter 20.)

[27]Except when $J = 2$, "one-tailed" tests are not meaningful when testing the null hypothesis in ANOVA. Directional tests are common in planned orthogonal contrasts (Section 17.16).

**TABLE 15.3** Summary of Consequences of Violation of Assumptions of the Fixed-Effects ANOVA.[a]

| | *Equal n's* | | *Unequal n's* | |
|---|---|---|---|---|
| *Type of Violation* | *Effect on $\alpha$* | *Effect on Power* | *Effect on $\alpha$* | *Effect on Power* |
| Nonindependence of errors | Nonindependence of errors seriously affects both the level of significance and power of the $F$-test whether or not $n$'s are equal. | | | |
| Non-normality: Skewness | Skewed populations have very little effect on either the level of significance or the power of the fixed-effects model $F$-test; distortions of nominal significance levels or power values are rarely greater than a few hundredths. (However, skewed populations can seriously affect the level of significance and power of *directional*—or "one-tailed"—tests.) | | | |
| Kurtosis | Actual $\alpha$ is less than nominal $\alpha$ when populations are leptokurtic (i.e., $\gamma_2 > 0$). Actual $\alpha$ exceeds nominal $\alpha$ for platykurtic populations. (Effects are slight.) | Actual power is less than nominal power when populations are platykurtic. Actual power exceeds nominal power when populations are leptokurtic. Effects can be substantial for small $n$. | Actual $\alpha$ is less than nominal $\alpha$ when populations are leptokurtic (i.e., $\gamma_2 > 0$). Actual $\alpha$ exceeds nominal $\alpha$ for platykurtic populations. (Effects are slight.) | Actual power is less than nominal power when populations are platykurtic. Actual power exceed nominal power when populations are leptokurtic. Effects can be substantial for small $n$'s. |
| Heterogeneous variances | Very slight effect on $\alpha$, which is seldom distorted by more than a few hundredths. Actual $\alpha$ seems always to be slightly increased over the nominal $\alpha$. | (No theoretical power value exists when variances are heterogeneous.) | $\alpha$ may be seriously affected. Actual $\alpha$ exceeds nominal $\alpha$ when smaller samples are drawn from more variable populations; actual $\alpha$ is less than nominal $\alpha$ when smaller samples are drawn from less variable populations. | (No theoretical power value exists when variances are heterogeneous.) |
| Combined non-normality and heterogeneous variances | Non-normality and heterogeneous variances appear to combine additively ("noninteractively") to affect either level of significance or power. (For example, the depressing effect on $\alpha$ of leptokurtosis could be expected to be counteracted by the elevating effect on $\alpha$ of having drawn smaller samples from the more variable, leptokurtic populations.) | | | |

[a]From Glass, Peckham, and Sanders (1972).

2. When the $n$'s are equal, violations of the homogeneity of variance assumption ($\sigma_1^2 = \sigma_2^2 = \ldots = \sigma_J^2$) have negligible consequences on the accuracy of the probability statements (type-I error) (see Figure 12.3) or power.[28] When the larger $\sigma_j^2$'s and $n_j$'s are paired, ANOVA yields conservative results, that is, actual $\alpha <$ nominal $\alpha$ (i.e., the actual probability of a type-I error is less than $\alpha$). When the larger $n_j$'s are associated with the smaller $\sigma_j^2$'s, ANOVA yields liberal results (i.e., actual $\alpha >$ nominal $\alpha$)[29]. Just as when testing the null hypothesis with $J = 2$ (the Welch $t'$ test, Section 12.11), similar procedures are available in ANOVA that do not assume homogeneity of variance (Section 15.25). These procedures are recommended for unbalanced designs in which the homogeneity of variance assumption is not tenable, especially if the ratio of the largest variance to the smallest variance differs greatly from 1.0.
3. The assumption of independence is necessary for accurate probability statements. The independence assumption is evaluated logically. Independence of observations requires that the observations within groups not be influenced by each other. Whenever the treatment is individually administered, observations are independent. But where treatments involve interaction among persons, such as "discussion" method and group counseling, the observations may influence each other. If the observations are analyzed as if the data were independent, the true probability of a type-I error is apt to be larger than the nominal $\alpha$. In other words, nonindependence of observations increases the probability that treatment effects will be claimed for ineffective treatments. (This concern is dealt with more fully in Section 19.22.)

## 15.25 THE WELCH AND BROWN-FORSYTHE MODIFICATIONS OF ANOVA: WHAT DOES ONE DO WHEN $\sigma^2$'s AND $n$'s DIFFER?

With unbalanced designs, ANOVA will yield accurate $p$-values only when the homogeneity of variance assumption is tenable. Procedures for testing this assumption are treated in Chapter 16. When $H_0$: $\sigma_1^2 = \sigma_2^2 \ldots = \sigma_J^2$ is false and the $n$'s are not equal, a modification of the standard ANOVA procedure is needed that does not assume homogeneity of variance. The Welch procedure (Section 12.11) can be extended to designs in which $J > 2$. When all population means are equal, the Welch statistic, $F'$ (Equation 15.20), has a sampling distribution that can be approximated by the central $F$-distribution even if the population variances are unequal:

$$F' = \frac{\sum_j w_j \left[ \frac{(\overline{X}_j - \overline{X}')^2}{J-1} \right]}{1 + \left[ \frac{2(J-2)}{J^2-1} \right] \sum_j \left[ \left(1 - \frac{w_j}{u}\right)^2 (n_j - 1) \right]} \quad \textbf{(15.20)}$$

where $w_j = n_j/s_j^2$, $u = \Sigma_j w_j$, and $\overline{X}' = \Sigma_j w_j \overline{X}_j / u$.

[28]This conclusion is correct within the degree of variance heterogeneity one is apt to encounter in practice.

[29]Recall that, other things being equal, $\alpha$ and $\beta$ are inversely related.

The critical value of $F'$ is found from Table F, using $\nu_B = J - 1$, and
$$1/\nu_W = [3/(J^2 - 1)]\Sigma_j[(1 - w_j/u)^2/(n_j - 1)].$$
A less well known, but better procedure[30] is the Brown-Forsythe (1974a) statistic, $F^*$:

$$F^* = \frac{\sum_j n_j(\bar{X}_j - \bar{X}_\bullet)^2}{\sum_j \left(1 - \frac{n_j}{n_\bullet}\right)s_j^2} \qquad \textbf{(15.21)}$$

where $F^*$ is distributed like a central $F$-distribution with $\nu_B = J - 1$, $1/\nu_W = \Sigma_j c_j^2/(n_j - 1)$, and $c_j = (1 - n_j/n_\bullet)s_j^2/[\Sigma_j(1 - n_j/n_\bullet)s_j^2]$. When $J = 2$, both $F'$ and $F^*$ are identical and equivalent to the Welch $t'$ (Section 12.11).

Obviously, we would like to avoid hand computation when using either of these procedures. Fortunately, they are available in the BMDP (Dixon, Brown, Engelman, Hill & Jennrich, 1988) statistical package.[31]

## 15.26 THE POWER OF THE *F*-TEST

Many studies in the behavioral and social sciences fail to find real differences between means because the design employed has insufficient power (see Table 12.4)—frequently less than .50 for a medium effect size (Sedlmeier & Gigerenzer, 1989). It should be standard procedure to obtain estimates of power for various effect sizes prior to initiating a research study so that one has a good chance of finding an effect, if indeed one exists. Unfortunately, this continues to be the exception rather than the rule (Sedlmeier & Gigerenzer, 1989).

Recall from Section 15.13 that the linear model for a one-factor, fixed-effects ANOVA is $X_{ij} = \mu + \alpha_j + \varepsilon_{ij}$. The power, $1 - \beta$, of a particular $F$-test in a one-factor ANOVA (i.e., the probability that $H_0$: $\mu_1 = \mu_2 = \ldots = \mu_J$ will be rejected when it is false) is a function of the following (see Section 11.12):

1. The magnitude of the differences among the population means. This is measured by their weighted (by $n_j$) effects, $n_j\alpha_j^2$, where $\alpha_j = \mu_j - \mu$, where $\mu$ is the grand mean of the variable $X$.
2. The error variance, the residual variance in $X$ not predicted using the parameters, $\mu$ and $\alpha_j$. In a one-factor ANOVA, the error variance is $\sigma_W^2 = \sigma_\varepsilon^2$.
3. The number of degrees of freedom associated with the numerator of the $F$-test, $MS_B$: $\nu_B = J - 1$.
4. The number of degrees of freedom associated with the denominator, "error term," of the $F$-test. In a one-factor ANOVA, $\nu_W = n_\bullet - J$.
5. The probability of a type-I error, $\alpha$. (Do not confuse the probability of a type-I error with $\alpha_j$, as defined in step 1.)

To determine the numerical value for power, one must first determine the *non-centrality* parameter, denoted by $\phi$:

---

[30]It is better because it can be used with ANOVA designs with two or more factors (Chapters 18–19).

[31]By the time this book is published, they will probably have found their way into other computer packages such as SPSS.

$$\phi = \sqrt{\frac{\sum_j n_j \alpha_j^2}{J\sigma_\varepsilon^2}} \quad \textbf{(15.22)}$$

If the design is balanced ($n_1 = n_2 = \ldots = n_J = n$), Equation 15.22[32] simplifies to:

$$\phi = \sqrt{\frac{n\sum_j \alpha_j^2}{J\sigma_\varepsilon^2}} \quad \textbf{(15.23)}$$

When $J = 2$, it has been shown (Hopkins & Hester, 1995) that the non-centrality parameter, $\phi$, is easily estimated from the hypothesized effect size, $\Delta$ (Section 12.8), and $n$:

$$\phi = \frac{\Delta}{2}\sqrt{n} \quad \textbf{(15.24)}$$

## 15.27 AN ILLUSTRATION

Suppose an experiment is being designed to test a treatment to improve the cognitive functioning level of environmentally impoverished children, who otherwise have an average IQ of 90, that is, the control group's expected mean is 90. If an expensive treatment (group 3) increases Wechsler IQ scores by an average of ten points, and an inexpensive treatment (group 2) increases IQ scores by five points, what is the power, that is, how likely is it that the researcher will come to the correct conclusion regarding the null hypothesis and reject it? Thus, $\mu_1 = 90$, $\mu_2 = 95$, and $\mu_2 = 100$. From the test's norms it is found that $\sigma = \sigma_\varepsilon = 15$. How large a sample is needed to have good power? Using Equation 15.23: $\sigma_\mu^2 = \Sigma_j(\mu_j - \mu)^2/J$, where $\mu$ is the grand mean (if the design is balanced, $\mu$ is the average of the $J$ means); in this illustration, $\mu = 95$.

$$\alpha_1 = 90 - 95 = -5;\ \alpha_1^2 = 25.$$

$$\alpha_2 = 95 - 95 = 0, \text{ and}$$

$$\alpha_3 = 100 - 95 = 5;\ \alpha_3^2 = 25.$$

Thus, $\Sigma\alpha_j^2 = 25 + 25 = 50$, $\sigma^2 = 225$, $J = 3$, and $\phi^2 = n(50)/[3(225)] = .0741n$, and $\phi = .272\sqrt{n}$.

If it is planned to have $n_1 = n_2 = n_3 = 40$, $\phi = .272\sqrt{40} = .272(.632) = 1.72$.

In addition, suppose one wishes to consider the power using only two groups, the con-

---

[32]Since $\sigma_\mu^2 = \Sigma\alpha_j^2/J$, Equation 15.23 can also be expressed as the ratio of the standard deviation of the $J$ means, $\sigma_\mu$, to the standard deviation of the observations within groups, $\sigma_\varepsilon$, weighted by $\sqrt{n}$: $\phi = \sqrt{n\sigma_\mu^2/\sigma_\varepsilon^2}$ or $\sqrt{n}(\sigma_\mu/\sigma_\varepsilon)$ (see Hopkins & Hester, 1995).

trol group and the expensive treatment. Since $\Delta = (100 - 90)/15 = .6667$, and $\Delta/2 = .333$, using Equation 15.24: $\phi = .333\sqrt{n}, \ = .333\sqrt{40} = 2.11$.

Once $\phi$ is known, the power of the $F$-test can be determined from Table G in the Appendix for $\alpha = .01$ (and $\alpha = .05$). The use of Table G requires some explanation and practice using the following steps.

1. Find the correct figure (family of curves) by using $\nu_B$; $\nu_B$ is given in the upper left-hand corner of each figure. In the first example $\nu_B = J - 1 = 2$, hence we will use the second figure in Table G.
2. Find the row of values along the base-axis that corresponds to the particular $\alpha$-value being used (.05 or .01). (In our example $\alpha = .05$ corresponds to the numerical values immediately below the grid.)
3. Locate the noncentrality parameter, $\phi$, that has been determined from Equation 15.22, 15.23, or 15.24 on the base-axis ($\phi = 1.72$ in the first example).
4. Read up from the $\phi$ value to the point where a vertical line above $\phi$ intersects with the value of $\nu_e$ ($=\nu_W$) in the set of curves associated with the $\alpha$ being used. (In the example $\nu_e = n_{\bullet} - J = 120 - 3 = 117$, and $\alpha = .05$.)
5. Read the value for power $(1 - \beta)$ on the vertical axis (in the example $\phi = 1.72$, and the curve for $\nu_e = 117$ would intersect at $1 - \beta \approx .65$)—the probability of making a type-II error is quite large ($\beta \approx .35$).

What is the power if only the expensive and control treatments are used? Using the figure for $\nu_B = 1$ (the first figure in Table G), enter $\phi = 2.11$ on the $\alpha = .05$ base axis and find that power is $1 - \beta \approx .84$. What is the power if $n_1 = n_2 = n$ is increased to 60? Then, $\nu_e = 118$ and $\phi = \sqrt{n}/3 = 7.746/3 = 2.58$, and at $\alpha = .05$, the power is about .975.

## 15.28 POWER WHEN $\sigma$ IS UNKNOWN

In many research situations, we do not have any way of obtaining a good estimate of $\sigma$ prior to the study. Perhaps groups are going to be compared on a measure that has never been used before. In such situations, it is useful to consider mean differences in standard deviation units. Suppose group 1 is a control treatment; we want to know the power of the experiment if treatment 3 is so effective that scores are increased by one standard deviation (an effect size of 1). Treatment 2 is presumed to fall midway between $\mu_1$ and $\mu_3$. In other words, $\mu_3$ exceeds $\mu_1$ by one standard deviation and exceeds $\mu_2$ by .50 standard deviations; thus, $\mu_2$ exceeds $\mu_1$ by $.5\sigma$. Expressed graphically:

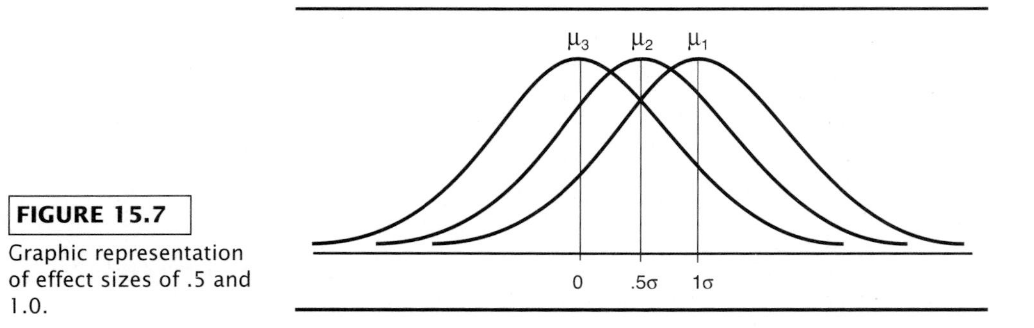


**FIGURE 15.7**

Graphic representation of effect sizes of .5 and 1.0.

If $n_1 = n_3 = 20$, and $n_2 = 40$, what is the power of the ANOVA $F$-test at $\alpha = .05$? Since the grand mean (Equation 4.9) = [20(0) + 40(.5) + 20(1)]/80 = .5, then $\alpha_1 = -.5$, $\alpha_2 = 0$, $\alpha_3 = +.5$, and $\Sigma\alpha^2 = .50$. Using Equation 15.22 with $J = 3$ and $\sigma_\varepsilon = 1$:

$$\sum_j n_j\alpha_j^2 = n_1\alpha_1^2 + n_2\alpha_2^2 + n_3\alpha_3^2$$

$$= 20(-.5)^2 + 40(0)^2 + 20(.5)^2 = 10, \text{ and}$$

$$\phi = \sqrt{\frac{\sum_j n_j\alpha_j^2}{J\sigma_\varepsilon^2}} = \sqrt{\frac{10}{3}} = 1.83$$

Reading the figure for $\nu_B = J - 1 = 2$ in Table G in the Appendix, we find that with $\alpha = .05$, and $\nu_e = n_\bullet - J = 80 - 3 = 77$, the power of the test is about .80. However, at $\alpha = .01$, the power is estimated (by extrapolation) to be only about .57.

## 15.29 A TABLE FOR ESTIMATING POWER WHEN $J = 2$

Estimates of power $(1 - \beta)$ for very small $(.1\sigma)$ to very large $(1\sigma)$ effect sizes, $\Delta$, (see Section 12.8) are given in Table 15.4 when $J = 2$ independent means are being compared via ANOVA (or the $t$-test). Power is given for various sample sizes ($n$ per group) and the commonly used values of $\alpha$. For example, if the effect size, $\Delta$, is .50 and $n = 50$, power is .46 at $\alpha = .01$, but .71 at $\alpha = .05$; if $n = 100$ and $\alpha = .05$, power increases to .94.

### An Example

The standard deviation for serum cholesterol levels in middle-aged men or women is approximately 50 units (mg/dl) = $\sigma$ (NCHS, 1977). We are planning to do a randomized experiment in which the experimental ($E$) group will begin a prescribed regimen of exercise and diet; the control ($C$) group is untreated. How large a sample will we need to find the effect of the treatment if, indeed, it lowers cholesterol level by 25 $(.5\sigma = \Delta)$ units? In Table 15.4, find the column that corresponds to an effect size of $.5\sigma$. Note if $n = 10$, we would have only .18 power for $\alpha_2 = .05$. Even if we relax $\alpha$ to .10, the power is only .30. In this situation, we could justify a one-tailed test since we can be confident that if there is a treatment effect, it will reduce cholesterol levels. We believe that there is no chance that our treatment will increase cholesterol levels; thus, with $\alpha_1 = .10$, our power would increase to .42 with $n = 10$. Although we have more than doubled power in going from $\alpha_2 = .05$ to $\alpha_1 = .10$, the odds are still greater than 1 in 2 that we will not find the treatment effect even if the treatment effect is $.5\sigma$ or 25 units. If we increased $n$ to 25, power is still only .68 at $\alpha_1 = .10$. We need at least 50 in the $E$ group and 50 in the $C$ group in order to have acceptable power: $1 - \beta = .89$ at $\alpha_1 = .10$.

If the treatment is extremely potent, we would not need as many subjects. Note that for a treatment effect of $1\sigma$, with $n = 15$, power is .86 with $\alpha_1 = .05$.

**TABLE 15.4** Power[a] for Various Effect Sizes for $J = 2$[b]

| | | *Effect Size* $(\Delta)$[c] | | | |
|---|---|---|---|---|---|
| *n per group* | $\alpha_2$[d] | $\Delta = .1\sigma$ | $\Delta = .25\sigma$ | $\Delta = .5\sigma$ | $\Delta = \sigma$ |
| | .01 | .01 | .01 | .03 | .10 |
| | .05 | .05 | .06 | .11 | .29 |
| 5 | .10 | .10 | .12 | .19 | .43 |
| | .20 | .13 | .17 | .27 | .54 |
| | .01 | .01 | .02 | .06 | .29 |
| | .05 | .05 | .08 | .18 | .57 |
| 10 | .10 | .10 | .15 | .30 | .71 |
| | .20 | .14 | .23 | .42 | .81 |
| | .01 | .01 | .02 | .09 | .50 |
| | .05 | .06 | .10 | .26 | .76 |
| 15 | .10 | .11 | .19 | .39 | .86 |
| | .20 | .15 | .27 | .52 | .92 |
| | .01 | .01 | .05 | .19 | .80 |
| | .05 | .06 | .14 | .42 | .94 |
| 25 | .10 | .12 | .24 | .56 | .97 |
| | .20 | .17 | .35 | .68 | .99 |
| | .01 | .02 | .09 | .46 | .99+ |
| | .05 | .07 | .24 | .71 | .99+ |
| 50 | .10 | .14 | .36 | .81 | .99+ |
| | .20 | .22 | .49 | .89 | .99+ |
| | .01 | .03 | .22 | .83 | .99+ |
| | .05 | .10 | .43 | .94 | .99+ |
| 100 | .10 | .18 | .56 | .97 | .99+ |
| | .20 | .29 | .68 | .99 | .99+ |
| | .01 | .05 | .48 | .99 | .99+ |
| | .05 | .16 | .69 | .99+ | .99+ |
| 200 | .10 | .27 | .79 | .99+ | .99+ |
| | .20 | .39 | .86 | .99+ | .99+ |
| | .01 | .11 | .78 | .99+ | .99+ |
| | .05 | .30 | .91 | .99+ | .99+ |
| 400 | .10 | .42 | .95 | .99+ | .99+ |
| | .20 | .55 | .97 | .99+ | .99+ |

[a]These values include only the probabilities of rejecting $H_0$ in the right direction (i.e., it excludes type-III errors).

[b]For $J = 3$ and $J = 4$ or power if the analysis of covariance is used; see Hopkins, Coulter, and Hopkins (1981).

[c]$\Delta = (\mu_1 - \mu_2)/\sigma$.

[d]To determine $\alpha_1$ for a one-tailed test, divide $\alpha_2$ by 2. For example, for $\alpha_1 = .05$, power is the same as for $\alpha_2 = .10$; for $\alpha_1 = .10$, use tabled values for $\alpha_2 = .20$.

## 15.30 THE NON-PARAMETRIC ALTERNATIVE: THE KRUSKAL-WALLIS TEST

The Kruskal-Wallis test can compare $J$ samples to see if there are differences among them that are too large to attribute to sampling error. The Kruskal-Wallis test makes no assumptions regarding normality in the populations sampled. It was once thought that it could be used in situations for which ANOVA is not robust (i.e., when there are great differences among variances and $n$'s), but now the evidence suggests that it may also fail to give accurate results when both $n$'s and $\sigma^2$'s differ greatly. Like the Mann-Whitney test (Section 12.17), the Kruskal-Wallis test ranks all of the observations in the composite distribution, then performs a "one-way ANOVA by ranks" to arrive at the test statistic, $H = SS_B/MS_{total}$. The quantities, $SS_B$ and $MS_{total}$ are obtained using the ranks (not the raw scores) as the dependent measures (where $MS_{total} = SS_{total}/\nu_{total}$). Special tables are referenced to obtain critical values of $H$.[33] Ordinarily, the results of ANOVA and the Kruskal-Wallis test do not differ greatly. Because of its greater power, and the robustness of ANOVA and the availability of the Welch and Brown-Forsythe procedures (which do not require the homogeneity of variance assumption, Section 15.25), the Kruskal-Wallis test is rarely the "method of choice," except perhaps when extreme outliers are present.[34]

Another non-parametric alternative for assessing differences in central tendency among $J$ groups is the chi-square median test (Section 13.14). Unfortunately, it is considerably less powerful than the Kruskal-Wallis test.

## 15.31 CHAPTER SUMMARY

If $J > 2$, performing several $t$-tests among the $J$ means is not recommended. When more than two means are to be compared, ANOVA should be used as an omnibus test of differences among the $J$ means: $H_0$: $\mu_1 = \mu_2 = \ldots = \mu_J$. When $J = 2$, ANOVA and the $t$-test are different paths to the same destination, and $F$ will always equal $t^2$.

ANOVA divides the total sum of squares ($SS_{total}$) in a set of observations into two sources of variation: (1) that which is determined entirely from differences between the $J$ means ($SS_B$), and (2) that which results entirely from differences among the $n$ observations within the $J$ groups ($SS_W$). When $SS_B$ and $SS_W$ are divided by their degrees of freedom ($\nu_B$ and $\nu_W$, respectively), two independent estimates of variance or "mean squares" are obtained, $MS_B$ and $MS_W$. When $H_0$ is true, both $MS_B$ and $MS_W$ estimate the same parameter, $\sigma^2$ (the variance of the observations in the population), and the $F$-ratio, $MS_B/MS_W$, has an expected value of approximately 1. The distribution of $F$-ratios when $H_0$ is true is termed the central $F$-distribution. If $H_0$ is false, the expected value of $MS_B$ increases and, consequently, the expected value of $F$ increases.

The linear model for the common one-factor ANOVA is $X_{ij} = \mu + \alpha_j + \varepsilon_{ij}$, where $\varepsilon_{ij} \sim NID(0, \sigma_\varepsilon^2)$. In ANOVA, it is assumed that the $\varepsilon$'s (the differences among the observations within a group) in the population (1) are normally distributed, (2) have equal variances, and (3) are independent. ANOVA is robust to violations of the normality assumptions (i.e., violations of statistical assumptions have negligible consequences on the probability of a type-

[33]See Conover (1980), Hollander and Wolfe (1971), and Siegel and Castellan (1988) for computational procedures and special tables.

[34]Other alternatives are available (Dixon & Massey, 1983) when extreme outliers are present (e.g., trimming and Winsorizing).

I error, $\alpha$, or a type-II error, $\beta$). ANOVA is also robust to the homogeneity of variance assumption in balanced designs; however, when the $n$'s are not equal, homogeneity of variance is necessary for accurate results. The Welch and Brown-Forsythe modifications of ANOVA are needed with unbalanced designs and heterogeneous variances.

The power of ANOVA is influenced by (1) the magnitude of the differences in the population means (i.e., $\Sigma\alpha_j^2$), (2) the number of groups, $J$, (3) the number of observations per group, $n$, and (4) the value of $\alpha$.

Non-parametric tests (Kruskal-Wallis and chi-square median tests) are less powerful than ANOVA.

## 15.32 CASE STUDY

A one-factor ANOVA was run using the HSB data set. Four racial groups (the independent variable) were compared on the dependent variables of (1) locus of control, (2) math achievement, and (3) self-concept measures. Sample output is given in Table 15.5. Below

**TABLE 15.5** ANOVA Output Using the High School and Beyond Data Set.

Variable LOCUS OF CONTROL (This is the dependent variable.)
By Variable RACE (This is the independent variable.)

***Analysis of Variance***

| *Source* | *D.F.* | *Sum of Squares* | *Mean Squares* | *F Ratio* | *p* |
|---|---|---|---|---|---|
| Between Groups | 3 | 4.074 | 1.3580 | 3.0538 | .0280 |
| Within Groups | 596 | 265.042 | .4447 | | |
| Total | 599 | 269.116 | | | |

| *Group* | *n* | *Mean* | *Standard Deviation* | *Standard Error* | *Min.* | *Max.* | *.95CI for Mean* |
|---|---|---|---|---|---|---|---|
| HISPANIC | 71 | –.118 | .691 | .082 | –1.78 | 1.36 | (–.282, .045) |
| ASIAN | 34 | .035 | .636 | .109 | –1.28 | 1.36 | (–.187, .257) |
| BLACK | 58 | .099 | .761 | .100 | –2.23 | 1.36 | (–.101, .300) |
| WHITE | 437 | .136 | .652 | .031 | –2.23 | 1.36 | (.075, .197) |
| Total | 600 | .097 | .670 | .027 | –2.23 | 1.36 | (.043, .150) |

Levene Test for Homogeneity of Variances, 2-tail significance: p = .352

Variable MATH
By Variable RACE

***Analysis of Variance***

| *Source* | *D.F.* | *Sum of Squares* | *Mean Squares* | *F Ratio* | *p* |
|---|---|---|---|---|---|
| Between Groups | 3 | 6705.12 | 2235.04 | 28.7158 | .0000 |
| Within Groups | 596 | 46388.59 | 77.83 | | |
| Total | 599 | 53093.72 | | | |

**TABLE 15.5** *(Continued)*

| *Group* | *n* | *Mean* | *Standard Deviation* | *Standard Error* | *Min.* | *Max.* | *.95CI for Mean* |
|---|---|---|---|---|---|---|---|
| HISPANIC | 71 | 45.77 | 8.156 | .9679 | 32.7 | 68.0 | (43.84, 47.70) |
| ASIAN | 34 | 57.66 | 9.779 | 1.6771 | 41.9 | 75.5 | (54.25, 61.07) |
| BLACK | 58 | 45.77 | 8.373 | 1.0994 | 33.4 | 67.1 | (43.57, 47.97) |
| WHITE | 437 | 53.19 | 8.905 | .4260 | 31.8 | 74.6 | (52.35, 54.03) |
| Total | 600 | 51.85 | 9.415 | .3844 | 31.8 | 75.5 | (51.09, 52.60) |

Levene Test for Homogeneity of Variances, 2-tail significance: p = .302

Variable SELFCONCEPT
By Variable RACE

***Analysis of Variance***

| *Source* | *D.F.* | *Sum of Squares* | *Mean Squares* | *F Ratio* | *p* |
|---|---|---|---|---|---|
| Between Groups | 3 | .995 | .3316 | .6651 | .5737 |
| Within Groups | 596 | 297.156 | .4986 | | |
| Total | 599 | 298.151 | | | |

| *Group* | *n* | *Mean* | *Standard Deviation* | *Standard Error* | *Min.* | *Max.* | *.95CI for Mean* |
|---|---|---|---|---|---|---|---|
| HISPANIC | 71 | .0396 | .6436 | .0764 | −1.67 | 1.19 | (−.113, .192) |
| ASIAN | 34 | −.1338 | .8147 | .1397 | −2.29 | 1.19 | (−.418, .150) |
| BLACK | 58 | .0705 | .9190 | .1207 | −2.62 | 1.19 | (−.171, .312) |
| WHITE | 437 | .0014 | .6741 | .0322 | −2.60 | 1.19 | (−.062, .065) |
| Total | 600 | .0049 | .7055 | .0288 | −2.62 | 1.19 | (−.052, .062) |

Levene Test of Homogeneity of Variances, 2-tail significance: p = .000

the ANOVA table, the output gives $\overline{X}$, $s$, $s_{\overline{X}}$, $X_{\min}$, $X_{\max}$, and the .95*CI*'s for $\mu$ for each group, followed by the results of the Levene test of homogeneity of variance. Note that the *n*'s for the four groups differ markedly; thus, the assumption of homogeneity of variance cannot be ignored.

**Locus of Control.** The Levene test[35] shows that $H_0$: $\sigma_1^2 = \sigma_2^2 = \sigma_3^2 = \sigma_4^2$ is tenable ($p = .352$); thus, the ANOVA results can be viewed as quite accurate; consequently, $H_0$: $\mu_1 = \mu_2 = \mu_3 = \mu_4$ can be rejected ($p = .028$). The differences among the four means are greater than one would expect from chance (sampling error) alone. Notice that the .95*CI*'s for the Hispanics and Whites do not overlap.[36] Perhaps the Hispanic students feel that they had less control of their destiny than certain of the other groups (although we will use

[35]Tests for homogeneity of variance are treated in Chapter 16.

[36]Overlapping *CI*'s do not indicate a lack of significant difference between two means, but nonoverlapping .95*CI*'s are a very conservative test that the difference between the two means is statistically significant ($p < .05$).

multiple comparison procedures in Chapter 17 to determine which means differ significantly from which other means).

**Mathematics.** Notice that the differences among the variances on the Mathematics measure are not significant ($p = .302$); therefore, the ANOVA allows $H_0$: $\mu_1 = \mu_2 = \mu_3 = \mu_4$ to be rejected ($p < .0001$).[37] The *CI* for the Asian mean does not overlap with any of the other group means, indicating its population mean is higher than that of the other groups. Multiple comparisons (Chapter 17) should be used to identify more precisely which pairs of means differ significantly.

**Self-concept.** For this measure, the Levene test finds that $H_0$: $\sigma_1^2 = \sigma_2^2 = \sigma_3^2 = \sigma_4^2$ is *not* tenable. Therefore, since the *n*'s vary greatly among the four groups, the *p*-value ($p = .5337$) yielded by ANOVA is not very accurate. Note, however, that the smaller groups tend to have somewhat larger standard deviations; hence, the *F*-test is liberal (the actual *p* is greater than the reported *p*)—if $H_0$ is not rejected with a liberal test, it will not be rejected with a more accurate test.[38] Nevertheless, because the *n*'s differ greatly and the homogeneity of variance assumption is not tenable, a computer program offering the Welch or Brown-Forsythe tests should be used to provide an accurate *p*-value.

## 15.33 SUGGESTED COMPUTER ACTIVITY

Using the EXERCISE data set, run a one-factor ANOVA using SMOKE as the factor and PUL_GAIN (i.e., PULSE_2 - PULSE_1) as the dependent variable. Compare the observed *F*-ratio with the *t*-ratio found in Section 12.20.[39]

Using the HSB data set, compare the WRTG means for the four ethnic groups.

## MASTERY TEST

1. Suppose pupils in grades seven, eight, nine, ten, eleven, and twelve ($J = 6$) were compared with respect to absenteeism. If ANOVA were used rather than multiple *t*-tests, the probability of a type-I error would be less. (T or F)
2. How many different *t*-tests would be required to make all possible comparisons of pairs of means in question 1? [$J(J - 1)/2$]
3. Write the null hypothesis for the omnibus *F*-test in question 1. (Use grade levels for the subscripts for the respective means.)
4. If ANOVA were performed and the critical *F*-values associated with $\alpha = .05$ were used, is the probability of a type-I error equal to .05 if $H_0$ is true?
5. If $H_0$ is true, if multiple *t*-tests are used, and if the critical value for *t* with $\alpha = .05$ is used, the probability of rejecting at least one of the 15 $H_0$'s is
   (a) slightly less than .05
   (b) .05
   (c) slightly more than .05
   (d) much greater than .05.
6. A "synonym" for sum of squares (*SS*) is
   (a) $\bar{X}$ (b) $\Sigma x_i^2$ (c) $\Sigma X_i^2$ (d) $(\Sigma X_i)^2$

[37]The printed $p = .0000$ on the output means $p < .00005$; the .0000 should be expressed as $p < .00001$. Likewise, $p = .000$ for the Levene test for the Self-concept measure is better represented as $p < .001$.

[38]For recommended procedures if $H_0$ had been rejected, see Section 15.25.

[39]Since $\sigma_B = 1$, $F = t^2$.

7. The degrees of freedom for $SS_B$ are

   (a) $J$ (b) $J-1$ (c) 1 (d) $n_{\bullet}-J$ (e) $J(n-1)$

8. The degrees of freedom for $SS_W$ are *not*

   (a) $J-1$ (b) $n_{\bullet}-J$ (c) $J(n-1)$ (d) $\Sigma_j v_j$

9. In ANOVA what is the numerator for the $F$-test?

   (a) $MS_B$ (b) $MS_W$

10. If $J = 3$ and $\overline{X}_1 = \overline{X}_2 = \overline{X}_3 = 11.0$, what will be the numerical value of the numerator of the $F$-test?

11. In question 10, what is the value of the grand mean, $\overline{X}_{\bullet}$?

12. In question 10, will $SS_{total} = SS_W$?

13. In ANOVA, if $H_0$: $\mu_1 = \mu_2 = \ldots = \mu_J$ is true, are the expected values of $MS_B$ and $MS_W$ both equal to $\sigma^2$?

14. If the observed $F$-ratio is 1.00 or less, will the null hypothesis be rejected at an $\alpha = .25$?

15. The means of the thirty-one persons in the experimental group and the thirty-one persons in the control group were compared using a $t$-test. The value of $t$ was 2.5. If ANOVA is performed on the same data, what will be the value of the $F$-ratio?

16. The critical value for $t$ in question 15 with $\alpha = .05$ is 2.00; what is the critical $F$-value ($_{.95}F_{1,60}$)?

*In questions 17 to 19 indicate which F-value will be smallest. Study Appendix Table F for trends.*

17. (a) $_{.90}F_{2,30}$ (b) $_{.95}F_{2,30}$ (c) $_{.99}F_{2,30}$

18. (a) $_{.95}F_{3,10}$ (b) $_{.95}F_{3,30}$ (c) $_{.95}F_{3,60}$

19. (a) $_{.95}F_{1,60}$ (b) $_{.95}F_{2,60}$ (c) $_{.95}F_{3,60}$

*Answer questions 20 to 39 below assuming that J, the number of groups, is 4.*

| *Source* | *SS* | *v* | *MS* | *F* |
|---|---|---|---|---|
| Between | 30 | ___ | ___ | — |
| Within | — | 60 | 2.00 | — |

20. What is the value of $v_B$?

21. What is the value of $MS_B$?

22. What is the $F$-ratio?

23. If $\alpha = .05$, what is the critical value for $F$?

24. Will $H_0$: $\mu_1 = \mu_2 = \mu_3 = \mu_4$ be rejected at $\alpha = .05$?

25. Can $H_0$ be rejected at $\alpha = .01$?

26. Can $H_0$ be rejected at $\alpha = .001$?

27. What is the total number of observations, $n$, in this example?

28. What is the value of $SS_{within}$?

29. What is the value of $SS_{total}$?

30. Will non-normality of $X$'s ordinarily lead to erroneous conclusions regarding the null hypothesis when ANOVA is used?

31. When using ANOVA with equal $n$'s, does one need to be concerned about the homogeneity-of-variance assumption?

32. If $n_1 \neq n_2 \neq n_3 \neq n_4$, should one be concerned about the $\sigma_1^2 = \sigma_2^2 = \sigma_3^2 = \sigma_4^2$ assumption?

33. If $n_1 > n_2 > n_3 > n_4$ and $\sigma_1^2 > \sigma_2^2 > \sigma_3^2 > \sigma_4^2$ and $H_0$ is rejected, is the conclusion suspect?

**34.** If the larger $n$'s are paired with smaller variances and $H_0$ is not rejected, is the conclusion suspect?

**35.** In which of these situations is the independence-of-$X$'s assumption less apt to be satisfied?

(a) When the treatment is administered separately to each individual
(b) When the treatment is administered to a group of individuals simultaneously

**36.** If n's are equal, is $\overline{X}_{\bullet} = \Sigma_j \overline{X}_j / J$?

**37.** Assuming $n_1 = n_2 = n_3 = n_4$, what is the average variance, $(s_1^2 + s_2^2 + s_3^2 + s_4^2)/4$, in the ANOVA table preceding question 20?

**38.** The mean of the standard deviations within the four groups would be roughly

(a) 1 (b) 1.5 (c) 2.0 (d) 2.5

**39.** If the ranges of scores within groups 1 through 4 are found to be 6, 5, 4, 5, is the value of $MS_W$ of 2.00 reasonable?

*For items 40–46, using the linear model for ANOVA:* $X_{ij} = \mu + \alpha_j + \varepsilon_{ij}$

**40.** The treatment effects are represented by the symbol ____; the assumptions of normality, homogeneity of variance, and independence pertain to the ____ term.

**41.** The assumption of normality, independence, and homogeneity of variance can be denoted by ____.

**42.** If $\mu_1 = 23$, $\mu_2 = 19$, and $\mu_3 = 18$, and the $n$'s are equal, $\mu =$ ____ and $\alpha_1 =$ ____.

**43.** If $X_{11} = 30$, $\varepsilon_{11} =$ ____.

**44.** If $n = 10$ and $\sigma_\varepsilon^2 = 7.5$, use Equations 15.18 and 15.19 to find $E(MS_W)$ and $E(MS_B)$.

**45.** If $s_1^2 = 6$, $s_2^2 = 5$, and $s_3^2 = 10$, $s_W^2 = MS_W =$ ____.

**46.** If $\alpha$ is changed from .05 to .01, power will be ____ (increased or decreased).

*If* $H_0$: $\mu_1 = \mu_2 = \ldots = \mu_J$ *is true, then (items 47–48):*

**47.** $\alpha_1 = \alpha_2 = \ldots = \alpha_J =$ ____; and $\sigma_\alpha^2 =$ ____.

**48.** $E(MS_B) = E(MS_W) =$ ____.

**49.** The noncentrality parameter $\phi$ used in determining power when the $n$'s are equal may be found from Equation 15.23:

$$\phi = \sqrt{\frac{n\Sigma\alpha_j^2}{J\sigma_\varepsilon^2}}$$

From Equation 15.23, supply the correct word (increases or decreases) in the following blanks. *Other things being equal*, power increases:

(a) as $n$ ____,
(b) as the variability among scores within the $J$ groups, $\sigma_\varepsilon^2$, ____.
(c) as the effect sizes for the $J$ groups, $\Sigma\alpha_j^2$, ____.

**50.** Which statistical treatment would you recommend to test the hypothesis that four sample means come from the same population when the sample sizes and variances differ greatly?

## PROBLEMS AND EXERCISES

**1.** Calculate the degrees of freedom for both $MS_B$ and $MS_W$ in each of the following instances:

(a) $J = 2, n = 4$ (b) $J = 5, n = 2$
(c) $J = 3, n_1 = 3, n_2 = 6, n_3 = 4$ (d) $J = 3, n_1 = 4, n_2 = 1, n_3 = 5$

**2.** Determine the critical value of $F = MS_B/MS_W$ for testing $H_0$ in each of the following instances:
(a) $J = 2$; $n = 6$; $\alpha = .01$ (b) $J = 5$; $n = 7$; $\alpha = .10$ (c) $J = 3$; $n_1 = 4$; $n_2 = 6$; $n_3 = 8$; $\alpha = .05$

**3.** Which one or more of the following statements are equivalent to the alternative hypothesis $H_1$ in the one-factor ANOVA?
(a) $\mu_j \neq \mu_{j'}$ for some $j$ and $j'$ (b) $\alpha_j \neq 0$ for some $j$'s
(c) $\sum_j (\mu_j - \mu)^2 \neq 0$ (d) $\sum_j \alpha_j^2 \neq 0$
(e) $\sum_j \alpha_j = 0$

**4.** Given only the following data in an ANOVA table, determine $MS_B$, $MS_W$, and $F$. State $H_0$; is it tenable with $\alpha = .10$?

| *Source* | *SS* | $\nu$ | *MS* | *F* |
|---|---|---|---|---|
| Between | 80 | 4 | | |
| Within | | | | |
| Total | 480 | 44 | | |

**5.** One study experimented with the order of cognitive "organizers" that structure the material for the learner. A group of thirty persons was randomly split into three groups of ten each. Group I received organizing material before studying instructional materials on mathematics; group II received the "organizer" after studying the mathematics; group III received the math materials but no organizing material. On a ten-item test over the mathematics covered, the following scores were earned:

| *Group I (Postorganizer)* | *Group II (Preorganizer)* | *Group III (NoOrganizer)* |
|---|---|---|
| 5 | 4 | 5 |
| 4 | 5 | 4 |
| 4 | 3 | 6 |
| 7 | 6 | 2 |
| 8 | 6 | 2 |
| 7 | 3 | 2 |
| 6 | 3 | 6 |
| 4 | 4 | 4 |
| 4 | 4 | 3 |
| 7 | 2 | 5 |
| $\bar{X}_j$: 5.60 | 4.00 | 3.90 |
| $s_j^2$: 2.49 | 1.78 | 2.54 |

Perform a one-factor ANOVA (see Figure 15.2 and Section 15.23; test the null hypothesis $H_0$: $\mu_1 = \mu_2 = \mu_3$ at $\alpha = .05$ and at $\alpha = .01$.

**6.** Ten samples of twenty scores each are drawn at random from a single normal population with mean $\mu$ and variance $\sigma^2$. The sample means of the ten samples have a variance of 2.40, that is:

$$s_{\bar{X}}^2 = \frac{\sum_j (\bar{X}_j - \bar{X}_{\bullet})^2}{J - 1} = 2.40$$

Find an estimate of $\sigma^2$, the variance of the original normal population sampled.

**7.** A study (Hakstian, 1971) was designed to determine whether the type of examination anticipated (essay, objective, or a combination of both) had an effect on performance on objective or essay tests. On a common assignment, one-third of a class of thirty-three students expected an objective test, one-third expected an essay test, and one-third expected both types of items. The actual examination consisted of both an objective and essay test over the common material. The analysis of variance for the objective test is given. (The means for the three groups were $\overline{X}_E = 27.3$, $\overline{X}_O = 27.2$, and $\overline{X}_C = 29.1$ for the students expecting objective, essay and combination, respectively.)

| *Source* | $\nu$ | *MS* | *F* |
|---|---|---|---|
| Between | 2 | 12.57 | .54 |
| Within | 30 | 23.35 | |

(a) What conclusion can be drawn from these results?
The ANOVA table for scores on the essay test is given:

| *Source* | $\nu$ | *MS* | *F* |
|---|---|---|---|
| Between | 2 | 259.49 | 1.44 |
| Within | 30 | 180.20 | |

(b) If $H_0$ is true, using Table F, estimate the probability of obtaining an $F$-ratio as large as 1.44.
(c) The three observed means on the essay test (graded anonymously) were as follows: $\overline{X}_O = 45.3$, $\overline{X}_E = 43.4$, and $\overline{X}_C = 52.6$. Recall that $s_{\overline{X}}^2 = s^2/n$; hence, $ns_{\overline{X}}^2 = s^2 = MS_B$. Thus, we can obtain an estimate of the population variance ($\sigma^2$) using only $n$ and $s_{\overline{X}}^2$. Compute $s_{\overline{X}}^2[s_{\overline{X}}^2 = \Sigma\hat{\alpha}_j^2/(J-1)]$, and estimate the population variance—that is, $ns_{\overline{X}}^2$. Compare the result with the mean square for between groups.

**8.** Calculators were randomly assigned to twenty students of the forty students in a statistics class. All students were instructed to work ten problems involving complex arithmetic operations. The mean of the calculator group was $\overline{X}_C = 6.40$; the mean of the hand-computation group was $\overline{X}_H = 5.90$; $\Sigma_j\Sigma_i X_{ij}^2$ was 1,662 and $\Sigma_j\Sigma_i X_{ij}$ was 246.

(a) Can $H_0$ be rejected at $\alpha = .10$? Perform an analysis of variance and present results in an ANOVA table.
(b) If instead of the one-factor ANOVA, a $t$-test had been employed to test $H_0$: $\mu_C = \mu_H$, the $t$-ratio would have been ____, and the critical $t$-value would have been ____.

**9.** (This problem is recommended only for students having access to a calculator because of the large amount of time that the arithmetic computation would require by hand. Use Equation 15.4 to obtain $SS_B$.) Fifth-grade students representing five ethnic groups from twenty-six school districts in Colorado were compared in school attitude (Hopkins, Kretke, Harms, Gabriel, Phillips, Rodriquez, & Averill, 1974). The means and $n$'s for each group were as follows:

| | *Blacks* | *Hispanics* | *American Indians* | *Orientals* | *White* | *Totals* |
|---|---|---|---|---|---|---|
| $\overline{X}_j$ | 54.9 | 55.8 | 54.5 | 55.1 | 55.6 | $\overline{X}_{\bullet} = 55.58$ |
| $n_j$ | 138 | 534 | 52 | 21 | 2,367 | $n_{\bullet} = 3{,}112$ |
| $\Sigma_i X_{ij}$ | 7,576 | 29,797 | 2,834 | 1,157 | 131,606 | |
| $s_j^2$ | 38.4 | 33.6 | 39.7 | 27.0 | 27.0 | |

**10.** Table 12.1 in Section 12.5 illustrates the independent $t$-test. Use the ANOVA procedures with these data to respond to the following:

(a) $MS_B$ = ____; $MS_W$ = ____; $F$ = ____; $p <$ ____
(b) How does $F$ compare with $t^2$?
(c) What is your conclusion regarding $H_0$ if $\alpha = .10$?

**11.** An investigator expects that the average math achievement in a school district on the annual criterion-referenced math tests can be increased 5% with a new instructional emphasis that monitors time-on-task. From previous years' results, it is known that $\mu \approx 80\%$ and $\sigma \approx 10\%$. If the new program if going to be field tested in one school with 100 students (who will be randomly assigned to either the $E$ or $C$ group), and if the researcher's expectations are correct,

(a) Compute power for the $F$-test with $\alpha_2 = .05$.
(b) Compare your result with those read from Table 15.4.
(c) Using Table 15.4, what is the power if $\alpha_1 = .05$ and $\alpha_1 = .10$, respectively?
(d) If the effect size is only one-half that which is expected, how many pupils must be in each group in order to have power $\approx .80$, even with a one-tailed test and taking a 5% chance of making a type-I error?

**12.** The null hypothesis, $H_0$: $\mu_1 = \mu_2 = \mu_3$, is to be tested with $n = 21$ ($n_{\bullet} = 63$). Suppose that, unknown to the researcher, $\mu_1 = 70$, $\mu_2 = 72$, and $\mu_3 = 74$, and $\sigma^2 = 24$.

(a) What is the power of the $F$-test under these conditions at $\alpha = .05$ and $\alpha = .01$?
(b) How large must $n$ be to have power $(1 - \beta)$ equal to .90 with $\alpha = .05$?

**13.** Unknown to the experimenter, the value of $\sigma^2$ is 20, and $\mu_1 = 10$, $\mu_2 = 15$, and $\mu_3 = 20$ in the three populations from which he has samples of size $n = 10$. What is the expected value of $MS_B$ in this experiment, that is, what would be the average value of $MS_B$ over an infinite number of replications of the same experiment?

**14.** Prove that $SS_W = \Sigma_j[\Sigma_i(X_{ij} - \overline{X}_j)^2]$ is equal to its computational formula $SS_W = \Sigma_j\Sigma_i X_{ij}^2 - \Sigma_j(\Sigma_i X_{ij})^2/n$. (*Hint:* First show that $\Sigma_i(X_{ij} - \overline{X}_j)^2$ equals $\Sigma_i X_{ij}^2 - (\Sigma_i X_{ij})^2/n$, as was done in Chapter 5. Then sum the $J$ sums of squares for each group across $j$.)

**15.** Prove that the value of $F = MS_B/MS_W$ in a one-way ANOVA with $J = 2$ equals the square of the value of $t$ for testing the significance of the difference between the two means, that is, prove that:

$$t^2 = \frac{(\overline{X}_1 - \overline{X}_2)^2}{\left[\dfrac{s_1^2 + s_2^2}{2}\right]\left(\dfrac{2}{n}\right)}$$

equals

$$F = \frac{n[(\overline{X}_1 - \overline{X}_{\bullet})^2 + (\overline{X}_2 - \overline{X}_{\bullet})^2]}{\dfrac{s_1^2 + s_2^2}{2}}$$

Start by noting that $\overline{X}_{\bullet} = (\overline{X}_1 + \overline{X}_2)/2$, and then manipulate the numerator of $F$ into the form $n(\overline{X}_1 - \overline{X}_2)^2/2$.

## ANSWERS TO MASTERY TEST

1. T
2. 15
3. $H_0$: $\mu_7 = \mu_8 = \mu_9 = \mu_{10} = \mu_{11} = \mu_{12}$
4. yes
5. (d)
6. (b)
7. (b)
8. (a)
9. (a)
10. 0; if $\overline{X}_1 = \overline{X}_2 = \ldots = \overline{X}_J$, $SS_B = 0$, and $MS_B = 0.0$
11. $\overline{X}_{\bullet} = 11.0$

12. yes, since $SS_B = 0$
13. yes
14. No; the expected value for $F$ when $H_0$ is true is approximately 1.
15. $(2.5)^2 = 6.25$ ($F = t^2$)
16. ${}_{.95}F_{1,60} = 4.00$ (when $J = 2$, $F = t^2$)
17. (a)
18. (c)
19. (c)
20. $\nu_B = J - 1 = 4 - 1 = 3$
21. $MS_B = SS_B/\nu_B = 30/3 = 10$
22. $F = MS_B/MS_W = 10/2 = 5.0$
23. ${}_{.95}F_{3,60} = 2.76$
24. yes; $F = 5 > 2.76 = {}_{.95}F_{3,60}$
25. yes; $F = 5 > 4.13 = {}_{.99}F_{3,60}$
26. no; $F = 5 < 6.17 = {}_{.999}F_{3,60}$
27. $n_{\bullet} = 64 = \nu_W + J$ (also, $n_{\bullet} = \nu_B + \nu_W + 1$)
28. 120 [$SS = (\nu)(MS)$]
29. 150 [$SS_{total} = SS_B + SS_W$)
30. no
31. no
32. yes, ANOVA is robust to violating homogeneity of variance assumption only when the $n$'s are equal.
33. no; when larger $n$'s and larger $\sigma^2$'s are associated, the probability of type-I error is even less than the nominal $\alpha$.
34. no; when larger $n$'s are associated with smaller variances, the probability of a type-I error is greater then the nominal $\alpha$. Hence, if $H_0$ is not rejected at nominal $\alpha$, it certainly would not be rejected at true $\alpha$.
35. (b)
36. yes
37. $MS_W = \Sigma s_j^2/J = 2.0$
38. b; since the average $s^2$ is 2.0, the average standard deviation within groups would be expected to be approximately $\sqrt{2}$.
39. yes; with $n = 16$, the range is expected to span 3–4 standard deviations (see Table 5.1).
40. $\alpha_j$, $\varepsilon_{ij}$
41. $NID \sim (0, \sigma_\varepsilon^2)$
42. 20, 3
43. 7
44. $E(MS_W) = 7.5$, $E(MS_B) = 7.5 + 10(14)/2 = 77.5$
45. 7
46. decreased
47. 0, 0
48. $\sigma^2$
49. (a) increases
    (b) decreases
    (c) increases
50. the Welch or Brown-Forsythe ANOVA procedure.

## ANSWERS TO PROBLEMS AND EXERCISES

1. (a) $\nu_B = 1$, $\nu_W = 6$
   (b) $\nu_B = 4$, $\nu_W = 5$
   (c) $\nu_B = 2$, $\nu_W = 10$
   (d) $\nu_B = 2$, $\nu_W = 7$
2. (a) ${}_{.99}F_{1,10} = 10.0$
   (b) ${}_{.90}F_{4,30} = 2.14$
   (c) ${}_{.95}F_{2,15} = 3.68$
3. (a) yes (b) yes (c) yes
   (d) yes (e) no
4. $H_0$: $\mu_1 = \mu_2 = \mu_3 = \mu_4 = \mu_5$

| *Source* | *SS* | $\nu$ | *MS* | *F* |
|---|---|---|---|---|
| Between | 80 | 4 | (20) | (2.0) |
| Within | (400) | (40) | (10) | |
| | 480 | 44 | | |

$2.0 < 2.09 = {}_{.90}F_{4,40}$; $H_0$ is tenable.

**5.** $SS_B = 10([-.5)^2 + (1.1)^2 + (-.6)^2] = 18.2$
$SS_W = 22.41 + 16.02 + 22.86 = 61.29$

| SV | SS | v | MS | F |
|---|---|---|---|---|
| Between | 18.2 | 2 | 9.10 | 4.01 |
| Within | 61.29 | 27 | 2.27 | |

Can reject $H_0$ at $\alpha = .05$, $4.01 > 3.37 = {}_{.95}F_{2,26}$.
Cannot reject $H_0$ at $\alpha = .01$, $4.01 < 5.53 = {}_{.99}F_{2,26}$.

**6.** Since $s_{\bar{X}}^2$ estimates $\sigma^2/n$, $ns_{\bar{X}}^2$ estimates $\sigma^2$. Hence, the estimate of $\sigma^2$ is $20(2.40) = 48.0$.

**7.** (a) The type of examination expected by the students had no discernible effect on performance on the objective test.
(b) $p \approx .25$, $({}_{.75}F_{2,30} = 1.45)$
(c)

$$s_{\bar{X}}^2 = \frac{(\bar{X}_O - \bar{X}_.)^2 + (\bar{X}_E - \bar{X}_.)^2 + (\bar{X}_C - \bar{X}_.)^2}{J-1}$$
$$= \frac{(45.3 - 47.1)^2 + (-3.7)^2 + (5.5)^2}{3-1}$$
$$= \frac{3.24 + 13.69 + 30.25}{2} = \frac{47.18}{2}$$
$$= 23.59;\ 11(23.59) = 259.49 = MS_B$$

**8.** (a) $SS_{total} = 1{,}662 - (246)^2/40 = 149.1$

$$SS_B = n\Sigma\hat{\alpha}_j^2;\ \hat{\alpha}_c = 6.40 - 6.15 = .25;$$
$$\hat{\alpha}_H = 5.90 - 6.15 = -.25$$
$$SS_B = 20[(.25)^2 + (-.25)^2] = 2.50$$
$$SS_W = SS_{total} - SS_B = 149.1 - 2.50 = 146.6$$

| SV | SS | v | MS | F |
|---|---|---|---|---|
| Between | 2.50 | 1 | 2.50 | .65 |
| Within | 146.6 | 38 | 3.86 | |
| Total: | 149.1 | 39 | | |

$F < 1$; therefore, $H_0$ is tenable $({}_{.90}F_{1,38} \approx 2.85)$.

(b) $t = \sqrt{F} = \sqrt{.65} = .81;\ {}_{.95}t_{38} = \sqrt{{}_{.90}F_{1,38}} = 1.69$

**9.**
$$SS_B = \Sigma n_j\hat{\alpha}_j^2;\ \hat{\alpha}_B = 54.9 - 55.58 = -.68\ \hat{\alpha}_C = .22;$$
$$\hat{\alpha}_I = -1.08;\ \hat{\alpha}_O = -.48;\ \hat{\alpha}_W = .02$$
$$SS_B = 138(-.68)^2 + 534(.22)^2 + 52(-1.08)^2 + 21(-.48)^2 + 2{,}367(.02)^2$$
$$SS_B = 63.81 + 25.84 + 60.65 + 4.84 + 0.95 = 156.1$$
$$SS_W = \Sigma SS_j = \Sigma v_j s_j^2 = 137(38.4) + 533(33.6) + 51(39.7) + 20(27.0) + 2366(27.0) = 89{,}616.3$$

| SV | SS | v | MS | F |
|---|---|---|---|---|
| Between | 156.1 | 4 | 39.03 | 1.353 |
| Within | 89,616.3 | 3,107 | 28.84 | |

$H_0$ is tenable—that is, differences in school attitude means are not statistically significant; indeed, $F = 1.353 > 1.35 = {}_{.75}F_{4,\infty}$, $p < .25$.

**10.** (a) $MS_B = 846.81$
$MS_W = 242.5$
$F = 3.49$
$p < .10$
(b) $F = t^2$ since $v_B = 1$
(c) $F = 3.49 > 2.88 \approx {}_{.90}F_{1,34}$; reject $H_0$ at $\alpha = .10$

**11.** (a) = .71 (b) same
(c) .81, .89 (d) about 200

**12.** (a) From Equation 15.23, the value of $\phi$ is $\sqrt{7/3} \approx 1.53$, and $v_B = J - 1 = 2$; $v_W = n_. - J = 60$. From Table G, the power of the $F$-test, $(1 - \beta)$, = .60 and .35 for $\alpha = .05$ and $\alpha = .01$, respectively.
(b) From Table G, ${}_{.05}\phi_{.90} = 2.1$ for $v_B = 2$ and $v_e = v_W = 60$; from Equation 15.23.
$n = 3(24)(2.1)^2/8 \approx 40$

**13.** (Equation 15.19A)

$$E(MS_B) = \sigma^2 + \frac{n\sum_j(\mu_j - \mu)^2}{(J-1)}$$
$$= 20 + 250 = 270$$

# 16

# INFERENCES ABOUT VARIANCES

## 16.1 INTRODUCTION

In empirical research, the investigator typically has the greatest interest in hypotheses that pertain to means, proportions, or correlation coefficients. On occasion, however, the interest concerns questions of variability, such as the following:

Are the individual differences in math achievement among boys greater than among girls?

Are year-to-year fluctuations in sales greater in luxury-type businesses than in businesses devoted to necessities?

Does participation in discussion groups lead to group consensus or does it tend to polarize attitudes?

More often tests of hypotheses about variances are performed to legitimize other analyses that rest on the assumption of equal variances in the various populations. Recall in the independent groups $t$-test that $\sigma_1^2 = \sigma_2^2$ is assumed.

In testing statistical hypotheses of the type $H_0$: $\sigma^2 = K$, a familiar family of sampling distributions will be employed, namely the chi-square, $\chi^2$, distributions. We will digress from the immediate question of testing $H_0$: $\sigma^2 = K$ to give an additional overview of the chi-square distribution.

## 16.2 CHI-SQUARE DISTRIBUTIONS[1]

Imagine a population of normally distributed, standardized $z$-scores ($\mu = 0$, $\sigma = 1$). Denote the square of this standard score, $z_i^2$, selected randomly from this normal distribution by $\chi_1^2$,

[1]Section 16.2 provides the rationale for the chi-square distribution; an understanding of the theory of the $\chi^2$ distribution is not essential to applying the procedures for testing hypotheses about variances.

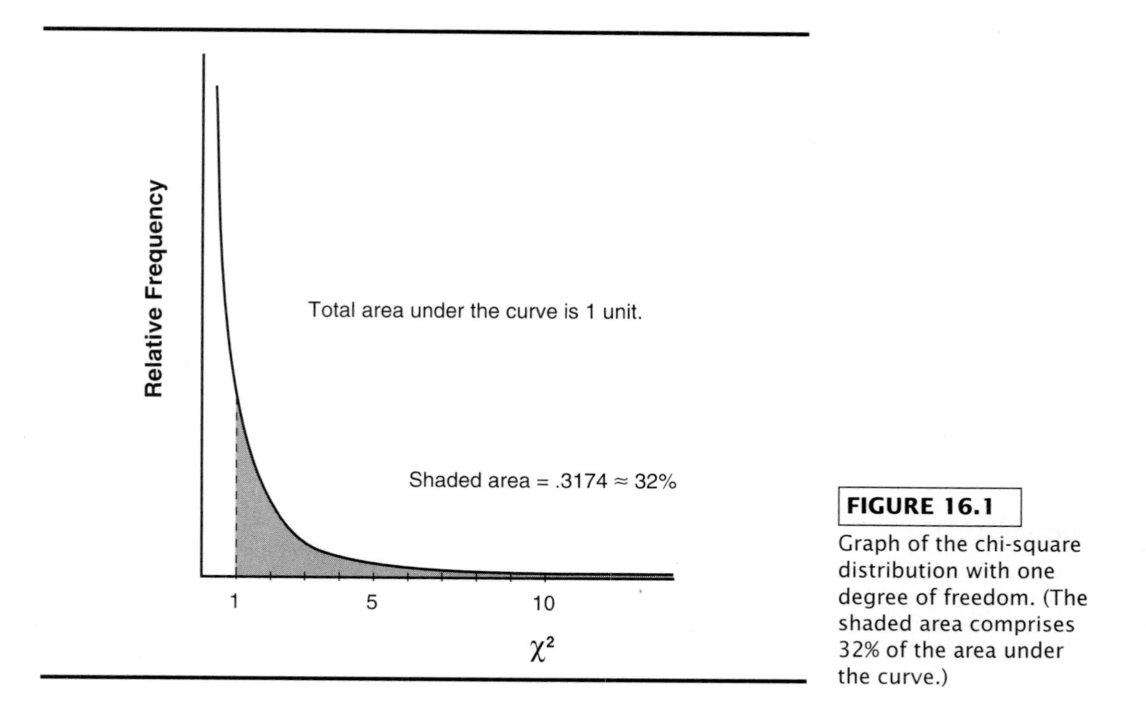


**FIGURE 16.1**
Graph of the chi-square distribution with one degree of freedom. (The shaded area comprises 32% of the area under the curve.)

where the exponent "$^2$" shows that the value has been squared; the subscript "$_1$" indicates that only one $z$-score is used to produce $\chi_1^2$:

$$\chi_1^2 = z_i^2 \qquad (16.1)$$

Because of the squaring, $\chi^2$ can never be negative. Suppose this process, of randomly selecting a $z$-value and squaring it, is repeated a million times. The frequency distribution of 1,000,000 $\chi_1^2$-values, the curve of the chi-square distribution with one degree of freedom, $\chi_1^2$, would be obtained. A graph of this distribution appears in Figure 16.1.[2]

As with the $z$ and $t$ distributions, the area under the curve for any $\chi^2$ distribution is set equal to one so that it is a probability distribution. For example, if a $z$-score is randomly selected and squared, the probability of obtaining a $\chi_1^2$-value above 1.00 equals the area under the curve that is to the right of 1.00. In Figure 16.1, .32 (32%) of the area under the curve lies to the right of $\chi^2 = 1$. Thus, the probability of obtaining a value of $z^2 = \chi_1^2$ that exceeds 1 is .32. In other words, 32% of the $z$-scores randomly selected from a normal distribution will have squares that exceed 1. Stated differently, the 68th percentile in the chi-square distribution with one degree of freedom equals 1.00, which can be written as: $_{.68}\chi_1^2 = 1.00$. $\chi_1^2$ denotes the chi-square distribution with one degree of freedom and .68

[2]The mathematical curve for the chi-square distribution was derived by Karl Pearson in 1900. The mathematical curve that is graphed in Figure 16.1 and that describes the distribution of $\chi_1^2$ has a complex formula given in Graybill (1961, p. 31).

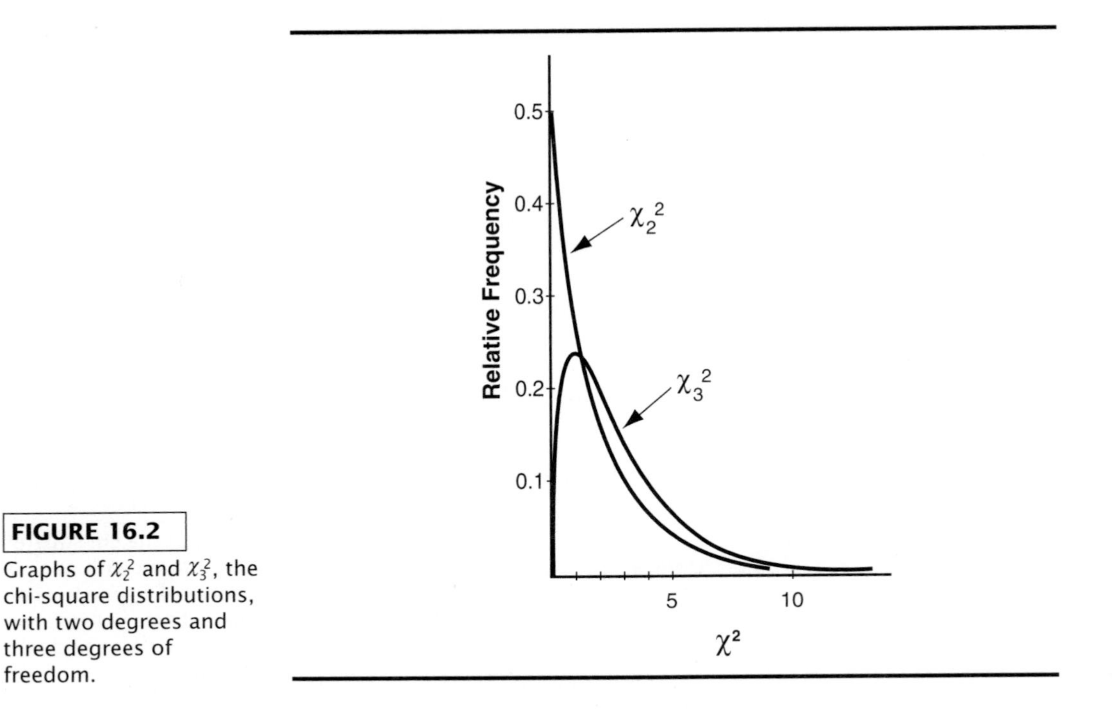


**FIGURE 16.2**

Graphs of $\chi_2^2$ and $\chi_3^2$, the chi-square distributions, with two degrees and three degrees of freedom.

denotes the 68th percentile of the distribution. Notice that if $|z| < 1$, then $z^2 < 1$; thus 68% of the $z^2$-scores (or $\chi_1{}^2$ values) will be less than 1. What is the value of ${}_{.95}\chi_1{}^2$? Since $\chi_1{}^2 = z^2$, if ${}_{.95}|z| = 1.96$, then ${}_{.95}\chi_1{}^2 = (1.96)^2 = 3.84$. Thus, the 95th percentile of $\chi_1{}^2$ is 3.84.

## 16.3 CHI-SQUARE DISTRIBUTIONS WITH $\nu > 1$: $\chi_2^2$ AND $\chi_3^2$

To understand the $\chi_2{}^2$ distribution, suppose that instead of randomly selecting a single $z$-score, we randomly draw two scores from the original normal distribution of $z$-scores. Define the first score as $z_1$, and the second as $z_2$. Now square $z_1$ and $z_2$ and sum the two $z^2$'s to form the quantity:

$$\chi_2^2 = z_1^2 + z_2^2 \quad \textbf{(16.2)}$$

This process could be repeated thousands of times with new pairs of $z$-scores. A frequency distribution of these $\chi_2^2$ scores could be constructed so that the area under the curve would be one unit. The resulting curve would look like the graph of the mathematical curve $\chi_2^2$ in Figure 16.2, the chi-square distribution with two degrees of freedom.

In like manner, three $z$-scores could be randomly selected, squared, and summed[3] to obtain $\chi_3^2$. Figure 16.2 also gives the graph of $\chi_3^2$.

---

[3] $z_1{}^2 + z_2{}^2 + z_3{}^2 = \Sigma_i z_i{}^2 = \chi_3{}^2$.

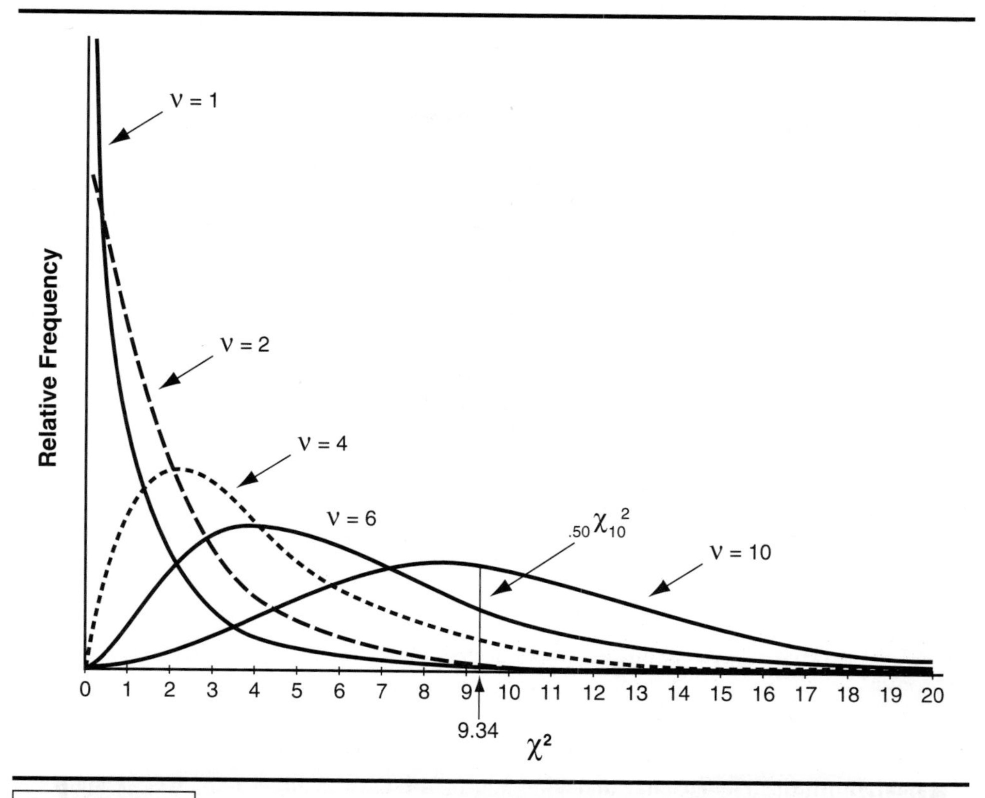


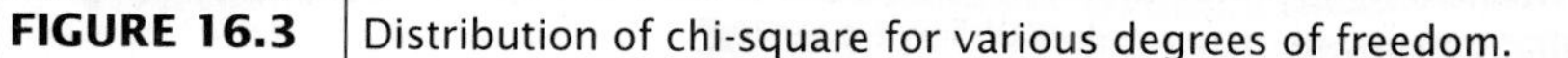

**FIGURE 16.3** Distribution of chi-square for various degrees of freedom.

## 16.4 THE CHI-SQUARE DISTRIBUTION WITH $\nu$ DEGREES OF FREEDOM, $\chi_\nu^2$

A chi-square distribution with $\nu$ degrees of freedom, $\chi_\nu^2$, is formed by adding the squares of $\nu$ randomly selected $z$-scores from a normal distribution:

$$\chi_\nu^2 = z_1^2 + z_2^2 + \ldots + z_\nu^2 = \sum_i z_1^2 \qquad \textbf{(16.3)}$$

Figure 16.3 illustrates the graphs of $\chi_\nu^2$ with $\nu = 1, 2, 4, 6$, and 10.

The area under each curve in Figure 16.3 is 1.00. Observe that half the area under $\chi_{10}^2$ lies above the point 9.34, that is, ${}_{.50}\chi_{10}^2 = 9.34$. Hence, the probability is .50 that the sum of the squares of ten $z$-scores randomly drawn from a normal distribution will exceed 9.34.

There is a different chi-square distribution for each integer value of $\nu$ (1, 2, 3, ...). The properties of the curve $\chi_\nu^2$ depend upon the value of $\nu$. The following facts describe the family of chi-square distributions:

1. The mean of a chi-square distribution with $\nu$ degrees of freedom is equal to $\nu$. For example, the expected (average) value of $\chi^2_{12}$ is 12.
2. The mode of $\chi^2_\nu$ is at the point $\nu - 2$ for $\nu \geq 2$.
3. The median $\chi^2_\nu$-value is approximately $(3\nu - 2)/3$ for $\nu \geq 2$.
4. The variance of $\chi^2_\nu$ is $2\nu$.
5. The skewness $\Omega$ of $\chi^2_\nu$ is $\sqrt{2/\nu}$. Every chi-square distribution is positively skewed, but the asymmetry decreases as $\nu$ increases. (Note in Table D that $\Omega$ is still evident (.2) even with $\nu = 50$.)
6. As $\nu$ becomes very large, $\chi^2_\nu$ approximates a normal distribution with mean $\nu$ and standard deviation $\sqrt{2\nu}$.

The 100 $p$th percentile in the chi-square distribution with $\nu$ degrees of freedom is denoted as ${}_p\chi^2_\nu$. The percentiles of the chi-square distribution play a prominent role in certain inferential statistical techniques. Various percentiles in chi-square distributions for $\nu = 1$ up to $\nu = 100$ appear in Table D of the Appendix. The following is an example of how Table D is read. Suppose you need to find the 95th percentile in the chi-square distribution with six degrees of freedom, that is ${}_{.95}\chi_6^2$. First, find the row for $\nu = 6$ in Table D. Second, locate the column for $p = .95$. At the intersection of the appropriate row and column, the number 12.59 is read. This is the value of ${}_{.95}\chi_6^2$, the 95th percentile of the chi-square distribution with six degrees of freedom. Locate this point in the $\chi_6^2$ distribution in Figure 16.3; notice that only a small portion of the area of the curve exceeds 12.59.

## 16.5 INFERENCES ABOUT THE POPULATION VARIANCE: $H_0$: $\sigma^2 = K$

1. The **hypothesis** to be tested is that a population has a variance $\sigma^2$ equal to some number $K$ versus the hypothesis that $\sigma^2$ is different from $K$:

$$H_0: \sigma^2 = K$$
$$H_1: \sigma^2 \neq K$$

2. The **assumption** is made that the variable $X$ has a *normal* distribution in the population and that a *random sample* of $n$ observations has been selected from which $\sigma^2$ will be estimated by $s^2$; the estimate has $\nu = n - 1$ degrees of freedom.
3. The **test statistic** for testing $H_0$ against $H_1$ is the chi-square ($\chi^2_\nu$) statistic:

$$\chi^2 = \frac{\nu s^2}{K}, \text{ where } \nu = n - 1. \quad \textbf{(16.4)}$$

4. When $H_0$ is true, the **sampling distribution** of $\chi^2$ in Equation 16.4 is the chi-square distribution with $\nu = n - 1$, that is, $\chi^2_\nu$; when $H_1$ is true and $K$ is equal to some number $L$ (different from zero), the sampling distribution of $\nu s^2/K$ will equal $L/K$ times $\chi_\nu^2$. For example, the graphs of $\nu s^2/10$ are drawn in Figure 16.4 for the cases in which $\sigma^2 = 10$ and $n = 9$, and for $\sigma^2 = 20$.

   If $H_0$: $\sigma^2 = 10$, and in a sample of $n = 9$ scores ($\nu = 8$), $s^2 = 21.40$, the value of the test statistic in Equation 16.4 would be:

$$\chi^2 = \frac{vs^2}{10} = \frac{8(21.40)}{10} = 17.12$$

Using Figure 16.4, we see that a value of the test statistic, $\chi^2$, as large as 17.12 is improbable when $\sigma^2 = 10$, but such values are common when $H_1$: $\sigma^2 = 20$ is true.

5. The **critical values** for testing $H_0$ against $H_1$ at the $\alpha$-level of significance are the $\alpha/2$ and $1 - (\alpha/2)$ percentile points in the chi-square distribution with $v = n - 1$, that is, ${}_{\alpha/2}\chi_v^2$ and ${}_{1-\alpha/2}\chi_v^2$.
6. The $1 - \alpha$ **confidence interval** for the parameter, $\sigma^2$, is:

$$\frac{vs^2}{{}_{1-\alpha/2}\chi_v^2} < \sigma^2 < \frac{vs^2}{{}_{\alpha/2}\chi_v^2} \qquad \textbf{(16.5)}$$

7. **Example.** For a sample of thirty congenitally blind pupils ages nine to fifteen, the standard deviation of the WISC Verbal IQ scores is 16.0 (Hopkins & McGuire, 1966), whereas for the sighted population, $\sigma = 15$. These data will be used to test the following hypotheses at the $\alpha_2 = .10$ level of significance:

$$H_0: \sigma^2 = (15)^2 = 225$$
$$H_1: \sigma^2 \neq 225$$

For the sample of thirty IQ scores, $s^2 = 256$ and $v = 29$. From Equation 16.4:

$$\chi^2 = \frac{29(256)}{225} = 33.00$$

is compared with the critical values obtained from Table D:

$${}_{.05}\chi_{29}^2 = 17.71 \text{ and } {}_{.95}\chi_{29}^2 = 42.56$$

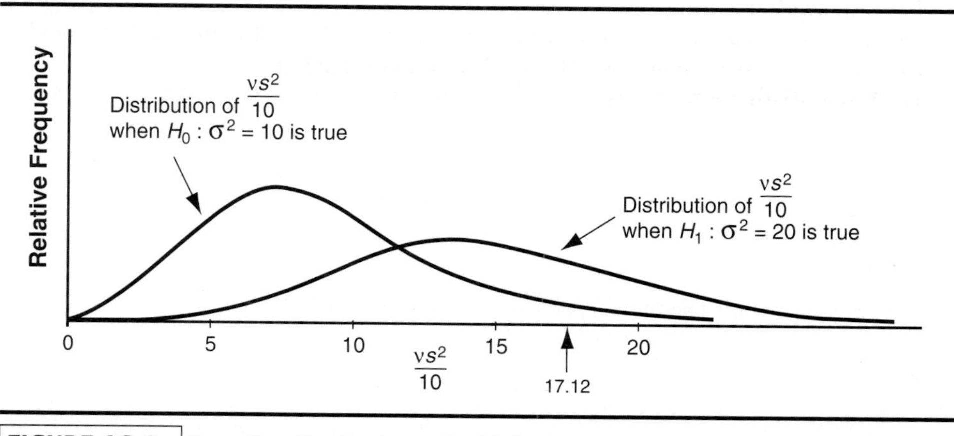


**FIGURE 16.4** Sampling distributions of $vs^2/\sigma^2$ when $H_0$: $\sigma^2 = 10$ is true and when $H_1$: $\sigma^2 = 20$ is true ($v = 8$).

Since the observed $\chi^2$ of 33.0 is greater than the lower critical value of 17.71, but less than the upper critical value of 42.56, the statistical hypothesis, $H_0$: $\sigma^2 = 225$ remains tenable ($p > .10$).[4]
The $.90CI$ on $\sigma^2$ is found by substituting the sample data into Equation 16.5:

$$\frac{\nu s^2}{_{1-\alpha/2}\chi^2} = \frac{(29)(56)}{42.56} < \sigma^2 < \frac{\nu s^2}{_{\alpha/2}\chi^2} = \frac{29(256)}{17.71}, \text{ or } 174 < \sigma^2 < 419$$

The variance of the blind population is not very precisely estimated because of the small sample ($n = 30$). Since $\sigma$ is more interpretable than $\sigma^2$ because the latter does not use the same metric as the original observation, it is more informative to take the square roots of the lower and upper limits of the confidence interval for $\sigma^2$ to form the confidence interval for $\sigma$; in this case, $\sigma$ is probably somewhere between $\sqrt{174} = 13.2$ and $\sqrt{419} = 20.5$, or the $.90CI$ for $\sigma$ is (13.2, 20.5).

8. Unlike hypothesis tests about means that use the $t$-distribution, the assumption of sampling from a normal population cannot be taken lightly when testing hypotheses about population variances (see Scheffé, 1959, Chapter 10). If the population is non-normal—particularly with respect to kurtosis—the probability of a type-I error can differ considerably from the nominal $\alpha$, as we shall see in Section 16.9. Testing for normality is treated in Section 13.11.

## 16.6 F-DISTRIBUTIONS[5]

Before considering procedures for testing if two variance estimates differ significantly, a brief introduction to the $F$-distribution will be helpful, since it is used in testing $H_0$: $\sigma_1^2 = \sigma_2^2$. Imagine that a chi-square value with ten degrees of freedom $\chi_{10}^2$ is formed from $z_1^2 + \ldots + z_{10}^2$. Now suppose a second, *independent* chi-square variable with five degrees of freedom $\chi_5^2$ is formed by sampling $z$-scores from a normal distribution, squaring, and summing the five $z_i^2$'s. The ratio called an *F-ratio* with ten and five degrees of freedom is formed as follows:

$$F_{\nu_1,\nu_2} = \frac{\dfrac{\chi_{\nu_1}^2}{\nu_1}}{\dfrac{\chi_{\nu_1}^2}{\nu_2}} = F_{10,5} = \frac{\dfrac{\chi_{10}^2}{10}}{\dfrac{\chi_5^2}{5}} \qquad \textbf{(16.6)}$$

$F$-distributions with $\nu_1$ degrees of freedom for the numerator and $\nu_2$ degrees of freedom for the denominator have the following properties:

1. They are unimodal. The mode is $[\nu_2(\nu_1 - 2)]/[\nu_1(\nu_2 + 2)]$ for $\nu_1 \geq 1$.

[4] If a one-tailed test had been planned with $H_1$: $\sigma^2 > 225$ and with $\alpha_1 = .10$, then the critical value, $_{.90}\chi_{29}^2$ equals 39.09.

[5] An understanding of the theory in Section 16.6, like Section 16.2, is not essential to make tests of $H_0$: $\sigma_1^2 = \sigma_2^2$.

**TABLE 16.1** Characteristics of Various F-distributions: $F_{v1,v2}$

| | | $v_1 = 1$ | | | $v_1 = 3$ | | | | $v_1 = 10$ | | | |
|---|---|---|---|---|---|---|---|---|---|---|---|---|
| $v_2$ | $\mu$ | $_{.50}F$ | $\Omega$ | $\sigma$ | Mode | $_{.50}F$ | $\Omega$ | $\sigma$ | Mode | $_{.50}F$ | $\Omega$ | $\sigma$ |
| 5 | 1.67 | .53 | .35 | 4.71 | .24 | .91 | .43 | 3.33 | .57 | 1.01 | .41 | 2.69 |
| 10 | 1.25 | .49 | .58 | 2.17 | .28 | .85 | .70 | 1.38 | .67 | 1.00 | .60 | .97 |
| 25 | 1.09 | .47 | .66 | 1.64 | .31 | .81 | .78 | .99 | .74 | .96 | .57 | .61 |
| 50 | 1.04 | .46 | .68 | 1.52 | .32 | .80 | .80 | .90 | .77 | .95 | .52 | .52 |
| 100 | 1.02 | .46 | .70 | 1.42 | .33 | .79 | .80 | .86 | .78 | .94 | .50 | .48 |
| $\infty$ | 1.00 | .46 | .71 | 1.41 | .33 | .79 | .80 | .82 | .80 | .93 | .44 | .45 |

| $v_1 = 25$ | | | | $v_1 = 100$ | | | | $v_1 = 500$ | | | |
|---|---|---|---|---|---|---|---|---|---|---|---|
| Mode | $_{.50}F$ | $\Omega$ | $\sigma$ | Mode | $_{.50}F$ | $\Omega$ | $\sigma$ | Mode | $_{.50}F$ | $\Omega$ | $\sigma$ |
| .66 | 1.12 | .41 | 2.49 | .70 | 1.14 | .41 | 2.39 | .71 | 1.15 | .41 | 2.36 |
| .76 | 1.04 | .59 | .83 | .82 | 1.06 | .58 | .75 | .83 | 1.07 | .57 | .73 |
| .85 | 1.00 | .52 | .46 | .91 | 1.02 | .49 | .37 | .92 | 1.03 | .49 | .34 |
| .88 | .99 | .53 | .37 | .94 | 1.01 | .39 | .26 | .96 | 1.02 | .36 | .23 |
| .90 | .98 | .36 | .33 | .96 | 1.00 | .29 | .21 | .98 | 1.01 | .25 | .16 |
| .92 | .97 | .29 | .28 | .98 | .99 | .14 | .14 | 1.00 | 1.00 | .07 | .06 |

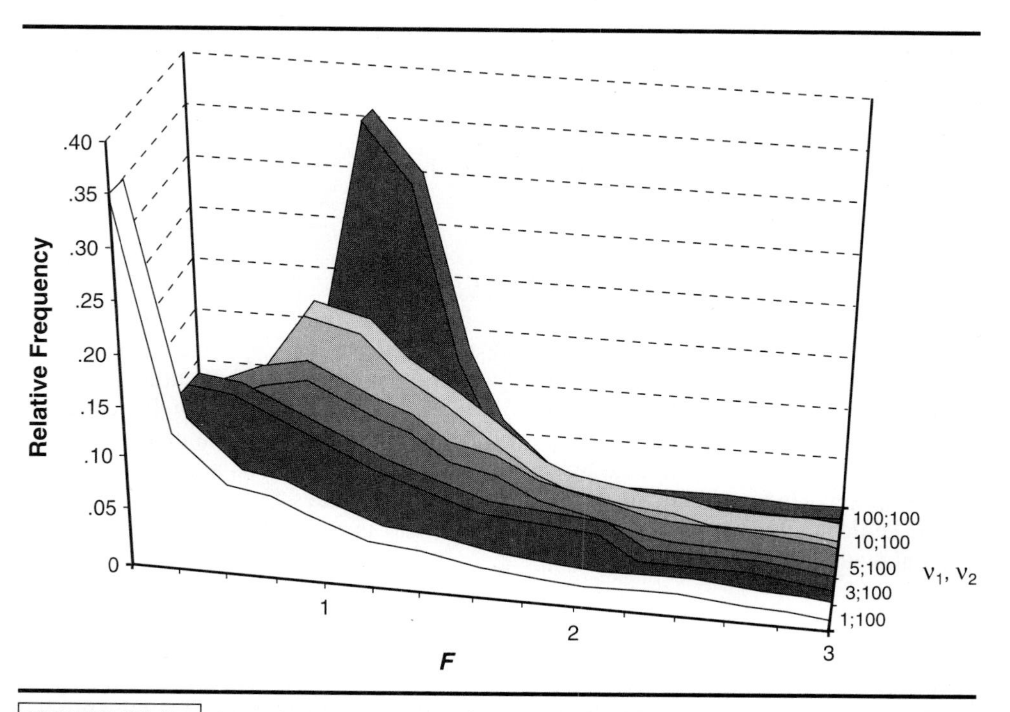


**FIGURE 16.5** Central F-distributions for $v_1 = 1, 3, 5, 10$ and 100, with $v_2 = 100$.

2. They are positively skewed.
3. They have a median of 1 when $\nu_1 = \nu_2$. If $\nu_2 > \nu_1$, the median $({}_{.50}F_{\nu_1,\nu_2})$ is less than 1.
4. They have a mean equal to $\nu_2/(\nu_2 - 2)$ for $\nu_2 > 2$. Thus, $\mu \approx 1$ when $\nu_2$ is large.
5. They have a variance equal to $[2\nu_2^2(\nu_1 + \nu_2 - 2)]/[\nu_1(\nu_2 - 4)(\nu_2 - 2)^2]$.

Descriptive data on selected $F$-distributions are given in Table 16.1 and Figure 16.5.

1. As $\nu_2$ increases, the mean of the $F$-distribution approaches its limit of 1; this average is unaffected by $\nu_1$.
2. As $\nu_2$ increases, the mode increases, but the median decreases.
3. The variance decreases as $\nu_2$ increases.
4. The distribution is skewed substantially unless both $\nu_1$ and $\nu_2$ are very large.

## 16.7 INFERENCES ABOUT TWO INDEPENDENT VARIANCES: $H_0$: $\sigma_1^2 = \sigma_2^2$

1. Testing the **hypothesis** that two variances are equal is much more common than testing the hypothesis that a population has a variance equal to some numerical value. Suppose you wish to test the hypothesis that the variances of populations 1 and 2 ($\sigma_1^2$ and $\sigma_2^2$) are equal:

$$H_0\text{: } \sigma_1^2 = \sigma_2^2$$
$$H_1\text{: } \sigma_1^2 \neq \sigma_2^2$$

2. It is **assumed** that a sample of size $n_1$ is drawn at random from a normal population with mean $\mu_1$ and variance $\sigma_1^2$. An *independent* random sample of size $n_2$ is drawn from a second normal population with mean $\mu_2$ and variance $\sigma_2^2$. The values of $\mu_1$ and $\mu_2$ are irrelevant in testing $H_0$.
3. The **test statistic** for testing $H_0$ against $H_1$ is the ratio, $F$, of the two sample variances:

$$F = \frac{s_1^2}{s_2^2} \qquad \textbf{(16.7)}$$

4. When $H_0$: $\sigma_1^2 = \sigma_2^2$ is true, the sampling distribution of $F = s_1^2/s_2^2$ is the $F$-distribution with $\nu_1 = n_1 - 1$ and $\nu_2 = n_2 - 1$. When $H_1$: $\sigma_1^2 \neq \sigma_2^2$ is true, the distribution of $s_1^2/s_2^2$ is equal to $\sigma_1^2/\sigma_2^2$ times the $F$-distribution with $\nu_1$ and $\nu_2$ degrees of freedom. For example, if $\sigma_1^2/\sigma_2^2 = 2$, the distribution of $s_1^2/s_2^2$ will look like the $F_{\nu_1,\nu_2}$-distribution in which the elements have been transformed by a multiplicative factor of 2; its mean and standard deviation would be double (Sections. 4.8 and 5.11) the values given in Table 16.1.
5. The **critical values** against which $F$ in Equation 16.7 is compared in testing $H_0$ against $H_1$ at the $\alpha_2$-level of significance are:

$${}_{\alpha/2}F_{\nu_1,\nu_2} \text{ and } {}_{1-\alpha/2}F_{\nu_1,\nu_2}$$

that is, the $100(\alpha/2)$ and $100[1 - (\alpha/2)]$ percentile points in the $F$-distribution with $\nu_1$ and $\nu_2$ degrees of freedom. For example if $\alpha = .10$, the 5th and 95th percentiles are the critical values. The upper percentile points in the $F$-distributions can be read directly from Table F. The lower percentile points are related to the upper percentiles in the manner denoted below.[6] Assuming $\alpha = .10$:

$$ {}_{.05}F_{\nu_2,\nu_1} = \frac{1}{{}_{.95}F_{\nu_1,\nu_2}} \quad \textbf{(16.8)} $$

The critical $F$-ratios in Table F are correct as they stand for a directional test (Section 11.13) of $H_0$: $\sigma_1^2 = \sigma_2^2$, in which the designation of group 1 is made prior to data collection. Thus $s_1^2$ will be placed in the numerator of Equation 16.7 even when it is smaller in value than $s_2^2$. Note, for example, if $\alpha_1 = .05$, $\nu_1 = 20$ and $\nu_2 = 40$, the critical $F$-ratio is ${}_{.95}F_{20,40} = 1.84$. Thus, if $s_1^2 = 200$ and $s_2^2 = 100$, then $F = 2.00$ and $H_0$: $\sigma_1^2 = \sigma_2^2$ is rejected at $\alpha_1 = .05$. However, what if $s_1^2 = 100$ and $s_2^2 = 200$? In that case, $F = .50$ and $H_0$ would have been judged tenable.

For nondirectional tests (e.g., $H_0$: $\sigma_1^2 = \sigma_2^2$ against $H_1$: $\sigma_1^2 \neq \sigma_2^2$), the use of Equation 16.8 to obtain the lesser critical $F$-ratio can be bypassed by defining the larger of the two sample variances as $s_1^2$; thus, the observed $F$-ratio will never take a value less than 1. However, the $\alpha$-value used in Table F must then be halved when a nondirectional test has not been employed. Thus, if $\alpha_2 = .05$, the observed ratio of the independent variances for two samples is 2.66, and the numerator and denominator have 10 and 15 degrees of freedom, respectively, the critical $F$-ratio is not ${}_{.95}F_{10,15} = 2.54$, but ${}_{.975}F_{10,15} = 3.06$; and in this example, $.05 < p < .10$, and $H_0$ remains tenable.

6. **Confidence intervals** set separately about each variance, using the procedures outlined in Section 16.5, are usually more meaningful than a confidence interval about the ratio of the two variances. Nevertheless, the .90 (or other $1 - \alpha$) confidence interval on the ratio of $\sigma_1^2$ to $\sigma_2^2$ can be constructed as follows:

$$ .90CI = {}_{.05}F_{\nu_2,\nu_1}\left(\frac{s_1^2}{s_2^2}\right) < \frac{\sigma_1^2}{\sigma_2^2} < {}_{.95}F_{\nu_2,\nu_1}\left(\frac{s_1^2}{s_2^2}\right) \quad \textbf{(16.9)} $$

Since Table F is constructed for one-tailed hypotheses concerning $\sigma_1^2$ and $\sigma_2^2$, where the numerator of the $F$-test is selected a priori, great care is required in obtaining the critical $F$-ratio for nondirectional hypotheses concerning $\sigma_1^2$ and $\sigma_2^2$. The Hartley (Section 16.8) and Bartlett (Section 16.9) tests are alternative methods for testing for homogeneity of variance that have the additional advantage of being able to test $J \geq 2$ variances.

7. **Example.** Are men more variable in height than women? Since we have no clear basis for making a direction hypothesis, we set $\alpha_2 = .05$ for testing the nondirectional test of $H_0$: $\sigma_M^2 = \sigma_F^2$. One study of 201 adult males and 206 adult females in the U.S. observed standard deviations of standing heights to be 6.69 cm (2.63″) and 5.47 cm (2.15″), respectively. The larger sample variance (6.69 cm) is placed in the numerator of Equation 16.7; thus, the test statistic, $F$, equals $(6.69)^2/(5.47)^2 = 1.496$.

---

[6]Notice that $\nu_1$ and $\nu_2$ switch positions, for example, ${}_{.05}F_{7,9} = 1/({}_{.95}F_{9,7}) = 1/4.82 = 0.21$.

The critical-$F$ is ${}_{.975}F_{200,205} \approx {}_{.975}F_{200,200} = 1.32$; since the observed $F$-ratio (1.50) exceeds the critical $F$-ratio (1.32), the null hypothesis can be rejected at $\alpha_2 = .05$. (Indeed, $H_0$ can be rejected at $\alpha_2 = .02$ since $1.496 > 1.39 = {}_{.99}F_{200,200}$.) The $.95CI$ on $\sigma_M^2/\sigma_F^2$ can be constructed using Equation 16.9. Equation 16.8 is used to find ${}_{.025}F_{200,205}$: ${}_{.025}F_{200,205} \approx 1/{}_{.975}F_{205,200} \approx 1/1.32 = .76$, and:

$$.95CI = .76(1.496) < \frac{\sigma_M^2}{\sigma_F^2} < 1.32(1.496)$$

$$= 1.14 < \frac{\sigma_M^2}{\sigma_F^2} < 1.98$$

$$.95CI = (1.14,\ 1.98)$$

Thus, the population variance of male heights, $\sigma_M^2$, is estimated to be at least 14%, and perhaps as much as 98%, greater than the population variance of females[7], $\sigma_F^2$.

8. In the past, it was customary to test $H_0$: $\sigma_1^2 = \sigma_2^2$ prior to performing a $t$-test of the hypothesis $H_0$: $\mu_1 - \mu_2 = 0$. The initial hypothesis is a statement of the homogeneous variances assumption. Textbooks of the time advised not to proceed with the conventional $t$-test (Section 12.4) if $s_1^2/s_2^2$ led to rejection of $H_0$: $\sigma_1^2 = \sigma_2^2$, since homogeneity of variance is assumed in the derivation of the $t$-test. Although such advice stemmed from an admirable concern for meeting the assumptions of the test employed, it proved to be unnecessary if $n_1 = n_2$ (see Figure 12.3). In other words, the $t$-test of $H_0$: $\mu_1 = \mu_2$ is robust with respect to the homogeneity of variance assumption when samples sizes are approximately equal.

   The assumption that $s_1^2$ and $s_2^2$ are derived from independent samples from populations that are *normally* distributed also underlies the $F$-test for homogeneity of variance (Equation 16.7). Unfortunately, unlike the normality assumption underlying the $t$-test of means, non-normality can have a moderate effect on the accuracy of tests of homogeneity of variance (Box, 1953; Glass, Peckham, & Sanders, 1972). In particular, the preliminary test of homogeneous variances is affected by non-normality of the populations (even though this non-normality is of no consequence to the validity of the $t$-test of $H_0$: $\mu_1 - \mu_2 = 0$). In a balanced design ($n_1 = n_2$), there is no reason to test $H_0$: $\sigma_1^2 = \sigma_2^2$, or to be concerned about violation of the homogeneity of variance assumption. Recall that the Welch and Brown-Forsythe tests (Sections 12.11 and 15.25) are safer tests for evaluating $H_0$: $\mu_1 = \mu_2 = \ldots = \mu_J$ with unbalanced designs.

## 16.8 TESTING HOMOGENEITY OF VARIANCE: HARTLEY'S $F_{max}$ TEST

There are several statistical tests for testing the hypothesis of homogeneity of variance (HOV), $H_0$: $\sigma_1^2 = \sigma_2^2 = \ldots = \sigma_J^2$. In Section 16.7, we saw that when $J = 2$ the ratio of the larger variance to the smaller variance has a central $F_{\nu_{larger}, \nu_{smaller}}$ distribution, where the criti-

[7]Expressed in terms of standard deviations: $\sigma_{Male}$ is somewhere between 7% and 41% greater than $\sigma_{Female}$.

cal $F$ is ${}_{1-\alpha/2}F_{\nu_{\text{larger}}, \nu_{\text{smaller}}}$ for $\alpha_2$. Frequently, there are more than two groups to be compared, that is, $J \geq 2$.

1. *Hartley's $F_{max}$ test* is a very simple and quick omnibus test of the **statistical hypothesis**, $H_0$: $\sigma_1^2 = \sigma_2^2 = \ldots = \sigma_J^2$, where each of the $J$ $s_j^2$'s is based on $n$ independent observations. The $F_{max}$ test is designed for situations where $n_1 = n_2 = \ldots = n_J$. The alternative hypothesis, $H_1$, is that at least one of the $J\sigma^2$'s differs from one or more of the others.
2. The sampling distribution of $F_{max}$ when $H_0$ is true **assumes** each of the $J$ variance estimates, $s_j^2$, is based on an independent random sample of $n$ observations from a population in which the observations are normally distributed.
3. The **test statistic** $F_{max}$ is the ratio of the largest $s_j^2$ to the smallest $s_j^2$ in the set of $J$ $s_j^2$'s.

$$F = \frac{s^2_{\text{largest}}}{s^2_{\text{smallest}}} \tag{16.10}$$

4. The **sampling distribution** of $F_{max}$ was derived by Hartley (1950).
5. **Critical values** for the $F_{max}$ test, ${}_{1-\alpha}F_{\max_{J},\, \nu_j}$ (where $\nu_j = n - 1$), are given in Table H for $\alpha = .05$ and $\alpha = .01$. Note that the table is entered using the degrees of freedom within each of the $J$ groups, $\nu_j = n - 1$.
6. When $J \geq 3$, confidence intervals are not very meaningful. **Confidence intervals** set separately about each variance, using the procedures outlined in Section 16.5, are usually more meaningful than a confidence interval about the ratio of the two variances. Equation 16.5 can be used to form *CI*'s for each of the $J$ variances.
7. **Example.** In Problem and Exercise 5 following Chapter 15: $s_1^2 = 2.49$, $s_2^2 = 1.78$, $s_3^2 = 2.54$, and $n_1 = n_2 = n_3 = n = 10$; thus, the values of $s^2_{\text{largest}}$ and $s^2_{\text{smallest}}$ are 2.54 and 1.78, respectively. From Equation 16.10:

$$F = \frac{s^2_{\text{largest}}}{s^2_{\text{smallest}}} = \frac{2.54}{1.78} = 1.43$$

From Table H, the critical $F_{max}$-value at $\alpha = .05$ for $J = 3$ and $\nu_j = n - 1 = 9$ is found to be ${}_{.95}F_{\max 3,9} = 5.34$; thus, $H_0$ is tenable ($p > .05$).
8. The $F_{max}$ test is less powerful than the Bartlett test (Section 16.9). In addition, it is designed for balanced designs. Its chief use is in situations where a quick and simple test is needed, such as when one is reading research that has ignored equal-population-variance issues.[8]

[8]The *Cochran test* is another common test of homogeneity of variance; it is very similar to the Hartley test; it uses the ratio $C$, where $C$ is the ratio of the largest of the $J$ variances compared to the sum of the $J$ variances: $C = s^2_{\text{largest}}/\Sigma_j s_j^2$. Like the Hartley, it requires a special table for obtaining critical values. The Cochran also has the serious limitation of requiring a balanced design. Recall from Figure 12.3 that a test of homogeneity of variance is needed to justify the $t$-test of means (as well as ANOVA, Chapter 15) only when the $n_j$'s differ—precisely the situation for which the Hartley and Cochran tests fail us!

## 16.9 TESTING HOMOGENEITY OF VARIANCE FROM *J* INDEPENDENT SAMPLES: THE BARTLETT TEST

The Bartlett test requires the use of logarithms; this impeded its use until the past decade or so when powerful and inexpensive hand calculators became available.[9] Unlike the $F_{max}$ omnibus HOV test, the Bartlett test can accommodate unequal $n$'s.

1. $H_0$: $\sigma_1^2 = \sigma_2^2 = \ldots = \sigma_J^2$; the alternative **hypothesis** is that at least one of the $J$ variances differs from at least one other.
2. It is **assumed** that a sample of $n_j$ observations was randomly and independently drawn from each of the normal populations.
3. The **test statistic** for testing $H_0$ against $H_1$ uses the chi-square distribution:[10]

$$\chi^2 = \nu_W \mathrm{Ln} s_W^2 - \sum_j \nu_j \mathrm{Ln} s_j^2 \quad \textbf{(16.11)}$$

where $\nu_j = n_j - 1$, $\nu_W = \Sigma_j \nu_j$, and $\mathrm{Ln}s_W{}^2$ is the natural logarithm of the within-group variance (see Equation 12.3).

4. When $\sigma_1{}^2 = \sigma_2{}^2 = \ldots = \sigma_J{}^2$ is true, the **sampling distribution** of the $\chi^2$ statistic obtained using Equation 16.11 is closely approximated by the chi-square distribution with $J - 1$ degrees of freedom. If $s_1{}^2 = s_2{}^2 = \ldots = s_J{}^2$, then $\Sigma_j \nu_j \mathrm{Ln}s_j^2 = \nu_W \mathrm{Ln}s_W^2$; otherwise, the latter term is larger, that is, $\nu_W \mathrm{Ln}s_W{}^2 \geq \Sigma_j \nu_j \mathrm{Ln}s_j^2$.
5. The **critical value** for $\chi^2$ at the $\alpha$-level of significance is ${}_{1-\alpha}\chi_\nu{}^2$, where $\nu = J - 1$ degrees of freedom.
6. **Confidence intervals** are not meaningful when $J > 2$ (see Equation 16.9 for $J = 2$). Equation 16.5 can be used to form the $CI$ for each $\sigma_j^2$.
7. **Example.** From the case study data the variance estimates given in Table 16.2 were obtained for each of five age groups. Is the heterogeneity greater within certain groups than within other groups? The computation of Bartlett's test ($\alpha$ =.05) is illustrated in Table 16.2. The observed $\chi^2$-value of 2.04 is less than the critical value of 9.49; thus, the

---

[9]Except for math and physical science majors, most students once learned, but promptly forgot, how to use Log tables ("mantissa," "characteristic," etc. . . . confusing, remember?). Hand calculators have rendered those nasty Log tables (along with the slide rule) obsolete. (Technology is not all bad.) The Bartlett test can be properly applied with little or no understanding of logarithms, even though the concept of logarithms is not particularly difficult.

The "Log" of a number, $N$, is simply the power (exponent) to which a certain fixed number (the "base") must be raised to yield $N$. "Common" logarithms use 10 as the base. The Log of 100 is 2 because $10^2 = 100$; and equivalently, Log100 = 2; or more explicitly, $\mathrm{Log}_{10}100 = 2$. The Log of 10 is 1; thus, numbers between 10 and 100 will have Logs that are greater than 1, but less than 2. More generally, the Log of a number $N$ is $p$ if $10^p = N$, or, $\mathrm{Log}N = p$.

"Natural" Logs use, not a base reference number of 10, but the "natural" number, "$e$" ($e$ = 2.718 ...). The natural Log ($\mathrm{Log}_e$ or Ln) of a number, $N$, is $x$ if $N = e^x$, that is $\mathrm{Ln}N = x$. The natural Log of 10 is 2.3026 because $e^{2.3026} = 2.718^{2.3026} = 10$. Scientific hand calculators yield the common Log of a number by entering the number, then pressing the [log] key; if instead, the key [ln] were pressed, the natural Log is given. Natural Logs can be easily converted to common Logs and vice versa: 2.3026Ln$N$ = Log$N$. It is nice to have been liberated from the pain and busywork of Log tables!

[10]Or the $F$-distribution, if Box's computation modification is used (as it is in SPSS programs).

null hypothesis is retained at the .05 level of significance. These data give no convincing evidence to suggest that the five age groups differ in heterogeneity with respect to cholesterol level.

8. The Bartlett test assumes the parent populations are normally distributed and yields accurate results when this assumption is met.[11] If distributions have positive kurtosis (i.e., are leptokurtic), the Bartlett test is liberal (i.e., the probability of a type-I error is greater than $\alpha$) (Hopkins & Weeks, 1990). If distributions have negative kurtosis (platykurtic curves, such as rectangular distributions), the Bartlett test is conservative, that is, it will reject a true $H_0$ with probability less than $\alpha$. If the non-normality is due to skewness, the Bartlett test is liberal, that is, it will reject a true $H_0$ with probability greater than $\alpha$ [because skewed distributions are also leptokurtic (Section 6.9)]. Thus, if $H_0$ is tenable and the distributions have positive kurtosis, one can be confident that $H_0$: $\sigma_1^2 = \sigma_2^2 = \ldots = \sigma_J^2$ remains tenable.

**TABLE 16.2** Computation of Bartlett's Test of Homogeneity of Variance: Cholesterol Levels for Five Age Groups.

| Group | $s$ | $s_j^2$ | $n_j$ | $\nu_j$ | $\nu_j s_j^2$ | $Lns_j^2$ | $\nu_j Ln\ s_j^2$ |
|---|---|---|---|---|---|---|---|
| 20–29 | 59.98 | 3,597.6 | 36 | 35 | 125,916.0 | 8.188 | 286.5808 |
| 30–39 | 57.36 | 3,290.2 | 45 | 44 | 144,767.5 | 8.099 | 356.3426 |
| 40–49 | 57.37 | 3,291.3 | 58 | 57 | 187,605.1 | 8.099 | 461.6455 |
| 50–59 | 66.80 | 4,462.2 | 44 | 43 | 191,876.3 | 8.403 | 361.3465 |
| 60–69 | 52.00 | 2,704.0 | 17 | 16 | 43,264.0 | 7.902 | 126.4398 |
| | | | 200 | 195 | 693,428.9 | | 1,592.355 |
| | | | ($n_\bullet$) | ($\nu_W$) | ($\Sigma_j \nu_j s_j$) | | ($\Sigma_j \nu_j$Ln $s_j^2$) |

$s_W^2 = \Sigma \nu_j s_j^2/\nu_W = 693{,}428.9/195 = 3{,}556.045$; Ln $s_W^2 = 8.1764$[12]

$\chi^2 = \nu_W \text{Ln}\ s_W^2 - \Sigma_j \nu_j \text{Ln}\ s_j^2$

$\chi^2 = 195(8.1764) - 1{,}592.355 = 2.0438$[13]

${}_{.95}\chi_4^2 = 9.49$; $H_0$: $\sigma_1^2 = \sigma_2^2 = \sigma_3^2 = \sigma_4^2$ is tenable[14]

[11] Some sources (e.g., Snedecor & Cochran, 1980) suggest that $n_j$ should be greater than 5 before the Bartlett test is used, but when the normality condition is present, the test provides accurate results for $n_j \geq 3$ (Weston, Marion, Durrand, & Hopkins, 1995).

[12] In Chapter 15, it was stated that an alias for "$s_W^2$" is "Mean Square Within" ($MS_W$), and an alias for "$\Sigma_j \nu_j s_j^2$" is "Sum of Squares Within." In a one-factor ANOVA, $MS_W$ is always computed; thus, the only additional computation required is to find the sum of the natural logs of the variance for each of the *J* groups.

[13] Actual $p = .84$ (from EXCEL spreadsheet).

[14] The $\chi^2$-value obtained from Equation 16.11 is very slightly positively biased, that is, it is inflated to a very small degree. If the computed $\chi^2$-value exceeds the critical $\chi^2$-value by only a small degree, you should correct for the bias by dividing the computed $\chi^2$ by (1 + A), where A = $\{1/[3(J-1)]\}[\Sigma_j(1/\nu_j) - (1/\nu_W)]$. For the data in Table 16.2, A = $\{1/[3(5-1)]\}[.1546 - (1/195)] = .01246$; hence, the $\chi^2$ obtained after correcting for bias = $\chi^2/(1 + A) = 2.0438/1.01246 = 2.019$. The correction is almost always superfluous, but should be programmed into any spreadsheet or computer program. The *F*-distribution is an alternative to the $\chi^2$ distribution for testing the null hypothesis for the Bartlett test; the procedure which employs the *F*-test is sometimes referred to as the "Bartlett-Box" test (SPSS, 1991, p. 181).

Fortunately, most non-normal distributions are skewed and, hence, are leptokurtic (Hopkins & Weeks, 1990). Consequently, if the Bartlett test finds the null hypothesis tenable, we can be confident that indeed it is.

## 16.10 OTHER TESTS OF HOMOGENEITY OF VARIANCE: THE LEVENE AND BROWN-FORSYTHE TESTS

The *Levene test* is equivalent to an ANOVA (or $t$-test when $J = 2$), not of the observations ($X_i$'s), but of the absolute deviations of the observations from the mean of their respective groups. In other words, if $\overline{X}_1 = 10$, a score of 14 becomes 4 ($|14 - 10| = 4$); likewise, a score of 3 becomes 7 ($|3 - 10|) = 7$). Obviously, the mean of the absolute deviations $\Sigma|\overline{X}_{ij} - \overline{X}_j|/n = (\Sigma|X - \overline{X}|/n = \Sigma|x|/n)$ will be larger for groups with greater heterogeneity. The Levene test has become popular (it is used almost exclusively in certain statistical computer programs) due to a fallacy—it is thought to be robust with respect to the normality assumption, but it is not (Weston, Marion, Durrand, & Hopkins, 1995). In addition, there is a critical flaw in the logic of using the Levene test to validate the HOV assumption for purposes of testing $H_0$: $\mu_1 = \mu_2$ via the $t$-test or ANOVA. Because the Levene uses ANOVA (or a $t$-test), it rests on the same HOV assumption (but now of the $|x_i|$'s, not the $X_i$'s)[15]. Consequently, the Levene test yields accurate probability statements only when the design is balanced (but when the design is balanced, the $t$-test and ANOVA are robust with respect to the HOV assumption, and no HOV preliminary test is needed when testing hypotheses about means). Furthermore, since the Levene $H_0$: $\sigma_1^2 = \sigma_2^2 = \ldots = \sigma_J^2$ employs absolute deviations, the distributions of the $|x|$'s are always extremely skewed (see Figure 6.6). Contrary to popular opinion, the Levene is at least as sensitive to non-normality as the Bartlett, Hartley, or Cochran tests. It is rarely the "test of choice" for testing $H_0$: $\sigma_1^2 = \sigma_2^2 = \ldots = \sigma_J^2$, and is included in the text only because it will be encountered in research literature.

A test that has been found to be quite insensitive to departures from normality (Conover, Johnson, & Johnson, 1981; Olejnik & Algina, 1987) was proposed by Brown and Forsythe[16] (1974b). The test is similar to the Levene test; it uses an ANOVA to compare the mean absolute value of the difference between each observation and its group *median*. The Brown-Forsythe (1974) test has been shown to give type-I error rates that are quite accurate (for $\alpha = .05$) even when parent populations differ substantially from the normal distribution in both skewness and kurtosis (Olejnik & Algina, 1987). If the sizes of the samples differ greatly, the test faces the same infinite regress assumption problem as does the Levene.[17] This problem can be obviated by using a test that does not assume homogeneity of variance of the $|x_{ij}|$'s (i.e., the absolute values of the deviations) across the $J$ groups. When $J = 2$, the

[15]Note that a test of homogeneity of variance of the $|x|$'s is needed to legitimize the Levene test assumption that the mean deviations for the $J$ populations are equal. To test the HOV assumption, the Levene would then need to test the hypothesis that the $J$ means of absolute deviation from the mean absolute deviation within each group are equal, a logical sequence of testing which continues ad infinitum.

[16]This a different test than the Brown-Forsythe test in Section 15.25.

[17]Another test that is thought to be relatively insensitive to departures from normality has been proposed by Scheffé (1959, pp. 83–87); this test is discussed and illustrated in Glass and Hopkins (1984, Section 16.23). When sample sizes differ substantially, Scheffé suggests randomly assigning observations to groups of approximately equal size for testing homogeneity of variance via ANOVA (absolute deviations from the median). This would solve the "infinite regress assumption" problem. Multiple comparison procedures (Chapter 17) would need to be used if the null hypothesis were rejected.

Welch $t'$ (Section 12.11) serves this purpose; when $J > 2$, the Welch $F'$ or the Brown-Forsythe $F^*$ (Section 15.25) tests can be used. If the $n$'s do not differ *greatly*, another acceptable option for purposes of testing $H_0$: $\sigma_1^2 = \sigma_2^2 = \ldots = \sigma_J^2$ is to randomly discard cases until the $n$'s are equal, then use the Brown-Forsythe test. If the distributions have positive kurtosis, the Brown-Forsythe is the method of choice. If the distributions do not differ markedly from a normal distribution, the Bartlett test is preferred.[18]

## 16.11 INFERENCES ABOUT $H_0$: $\sigma_1^2 = \sigma_2^2$ WITH PAIRED OBSERVATIONS

1. As in Section 16.7, the null **hypothesis** being tested here is that the two variance parameters, $\sigma_1^2$ and $\sigma_2^2$, are equal:

$$H_0: \sigma_1^2 = \sigma_2^2$$
$$H_1: \sigma_1^2 \neq \sigma_2^2$$

2. It is **assumed** that the population distributions of paired observations, $X_1$ and $X_2$, are normally distributed. Since the observations are paired, a non-zero correlation ($\rho_{12}$) is expected. (The values of $\mu_1$ and $\mu_2$ are irrelevant here.) A common example of paired observations results when pretest and posttest scores are obtained on the same group of persons.
3. The **test statistic** used in testing $H_0$ against $H_1$ is:

$$t = \frac{s_1^2 - s_2^2}{\sqrt{\frac{4s_1^2 s_2^2}{n-2}(1 - r_{12}^2)}} = \frac{s_1^2 - s_2^2}{2s_1 s_2 \sqrt{\frac{1 - r_{12}^2}{\nu}}} \quad (16.12)$$

where $s_1^2$ and $s_2^2$ are the sample variances of the observations in samples 1 and 2, respectively, $n$ is the number of *pairs* of observations, and $r_{12}$ is the correlation coefficient between the paired observations for the sample of $n$ pairs.
4. When $H_0$: $\sigma_1^2 = \sigma_2^2$ is true, the **sampling distribution** of $t$ in Equation 16.12 is Student's $t$-distribution with $\nu = n - 2$ degrees of freedom.
5. The critical values for testing $H_0$ against $H_1$ at the $\alpha$-level of significance are:

$$_{\alpha/2}t_\nu \text{ and } _{1-\alpha/2}t_\nu, \text{ or } |t_\nu| = {}_{1-\alpha/2}t_\nu$$

6. A **confidence interval** for $\sigma_1^2$ or $\sigma_2^2$ can be obtained using the procedures described in Section 16.5.
7. **Example:** Table 5.2 gives the standard deviations for systolic blood pressure (SBP = $X_1$) and diastolic blood pressure (DBP = $X_2$) for the 200 persons in the case study: $s_1 = 16.7$ and $s_2 = 10.0$. Table 7.11 reports the correlation between SBP and DBP: $r_{12} = .80$. Since

[18]Note that neither the Levene nor the Brown-Forsythe test checks the homogeneity of variance assumption *directly*; although highly unlikely, it is possible for variances to be heterogeneous and yet have the mean absolute differences from group means (or medians) equal, and vice-versa.

both measures were obtained on the same individuals, the observations are paired and not independent. These data will be used in the right-hand expression of Equation 16.12 to test $H_0$: $\sigma_1^2 = \sigma_2^2$ at $\alpha_2 = .01$: $s_1^2 = (16.7)^2 = 278.89$ and $s_2^2 = (10.0)^2 = 100.00$, $n = 200$, $\nu = 198$, and $r_{12} = .80$.

$$t = \frac{278.89 - 100.00}{2(16.7)(10.0)\sqrt{\frac{1-(.80)^2}{198}}} = \frac{178.89}{334(.04264)} = \frac{178.89}{14.24} = 12.56$$

The critical value for $|t|$ with which the obtained $t$ of 12.56 is compared when $\alpha_2 = .01$ is found in Table C: ${}_{.995}t_{198} \approx {}_{.995}t_{200} = 2.601$; thus, the null hypothesis is rejected. Indeed, $H_0$ can be easily rejected even at the .001 level (12.56 > 3.340).

The .95*CI*'s for $\sigma_1$ and $\sigma_2$ are (9.2, 10.9) and (15.4, 18.2), respectively. We see that the evidence is convincing that in the population sampled the variability in the SBP measures, $\sigma_1^2$, is greater than the variability in the DBP measures, $\sigma_2^2$. The probability of obtaining a value of $t$ as discrepant from zero as that obtained is much less than .001 if $\sigma_1^2$ is truly equal to $\sigma_2^2$.

## 16.12 RELATIONSHIPS AMONG THE NORMAL, $t$, $\chi^2$, AND $F$-DISTRIBUTIONS

The $t$, $\chi^2$, and $F$-distributions are all derived from the normal distribution. In each instance, sampling from a normal distribution underlies the new distribution. For example, a chi-square variable is formed by summing squared $z$-scores from the unit-normal distribution. Chi-square distributions are combined to form $F$-distributions. The relationships among the various families of distributions will be made explicit in this section.

It was noted earlier that a $t$-distribution with $\nu = \infty$ is the normal distribution.[19] Consider, then, the *square* of the $t$-variable with $\nu$ degrees of freedom:

$$t_\nu^2 = \frac{z^2}{\frac{\chi_\nu^2}{\nu}} \quad \textbf{(16.13)}$$

The numerator of Equation 16.13, $z^2$, is divided by 1, which is a chi-square distribution with $\nu = 1$; the denominator is an independent chi-square variable divided by its degrees of freedom. Stated in different form:

$$t_\nu^2 = \frac{\frac{\chi_1^2}{1}}{\frac{\chi_\nu^2}{\nu}} \quad \textbf{(16.14)}$$

[19]Stated more mathematically: In the limit as $\nu$ approaches $\infty$, the $t$-distribution approaches the normal distribution.

Equation 16.14 is now recognized as the central $F$-distribution with 1 and $\nu$ degrees of freedom in the numerator and denominator, respectively. Therefore, the square of a $t$-variable with $\nu$ degrees of freedom is an $F$-variable with 1 and $\nu$ degrees of freedom.

It is more difficult to prove another interesting relationship, which shall simply be stated: Any $F$-distribution with $\nu$ degrees of freedom for the numerator and infinite degrees of freedom for the denominator is the same as the $\chi^2_\nu$ distribution divided by the constant[20] $\nu$, that is:

$$F_{\nu,\infty} = \frac{\chi^2_\nu}{\nu} \quad \textbf{(16.15)}$$

The $p$th percentile in the $\chi^2_\nu$ distribution is the same as the $p$th percentile in the $\nu(F_{\nu,\infty})$ distribution. However, if the $p$th percentile in the $t$-distribution with $\nu$ degrees of freedom is squared, ${}_pt_\nu^2$, the $|2p - 1|$ percentile in the distribution, ${}_{(2p-1)}F_{1,\nu}$, is obtained. For example, the 95th percentile of the $t_\nu$-distribution is the $2(.95) - 1 = .90 =$ 90th percentile of the $t_\nu^2 = F_{1,\nu}$-distribution. (This is true because 5% of the cases exceed the 95th percentile in $t_\nu$ and 5% lie below the 5th percentile. When the $t$ values are squared both the top 5% and the bottom 5% take on a positive sign; hence, 10% of the values in $F_{1,\nu}$ exceed the square of ${}_{.95}t_\nu$.)

## 16.13 CHAPTER SUMMARY

There are two purposes in testing for homogeneity of variance, $H_0$: $\sigma_1^2 = \sigma_2^2 = \ldots = \sigma_J^2$: (1) for the obvious reason, that is, to decide whether one population is more variable than another population, and (2) to assess the tenability of the assumption of homogeneity of variance, which is required for the $t$-test of means, ANOVA, and certain other statistical tests. For practical purposes, violation of the assumption of homogeneity of variance can be disregarded when testing mean differences *only* when sample sizes for each group are equal (see Figure 12.3).

The chi-square distribution is employed for testing $H_0$: $\sigma^2 = K$, for setting a confidence interval for $\sigma^2$ or $\sigma$, and in testing $H_0$: $\sigma_1^2 = \sigma_2^2 = \ldots = \sigma_J^2$ when the Bartlett test is used. The mean of a $\chi^2$-distribution with $\nu$ degrees of freedom is $\nu$, but the most probable (modal) $\chi^2$-value is $\nu - 2$ for $\nu > 1$. The $\chi^2$-distribution is positively skewed, but the skewness decreases as $\nu$ increases. In testing $H_0$: $\sigma^2 = K$, the test statistic $\chi^2 = \nu s^2/\sigma^2$ has $\nu = n - 1$ degrees of freedom, and a critical value of ${}_{1-\alpha}\chi_\nu^2$.

The $F$-distribution is the distribution of the ratio of two independent variance estimates, $s_1^2/s_2^2$; it is used to test $H_0$: $\sigma_1^2 = \sigma_2^2$. Table F gives critical $F$-values for directional (one-tailed) hypotheses, for example, $H_1$: $\sigma_1^2 > \sigma_2^2$, in which sample 1 is predicted to have the larger variance. If *nondirectional* tests of the two independent variances are made, the $\alpha$-value used to obtain critical values in Table F must be *halved*; critical values for all test statistics are always larger with two-tailed tests than with one-tailed tests.

The Bartlett test can test for homogeneity of variance for any number of independent groups, $J$, with equal or unequal $n$'s. The Hartley $F_{max}$ and the Cochran tests of homogeneity of variance require equal $n$'s. The Levene test has a flawed rationale when the $n$'s are not equal, but can be used with tests that do not assume the population variances of the absolute deviations are equal (Section 15.25). The Brown-Forsythe test of homogeneity of variance

[20]The proof depends on the fact that the ratio $\chi\nu^2/\nu = 1$ in the limit as $\nu \rightarrow \infty$.

is similar to the Levene except that the dependent measure is the absolute value of the deviations of each score from the median of its group. For paired observations, a special $t$-test (Equation 16.12) is used to test $H_0$: $\sigma_1^2 = \sigma_2^2$.

All methods of testing for homogeneity of variance assume that the parent populations are normally distributed. Unfortunately, unlike the $t$-test of means in Chapter 12, these tests are not robust when the distributions do not have normal kurtosis ($\gamma_2 = 0$). Leptokurtosis increases the probability of a type-I error; for example, with $\alpha$ set at .05, a true null hypothesis will be rejected in more than 5% of its applications. Consequently, the Bartlett test and other related tests for homogeneity of variance are liberal (i.e., the true $\alpha$ is greater than the nominal $\alpha$) when there is positive kurtosis (i.e., with leptokurtic distributions), and conservative if there is negative kurtosis (i.e., with platykurtic distributions). Highly skewed distributions are also leptokurtic and result in liberal tests. Consequently in such situations, if the Bartlett test does not reject $H_0$, one can be confident that $\sigma_1^2 = \sigma_2^2 = \ldots = \sigma_J^2$ is tenable. The Brown-Forsythe test is less sensitive to departures from normality than the other tests.

## 16.14 CASE STUDY AND COMPUTER ACTIVITY

The Levene test (although it is not the best choice when $n_1 \neq n_2$) is used to test $H_0$: $\sigma_1^2 = \sigma_2^2$ by many popular software programs, including the SPSS and BMDP computer programs; it was used in our SPSS computer analysis of the case study data in Section 12.19. With reference to that computer output, use Equation 16.7 to make a one-tailed test[21] of the $H_0$: $\sigma_1^2 = \sigma_2^2$ for cholesterol level for the two coronary groups with $\alpha_1 = .05$. What is the critical value of $F$?[22] Compare your obtained $p$-value with that for the Levene test (see Section 12.19) after converting the Levene two-tailed $p$ to a one-tailed $p$[23] by dividing it by 2.

Are systolic and diastolic blood pressures equally variable for the case study group? Which equation is appropriate to test the $H_0$: $\sigma_1^2 = \sigma_2^2$? With reference to Tables 5.2 and 7.11, find the needed data and use Equation 13.12 to make a nondirectional test of $H_0$: $\sigma_1^2 = \sigma_2^2$ for this group.[24] Why is homogeneity of variance less critical with the paired $t$-test than with the independent $t$-test?[25]

## MASTERY TEST

1. When can the assumption $\sigma_1^2 = \sigma_2^2$ be disregarded in making a $t$-test for differences between independent means?

---

[21] It is anticipated that the coronary incident group ("1") has the greater variance in cholesterol measures.

[22] Since we a making a one-tailed test, the critical $F$ at $\alpha_1 = .05$ from Table F is ${}_{.95}F_{24,174} \approx 1.61$ (using EXCEL, the precise critical value is found to be 1.580) $> F = (76.12)^2/(62.33)^2 = 1.49$, the null hypothesis is tenable ($.10 > p > .05$) (the precise value of $p$ is .075). If a two-tailed test were employed here, the critical $F$-value is ${}_{.975}F_{24,174} \approx {}_{.975}F_{24,120} = 1.76$.

[23] When a one-tailed test is employed, but a two-tailed $p$ is produced by the computer printout, divide the $p$-value by 2 to get the correct value of $p$ (assuming, of course, that the difference is in the direction that was predicted.) For the Levene, $p = .366/2 = .183$.

[24] $t = (278.89 - 100)/2(16.7)(10)\sqrt{[(1-.80^2)/198]} = 178.89/14.242 = 12.56, p < .001$. See Section 16.11.

[25] Because the two means are always based on the same $n$ with the paired $t$-test, the test is robust with respect to the homogeneity of variance condition.

2. If $n_1 = n_2$, why might one be interested in testing $H_0$: $\sigma_1^2 = \sigma_2^2$?
3. What is the name of the distribution that is formed by the ratio of two independent estimates of $\sigma^2$, that is, $s_1^2/s_2^2$?

*For questions 4 to 7, which distribution, F, t, or $\chi^2$, is ordinarily used for testing the given hypothesis?*

4. $H_0$: $\sigma^2 = 225$?
5. $H_0$: $\sigma_1^2 = \sigma_2^2$, when the variance estimates are independent?
6. $H_0$: $\sigma_1^2 = \sigma_2^2$, when the variance estimates are paired?
7. $H_0$: $\sigma_1^2 = \sigma_2^2 = \ldots = \sigma_J^2$, using the Bartlett test?
8. Tests of homogeneity are generally robust with respect to the assumption of normality. (T or F)
9. If populations are leptokurtic (have positive kurtosis), Hartley's and Bartlett's tests results in more type-I errors than $\alpha$ would indicate. (T or F)
10. If parent populations are highly skewed, they also tend to have positive kurtosis (leptokurtosis). (T or F)
11. If a parent population is skewed, the Bartlett test will be

    (a) conservative (b) liberal
12. For a directional test of variances (e.g., $H_1$: $\sigma_1^2 > \sigma_2^2$), are the critical values in Table F correct for testing $H_0$: $\sigma_1^2 = \sigma_2^2$? For two-tailed tests, critical values of test statistics such as $F$ are ______ (larger or smaller) than for one-tailed tests.
13. If $\nu_1 < \nu_2$, the median value of the $F$-distribution ${}_{.50}F_{\nu1,\nu2}$ is (use Table 16.1) > 1, 1, or < 1?

*Which of the distributions, F, t, and $\chi^2$, have the characteristics suggested in questions 14 to 21?*

14. Skewed negatively
15. Skewed positively
16. Always symmetrical
17. Has an expected value of approximately 1
18. $E(?) = 0$
19. Has a median value of 1 when $\nu_1 = \nu_2$
20. $E(?) = \nu$
21. The distribution more closely resembles a normal distribution as degrees of freedom increase.
22. Compare ${}_{.975}t_5$ with ${}_{.95}F_{1,5}$. Is ${}_{1-\alpha/2}t_\nu = \sqrt{{}_{1-\alpha}F_{1,\nu}}$ ?
23. Does ${}_{.95}\chi_1^2 = {}_{.975}z^2$?
24. Explain why the Hartley, the Levene, the Brown-Forsythe, or the Cochran HOV tests are not recommended as checks on the homogeneity of variance assumption prior to testing $H_0$: $\mu_1 = \mu_2 = \ldots = \mu_J$?
25. You have an unbalanced ANOVA design and the $J$ distributions are highly skewed. The Bartlett HOV test yields $p = .13$. Is the HOV assumption tenable?

## PROBLEMS AND EXERCISES

1. In the case study, it was found that for a sample of $n = 200$ individuals the standard deviation of cholesterol measure was 65.0 (see Table 5.2). Assuming this to be a random sample, give the $.90CI$ for $\sigma$.

**2.** In one study, the authors found that the standard deviation of reading grade equivalent (GE) scores for the eighty-one students who completed an experimental primary curriculum was $.93 = s_1$. The corresponding parameter given in the test manual was 1.00.

(a) Assuming the eighty-one students were a random sample, does the experimental curriculum appear to significantly reduce ($\alpha_2 = .10$) individual differences?

(b) Treating the eighty-one students as a random sample, set the .90 *CI* for $\sigma_1^2$.

(c) For 103 comparable students in a conventional curriculum, the standard deviation was $1.08 = s_2$. If, before the study, it had been predicted that $\sigma_2^2 > \sigma_1^2$, test $H_0$: $\sigma_2^2 = \sigma_1^2$ with $\alpha_1 = .05$.

**3.** The mean and standard deviation of IQ scores for the 195 girls and the 209 boys in the fifth grade of a school district are given.

| | *Boys* | *Girls* |
|---|---|---|
| $\bar{X}_j$ | 99.7 | 99.2 |
| $s_j$ | 15.5 | 14.3 |

(a) Test $H_0$: $\sigma_B^2 = \sigma_G^2$ using the *F*-test with $\alpha_2 = .10$.

(b) Since $n_B \neq n_G$, would a *t*-test of $H_0$: $\mu_1 = \mu_2$ be seriously in error if the variances are not homogeneous?

(c) Could the $H_0$ in part (a) above have been tested using the Bartlett test?

**4.** In one study, 543 sixth-grade students were retested with a social studies test that they had taken one year earlier as fifth graders. The observed correlation between the two sets of scores was .79, with $s_5 = 7.60$ and $s_6 = 7.91$. Test $H_0$: $\sigma_6^2 = \sigma_5^2$, with $\alpha = .05$.

**5.** Suppose the variances in GPA for 101 students drawn randomly from grades ten, eleven, and twelve are .25, .20, and .16, respectively. Is $H_0$: $\sigma_{10}^2 = \sigma_{11}^2 = \sigma_{12}^2$ tenable at $\alpha = .10$, using the Bartlett test?

**6.** The stereotypes of Mexican Americans by 63 White and 27 Mexican American students were compared in problem 7(b), following Chapter 12. The variance of the White's scores was 112.4; the variance of the Mexican Americans was 53.2. Were the perceptions among the Mexican American students more homogeneous? Use the *F*-test, with $\alpha_2 = .05$.

**7.** Test $H_0$: $\sigma_1^2 = \sigma_2^2 = \sigma_3^2$ in problem 5 in Problems and Exercises following Chapter 15 using (a) the Bartlett test, and (b) the Hartley $F_{max}$ test. Let $\alpha = .10$.

**8.** If ${}_{.95}F_{2,10} = 4.10$, ${}_{.95}F_{10,2} = ?$

**9.** The mean of the chi-square distribution with $\nu$ degrees of freedom is $\nu$. The mode is at $\nu - 2$ for $\nu > 2$. The chi-square distribution is positively skewed. Recall from Equation 4.11 that the mode is estimated by $3\text{Mdn} - 2\bar{X}$.

(a) If $\nu = 10$, estimate ${}_{.50}\chi_{10}^2$. Compare this value with that from Table D.

(b) Is the median of the chi-square distribution with $\nu$ degrees of freedom above, below, or equal to $\nu$?

**10.** For very large $\nu$, the chi-square distribution with $\nu$ degrees of freedom approximates a normal distribution. The mean and standard deviation are $\nu$ and $\sqrt{2\nu}$ respectively, regardless of the value of $\nu$. For $\nu = 50$, find the 95th percentile in the chi-square distribution from Table D and compare it with the 95th percentile in a normal distribution with mean $\nu = 50$ and standard deviation $\sqrt{2\nu} = \sqrt{100}$.

**11.** Prove that the variance of the *t*-distribution with $\nu$ degrees of freedom is $\nu/(\nu - 2)$. Hint: $t_\nu^2$ is the same as the *F*-distribution with 1 and $\nu$ degrees of freedom. Since $E(t_\nu) = 0$, and $\sigma_t^2 = E[t - E(t)]^2$, the variance of $t_\nu$ is $E(t_\nu^2)$.

## ANSWERS TO MASTERY TEST

1. When $n_1 = n_2$.
2. When one is interested in comparing variances as an inferential question in its own right.
3. $F$-distribution
4. $\chi^2$ (or $F$)
5. $F$
6. $t$
7. $\chi^2$ (or $F$)
8. F
9. T
10. T
11. (b)
12. yes, larger
13. $< 1$
14. none of these
15. $F$ and $\chi^2$
16. $t$
17. $F$
18. $t$
19. $F$
20. $\chi^2$
21. $t$, $F$, and $\chi^2$
22. $(2.015)^2 = 4.06$, yes
23. Yes, for example, $3.841 = (1.96)^2$.
24. These HOV tests yield accurate $p$-values only for balanced ANOVA designs, and HOV tests are not needed when designs are balanced.
25. Since the test is liberal (actual $p >$ nominal $p$, i.e., actual $p > .13$), the HOV assumption is tenable.

## ANSWERS TO PROBLEMS AND EXERCISES

1. (60.1, 70.9)
2. (a) No, $\chi^2 = 69.19$; ${}_{.05}\chi_{80}^2 = 60.34$, ${}_{.95}\chi_{80}^2 = 101.9$
   (b) $(69.19/{}_{.05}\chi_{80}^2, 69.19/{}_{.95}\chi_{80}^2) = (69.19/60.34, 69.19/101.9) = (1.15, .68)$ or $1.15 > \sigma^2 > .68$
   (c) $F = (1.08)2/(.93)^2 = 1.349$; ${}_{.95}F_{102,80} \approx {}_{.95}F_{100,60} = 1.48$, $H_0$ is tenable.
3. (a) $F = (15.5/14.3)^2 = 1.175$; ${}_{.95}F_{208,194} \approx {}_{.95}F_{200,200} = 1.26$; $H_0$ is tenable, $p > .05$.
   (b) No, because $n_B/n_G \approx 1$; see Figure 12.3
   (c) yes
4. $$t = \frac{(7.91)^2 - (7.60)^2}{2(7.91)(7.60)\sqrt{[1-(.79)^2]/541}} = \frac{4.81}{3.17} = 1.52 < 1.96 = {}_{.975}t_{541};$$
   $H_0$ is tenable; $p > .05$
5. $\chi^2 = [300(-1.5929) - (-482.83)]/1.0044 = 4.94 > 4.605 = {}_{.90}\chi_2^2$; reject $H_0$ at .10 level.
6. $F = 112.4/53.2 = 2.11 > 2.08 \approx {}_{.975}F_{62,26}$; reject $H_0$ at the .05 level.
7. (a) $\chi^2 = .34$; $1.39 = {}_{.50}\chi_2^2$; $p > .50$
   (b) $F_{max} = 1.43 < 5.34 = {}_{.95}F_{max_{3,9}}$; $p > .05$
8. $1/4.10 = .244$
9. (a) $9.33 \approx 9.34 = {}_{.50}\chi_{10}^2$
   (b) below
10. ${}_{.95}\chi_{50}^2 = 67.51 \approx 50 + 1.645(10) = 66.45$
11. $\sigma_t^2 = E(t_\nu^2) = E(F_{1,\nu}) = \nu/(\nu - 2)$

# MULTIPLE COMPARISONS AND TREND ANALYSIS

## 17.1 INTRODUCTION

The omnibus $F$-test in an analysis of variance (ANOVA) is a test of the hypothesis that the population means of all $J$ groups are equal, that is, $H_0$: $\mu_1 = \mu_2 = \ldots = \mu_J$. One of two possible statistical conclusions follows an ANOVA: Either $H_0$ is accepted, or it is rejected. If there are only two means being compared, multiple comparisons are superfluous. However, if $H_0$ is rejected and $J > 2$, the conclusion, "not all $J$ population means are equal," only allows us to open the door to look further. The rejection of the null hypothesis does not mean that all differences among the means are significant, nor does this indicate which means differ significantly from which other means. The omnibus $F$-test is a decision point:[1] If the $F$-test is not statistically significant, sampling error can be viewed as a plausible explanation (hypothesis) for the pattern of differences that was observed among the $J$ means, but if $H_0$ is rejected, a search for which differences among the means are significant is called for. These search procedures are termed *multiple comparisons* (MC) techniques.

From a historical perspective, MC procedures are a relatively recent addition to the statistical arsenal. Most MC techniques were developed during the 1950s, although their use in behavioral research was rare prior to the 1960s.

Prior to the availability of MC techniques, the $t$-test was used following a rejection of $H_0$ in ANOVA when comparing three or more means, but the $t$-test does not take into account how many groups (or means) are in the set. Clearly, if one draws $J = 10$ random samples from the same parent population and compares the two most extreme means using the $t$-test, the observed $t$-ratio will exceed the critical $t$-ratio far more often than the probability denoted by the nominal value of alpha. When $J > 2$, the probability of a type-

[1]Except in trend analysis (Section 17.19) and other planned orthogonal contrasts (Section 17.16).

**TABLE 17.1** Sample Problem for Multiple Comparisons Illustrations: A One-Factor ANOVA with $J = 7$ Groups with $n = 20$ per Group.

A.

| *Source* | $\nu$ | *MS* | *F* |
|---|---|---|---|
| Between (Treatments) | 6 | 467 | 2.25* |
| Within (Error) | 133 | 207 | |

$^{*}p < .05$, ${}_{.95}F_{6,133} \approx 2.17$

B.

| *Advanced Organizer (AO)* | | | | | *No AO* | |
|---|---|---|---|---|---|---|
| *AO Before* | | | *AO After* | | *Control* | *"Read Carefully"* |
| *Answers Provided for AO?* | | | | | | |
| *Yes* | *Yes* | *No* | *Yes* | *No* | | |
| *Blocked* | *Interspersed* | | | | | |
| 36 | 35 | 30 | 40 | 43 | 33 | 42 |
| $\bar{X}_4$ | $\bar{X}_5$ | $\bar{X}_7$ | $\bar{X}_3$ | $\bar{X}_1$ | $\bar{X}_6$ | $\bar{X}_2$ |

I error will be larger than .05 when the nominal value of .05 is set for alpha (Section 15.2).[2]

There are several multiple comparison procedures available. The seven most useful will be developed in this chapter.

## An Example

One study examined the effects of "advance organizers" (interspersed questions designed to produce a mental set that facilitates the comprehension of assigned reading). There were $n = 20$ subjects randomly assigned to each of the $J = 7$ groups; the researcher set $\alpha = .10$. Panel A of Table 17.1 gives the ANOVA table. The $F$-ratio of 2.25 allows the null hypothesis ($H_0$: $\mu_1 = \mu_2 = \mu_3 = \mu_4 = \mu_5 = \mu_6 = \mu_7$) to be rejected ($p < .05$). The next step following the rejection of the null hypothesis is to select a MC procedure to find which means differ significantly from which other means.

Five groups received the advance organizer (AO) and two groups did not (see Panel B of Table 17.1). One of the two "No-AO" groups was given special instructions to read

[2]The procedure of performing multiple $t$-tests following an ANOVA is also commonly known as the "least-significant difference" ($LSD$) method: $LSD$ = (critical-$t$)$s_{\bar{X}_1-\bar{X}_2} = ({}_{1-\alpha/2}t_{\nu_e})s_{\bar{X}_1-\bar{X}_2}$, where $s_{\bar{X}_1-\bar{X}_2} = \sqrt{MS_W(2/n)}$ with a balanced design. In the example in Table 17.1 with $\alpha = .05$, $LSD = ({}_{.975}t_{133})s_{\bar{X}_1-\bar{X}_2} = 1.98\sqrt{20.7} = 9.01$. Any difference between a pair of means greater than 9.01 is judged to be statistically significant by the $LSD$ method. For $C$ independent $t$-tests the probability of at least one type-I error is $\alpha_\Sigma = 1 - (1 - \alpha)^C$ (see Section 17.14). In Table 17.1 there are $C = 21$ possible pairwise comparisons. If the contrasts were independent and alpha were set at .05, the probability of at least one type-I error would be $\alpha_\Sigma = 1 - (.95)^{21} = .66$. The dependency among multiple $t$-tests makes it impossible to determine the probability of a type-I error precisely.

carefully. Of the five groups receiving the AO, three of the groups received the AO before reading the material, the other two received the organizer after reading. Within each of the "AO Before" and "AO After" subsets of groups, one group did not receive answers to the AO questions.

MC computations are facilitated if the means are denoted by their magnitude. The seven means in Table 17.1 have been ordered by subscripts from the largest ($\bar{X}_1$) to the smallest ($\bar{X}_7$).

## 17.2 TESTING ALL PAIRS OF MEANS: THE STUDENTIZED RANGE STATISTIC, *q*

The typical situation in which MC methods are used is one in which the researcher wishes to compare each mean with each and every other mean, that is, all possible pairwise comparisons. The maximum number of possible simple or pairwise contrasts ($C$) among $J$ means is:

$$C = \frac{J(J-1)}{2} \qquad (17.1)$$

If school attendance rates are compared for all twelve grade levels of a school district, there would be 12(11)/2 = 66 possible pairwise contrasts, or 66 unique hypotheses involving two means. In Table 17.1, can you identify the 7(6)/2 = 21 possible pairwise contrasts in the example? With $\alpha = .10$ and when $H_0$ is true, it is unlikely that we would not make at least one type-I error in the 21 tests.

Recall from Chapter 5 (Section 5.13) that in a normal distribution as the number of observations ($n$) in a sample increases the magnitude of the range also increases. The same is true for a sample of means: In a set of $J$ means each based on a random sample of $n$ observations drawn from the same population, the magnitude of the difference between the largest mean, $\bar{X}_1$, and the smallest mean, $\bar{X}_J$, increases as the number of means ($J$) increases. The method of choice for testing all possible pairwise contrasts makes use of the *studentized range statistic*, $q$. Several multiple comparison procedures are based on the test statistic, $q$. Unlike multiple $t$-tests (*LSD*), the critical value of the studentized range statistic ($q$) is influenced by $J$, the number of means in the set. The numerical value of $q$ is the difference between the larger and the smaller of two sample means, $\bar{X}_1 - \bar{X}_J$, expressed in units of the standard error of the mean, $s_{\bar{X}}$:

$$q = \frac{\bar{X}_1 - \bar{X}_J}{s_{\bar{X}}} \qquad (17.2)$$

where $\bar{X}_1 > \bar{X}_J$, and

$$s_{\bar{X}} = \sqrt{\frac{MS_{\text{error}}}{n}} \qquad (17.3)$$

The value of $MS_{\text{error}}$ ($MS_e$) in Equation 17.3 is the denominator of the $F$-test; in a one-factor ANOVA (or fixed-effects ANOVA, Chapter 18), $MS_e$ is always $MS_{\text{within}}$. In more complex ANOVA designs, such as those considered in Chapters 18 and 19, $MS_{\text{error}}$, the denominator of the $F$-test that tests a given null hypothesis, is not always $MS_{\text{within}}$.

If the $J$ $n$'s are not equal,[3] the value of $s_{\overline{X}}$ for comparing pairs of means can be estimated from Equation 17.4:

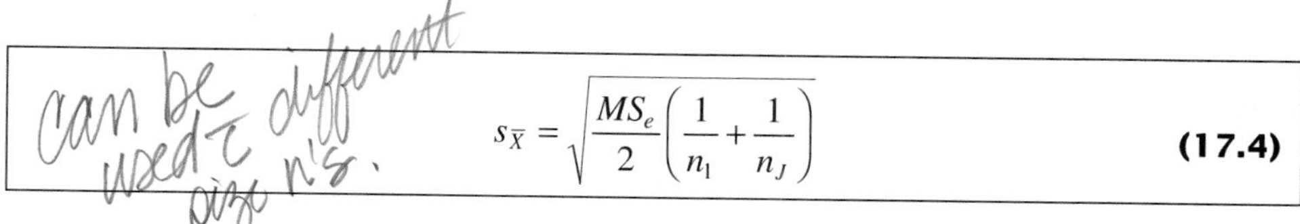

$$s_{\overline{X}} = \sqrt{\frac{MS_e}{2}\left(\frac{1}{n_1} + \frac{1}{n_J}\right)} \qquad \textbf{(17.4)}$$

where $n_1$ and $n_J$ are the numbers of observations on which the larger mean, $\overline{X}_1$, and the smaller mean, $\overline{X}_J$, are based.

## 17.3 THE TUKEY METHOD OF MULTIPLE COMPARISONS

The Tukey MC method begins by testing the largest pairwise difference in the set of $J$ means, that is, by testing $H_0$: $\mu_1 - \mu_J = 0$. Since the means are ranked in order of their size (denoted by subscripts from 1 to $J$), $\overline{X}_1$ is the largest mean and $\overline{X}_J$ is the smallest mean. In the example in Table 17.1, the first hypothesis to be tested is $H_{01}$: $\mu_1 - \mu_7 = 0$. With alpha = .10, is $H_{0_1}$ tenable? Using Equation 17.2, the numerical value of the studentized range statistic, $q_1$, is:

$$q_1 = \frac{(\overline{X}_1 - \overline{X}_7)}{s_{\overline{X}}}$$

where, from Equation 17.3, the value of the standard error of the mean, $s_{\overline{X}}$, is:

$$s_{\overline{X}} = \sqrt{\frac{MS_W}{n}} = \sqrt{\frac{207}{20}} = 3.217$$

Hence:

$$q_1 = \frac{(43-30)}{3.217} = 4.04$$

The critical $q$-value is found from Table I in the Appendix by locating the intersection of (1) the *column* for the number of means in the set, $r$ (no relation to the correlation coefficient—for the Tukey method, the value of $r$ is always $J$), (2) the *row* for $\nu_e$, the degrees of

[3] In the derivation of the studentized range statistic, all $J$ means are assumed to be based on the same number of observations so that $\sigma^2_{\overline{X}_1} = \sigma^2_{\overline{X}_2} = \ldots = \sigma^2_{\overline{X}_J}$ will be true when $\sigma_1^2 = \sigma_2^2 = \ldots = \sigma_J^2$. The modification proposed by Kramer (1956) given as Equation 17.4 is logical and has been shown to yield accurate results with unequal $n$'s (Smith, 1971; Myette & White, 1982). (The mathematical basis for the studentized range with unequal $n$'s is treated by Hochberg, 1975; and Spjotvoll & Stoline, 1973.)

**TABLE 17.2** Tukey Multiple Comparisons for the Sample Problem (Table 17.1).

| | *Ordered Means* | | | | | | |
|---|---|---|---|---|---|---|---|
| **A.** | $\overline{X}_1$ 43 | $\overline{X}_2$ 42 | $\overline{X}_3$ 40 | $\overline{X}_4$ 36 | $\overline{X}_5$ 35 | $\overline{X}_6$ 33 | $\overline{X}_7$ 30 |
| **B.** $\hat{\Delta}_j$: | (.90) | (.83) | (.70) | (.42) | (.35) | (.21) | ... |

**C.** $q_1 = \dfrac{\overline{X}_1 - \overline{X}_7}{s_{\overline{X}}}$; $s_{\overline{X}} = \sqrt{\dfrac{MS_w}{n}} = \sqrt{\dfrac{207}{20}} = 3.217$

$$q_1 = \frac{43-30}{3.217} = 4.04;\ p < .10,\ {}_{.90}q_{133,7} \approx 3.86$$

$$q_2 = \frac{\overline{X}_1 - \overline{X}_6}{s_{\overline{X}}} = \frac{43-33}{3.217} = 3.11,\ p > .10$$

$$q_3 = \frac{\overline{X}_2 - \overline{X}_7}{s_{\overline{X}}} = \frac{42-30}{3.217} = 3.73,\ p > .10$$

freedom for $MS_e$,[4] *and* (3) the row for alpha, .10 in our example. Thus, the critical $q$-value for $J = 7$, $\nu_e = 133$ (use the closest, but smaller tabled value of $\nu_e$—in this instance, 120), and alpha =.10 is 3.86 (${}_{.90}q_{133,7} \approx {}_{.90}q_{120,7} = 3.86$). The computation for $q_1$ is shown in Panel C of Table 17.2. Since the observed value of $q_1$ of 4.04 exceeds the critical $q$-value of 3.86, the null hypothesis, $H_{0_1}$: $\mu_1 - \mu_7 = 0$, can be rejected at the .10 level, and it can be concluded that the mean of population 1 is greater than the mean of population 7. (Since ${}_{.95}q_{133,7} \approx {}_{.95}q_{120,7} = 4.24$, the null hypothesis cannot be rejected at the .05 level.)

If the difference between the extreme-most means had not been significant, the tests of the $H_0$'s for differences between other pairs of means would have been superfluous. Since the largest difference in means was significant, one proceeds to test the second-largest difference involving $\overline{X}_1$, that is $\overline{X}_1$ vs. $\overline{X}_{J-1}$, or $H_{0_2}$: $\mu_1 - \mu_6 = 0$. Panel C of Table 17.2 shows that $q_2 = 3.11$, which is less than the critical-$q$ of 3.86; hence, there are no significant differences among the set of means $\overline{X}_1$, $\overline{X}_2$, $\overline{X}_3$, $\overline{X}_4$, $\overline{X}_5$, and $\overline{X}_6$.

After a nonsignificant range has been encountered involving the largest mean, one proceeds to take the next-largest mean, $\overline{X}_2$, and test it against the smallest mean, $\overline{X}_J$, that is, $H_{0_3}$: $\mu_2 - \mu_7 = 0$. The computed value of the studentized range for this comparison, $q_3$, is shown in Panel C to be $q_3 = 12/3.217 = 3.73$; this is less than the critical $q$-value of 3.86, thus $H_0$: $\mu_2 = \mu_7$ is tenable. Since there remains no pair of means that is not within a non-significant range of means, no further hypotheses need to be tested. In other words, if a difference in means of 12 is not large enough to be significant, it is pointless to test differences that are less than 12.

When the $n$'s are equal, the Tukey method can be simplified for hand computation by finding the *minimum* difference between means necessary to reject the null hypothesis. This minimum difference is termed *honest significant difference* (*HSD*). By inserting the critical $q$-value (${}_{1-\alpha}q_{\nu e,J}$) from Table I into Equation 17.2 and rearranging the equation, the value of *HSD* is obtained.

[4] $\nu_e = \nu_W$, except for some "mixed-model" ANOVA designs considered in Chapter 19.

$$HSD = (\text{critical-}q)s_{\overline{X}} \qquad (17.5)$$

For example, from Table I with alpha =.10, $J = 7$, and with 133 degrees of freedom, the critical value of $q$ is found to be 3.86; thus: $HSD = 3.86s_{\overline{X}} = (3.86)(3.217) = 12.42$. Only one pair of means ($\overline{X}_1 - \overline{X}_7 = 13$) differs as much as 12.42, thus, this is the only pair of means that differs significantly.

## 17.4 THE EFFECT SIZE OF MEAN DIFFERENCES

The effect size (Section 12.8) of a difference in means can be estimated by Equation 17.6:

$$\hat{\Delta}_j = \frac{\overline{X}_j - \overline{X}_J}{s_W} \qquad (17.6)$$

where $s_W = \sqrt{MS_W}$. In Panel B of Table 17.2, the largest effect size, $\hat{\Delta}_1$, is shown to be .90: $\hat{\Delta}_1 = (\overline{X}_1 - \overline{X}_7)/\sqrt{MS_W} = (43-30)/\sqrt{207} = 13/14.4 = .90$ (or $.90\hat{\sigma}$).

The effect-size metric is a useful descriptive estimate of the magnitude of the difference between means when the dependent variable has an arbitrary numerical scale (as with most measures in behavioral research, but unlike most measures in the physical and biological sciences). The effect size metric should not be limited to only those differences that are statistically significant (Glass, McGaw & Smith, 1981). To express the magnitude of the mean differences, the effect size for each mean using the lowest mean, $\overline{X}_7$, as the point of reference is given in parentheses in Panel B of Table 17.2. The effect size between any other pair of means is simply the difference between their respective $\hat{\Delta}_j$'s. For example, the estimated effect size between groups 2 and 6 is $\hat{\Delta}_2 - \hat{\Delta}_6 = .83 - .21 = .62$. Since the associated $H_0$ is tenable, the estimate of the effect size is not significantly different from 0.

## 17.5 THE BASIS FOR TYPE-I ERROR RATE: CONTRAST VERSUS FAMILY

In previous chapters, as in most other statistical applications, alpha pertains to the probability of a type-I error for a particular, explicit hypothesis. With MC methods, however, there is a choice between a type-I error rate per contrast (or specified hypothesis), $\alpha$, or a type-I error rate for a set or family[5] of $C$ contrasts, $\alpha_\Sigma$.[6]

Two of the seven MC methods presented in this chapter base the probability of a type-I error (alpha) on the individual contrast; the other five MC techniques consider the set of $C$ contrasts as a family and base the type-I error rate on the entire set or family. The Tukey

[5]The term "experiment-wise" error rate is commonly used synonymously with family error rate, but this terminology is confusing when there are two or more factors in the ANOVA (Chapter 18). Following Miller (1966, 1977), we will consistently use the expression "family" error rate, or error rate per family. The terms contrast and comparison are also synonymous (O'Neill & Wetherill, 1971).

[6]Multiple comparison hypotheses are usually nondirectional. A family-based type-I error rate for directional hypotheses is denoted by $\alpha_{\Sigma_1}$, otherwise $\alpha_\Sigma = \alpha_{\Sigma_2}$.

method (Section 17.3) uses a family-based type-I error rate; thus, the probability of a type-I error in one or more of the $C = J(J - 1)/2 = 21$ pairwise contrasts is alpha (in the example, .10). Certain other MC methods (like the Newman-Keuls, Section 17.6) set the risk of a type-I error of $\alpha$ for each contrast tested.

Which type of error rate is preferable is a matter of opinion and controversy. In the long run, the contrast-based error rate has greater power, but makes more type-I errors. Conversely, the family error rate results in fewer type-I errors, but more type-II errors. The rationale for a family error-rate is weakened by the arbitrariness of the decision as to what constitutes a family,[7] especially when there are two or more factors in the design (Chapter 18). The authors, like Miller (1966, 1977), feel that the contrast-based error rate is advantageous for most applications since it is consistent with the rationale that researchers employ for almost all other hypotheses that they test and it does not suffer from the conservativeness (and loss of power) of the family error rate, especially when $J$ is large.

## 17.6 THE NEWMAN-KEULS METHOD

The Newman-Keuls[8] (NK) method of multiple comparisons is very similar to the Tukey method, except that it uses a per-contrast type-I error rate. Each pairwise hypothesis that is tested has a probability, $\alpha$, of a type-I error. The NK procedure is identical to that outlined in Table 17.2, except that the critical value of $q$ depends on the number of the means, $r$ (for range), in the set of means being considered in the particular comparison being made. For the initial hypothesis tested (that is, when the largest and smallest of the set of $J$ means are being compared, $H_0$: $\mu_1 - \mu_J$), the Tukey and NK procedures are identical. If this $H_0$ is not rejected, then all null hypotheses for every other pair of means are tenable. However, if the initial $H_0$ is rejected (as it was in the example in Table 17.2), the two procedures differ with respect to the critical value of $q$ for all other contrasts. For the NK procedure, the critical $q$-value is not ${}_{1-\alpha}q_{\nu_e,J}$, but ${}_{1-\alpha}q_{\nu_e,r}$, where $r$ is the number of means in the set being compared in the particular hypothesis being tested. For $q_2$ and $q_3$ of Table 17.3, $r$ is 6. The range rationale is employed with both methods: Whenever one finds a subset of means for which the difference between the largest and smallest means is not significant, no further comparisons are made within this subset of means.

The NK method is outlined below and is illustrated in Table 17.3.

1. The initial step is identical with the Tukey method (Equation 17.2): In the set of $J$ means, the largest mean, $\overline{X}_1$, is compared with the smallest mean, $\overline{X}_J$. If this difference is not significant at the specified alpha (.10 in the example), no further hypotheses are tested and all null hypotheses are tenable.
2. If the hypothesis for the extreme-most means is rejected (as it is in Table 17.3), the mean of group 1 is contrasted with the mean of group $J - 1$ ($\overline{X}_6$ in the example). The critical $q$-value is based on $r = J - 1$. In Panel C of Table 17.3, $H_{0_2}$: $\mu_1 - \mu_6 = 0$ cannot be rejected: $q = 3.11 < {}_{.90}q_{133,6} \approx 3.71$. If this hypothesis had been rejected, group 1 would have

[7]For example, in factorial ANOVA (Chapters 18–19), a per-contrast error rate is ordinarily used to test each main effect and interaction, rather than a family error rate for the entire package of main effects and interactions. Indeed, each $F$-test is a special case of planned orthogonal contrasts (Section 17.16). Miller (1966, p. 35) observed, "There are no hard-and-fast rules for where the family lines should be drawn, and the statistician must rely on his own judgment for the problem at hand. Large single experiments cannot be treated as a whole (family) without an unjustifiable loss in sensitivity."

[8]Also termed the Student-Newman-Keuls method.

**TABLE 17.3** Newman-Keuls Multiple Comparisons for the Sample Problem (Table 17.1).

| | *Ordered Means* | | | | | | |
|---|---|---|---|---|---|---|---|
| A. | $\bar{X}_1$ 43 | $\bar{X}_2$ 42 | $\bar{X}_3$ 40 | $\bar{X}_4$ 36 | $\bar{X}_5$ 35 | $\bar{X}_6$ 33 | $\bar{X}_7$ 30 |
| B. $\hat{\Delta}_j$: | (.90) | (.83) | (.70) | (.42) | (.35) | (.21) | ... |

C.

$$q_1 = \frac{\bar{X}_1 - \bar{X}_7}{s_{\bar{X}}};\ s_{\bar{X}} = \sqrt{\frac{MS_w}{n}} = \sqrt{\frac{207}{20}} = 3.217$$

$$q_1 = \frac{43-30}{3.217} = 4.04;\ p < .10,\ {}_{.90}q_{133,7} = 3.86$$

$$q_2 = \frac{\bar{X}_1 - \bar{X}_6}{s_{\bar{X}}} = \frac{43-33}{3.217} = 3.11,\ p > .10;\ {}_{.90}q_{133,6} \approx 3.71$$

$$q_3 = \frac{\bar{X}_2 - \bar{X}_7}{s_{\bar{X}}} = \frac{42-30}{3.217} = 3.73,\ p < .10;\ {}_{.90}q_{133,6} \approx 3.71$$

$$q_4 = \frac{\bar{X}_3 - \bar{X}_7}{s_{\bar{X}}} = \frac{40-30}{3.217} = 3.11,\ p > .10,\ {}_{.90}q_{133,5} \approx 3.52$$

been tested against group $J - 2$, and $J - 3$, and so on, until a nonsignificant range is encountered. There is no significant difference between any two means within a nonsignificant range. The subset of means, $\bar{X}_1$ through $\bar{X}_6$, is underscored to denote that there is no significant difference between any pair of means in this subset. Note that the only difference at step two between the Tukey and NK methods is that the NK has a smaller critical $q$-value.

3. If the means of groups 2 and $J$ are not underscored by a common line, one proceeds to test the second-largest mean, $\bar{X}_2$, against the mean of group $J$. In Panel C of Table 17.3, $q_3$ is found to be 3.73, which is larger than the critical $q$-value of 3.71; thus, $H_{0_3}$: $\mu_2 - \mu_7 = 0$ is rejected at the .10 level. Note, however, in step 2 that one does not proceed to test group 2 against group $J - 1 = 6$ because groups 2 and 6 are within a nonsignificant range; hence, no further hypotheses are tested among means within this subset.
4. If the third-largest mean, $\bar{X}_3$, and the smallest mean, $\bar{X}_J$, are not underscored by a common line, one proceeds to test pairs of means within this subset until a nonsignificant range is found. In Panel C of Table 17.3, for $H_{0_4}$: $\mu_3 - \mu_J = 0$, $q_4 = 3.11$, which is less than the critical $q$-value (3.52) with $r = 5$. No further null hypotheses are tested because the remaining means fall within a nonsignificant range.

Unlike the $t$-test of two means, the Tukey and Newman-Keuls multiple comparison methods illustrate that the difference between means needed for statistical significance with MC techniques is influenced by the parameter $J$.

## 17.7 THE TUKEY AND NEWMAN-KEULS METHODS COMPARED

Both the Tukey and the NK methods employ the studentized range statistic, $q$. The principal difference between them is that the Tukey procedure uses a family-based alpha, $\alpha_\Sigma$, whereas the NK method risks a type-I error with probability $\alpha$ for each null hypothesis that is tested. Consequently, the NK method will have greater power than the Tukey method, except for the initial comparisons, where the two procedures are identical. After the initial comparison hurdle, the NK method is more likely to reject subsequent $H_0$'s than the Tukey procedure, as illustrated in Tables 17.3 and 17.2. Notice that the critical value for $q$ with the Tukey method is 3.86 for all comparisons, whereas for the NK method, the critical $q$-values decrease progressively: 3.86, 3.71, 3.52, 3.28, 2.93, to 2.34, when there are $r = 7, 6, 5, 4, 3,$ and 2 means, respectively, in the set of means being compared. The authors concur with Miller's (1966, p. 88) observation in his authoritative treatment of multiple comparisons, that:

> The Newman-Keuls [significance] levels provide a high degree of protection for the entire [omnibus] null hypothesis, and this is the multiple range test this author favors. Moreover, it does not suffer from the conservatism of the Tukey test caused by utilizing just a single critical value.[9]

## 17.8 THE DEFINITION OF A CONTRAST

To describe, use, and properly evaluate other MC methods, in addition to understanding the distinction between a contrast-based and a family-based type-I error rate, it is necessary to understand (1) the formal definition of a contrast, (2) the distinction between simple and complex contrasts, and (3) the meaning of planned versus post-hoc contrasts. These matters are treated prior to dealing with other MC techniques.

Central to the use of MC methods is the notion of a contrast. A contrast represents the mean difference between two subsets of means. There may be only one mean in each subset, as in the pairwise contrast employed with the Tukey and NK methods, or there may be as many as $J - 1$ means in one of the subsets. Obviously, there are several possible contrasts when there are three or more means.

**Definition.** A contrast $\psi$ among the $J$ population means is a linear combination:

$$\psi = \sum_j c_j\mu_j = c_1\mu_1 + c_2\mu_2 + \ldots + c_J\mu_J \qquad \textbf{(17.7)}$$

such that the sum of contrast coefficients,[10] $\Sigma_j c_j = 0$. In terms of unbiased estimators:

$$\hat{\psi} = \sum_j c_j\overline{X}_j = c_1\overline{X}_1 + c_2\overline{X}_2 + \ldots + c_J\overline{X}_J \qquad \textbf{(17.7A)}$$

[9]We have chosen not to include two multiple range MC methods that in our opinion are rarely, if ever, the MC method of choice. One, suggested by Tukey, uses a critical $q$-value that is the average of the critical $q$-values for the Tukey and NK methods (see O'Neill & Wetherill, 1971, p. 226). Another common method is that suggested by Duncan and popularized by Edwards (1960), "Duncan's new multiple range test," in which the true value for alpha increases as $J$ increases. With the Duncan method, the alpha for the largest observed pairwise difference in means is $1 - (1 - \alpha)^{J-1}$, or in our example with $J = 7$ and $\alpha = .10$, the probability of a type-I error when comparing the most extreme means is $1 - (.90)^6 = .47$. The authors concur with Miller (1966, p. 87) that "... this violates the spirit of what simultaneous inference is all about, namely to protect a multi-parameter null hypothesis from any false declaration [conclusion] due to the large number of declarations required."

[10]The contrast coefficients, $c_j$'s, are not to be confused with $C$, the number of contrasts.

The contrast coefficients, $c_1 + c_2 \ldots + c_J$, are simply positive and negative numbers that define the particular hypotheses to be tested. The interpretation of a contrast is enhanced if the positive $c_j$'s sum to +1 and the negative $c_j$'s sum to –1.[11]

## 17.9 SIMPLE VERSUS COMPLEX CONTRASTS

The difference between any two means is a simple contrast. For example, if $\psi = \mu_3 - \mu_6$, the contrast coefficients for groups 3 and 6 are 1 and –1, respectively, with all other $c_j$'s being equal to 0 (since these groups are irrelevant in this contrast). Contrasts that involve only two means, each mean having a contrast coefficient of either +1 or –1, are said to be *simple* or *pairwise contrasts*. If $J = 2$, there is only one possible contrast, $\mu_1 - \mu_2$ (or $\mu_2 - \mu_1$); if $J = 3$, there are three simple contrasts, $\mu_1 - \mu_2$, $\mu_1 - \mu_3$, and $\mu_2 - \mu_3$. Contrasts 1, 2, and 3 of Panel C of Table 17.2 are simple contrasts. The null hypothesis states that the value of the parameter for every contrast is 0, that is, $H_0$: $\psi = 0$. The unbiased estimator of the contrast parameter is given in Equation 17.7A. The numerical value of each contrast for simple contrasts is the difference in the two sample means. The value of the contrast will be tested (by a *t*-test, or a near relative) to see if the observed value of the contrast differs significantly from the hypothesized value of 0.

*Complex contrasts* involve three or more means. The contrast, $\psi = \frac{1}{2}\mu_1 + \frac{1}{2}\mu_2 - \mu_3$, is a contrast involving three means; the implicit $H_0$ is that $\mu_3$ equals the average of $\mu_1$ and $\mu_2$. The significance test will respond to the question, "Is the average of means of groups 1 and 2 significantly different from the mean of group 3?"

Each contrast ($\psi_c$) is designed to answer a specific question in a research study. Six meaningful contrasts related to the example in Table 17.1 are given below and expressed via statistical symbols in Panel A of Table 17.4. Note that the corresponding null hypothesis is implicit from each contrast:

$\psi_1$: Is the effect of the AO when positioned before the reading selection different from the effect when positioned after the selection, when answers are not supplied?

$\psi_2$: Is there a difference in the means of the two non-AO groups, that is, do the special directions to "read carefully" have an effect?

$\psi_3$: When the AO is positioned after the reading selection, does having answers to the questions have an effect on the mean?

$\psi_4$: When the AO is positioned before the reading selection, does having answers to the questions have an effect on the mean?

$\psi_5$: Is the mean of the groups having the AO before the reading different from the mean of the groups having the AO after the reading?

$\psi_6$: Is the mean of the groups having the AO different from the mean of the groups that did not receive the AO?

The numerical estimates of these contrasts ($\hat{\psi}_j$'s) are defined in Panel B of Table 17.4. Note that $\hat{\psi}_j$ is a difference between two averages, the mean of the groups having positive $c$'s versus the mean of the groups with negative $c$'s.[12]

---

[11]This convention also allows the Tukey method to be used with complex contrasts (Guenther, 1964), although there are usually better MC alternatives for complex contrasts (Hopkins & Anderson, 1973).

[12]The effect size of a contrast, $\hat{\psi}_c$, is $\hat{\Delta}_c = \hat{\psi}_c / s_W$ (see Section 17.4).

**TABLE 17.4** Six Illustrative Contrasts from the Sample Experiment (from Table 17.1).

| | *Group Means* | | | | | | |
|---|---|---|---|---|---|---|---|
| | $\overline{X}_1$ | $\overline{X}_2$ | $\overline{X}_3$ | $\overline{X}_4$ | $\overline{X}_5$ | $\overline{X}_6$ | $\overline{X}_7$ |
| | 43 | 42 | 40 | 36 | 35 | 33 | 30 |
| **A.** *Contrasts:* $\hat{\psi} = \sum_j c_j \overline{X}_j,\ H_0: \psi = 0$ | *Contrast Coefficients* | | | | | | |
| $\psi_1$: $\mu_1 - \mu_7$ | 1 | 0 | 0 | 0 | 0 | 0 | −1 |
| $\psi_2$: $\mu_2 - \mu_6$ | 0 | 1 | 0 | 0 | 0 | −1 | 0 |
| $\psi_3$: $\mu_1 - \mu_3$ | 1 | 0 | −1 | 0 | 0 | 0 | 0 |
| $\psi_4$: $\frac{1}{2}\mu_4 + \frac{1}{2}\mu_5 - \mu_7$ | 0 | 0 | 0 | ½ | ½ | 0 | −1 |
| $\psi_5$: $\frac{1}{2}\mu_1 + \frac{1}{2}\mu_3 - \frac{1}{3}\mu_4 - \frac{1}{3}\mu_5 - \frac{1}{3}\mu_7$ | ½ | 0 | ½ | −⅓ | −⅓ | 0 | −⅓ |
| $\psi_6$: $\frac{1}{5}\mu_1 + \frac{1}{5}\mu_3 + \frac{1}{5}\mu_4 + \frac{1}{5}\mu_5 + \frac{1}{5}\mu_7 - \frac{1}{2}\mu_2 - \frac{1}{2}\mu_6$ | ⅕ | −½ | ⅕ | ⅕ | ⅕ | −½ | ⅕ |

**B.**

$$\hat{\psi}_1 = \overline{X}_1 - \overline{X}_7 = 43 - 30 = 13.0$$
$$\hat{\psi}_2 = 42 - 33 = 9.0$$
$$\hat{\psi}_3 = 43 - 40 = 3.0$$
$$\hat{\psi}_4 = (36 + 35)/2 - 30 = 5.5$$
$$\hat{\psi}_5 = (43 + 40)/2 - (36 + 35 + 30)/3 = 7.83$$
$$\hat{\psi}_6 = (43 + 40 + 36 + 35 + 30)/5 - (42 + 33)/2 = -.7$$

**C.**

$$s_{\hat{\psi}_1} = \sqrt{MS_e\left(\frac{\sum_j c_j^2}{n_j}\right)} = \sqrt{207\left(\frac{2}{20}\right)} = 4.550;\ s_{\hat{\psi}_1} = s_{\hat{\psi}_2} = s_{\hat{\psi}_3} = 4.550 = s_{\overline{X}-\overline{X}}$$

$$s_{\hat{\psi}_4} = \sqrt{207\left(\frac{1.5}{20}\right)} = 3.940;\ s_{\hat{\psi}_5} = \sqrt{207\left(\frac{.833}{20}\right)} = 2.937;\ s_{\hat{\psi}_6} = \sqrt{207\left(\frac{.7}{20}\right)} = 2.692$$

**D.**

$$t_{\hat{\psi}} = \frac{\hat{\psi}}{s_{\hat{\psi}}};\ t_{\hat{\psi}_1} = \frac{13.0}{4.550} = 2.857$$
$$t_{\hat{\psi}_2} = \frac{9.0}{4.55} = 1.978$$
$$t_{\hat{\psi}_3} = .659$$
$$t_{\hat{\psi}_4} = 1.396$$
$$t_{\hat{\psi}_5} = 2.666$$
$$t_{\hat{\psi}_6} = -.260$$

## 17.10 THE STANDARD ERROR OF A CONTRAST

The remaining MC methods of this chapter use a $t$-ratio as the test statistic: the ratio of the estimate of the contrast, $\hat{\psi}$, to its estimated standard error, $s_{\hat{\psi}}$: $t_{\hat{\psi}} = \hat{\psi}/s_{\hat{\psi}}$. The standard error of a contrast is given by Equation 17.8:

$$s_{\hat{\psi}} = \sqrt{MS_e\left(\frac{c_1^2}{n_1} + \frac{c_2^2}{n_2} + \ldots + \frac{c_J^2}{n_J}\right)} \quad \textbf{(17.8)}$$

where $MS_e$ is the error mean square (the denominator of the $F$-test in the ANOVA, usually $MS_W$).

In Equation 17.8, $c_j$ is the contrast coefficient for the mean, $\overline{X}_j$, and $n_j$ is the number of observations on which this mean is based. Equation 17.8 can also be expressed as:

$$s_{\hat{\psi}} = \sqrt{\frac{MS_e \sum_j c_j^2}{n_j}} \quad \textbf{(17.8A)}$$

If the design is balanced (i.e., $n_1 = n_2 = \ldots = n_J$), the value of $s_\psi$ is simplified further, as shown in Equation 17.8B:

$$s_{\hat{\psi}} = \sqrt{\left(\frac{MS_e}{n}\right)\sum_j c_j^2} \quad \textbf{(17.8B)}$$

For pairwise contrasts, with a balanced design:

$$s_{\hat{\psi}} = \sqrt{\left(\frac{MS_e}{n}\right)\sum_j c_j^2} = s_{\overline{X}}\sqrt{2} \quad \textbf{(17.8C)}$$

In the example in Table 17.4, the standard error of the simple contrast $\psi_1$ is (see Panel C) 4.550. Since the design is balanced, all other pairwise contrasts (e.g., contrasts 2 and 3) will have the same value for their estimated standard error. Complex contrasts will have smaller standard errors. The more means that are involved in the contrast, the smaller will be the standard error of the contrast. For example, the standard error for contrast 6 found from Equation 17.8 is (see Panel C of Table 17.4):

$$s_{\hat{\psi}_6} = \sqrt{\frac{207[(.2)^2 + (-.5)^2 + (.2)^2 + (.2)^2 + (.2)^2 + (-.5)^2 + (.2)^2]}{20}} = \sqrt{207\left(\frac{.7}{20}\right)} = 2.692$$

Standard errors for the other contrasts are given in Panel C in Table 17.4.

## 17.11 THE *t*-RATIO FOR A CONTRAST

The $t$-ratio for a contrast is simply the ratio of the estimated value of the contrast, $\hat{\psi}$, to its standard error, $s_{\hat{\psi}}$:

$$t = \frac{\hat{\psi}}{s_{\hat{\psi}}} \quad \textbf{(17.9)}$$

The $t$-ratios for the six contrasts specified in Panel A of Table 17.4 are given in Panel D. Whether these $t$-ratios achieve statistical significance depends on which MC method is used. Each MC has different critical values for $t$ resulting from different restrictions and conditions that are imposed. In other words, the computations in Table 17.4 are not dependent on which MC method is employed. The difference in the conditions imposed by the various MC methods produce different critical values. Before considering the remaining methods, a clarification of the distinction between *planned* and *post hoc* contrasts is needed.

## 17.12 PLANNED VERSUS POST HOC COMPARISONS

An important distinction must be made between the MC methods that are *planned* or use *a priori* contrasts versus those that allow *post hoc* or *a posteriori* contrasts. In planned contrasts, the hypotheses (contrasts) to be tested must be specified *prior* to data collection. Other things being equal, MC methods that employ planned comparisons are more powerful than post hoc methods if a relatively small subset of contrasts is needed to address the questions of interest. The distribution theory and probability statements for planned MC methods are valid only if the user cannot be influenced by the data in the choice of which hypotheses are to be tested. The rationale for planned contrasts is similar to that for one-tailed $t$-tests: To be valid, the decision must be made a priori. Post hoc MC techniques do not require advance specification of the hypotheses (contrasts) to be tested. The Tukey and Newman-Keuls MC methods are considered to be post hoc methods since there is no restriction on which pairs of means will be contrasted. As in the case of one-tailed versus two-tailed tests, greater power ordinarily accrues to the use of planned MC methods.

## 17.13 DUNN (BONFERRONI) METHOD OF MULTIPLE COMPARISONS

The Dunn (1961) MC method uses the *Bonferroni inequality* (Equation 17.10, see Snedecor and Cochran, 1980, pp. 115–117) for determining the critical value of $t$. The probability of a type-I error in the family (Section 17.5) of $C$ independent or dependent contrasts[13] is:

$$\alpha_{\Sigma} \leq \alpha_1 + \alpha_2 + \ldots + \alpha_C \quad \textbf{(17.10)}$$

For example, it is evident from Equation 17.10 that if five significance tests are conducted, each with $\alpha = .01$, the probability of one or more type-I errors is not more than .05. The Dunn MC procedure requires that all $C$ contrasts be planned (Section 17.12), and defines

[13]The Bonferroni inequality can be used to estimate the maximum probability of a type-I error in any set of significance tests, not just those involving means.

the $C$ contrasts as a family that is the basis for $\alpha_\Sigma$. The critical value of $t$, ${}_{1-\alpha/2}t_{\nu_e,C}$, for all $C$ contrasts is given in Table L in the Appendix. Note that, as you would expect, the critical values of $t$ increase as $C$ increases. For example, with $\alpha_\Sigma = .10$, $\nu_e = 120$, and $C = 6$ (as in Table 17.4), the critical $t$-value is 2.411, but if $C = 20$, the critical $t$-value $\approx 2.843 = {}_{.90}t_{120,20}$. When the absolute values of the $t$-ratios for each of the $C = 6$ contrasts in Table 17.4 are compared with the critical $t$-value of 2.411, two of the null hypotheses (for contrasts 1 and 5) can be rejected. For the other four contrasts (2, 3, 4, and 6), $H_0$ cannot be rejected.

The Dunn MC method is very flexible; it allows any number of simple or complex contrasts, and uses a type-I error rate based on the family of $C$ contrasts. Its relative advantages and disadvantages in comparison to other MC procedures will be reviewed after other methods are presented.[14]

## 17.14 DUNNETT METHOD OF MULTIPLE COMPARISONS

The Dunnett MC method is tailor-made for the situation where the plan is to compare each of the $J - 1$ means with one, and only one, predesignated mean (usually the mean of the control group). Thus with the Dunnett method, it is assumed that there are $C = J - 1$ planned pairwise contrasts—each contrast is against the mean of the predesignated control group, $\overline{X}_*$.

$$t_{\hat{\psi}_c} = \frac{\overline{X}_j - \overline{X}_*}{s_{\hat{\psi}_c}} \qquad \textbf{(17.11)}$$

The critical $t$ values, ${}_{1-\alpha/2}t_{\nu_e,C}$ $(C = J - 1)$, for the Dunnett method are given in Table M in the Appendix. If the Dunnett method is used to compare the mean of the control group ($\overline{X}_6$) with each of the other $C = J - 1 = 6$ group means, the critical value for the $t$-ratio for each of the six planned contrasts with $\alpha_\Sigma = .10 \approx 2.32 = {}_{.90}t_{120,6}$.

Although the Dunn method could be used to test these same $C = J - 1 = 6$ planned contrasts, it is slightly less powerful than the Dunnett for this family of prespecified contrasts. The critical $t$-values for the sample problem with $\alpha_\Sigma = .10$, $C = 6$, and $\nu_e = 133$ are 2.32 and 2.41 for the Dunnett and Dunn MC methods, respectively.

In the example in Panel C of Table 17.4, $s_{\hat{\psi}} = 4.55$; thus, if $\overline{X}_6$ (the control group) had been predesignated as $\overline{X}_*$, the $t$-ratio for testing the null hypothesis, $H_0$: $\mu_1 - \mu_6 = 0$ would be $t = (43 - 33)/4.55 = 2.20$. This is below the critical $t$-ratio of 2.32; thus, the null hypothesis cannot be rejected. The $t$-ratios for the other simple contrasts would be less than 2.20; thus, if the Dunnett MC method were employed, none of these six null hypotheses ($H_0$: $\mu_j - \mu_*$) would be rejected.[15]

---

[14]The Sidak $t$ MC method is essentially equivalent to the Dunn method, but less widely used. It determines its critical $t$ using $\alpha = 1 - (1-\alpha_\Sigma)^{1/C}$, which is slightly smaller than the critical $t$ using the Bonferroni inequality: $\alpha = \alpha_\Sigma/C$. It is used in Table M.

[15]In actual research applications, the optimal MC method for the questions of interest should be selected and used. In this chapter, the various MC methods are all used with the sample problem so that the results can be compared.

## 17.15 SCHEFFÉ METHOD OF MULTIPLE COMPARISONS

The Scheffé method[16] is the most widely presented MC method in textbooks of statistical methods and in applied research studies; ironically, it is rarely the MC method of choice for the questions of interest. The Scheffé method is a very flexible post hoc MC method. It defines the family of contrasts as the family of all possible simple and complex contrasts, and employs a family-based type-I error rate $\alpha_\Sigma$. As a consequence of such latitude, the critical $t$-value for the Scheffé method is large (and the power less) relative to the other MC methods that have been presented, especially as the number of means, $J$, increases. One can be certain, however, that if the omnibus $F$-test is significant at a given alpha level, that at least one contrast will also be significant when the Scheffé MC method is used (Scheffé, 1959), and that if the $F$-test is not significant, then no Scheffé contrast will be significant.

The critical $t$-ratio with the Scheffé method is:

$$ {}_{1-\alpha/2}t_{\nu_W,J} = \sqrt{(J-1)_{1-\alpha}F_{\nu_B,\nu_W}} \qquad \textbf{(17.12)} $$

where $\nu_B = J - 1$, and $\nu_W$ is the degrees of freedom associated with $MS_e$.

In the example in Table 17.4, the critical $t$-ratio for all contrasts for the Scheffé MC method with $\alpha_\Sigma = .10$ is found from Equation 17.12 to be:

$$ {}_{.90}t_{133,7} = \sqrt{(7-1)_{.90}F_{6,133}} \approx \sqrt{6(1.82)} = 3.30 $$

Notice that if the Scheffé method were employed in the sample problem, none of the contrasts specified in Table 17.4 would have approached statistical significance (see Panel D).

The unique advantage of the Scheffé MC method is that it can be used for "data snooping"—for making any simple or complex contrasts even after inspecting the means. For example, is the mean of the three largest means in Table 17.4 significantly larger than the mean of the two groups having the lowest means?

$$ H_0\text{: } \psi_7 = (\mu_1 + \mu_2 + \mu_3)/3 - (\mu_6 + \mu_7)/2 = 0 $$

The estimated value of this contrast ($\hat{\psi}_7$) is:

$$ \psi_7 = (43 + 42 + 40)/3 - (33 + 30)/2 = 41.67 - 31.50 = 10.17 $$

Note that (see Panel C of Table 17.4):

$$ s_{\hat{\psi}_7} = s_{\hat{\psi}_5} = 2.94 $$

Thus,

$$ t_{\hat{\psi}_7} = 10.17/2.94 = 3.46 $$

[16]This method is also called $F$-projections (Miller, 1966) and the $S$-method (Scheffé, 1959).

which is greater than the critical $t$-value of 3.30 for the Scheffé MC method; therefore, this null hypothesis can be rejected at $\alpha_\Sigma = .10$. Try your hand at interpreting this difference—the contrast has little apparent meaningfulness.

The flexibility of the Scheffé method that allows post hoc data snooping for any number of contrasts causes it to be a very conservative and inefficient procedure in the usual research circumstance in which there is interest in only a limited subset of possible contrasts, such as all pairwise contrasts. As Miller (1966, p. 54) observed:

> The great versatility of the Scheffé technique is at the same time its major drawback. Although data-snooping with $F$-projections [Scheffé] is an intellectually nice idea, it does not seem to be of much practical importance. For a pre-specified subset of the possible contrasts, the Dunn method will usually be more powerful than the Scheffé method.

When testing only all possible pairwise contrasts, the Tukey or Newman-Keuls methods are more sensitive, especially as $J$ increases.

## 17.16 PLANNED ORTHOGONAL CONTRASTS

When a researcher can accept the constraints imposed by *planned orthogonal contrasts* (POC), they are the most powerful tests of mean differences. The POC method employs a contrast-based type-I error rate, $\alpha$. The notion of a planned contrast was treated in Section 17.12; the concept of *orthogonality* will now be considered.

In the POC method, the sum of squares between groups, $SS_B$, is decomposed into $\nu_B = J - 1$ orthogonal (i.e., mathematically independent, mutually exclusive) parts. Each part is associated with a contrast. Thus, the $J - 1$ possible orthogonal contrasts contain unique, non-overlapping information.

In balanced (equal $n$) designs, the two contrasts $\psi$ and $\psi'$ are orthogonal when the products of the corresponding contrast coefficients sum to zero:[17]

$$\sum_j c_j c_j' = c_1 c_1' + c_2 c_2' + \ldots + c_J c_J' = 0 \qquad \textbf{(17.13)}$$

For example, for contrasts 1 ($\psi_1$) and 2 ($\psi_2$) in Table 17.4:

$$\sum_j c_{j1} c_{j2} = (1)(0) + (0)(1) + (0)(0) + (0)(0) + (0)(0) + (0)(-1) + (-1)(0) = 0;$$

thus, the contrasts $\psi_1$ and $\psi_2$ are orthogonal. What about contrasts $\psi_1$ and $\psi_3$? Note that:

$$\sum_j c_{j1} c_{j3} = (1)(1) + (0)(0) + (0)(-1) + (0)(0) + (0)(0) + (0)(0) + (-1)(0) = 1;$$

hence, $\psi_1$ and $\psi_3$ are not orthogonal. Since $\psi_1$, $\psi_2$, and $\psi_3$ are not orthogonal, the conditions required for use of the POC method are not met. Although contrasts 1 and 2 and contrasts 2 and 3 are orthogonal, *each* contrast must be orthogonal to *every other* contrast to achieve the condition of orthogonality of the set of contrasts. POC is the MC method of choice only

[17] When the $n$'s are not equal, orthogonality is maintained when $\Sigma_j c_{ij} c_{ij}'/n_j = 0$ (Winer et al., 1991, p. 143). Thus, contrasts are rarely purely orthogonal with unbalanced designs. In practice, the meaningfulness of the contrasts must be preserved even if some departure from orthogonality results.

when (1) all research questions can be answered by $C = J - 1$ or fewer contrasts, and (2) all $C$ contrasts are orthogonal.

For POC, the critical value is the central $t$-ratio found in Table C in the Appendix, where $\nu_e$ ($\nu_W$) is the degrees of freedom for $MS_e$ ($MS_W$), that is, ${}_{1-\alpha/2}t_\nu$, where $\alpha$ is the probability of a type-I error for each contrast. With $\alpha = .10$, the critical $t$-value is ${}_{.95}t_{133} \approx {}_{.95}t_{120} = 1.658$.[18]

Using the example in Table 17.4, five of the six contrasts (contrasts 2–6) are orthogonal. For purposes of illustration, assume that these contrasts were decided upon prior to the study. Two of the five orthogonal contrasts (contrasts 2 and 5) achieve statistical significance when the POC method is used, whereas for the other three (contrasts 3, 4, and 6), the null hypothesis is tenable. Although contrast 1 would have been significant, it could not legitimately be included in the POC analysis since it is not orthogonal to the other contrasts.

The requirement that the contrasts be both planned and orthogonal makes the POC method conceptually and procedurally very different from multiple $t$-tests, even though the critical $t$-ratio employed is the same.

## 17.17 CONFIDENCE INTERVALS FOR CONTRASTS[19]

The $1 - \alpha$ confidence interval ($CI$) for $\mu_j - \mu_j'$ using the Tukey method is:

$$(\overline{X}_j - \overline{X}_{j'}) \pm HSD \qquad \textbf{(17.14)}$$

where (see Equation 17.5) $HSD$ = (critical-$q$)$s_{\overline{X}}$. Thus, in Table 17.2, the $.90CI$ for the difference in the mean of population 1 and the mean of population 7 (i.e., contrast 1 in Table 17.4) is (from Equation 17.14):

$$13 \pm (3.86)(3.217) = 13 \pm 12.42 \text{ or } (.58, 25.42).$$

For the MC methods for which the $t$-distribution is used, the $.90CI$ for a contrast $\psi$ is:

$$\hat{\psi} \pm (\text{critical-}t)s_{\hat{\psi}} \qquad \textbf{(17.15)}$$

The critical $t$-ratios for the various MC methods (using alpha =.10) for the sample problem were determined earlier when the null hypotheses were being tested:

$$\text{Dunn: } {}_{.95}t_{\nu_e,C}$$

$$\text{Dunnett: } {}_{.95}t_{\nu_e,J-1}$$

$$\text{Scheffé: } \sqrt{(J-1)\,{}_{.90}F_{J-1,\nu_e}}$$

$$\text{POC: } {}_{.95}t_{\nu_e} = \sqrt{{}_{.90}F_{1,\nu_e}}$$

---

[18]Using the TINV "paste function" of EXCEL, the exact critical $t$-value is found to be 1.656, which is trivially different from 1.658.

[19]The Newman-Keuls and Duncan (see Section 17.7 footnote) methods do not lend themselves to interval estimation.

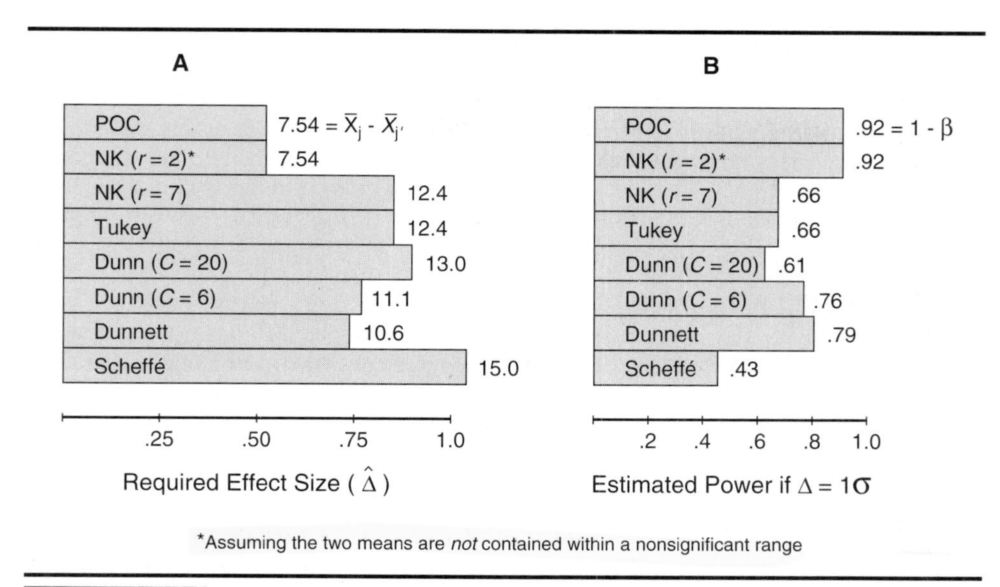


**FIGURE 17.1** Minimum difference between two means needed to reject $H_0$ (Panel A) and estimated power for an effect size of $1\sigma$ (Panel B) $H_0$: $\mu_j = \mu_{j'}$ at the .10 level for various multiple comparison methods using the data in Table 17.1 ($J = 7$, $MS_e = 207$, $\nu_e = 133$, $s_{\hat{\psi}} = 4.55$, $s_{\bar{X}} = 3.217$).

The relative sizes of the confidence intervals for pairwise contrasts for the various MC methods are illustrated in Panel A of Figure 17.1. The length of each bar is the minimum difference for a pairwise contrast required for statistical significance at the .10 level (i.e., each bar is one-half the width of the .90*CI*) for the sample problem.

## 17.18 RELATIVE POWER OF MULTIPLE COMPARISON TECHNIQUES

Notice that the mean difference required for significance for the various MC methods varies greatly. Observe in Panel A of Figure 17.1 that:

1. The POC method requires the smallest mean difference for statistical significance.
2. The NK and the POC methods require the identical difference for significance between adjacent, ordered means (of course, the NK method will never reach or allow this comparison if the two means fall within a nonsignificant range).
3. The initial comparison ($\bar{X}_1$ vs. $\bar{X}_J$) for the Tukey and NK methods is the same.
4. The Tukey is slightly more powerful than the Dunn method if all pairwise contrasts are planned ($C = 21$).
5. The Dunn method requires a slightly larger mean difference for $J - 1 = 6$ planned contrasts than does the Dunnett.
6. The Scheffé technique requires a much larger difference than any of the other MC methods for simple contrasts. The Scheffé method becomes increasingly conservative, and lacking in power, as $J$ increases.

To demonstrate further the relative power of the various MC techniques, assume for purposes of illustration that the difference between two population means is 10. Using the design in Table 17.1, the estimated power of the various MC methods for correctly rejecting the pairwise null hypothesis is given in Panel B of Figure 17.1. Notice that the Scheffé method is much less powerful than the other procedures. Although the POC method is much more powerful than the other techniques, the conditions of requiring contrasts to be planned and orthogonal greatly restricts its utility.

## 17.19 TREND ANALYSIS

Trend analysis is similar to planned orthogonal comparisons, but it is ordinarily used in lieu of multiple comparisons when there is a continuum underlying the $J$ levels of the factor. When persons are grouped into levels of a factor such as age, grade, IQ, or SES, by using trend analysis, one can examine statistically the shape of the curve that results when the means of the dependent variable, $\bar{Y}_j$, are plotted for the $J$ levels of the factor (independent variable).[20] In such situations, the use of trend analysis is usually more informative than multiple comparisons. Indeed, MC methods often fragment the whole configuration into seemingly contradictory parts when the $J$ levels of the factor represent a continuum. For example, suppose persons are classified into very low (1), low (2), medium (3), high (4), and very high (5) levels of the factor "Anxiety," the omnibus $F$-test for $H_0$: $\mu_1 = \mu_2 = \ldots = \mu_5$ is rejected, and all pairwise comparisons are performed with the following result: $H_0$: $\mu_1 = \mu_5$ is rejected, but all the other $H_0$'s are tenable. It is implausible that the effects of anxiety appear abruptly and that there is only a difference between levels 1 and 5. More likely, the difference among all levels would have been significant if the power were greatly increased.

When the levels of a factor can be ordered, the use of multiple comparisons can make the findings seem fragmented and illogical. A trend analysis, however, can illuminate the nature of the relationship among the $J$ levels of the independent variable, $X$, and the dependent variable, $Y$. Trend analysis allows one to assess whether the relationship between $X$ and $Y$ is linear or has a nonlinear pattern. If nonlinear, trend analysis identifies the general shape of the best fitting regression (trend) line of $Y$ on $X$.

Trend analysis uses "orthogonal polynomials" to fit the trend line of the $J$ means. A polynomial is a mathematical equation that contains powers of the variable $X$ greater than one. For example:

$Y = a + bX$ is a linear or first-degree equation,

$Y = a + bX + cX^2$ is a quadratic or second-degree equation,

$Y = a + bX + cX^2 + dX^3$ is a cubic or third-degree equation, and so on.

The general algebraic expression for an orthogonal polynomial in a trend analysis for a factor $X$ of $J$ levels is:

$$Y = a + bX + cX^2 + dX^3 + \ldots + qX^{J-1} \qquad \textbf{(17.16)}$$

[20]In trend analysis, as in regression analysis (Chapter 8) and the analysis of covariance (Chapter 21), the dependent variable is denoted by $Y$ and the independent variable by $X$.

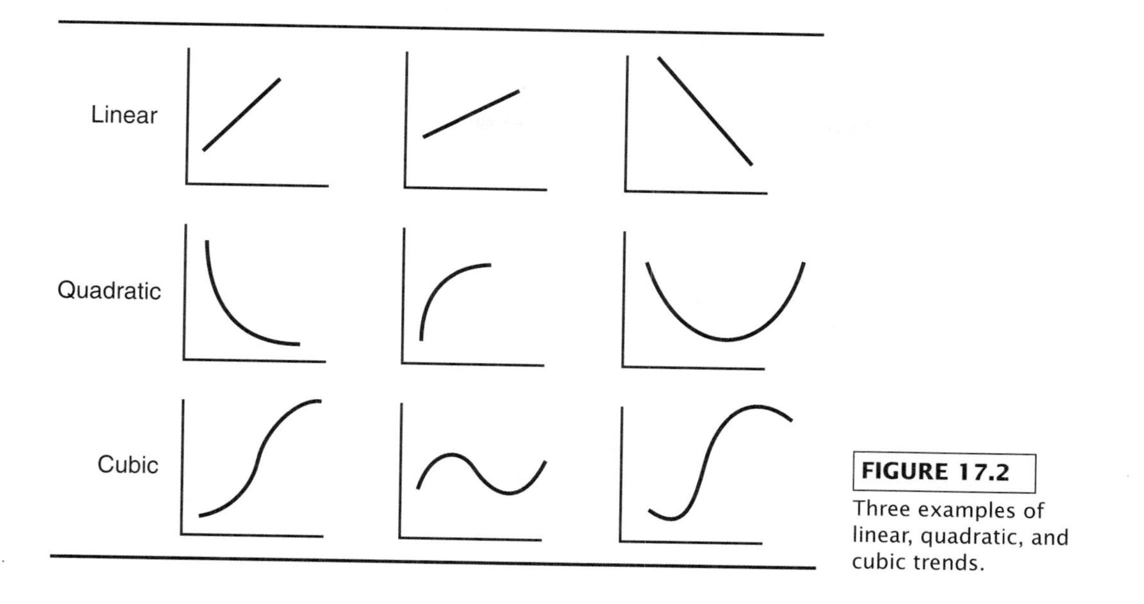


**FIGURE 17.2**
Three examples of linear, quadratic, and cubic trends.

Examples of linear, quadratic, and cubic trends are illustrated in Figure 17.2.

As with POC, there are $C = J - 1$ possible trends that can be evaluated; indeed, trend analysis is a special subset of planned orthogonal contrasts. Trend analysis determines whether each term in Equation 17.16 contributes unique information—if it does not, $H_0$ for that trend is tenable. The correlation ratio, $\eta^2$, (Section 8.27) describes the proportion of variance in $Y$ that is explicable or predictable from the orthogonal polynomial (curvilinear regression), whereas $r^2$ denotes the proportion of variance explicable from the first-degree (linear) equation ($a + bX$) alone. If there is no curvilinear relationship between the independent and dependent variables in the population, the second and higher degree equations will not significantly improve the prediction of $Y$, that is, the degree of improvement will not be statistically significant and can be interpreted to be the result of sampling error, except when a type-I error is made.

The example in Table 17.5 confirms that trend analysis is just a special application of planned orthogonal contrasts.[21] The example is from Table 8.5 (Section 8.27) in which $n = 4$ persons in each of $J = 7$ age groups are tested on psychomotor performance. The ANOVA table in Panel A of Table 17.5 shows that the means of the seven age groups differ significantly. Is there a trend in the pattern of mean differences? Is there a linear trend among the seven means, that is, can a straight (linear) regression line predict the $J$ means significantly better than the grand mean $\overline{Y}_{\bullet} = 9.64$—is $H_0$: $\psi_{\text{linear}} = 0$ tenable?

A second and *independent* question is whether or not a quadratic component (a smooth curved line with a single bend, e.g., a parabola) can account for a significant amount of variance in the $\overline{Y}_j$'s over and above that provided by the grand mean and the linear contrast—is $H_0$: $\psi_{\text{quadratic}} = 0$ tenable? Notice that the orthogonality criterion defined in Equa-

[21]Unlike POC's, the numerical values of these trend analysis contrasts are not interpreted as a difference between the means of two subsets of means; consequently, whole numbers are used for contrast coefficients to simplify the computations.

tion 17.13 is met by the linear and quadratic contrasts given in Panel B of Table 17.5: The sum of the products of their corresponding coefficients is 0:

$$(-3)(5) + (-2)(0) + (-1)(-3) + (0)(-4) + (1)(-3) + (2)(0) + (3)(5) = 0$$

Similarly, a third and independent question asks if there is a significant cubic component—will a regression line that allows two bends better fit the data than a straight line and/or a quadratic curve with a single bend? Look at the scatterplot of the data in Figure 8.9 in Section 8.27. There does not appear to be a significant linear component (note that $r = -.077$). The means seem to increase up to a point, then begin to decline; this suggests that there is a quadratic component. There is not a second change of direction, which suggests that there is no cubic component in the relationship. These apparent trends should be evaluated for statistical significance to guard against overinterpretation. Notice that, unlike POC's, the contrast coefficients do not have to be constructed; they are found in Table N in the Appendix. Panel B in Table 17.5 gives the $J = 7$ contrast coefficients for $\psi_{\text{linear}}$, $\psi_{\text{quadratic}}$, and $\psi_{\text{cubic}}$. Higher order trends could also be tested, but such complex trends are rarely expected. The contrast coefficients are given for only the first five trends in Table N. Notice in Panel D of Table 17.5 that the numerical values for $MS_{\text{linear}}$ and $MS_{\text{cubic}}$ are very small (only .32 and .67), whereas $MS_{\text{quadratic}}$ is much larger (24.11).

## 17.20 SIGNIFICANCE OF TREND COMPONENTS

Are the trend contrasts large enough to reject $H_0$: $\psi = 0$? Equation 17.9 can be expressed as Equation 17.17 and used to make a $t$-test for each of the trends (contrasts):

$$t_{\hat{\psi}} = \frac{\hat{\psi}}{s_{\hat{\psi}}} = \frac{\hat{\psi}}{\sqrt{\dfrac{MS_e \Sigma c_j^2}{n}}} \quad \textbf{(17.17)}$$

The statistical significance of the contrast is often evaluated using the $F$-test that is mathematically equivalent to $t^2$ found using Equation 17.17. The $F$-ratio for a trend (or contrast) is the ratio of the mean square for the trend, $MS_{\hat{\psi}}$, divided by $MS_e$ ($MS_W$), where:

$$MS_{\hat{\psi}} = \frac{\hat{\psi}^2}{\dfrac{\Sigma c_j^2}{n}} \quad \textbf{(17.18)}$$

(Notice that the value of $\Sigma c_j^2$ is also given in Table N.) If the observed $F$-ratio, $F = MS_\psi / MS_e$, is larger than the critical $F$ $({}_{1-\alpha}F_{1,\nu_e})$, then $H_0$: $\psi = 0$ is rejected.

The $F$-tests for the linear, quadratic, and cubic trends are given in Panel D of Table 17.5. Notice that only the quadratic component is significant.[22] The findings from the trend analysis are given in the ANOVA table in Panel E of Table 17.5.

[22]If it is desired to express the curvilinear relationship via a mathematical equation, SPSS's curve estimating procedure can be used. the equation of the curved line in Figure 17.4 (mean cholesterol level with age) is $\hat{Y}_i = 62.65 + 8.33X_i - 8.33X_i - .068X_1^2$. The statistical particulars are given in Scedecor and Cochran (1980, pp. 404–407).

**TABLE 17.5** Means for Seven Age Levels on Psychomotor Test (Data from Table 8.5).

**A. *ANOVA Table***

| *Source* | *SS* | *v* | *MS* | *F* | $p^a$ |
|---|---|---|---|---|---|
| Age (between) | 29.43 | 6 | 4.905 | 4.12 | .007 |
| Error (within) | 25.00 | 21 | 1.190 | | |
| Total | 54.43 | $27 = n_{\bullet} - J$ | | | |

**B. *Means:***

| | $\bar{Y}_1$ (8.5) | $\bar{Y}_2$ (9.5) | $\bar{Y}_3$ (10.5) | $\bar{Y}_4$ (11.5) | $\bar{Y}_5$ (10.0) | $\bar{Y}_6$ (9.0) | $\bar{Y}_7$ (8.5) | |
|---|---|---|---|---|---|---|---|---|
| Contrast Coefficients: | $c_1$ | $c_2$ | $c_3$ | $c_4$ | $c_5$ | $c_6$ | $c_7$ | $\Sigma c_j^2$ |
| $\psi_{\text{linear}}$ | −3 | −2 | −1 | 0 | 1 | 2 | 3 | 28 |
| $\psi_{\text{quadratic}}$ | 5 | 0 | −3 | −4 | −3 | 0 | 5 | 84 |
| $\psi_{\text{cubic}}$ | −1 | 1 | 1 | 0 | −1 | −1 | 1 | 6 |

**C. *Estimated Contrasts***

$$\hat{\psi}_{\text{linear}} = (-3)(8.5) + (-2)(9.5) + (-1)(10.5) + (0)(11.5) + (1)(10.0) + (2)(9.0) + (3)(8.5) = -1.5$$
$$\hat{\psi}_{\text{quadratic}} = (5)(8.5) + (-3)(10.5) + (-4)(11.5) + (-3)(10.0) + (5)(8.5) = -22.5$$
$$\hat{\psi}_{\text{cubic}} = -8.5 + 9.5 + 10.5 - 10.00 - 9.0 + 8.5 = 1.0$$

**D. *Significance Tests of Contrasts***

$$MS_{\hat{\psi}} = \frac{\hat{\psi}_k^2}{\frac{\Sigma c_j^2}{n}}, \quad MS_{\hat{\psi}_{\text{linear}}} = \frac{(-1.5)^2}{\frac{28}{4}} = \frac{2.25}{7} = .32$$

$$F_{\hat{\psi}_{\text{linear}}} = \frac{MS_{\hat{\psi}_{\text{linear}}}}{MS_e} = \frac{.32}{1.19} = .27, \quad {}_{.75}F_{1,21} = 1.40, \ p > .25$$

$$MS_{\hat{\psi}_{\text{quadratic}}} = \frac{(-22.5)^2}{\frac{84}{4}} = 24.11, \ F_{\hat{\psi}_{\text{quadratic}}} = \frac{24.11}{1.19} = 20.26, \quad {}_{.999}F_{1,21} = 14.8, \ p < .01,$$

$$MS_{\hat{\psi}_{\text{cubic}}} = \frac{(1.0)^2}{\frac{6}{4}} = .67, \ F_{\hat{\psi}_{\text{cubic}}} = \frac{.67}{1.19} = .56, \ p > .25$$

**E. *Trend Analysis Summary***

| *Source* | *SS* | *v* | *MS* | *F* | $p^a$ |
|---|---|---|---|---|---|
| Age | 29.43 | 6 | 4.905 | 4.12 | .007 |
| Linear | .32 | 1 | .32 | .27 | .61 |
| Quadratic | 24.11 | 1 | 24.11 | 20.26 | .0002 |
| Cubic | .67 | 1 | .67 | .56 | .46 |
| Remainder[b] | 4.33 | 3 | 1.44 | 1.21 | .33 |
| Error (within) | 25.00 | 21 | 1.190 | | |

[a]From computer.

[b]This is an aggregate of quartic and other higher order curvilinear trends:
$SS_{\text{remainder}} = SS_B - SS_{\text{linear}} - SS_{\text{quadratic}} - SS_{\text{cubic}} = 29.43 - .32 - 24.11 - .67 = 4.33.$

The sum of squares for the remaining components for the three higher order (quartic, etc.) trends can be aggregated and tested as a composite by subtracting the sum of squares accounted for by the three trends that have been evaluated (.32 + 24.11 + .67 = 25.10) from $SS_{\text{between}}$ (= $SS_{\text{age}}$ = 29.43) to yield $SS_{\text{remainder}}$ (29.43 – 25.10 = 4.33). The remainder has $J - 1 - 3 = 3$ degrees of freedom. The mean square for the remainder is shown in Panel E to be 1.44 (= 4.33/3). The $F$-test for the composite of the remaining higher order trends is given in the fifth line of the ANOVA table in Panel E of Table 17.5. Since $F = 1.44/1.19 = 1.21$ and $p > .33$, it does not appear that there are higher order trends.[23]

## 17.21 RELATION OF TRENDS TO CORRELATION COEFFICIENTS

There is a close parallel between the linear trend and the Pearson product-moment correlation coefficient, $r_{YX}$:

$$r^2 = \frac{SS_{\text{linear}}}{SS_{\text{total}}} \tag{17.19}$$

where $SS_{\text{linear}} = MS_{\text{linear}}$ since for each trend (and planned orthogonal contrast) $\nu = 1$. In the example, using the results summarized in Table 17.5:

$$r^2 = \frac{SS_{\text{linear}}}{SS_{\text{total}}} = \frac{.32}{54.43} = 0.0058, \text{ and } r = \pm\,.077$$

which agrees with the $r$ of –.077 found in Section 8.27.

Likewise:

$$\hat{\eta}^2_{Y.X} = \frac{SS_{\text{between}}}{SS_{\text{total}}} = \frac{29.43}{54.43} = .541 \tag{17.20}$$

which agrees with the value for $\eta^2_{Y.X}$ that was found in Section 8.27. $\eta^2_{Y.X}$ defines the proportion of variance explained by the independent variable $X$; this is a composite of all the $J - 1$ trends.

Note in Panel E of Table 17.5 that the $F$-ratio of 4.12 for the Age (between) effect is identical to the test for $H_0$: $\eta^2_{Y.X} = 0$ in Section 14.20. Similarly, the $F$-test for nonlinearity of regression in Section 14.21 yields $F = 4.89$, which is identical to testing the remaining $J - 2$ trend components after the linear component has been removed, that is:

$$SS_{\text{nonlinear}} = SS_{\text{between}} - SS_{\text{linear}} = 29.43 - .32 = 29.11$$

---

[23] Some writers advocate a significant $F$-test of the remainder at each step before exploring further trends. We advocate this only after a priori contrasts have been examined individually. The logic is identical to that for POC's in relation to the omnibus $F$-test. The $SS_{\hat{\psi}} = MS_{\hat{\psi}}$ for the fourth, fifth, and sixth-order terms, if tested individually, are 3.14 ($p = .12$), .01 ($p = .93$), and 1.18 ($p = .33$), which sum to 4.33 = $SS_{\text{remainder}}$.

and:

$$MS_{\text{nonlinear}} = \frac{SS_{\text{nonlinear}}}{(J-2)} = \frac{29.11}{(7-2)} = 5.82$$

and:

$$F = \frac{MS_{\text{nonlinear}}}{MS_e} = \frac{5.82}{1.19} = 4.89$$

which is greater than the critical $F$ ($_{.999}F_{5,133} \approx 4.42$); thus, there is a significant nonlinear relationship between $X$ and $Y$.

## 17.22 ASSUMPTIONS OF MC METHODS

All methods discussed in this chapter have the same assumptions of normality, homogeneity of variance, and independence that are made for the $t$-test and ANOVA.

The MC methods appear to be robust to departures from normality, but cannot be presumed to be robust to large departures from homogeneity of variance (Petrinovich & Hardyck, 1969). Consequently, the HOV assumption should be tested when using MC methods even if the design is balanced. If variances are very heterogeneous, the Welch quasi-$t'$ or Brown-Forsythe tests can be used for pairwise testing, setting $\alpha$ more stringently (e.g., $\alpha = .01$) or use the Bonferroni inequality (Equation 17.10) to make allowance for the fact that several $H_0$'s are to be tested.[24]

## 17.23 MULTIPLE COMPARISONS AMONG OTHER STATISTICS

The large sample[25] method described by Marascuilo (1966) defines a contrast similar to, but more general than, Equation 17.7:

$$\hat{\psi} = \sum_j c_j \hat{\theta}_j \qquad \textbf{(17.21)}$$

where $\hat{\theta}_j$ represents any of $J$ independent statistics ($p$, $r$, $\overline{X}$, $Md$, etc.) and $\Sigma_j c_j = 0$. The estimated variance of the contrast, $\sigma_{\hat{\psi}}^2$, is the sum of the variances of the statistics involved in the contrast, weighted by the contrast coefficients:

[24]A large sample MC test that does not assume homogeneity of variance (Marascuilo, 1966) is given in Section 17.23. This procedure is not very powerful (Hopkins & Anderson, 1973; Hochberg, 1976) for pairwise contrasts among means. A modification by Levy (1975, 1977) is less conservative.

[25]A large sample statistical test is one in which the test requires knowledge of a parameter that is not known, but, because $n$ is large, the sampling error in the estimate of that parameter is viewed as negligible.

**TABLE 17.6** Illustration of Multiple Comparison among Proportions.

| | Group 1 | Group 2 | Group 3 |
|---|---|---|---|
| $P_j$: | .25 | .20 | .49 |
| $n_j$: | 40 | 60 | 200 |
| $\hat{\sigma}^2_{p_j} = \dfrac{p_j(1-p_j)}{n_j}$ | .00469 | .00267 | .00125 |

$$\psi_1 : \pi_1 - \pi_3;\ \hat{\psi}_1 = .25 - .49 = -.24;\quad \hat{\sigma}^2_{\hat{\psi}_1} = .00469 + .00125 = .00594$$

$$\psi_2 : \pi_1 - \pi_2;\ \hat{\psi}_2 = .25 - .20 = .05;\quad \hat{\sigma}^2_{\hat{\psi}_2} = .00736$$

$$\psi_3 : \pi_2 - \pi_3;\ \hat{\psi}_3 = .20 - .49 = -.29;\quad \hat{\sigma}^2_{\hat{\psi}_2} = .00392$$

$$\chi^2_{\hat{\psi}_1} = \frac{\hat{\psi}_1^2}{\hat{\sigma}^2_{\hat{\psi}_1}} = \frac{(-.24)^2}{.00594} = 9.70 > 9.21 =_{.99} \chi^2_2, p < .01$$

$$\chi^2_{\hat{\psi}_2} = \frac{(.05)^2}{.00736} = .34, p > .80$$

$$\chi^2_{\hat{\psi}_3} = \frac{(-.29)^2}{.00392} = 21.45 > 13.82 =_{.999} \chi^2_2, p < .001$$

$$\hat{\sigma}^2_{\hat{\psi}} = \sum_j c_j^2 \hat{\sigma}^2_{\hat{\theta}_j} \qquad \textbf{(17.22)}$$

for pairwise contrasts, $c_j^2 = 1$, hence $\hat{\sigma}_{\hat{\psi}}^2 = \Sigma_j \hat{\sigma}_{\hat{\theta}_j}^2$.

If $n$ is large, the ratio $\psi^2/\hat{\sigma}_{\hat{\psi}}^2$ has an approximate $\chi^2$-distribution with $\nu = J - 1$:

$$\chi^2 = \frac{\hat{\psi}^2}{\hat{\sigma}^2_{\hat{\psi}}} \qquad \textbf{(17.23)}$$

The critical value for the *family*[26] of any number of contrasts is ${}_{1-\alpha}\chi_{\nu}^2$.

The technique is illustrated in Table 17.6 using the proportions from three groups: $p_1 = .25$, $n_1 = 40$, $p_2 = .25$, $n_2 = 60$, $p_3 = .49$, and $n_3 = 200$. Note that $H_0$: $\pi_1 = \pi_2$ was tenable at $\alpha_\Sigma = .05$, whereas $H_0$: $\pi_1 = \pi_3$ and $H_0$: $\pi_2 = \pi_3$ were rejected.[27]

[26] Levy's (1975, 1977) modification increases the power of the tests by limiting the comparisons to only pairwise contrasts.

[27] Although the authors have never seen it used for this purpose, another satisfactory alternative is to use methods appropriate for comparing two statistics (such as chi-square), and use the Bonferroni inequality to obtain the critical value for the test statistic.

## 17.24 CHAPTER SUMMARY AND CRITERIA FOR SELECTING A MULTIPLE COMPARISON METHOD

There are several multiple comparison methods; the methods will often yield very different results. Some MC methods require planned (a priori) contrasts (Dunn, Dunnett, and planned orthogonal contrasts) while others are post hoc (Tukey, Newman-Keuls, Scheffé, and Marascuilo). The MC methods also differ with respect to the basis for $\alpha$; POC and NK use the contrast as the basis; the others have a family-based significance level, $\alpha_\Sigma$. MC methods using contrast-based $\alpha$ will tend to have greater power, but have less protection against type-I errors. All methods except Marascuilo's assume homogeneity of variances; this assumption should be tested especially if the $n$'s are not equal. Other distinctions are reviewed in the decisions in the schema in Figure 17.3.

1. The large-sample method described by Marascuilo (1966) can be used when making MC's among correlation coefficients, proportions, and other statistics.
2. If the $J$ levels are levels on an ordered continuum, such as age, grade, and trials, use trend analysis.
3. Make planned orthogonal contrasts if they will test the relevant hypotheses (often this will not be the case). Each comparison will have the contrast as the base for $\alpha$. If the contrasts are not planned, do an ANOVA (step 6).
4. If all comparisons of interest contrast the control group with each of the other $J - 1$ groups, use the Dunnett procedure. Using the Dunnett technique, the probability of a type-I error is $\alpha_\Sigma$ for the set of $J - 1$ tests.
5. If the number of comparisons, $C$, is not large (e.g., $C < (J - 1)/4$), use the Dunn test.[28] The Dunn test is appropriate for simple contrasts involving only two means (i.e., a pair of means) and complex contrasts involving more than two means. If $C$ is large, do an ANOVA.
6. Compare the $F$-ratio differences among the means obtained in the ANOVA with the critical $F$-value required for significance. If $H_0$ cannot be rejected, one ordinarily does not look further for mean differences. If the omnibus $F$ is not significant, it is tantamount to concluding that all differences among all means are attributable to random sampling error.[29]
7. If only pairwise comparisons are to be made and a contrast-based $\alpha$ is desired, use NK.
8. If only $C = J(J - 1)/2$ pairwise comparisons are of interest and a family-based $\alpha$ is desired, the Tukey method should be used, since it is more powerful than the Dunn and Scheffé methods under such conditions (Scheffé, 1959, p. 76). If the number of hypotheses to be tested, $C$, is less than $J(J - 1)/2$, the Dunn (1961) method will usually be more powerful than either the Tukey or the Scheffé method.
9. If comparisons between complex combinations of means are desired, the Dunn method usually has more power than Scheffé, unless $C$ is very large.
10. The Scheffé is rarely the MC method of choice except for "data snooping."

[28] Tables 4 to 6 in Dunn (1961) provide precise figures for various $J$, $\alpha$, and $\nu_e$ combinations for which the Dunn method is more powerful than the Scheffé method.

[29] Strictly speaking, none of the methods is contingent upon a significant omnibus $F$-test. Indeed, this recommendation makes the MC tests somewhat conservative (Myette & White, 1982). This sequence is logical, however, since the omnibus $F$-test is more powerful than the MC tests it precedes.

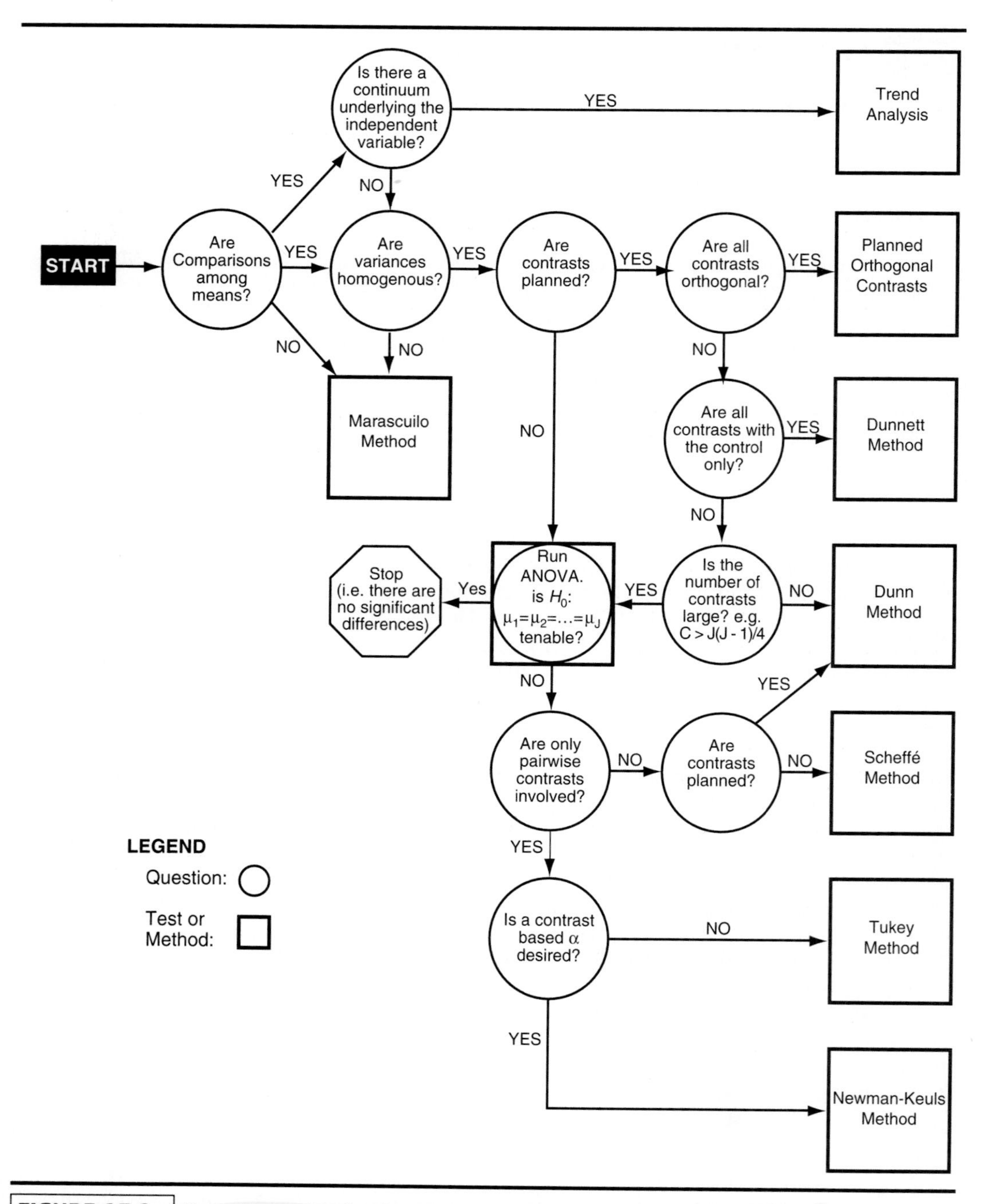


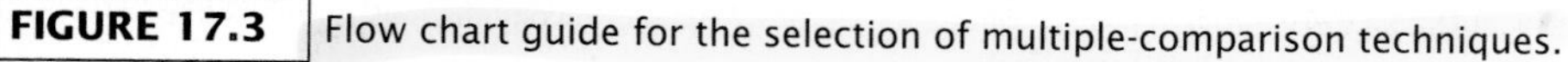
**FIGURE 17.3** Flow chart guide for the selection of multiple-comparison techniques.

## 17.25 CASE STUDY

**Multiple Comparisons.** In the Case Study following Chapter 15 (Section 15.32), a one-factor ANOVA found a significant difference ($p = .028$) among the means of the four ethnic groups on the locus of control variable (see Figure 15.7). Without multiple comparisons, we were unable to determine which of the four means differed from which other means. Table 17.7 gives the output when the Newman-Keuls method is used to make all

**TABLE 17.7** Multiple Comparison Computer[30] Output for the HSB Data Set.

Variable LOCUS LOCUS OF CONTROL
By Variable RACE

***Analysis of Variance***

| *Source* | *D.F.* | *Sum of Squares* | *Mean Squares* | *F Ratio* | *p* |
|---|---|---|---|---|---|
| Between Groups | 3 | 4.0740 | 1.3580 | 3.0538 | .0280 |
| Within Groups | 596 | 265.0418 | .4447 | | |
| Total | 599 | 269.1158 | | | |

| *Group* | *n* | *Mean* | *Standard Deviation* | *Standard Error* | *Min.* | *Max.* | *.95CI for Mean* |
|---|---|---|---|---|---|---|---|
| HISPANIC | 71 | −.1180 | .6906 | .0820 | −1.78 | 1.36 | (−.282, .045) |
| ASIAN | 34 | .0347 | .6363 | .1091 | −1.28 | 1.36 | (−.187, .257) |
| BLACK | 58 | .0993 | .7612 | .1000 | −2.23 | 1.36 | (−.101, .300) |
| WHITE | 437 | .1358 | .6519 | .0312 | −2.23 | 1.36 | (.075, .197) |
| Total | 600 | .0965 | .6703 | .0274 | −2.23 | 1.36 | (.043, .150) |

Levene Test[31] for Homogeneity of Variances

| *Statistic* | *df1* | *df2* | *2-tailed Sig.* |
|---|---|---|---|
| 1.0924 | 3 | 596 | .352 |

Multiple Range Test: Newman-Keuls test with significance level .050

(*) Indicates significant differences between groups

| Mean | RACE | HISPANIC | ASIAN | BLACK | WHITE |
|---|---|---|---|---|---|
| −.1180 | HISPANIC | | | | |
| .0347 | ASIAN | | | | |
| .0993 | BLACK | | | | |
| .1358 | WHITE | * | | | |

[30]From the SPSS ONEWAY program.

[31]The Bartlett test is preferred in this situation because the $n$'s differ greatly; its $p$-value is .57.

**TABLE 17.8** Trend Analysis Output[32] for Cholesterol Level with Age.

*ONEWAY*

Variable CHOLES Serum Cholesterol—Mg per DL
By Variable AGELEVEL

***Analysis of Variance***

| *Source* | *D.F.* | *Sum of Squares* | *Mean Squares* | *F Ratio* | *p* |
|---|---|---|---|---|---|
| Between Groups | 4 | 146779.55 | 36694.89 | 10.295 | .0000 |
| Linear Term | 1 | 135763.67 | 135763.67 | 38.089 | .0000 |
| Deviation from Linear | 3 | 11015.89 | 3671.96 | 1.0302 | .3803 |
| Quadratic Term | 1 | 10508.75 | 10508.75 | 2.948 | .0876 |
| Deviation from Quad. | 2 | 507.14 | 253.57 | .0711 | .9314 |
| Cubic Term | 1 | 213.37 | 213.37 | .0599 | .8070 |
| Deviation from Cubic | 1 | 293.77 | 293.77 | .0824 | .7744 |
| Quartic Term | 1 | 293.77 | 293.77 | .0824 | .7744 |
| Within Groups | 195 | 695052.03 | 3564.37 | | |
| Total | 199 | 841831.58 | | | |

| *Group* | *n* | *Mean* | *Standard Deviation* | *Standard Error* | *Min.* | *Max.* | *.95CI for Mean* |
|---|---|---|---|---|---|---|---|
| Grp 1 | 36 | 235.86 | 59.98 | 10.00 | 135 | 386 | (215.6, 256.2) |
| Grp 2 | 45 | 274.07 | 57.36 | 8.55 | 166 | 403 | (256.8, 291.3) |
| Grp 3 | 58 | 294.69 | 57.37 | 7.53 | 172 | 520 | (279.6, 309.8) |
| Grp 4 | 44 | 311.48 | 66.80 | 10.07 | 178 | 474 | (291.2, 331.8) |
| Grp 5 | 17 | 317.71 | 52.00 | 12.85 | 243 | 420 | (290.5, 345.0) |
| Total | 200 | 285.11 | 65.04 | 4.60 | 135 | 520 | (276.0, 294.2) |

Levene Test for Homogeneity of Variances

| *Statistic* | *df1* | *df2* | *2-tailed Sig.* |
|---|---|---|---|
| .419 | 4 | 195 | .795 |

possible pairwise comparisons. Note that there is only one "*", indicating that only one of the pairwise comparisons was statistically significant; the White mean was significantly greater than the Hispanic mean. Although the Levene test found that the homogeneity of variance assumption was tenable, the Bartlett test is a better choice since the Levene test is equivocal when *n*'s differ greatly, as they do here.[33] Assuming representative samples, we can be confident that the population means of these two populations differ, but we cannot be confident that the means of any other contrasts differ.

[32]From the SPSS ONEWAY program.

[33]The homogeneity of variance assumption was also found to be tenable using the Bartlett test ($\chi^2 = 2.94$, $p = .57$).

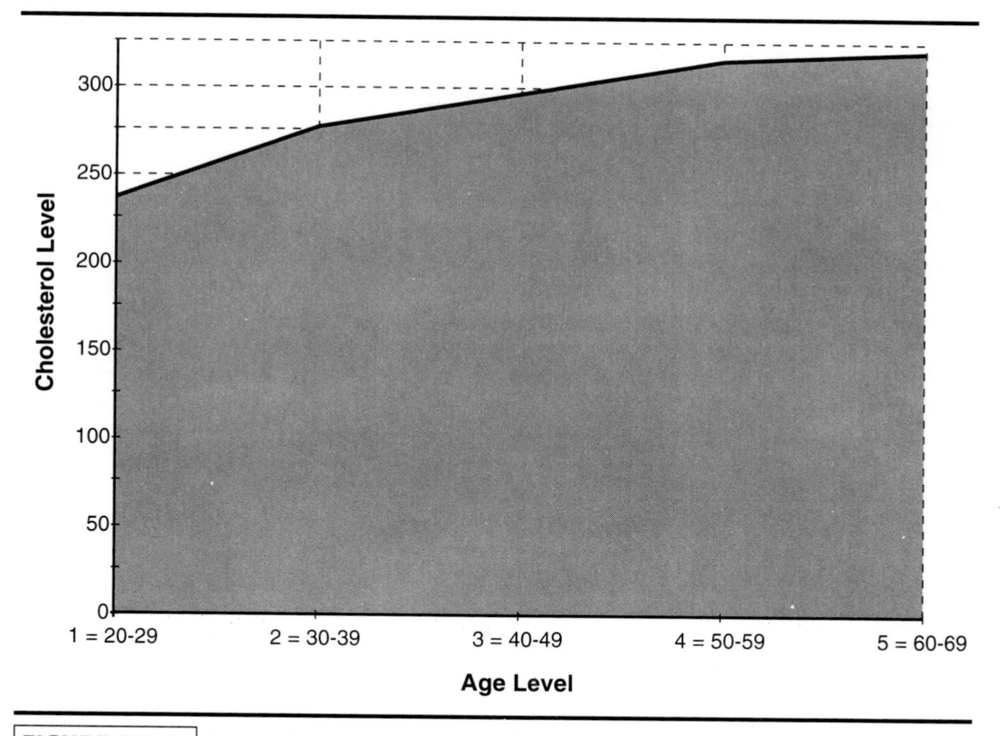


**FIGURE 17.4** Graph of Mean Cholesterol Level for Five Age Groups.

**Trend Analysis.** In the Chapman data set, a correlation of .41 was found between age and cholesterol level (Table 7.11, Section 7.29); age and cholesterol level are related, but let us examine the relationship more closely. Is the increase in cholesterol level constant across age, or is there some nonlinear relationship, for example, is there an increase up to a certain age at which cholesterol level reaches a plateau? As the $n$'s within the various age levels are not large, we will set $\alpha = .10$ to increase our power for finding real effects. Table 17.8 gives a computer output for the trend analysis of cholesterol level with age level (1 = 20–29, 2 = 30–39, 3 = 40–49, 4 = 50–59, and 5 = 60–69). The $r = .41$ has already informed us that there is a definite linear trend, consistent with the linear term in the trend analysis.[34] The graph in Figure 17.4 shows the increase in cholesterol means with age. Notice that cholesterol levels do seem to be reaching a plateau as age increases; this is confirmed by the quadratic effect ($p$ = .0876). The graph illustrates why there were no cubic or quartic trends. Thus, we concluded that not only does cholesterol level increase between ages 20 to 70, but the rate of the increase is greater in the earlier decades.

Although the computer's choice of the Levene test for homogeneity of variance could

[34]From Equation 17.19: $r^2 = SS_{\text{linear}}/SS_{\text{total}} = 135{,}763.67/841{,}831.58 = .1613$, $r = .401$. The difference between the $r$'s of .41 versus .40 is due to the fact that in the trend analysis the correlation is between the age levels (1–5) rather than the precise ages. The slight loss in information in the groupings caused the slight drop in $r$.

have been improved (because the $n$'s are not equal), the results from the Bartlett test using these data (Table 16.2, Section 16.9) were consistent with the Levene ($p = .84$).

## 17.26 SUGGESTED COMPUTER ACTIVITY

Using the EXERCISE data set, create four groups: male smokers, female smokers, male nonsmokers, and female nonsmokers. Run a one-factor ANOVA followed by planned orthogonal contrasts using PUL_GAIN (PULSE_2 - PULSE_1) as the dependent variable. Then (1) compare smokers and nonsmokers, (2) compare males versus females, and (3) find the remaining contrast that is orthogonal to 1 and 2.[35]

## MASTERY TEST

**1.** If a $t$-test is used to compare the largest mean with the smallest mean in a set of five means, which of the following is true? The probability of a type-I error is

(a) greater than
(b) equal to
(c) less than

the $\alpha$ associated with the critical $t$-value.

**2.** Are multiple $t$-tests recommended for locating significant differences when more than two means are involved?

**3.** If ten hypotheses are tested and the probability of a type-I error in any one (or more) of the $H_0$'s is $\leq .05$, the error rate is

(a) per comparison $\alpha$.
(b) per the family of ten contrasts, $\alpha_\Sigma$.

**4.** In making all pairwise comparisons among five means, MC methods that use a family type-I error rate, $\alpha_\Sigma$, will tend to make ____ (fewer or more) type-I errors and ____ (fewer or more) type-II errors than MC methods that employ a contrast-based type-I error rate, $\alpha$.

**5.** After inspecting the data, is it appropriate for a researcher to decide which "planned contrasts: he or she will make?

**6.** What is the distinction between $\psi$ and $\hat{\psi}$?

**7.** Which of these is not a valid contrast?

(a) $\hat{\psi}_1 = \bar{X}_2 - \bar{X}_3$
(b) $\hat{\psi}_2 = \bar{X}_1 + \bar{X}_2 + \bar{X}_3 = 0$
(c) $\hat{\psi}_3 = -\bar{X}_1/2 + \bar{X}_2 - \bar{X}_3/2$
(d) $\hat{\psi}_4 = \bar{X}_1 - \bar{X}_2 - \bar{X}_3 + \bar{X}_4$
(e) $\hat{\psi}_5 = \bar{X}_1 - (\bar{X}_2 + \bar{X}_3 + \bar{X}_4)/3$

**8.** Which of the valid contrasts above are "complex contrasts?"

**9.** What is the null hypothesis implicit in question 7c?

**10.** Are these contrasts in question 7 orthogonal?

(a) a and c
(b) a and d
(c) a and e
(d) c and e
(e) d and e

[35]We will have occasion to deal further with contrast three following Chapter 18.

11. Which contrast in question 7 could be used in comparing the freshmen mean with the average mean from the sophomores, juniors, and seniors?

*Indicate which of the following methods is the proper MC method in the situations described in questions 12 to 17.*

(a) Dunnett method
(b) Newman-Keuls method
(c) planned orthogonal contrasts
(d) Scheffé method
(e) Tukey method
(f) Dunn method
(g) Marascuilo method

12. If a family error rate, $\alpha_\Sigma$, is desired and all hypotheses involved only pairs of means (not complex contrasts), which method should one select?
13. If $J = 6$ and hypotheses $H_{0_1}$: $\mu_1 = \mu_2$, $H_{0_2}$: $\mu_3 = \mu_4$, and $H_{0_3}$: $\mu_1 + \mu_2 = \mu_3 + \mu_4$ were to be tested, which would probably be employed?
14. Which methods use a type-I error rate per comparison (contrast)?
15. If one were only interested in comparing $\overline{X}_1$, $\overline{X}_3$, $\overline{X}_4$, and $\overline{X}_5$ with $\overline{X}_2$, which method would probably be selected?
16. To go "data snooping," which method is most general and makes fewest assumptions?
17. To make multiple comparisons among several independent proportions or correlation coefficients, which one would be chosen?
18. In which of these ways does the Scheffé method differ from POC, for example, to test the $H_0$ in question 7c?
    (a) in the coefficients employed for a given contrast
    (b) in computing the value of $\hat{\psi}$
    (c) in calculating $t$ (or $F$)
    (d) in the critical value for the test statistic
19. The Newman-Keuls and Tukey tests always give the identical result in testing a hypothesis for a contrast when:
    (a) $J = 3$
    (b) comparing the extreme-most means
    (c) $r = 2$ (range of ordered mean = $r$)
    (d) when $n$ is large
20. The assumption $\sigma_1^2 = \sigma_2^2 = \ldots = \sigma_J^2$ can be disregarded in making multiple comparisons if $n_1 = n_2 = \ldots = n_J$. (T or F)
21. Which method does not assume homogeneity of variance?
22. Which method is best for planned complex, nonorthogonal contrasts?

*The figure below is from a recent review of the literature on the relationship between hours of television viewing (weekly) and school achievement for students in grades K through 12 (Williams et al., 1982). If a trend analysis were performed on these data, does it appear that there would be:*

23. A linear trend?
24. A cubic trend?
25. A quartic (fourth-degree) trend?

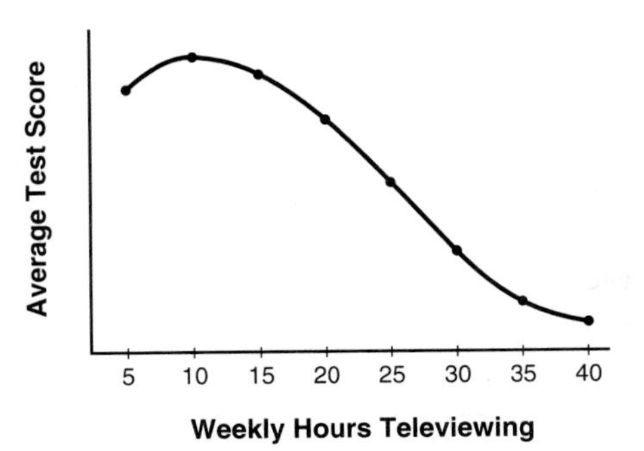

*The figures below depict the national trends in average high school GPA and ACT (college admission test) scores during 1970–1992.*

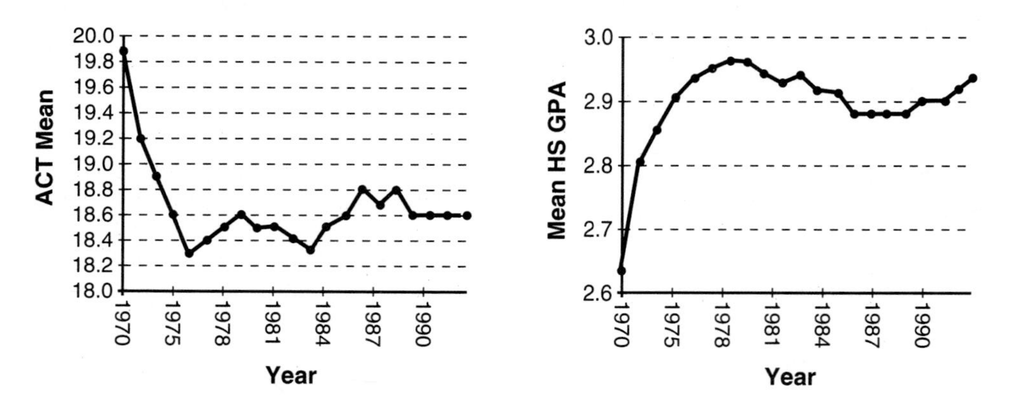


26. Which trend lines reflect a linear trend (linear component would be significant in a trend analysis)?
27. Is the nature of the linear trend in the two graphs logically congruent?
28. Which trend lines reflect a quadratic trend?
29. Which line most clearly reflects a possible cubic trend?
30. How many orthogonal trends (including the linear, quadratic, and cubic trends), could be evaluated statistically in each figure?

## PROBLEMS

*Use the following data for problems 1–5 (see problem 5 following Chapter 15).*

| *Source* | $\nu$ | *MS* | *F* | *p* |
|---|---|---|---|---|
| Between | 2 | 9.10 | 4.01 | .03 |
| Within | 27 | 2.27 | | |

| *Postorganizer Group* | *Preorganizer Group* | *No organizer Group* |
|---|---|---|
| $\overline{X}_1 = 5.6$ | $\overline{X}_2 = 4.0$ | $\overline{X}_3 = 3.9$ |

1. For the balanced design above ($n = 10$), use planned orthogonal contrasts with $\alpha = .05$, to test (a) whether the means of the two "organizer" groups differ from the "no organizer" group, and (b) the difference between the means of the two organizer groups.
2. If the two null hypotheses in the problem 1 were tested using the Scheffé method, would both be tenable with $\alpha_\Sigma = .05$?
3. Use the Dunn method to test $H_0$: $\psi = 0$ for the two contrasts.
4. Use the Tukey method to test all pairwise contrasts.
5. If the Newman-Keuls method were used, would the results agree with those of the Tukey method?

**6.** Four methods of teaching percentage (case method, formula method, equation method, unitary analysis method) were compared (Sparks, 1963). Twenty-eight sixth-grade classes were randomly assigned to the four methods; seven classes studied under each method. The observational unit was the mean of each class, that is, $n_{\bullet} = 28$. At the conclusion of the teaching unit, a forty-five-item test on computing percentages were administered to each class. The following means were obtained, each based on seven observations:

*Average test scores for each class*

| *Case Method* | *Formula Method* | *Equation Method* | *Unitary Analysis Method* |
|---|---|---|---|
| $\overline{X}_4 = 41.5\%$ | $\overline{X}_3 = 47.2\%$ | $\overline{X}_2 = 61.9\%$ | $\overline{X}_1 = 72.3\%$ |

(a) Fill in the blanks in the ANOVA table:

| *Source* | $\nu$ | *MS* | *F* |
|---|---|---|---|
| Between (Treatments) | | 1366.6 | |
| Within (Error) | | 85.8 | |

(b) Can $H_0$: $\mu_1 = \mu_2 = \mu_3 = \mu_4$ be rejected at $\alpha = .01$?
(c) Use the NK method of multiple comparison at $\alpha = .01$ to find any untenable null hypotheses involving pairs of means.
(d) Summarize the results using the underscoring procedure.

## EXERCISES

*Given one factor ANOVA with five randomly-assigned treatment groups and $n_1 = n_2 = \ldots = n_5 = 9$. The definitions of the five groups are given.*

*Group 1. Frequently tested pupils with positive feedback* ($\overline{X}_1 = 65$)
*Group 2. Infrequently tested pupils with positive feedback* ($\overline{X}_2 = 54$)
*Group 3. Frequently tested pupils with negative feedback* ($\overline{X}_3 = 50$)
*Group 4. Control* ($\overline{X}_4 = 47$)
*Group 5. Infrequently tested pupils without feedback* ($\overline{X}_5 = 43$)

*An ANOVA summary table is given.*

| *Source* | *SS* | $\nu$ | *MS* | *F* | $p^a$ |
|---|---|---|---|---|---|
| Treatments | 2545.2 | 4 | 636.3 | 6.3 | <.001 |
| Error | 4000 | 40 | 100 | | |

[a] ${}_{.99}F_{4,40} = 5.70$

**1.** How many planned orthogonal contrasts are possible?

**2.** Could you have legitimately inspected the means prior to your selection of which $J - 1$ orthogonal contrasts should be tested?

**3.** Suppose you wished to test $H_0$: $\mu_1 - \mu_3 = 0$; what are the coefficients for this contrast ($\hat{\psi}_1 = \overline{X}_1 - \overline{X}_3$)?

**4.** Distinguish $\hat{\psi}$ from $\psi$.

5. Suppose you also had good reason to test $H_0$: $\mu_1 = \mu_5$. Would this be orthogonal with $\hat{\psi}_1$?
6. In addition to $\hat{\psi}_1$, give the coefficients to contrast the frequently versus the infrequently tested groups ($\hat{\psi}_2$).
7. What is $H_0$ for $\hat{\psi}_3$ that has contrast coefficients of ¼, ¼, ¼, –1, and ¼?
8. Is $\hat{\psi}_2$ orthogonal with $\hat{\psi}_1$? with $\hat{\psi}_3$?
9. $\hat{\psi}_1 = ?$, $s_{\hat{\psi}_1} = ?$, $t_{\hat{\psi}_1} = ?$
10. For planned orthogonal contrasts, the critical $t$-value ($\alpha = .01$) in this problem is ____.
11. Is $H_0$: $\psi_1 = 0$ rejected with $\alpha = .01$?
12. Using the Scheffé method, could the identical procedure be used to obtain $t_{\hat{\psi}1}$?
13. For $H_0$: $\psi_1 = 0$, the Scheffé method would have a critical $t$-value of $\sqrt{(J-1)(_{.99}F_{J-1,v_e})} = ?$
14. How does the critical $t$-value for the Scheffé method compare with that for a planned orthogonal comparison? (See exercises 10 and 13.)
15. Does the Scheffé approach require orthogonality among the $C$ contrasts?
16. Does the Scheffé method use a contrast-based or a family-based type-I error rate?
17. For the planned orthogonal contrasts, would the critical $t$-value (2.70) be the same for each $(J - 1) = 4$ possible orthogonal contrasts?
18. Would the critical $t$-value for the $S$-method be constant for all the possible contrasts? In the sample problem, can we be certain that at least one contrast somewhere in the set of possible contrasts would reject $H_0$: $\psi = 0$ at $\alpha_\Sigma = .01$?
19. If the experimenter selected the Tukey method, the distribution theory involves the studentized range statistic, denoted by ____.
20. For the Tukey method, what is the critical value ($\alpha = .01$) for each comparison?
21. $s_{\overline{X}} = \sqrt{MS_e / n} = \sqrt{\quad} =$ ____.
22. Since the critical $q$-value is the same for all comparisons with the Tukey method, the minimum mean difference needed to reject $H_0$ (termed the honest significance difference, $HSD$) is $HSD = (_{1-\alpha}q_{J,v_e})s_{\overline{X}}$ or $HSD$(____)(____) = ____, when $\alpha_\Sigma = .01$.
23. From the following matrix of pairwise differences between means, which $H_0$'s between pairs of means allow the associated $H_0$'s to be rejected at the .01 level, using $HSD$?

| | | *Smaller Mean, $\overline{X}_J$* | | | |
|---|---|---|---|---|---|
| | | $\overline{X}_2$ | $\overline{X}_3$ | $\overline{X}_4$ | $\overline{X}_5 = 43$ |
| *Larger* | $65 = \overline{X}_1$ | 11 | 15 | 18 | 22 |
| *Mean,* | $54 = \overline{X}_2$ | | 4 | 7 | 11 |
| $\overline{X}_J$ | $50 = \overline{X}_3$ | | | 3 | 7 |
| | $47 = \overline{X}_4$ | | | | 4 |

24. The Newman-Keuls method, unlike the Tukey method (but like planned orthogonal contrasts), employs a type-I error rate, $\alpha$, per ____.
25. The NK method has ____ different critical values for $q$.
26. The minimum mean difference required to reject $H_0$: $\mu_1 = \mu_J$ for the extreme-most means is identical for the ____ and ____ methods.
27. Is this always the case when $r = J$?
28. Therefore, for $\alpha_\Sigma = .01$ and $r = 5$, a difference between $\overline{X}_5$ and $\overline{X}_1$ of ____ is needed to reject $H_0$ (see exercise 22).

**29.** Which $H_0$ was rejected for NK that was not with the Tukey method?

**30.** For the NK method, complete the summary figure using the underscoring procedure (any two means *not* underlined by the *same* line differ significantly at the .01 level).

$\bar{X}_1 \quad \bar{X}_2 \quad \bar{X}_3 \quad \bar{X}_4 \quad \bar{X}_5$

**31.** If the Dunnett method has been used to compare each of the $J - 1$ means with the control group ($\bar{X}_4$), $\psi$: $\mu_j - \mu_c$, the critical $t$-ratio (at $\alpha_\Sigma = .01$) would have been ____, and $s_\psi$ = ____ (see exercise 9); hence, for the Dunnett method, min. ($\bar{X}_j - \bar{X}_c$) = ____. Which of the four $H_0$'s could have been rejected with $\alpha_\Sigma = .01$?

**32.** If only ten of the possible comparisons were of interest, and some contrasts were complex, one would probably use the ____ method. The critical $t$-ratio ($\alpha_\Sigma = .01$) would be ____, and for the pairwise contrasts, min. ($\bar{X}_j - \bar{X}_{j'}$) would be ____.

**33.** If the number of comparisons were limited to five, for the Dunn method, min. ($\bar{X}_j - \bar{X}_{j'}$) = ____, ($\alpha_\Sigma = .01$).

**34.** The sensitivity of the various MC procedures can be seen from the relative values of min. ($\bar{X}_j - \bar{X}_{j'}$) to reject $H_0$: $\mu_j = \mu_{j'}$. At $\alpha = .01$,

(a) POC: $({}_{1-\alpha/2}t_{\nu_e})(s_{\hat{\psi}})$ = (____)(____) = ____ (see exercise 9).
(b) Scheffé method: $\sqrt{(J-1)_{1-\alpha}F_{J-1,\nu_e}}\,(s_{\hat{\psi}})$ = (____)(____) = ____ (see exercise 13).
(c) Tukey method: $({}_{1-\alpha}q_{J,\nu_e})(s_{\bar{X}})$ = ____ (see exercise 22).
(d) NK ($r = J$): $({}_{1-\alpha}q_{\nu_e,J})(s_{\bar{X}})$ = ____ (see exercise 26).
(e) NK ($r = 2$): $({}_{1-\alpha}q_{\nu_e,2})(s_{\bar{X}})$ = (____)(____) = ____ (see exercise 28).
(f) Dunn ($K = 10$): $({}_{1-\alpha/2}t_{\nu_e,C})(s_{\hat{\psi}})$ = ____ (see exercise 31).
(g) Dunn ($K = 5$): ____, (see exercise 33).
(h) Dunnett: $({}_{1-\alpha/2}t_{\nu_e,J})(s_{\hat{\psi}})$ = (____)(____) = ____ (see exercise 31).

## ANSWERS TO MASTERY TEST

**1.** (a)
**2.** no
**3.** (b)
**4.** fewer, more
**5.** No, a planned contrast must be a priori.
**6.** $\psi$ is a parameter, $\hat{\psi}$ is a statistic (estimate).
**7.** (b)
**8.** (c), (d), (e)
**9.** $H_0$: $\mu_2 - (\mu_1 + \mu_3)/2 = 0$ or $\mu_2 = (\mu_1 + \mu_3)/2$.
**10.** (a) no
(b) yes
(c) yes
(d) no
(e) no
**11.** (e)
**12.** (e)
**13.** (c)
**14.** (b), (c)
**15.** (a)
**16.** (d)
**17.** (g)
**18.** (d)
**19.** (b)
**20.** F
**21.** Marascuilo
**22.** Dunn
**23.** yes
**24.** yes
**25.** no
**26.** both
**27.** No; a downward trend (negative $r$ with year) for the ACT, but an upward trend with GPA.
**28.** both
**29.** GPA
**30.** $J - 1 = 6$

## ANSWERS TO PROBLEMS

1. (a) $\hat{\psi}_1 = \frac{1}{2}\overline{X}_1 + \frac{1}{2}\overline{X}_2 - \overline{X}_3 = .90,$

   $s_{\hat{\psi}_1} = \sqrt{2.27(.5^2/10 + .5^2/10 + 1/10)}$

   $= .584$

   $t_{\hat{\psi}_1} = .90/.584 = 1.54$

   ${}_{.95}t_{27} = 2.05,\ \hat{\psi}_1$ not significant

   (b) $\hat{\psi}_2 = 5.6 - 4.0 = 1.6,$

   $s_{\hat{\psi}_2} = \sqrt{2.27(.2)} = .674$

   $t_{\hat{\psi}_2} = 1.6/.674 = 2.37,\ p < .02$

   (c) $s_{\overline{X}} = \sqrt{85.8/7} = 3.50$

   $q_1 = (\overline{X}_1 - \overline{X}_4)/s_{\overline{X}}$

   $= (72.3 - 41.5)/3.50$

   $= 8.80,\ p < .01$

   $q_2 = (72.3 - 47.2)/3.50$

   $= 7.17,\ p < .01$

   $q_3 = (72.3 - 61.9)/3.50$

   $= 2.97 < 3.96 = {}_{.99}q_{24,2},$

   $p > .01$

   $q_4 = (61.9 - 41.5)/3.50 = 5.83 > 4.54$

   $= {}_{.99}q_{24,3};\ p < .01$

   $q_5 = (61.9 - 47.2)/3.50 = 4.20 > 3.96$

   $= {}_{.99}q_{24,3};\ p < .01$

   $q_6 = (47.2 - 41.5)/3.50 = 1.63 < 3.96$

   $= {}_{.99}q_{24,3};\ p > .10$

   (d) $\overline{X}_1\,\overline{X}_2\,\overline{X}_3\,\overline{X}_4$, that is, all differences between means are significant except $X_1$ versus $X_2$ and $X_3$ versus $X_4$.

2. Yes, $\sqrt{(3-1)\,{}_{.95}F_{2,27}} \approx \sqrt{2(3.37)} = 2.60.$
3. For Dunn, ${}_{.975}t_{27,2} \approx 2.38$, both $H_{0_1}$: $\psi_1 = 0$ and $H_{0_1}$: $\psi_2 = 0$ are tenable.
4. $s_{\overline{X}} = \sqrt{2.27/10} = .476,$

   $q_1 = (\overline{X}_1 - \overline{X}_3)/s_{\overline{X}} = 1.70/.476$

   $= 3.55 > {}_{.95}q_{27,3} \approx 3.53$

   $q_2 = (\overline{X}_1 - \overline{X}_2)/s_{\overline{X}} = 1.6/4.76$

   $= 3.36,$

   and $q_3 = (\overline{X}_2 - \overline{X}_3)/s_{\overline{X}} = .1/.476$

   $= .21$ are not significant.
5. No, $q_2 = 3.36 > {}_{.95}q_{27,2} \approx 2.92, p < .05$; $q_3$ is not significant
6. (a) $\nu_B = 3$, $\nu_e = 24$, $F = 15.93$
   (b) yes; $15.93 > 4.72 = {}_{.99}F_{3,24}$

## ANSWERS TO EXERCISES

1. $J - 1 = 4$
2. No, a priori rationale would no longer apply.
3. 1, 0, –1, 0, 0; (or –1, 0, 1, 0, 0)
4. $\hat{\psi}$ is an *estimate* of the parameter $\psi$.
5. no (see Equation 17.12)
6. ½, –½, ½, 0, –½
7. $H_0$: $(\mu_1 + \mu_2 + \mu_3 + \mu_5)/4 - \mu_4 = 0.$
8. yes, yes
9. $\hat{\psi}_1 = 65 - 50 = 15;$

   $s_{\hat{\psi}} = \sqrt{100(1/9 + 1/9)} = 4.71$

   $t_{\hat{\psi}_1} = 3.18$
10. ${}_{.995}t_{40} = 2.70$
11. yes, $p < .01$
12. yes
13. $\sqrt{4({}_{.99}F_{4,40})} = \sqrt{4(3.83)} = 3.91$
14. It is much larger (3.91 versus 2.70).
15. No, any conceivable contrast is allowable.
16. family-based $\alpha_\Sigma$
17. yes
18. yes; yes (since $p < .01$ for $F$-test)
19. $q$
20. 4.93
21. $\sqrt{100/9} = 10/3 = 3.33$

**22.** (4.93)(3.33) = 16.4. Therefore, in using the Tukey-method, every $\hat{\psi}$ (usually a difference between a pair of means) greater than 16.4 would be judged significant, and $H_0$: $\psi = 0$ rejected at the .01 level.
**23.** $H_0$: $\mu_1 = \mu_5$, and $H_0$: $\mu_1 = \mu_4$
**24.** contrast
**25.** $J - 1$
**26.** Tukey and Newman-Keuls
**27.** yes
**28.** 16.4
**29.** $H_0$: $\mu_1 = \mu_3$
**30.** $\bar{X}_1 \bar{X}_2 \bar{X}_3 \bar{X}_4 \bar{X}_5$
**31.** 3.19; 4.71; (3.19)(4.71) = 15.0, only $H_0$: $\mu_1 = \mu_4$ would be rejected.
**32.** Dunn, $_{.995}t_{40,10}$ = 3.549 (3.549)(4.71) = 16.7
**33.** $_{.995}t_{40,5}$ = 3.305, (3.305)(4.71) = 15.6
**34.** (a) (2.70)(4.71) = 12.7
(b) (3.91)(4.71) = 18.4
(c) (4.93)(3.33) = 16.4
(d) same as Tukey method: 16.4
(e) 12.7
(f) 16.7
(g) 15.6
(h) 15.0

# 18

# TWO- AND THREE-FACTOR ANOVA: An Introduction to Factorial Designs

## 18.1 INTRODUCTION

In Chapter 15, the rationale for one-factor analysis of variance (ANOVA) was considered, along with procedures for testing whether or not the differences among two or more means were within chance expectations (sampling error). However, ANOVA is not limited to a single independent variable; the special richness of ANOVA designs is evidenced when there are *two or more independent variables* (factors). If a two-factor ANOVA design is employed, three different hypotheses are testable. Two of these hypotheses pertain to the effect of each factor viewed separately (main effects); these hypotheses are essentially the same as the hypothesis for a one-factor ANOVA design (Chapter 15):

1. Whether the $J$ means of factor $A$ are equal in the population ($H_{0_1}$: $\mu_{1\bullet} = \mu_{2\bullet} = \ldots = \mu_{J\bullet}$).
2. Whether the $K$ means of factor $B$ are equal in the population ($H_{0_2}$: $\mu_{\bullet 1} = \mu_{\bullet 2} = \ldots = \mu_{\bullet K}$).[1]

The third hypothesis pertains to a new and important concept, statistical interaction, that is, whether the two factors operate independently or whether there is an *interaction* between factors $A$ and $B$: Are there certain combinations of the two factors that produce different effects from what would be expected from the two factors considered separately? For example, suppose the factors in a two-factor ANOVA design are treatment ($E$ vs. $C$) and gender ($M$ vs. $F$). If the difference between the $E$ and $C$ means is the same for males as it is for females, there is no interaction between the two factors. On the other hand, if the treatment has a greater effect for one sex than it does for the other, there would be a treatment-by-gender interaction. The concept of interaction is of central importance in this and subsequent chapters.

---

[1]Consistent with previous use, the "dot" subscripts denote aggregation; for example, $\mu_{2\bullet}$ is the mean of level 2 of factor $A$ with all levels of factor $B$ aggregated. If there are 3 levels of factor $B$ and 2 levels of factor $A$, and $\mu_{11} = 10$, $\mu_{12} = 20$, and $\mu_{13} = 9$, then $\mu_{1\bullet} = 13$; and if $\mu_{11} = 10$ and $\mu_{21} = 20$, then $\mu_{\bullet 1} = 15$ (see Section 18.7 for further discussion of notation).

The two-factor ANOVA design is the simplest of multiple-factor ANOVA designs. The procedures and concepts this design employs are essential building blocks for more complex ANOVA designs.

## 18.2 THE MEANING OF INTERACTION[2]

In addition to interest in whether a treatment (independent variable) has an effect on the criterion (dependent variable), there is usually interest in whether the treatment is equally effective for certain types of individuals. For example:

Is the treatment effect different for females than for males?

Is the new method more effective for high- than for low-ability students?

Is the sex difference on some variable (e.g., math achievement) greater for certain nationalities than for others?

An interaction between two factors is said to exist if the mean differences among the levels of factor $A$ are not constant across levels (categories) of factor $B$. For example, suppose two methods of teaching are being compared. If one teaching method is better for boys but the other method is better for girls, there is an interaction between the two factors, teaching method and gender. Alternately, if one method is much better for boys, but only slightly better for girls, there is an interaction between teaching method and gender. Stated differently, if the gender difference is greater within method $E$ than within method $C$, there is a method-by-gender interaction.

### Interaction Examples

In recent years, behavioral and educational research has become increasingly concerned with assessing interaction effects. Following are three examples of studies in which the interaction hypothesis is of particular interest.

In a study of test-wiseness, two types of questions (multiple-choice and free-response) are given to two ethnic groups (American and Indonesian students). The principal research question is not concerned with either of the two main effects—whether the mean scores for the two nationalities differ, or whether mean scores differed on multiple-choice questions versus free-response items. The research question focused on the possible interaction between nationality and type of item. Does one nationality perform *relatively* better on one type of item than they do on the other type of item—that is, is there an interaction between the two factors, nationality and item type? If the difference between the means for the two nationality groups is the same for both types of item, there is no interaction between the two factors. However, for example, if the mean difference between nationalities is significantly greater for multiple-choice items than for free-response items, an interaction between nationality and item type is said to exist.

In a learning experiment, the effects of immediate versus delayed reinforcement on vocabulary acquisition were compared for pupils of low and middle socioeconomic status

[2]The concept of the interaction of two independent variables is due to the famed English statistician and geneticist, Sir Ronald Fisher. Fisher's concepts of experimental control through randomization and the study of the effects of several factors and their interactions simultaneously successfully overthrew the "change one variable while holding all others constant" orthodoxy of experimental agriculture in the early 1900s. See Fisher (1925) and Stanley (1966).

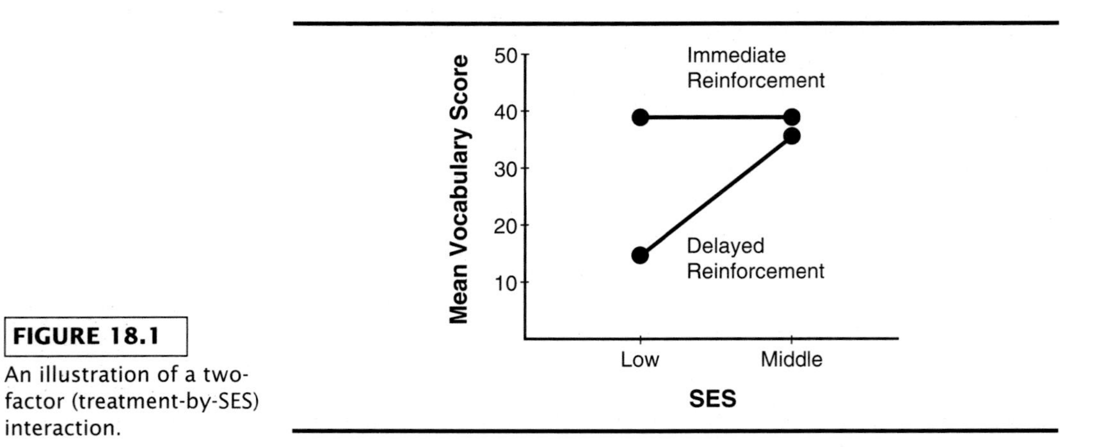


**FIGURE 18.1**

An illustration of a two-factor (treatment-by-SES) interaction.

(SES). The researcher expected to find an interaction between the factors, treatment (timing of reinforcement) and SES. It was hypothesized that delay of gratification is more characteristic of middle SES families; hence, a smaller difference was expected between immediate and delayed reinforcement for middle SES students than for low SES students. A graphic illustration of the researcher's hypothesis is given in Figure 18.1, with hypothetical means on the dependent variable for each of the four combinations (cells) of the two factors, treatment and SES. A two-factor (treatment × SES) analysis of variance on the data collected would be employed to determine whether the hypothesized treatment-by-SES interaction is tenable.

A third interaction example is taken from a bilingual-bicultural study. The two factors are teacher ethnicity and pupil ethnicity. All Anglo and Hispanic pupils were taught in Spanish by a Hispanic teacher for half the school day, and an Anglo teacher for the other half. Each teacher independently rated each of his or her Hispanic and Anglo students using a behavior rating scale designed to assess "adaptive behavior." No significant difference was found between the means of the Anglo and Hispanic teachers (the teacher ethnicity factor). In addition, the means for the Hispanic and Anglo students did not differ significantly, that is, both null hypotheses for the two main effects (teacher ethnicity and pupil ethnicity) were tenable. However, there was a highly significant interaction between the teacher ethnicity and pupil

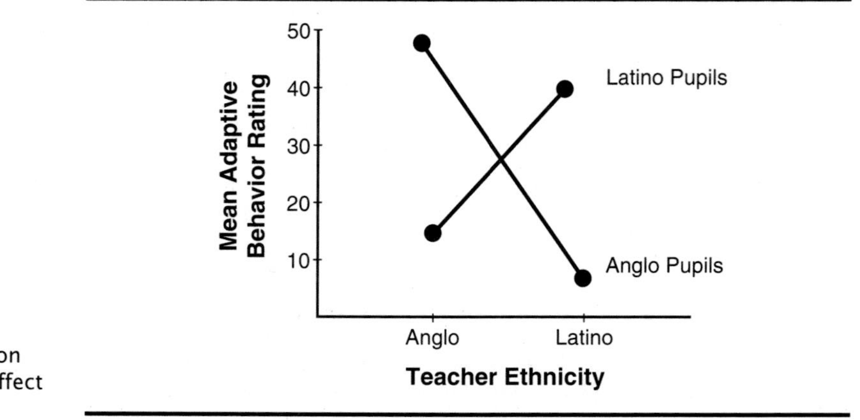


**FIGURE 18.2**

An illustration of a significant interaction with neither main effect being significant.

ethnicity factors, as shown in Figure 18.2. The interaction shows that the two factors are *not* independent. Hispanic teachers rated the behavior of Hispanic students as more adaptive than the Anglo students, whereas the pattern was reversed for the Anglo teachers.[3]

## 18.3 INTERACTION AND GENERALIZABILITY: FACTORS DO NOT INTERACT

The *absence of interaction* is the statistical justification for *generalizability*. If there is no interaction between two factors, the overall difference among the means of the levels for one factor is more or less constant across all levels of the second factor. If there is no interaction between a treatment factor and a relevant characteristic of the subjects (e.g., gender), the overall treatment effect can be generalized to both sexes without qualification. However, if two factors interact, the generalization of the main effects must be qualified. Often a second factor is included in a research design, not because interaction is expected, but because the absence of interaction provides an empirical springboard for generalizing any treatment effect to all levels of the second factor. For example, consider a hypothetical study in which two instructional methods ($E$ and $C$—experimental and control) are compared on students in a community with above average IQ's. If the study contrasted only the means for the experimental and control groups (i.e., used a $t$-test or a one-factor ANOVA), the findings cannot be safely generalized to low ability pupils since they are only a small proportion of the sample. However, if a two-factor (treatment-by-ability) design is employed with several levels of the ability factor, the treatment-by-ability interaction can be statistically evaluated, as shown in Figure 18.3. In other words, in addition to comparing the means of the $E$ and $C$ groups, we can determine whether the treatment effect (the difference between $E$ and $C$ means, if any) is uniform across all ability levels; we can determine whether or not there is a significant interaction between treatment and ability level.

Study Figure 18.3 to confirm that although there are treatment and ability main effects, there is no interaction. Notice that the difference in $E$ and $C$ means is approximately the same for all ability (IQ) levels—the treatment effect does not interact with IQ level. It is obvious that, even though the $E$ and $C$ groups may have had mean IQ's of 110 or so, the study is relevant for average or even below-average students, since the treatment effect was constant across the various IQ levels.

Suppose the ability factor in Figure 18.3 is replaced by a teacher factor—six teachers each used method $E$ with one random class of students and the method $C$ with another random class. It is then possible to assess statistically whether the $E$ method (or $C$ method) is superior for all teachers, or whether the efficacy of the treatment varies with (i.e., interacts with) the particular teacher involved. If there is no treatment-by-teacher interaction, one can conclude that the $E$ method will result in superior performance with other teachers like those represented in the study.[4] If results like those represented in Figure 18.3 were obtained for each teacher, there would be no treatment-by-teacher interaction.

---

[3]We do not know whether the findings result from prejudice or whether there is more adaptive behavior when there is a common ethnicity of the teacher and the pupil.

[4]Indeed, a three-factor (treatment-by-teacher-by-IQ) ANOVA design could be employed (Section 18.20). Using this design, the treatment-by-IQ and treatment-by-teacher interactions would be tested in the same analysis, as well as the three-factor interaction (treatment-by-teacher-by-IQ). In the illustration, the absence of a significant three-factor interaction would indicate that the pattern of results for treatment and IQ level was uniform across all teachers.

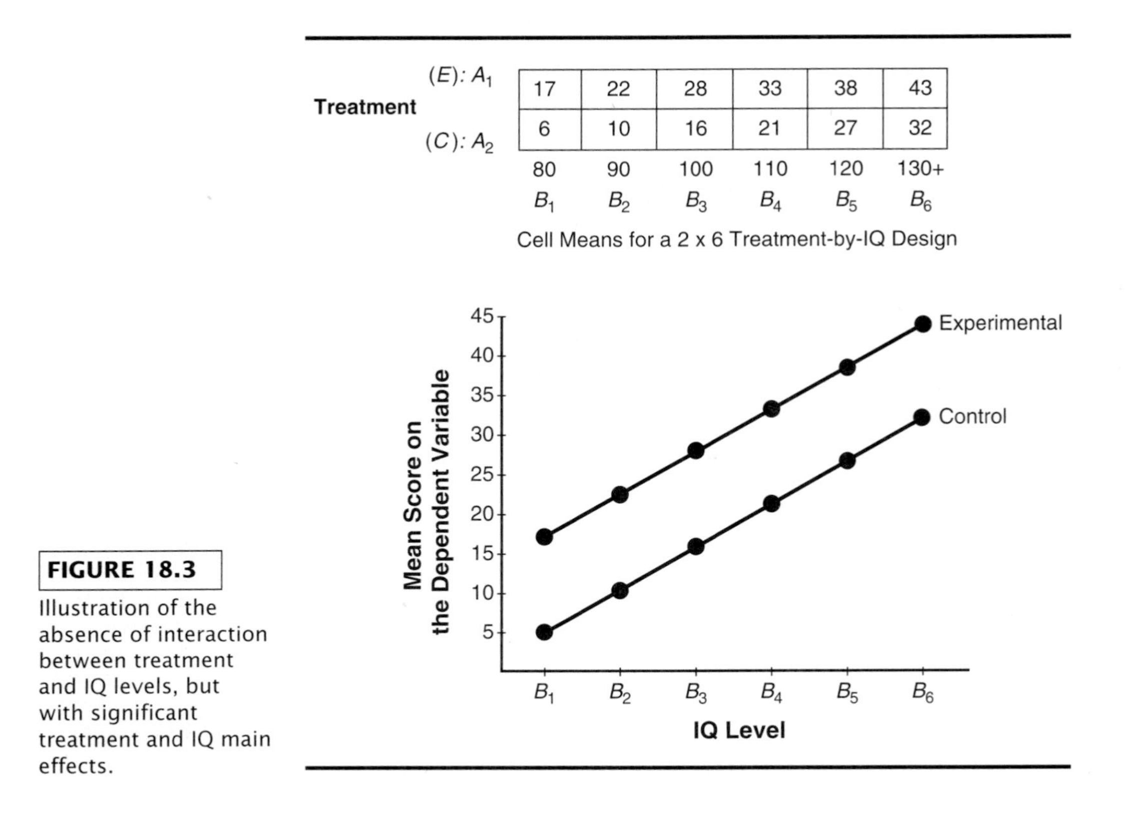

| Treatment | | | | | | |
|---|---|---|---|---|---|---|
| (E): $A_1$ | 17 | 22 | 28 | 33 | 38 | 43 |
| (C): $A_2$ | 6 | 10 | 16 | 21 | 27 | 32 |
| | 80 | 90 | 100 | 110 | 120 | 130+ |
| | $B_1$ | $B_2$ | $B_3$ | $B_4$ | $B_5$ | $B_6$ |

Cell Means for a 2 x 6 Treatment-by-IQ Design



**FIGURE 18.3**
Illustration of the absence of interaction between treatment and IQ levels, but with significant treatment and IQ main effects.

## 18.4 INTERACTION AND GENERALIZABILITY: FACTORS INTERACT

Suppose a study finds that "new math," $E$, results in higher scores than conventional math, $C$, on a math attitude inventory for bright students, but lower scores for low ability students. There is no method effect for students of average ability. Hypothetical cell means are given for the method-by-ability ANOVA design in Figure 18.4.

Notice that if one used only a $t$-test or a one-factor ANOVA, no treatment effect would be found (in the hypothetical example, the means of both methods would be the same).[5] Without a factorial design, one would mistakenly conclude that the two methods make no difference on math attitude. The data in Figure 18.4 demonstrate that there were definite differential method effects depending on the ability level of the student.

The interaction question is not directly concerned with whether there are overall differences in average interest level, either between conventional and "new math," or between bright, average, and low ability students. Questions about overall differences among row or column means are questions about main effects. The interaction null hypothesis is that the effect, if any, of factor $A$ does not depend on factor $B$, that is, mean differences among the levels of factor $A$ are constant across all levels of factor $B$. If the $A \times B$ interaction is not

[5]Assuming a balanced design, that is, the $n$ for each of the six cells is the same.

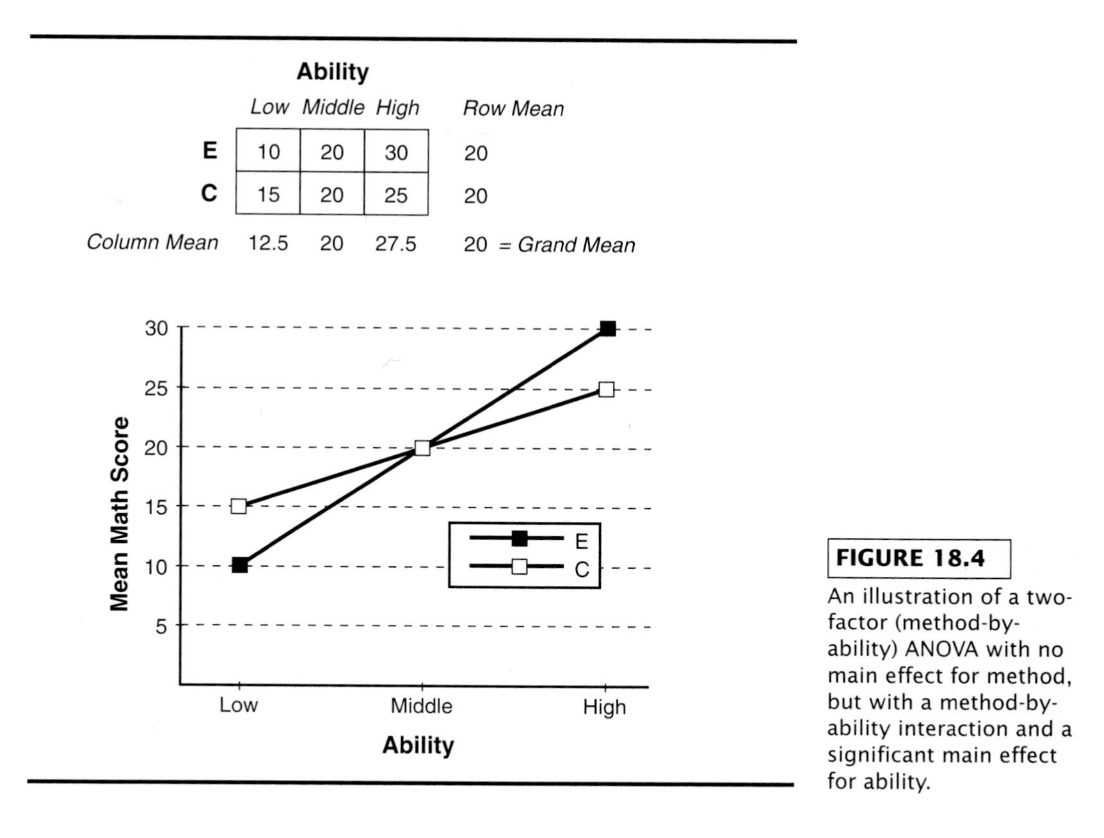


**FIGURE 18.4**

An illustration of a two-factor (method-by-ability) ANOVA with no main effect for method, but with a method-by-ability interaction and a significant main effect for ability.

significant, there is empirical support for generalizing the overall effect of factor *A* to all levels of factor *B* without qualification.

It should be clear that the examination of interaction between treatment and various subject characteristics (i.e., personological or organismic variables) contributes substantially to the generalizability of a study. If an interaction between two factors (e.g., treatment and ability) is not significant, the overall pattern of mean differences on factor *A* is constant for each level of factor *B*. In many research studies, although an interaction is not expected, ancillary factors are often included so that the generalizability of the study can be empirically assessed.

If an interaction is significant, it should be graphed, as illustrated in Figures 18.1–18.4, and studied so that the proper interpretation can be made.

## 18.5 INTERPRETING MAIN EFFECTS WHEN INTERACTION IS PRESENT

A two-factor interaction will be illustrated by using hypothetical data from a large sample in an ESP experiment. There are two levels of the treatment factor: Level 1 is the experimental (*E*) group, which attempted to receive a mentally transmitted message, and level 2 is the control (*C*) group. Suppose in this study that the null hypothesis, $H_0$: $\mu_1 = \mu_2$, was

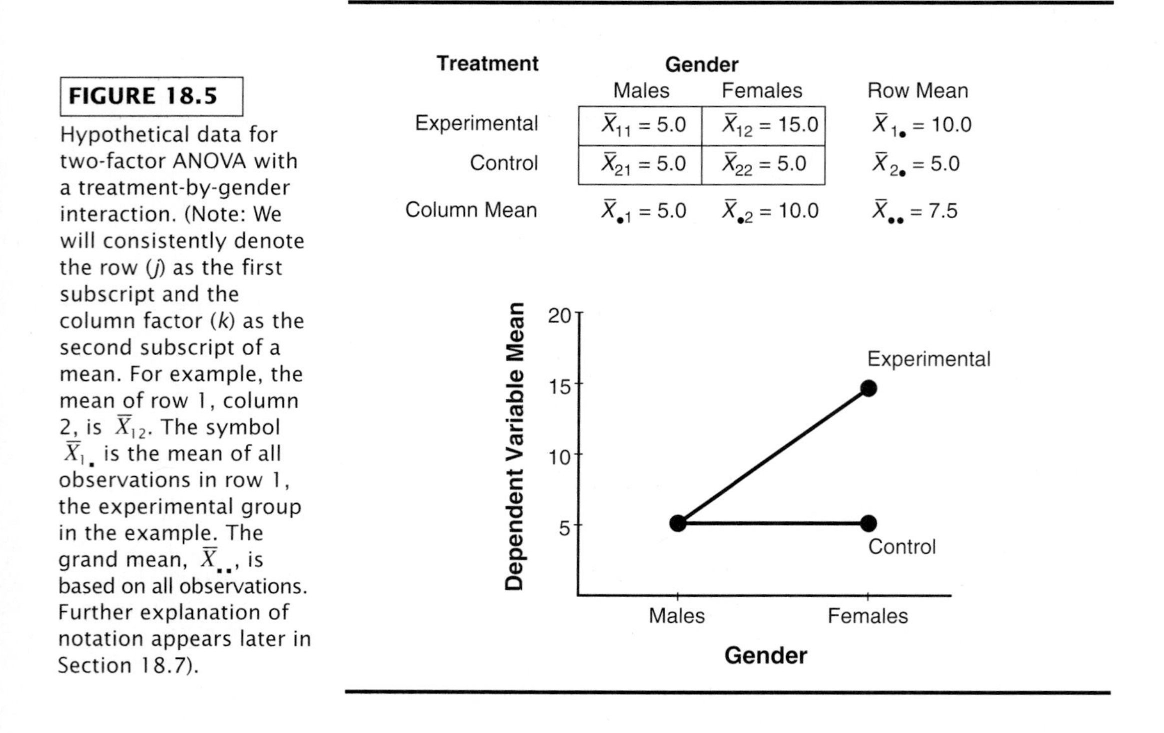

| Treatment | Gender | | |
|---|---|---|---|
| | Males | Females | Row Mean |
| Experimental | $\bar{X}_{11} = 5.0$ | $\bar{X}_{12} = 15.0$ | $\bar{X}_{1\bullet} = 10.0$ |
| Control | $\bar{X}_{21} = 5.0$ | $\bar{X}_{22} = 5.0$ | $\bar{X}_{2\bullet} = 5.0$ |
| Column Mean | $\bar{X}_{\bullet 1} = 5.0$ | $\bar{X}_{\bullet 2} = 10.0$ | $\bar{X}_{\bullet\bullet} = 7.5$ |



**FIGURE 18.5**

Hypothetical data for two-factor ANOVA with a treatment-by-gender interaction. (Note: We will consistently denote the row ($j$) as the first subscript and the column factor ($k$) as the second subscript of a mean. For example, the mean of row 1, column 2, is $\bar{X}_{12}$. The symbol $\bar{X}_{1\bullet}$ is the mean of all observations in row 1, the experimental group in the example. The grand mean, $\bar{X}_{\bullet\bullet}$, is based on all observations. Further explanation of notation appears later in Section 18.7).

rejected. Does it necessarily follow that treatment $E$ had an effect on all persons in the experimental group? Certainly not, as is evident from Figure 18.4. It is possible that only certain persons in the $E$ group were "sensitive" to the treatment. Perhaps ESP is a sex-linked trait and appears only in females. Notice that if females were capable of ESP and males were not, the mean of the experimental group taken as a whole would exceed the control group mean as a consequence of the higher female scores. This is illustrated graphically in Figure 18.5. If the mean of the females in the $E$ group ($\bar{X}_{12} = 15.0$) exceeds the mean of the females in the $C$ group ($\bar{X}_{22} = 5.0$), the mean of the experimental group ($\bar{X}_{1\bullet} = 10.0$) will exceed the control group mean ($\bar{X}_{2\bullet} = 5.0$) even if the males in each of the $E$ and $C$ groups had equal means ($\bar{X}_{11} = 5.0$, $\bar{X}_{21} = 5.0$).

If only a one-factor ANOVA design had been employed for the data represented in Figure 18.5, the null hypothesis for the treatment effect, $H_0$: $\mu_E = \mu_C$, would have been rejected on the basis of $\bar{X}_E = 10.0$ and $\bar{X}_C = 5.0$.[6] However, using the treatment-by-gender design, we can discover that ESP is a sex-linked trait. If a two-factor design were employed, the pattern of results would be illuminated, as depicted in Figure 18.5. Since the treatment effect is not the same for both sexes, a treatment-by-gender interaction exists.

In many research studies, interactions go undetected because of the failure to employ factorial designs, designs that examine the effects of two or more factors (independent variables) simultaneously. An interaction exists when the difference in row means is not the same across all levels of the column factor, and vice versa. Notice in Figure 18.5 that the treatment

[6]Unless the sample size was so small that the power was extremely low.

**TABLE 18.1** Two-Factor ANOVA Table for the Hypothetical Data in Figure 18.4 (assuming $n = 6$ and $MS_W = 100$).

| *Source* | *SS* | *v* | *MS* | *F* | *p* | $H_0$ |
|---|---|---|---|---|---|---|
| Method (*M*) | 0 | 1 | 0 | 0 | >.99 | $H_{0_1}$: $\mu_{1\bullet} = \mu_{2\bullet}$ |
| Ability (*A*) | 950 | 2 | 475 | 4.75 | .016 | $H_{0_2}$: $\mu_{\bullet 1} = \mu_{\bullet 2} = \mu_{\bullet 3}$ |
| $M \times A$ | 850 | 2 | 425 | 4.25 | .023 | $H_{0_3}$: $\mu_{11} - \mu_{21} = \mu_{12} - \mu_{22} = \mu_{13} - \mu_{23}$ |
| Within | 3000 | 30 | 100 | | | |

factor interacts with the sex factor because an unbiased estimate of the treatment effect is 0 for males ($\overline{X}_{11} - \overline{X}_{21} = 0$), but is 10 for females ($\overline{X}_{12} - \overline{X}_{22} = 10$). On the other hand, if $\mu_{11} - \mu_{21} = \mu_{12} - \mu_{22}$, that is, the difference between the *E* and *C* means were the same for males and females, there would be no interaction between the two factors, treatment and sex.

## 18.6 STATISTICAL SIGNIFICANCE AND INTERACTION

The question of the statistical significance of interaction questions (hypotheses) are answered by means of an *F*-test. An ANOVA for the hypothetical data in Figure 18.4, assuming six observations per cell and an average within-cell variance ($MS_W$) of 100, is shown in Table 18.1, along with the corresponding three null hypotheses being tested.

Null hypotheses $H_{0_1}$ and $H_{0_2}$ represent main effects, whereas $H_{03}$ represents the hy-pothesis regarding the interaction. The illustrative data represented in Figure 18.4, evaluated for statistical significance in the ANOVA table (Table 18.1), demonstrate that when a significant treatment-by-ability interaction exists, the interaction influences the interpretation of the main effects. It is certainly true that, considering all the data as a whole, it can be concluded that $H_{0_1}$: $\mu_{1\bullet} = \mu_{2\bullet}$ is tenable ($p > .99$).[7] It also can be concluded that $H_{0_2}$: $\mu_{\bullet 1} = \mu_{\bullet 2} = \mu_{\bullet 3}$ is untenable and can be rejected—ability and math attitudes are related ($p = .016$). It is evident that a more precise and meaningful conclusion can be reached when the design allows the treatment-by-ability interaction to be considered—method *E* is better for bright students and method *C* is superior for low ability students.

The design in this example can be described as a $2 \times 3$ method-by-ability design. There are two levels (*E* and *C*) of the method factor and three levels (low, middle, and high) of the ability factor.

## 18.7 DATA LAYOUT AND NOTATION

Consider an experiment that uses a two-factor design in which three methods of teaching beginning reading are compared for boys and girls. The pupils involved in this experiment can be classified in two ways: with respect to the teaching method under which they study (factor *A*) and by their gender (factor *B*). Factor *A*, teaching method, has three levels and

[7]Our example is not representative for the method factor; in practice, the expected value of an *F*-ratio is ≈ 1 when $H_0$ is true (and virtually never 0). Our example is primarily for conceptual purposes, to eliminate any main effect for the method factor.

| | $B_1$ *(boy)* | | $B_2$ *(girl)* | | *Row Means* | |
|---|---|---|---|---|---|---|
| | $\overline{X}_{11}$ | $X_{111}$<br>$X_{211}$<br>$X_{311}$<br>$X_{411}$ | $\overline{X}_{12}$ | $X_{112}$<br>$X_{212}$<br>$X_{312}$<br>$X_{412}$ | $\overline{X}_{1\bullet}$ | |
| Row Factor *A* (Method) | $\overline{X}_{21}$ | $X_{121}$<br>$X_{221}$<br>$X_{321}$<br>$X_{421}$ | $\overline{X}_{22}$ | $X_{122}$<br>$X_{222}$<br>$X_{322}$<br>$X_{422}$ | $\overline{X}_{1\bullet}$ | |
| | $\overline{X}_{31}$ | $X_{131}$<br>$X_{231}$<br>$X_{331}$<br>$X_{431}$ | $\overline{X}_{32}$ | $X_{132}$<br>$X_{232}$<br>$X_{332}$<br>$X_{432}$ | $\overline{X}_{1\bullet}$ | |
| *Column Means* | | | $\overline{X}_{\bullet 1}$ | | $\overline{X}_{\bullet 2}$ | $\overline{X}_{\bullet\bullet}$ |

**FIGURE 18.6** Layout of data in a 3 × 2 two-factor ANOVA design with four observations per cell ($X_{ijk}$ notation, where $j = 1, 2, 3$ for method, $k = 1, 2$ for gender and $i = 1, 2, 3, 4$ for pupil within method-gender group).

factor *B*, gender, has two levels. Since a sample of both boys and girls use each method, six unique combinations of the levels of the two factors are possible. Suppose the outcome variable in this experiment is reading comprehension, *X*. Observations, $X_{ijk}$, are taken by administering a standardized measure of reading comprehension. If four boys and four girls were taught to read by each of the three methods, the data could be represented as shown in Figure 18.6.

## Notation

Since there are two factors, two subscripts are necessary to identify cell means ($\overline{X}_{jk}$). Let the *j* subscript denote the row (method) factor, and let the *k* subscript represent the column (sex) factor.

Dots represent aggregation. For example, the mean of all observations in row 1 is $\overline{X}_{1\bullet}$. The dot subscript indicates that the row mean $\overline{X}_{1\bullet}$ is based on all the observations in row 1. The grand mean $\overline{X}_{\bullet\bullet}$ is based on all observations—all rows and all columns, and hence the grand mean has dots for subscripts *j* and *k*. $\overline{X}_{\bullet\bullet}$ is based on all $n_{\bullet\bullet}$ observations. With a little practice, the dot notation can be used without confusion.

A total of twenty-four pupils participated in our hypothetical experiment. Find $X_{111}$ in Figure 18.6; it represents the reading comprehension test score of the first ($i = 1$) boy ($k = 1$) with whom method 1 ($j = 1$) was used. Locate $X_{432}$—the fourth ($i = 4$) girl ($k = 2$) in method 3 ($j = 3$). In other words, the "3" stands for the method, the "2" for the sex (male–1, female–2), and the "4" designates the arbitrarily labeled fourth pupil in the group of four girls in method 3.

A general observation in a two-factor ANOVA design is denoted by $X_{ijk}$ where *j* is a subscript for factor *A* and takes on the values 1, 2, …, *J*; *k* is the subscript for factor *B* and takes on the values 1, 2, ..., $K$; and $i$ is the subscript that identifies the particular replicate (observation) within a cell of the design and takes on the values 1, 2, ..., $n$. As a final example, the score of the third ($i = 3$) girl ($k = 2$) studying under the first method ($j = 1$) is denoted $X_{312}$. To summarize, in $X_{ijk}$:[8]

$i = 1, 2, \ldots, n$ for observations "nested within cells"

$j = 1, 2, \ldots, J$ for factor $A$, and

$k = 1, 2, \ldots, K$ for factor $B$.

## 18.8 A MODEL FOR THE DATA

Our interest in gathering the data is to determine how the mean scores on the outcome variable vary with the levels of the two factors, that is, whether boys score higher than girls, whether method $E$ gives higher scores than method $C$, and so on. Toward this end, we shall now devise a fairly abstract model—a generalization of the model that was used with the one-factor ANOVA (Sections 15.13 and 15.14)—to explain how the data are related to factors $A$ and $B$.

The fixed model for data in a two-factor ANOVA involves two terms for main effects: $\alpha_j$ which describes the effect of the $j$th level of factor $A$[9] ($\alpha_j = \mu_{j\bullet} - \mu$), and $\beta_k$ which describes the effect of the $k$th level of factor $B$ ($\beta_k = \mu_{\bullet k} - \mu$). As in Equation 15.10, $\mu_{\bullet\bullet} = \mu$ is the grand mean—the mean of all observations; $\varepsilon_{ijk}$ is the difference between the score, $X_{ijk}$, and ($\mu + \alpha_j + \beta_k$). The discussion to follow assumes that the design is balanced—there are $n$ observations in each of the $JK$ cells. Under this model, a score $X_{ijk}$ would be represented as in Equation 18.1:[10]

$$X_{ijk} = \mu + \alpha_j + \beta_k + \varepsilon_{ijk} \qquad \textbf{(18.1)}$$

For example, adult males in general tend to be 69 inches tall ($\mu = 69$). Suppose feeding them yoghurt tends to add 1 inch $= \alpha_1$ to their height, and sleeping on a hard mattress tends to add .5 inch $= \beta_1$ to their height. If one's unique history (environmental influences and heredity) explains the remainder ($\varepsilon_{111} = X_{111} - (\mu + \alpha_1 + \beta_1)$), then if Joe is 66 inches tall, eats yoghurt, and sleeps on a hard mattress: $\varepsilon_{111} = 66 - (69 + 1 + .5) = -4.5$; hence:

$$X_{ijk} = \mu + \alpha_j + \beta_k + \varepsilon_{ijk} = 69 + 1 + .5 - 4.5 = 66$$

A more useful and widely applicable model for the data in a two-factor ANOVA is slightly more complex. It differs from Equation 18.1 by a term that denotes the result of the

[8]The subscripts are arranged $ijk$ so that the left-most subscript can remain $i$ and always denote the observation number; the subscript $j$ is always associated with the first factor, $A$; and $k$ is always associated with the second factor, $B$.

[9]Do not confuse this use of the symbols "$\alpha$" and "$\beta$" with their meaning when used to represent probabilities of type I and type II errors.

[10]A more explicit notation is unnecessary: $X_{ijk} = \mu_{\bullet\bullet} + \alpha_{j\bullet} + \beta_{\bullet k} + \varepsilon_{ijk}$.

unique effect of *combining* level $j$ of factor $A$ with level $k$ of factor $B$. "Unique" in this context means any special outcome (+ or –) resulting from the particular combination: level $j$ of $A$ with level $k$ of $B$—an effect that is not simply the sum or the product of $\alpha_j$ and $\beta_k$. If there is a unique effect for the particular $jk$ combination, a new term, $\alpha\beta_{jk}$,[11] is needed to describe the scores in the $jk$th cell. Such a term is called an interaction term. If an interaction term is needed in the model to accurately describe the scores, then knowing the general effect of level $j$ of $A$ and of level $k$ of $B$ is not enough to predict the mean of cell $jk$.

The expanded model, upon which the analyses in this chapter are based, is:

$$X_{ijk} = \mu + \alpha_j + \beta_k + \alpha\beta_{jk} + \varepsilon_{ijk} \quad \textbf{(18.2)}$$

Without any loss of generality, the $\alpha$, $\beta$, and $\alpha\beta$ terms in the model are defined such that they sum to zero over both $j$ and $k$, that is, $\Sigma_j\alpha_j = \Sigma_k\beta_k = \Sigma_j\alpha\beta_{jk} = \Sigma_k\alpha\beta_{jk} = 0$. Recall that the $\alpha\beta_{jk}$ term is not the product of $\alpha_j$ and $\beta_k$; $\alpha\beta_{jk}$ represents the interaction effect of level $j$ of factor $A$ with level $k$ of factor $B$.

## 18.9 LEAST-SQUARES ESTIMATION OF THE MODEL

With data in hand and having adopted a particular model to explain them, the task of relating the data to the model remains. What features of the data influence the value of $\mu$ in Equation 18.2? How can the data be used to estimate the values of the $\alpha_j$'s, the $\beta_k$'s, and the $\alpha\beta_{jk}$'s?

This is the same general problem faced in Chapter 8 when $Y$ is predicted from $X$ by means of a straight line, or when there are differences between factor levels in a one-factor ANOVA (Sections 15.13 and 15.14). The model in Equation 18.2 is fit to the data so that the *least-squares criterion* is satisfied. The criterion of least squares is as follows: (1) values are substituted into Equation 18.2 for $\mu$, $\alpha_1, \ldots, \alpha_J$, $\beta_1, \ldots, \beta_K$, $\alpha\beta_{11}, \ldots, \alpha\beta_{JK}$; (2) these values along with the data $X_{ijk}$ determine, by subtraction, estimated values for the $nJK$ errors, $\varepsilon_{ijk}$; (3) when the sum of the squared errors so determined is at a minimum, the least-squares estimates of $\mu$, the $\alpha_j$'s, the $\beta_k$'s, and the $\alpha\beta_{jk}$'s have been found.

For example, twelve scores are gathered in a simple $2 \times 3$ design, with $n$ equal to 2, as shown in Figure 18.7. The model in Equation 18.2 is postulated for the data:

$$X_{ijk} = \mu + \alpha_j + \beta_k + \alpha\beta_{jk} + \varepsilon_{ijk}$$

where $i = 1, 2$; $j = 1, 2$; and $k = 1, 2, 3$.

The hypothetical main and interaction effects represented in the data in the model are shown in the upper portion of Figure 18.7. For example, the model views the first observation in level 1 of factor $A$ and level 2 of factor $B$ as:

$$X_{112} = \mu + \alpha_1 + \beta_2 + \alpha\beta_{12} + \varepsilon_{112}$$

Rearranging Equation 18.2, it is evident that:

[11] Do not read "$\alpha\beta_{jk}$" as the product of $\alpha_j$ and $\beta_k$.

$$\varepsilon_{ijk} = X_{ijk} - (\mu + \alpha_j + \beta_k + \alpha\beta_{jk}) \quad \textbf{(18.3A)}$$

Using the example directly above:

$$\varepsilon_{112} = X_{112} - (\mu + \alpha_1 + \beta_2 + \alpha\beta_{12})$$

The minimum value for the sum of squared errors is produced by the following least-squares estimates of the parameters of the model:

$$\hat{\mu} = \overline{X}_{\bullet\bullet} = 4.0$$

$$\hat{\alpha}_1 = \overline{X}_{1\bullet} - \overline{X}_{\bullet\bullet} = 2.5 - 4.0 = -1.5$$

$$\hat{\alpha}_2 = \overline{X}_{2\bullet} - \overline{X}_{\bullet\bullet} = 5.5 - 4.0 = 1.5$$

$$\hat{\beta}_1 = \overline{X}_{\bullet 1} - \overline{X}_{\bullet\bullet} = 5.0 - 4.0 = 1.0$$

$$\hat{\beta}_2 = \overline{X}_{\bullet 2} - \overline{X}_{\bullet\bullet} = 3.0 - 4.0 = -1.0$$

$$\hat{\beta}_3 = \overline{X}_{\bullet 3} - \overline{X}_{\bullet\bullet} = 4.0 - 4.0 = 0$$

$$\widehat{\alpha\beta}_{11} = \overline{X}_{11} - (\overline{X}_{\bullet\bullet} + \alpha_1 + \beta_1) = 3.0 - (4.0 - 1.5 + 1) = -.5$$

$$\widehat{\alpha\beta}_{12} = \overline{X}_{12} - (\overline{X}_{\bullet\bullet} + \alpha_1 + \beta_2) = 2.0 - (4.0 - 1.5 - 1) = .5$$

$$\widehat{\alpha\beta}_{13} = \overline{X}_{13} - (\overline{X}_{\bullet\bullet} + \alpha_1 + \beta_3) = 2.5 - (4.0 - 1.5 + 0) = 0$$

$$\widehat{\alpha\beta}_{21} = \overline{X}_{21} - (\overline{X}_{\bullet\bullet} + \alpha_2 + \beta_1) = 7.0 - (4.0 + 1.5 + 1) = .5$$

$$\widehat{\alpha\beta}_{22} = \overline{X}_{22} - (\overline{X}_{\bullet\bullet} + \alpha_2 + \beta_2) = 4.0 - (4.0 + 1.5 - 1) = -.5$$

$$\widehat{\alpha\beta}_{23} = \overline{X}_{23} - (\overline{X}_{\bullet\bullet} + \alpha_2 + \beta_3) = 5.5 - (4.0 + 1.5 + 0) = 0$$

Least-squares estimates of the twelve parameters are given in the lower portion of Figure 18.7. If these parameter estimates are used, the $\varepsilon$'s (Equation 18.3A) are estimated by $e$'s, as defined in Equation 18.3B:

$$e_{ijk} = X_{ijk} - (\hat{\mu} + \hat{\alpha}_j + \hat{\beta}_k + \widehat{\alpha\beta}_{jk}) \quad \textbf{(18.3B)}$$

For example,

$$e_{111} = X_{111} - (\hat{\mu} + \hat{\alpha}_1 + \hat{\beta}_1 + \widehat{\alpha\beta}_{11}) = 2 - (4.0 - 1.5 + 1 - .5) = -1.$$

In like manner the other eleven $e_{ijk}$'s could be estimated: $e_{211} = 1$, $e_{112} = -1$, $e_{212} = 1$, $e_{113} = -.5$, $e_{213} = .5$, $e_{121} = -1$, $e_{221} = 1$, $e_{122} = 1$, $e_{222} = -1$, $e_{123} = -.5$, $e_{223} = .5$.

The sum of the squared estimated errors (obtained using Equation 18.3B) is equal to 9.0 ($\Sigma e_{ijk}^2 = 9.0$); thus, 9.0 is the smallest possible value for the sum of the squared errors. Table 18.2 gives the least-squares estimates of the terms in the model for the data both in terms of the parameters and least-squares estimates of the parameters.

| | $B_1$ | $B_2$ | $B_3$ | *Row Means* |
|---|---|---|---|---|
| $A_1$ | $X_{111} = 2$<br>$X_{211} = 4$<br>$\overline{X}_{11} = 3.0$ | $X_{112} = 2$<br>$X_{212} = 3$<br>$\overline{X}_{12} = 2.0$ | $X_{113} = 2$<br>$X_{213} = 2$<br>$\overline{X}_{13} = 2.5$ | $\overline{X}_{1\bullet} = 2.5$ |
| $A_2$ | $X_{121} = 6$<br>$X_{221} = 8$<br>$\overline{X}_{21} = 7.0$ | $X_{122} = 5$<br>$X_{222} = 3$<br>$\overline{X}_{22} = 4.0$ | $X_{123} = 5$<br>$X_{223} = 6$<br>$\overline{X}_{23} = 5.5$ | $\hat{X}_{2\bullet} = 5.5$ |
| *Column Means* | $\overline{X}_{\bullet 1} = 5.0$ | $\overline{X}_{\bullet 2} = 3.0$ | $\overline{X}_{\bullet 3} = 4.0$ | $\overline{X}_{\bullet\bullet} = 4.0$ |

| | | | | *Row Effects* |
|---|---|---|---|---|
| | $\widehat{\alpha\beta}_{11} = -.5$ | $\widehat{\alpha\beta}_{12} = .5$ | $\widehat{\alpha\beta}_{13} = 0$ | $\hat{\alpha}_1 = -1.5$ |
| | $\widehat{\alpha\beta}_{21} = .5$ | $\widehat{\alpha\beta}_{22} = -.5$ | $\widehat{\alpha\beta}_{23} = 0$ | $\hat{\alpha}_2 = 1.5$ |
| *Column Effects* | $\hat{\beta}_1 = 1.0$ | $\hat{\beta}_2 = -1.0$ | $\hat{\beta}_3 = 0.0$ | $\hat{\mu} = 4.0$ |

**FIGURE 18.7** Illustration of estimating effects in a 2 × 3 ANOVA design.

## 18.10 STATEMENT OF NULL HYPOTHESES

Note in Figure 18.6 that factor $B$ is gender; if this factor were disregarded, the data would be identical to those gathered in a one-factor experiment comparing three teaching methods. Each level of factor $A$ has eight observations, and the one-factor ANOVA model is appropriate for a statistical inferential test of the hypothesis that the three population means underlying the teaching methods are equal. This null hypothesis, namely that the population means for the three teaching methods are equal, is identical to the null hypothesis for the method factor in the two-factor ANOVA. Specifically, we are interested in whether the data gathered in a two-factor ANOVA support or run counter to a decision to accept as tenable the statement $H_0$: $\mu_{1\bullet} = \mu_{2\bullet} = \mu_{3\bullet}$. In any two-factor ANOVA, the null hypothesis for factor $A$ $(H_{0_1})$[12] can be stated as follows:

$$H_{0_1}: \mu_{1\bullet} = \mu_{2\bullet} = \ldots = \mu_{J\bullet}$$

Notice that the equality of the $J$ population means for the $J$ levels of factor $A$ has implications that can be used to state $H_{0_1}$ in several equivalent forms. Since, when $i = 1, 2, \ldots, n$ for every $jk$th factor-level combination, $\mu$ is the average of the $JK$ population means (the cell means), equality of the $\mu_j$'s implies that each $\mu_{j\bullet}$ equals $\mu$. If each $\mu_{j\bullet} = \mu$, then $\mu_{j\bullet} - \mu = 0$ for the $J$ levels of factor $A$. Since $\alpha_j$, the main effect for level $j$ of factor $A$, is equal to $\mu_{j\bullet} - \mu$, all

[12]Since there are three null hypotheses in a two-factor ANOVA, they are distinguished by subscripts: $H_{0_1}$, $H_{0_2}$, and $H_{0_3}$.

**TABLE 18.2** Least-Squares Estimation in the Two-Factor, Fixed Effects, 2 × 3 ANOVA Model.

| *Term in model* | *Parameter* | *Least-squares estimate* |
|---|---|---|
| $\mu$ | $\mu$ | $\hat{\mu} = \overline{X}_{\bullet\bullet}$ |
| $\alpha_1$ | $\mu_{1\bullet} - \mu$ | $\hat{\alpha}_1 = \overline{X}_{1\bullet} - \overline{X}_{\bullet\bullet}$ |
| $\alpha_2$ | $\mu_{2\bullet} - \mu$ | $\hat{\alpha}_2 = \overline{X}_{2\bullet} - \overline{X}_{\bullet\bullet}$ |
| $\beta_1$ | $\mu_{\bullet 1} - \mu$ | $\hat{\beta}_1 = \overline{X}_{\bullet 1} - \overline{X}_{\bullet\bullet}$ |
| $\beta_2$ | $\mu_{\bullet 2} - \mu$ | $\hat{\beta}_2 = \overline{X}_{\bullet 2} - \overline{X}_{\bullet\bullet}$ |
| $\beta_3$ | $\mu_{\bullet 3} - \mu$ | $\hat{\beta}_3 = \overline{X}_{\bullet 3} - \overline{X}_{\bullet\bullet}$ |
| $\alpha\beta_{11}$ | $\mu_{11} - (\mu + \alpha_1 + \beta_1)$ | $\widehat{\alpha\beta}_{11} = \overline{X}_{11} - (\overline{X}_{\bullet\bullet} + \alpha_1 + \beta_1)$ |
| $\alpha\beta_{12}$ | $\mu_{12} - (\mu + \alpha_1 + \beta_2)$ | $\widehat{\alpha\beta}_{12} = \overline{X}_{12} - (\overline{X}_{\bullet\bullet} + \alpha_1 + \beta_2)$ |
| $\alpha\beta_{13}$ | $\mu_{13} - (\mu + \alpha_1 + \beta_3)$ | $\widehat{\alpha\beta}_{13} = \overline{X}_{13} - (\overline{X}_{\bullet\bullet} + \alpha_1 + \beta_3)$ |
| $\alpha\beta_{21}$ | $\mu_{21} - (\mu + \alpha_2 + \beta_1)$ | $\widehat{\alpha\beta}_{21} = \overline{X}_{21} - (\overline{X}_{\bullet\bullet} + \alpha_2 + \beta_1)$ |
| $\alpha\beta_{22}$ | $\mu_{22} - (\mu + \alpha_2 + \beta_2)$ | $\widehat{\alpha\beta}_{22} = \overline{X}_{22} - (\overline{X}_{\bullet\bullet} + \alpha_2 + \beta_2)$ |
| $\alpha\beta_{23}$ | $\mu_{23} - (\mu + \alpha_2 + \beta_3)$ | $\widehat{\alpha\beta}_{23} = \overline{X}_{23} - (\overline{X}_{\bullet\bullet} + \alpha_2 + \beta_3)$ |

$\alpha_j$'s = 0 when the null hypothesis is true. The following statements are equivalent ways of stating the null hypothesis for factor *A*:

1. $H_{0_1}\colon \mu_{1\bullet} = \ldots = \mu_{J\bullet}$
2. $H_{0_1}\colon \Sigma_j(\mu_{j\bullet} - \mu)^2 = 0$
3. $H_{0_1}\colon \alpha_1 = \alpha_2 = \ldots = \alpha_J = 0$
4. $H_{0_1}\colon \Sigma_j\alpha_j^2 = 0$

The development of the statement of the null hypothesis for factor *B* is perfectly analogous to the $H_0$'s for factor *A*. Specifically, the interest in factor *B* is whether the null hypothesis (that the *K* population means for the levels of factor *B* are all equal) can be rejected. The following statements are equivalent ways of stating the null hypothesis for factor *B*:

1. $H_{0_2}: \mu_{\bullet 1} = \mu_{\bullet 2} = \ldots = \mu_{\bullet K}$
2. $H_{0_2}: \sum_k (\mu_{\bullet k} - \mu)^2 = 0$
3. $H_{0_2}: \beta_1 = \beta_2 = \ldots = \beta_K = 0$
4. $H_{0_2}: \sum_k \beta_k^2 = 0$

Except when there are two levels of a factor, there are several ways in which the null hypothesis about a main effect, that is, about a single factor, can be false. For factor *A*, $\mu_1$ could equal 20.0 and the remaining $\mu_j$ 's could equal 25.0, for example; or $\mu_{1\bullet} = \mu_{2\bullet} = 16.65$ and $\mu_{3\bullet} = \mu_{4\bullet} = 17.80$. In both instances, $H_0$ is false. All that it takes for $H_0$ to be false is for at least two population means to be unequal. The decision faced in an ANOVA is whether one should continue to view the null hypothesis as plausible, or whether $H_0$ should be rejected and the alternative hypothesis $H_1$ be accepted. The alternative hypothesis, can be stated in the following equivalent ways for factor $A$:

1. $H_1: \mu_{j\bullet} \neq \mu_{j\bullet*}$, where $j \neq j*$
2. $H_1: \sum_j (\mu_{j\bullet} - \mu)^2 \neq 0$
3. $H_1: \alpha_j \neq 0$ for at least one $j$
4. $H_1: \sum_j \alpha_j^2 \neq 0$

All of the above statements are equivalent and will be true if, and only if, the null hypothesis for factor $A$ is false. Hence, if $H_0$ is rejected, $H_1$ is accepted automatically. The form of the alternative hypothesis for factor $B$ is perfectly analogous to the form of $H_1$ for factor $A$.

There remains one hypothesis of interest—that concerning the interaction terms, $\alpha\beta_{jk}$. In Sections 18.2 to 18.5, attention was directed toward two sets of conditions: (1) Where the two factors do not interact, the graph of the population means produces parallel lines; (2) There is an interaction between the two factors, and the graph of the population means produces nonparallel lines.

In Section 18.3, it was seen that no interaction exists between factors $A$ and $B$ if the line graph of the means has the same profile for the two factors. If this is the case, the mean of any cell ($\mu_{jk}$) will (as shown in Table 18.2), equal:

$$\mu_{jk} = \mu + (\mu_{j\bullet} - \mu) + (\mu_{\bullet k} - \mu) = \mu + \alpha_j + \beta_k$$

Stated differently, if there is no interaction between the two factors:

$$\mu_{jk} = \mu_{j\bullet} + \mu_{\bullet k} - \mu$$

If there is no interaction, then for all the $\mu_{jk}$'s:

$$\mu_{jk} - \mu_{j\bullet} - \mu_{\bullet k} + \mu = 0$$

Alternately, in terms of the model in Equation 18.2:

$$\alpha\beta_{jk} = 0 \text{ for all } j \text{ and } k$$

If the lines in the graph of the population cell means are not parallel, then at least one $\alpha\beta_{jk}$ is not equal to zero. Hence, parallel lines in the graph of the $JK$ population means correspond to all of the $\alpha\beta_{jk}$'s equaling zero (and $H_0$ is true); when the lines in an interaction graph are not parallel, then all the $\alpha\beta_{jk}$'s do not equal zero. There are several ways of stating the null hypothesis $H_0$ and the alternative hypothesis $H_1$ about the interaction effects. Table 18.3 illustrates several equivalent ways in which $H_0$ and $H_1$ can be expressed.

In summary, in the two-factor ANOVA, there are three null hypotheses (and the corresponding three alternative hypotheses) that are typically of interest : (1) $H_{0_1}$ for factor $A$, (2) $H_{0_2}$ for factor $B$, and (3) $H_{0_3}$ for the interaction of factors $A$ and $B$. In the remaining sections of this chapter, the data gathered in a two-factor experiment are brought to bear on the decision to reject the null hypotheses for factor $A$, factor $B$, and for the interaction of $A$ and $B$.

**TABLE 18.3** Equivalent Expressions of the Interaction Hypotheses in Two-Factor ANOVA.[13]

| *Equivalent statements of $H_0$ for the interaction of A and B* | *Equivalent statements of $H_1$ for the interaction of A and B* |
|---|---|
| 1. $H_{0_3}: \text{all } (\mu_{jk} - \mu_{j\bullet} - \mu_{\bullet k} + \mu) = 0$ | 1. $H_1: \mu_{jk} - \mu_{j\bullet} - \mu_{\bullet k} + \mu \neq 0$ for at least one $\mu_{jk}$ |
| 2. $H_{0_3}: \text{all } \alpha\beta_{jk} = 0$ | 2. $H_1: \alpha\beta_{jk} \neq 0$ for at least one $\alpha\beta_{jk}$ |
| 3. $H_{0_3}: \sum_k \sum_j (\mu_{jk} - \mu_{j\bullet} - \mu_{\bullet k} + \mu)^2 = 0$ | 3. $H_1: \sum_k \sum_j (\mu_{jk} - \mu_{j\bullet} - \mu_{\bullet k} + \mu)^2 \neq 0$ |
| 4. $H_{0_3}: \sum_k \sum_j \alpha\beta_{jk}^2 = 0$ | 4. $H_1: \sum_k \sum_j \alpha\beta_{jk}^2 \neq 0$ |

## 18.11 SUMS OF SQUARES IN THE TWO-FACTOR ANOVA

As with one-factor ANOVA, inferential tests of the three null hypotheses in the two-factor ANOVA employ sums of squares, degrees of freedom, mean squares, expected mean squares, and $F$-ratios.

There are four sources of variation in a two-factor ANOVA: (1) variation resulting from difference among the $J$ means for factor $A$, (2) variation resulting from difference among the $K$ means for factor $B$, (3) variation due to the interaction of $A$ and $B$, and (4) variation of the observations "within" cells. We shall define the sum of squares for each source of variation. It will be assumed throughout that the design is balanced, that is, the number of observations in all cells is the same: $n_{11} = n_{21} = \ldots = n_{JK} = n$.

### Total Sum of Squares

The total sum of squares in the set of $n_{\bullet\bullet}$ scores in a two-factor ANOVA is the sum of the squared difference between each score and the grand mean, as indicated in Equation 18.4:

$$SS_{\text{total}} = \Sigma_k \Sigma_j \Sigma_i (X_{ijk} - \overline{X}_{\bullet\bullet})^2 = \Sigma_k \Sigma_j \Sigma_i x_{ijk}^2 \qquad \textbf{(18.4)}$$

$SS_{\text{total}}$ can be analyzed into four independent (orthogonal) components which, when divided by their respective degrees of freedom, yield four independent estimates of the variance in the population, thus the expression analysis of variance. We first obtain the values of the sums of squares which will be used to obtain an estimate of the population variance.

### Sum of Squares for Factor *A*

The sum of squares for factor $A$, denoted $SS_A$, is simply $nK = n_{j\bullet}$ multiplied by the sum of the squared least-squares estimates of the $\alpha_j$'s:

$$SS_A = nK \sum_j \hat{\alpha}_j^2 = nK \sum_j (\overline{X}_{j\bullet} - \overline{X}_{\bullet\bullet})^2 \qquad \textbf{(18.5)}$$

[13]Recall that $\alpha\beta_{jk}$ is not a product of $\alpha_j$ and $\beta_k$; note also that $\alpha\beta_{jk}^2 = (\alpha\beta_{jk})^2$.

Note in Equation 18.5 that each $\overline{X}_{j\bullet}$ is based on $nK$ observations.

Recall that $\alpha_j = \mu_{j\bullet} - \mu$ is estimated by the row mean of level $j$ minus the grand mean, that is, $\hat{\alpha}_j = \overline{X}_{j\bullet} - \overline{X}_{\bullet\bullet}$. The sum of squares for $\hat{\alpha}_j$ is $nK\hat{\alpha}_j^2$. The sum aggregated across all $J$ levels of $A$ of these squared estimates, $nK\hat{\alpha}^2$ (Equation 18.5) is the "sum of squares for factor $A$," denoted as $SS_A$.

### Sum of Squares for Factor B

The sum of squares for factor $B$ is $nJ = n_{\bullet k}$ times the sum of the squared least-squares estimates of the $\beta_k$'s:

$$SS_B = nJ\sum_k \hat{\beta}_k^2 = nJ\sum_k(\overline{X}_{\bullet k} - \overline{X}_{\bullet\bullet})^2 \quad \textbf{(18.6)}$$

Notice that $nJ$ is the number of scores averaged to obtain $\overline{X}_{\bullet k}$ just as $nK$ was the number of scores averaged to obtain $\overline{X}_{j\bullet}$.

### Sum of Squares for the A × B Interaction

The interaction sum of squares is:

$$SS_{AB} = n\sum_k\sum_j \widehat{\alpha\beta}_{jk}^2 = n\sum_k\sum_j[\overline{X}_{jk} - (\overline{X}_{\bullet\bullet} + \hat{\alpha}_j + \hat{\beta}_k)]^2 \quad \textbf{(18.7)}$$

Notice as before that $n$ is the number of scores averaged to obtain $\overline{X}_{jk}$.

### Sum of Squares "Within" Cells

The sum of squares within cells (or just "within" for short) is denoted by $SS_W$. If the difference between each observation and the mean of the cell of which it is a member is squared, and summed for all $nJK$ observations, the result is $SS_W$:

$$SS_W = \sum_k\sum_j\sum_i(X_{ijk} - \overline{X}_{jk})^2 = \sum_k\sum_j\sum_i x_{ijk}^2 \quad \textbf{(18.8)}$$

Since $SS_{total} = SS_A + SS_B + SS_{AB} + SS_W$, it is sometimes useful to obtain $SS_W$ indirectly using Equation 18.9:

$$SS_W = SS_{total} - SS_A - SS_B - SS_{AB} \quad \textbf{(18.9)}$$

The meaning of these four sums of squares will become clearer when the corresponding mean squares and their expected values are considered in the following sections.

## 18.12 DEGREES OF FREEDOM

Each of the four independent sums of squares in the two-factor ANOVA is converted into a variance estimate (mean square) by dividing it by its degrees of freedom. The degrees of freedom for a given sum of squares are the number of least-squares estimates of effects that comprise the sum of squares minus the number of independent linear restrictions placed on these estimates. This is a difficult and abstract notion, and it will be discussed in some detail.

$SS_A$ is calculated from the $J$ least-squares estimates $\hat{\alpha}_1, \hat{\alpha}_2, \ldots, \hat{\alpha}_J$. It was natural and less restrictive to specify in the model in Equation 18.2 that $\alpha_1 + \alpha_2 + \ldots + \alpha_J = 0$. Furthermore, it is necessary to assume that $\hat{\alpha}_1 + \hat{\alpha}_2 + \ldots + \hat{\alpha}_J = 0$ before the solution to the mathematical criterion of least-squares estimation can be found. Indeed, as they must, the least-squares estimates of the effects ($\alpha_j$'s) satisfy this restriction, that is, $\hat{\alpha}_1 + \hat{\alpha}_2 + \ldots + \hat{\alpha}_J = 0$:

$$\sum_j \hat{\alpha}_j = \sum_j (\overline{X}_{j\bullet} - \overline{X}_{\bullet\bullet}) = 0$$

because in a balanced design, $\overline{X}_{\bullet\bullet}$ is the mean of the $J$ means, $\overline{X}_{j\bullet}$.

There are $J$ least-squares estimates in the calculation of $SS_A$, and they must conform to the single linear restriction that their sum be zero. Hence, the degrees of freedom for $SS_A$ are $J - 1$. An exactly analogous line of reasoning leads to the correct conclusion that $SS_B$ has degrees of freedom equal to $K - 1$.

The calculation of $SS_{AB}$ involves the $JK$ least-squares estimates of the $\alpha\beta_{jk}$ terms. The restrictions it is necessary to impose on these estimates to solve the least-squares problem are that summing the estimates across rows for any given column yields a sum of zero and summing the estimates across the columns for any given row yields a sum of zero, that is:

$$\sum_k \widehat{\alpha\beta}_{jk} = 0 \text{ for each } j \tag{18.10}$$

$$\sum_j \widehat{\alpha\beta}_{jk} = 0 \text{ for each } k \tag{18.11}$$

The conditions in Equation 18.10 are $J$ in number; there are $K$ restrictions represented in Equation 18.11. Not all $J + K$ of these restrictions are independent, however. Namely, given the restrictions in Equation 18.10 and knowing that $\Sigma_j\, \alpha\beta_{jk}$ equals zero for $k = 1, \ldots, K - 1$, it must necessarily follow that $\Sigma_j \alpha\beta_{jK} = 0$. Hence, only $J + K - 1$ of the linear restrictions on the $JK$ values of $\alpha\beta_{jk}$ are independent. Therefore, the degrees of freedom for the interaction $SS_{AB}$, are $JK - (J + K - 1) = JK - J - K + 1$, which can be factored into $(J - 1)(K - 1)$.

The sum of squares within cells, $SS_W$, is actually the sum of the squares of the $nJK$ least-squares estimates of the $\varepsilon$-terms in the model in Equation 18.2. Any single $e_{ijk}$ is estimated by $e_{ijk} = X_{ijk} - \overline{X}_{jk}$. Since $e_{ijk}$ is the deviation of a score from the mean of its cell, the sum of the $n$ $e_{ijk}$-values within each cell is zero. Thus, there are $JK$ independent linear restrictions on the $nJK$ values of $e_{ijk}$. Consequently, the degrees of freedom associated with $SS_W$ are $nJK - JK = JK(n - 1)$.

| Row number | Column number 1 | 2 | 3 | Row sums |
|---|---|---|---|---|
| 1 | 1 | | | 7 |
| 2 | | 4 | | |
| Column sums | 4 | 6 | | 16 |

**FIGURE 18.8**

An illustration of linear restriction.

The preceding results are summarized where there are $J$ levels of factor $A$, $K$ levels of factor $B$, and $n$ observations within each $JK$ combination.

| *Sum of squares* | *Degrees of freedom* |
|---|---|
| $SS_A$ | $J - 1$ |
| $SS_B$ | $K - 1$ |
| $SS_{AB}$ | $(J - 1)(K - 1)$ |
| $SS_W$ | $JK(n - 1)$ |

Now look at a very simple example of linear restrictions using the data in the $2 \times 3$ table in Figure 18.8. Try filling in the four missing cell entries and the missing row and column sum. If the number of degrees of freedom is the number of cells (here, $2 \times 3 = 6$) minus the number of independent linear restrictions on the data ($J + K - 1 = 4$), how many degrees of freedom are there for a table of this type? Notice two cell entries are *free* to vary. This is analogous to the degrees of freedom for the interaction of factor $A$ with factor $B$ in a $2 \times 3$ factorial design. For that ANOVA, the cell entries are interaction residuals, the six $\alpha\beta$ sum to zero, and every row sum and column sum is zero.

## 18.13 MEAN SQUARES

From each sum of squares, a mean square ($MS$) or variance estimate can be obtained, which is the ratio of the sum of squares ($SS$) to its degrees of freedom ($\nu$), that is, $MS = SS/\nu$:

$$MS_A = \frac{SS_A}{J-1}, \quad MS_B = \frac{SS_B}{K-1}, \quad MS_{AB} = \frac{SS_{AB}}{(J-1)(K-1)}, \quad MS_W = \frac{SS_W}{JK(n-1)}$$

As in the one-factor ANOVA, the ratios of $MS_A$, $MS_B$, and $MS_{AB}$ to $MS_W$ yield three $F$-ratios—the final calculations leading toward significance tests of the null hypotheses.

## 18.14 ILLUSTRATION OF COMPUTATION FOR THE TWO-FACTOR ANOVA

In this section, the computational formulas are applied to find the sums of squares and mean squares. For a two-factor ANOVA design in which factor $A$ has $J$ levels, factor $B$ has $K$ levels, and each of the $JK$ cells contains $n$ observations, the four sums of squares can be obtained most conveniently from the formulas used in Table 18.4.

**TABLE 18.4** Computation Illustration of a Two-Factor ANOVA with $n = 32$ Observations per Cell.

| | *Factor B: SES* | | | |
|---|---|---|---|---|
| | *Lower* $B_1$ | *Middle* $B_2$ | *Upper* $B_3$ | *A (Row) Effect* |
| *Public School* $A_1$ | $\bar{X}_{11} = 48.518$<br>$s_{11}^2 = 99.91$<br>$\widehat{\alpha\beta}_{11}{}^b = -.234$ | $\bar{X}_{12} = 51.796$<br>$s_{12}^2 = 100.19$<br>$\widehat{\alpha\beta}_{12} = -.307$ | $\bar{X}_{13} = 55.222$<br>$s_{13}^2 = 80.59$<br>$\widehat{\alpha\beta}_{13} = .542$ | $\bar{X}_{1.} = 51.845$<br>$\alpha_1 = -1.376^a$<br>$n_{1.} = nK = 96$ |
| *Private School* $A_2$ | $\bar{X}_{21} = 51.738$<br>$s_{21}^2 = 53.86$<br>$\widehat{\alpha\beta}_{21} = .234$ | $\bar{X}_{22} = 55.162$<br>$s_{22}^2 = 53.48$<br>$\widehat{\alpha\beta}_{22} = .308$ | $\bar{X}_{23} = 56.889$<br>$s_{23}^2 = 51.92$<br>$\widehat{\alpha\beta}_{23} = -.542$ | $\bar{X}_{2.} = 54.596$<br>$\alpha_2 = 1.376$ |
| *B (Column) Effect* | $\bar{X}_{.1}{}^c = 50.127$<br>$\hat{\beta}_1 = -3.093$ | $\bar{X}_{.2} = 53.478$<br>$\hat{\beta}_2 = .258$ | $\bar{X}_{.3} = 56.066$<br>$\hat{\beta}_3 = 2.835$ | $\bar{X}_{..} = 53.221$<br>$n_{..} = nJK = 192$ |

$n_{1.} = nJ = 64$

1. *Compute* $SS_A = nK\Sigma_j \hat{\alpha}_j^2$ (Equation 18.5)
$= 32(3)[(-1.376)^2 + (1.376)^2] = 96(1.892 + 1.892) = 363.282$
2. *Compute* $SS_B = nJ\Sigma_k \hat{\beta}_k^2$ (Equation 18.6)
$=32(2)[(-3.093)^2 + (.258)^2 + (2.834)^2] = 64(9.567 + .067 + 8.036) = 1{,}130.88$
3. *Compute* $SS_{AB} = n\Sigma_k\Sigma_j(\widehat{\alpha\beta}_{jk})^2$ (Equation 18.7)
$= 32[(-.234)^2 + (.234)^2 + (-.307)^2 + (.307)^2 + (.542)^2 + (-.542)^2] = 43.961$
4. *Compute* $MS_W = \Sigma_k\Sigma_j s_{jk}^2/JK = 439.95/6 = 73.325$
5. *Construct ANOVA table:*

| *Source* | *SS* | $\nu$ | $MS^d$ | $F$ | $p^e$ |
|---|---|---|---|---|---|
| School Type ($T$) | 363.282 | 1 | 363.282 | 4.954 | <.05 |
| SES ($S$) | 1,130.880 | 2 | 565.440 | 7.711 | <.01 |
| $T \times S$ | 43.961 | 2 | 21.980 | .300 | >.25 |
| Within | 13,638.45 | 186 | 73.325 | | |

[a] $\hat{\alpha}_1 = \bar{X}_{1.} - \bar{X}_{..}$; $\hat{\alpha}_j = \bar{X}_{j.} - \bar{X}_{..}$
[b] $\widehat{\alpha\beta}_{11} = \bar{X}_{11} - (\bar{X}_{..} + \hat{\alpha}_1 + \hat{\beta}_1)$; $\widehat{\alpha\beta}_{jk} = \bar{X}_{jk} - (\bar{X}_{..} + \hat{\alpha}_j + \hat{\beta}_k)$
[c] $\hat{\beta}_1 = \bar{X}_{.1} - \bar{X}_{..}$; $\hat{\beta}_k = \bar{X}_{.k} - \bar{X}_{..}$
[d] Alternatively, *MS*-values can be computed directly from effects:
$MS_A = nK\Sigma_j\alpha_j^2/(J-1)$; $MS_B = nJ\Sigma_k\beta_k^2/(K-1)$; $MS_{AB} = n\Sigma_j\Sigma_k(\alpha\beta_{jk})^2/[(J-1)(K-1)]$
[e] Most ANOVA software will give precise values of p: .027, .0006, and .741 for $T$, $S$, and $T \times S$, respectively.

The High School and Beyond (HSB) national study compared the academic achievement of representative samples of high school seniors attending public and private schools in various content areas. Since the two populations could differ in socioeconomic status (SES), samples were taken from lower, middle, and upper SES levels in both types of school. Raw scores were converted to $T$-scores.[14] The $T$-score means and variances on the measure of writing proficiency for each of the $2 \times 3$ cells in the School-type by SES design are given in Table 18.4, each cell having $n = 32$ students.

## Sum of Squares

In step 1 of Table 18.4, the sum of squares for factor $A$, $SS_A$, is determined: The *effect* of each level of factor $A$ ($\hat{\alpha}_1 = \bar{X}_{1\bullet} - \bar{X}_{\bullet\bullet}$, and $\hat{\alpha}_2 = \bar{X}_{2\bullet} - \bar{X}_{\bullet\bullet}$) is squared, and their sum is multiplied by the number of observations on which each mean is based ($nK = 96$) to obtain $SS_A$. The procedure is parallel for finding $SS_B$ in step 2. In step 3, the sum of squares for the interaction, $SS_{AB}$, is determined by squaring the effect of each cell, $\widehat{\alpha\beta}$, then multiplying their sum by $n$. In step 4, $MS_W$, the mean of the $JK$ cell variances is computed (in balanced designs: $MS_W = \Sigma_k\Sigma_j s_{jk}^2/JK$).

## Degrees of Freedom and Mean Squares

In step 5, each of the sums of squares is divided by its respective degrees of freedom to obtain mean squares; the degrees of freedom for a main effect are one less than the number of levels of that factor. The degrees of freedom for an interaction are simply the *product* of the $\nu$'s for all the factors involved. In the example, the treatment factor (type of school) has 1 degree of freedom, but the SES factor has 2 degrees of freedom; hence, the $A \times B$ interaction has $1 \times 2 = 2$ degrees of freedom. The degrees for freedom for "within" are the total number of cells ($JK$) multiplied by the number of degrees of freedom per cell ($n - 1$): $\nu_W = JK(n - 1)$.[15] The resulting mean squares are given in the ANOVA table in Table 18.4.

## *F*-Tests

If the null hypotheses for the two main effects and the interaction are true, the expected values of each of these four $MS$-values are equal to $\sigma^2$, the variance of observations in the parent population. Stated differently, if all null hypotheses are true, sampling error accounts for all the differences among the four mean square values in the ANOVA table in Table 18.4. However, if the null hypothesis for a source of variation (e.g., type of school, SES, or the interaction) is false, the expected $MS$-value for this source will increase, and hence the expected value for the $F$-ratio will increase. The bases for the $F$-test are treated more fully in Section 18.15.

In a one-factor ANOVA, $MS_A$ is divided by $MS_W$ to obtain the $F$-ratio to test $H_0$: $\mu_1 = \mu_2 = \ldots = \mu_J$. In a two-factor, fixed-effects ANOVA, the $MS$ for the two main effects ($MS_A$ and $MS_B$) and the mean square for the $AB$ interaction ($MS_{AB}$) are each divided by the average within-cell variance ($MS_W$) to obtain an $F$-ratio. The $F$-ratio to determine whether or not the null hypothesis for that source is tenable.

[14] Only a portion of the total sample is used for our illustration; hence, the grand mean and standard deviation in Table 18.4 are not exactly 50 and 10, respectively.

[15] Equivalently, $\nu_W = n_{\bullet\bullet} - JK$.

The $F$-tests in the ANOVA table in Table 18.4 indicate that two of the null hypotheses can be rejected—the two main effects were statistically significant (i.e., the $F$-ratios are greater than the critical $F$ of 3.92).[16] The private school mean was higher than the public school mean—the difference in means was greater than would be expected from chance (i.e., $H_{0_1}$ is rejected, $p < .05$). The fact that the interaction was not significant shows that at each of the three SES levels, the private school mean was higher. The differences among the means of the three SES levels were also greater than would be expected from sampling error (i.e., $H_{0_2}$ is rejected, $p < .01$).

## 18.15 EXPECTED VALUES OF MEAN SQUARES

The computational aspects of the two-factor ANOVA have been illustrated, but what is the purpose of the computations? What is the rationale underlying the $F$-test? A statistical inferential test is desired for deciding whether the data allow the null hypotheses to remain tenable, or whether they must be rejected. As was true in the one-factor ANOVA, expected values reveal how the mean squares bear on the truth of the three null hypotheses.

### $E(MS_W)$

The expected value of $MS_W$ is the mean of its sampling distribution. Another way to look at $E(MS_W)$ is that it is the variance of the population from which the observations in any one cell of the two-factor ANOVA design are assumed to have been sampled, given that the variance of the population from which the $n$ observations in any cell have been sampled is equal to $\sigma^2$. In other words, the variance of each of the populations underlying each of the $JK$ cells is equal to the same value, $\sigma^2$. This is an extension to the two-factor ANOVA of the assumption of homogeneous variances in the one-factor ANOVA.

If the $n$ observations in the $jk$th cell are assumed to have been drawn from a population with variance $\sigma^2$, then $E(s_{jk}^2) = \sigma^2$. $MS_W$ has the following form:

$$MS_W = \frac{SS_W}{\nu_W} = \frac{\sum_k \sum_j \sum_i (X_{ijk} - \overline{X}_{jk})^2}{JK(n-1)} = \frac{\sum_k \sum_j \sum_i x_{ijk}^2}{JK(n-1)} \qquad (18.12)$$

In a balanced ANOVA design, $MS_W$ is the average of the $JK$ within cell variances:

$$MS_W = \frac{\sum_k \sum_j s_{jk}^2}{JK} \qquad (18.13)$$

For example, in Table 18.4 notice that:

---

[16]When the actual degrees of freedom are not found in the table, use the closest, but lower value, to be conservative, that is, ${}_{.95}F_{1,186} \approx {}_{.95}F_{1,120} = 3.92$. Better yet, obtain the exact critical value of $F$ (or $p$) using computer software: ${}_{.95}F_{1,186} = 3.89$. In actual practice, the computer prints out the actual $p$-values, obviating the need for an $F$-table.

$$MS_W = \frac{(s_{11}^2 + s_{12}^2 + s_{13}^2 + s_{21}^2 + s_{22}^2 + s_{23}^2)}{JK} = \frac{(99.91 + 100.19 + \ldots + 51.92)}{6} = 73.325$$

The expected value of $MS_W$, $E(MS_W)$ is an unbiased estimate of the parameter, $\sigma_\varepsilon^2$ (or simply, $\sigma^2$)—the average value of an infinite number of $MS_W$-values, each one obtained from an independent replication of the same two-factor ANOVA design ($J$ levels of factor $A$, $K$ levels of factor $B$, and $n$ cases in each of the $JK$ cells). In the $2 \times 3$ design in Table 18.4, the value of $MS_W$ was 73.325. This is just one of a hypothetically infinite population of $MS_W$-values that could be generated by replicating the same school-type by SES ANOVA with a new set of students, randomly drawn from the populations. We do not know whether 73.325 is somewhat above or below the average value of $MS_W$ ($\sigma^2$), but it is an unbiased estimate:

$$E(MS_W) = \sigma^2 \qquad \textbf{(18.14)}$$

### $E(MS_A)$

From a single experiment (i.e., one replication of an experiment), one value of $MS_A$ can be calculated. Equation 18.15 gives the algebraic formula for $E(MS_A)$ in terms of the parameters of the model in Equation 18.2. Unlike $MS_W$, it does not estimate a single parameter (see Eq. 18.14), but is a composite:

$$E(MS_A) = \sigma_\varepsilon^2 + \frac{nK\sum_j \alpha_j^2}{J-1} = \sigma_\varepsilon^2 + nK\sigma_\alpha^2 \qquad \textbf{(18.15)}$$

where $nK = n_{j\bullet}$, $\sigma^2 = \sigma_\varepsilon^2$ is the variance of the error term in Equations 18.3A–B and is estimated by $MS_W$, and $\alpha_j$ is the main effect of the $j$th level of factor $A$, that is, $\alpha_j = \mu_{j\bullet} - \mu$, and $\sigma_\alpha^2 = \Sigma_j\alpha_j^2/(J-1)$.

In Table 18.4, suppose that, unknown to the researcher, the true value of $\sigma_\varepsilon^2$ (the parameter estimated by the within cell mean square) is 75, and that $\mu_{1\bullet} = 50$ and $\mu_{2\bullet} = 54$. Since $\mu = \frac{1}{2}(50 + 54) = 52$, the effect of level 1 of factor $A$ is $\alpha_1 = 50 - 52 = -2$ and $\alpha_2$ is $54 - 52 = 2$.[17] Substituting these values and $J = 2$ and $n = 32$ into Equation 18.15 yields:

$$E(MS_A) = 75 + \frac{32(3)[(-2)^2 + (2)^2]}{2-1} = 75 + 768 = 843$$

The preceding calculations were performed only for instructional purposes—to illustrate the nature of the terms in Equation 18.15. In practice, one never actually calculates a value for $E(MS_A)$—this would require knowledge of parameters (which typically only God knows). What is important is to note the relationship between the expression for $E(MS_A)$ and the truth or falsity of the null hypothesis about factor $A$. Notice that the fourth of several equivalent statements of $H_{0_1}$ for factor $A$ in Section 18.10 is $H_{0_1}$: $\Sigma_j\alpha_j^2 = 0$.

The quantity hypothesized to be zero in $H_{0_1}$ for factor $A$ is the same quantity that ap-

[17]These alphas are not to be confused with probabilities of type-I error.

pears in the numerator of the second term for $E(MS_A)$. Thus, if $H_0$ is true—which means that $\Sigma_j \alpha_j^2 = 0$ (i.e., $\alpha_1 = \alpha_2 = \ldots \alpha_J = 0$)—then:

$$E(MS_A) = \sigma_\varepsilon^2 + nK\sigma_\alpha^2 = \sigma_\varepsilon^2 + nK(0) = \sigma_\varepsilon^2$$

On the other hand, if $H_{0_1}$ is false, then $\sigma_\alpha^2 > 0$, hence:

$$E(MS_A) = \sigma_\varepsilon^2 + nK\sigma_\alpha^2 > \sigma_\varepsilon^2$$

This is an important relationship to understand; it provides the rationale for the $F$-test, $MS_A/MS_W$. If $H_{0_1}$ is *true, both* $MS_A$ and $MS_W$ have the *same* expected value ($\sigma_\varepsilon^2$), but if $H_{0_1}$ is *false*, the value of $MS_A$ is expected to be *larger* than $\sigma_\varepsilon^2 = E(MS_W)$.

### $E(MS_B)$

The expected value of $MS_B$ is:

$$E(MS_B) = \sigma_\varepsilon^2 + \frac{nJ\sum_k \beta_k^2}{K-1} = \sigma_\varepsilon^2 + nJ\sigma_\beta^2 \qquad \textbf{(18.16)}$$

The null hypothesis for the main effect of factor $B$ is $H_{0_2}$: $\Sigma_k \beta_K^2 = 0$. If $H_{0_2}$ for factor $B$ is *true*, then:

$$E(MS_B) = \sigma_\varepsilon^2 + nJ\sigma_\beta^2 = \sigma_\varepsilon^2 + nJ(0) = \sigma_\varepsilon^2$$

If $H_{0_2}$ for factor $B$ is true, the expected value of $MS_B$ equals $\sigma_\varepsilon^2 = E(MS_W)$; $MS_B$ will tend to be larger than $MS_W$ when $H_{0_2}$ for factor $B$ is false.

### $E(MS_{AB})$

The expected value of $MS_{AB}$ is:

$$E(MS_{AB}) = \sigma_\varepsilon^2 + n\sum_k\sum_j(\alpha\beta_{jk})^2 = \sigma_\varepsilon^2 + n\sigma_{\alpha\beta}^2 \qquad \textbf{(18.17)}$$

The null hypothesis for the interaction of factors $A$ and $B$ can be stated as $H_{0_3}$: $\Sigma_j\Sigma_k(\alpha\beta_{jk})^2 = 0$. Thus, if, for the interaction of $A$ and $B$, $H_{0_3}$ is *true*, then $E(MS_{AB})$ equals $\sigma_\varepsilon^2$; if $H_{0_3}$ is *false*, then $E(MS_{AB}) > \sigma_\varepsilon^2$. These relationships are summarized in Table 18.5.

The ratio of the value of $MS_A$ to $MS_W$ bears on the probability that $H_{0_1}$: $\Sigma_j \alpha_j^2 = 0$. If $H_{0_1}$ is true, then $MS_A$ and $MS_W$ have the same expected value; if $H_{0_1}$ is false, then $MS_A$ has an expected value larger than $\sigma_\varepsilon^2$, but the expected value of $MS_W$ remains $\sigma_\varepsilon^2$. If $MS_A$ proves to be much larger than $MS_W$ in a particular analysis, one is drawn to the conclusion that $H_{0_1}$ is false; if $MS_A$ and $MS_W$ are about the same size in a particular replication of the experiment, it is reasonable to conclude that they both may be estimating the same quantity, $\sigma_\varepsilon^2$, which is the case when $H_{0_1}$ is true. Comparisons of either $MS_B$ or $MS_{AB}$ with $MS_W$ bear on the truth

**TABLE 18.5** Relationships between Null Hypothesis and Expected Values of Mean Squares.

| *Source of Variation* | *Mean square* | *Expected mean square when $H_0$ is true* | *Expected mean square when $H_0$ is false*[a] |
|---|---|---|---|
| Factor $A$ | $MS_A$ | $\sigma_\varepsilon^2$ | $\sigma_\varepsilon^2 + nK\sigma_\alpha^2$ |
| Factor $B$ | $MS_B$ | $\sigma_\varepsilon^2$ | $\sigma_\varepsilon^2 + nJ\sigma_\beta^2$ |
| Interaction of $A$ and $B$ | $MS_{AB}$ | $\sigma_\varepsilon^2$ | $\sigma_\varepsilon^2 + n\sigma_{\alpha\beta}^2$ |
| Within cells | $MS_W$ | $\sigma_\varepsilon^2$ | $\sigma_\varepsilon^2$ |

[a]More explicitly, $\sigma_\alpha^2 = \Sigma_j\alpha_j^2/(J-1)$; $\sigma_\beta^2 = \Sigma_k\beta_k^2/(K-1)$; $\sigma_{\alpha\beta}^2 = \Sigma_k\Sigma_j\alpha\beta_{jk}^2/[(J-1)(K-1)]$.

or falsity of the null hypotheses about the main effect of $B$ and the $A \times B$ interaction, in the same manner that comparing $MS_A$ with $MS_W$ tells us something about the plausibility that the null hypothesis for factor $A$ is true. The matter of deciding when $MS_A$, $MS_B$, or $MS_{AB}$ is sufficiently larger than $MS_W$ to allow $H_0$ to be rejected is addressed in the next section.

## 18.16 THE DISTRIBUTION OF THE MEAN SQUARES

Before proceeding to the question of the distributions of the four mean squares in a two-factor ANOVA design, the nature of the statistical inference one makes in this situation needs to be clarified. In the two-factor design in Section 18.4, thirty-two observations were taken in each of the $2 \times 3 = 6$ cells of the design. These 192 observations are considered to have been randomly drawn from six hypothetical populations (one for each cell); theoretically, there are an infinite number of observations for each of these six populations.[18] The 192 observations in Table 18.4 will be called one *replication* of the experiment. This replication produced the following mean squares: $MS_A = 363.282$, $MS_B = 565.440$, $MS_{AB} = 21.980$, and $MS_W = 73.325$. A second replication of the study could be obtained; this second replication would yield somewhat different values for each of the four mean squares. Conceptually, third, fourth, fifth, and so on replications of the experiment could be run, and each replication would produce its own set of four mean squares. Now the question is, what will be the sampling distribution of the $MS$ values obtained from an infinite number of replications of the experiment?

Before answering this question, it is necessary to add an assumption to our model in Equation 18.2. In Section 18.14, it was necessary to assume that the variances of the hypothetical populations underlying the $JK$ cells of the experiment all have the same variance, $\sigma_\varepsilon^2 = \sigma^2$. To these assumptions, it is necessary to add the assumption that these populations are normally distributed in order for the mathematics to be tractable.

### The Distribution of $MS_W$

With the addition of the normality assumption, the $n$ observations in any cell, the $jk$th cell, constitute a random sample from a normal distribution with mean $\mu_{jk}$ and variance $\sigma^2 = \sigma_\varepsilon^2$. Each cell variance $s_{jk}^2$ is an unbiased estimator of $\sigma^2$. Furthermore:

[18]Of course, the null hypothesis contends that the six populations have the same means and variances.

$$\frac{s_{jk}^2}{\sigma_\varepsilon^2} \sim \frac{\chi_{n-1}^2}{n-1} = \frac{\chi_\nu^2}{\nu}$$

In other words, $s_{jk}^2/\sigma_\varepsilon^2$ has a distribution equal to the chi-square distribution ($\nu = n - 1$) divided by $n - 1$. This statement is true for the $JK$ independent cell variances $s_{jk}^2$. From the additive property of chi-square variables:

$$\sum_j \sum_k \frac{s_{jk}^2}{\sigma_\varepsilon^2} \sim \frac{\chi_{n-1}^2}{n-1} + \ldots + \frac{\chi_{n-1}^2}{n-1} \sim \frac{\chi_{JK(n-1)}^2}{n-1}$$

Dividing the preceding quantities by $JK$ yields:

$$\frac{\sum_j \sum_k \frac{s_{jk}^2}{\sigma_\varepsilon^2}}{JK} = \frac{MS_\text{W}}{\sigma_\varepsilon^2} \sim \frac{\chi_{JK(n-1)}^2}{JK(n-1)}$$

$MS_\text{W}/\sigma_\varepsilon^2$ has a chi-square distribution, $\nu = JK(n - 1)$ divided by $\nu$. In Table 18.4, where $J = 2$, $K = 3$, and $n = 32$, $\nu = (2)(3)(32 - 1) = 186$. Suppose the value of $\sigma_\varepsilon^2$ is 75, then $MS_\text{W}/75 \sim \chi_{186}^2/186$, and the observed value of $MS_\text{W} = 73.325$ is a single observation from a chi-square distribution ($\nu = 186$) that has been rescaled by division by 186.

## The Distribution of $MS_A$

One must consider two cases in this instance: the distribution of $MS_A$ when $H_0$: $\Sigma\alpha_j^2 = 0$ is true and when $H_0$ is false. If $H_0$ is true, then:

$$\frac{MS_\text{A}}{\sigma_\varepsilon^2} \sim \frac{\chi_{J-1}^2}{J-1}$$

that is, $MS_A/\sigma_\varepsilon^2$ has a distribution over complete replications of the two-factor design that is the chi-square distribution ($\nu = J - 1$) divided by $J - 1$.

If $H_0$ is false, then $MS_A/\sigma_\varepsilon^2$ has what is called a *noncentral chi-square distribution* ($\nu = \text{J} - 1$) divided by $J - 1$. The noncentral chi-square distribution with $\nu = J - 1$ is a mathematical curve that has a higher mean and is generally to the right of the chi-square distribution ($\nu = J - 1$). The relationship of the chi-square distribution to the noncentral chi-square distribution is illustrated in Figure 18.9.

When $H_0$ is false, the values of $MS_A$ tend to be larger than those of $MS_A$ when $H_0$ is true. This is reflected in the displacement to the right of the noncentral chi-square distribution. The larger the value of $\Sigma\alpha_j^2$, the further to the right of $\chi_{J-1}^2/(J - 1)$ the values of $MS_A/\sigma_\varepsilon^2$ will be displaced. Thus, the noncentral chi-square distribution in Figure 18.9 is for one particular value of $\Sigma\alpha_j^2$ only; there exists a separate noncentral $\chi^2$ distribution for each value of $\Sigma\alpha_j^2$.

## The Distribution of $MS_B$

The distributional statements that can be made about $MS_B$ are quite analogous to those for $MS_A$. If $H_0$: $\Sigma_k\beta_k^2 = 0$ is true, then:

$$\frac{MS_\text{B}}{\sigma_\varepsilon^2} \sim \frac{\chi_{K-1}^2}{K-1}$$

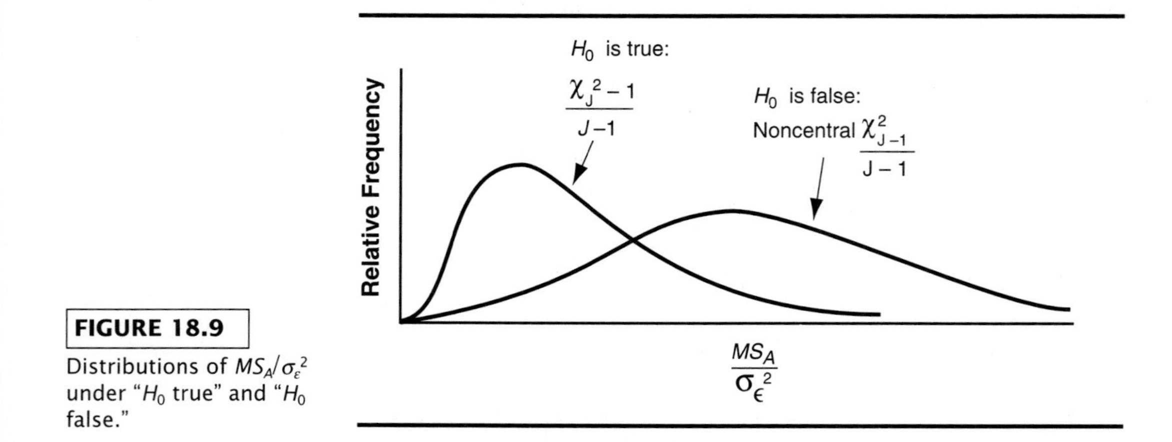


**FIGURE 18.9**

Distributions of $MS_A/\sigma_\varepsilon^2$ under "$H_0$ true" and "$H_0$ false."

If $H_0$ is false, then $MS_B/\sigma_\varepsilon^2$ has a noncentral chi-square distribution ($\nu = K - 1$) divided by $K - 1$.

### The Distribution of $MS_{AB}$

If $H_0$: $\Sigma_k\Sigma_j\alpha\beta_{jk}^2 = 0$, that is, if there is no interaction between factors $A$ and $B$, then:

$$\frac{MS_{AB}}{\sigma_\varepsilon^2} \sim \frac{\chi^2_{(J-1)(K-1)}}{(J-1)(K-1)}$$

$MS_{AB}/\sigma_\varepsilon^2$ has a chi-square distribution, $\nu = (J-1)(K-1)$, divided by $(J-1)(K-1)$.

Again, if the null hypothesis about the interaction of $A$ and $B$ is false, $MS_{AB}/\sigma_\varepsilon^2$ has a noncentral chi-square distribution, $\nu = (J-1)(K-1)$, divided by $(J-1)(K-1)$.

The facts can now be combined into the major results of this section. Recall that the ratio of two independent chi-square variables, each divided by its own degrees of freedom, has an $F$-distribution (see Section 16.6).

Suppose that $H_0$: $\Sigma\alpha_j^2 = 0$ is true; then $MS_A/\sigma_\varepsilon^2 \sim \chi_{J-1}{}^2/(J-1)$. Regardless of whether $H_0$ is true or false, $MS_W/\sigma_\varepsilon^2$ has a chi-square distribution divided by $JK(n-1)$. Now:

$$\frac{\dfrac{MS_A}{\sigma_\varepsilon^2}}{\dfrac{MS_W}{\sigma_\varepsilon^2}} \sim F_{J-1,JK(n-1)}$$

Notice that;

$$\frac{\dfrac{MS_A}{\sigma_\varepsilon^2}}{\dfrac{MS_W}{\sigma_\varepsilon^2}} = \frac{MS_A}{MS_W} \sim F_{J-1,JK(n-1)}$$

Fortunately, $\sigma_\varepsilon^2$ can be eliminated without having to know its actual value.

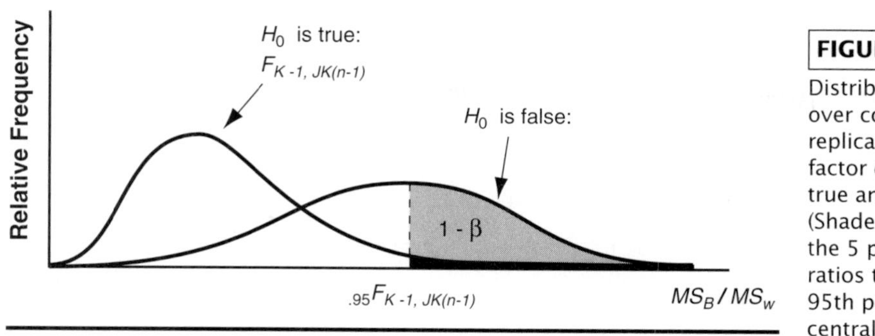


**FIGURE 18.10**
Distribution of $MS_B/MS_W$ over complete replications of the two-factor design when $H_0$ is true and when it is false. (Shaded portion contains the 5 percent of the ratios that exceed the 95th percentile in the central $F$-distribution.)

The ratio of $MS_A$ to $MS_W$ has an $F$-distribution with $J - 1$ and $JK(n - 1)$ degrees of freedom when $H_0$ is true. Thus, if the value of $MS_A/MS_W$ for a replication of a two-factor experiment looks like a "typical" observation from the distribution $F_{J-1,JK(n-1)}$—by "typical" meaning that $MS_A/MS_W$ does not exceed the 90th, 95th, or 99th percentile of that distribution—one is inclined to think that $H_0$ is tenable. On the other hand, if $H_0$ is false, then the value of $MS_A$ is expected to be larger than the value of $MS_W$. Hence, if a very large value of $MS_A/MS_W$ is obtained—a value that seems not to have been drawn from $F_{J-1,JK(n-1)}$ since it exceeds the 99th percentile of that distribution—then $H_0$ is probably false.

When $H_0$: $\Sigma\beta_k^2 = 0$ is true:

$$\frac{\dfrac{MS_B}{\sigma_\varepsilon^2}}{\dfrac{MS_w}{\sigma_\varepsilon^2}} = \frac{MS_B}{MS_w} \sim F_{K-1,JK(n-1)}$$

When $H_0$: $\Sigma\Sigma\alpha\beta_{jk}^2 = 0$ is true, then:

$$\frac{\dfrac{MS_{AB}}{\sigma_\varepsilon^2}}{\dfrac{MS_w}{\sigma_\varepsilon^2}} = \frac{MS_{AB}}{MS_w} \sim F_{(J-1)(K-1),JK(n-1)}$$

The effect of a false null hypothesis about either the main effects of factor $B$ or the interaction effects of $A$ and $B$ is to increase $MS_B$ or $MS_{AB}$ without systematically increasing $MS_W$, thus producing a distribution, over complete replications of the design, of mean squares that is displaced to the right of the $F$-distribution. These relationships are illustrated for factor $B$ in Figure 18.10. Note that the proportion of the noncentral $F$-distribution that exceeds the critical $F$-value (the vertical dashed line) is the power (the probability of not making a type-II error), $1 - \beta$.

## 18.17 HYPOTHESIS TESTS OF THE NULL HYPOTHESES

The discussion to this point has led to three ratios of mean squares that will be called $F$-ratios:

$$F_A = \frac{MS_A}{MS_W} \qquad F_B = \frac{MS_B}{MS_W} \qquad F_{AB} = \frac{MS_{AB}}{MS_W}$$

For the data in Table 18.4, these $F$-ratios have the following values:

$$F_A = 363.282/73.325 = 4.954$$

$$F_B = 565.440/73.325 = 7.711$$

$$F_{AB} = 21.980/73.325 = .300$$

These $F$-tests follow the pattern of the $F$-test in the one-factor ANOVA. The $F$-test will be illustrated with the main effects of factor $A$. First, one sets a value for alpha—the level of significance $\alpha$, which is the probability of rejecting $H_0$ when it is in fact true. The $\alpha$ so chosen determines a critical region, that is, the minimum value of the ratio $MS_A/MS_W$ that will lead one to reject $H_0$. This critical region includes all numbers greater than the $100(1-\alpha)$ percentile in the distribution $F_{J-1,JK(n-1)}$, that is, all values larger than ${}_{1-\alpha}F_{J-1,JK(n-1)}$. If the calculated value of $F_A = MS_A/MS_W$ exceeds the critical value ${}_{1-\alpha}F_{J-1,JK(n-1)}$, then $H_0$ is rejected. If $F_A$ is less than the critical $F$-value, $H_0$ is not rejected. The example in Table 18.4 can be used to illustrate the hypothesis tests. There it was found that $F_A = 4.954$. If $H_0$ were true, the distribution of $F_A$ over repeated complete replications of the $2 \times 3$ design would describe an $F$-distribution with 1 (i.e., $J-1$) and 186 [i.e., $JK(n-1)$] degrees of freedom. Obviously, we do not wish to make a type-I error and conclude erroneously that $H_0$ is false when in fact it is true. Indeed, we wish to adopt a decision rule for choosing between $H_0$ and the alternative hypothesis, $H_1$, that will lead to an erroneous decision to reject $H_0$ in favor of $H_1$ only rarely, for example, one time in 20 or .05. Hence, we adopt the conventional risk of $\alpha = .05$ of committing a type-I error—rejecting $H_0$ when it is true. Since the only evidence in favor of $H_1$ is a large value of $F_A$, the entire critical region of the test should be placed in the upper tail of the distribution $F_{1,186}$; hence, the critical value for the test becomes ${}_{.95}F_{1,186}$. From Table F in the Appendix, the 95th percentile in the $F$-distribution with 1 and 186 degrees of freedom is approximately 3.92.[19] Any $F$-ratio $F_A$ exceeding 3.92 will be taken to be evidence that the null hypothesis is false. This statement constitutes the decision rule of the hypothesis test. If in reality $H_0$ is true, this decision rule will have a probability of $\alpha =$ .05 of falsely rejecting $H_0$. Such is the magnitude of the risk one takes in agreeing to reject $H_0$ if $F_A$ is greater than 3.92. For the data in Table 18.4, the value of $F_A$ is 4.954. Since this $F$-ratio is greater than the critical value of 3.92, the null hypothesis is rejected. The position of this $F$-ratio relative to the central $F$-distribution—the distribution $F_A$ would follow if $H_0$ were true—is illustrated in Figure 18.11. We conclude that the difference between the two sample means $\bar{X}_{1\bullet}$ and $\bar{X}_{2\bullet}$ is significantly different at the .05 level. The mean of Population 2 (private schools) is greater than the mean of Population 1 (public schools) on this dependent variable (writing ability).

The $F$-test procedure of the null hypothesis for factor $B$ is parallel to that for factor $A$. The $F$-ratio for factor $B$ equals 7.711, well above the critical value, ${}_{.95}F_{2,\,186} \approx {}_{.95}F_{2,\,120} =$ 3.07, hence $H_0$ for factor $B$ can be rejected. Indeed, since the obtained $F$-ratio is greater than $7.32 \approx {}_{.999}F_{2,\,186}$, this null hypothesis can be rejected at the .001 level—the probability of observing an $F$-ratio greater than 7.32 when $H_0$ is true is less than 1 in 1,000. Thus, we can

[19] Recall that when the actual degrees of freedom are not tabled, use the closest, but lower, value to be conservative. Exact values can be obtained from computer software (e.g., EXCEL).

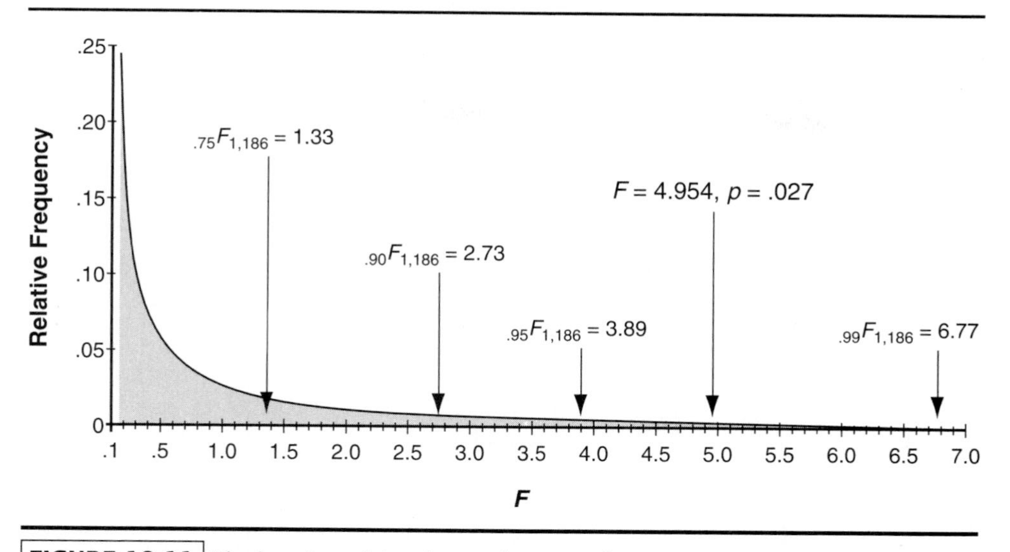


**FIGURE 18.11** The location of the observed $F$-ratio of 4.954 in the central $F$-distribution with 1 and 186 degrees of freedom.

be very confident that the population means represented by the three levels of factor $B$ are not equal, that is, SES and writing ability are related.

Figure 18.12 gives a graph of the means, $\overline{X}_{jk}$'s, that are involved with the interaction mean square for factors $A$ and $B$. It appears from the figure that the private-public school difference is less for students of upper SES than for middle and lower SES. To assess whether this conclusion is warranted, the $A \times B$ interaction must be tested to see if sampling error alone can account for any irregularity in the configuration. The rationale for the $F$-test of the null hypothesis about the interaction of factors $A$ and $B$ is parallel to that for the main

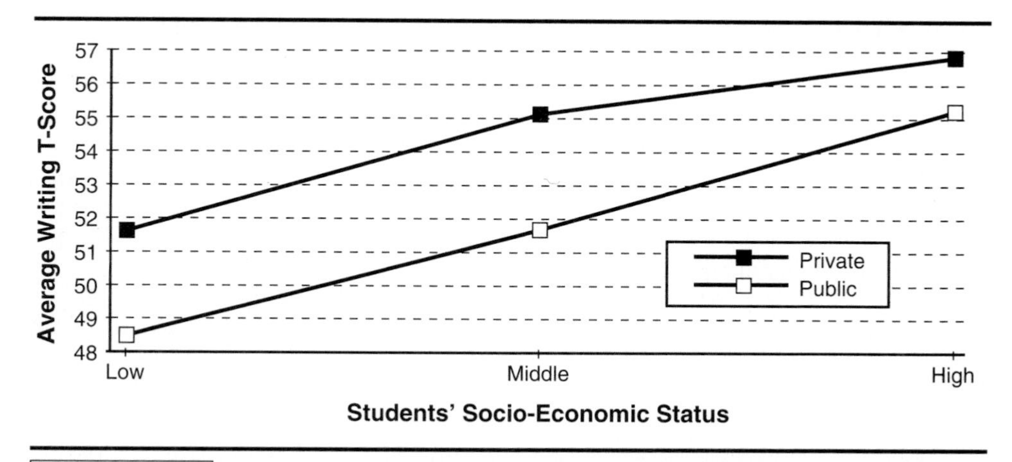


**FIGURE 18.12** Graph associated with the Type-of-School by SES interaction (Table 18.4).

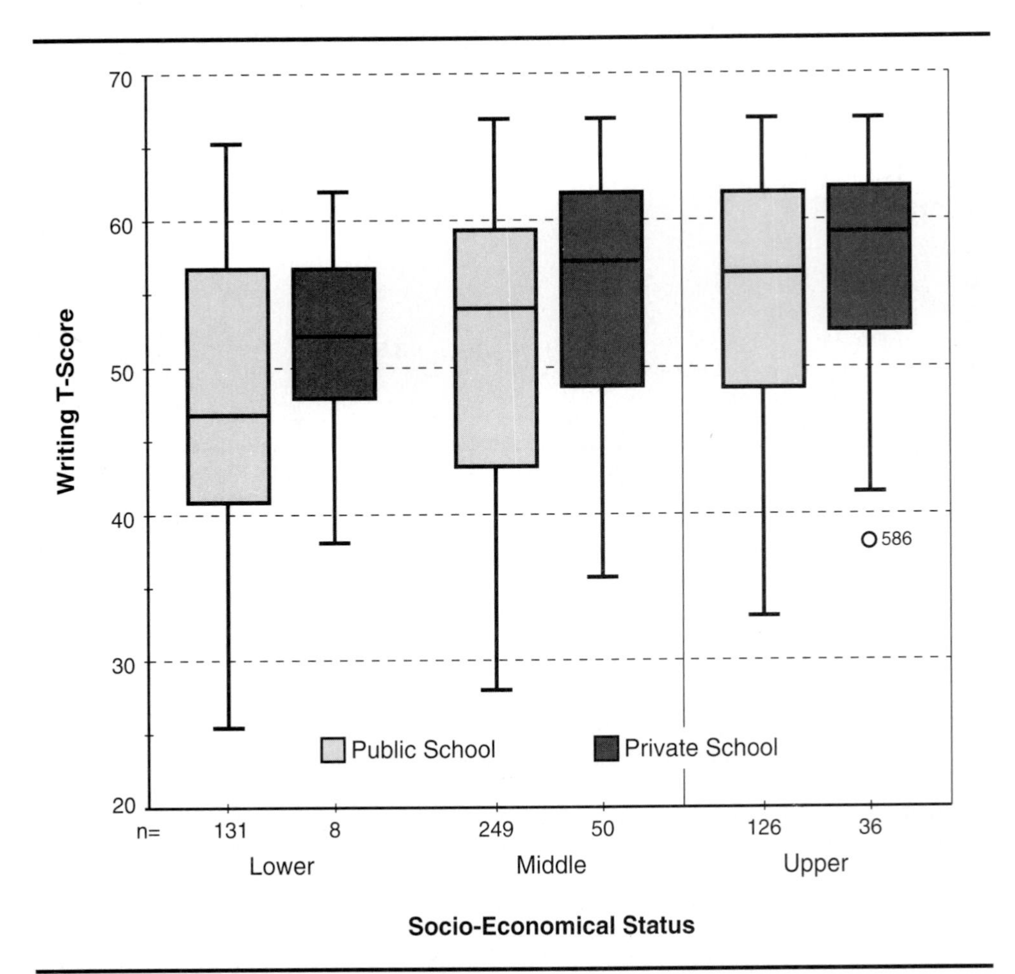

**FIGURE 18.13** The Type-of-School by SES interaction graphed using box plots.

effects. If there is no interaction ($H_0$ is true), then $F_{AB}$ has an $F$-distribution with $(J - 1)(K - 1) = 2$ and $JK(n - 1) = 186$ degrees of freedom. The value of $F_{AB}$ is $21.980/73.325 = .300$,[20] well below the critical $F$ of 3.07. It appears plausible to regard an $F$-ratio of .300 as having been drawn at random from the central $F$-distribution, $F_{2,186}$—to conclude that the data do not refute the null hypothesis for the $AB$ interaction. The conclusion is tenable that the difference in school type is constant across all three SES levels.

Figure 18.12 illustrates a conventional interaction graph. Notice, however, that the box-and-whisker interaction graph in Figure 18.13 gives a more complete picture of the relevant information. Notice the negative skewness in the distribution of scores for upper SES students (especially those in private schools), suggesting that the measure lacked ad-

[20]Even though the average (expected) $F$-ratio when $H_0$ is true is $\approx 1.0$ [actually $E(F) = \nu_2/(\nu_{2-2})$, see Section 16.6], approximately half of $F$-ratios will be below 1.0 when $H_0$ is true.

equate ceiling for distinguishing between excellent and outstanding writing skills. This probably explains why the two means are closer for the higher SES students than at the other SES levels. (Note that an outlier, case 586, was also identified in the graph.)

## 18.18 DETERMINING POWER IN FACTORIAL DESIGNS

Procedures for determining power for a one-factor ANOVA were treated in Sections 15.26 to 15.29. The procedures for balanced designs having two or more factors are very similar: The $n$ in Equation 15.22 is the number of observations on which each of the $J$ means for the factor in question is based, $n_{J\bullet}$. In Table 18.4, each row mean, $\overline{X}_{j\bullet}$, is based on $nK = 32(3) = 96$ observations; thus, the value for $n$ in Equation 15.22 would be 96; $J$, $\alpha_j$, and $\sigma_\varepsilon^2$ are unchanged in definition. In estimating power, the error variance, $\sigma_\varepsilon^2$, is the denominator of the $F$-test for testing the factor in question, which is ($MS_W$ when all factors are fixed;[21] hence, $MS_W$ and $MS_{error}$ are often synonymous, as they are in the example in Table 18.4. Equation 15.22 extended to a two-factor ANOVA becomes for the $A$ and $B$ main effects, respectively:

$$\phi_\alpha = \sqrt{\frac{nK\sum_j \alpha_j^2}{J\sigma_\varepsilon^2}} \quad \textbf{(18.18A)}$$

$$\phi_\beta = \sqrt{\frac{nJ\sum_k \beta_k^2}{K\sigma_\varepsilon^2}} \quad \textbf{(18.18B)}$$

Suppose in a $4 \times 3$ ANOVA design that factor $A$ is age level and factor $B$ is treatment (anxiety conditions). If anxiety-reducing conditions ($B_1$) increase performance by $.25\sigma$ ($\beta_1 = \mu_{\bullet 1} - \mu = .25\sigma$), neutral conditions ($B_2$) have no effect on performance ($\beta_2 = 0$), and anxiety-producing conditions decrease performance by $.25\sigma$ ($\beta_3 = -.25\sigma$), estimate the power for detecting the $B$ main effect if there are $n = 12$ subjects per cell with $\alpha = .05$. Using the $z$-score metric (Section 15.28), $\sigma_\varepsilon^2 = 1$, $\beta_1 = .25$, $\beta_2 = 0$, $\beta_3 = -.25$, $n_{\bullet k} = nJ = (4)(12) = 48$, and $K = 3$. Hence, form Equation 18.18B:

$$\phi_\beta = \sqrt{\frac{nJ\sum_k \beta_k^2}{K\sigma_\varepsilon^2}} = \sqrt{\frac{48[(.25)^2 + 0 + (-.25)^2]}{(3)(1)}} = \sqrt{2} = 1.414$$

From Appendix Table G ($\nu_B = 2$), with $\alpha = .05$ and $\nu_e = nJK - JK = [(12)(4)(3) - (4)(3)] = 132$, power would be estimated to be approximately .56.[22]

[21] The distinction between fixed and random factors is treated in Section 19.2.

[22] The procedures for estimating the power for detecting an interaction are closely parallel. The noncentrality parameter for an interaction in a two-factor ANOVA design is:

$\phi_{\alpha\beta} = \sqrt{n\sum_j\sum_k \beta_{jk}^2 / JK\sigma_\varepsilon^2}$ See Cohen (1988) for computational examples.

## 18.19 MULTIPLE COMPARISONS IN FACTORIAL ANOVA DESIGNS

As in the one-factor ANOVA, the rejection of a null hypothesis about a main effect implies only that not all of the population means for the levels of that factor are equal. Obviously, if there are only two levels of a factor, multiple comparison (MC) procedures are superfluous. However, if there are three or more levels of any factor associated with a significant main effect, multiple comparison procedures are required to determine which of the pairs of sample means show differences large enough to permit the conclusion that the associated population means differ.

The MC procedures described in Chapter 17 extend logically to each fixed ANOVA factor, the only difference being that the $n$'s in the equations are the $n$'s for the marginal means for the factor being examined, that is, the number of observations on which the means being compared are based. Although the assumption of homogeneity of variance can be ignored in the ANOVA because of ANOVA's robustness when cell sizes are equal, multiple comparisons are more definitive if the assumption is tenable. In Table 18.4, $F_{max} = 100.19/51.92 = 1.93 < {}_{.95}F_{max_{30,6}} = 2.91 \pm {}_{.95}F_{max_{31,6}}$; thus, the assumption of homogeneity of variance is tenable.

The MC procedures will be illustrated using the school type by SES design in Table 18.4. Since there are only two levels of factor $A$, multiple comparisons are not needed. Factor $B$ had three levels, and $H_0$ for the main effect was rejected. Since the three levels are ordered, not categorical, trend analysis (Section 17.19) is preferable to multiple comparisons. The definition of a contrast (Equation 17.7; Section 17.8) involving the means of factor $B$ is:

$$\hat{\psi} = \sum_k c_k \overline{X}_{\bullet k} = c_1\overline{X}_{\bullet 1} + c_2\overline{X}_{\bullet 2} + c_3\overline{X}_{\bullet 3}$$

The standard error of contrasts (Equation 17.8A; Section 17.10) among means of factor $B$ is:

$$s_{\hat{\psi}} = \sqrt{\frac{MS_e \sum_k c_k^2}{nJ}} \quad \text{and } t = \frac{\hat{\psi}}{s_{\hat{\psi}}}$$

(Equation 17.9; Section 17.11) where $MS_e = MS_W$[23], and $n_{\bullet k} = nJ$. The degrees of freedom for the critical $t$-value for a contrast will be $\nu_e$; in Table 18.4, $\nu_e = 186$. The contrast coefficients for a trend analysis are given in Table N in the Appendix. For $J = 3$, the contrast coefficients are:

| | $B_1$ | $B_2$ | $B_3$ |
|---|---|---|---|
| *Linear* | –1 | 0 | 1 |
| *Quadratic* | 1 | –2 | 1 |

[23]Up to this point is has been unnecessary to distinguish between $MS_W$ and $MS_e$, because $MS_W$ has been the proper denominator ("the error term") for all $F$-tests up to this point. Beginning with Chapter 19, this is not always the case.

Hence,

$$\hat{\psi}_{\text{linear}} = \sum_k c_k \overline{X}_{\bullet k} = c_1\overline{X}_{\bullet 1} + c_2\overline{X}_{\bullet 2} + c_3\overline{X}_{\bullet 3}$$
$$= (-1)(50.127) + (0)(53.478) + (1)(56.055) = -50.127 + 56.055$$
$$= 5.928$$

$$s_{\hat{\psi}} = \sqrt{\frac{MS_e \sum_j c_j^2}{nJ}} = \sqrt{\frac{73.325[(-1)^2 + (0)^2 + (1)^2]}{(32)(2)}}$$
$$= 1.514$$

and

$$t = \frac{\hat{\psi}}{s_{\hat{\psi}}} = \frac{5.928}{1.514} = 3.915.$$

Since trend components are a special case of planned orthogonal contrasts, the critical values for $t$ are found in Table C. Since the observed $t$-ratio is greater than the critical $t \approx 3.37$ for $\alpha = .001$ and $\nu = 186$, the linear trend in the three means is highly significant.[24] The linear trend is readily apparent in Figures 18.12 and 18.13.

Recall that each trend assesses unique (orthogonal) information; hence, they are entirely independent, and any combination of trends is possible. Is there a nonlinear (quadratic) trend? For example if $\mu_L < \mu_M = \mu_U$, a linear trend and a quadratic trend would be present:

$$\hat{\psi}_{\text{quadratic}} = \sum_k c_k \overline{X}_{\bullet k} = c_1\overline{X}_{\bullet 1} + c_2\overline{X}_{\bullet 2} + c_3\overline{X}_{\bullet 3}$$
$$= (1)(50.127) + (-2)(53.478) + (1)(56.055) = 50.127 - 106.956 + 56.055$$
$$= -.774$$

$$s_{\hat{\psi}} = \sqrt{\frac{MS_e \sum_k c_k^2}{nJ}} = \sqrt{\frac{73.325[(1)^2 + (-2)^2 + (1)^2]}{(32)(2)}}$$
$$= 2.628$$

and

$$t = \frac{\hat{\psi}}{s_{\hat{\psi}}} = \frac{-.774}{2.628} = -.294$$

Obviously, $t$ is not significant, since it is well below the critical value, ${}_{.975}t_{186} \approx 1.98$; indeed, $p > .50$. The hypothesis that there is no quadratic trend in the mean is supported (tenable).

If the three means had not had an underlying continuum (e.g., three ethnic groups

[24]If the $F$-test had been used to test the trend components, as in Table 17.5, its value would be equal to the square of the observed $t$-ratio. Recall that when $\nu_B = 1$, $t^2 = F$.

instead of the SES groups), multiple comparisons would have been employed to discover significant differences among the $K$ means. The above procedure would have been the same (except for the contrast coefficients) for the POC, Dunn, Dunnett, and Scheffé methods. The Newman-Keuls and Tukey procedures employ the studentized range statistic (Equation 17.2):

$$q_1 = \frac{(\overline{X}_{\bullet 3} - \overline{X}_{\bullet 1})}{s_{\overline{X}}}$$

where:

$$s_{\overline{X}} = \sqrt{\frac{MS_e}{nJ}} = \sqrt{\frac{73.325}{64}} = 1.070$$

Thus, $q_1 = (56.055 - 50.127)/1.070 = 5.54$, which is greater than the critical value for $q$ found in Table I at $\alpha = .001$ $({}_{.999}q_{186,3} \approx 5.21)$.[25]

## 18.20 CONFIDENCE INTERVALS FOR MEANS IN TWO-FACTOR ANOVA

Confidence intervals about marginal ($\overline{X}_{j\bullet}$ and $\overline{X}_{\bullet k}$) and cell ($\overline{X}_{jk}$) means follow the procedures given in Section 11.18:

$$(1-\alpha)CI \text{ for } \mu = \overline{X} \pm {}_{1-\alpha/2}t_\nu s_{\overline{X}}$$

where $s_{\overline{X}} = \sqrt{MS_e/\text{“}n\text{”}}$, where "$n$" represents the number of observations on which $\overline{X}$ is based. Thus, to set a confidence interval for public schools, $\mu_{1\bullet}$, in Table 18.4:

$$s_{\overline{X}} = \sqrt{\frac{MS_e}{nK}} = \sqrt{\frac{73.325}{96}} = .874^{26}$$

$${}_{.975}t_{186} = 1.973^{27}$$

$$.95CI = 51.845 \pm 1.973(.874) = 51.845 \pm 1.724 = (50.12,\ 53.57)$$

For private schools, only the value of $\overline{X}$ changes; thus $54.596 \pm 1.724$, or $.95CI$ for $\mu_2 = (52.87, 56.32)$.[28]

---

[25]The associated $q$-values for $H_{0_2}$: $\mu_2 = \mu_3$ and $H_{0_3}$: $\mu_1 = \mu_2$ are 2.40 and 3.12, which do not allow these hypotheses to be rejected using the Tukey method (and only $H_{0_3}$ is to be rejected at $\alpha = .05$ with the Newman-Keuls method). This illustrates the advantage of trend analysis over multiple comparisons when the means are ordered. No doubt both $H_{0_2}$ and $H_{0_3}$ would be rejected with greater power.

[26]Notice that the value of $s_{\overline{X}}$ for factor $A$ is less than that found for factor $B$ (in Section 18.18) because each mean is based on more observations (96 rather than 64).

[27]When setting confidence intervals, exact critical values are desirable. Exact critical values are available in EXCEL and most other spreadsheet programs.

[28]Note that overlapping $.95CI$'s do not mean that the means do not differ significantly. If $.68CI$'s are used, means that differ significantly for $\alpha = .05$ will have nonoverlapping $.68CI$'s; if $.68CI$'s are used, nonoverlapping means would differ by at least $2s_{\overline{X}} \approx 1.414 s_{\overline{X}_1 - \overline{X}_2}$, significant at about the $\alpha_2 = .16$ (or $\alpha_1 = .08$) level.

For the SES (factor $B$) means, the value of $s_{\bar{X}}$ was found in Section 18.19 to be 1.070; the critical $t$-value is the same as above (1.973). Thus, .95*CI*'s can be formed for the three SES levels by adding and subtracting (1.973)(1.073) = ±2.11 points from each mean.

Confidence intervals about cell means are helpful in interpreting interaction, but approximate .68*CI*'s are usually appropriate to avoid being overly conservative.[29] For cell means, $s_{\bar{X}} = \sqrt{MS_e / n} = \sqrt{73.325/32} = 1.514$, that is, ±1.514 about each cell means approximates the .68 confidence interval. (As an illustration of this procedure, see Figure 18.14 of Section 18.23, where the .68 CI's for cell means are represented graphically.[30])

## 18.21 THREE-FACTOR ANOVA

Once the concepts of two-factor ANOVA are mastered, the building blocks are in place for ANOVAs with three and more factors. Indeed, the only new concept in the transition from a two-factor to a three-factor ANOVA is the three-factor interaction. The key to understanding a three-factor interaction is to view it as addressing the question, "Is the $A \times B$ interaction constant across all levels of factor $C$?" For example, if method $E$ is better for bright students, but method $C$ is superior for lower scoring students, there is a method-by-ability interaction. However, do both boys and girls have the same pattern? This is the three-factor interaction question—is the two-factor interaction generalizable across both genders?

In a balanced design all sources of variation are orthogonal. This indicates that the three-factor interaction is independent of the two-factor interactions. In other words, whether there is a three-factor interaction does not depend on the existence of any two-factor interaction. The three-factor interaction asks, "Is the $A \times B$ pattern, regardless of whether the interaction zero or large, constant across all levels of factor $C$?" (Or, "Is the $A \times C$ pattern constant across all levels of $B$, and so on?") The example in Table 18.6 will be interpreted to illustrate the meaning of two- and three-factor interactions.

## 18.22 THREE-FACTOR ANOVA: AN ILLUSTRATION

To assess the effects of anxiety on test performance, three sets of instructions to examinees were used: (1) instructions designed to reduce anxiety, (2) neutral (standard) directions, or (3) directions designed to produce anxiety. Students were classified by sex, then randomly assigned to one of the three test instructions conditions: $A_1$ (anxiety-reducing), $A_2$ (neutral), $A_3$ (anxiety-producing). Within each level of factor $A$, 10 males and 10 females took a standardized verbal ability test ($T_1$) and 10 other males and 10 other females took a standardized math ability test ($T_2$) previously calibrated to be of the same difficulty level as the verbal test.[31]

The basic statistical model for the analysis of the data is a balanced $J = 3 \times K = 2 \times L = 2$,

---

[29]If you think this is too risky—not sensitive enough to type-I errors—consider the conventional interaction graph that includes no information about the sampling error associated with cell means! SPSS for Windows will give interaction graphs with *CI*'s about the cell means.

[30]In Figure 18.14, the .68 CI's for boys would overlap and are left incomplete. The within-cells variance, $MS_W$, in factorial designs should not be used in effect size computations; sigma should be estimated by the standard deviation of the reference group (public school students) taken as a whole (for example, in Figure 18.14, for the public school sample, $s = 9.96$ (see Equation 5.8).

[31]The use of standard scores could have accomplished the same purpose.

anxiety-condition ($A$) by test type ($T$) by sex ($S$), design.[32] For the three-factor ANOVA design the statistical model is: $X_{ijkl} = \mu + \alpha_j + \beta_k + \gamma_l + \alpha\beta_{jk} + \alpha\gamma_{jl} + \beta\gamma_{kl} + \alpha\beta\gamma_{jkl} + \varepsilon_{ijkl}$, when $X_{ijkl}$ is the $i$th replicate (score) in cell $jkl$. The unbiased estimators of the parameters in the model are

$$\hat{\alpha}_j = \overline{X}_{j\bullet\bullet} - \overline{X}_{\bullet\bullet\bullet}$$

$$\hat{\beta}_k = \overline{X}_{\bullet k\bullet} - \overline{X}_{\bullet\bullet\bullet}$$

$$\hat{\gamma}_l = \overline{X}_{\bullet\bullet l} - \overline{X}_{\bullet\bullet\bullet}$$

$$\widehat{\alpha\beta}_{jk} = \overline{X}_{jk\bullet} - (\overline{X}_{\bullet\bullet\bullet} + \hat{\alpha}_j + \hat{\beta}_k)$$

$$\widehat{\alpha\gamma}_{jl} = \overline{X}_{j\bullet l} - (\overline{X}_{\bullet\bullet\bullet} + \hat{\alpha}_j + \hat{\gamma}_l)$$

$$\widehat{\beta\gamma}_{kl} = \overline{X}_{\bullet kl} - (\overline{X}_{\bullet\bullet\bullet} + \hat{\beta}_k + \hat{\gamma}_l)$$

$$\widehat{\alpha\beta\gamma}_{jkl} = \overline{X}_{jkl} - (\overline{X}_{\bullet\bullet\bullet} + \hat{\alpha}_j + \hat{\beta}_k + \hat{\gamma}_l + \alpha\beta_{jk} + \alpha\gamma_{jl} + \beta\gamma_{kl})$$

The sum of each of the seven orthogonal effects is zero.

The twelve cell means and variances, as well as the estimates of the anxiety main effect, $\hat{\alpha}_j$'s, are given in panel I of Table 18.6. The three different combinations ($A \times T$, $A \times S$, and $T \times S$) of two-factor means are given in panel II, along with the estimates of the gender and test type main effects $\hat{\beta}_k$'s and $\hat{\gamma}_l$'s.

**TABLE 18.6** Computation Illustration of a Three Factor ANOVA with $n = 10$ Observations per Cell.

| | | $T_1$ | | $T_2$ | | |
|---|---|---|---|---|---|---|
| *I. $A \times T \times S$* | | $S_1$ (M) | $S_2$ (F) | $S_1$ (M) | $S_2$ (F) | $\overline{X}_{\bullet\bullet\bullet} = 13.00$ |
| $A_1$ | $\overline{X}_{jkl}$ | 12.7 | 14.0 | 16.0 | 10.5 | $13.30 = \overline{X}_{1\bullet\bullet}$ |
| | $\widehat{\alpha\beta\gamma}$ | −.65 | .65 | .65 | −.65 | $.30 = \hat{\alpha}_1$ |
| | $s^2_{jkl}$ | 28.1 | 25.0 | 20.3 | 18.5 | |
| $A_2$ | $\overline{X}_{jkl}$ | 13.0 | 13.2 | 12.6 | 10.2 | $12.25 = \overline{X}_{2\bullet\bullet}$ |
| | $\widehat{\alpha\beta\gamma}$ | .40 | −.40 | −.40 | −.40 | $-.75 = \hat{\alpha}_2$ |
| | $s^2_{jkl}$ | 22.1 | 26.0 | 23.0 | 25.0 | |
| $A_3$ | $\overline{X}_{jkl}$ | 12.1 | 16.3 | 12.2 | 13.2 | $13.45 = \overline{X}_{3\bullet\bullet}$ |
| | $\widehat{\alpha\beta\gamma}$ | .25 | −.25 | −.25 | .25 | $.45 = \hat{\alpha}_3$ |
| | $s^2_{jkl}$ | 27.0 | 39.7 | 43.6 | 29.2 | |

[32]It is easier to keep the factors identified if, instead of $A$, $B$, et cetera, the initial letter of the factor name is used.

| **TABLE 18.6** | *(Continued)* |
|---|---|

*II. A × T*

| | | $T_1$ | $T_2$ |
|---|---|---|---|
| $A_1$ | $\bar{X}_{jk\bullet}$ | 13.35 | 13.25 |
| | $\widehat{\alpha\beta}$ | −.50 | .50 |
| $A_2$ | $\bar{X}_{jk\bullet}$ | 13.10 | 11.40 |
| | $\widehat{\alpha\beta}$ | .30 | −.30 |
| $A_3$ | $\bar{X}_{jk\bullet}$ | 14.20 | 12.70 |
| | $\widehat{\alpha\beta}$ | .20 | −.20 |
| | | $13.55 = \bar{X}_{\bullet 1\bullet}$ | $12.45 = \bar{X}_{\bullet 2\bullet}$ |
| | | $.55 = \hat{\beta}_1$ | $-.55 = \hat{\beta}_2$ |

*A × S*

| | | $S_1$ | $S_2$ |
|---|---|---|---|
| $A_1$ | $\bar{X}_{j\bullet l}$ | 14.35 | 12.25 |
| | $\widehat{\alpha\gamma}$ | .95 | −.95 |
| $A_2$ | $\bar{X}_{j\bullet l}$ | 12.80 | 11.70 |
| | $\widehat{\alpha\gamma}$ | .45 | −.45 |
| $A_3$ | $\bar{X}_{j\bullet l}$ | 12.15 | 14.75 |
| | $\widehat{\alpha\gamma}$ | −1.40 | 1.40 |
| | | $13.10 = \bar{X}_{\bullet\bullet 1}$ | $12.90 = \bar{X}_{\bullet\bullet 2}$ |
| | | $.10 = \hat{\gamma}_1$ | $-.10 = \hat{\gamma}_2$ |

*T × S*

| | | $S_1$ | $S_2$ |
|---|---|---|---|
| $T_1$ | $\bar{X}_{\bullet kl}$ | 12.60 | 14.50 |
| | $\widehat{\beta\gamma}$ | −1.05 | 1.05 |
| $T_2$ | $\bar{X}_{\bullet kl}$ | 13.60 | 11.30 |
| | $\widehat{\beta\gamma}$ | 1.05 | −1.05 |

III. *Computations*

1. $SS_A = nKL\Sigma_j \hat{\alpha}_j^2 = 10(2)(2)[(.30)^2 + (-.75)^2 + (.45)^2] = 40(.855) = 34.20$
2. $SS_T = nJL\Sigma_k \hat{\beta}_k^2 = 10(3)(2)[(.55)^2 + (-.55)^2] = 60(.605) = 36.30$
3. $SS_S = nJK\Sigma_l \hat{\gamma}_l^2 = 10(3)(2)[(.10)^2 + (-.10)2] = 60(.02) = 1.20$
4. $SS_{AT} = nL\Sigma_k\Sigma_j(\widehat{\alpha\beta}_{jk})^2 = 10(2)[(-.5)^2 + (.5)^2 + (.3)^2 + (-.3)^2 + (.20)^2 + (-.2)^2] = 15.2$
5. $SS_{AS} = nK\Sigma_l\Sigma_j(\widehat{\alpha\gamma}_{jl})^2 = 10(2)[(.95)^2 + (-.95)^2 + (.45)^2 + (-.45)^2 + (-1.4)^2 + (1.4)^2] = 122.6$
6. $SS_{TS} = nJ\Sigma_l\Sigma_k(\widehat{\beta\gamma}_{lk})^2 = 10(3)[(-1.05)^2 + (1.05)^2 + (1.05)^2 + (-1.05)^2] = 132.30$
7. $SS_{ATS} = n\Sigma_l\Sigma_k\Sigma_j(\widehat{\alpha\beta\gamma}_{jlk})^2 = 10[(-.65)^2 + (.65)^2 + (.65)^2 + (-.65)^2 + (.4)^2 + (-.4)^2 + (-.4)^2 + (.4)^2 + (.25)^2 + (-.25)^2 + (-.25)^2 + (.25)^2] = 25.80$
8. $MS_W = \Sigma_l\Sigma_k\Sigma_j s_{jkl}^2/JKL = (28.1 + 22.1 + \ldots + 29.2)/12 = 327.5/12 = 27.29$

*IV. ANOVA Table*

| *Source* | *SS*[33] | *ν* | *MS* | *F* | *p*[34] |
|---|---|---|---|---|---|
| Anxiety Conditions (*A*) | 34.20 | 2 | 17.10 | .63 | .53 |
| Test (*T*) | 36.30 | 1 | 36.30 | 1.33 | .25 |
| Sex (*S*) | 1.20 | 1 | 1.20 | .04 | .84 |
| *AT* (or *A* × *T*) | 15.20 | 2 | 7.60 | .28 | .76 |
| *AS* | 122.60 | 2 | 61.30 | 2.25 | .11 |
| *TS* | 132.30 | 1 | 132.30 | 4.85 | .03 |
| *ATS* | 25.80 | 2 | 12.90 | .47 | .63 |
| Within (*error*) | 2,947.50 | 108 | 27.29 | | |

[33] *SS* values are of little interest; they are often excluded from ANOVA tables; $SS = \nu MS$.

[34] From computer output.

## 18.23 THREE-FACTOR ANOVA COMPUTATION[35]

Using the data in panel I, the computations of a three-factor ANOVA are illustrated.[36] In step 1, the sum of squares for the anxiety main effect, $SS_A$, is obtained using the $\hat{\alpha}_j$'s estimates found in panel I (see Table 18.2 for the formulas for the $\hat{\alpha}_j$'s, e.g., $\hat{\alpha}_1 = \bar{X}_{1..} - \bar{X}_{...} = 13.30 - 13.00 = .30$). The sum of squares for the test content ($SS_T$) and sex ($SS_S$) main effects are computed similarly using the $\hat{\beta}_k$ and $\hat{\gamma}_l$ estimates found in panel II. The sum of squares for the three two-factor interactions ($SS_{AT}$, $SS_{AS}$, and $SS_{TS}$) can proceed as if three separate two-factor ANOVA's had been performed using the $\widehat{\alpha\beta}_{jk}$, $\widehat{\alpha\gamma}_{jl}$, and $\widehat{\beta\gamma}_{kl}$ estimates [see Table 18.2 for the relevant formulas, e.g., $\widehat{\alpha\beta}_{11} = \bar{X}_{11.} - (\bar{X}_{...} + \hat{\alpha}_1 + \hat{\beta}_1) = 13.35 - (13.00 + .30 + .55) = -.50$] as shown in panel II.

Only two remaining sources of variation are undetermined: (1) that for the three-factor ($A \times T \times S$) interaction, and (2) within cells. The rationale for the computation of the three-factor interaction is a logical extension of the procedures used in determining a two-factor interaction. The mean of each cell is predicted using the estimates of effects. For example, the mean of the cell that represents level 1 of factors $A$, $T$, and $S$ from the model is predicted to be:

$$\begin{aligned}\mu_{111} &= \bar{X}_{...} + \hat{\alpha}_1 + \hat{\beta}_1 + \hat{\gamma}_1 + \widehat{\alpha\beta}_{11} + \widehat{\alpha\gamma}_{11} + \widehat{\beta\gamma}_{11} \\ &= 13.00 + .30 + .10 + .55 + (-.55) + .95 + (-1.05) = 13.35\end{aligned}$$

The difference between the observed mean of this cell (12.7) and 13.35 represents the three-factor interaction component, $\widehat{\alpha\beta\gamma}_{111}$, used in step 7 to compute $SS_{ATS}$.

$$\widehat{\alpha\beta\gamma}_{111} = \bar{X}_{111} - (\bar{X}_{...} + \hat{\alpha}_1 + \hat{\beta}_1 + \hat{\gamma}_1 + \widehat{\alpha\beta}_{11} + \widehat{\alpha\gamma}_{11} + \widehat{\beta\gamma}_{11}) = 12.7 - 13.35 = -.65$$

If cell means are predictable from the main effects and the two-factor interaction effects, obviously there is no three-factor interaction. The essence of the three-factor interaction is that there are unique effects associated with particular three-factor combinations. The computation of $SS_{ATS}$ is illustrated in step 7 in panel III of Table 18.6. The procedure for finding $MS_W$ is parallel to that for a two-factor ANOVA: In a balanced design, $MS_W$ is the mean of the $JKL = (3)(2)(2) = 12$ cell variances, as shown in step 8 of panel III of Table 18.6.

The degrees of freedom associated with $MS_W$, $\nu_W$, $= JKL(n - 1)$, or in the example, $(3)(2)(2)(10 - 1) = 108$. Stated differently, $\nu_W$ equals the number of cells ($JKL$) times the degrees of freedom per cell ($n - 1$).

### Results

The ANOVA table for the three-factor ANOVA is given in panel IV of Table 18.6. None of the three main effects (anxiety conditions, test-type, or sex) is significant. The differences among the means of the three anxiety conditions ($\bar{X}_{1..} = 13.30$, $\bar{X}_{2..} = 12.25$, and $\bar{X}_{3..} = 13.45$) do not approach statistical significance ($F = .63, p > .25$). Neither is the overall mean of the verbal test ($\bar{X}_{.1.} = 13.55$) significantly different from the overall mean of the math

---

[35]In practice, hand-computation of multi-factor ANOVA designs is rare (and not recommended); the computations in Table 18.6 are given so that the procedure can be observed at close range.

[36]Although the assumption of homogeneity of variance among the twelve cells is not required because of ANOVA's robustness, the assumption is tenable: $F_{max} = 43.6/18.5 = 2.36 < 10.7 = {}_{.95}F_{max_{9,6}}$, and $p > .05$.

test ($\bar{X}_{\bullet 2 \bullet}$ = 12.45). Thirdly, the difference in the means for the two sexes averaged across the two other factors is not significant ($\bar{X}_{\bullet\bullet 1}$ = 13.10 versus $\bar{X}_{\bullet\bullet 2}$ = 12.90). The *AT* and *AS* two-factor interactions were not statistically significant.

Recall that the absence of a two-factor interaction supports the generalizability of the pattern among the means of factor 1 across the levels of factor 2 (Section 18.3). Consequently, the absence of an *AT* interaction indicates that the overall pattern among the means (in this case, small, nonsignificant differences) on factor *A* (anxiety conditions) was evident for both test content (verbal and math). Likewise, the absence of a significant *AS* interaction shows that the overall pattern of means for the two sexes (factor *S*) can be generalized across the three levels of factor *A*.

The only significant effect is the *TS* interaction; the significant *TS* interaction indicates that the difference between the male and female means is not constant across factor *T*, test content. The *TS* interaction is graphed in Figure 18.14 to illuminate the nature of the interaction. The interaction shown in Figure 18.14 reveals a familiar pattern: Superior performance of females on verbal tests and better performance by males on math tests. "Wings" extend one $s_{\bar{X}}$ above and below each mean (except where overlap would result in confusion); note the performance difference in females was greater than that for males.

## 18.24 THE INTERPRETATION OF THREE-FACTOR INTERACTIONS

The three-factor (*ATS*) interaction was not significant. The null hypothesis of the three-factor interaction is tenable. The most direct way to interpret a three-factor interaction is to view it as the generalizability of a two-factor configuration across the levels of the third factor, for example, is the *TS* interaction influenced by the anxiety condition—does the pattern depicted in Figure 18.14 vary depending on the level of factor *A*? The absence of a significant *ATS* interaction indicates that the *TS* configuration in Figure 18.14 is not signifi-

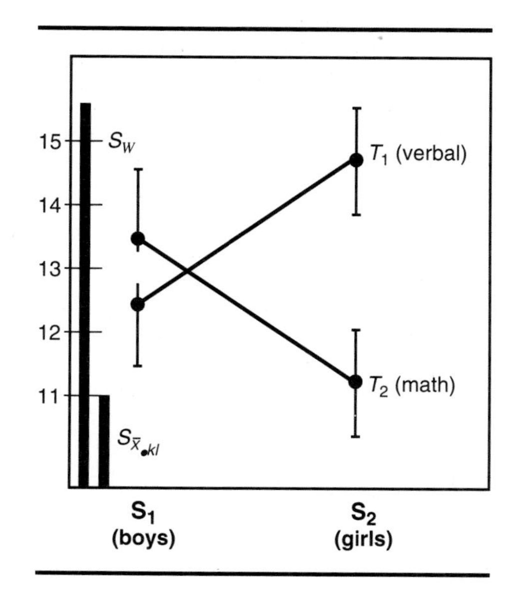

**FIGURE 18.14**

A graph of the sex by type-of-test interaction.

cantly affected by the anxiety treatment—the *TS* interaction does not have to be qualified regarding which level of factor *A* is involved.

In reference to Figure 18.12, suppose a third factor, grade level, were added to the school type by SES design. If the configuration shown in Figure 18.12 was not consistent across grade levels, there would be a three-way (school type-by-SES-by-grade level) interaction. That is, the pattern of the two-way interaction between school type and SES for one grade level would differ from that of one or more other grade levels.

## 18.25 CONFIDENCE INTERVALS IN THREE-FACTOR ANOVA

If we bear in mind that the $n$ and the degrees of freedom associated with the standard error of a mean, $s_{\overline{X}}$, and the critical $t$-value (Equations 11.8 to 11.9) pertain to the *number of observations* on which the *particular mean* in question is based, the application of confidence intervals to cell means or other subgroup means is direct. The value of $s_{\overline{X}}$ needed to set *CI*'s about the factor level means for any factor in Table 18.6 is:

$$s_{\overline{X}} = \sqrt{\frac{MS_e}{"n"}}$$

where "$n$" = $nKL$ for factor $A$ means, $nJL$ for factor $B$ means, and $nJK$ for factor $C$ means. Since in Table 18.6, $J = 3$ and $K = L = 2$, the number of observations on which each of the means for factor $A$ is based is $10(2)(2) = 40$; thus:

$$s_{\overline{X}} = \sqrt{\frac{27.29}{40}} = .826$$

To set confidence intervals about the level means for factors $T$ and $S$, each of these means is based on $10(3)(2) = 60$ observations, and:

$$s_{\overline{X}} = \sqrt{\frac{27.29}{60}} = .674$$

Note that the *CI*'s about the three means for factor $A$ will be $.826/.674 = 1.23$ times as wide as those for factors $S$ and $T$ because each $A_j$ mean is based on only forty scores, whereas each $S_k$ mean and each $T_l$ mean is based on sixty observations.

The *CI*'s about cell means will be much larger than about level means because each cell mean is based on only $n = 10$ observations:

$$s_{\overline{X}} = \sqrt{\frac{27.29}{10}} = 1.65$$

## 18.26 HOW FACTORIAL DESIGNS INCREASE POWER

Even if one is not interested in a particular factor or its interaction with other factors, the inclusion of the factor in the design is often advisable because it can increase the power for identifying the effects of principal interest. For example, if a one-factor ANOVA were performed on the factor $A$ for the data in Table 18.4 the ANOVA table in Table 18.7 would be the result.

**TABLE 18.7** ANOVA Table for the Data in Table 18.4 if analyzed as a One-Factor ANOVA for Factor *A* (School Type).

| *Source* | *SS* | *ν* | *MS* | *F* | *p* |
|---|---|---|---|---|---|
| School type (*T*) | 363.282 | 1 | 363.282 | 4.66 | .032 |
| Within[37] | 14,813.291 | 190 | 77.96 | | |

Notice from Table 18.7 that the mean square for factor *A*, 363.282, is not influenced by whether a second factor, *B*, was included in the design. This is always the case with balanced designs. In one-factor ANOVA, all variance not associated with the main effect becomes within (error) variance (see Equation 15.10), with no effect on the mean square for the main effect.

Notice the *F*-ratio for the *A* effect in the one-factor ANOVA dropped from 4.954 (in Table 18.4) to 4.66 (in Table 18.7) because the within (error) variance was slightly larger and the *F*-ratio slightly lower in the one-factor ANOVA than in the two-factor ANOVA (the associated *p*-value increased from .028 and .032). Whenever a second factor is related to the dependent variable or interacts with the first factor, the $MS_W$ for the two-factor ANOVA will be less than for a one-factor ANOVA, and the *F*-ratio for the first factor will be larger in the two-factor design than in a one-factor design. If SES had been more highly related to the dependent variable (or its interaction with factor *A* stronger) the differences in the associated *F*-ratios and corresponding *p*-values would have been greater than those illustrated.[38] For example, consider the ANOVA table in Problems and Exercises 8 of this chapter. The *F*-ratio of 6.50 would have been only 4.82 if a one-factor (treatment) design had been employed. However, if the null hypotheses for the second factor and the interaction are true, the value of $MS_W$ (and associated *F*'s and *p*'s) will change little. For example, if a one-factor ANOVA is performed on the factor *A* in Table 18.4, the values of $MS_W$ in the two-factor and one-factor ANOVA's differ trivially.

## 18.27 FACTORIAL ANOVA WITH UNBALANCED DESIGNS

When cell frequencies are unequal in *factorial designs*, complications arise in the analysis of such data. If the procedures in Table 18.4 were followed with unequal *n*'s, the sums of squares calculated directly (i.e., none of the *SS*'s was obtained by subtraction) would not add up to the $SS_{total}$; the *SS*'s associated with the various effects are no longer independent (orthogonal, Section 17.16). This nonorthogonality leads to *F*-tests for confounded effects unless certain adjustments are made. The complications are relatively minor if the differences in the cell *n*'s are small. If the cell sizes are proportional, the problems can also be minor (Winer, Brown, & Michels, 1991, Section 520). The situation becomes problematic, however, when two factors are substantially correlated (for example, race and SES), and the

[37]With the SES factor ignored, the *SS* for *S*, $T \times S$, and within are aggregated into the augmented within sum of squares: 1,130.880 + 43.961 + 13,638.45 = 14,813.29; and the augmented degrees of freedom within = 2 + 2 + 186 = 190.

[38]A rare exception could occur if the second factor greatly reduced the degrees of freedom for $MS_e$, $\nu_e$. For example, if $J = 2$ and $K = 5$, and $nJK = 20$, the critical *F* for a two-factor design with $\alpha = .05$ is ${}_{.95}F_{1,10} = 4.96$, and for a one-factor ANOVA is ${}_{.95}F_{1,18} = 4.41$. This increase in critical value for *F* could offset the larger observed *F*-ratio.

cell frequencies are disproportional. (The situation is identical to evaluating independent variables in multiple regression when they are correlated.)

What, then, is the analysis-of-choice in such situations? The most common alternative is to utilize multiple regression techniques[39] with "dummy variables." The investigator must be careful, however, to insure that the question addressed statistically is, indeed, the same question that the research wishes to answer. There are several different models relating to various orders for estimating the unknown parameters. In such situations, one may wish to consult a statistician. As a general rule, the authors favor the most conservative alternative in which the effect being tested is required to add *unique* information with respect to all other parameters in the model.

## 18.28 CHAPTER SUMMARY

ANOVA is a very useful statistical model; the effects of the two or more independent variables (factors) can be assessed separately and simultaneously. In this chapter, two- and three-factor ANOVA have been considered—the simplest examples of a factorial design.

In addition to testing main effects, ANOVA can identify interactions between factors. If there are particular combinations of two factors that result in performance above or below what would be expected by considering the two factors separately, the factors are said to interact. The absence of interaction indicates that the pattern of results on factor $A$ is constant across all levels of factor $B$; the results for factor $A$ are consistent across all of the categories of factor $B$.

Significant interactions should be graphed to clarify the nature of the relationships. Three-factor interaction assesses the generalizability of two-factor configurations across all of the levels of the third factor.

In addition to detecting interaction and assessing generalizability, factorial designs usually are more powerful than one-factor ANOVA designs. The gain in power results when either (1) the second factor is related to the dependent variable or (2) there is an interaction between the factors.

In ANOVA with two or more factors it is assumed that the observations within each cell are independent and are a random sample from a population of observations that is normally distributed. It is further assumed that the cell variances in the population are equal. ANOVA is quite robust to non-normality and, if the design is balanced, to violations of the homogeneity of variance assumption.

The procedures for two-factor ANOVA extend to ANOVA designs having three or more factors. In a balanced ANOVA, the mean squares for all main effects and interactions are orthogonal; hence, each effect is assessing unique, non-redundant information. Any combination of significant effects is possible. In an unbalanced ANOVA, the effects are not orthogonal and the analyses and interpretations are much more complex.

## 18.29 CASE STUDY AND COMPUTER ACTIVITY

Using the EXERCISE data set, run a two-factor (SMOKE by SEX) ANOVA. Compare the $p$-values with the $p$-values from the three planned orthogonal contrast in Section 17.26.[40]

[39] This is the default option in SPSS ANOVA and MANOVA procedures.

[40] They should be identical.

(The interaction test is equivalent to the third contrast.) Compare the $p$-value for testing the SMOKE and SEX main effects with those from the $t$-test in Section 12.20. Why do the $p$'s for the same $H_0$'s differ?[41]

## MASTERY TEST

*For questions 1 to 10, suppose a study was made of attendance of elementary, junior high, and senior high school students for three ethnic groups (I, II, and III).*

1. If a two-factor ANOVA were used, what are the two independent variables?
2. What is the dependent variable?
3. How many levels (categories) are there of each factor?
4. The design can be described as a ____ design.

   (a) $2 \times 2$  (d) $3 \times 2$
   (b) $2 \times 3$  (e) $3 \times 4$
   (c) $3 \times 3$

5. Portions of the ANOVA table from the analysis are given. Complete the table.

| *Source of Variation* | *SS* | $\nu$ | *MS* | *F* |
|---|---|---|---|---|
| School level ($S$) | 900 | | | |
| Ethnicity ($E$) | | 2 | 250 | |
| $S \times E$ | 1,200 | | | |
| Within | 44,500 | 891 | | |

6. What are the critical $F$-values for the two main effects and for the interaction with $\alpha = .05$, $\alpha = .01$, and $\alpha = .001$?
7. Can the null hypotheses for the two main effects be rejected? At what level of significance?
8. Does the $F$-test for the $S \times E$ interaction indicate that the attendance trend did not follow the same pattern for the three ethnic groups, that is, is the $S \times E$ interaction statistically significant? Can the null hypothesis be rejected at $\alpha = .001$?
9. Which of the following figures (a), (b), or (c), is *consistent* with all the information in the ANOVA table in question 5?

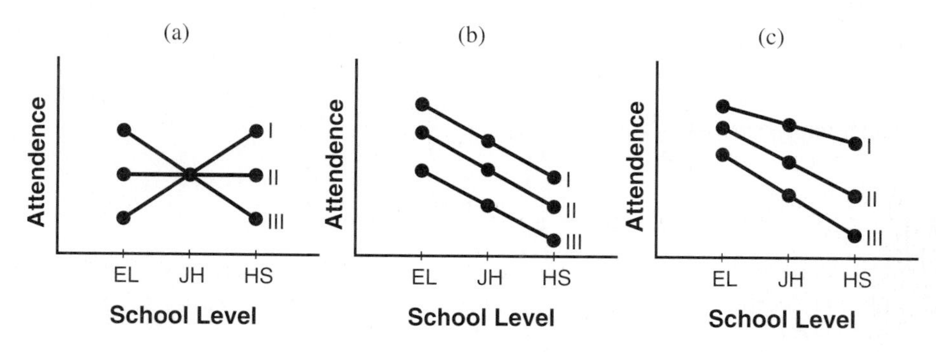


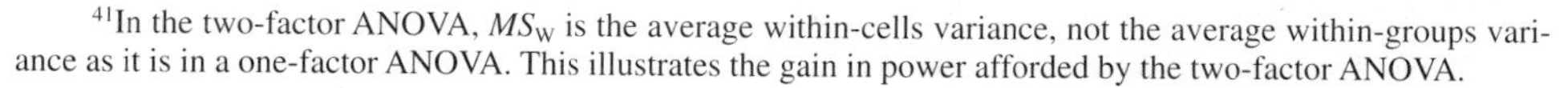
[41]In the two-factor ANOVA, $MS_W$ is the average within-cells variance, not the average within-groups variance as it is in a one-factor ANOVA. This illustrates the gain in power afforded by the two-factor ANOVA.

**10.** If a one-factor ANOVA had been performed comparing the three school levels, are the following true or false?

(a) The $F$-ratio for school level would have been less.
(b) The interaction of school level and ethnicity would not be tested.

**11.** Which of the following are advantages of a two-factor ANOVA over a one-factor ANOVA?

(a) The denominator of the $F$-test is increased.
(b) The generalizability of the results is enhanced.
(c) Interaction between factors can be identified.
(d) Power is often increased.

**12.** Given a $2 \times 4$, $A \times B$ ANOVA:

$$SS_{\text{total}} = 100$$
$$SS_A + SS_B + SS_{AB} = 50$$
$$SS_A = 25$$
$$SS_B = 10$$

(a) What is the value of $SS_{\text{within}}$?
(b) What is the value of $SS_{A \times B}$?
(c) What are the degrees of freedom for the $A \times B$ interaction?
(d) What is $MS$ for the $A \times B$ interaction?

**13.** Among $n_{\bullet 1}$, $n_{1\bullet}$ and $n_{\bullet\bullet}$, which is the largest?

**14.** Graph the interaction of factor $B$, traditional orthography (TO) versus initial teaching alphabet (ITA), and factor $A$, sex, from the following cell means (expressed in grade-placement units) on a standardized reading test. Does the interaction appear to be significant?

| | | *Orthography* | |
|---|---|---|---|
| | | *$B_1$(TO)* | *$B_2$(ITA)* |
| *Sex* | Boys $A_1$ | $\bar{X}_{11} = 4.6$ | $\bar{X}_{12} = 4.5$ |
| | Girls $A_2$ | $\bar{X}_{21} = 4.9$ | $\bar{X}_{22} = 4.8$ |

**15.** The following figure represents cell, row, and column *population* means (parameters) in a two-factor ANOVA design.

| | | *Factor B* | | | |
|---|---|---|---|---|---|
| | | *$B_1$* | *$B_2$* | *$B_3$* | |
| Factor $A$ | $A_1$ | $\mu_{11} = 16$ | $\mu_{12} = 11$ | $\mu_{13} = 6$ | $\mu_{1\bullet} = 11$ |
| | $A_2$ | $\mu_{21} = 4$ | $\mu_{22} = 9$ | $\mu_{23} = 14$ | $\mu_{2\bullet} = 9$ |
| | | $\mu_{\bullet 1} = 10$ | $\mu_{\bullet 2} = 10$ | $\mu_{\bullet 3} = 10$ | $\mu_{\bullet\bullet} = \mu = 10$ |

(a) Is $H_{0_1}$: $\Sigma\alpha_j^2 = 0$?
(b) Is $H_{0_2}$: $\Sigma\beta_k^2 = 0$?
(c) Is $H_{0_3}$: $\Sigma_k\Sigma_j(\alpha\beta_{jk})^2 = 0$?

**16.** Which hypotheses in question 15 pertain to main effects and which to interaction?

**17.** In question 9, figure (a), is the null hypothesis tenable for: (a) the school effect level? (b) the ethnicity effect? (c) the interaction?

**18.** For the data in question 14, assuming a balanced design, give the numerical values for

(a) $\hat{\alpha}_1$, $\hat{\alpha}_2$, $\hat{\beta}_1$, $\hat{\beta}_2$, $\bar{X}_{\bullet\bullet}$

(b) Estimate $\widehat{\alpha\beta}_{11}$, $\widehat{\alpha\beta}_{jk} = \bar{X}_{jk} - (\bar{X}_{\bullet} + \hat{\alpha}_j + \hat{\beta}_k)$

**19.** Assuming the ANOVA table in question 5 is from a balanced (equal $n$) design,

(a) what is the value of $s_{\bar{X}_{j\bullet}} = \sqrt{MS_e / n_{j\bullet}}$ ?

(b) if $\bar{X}_{2\bullet} = 10$, give the .95 $CI$ for $\mu_{2\bullet}$.

**20.** How does the $F$-ratio for the school-level effect in question 5 compare with what it would have been in a one-factor ANOVA?

**21.** In question 5 $(s_{11}^2 + s_{12}^2 + \ldots + s_{33}^2)/9 = ?$

**22.** In a two-factor ANOVA, the $JK$ within-cell variance estimates (the $s_{ij}^2$'s are assumed to be from the same population, that is, $H_0$: $\sigma_{11}^2 = \sigma_{12}^2 = \ldots = \sigma_{JK}^2$. Generalizing from Chapter 15, when can this assumption be ignored? Which tests (presented in this text) could be used to test this assumption?

**23.** In question 15, if $\sigma_\varepsilon^2 = 60$ and $n = 10$,

(a) what is the expected value of $MS_A$: $E(MS_A) = \sigma_\varepsilon^2 + nK\Sigma\alpha_j^2/(J-1)$?

(b) what is the value of $E(MS_B)$?

(c) what is the value of $E(MS_W)$?

**24.** In question 14, if $n = 50$ and $MS_W = 2.0$, what is the .90 $CI$ for $\mu_{22}$?

## PROBLEMS AND EXERCISES

**1.** Using a two-factor ANOVA, analyze the following scores on a fifty-item vocabulary test administered to twenty-four students of high and average intelligence after one year of studying a foreign language under one of three methods with $\alpha = .01$ (see Table 18.4 for computational steps).

| | | *Method* | | |
|---|---|---|---|---|
| | | *Aural-Oral Method (A)* $B_1$ | *Translation Method (T)* $B_2$ | *Combined Method (C)* $B_3$ |
| High (IQ ≥ 115) | $A_1$ | 37<br>30<br>26<br>31 | 27<br>24<br>22<br>19 | 20<br>31<br>24<br>21 |
| Average (IQ ≤ 114) | $A_2$ | 32<br>19<br>37<br>28 | 20<br>23<br>14<br>15 | 17<br>18<br>23<br>18 |

**2.** Perform the Tukey HSD multiple comparisons for the method effect of problem 1.

(a) $s_{\bar{X}_{\bullet k}} = \sqrt{MS_W / n_{\bullet k}} = ?$

(b) For $\alpha = .05$, what is $\text{HSD}_{.05} = {}_{1-\alpha}q_{v_e,J}(s_{\bar{X}})$?

(c) Which null hypotheses for difference in means can be rejected?

3. A researcher is studying the effects on learning of inserting questions into instructional materials. There is some doubt whether these questions would be more effective preceding or following the passage about which the question is posed. In addition, the researcher wonders if the effect of the position of the questions is the same for factual questions and for questions that require the learner to compose a thoughtful and original response. A group of twenty-four students is split at random into four groups of six students each. One group is assigned to each of the four combinations of factor $B$, "position of question (before versus after the passage)," and factor $A$, "type of question (factual versus thought-provoking)." After ten hours of studying under these conditions, the twenty-four students are given a fifty-item test on the content of the instructional materials. The following test scores are obtained. (Round means to two decimal places.)

| | | *Position of Question* | | | |
|---|---|---|---|---|---|
| | | *Before* $B_1$ | | *After* $B_2$ | |
| *Nature of Question* | Fact $A_1$ | 19 | 23 | 31 | 28 |
| | | 29 | 26 | 26 | 27 |
| | | 30 | 17 | 35 | 32 |
| | Thought $A_2$ | 27 | 21 | 36 | 29 |
| | | 20 | 26 | 39 | 31 |
| | | 15 | 24 | 41 | 35 |

(a) Perform a two-factor ANOVA on the data. Test the null hypotheses for both main effects and the interaction effect with $\alpha = .10$.

(b) Graph the interaction using the procedure illustrated in Figure 18.14; place the nature-of-the-question factor on the abscissa.

4. A study by Carrier and Titus (1981) investigated the effects of pretraining in notetaking on learning from lectures. A second factor was the mode of test expected: One-third of the students were told they would be given a multiple-choice test, another third, an essay test; the final third were told only that they would be tested. A thirty-five-item objective test and an essay test were given following the lecture. Means and standard deviations for the 2 × 3 ANOVA design are given for the objective test.

(a) Perform the ANOVA assuming $n = 16$ students were randomly assigned to each cell, with $\alpha = .10$ for both main effects and the interaction.

(b) Graph the interaction to facilitate its interpretation.

(c) Use the Hartley $F_{max}$ test to test whether the heterogeneity of scores is affected by the treatment combinations ($\alpha = .05$).

| | | *Mode-of-Test Expected* | | |
|---|---|---|---|---|
| | | *MS* | *Essay* | *Unspecified* |
| *Treatment* | Pretrained ($E$) | $\bar{X}_{11} = 28.1$<br>$s_{11} = 3.5$ | $\bar{X}_{12} = 23.6$<br>$s_{12} = 6.6$ | $\bar{X}_{13} = 25.3$<br>$s_{13} = 4.8$ |
| | Not Pretrained ($C$) | $\bar{X}_{21} = 25.1$<br>$s_{21} = 5.0$ | $\bar{X}_{22} = 26.6$<br>$s_{22} = 5.5$ | $\bar{X}_{23} = 26.7$<br>$s_{23} = 4.9$ |

5. For each of the following arrangements of data, graph the interaction of factor B, sex, with factor

A, treatments. Place factor B on the abscissa so that each treatment level yields one line in the graph. In each case indicate whether or not the two factors appear to interact.

(a)

| | | *Male* | *Female* |
|---|---|---|---|
| Treatments | 1 | $\overline{X}_{11} = 18.65$ | $\overline{X}_{12} = 21.68$ |
| | 2 | $\overline{X}_{21} = 25.20$ | $\overline{X}_{22} = 14.17$ |
| | 3 | $\overline{X}_{31} = 16.44$ | $\overline{X}_{32} = 17.89$ |

(b)

| | | *Male* | *Female* |
|---|---|---|---|
| Treatments | 1 | $\overline{X}_{11} = 19.63$ | $\overline{X}_{12} = 14.81$ |
| | 2 | $\overline{X}_{21} = 10.21$ | $\overline{X}_{22} = 13.55$ |

(c)

| | | *Male* | *Female* |
|---|---|---|---|
| Treatments | 1 | $\overline{X}_{11} = 9.43$ | $\overline{X}_{12} = 13.95$ |
| | 2 | $\overline{X}_{21} = 11.06$ | $\overline{X}_{22} = 15.58$ |

**6.** In one study, a group of 240 sixth-grade pupils were randomly assigned to one of two levels of reading difficulty: "grade six reading difficulty" or "grade three reading difficulty." The pupils read a chapter in a science text at either the third-grade or sixth-grade reading difficulty level. A 129-item multiple-choice test was administered at the end of the experiment to assess comprehension. Within both levels of reading difficulty, pupils were classified as either high, average, or low scorers on the reading section of the Stanford Achievement Test. The following data were obtained for the two levels of reading difficulty and three levels of reading achievement:

| | | *Reading Difficulty* | |
|---|---|---|---|
| | | *Grade 6* | *Grade 3* |
| *Reading Achievement* | High | $n = 40$<br>$\overline{X}_{11} = 89.93$<br>$s_{11} = 12.02$ | $n = 40$<br>$\overline{X}_{12} = 93.89$<br>$s_{12} = 13.02$ |
| | Average | $n = 40$<br>$\overline{X}_{21} = 70.79$<br>$s_{21} = 14.76$ | $n = 40$<br>$\overline{X}_{22} = 72.55$<br>$s_{22} = 15.90$ |
| | Low | $n = 40$<br>$\overline{X}_{31} = 52.09$<br>$s_{31} = 11.30$ | $n = 40$<br>$\overline{X}_{32} = 56.84$<br>$s_{32} = 12.21$ |

(a) Perform a two-factor ANOVA on these data. Test all three null hypotheses at the .05 level of significance (*Hint:* $MS_W$ is the average of the six within-cell *variances*.)

(b) If the scores had been converted to percent-correct scores before the ANOVA, how would the ANOVA results have differed?

**7.** The following figure is based on three years of test results from National Assessments in Science. The results are given for three age levels (9, 13, and 17) and by content area (physical versus biological science). Each mean is based on a large, nationally representative sample. Assume a three-factor ANOVA was used to analyze these data.

(a) Identify the three factors.

(b) What is the dependent variable?

(c) Does the content-area ($C$) main effect appear to be significant?

(d) Does the year ($Y$) main effect (I, II, III) appear to be significant (i.e., is an "achievement decline" evident in the data?)?

(e) Aggregate the results to construct the year-by-content ($YC$) interaction graph. (Place "year" on the $x$-axis.)

(f) Does the $YC$ interaction appear to be significant? Explain. (Recall that the $n$'s are large.)

(g) Does the $YCA$ interaction appear to be significant? Explain.

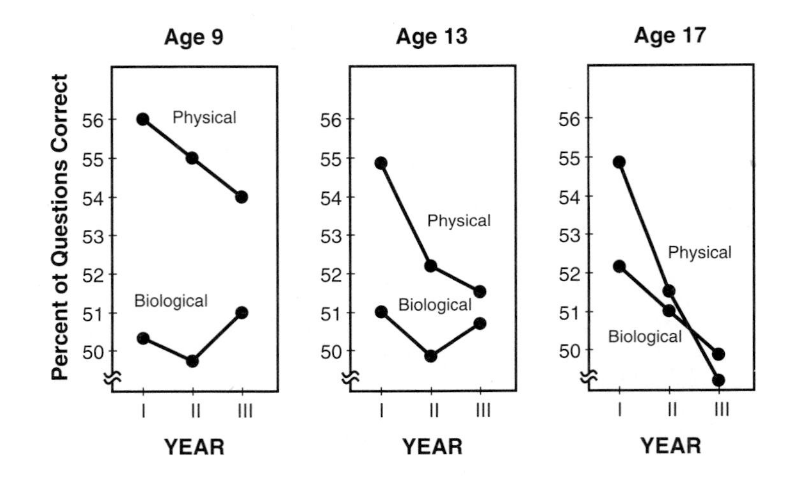


**8.** Given are the results of a three-factor ANOVA with five observations per cell ($n = 5$) (Hopkins & Kretke, 1976).

(a) Give the ANOVA table that would have resulted if the ethnicity factor had been ignored ($n$ = 10).

(b) Give the ANOVA table if both ethnicity and sex had been ignored ($n = 20$).

(c) Was power lost as $n$/cell decreased?

***A Treatments-by-Sex-by-Ethnicity ANOVA of The Sixty Observations from Three Treatment Groups.***

| *Source* | *SS* | $\nu$ | *MS* | *F* |
|---|---|---|---|---|
| Treatment ($T$) | 520.00 | 2 | 260.00 | 6.50 |
| Sex ($S$) | 60.00 | 1 | 60.00 | 1.50 |
| Ethnicity ($E$) | 240.00 | 1 | 240.00 | 6.00 |
| $T \times S$ | 120.00 | 2 | 60.00 | 1.50 |
| $T \times E$ | 280.00 | 2 | 140.00 | 3.50 |
| $S \times E$ | 93.75 | 1 | 93.75 | 2.34 |
| $T \times S \times E$ | 360.00 | 2 | 180.00 | 4.50 |
| Within | 1920.00 | 48 | 40.00 | |

**9.** Suppose prior to performing the study reported in the previous question that you were to estimate the power for detecting the treatment effect under conditions such that the treatment means, expressed as z-scores in the untreated population, were $\mu_{1\bullet\bullet} = -.5$, $\mu_{2\bullet\bullet} = 0$, and $\mu_{3\bullet\bullet} = .5$, and $\alpha = .05$.

## ANSWERS TO MASTERY TEST

1. school level and ethnicity
2. attendance
3. three levels of ethnicity and three of school type
4. (c)
5.

| *Source* | *SS* | *v* | *MS* | *F* |
|---|---|---|---|---|
| School level (*S*) | 900 | 2 | 450 | 9.0 |
| Ethnicity (*E*) | 500 | 2 | 250 | 5.0 |
| $S \times E$ | 1,200 | 4 | 300 | 6.0 |
| Within | 44,550 | 891 | 50 | |

6. ${}_{.95}F_{2,891} \approx 3.00$; ${}_{.95}F_{4,891} \approx 2.38$
   ${}_{.99}F_{2,891} \approx 4.62$; ${}_{.99}F_{4,891} \approx 3.34$
   ${}_{.999}F_{2,891} \approx 6.95$; ${}_{.999}F_{4,891} \approx 4.65$
7. Yes, $H_{0_1}: \mu_E = \mu_J = \mu_S$ can be rejected at $\alpha = .001$; $9.0 > 6.95$; $p < .001$. $H_{0_2}: \mu_I = \mu_{II} = \mu_{III}$ can be rejected at $\alpha = .01$; $5.0 > 4.62$; $p < .01$.
8. Yes, $F = 6.0 > 4.65 \approx {}_{.999}F_{4,891}$; $p < .001$. Yes, the null hypothesis can be rejected with $\alpha = .001$.
9. Only Figure C is consistent with the ANOVA table. (Figure A has no main effects for factors *A* and *B*; Figure B has no $A \times B$ interaction.)
10. (a) True (the numerator of the *F*-ratio would remain unchanged, but the denominator of the *F*-ratio would have increased):

$$MS_W = \frac{500 + 1,200 + 44,500}{2 + 4 + 900} = 51.45$$

$$F = \frac{450}{51.45} = 8.75$$

    (b) true
11. (b), (c), and (d)
12. (a) $SS_{\text{within}} = SS_{\text{total}} - (SS_A + SS_B + SS_{AB}) = 100 - 50 = 50$
    (b) $SS_{A\times B} = 50 - 25 - 10 = 15$
    (c) $(J-1)(K-1) = (2-1)(4-1) = 3$
    (d) $MS = \frac{SS}{v} = \frac{15}{3} = 5$
13. $n_{\bullet\bullet}$ is the largest; $n_{\bullet\bullet}$ is the total number of all observations, whereas $n_{\bullet 1}$ is the total from column 1 and $n_{1\bullet}$ is the total in row 1.
14. no

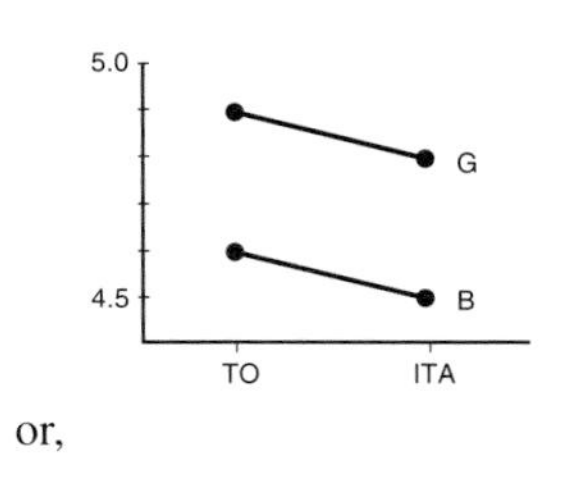


or,

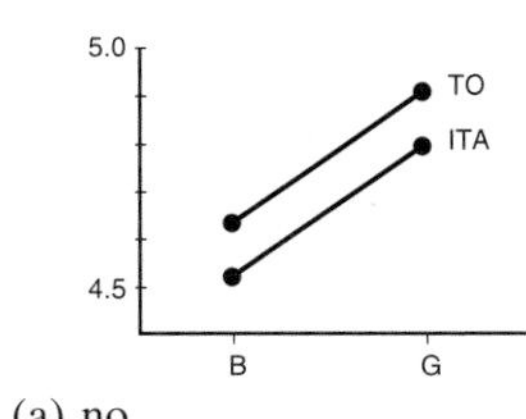


15. (a) no
    (b) yes
    (c) no
16. $H_{0_1}$ and $H_{0_2}$ pertain to main effects; the interaction null hypothesis is represented by $H_{0_3}$.
17. (a) yes (b) yes (c) no
18. (a) $\bar{X}_{1\bullet} = 4.55$, $\bar{X}_{2\bullet} = 4.85$, $\bar{X}_{\bullet\bullet} = 4.70$, $\bar{X}_{\bullet 1} = 4.75$, and $\bar{X}_{\bullet 2} = 4.65$, thus $\hat{\alpha}_1 = \bar{X}_{1\bullet} - \bar{X}_{\bullet\bullet} = -.15$, $\hat{\alpha}_2 = .15$, $\hat{\beta}_1 = .05$, $\hat{\beta}_2 = -.05$
    (b) $\widehat{\alpha\beta}_{11} = 4.60 - 4.70 - (-.15) - .05 = 0$
19. (a) $s_{\bar{X}_{j\bullet}} = \sqrt{50/300} = .41$
    (b) $10 \pm (1.96)(.41) = 10 \pm .80$, or (9.20, 10.80)
20. It is larger.
21. $MS_W = 50$

22. When $n_{jk}$'s are equal; Bartlett, Hartley, or Scheffé tests

23. (a) $E(MS_A) = 60 + 10(3)[(1)^2 + (-1)^2]/(2 - 1) = 120$
 (b) 60
 (c) 60

24. $s_{\bar{X}_{22}} = \sqrt{MS_W / n} = \sqrt{2.0/50} = .20$; $.90CI = 4.80 \pm (1.68)(.20) = 4.80 \pm .34$, or (4.46, 5.14)

## ANSWERS TO PROBLEMS AND EXERCISES

1.

*Method*

| | | $B_1$ | $B_2$ | $B_3$ | *A Means* | |
|---|---|---|---|---|---|---|
| | $A_1$ | $\bar{X}_{11} = 31.0$<br>$s_{11}^2 = 20.67$ | $\bar{X}_{12} = 23.0$<br>$s_{12}^2 = 11.33$ | $\bar{X}_{13} = 24.0$<br>$s_{13}^2 = 24.67$ | $\bar{X}_{1\bullet} = 26.0$<br>$\hat{\alpha}_1 = 2$ | |
| *IQ* | $A_2$ | $\bar{X}_{21} = 29.0$<br>$s_{21}^2 = 58.00$ | $\bar{X}_{22} = 18.0$<br>$s_{22}^2 = 18.00$ | $\bar{X}_{23} = 19.0$<br>$s_{23}^2 = 7.33$ | $\bar{X}_{2\bullet} = 22.0$<br>$\hat{\alpha}_2 = -2$ | $(n_{j\bullet} = 12)$ |
| *B Means* | | $\bar{X}_{\bullet 1} = 30.0$<br>$\hat{\beta}_1 = 6$ | $\bar{X}_{\bullet 2} = 20.5$<br>$\hat{\beta}_2 = -3.5$ | $\bar{X}_{\bullet 3} = 21.5$<br>$\hat{\beta}_3 = -2.5$ | $\bar{X}_{\bullet\bullet} = 24.0$<br>$(n_{\bullet\bullet} = 24)$ | |

$(n_{\bullet k} = 8)$

$$SS_A = nK \sum_j \hat{\alpha}_j^2 = 12[(2)^2 + (-2)^2] = 96;\ MS_A = 96$$

$$SS_B = nJ \sum_k \hat{\beta}_k^2 = 8[(6)^2 + (-3.5)^2 + (-2.5)^2] = 436;\ MS_B = 218$$

$$SS_{AB} = n \sum_k \sum_j \widehat{\alpha\beta}_{jk}^2 = 4\left[(-1)^2 + (.5)^2 + (.5)^2 + (1)^2 + (-.5)^2 + (-.5)^2\right]$$

$$SS_{AB} = 12;\ MS_{AB} = \frac{12}{2} = 6$$

$$MS_W = \frac{\sum_k \sum_j s_{jk}^2}{JK} = \frac{20.67 + \ldots + 7.33}{6} = 23.3$$

| *Source* | *v* | *MS* | *F* |
|---|---|---|---|
| *A* | 1 | 96 | 4.12[a] |
| *B* | 2 | 218 | 9.36[b] |
| $A \times B$ | 2 | 6 | .26 |
| Within | 18 | 23.3 | |

[a] $p < .10$; ${}_{.90}F_{1,18} = 3.01$, ${}_{.95}F_{1,18} = 4.41$, ${}_{.99}F_{2,18} = 6.01$, ${}_{.999}F_{2,18} = 10.4$

[b] $p < .01$

2. (a) $s_{\bar{X}_{\bullet k}} = \sqrt{23.3/8} = 1.71$
 (b) ${}_{.95}q_{18,3} = 3.61$, $HSD_{.05} = (3.61)(1.71) = 6.17$
 (c) $\bar{X}_A - \bar{X}_T = 30.0 - 20.5 = 9.5$; reject $H_{0_1}$
 $\bar{X}_A - \bar{X}_C = 30.0 - 21.5 = 8.5$; reject $H_{0_2}$
 $\bar{X}_C - \bar{X}_T = 21.5 - 20.5 = 1.0$; $H_{0_3}$ is tenable.

**3.** (a)

| | $B_1$ | $B_2$ | $A$ *Means* |
|---|---|---|---|
| $A_1$ | $\bar{X}_{11} = 24.00$<br>$s_{11}^2 = 28.00$ | $\bar{X}_{12} = 29.83$<br>$s_{12}^2 = 11.77$ | $\bar{X}_{1\bullet} = 26.92$<br>$\hat{\alpha}_1 = -.87$ |
| $A_2$ | $\bar{X}_{21} = 22.17$<br>$s_{21}^2 = 19.77$ | $\bar{X}_{22} = 35.17$<br>$s_{22}^2 = 20.97$ | $\bar{X}_{2\bullet} = 28.67$<br>$\hat{\alpha}_2 = .87$ |
| $B$ *Means* | $\bar{X}_{\bullet 1} = 23.08$<br>$\hat{\beta}_1 = -4.71$ | $\bar{X}_{\bullet 2} = 32.50$<br>$\hat{\beta}_2 = 4.71$ | $\bar{X}_{\bullet\bullet} = 27.79$<br>$(n_{\bullet\bullet} = 24)$ |

$(n_{\bullet k} = 12)$

1. $SS_A = 12[(-.87)^2 + (.87)^2] = 18.17$; $MS_A = 18.17$
2. $SS_B = 12[(-4.71)^2 + (4.71)^2] = 532.42$; $MS_B = 532.42$
3. $SS_{AB} = n\sum_k \sum_j \widehat{\alpha\beta}_{jk}^2 = 6\left[(1.79)^2 + (-1.8)^2 + (-1.78)^2 + (1.8)^2\right] = 77.11$; $MS_{AB} = 77.11$
4. $MS_W = (28.00 + 19.77 + 11.77 + 20.97)/4 = 20.13$

| *Source* | $\nu$ | *MS* | *F* |
|---|---|---|---|
| *A* (Question) | 1 | 18.17 | .90 |
| *B* (Position) | 1 | 532.42 | 26.45[a] |
| $A \times B$ | 1 | 77.11 | 3.83[b] |
| Within | 20 | 20.13 | |

[a] $p < .001$

[b] $p < .10$

(b) $s_{\bar{X}} = \sqrt{20.13/6} = 1.83$

$s_w = \sqrt{20.13} = 4.49$

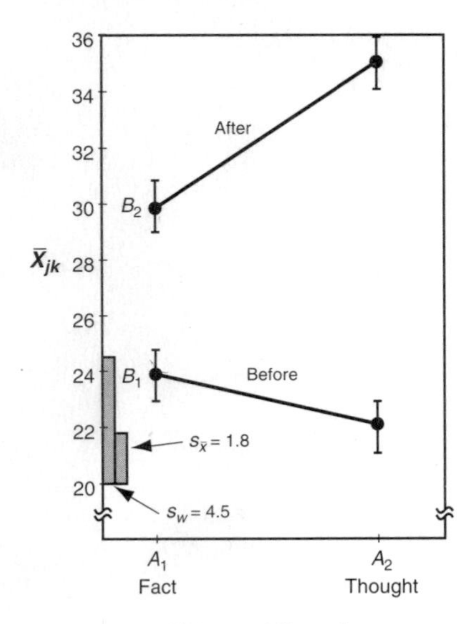


**4.** (a)

| *Source* | $\nu$ | *MS* | *F* |
|---|---|---|---|
| Treatment (*T*) | 1 | 5.08 | .19 |
| Mode (*M*) | 2 | 18.24 | .69 |
| $T \times M$ | 2 | 77.30 | 2.93[a] |
| Within | 90 | 26.35 | |

[a] $p < .10$

(c) $F_{max} = (6.6)^2/(3.5)^2 = 3.56$ not significant at the .05 level.

**5.** Case *a*, yes; case *b*, yes; case *c* no.

**6.** (a) ANOVA table:

| *Source* | $\nu$ | *MS* | *F* |
|---|---|---|---|
| Reading achievement (*A*) | 2 | 28,103.97 | 158.86[a] |
| Reading difficulty (*D*) | 1 | 730.81 | 4.13[b] |
| $A \times D$ | 2 | 48.02 | 0.27 |
| Within | 234 | 176.91 | |

[a] $p < .001$

[b] $p < .05$

(b) Since $X\% = (X/129) = .775X$, $s_{\%}^2 = (.775)^2 s^2 = .60s^2$ (Section 5.11); hence, all *MS*-values would be .60 of their value in the preceding ANOVA table. The *F*-ratios would be unchanged, as with any linear transformation of *X*.

**7.** (a) year (*Y*), age (*A*), and content-area (*C*)
(b) percent-correct score on the science test
(c) yes, ($\bar{X}_{\text{phys.}} > \bar{X}_{\text{biol.}}$)
(d) yes, ($\bar{X}_{\text{I}} > \bar{X}_{\text{II}} > \bar{X}_{\text{III}}$)
(e)

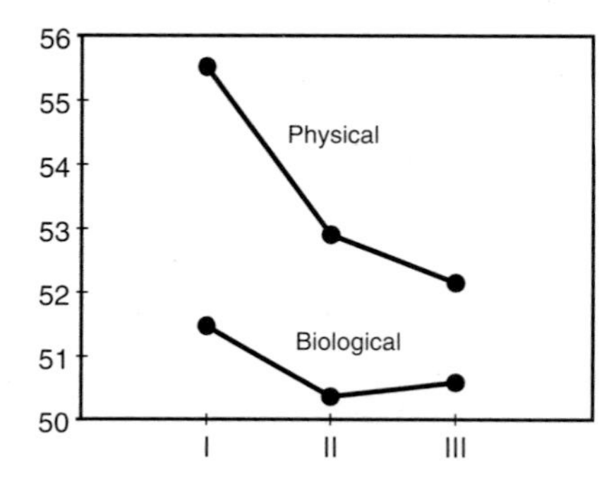


(f) Yes; the *difference* between the content-area means decreased progressively between I and III.
(g) Yes; at age seventeen performance has steadily decreased in both physical and biological science, whereas at ages nine and thirteen the III biological science scores "rebounded" to the I levels. Thus, an achievement decline in physical science is evidenced at all three age levels, but in biological science only at age seventeen.

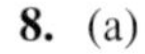

**8.** (a)

| *Source* | *SS* | *v* | *MS* | *F* |
|---|---|---|---|---|
| Treatments (*T*) | 520.00 | 2 | 260.00 | 4.85 |
| Sex (*S*) | 60.00 | 1 | 60.00 | 1.12 |
| $T \times S$ | 120.00 | 2 | 60.00 | 1.12 |
| Within | 2893.75 | 54 | 53.59 | |

(b)

| *Source* | *SS* | *v* | *MS* | *F* |
|---|---|---|---|---|
| Treatments (*T*) | 520.00 | 2 | 260.000 | 4.82 |
| Within | 3073.75 | 57 | 53.925 | |

(c) No, on the contrary—$MS_W$ is much less in three-factor ANOVA where $n = 5$.

**9.** $\phi = \sqrt{\frac{20[(-.5)^2 + 0 + (.5)^2]}{(3)1}} = 1.83,$

and from Table G, power $\approx .80$.

# MULTI-FACTOR ANOVA DESIGNS: Random, Mixed, and Fixed Effects

## 19.1 INTRODUCTION

This chapter has two major purposes: (1) to present the rationale for the random-effects ANOVA model, and (2) to introduce the mixed-effects (or mixed) ANOVA model (a combination of the fixed and random ANOVA models). In addition, advanced ANOVA applications that include nested factors will be considered.[1]

## 19.2 THE RANDOM-EFFECTS ANOVA MODEL

The random-effects analysis of variance model differs in certain respects from the fixed-effects ANOVA model of Chapters 15 and 18. Fortunately, there are many similarities between the techniques seen in Chapters 15 and 18 and those to be presented here which will substantially facilitate learning the material in this chapter. The model that will now be developed is called the *random* or *random-effects* analysis of variance model (in contrast to the fixed-effects ANOVA model in Chapters 15 and 18). It is easier to grasp the meaning of random effects when they can be contrasted with fixed effects. In the fixed ANOVA model, the primary interest was in making statistical inferences about the set of main effects $\alpha_1, \ldots, \alpha_J$. The inference to be made was from a set of a sample of $n$ observations from each of the $J$ populations. In theory, for each of an infinite number of replications of the experiment, there were $n$ persons within each of $J$ levels. The interest was solely in the $J$ means in the population—or equivalently, the $J$ main effects. Only replications of the experiment in which the same $J$ levels (groups or treatments) appeared were considered. In a sense, then, the $J$ levels in the population were "fixed" or explicitly denoted. By contrast, with a random factor, the sample of $J$ levels in each replication of the experiment is viewed as varying

[1]The concepts of this chapter are challenging. Most persons will need to read and study the material carefully before mastery is sufficient for application.

Fixed-effects model ($J = 3$)
$X_{ij} = \mu + \alpha_j + \varepsilon_{ij}$
Main effects: $\alpha_1, \alpha_2, \alpha_3$.

| *Replication of experiment* | *Main effects present in replication* |
|---|---|
| 1 | $\alpha_1, \alpha_2, \alpha_3$ |
| 2 | $\alpha_1, \alpha_2, \alpha_3$ |
| 3 | $\alpha_1, \alpha_2, \alpha_3$ |

Random-effects model ($J = 3$)
$X_{ij} = \mu + a_j + \varepsilon_{ij}$
Main effects: $a_1, a_2, a_\infty$

| *Replication of experiment* | *Main effects present in replication* |
|---|---|
| 1 | $a_5, a_{31}, a_8$ |
| 2 | $a_{16}, a_3, a_9$ |
| 3 | $a_{21}, a_{11}, a_{50}$ |

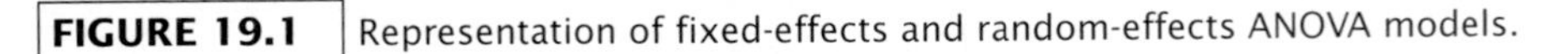

**FIGURE 19.1** Representation of fixed-effects and random-effects ANOVA models.

randomly across replications; for example, levels A, B, and C will be randomly selected (sampled) when I do the study, whereas when you replicate the study, you might have levels D, E, and F.

This procedure is applicable when one is interested in the amount of variance in the means of a large collection of levels, only a few of which could be employed in one experiment. For a given experiment, a sample of $J$ levels could be randomly selected from a population of levels and then samples of size $n$ observations could be randomly selected from each level. If the experiment were run again, the levels would not be "fixed"—the same $J$ levels would not be represented again; rather, a different random sample of $J$ levels would be used.

As there were effects of the form $\alpha_j = \mu_j - \mu$ in the fixed-effects model, so are there effects of the form $a_j = \mu_j - \mu$ for this new model.[2] The complete set of $J$ $\alpha_j$'s is present in every replication of the fixed-effects ANOVA; in the random-effects ANOVA, only a random sample of the $a_j$ effects is present in any replication of the study, hence the name random or random-effects ANOVA model. Figure 19.1 illustrates this distinction between the fixed-effects and random-effects models.

A study by Bennet (1972) illustrates the random-effects ANOVA model. He studied the magnitude of the teacher effect on first-grade pupils' reading performance, asking how much of the variance among pupils' end-of-year reading scores is attributable to differences among teachers? The random ANOVA model addresses how much the $\mu_j$'s differ—how variable are the $a_j$'s? The variance of the $\hat{\mu}_j$'s estimates the differences among $\mu_j$'s.

To conceptualize the random-effects model, assume that there is an infinite population of teachers, each having a mean score equal to $\mu_j$. Denote the average of all these $\mu_j$'s by $\mu$. The $i$th student earns a score of $X_{ij}$ with the $j$th teacher. The difference between the $i$th student's score with teacher $j$ and the mean of all students' scores for that teacher is denoted by $\varepsilon_{ij}$. Therefore:

$$X_{ij} = \mu_j + \varepsilon_{ij} \quad \textbf{(19.1)}$$

[2]In contrast to the use of lowercase Greek letters for fixed effects, random effects are commonly denoted by lowercase Roman letters.

where $X_{ij}$ is the reading score for student $i$ in level $j$ of the factor, that is, "teacher $j$," $\mu_j$ is the mean of all students' scores for the $j$th level of the random factor, and $\varepsilon_{ij}$ is the deviation of the $i$th student's score from the mean of all students' scores at the $j$th level of the factor.

The model in Equation 19.1 will be altered in form by deviating the $\mu_j$'s around $\mu$, the mean of all the $\mu_j$'s, as follows:

$$X_{ij} = \mu + (\mu_j - \mu) + \varepsilon_{ij} \quad \textbf{(19.2)}$$

A simplification of the notation in Equation 19.2 puts the random-effects ANOVA model into its customary form:

$$X_{ij} = \mu + a_j + \varepsilon_{ij} \quad \textbf{(19.3)}$$

where $a_j = \mu_j - \mu$, and $\varepsilon_{ij} = X_{ij} - \mu_j$.

Suppose that $\mu$, the mean reading test score of all students in the student population over all teachers in the population of teachers, is 30; and suppose that the population of students would average four points above 30 if they had teacher number 9, that is, $a_9 = 4$. Finally suppose that the fourth student scored eight points below the average of all students having teacher 9, that is, $\varepsilon_{49} = -8$. If the model in Equation 19.3 holds, the test score of the fourth student will be

$$X_{ij} = \mu + \text{a}_j + \varepsilon_{ij}$$
$$X_{49} = \mu + \text{a}_9 + \varepsilon_{49} = 30 + 4 - 8 = 26$$

Initially, the interest was in the variance of the $\mu_j$'s. How has this concern changed now that the $\mu_j$'s have been eliminated from the model? Since $a_j$ is simply $\mu_j$ minus a constant $\mu$, the variance of the $\mu_j$'s is the same as the variance of the $a_j$'s (Section 5.10). Thus, differences in scores due to differential teacher effects will be reflected in the variance of the $a_j$'s, in other words, in $\sigma_a^2$.

## 19.3 ASSUMPTIONS OF THE RANDOM ANOVA MODEL

Before proceeding to estimate $\sigma_a^2$ and making statistical inferential statements about it, it is necessary to make some assumptions about the model in Equation 19.3:

1. The random-effects, $a_j$'s, are independent and normally distributed with a mean of zero and a variance of $\sigma_a^2$, that is, $\text{a} \sim NID(0, \sigma_a^2)$.
2. The error components, $\varepsilon_{ij}$'s, are independent and normally distributed with mean zero and variance $\sigma_\varepsilon^2$, that is, $\varepsilon \sim NID(0, \sigma_\varepsilon^2)$.

These assumptions have several implications for the study of teacher effects. If the random-effects model is an accurate description of the data in the study of teacher effects, then:

1. The means ($\mu_j$'s) of populations of students' scores for all teachers in the population are normally distributed around $\mu$ and have a variance of $\sigma_a^2$. Since $a_j = \mu_j - \mu$, the $a_j$'s

should have a normal distribution around zero with a variance of $\sigma_a^2$. The effect $a_j$ is estimated by: $\hat{a}_j = \overline{X}_j - \overline{X}_{\bullet}$

2. The reading test scores $X_{ij}$ for all students for a given teacher (the $j$th teacher) are normally distributed around a mean of $\mu_j$ with variance $\sigma_\varepsilon^2$. Since $\varepsilon_{ij} = X_{ij} - \mu_j$, $\varepsilon_{ij}$ will be normally distributed around zero with variance $\sigma_\varepsilon^2$. This is assumed to be true for all values of $j$ (i.e., for all teachers)—this is the homogeneity of variance assumption. $\varepsilon_{ij}$ is estimated by $e_{ij} = X_{ij} - \overline{X}_j$.

## 19.4 AN EXAMPLE

Procedures for estimating both $\sigma_a^2$ and $\sigma_\varepsilon^2$ from data are needed. The problem is estimating the variability in reading scores due to teachers, $\sigma_a^2$, and the variance among students having the same teacher, $\sigma_\varepsilon^2$.

Theoretically, data are gathered in a two-tiered sampling plan. First, $J$ levels of the random ANOVA factor are randomly drawn. For example, $J = 5$ teachers are randomly selected from the population of teachers. Just as random sampling of persons from a population permits generalizations to the population of persons, randomly sampling levels of a factor allows generalization to a population of levels of the factor. Second, a random sample of $n$ observations is drawn from the populations in each of the $J$ levels. Theoretically, there is an infinite number of students for each teacher, even though perhaps only twenty or thirty are currently experimentally accessible. In the example, $n = 7$ students are randomly drawn for each of the $J = 5$ teachers.[3]

In the hypothetical study $J = 5$, therefore 5 $a_j$'s and $Jn = 35$ $\varepsilon_{ij}$'s have been sampled. The scores on a reading test are given in Table 19.1.

**TABLE 19.1** Hypothetical Data from a Study of Teacher Effects on Pupils' Reading Test Scores.

| *Teacher (j)* | | | | |
|---|---|---|---|---|
| *1* | *2* | *3* | *4* | *5* |
| $X_{11} = 35$ | $X_{12} = 36$ | $X_{13} = 28$ | $X_{14} = 27$ | $X_{15} = 32$ |
| $X_{21} = 32$ | $X_{22} = 32$ | $X_{23} = 27$ | $X_{24} = 16$ | $X_{25} = 34$ |
| $X_{31} = 41$ | $X_{32} = 34$ | $X_{33} = 23$ | $X_{34} = 40$ | $X_{35} = 26$ |
| $X_{41} = 42$ | $X_{42} = 40$ | $X_{43} = 15$ | $X_{44} = 32$ | $X_{45} = 28$ |
| $X_{51} = 31$ | $X_{52} = 37$ | $X_{53} = 29$ | $X_{54} = 36$ | $X_{55} = 23$ |
| $X_{61} = 36$ | $X_{62} = 44$ | $X_{63} = 28$ | $X_{64} = 38$ | $X_{65} = 36$ |
| $X_{71} = 35$ | $X_{72} = 42$ | $X_{73} = 33$ | $X_{74} = 22$ | $X_{75} = 28$ |
| $\overline{X}_1 = 36.00$ | $\overline{X}_2 = 37.86$ | $\overline{X}_3 = 26.14$ | $\overline{X}_4 = 30.14$ | $\overline{X}_5 = 29.57$ |
| $s_1^2 = 17.33$ | $s_2^2 = 18.81$ | $s_3^2 = 32.81$ | $s_4^2 = 78.81$ | $s_5^2 = 21.29$ |

[3]Restricting the $n$'s to be equal is not a matter of convenience here; the methods of this section have never been fully developed for the unequal $n$'s case.

The computations for the one-factor random-effects ANOVA are identical to the one-factor fixed-effects ANOVA (Chapter 15).[4] The variance of the $J$ sample means, $\overline{X}_1, \ldots, \overline{X}_J$, is used to estimate the variance of the $\mu_j$'s, $\sigma_a^2$. Similarly, the variance of the $X_{ij}$'s for each teacher yields an estimate of $\sigma_\varepsilon^2$.

## 19.5 MEAN SQUARE WITHIN, $MS_W$

As in the fixed-effects ANOVA model (Chapters 15 and 18), each of the $J$ samples of scores produces a variance $s_j^2$ that is an unbiased estimator of $\sigma_\varepsilon^2$ (or simply $\sigma^2$), the variance of the population of scores for each teacher (level). Since the $n$'s are equal, the average of these $J$ sample variances is the best estimator available for $\sigma_\varepsilon^2$ (Section 15.8). The average within sample variance is called $MS_W$, the mean-square within:

$$MS_W = \frac{s_1^2 + \ldots + s_J^2}{J} = \frac{\sum_j \sum_i (X_{ij} - \overline{X}_j)^2}{J(n-1)} = \frac{\sum_j \sum_i x_{ij}^2}{J(n-1)} = \frac{SS_W}{\nu_W} \qquad \textbf{(19.4)}$$

$MS_W$ estimates $\sigma_\varepsilon^2$ with the following properties:

1. The expected value of $MS_W$ is equal to $\sigma_\varepsilon^2$, that is, $E(MS_W) = \sigma_\varepsilon^2$. Thus, $MS_W$ is an unbiased estimator of $\sigma_\varepsilon^2$, the variance of scores within each factor level.
2. The sampling distribution of $MS_W$ based on an infinite number of replications for the $J$ levels and $n$ random observations within each level, is given by:

$$MS_W \sim \sigma^2 \frac{\chi^2_{J(n-1)}}{J(n-1)} = \frac{\chi^2_{\nu_e}}{\nu_e} \sigma^2$$

that is, the sampling distribution of $MS_W$ is $\sigma_\varepsilon^2$ times a chi-square distribution with $J(n-1)$ degrees of freedom divided by $J(n-1)$.

It is simple to prove that the expected value of $MS_W$ is $\sigma_\varepsilon^2$ if one remembers that the expected value of $\chi_{\nu e}^2$ is simply $\nu_e$ (Section 16.4):

$$E(MS_W) = E\left[\frac{\sigma_\varepsilon^2 \chi^2_{\nu_e}}{\nu_e}\right] = \frac{\sigma_\varepsilon^2 \nu_e}{\nu_e} = \sigma_\varepsilon^2 \qquad \textbf{(19.5)}$$

## 19.6 MEAN SQUARE BETWEEN, $MS_{\text{BETWEEN}}$

Recall from Chapters 15 and 18 that in balanced ANOVA designs, $MS_{\text{Between}}$, the mean square between groups, is 0 if $\overline{X}_1 = \ldots = \overline{X}_J$; $MS_{\text{Between}}$ is determined solely by differences among the means of the $J$ groups, weighted by $n$. $MS_{\text{Between}}$ is used in estimating[5] $\sigma_a^2$ (the

---

[4]Computations for fixed and random-effects ANOVA differ when two or more factors are employed.

[5]Capital letters denote fixed factors; lower-case letters represent random factors. To avoid confusing with factor $B$, $MS_{\text{Between}}$ will be used (rather than $MS_B$).

variance of the population of $a_j$'s or, equivalently, the variance of the population of $\mu_j$'s). Since (see Equation 15.8A)

$$MS_{\text{Between}} = \frac{SS_{\text{Between}}}{\nu_{\text{Between}}} = \frac{n\sum_j(\bar{X}_j - \bar{X}_\bullet)^2}{J-1} = \frac{n\sum_j \hat{\alpha}_j^2}{J-1} \quad \textbf{(19.6)}$$

that is, $MS_{\text{Between}}$ is $n$ times the variance ($s_{\bar{X}}^2$) of the sample of $J$ means, $\bar{X}_1, \ldots, \bar{X}_J$; that is, $MS_{\text{Between}} = ns_{\bar{X}}^2$.

It can be shown that the expected value of $MS_{\text{Between}}$ has the following form:

$$E(MS_{\text{Between}}) = \sigma_\varepsilon^2 + n\sigma_a^2 \quad \textbf{(19.7)}$$

that is, the average $MS_{\text{Between}}$ value from an infinite number of independent replications of the same study with $J$ randomly chosen levels with $n$ randomly chosen observations at each level is $\sigma_\varepsilon^2$ (the same variance that is estimated by $MS_W$) plus $n$ times the variance of the population of $a_j$'s (which is the same as the variance of the population of $\mu_j$'s as shown in Equation 19.6).

Thus, $MS_{\text{Between}}$ estimates all that $MS_W$ estimates and more. The something "more" is $n$ times the quantity of interest $\sigma_a^2$. However, if $\sigma_a^2 = 0$, then $MS_{\text{Between}}$ and $MS_W$ are two independent estimates of the same parameter, $\sigma_\varepsilon^2$.

The sampling distribution of $MS_{\text{Between}}$ is

$$MS_{\text{Between}} \sim (\sigma_\varepsilon^2 + n\sigma_a^2)\frac{\chi_{J-1}^2}{J-1} \quad \textbf{(19.8)}$$

that is, over repeated random samples of $J \times n$ data points (in which both factor levels and observations within levels are sampled), the sampling distribution of $MS_{\text{Between}}$ is that of chi-square with $J - 1$ degrees of freedom multiplied by the constant $(\sigma_\varepsilon^2 + n\sigma_a^2)/(J - 1)$. Unlike the fixed-effects model, $MS_{\text{Between}}$ has a sampling distribution that is a constant times the chi-square distribution *even* when there are differences among the $\mu_j$'s.

In Table 19.2, the calculations of $MS_{\text{Between}}$ and $MS_W$ are illustrated using the data in Table 19.1. In Table 19.2, the best estimate of $\sigma_\varepsilon^2 = \sigma^2$, the variance of the reading test scores in the population of students except for teacher effects is $MS_W$, which equals $33.81 = \sigma_\varepsilon^2$.

## 19.7 THE VARIANCE COMPONENT, $\sigma_a^2$

The grand mean ($\bar{X}_\bullet$) of all five groups in Tables 19.1 and 19.2 is 31.94. If $\sigma_a^2 = 0$, scores on the reading test for the population of students being sampled are assumed to be normally distributed around $\mu$, estimated in Table 19.2 to be 31.94. The standard deviation is estimated by $\sqrt{MS_W} = \sqrt{33.81} = 5.82$.

The value of $MS_{\text{Between}}$ is an estimate of $\sigma_\varepsilon^2 + n\sigma_a^2$ (Equation 19.7). An unbiased esti-

**TABLE 19.2** Illustration of Calculation of $MS_{\text{Between}}$ and $MS_{\text{W}}$ on the Data in Table 19.1, where $J = 5$ and $n = 7$.

| | *Teacher (j)* | | | | | |
|---|---|---|---|---|---|---|
| | *1* | *2* | *3* | *4* | *5* | |
| $\sum_i X_{ij}$: | 252 | 265 | 183 | 211 | 207 | |
| $\overline{X}_j$: | 36.00 | 37.86 | 26.14 | 30.14 | 29.57 | $\overline{X}_{\bullet} = 31.94$ |
| $\hat{a}_j = \overline{X}_j - \overline{X}_{\bullet}$: | 4.06 | 5.92 | −5.80 | −1.80 | −2.37 | |
| $\sum_i x_{ij}^2$: | 104.00 | 112.86 | 196.86 | 472.86 | 127.74 | |
| $s_j^2$: | 17.33 | 18.81 | 32.81 | 78.81 | 21.29 | |

$$SS_{\text{Between}} = n\sum_j \hat{a}_j^2 = 7[(4.06)^2 + (5.92)^2 + \ldots + (-2.37)^2] = 7(94.027) = 658.19$$

$$MS_{\text{Between}} = \frac{SS_{\text{B}}}{J-1} = \frac{658.19}{4} = 164.55 \text{ (Equation 19.6)}$$

$$MS_{\text{W}} = \frac{\sum_j s_j^2}{J} = \frac{(17.33 + 18.81 + \ldots + 21.29)}{5} = \frac{169.05}{5} = 33.81$$

***ANOVA Table***

| *Source* | *v* | *MS* | *F* | *Variance Component* |
|---|---|---|---|---|
| Between (Teachers) | 4 | 164.55 | 4.87* | $18.68 = \hat{\sigma}_a^2$ |
| Within | 30 | 33.81 | | $33.81 = \hat{\sigma}_\varepsilon^2$ |

*$p < .01$

mate of the variance in teachers' means, $\sigma_a^2$, can be obtained from $MS_B$ and $MS_{\text{W}}$ in the following manner:

$$E\left[\frac{MS_{\text{Between}} - MS_{\text{W}}}{n}\right] = \frac{E(MS_{\text{Between}}) - E(MS_{\text{W}})}{n} = \frac{(\sigma_\varepsilon^2 + n\sigma_a^2) - \sigma_\varepsilon^2}{n} = \frac{ns_a^2}{n} = \sigma_a^2 \quad \textbf{(19.9)}$$

An unbiased estimate of $\sigma_a^2$ is $\sigma_a^2 = (MS_{\text{Between}} - MS_{\text{W}})/n$. The $F$-test in Table 19.2 shows that teacher differences were statistically significant. The *variance component* $\sigma_a^2$ estimates the magnitude of the source of variation (effect).

For the data in Table 19.1:

$$\hat{\sigma}_a^2 = \frac{MS_{\text{Between}} - MS_{\text{W}}}{n} = \frac{164.55 - 33.81}{7} = 18.68$$

Thus, the estimate of the variance of the means of the population of teachers, that is, the variance component, $\sigma_a^2$ equals 18.68. The standard deviation of these population means is estimated to be $\sqrt{18.68} = 4.32$.

This estimate of $\sigma_a^2$ has some meaning by itself. For example, if the metric in the preceding example were converted to grade-equivalents in months by using a table of norms, and a $\sigma_a^2$ of 4.32 was equivalent to 2.5 months, this would show that the size of the teacher effect is substantial; students having a teacher whose $a_j$ is one $\sigma_a$ above the mean of the population of teachers will average about 2.5 months higher than the students having a teacher who is at the mean.[6] When the metric is arbitrary, such as raw scores on a test or inventory, $\sigma_a^2$ acquires meaning when compared with $\sigma_W^2$. In our example, $\sigma_a^2/\sigma_W^2$ is 18.68/33.81 = 0.55. In statistical parlance, it is said that the variance associated with the teacher factor is about half as great as the variance among the test scores of students having the same teacher (within teachers).

If $MS_W$ is larger than $MS_{Between}$—which, because of sampling error, does happen occasionally—the estimate $\sigma_a^2$ of $\sigma_a^2$ would be negative. However, a variance can never be negative. Thus, if ever a negative estimate of $\sigma_a^2$ is obtained, it is replaced by zero.

## 19.8 CONFIDENCE INTERVAL FOR $\sigma_a^2/\sigma_\varepsilon^2$

The questions of inferential interest in the one-way random-effects ANOVA model include (1) How can a confidence interval for $\sigma_a^2/\sigma_\varepsilon^2$ be established around $\hat{\sigma}_a^2/\hat{\sigma}_\varepsilon^2$? (2) How can the hypothesis that $\sigma_a^2 = 0$ be tested?[7]

The $1 - \alpha$ confidence interval on $\sigma_a^2/\sigma_\varepsilon^2$ is given in Equation 19.10. The probability of:

$$\left\{\frac{1}{n}\left[\frac{MS_{Between}}{MS_W}\left(\frac{1}{{}_{1-(\alpha/2)}F_{J-1,J(n-1)}}\right)-1\right] \le \frac{\sigma_a^2}{\sigma_\varepsilon^2} \le \frac{1}{n}\left[\frac{MS_{Between}}{MS_W}\left(\frac{1}{{}_{\alpha/2}F_{J-1,J(n-1)}}\right)-1\right]\right\} = 1-\alpha \qquad \textbf{(19.10)}$$

Both the $100[1-(\alpha/2)]$ and the $100(\alpha/2)$ percentiles in $F_{J-1,J(n-1)}$ are required in Equation 19.10. Recall that:

$$ {}_{\alpha/2}F_{J-1,J(n-1)} = \frac{1}{{}_{1-(\alpha/2)}F_{J(n-1),J-1}} \qquad \textbf{(19.11)}$$

To construct the 95% confidence interval on $\sigma_a^2/\sigma_\varepsilon^2$ for the data in Table 19.1, find (from Table F in the Appendix) the value of ${}_{.975}F_{4,30} = 3.25$. Next, the value of ${}_{.025}F_{4,30}$, the other required percentile, is calculated using Equation 19.11.

$$ {}_{.025}F_{4,30} = \frac{1}{{}_{.975}F_{30,4}} = \frac{1}{8.46} = 0.12$$

[6]These data are hypothetical. Using fifty-one teachers, Bennet (1972) estimated the variance component for teachers at grade one to be .04 to .16 or $\hat{\sigma}_a = .2$ to .4 grade equivalents.

[7]Unfortunately, the techniques for setting a confidence interval for $\hat{\sigma}_a^2$ cannot be derived in a straightforward manner from the original model. Approximate techniques are available; however, they are quite complex (see Scheffé, 1959, pp. 231–35; and Collins, 1970).

Substituting the two percentiles along with the values of $MS_{\text{Between}}$, $MS_W$, and $n$ into Equation 19.10 yields the 95% confidence interval on $\sigma_a^2/\sigma_\varepsilon^2$:

$$\frac{1}{7}\left[\frac{164.55}{33.81}\left(\frac{1}{3.25}\right)-1\right]=.071,\quad \frac{1}{7}\left[\frac{164.55}{33.81}\left(\frac{1}{0.12}\right)-1\right]=5.65$$

The 95% confidence interval on $\sigma_a^2/\sigma_\varepsilon^2$ extends from .071 to 5.65. The wide band shows that $\hat{\sigma}_a^2/\hat{\sigma}_\varepsilon^2$ is a very crude estimate of $\sigma_a^2/\sigma_\varepsilon^2$. The *CI* shows that $\sigma_a^2$ could be anywhere from less than one-tenth as large as, to over five times as large as $\sigma_\varepsilon^2$. Both $J$ and $n$ must be fairly large to produce stable and accurate estimates of $\sigma_a^2$ and $\sigma_\varepsilon^2$, or a narrow *CI* for $\sigma_a^2/\sigma_\varepsilon^2$. Testing the null hypothesis $H_0$: $\sigma_a^2 = 0$ is usually not of as much interest as was the corresponding test in the fixed model, $H_0$: $\Sigma\alpha_j^2 = 0$.

It is often implausible for all levels of a factor to have the same population mean, as must be true if $H_0$: $\sigma_a^2 = 0$ is true. Hence, when the random ANOVA model is applied, in addition to testing whether $\sigma_a^2 = 0$ is tenable, interest will usually center on estimating the value of $\sigma_a^2$. The procedure for testing $H_0$: $\sigma_a^2 = 0$ is similar to that for testing $H_0$: $\Sigma\alpha_j^2 = 0$. If $F = MS_{\text{Between}}/MS_W$ exceeds ${}_{1-\alpha}F_{J-1,J(n-1)}$, $H_0$: $\sigma_a^2 = 0$ can be rejected at the $\alpha$-level of significance. For example, with the data in Table 19.2, $F = MS_{\text{Between}}/MS_W = 164.55/33.81 = 4.87$, which exceeds 4.02, the 99th percentile in $F_{4,30}$. Thus, $H_0$: $\sigma_a^2 = 0$ can be rejected with $\alpha = .01$.

For all values of $\sigma_a^2$, the noncentral sampling distribution of $F = MS_{\text{Between}}/MS_W$ is given by

$$F = \frac{MS_{\text{Between}}}{MS_W} \sim \left(1+\frac{n\sigma_a^2}{\sigma_\varepsilon^2}\right)F_{J-1,J(n-1)} \qquad \textbf{(19.12)}$$

## 19.9 SUMMARY OF RANDOM ANOVA MODEL

Several major points developed in this section about the balanced one-factor random-effects ANOVA model are summarized in Table 19.3.

In the fixed-effects model, $X_{ij} = \mu + \alpha_j + \varepsilon_{ij}$, the assumption $\varepsilon_{ij} \sim NID(0, \sigma_\varepsilon^2)$ is made. In the random model, $X_{ij} = \mu + a_j + \varepsilon_{ij}$, the additional assumption $a_j \sim NID(0, \sigma_a^2)$ is made. Thus, with the random-effects ANOVA model, one must deal with the assumptions of normality, homogeneity of variance, and independence for two components—both for the $a_j$'s and the $\varepsilon_{ij}$'s.

**TABLE 19.3** Summary of the One-Factor Random-Effects ANOVA.

| *Source of Variation* | *v* | *MS* | *E(MS)* | *Estimated Variance Component* ($\sigma^2$) |
|---|---|---|---|---|
| Between levels | $J-1$ | $n\sum_j \hat{a}_j^2/(J-1)$ | $\sigma_\varepsilon^2 + n\sigma_a^2$ | $\hat{\sigma}_a^2 = \dfrac{MS_{\text{Between}} - MS_W}{n}$ |
| Within levels | $J(n-1)$ | $\sum_j s_j^2/J$ | $\sigma_\varepsilon^2$ | $\hat{\sigma}_\varepsilon^2 = MS_W$ |

In Chapter 15, it was seen that the consequences of non-normality on the validity of the fixed-effects ANOVA are negligible; in addition, heterogeneous variances have trivial practical consequences on the accuracy of inferences in the fixed-effects model if the $n$'s are equal. Less is known about the empirical consequences of violating the second set of assumptions in the random-effects ANOVA model. As with the $\varepsilon$'s, it is likely that the consequences of not meeting the assumptions regarding the $a_j$'s are less serious as the number of levels of the random factor, $J$, increases.

## 19.10 THE MIXED-EFFECTS ANOVA MODEL

The third and final analysis of variance model that will be dealt with is a combination of the fixed-effects and the random-effects models. This union of the two models into a mixed model is particularly useful in experimental research.

As the name *mixed-effects model* suggests, the mixed model involves at least one fixed and at least one random factor. The simplest form of the model describes data gathered in a two-factor design, similar in appearance to the two-factor fixed model of Chapter 18. One factor (e.g., the row factor) comprises a set of $J$ fixed effects ($\alpha$'s); the column factor is a random sample of $K$ random effects ($b$'s) that are assumed to be a random sample from an infinite population of normally distributed effects. Consider the randomized experiment (based on Roney, 1975) in which two methods designed to increase the enjoyment of reading were compared with a control (conventional) condition. The experiment was designed as follows: Ten teachers were randomly sampled to participate; each randomly selected seven pupils ($n = 7$) for each of the three instructional methods that were independently implemented. The dependent variable was a measure of reading attitude. Each observation in the study can be represented by $X_{ijk}$, where $j$ ranges over rows (methods) from 1 to 3, $k$ ranges over columns (teachers) from 1 to 10, and $i$ ranges over observations within cells (pupils) from 1 to 7. More generally, $j = 1, \ldots, J$; $k = 1, \ldots, K$; and $i = 1, \ldots, n$. The notation is equivalent to that for the two-factor fixed-effects ANOVA of Chapter 18. The means and variances of the seven students in each of the three methods for each of the ten teachers are given in Table 19.4 in Section 19.12.

The two-factor design in Table 19.4 presents two sets of main effects, $\alpha$'s and b's, plus an interaction effect, $\alpha b$. The two main effects are method, factor $M$, and teacher, factor $t$.[8] Clearly, it is not sensible to consider the three methods as samples from a large population of methods; the researcher is not interested in generalizing to a hypothetical population of other methods from which these methods were sampled; he wanted to see if either of the two methods is superior to the control (conventional) condition—his research question focused on the question of whether one of these three methods is superior (or inferior) to either of the others. Therefore, factor $M$ is considered fixed. On the other hand, the ten teachers in the experiment can be viewed as a random sample of teachers from a population; more importantly, the researcher did not want the results of the study to be generalizable *only* to the ten teachers of the experiment (which would be the case if teachers were considered as a fixed factor). One hopes that the conclusion about the relative superiority of the methods is generalizable beyond these ten teachers, that is, to the population of teachers from which these ten were sampled. Therefore, the ten teachers are viewed as a random sample of levels of the random-effects factor, $t$. Thus, in this mixed-model design, a fixed

---

[8]Lowercase letters serve as abbreviations for random factors; capital letters denote fixed factors.

**TABLE 19.4** Computations for a Two-Factor Mixed Model ANOVA: There are 3 = $M$ Levels of the Fixed Factor (Method) that Cross the 10 = $T$ Levels of the Random Factor (Teacher) [$n$ = 7].

| | | TEACHER | | | | | | | | | | Method Mean | Method Effect | |
|---|---|---|---|---|---|---|---|---|---|---|---|---|---|---|
| METHOD | | $t_1$ | $t_2$ | $t_3$ | $t_4$ | $t_5$ | $t_6$ | $t_7$ | $t_8$ | $t_9$ | $t_{10}$ | $\overline{X}_j$ | $\hat{\alpha}_j$ | $\hat{\alpha}_j^2$ |
| $M_1$ | $\overline{X}$ | 20 | 19 | 21 | 16 | 14 | 10 | 15 | 13 | 15 | 7 | 15.00 | 1.97 | 3.8678 |
| | $s^2$ | 55 | 22 | 33 | 50 | 27 | 33 | 44 | 34 | 77 | 29 | | | |
| $M_2$ | $\overline{X}$ | 15 | 15 | 12 | 16 | 15 | 12 | 10 | 12 | 10 | 8 | 12.50 | –.53 | .28 |
| | $s^2$ | 21 | 40 | 64 | 45 | 32 | 44 | 33 | 34 | 19 | 54 | | | |
| $M_3$ | $\overline{X}$ | 15 | 14 | 12 | 14 | 6 | 11 | 13 | 10 | 15 | 6 | 11.60 | –1.43 | 2.0544 |
| | $s^2$ | 41 | 19 | 12 | 41 | 50 | 35 | 29 | 40 | 27 | 16 | | | |
| Teacher Mean | $\overline{X}$ | 16.7 | 16.0 | 15.0 | 15.3 | 11.7 | 11.0 | 12.7 | 11.7 | 13.3 | 7.0 | 13.03 | $\Sigma\hat{\alpha}_j^2 = 6.207$ | |
| Teacher Effect | $\hat{b}_k$ | 3.63 | 2.97 | 1.97 | 2.30 | –1.37 | –2.03 | –.37 | –1.37 | .30 | –6.03 | | | |
| | $\hat{b}_k^2$ | 13.20 | 8.801 | 3.868 | 5.290 | 1.868 | 4.134 | .134 | 1.868 | .090 | 36.40 | $75.656 = \Sigma\hat{b}_k^2$ | | |

***ANOVA Table***

| SV | SS | $\nu$ | MS | F | p | $\hat{\sigma}^2$ | E(MS) | |
|---|---|---|---|---|---|---|---|---|
| Method ($M$) | 434.5 | 2 | 217.2 | 4.99 | .019 | | $\sigma^2_{p:tM} + n\sigma^2_{Mt} + nT\sigma^2_M$ | $= \sigma^2_{p:tM} + 7\sigma^2_{Mt} + 70\sigma^2_M$ |
| Teacher ($t$) | 1588.8 | 9 | 176.5 | 4.81 | .000 | 6.66 | $\sigma^2_{p:tM} + nM\sigma^2_t$ | $= \sigma^2_{p:tM} + 21\sigma^2_t$ |
| M × t | 783.5 | 18 | 43.53 | 1.19 | .276 | 0.98 | $\sigma^2_{p:tM} + n\sigma^2_{Mt}$ | $= \sigma^2_{p:tM} + 7\sigma^2_{Mt}$ |
| Within ($p:tM$)* | 6600.0 | 180 | 36.67 | | | 36.67 | $\sigma^2_{p:tM}$ | $= \sigma^2_{p:tM}$ |
| total | 9406.8 | 209 | | | | | | |

*The "$p:tM$" notation will be clarified in Section 19.14.

factor (method) crosses a random factor (teachers). The structural model postulated for the observations in this design in Equation 19.13 is aptly named the *mixed-effects model*:

$$X_{ijk} = \mu + \alpha_j + b_k + \alpha b_{jk} + \varepsilon_{ijk} \quad \textbf{(19.13)}$$

where $X_{ijk}$ is the $i$th observation in the $jk$th cell, $\mu$ is the grand population mean of all observations, $\alpha_j$ is the effect $(\mu_j - \mu)$ of the $j$th level of the fixed factor, $b_k$ is the effect $(\mu_k - \mu)$ of the $k$th level of the random factor, $\alpha b_{jk}$ is the interaction effect $[\mu_{jk} - (\mu + \alpha_j + b_k)]$ of the $jk$th combination of the fixed and random factors, and $\varepsilon_{ijk}$ is the within or residual component that accounts for variation of observations within the $jk$th cell. The following restrictions (not assumptions) are placed on the terms of the mixed-effects model in Equation 19.13:

1. $\Sigma_j \alpha_j = 0$.
2. The population mean of the infinite number of $b_k$'s—only ten of which are present in the instructional methods experiment—is zero.
3. $\alpha b_{1k} + \alpha b_{2k} + \ldots + \alpha b_{JK} = 0$ for all $K$.
4. The population of the infinite set of $\alpha b_{jk}$'s for a single $j$ (row) has a mean of zero.

These restrictions imply that if the fixed effects and interaction effects are summed across the three rows of the data in Table 19.4, they will "add out," that is, sum to zero. However, summing across the columns of the design to obtain a particular row mean, for example, will not cause the $K$ values of $b_k$ or the $K$ values of $\alpha b_{jk}$ to sum to zero.

Suppose the means of methods 1 and 2 are compared. These two means, $\overline{X}_{1\bullet}$ and $\overline{X}_{2\bullet}$, have the following structure in terms of the model in Equation 19.13:

$$\begin{aligned}\overline{X}_{1\bullet} &= \frac{1}{Kn}\left[\sum_k \sum_i (\mu + \alpha_1 + b_k + \alpha b_{1k} + \varepsilon_{i1k})\right] \\ &= \mu + \alpha_1 + \overline{b}_\bullet + \overline{\alpha b}_{1\bullet} + \overline{\varepsilon}_{1\bullet}\end{aligned}$$

where:

$$\overline{b}_\bullet = \frac{\sum_k b_k}{K} \quad \overline{\alpha b}_{1\bullet} = \frac{\sum_k \alpha b_{1k}}{K}$$

and:

$$\begin{aligned}\overline{\varepsilon}_{1\bullet} &= \frac{\sum_k \sum_i \varepsilon_{i1k}}{nK} \\ \overline{X}_{2\bullet} &= \mu + \alpha_2 + \overline{b}_\bullet + \overline{\alpha b}_{2\bullet} + \overline{\varepsilon}_{2\bullet}\end{aligned}$$

The difference between $\overline{X}_{1\bullet}$ and $\overline{X}_{2\bullet}$ is:

$$\overline{X}_{1\bullet} - \overline{X}_{2\bullet} = (\hat{\alpha}_1 - \hat{\alpha}_2) + (\overline{\alpha b}_{1\bullet} - \overline{\alpha b}_{2\bullet}) + (\overline{\varepsilon}_{1\bullet} - \overline{\varepsilon}_{2\bullet})$$

Since the $\alpha b$'s do not necessarily sum to zero across the $K$ columns and because a replication of the experiment with a different set of $K$ random effects would produce different values of $\overline{\alpha b}_{1\bullet}$ and $\overline{\alpha b}_{2\bullet}$, the sampling variance of the difference between $\bar{X}_{1\bullet} - \bar{X}_{2\bullet}$ will contain a component for the interaction effects, $\alpha b$. This fact will be fully appreciated when the expected values of mean squares for the mixed model are discussed. Before that subject though, the assumptions which must be made about the mixed model of Equation 19.13 need to be stated.

## 19.11 MIXED-MODEL ANOVA ASSUMPTIONS

The following assumptions are made about the terms of the model in Equation 19.13:

$$X_{ijk} = \mu + \alpha_j + b_k + \alpha b_{jk} + \varepsilon_{ijk}$$

1. The random effects, $b_k = \mu_k - \mu$, are normally distributed with a mean of zero and a variance of $\sigma_b^2$.
2. The interaction effects, $\alpha b_{jk}$, are normally distributed over $k$ for each $j$ with a mean of zero and a variance of $\sigma_{\alpha b}^2$.
3. The error components $\varepsilon_{ijk}$, are distributed normally and independently of the $b$'s and $\alpha b$'s with a mean of zero and a variance of $\sigma_\varepsilon^2$.

When testing $H_0$ for the fixed main effect, there is a fourth assumption, *sphericity*. If the population variances are equal, and the correlations are equal, sphericity is obtained.

4. The essence of the sphericity assumption can best be visualized by assuming all levels of the fixed factor have the same variance in the population; then, sphericity will exist if the correlations between all pairs of levels are equal.

When the sphericity assumption is violated, the $F$-test for the fixed effect becomes somewhat liberal, that is, true $\alpha >$ nominal $\alpha$ (e.g., the true probability of a type-I error is greater than $\alpha$). The error in the probability statement is rarely large, however (Collier et al., 1967). When the condition is not met, adjustments can be made to make the $p$ value more accurate.[9]

### Null Hypotheses

The null hypotheses about the fixed effect ($\alpha$) and the random main effect (b) and the interaction in the two-factor mixed ANOVA model are:

1. $H_{0_1}: \sum_j \alpha_j^2 = 0$ (versus $H_1: \sum_j \alpha_j^2 \neq 0$)
2. $H_{02}: \sigma_b^2 = 0$ (versus $H_1: \sigma_b^2 \neq 0$)
3. $H_{03}: \sigma_{Ab}^2 = 0$ (versus $H_1: \sigma_{Ab}^2 \neq 0$)

## 19.12 MIXED-MODEL ANOVA COMPUTATION

The computations of the mean squares and degrees of freedom are identical in the fixed, random, and mixed ANOVA models. The fixed and mixed ANOVA models part company

[9] The condition of sphericity is considered more fully in Chapter 20, along with adjustments when it is not achieved.

only when $F$-ratios are to be formed. The computations in the two-factor mixed model for $SS$, $\nu$, and $MS$ are presented in Table 19.4.

As in the fixed ANOVA model, the expected values of mean squares for the various effects determine the appropriate denominator of the $F$-test—the ratio of two independent variance estimates (mean squares). The expected mean square values[10] corresponding to the experiment in Table 19.4 are given in the lower right-hand portion of Table 19.4. Notice that the expected mean square for the fixed factor (method) has three components in the mixed ANOVA model (see Table 19.4), whereas in the fixed ANOVA model it has only two components (see Table 18.5).

If both factors are fixed, the expected mean square for the fixed main effect $A$ is:

$$E(MS_A) = \sigma_\varepsilon^2 + nK\sigma_A^2 \quad \textbf{(19.14)}$$

If factor $A$ is fixed, but factor $b$ is random, the interaction component $n\sigma_{\alpha b}^2$ is an additional component:

$$E(MS_A) = \sigma_\varepsilon^2 + nK\sigma_A^2 + n\sigma_{Ab}^2 \quad \textbf{(19.15)}$$

Notice by comparing the $E(MS)$'s in Table 19.4 with those in Table 18.5, that the $E(MS)$'s in the two models are identical for three sources of variation: (1) the main effect for the *random* factor, (2) the two-factor interaction, and (3) the within cells variability (i.e., persons within cells).

First consider the problem of testing the null hypothesis for the fixed factor in Table 19.4—the main effect ($M$). The null hypothesis contends that all the $\alpha_j$'s are zero (or equivalently, $H_0$: $\mu_1 = \mu_2 = \mu_3$). With the fixed model, this $H_0$ is tested by dividing the mean square for the fixed factor ($MS_M$) by the within cell variance ($MS_W$) to obtain the $F$-ratio. Notice in Table 19.4 that by comparing the $E(MS)$[11] values for $MS_M$ and $MS_W$ (see the lower right-hand portion of Table 19.4) that the ratio $MS_M/MS_W$ does *not* bear *solely* on the question of whether the variance among the population means for the three methods is 0. The three population means could be equal and yet $MS_M/MS_W$ might be large because of a strong interaction component, $\sigma_{Mt}^2$. The *difference* between $MS_M$ and $MS_W$ is an aggregate of two effects, $nT\sigma_M^2 + n\sigma_{Mt}^2$ (not just $nT\sigma_M^2$, as in the two-factor fixed model described in Table 18.4).

Notice in Table 19.4 that $E(MS_M)$ differs from $E(MS_{Mt})$ *only* by $nT\sigma_M^2$ (or $70\sigma_M^2$—cf. lines $M$ versus $Mt$), the effect to be tested. Thus, the size of the discrepancy between $MS_M$ and $MS_{Mt}$, reflected in the ratio of $MS_M$ to $MS_{Mt}$, reflects the magnitude of the component, $70\sigma_M^2$. More specifically, given the assumptions of the mixed-effects model, $F = MS_M/MS_{Mt}$ will have the $F$-distribution with $(M - 1)$ and $[(M - 1)(T - 1)]$ degrees of freedom when $H_0$: $\mu_1 = \mu_2 = \mu_3$ is true. *However*, if $H_0$ is *not* true, $E(MS_M) > E(MS_{Mt})$; the expected value of $F = MS_M/MS_{Mt}$ will increase; and the probability will increase that the observed value of $F$ will be greater than the critical value of $F$ $({}_{1-\alpha}F_{(M-1),[(M-1)(T-1)]})$.

[10]That is, the average $MS$-values that would result if the experiment were replicated an infinite number of times with different random samples of teachers and pupils each time, but the same three experimental treatments.

[11]In the expected mean square expressions, the initial letter of the factor identifies the factor, which will show up either as a subscript or as a coefficient.

It is counterintuitive, but nevertheless true, that testing the null hypothesis for the *random* factor, $H_0$: $\sigma_b^2 = 0$ is *identical* to testing $H_0$ when both factors are *fixed*. If $H_0$ is true, the value of the ratio for testing the teacher effect ($F = MS_T/MS_W$) follows the central $F$-distribution with the associated degrees of freedom, $T-1$ and $MT(n-1)$: ${}_{1-\alpha}F_{(T-1),[MT(n-1)]}$.

## Variance Components

Variance components, $\hat{\sigma}^2$, are typically reported for those sources of variation that involve a *random factor* (in Table 19.4 variance components are given in the $\hat{\sigma}^2$ column of the ANOVA table). The value of $\hat{\sigma}^2$ is an estimate of the variance in the means for the population of levels for the random effect. When a source of variation represents a random effect (i.e., at least one random element is present in the source of variation), an unbiased estimate of the numerical value of the *variance component* can be obtained using simple algebra. For example, the variance component for teachers is:

$$\hat{\sigma}_t^2 = \frac{MS_t - MS_W}{nM} = \frac{176.5 - 36.67}{7(3)} = 6.66$$

Stated differently, an estimate of the population standard deviation for the distribution of teacher means within a given method (and with the sampling error associated with pupils eliminated) is $2.58 = \sqrt{6.66}$.

Expected mean squares help define the estimation of the variance component $\sigma_{MT}^2$; the variance component for the $M \times T$ interaction is estimated by:

$$\hat{\sigma}_{Mt}^2 = \frac{MS_{Mt} - MS_W}{n} = \frac{43.53 - 36.67}{7} = .98$$

That is, .98 is an estimate of the variance in the cell residuals—the differences between cells means and the means predicted from the grand means plus the teacher and method effects. Notice that the variance component for the interaction (.98) is much less than for the teacher main effect (6.66).[12] In other words, the differences among the teachers were much larger than the differential effectiveness of the methods within teachers.

## Testing $H_0$'s

For the data in Table 19.4, the three null hypotheses mentioned have been tested using the conventional risk of a type-I error ($\alpha = .05$). The results appear in the ANOVA table in Table 19.4. The main effect for the fixed (method) effect is statistically significant ($p = .019 < \alpha = .05$). The differences among the means of the dependent variable for these three instructional methods are too great to be attributed to sampling error—there are method effects that can be generalized to the populations of teachers and students that are sampled in this study.

The random (teacher) factor is statistically significant—differences among teachers were significant beyond the .001 level.[13]

---

[12]The $1-\alpha$ confidence interval on $\sigma_T^2/\sigma_{tM}^2$ can be constructed by using Equation 19.10 of Section 19.8; $F_{K-1,JK(n-1)}$ is substituted for $F_{J-1,J(n-1)}$ in that equation.

[13]Computer printouts such as ".000" simply mean $p < .0005$. Values such as ".000" or ".0000" are best replaced by "< .001" and "< .0001," respectively.

The null hypothesis for the method-by-teacher interaction ($H_0$: $\sigma^2_{Mt} = 0$) is tested by referring the observed $F$-ratio, $F = MS_{Mt}/MS_W$, to the $F$-distribution with degrees of freedom of $(M-1)(T-1)]$ and $MT(n-1)$ in the numerator and denominator, respectively. The $M \times T$ interaction was not significant ($p = .276$)—teachers with higher (or lower) means tended to be higher (or lower) regardless of the method. Stated differently, the shape of the *profiles* for the teacher did not evidence differences greater than would be expected from sampling error.

Of course, as with any study, the teachers and pupils need to be clearly defined on relevant variables. The explicit definition of the sample of teachers and pupils is the clearest indication of the populations to which the results can be generalized.[14]

## 19.13 MULTIPLE COMPARISONS IN THE TWO-FACTOR MIXED MODEL

*Multiple comparisons* (and trend analysis) are applied only to *fixed* factors. The procedures are the same as those presented in Chapters 17 and 18. The only difference as ANOVA designs become more complex is that the error mean square, $MS_e$, in the formulas for multiple comparisons given in Chapter 17 denotes the denominator of the $F$-test for the fixed factor—in Table 19.4, $MS_e = MS_{Mt}$; similarly, $\nu_e = \nu_{Mt}$.

Since the $H_0$ for the method main effect was significant, a post hoc multiple comparison method, such as the Newman-Keuls (Section 17.6) can be employed to find which of the three means differs significantly from which of the others. Using the Newman-Keuls with $\alpha = .05$ and Equations 17.2 and 17.3:

$$q_1 = \frac{\bar{X}_{\text{largest}} - \bar{X}_{\text{smallest}}}{s_{\bar{X}}} = \frac{\bar{X}_1 - \bar{X}_3}{s_{\bar{X}}}$$

where

$$s_{\bar{X}} = \sqrt{\frac{MS_e}{n\text{T}}} = \sqrt{\frac{43.53}{70}} = .789$$

thus,

$$q_1 = \frac{15.00 - 11.60}{.789} = 4.31$$

[14]Although, in theory, both teachers and pupils are randomly sampled from defined populations of teachers and pupils, in practice this is usually logistically impossible. Indeed, in experimental studies the target population cannot be randomly sampled. For example, in an experiment using two methods of instruction in grade one, the population to which one wishes to generalize includes next year's first graders who obviously cannot be part of the population being randomly sampled. A common compromise is to find experimentally accessible teachers and pupils that are as representative as possible, and then define them explicitly on as many variables as possible to better define the populations of inference.

The value of $q_1$ (4.31) is larger than the critical $q$-value found in Table I ($_{.95}q_{18,3} = 3.61$); thus, $H_{0_1}$: $\mu_1 - \mu_3 = 0$ is rejected. However, the null hypothesis cannot be rejected at the .01 level since $4.31 < 4.70 = {}_{.99}q_{18,3}$.

Note that to obtain $s_{\overline{X}}$, the value of $nT = 70$ (the number of observations on which each mean is based) is used: The error mean square (i.e., the denominator of the $F$-test for that effect) is divided by the number of observations on which the means being compared are based. Note in Table 19.4 that this is the value for the coefficient for the main effect of the respective variance component ($70\sigma_M^2$). The multiple comparison procedures given in Chapter 17 can be extended to balanced ANOVA designs of any number of factors, bearing in mind that (1) $MS_{\text{error}}$ in the formulas is the denominator (error term) that is used in the $F$-ratio to test that main effect, and (2) to obtain the appropriate value of $s_{\overline{X}}$, $MS_e$ is divided by the number of observations on which each of the means being compared is based.[15]

Since $H_{0_1}$: $\mu_1 = \mu_3$ is rejected, we proceed to test $H_{0_2}$: $\mu_1 = \mu_2$ and find:

$$q_2 = \frac{\overline{X}_1 - \overline{X}_2}{s_{\overline{X}}} = \frac{15.0 - 12.5}{.789} = 3.17$$

From Appendix Table I, the critical value for adjacent means is found to be 2.97; therefore, $H_{0_2}$ can be rejected at the .05 level—method 1 is superior to method 2 (as well as to method 3). $H_{0_3}$: $\mu_2 = \mu_3$ is tenable ($q_3 = 1.14$).

## 19.14 CROSSED AND NESTED FACTORS

All of the factors that have been considered up to this point have been crossed factors;[16] two factors are *crossed* if every combination of the levels of both factors is found. In some designs, factors are not crossed, but one factor is *nested* within another factor. If all methods are used in all schools of an experiment, then methods and schools are crossed. However, if method $E$ is used in schools 1 and 2, and method $C$ is used in schools 3 and 4, schools are nested within methods. Counties are nested within states; schools are nested within school districts; teachers are usually nested within schools.[17]

The experiment depicted in Table 19.4 did not tell the whole story. Teachers 1–5 taught in school 1, and teachers 6–10 taught in school 2—teachers were nested within schools.[18] The design given in Table 19.5 uses the factors of method, school, and teacher, and illustrates crossed and nested factors. The factors of school and method are crossed because each of the five methods appears with each of the two schools—there are $2 \times 5 = 10$ unique combinations of factors $s$ and $M$. (The number of levels of each factor will be denoted by the

[15]For example, if one were to make multiple comparisons among the means of the ten teachers, $s_{\overline{X}} = \sqrt{MS_e / nM} = \sqrt{36.67/21} = 1.32$.

[16]Except the "within" source of variation, which has been nested within all other factors.

[17]If, however, in the unlikely event that the same teachers taught in both schools (as, for example, would be the case if teachers were assigned to one school in the morning and to the other school in the afternoon), teachers would not be nested within schools, but would cross schools.

[18]Notice the two levels of the school factor are like two nests, each nest having three eggs (teachers); thus, teachers are said to be nested within schools.

**TABLE 19.5** A Three-Factor Mixed Model ANOVA: Three Methods ($M = 3$) Used by Five Teachers ($T = 5$) Nested within Two Schools ($S = 2$) and ($n = 7$) Pupils Are Nested within Teacher and School).

| METHOD | | $s_1$ $t_1$ | $s_1$ $t_2$ | $s_1$ $t_3$ | $s_1$ $t_4$ | $s_1$ $t_5$ | $s_2$ $t_6$ | $s_2$ $t_7$ | $s_2$ $t_8$ | $s_2$ $t_9$ | $s_2$ $t_{10}$ | Method Mean $\overline{X}$ | Method Effect $\hat{\alpha}_j$ | $\hat{\alpha}_j^2$ |
|---|---|---|---|---|---|---|---|---|---|---|---|---|---|---|
| $M_1$ | $\overline{X}$ | 20 | 19 | 21 | 16 | 14 | 10 | 15 | 13 | 15 | 7 | 15.00 | 1.97 | 3.868 |
| | $s^2$ | 55 | 22 | 33 | 50 | 27 | 33 | 44 | 34 | 77 | 29 | | | |
| $M_2$ | $\overline{X}$ | 15 | 15 | 12 | 16 | 15 | 12 | 10 | 12 | 10 | 8 | 12.50 | –.53 | .284 |
| | $s^2$ | 21 | 40 | 64 | 45 | 32 | 44 | 33 | 34 | 19 | 54 | | | |
| $M_3$ | $\overline{X}$ | 15 | 14 | 12 | 14 | 6 | 11 | 13 | 10 | 15 | 6 | 11.60 | –1.43 | 2.054 |
| | $s^2$ | 41 | 19 | 12 | 41 | 50 | 35 | 29 | 40 | 27 | 16 | | | |
| School Mean | $\overline{X}$ | | | 14.93 | | | | | 11.13 | | | 13.03 | $\Sigma\hat{\alpha}_j^2 = 6.21$ | |
| School Effect | $\hat{b}_k$ | | | 1.90 | | | | | –1.90 | | | | | |
| | $\hat{b}_k^2$ | | | 3.61 | | | | | 3.61 | | | $7.22 = \Sigma\hat{b}_k^2$ | | |
| Teacher Mean | $\overline{X}$ | 16.7 | 16.0 | 15.0 | 15.3 | 11.7 | 11.0 | 12.7 | 11.7 | 13.3 | 7.0 | | | |
| Teacher Effect ($t{:}s$) | $\widehat{c{:}b}$ | 1.7 | 1.1 | .1 | .4 | –3.3 | –.1 | 1.5 | .5 | 2.2 | –4.1 | | | |
| | $\widehat{c{:}b}^2$ | 3.0 | 1.1 | .0 | .2 | 10.7 | .0 | 2.4 | .3 | 4.8 | 17.1 | $39.56 = \Sigma\widehat{c{:}b}^2$ | | |

***ANOVA Table***

| SV | SS | $v$ | MS | F | p | $\sigma^2$ | E(MS) | |
|---|---|---|---|---|---|---|---|---|
| Method ($M$) | 434.5 | 2 | 217.2 | 2.11 | .321 | | $\sigma^2_{p:tsM} + n\sigma^2_{Mt:s} + nT\sigma^2_{Ms} + nTM\sigma^2_s$ | $= \sigma^2_{p:tsM} + 7\sigma^2_{MTt:s} + 35\sigma^2_{Ms} + 70\sigma^2_M$ |
| School ($s$) | 758.1 | 1 | 758.1 | 7.30 | .027 | 6.23 | $\sigma^2_{p:tsM} + nM\sigma^2_{t:s} + nTM\sigma^2_s$ | $= \sigma^2_{p:tsM} + 21\sigma^2_{t:s} + 105\sigma^2_s$ |
| Teacher ($t{:}s$) | 830.7 | 8 | 103.8 | 2.83 | .006 | 3.20 | $\sigma^2_{p:tsM} + nM\sigma^2_{t:s}$ | $= \sigma^2_{p:tsM} + 21\sigma^2_{t:s}$ |
| M × s | 205.8 | 2 | 102.9 | 2.85 | .087 | 1.91 | $\sigma^2_{p:tsM} + n\sigma^2_{Mt:s} + nT\sigma^2_{Ms}$ | $= \sigma^2_{p:tsM} + 7\sigma^2_{Mt:s} + 35\sigma^2_{Ms}$ |
| M × $t{:}s$ | 577.7 | 16 | 36.11 | 0.98 | .475 | 0* | $\sigma^2_{p:tsM} = n\sigma^2_{Mt:s}$ | $= \sigma^2_{p:tsM} + 7\sigma^2_{Mt:s}$ |
| Within ($p{:}tM$) | 6600.0 | 180 | 36.67 | | | 36.67 | $\sigma^2_{p:tsM}$ | $= \sigma^2_{p:tsM}$ |
| total | 9406.8 | 209 | | | | | | |

*When the computed value for a variance component is negative (here, –.08), the variance component is set to zero.

capital letter that identifies that factor. As a mnemonic aid, letters representing fixed factors will be italicized; letters representing random factors will not, $M = 3$, $S = 2$, and $T = 5$). Each teacher uses each method; thus, the factors of teacher and method are also crossed—there are $5 \times 2 = 10$ combinations. Notice, however, that teachers and schools do not cross: Teachers are nested within schools.

More generally, a factor $A$ is said to be nested within a factor $B$ if each level of factor $A$ (the nested factor) appears in only one level of factor $B$. In the study represented in Table 19.5, teachers are nested within schools. Each teacher is assigned to only one school; thus, teachers ($t$) are said to be nested within schools ($s$); this is denoted as $t{:}s$, where ":" is read "is nested within." Since teacher 1 ($t_1$) teaches only at school 1 ($s_1$), $t_1$ is not found within school 2 in Table 19.5. The fact that the teacher subscripts, 1, 2, and 3, are not repeated at school 2 shows that three different teachers (4, 5, and 6) appear at school 2. The design in Table 19.5 is a three-factor design, but only two of the factors, method ($M$) and school ($s$) are completely crossed; the third factor, teacher ($t$), is nested within school—the three factors (or sources of variation) can be denoted as $M$, $s$, and $t{:}s$.

In practice, *nested factors* are almost always *random* factors (like the teacher factor in this example). The converse is not true however—both fixed and random factors are frequently crossed. In the design in Table 19.5, the richest generalization is yielded when both teachers and schools are viewed as random effects so that the findings can be generalized beyond these particular teachers and schools to the populations of schools and teachers from which they can be viewed as representative samples.

Actually, an undesignated nested factor has been carried along in all previous ANOVA applications (although it ordinarily is not designated as a factor). In all examples given in Chapters 15 and 18, the replicate factor (usually persons) is nested within all other factors. Indeed, the "within" factor is a less explicit designation of the fact that persons are nested within all other factors. For example, "within" in Table 15.2 is "persons nested within treatments ($p{:}T$)"; in Table 18.1, "within" is "persons nested within factors $A$ and $M$ ($p{:}AM$)"; in Table 18.6 "within" is "persons nested within (fixed) factors $A$, $S$, and $T$, ($p{:}AST$)." Although the use of "within" as a source of variation is conventional, it is better practice to make this source of variation explicit.

## 19.15 COMPUTATION OF SUMS OF SQUARES FOR NESTED FACTORS[19]

To estimate the method effect in Table 19.5, each method mean is based on $nTS = (7)(5)(2) = 70$; thus,

$$SS_M = 70\Sigma_m \hat{\alpha}_m^2 = 70[(1.97)^2 + (-.53)^2 + (-1.43)^2] = 70(6.2) = 434.5.$$

In estimating the school effect, each school mean is based on $nTM = (7)(5)(3) = 105$ observations, therefore $SS_S = 105\Sigma_s \hat{b}_s^2$. The procedure is similar with nested effects. The sum of squares for a nested effect, $t{:}s$, can be computed directly, that is, $SS_{t:s} = nM\Sigma_t \hat{c}_{t:s}^2$ where $nM$ is the number of observations on which each of the $t$ means is based. For example, in Table 19.5, the sum of squares for the $t{:}s$ effect (teacher-within-school, $\hat{c}_{t:s}$) is the number of

[19]The computations are given only to illustrate the process, and are not per se critically important objectives of this text. Standard statistical software packages will do the work if given the correct input. In previous examples, the direct computation of $MS$'s has been emphasized: in Table 19.5 $SS$'s are illustrated.

observations per teacher ($nM = (7)(3) = 21$) times the sum of the squared effects, where the estimated effects are $\hat{c}_{t:s} = \overline{X}_{\bullet t:s} - (\overline{X}_{\bullet\bullet\bullet} + \hat{b}_s)$; thus, $SS_{t:s} = 21\Sigma_t\hat{c}^2_{t:s}$. The estimated teacher-within-method effects, $\hat{c}_{t:s}$, are given in line 14 of Table 19.5.[20]

## 19.16 DETERMINING THE SOURCES OF VARIATION IN THE ANOVA TABLE

Computer output from a program that handles nested effects will have the sources of variation listed. Nevertheless, in the planning stage of a study, it is useful to know which effects will, and will not, be tested. Each line in an ANOVA table corresponds to an effect—a source of variation in the model. There is an effect for each factor (main effects), and each unique combination of factors (interactions). A factor that is nested (e.g., teachers in Table 19.5) interacts only with other factors that cross it. For the design shown in Table 19.5, there is no source of variation for a school-by-teacher interaction because teachers are nested within school. A source of variation for each component in the statistical model (Equation 19.16) is found in the ANOVA table.

$$X_{itsm} = \mu + \alpha_m + b_s + c_{t:s} + \alpha b_{ms} + \alpha c_{mt:s} + \varepsilon_{i:tsm} \qquad (19.16)$$

where, $\mu = \overline{X}_{\bullet\bullet\bullet}$, $\alpha_m = \overline{X}_{\bullet\bullet m} - \overline{X}_{\bullet\bullet\bullet}$, $b_s = \overline{X}_{\bullet s\bullet} - \overline{X}_{\bullet\bullet\bullet}$, $c_{t:s} = \overline{X}_{t:s\bullet} - (\overline{X}_{\bullet\bullet\bullet} + b_s)$, $\alpha b_{ms} = \overline{X}_{\bullet ms} - (\overline{X}_{\bullet\bullet\bullet} + \alpha_m + b_s)$, $\alpha c_{mt:s} = \overline{X}_{mt:s} - (\overline{X}_{\bullet\bullet\bullet} + \alpha_m + c_{t:s})$, and $\varepsilon_{i:tsm} = X_{itms} - \overline{X}_{tms}$. In Table 19.5, $i$ varies from 1 to $7 = n$, $t$ varies from 1 to $5 = T$, $s$ varies from 1 to $2 = S$, and $m$ varies from 1 to $3 = M$.

## 19.17 DEGREES OF FREEDOM FOR NESTED FACTORS

If a factor is nested, its degrees of freedom are the number of nests, $U$, times the degrees of freedom per nest (one less than the number of observations per nest), that is, $U(n - 1)$. In Table 19.5, five teachers ($T = 3$) are nested within each of two schools ($S = 2$); hence, the degrees of freedom for the $t{:}s$ source of variation are $S(T - 1) = 2(5 - 1) = 8$ (see $T$ and $S$ in Table 19.5). For pupils, $p{:}tsM$, where there are 5, 2, and 3 levels, respectively, for factors $t$, $s$, and $M$, the number of nests is the product of the number of levels of factors $t$, $s$, and $M$,

[20]Many ANOVA programs (e.g., SPSS ANOVA) do not accommodate nested factors. However, if the design is balanced and the data are analyzed as if all factors were crossed, the various sums of squares can be rather easily aggregated from the ANOVA table output to obtain the sum of squares for the nested effects using the "trick" below. The rule for aggregation from such ANOVA tables is: The sum of squares for any effect that is nested includes itself plus all interactions of itself with the factor(s) under which it is nested. Thus:

$SS_{A:B} = SS_A + SS_{AB}$

$SS_{AB:C} = SS_{AB} + SS_{ABC}$

$SS_{A:BC} = SS_A + SS_{AB} + SS_{AC} + SS_{ABC}$

$SS_{AB:CD} = SS_{AB} + SS_{ABC} + SS_{ABD} + SS_{ABCD}$

(The associated degrees of freedom are aggregated in the same way.)

The data in Table 19.5 could be analyzed as if it were a three-factor fully crossed ANOVA (as in Table 18.6, Section 18.22). Then $SS_t$ and $SS_{ts}$ would be aggregated to obtain $SS_{t:s}$, which divided by $\nu_t + \nu_{ts}$ yields $MS_{t:s}$. Likewise, $SS_{Mt:s} = SS_{Mt} + SS_{MTs}$, and $\nu_{Mt:s} = \nu_{tM} + \nu_{Mts}$.

that is, $U = (5)(2)(3) = 30$. Thus, since there are seven ($n = 7$) pupils per nest, the degrees of freedom for $p{:}tsM$ are $TSM(n - 1) = (30)(7 - 1) = 180$ (see Table 18.5).

As with crossed factors, $\nu$ for any interaction is the product of the $\nu$'s for the participating factors. For example in Table 19.5, for the method-teacher ($Mt{:}s$) interaction, there are $(M - 1)(S)(T - 1) = (2)(2)(5 - 1) = 16$ degrees of freedom (see Table 18.5).

## 19.18 DETERMINING EXPECTED MEAN SQUARES

As designs become more complex, the $E(MS)$ for each source of variation is needed to determine the proper error term (denominator) for the $F$-test for a given effect.[21] The expected mean square is also needed to determine variance components for random effects. Several methods provide guidelines for finding entries in an ANOVA table (Millman & Glass, 1967; Cornfield & Tukey, 1956). The simplest method (Hopkins, 1976) requires only two rules, but the first rule must be practiced on several designs in order to be mastered.

1. The *components* (addends) of an expected mean square for any source of variation are the specified effect (a main effect or interaction, i.e., source of variation) plus (a) the interaction of the specified effect with any random effect (including combinations of random effects) and (b) any random effect nested within the specified effect.

In a one-factor ANOVA in which $n$ persons are nested within each of the $M$ methods, the $E(MS)$ for the method effect includes the method component ($\sigma_M^2$) plus the variance from the random effect (persons), which is nested within method, $\sigma_{p:M}^2$ (or $\sigma_{\text{within}}^2 = \sigma_\varepsilon^2$). In Table 18.3 there are two fixed factors, $M$ and $A$; persons, a random effect, are nested within cells ($p{:}MA$); thus, the $E(MS)$ for factor $M$ includes the variance component for factor $M$ ($\sigma_M^2$), plus the component for persons $\sigma_{p:MA}^2$. The procedures for determining $E(MS)$'s are best learned inductively, using examples. Study the examples in Tables 19.4 and 19.5.

Since it is the subscripts that define the proper error term for an effect, notation can be simplified by ignoring coefficients and $\sigma^2$ symbols. In a design in which the fixed effect, $A$, crosses random effects[22] $b$ and $c$, the $E(MS)$ for the $A$ effect is $A + Ab + Ac + Abc$—it includes the $A$ component, plus all of the interactions of $A$ with $b$ and/or $c$ ($\sigma_A^2 + \sigma_{Ab}^2 + \sigma_{Ac}^2 + \sigma_{Abc}^2$). Note that each $E(MS)$ component for the mean square for factor $A$ included the specified effect, $A$, plus a term for each random factor and combination of random factors that crossed the specified effect. Similarly, with the same design, the $E(MS)$ for the $Ab$ interaction is $Ab + Abc$ ($\sigma_{Ab}^2 + \sigma_{Abc}^2$). If random factor $b$ is nested within $A$, but crosses random effect $c$, the $E(MS)$ for $A$ is $A + b{:}A + Ac + cb{:}A$ ($\sigma_A^2 + \sigma_{b:A}^2 + \sigma_{Ac}^2 + \sigma_{cb:A}^2$). If random effect $c$ is nested within random effect $b$ which is nested within fixed effect $A$, the $E(MS)$ for factor $A$ becomes $A + b{:}A + c{:}bA$ ($\sigma_A^2 + \sigma_{b:A}^2 + \sigma_{Ac}^2 + \sigma_{cb:A}^2$). Note that in each instance each component included the specified effect, $A$, plus $A$ associated with a unique effect involving random factors.[23]

---

[21]Many ANOVA programs assume all factors are fixed, but if you can determine the expected mean square for an effect, you can quickly identify the correct denominator for the $F$-test and compute the correct $F$-ratio. In balanced ANOVA designs, the mean squares are not influenced by fixed versus random designations, but the denominator of the $F$-test is changed for certain (fixed) effects.

[22]Recall that capital letters denote fixed factors, and lower-case letters, random factors.

[23]Only a few computer programs currently produce expected mean squares for various sources of variation. Increasingly, programs will no doubt ask the user to designate factors as fixed or random from which the $E(MS)$'s can be produced by algorithm.

2. The *coefficient* for any component[24] is the product of the number of levels of all factors *not* denoted in the variance subscript for that component.

Thus, in Table 19.5, the within component ($\sigma^2_{p:tsM}$) has a coefficient of 1 because all factors (including pupils) appear in the subscript. Likewise, the coefficient for the method component ($\sigma^2_M$) has the coefficient of $nTS$, or (7)(5)(2) = 70, since $p$,[25] $t$, and $s$ do not appear in the subscript of the effect, $\sigma^2_M$. Stated differently, the coefficient for any component is the number of observations on which each of the means directly involved in the component is based. Thus, for $\sigma^2_M$, each of the $M = 3$ means is based on 70 observations; hence, the coefficient of $\sigma^2_M$ is 70. The numerical values of the coefficients of the variance component are necessary to find the value of $\hat{\sigma}^2$ (see Table 19.5).

## 19.19 ERROR MEAN SQUARES IN COMPLEX ANOVA DESIGNS

The general form of an $F$-test is $F = (A + B)/B$, or $F = (A + B + C)/(B + C)$, et cetera. Note that the denominator of the $F$-test includes every component contained in the numerator *except* the effect to be tested. The null hypothesis states that the component to be tested has zero variance; hence, when the null hypothesis is true, the numerator and denominator are two independent estimates of the same parameter, for example, the null hypothesis for factor $a$ is $H_0$: $\sigma_a^2 = 0$.

In Table 19.5, the expected value for the $t{:}s$ mean square includes $\sigma^2_{p:tsM}$ in addition to $21\sigma^2_{t:s}$; thus, the ratio $MS_{t:s}/MS_{p:tsM}$ produces the $F$-ratio for testing whether there are differences among the means for the teachers within the same schools. Note also that $MS_{t:s}$ is the error term for testing the school effect, since its $E(MS)$ includes all components for the school effect (the numerator) except the one to be tested, $\sigma_s^2$. Confirm that the error term for testing the method ($M$) effect is the mean square for $M \times s$ interaction. For testing the school ($s$) effect, the denominator of the $F$-test is the mean square for $t{:}s$. Confirm that to test the $t{:}s$, $Ms$, and $Mt{:}s$ effects, the error terms are the mean squares associated with the $p{:}tsM$, $Mt{:}s$, and $p{:}tsM$ sources of variation, respectively.[26]

## 19.20 THE INCREMENTAL GENERALIZATION STRATEGY: INFERENTIAL "CONCENTRIC CIRCLES"

Notice in Table 19.5 that the error mean square for the $F$-test for the method effect has only 2 degrees of freedom. Consequently, the critical $F$ for the method effect is large (i.e., ${}_{.95}F_{2,2} = 19.0$); large critical $F$'s also mean less power. With mixed-model ANOVA designs, fixed

[24]The coefficients are needed only when variance components are to be determined (Section 19.12). The coefficients are not required for the purpose of defining the ingredients of the $E(MS)$ for effects, and, hence, for selecting the correct denominator (error term) for making $F$-tests that are appropriate for the desired inferences.

[25]To maintain consistency with previous notation, $n$ will continue to represent the number of persons within each cell of a balanced design.

[26]If a design contains two random effects that cross, there will be no appropriate $F$-ratio for testing certain effects; in such cases follow the incremental inference strategy described in Section 19.20. Approximate ("quasi-$F$") methods are sometimes applicable (see, e.g., Winer et al., 1991, pp. 374–377), but are best done after safer, albeit more limited, inferences are addressed.

effects often have error terms with few degrees of freedom. This is especially unfortunate because the principal research interest lies in the fixed effects (e.g., treatment)—the random factors are usually of ancillary interest and are included to address questions of external validity.[27] In Table 19.5, the method effect has a nonsignificant $F$-ratio of 2.11, and $p = .321 > .05 = \alpha$; yet, in Table 19.4 using the same data, but ignoring the school factor, these same data produced a significant method effect ($p = .019$)—an effect that was generalizable to the populations of pupils and teachers![28] How can a significant and generalizable effect suddenly disappear? Explicating the school factor adds rigor to the analysis by addressing inferential questions directly (rather than gratuitously), yet the price was the loss of statistical significance of the method effect! Behind this paradox lies a latent and fundamentally important issue in statistical inference: Real but ignored random factors are implicitly treated as fixed effects. Readers of research need to keep this in mind as they ponder questions of generalizability. As a practical matter, how are researchers to deal rationally and fairly with data that involve random factors, given that the more careful and rigorous they are about making their statistical analyses congruent with the desired inferences, the less likely they are to have findings that achieve statistical significance?

There is a second problem with statistical orthodoxy: It can occasionally result in incredible and logically untenable conclusions. For example, in one study (see Hopkins, 1983), the method effect was statistically significant when teachers were treated as a random effect, but the effect was not significant if teachers were treated as a fixed factor! Certainly, if one cannot generalize method effects implemented by the teachers in the study (the only teachers on whom data are available), to a different sample of students how can one safely generalize method effects to the population of teachers? Such implausible results must be type-I errors.[29] Such illogical, inferential predicaments can be prevented by the incremental inference strategy (Hopkins, 1983) that employs "*concentric circles*" of inference (see Figure 19.2).

First, the data are analyzed treating all factors (except the replication factor, typically subjects) as fixed. This analysis loop assesses whether the findings are strong enough to allow generalization to other subjects—the population of subjects sampled in the study (see universe (circle) #1 in Figure 19.2). Then, *if*, and only if, significance is obtained in this limited circle (universe of inference), is the inference to universe #2 considered, by defining a second factor as random (if indeed the factor is a random factor in the desired universe of inference) to see if the findings are generalizable to the desired universe of inference.

For example, in Table 19.5, one would initially treat pupils as a random effect and schools and teachers as fixed factors, then *if* effects are significant (universe #1), a second loop of analyses is conducted that treats teachers as a random factor. This loop assesses whether the findings are generalizable to the populations of pupils *and* teachers (universe #2). Finally, if a finding continues to be significant, a third loop of analyses is conducted that treats schools as a random factor to see if findings are generalizable to the populations of pupils, teachers, *and* schools (universe #3).

---

[27]It is counterintuitive, but nevertheless true, that in a design having one random factor the expected mean squares for the random effects (the main effect for that factor and the interactions of that factor with fixed factors) are not affected, but the $E(MS)$ for all fixed effects are affected.

[28]Note that whenever the error mean square changes in ANOVA, it will also change accordingly for multiple comparison purposes.

[29]These are the situations in which the computed variance component for the denominator of the $F$-test would be negative. If we use rational judgment to "better estimate" the variance component as 0, we should apply the same reasoning to prevent type-I errors.

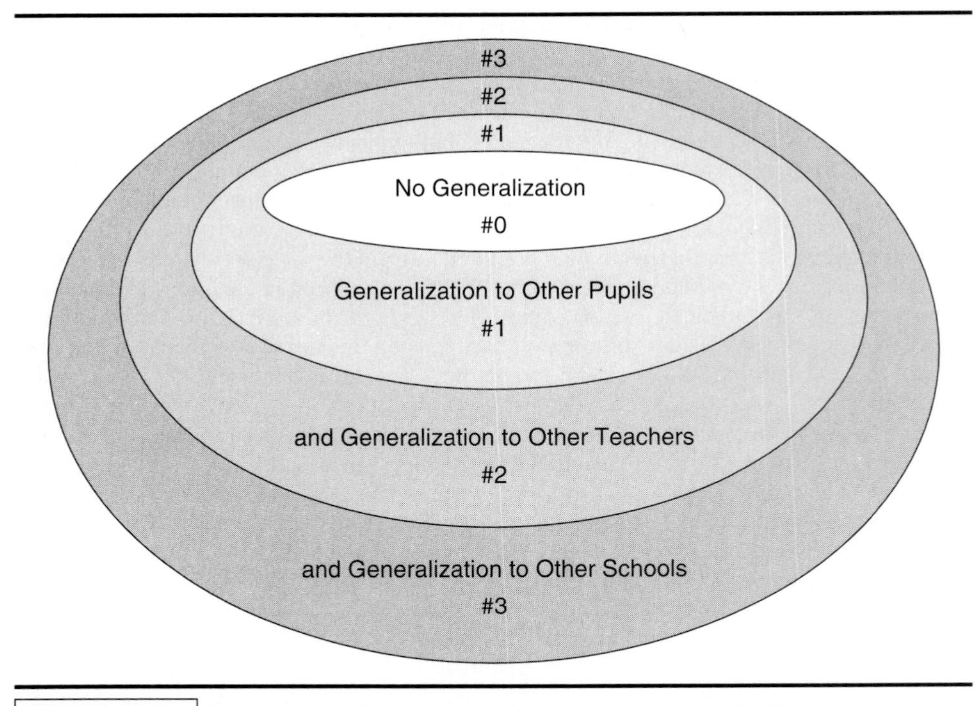


**FIGURE 19.2** Concentric circles representing various universes of inference.

For example, in the initial analysis of the data in Table 19.5, the null hypothesis that is tested for the method ($M$) effect pertains to the question: "Can the method effect be generalized to universe #1—other students (e.g., to next year's students) in these schools with these teachers?" Note that, in this conclusion, both teachers and schools are fixed. If this inferential hurdle is jumped ($H_0$ is rejected), the method effect that is tested in loop #2 is: "Can the method effect be generalized to universe #2—to other students *and* teachers in these schools?" The inferential question regarding universe #3 (when there is one) is then asked for those effects for which $H_0$ has been rejected in universes #1 and #2. The effect that is tested then becomes: "Can the method effect be generalized to universe #3—to other students *and* other teachers *and* other schools?" Stated differently, the students are viewed as a random sample of the population of students *and* the teachers are viewed as a random sample of the population of teachers *and* the schools are viewed as a random sample of the population of schools to *all* (students, teachers, and schools) of which one wishes to generalize.

This incremental inferential strategy has the advantage of assessing in a step-by-step sequence the extent to which the results are generalizable to specific universes of inference, rather than settling for a single universe of inference (and the universe for which power is often quite limited due to the small $\nu$ in the denominator of the $F$-test).[30]

[30]The incremental inference strategy also provides more credible information about inferences from complex ANOVA designs that rest on fragile inferential grounds ("quasi-$F$")—designs that do not yield the proper error term for an effect, and for which the error mean square must be constructed from variance components.

**TABLE 19.6** Expected Mean Squares in the Incremental Inference Strategy for ANOVA Design in Table 19.5 for Inferential Concentric Circles 0–3.

| | *E(MS)* | | | | |
|---|---|---|---|---|---|
| | *All factors (including students) are fixed* (#0) | *Pupils are random* (#1) | *Teachers are also random* (#2) | *Schools are also random* (#3) | *Computed MS* |
| Method (*M*) | $nTS\sigma_M^2$ | $+ \sigma^2_{p:TSM}$ | $+ n\sigma^2_{Mt:S}$ | $+ nT\sigma^2_{Ms}$ | 217.2 |
| School (*s*) | $nTM\sigma_S^2$ | $+ \sigma^2_{p:TSM}$ | $+ nM\sigma^2_{t:S}$ | | 758.1 |
| Teacher (*t:s*) | $nM\sigma^2_{T:S}$ | $+ \sigma^2_{p:TSM}$ | | | 103.8 |
| $M \times s$ | $nT\sigma^2_{MS}$ | $+ \sigma^2_{p:TSM}$ | $+ nn\sigma^2_{Mt:S}$ | | 102.9 |
| $M \times t{:}s$ | $n\sigma^2_{MT:S}$ | $+ \sigma^2_{p:TSM}$ | | | 36.11 |
| Within (*p:tsM*) | $\sigma^2_{p:TSM}$ | | | | 36.67 |

Table 19.6 gives the *E*(*MS*)'s for the various sources of variation found in Table 19.5 when all factors are fixed (universe #0), when one effect (pupils) is random (universe #1), when two effects (students and teachers) are random (universe #2), and when three effects (students, teachers, and schools) are random (universe #3).

In universe #0, there is no random source of variation, hence the data are viewed as parameters, and there is no inference to other pupils, teachers, or schools. The research is viewed as a *descriptive* study; no question of generalizability is addressed.

Universe #1 represents the classical ANOVA (and *t*-test) applications (the type that is the default for most ANOVA computer programs). With school and teacher factors defined as fixed, the question that is addressed is whether the findings are generalizable to the population of students sampled in the study in *these* two schools and with *these* ten teachers. The *F*-test for each effect is formed by dividing the value of its *MS* by the common error term—the within cell mean square ($MS_W = MS_{p:TSM} = 36.67$). In this restricted universe of inference (#1), the *F*-ratios (and *p*-values) for the various effects become: method ($F = 5.92$, $p = .0032$), school ($F = 20.7$, $p < .0001$), teacher (within method) ($F = 2.83$, $p = .0055$), $M \times s$ ($F = 2.81$, $p = .0631$), and *Mt:s* ($F = .98$, $p = .475$). Note that the method (*M*), school (*s*), and teacher-within-school effects (*t:s*) are all generalizable to the population of students. The $H_0$'s for the $M \times s$ and *Mt:s* effects are tenable.

If in addition to pupils, teachers are also viewed as a random sample from a larger population of teachers to which one wishes to generalize (universe #2), the *F*-ratios for certain effect are altered: method (*M*), school (*s*), and the $M \times s$ interaction (see *E*(*MS*)'s in Table 19.6). Since the $M \times s$ interaction was not significant in universe #1 (with the teacher factor regarded as fixed), it is not tested in any subsequent loop.[31] In universe #2, the method (*M*) effect continues to be significant ($F = 6.01$, $p = .025$); this legitimizes the inference of method differences to the associated populations of pupils and teachers. The school (*s*) effect also continues to be significant in universe #2, although the associated *p*-value drops considerably ($F = 7.30$, $p = .027$); school differences are expected even if a different sample of teachers (and students) were involved.

[31] If it were tested, $F = 2.85$, and $p = .0873$.

If schools are also viewed as a random factor (universe #3), the method effect is no longer significant ($F = 2.11$, $p = .321$)—as was found in the orthodox analysis given in Table 19.5.

What has been gained from the incremental strategy? Significant method effects were found that were generalizable to populations of pupils and teachers, which would have been latent in the orthodox analysis given in Table 19.5. The method findings were not robust enough to confidently generalize the method effects to all schools in the population of schools. Since the effect was tested with only two degrees of freedom in the error term, with a larger sample of schools (and more power) the findings might be found to be generalizable. At any rate, we are far less likely to believe the null hypothesis than if only the analysis shown in Table 19.5 had been performed.

## 19.21 MODEL SIMPLIFICATION AND POOLING

An analysis alternative (or complement) to the incremental inference strategy is based on logic (not mathematics). In certain situations, like that in Table 19.5, the critical-$F$ for certain effects can be large because the error terms have few degrees of freedom. In such situations, some data analysts (e.g., Green & Tukey, 1960; Winer et al., 1991) recommend that the ANOVA model be evaluated to see if it can be simplified (unless significance was obtained without simplification). If the model can be simplified, any effect having an $F$-ratio below 1 (or below some other critical $F$-value, such as that for $\alpha = .25$) can be dropped from the model.[32]

In Table 19.5, the $Mt{:}s$ effect has an $F$-ratio less than 1; thus, $H_0$ is tenable and it is reasonable to view $\sigma^2_{Mt:s} = 0$. Consequently, logic suggests that this component can be deleted from the model—from the $E(MS)$'s for the various effects. The expected consequence is that the critical-$F$ for certain effects will decrease because an error term with more degrees of freedom can be found. For example, in universe #2 in Table 19.6, the denominator for the method ($M$) effect is $Mt{:}s$ (method-by-teacher-within-school interaction), which has only 16 degrees of freedom. If $\sigma^2_{Mt:s} = 0$, then $\sigma^2_{p:tsM}$ is a proper error term for the $F$-test for the method effect; thus, the critical-$F$ drops from $_{.95}F_{2,16} = 3.63$ to $_{.95}F_{2,180} = 3.05$. Although in this example, nothing is changed, if the $F$-ratio had been less than 3.63 but greater than 3.05, model simplification would have allowed a basis for rejecting the null hypothesis.

Since $H_0$ for the $M \times s$ interaction is suspect ($p = .09$), it should not be dropped from the model. However, if the results had been different (e.g., $p > .25$), and both $Mt{:}s$ and $Ms$ components could have been deleted from the model, the change in the critical $F$-value for the method effect would have been dramatic ($_{.95}F_{2,2} = 19.0$ versus $_{.95}F_{2,180} = 3.05$) in universe #3.

In many instances (as with the $M \times s$ effect here), however, pooling is not an option because the observed $F$-ratios substantially exceed 1.0, and the model cannot be legitimately simplified. Since model simplification rests on logic (and not mathematical statistics) when it is employed, the results should be given before and after so that readers can make their own evaluations of the conclusions.[33]

---

[32]The larger the value of $\alpha$, the safer the model simplification or pooling strategy.

[33]Some advocate that, after model simplification, all sources of variation that have the same components be *pooled* to form an error term with more degrees of freedom. This probably should be done only for sources of variation that have $F$'s > 1, and that will not lower the value of the resulting error mean square.

## 19.22 THE EXPERIMENTAL UNIT AND THE OBSERVATIONAL UNIT

In the analysis of experiments, a distinction must be made between the observational unit in the statistical analysis and the experimental unit. *Observational* units are the units on which the data (the actual numbers) that one considers to be outcomes of the study are obtained. The number of observational units in a statistical analysis is greater (by 1) than the total number of degrees of freedom from all the sources of variation in the ANOVA table. The *experimental* unit is that entity that is allocated to a treatment independently of the other entities. It may contain several observation units (Addelman, 1970) as, for example, when classrooms are randomly assigned to treatments but there are several students within the classroom. In repeated-measures designs (Chapter 20), the experimental unit is usually a person and the observational unit is a score on a trial or test or some other dependent measure.

There has been much confusion about the proper method of analysis in studies in which there are several observational units (e.g., students) per experimental unit (e.g., classes) (Hopkins, 1982). The most common recommendation in such situations has been to compute the class (or group) mean and make the observational unit identical with the experimental unit.

Three methods of analysis will be compared using data from a study (DeRosia, 1980) in which two methods of instruction are contrasted. Three teachers are nested within each method, and twenty-five students are nested within each teacher. If the teacher factor is ignored in the analysis, the implicit model for the score for the $i$th student ($i = 1, \ldots, n$) in the $m$th ($m = 1, \ldots, M$) method is

$$X_{im} = \mu + \alpha_m + \varepsilon_{i:m} \qquad \textbf{(Model A)}$$

The assumptions of normality, homogeneity of variance, and independence pertain to the $\varepsilon$'s, that is, $\varepsilon_{i:m} \sim NID(0, \sigma_\varepsilon^2)$ (i.e., within each of the $M$ methods, the errors, $\varepsilon$'s, are normally and independently distributed and have a mean of 0, and a common variance, $\sigma_\varepsilon^2$). The expected mean squares $E(MS)$ for Model A are given in panel A of Table 19.7; the right-hand portion of panel A gives the results of the analysis of the data using Model A. Analyses such as this that use scores from individual students have been widely criticized since Lindquist (1940) because the method and teacher effects are inextricably confounded; it is included here for purposes of comparison. Any difference in "method" means may be due to teacher or method difference or both. The results using Model A are shown in panel A of Table 19.7.

If, instead of using student scores as the observational unit, class means for the T teachers (t = 1, ..., T) were employed, the model becomes

$$X_{tm} = \mu + \alpha_m + b_{t:m} \qquad \textbf{(Model B)}$$

where $b_{t:m} \sim NID(0, \sigma_b^2)$. This is the model advocated by Lindquist (1940) and Campbell and Stanley (1966) for studies in which the treatment is group oriented and can result in non-independence among the students' scores. The $E(MS)$'s for Model B along with the analysis using Model B are found in panel B of Table 19.7. Notice that the "highly significant"

**TABLE 19.7** Expected Mean Squares for a Balanced ANOVA Design (and Illustrative Analyses) in Which $n$ Pupils are Nested within $T$ Teachers, Which Are Nested within $M$ Methods, Using Three Models (from Hopkins, 1982).

| *SV* | $\nu$ | $E(MS)$ | Example $\nu$ | Example *MS* | Example *F* |
|---|---|---|---|---|---|
| A. [Model A: $X_{im} = \mu + \alpha_m + \varepsilon_{i:m}$] | | | | | |
| Methods ($M$) | $M - 1$ | $\sigma^2_{p:M} + n\sigma^2_M$ | 1 | 2,814.6 | 7.69[a] |
| Pupils nested within method ($p:M$) | $M(n - 1)$ | $\sigma^2_{p:M}$ | 148 | 366.2 | |
| B. [Model B: $X_{tm} = \mu + \alpha_m + b_{t:m}$] | | | | | |
| Methods ($M$) | $M - 1$ | $\sigma^2_{t:M} + T\sigma^2_M$ | 1 | 112.6 | 1.99 |
| Teachers nested within method ($t:M$) | $M(T - 1)$ | $\sigma^2_{t:M}$ | 4 | 56.5 | |
| C. [Model C: $X_{itm} = \mu + \alpha_m + b_{t:m} + \varepsilon_{i:tm}$] | | | | | |
| Methods ($M$) | $M - 1$ | $\sigma^2_{p:tM} + n\sigma^2_{t:M} + nT\sigma^2_M$ | 1 | 2,814.6 | 1.99 |
| Teachers nested within method ($t:M$) | $M(T - 1)$ | $\sigma^2_{p:tM} + n\sigma^2_{t:M}$ | 4 | 1,412.7 | 4.19[a] |
| Pupils nested within teachers and methods ($p:tM$) | $MT(n - 1)$ | $\sigma^2_{p:tM}$ | 144 | 337.1 | |

[a]$p < .01$

($p = .006$) methods effect that was found when Model A (panel A) was used disappears ($p = .231$) when Model B is employed.

When there are several observational units per experimental unit, *both* $b_{t:m}$ and $\varepsilon_{i:tm}$ should be included in the model. Since both types of errors include sampling error due to factors unknown to or beyond the control of the experimenter, neither should be deleted from the model at the whim of the experimenter. Model C incorporates components both for teachers (or classes) and students; both are viewed as random effects because the desired inference is to a population of teachers that was sampled as well as to a population of students sampled. The linear model for the design in which $n$ students are nested within $T$ teachers who, in turn, are nested within $M$ methods is:

$$X_{itm} = \mu + \alpha_m + b_{t:m} + \varepsilon_{i:tm} \qquad \textbf{(Model C)}$$

In Model C, there are two sets of assumptions, that is, $\varepsilon_{i:tm} \sim NID(0, \sigma_\varepsilon^2)$ and $b_{t:m} \sim NID(0, \sigma_b^2)$. In other words, since teachers are properly viewed as a random effect, a second layer of assumptions is required in the desired universe of inference. If scores from individual students are used as observational units and the data are analyzed using Model C (students are nested within teachers who are nested within methods), and if teachers are appropriately designated as a random factor, the expected mean squares for the effects are given in panel C of Table 19.7. The analysis of the sample data using Model C is given in the right-hand portion of panel C in Table 19.7.

It is apparent from Table 19.7 that, for balanced designs, the $F$-ratio for the methods effect is the same whether the class means or individual observations are used, since the methods mean square would be divided by the teachers within-methods mean square ($t:M$)

in both instances. Even though the mean squares for methods in Models B and C will differ (by a factor of $n$), the $F$-ratios for treatment will be identical in the two analyses, and these $F$'s will have identical degrees of freedom and critical $F$'s.

Note that if the proper ANOVA model is employed, the question of the proper unit of analysis is taken care of implicitly. When the proper ANOVA model is used, although the analyses are identical as far as the method effect is concerned, the analyses using individual students in Model C are preferred because the hypothesis concerning the teacher within-method effect can be evaluated. In addition, by retaining individual scores in the analysis, the researcher can consider incorporating personological variables into the design so that interactions of these factors with treatment effects can be evaluated. These interactions speak directly to critical generalizability questions. An additional advantage of Model C is that it allows the incremental inference strategy or model simplification (or pooling) to be considered.

## 19.23 CHAPTER SUMMARY

When the levels of a factor represented in a study do not exhaust the levels in the population, but are viewed as a sample of the levels in the population, the factor is said to be random, not fixed. The levels of a random factor are assumed to be normally distributed.

In addition to $F$-tests for random effects, variance components are ordinarily calculated to estimate the variance among the means of the various levels in the population. Multiple comparisons and trend analysis (Chapter 17) are meaningful only for fixed factors.

When a random factor and a fixed factor cross, the resulting model is said to be mixed ANOVA model. Although the procedures for determining mean squares for the various sources of variation are unaffected by whether factors are fixed or random, the associated $F$-ratios for fixed effects will change in the mixed model. The error mean square (error term) for any source of variation is defined by its expected mean square; the denominator of the $F$-test for that effect contains all the components of the numerator except for the effect to be tested. The expected mean square for any effect includes, in addition to itself, a component for any random effect that either crosses that effect, or is nested within that effect. Expected mean squares are also needed to compute variance components; variance components should be estimated for random effects.

Most ANOVA factors are crossed (i.e., each level of every factor appears in combination with each level of every other factor). When each level of a factor $b$ appears only within one level of another factor $A$, factor $b$ is said to be nested within factor $A$, that is, $b{:}A$. If $b{:}A$, the $A \times b$ interactions cannot be evaluated. Nested factors are usually random factors.

With mixed-model ANOVA designs, the incremental inference strategy is recommended: The initial analysis views all factors as fixed. For effects that are significant in this universe of inference, other factors that are random in the desired universe of inference are sequentially analyzed as random.

## 19.24 CASE STUDY/APPLICATION

An experimental study (Bleakley, Westerberg, & Hopkins, 1988) was done to assess the effect of the sex of the main character [character sex ($C$)] of short stories on the interest level of the stories for upper elementary pupils. It was hypothesized that the factor of character sex would interact with the sex of the reader [reader sex ($R$)]. To control for the intrinsic interest level among the novel stories, each story was edited into two versions that were identical except that the sex of the protagonist was male in one version and female in the other. The reading ability level of the student [reader ability ($A$)] was also included. Three stories were selected for each of three story types (mystery, humor, and adventure) [type of story ($T$)] since the effects of factor $C$ may differ depending on the type of reading content.

The sample of 540 pupils[34] was stratified by sex and reading ability, then the 18 various story versions (three mystery, three humor, and three adventure, each with a male and a female protagonist) were randomly assigned to the students such that a balanced design was achieved with $n = 5$ pupils per cell. After reading the story, each student completed an eight question inventory designed to assess the story's interest level for the pupil.

Answer the following questions that pertain to this ANOVA design.

a. How many factors are there? Identify them by letter abbreviation.[35]
b. Which factors are fixed (in the desired universe of inference)?[36]
c. Which factor is random? Is it nested?[37]
d. If the incremental inference strategy is employed, what will be the error term for testing all other effects in the first universe of inference?[38]
e. If story is viewed as a random effect in the second concentric circle, what *additional* component will be included in the $E(MS)$ for the $R$, $T$, $R \times C$, and $R \times s{:}T$ sources of variation?[39]
f. How many degrees of freedom are there for the five main effects (C, $R$, $A$, $T$, and $s{:}T$)?[40]
g. How many degrees of freedom are there for the $R \times C$, $R \times C \times T$, and the $R \times C \times s{:}T$ interactions?[41]

The ANOVA table from this study is given in Table 19.8.

h. For *these* stories, did the mean interest rating differ depending on the sex of the main character ($\alpha = .05$)? Is this finding generalizable to other stories like these?[42]
i. For *these* stories, did the mean interest rating for females differ from that for males? Is this finding generalizable to other stories like these?[43]
j. Did the high ability readers tend to report greater interest in the stories than the low ability readers for these stories? Why was this question not addressed in universe #2 (where stories were defined as a random factor)?[44]
k. Did the average reader interest level differ for the three types of stories? Is this generalization limited to these stories?[45]

---

[34]A few students were randomly dropped to achieve a balanced design.

[35]Five factors: Character sex ($C$), Reader sex ($R$), Ability ($A$), type of story ($T$), and story ($s$).

[36]$C, R, A, T$.

[37]Story; yes, within type of story ($s{:}T$). Pupils are nested within all factors.

[38]The within cell variance, the mean square for pupils nested within all other factors ($p{:}sTARC$).

[39]The components $nCA\sigma^2_{Rs:T}$, $nCAR\sigma^2_{s:T}$, $nA\sigma^2_{RCs:T}$, and none, respectively.

[40]For $C$: 1, $R$: 1, $A$: 2, $T$: 2, and 6 for $s{:}T$.

[41]1, 2, and 6, respectively.

[42]Yes (although not evident from Table 19.8, it is higher for male protagonist: 50.2 vs. 48.5); no ($p = .104$).

[43]Yes (although not evident from the ANOVA table, the females had the higher mean, 50.4 vs. 48.2, effect size ≈ .2); yes (although the significance level drops from .008 to .026).

[44]No ($p = .068$); because if a finding is not significant in universe #1, it is logically implausible for it to be significant in universe #2 (if it were computed: $F = 2.24$, $p = .149$).

[45]Yes; no, it is not limited (although $p$ increased from .0000018 to .007).

**TABLE 19.8** ANOVA Table for a Five-Factor Mixed-Model Design.

| | | | | | *Universe #1* | | *Universe #2 (Story random)* | | | |
|---|---|---|---|---|---|---|---|---|---|---|
| | *Source of Variation* | *SS* | $v$ | *MS* | *F* | *p* | *F* | *p* | $MS_{error}$ | $\sigma^2$ |
| 1 | Character sex ($C$) | 370.02 | 1 | 370.02 | 4.21 | **.043** | 3.67 | .104 | $C \times s{:}T$ | |
| 2 | Reader sex ($R$) | 651.2 | 1 | 651.20 | 7.40 | **.008** | 8.56 | .026 | $R \times s{:}T$ | |
| 3 | Ability level ($A$) | 488.08 | 2 | 244.04 | 2.77 | .068 | * | | $A \times s{:}T$ | |
| 4 | Type of story ($T$) | 2719.22 | 2 | 1359.61 | 15.45 | **.0000018** | 12.47 | **.007** | $s{:}T$ | |
| 5 | Story ($s{:}T$) | 654.18 | 6 | 109.03 | 1.24 | .294 | | .294 | | .35 |
| 6 | $C \times R$ | 2252.98 | 1 | 2252.98 | 25.60 | **.0000023** | 14.69 | **.009** | $C \times R \times s{:}T$ | |
| 7 | $C \times A$ | 16.24 | 2 | 8.12 | .09 | .912 | * | | $C \times A \times s{:}T$ | |
| 8 | $C \times T$ | 118.34 | 2 | 59.17 | .67 | .513 | * | | $C \times s{:}T$ | |
| 9 | $C \times s{:}T$ | 605.22 | 6 | 100.87 | 1.15 | .343 | | .343 | | .43 |
| 10 | $R \times A$ | 133.12 | 2 | 66.56 | .76 | .472 | * | | $R \times A \times s{:}T$ | |
| 11 | $R \times T$ | 164.02 | 2 | 82.01 | .93 | .398 | * | | $R \times s{:}T$ | |
| 12 | $R \times s{:}T$ | 456.66 | 6 | 76.11 | .86 | .524 | | .524 | | 0† |
| 13 | $A \times T$ | 132.76 | 4 | 33.19 | .38 | .824 | * | | $A \times s{:}T$ | |
| 14 | $A \times s{:}T$ | 1306.92 | 12 | 108.91 | 1.24 | .271 | | .271 | | 1.05 |
| 15 | $C \times R \times A$ | 9.16 | 2 | 4.58 | .05 | .949 | * | | $C \times R \times A \times s{:}T$ | |
| 16 | $C \times R \times T$ | 99.82 | 2 | 49.91 | .57 | .569 | * | | $C \times R \times s{:}T$ | |
| 17 | $C \times R \times s{:}T$ | 920.34 | 6 | 153.39 | 1.74 | .120 | | .120 | | 4.36 |
| 18 | $C \times A \times T$ | 617.96 | 4 | 154.49 | 1.76 | .145 | * | | $C \times A \times s{:}T$ | |
| 19 | $C \times A \times s{:}T$ | 851.52 | 12 | 70.96 | .81 | .643 | | .643 | | 0† |
| 20 | $R \times A \times T$ | 170.4 | 4 | 42.60 | .48 | .747 | * | | $R \times A \times s{:}T$ | |
| 21 | $R \times A \times s{:}T$ | 1098.6 | 12 | 91.55 | 1.04 | .420 | | .420 | | .36 |
| 22 | $C \times R \times A \times T$ | 527.84 | 4 | 131.96 | 1.50 | .209 | * | | $C \times R \times A \times s{:}T$ | |
| 23 | $C \times R \times A \times s{:}T$ | 603.72 | 12 | 50.31 | .57 | .859 | | .859 | | 0† |
| 24 | Within ($p{:}CRAsT$) | 38011.7 | 432 | 87.99 | | | | | | 87.99 |
| | total | 52980 | 539 | | | | | | | |

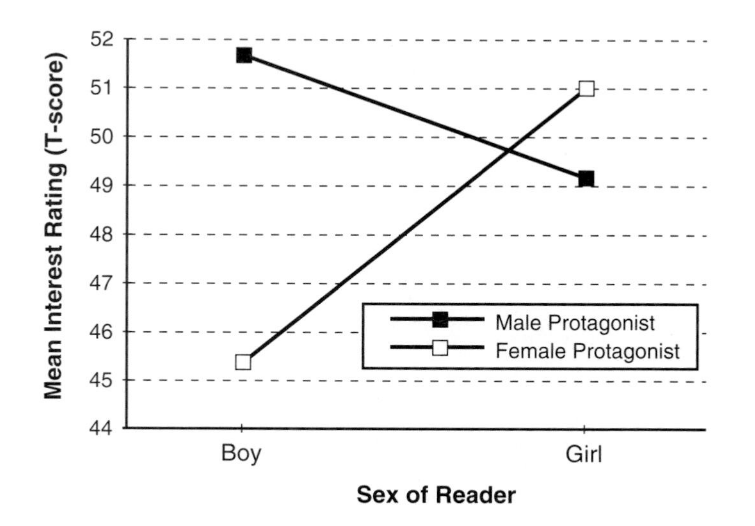


*$F$-ratio not computed for universe #2 because the null hypothesis in universe #1 was not rejected.

†Computed value of variance component was negative.

l. Were certain stories within a given story type more interesting than others of the same type?[46]
m. Which source of variation reveals whether boys prefer "boy" stories and girls prefer "girl" stories? Was the finding generalizable to the populations of stories like these?[47]
n. The figure in Table 19.8 gives the graph for the $C \times R$ interaction. Was this configuration generalizable to all three ability levels? Did the pattern differ depending on the type of story? Was the same pattern evident on all the stories within type of story?[48]
o. In question (i) above, it was found that the mean reader interest level was higher for females than for males. Was this pattern consistent (1) across all three ability levels, and (2) for all three story types?[49]
p. Which sources of variation had no change in their $F$-ratios between universe #1 and universe #2?[50]
q. If ability level had been ignored, other things being the same, how many sources of variation would be eliminated from the ANOVA table? Which sources of variation would change as a result of ignoring the ability factor? The $\nu_W$ would increase by how many? None of the sources of variation involving ability even approached significance; this being the case would you expect the value of $MS_{\text{Within}}$ to differ substantially after all the sources of variation involving ability were pooled into the new within ($p{:}CRsT$)?[51]
r. What distinguishes those sources of variation for which a variance component is, and is not, given (column $\hat{\sigma}^2$)?[52]
s. What pattern (and implication) is evident in the $F$-ratio for those effects in column $\hat{\sigma}^2$ that have a value of "0" for $\hat{\sigma}^2$?[53]
t. Other than the variance component for individual differences within cells ($\hat{\sigma}^2_{p:CRAsT}$), which effect has the largest value for the estimated variance component? Compare its value for $p$ with the $p$-values associated with the other variance components.[54]

## MASTERY TEST

1. Which of the following factors would almost always be viewed as fixed?
   (a) Teachers (b) Raters (c) Treatments (d) Schools
2. In the random model $X_{ij} + a_j + \varepsilon_{ij}$ which of the components are assumed to be normally distributed?

---

[46]No ($p = .294$).

[47]$C \times R$, yes.

[48]Yes, no, yes.

[49]Yes, for the $R \times A$ interaction, $p = .472$; for the $R \times T$ interaction, $p = .398$.

[50]Those which contain the factor, story, that was defined as a random factor.

[51]Twelve effects would be eliminated. $MS_{\text{within}}$ would change from $MS_{p:CRAsT}$ to $MS_{p:CRST}$. $\nu_W$ would increase by 72. In this example, the value of $MS_{\text{within}}$ would not change much because the effects involving ability have an average $F$-ratio $\approx 1$. A second dependent variable, reading comprehension, was employed in the same study; if the ability factor had been ignored, the value of $MS_{\text{within}}$ would have increased 76% (from 55.5 to 97.8), and the $F$-ratios for all effects (not involving ability) would have decreased dramatically in universe #1 (see Section 18.25).

[52]They are random effects, that is, those given all contain the "ingredient" $s$ (story).

[53]They all have $F$-ratios that are less than 1.0 (i.e., they were set equal to 0 because the computations yielded a negative value).

[54]$C \times R \times s{:}T$; it has the smallest $p$-value.

**3.** Does the random model in question 2 assume that $\sigma_a^2 = \sigma_\varepsilon^2$?

**4.** If a factor is random, one ordinarily would

(a) determine the variance component for that factor.
(b) perform multiple comparisons on that factor if $H_0$ is rejected.
(c) perform a trend analysis on that factor if $H_0$ is rejected.

**5.** A Treatment by school ANOVA design (in the desired universe of inference) is an example of a

(a) fixed model.
(b) mixed model.
(c) random model.

**6.** If certain teachers employ method *E* and other teachers employ method *C*,

(a) teachers are nested within method.
(b) teachers cross methods.
(c) methods are nested within teachers.

**7.** Which of the following notations denotes that teachers ($t$) are nested within method ($M$)?

(a) $M{:}t$ (b) $t \times M$ (c) $M \times t$ (d) $t{:}M$

**8.** Are $A \times B$ and $B \times A$ synonymous?

**9.** Are $A{:}B$ and $B{:}A$ synonymous?

**10.** If a factor is nested, it is almost always a ____ (fixed or random) factor.

**11.** Which of the following would rarely, if ever, be considered random factors?

| (a) method | (b) experimenter | (c) test items | (d) sex |
|---|---|---|---|
| (e) school | (f) teacher | (g) school district | (h) type of school |
| (i) SES | (j) ability level | (k) rater (judge) | (l) person |

**12.** If factor $a$ is a random factor and $a_j = \mu_j - \mu$, which of the following is *not* assumed?

(a) $\sigma_a^2 = 0$. (b) The $a_j$'s are normally distributed. (c) The $a_j$'s are independent.

**13.** The interaction of two factors, *A* and *B*, can be assessed only if

(a) both factors are fixed.
(b) both factors are random.
(c) factor *A* is nested with factor *B*.
(d) factor *B* is nested within factor *A*.
(e) factors *A* and *B* cross.

**14.** In a balanced two-factor ANOVA design in which persons ($p$) are nested within both factors, *A* and *B*, *a more explicit* notation of the "within" source of variation is

(a) $p{:}A$ (b) $p{:}B$ (c) $p{:}AB$ (d) $AB{:}p$

**15.** Are the computations and *F*-tests in a *one-factor* random ANOVA model identical with those in a one-factor fixed model?

**16.** If the $H_0$ being tested is true, are the expected values of the numerator and the denominator of the proper *F*-test equal?

**17.** Is the expected value of *F* equal to 0 when $H_0$ is true?

**18.** In a factorial ANOVA design, are the computed values of the mean squares affected by whether or not one or more of the factors is random? Are the *F*-ratios for all effects the same?

*Items 19–28 pertain to an ANOVA design in which pupil outcomes from a highly structure kindergarten curriculum (E) were compared with the conventional kindergarten curriculum (C) on a comprehensive measure of cognitive, affective, and social measures. Six teachers used each curriculum for both morning (AM) and afternoon (PM) classes. The data used is from twenty (n = 20) randomly selected pupils within each class.*

| | Teacher | AM | PM |
|---|---|---|---|
| Method $E$ | $t_1$ | | |
| | $t_2$ | | |
| | $t_3$ | | |
| | $t_4$ | | |
| | $t_5$ | | |
| | $t_6$ | | |
| Method $C$ | $t_7$ | | |
| | $t_8$ | | |
| | $t_9$ | | |
| | $t_{10}$ | | |
| | $t_{11}$ | | |
| | $t_{12}$ | | |

*The ANOVA table given below pertains to this study. The E(MS) are for the desired universe of inference.*

| *SV* | *E(MS)* | $\nu$ | *MS* | *F* | *p* |
|---|---|---|---|---|---|
| Method ($M$) | $\sigma^2_{p:tMA} + 40\sigma^2_{t:M} + 240\sigma_M^2$ | 1 | 2505 | ____ | ____ |
| Teacher ($t{:}M$) | $\sigma^2_{p:tMA} + 40\sigma^2_{t:M}$ | 10 | 3488 | ____ | <.001 |
| AM/PM ($A$) | $\sigma^2_{p:tMA} + 20\sigma^2_{At:M} + 240\sigma_A^2$ | 1 | 3218 | ____ | ____ |
| $M \times A$ | $\sigma^2_{p:tMA} + 20\sigma^2_{At:M} + 120\sigma_{AM}^2$ | 1 | 95 | ____ | ____ |
| A $\times$ $t{:}M$ | $\sigma^2_{p:tMA} + 20\sigma^2_{At:M}$ | ____ | 264 | .85 | >.25 |
| $p{:}tMA$ (within) | $\sigma^2_{p:tMA}$ | 456 | 310 | | |

**19.** Complete the missing value for degrees of freedom.

**20.** The ____ factor is nested within ____?

**21.** In the desired universe of inference, is the design a fixed or mixed ANOVA model? Which factors are fixed?

**22.** Use the incremental universe of inference analysis strategy (Section 19.20) and see if the findings are generalizable to other students for *these same teachers* (universe #1). As a consequence of viewing teachers as a fixed rather than random factor, the expected mean square of which sources of variation (effects) will change? [Put parentheses around the *E*(*MS*) components for these effects that will be excluded in universe #1.] The error term (denominator) for all *F*-tests in universe #1 is ____.

**23.** Complete the *F*-tests and give corresponding *p*-values ($p < .25$, $< .05$, $< .01$, or $< .001$) for all main effects and interactions in universe #1. Which null hypotheses can be rejected ($\alpha = .05$)?

**24.** Although the means are not given, the significant difference between the *E* and *C* means favored the *E* classes. Did the *E* classes tend to be superior for both morning and afternoon classes for these teachers?

**25.** The afternoon classes outperformed the morning classes; were there significant exceptions to this pattern for certain teachers, for example, was the pattern reversed from some teachers? Did the teachers with high means for AM classes also tend to have high means in their PM classes?

26. *Within* each of the methods, were there significant difference among the teachers?
27. Now view teachers as a random factor (universe #2). The error term for testing the method effect now becomes the mean square for ____. Can the superiority of the $E$ method be safely generalized to other teachers?
28. In universe #2, the $F$-ratios for which other main effect changes? Give the $F$-ratio for this effect for universe #2. The critical $F$ is based on ____ and ____ degrees of freedom. Can $H_0$ rejected? ($p$ ____ ____). Is the pattern of higher means in the afternoon classes generalizable to other teachers like those participating in the study?
29. Will the $A \times t{:}M$ effect be tested in universe #2? Why?
30. Estimate the variance component for teachers ($\sigma^2_{t:M}$).
31. If the $M$ effect had been significant, and there had been, not two, but three methods, would one use multiple comparisons or a trend analysis? In universe #2, the error mean square for this purpose is the $MS$ value for ____.
32. If teachers were randomly assigned to experimental and control groups, and scores from twenty students per class are used in the analysis, the observational unit is the ____ and the experimental unit is the ____.
33. The smallest unit which is independent assigned to treatment condition is the ____ (observational or experimental) unit. Must the observational unit be the same as the experimental unit in order for the statistical analysis to be valid?
34. Table 19.7 demonstrates that if the ANOVA design is balanced, the statistical tests for the method main effect give identical results irrespective of whether the observational unit is the teacher, or student [if classes (teachers), and students are viewed as random effects]. (T or F)

## PROBLEMS AND EXERCISES

1. A random sample of ten judges was drawn from a population of judges. Each judge evaluated a randomly assigned sample of $n$ = 20 science projects for creativity using a 7-point scale. The analysis of variance yielded the following results:

| *SV* | $\nu$ | *MS* | *E(MS)* |
|---|---|---|---|
| Judge ($j$) | 9 | 60 | $\sigma^2_{p:j} + 20\sigma^2_j$ |
| Projects ($p{:}j$) | 190 | 10 | $\sigma^2_{p:j}$ |

(a) Are some judges more lenient in their ratings than others?
(b) Estimate the variance component for judges, $\sigma^2_j$.
(c) Compare the sizes of $\sigma^2_{p:j}$ and $\sigma^2_j$.

2. Criteria for a population of words are specified, and the 30,000 spelling words in this population is identified. A test publisher is interested in how much variability ($\sigma^2_t$) is to be expected among 100-item (randomly selected) spelling tests formed from the pool of 30,000 words. (The total number of possible 100-item tests equal to the combinations of 30,000 items taken 100 at a time is incredibly large; see Equation 9.10, Section 9.9.) A researcher constructs six 100-item spelling tests by randomly sampling items from the item pool. Thus, the $J$ = 6 tests ($t$) can be considered to be randomly sampled from the population of all possible 100-item tests, and $t_j = \mu_j - \mu$. Each test is given to an independent random sample of $n$ = 25 pupils. The following results are obtained for the six tests:

| | *Test (j)* | | | | | | |
|---|---|---|---|---|---|---|---|
| | *1* | *2* | *3* | *4* | *5* | *6* | |
| $\bar{X}_j$: | 48.4 | 51.7 | 52.3 | 47.3 | 49.4 | 50.9 | $\bar{X}_{\bullet} = 50.0$ |
| $s_j^2$: | 101.8 | 94.9 | 106.3 | 102.1 | 95.8 | 99.0 | $\sum_j s_j^2 / J = 10.0$ |
| $t_j$: | −1.6 | 1.7 | 2.3 | −2.7 | −.6 | .9 | |

(a) Using the one-factor random-effects ANOVA, give the two sources of variation, $t$ and $p{:}t$, the respective $\nu$'s, and their $E(MS)$'s (see Table 19.3).

(b) Estimate the variance among the population of spelling test means, $\sigma_t^2$, and the variance of pupils' scores within a spelling test, $\sigma_{p:t}^2$.

**3.** At the end of the school year in each of four randomly selected schools ($s$), two first grade classes ($c$) were randomly selected. Within each class, ten boys and ten girls ($G$) were randomly selected, half of which are randomly assigned to treatment ($T$) $E$ (parental guided reading) and $C$ (control).

(a) How many students are involved in the study?

(b) In the desired universe of inference, which factors (in addition to pupils) are random effects, and which are fixed effects?

(c) What is a more explicit denotation of the "within" source of variation?

(d) In universe #1, view pupils as the only random source of variation; list the various sources of variation for this design, and give the degrees of freedom and $E(MS)$ for each.

(e) In universe #2, view classes as a random effect. Which sources of variation will have an additional component? Add this component in parentheses.

(f) In universe #3, also view schools as a random effect. Which sources of variation will have an additional component? Add this component in brackets.

**4.** In a two-factor random-effects ANOVA with $J$ levels of factor $a$, $K$ levels of factor $b$, and $n$ observations per cell, the expected values of the mean squares are:

$$E(MS_a) = \sigma^2 + n\sigma_{ab}^2 + nK\sigma_a^2$$

$$E(MS_b) = \sigma^2 + n\sigma_{ab}^2 + nJ\sigma_b^2$$

$$E(MS_{ab}) = \sigma^2 + n\sigma_{ab}^2$$

$$E(MS_W) = \sigma^2$$

Find the combination of the mean squares that proves an unbiased estimator of $\sigma_a^2$ and $\sigma_{ab}^2$. (*Hint*: Notice how $\sigma_b^2$ is estimated.) $E(MS_b - MS_{ab}) = (\sigma^2 + n\sigma_{ab}^2 + nJ\sigma_b^2) - (\sigma^2 + n\sigma_{ab}^2) = nJ\sigma_b^2$, thus, $\sigma_b^2 = (MS_b - MS_{ab})/nJ$

## ANSWERS TO MASTERY TEST

1. (c)
2. $a_j$ and $\varepsilon_{ij}$
3. No
4. (a)
5. (b)
6. (a)
7. (d)
8. yes
9. no
10. random
11. (a), (d), (h), (i), (j)
12. (a)
13. (e)
14. (c)
15. yes
16. yes
17. No, $E(F) \approx 1$; more precisely, $E(F) = \nu_e/(\nu_e - 2)$.

18. no, no
19. 10
20. teacher, method
21. mixed method and AM/PM
22. $M$, $A$, $M \times A$; $40\sigma^2_{t:M}$, $20\sigma^2_{At:M}$, and $120\sigma\sigma^2_{At:M}$, respectively; $MS_W = 310$
23. $F$-ratios (top to bottom): 8.08, 11.25, 10.38, .31; $p < .01$, $< .001$, $< .01$, $> .25$, respectively; $H_0$'s for $M$, $t:M$, and $A$ are rejected.
24. yes
25. no, yes
26. yes
27. $t:M$ or 3488, no ($F = .72$, $p > .25$)
28. $A$, $F = 12.19$, 1 and 10, yes ($p < .01$)
29. no, effects that are not significant in universe #1 are not tested in universe #2.
30. $\hat{\sigma}^2_{t:M} = (3488 - 310)/40 = 79.45$
31. multiple comparisons, $t:M$ (or 3488)
32. pupil, class
33. experimental, no
34. true

## ANSWERS TO PROBLEMS AND EXERCISES

1. (a) yes, $F = 6.0$, $p < .001$; (b) $\sigma_j^2 = (60 - 10)/20 = 2.5$; (c) $\sigma_j^2 = 2.5$, $\sigma^2_{p:t} = 10$. The variance for projects is four times as great as the variance among the judges.
2. (a)

| *Source* | $v$ | *E(MS)* |
|---|---|---|
| Test ($t$) | 5 | $\sigma^2_{p:t} + 25\sigma t^2$ |
| Pupils ($p:t$) | 144 | $\sigma^2_{p:t}$ |

(b) $\sigma^2_{p:t} = MS_W = 100$, $\sigma_t^2 = (MS_t - MS_W)/n$, $MS_t = ns_{\overline{X}}^2 = 25(3.84) = 96.0$, $(96 - 100)/25 = -.16$; set to zero.

3. (a) $n \times G \times C \times S \times T = 5 \times 2 \times 2 \times 4 \times 2 = 160$. (b) school and class, treatment and gender. (c) $MS_W = MS_{p:GcsT}$.
(d) (e) (f)

| | *SV* | $v$ | *E(MS)* | |
|---|---|---|---|---|
| Treatment ($T$) | 1 | $\sigma_W^2 + 80\sigma_T^2$ | $+ (10\sigma^2_{Tc:s})$ | $+ [20\sigma^2_{Ts}]$ |
| Gender ($G$) | 1 | $\sigma_W^2 + 80\sigma_g^2$ | $+ (10\sigma^2_{Gc:s})$ | $+ [20\sigma^2_{Gs}]$ |
| School ($s$) | 3 | $\sigma_W^2 + 40\sigma_s^2$ | $+ (20\sigma^2_{c:s})$ | |
| Class ($c:s$) | 4 | $\sigma_W^2 + 20\sigma^2_{c:s}$ | | |
| $T \times G$ | 1 | $\sigma_W^2 + 40\sigma^2_{TG}$ | $+ (5\sigma^2_{TGc:s})$ | $+ [10\sigma^2_{TGs}]$ |
| $T \times s$ | 3 | $\sigma_W^2 + 20\sigma^2_{Ts}$ | $+ (10\sigma^2_{Tc:s})$ | |
| $T \times c:s$ | 4 | $\sigma_W^2 + 10\sigma^2_{Tc:s}$ | | |
| $G \times s$ | 3 | $\sigma_W^2 + 20\sigma^2_{Gs}$ | $+ (10\sigma^2_{Gc:s})$ | |
| $G \times c:s$ | 4 | $\sigma_W^2 + 10\sigma^2_{Gc:s}$ | | |
| $T \times G \times s$ | 3 | $\sigma_W^2 + 10\sigma^2_{TGs}$ | $+ (5\sigma^2_{TGc:s})$ | |
| $T \times G \times c:s$ | 4 | $\sigma_W^2 + 5\sigma^2_{TGc:s}$ | | |
| within ($p:GcsT$) | 128 | $\sigma_W^2$ | | |

4. $$\hat{\Sigma}^2_{\hat{a}} = \frac{E(MS_a) - E(MS_{ab})}{nK}$$
$$\hat{\Sigma}^2_{\hat{ab}} = \frac{E(MS_{ab}) - E(MS_W)}{n}$$

# REPEATED-MEASURES ANOVA

## 20.1 INTRODUCTION

The mixed-effects ANOVA model with $n = 1$ (i.e., one observation per cell) is frequently encountered in research and is commonly known as a *repeated-measures* design. For example, each person (or other observational unit) in a group may be observed on the *same* variable on several different occasions. Alternately, scores on several *different* measures that express performance using the same metric (such as standard scores or grade equivalents) may be available on each subject. ANOVA designs of this type are commonly described as a *repeated-measures* design[1] because the dependent measures on the experimental units (e.g., persons or whatever variable defines the levels of a random factor—teachers, schools, businesses) occur several times, not just once.

In learning experiments, subjects typically receive a score on each of several trials; in such designs, *trials* is the repeated-measures factor. In developmental and other longitudinal studies, the same subjects are assessed periodically on certain variables (e.g., height, reaction time, cholesterol levels, cognitive style, etc.) to discover developmental patterns. In such studies, the repeated-measures factor is age.

In the High School and Beyond study, all results on the various achievement tests were expressed as $T$-scores. A repeated-measures ANOVA could be run on some group (Asians, private school students, females, etc.) to see if their profile of means was flat (as the null hypothesis states), or whether there are significant peaks or valleys.

## 20.2 A SIMPLE REPEATED-MEASURES ANOVA

The simplest example of a repeated-measures design is one in which there are two main effects, subjects (or whatever the unit on which observations are made) and measures. The

[1]In some sources, they are described as split-plot designs. EXCEL's "Anova: Two-factor without Replication" counts persons as a factor, and can be used to analyze designs like that given in Table 20.1.

subjects factor is a random factor (because we wish to generalize the results from our sample to other subjects—actually to the population); the repeated-measures factor is typically a fixed effect such as trial or another ordered variable such as age. An observation in the simple repeated-measures ANOVA model will be denoted by $X_{st}$, denoting the $t$th measure for the $s$th subject:[2]

$$X_{st} = \mu + a_s + \beta_t + a\beta_{st} + \varepsilon_{st} \quad \textbf{(20.1)}$$

Suppose there are five measures for each of ten subjects, (i.e., $S = 10$ levels of the random factor *Subjects*, and $T = 5$ levels of the fixed *Trials* factor), as shown in the upper portion of Table 20.1. The sum of squares for the row factor (subjects), the column factor (trials), and for the interaction (subjects-by-trials, $s \times T$) can all be calculated using the computational formulas in Chapter 19 (Table 19.4), noting that the number of observations per cell is 1.[3] Since $n = 1$, there are $ST(n - 1) = 0$ degrees of freedom for the within cells variation; obviously, there can be no within cell variance with $n = 1$—the single observation in each cell is also the mean of the cell. Table 20.1 is edited output from the spreadsheet *EXCEL*'s repeated-measures ANOVA.

The ANOVA table and expected mean squares for the three sources of variation appear in the middle section of Table 20.1. The expected mean square for the trials factor is $\sigma_{sT}^2 + S\sigma_T^2$(see Table 20.1); the expected mean square for the $s \times T$ interaction is $\sigma_{sT}^2$ (cf. cell G21), thus the $F$-ratio for the trials factor is $MS_T/MS_{sT}$ 65.95/.372 = 177.18. The $F = MS_T/MS_{sT}$ can be compared with ${}_{1-\alpha}F_{(T-1),[(T-1)(S-1)]}$ to test $H_0$ at the $\alpha$-level of significance. The null hypothesis for the interaction cannot be tested since $\sigma_\varepsilon^2$ is not available.[4]

## 20.3 REPEATED-MEASURES ASSUMPTIONS

In addition to the usual ANOVA assumptions (independence of observation between subjects, and homogeneity of variance and normality of error), an additional assumption is

---

[2]For mnemonic purposes, the first letter of a factor is often used to denote that factor (rather than the generic $A$ and $B$, or $J$ and $K$). Fixed factors are denoted by Greek letters; roman letters indicate random factors.

[3]The mean squares for the two main effects can be computed directly, recalling that the mean square (variance estimate) for an effect is the variance error of the level means for that factor multiplied by the number of observations on which each of the level means is based. For the mean square for subjects: the variance error of the ten subject means is .5956, thus $MS_{\text{subjects}} = T(.5956) = 5(.5956) = 2.978$. The mean square for trials is the number of subjects (10) multiplied by $s_{\overline{X}}^2 = 10(6.595) = 65.95$. The sum of squares for the interaction can be obtained by subtracting the sum of squares for each of the two main effects from the total sum of squares, where $SS_{sT} = SS_{\text{total}} - SS_s - SS_T$, and $SS_{\text{total}} = \Sigma_j\Sigma_k(X_{jk} - \overline{X}_{\bullet\bullet})^2$

[4]In theory, the observation within each cell is viewed as a random sample of $n = 1$ observation from a population of observations with variance $\sigma_\varepsilon^2$. Since there is only one score per cell, the within-cell variance $\sigma_\varepsilon^2$ cannot be estimated directly and is excluded from the $E(MS)$'s in Table 20.1; $\sigma_\varepsilon^2$ is confounded with $\sigma_{sT}^2$. It is possible to test $H_0$:$\sigma_{sT}^2 = 0$, by using a "test of non-additivity" devised by Tukey (Hays, 1988, pp. 512–525; Winer et al., 1991, pp. 352–354). This test is also incorporated as an option on several statistical software packages. For the data in Table 20.1 the condition of additivity (no interaction) is tenable ($p > .10$).

The "Subjects" factor is usually not tested; there is no mean square with the proper expected value. Since the $E(MS)$ for the $s \times T$ interaction is at least as large as $\sigma_\varepsilon^2$ (the proper error term), if a test of the Subjects factor is desired, $F = MS_s/MS_{sT}$ can be used as a conservative test (that is, if this null hypothesis is tenable, $MS_{sT}$ can be viewed as an estimate of the $\sigma_\varepsilon^2$). For example, the $F$-ratio ($F = 2.978/3.72 = 8.01$) for "Subjects" in Table 20.1 is a conservative estimate because $MS_{sT}$ is a composite of interaction ($\sigma_{sT}^2$) and within-cell ($\sigma_\varepsilon^2$) variance.

**TABLE 20.1** A Simple Repeated-Measures ANOVA: Ten Subjects Observed on Five Measures

| | | Trials | | | | | Subject Mean | Subject Effect | |
|---|---|---|---|---|---|---|---|---|---|
| | Subjects | $T_1$ | $T_2$ | $T_3$ | $T_4$ | $T_5$ | $\bar{X}_{s\bullet}$ | $\hat{a}_s$ | $\hat{a}_s^2$ |
| | $s_1$ | 1 | 2 | 4 | 5 | 6 | 3.6 | –.8 | .64 |
| | $s_2$ | 1 | 1 | 3 | 5 | 6 | 3.2 | –1.2 | 1.44 |
| | $s_3$ | 1 | 2 | 5 | 7 | 6 | 4.2 | –.2 | .04 |
| | $s_4$ | 2 | 1 | 4 | 6 | 7 | 4.0 | –.4 | .16 |
| | $s_5$ | 3 | 3 | 5 | 8 | 8 | 5.4 | 1.0 | 1.00 |
| | $s_6$ | 2 | 2 | 4 | 7 | 8 | 4.6 | .2 | .04 |
| | $s_7$ | 1 | 3 | 4 | 6 | 7 | 4.2 | –.2 | .04 |
| | $s_8$ | 0 | 2 | 5 | 7 | 8 | 4.4 | .0 | .00 |
| | $s_9$ | 3 | 3 | 6 | 8 | 9 | 5.8 | 1.4 | 1.96 |
| | $s_{10}$ | 2 | 2 | 4 | 7 | 8 | 4.6 | .2 | .04 |
| *Trial Mean* | $\bar{X}_{\bullet t}$ | 1.6 | 2.1 | 4.4 | 6.6 | 7.3 | 4.4 | | $\Sigma\hat{a}_s^2 = 5.36$ |
| *Trial Effect* | $\hat{\beta}_t$ | –2.8 | –2.3 | .0 | 2.2 | 2.9 | | | |
| | $\hat{\beta}_t^2$ | 7.84 | 5.29 | 0.0 | 4.84 | 8.41 | $26.38 = \Sigma\hat{\beta}_t^2$ | | |

***ANOVA Table***

| *Source of Variation* | *SS* | ν | *MS* | *F* | *p* | *E(MS)* |
|---|---|---|---|---|---|---|
| Subjects ($s$) | 26.8 | $S - 1 = 9$ | 2.978 | | | $T\sigma_s^2$ |
| Trials ($T$) | 263.8 | $T - 1 = 4$ | 65.950 | 177.18 | <.001 | $\sigma_{sT}^2 + S\sigma_T^2$ |
| $s \times T$ | 13.4 | 36 | .372 | | | $\sigma_{sT}^2$ |
| Total | 304 | 49 | | | | |

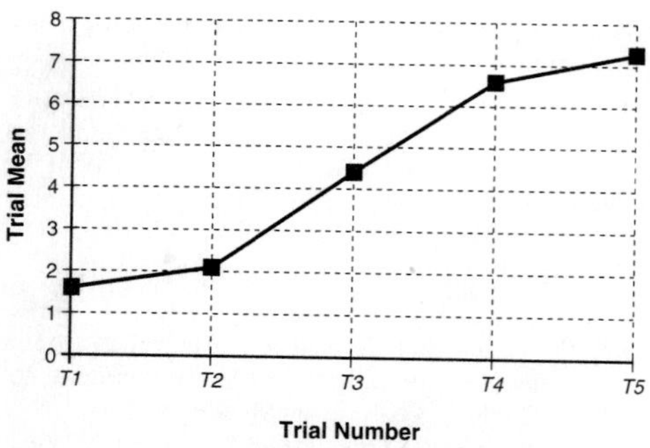


***Trend Analysis***

| *SV* | ν | *MS* | *F* | *p* |
|---|---|---|---|---|
| Linear | 1 | 252.81 | 506.7 | <.001 |
| error (1) | 9 | .499 | | |
| Quadratic | 1 | .064 | .119 | .738 |
| error (2) | 9 | .540 | | |
| Cubic | 1 | 10.89 | 34.88 | <.001 |
| error (3) | 9 | .312 | | |
| Quatric | 1 | .036 | .260 | .622 |
| error (4) | 9 | .137 | | |

made in repeated-measures ANOVA, sphericity. If the $T$ levels of the fixed repeated-measures factor have homogeneity of variance ($\sigma_1^2 = \ldots = \sigma_T^2$) and all correlations between pairs of levels are equal ($\rho_{12} = \rho_{13} = \ldots = \rho_{(T-1)T}$), then $F = MS_T/MS_{sT}$ will have a central $F$-distribution with $T-1$ and $(T-1)(S-1)$ degrees of freedom when $H_0$: $\mu_1 = \ldots = \mu_T$ is true. These conditions (compound symmetry) are *sufficient* to give correct probability statements in repeated-measures designs, but in recent years have been shown to be more restrictive than necessary. Huynh and Feldt (1970, 1979) demonstrated that the assumption of *sphericity* (that variances of *differences* for all pairs of levels of the repeated-measures factor are equal)[5] is sufficient to obtain central $F$-distributions with the nominal degrees of freedom. The condition of compound symmetry is, however, more intuitive than the *necessary* and *sufficient* condition of sphericity. Although the sphericity rationale is complex, its practical application does not require mathematical understanding.[6]

When the sphericity assumption is violated, the actual probability of a type-I error is greater than the purported $p$-value (i.e., $\alpha > p$). When correlations among the pairs of levels of the fixed factor are heterogeneous, or when the variances for the levels are heterogeneous, special correction procedures can be employed to insure that the probability of a type-I error is not greater than claimed. The absence of sphericity results in sampling distributions of $F = MS_T/MS_{sT}$ that have fewer degrees of freedom than given in the ANOVA table (i.e., less than $(T-1)$ and $(T-1)(S-1)$.[7]

Huynh and Feldt proposed a measure, epsilon ($\varepsilon$), that describes the degree of departure from the sphericity assumption. When sphericity is evidenced, $\hat{\varepsilon}$ is 1.0; at worst, $\hat{\varepsilon}$ is $1/(T-1)$ (i.e, the $\nu$ for the repeated-measures factor is reduced from $T-1$ to 1). In other words, $1 \geq \hat{\varepsilon} \geq 1/(T-1)$, and the degrees of freedom for the repeated-measures factors is $\hat{\varepsilon}(T-1)$. The value of epsilon can be used to compensate for the absence of sphericity by adjusting the associated degrees of freedom for effects that involve the repeated-measures factor.[8] Using the Huynh-Feldt adjustment, the critical $F$-value used to test the main effect for the repeated-measures factor $T$ becomes ${}_{1-\alpha}F_{\varepsilon(T-1),[\varepsilon(T-1)(S-1)]}$. For the data in Table 20.1 the value of epsilon is 1, indicating that the sphericity assumption was not violated, therefore no correction in the $\nu$'s is needed. If the correlations among the various pairs of trials had differed greatly, the variances of the mean *differences* between pairs of levels would have been dissimilar, the value of the epsilon would have been less than 1, and the critical $F$ would have increased accordingly.

The Huynh-Feldt correction is finding its way into standard statistical programs for

---

[5]This is tested by "Mauchley's test of sphericity" (Winer et al., 1991); it is included in BMDP, SPSS and certain other statistical software packages. This test is not very powerful with small samples, and is overly sensitive when $n$ is large (Dixon et al., 1988). We recommend using the Huynh-Feldt epsilon adjustment to degrees of freedom for establishing critical values of $F$.

[6]See Appendix D7 in Hays (1988), or Winer et al. (1991, pp. 239–261).

[7]Box (1954) and Greenhouse and Geisser (1959) have demonstrated that, *at worst*, the degrees of freedom for the critical $F$ for testing the repeated-measures factor $T$ are 1 and $S-1$, that is, ${}_{1-\alpha}F_{1,S-1}$. Greenhouse and Geisser proposed a procedure by which the degree of departure from the compound symmetry condition is measured and used to correct the critical $F$-values (by lowering the associated degrees of freedom). Huynh and Feldt (1979) have shown that the Greenhouse-Geisser procedure is unnecessarily conservative.

[8]Box also devised a different epsilon measure (popularized by Greenhouse and Geisser), that describes the degree of departure from compound symmetry. In Table 20.1 the value of epsilon is .800, thus the adjusted degrees of freedom are .80(4) = 3.2 and .80(36) = 28.8, and the critical-$F$ (rounding $\nu$ downward) is $2.95 = {}_{.95}F_{3,28}$. The Huynh-Feldt epsilon measure provides less conservative (and more accurate) estimates of the probability of a type-I error that reflect the degree of departure from sphericity; for the data in Table 20.1, the Huynh-Feldt epsilon value is 1, legitimizing the use of the nominal critical-$F$ value of $2.63 = {}_{.95}F_{4,36}$.

repeated-measures AVOVAs. In practice, probability statements using the nominal degrees of freedom, $(T-1)$ and $(T-1)(S-1)$, are rarely seriously underestimated (Collier, Baker, Mandeville, & Hays, 1967), nevertheless, the method-of-choice for the analysis of repeated-measures ANOVA is to use the $p$-values yielded by the Huynh-Feldt adjustment.[9] When there are only two levels of the repeated-measures factor, the sphericity (and compound symmetry) condition will always be met. When there is just one off-diagonal element (or correlation), heterogeneity in the covariance matrix is impossible.

## 20.4 TREND ANALYSIS ON REPEATED-MEASURES FACTORS[10]

In repeated-measure designs, the levels of the repeated-measures factor are often ordered (i.e., the levels represent an ordinal or interval scale) as in Table 20.1. Trend analysis[11] is usually more informative than multiple comparisons[12] when a continuum underlies the repeated-measures factor. Recall from Chapter 17 (Sec. 17.19) that trend analysis is a special application of planned orthogonal contrasts, and is appropriate even when the $F$-test for the main effect is not statistically significant.

The interpretations of the trends were described in Sec. 17.19. Note in the trend analysis table in Table 20.1 that both the linear and cubic trends are significant, but the quadratic and quartic trends are not. These linear and cubic trends common in learning studies are evident from the trend line shown in the graph in Table 20.1.

It should be noted that the trend analysis illustrated in Table 20.1 uses a different error mean square for each trend. No assumption of compound symmetry or sphericity is necessary for this type of trend analysis.[13]

## 20.5 ESTIMATING RELIABILITY VIA REPEATED-MEASURES ANOVA

If an outcome measure represents only measurement error, any real treatment effects will be missed. A measure must have some reliability if it is to have any validity; if the dependent variable contains nothing but measurement error, its reliability coefficient will be 0.[15] It is good practice to estimate and report reliability coefficients for the outcome measures, especially when they are developed by the researcher. For example, one research study com-

---

[9]Another alternative is to use a multivariate analysis of variance procedure (MANOVA) that makes less restrictive assumptions (but has less power than the repeated-measures ANOVA when ANOVA's assumptions are met (see Section 20.10).

[10]Analyses like this (and most others in this and subsequent chapters) are too time-consuming and too likely to result in computational errors to do by hand. Any good statistical software package will have a trend analysis procedure for repeated-measures ANOVA.

[11]Termed "orthogonal polynomial contrasts" by some computer programs.

[12]For example, if the Tukey method were used, the differences between the means of trials 1 and 2, and between trials 4 and 5 would not have been sufficient to reject $H_0$.

[13]If the sphericity assumption is tenable, the $SS$'s and $\nu$'s for the error terms can be pooled so that the critical-$F$ can be reduced due to the increase in degrees of freedom. Rarely, however, will this procedure alter a conclusion.

[14]Section 20.5 is an instructional cul-de-sac; we will return to the main road in Section 20.6.

[15]It is probably unfortunate that measurement theory is typically taught in special courses, and ignored in statistics courses. Measurement and statistics interface at many points.

pared two instructional methods on a reading comprehension test that was so easy that virtually every student answered all the questions correctly (resulting in a very low reliability coefficient); obviously, no difference will be found between the methods on such a measure even if one method is much better than the other.

The reliability coefficient describes the degree to which scores on a measure represent something other than measurement error. The proportion of error variance in the dependent measure is $1 - \rho_{XX}$ (where $\rho_{XX}$ is the reliability coefficient of the measure). If two sets of parallel measures agree perfectly, $\rho_{XX} = 1.00$. If examinees are unmotivated and mark answers without reading the questions, the differences among the subjects will represent only measurement error.

Suppose (for purposes of illustrating the computation of reliability) that the levels of the repeated-measures factor in the data in Table 20.1 represented, not trials, but items on a test or inventory (or independent ratings given by each of five raters). The reliability coefficient for the subjects' total (or average)[16] scores, can be estimated from Equation 20.2. The *reliability coefficient* of a measure estimates the correlation between the observed scores and the score on a parallel form of the measure:

$$\hat{\rho}_{XX} = 1 - \frac{MS_{sT}}{MS_s} \qquad \textbf{(20.2)}$$

where, $MS_{sT}$ is the $s \times T$ interaction mean square (often labeled *residual*), and $MS_s$ is the mean square *between* subjects (persons, examinees, ratees, or whatever unit is being measured). Thus, using Equation 20.2, the reliability coefficient of the total scores in Table 20.1 is $\hat{\rho}_{XX} = 1 - .372/2.978 = .875$.[17]

## Reliability and Length: The Spearman-Brown Formula

If the length of a measure is changed, the reliability coefficient of the new measure ($\rho'_{XX}$), assuming that the new set of items samples the same universe of content as the original set of items, can be estimated from the *Spearman-Brown* formula (Equation 20.3).

$$\rho'_{XX} = \frac{L\rho_{XX}}{1+(L-1)\rho_{XX}} \qquad \textbf{(20.3)}$$

---

[16]Since average score is a linear transformation of total score, the reliability coefficient is the same for each.

[17]The use of ANOVA to estimate the reliability of a measure was first proposed by Hoyt, and is sometimes described as Hoyt reliability. The reliability coefficient given by Equation 20.2 is identical to the widely used "Cronbach's alpha," $\rho_\alpha$ (although the formula for Cronbach's alpha does not require an ANOVA):

$$\rho_\alpha = \left(\frac{K}{K-1}\right)\left(1 - \sum_k \frac{\sigma_K^2}{\sigma^2}\right)$$

where the measure is composed of $K$ parts (items, ratings, etc.), $\Sigma^2_{k\sigma k}$ is the sum of the variance of the $K$ parts (trials in Table 20.1), and $\sigma^2$ is the variance of the total scores. In Table 20.1, the variances of each of the five parts are .933, .544, .711, 1.156, and 1.122 (which sum to 4.466), and the variance of total scores is 14.89, thus, $\rho_\alpha = 5/4(1 - 4.466/14.89) = .875$, which is identical with the value given by Equation 20.2.

The reliability estimated via Equation 20.2 has been shown to be the mean of all possible split-half reliability coefficients. It has been demonstrated (Cronbach & Azuma, 1962) that reliability estimated by Cronbach's alpha coefficient is a good estimate of parallel form reliability for unspeeded tests. (See Hopkins, Stanley, & Hopkins, 1990, Chapter 5 for an elementary introduction to reliability theory.)

where $\rho_{XX}$ is the reliability coefficient for the original measure, and $L$ is the *ratio* of the new length to the original length. For the data in Table 20.1, the reliability coefficient calculated using Equation 20.2 indicates that the measure was quite reliable ($.875 = 1 - .372/2.978$). Equation 20.3 can be used to estimate the reliability of the measure if it were shortened to three items ($L = 3/5 = .60$): $\rho'_{XX} = .6(.875)/[1 - .4(.875)] = .808$. Note that a highly reliable measure can often be shortened considerably with less loss of reliability than one might expect.[18] The Spearman-Brown formula assumes that the additional items or raters are of the same type (technically, that they are random samples from the same population of content, or raters).

## 20.6 REPEATED-MEASURES DESIGNS WITH A BETWEEN-SUBJECTS FACTOR

Repeated-measures ANOVA designs often include factors within which the subjects are nested. Effects associated with the repeated-measures factor (the factor or factors that subjects cross) are termed within-subjects effects. Effects pertaining only to factors within which subjects are nested are described as between-subjects effects. In previous chapters, all effects were between-subjects effects (i. e., the subjects were nested within all the factors).

In within-subject effects, subjects serve as their own controls; it is analogous to the paired $t$-test in this way (except that more than two measures can be involved). If there is a correlation between scores on the repeated-measures factor, the denominator of the $F$-test is reduced accordingly. Because of this, the magnitude of the mean differences needed to achieve statistical significance is reduced (and power is increased). Stated differently, the power for testing within-subjects effects is generally greater than the power for testing between-subjects effects.

The simplest ANOVA design that has both kinds of effects is obvious: a design with one between-subjects factor and one within-subjects factor. For example, one study (Omey, 1987) administered four measures of different Piagetian conservation tasks (liquid, mass, weight, volume) to deaf children. The children were classified into one of two different types of communication modes: consistent (the child's environment consisted of only *one* mode of communication—oral or manual) versus inconsistent (the child's environment was characterized by two modes of communication). There were sixteen subjects in each of the two communication mode groups. All subjects were tested on each of the four conservation tasks. Note that the subjects were nested within the communication mode factor, but crossed the four levels of the task factor; both the communication mode and the tasks factors are fixed—there was no intent to generalize to any other communication modes or types of conservation tasks. Subjects are a random effect because generalization to other children like those represented in the study was desired.

Table 20.2 gives the $E(MS)$'s and ANOVA results from the $2 \times 4$ communication mode by conservation task ANOVA (with subjects nested within communication mode). Note in

[18]Historically, a common method of estimating reliability has been to divide a test into two halves (usually odd and even numbered items or raters), then find the correlation between the two halves. This correlation estimates what the reliability of the measure would be if it were *one-half* its current length. The Spearman-Brown formula can then be used to obtain the corrected reliability estimate: If a measure is doubled in length the Spearman-Brown formula becomes $\rho'_{XX} = 2\rho_{XX}/(1 + \rho_{xx})$.

Suppose two raters judge the quality of an essay and have ratings that correlate .50; using the equation above, the reliability of the average of the two ratings is $2(.50)/(1 + .5) = .67$. Can you confirm that the reliability of the average rating if four raters are used is .80?

**TABLE 20.2** ANOVA Table for a Repeated-Measures Design with One Between-Subjects Factor.

| *Source of Variation* | ν | *E(MS)* |
|---|---|---|
| *Between Subjects* | | |
| 1 Communication mode (*C*) | $C-1 = 1$ | $\sigma^2_{s:C} + nT\sigma^2_C$ |
| 2 Subjects:*C* (*s:C*) | $C(n-1) = 30$ | $\sigma^2_{s:C}$ |
| *Within Subjects* | | |
| 3 Tasks (*T*) | $T-1 = 3$ | $\sigma^2_{Ts:C} + nC\sigma^2_T$ |
| 4 $C \times T$ | $(C-1)(T-1) = 3$ | $\sigma^2_{Ts:C} + n\sigma^2_{CT}$ |
| 5 $T \times s{:}C$ | $(T-1)(n-1)C = 90$ | $\sigma^2_{Ts:C}$ |

| | | | | | | | Huynh-Feldt Adjustment | |
|---|---|---|---|---|---|---|---|---|
| *Source of Variation* | *SS* | ν | *MS* | *F* | *p* | $MS_{error}$ | υ | *p* |
| *Between Subjects* | 347.99 | 31 | | | | | | |
| 1 Communication mode (*C*) | 76.57 | 1 | 76.57 | 8.46 | .007 | *s:C* | | |
| 2 Subjects:*C* (*s:C*) | 271.42 | 30 | 9.05 | $= \sigma^2_{s:C}$ | | | | |
| *Within Subjects* | 230.73 | 96 | | | | | ($\hat{\varepsilon} = .845$) | |
| 3 Tasks (*T*) | 24.32 | 3 | 8.11 | 3.63 | .016 | $T \times$ s:C | 2.54* | .017 |
| 4 $C \times T$ | 5.52 | 3 | 1.84 | .82 | .484 | $T \times$ s:C | 2.54 | .484 |
| 5 $T \times s{:}C$ | 200.89 | 90 | 2.23 | $= \hat{\sigma}^2_{Ts:C}$ | | | | |
| total | 578.72 | 127 | | | | | | |

*Round fractional degrees of freedom upward

*Multiple Comparisons on the Task Factor*

$MS_{\text{error}} = MS_{T \times s:C} = 2.23,\ s_{\bar{X}} = .263$

*Means*

| *Mass* | *Volume* | *Weight* | *Liquid* |
|---|---|---|---|
| 4.75 | 4.22 | 4.03 | 3.53 |

$q_1 = (4.75 - 3.53)/.263 = 4.64,\ p < .01$

$q_2 = (4.75 - 4.03)/.263 = 2.73,\ p > .10$

$q_3 = (4.22 - 3.53)/.263 = 2.62,\ p > .10$

the top portion of Table 20.2 that components of the expected mean squares for each effect (cf. Section 19.18) are (1) the effect itself, plus (2) the effect in a nested or crossed combination with the random effect (subjects). Note from the expected mean squares that the between-subjects and the within-subjects effects have different error terms. As previously noted, the error mean squares for the within-subjects effects are ordinarily smaller than the error mean squares for the between subjects.

The mean for the students in the consistent communication mode group was significantly higher than that for subjects in the inconsistent group ($p = .007$). The absence of a significant $C \times T$ interaction shows that this pattern was consistent across all four of the conservation tasks.

The computed Huynh-Feldt epsilon[19] value (.845) was less than 1.00, showing that the sphericity condition was not completely achieved, thus the degrees of freedom (and the associated $p$-values) for all effects involving the repeated-measures factor (tasks) should be adjusted accordingly (see last column of middle section of Table 20.2)—in this instance, the $T$, $C \times T$, and $T \times s{:}C$ effects. Note that the adjustment does not affect the observed $F$-ratios; only the critical-$F$'s and $p$-values are affected. The changes in the $p$-values are negligible; e. g., for the tasks factor, .022 versus .016. If the data set had differed dramatically from the sphericity condition (e.g., some tasks correlated positively, and others negatively) the differences in $p$-values would have been greater. The small differences among $p$-values apparent in Table 20.2 is common with real data.

The differences among the four task means was too large to be attributed to sampling error. To find on which conservation tasks the performance was more and less successful, the Newman-Keuls method is illustrated in the lower portion of Table 20.2. The procedures are the same as those given in Chapter 17, bearing in mind that $MS_{\text{error}}$ ($MS_{\text{error}} = 2.23$) is the denominator for testing the task main effect, here $MS_{T \times s:C}$ (sometimes expressed as $MS_{Ts:C}$ or $MS_{Ts(C)}$). The error mean square is divided by the number of *observations* on which each mean is based (here, $nC = 32$) to obtain $s_{\bar{x}} : s_{\bar{x}} = \sqrt{2.23/32} = .263$. Note that the only reliable difference between means was between the extremes; the deaf children had less success with conservation of liquid than with conservation of mass. The absence of the $C \times T$ interaction indicates that this pattern was evident for children in both communication mode groups.

## 20.7 REPEATED-MEASURES ANOVA WITH TWO BETWEEN-SUBJECTS FACTORS

Any number of between-subjects factors can be included in a repeated-measures ANOVA, be they fixed or random, nested or crossed. In the study given in Table 20.2, we ignored one of the between-subjects factors (age) to keep the initial example simple. Actually, students at four age levels were involved: 9, 11, 13, and 15. At each age level, there were four deaf students for each of the two communication modes. Thus, the ANOVA design is a $2 \times 4 \times 4$ communication mode-by-age-by-conservation task design, with subjects nested within communication mode and age, but crossing tasks. The results of this analysis are given in Table 20.3.

Notice that the $F$-ratios for the effects in Table 20.2 have become somewhat larger in Table 20.3; the numerators remain unchanged, but the denominators are reduced because

---

[19]Provided by the computer program; hand computation is not recommended.

**TABLE 20.3** ANOVA Table for a Repeated-Measures Design with Subjects Nested within Two Between-Subjects Factors.

| *Source of Variation* | *SS* | $\nu$ | *MS* | *F* | *p* | $MS_{error}$ | *E(MS)* |
|---|---|---|---|---|---|---|---|
| *Between Subjects* | 347.99 | 31 | | | | | |
| 1 Communication mode (*C*) | 76.57 | 1 | 76.57 | 11.05 | .003 | *s:CA* | $\nu^2_{s:CA} + nTA\nu^2_c$ |
| 2 Age level (*A*) | 84.77 | 3 | 28.26 | 4.08 | .018 | *s:CA* | $\nu^2_{s:CA} + nTC\nu_A{}^2$ |
| 3 C × *A* | 20.34 | 3 | 6.78 | .98 | .419 | *s:CA* | $\nu^2_{s:CA} + nT\nu^2_{CA}$ |
| 4 Subjects:*CA* (*s:CA*) | 166.31 | 24 | 6.93 | | | | $\nu^2_{s:CA}$ |
| *Within Subjects* | 230.74 | 96 | | | | | |
| 5 Task (*T*) | 24.32 | 3 | 8.11 | 3.83 | .013 | *T* × *s:CA* | $\sigma^2_{T\,s:CA} + nCA\nu^2_T$ |
| 6 *C* × *T* | 5.52 | 3 | 1.84 | .87 | .461 | *T* × *s:CA* | $\sigma^2_{T\,s:CA} + nA\nu^2_{CT}$ |
| 7 *A* × *T* | 39.01 | 9 | 4.33 | 2.05 | .046 | *T* × *s:CA* | $\sigma^2_{T\,s:CA} + nC\sigma^2_{AT}$ |
| 8 *C* × *A* × *T* | 9.45 | 9 | 1.05 | .50 | .873 | *T* × *s:CA* | $\sigma^2_{T\,s:CA} + n\sigma^2_{CAT}$ |
| 9 *T* × *s:CA* | 152.44 | 72 | 2.12 | | | | $\sigma^2_{T\,s:CA}$ |
| total | 578.73 | 127 | | | | | |

*Trend Analysis on Age Factor*

$MS_{\text{error}} = MS_{s:CA} = 6.93$ $\quad s_{\overline{X}} = .4654$ (Equation 17.8B)

| | *Age* | | | | | | | |
|---|---|---|---|---|---|---|---|---|
| | *9* | *11* | *13* | *15* | $\hat{\varphi}$ | $s_{\hat{\varphi}}$ | $t_{\hat{\varphi}}$ | *p* |
| *Means* | 3.0625 | 3.625 | 4.90625 | 4.9375 | | | | |
| *linear coefficients* | –3 | –1 | 1 | 3 | 6.906 | 2.081 | 3.318 | .003 |
| *quadratic coefficients* | 1 | –1 | –1 | 1 | –.531 | .931 | –.571 | .573 |
| *cubic coefficients* | –1 | 3 | –3 | 1 | –1.969 | 2.081 | –9.46 | .354 |

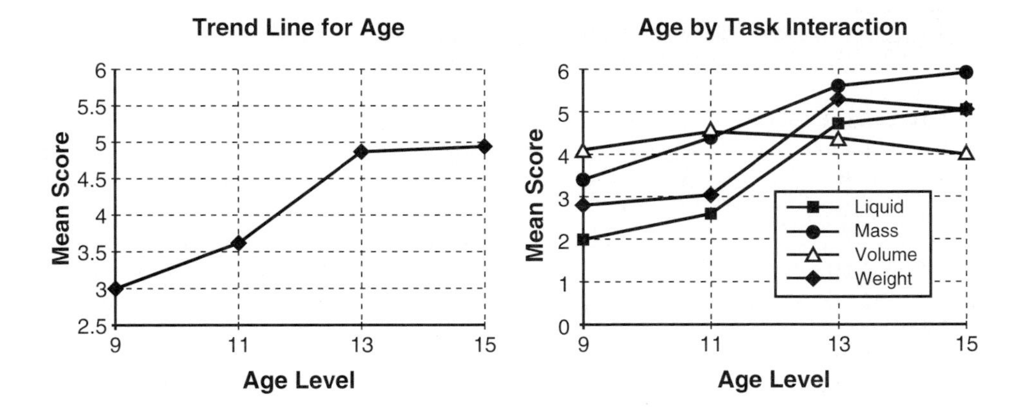

there are significant effects associated with the additional factor, age.[20] The Huynh-Feldt epsilon value in this design was 1.0; thus, no adjustments in the degrees of freedom values are required.

The lack of a significant $C \times A$ interaction indicates that the difference between the two communication mode groups (favoring the consistent group) was uniform across the four age levels—the difference was not influenced by the age of the students. The significant $A \times T$ interaction indicates that the pattern of differences among the means of the four types of conservation tasks was not consistent across age level. The interaction graph in the lower right of Table 20.3 shows that three of the four conservation tasks followed a similar pattern with age level. The conservation of volume, however, did not show this pattern for these subjects, hence the significant $A \times T$ interaction. The absence of the $C \times A \times T$ interaction indicates that the $A \times T$ interaction generalizes to subjects in both communication mode groups.

## 20.8 TREND ANALYSIS ON BETWEEN-SUBJECTS FACTORS

In Table 20.3, the age factor was significant as expected. Since a continuum underlies this factor, a trend analysis is preferable to multiple comparisons. The procedures are given in Chapter 17. Note, however, that to obtain $s_{\bar{X}}$, $MS_{\text{error}}$ (i. e., $MS_{s:CA}$) is divided by the number of *observations* (not persons) on which each mean is based: $s_{\bar{X}} = \sqrt{MS_{s:CA} / nCT} = \sqrt{6.93/32}$. The contrast coefficients are found in Table N of the Appendix; Equation 17.7A gives $\hat{\psi}$ (the numerical value of the contrast), and Equation 17.8B gives $s_{\hat{\psi}}$ (the standard error of the contrast). The $t$-ratio for each contrast is $\hat{\psi}/s_{\hat{\psi}}$; each contrast has degrees of freedom of the error mean square (here, 24). Only the linear trend is inferentially reliable ($p = .003$). Although the configuration in the lower left of Table 20.3 may appear to reveal a cubic trend, the $p$-value of .354 for the cubic trend indicates that no such trend can be safely inferred.

## 20.9 REPEATED-MEASURES ANOVA WITH TWO WITHIN-SUBJECTS FACTORS AND TWO BETWEEN-SUBJECTS FACTORS

Repeated-measures designs can have any number of between-subjects or within-subjects factors. These factors can be random or fixed, and crossed or nested.[21]

---

[20]To perform multiple comparisons on the tasks factor in Table 20.3, the only difference in procedure from that illustrated in Table 20.2 is that the error mean square would have a slightly smaller value (2.12 vs. 2.23); hence $\sigma_{\bar{X}}$ would be slightly smaller (.257 vs. 263). Although the computed $q$-values for contrasts would be slightly larger, the critical $q$-values would also be slightly larger because of the change in $\nu$ associated with the error mean square (24 vs. 30). For additional examples, see Keselman, Keselman, and Shaffer (1991), Keselman, Lix, and Keselman (1993), and Hoppe (1993).

[21]Most ANOVA software programs have defaults that treat all factors as crossed and fixed effects. Special instructions can usually be given that will override these designations. When this is not an option, one can easily obtain the correct $F$-ratios if one has mastered the rules for determining $E(MS)$'s (Section 19.18), because random versus fixed designations do not affect the observed mean squares for the effects. When a crossed factor is analyzed as if it were nested, the $SS$'s and $\nu$'s for certain effects must be aggregated (Section 19.15). The incremental inferential strategy (Section 19.20) is recommended, especially in complex mixed-model ANOVA designs in which the error mean square must be constructed from variance components (cf. Winer et al., 1991, pp. 374-382).

Our final analysis[22] will employ a second within group factor that has been ignored up to this point. In the Omey (1987) study, two different modes of response were employed (recognition and explanation). Table 20.4 gives the analysis for this design. Note that there are now four different error terms.

Each error mean square that involves a repeated-measures factor rests on a different sphericity condition. Notice that Table 20.4 gives the Huynh-Feldt epsilon values. Since there are only two levels of the mode of response ($M$) factor, no adjustment is needed (epsilon is always 1.0). For the task ($T$) factor, the value of epsilon is also 1.0, indicating that the data satisfy the sphericity condition. For the effects associated with $T \times M$, the sphericity condition is also essentially satisfied ($\hat{\varepsilon} = .989$).

The addition of the mode-of-response factor adds ten sources of variation and eight statistical hypotheses to the analysis. The main effect for the mode-of-response within-subjects factor was significant ($p = .003$); the mean score was lower when the subjects had to answer questions expressively. This pattern was evident for subjects in both communication mode groups (note $p = .133$ for the $C \times M$ interaction), and on all four types of conservation tasks ($T \times M$, $p = .140$). The significant $A \times M$ interaction ($p = .022$) is graphed, showing that only at the younger ages did the deaf students perform less well when required to explain their answers. Note the misleading inference that could have resulted had the age factor been ignored.

The $C \times A \times M$ ($p = .140$) and $T \times A \times M$ ($p = .864$) effects were not significant, allowing generalizability of the pattern represented in the $A \times M$ interaction to both communication mode groups and across all four conservation tasks. The absence of the four-factor $T \times C \times A \times M$ interaction indicates that these three-factor patterns did not change across the levels of the fourth factor.

## 20.10 REPEATED-MEASURES ANOVA VERSUS MANOVA

The questions addressed by repeated-measures ANOVA can also be addressed by multivariate analysis of variance (MANOVA). MANOVA does not require the sphericity condition, and thus yields accurate type-I error probabilities even when this condition is violated. However, as Stevens (1986, p. 414) stated, "In terms of controlling type I error, there is no real basis for preferring the multivariate approach, since use of the modified univariate test (i. e., multiplying the degrees of freedom by $\hat{\varepsilon}$) yields an 'honest' error rate." The other criteria of power and "user-friendliness," then, are the bases for choice. When the sphericity condition is attained (or approximated), repeated-measures ANOVA is more powerful (Davidson, 1972). As a guideline, if $\hat{\varepsilon}$ is .75 or more, repeated-measures ANOVA is the method of choice. With real data sets, this will usually be the case. Repeated-measures ANOVA is more user-friendly (O'Brien & Kaïser, 1985) unless one has special course work or study in multivariate statistics.

---

[22]In practice, this is the only analysis that would be performed; it answers all the questions of the previous analyses, and addresses them with equal or greater power. The sequential analyses (Tables 20.2 and 20.3) were given for instructional purposes.

**TABLE 20.4** ANOVA Table for a Repeated-Measures Design with Subjects Nested within Two Between-Subjects Factors and Crossing Two Within-Subjects Factors.

| Source of Variation | SS | $v$ | MS | F | p | $MS_{error}$ | Huynh-Feldt Adjustment $v$ | Huynh-Feldt Adjustment p |
|---|---|---|---|---|---|---|---|---|
| *Between Subjects* | 174.01 | 31 | | | | | | |
| 1 Communication mode ($C$) | 38.29 | 1 | 38.29 | 11.05 | .003 | $s{:}CA$ | | |
| 2 Age level ($A$) | 42.39 | 3 | 14.13 | 4.08 | .018 | $s{:}CA$ | | |
| 3 $C \times A$ | 10.17 | 3 | 3.39 | .98 | .419 | $s{:}CA$ | | |
| 4 Subjects:$CA$ ($s{:}CA$) | 83.16 | 24 | 3.47 | $= \hat{\sigma}^2_{s:CA}$ | | | | |
| *Within Subjects* | 137.87 | 224 | | | | | | |
| 5 Task ($T$) | 12.17 | 3 | 4.06 | 3.83 | .013 | $T \times s{:}CA$ | 3 | .013 |
| 6 $C \times T$ | 2.76 | 3 | .92 | .87 | .461 | $T \times s{:}CA$ | 3 | .461 |
| 7 $A \times T$ | 19.5 | 9 | 2.17 | 2.05 | .046 | $T \times s{:}CA$ | 9 | .046 |
| 8 $C \times A \times T$ | 4.72 | 9 | .52 | .50 | .873 | $T \times s{:}CA$ | 9 | .873 |
| 9 $T \times s{:}CA$ | 76.22 | 72 | 1.06 | $= \hat{\sigma}^2_{Ts:CA}$ | | | 72 | ($\hat{\varepsilon} = 1.0$) |
| 10 Mode of Response ($M$) | 2.07 | 1 | 2.07 | 10.66 | .003 | $M \times s{:}CA$ | | |
| 11 $C \times M$ | .47 | 1 | .47 | 2.42 | .133 | $M \times s{:}CA$ | | |
| 12 $A \times M$ | 2.26 | 3 | .75 | 3.88 | .022 | $M \times s{:}CA$ | | |
| 13 $C \times A \times M$ | 1.17 | 3 | .39 | 2.01 | .140 | $M \times s{:}CA$ | | |
| 14 $M \times s{:}CA$ | 4.66 | 24 | .19 | $= \hat{\sigma}^2_{Ms:CA}$ | | | | |
| 15 $T \times M$ | .110 | 3 | .037 | .25 | .864 | $T \times M \times s{:}CA$ | 2.97 | .864 |
| 16 $T \times C \times M$ | .320 | 3 | .107 | .72 | .545 | $T \times M \times s{:}CA$ | 2.97 | .545 |
| 17 $T \times A \times M$ | .500 | 9 | .056 | .37 | .944 | $T \times M \times s{:}CA$ | 8.90 | .944 |
| 18 $T \times C \times A \times M$ | .220 | 9 | .024 | .16 | .997 | $T \times M \times s{:}CA$ | 8.90 | .997 |
| 19 $T \times M \times s{:}CA$ | 10.72 | 72 | .149 | $= \hat{\sigma}^2_{TMs:CA}$ | | | 71.21 | ($\hat{\varepsilon} = .989$) |
| total | 311.88 | 255 | | | | | | |

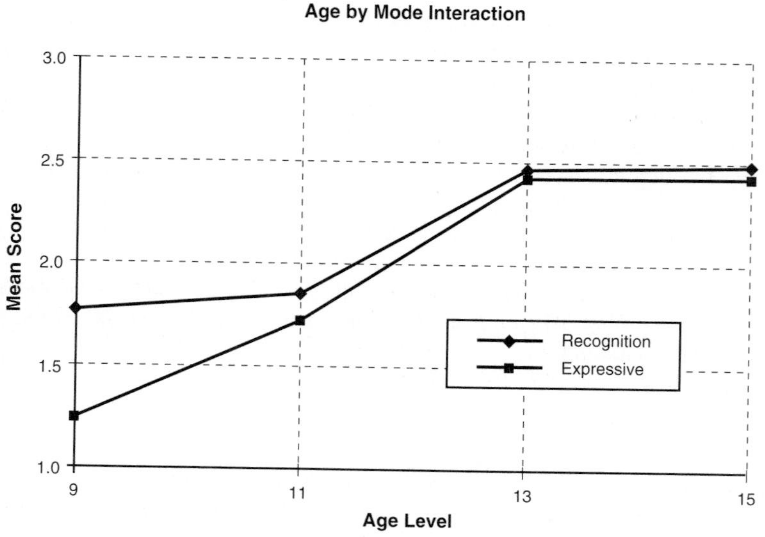

**Age by Mode Interaction**

## 20.11 CHAPTER SUMMARY

Repeated-measures ANOVA designs are often much more powerful than completely randomized designs because variance due to individual differences is removed from the error terms of the within-subjects effects. The increase in power is a major appeal of repeated-measures ANOVA, when logistically possible. There are many instances, however, where a subject cannot receive more than one treatment.

Repeated-measures ANOVA is called for when there are two or more observations of the same type on each subject. Repeated-measures ANOVA is a special case of a mixed-model ANOVA: The subjects factor is a random effect that crosses a fixed effect. In repeated-measures ANOVA, there is a single observation in each cell, consequently there is no within-cell variation.

When there are only two levels of the repeated-measures factor, the sphericity and compound symmetry conditions will always be met. If the levels of the repeated-measures factor have variance parameters that are equal, and the scores on each level correlate equally with the scores on any other level, the sphericity and compound symmetry conditions will be met. The method of choice for repeated-measures ANOVA designs includes the use of the Huynh-Feldt epsilon value to adjust the degrees of freedom for the within-subjects effects. The epsilon value becomes less than 1.0 when the sphericity condition is violated; the practical consequence of its use is to increase the critical value of $F$ when the data fail to satisfy the sphericity assumption.

When there is a continuum underlying the levels of the repeated-measures factor, a trend analysis is suggested. Since trend analysis is a special case of planned orthogonal contrasts, it can be performed independently of the test of the main effect (although usually the main effect will be significant if any of the trends are significant). The trend analysis does not require the data to meet the sphericity conditions.

When the levels of the repeated-measure are parts of a whole, such as items, subtests, or raters, the reliability of the total or average scores can be obtained from the mean squares provided by the ANOVA table. The Spearman-Brown formula can estimate the expected change in reliability if the length of a measure (or the number of raters) is changed.

There can be any number of between-subjects and within-subjects factors. Each can be defined as fixed or random.

Because of its greater power, repeated-measures ANOVA is preferable to MANOVA except when the sphericity condition is seriously violated.

## 20.12 CASE STUDY

Using the High School and Beyond data set, a repeated-measures ANOVA was performed. The between-subjects factors were school-type (public vs. private) and gender; content area (reading, math, science, and writing) was the within-subjects factor. In other words, students were nested within school type and gender, but crossed content area. Table 20.5 summarizes this analysis.[23]

[23]Unlike the analysis given in the previous tables, this is not a balanced design, thus, the effects are not completely independent (orthogonal). The option (Section 18.26) of using only the unique (non-redundant) portion of the effect is used in Table 20.5; this is usually the default option in computer programs.

**TABLE 20.5** ANOVA Table for a Repeated-Measures Design with Subjects Nested within Two Between-Subjects Factors and Crossing Two Within-Subjects Factors

| Source of Variation | SS | v | MS | F | p | $MS_{error}$ | Huynh-Feldt Adjustment v | Huynh-Feldt Adjustment p |
|---|---|---|---|---|---|---|---|---|
| *Between Subjects* | | | | | | | | |
| 1 School Type ($T$) | 2501.5 | 1 | 2501.5 | 9.12 | .003 | $s{:}TG$ | | |
| 2 Gender ($G$) | 204.87 | 1 | 204.87 | .75 | .388 | $s{:}TG$ | | |
| 3 $T \times G$ | 484.16 | 1 | 484.16 | 1.77 | .184 | $s{:}TG$ | | |
| 4 Students:$TG$ ($s{:}TG$) | 163426 | 596 | 274.20 | $= \hat{\sigma}^2_{s:TG}$ | | | | |
| *Within Subjects* | | | | | | | | |
| 5 Content Area ($C$) | 132.27 | 3 | 44.09 | 1.40 | .241 | $T \times s{:}TG$ | 3 | .241 |
| 6 $T \times C$ | 126.36 | 3 | 42.12 | 1.34 | .260 | $T \times s{:}TG$ | 3 | .260 |
| 7 $G \times C$ | 1991.7 | 3 | 663.90 | 21.09 | .0000 | $T \times s{:}TG$ | 3 | .000 |
| 8 $T \times G \times C$ | 65.32 | 3 | 21.77 | .69 | .557 | $T \times s{:}TG$ | 3 | .557 |
| 9 $C \times s{:}TG$ | 56277.4 | 1788 | 31.48 | $= \hat{\sigma}^2_{Cs:TG}$ | | | 1788 | ($\hat{\varepsilon} = 1.0$) |

*Content Area Means*

| | Reading | Math | Science | Writing |
|---|---|---|---|---|
| *Males* | 52.4 | 52.4 | 53.2 | 49.8 |
| *Females* | 51.5 | 51.4 | 50.5 | 54.6 |

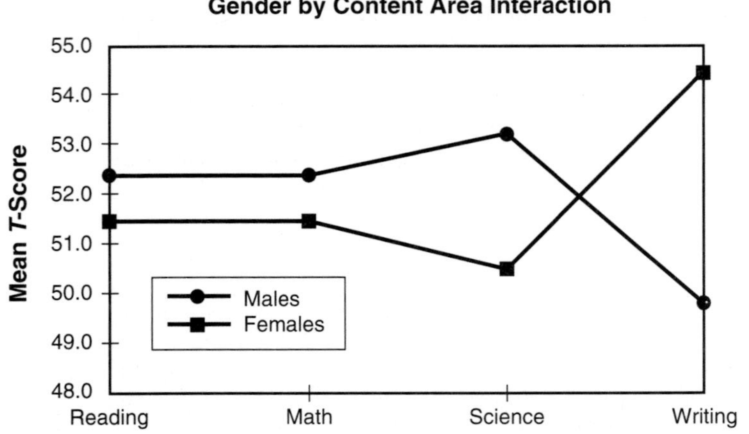

Check your literacy of reading repeated-measures ANOVA tables by using Table 20.5 to answer the following questions.

1. (a) Was the sphericity condition violated by this data set? (b) Are the columns for the Huynh-Feldt adjustment superfluous in this instance?[24]
2. (a) Did the means of the two school types differ significantly? (b) From the ANOVA table is it evident which of the two means is higher? (c) How often would one get a difference as large as that which was observed if $H_0$ were true? (d) Was this difference similar for both males and females? (e) Was this difference significantly greater in certain content areas than in others?[25]
3. (a) What does the lack of a significant main effect for gender mean? (b) What does the significant $G \times C$ interaction reveal? (c) The gender difference is greatest in which content area? (d) If two graphs like that in Table 20.5 were constructed, one for private school students and another for public school students, would they look similar? How do you know?[26]
4. In this situation, why does one not expect a significant main effect for content area?[27]
5. Determine the expected mean square for the school type effect, and for the $T \times C$ interaction.[28]

## 20.13 SUGGESTED COMPUTER ACTIVITY

Using the EXERCISE data set, run a repeated-measures ANOVA with two between-subjects factors (SMOKE and SEX), and one within-subjects factor (PULSE_1 and PULSE_2). Express each hypothesis that is tested in non-statistical language.

Run a $2 \times 2$ SMOKE by SEX ANOVA with PUL_GAIN as the dependent measure, and compare the results—is the meaning consistent?

## MASTERY TEST

**1.** In a longitudinal study in which a $101 \times 5$, subjects-by-age level ANOVA is performed, how many between-subjects sources of variation will there be in the ANOVA table? How many within-subjects sources of variation will there be? How many degrees of freedom will the interaction have?

---

[24](a) No, $\hat{\varepsilon} = 1.0$; (b) Yes.

[25](a) Yes; (b) No (the observed means were 53.54 and 51.60 for private and public school students, respectively); (c) Approximately 3 replications in 1,000; (d) Yes; (e) No ($T \times G$ and $T \times C$ interactions were not significant).

[26](a) That the gender difference between the *average* across all four content was not statistically significant; (b) That the magnitude or pattern of gender differences differs among the content areas; (c) Writing (since we are using $T$-scores, we know that the effect size is approximately .5 standard deviation); (d) Yes, because the $T \times G \times C$ was not significant, indicating that the $G \times C$ configuration generalizes across levels of the T (school type) factor.

[27]Because the raw scores for each content area were converted to a common standard score metric, $T$-scores. Indeed, if this were the entire data set (rather than a random sample of 600 from the entire data set), the mean square would have been zero.

[28]The only random effect is students ($s{:}TG$), and students are nested within school type, thus the expected mean square for school type is $\sigma^2_{s:TG} + nGC\sigma_T^2$. Content area crosses the random effect, thus the expected mean square for school type is $\sigma^2_{s:TG} + nGC\sigma_T^2$.

2. For the age level factor, which is more appropriate, multiple comparisons or trend analysis? How many different orthogonal trends can be tested?
3. Does a trend analysis of the repeated-measures factor require sphericity?
4. When is trend analysis inappropriate for comparisons among three or more levels of the repeated-measures factor? What should be used?
5. Why is there not "within cell" variation in repeated-measures ANOVA designs?
6. Suppose you find the reliability coefficient for a ten-item attitude inventory is .50; estimate the reliability if ten more items are added.
7. In the previous item, what assumption is made about the ten additional items?
8. Suppose that an essay test given to a group of students. The essays are independently and anonymously judged by five readers. The essay tests, when read by five raters were found to have a reliability coefficient of .80. Estimate the reliability if only a single reader is used.
9. Suppose you are going to compare two groups on three dependent variables. Raw scores on the three outcome measures (reading comprehension, reading vocabulary, and reading attitude) have been converted to *T*-scores. Do you expect the data to satisfy the sphericity condition? Why?
10. The error mean square for within-subjects effects tends to be smaller than for between-subjects effects. (T or F)
11. If a study used a repeated-measures ANOVA with data that do not satisfy the sphericity condition, and reported the *p*-value yielded by the unadjusted degrees of freedom, the true probability of a type-I error is ______ ($>, =, <$) $p$.
12. When the Huynh-Feldt epsilon value is .75, the degrees of freedom are adjusted for which effects?

    (a) between-subjects (b) within-subjects (c) both
13. If the $E(MS)$ for an effect is $\sigma^2_{sM} + \sigma^2_{M}$, the error mean square for testing the $M$ main effect will be which source of variation?
14. Did the mean square for the main effect for factor $C$ change between ANOVA designs represented in Tables 20.2 and 20.3?
15. Why is the $F$-ratio for the main effect for factor $C$ greater in Table 20.3 than in Table 20.2?
16. Variance components should be reported for which effects?

    (a) random effects (b) fixed effects (c) both
17. In an ANOVA design in which the repeated-measures factor is age, crossed with the between-subjects factors of treatment and ability level, subjects are nested within ______, and cross ______.

    (a) age (b) treatment (c) ability (d) both treatment and ability
18. In repeated-measures ANOVA, there is never a problem with violating the sphericity assumption if there are ______ levels of the repeated-measures factor.
19. From the gender means given in the middle portion of Table 20.5, estimate the effect size for the gender difference on the science test.
20. In Table 20.5, there was a gender by content area ($G \times C$) interaction. Since the configuration given in the interaction graph was similar for both private and public school students, there was no ___ × ___ × ___ interaction.
21. A repeated-measures ANOVA is a special type of which ANOVA model?

    (a) fixed (b) mixed (c) random
22. Given a study with five age levels as the repeated-measures factor, and given $\hat{\varepsilon} = .75$, the numerator for the *adjusted* critical $F$ for the main effect for the age factor has how many degrees of freedom?

**23.** If the ANOVA table for the study in the previous item shows the error mean square for testing the age factor ($A$) to have $(A-1)(n-1)$ degrees of freedom, and if $n = 21$ and $\hat{\varepsilon} = .75$, the denominator for the *adjusted* critical-$F$ for the age factor has how many degrees of freedom?

**24.** In which of these situations would repeated-measures ANOVA have the greatest power advantage over MANOVA?

(a) $\hat{\varepsilon} = .50$ (b) $\hat{\varepsilon} = .75$ (c) $\hat{\varepsilon} = 1.0$

**25.** In the design below, how many within-subjects and between-subjects factors are there? Persons are nested within _____, but cross ______. Which factor is certainly a fixed effect?

| | | *Grade Level* | | |
|---|---|---|---|---|
| | *Pupil* | *1* | *2* | *3* |
| *School A* | $p_1$ | ___ | ___ | ___ |
| | $p_2$ | ___ | ___ | ___ |
| | $p_3$ | ___ | ___ | ___ |
| | $p_4$ | ___ | ___ | ___ |
| | $p_5$ | ___ | ___ | ___ |
| | $p_6$ | ___ | ___ | ___ |
| *School B* | $p_7$ | ___ | ___ | ___ |
| | $p_8$ | ___ | ___ | ___ |
| | $p_9$ | ___ | ___ | ___ |
| | $p_{10}$ | ___ | ___ | ___ |
| | $p_{11}$ | ___ | ___ | ___ |
| | $p_{12}$ | ___ | ___ | ___ |

## PROBLEMS AND EXERCISES

**1.** In one study the writing ability of 646 students, based on five writing samples, is independently rated by five raters (see Hopkins, 1983). The ANOVA table is given below:

| *Source* | $v$ | *MS* |
|---|---|---|
| Student ($s$) | 645 | 3.36 |
| Rater ($r$) | 4 | 11.89 |
| $s \times r$ | 2580 | .266 |

(a) Indicate whether, in the desired universe, the student and rater factors are fixed or random.
(b) Give the $E(MS)$ for the $s$, $r$, and $s \times r$ effects.
(c) Act on the $H_0$'s: $\sigma_s^2 = 0$, and $\sigma_r^2 = 0$.
(d) Give the variance components for each of the three effects.
(e) Estimate the reliability coefficient of the students' scores, based on the average of the five raters.
(f) Estimate the reliability of the students' scores, if students' scores are based on just one rater.
(g) What effect on the reliability of the writing ability measure would result if the number of writing samples were reduced from five to two?

**2.** In Table 12.3, consider the "Persons" to be a random factor and the "Verbal IQ versus Performance IQ" to be a fixed factor. Using the repeated-measures ANOVA model, test the null hypothesis at the .05 level that the populations of Verbal and Performance IQ's have the same mean for neurologically handicapped children. Does the $F$-test lead to the same decision that would be arrived at if a dependent-groups $t$-test of the hypothesis $\mu_2 = \mu_2$ were made? Compare $F$ with $t^2$, and $_{.99}F_{1,9}$ with $_{.995}t_9$. (Computation procedures are illustrated in Table 20.1) Could the condition of sphericity be violated in this example?

3. Scores on the Information, Vocabulary, Digit Span, and Block Design subtests of the Wechsler Intelligence Scale for Children are tabulated for a group of twelve neurologically handicapped children.

| | | Test | | | | Person Sum | Person Mean | Person Effect |
|---|---|---|---|---|---|---|---|---|
| | Person ($p$) | Infor-mation | Vocab-ulary | Digit Span | Block Design | $\Sigma_t X_{pt}$ | $\overline{X}_{p\bullet}$ | $\hat{a}_p$ |
| | 1 | 7 | 8 | 7 | 7 | 29 | 7.25 | −2.50 |
| | 2 | 5 | 10 | 8 | 12 | 35 | 8.75 | −1.00 |
| | 3 | 9 | 11 | 9 | 11 | 40 | 10.00 | .25 |
| | 4 | 17 | 18 | 9 | 13 | 57 | 14.25 | 4.50 |
| | 5 | 4 | 7 | 7 | 9 | 27 | 6.75 | −3.00 |
| | 6 | 6 | 9 | 8 | 11 | 34 | 8.50 | −1.25 |
| | 7 | 11 | 11 | 7 | 7 | 36 | 9.00 | −.75 |
| | 8 | 10 | 14 | 12 | 7 | 43 | 10.75 | 1.00 |
| | 9 | 8 | 11 | 7 | 13 | 39 | 9.75 | .00 |
| | 10 | 12 | 11 | 5 | 9 | 37 | 9.25 | −.50 |
| | 11 | 13 | 16 | 6 | 18 | 53 | 13.25 | 3.50 |
| | 12 | 11 | 10 | 11 | 6 | 38 | 9.50 | −.25 |
| Test Sum: | $\Sigma_p X_{pt}$ | 113 | 136 | 96 | 123 | $468 = \Sigma_t \Sigma_p X_{pt}$ | | |
| Test Means: | $\overline{X}_{\bullet p}$ | 9.417 | 11.333 | 8.00 | 10.25 | $9.75 = \overline{X}_{\bullet\bullet}$ | | |
| Test Effect: | $\hat{\beta}_t$ | −.333 | 1.583 | −1.75 | .50 | $5{,}078 = \Sigma_t \Sigma_p X_{pt}^2$ | | |

*WISC subtest scores are scaled to a mean of 10 and a standard deviation of 3 for general population. It has often been asserted that patterns of subtest scores on the WISC can be used to diagnose neurological handicaps.*

(a) Test the null hypothesis that the twelve test scores above were randomly sampled from four normal distributions with the same mean, with $\alpha = .05$. The design should be regarded as a repeated-measures design.

(b) If multiple comparisons were to be made among subtests, what is the numerical value of "$MS_e$"?

4. Twenty raters are drawn at random from a population of raters. Thirty-two ratees are drawn at random from a population of ratees. The eight traits of interest for this particular study are rated. Each of the twenty raters rated each of the thirty-two ratees once on each of the eight traits.

(a) How many ratings does this study yield?

(b) Which factors represent "random" effects and which "fixed?" Are any factors "nested" within any other factors?

(c) How many sources of variation are there in these ratings? List them and the associated $\nu$'s.

(d) Work out all the expected mean squares for this design and indicate the appropriate error mean squares for each effect.

(e) Provide the formulas for estimating the variance component, $\hat{\sigma}_r^2$.

5. Two raters who were Democrats and two raters who were Republicans each rated three ratees who were prominent Democrats and three ratees who were prominent Republicans on each of

the four different traits. This yielded a total of $2 \times 2 \times 2 \times 3 \times 4 = 96$ ratings. The design is shown. There are five factors, two of which are nested.

| | | *Trait rated* | | | | | | | | | | | | | | | | |
|---|---|---|---|---|---|---|---|---|---|---|---|---|---|---|---|---|---|---|
| | | *Intelligence* | | | | *Honesty* | | | | *Friendliness* | | | | *Generosity* | | | | |
| | | *D* | | *R* | | *D* | | *R* | | *D* | | *R* | | *D* | | *R* | | *Party of rater* |
| *Party of ratee* | *Ratee number* | *1* | *2* | *3* | *4* | *1* | *2* | *3* | *4* | *1* | *2* | *3* | *4* | *1* | *2* | *3* | *4* | *Rater number* |
| | 1 | 7 | 6 | 8 | 7 | 8 | 2 | 8 | 7 | 5 | 1 | 8 | 2 | 5 | 0 | 10 | 5 | |
| *R* | 2 | 7 | 7 | 6 | 7 | 7 | 6 | 6 | 6 | 6 | 6 | 9 | 1 | 5 | 6 | 8 | 2 | |
| | 3 | 6 | 6 | 4 | 5 | 8 | 9 | 8 | 6 | 10 | 5 | 9 | 8 | 9 | 5 | 10 | 6 | |
| | 4 | 8 | 8 | 6 | 6 | 9 | 10 | 3 | 1 | 8 | 8 | 7 | 6 | 9 | 7 | 4 | 4 | |
| D | 5 | 8 | 5 | 6 | 7 | 9 | 5 | 4 | 4 | 5 | 1 | 4 | 1 | 9 | 1 | 3 | 1 | |
| | 6 | 5 | 4 | 3 | 3 | 7 | 8 | 1 | 0 | 7 | 7 | 8 | 4 | 7 | 8 | 0 | 0 | |

(a) Identify the two nested factors. Within what is each such factor nested?
(b) Do the nested factors cross any other factors? Which ones?
(c) Which factors does the "political party of rater" factor cross?
(d) Which of the factors were probably considered as each having had its levels drawn randomly from an infinite (hypothetical) population of levels?
(e) $\hat{\sigma}^2_{(\text{party of rater} \times \text{party of ratee})}$ contributed must to variation of the ratings. Would you have expected this result in advance of the rating procedure? What does this interaction probably mean?
(f) The second largest estimated component of variance was that for party of rater × party of ratee × trait. What does this three-factor interaction mean? (One sometimes sees a three-factor interaction referred to as a "second-order" interaction, because a zero-order "interaction" would be a main effect, not interacting with anything. Thus, a two-factor interaction, such as that in part e, may be called a "first-order" interaction.)

## ANSWERS TO MASTERY TEST

1. 1 (Age); 2 (Subjects, and the Subjects × Age interaction); $100 \times 4 = 400$
2. trend analysis, 4
3. no, each trend has a unique error mean square
4. when the levels represent a categorical (nominal) variable; multiple comparisons
5. because there is only one observation in each cell
6. $L = 2$; $\hat{\rho}'_{XX} = 2(.50)/(1+.50) = .67$
7. the new items are like the original ten items, that is, the new items are from the same universe of content
8. $L = .2$; $\hat{\rho}'_{XX} = .2(.80)/[1+(.2-1).80] = .16/.36 = .44$
9. no; the correlation between the two cognitive measures will be much higher than the correlations between the affective and the cognitive variables
10. T (unless there is no correlation between levels of the repeated-measures factor)
11. greater than
12. (b)
13. $\sigma^2_{sM}$
14. no
15. The $F$-ratio is greater because the addi-

tional factor, age, was related to the dependent measure. (The $F$-ratios for effects involving age tended to be greater than 1.0.)

**16.** (a)

**17.** (d) both treatment and ability, (a) age

**18.** two

**19.** Since the scores are expressed as $T$-scores, $\sigma \approx 10$, thus the effect size is estimated to be $2.7/10 = .27$.

**20.** $T \times G \times C$

**21.** (b)

**22.** $M - 1 = 4$; $.75(4) = 3$

**23.** 60

**24.** (c)

**25.** one within- and one between-subjects factor; school, grade level; grade level

## ANSWERS TO PROBLEMS AND EXERCISES

**1.** (a) Both are random.
(b) For $s$: $\sigma_{sr}^2 + R\sigma_s^2$; for $r$: $\sigma_{sr}^2 + S\sigma_r^2$; for $s \times r$: $\sigma_{sr}^2$.
(c) Both are rejected ($p < .001$): $F_s = 3.36/.266 = 12.6$; $F_r = 44.7$
(d) $\hat{\sigma}_{sr}^2 = .266$, $\hat{\sigma}_s^2 = (3.36 - .266)/5 = .62$; $\hat{\sigma}_r^2 = (11.89 - .266)/646 = .018$
(e) $\rho'_{xx} = 1 - .266/3.36 = .92$
(f) $L = .2$; for 1 rater: $\rho'_{xx} = [.20(.92)]/[1 - .8(.92)] \approx .70$
(g) It would be reduced substantially (for precise effect, see Hopkins, 1983).

**2.** $F = 10.96 = (3.31)^2$; ${}_{.99}F_{1,9} = 10.56 = (3.25)^2 = {}_{.995}t_9$. No, because there is only one covariance term.

**3.** (a)

| *Source* | *SS* | *ν* | *MS* | *F* |
|---|---|---|---|---|
| Test ($T$) | 71.15 | 3 | 23.72 | 3.39* |
| Person ($p$) | 209.00 | 11 | 19.00 | |
| $T \times p$ | 230.82 | 33 | 6.99 | |

*$p < .05$

(b) 6.69

**4.** (a) $20 \times 32 \times 8 = 5{,}120$
(b) *raters* and *ratees* are random factors; *trait* is a fixed factor. This is a fully crossed design—there is no nested factor.
(c) 7: raters ($r$), $R - 1 = 19$; ratees ($p$), $P - 1 = 31$; Traits ($T$), $T - 1 = 7$; $r \times p = 589$, $r \times T = 133$, $p \times T = 217$, $r \times p \times T = 4{,}123$

(d)

| *E(MS)* | | | | | | | ν | *Error MS* |
|---|---|---|---|---|---|---|---|---|
| $E(MS_r)$ | $= \sigma_\varepsilon^2$ | | $+8\sigma_{rp}^2$ | | | $+ 256\sigma_r^2$ | $r - 1 = 19$ | $MS_{rp}$ |
| $E(MS_p)$ | $= \sigma_\varepsilon^2$ | | $+8\sigma_{rp}^2$ | | | $+ 160\sigma_p^2$ | $p - 1 = 31$ | $MS_{rp}$ |
| $E(MS_T)$ | $= \sigma_\varepsilon^2$ | $+ \sigma_{rpT}^2$ | | $+32\sigma_{rT}^2$ | $+20\sigma_{pT}^2$ | $+ 640\sigma_T^2$ | $T - 1 = 7$ | None |
| $E(MS_{rp})$ | $= \sigma_\varepsilon^2$ | | $+8\sigma_{rp}^2$ | | | | $(19)(31) = 589$ | None |
| $E(MS_{rT})$ | $= \sigma_\varepsilon^2$ | $+ \sigma_{rpT}^2$ | | $+32\sigma_{rT}^2$ | | | $(19)(7) = 133$ | $MS_{rpT}$ |
| $E(MS_{pT})$ | $= \sigma_\varepsilon^2$ | $+ \sigma_{rpT}^2$ | | | $+20\sigma_{pT}^2$ | | $(31)(7) = 217$ | $MS_{rpT}$ |
| $E(MS_{rpT})$ | $= \sigma_\varepsilon^2$ | $+ \sigma_{rpT}^2$ | | | | | $(19)(31) = 4{,}123$ | None |

(e) $\sigma_r^2 = (MS_r - MS_{rp})/256$

**5.** (a) rater is nested within political party; ratee is nested within political party
(b) rater crosses ratee, political party of ratee, and trait; ratee crosses rater, political party of rater, and trait
(c) trait, party of ratee, and ratee (i.e., everything but rater)
(d) rater and ratee
(e) raters are biased in favor of ratees of their own political party
(f) raters' bias in favor of their own party was not uniform across traits

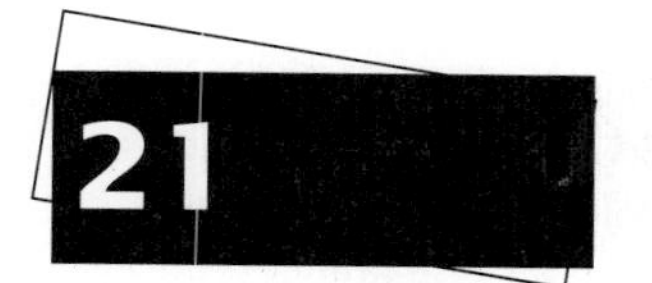

# AN INTRODUCTION TO THE ANALYSIS OF COVARIANCE

## 21.1 THE FUNCTIONS OF ANCOVA

The analysis of covariance (ANCOVA) is a method of statistical analysis devised by Fisher in 1932 that combines the analysis of variance with regression analysis (Chapter 8). Any ANOVA design can become an ANCOVA design by the addition of a concomitant variable, called a *covariate*. ANCOVA has two purposes: (1) increase statistical power, and/or (2) reduce bias, that is, to statistically equate groups on one or more variables. ANCOVA can often increase the power of an ANOVA analysis, but its ability to remove bias in nonrandomized experiments is imperfect and fraught with technical difficulties. Novices often initially view ANCOVA as the messiah of statistical methods; it sometimes has been asked to give signs and perform wonders, to reveal the truth amidst a bewildering array of uncontrolled and poorly measured confounding variables.

Some have mistakenly assumed that ANCOVA, in effect, transforms quasi experiments into randomized experiments. In reality, ANCOVA is never able to make the results of a quasi experiment[1] as definitive as those of randomized experiments.

### An Illustration

An experiment is performed in grade six of twenty elementary schools of a large school district. Ten of the schools are randomly designated to be the sites for adoption of a computer-assisted instruction program in writing—method *E*. The other ten elementary schools continue to use the district's traditional language arts curriculum. At the end of the school year, all students in all twenty schools are given a common assignment designed to measure writing performance. The students' writing samples are randomly ordered and indepen-

[1]Studies in which the experimental units are not randomly assigned to treatments, but are taken as they occurred naturally. ANCOVA can reduce, but not entirely elıminate, selection threats to the interval validity of quasi-experimental studies.

dently and anonymously evaluated by two writing specialists using carefully defined criteria. The maximum score is 100. There are 50 to 120 sixth-grade pupils in each school; but, since the school itself (along with its teachers, administrators, surrounding neighborhoods, and the like) was randomly designated as either $E$ or $C$ (the two experimental conditions), the school is the experimental unit.[2] The twenty school means of sixth-grade pupils' writing scores will be used as the observational unit in the statistical analysis. The data collected in the experiment are reproduced in Table 21.1, and will be analyzed using both ANOVA and ANCOVA so that their differences can be illustrated.

## 21.2 ANOVA RESULTS

An analysis of variance will be performed on the dependent variable $Y$ so that the ANOVA results can be compared with those that will be obtained from the ANCOVA. In ANCOVA, as in multiple regression (Chapter 8) and trend analysis (Section 17.19), the dependent variable is usually designated by $Y$ (and the covariate by $X$); to avoid confusion when comparing results, $Y$ will be used to denote the dependent variable in both the ANOVA and ANCOVA. The usual one factor fixed-effects ANOVA (Equation 15.10; Section 15.13) model is:

$$Y_{ij} = \mu + \alpha_j + \varepsilon_{ij} \quad \textbf{(21.1)}$$

where, the customary assumptions (Section 15.24) of homogeneously, independently, and normally distributed errors, $\varepsilon_{ij}$, are made, that is, $\varepsilon \sim \text{NID}(0, \sigma_\varepsilon^2)$. The ANOVA results are given in panel B of Table 21.1.

The mean square for the method effect is 1.44 (= $F$) times as large as the mean square for schools nested within method ($s{:}M$). This $F$-ratio of 1.44 is less than the critical $F$-value ($_{.95}F_{1,18} = 4.41$); hence, the null hypothesis ($H_0$: $\mu_1 = \mu_2$) cannot be rejected.

## 21.3 ANCOVA MODEL

The ANOVA results in Table 21.1 will now be compared with an ANCOVA on the same data. ANCOVA can be used to reduce unpredictable variance in the ANOVA model (Equation 21.1). The error $\varepsilon_{ij}$ using the ANOVA model represents the deviation of the mean of a school from the mean of all schools *within* its same treatment group ($E$ or $C$); for example, the model predicts the value for each $E$ school to be:

$$\hat{\mu} + \hat{\alpha}_1 = \overline{Y}_{\bullet} + \hat{\alpha}_1 = \overline{Y}_1$$

---

[2] In practice, the teacher factor should be included in the design, and the scores of individual students would ordinarily serve as the observational unit (Section 19.22), but this would complicate the illustration. Students would be nested within both teachers and schools, and schools would be designated as a random factor. When the design is balanced, the results for the treatment effect in both analyses would be identical when school is properly designated as a random factor (Hopkins, 1982). The use of students' scores as the observational units allows the examination of possible interactions of the treatment with learner characteristics such as ability level and sex. To avoid unnecessary complexity in notation, since the school means are the observational unit in the example, they will be denoted by $Y_{ij}$, not $\overline{Y}_{ij}$.

**TABLE 21.1** School Means and ANOVA for a Hypothetical Experiment Comparing Ten Experimental (*E*) Schools with Ten Control (*C*) Schools on the Writing Measure ($n = 10$).

A.

| | *E Schools* | | *C Schools* |
|---|---|---|---|
| | 77.63 | | 64.10 |
| | 74.13 | | 43.67 |
| | 67.20 | | 50.40 |
| | 78.23 | | 84.33 |
| | 57.93 | | 44.93 |
| | 57.65 | | 71.43 |
| | 83.30 | | 71.10 |
| | 73.90 | | 44.57 |
| | 45.90 | | 68.23 |
| | 64.83 | | 68.47 |
| $\overline{Y}_1 =$ | 68.070 | $\overline{Y}_2 =$ | 61.123 |
| $s_1^2 =$ | 134.60 | $s_2^2 =$ | 201.50 |

B. ANOVA Table

| *Source* | *SS* | *v* | *MS* | *F* | *p* |
|---|---|---|---|---|---|
| Methods (*M*) | 241.30 | 1 | 241.30 | 1.44 | .246 |
| Within (*s*:*M*)[3] | 3,024.94 | 18 | 168.05 | | |
| total | 3,266.24 | 19 | | | |

For example, the error component for the second school in method *E* is $\hat{\varepsilon}_{21} = Y_{21} - \overline{Y}_{1}$. Note that $\hat{\varepsilon}$ is the residual or error of estimate (Section 8.7) when the sole predictor variable is method of instruction.

If absolutely nothing is known about the twenty schools except which ten are in the *E* group and which ten are in the *C* group, then the variance of the errors, $\hat{\varepsilon}_{ij}$'s, is the mean square within (i. e., the variance among schools within method) from the ANOVA given in Table 21.1.

It is often the case, however, that some measure, *X*, of the observational units (school IQ means in this illustration) correlates with the dependent variable, *Y*. The use of this variable, together with the method variable, can improve the accuracy in predicting *Y*; and, thus, decrease the residuals and, therefore, the error variance. It is reasonable to expect, for example, that schools with higher mean scores on the scholastic aptitude measure (IQ) will tend to have higher mean scores on the achievement test than schools of lower IQ means. School means in IQ[4] (*X*) and writing (*Y*) are given in panel A of Table 21.2. Thus, since *X* (the covariate)[5] and *Y* (the dependent variable) are correlated, the inclusion of *X* in the

[3]Within = schools nested within method (*s*:*M*).

[4]In this illustration, assume that *X* represents the mean score on a standardized scholastic aptitude test that was given *prior* to the treatment. Covariates that could be affected by the treatment must be obtained before the treatment to avoid confounding.

[5]Also termed "covariable" and "concomitant variable" in some sources.

model can be used to reduce the magnitude of the error, and thus reduce the denominator of the $F$-test. Consequently, the error $\hat{\varepsilon}_{ij}$ in the ANOVA model (Equation 21.1) can be separated into two independent, additive portions:

$$\hat{\varepsilon}_{ij} = \hat{\beta}_W(X_{ij} - \overline{X}_\bullet) + \hat{\varepsilon}'_{ij} \quad \textbf{(21.2)}$$

where $\hat{\beta}_W$ is an estimate of the regression coefficient that describes the relationship of $X$ to $Y$, $X_{ij} - \overline{X}_\bullet$ is the deviation of the $i$th observation ($X_{ij}$) on the covariate from the covariate grand mean ($\overline{X}_\bullet$), and the resulting residuals are normally distributed and have a common variance within groups. The new error, $\varepsilon'$, represents that portion of the error in the ANOVA model, $\varepsilon$, that remains when the variance in that portion of the $\varepsilon$'s related to the covariate is removed. In other words, in ANCOVA, the error in an observation ($Y_{ij}$) is the residual when the treatment group ($E$ or $C$) and the covariate are used as predictors, as in multiple regression (Chapter 8). The fixed effects ANOVA model then becomes the fixed-effects analysis of covariance (ANCOVA) model:

$$Y_{ij} = \hat{\mu} + \hat{\alpha}_j + \hat{\beta}_W(X_{ij} - \overline{X}_\bullet) + \varepsilon'_{ij} \quad \textbf{(21.3)}$$

or, expressed differently:

$$Y_{ij} - \hat{\beta}_W(X_{ij} - \overline{X}_\bullet) = \hat{\mu} + \hat{\alpha}_j + \varepsilon'_{ij} \quad \textbf{(21.3A)}$$

Equation 21.3A shows that ANCOVA can be viewed as an ANOVA (Equation 21.1) in which the dependent variable is not $Y$, but the *difference* in $Y$ and the $Y$-value predicted from the covariate (i.e., $Y_{ij} - \hat{\beta}_W(X_{ij} - \overline{X}_\bullet)$). The value of $\hat{\beta}_W$ in the ANCOVA model represents the relationship between $X$ and $Y$ *within* the treatment groups. ANCOVA makes the assumption that the regression of $Y$ on $X$ is the same for each treatment condition, that is, $\beta_1 = \beta_2 = \ldots = \beta_J = \beta_W$. This means that the *slopes* when $Y$ is regressed on $X$ within each of the $J$ groups ($\beta_j$) differ only because of sampling error, that is, $E(b_1) = E(b_2) = \ldots = E(b_J) = \beta_W$. Research suggests that ANCOVA is relatively robust with respect to violations of this assumption (Glass, Peckham, & Sanders, 1972).

The absolute value of the error ($\varepsilon'$) in ANCOVA (Equation 21.3) will be smaller than the error ($\varepsilon$) in ANOVA (Equation 21.1), except when the covariate is irrelevant, that is, when $\rho_{XY} = 0$. Consequently, a one-factor ANCOVA is expected to yield a more powerful test of the treatment effects than a one-factor ANOVA. Notice in panel C of Table 21.2 how the dependent variable $Y$ and the covariate $X$ are highly correlated within each of the two groups: $r$ is +.931 within the $E$ group and +.805 within the $C$ group—the average IQ's of the schools are closely related to the writing means of the schools.[6] Making use of this relationship will allow ANCOVA to result in a more powerful test of $H_0$: $\mu_1 = \mu_2$ than ANOVA.

Notice that the ANOVA of the sample data (in panel B of Table 21.1) did not reveal a significant treatment effect; the estimated treatment effects $\hat{\alpha}_1$ and $\hat{\alpha}_2$ were not reliably

[6]When school is the observational unit, the correlations among cognitive measures will be much higher than when the observational unit is the individual student (Section 7.18).

different from 0, that is, $H_0$: $\mu_1 - \mu_2 = 0$ remained tenable. However, since the errors in the ANCOVA model are smaller and have less variance than those in ANOVA, the probability of rejecting a false null hypothesis will increase. In other words, the proper use of ANCOVA can reduce the chance of a type-II error without changing the probability of a type I error.

## 21.4 ANCOVA COMPUTATIONS: $SS_{total}$

To test the null hypothesis, $H_0$: $\mu_1 = \mu_2 = \ldots = \mu_J$, the sums of squares for each effect must be adjusted for the effects of the covariate. Recall that the proportion of variance (or sum of squares) in variable $Y$ that is predictable from variable $X$ is described by $r^2$. Thus, the adjusted total sum of squares ($SS'_{total}$) can be obtained using Equation 21.4:

$$SS'_{total} = SS_{total}(1 - r^2_{total}) \quad \textbf{(21.4)}$$

where $SS_{total}$ is the total sum of squares obtained using ANOVA (i.e., the unadjusted $\Sigma y^2$) and $r_{total}$ is the correlation between the covariate, $X$, and the dependent variable, $Y$, for all $nJ$ pairs of observations taken together (i.e., treatment group membership is ignored).

If Equation 7.4 is employed to compute the correlation between $X$ and $Y$ for the twenty pairs of scores in Table 21.2, the result is $r_{total}$. In the right-hand portion of panel A of Table 21.2, $r_{total}$ was found to be .7105. In Table 21.1, the total sum of squares from the ANOVA of $Y$, $\Sigma y^2_{total}$, was shown to be 3,266.24. In panel D of Table 21.2, Equation 21.4 is used to find the adjusted total sum of squares for ANCOVA:

$$SS'_{total} = SS_{total}(1 - r^2_{total}) = (3{,}266.24)[1 - (.7105)^2] = 1{,}617.41$$

## 21.5 THE ADJUSTED WITHIN SUM OF SQUARES, $SS'_W$

The adjusted within sum of squares, $SS'_W$ is given by Equation 21.5:

$$SS'_W = SS_W(1 - r^2_W) \quad \textbf{(21.5)}$$

where $SS_W$ is the unadjusted sum of squares (from the ANOVA) and $r_W$ is the *within* groups (pooled) correlation coefficient between $X$ and $Y$.

Before the equation for determining $r_W$ is given, for simplicity in notation let:[7]

$$\Sigma xy_W = \Sigma xy_1 + \Sigma xy_2 + \ldots + \Sigma xy_J$$
$$\Sigma x^2_W = \Sigma x_1^2 + \Sigma x_2^2 + \ldots + \Sigma x_J^2$$
$$\Sigma y^2_W = \Sigma y_1^2 + \Sigma y_2^2 + \ldots + \Sigma y_J^2$$

[7] More explicitly, $\Sigma xy_W = \Sigma_j \Sigma_i x_{ij} y_{ij}$; $\Sigma x_W{}^2 = \Sigma_j \Sigma_i x_{ij}{}^2$; and $\Sigma y_W{}^2 = \Sigma_j \Sigma_i y_{ij}{}^2$.

Then:

$$r_W = \frac{\Sigma xy_W}{\sqrt{(\Sigma x_W^2)(\Sigma y_W^2)}} \quad \textbf{(21.6)}$$

In the right-hand portion of panel C in Table 21.2, $r_W$ is found to equal .8517, and in panel D, $SS'_W$ is found to equal 830.88.

## 21.6 THE ADJUSTED SUM OF SQUARES BETWEEN GROUPS, $SS'_B$

The adjusted sum of squares from between treatments, $SS'_B$, is the difference between $SS'_{total}$ and $SS'_W$; $SS'_B$ must be computed indirectly using Equation 21.7:

$$SS'_B = SS'_{total} - SS'_W \quad \textbf{(21.7)}$$

In panel D of Table 21.2, $SS'_B$ is found to equal 786.71.

## 21.7 DEGREES OF FREEDOM IN ANCOVA AND THE ANCOVA TABLE

The degrees of freedom in ANCOVA are identical to those in ANOVA with one exception: One degree of freedom is lost from the within source of variation for the covariate. If there is more than one covariate, one degree of freedom is lost for each covariate.

If the null hypothesis is true ($H_0$: $\alpha_1 = \alpha_2 = \ldots = \alpha_j = 0$), then the ratio of the adjusted mean squares, $MS'_B/MS'_W$ will have a central $F$-distribution with $J - 1$ and $n_{\bullet} - J - 1$ degrees of freedom.[8]

The ratio of $MS'_B$ to $MS'_W$ in panel E of Table 21.2 is found to be 16.10, which exceeds the 99.9th percentile in the central $F$-distribution ($_{.999}F_{1,17} = 15.7$); thus, the null hypothesis of zero method effects is rejected. The results of the ANCOVA are summarized in a table like that used to report ANOVA results in panel E of Table 21.2.

Recall that when the same data were analyzed by an ANOVA (Table 21.1), without taking the correlation between $X$ (IQ) and $Y$ (writing) into account, the null hypothesis could not be rejected ($p = .246$). By removing from the error in Equations 21.1 and 21.2 that portion which was predictable from $X$, a more powerful test of the difference between the means for the two treatment groups was obtained, and the null hypothesis was rejected at the .001 level of significance.[9]

---

[8] More generally, $\nu_e = n_{\bullet} - J - C$, where $C$ is the number or covariates.

[9] Sometimes the covariate(s) is listed as a source of variation in the summary table. The sum of squares explained by the covariates is the difference between $SS_{total}$ and $SS'_{total}$. In the example, $SS_{covariates} = 3266.24 - 1617.59 = 1{,}648.65$, and $MS_{covariates} = SS_{covariates}/C$, where $C$ is the number of covariates. In the example in Table 21.2, $C = 1$; thus, $MS_{covariates} = 1{,}648.65$. The test of the hypothesis, $H_0$: $\rho_{total} = 0$, is $F = MS_{covariates}/MS_W = 1{,}648.65/48.88 = 33.73$, $p < .001$, indicating that the covariate reduced the error by a significant amount.

**TABLE 21.2** School Means and ANCOVA on the Writing Measure (*Y*) and the Ability Test (*X*) for the 20 Schools in the Hypothetical Curriculum Experiment.

A.

| E Schools ($n = 10$) | | C Schools ($n = 10$) | | |
|---|---|---|---|---|
| *X* | *Y* | *X* | *Y* | Total ($n_{\bullet} = 20$) |
| 105.7 | 77.63% | 101.2 | 64.10% | $\bar{X}_{\bullet} = 100.63$ $\bar{Y}_{\bullet} = 64.597$ |
| 100.3 | 74.13 | 97.6 | 43.67 | $\Sigma x^2_{\text{total}} = 796.48$ |
| 94.3 | 67.20 | 96.4 | 50.40 | $\Sigma y^2_{\text{total}} = 3{,}266.24$ |
| 18.7 | 78.23 | 109.6 | 84.33 | $\Sigma xy_{\text{total}} = 1{,}145.97$ |
| 93.1 | 57.93 | 94.0 | 44.93 | $r_{\text{total}} = .7105$ |
| 96.7 | 57.65 | 105.4 | 71.43 | |
| 106.9 | 83.30 | 102.4 | 71.10 | |
| 100.3 | 73.90 | 100.6 | 44.57 | |
| 86.5 | 45.90 | 104.2 | 68.23 | |
| 96.1 | 64.83 | 112.6 | 68.47 | |

B.

| | | | | |
|---|---|---|---|---|
| $\bar{X}_1 = 98.86$ | $\bar{Y}_1 = 68.070\%$ | $\bar{X}_2 = 102.40$ | $\bar{Y}_2 = 61.123\%$ | |
| $s_X^2 = 47.94$ | $s_Y^2 = 134.60$ | $s_X^2 = 33.60$ | $s_Y^2 = 201.50$ | $\Sigma y^2_{\text{W}} = 3{,}024.94$ |
| $\Sigma x_1^2 = 431.42$ | $\Sigma y_1^2 = 1{,}211.44$ | $\Sigma x_2^2 = 302.40$ | $\Sigma y_2^2 = 1{,}813.50$ | $\Sigma x^2_{\text{W}} = 733.82$ |

C. $\Sigma xy_1 = 672.78$ $\quad \Sigma xy_2 = 596.10$ $\quad \Sigma xy_{\text{W}} = 1{,}268.88$

$r_1 = .931$ $\quad r_2 = .805$ $\quad r_{\text{W}} = \dfrac{\Sigma xy_{\text{W}}}{\sqrt{(\Sigma x^2_{\text{W}})(\Sigma y^2_{\text{W}})}} = .8517$

D.

$$SS'_{\text{total}} = SS_{\text{total}}(1 - r^2_{\text{total}}) = 3{,}266.24[1 - (.7105)^2] = 1{,}617.41$$

$$SS'_{\text{W}} = SS_{\text{W}}(1 - r^2_{\text{W}}) = 3{,}024.94[1 - (.8517)^2] = 830.88$$

$$SS_{\text{B}} = SS'_{\text{total}} - SS'_{\text{W}} = 1617.41 - 830.88 = 786.53$$

E.

| *Source* | *SS'* | *v* | *MS'* | *F* | *p* |
|---|---|---|---|---|---|
| Between | 786.53 | 1 | 786.71 | 16.10 | < .001 |
| Within | 830.88 | 17 | 48.88 | | |
| Total | 1,617.41 | 18 | | | |

F.

$$b_{\text{W}} = \frac{\Sigma xy_{\text{W}}}{\Sigma x^2_{\text{W}}} = \frac{1{,}268.88}{733.82} = 1.73; \quad \bar{Y}'_j = \bar{Y}_j - b_{\text{w}}(\bar{X}_j - \bar{X}_{\bullet})$$

$$\bar{Y}'_1 = 68.070 - 1.73(98.86 - 100.63) = 71.132$$

$$\bar{Y}'_2 = 61.123 - 1.73(102.40 - 100.63) = 58.061$$

G.

$$s^2_{\bar{Y}'} = MS'_{\text{W}}\left[\frac{1}{n} + \frac{(\bar{X}_j - \bar{X}_{\bullet})^2}{\Sigma x^2_{\text{w}}}\right] = 48.88\left[\frac{1}{10} + \frac{(98.86 - 100.63)^2}{733.82}\right] = 5.097$$

$$s_{\bar{Y}'} = 2.258$$

$$.90CI \text{ for } \mu_1: \bar{Y}'_1 \pm {}_{.95}t_8 s_{\bar{Y}'} = 71.132 \pm (1.860)(2.258) = 71.132 \pm 4.199 = (66.93,\ 75.33)$$

$$.90CI \text{ for } \mu_2: \bar{Y}'_2 \pm 4.199 = (58.061 \pm 4.199) = (53.86,\ 62.26)$$

## 21.8 ADJUSTED MEANS, $\overline{Y}'_j$

To interpret the ANCOVA results properly, one needs to know the adjusted mean of each group (the predicted mean if the group's covariate mean, $\overline{X}_j$, had been equal to the grand mean on the covariate, $\overline{X}_\bullet$). The adjusted mean of group $j$, $\overline{Y}'_j$, is:

$$\overline{Y}_j' = \overline{Y}_j - b_W(\overline{X}_j - \overline{X}_\bullet) \qquad \textbf{(21.8)}$$

where $\overline{Y}_j$ is the unadjusted mean of group $j$ on $Y$ (the dependent variable), $\overline{X}_j$ is the mean of group $j$ on $X$ (the covariate), $\overline{X}_\bullet$ is the grand mean on the covariate, and $b_W$ is the estimate of $\beta_W$, the slope (regression coefficient):[10]

$$b_W = \frac{\Sigma xy_W}{\Sigma x_W^2} \qquad \textbf{(21.9)}$$

The computation of $b_W$ and the adjusted means $\overline{Y}'_1$ and $\overline{Y}'_2$ is illustrated in panel F of Table 21.2. Notice that the difference between the adjusted means, $\overline{Y}'_1 - \overline{Y}'_2 = 71.13 - 58.06 = 13.07$, is much greater than the difference in unadjusted means, $\overline{Y}_1 - \overline{Y}_2 = 68.07 - 61.12 = 6.95$. In other words, if both the $E$ and $C$ groups had the identical mean IQ of 100.63, the mean of the $E$ group would be predicted to be 71.13 which is 13.07 higher[11] than the predicted mean of the $C$ group (58.06).

In the example, the main effect for method after being adjusted for the covariate (Table 21.2) is slightly larger than the unadjusted ANOVA main effect (Table 21.1). Although the $E$ schools scored higher on the writing measure than the $C$ schools (presumably because of the superiority of the $E$ curriculum), they had to overcome a very slight disadvantage in mean IQ. On the other hand, if there had been a large covariate (IQ) difference favoring the $E$ group, the ANCOVA adjusted main effects would have been substantially smaller than the ANOVA unadjusted effects. In any event, for randomized experiments the adjustment of the means through covariance analysis will ordinarily be small when $n$ is large, since the random assignment to treatments makes the groups only randomly different on the covariate. When $\overline{X}_j - \overline{X}_\bullet$ is quite small, the adjusted means will differ little from the unadjusted means. When $n$ is small, the adjusted and unadjusted means can differ considerably, even when units are randomly assigned to treatments.[12] The more important consequence of using a relevant covariate, especially in experimental studies, is that it reduces error variance, and thus increases precision of estimates and the power of hypothesis tests. The relationship between the variance of $\varepsilon'$ and $\varepsilon$ is described in Equation 21.10:

---

[10]For a balanced design, an alternative formula is: $b_W = r_W\sqrt{ms_W / s_{W_x}^2}$ where $MS_W$ and $s_{W_x}^2$ are the average within-groups variances on $Y$ and $X$, respectively.

[11]To quantify effect size (Section 12.8), one should not use $MS_W$, but continue to use the unadjusted $s_C$ (or $\sqrt{MS_W}$ if $s_C$ is not available).

[12]The difference of 3.56 points in covariate means in Table 21.2 ($\overline{X}_1 = 98.86$ and $\overline{X}_2 = 102.40$) is well within the difference that would be expected from chance when $n = 10$. The difference would not be statistically significant ($F = 1.54$, $p > .20$).

$$\sigma_{\varepsilon'}^2 = \sigma_{\varepsilon}^2(1-\rho_W^2)\left[1+\frac{1}{\nu_e-2}\right] \qquad \textbf{(21.10)}$$

where $\nu_e$ is the degrees of freedom for the error mean square in an ANOVA. If $\nu_e$ is large:

$$\sigma_{\varepsilon'}^2 \approx \sigma_{\varepsilon}^2(1-\rho_W^2) \qquad \textbf{(21.10A)}$$

or

$$MS'_W \approx MS_W(1-r_W^2) \qquad \textbf{(21.10B)}$$

$MS'_W$ is the error variance for ANCOVA; $MS_W$ is the error variance for the corresponding ANOVA; and $r_W$ is the correlation of $X$ and $Y$ within groups. Notice, for example, that if the covariate and the dependent variable are correlated, $MS'_W$ is less than $MS_W$ (Equation 21.10B); indeed, if $r_W = .7$, $MS'_W$ will be approximately one-half the value of $MS_W$.

## 21.9 CONFIDENCE INTERVALS AND MULTIPLE COMPARISONS FOR ADJUSTED MEANS

In setting confidence intervals, one cannot use $MS'_W$ directly; the error variance must be increased by a factor which represents the degree of extrapolation employed. In other words, when the adjusted means differ substantially from the unadjusted means, there is more sampling error involved than when the amount of adjustment is small:

$$s_{\bar{Y}'}^2 = MS'_W\left[\frac{1}{n}+\frac{(\bar{X}_j-\bar{X}_{\bullet})^2}{\Sigma x_W^2}\right] \qquad \textbf{(21.11)}$$

where $\Sigma x_W^2 = \Sigma_j\Sigma_i(X_{ij} - \bar{X}_j)^2$, and

$$.90CI: \bar{Y}'_j \pm {}_{.95}t_{\nu_j} s_{\bar{Y}'}^2 \qquad \textbf{(21.12)}$$

where $\nu_j = n_j - 2$.

In panel G of Table 21.2, the .90 confidence intervals for the population means, $\mu_E$ and $\mu_C$, were found to be (66.93, 75.33) and (53.86, 62.26). Thus, we can say with 90% confidence that the population mean for the experimental group could be as low as 66.93 or as high as 75.33; in contrast, the population mean for the control population is probably between 53.86 and 62.26.

For making multiple comparisons, the error mean square must be adjusted to reflect the magnitude of extrapolations among the $J$ means:

$$MS''_{W} = MS''_{W}\left[1+\frac{\Sigma x_B^2}{(J-1)\Sigma x_W^2}\right] \quad \textbf{(21.13)}$$

where $\Sigma x_B^2$ and $\Sigma x_W^2$ are the between and within sums of squares, respectively, on the covariate $X$.[13] Note in Equation 21.13 that $MS''_W$ will exceed $MS'_W$ to the extent that the $J$ covariate means differ (i.e., the value of $\Sigma x_B^2$).

## 21.10 ANCOVA ILLUSTRATED GRAPHICALLY

The sense in which covariance analysis adjusts $Y$ for concomitant variation in $X$, and thus predicts what might have been seen in $Y$ if all groups were equal in terms of $X$, is illuminated by Figure 21.1. The data from the elementary school writing experiment are graphed and various features of the ANCOVA are depicted.

Figure 21.1 depicts the data in Table 21.2. The value of the covariate $X$ is given along the $X$-axis and the corresponding value of the dependent variable $Y$ is shown on the $Y$-axis. Notice that group $C$ has a slightly higher average on the covariate (IQ) than the $E$ group (102.4 versus 98.86), even though the difference is known to be due entirely to sampling error because the schools were randomly assigned to the $E$ or $C$ groups.

Each school is represented as a dot in the scatter plot. To visually organize the data belonging to each group, the $E$ schools are denoted by solid dots "•", and the $C$ schools by open dots "∘". The unadjusted means $\bar{Y}_1$ and $\bar{Y}_2$ are shown on the $Y$-axis. Recall from Table 21.1 that the ANOVA procedures indicated that the difference in the unadjusted means was not statistically significant. The denominator in the ANOVA is the average within-group variance $MS_W = s_W^2 = (s_1^2 + s_2^2)/2 = (134.60 + 201.50)/2 = 168.05$. $MS_W$ is approximately equal to the mean of the squared residuals, $x_{ij}^2 = (X_{ij} - \bar{X}_j)^2$, within the two groups.

Examination of the "•" points reveals a high correlation between $X$ and $Y$ within the $E$ group: $r_1 = .931$. The correlation is also high within the $C$ group: $r_2 = .805$. Pooling the information with each of the two groups, the within-group correlation, $r_W$, was found to be .852.

ANCOVA assumes $\beta_1 = \beta_2$; thus, any difference between the regression slope in groups 1 and 2, that is, $b_1$ versus $b_2$, is viewed as sampling error. Pooling $\Sigma xy_1$ and $\Sigma xy_2$ to obtain $\Sigma xy_W$, and $\Sigma x_1^2$ and $\Sigma x_2^2$ to obtain $\Sigma x_W^2$ provides the information needed for the best (least squares) estimate of the regression coefficient in the population, $b_W = \Sigma xy_W/\Sigma x_W^2 = 1.73$. Thus, for each unit that $\bar{X}_1$ is below $\bar{X}_{\bullet}$, $\bar{Y}_1$ is adjusted upward by 1.73 points. Conversely, since $\bar{X}_2 - \bar{X}_{\bullet} = 1.77$, $\bar{Y}'_2$ will be $(1.73)(1.77) = 3.06$ points less than $\bar{Y}_2$: $\bar{Y}'_2 = 61.12 - 3.06 = 58.06$. In other words, $b_W$ is used to estimate what the $\bar{Y}_j$'s would have been if the covariate means of both groups ($\bar{X}_1$ and $\bar{X}_2$) were precisely equal.

[13] Since there are only two means in the illustration, multiple comparisons are superfluous. Nevertheless, to illustrate the use of Equation 21.13, the error mean square for multiple comparisons is: $MS''_W = 48.88\ \{1 + 62.66/[(2-1)733.82]\} = 53.05$, where $\Sigma x_B^2 = \Sigma x_{total}^2 - \Sigma x_W^2 = 796.48 - 733.82 = 62.66$.

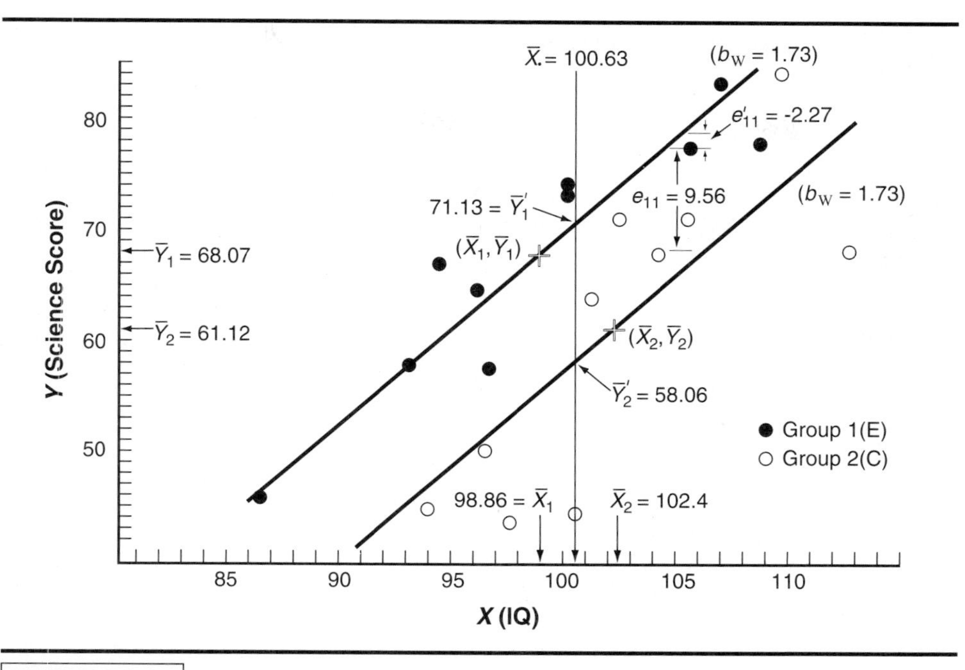


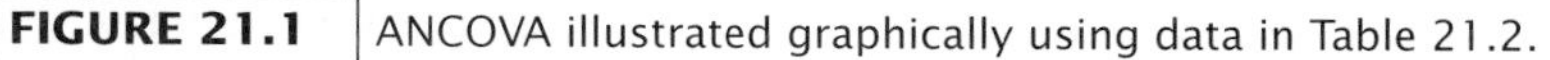
**FIGURE 21.1** ANCOVA illustrated graphically using data in Table 21.2.

In ANOVA, error for school 1 in group 1 is $e_{11} = Y_{11} - \bar{Y}_1 = 77.63 - 68.07 = 9.56$. The square of these residuals for all ten schools within each group, summed for both groups is $SS_W$. In ANCOVA, however, the error $e'_{11}$ is the *residual* for school 1—the distance from $Y_{11}$ to the regression line for group 1, that is, $e'_{11} = Y_{11} - Y'_{11}$, where $Y'_{11} = \bar{Y}_1 + b_W(X_{11} - \bar{X}_1) = 68.07 + 1.73(105.7 - 98.86) = 79.90$; thus, $e'_{11} = 77.63 - 79.90 = -2.27$, which is much less than the $e_{11}$ of 9.5 in ANOVA. (Locate $e_{11}$ and $e'_{11}$ in Figure 21.1.) Stated differently, $e'_{11}$ is the vertical distance from $Y_{11}$ to the regression line with slope $b_W$ that passes through the centroid of its group ($\bar{X}_1$, $\bar{Y}_1$). The centroid for each group is marked "+" in Figure 21.1.

When $X$ and $Y$ correlate, the residuals from ANCOVA will be smaller than from ANOVA; thus, the sum of the squared residuals in ANCOVA ($SS'_W$) will be less than the sum of the squared residuals in ANOVA ($SS_W$); consequently, $MS'_W$ will be smaller than $MS_W$, and the ANCOVA will be more powerful than the ANOVA.[14] $MS'_W$ is analogous to the square of the standard error of estimate (Section 8.10), that is, $MS'_W \approx s_Y^2(1 - r_W^2)$.

The $F$-ratio of the adjusted between treatment mean square $MS'_B$ to the adjusted within mean square $MS'_W$ provides a test of the hypothesis that treatment means on $Y$ would be equal if the groups had equal means on $X$.

[14]If $r_W$ is near zero, it is theoretically possible for $MS'_W$ to be slightly larger than $MS_W$, since the degrees of freedom are one less for $MS'_W$. This is virtually never the case unless one is using irrelevant variables as covariates.

## 21.11 ANCOVA ASSUMPTIONS

All the assumptions made regarding errors, $\varepsilon_{ij}$, as defined in the ANOVA model in Equation 21.1 (Equation 15.10, see Sections 15.8, 15.13, 15.20, 15.25), are made for the adjusted errors, $\varepsilon'_{ij}$, in the ANCOVA model in Equation 21.2, that is, $\varepsilon'_{ij} \sim NID(0, \sigma_{\varepsilon'}^2)$. The general precautions that have been given regarding ANOVA (Section 15.24) should be observed in ANCOVA (Cochran, 1957; Glass, Peckham, & Sanders, 1972; Ragosa, 1980). Note that, in testing for normality or heterogeneity of variance, the "observations" for each of the $J$ groups are the residuals about the regression line with slope $b_W$ that passes through the centroid ($\bar{X}_j$, $\bar{Y}_j$) of each group.

ANCOVA makes three additional assumptions that involve the regression of $Y$ on $X$.

1. The regression lines for each group are assumed to be parallel, that is, $\beta_1 = \beta_2 = \ldots = \beta_j = \beta_W$. If this parallel regression lines assumption is violated, the covariance adjustment may still improve the precision, but the meaning of the adjusted means becomes cloudy. Violation of the parallel regression slopes assumption appears to not be serious in one-factor fixed-effects experiments that use ANCOVA (Glass, Peckham, & Sanders, 1972). Heterogeneity of regression coefficients will result when there is an interaction between treatment and the covariate. For example, in Figure 18.4 view ability as a covariate and observe that the treatment-by-ability interaction would result in nonparallel regression lines.[15]

   To test whether the slopes of the $J$ regression lines are from the same population, that is, $H_0$: $\beta_1 = \beta_2 = \ldots = \beta_J = \beta_W$, the sum of squares due to the variation among $b_1$, $b_2$, $\ldots$, $b_J$ is found by finding the squared residuals within each of the $J$ groups, allowing each group to determine its own least-squares regression line with slope $b_j$:

$$SS'_{W_j} = \sum_j \left[ \sum_i y_{ij}^2 (1 - r_j^2) \right]$$

In the curriculum experiment in Table 21.2:

$$\begin{aligned} SS'_{W_j} &= \Sigma y_1^2 (1 - r_1^2) + \Sigma y_2^2 (1 - r_2^2) \\ &= 1,211.44[1 - (.931)^2] + 1,813.50[1 - (.805)^2] \\ &= 161.41 + 638.31 = 799.72 \end{aligned}$$

Only when $b_1 = b_2$, does $SS'_{Wj}$ equal $SS'_W$; the difference between $SS'_W$ and $SS'_{Wj}$ is due to the difference in the $b_j$'s. The sum of squares accruing from variance in the $b_j$'s, $SS_{\sigma_B}$, is:

$$SS_{\sigma_B} = SS'_W - SS'_{W_j} = 830.88 - 799.72 = 31.16$$

and,

[15]There are ANCOVA models (Huitema, 1980, chapter 13) which do not assume parallel regression lines and allow each of the $J$ groups to use its own regression coefficient, $b_j$, to adjust its mean. A difficulty with these procedures is that the difference in the adjusted means depends on the value of the covariate at which comparisons are made (see Ragosa, 1980).

$$F = \frac{\dfrac{SS_{\sigma_B}}{J-1}}{\dfrac{SS'_{Wj}}{J(n-2)}} = \frac{\dfrac{31.16}{2-1}}{\dfrac{799.72}{2(8)}} = \frac{31.16}{49.98} = .62$$

Therefore, $H_0$: $\beta_1 = \beta_2$ is tenable.

2. The covariance procedure assumes that the correct form of the regression equation has been fitted. Virtually all ANCOVA applications assume a linear relationship between $X$ and $Y$. Nonlinearity will result in biased estimates of effects; the magnitude of the bias depends on the true form of the relationship between $X$ and $Y$. The bias will be least severe when subjects are randomly assigned to groups. The randomization ensures that the usual interpretations of standard errors and tests of significance are not seriously weakened, although fitting the correct form of regression would presumably give a larger increase in precision. The danger of misleading results is much greater when there are real differences among treatment groups on the covariate. Fortunately, most cognitive and psychomotor variables are linearly related, and unless the measurement procedures are faulty (e.g., a test that lacks ceiling), the linear regression model works well in most applications. In some instances, curvilinear relationships can be made linear by mathematical transformations (Section 8.28) of either the dependent variable $Y$ or the covariate $X$ or both (see Li, 1964, for treatment of curvilinear ANCOVA).
3. An assumption in the usual ANCOVA model that is not widely recognized is that the covariate is fixed (Section 8.25) and contains no measurement error. Lord (1963) showed how large errors in the covariate can produce misleading results. The effects of the less than perfectly reliable covariate are often predictable so the nature of the bias in the adjustment can be considered in any interpretation. It should be emphasized that, to the extent the covariate is unreliable, the groups will not be truly equated on the covariate. Measurement error will decrease the observed correlation between $X$ and $Y$, and hence the slope, $b_W$, and will affect the adjusted means.

## 21.12 ANCOVA PRECAUTIONS

Two or more groups differing on some characteristic (such as age, IQ, or pretest) can be studied to discover whether or not there is a significant difference among the groups on the dependent variable when the groups are "statistically equated" on the characteristic(s) on which they differ. Examples where randomized experiments are not practical or possible include studies contrasting cultures, states, and social classes. In quasi-experimental studies, it is widely realized that an observed association, even if statistically significant, may be due wholly or partly to other uncontrolled variables on which the groups differ. A common device has been to match the groups for the disturbing variables thought to be most important. This matching often results in serious problems (Section 12.15; Hopkins, 1969). In the same way, the $X$-variables can be treated as covariates and ANCOVA can be employed to remove, at least partly, the influence of the $X$-variables.

Unfortunately, quasi-experimental studies are subject to difficulties of interpretation from which randomized experiments are free. Although ANCOVA has been skillfully applied, one can never be sure that bias is not present from some confounding variable that was overlooked. Indeed, unless the covariate is perfectly reliable, ANCOVA does not remove all the bias due to $X$ itself. In true experiments, the effects of all variables measured and unmeasured, real and illusory, are distributed among the groups by the randomization in a way that is taken into account in the standard tests of significance. There is no such safeguard in the absence of randomization.

Second, when the $X$-variables show real differences among groups—the case in which adjustment is needed most—covariance adjustments involve a degree of extrapolation. To illustrate by an extreme case, suppose that one were adjusting for differences in parents' education in a comparison of the achievement of delinquents and nondelinquents. Suppose the mean education levels were 10 and 13 for the two groups. The covariance would adjust the results so that they allegedly applied to a mean education level of 11.5, although 11.5 is not representative for either group.

Two consequences of this extrapolation should be noted. Unless the statistical assumption of linear and homogeneous regression holds in the region in which observations are lacking, covariance will not remove all the bias and in practice may remove only a small part of it. Second, even if the regression is valid for the extrapolation, the standard errors of the adjusted means become large (Equation 21.11) because the standard error formula in an ANCOVA takes into account the degree to which extrapolation ( $\overline{X}_j - \overline{X}_{\bullet}$) is involved. Consequently, the adjusted differences may become insignificant statistically merely because the adjusted comparisons are of low precision.

When groups differ widely on some confounding variable $X$, these difficulties imply that the interpretation of an adjusted analysis is speculative rather than definitive. While there is no sure way out of the difficulty, two precautions are worth observing. Consider what internal evidence exists to indicate whether or not the regression is valid in the region of extrapolation. Sometimes the fitting of a more complex regression formula serves as a partial check. Examine the confidence intervals for the adjusted group means (Section 21.9), particularly when the differences are nonsignificant after adjustment. Confidence limits for the adjusted means will reveal the degree of precision of the adjusted comparison.

Researchers are frequently tempted to try to make ANCOVA compensate for the lack of randomization, that is, to equate groups on selected variables. ANCOVA is generally not up to the job it is asked to perform; what is worse, its defects may be hidden.[16] If the covariate $X$ is measured after the treatment is applied (e.g., suppose $X$ stood for IQ scores of sixth graders and it was measured on the same day that the achievement test was given), then if $E$ also increased students IQ scores, the ANCOVA is likely to remove from the main effects on $Y$ some of the effects that should be credited to the treatment. For this reason, it is recommended that covariate $X$ be observed before treatments are applied, if it can be affected by the treatments.

## 21.13 COVARYING VERSUS STRATIFYING

If the covariate is obtained prior to the treatment, an alternative design and alternative analysis strategy should be considered by the experimenter. An ANOVA of simple gain scores (e.g., posttest-pretest) is a simple alternative, but will be less powerful than ANCOVA.[17]

---

[16]For an even more cautious perspective on the use of ANCOVA in quasi experiments, see Reichardt (1979) and Cronbach et al. (1977).

[17]If the covariate and the dependent variable do not employ a common metric (e.g., IQ and grade equivalents), both distributions can be transformed to $T$-scores (Section 6.7) using the composite $X$ and composite $Y$ distributions.

The measure to serve as the covariate, $X$, can also be used to form $K$ levels of an ancillary factor. To maintain a balanced design, the levels are defined so that the same number of subjects will be in each level. In experimental studies, each of the $nJ$ subjects within each level should be assigned randomly to each of the $J$ conditions. If this design is employed, the data are analyzed as a factorial design. This design is generally preferable to ANCOVA because, in addition to increasing power, the interaction between the factors can be tested. If the experimenter's sole interest is to minimize the error mean square for purposes of increasing power (Equation 21.10B), ANCOVA becomes more powerful when the covariate and the dependent variable correlate highly (e.g., above .6).[18]

In randomized experiments where the bias-reducing function of ANCOVA is not needed, the two-factor ANOVA (stratifying on $X$) is preferred to ANCOVA, primarily because it yields additional useful information regarding the generalizability of the treatment effects across the various levels of the second factor, $X$. In addition, the factorial design works well even when the relationship between $X$ and the dependent variable $Y$ is not linear. ANCOVA also has the disadvantage of additional assumptions and related computational complexity. On the other hand, loss of experimental subjects creates even greater problems for randomized blocks and factorial designs than for ANCOVA, since in the former case nonorthogonal designs will result. Frequently, ANCOVA and factorial designs are combined as in problem 1 of the Problems and Exercises following this chapter. More complex applications of ANCOVA, where there are two or more covariates in combination with factorial designs, are found in Keppel (1982), Kirk (1982), Winer, Brown, and Michels (1991), and especially Huitema (1980).

## 21.14 CHAPTER SUMMARY

ANCOVA is an integration of ANOVA and multiple regression. It has two principal functions: (1) to increase power and (2) to reduce bias. Although typically there is one covariate, the number of covariates is not limited. In practice, there is usually little gain after the best two or three covariates. The average variance within groups (or cells in factorial designs) from ANOVA, $MS_W$, is reduced in ANCOVA, $MS'_W$, to approximately $MS_W(1 - r_W^2)$, where $r_W$ is the within-groups (or within-cells) correlation between the dependent variable $Y$ and the covariate $X$ (or optimally weighted covariates, when there are more than one).

Although ANCOVA can reduce bias, it can never remove all possible sources of confounding. The credibility of ANCOVA findings is reduced when the amount of extrapolation is large (i.e., the adjusted and unadjusted means differ considerably). The ANCOVA model assumes that within each of the $J$ groups or cells, the errors are independent, normally distributed, and have common variance. The covariate is assumed to be linearly related to the dependent variable and the slopes of regression lines within each of the $J$ groups or $JK$ cells differ randomly only from a common slope (regression coefficient), $\beta_W$. The covariate is also assumed to be a fixed factor containing no measurement error. The extent to which the covariate is unreliable is the extent to which the statistical compensation for bias in that variable will be imperfect. In randomized experiments, it is usually preferable to create an additional factor by stratifying on $X$ than to use $X$ as a covariate. Although when $\rho_{XY}$ is high, ANCOVA will have somewhat more power than the factorial ANOVA, but the factorial ANOVA provides important information regarding questions of generalizability.

---

[18]See Feldt (1958) to determine the optimal number of levels of $X$ and cell size ($n$), given $\rho_{XY}$ and the total number of subjects available.

## 21.15 CASE STUDY

The High School and Beyond data set was used to illustrate and contrast ANOVA and ANCOVA. Parallel results are given in Table 21.3 for both the ANOVA and ANCOVA to facilitate comparisons. Apply your understanding of the concepts by responding to the following questions.

**TABLE 21.3** Two-Factor ANOVA And ANCOVA Results for Math Scores in the High School and Beyond Data Set.

| | *ANOVA* | | | | *ANCOVA* | | | |
|---|---|---|---|---|---|---|---|---|
| *Source* | $\nu$ | *MS* | *F* | *p* | $\nu$ | *MS'* | *F* | *p* |
| School Type (*T*) | 1 | 592.6 | 6.76 | .010 | 1 | 159.3 | 2.24 | .138 |
| Gender (*G*) | 1 | 286.1 | 3.26 | .071 | 1 | 172.1 | 2.15 | .143 |
| $T \times G$ | 1 | 155.5 | 1.77 | .184 | 1 | 183.0 | 2.28 | .131 |
| Within[25] ($s{:}TG$) | 596 | 87.73 | | | 595 | 80.17 | | |
| Covariate (SES) | | | | | 1 | 4587 | 57.2 | <.001 |

1. The __ × __ School Type (*T*) by Gender (*G*) ANOVA design finds that the mean math scores are significantly different for private and public school students ($p =$ ____). From the ANOVA table, is it evident which mean is higher? Is this pattern evidenced for both sexes? ____ (i.e., the null hypothesis for the ____ is tenable).[19]
2. ANCOVA is used to assess whether there is a reliable difference between the private and public school means, for students having the same value on the ____ measure. Notice the error mean square in ANOVA (____) became smaller in ANCOVA (____). Use Equation 21.10B to estimate the within cell correlation between the SES and math scores. Is the covariate relevant—is SES significantly related to math performance?[20]
3. The fact that SES is shown to be a relevant covariate indicates that ANCOVA will have greater power than ANOVA, that is, an increased probability of rejecting the null hypothesis when $H_0$ is ____. This being the case, can we say that, when ANCOVA is used, the main effects always will be more significant (i.e., have larger *F*-ratios and smaller *p*-values), than if ANOVA were used? Why? The gain in power from ANCOVA versus ANOVA is reflected in a ____ (smaller or larger) value for the denominator for the *F*-tests.[21]
4. If the null hypothesis is true, and the study was replicated many times, how often would the difference in adjusted means be as large as that observed with these data? For students who are the same on the SES measure, the mean difference in math scores ____ (is or is not) great enough to be statistically reliable. Can this finding be safely generalized to other achievement areas?[22]

---

[19] 2 × 2; .01; no (It was the mean of the private school students.); yes; $T \times G$ interaction

[20] SES; 87.73; 80.17; Yes, $p < .001$; $r_W^2 \approx 1 - 80.17/87.73$, $r_W \approx .28$; Yes, $p < .001$.

[21] false; no; the bias on the covariate can result in lower *p*-values, as in Table 21.3; smaller.

[22] approximately one replication in fourteen ($p = .138$); is not; no (In fact, even when covarying on SES, the mean of the private schools is higher in certain achievement areas.).

5. Descriptive statistics show that the mean math scores for the males were higher. Was the difference large enough to reject the null hypothesis ($H_0$: ____)? Give a rationale for how ANOVA and ANCOVA yield a consistent conclusion for the gender main effect, unlike the school type main effect.[23]
6. For these data, the math means for the private and public school students were 54.01 and 51.45, respectively. On the SES measure, the means for the private and public school students were 2.11 and 1.98, respectively; the grand SES mean was 2.04, with $b_W$ = 3.976. Use Equation 21.8 to find the adjusted means.[24] Express the difference in adjusted means as and effect size. (Use the standard deviation of public school students on the math test, $s_C = 9.58$, as the estimate of sigma.)

## 21.16 SUGGESTED COMPUTER ACTIVITY

Using the EXERCISE data set, run a two-factor (SMOKE by SEX) ANCOVA, covarying on PULSE_1, with PULSE_2 serving as the dependent measure. Create a new variable, change in pulse rate, by subtracting PULSE_1 from PULSE_2, and run a SMOKE by SEX two-factor ANOVA and compare the results.

## MASTERY TEST

1. ANCOVA removes the need for random assignment of subjects to treatments, that is, ANCOVA often makes the results from a quasi experiment as definitive as findings from a randomized experiment. (T or F)
2. When the covariate correlates +.5 with the dependent variable, the adjusted mean square within, $MS'_W$, will be approximately 25% less than the $MS_W$ from ANOVA. (T or F)
3. In question 2, the ratio $MS'_W/MS_W \approx$ ____.
4. Can the mean square for a main effect from ANCOVA ($MS_B'$) be less than the mean square for that main effect from ANOVA ($MS_B$)?
5. Will the $F$-ratio for the treatment main effects always be larger when ANCOVA is used rather than ANOVA?

*Which of these (questions 6 to 9) are assumptions of ANCOVA? (T or F)*

6. The within-groups regression slopes for the $J$ groups are equal.
7. The errors are normally distributed, have common variance across groups, and are independent.
8. The covariate is a fixed variable without measurement error.
9. The dependent variable contains no measurement error.
10. ANCOVA results have greatest credibility when the groups being compared on $Y$ differ little on the covariate $X$. (T or F)

---

[23]no, $H_0$: $\mu_M = \mu_F$; As expected, the males and females do not differ in SES, thus the adjusted and unadjusted means on the math tests are about the same. The private school students are somewhat higher in SES, thus, the difference in their math means that is explicable by this SES difference is removed in the ANCOVA, making their adjusted math means differ less than their unadjusted means.

[24]The adjusted math means are 53.73 and 51.69 for private and public school students, respectively. Effect size: $\hat{\Delta} = (53.73 - 51.69)/9.58 = .21$

[25]Within = $s{:}TG$ (students nested within the factors of gender and school type).

*Use Figures A, B, and C to answer questions 11 to 20:* • = *E*, ○ = *C*.

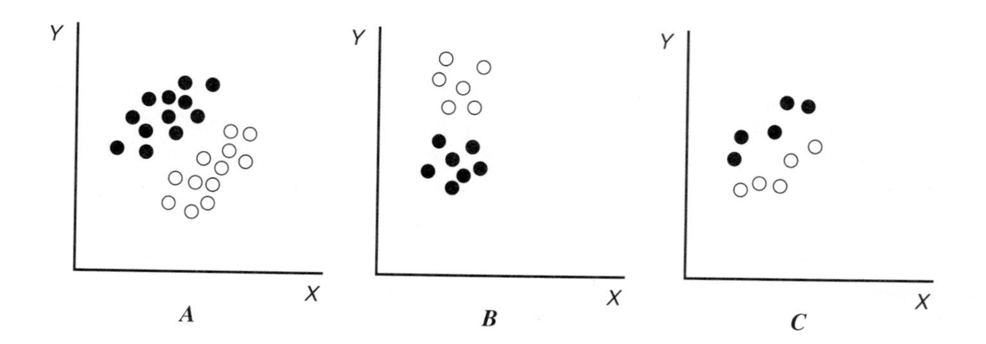


**11.** Which figure is least apt to be the result in a randomized experiment?
**12.** In which figure would the ANOVA and ANCOVA results be highly similar?
**13.** The within-groups correlation in Figure B is approximately ____.
**14.** In which figure would $MS'_W/MS_W$ be least?
**15.** In which figure would the adjusted means differ by more than the unadjusted means?
**16.** What is the value of $n$ in Figure C?
**17.** In which figure is $\bar{Y}'_C > \bar{Y}'_E$?
**18.** In which figure(s) does the relationship between $X$ and $Y$ (within groups) appear to be linear?
**19.** Making "visual" allowance for sampling error, does $\beta_E = \beta_C$ appear tenable in all figures?
**20.** Do the residuals $e'_{ij}$ appear to be heterogenous in any figure?

## PROBLEMS AND EXERCISES

*The following gives the results of both an ANOVA and ANCOVA on the same data set. Subjects were classified by learning style (auditory, visual, and mixed) and sex, then randomly assigned to one of three treatments. Observations were randomly discarded from some cells to achieve a balanced design with n = 5 persons per cell. In the ANCOVA, scores on a reading test served as the covariate.*

| | ANOVA | | | ANCOVA | | |
|---|---|---|---|---|---|---|
| *Source* | $\nu$ | *MS* | *F* | $\nu$ | *MS'* | *F* |
| Treatment (*T*) | 2 | 661.11 | 21.34[a] | 2 | 713.87 | 26.13[a] |
| Learning Style (*L*) | 2 | 109.98 | 3.55 | 2 | 4.37 | .16 |
| Sex (*S*) | 1 | 48.02 | 1.55 | 1 | 62.84 | 2.30 |
| *TL* | 4 | 4.33 | .14 | 4 | 10.38 | .38 |
| *TS* | 2 | 5.58 | .18 | 2 | 5.46 | .20 |
| *LS* | 2 | 23.54 | .76 | 2 | 32.51 | 1.19 |
| *TLS* | 4 | 4.34 | .14 | 4 | 7.92 | .29 |
| Within (*p*: *SLT*) | 72 | 30.98 | | 71 | 27.32 | |

[a] $p < .001$

1. (a) Do the adjusted means for the three treatment groups appear to differ greatly from the unadjusted means?
   (b) Do the adjusted means for the three learning styles appear to differ less than the unadjusted means? What is the explanation?
   (c) Did the ANCOVA result in a more powerful analysis than ANOVA?
   (d) Estimate the "average" correlation between $X$ and $Y$ within the eighteen cells, that is, $r_W$.
   (e) Estimate the standard error of estimate (Section 8.10) using the three predictors: learning style, sex, and covariate $X$ (reading test scores). (*Hint:* The standard error of estimate is the standard deviation of residuals within cells.)
2. Suppose there are three intact groups ($A$, $B$, $C$) and each was given a treatment. They were pretested ($X$) before the treatment and posttested following the treatment. Graph the data using $a$, $b$, and $c$ (not dots) to denote observations.

***Treatment***

| A | | B | | C | | |
|---|---|---|---|---|---|---|
| $X$ | $Y$ | $X$ | $Y$ | $X$ | $Y$ | $\bar{X}_{\bullet} = 14.0$ $\bar{Y}_{\bullet} = 14.0$ |
| 2 | 5 | 14 | 7 | 20 | 20 | $\Sigma x^2_{total} = 818$ |
| 4 | 8 | 16 | 8 | 18 | 22 | $\Sigma y^2_{total} = 846$ |
| 5 | 7 | 15 | 10 | 23 | 26 | $r_{total} = .841$ |
| 8 | 9 | 19 | 13 | 25 | 28 | |
| 6 | 11 | 11 | 12 | 24 | 24 | |
| 5.0 | 8.0 | 15.0 | 10.0 | 22.0 | 24.0 | |
| $s^2_{X_1} = 5.0$ | $s^2_{Y_1} = 5.0$ | $s^2_{X_2} = 8.5$ | $s^2_{Y_2} = 6.5$ | $s^2_{X_3} = 8.5$ | $s^2_{Y_3} = 10.0$ | $\Sigma x^2_W = 88$ |
| $\Sigma^2_{x_1} = 20$ | $\Sigma^2_{y_1} = 20$ | $\Sigma^2_{x_2} = 34$ | $\Sigma^2_{y_2} = 26$ | $\Sigma^2_{x_3} = 34$ | $\Sigma^2_{y_3} = 40$ | $\Sigma y^2_W = 86$ |
| $\Sigma xy_1 = 15$ | | $\Sigma xy_2 = 5$ | | $\Sigma xy_3 = 30$ | | $\Sigma xy_W = 50$ |
| $r_1 = .75$ | | $r_2 = .168$ | | $r_3 = .813$ | | |

   (a) $r_W^2 =$ _____.
   (b) $SS_W =$ _____.
   (c) $SS'_W =$ _____, $MS'_W =$ _____.
   (d) $SS_{total} =$ _____, $SS'_{total} =$ _____.
   (e) $SS'_B =$ _____, $MS'_B =$ _____.
   (f) Construct an ANCOVA table. Is $H_0$ tenable using ANCOVA ($\alpha = .01$)?
   (g) Using $b_W =$ _____, adjust the three means.
   (h) Set a .90 $CI$ around each mean. Why is the confidence interval for $\mu_B$ so much narrower than for $\mu_A$ and $\mu_C$?
   (i) Show the adjusted means on a graph.
   (j) Why might one lack confidence in the conclusions from this study?
3. One study (Gehler, 1979) compared a highly structured instructional approach ($E$) in kindergarten to the conventional method ($C$) on the end-of-year class performance on a composite measure $Y$ of cognitive perceptual and psychomotor kindergarten objectives. The experimental method of emphasized behavioral objectives, diagnosis and prescription, and criterion-referenced assessment. Eight kindergarten teachers taught using the $E$ method, and eight others served as control teachers. To help control for differences in teacher quality, a confidential rating of teacher quality was obtained on each teacher (maximum possible score of 100), which served as covariate $X$. Quality ratings ($X$) and class means ($Y$) for the sixteen teachers are given below.

| E (n = 8) | | C (n = 8) | |
|---|---|---|---|
| X | Y | X | Y |
| 65 | 105.8 | 96 | 129.1 |
| 52 | 111.0 | 61 | 113.1 |
| 76 | 95.3 | 77 | 90.8 |
| 81 | 109.6 | 68 | 114.1 |
| 99 | 111.3 | 76 | 121.6 |
| 82 | 118.4 | 84 | 120.7 |
| 95 | 122.8 | 65 | 118.1 |
| 79 | 119.7 | 94 | 115.4 |

(a) Perform an ANOVA on the dependent variable $Y$.
(b) Perform an ANCOVA on the dependent variable $Y$.
(c) Contrast the ANOVA and ANCOVA results.
(d) Were there significant differences between the two groups in teacher quality ratings? What could account for such a small $F$-ratio?
(e) Express $\bar{Y}'_E - \bar{Y}'_C$ as an effect size, $\hat{\Delta} = (\bar{Y}'_E - \bar{Y}'_C)/s_W$.

## ANSWERS TO MASTERY TEST

1. F
2. T
3. .75
4. yes
5. no
6. T
7. T
8. T
9. F
10. T
11. A
12. B
13. 0
14. C
15. A
16. 5
17. B
18. A, B, and C
19. yes
20. no

## ANSWERS TO PROBLEMS AND EXERCISES

**1.** (a) No ($MS'_T$ and $MS_T$ do not differ greatly.)
(b) Yes ($MS_L$ is much greater than $MS'_L$)
(c) Yes ($MS_W > MS'_W$)
(d) (a) $MS'_W = (MS_W)(1 - r_W^2)$; $r_W = .34$.
(e) $s_{Y.X} = \sqrt{MS'_W} = \sqrt{27.32} = 5.23$

**2.** (a) $r_W^2 = \dfrac{(\Sigma xy_W)^2}{(\Sigma x_W^2)(\Sigma y_W^2)} = \dfrac{(50)^2}{(88)(86)} = .330$
(b) 86
(c) $SS'_W = SS_W(1 - r_W^2) = 86(1 - .330) = 57.62$; $MS'_W = 57.62/11 = 5.238$
(d) 846, 247.64
(e) $SS'_B = SS'_{total} - SS'_W = 190.02$; 95.01

(f)

| *Source* | *SS'* | *v* | *MS'* | *F* |
|---|---|---|---|---|
| Between | 190.02 | 2 | 95.01 | 18.13 |
| Within | 57.62 | 11 | 5.24 | |

$>7.21 = {}_{.99}F_{2,11}$; $H_0$ rejected

(g) $b_W = \Sigma xy_W/\Sigma x_W^2 = 50/88 = .568$; $\overline{Y}'_A = \overline{Y}_A - b_W(\overline{X}_A - \overline{X}_{\bullet}) = 8.0 - (.568)(5 - 14) = 13.112$, $\overline{Y}'_B = 9.432$, $\overline{Y}'_C = 19.456$

(h) $s^2_{\overline{Y}'_A} = MS'_W[1/n + (\overline{X}_A - \overline{X}_{\bullet})^2/\Sigma x_W^2] = 5.238[1/5 + (5 - 14)^2/88] = 5.869$, $s_{\overline{Y}'_A} = 2.423$.

.90 $CI$ for $\mu_A$: $\overline{Y}'_A \pm {}_{.95}t_3 s_{\overline{Y}'_A} = 13.112 \pm (2.353)(2.423) = 13.112 \pm 5.70$ or (7.41, 18.81)

$s^2_{\overline{Y}'_B} = 5.238\ [1/5 + 1/88] = 1.107$, $s_{\overline{Y}'_B} = 1.052$; .90 $CI$ for $\mu_B = 9.432 \pm (2.353)(1.052) = 9.432 \pm 2.48$ or (6.95, 11.91)

$s_{\overline{Y}'_C} = 2.204$; .90 $CI$ for $\mu_C = 19.456 \pm 5.19$ or (14.27, 24.65)

Because $\overline{X}_B$ differs little from $\overline{X}_1$, extrapolation error is minimal in group $B$, but large in groups $A$ and $C$.

(j) Because of the large amount of extrapolation required in groups $A$ and $C$.

**3.** (a)

| *Source* | *SS* | *v* | *MS* | *F* |
|---|---|---|---|---|
| Between | 52.56 | 1 | 52.56 | .52 |
| Within | 1,414.56 | 14 | 101.04 | |

(b)

| *Source* | *SS'* | *v* | *MS'* | *F* |
|---|---|---|---|---|
| Between | 59.27 | 1 | 59.27 | .61 |
| Within | 1,265.46 | 13 | 97.34 | |

$\overline{Y}'_E = 111.62$, $\overline{Y}'_C = 115.48$

(c) The ANOVA and ANCOVA results are very similar because (1) $\overline{X}_E$ and $\overline{X}_C$ are very similar, and (2) $r_W$ is very low. No.

(d)

| *Source* | *SS* | *v* | *MS* | *F* |
|---|---|---|---|---|
| Between | 4.00 | 1 | 4.00 | .02 |
| Within | 2,779.76 | 14 | 198.55 | |

No. Perhaps the experimenter did not randomly assign teachers to a group, but made the two groups more comparable than would have been expected from random assignment.

(e) $\hat{\Delta} = \dfrac{(111.69 - 115.48)}{\sqrt{101.23}} = -.38$

# TABLES

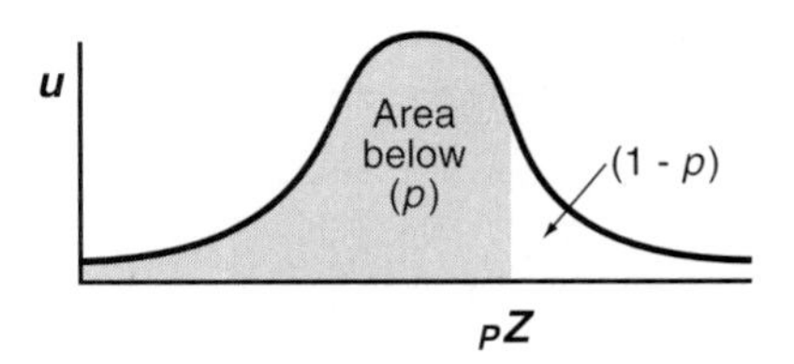


**TABLE A** Areas of the Unit-Normal ($z$) Distribution.

| $z^a$ | Proportion of Area: Below $z^b$ | Proportion of Area: Above $z$ | Ordinate $u$ |
|---|---|---|---|
| **0.000** | **.5000** | **.5000** | **.3989** |
| 0.01 | .5040 | .4960 | .3989 |
| 0.02 | .5080 | .4920 | .3989 |
| 0.03 | .5120 | .4880 | .3988 |
| 0.04 | .5160 | .4840 | .3986 |
| 0.05 | .5199 | .4801 | .3984 |
| 0.06 | .5239 | .4761 | .3982 |
| 0.07 | .5279 | .4721 | .3980 |
| 0.08 | .5319 | .4631 | .3977 |
| 0.09 | .5359 | .4641 | .3973 |
| 0.10 | .5398 | .4602 | .3970 |
| 0.11 | .5438 | .4562 | .3965 |
| 0.12 | .5478 | .4522 | .3961 |
| **0.126** | **.5500** | **.4500** | **.3958** |
| 0.13 | .5517 | .4483 | .3956 |
| 0.14 | .5557 | .4443 | .3951 |
| 0.15 | .5596 | .4404 | .3945 |
| 0.16 | .5636 | .4364 | .3939 |
| 0.17 | .5675 | .4325 | .3932 |
| 0.18 | .5714 | .4286 | .3925 |
| 0.19 | .5753 | .4247 | .3918 |
| 0.20 | .5793 | .4207 | .3910 |
| 0.21 | .5832 | .4168 | .3902 |
| 0.22 | .5871 | .4129 | .3894 |
| 0.23 | .5910 | .4090 | .3885 |
| 0.24 | .5948 | .4052 | .3876 |
| 0.25 | .5987 | .4013 | .3867 |
| **0.253** | **.6000** | **.4000** | **.3863** |
| 0.26 | .6026 | .3974 | .3857 |
| 0.27 | .6064 | .3936 | .3847 |
| 0.28 | .6103 | .3897 | .3836 |
| 0.29 | .6141 | .3859 | .3825 |
| 0.30 | .6179 | .3821 | .3814 |
| 0.31 | .6217 | .3783 | .3802 |
| 0.32 | .6255 | .3745 | .3790 |
| 0.33 | .6293 | .3707 | .3778 |
| 0.34 | .6331 | .3669 | .3765 |
| 0.35 | .6368 | .3632 | .3752 |
| 0.36 | .6406 | .3594 | .3739 |
| 0.37 | .6443 | .3557 | .3725 |
| 0.38 | .6480 | .3520 | .3712 |
| **0.385** | **.6500** | **.3500** | **.3704** |
| 0.39 | .6517 | .3483 | .3697 |
| 0.40 | .6554 | .3446 | .3683 |
| 0.41 | .6591 | .3409 | .3668 |
| 0.42 | .6628 | .3372 | .3653 |
| 0.43 | .6664 | .3336 | .3637 |
| 0.44 | .6700 | .3300 | .3621 |
| 0.45 | .6736 | .3264 | .3605 |
| 0.46 | .6772 | .3228 | .3589 |
| 0.47 | .6808 | .3192 | .3572 |
| 0.48 | .6844 | .3156 | .3555 |
| 0.49 | .6879 | .3121 | .3538 |
| 0.50 | .6915 | .3085 | .3521 |
| 0.51 | .6950 | .3050 | .3503 |
| 0.52 | .6985 | .3015 | .3485 |
| **0.524** | **.7000** | **.3000** | **.3477** |
| 0.53 | .7019 | .2981 | .3467 |
| 0.54 | .7054 | .2946 | .3448 |
| 0.55 | .7088 | .2912 | .3429 |
| 0.56 | .7123 | .2877 | .3410 |
| 0.57 | .7157 | .2843 | .3391 |
| 0.58 | .7190 | .2810 | .3372 |
| 0.59 | .7224 | .2776 | .3352 |
| 0.60 | .7257 | .2743 | .3332 |
| 0.61 | .7291 | .2709 | .3312 |
| 0.62 | .7324 | .2676 | .3292 |
| 0.63 | .7357 | .2643 | .3271 |
| 0.64 | .7389 | .2611 | .3251 |
| 0.65 | .7422 | .2578 | .3230 |
| 0.66 | .7454 | .2546 | .3209 |
| 0.67 | .7486 | .2514 | .3187 |
| **0.674** | **.7500** | **.2500** | **.3179** |
| 0.68 | .7517 | .2483 | .3166 |
| 0.69 | .7549 | .2451 | .3144 |
| 0.70 | .7580 | .2420 | .3123 |

[a] If $z$ is negative, interchange the "area" columns, for example, if $z = -.10$, then .4602 of the area under the normal curve is below that point.

[b] Percentile points are commonly denoted as $_{p}z$; thus, the 60th percentile is denoted $_{.60}z$ and equals .253. Commonly used percentiles are given in boldface type.

**TABLE A** *Continued*

| | *Proportion of Area* | | |
|---|---|---|---|
| *z*[a] | *Below z*[b] | *Above z* | *Ordinate u* |
| 0.71 | .7611 | .2389 | .3101 |
| 0.72 | .7642 | .2358 | .3079 |
| 0.73 | .7673 | .2327 | .3056 |
| 0.74 | .7704 | .2296 | .3034 |
| 0.75 | .7734 | .2266 | .3011 |
| 0.76 | .7764 | .2236 | .2989 |
| 0.77 | .7794 | .2206 | .2966 |
| 0.78 | .7823 | .2177 | .2943 |
| 0.79 | .7852 | .2148 | .2920 |
| 0.80 | .7881 | .2119 | .2897 |
| 0.81 | .7910 | .2090 | .2874 |
| 0.82 | .7939 | .2061 | .2850 |
| 0.83 | .7967 | .2033 | .2827 |
| 0.84 | .7995 | .2005 | .2803 |
| **0.842** | **.8000** | **.2000** | **.2799** |
| 0.85 | .8023 | .1977 | .2780 |
| 0.86 | .8051 | .1949 | .2756 |
| 0.87 | .8078 | .1922 | .2732 |
| 0.88 | .8106 | .1894 | .2709 |
| 0.89 | .8133 | .1867 | .2685 |
| 0.90 | .8159 | .1841 | .2661 |
| 0.91 | .8186 | .1814 | .2637 |
| 0.92 | .8212 | .1788 | .2613 |
| 0.93 | .8238 | .1762 | .2589 |
| 0.94 | .8264 | .1736 | .2565 |
| 0.95 | .8289 | .1711 | .2541 |
| 0.96 | .8315 | .1685 | .2516 |
| 0.97 | .8340 | .1660 | .2492 |
| 0.98 | .8365 | .1635 | .2468 |
| 0.99 | .8389 | .1611 | .2444 |
| 1.00 | .8413 | .1587 | .2420 |
| 1.01 | .8438 | .1562 | .2396 |
| 1.02 | .8461 | .1539 | .2371 |
| 1.03 | .8485 | .1515 | .2347 |
| **1.036** | **.8500** | **.1500** | **.2333** |
| 1.04 | .8508 | .1492 | .2323 |
| 1.05 | .8531 | .1469 | .2299 |
| 1.06 | .8554 | .1446 | .2275 |
| 1.07 | .8577 | .1423 | .2251 |
| 1.08 | .8599 | .1401 | .2227 |
| 1.09 | .8621 | .1379 | .2203 |
| 1.10 | .8643 | .1357 | .2179 |
| 1.11 | .8665 | .1335 | .2155 |
| 1.12 | .8686 | .1314 | .2131 |
| 1.13 | .8708 | .1292 | .2107 |
| 1.14 | .8729 | .1271 | .2083 |
| 1.15 | .8749 | .1251 | .2059 |
| 1.16 | .8770 | .1230 | .2036 |
| 1.17 | .8790 | .1210 | .2012 |
| 1.18 | .8810 | .1190 | .1989 |

| | *Proportion of Area* | | |
|---|---|---|---|
| *z*[a] | *Below z*[b] | *Above z* | *Ordinate u* |
| 1.19 | .8830 | .1170 | .1965 |
| 1.20 | .8849 | .1151 | .1942 |
| 1.21 | .8869 | .1131 | .1919 |
| 1.22 | .8888 | .1112 | .1895 |
| 1.23 | .8907 | .1093 | .1872 |
| 1.24 | .8925 | .1075 | .1849 |
| 1.25 | .8944 | .1056 | .1826 |
| 1.26 | .8962 | .1038 | .1804 |
| 1.27 | .8980 | .1020 | .1781 |
| 1.28 | .8997 | .1003 | .1758 |
| **1.282** | **.9000** | **.1000** | **.1754** |
| 1.29 | .9015 | .0985 | .1736 |
| 1.30 | .9032 | .0968 | .1714 |
| 1.31 | .9049 | .0951 | .1691 |
| 1.32 | .9066 | .0934 | .1669 |
| 1.33 | .9082 | .0918 | .1647 |
| 1.34 | .9099 | .0901 | .1626 |
| **1.341** | **.9100** | **.0900** | **.1623** |
| 1.35 | .9115 | .0885 | .1604 |
| 1.36 | .9131 | .0869 | .1582 |
| 1.37 | .9147 | .0853 | .1561 |
| 1.38 | .9162 | .0838 | .1539 |
| 1.39 | .9177 | .0823 | .1518 |
| 1.40 | .9192 | .0808 | .1497 |
| **1.405** | **.9200** | **.0800** | **.1487** |
| 1.41 | .9207 | .0793 | .1476 |
| 1.42 | .9222 | .0778 | .1456 |
| 1.43 | .9236 | .0764 | .1435 |
| 1.44 | .9251 | .0749 | .1415 |
| 1.45 | .9265 | .0735 | .1394 |
| 1.46 | .9279 | .0721 | .1374 |
| 1.47 | .9292 | .0708 | .1354 |
| **1.476** | **.9300** | **.0700** | **.1342** |
| 1.48 | .9306 | .0694 | .1334 |
| 1.49 | .9319 | .0681 | .1315 |
| 1.50 | .9332 | .0668 | .1295 |
| 1.51 | .9345 | .0655 | .1276 |
| 1.52 | .9357 | .0643 | .1257 |
| 1.53 | .9370 | .0630 | .1238 |
| 1.54 | .9382 | .0618 | .1219 |
| 1.55 | .9394 | .0606 | .1200 |
| **1.555** | **.9400** | **.0600** | **.1191** |
| 1.56 | .9406 | .0594 | .1182 |
| 1.57 | .9418 | .0582 | .1163 |
| 1.58 | .9429 | .0571 | .1145 |
| 1.59 | .9441 | .0559 | .1127 |
| 1.60 | .9452 | .0548 | .1109 |
| 1.61 | .9463 | .0537 | .1092 |
| 1.62 | .9474 | .0526 | .1074 |
| 1.63 | .9484 | .0516 | .1057 |

**TABLE A** *Continued*

| | Proportion of Area | | |
|---|---|---|---|
| $z^a$ | Below $z^b$ | Above $z$ | Ordinate $u$ |
| 1.64 | .9495 | .0505 | .1040 |
| **1.645** | **.9500** | **.0500** | **.1031** |
| 1.65 | .9505 | .0495 | .1023 |
| 1.66 | .9515 | .0485 | .1006 |
| 1.67 | .9525 | .0475 | .0989 |
| 1.68 | .9535 | .0465 | .0973 |
| 1.69 | .9545 | .0455 | .0957 |
| 1.70 | .9554 | .0446 | .0940 |
| 1.71 | .9564 | .0436 | .0925 |
| 1.72 | .9573 | .0427 | .0909 |
| 1.73 | .9582 | .0418 | .0893 |
| 1.74 | .9591 | .0409 | .0878 |
| 1.75 | .9599 | .0401 | .0863 |
| **1.751** | **.9600** | **.0400** | **.0861** |
| 1.76 | .9608 | .0392 | .0848 |
| 1.77 | .9616 | .0384 | .0833 |
| 1.78 | .9625 | .0375 | .0818 |
| 1.79 | .9633 | .0367 | .0804 |
| 1.80 | .9641 | .0359 | .0790 |
| 1.81 | .9649 | .0351 | .0775 |
| 1.82 | .9656 | .0344 | .0761 |
| 1.83 | .9664 | .0338 | .0748 |
| 1.84 | .9671 | .0329 | .0734 |
| 1.85 | .9678 | .0322 | .0721 |
| 1.86 | .9686 | .0314 | .0707 |
| 1.87 | .9693 | .0307 | .0694 |
| 1.88 | .9699 | .0301 | .0681 |
| **1.881** | **.9700** | **.0300** | **.0680** |
| 1.89 | .9706 | .0294 | .0669 |
| 1.90 | .9713 | .0287 | .0656 |
| 1.91 | .9719 | .0281 | .0644 |
| 1.92 | .9726 | .0274 | .0632 |
| 1.93 | .9732 | .0268 | .0620 |
| 1.94 | .9738 | .0262 | .0608 |
| 1.95 | .9744 | .0256 | .0596 |
| **1.960** | **.9750** | **.0250** | **.0584** |
| 1.97 | .9756 | .0244 | .0573 |
| 1.98 | .9761 | .0239 | .0562 |
| 1.99 | .9767 | .0233 | .0551 |
| 2.00 | .9772 | .0228 | .0540 |
| 2.01 | .9778 | .0222 | .0529 |
| 2.02 | .9783 | .0217 | .0519 |
| 2.03 | .9788 | .0212 | .0508 |
| 2.04 | .9793 | .0207 | .0498 |
| 2.05 | .9798 | .0202 | .0488 |
| **2.054** | **.9800** | **.0200** | **.0484** |
| 2.06 | .9803 | .0197 | .0478 |
| 2.07 | .9808 | .0192 | .0468 |
| 2.08 | .9812 | .0188 | .0459 |
| 2.09 | .9817 | .0183 | .0449 |
| 2.10 | .9821 | .0179 | .0440 |
| 2.11 | .9826 | .0174 | .0431 |
| 2.12 | .9830 | .0170 | .0422 |
| 2.13 | .9834 | .0166 | .0413 |
| 2.14 | .9838 | .0162 | .0404 |
| 2.15 | .9842 | .0158 | .0396 |
| 2.16 | .9846 | .0154 | .0387 |
| 2.17 | .9850 | .0150 | .0379 |
| 2.18 | .9854 | .0146 | .0371 |
| 2.19 | .9857 | .0143 | .0363 |
| 2.20 | .9861 | .0139 | .0355 |
| 2.21 | .9864 | .0136 | .0347 |
| 2.22 | .9868 | .0132 | .0339 |
| 2.23 | .9871 | .0129 | .0332 |
| 2.24 | .9875 | .0125 | .0325 |
| 2.25 | .9878 | .0122 | .0317 |
| 2.26 | .9881 | .0119 | .0310 |
| 2.27 | .9884 | .0116 | .0303 |
| 2.28 | .9887 | .0113 | .0297 |
| 2.29 | .9890 | .0110 | .0290 |
| 2.30 | .9893 | .0107 | .0283 |
| 2.31 | .9896 | .0104 | .0277 |
| 2.32 | .9898 | .0102 | .0270 |
| **2.326** | **.9900** | **.0100** | **.0267** |
| 2.33 | .9901 | .0099 | .0264 |
| 2.34 | .9904 | .0096 | .0258 |
| 2.35 | .9906 | .0094 | .0252 |
| 2.36 | .9909 | .0091 | .0246 |
| 2.37 | .9911 | .0089 | .0241 |
| 2.38 | .9913 | .0087 | .0235 |
| 2.39 | .9916 | .0084 | .0229 |
| 2.40 | .9918 | .0082 | .0224 |
| 2.41 | .9920 | .0080 | .0219 |
| 2.42 | .9922 | .0078 | .0213 |
| 2.43 | .9925 | .0075 | .0208 |
| 2.44 | .9927 | .0073 | .0203 |
| 2.45 | .9929 | .0071 | .0198 |
| 2.46 | .9931 | .0069 | .0194 |
| 2.47 | .9932 | .0068 | .0189 |
| 2.48 | .9934 | .0066 | .0184 |
| 2.49 | .9936 | .0064 | .0180 |
| 2.50 | .9938 | .0062 | .0175 |
| 2.51 | .9940 | .0060 | .0171 |
| 2.52 | .9941 | .0059 | .0167 |
| 2.53 | .9943 | .0057 | .0163 |
| 2.54 | .9945 | .0055 | .0158 |
| 2.55 | .9946 | .0054 | .0154 |
| 2.56 | .9948 | .0052 | .0151 |
| 2.57 | .9949 | .0051 | .0147 |
| **2.576** | **.9950** | **.0050** | **.0145** |

**TABLE A** *Continued*

| | *Proportion of Area* | | |
|---|---|---|---|
| $z^a$ | *Below* $z^b$ | *Above z* | *Ordinate u* |
| 2.58 | .9951 | .0049 | .0143 |
| 2.59 | .9952 | .0048 | .0139 |
| 2.60 | .9953 | .0047 | .0136 |
| 2.61 | .9955 | .0045 | .0132 |
| 2.62 | .9956 | .0044 | .0129 |
| 2.63 | .9957 | .0043 | .0126 |
| 2.64 | .9959 | .0041 | .0122 |
| 2.65 | .9960 | .0040 | .0119 |
| 2.66 | .9961 | .0039 | .0116 |
| 2.67 | .9962 | .0038 | .0113 |
| 2.68 | .9963 | .0037 | .0110 |
| 2.69 | .9964 | .0036 | .0107 |
| 2.70 | .9965 | .0035 | .0104 |
| 2.71 | .9966 | .0034 | .0101 |
| 2.72 | .9967 | .0033 | .0099 |
| 2.73 | .9968 | .0032 | .0096 |
| 2.74 | .9969 | .0031 | .0093 |
| 2.75 | .9970 | .0030 | .0091 |
| 2.76 | .9971 | .0029 | .0088 |
| 2.77 | .9972 | .0028 | .0086 |
| 2.78 | .9973 | .0027 | .0084 |
| 2.79 | .9974 | .0026 | .0081 |
| 2.80 | .9974 | .0026 | .0079 |
| 2.81 | .9975 | .0025 | .0077 |
| 2.82 | .9976 | .0024 | .0075 |
| 2.83 | .9977 | .0023 | .0073 |
| 2.84 | .9977 | .0023 | .0071 |
| 2.85 | .9978 | .0022 | .0069 |
| 2.86 | .9979 | .0021 | .0067 |
| 2.87 | .9979 | .0021 | .0065 |
| 2.88 | .9980 | .0020 | .0063 |
| 2.89 | .9981 | .0019 | .0061 |
| 2.90 | .9981 | .0019 | .0060 |
| 2.91 | .9982 | .0018 | .0058 |
| 2.92 | .9982 | .0018 | .0056 |
| 2.93 | .9983 | .0017 | .0055 |
| 2.94 | .9984 | .0016 | .0053 |
| 2.95 | .9984 | .0016 | .0051 |
| 2.96 | .9985 | .0015 | .0050 |
| 2.97 | .9985 | .0015 | .0048 |
| 2.98 | .9986 | .0014 | .0047 |
| 2.99 | .9986 | .0014 | .0046 |
| 3.00 | .99865 | .00135 | .0044 |
| 3.01 | .99869 | .00131 | .00430 |
| 3.02 | .99874 | .00126 | .00417 |
| 3.03 | .99878 | .00122 | .00405 |
| 3.04 | .99882 | .00118 | .00393 |
| 3.05 | .99886 | .00114 | .00381 |
| 3.06 | .99889 | .00111 | .00370 |
| 3.07 | .99893 | .00107 | .00358 |

| | *Proportion of Area* | | |
|---|---|---|---|
| $z^a$ | *Below* $z^b$ | *Above z* | *Ordinate u* |
| 3.08 | .99896 | .00104 | .00348 |
| 3.09 | .99900 | .00100 | .00337 |
| **3.0902** | **.99900** | **.001000** | **.00337** |
| 3.10 | .99903 | .00097 | .00327 |
| 3.11 | .99906 | .00094 | .00317 |
| 3.12 | .99910 | .00090 | .00307 |
| 3.13 | .99913 | .00087 | .00298 |
| 3.14 | .99916 | .00084 | .00288 |
| 3.15 | .99918 | .00082 | .00279 |
| 3.16 | .99921 | .00079 | .00271 |
| 3.17 | .99924 | .00076 | .00262 |
| 3.18 | .99926 | .00074 | .00254 |
| 3.19 | .99929 | .00071 | .00246 |
| 3.20 | .99931 | .00069 | .00238 |
| 3.21 | .99934 | .00066 | .00231 |
| 3.22 | .99936 | .00064 | .00224 |
| 3.23 | .99938 | .00062 | .00216 |
| 3.24 | .99940 | .00060 | .00210 |
| 3.25 | .99942 | .00058 | .00203 |
| 3.26 | .99944 | .00056 | .00196 |
| 3.27 | .99946 | .00054 | .00190 |
| 3.28 | .99948 | .00050 | .00184 |
| 3.29 | .99950 | .00050 | .00178 |
| **3.2905** | **.999500** | **.000500** | **.00178** |
| 3.30 | .99951 | .00048 | .00172 |
| 3.31 | .99953 | .00047 | .00167 |
| 3.32 | .99955 | .00045 | .00161 |
| 3.33 | .99957 | .00043 | .00156 |
| 3.34 | .99958 | .00042 | .00151 |
| 3.35 | .99960 | .00040 | .00146 |
| 3.36 | .99961 | .00039 | .00141 |
| 3.37 | .99962 | .00038 | .00136 |
| 3.38 | .99964 | .00036 | .00132 |
| 3.39 | .99965 | .00035 | .00127 |
| 3.40 | .99966 | .00034 | .00123 |
| 3.41 | .99968 | .00032 | .00119 |
| 3.42 | .99969 | .00031 | .00115 |
| 3.43 | .99970 | .00030 | .00111 |
| 3.44 | .99971 | .00029 | .00107 |
| 3.45 | .99972 | .00028 | .00104 |
| 3.46 | .99973 | .00027 | .00100 |
| 3.47 | .99974 | .00026 | .00097 |
| 3.48 | .99975 | .00025 | .00094 |
| 3.49 | .99976 | .00024 | .00090 |
| 3.50 | .99977 | .00023 | .00087 |
| 3.51 | .99978 | .00022 | .00084 |
| 3.52 | .99978 | .00022 | .00081 |
| 3.53 | .99979 | .00021 | .00079 |
| 3.54 | .99980 | .00020 | .00076 |
| 3.55 | .99981 | .00019 | .00073 |

**TABLE A** *Continued*

| | *Proportion of Area* | | |
|---|---|---|---|
| $z^a$ | *Below* $z^b$ | *Above z* | *Ordinate u* |
| 3.56 | .99981 | .00019 | .00071 |
| 3.57 | .99982 | .00018 | .00068 |
| 3.58 | .99983 | .00017 | .00066 |
| 3.59 | .99983 | .00017 | .00063 |
| 3.60 | .99984 | .00016 | .00061 |
| 3.61 | .99985 | .00015 | .00059 |
| 3.62 | .99985 | .00015 | .00057 |
| 3.63 | .99986 | .00014 | .00055 |
| 3.64 | .99986 | .00014 | .00053 |
| 3.65 | .99987 | .00013 | .00051 |
| 3.66 | .999873 | .000126 | .00049 |
| 3.67 | .999879 | .000121 | .00047 |
| 3.68 | .999883 | .000117 | .00046 |
| 3.69 | .999888 | .000112 | .00044 |
| 3.70 | .999892 | .000108 | .00042 |
| 3.71 | .999896 | .000104 | .00041 |
| **3.719** | **.9999000** | **.000100** | **.00040** |
| 3.72 | .999900 | .000100 | .00039 |
| 3.73 | .999904 | .000096 | .00038 |
| 3.74 | .999908 | .000092 | .00037 |
| 3.75 | .999912 | .000088 | .00036 |
| 3.76 | .999915 | .000085 | .00034 |
| 3.77 | .999918 | .000082 | .00033 |
| 3.78 | .999922 | .000078 | .00031 |
| 3.79 | .999925 | .000075 | .00030 |
| 3.80 | .999928 | .000072 | .00029 |
| 3.81 | .999931 | .000070 | .00028 |

| | *Proportion of Area* | | |
|---|---|---|---|
| $z^a$ | *Below* $z^b$ | *Above z* | *Ordinate u* |
| 3.82 | .999933 | .000067 | .00027 |
| 3.83 | .999936 | .000064 | .00026 |
| 3.84 | .999939 | .000062 | .00025 |
| 3.85 | .999941 | .000059 | .00024 |
| 3.86 | .999943 | .000057 | .00023 |
| 3.87 | .999946 | .000054 | .00022 |
| 3.88 | .999948 | .000052 | .00021 |
| 3.89 | .999950 | .000050 | .00021 |
| **3.891** | **.9999500** | **.000050** | **.00021** |
| 3.90 | .999952 | .000048 | .00020 |
| 3.91 | .999954 | .000046 | .00019 |
| 3.92 | .999956 | .000044 | .00018 |
| 3.93 | .999958 | .000043 | .00018 |
| 3.94 | .999959 | .000041 | .0017 |
| 3.95 | .999961 | .000039 | .00016 |
| 3.96 | .999963 | .000038 | .00016 |
| 3.97 | .999964 | .000036 | .00015 |
| 3.98 | .999966 | .000035 | .00014 |
| 3.99 | .999967 | .000033 | .00014 |
| 4.00 | .999968 | .000032 | .00013 |
| **4.265** | **.9999900** | **.0000100** | **.0000448** |
| 4.417 | .9999950 | .0000050 | .0000231 |
| 4.50 | .9999966023 | .0000033977 | .0000160 |
| 5.00 | .9999997133 | .0000002867 | .00000149 |
| 5.327 | .9999999500 | .0000000500 | .00000027 |
| 5.50 | .9999999810 | .0000000190 | .00000011 |
| 6.00 | .9999999990 | .0000000010 | .000000006 |

**TABLE B** Random Digits.[a]

| | | | | | | | | | | | | | | | | | | | |
|---|---|---|---|---|---|---|---|---|---|---|---|---|---|---|---|---|---|---|---|
| 60 | 36 | 59 | 46 | 53 | 35 | 07 | 53 | 39 | 49 | 42 | 61 | 42 | 92 | 97 | 01 | 91 | 82 | 83 | 16 |
| 83 | 79 | 94 | 24 | 02 | 56 | 62 | 33 | 44 | 42 | 34 | 99 | 44 | 13 | 74 | 70 | 07 | 11 | 47 | 36 |
| 32 | 96 | 00 | 74 | 05 | 36 | 40 | 98 | 32 | 32 | 99 | 38 | 54 | 16 | 00 | 11 | 13 | 30 | 75 | 86 |
| 19 | 32 | 25 | 38 | 45 | 57 | 62 | 05 | 26 | 06 | 66 | 49 | 76 | 86 | 46 | 78 | 13 | 86 | 65 | 59 |
| 11 | 22 | 09 | 47 | 47 | 07 | 39 | 93 | 74 | 08 | 48 | 50 | 92 | 39 | 29 | 27 | 48 | 24 | 54 | 76 |
| 31 | 75 | 15 | 72 | 60 | 68 | 98 | 00 | 53 | 39 | 15 | 47 | 04 | 83 | 55 | 88 | 65 | 12 | 25 | 96 |
| 88 | 49 | 29 | 93 | 82 | 14 | 45 | 40 | 45 | 04 | 20 | 09 | 49 | 89 | 77 | 74 | 84 | 39 | 34 | 13 |
| 30 | 93 | 44 | 77 | 44 | 07 | 48 | 18 | 38 | 28 | 73 | 78 | 80 | 65 | 33 | 28 | 59 | 72 | 04 | 05 |
| 22 | 88 | 84 | 88 | 93 | 27 | 49 | 99 | 87 | 48 | 60 | 53 | 04 | 51 | 28 | 74 | 02 | 28 | 46 | 17 |
| 78 | 21 | 21 | 69 | 93 | 35 | 90 | 29 | 13 | 86 | 44 | 37 | 21 | 54 | 86 | 65 | 74 | 11 | 40 | 14 |
| 41 | 84 | 98 | 45 | 47 | 46 | 85 | 05 | 23 | 26 | 34 | 67 | 75 | 83 | 00 | 74 | 91 | 06 | 43 | 45 |
| 46 | 35 | 23 | 30 | 49 | 69 | 24 | 89 | 34 | 60 | 45 | 30 | 50 | 75 | 21 | 61 | 31 | 83 | 18 | 55 |
| 11 | 08 | 79 | 62 | 94 | 14 | 01 | 33 | 17 | 92 | 59 | 74 | 76 | 72 | 77 | 76 | 50 | 33 | 45 | 13 |
| 52 | 70 | 10 | 83 | 37 | 56 | 30 | 38 | 73 | 15 | 16 | 52 | 06 | 96 | 76 | 11 | 65 | 49 | 98 | 93 |
| 57 | 27 | 53 | 68 | 98 | 81 | 30 | 44 | 85 | 85 | 68 | 65 | 22 | 73 | 76 | 92 | 85 | 25 | 58 | 66 |
| 20 | 85 | 77 | 31 | 56 | 70 | 28 | 42 | 43 | 26 | 79 | 37 | 59 | 52 | 20 | 01 | 15 | 96 | 32 | 67 |
| 15 | 63 | 38 | 49 | 24 | 90 | 41 | 59 | 36 | 14 | 33 | 52 | 12 | 66 | 65 | 55 | 82 | 34 | 76 | 41 |
| 92 | 69 | 44 | 82 | 97 | 39 | 90 | 40 | 21 | 15 | 59 | 58 | 94 | 90 | 67 | 66 | 82 | 14 | 15 | 75 |
| 77 | 61 | 31 | 90 | 19 | 88 | 15 | 20 | 00 | 80 | 20 | 55 | 49 | 14 | 09 | 96 | 27 | 74 | 82 | 57 |
| 38 | 68 | 83 | 24 | 86 | 45 | 13 | 46 | 35 | 45 | 59 | 40 | 47 | 20 | 59 | 43 | 94 | 75 | 16 | 80 |
| 25 | 16 | 30 | 18 | 89 | 70 | 01 | 41 | 50 | 21 | 41 | 29 | 06 | 73 | 12 | 71 | 85 | 71 | 59 | 57 |
| 65 | 25 | 10 | 76 | 29 | 37 | 23 | 93 | 32 | 95 | 05 | 87 | 00 | 11 | 19 | 92 | 78 | 42 | 63 | 40 |
| 36 | 81 | 54 | 36 | 25 | 18 | 63 | 73 | 75 | 09 | 82 | 44 | 49 | 90 | 05 | 04 | 92 | 17 | 37 | 01 |
| 64 | 39 | 71 | 16 | 92 | 05 | 32 | 78 | 21 | 62 | 20 | 24 | 78 | 17 | 59 | 45 | 19 | 72 | 53 | 32 |
| 04 | 51 | 52 | 56 | 24 | 95 | 09 | 66 | 79 | 46 | 48 | 46 | 08 | 55 | 58 | 15 | 19 | 11 | 87 | 82 |
| 83 | 76 | 16 | 08 | 73 | 43 | 25 | 38 | 41 | 45 | 60 | 83 | 32 | 59 | 83 | 01 | 29 | 14 | 13 | 49 |
| 14 | 38 | 70 | 63 | 45 | 80 | 85 | 40 | 92 | 79 | 43 | 52 | 90 | 63 | 18 | 38 | 38 | 47 | 47 | 61 |
| 51 | 32 | 19 | 22 | 46 | 80 | 08 | 87 | 70 | 74 | 88 | 72 | 25 | 67 | 36 | 66 | 16 | 44 | 94 | 31 |
| 72 | 47 | 20 | 00 | 08 | 80 | 89 | 01 | 80 | 02 | 94 | 81 | 33 | 19 | 00 | 54 | 15 | 58 | 34 | 36 |
| 05 | 46 | 65 | 53 | 06 | 93 | 12 | 81 | 84 | 64 | 74 | 45 | 79 | 05 | 61 | 72 | 84 | 81 | 18 | 34 |
| 39 | 52 | 87 | 24 | 84 | 82 | 47 | 42 | 55 | 93 | 48 | 54 | 53 | 52 | 47 | 18 | 61 | 91 | 36 | 74 |
| 81 | 61 | 61 | 87 | 11 | 53 | 34 | 24 | 42 | 76 | 75 | 12 | 21 | 17 | 24 | 74 | 62 | 77 | 37 | 07 |
| 07 | 58 | 61 | 61 | 20 | 82 | 64 | 12 | 28 | 20 | 92 | 90 | 41 | 31 | 41 | 32 | 39 | 21 | 97 | 63 |
| 90 | 76 | 70 | 42 | 35 | 13 | 57 | 41 | 72 | 00 | 69 | 90 | 26 | 37 | 42 | 78 | 46 | 42 | 25 | 01 |
| 40 | 18 | 82 | 81 | 93 | 29 | 59 | 38 | 86 | 27 | 94 | 97 | 21 | 15 | 98 | 62 | 09 | 53 | 67 | 87 |
| 34 | 41 | 48 | 21 | 57 | 86 | 88 | 75 | 50 | 87 | 19 | 15 | 20 | 00 | 23 | 12 | 30 | 28 | 07 | 83 |
| 63 | 43 | 97 | 53 | 63 | 44 | 98 | 91 | 68 | 22 | 36 | 02 | 40 | 08 | 67 | 76 | 37 | 84 | 16 | 05 |
| 67 | 04 | 90 | 90 | 70 | 93 | 39 | 94 | 55 | 47 | 94 | 45 | 87 | 42 | 84 | 05 | 04 | 14 | 98 | 07 |
| 79 | 49 | 50 | 41 | 46 | 52 | 16 | 29 | 02 | 86 | 54 | 15 | 83 | 42 | 43 | 46 | 97 | 83 | 54 | 82 |
| 91 | 70 | 43 | 05 | 52 | 04 | 73 | 72 | 10 | 31 | 75 | 05 | 19 | 30 | 29 | 47 | 66 | 56 | 43 | 82 |

[a]From *A Million Random Digits With 100,000 Normal Deviates* (New York: Free Press, 1955), by permission of the RAND Corporation.

T-table

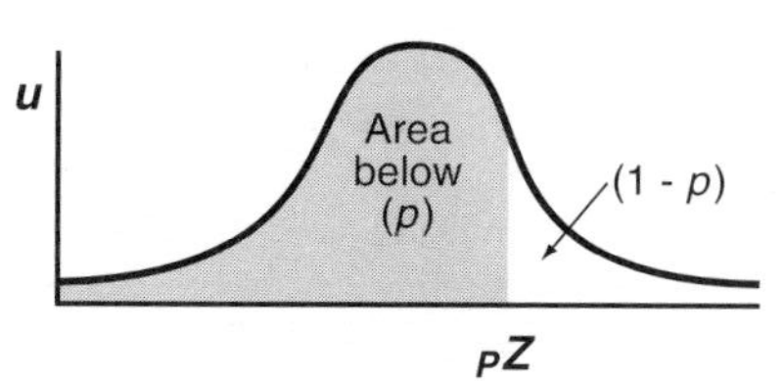


**TABLE C** Percentile Points of $t$-Distribution.[a, b]

| $v$ | | | $\alpha_1 = .10$ | $\alpha_1 = .05$ | $\alpha_1 = .025$ | $\alpha_1 = .01$ | $\alpha_1 = .005$ | $\alpha_1 = .001$ | $\alpha_1 = .0005$ | | Kurtosis |
|---|---|---|---|---|---|---|---|---|---|---|---|
| | | | | $\alpha_2 = .10$ | $\alpha_2 = .05$ | $\alpha_2 = .02$ | $\alpha_2 = .01$ | $\alpha_2 = .002$ | $\alpha_2 = .001$ | | |
| $v$ | $_{.75}t$ | $_{.80}t$ | $_{.90}t$ | $_{.95}t$ | $_{.975}t$ | $_{.99}t$ | $_{.995}t$ | $_{.999}t$ | $_{.9995}t$ | $v$ | $\gamma_2$ |
| **1** | 1.000 | 1.376 | 3.078 | 6.314 | 12.706 | 31.821 | 63.657 | 318.309 | 636.619 | **1** | |
| **2** | .816 | 1.061 | 1.886 | 2.920 | 4.303 | 6.965 | 9.925 | 22.327 | 31.598 | **2** | |
| **3** | .765 | .978 | 1.638 | 2.353 | 3.182 | 4.541 | 5.841 | 10.214 | 12.924 | **3** | |
| **4** | .741 | .941 | 1.532 | 2.132 | 2.776 | 3.747 | 4.604 | 7.173 | 8.610 | **4** | |
| **5** | .727 | .920 | 1.476 | 2.015 | 2.571 | 3.365 | 4.032 | 5.893 | 6.869 | **5** | 6 |
| **6** | .718 | .906 | 1.440 | 1.943 | 2.447 | 3.143 | 3.707 | 5.208 | 5.959 | **6** | 3 |
| **7** | .711 | .896 | 1.415 | 1.895 | 2.365 | 2.998 | 3.499 | 4.785 | 5.408 | **7** | 2 |
| **8** | .706 | .889 | 1.397 | 1.860 | 2.306 | 2.896 | 3.555 | 4.501 | 5.041 | **8** | 1.5 |
| **9** | .703 | .883 | 1.383 | 1.833 | 2.262 | 2.821 | 3.250 | 4.297 | 4.781 | **9** | 1.2 |
| **10** | .700 | .879 | 1.372 | 1.812 | 2.228 | 2.764 | 3.169 | 4.144 | 4.587 | **10** | 1.0 |
| **11** | .697 | .876 | 1.363 | 1.796 | 2.201 | 2.718 | 3.106 | 4.025 | 4.437 | **11** | .86 |
| **12** | .695 | .873 | 1.356 | 1.782 | 2.179 | 2.681 | 3.055 | 3.930 | 4.318 | **12** | .75 |
| **13** | .694 | .870 | 1.350 | 1.771 | 2.160 | 2.650 | 3.012 | 3.852 | 4.221 | **13** | .67 |
| **14** | .692 | .868 | 1.345 | 1.761 | 2.145 | 2.624 | 2.977 | 3.787 | 4.140 | **14** | .60 |
| **15** | .691 | .866 | 1.341 | 1.753 | 2.131 | 2.602 | 2.947 | 3.733 | 4.073 | **15** | .55 |
| **16** | .690 | .865 | 1.337 | 1.746 | 2.120 | 2.583 | 2.921 | 3.686 | 4.015 | **16** | .50 |
| **17** | .689 | .863 | 1.333 | 1.740 | 2.110 | 2.567 | 2.898 | 3.646 | 3.965 | **17** | .46 |
| **18** | .688 | .862 | 1.330 | 1.734 | 2.101 | 2.552 | 2.878 | 3.610 | 3.922 | **18** | .42 |
| **19** | .688 | .861 | 1.328 | 1.729 | 2.093 | 2.539 | 2.861 | 3.579 | 3.883 | **19** | .40 |
| **20** | .687 | .860 | 1.325 | 1.725 | 2.086 | 2.528 | 2.845 | 3.552 | 3.850 | **20** | .38 |

**TABLE C** *Continued*

| $\nu$ | $_{.75}t$ | $_{.80}t$ | $\alpha_1 = .10$<br>$_{.90}t$ | $\alpha_1 = .05$<br>$\alpha_2 = .10$<br>$_{.95}t$ | $\alpha_1 = .025$<br>$\alpha_2 = .05$<br>$_{.975}t$ | $\alpha_1 = .01$<br>$\alpha_2 = .02$<br>$_{.99}t$ | $\alpha_1 = .005$<br>$\alpha_2 = .01$<br>$_{.995}t$ | $\alpha_1 = .001$<br>$\alpha_2 = .002$<br>$_{.999}t$ | $\alpha_1 = .0005$<br>$\alpha_2 = .001$<br>$_{.9995}t$ | $\nu$ | Kurtosis<br>$\gamma_2$ |
|---|---|---|---|---|---|---|---|---|---|---|---|
| **21** | .686 | .859 | 1.323 | 1.721 | 2.080 | 2.518 | 2.831 | 3.527 | 3.819 | **21** | .35 |
| **22** | .686 | .858 | 1.321 | 1.717 | 2.074 | 2.508 | 2.819 | 3.505 | 3.792 | **22** | .33 |
| **23** | .685 | .858 | 1.319 | 1.714 | 2.069 | 2.500 | 2.807 | 3.485 | 3.767 | **23** | .32 |
| **24** | .685 | .857 | 1.318 | 1.711 | 2.064 | 2.492 | 2.797 | 3.467 | 3.745 | **24** | .30 |
| **25** | .684 | .856 | 1.316 | 1.708 | 2.060 | 2.485 | 2.787 | 3.450 | 3.725 | **25** | .29 |
| **26** | .684 | .856 | 1.315 | 1.706 | 2.056 | 2.479 | 2.779 | 3.435 | 3.707 | **26** | .27 |
| **27** | .684 | .855 | 1.314 | 1.703 | 2.052 | 2.473 | 2.771 | 3.421 | 3.690 | **27** | .26 |
| **28** | .683 | .855 | 1.313 | 1.701 | 2.048 | 2.467 | 2.763 | 3.408 | 3.674 | **28** | .25 |
| **29** | .683 | .854 | 1.311 | 1.699 | 2.045 | 2.462 | 2.756 | 3.396 | 3.659 | **29** | .24 |
| **30** | .683 | .854 | 1.310 | 1.697 | 2.042 | 2.457 | 2.750 | 3.385 | 3.646 | **30** | .23 |
| **35** | .682 | .852 | 1.306 | 1.690 | 2.030 | 2.438 | 2.724 | 3.340 | 3.591 | **35** | .19 |
| **40** | .681 | .851 | 1.303 | 1.684 | 2.021 | 2.423 | 2.704 | 3.307 | 3.551 | **40** | .17 |
| **50** | .680 | .849 | 1.299 | 1.676 | 2.008 | 2.403 | 2.678 | 3.261 | 3.496 | **50** | .13 |
| **60** | .679 | .848 | 1.296 | 1.671 | 2.000 | 2.390 | 2.660 | 3.232 | 3.460 | **60** | .11 |
| **70** | .678 | .847 | 1.294 | 1.667 | 1.994 | 2.381 | 2.648 | 3.211 | 3.435 | **70** | .09 |
| **80** | .678 | .847 | 1.293 | 1.665 | 1.990 | 2.374 | 2.638 | 3.195 | 3.416 | **80** | .08 |
| **90** | .678 | .846 | 1.291 | 1.662 | 1.987 | 2.368 | 2.632 | 3.183 | 3.402 | **90** | .07 |
| **100** | .677 | .846 | 1.290 | 1.661 | 1.984 | 2.364 | 2.626 | 3.174 | 3.380 | **100** | .06 |
| **120** | .677 | .845 | 1.289 | 1.658 | 1.980 | 2.358 | 2.617 | 3.160 | 3.373 | **120** | .05 |
| **200** | .676 | .844 | 1.286 | 1.653 | 1.972 | 2.345 | 2.601 | 3.131 | 3.340 | **200** | .03 |
| **300** | .676 | .843 | 1.285 | 1.650 | 1.968 | 2.339 | 2.592 | 3.118 | 3.323 | **300** | .02 |
| **400** | .676 | .843 | 1.284 | 1.649 | 1.966 | 2.336 | 2.588 | 3.111 | 3.315 | **400** | .015 |
| **500** | .676 | .843 | 1.284 | 1.648 | 1.965 | 2.334 | 2.586 | 3.107 | 3.310 | **500** | .012 |
| **1000** | .675 | .842 | 1.283 | 1.647 | 1.962 | 2.330 | 2.581 | 3.098 | 3.301 | **1000** | .006 |
| $\infty$ | .674 | .842 | 1.282 | 1.645 | 1.960 | 2.326 | 2.576 | 3.090 | 3.291 | $\infty$ | 0 |

[a]Table C is adapted from Table III of Fisher and Yates: *Statistical Tables for Biological, Agricultural and Medical Research,* published by Oliver & Boyd Ltd., Edinburgh, and by permission of the authors and publishers. (Certain corrections and additions from Federighi (1959); other values were calculated by Geroge Kretke.)

[b]The lower percentiles are related to the upper percentiles which are tabulated by the equation $_pt_\nu = -_{1-p}t_\nu$. Thus, the 10th percentile in the *t*-distribution with $\nu = 15$ equals the negative of the 90th percentile in the same distribution, that is, $_{.10}t_{15} = -1.341$. *Critical values* for nondirectional ($\alpha_2$) tests are: $|_{1-\alpha/2}t|$; for directional ($\alpha_1$) tests: $_{1-\alpha}t$. Thus, with $\alpha_2 = .05$ and $\nu = 20$: $|2.086|$; for $\alpha_1 = .05$ and $\nu = 20$, $|t| = 1.725$.

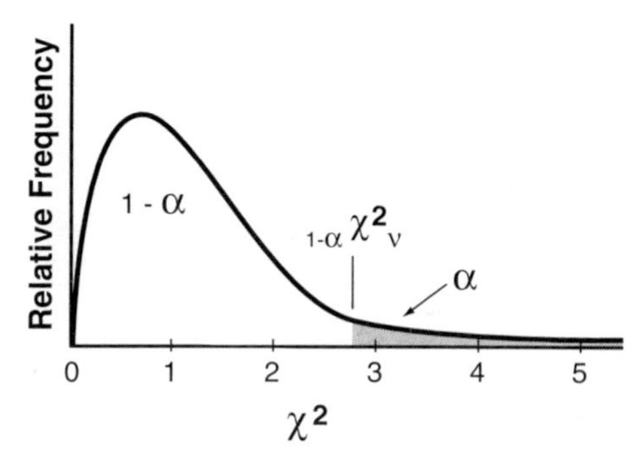


**TABLE D** Percentile Points of Chi-Square Distributions[a]: ${}_p\chi^2_\nu = {}_{1-\alpha}\chi^2_\nu$.

| $\nu$ | $p$ = .01 | .02 | .05 | .10 | .20 | .30 | .50 | .70 | .80 | .90 | .95 ($\alpha$ = .05) | .98 | .99 ($\alpha$ = .01) | .999 | $\nu$ | *Mode* | *Skewness* $\Omega K$ | *Kurtosis* $\gamma_2$ |
|---|---|---|---|---|---|---|---|---|---|---|---|---|---|---|---|---|---|---|
| **1** | .00016 | .00063 | .00393 | .0158 | .0642 | .148 | .455 | 1.07 | 1.64 | 2.71 | 3.84 | 5.41 | 6.64 | 10.83 | **1** | | | 12.0 |
| **2** | .0201 | .0404 | .103 | .211 | .446 | .713 | 1.39 | 2.41 | 3.22 | 4.60 | 5.99 | 7.82 | 9.21 | 13.82 | **2** | | 1.00 | 6.0 |
| **3** | .115 | .185 | .352 | .584 | 1.00 | 1.42 | 2.37 | 3.66 | 4.64 | 6.25 | 7.82 | 9.84 | 11.34 | 16.27 | **3** | 1 | .82 | 4.0 |
| **4** | .297 | .429 | .711 | 1.06 | 1.65 | 2.20 | 3.36 | 4.88 | 5.99 | 7.78 | 9.49 | 11.67 | 13.28 | 18.47 | **4** | 2 | .71 | 3.0 |
| **5** | .554 | .752 | 1.14 | 1.61 | 2.34 | 3.00 | 4.35 | 6.06 | 7.29 | 9.24 | 11.07 | 13.39 | 15.09 | 20.52 | **5** | 3 | .63 | 2.4 |
| **6** | .872 | 1.13 | 1.64 | 2.20 | 3.07 | 3.83 | 5.35 | 7.23 | 8.56 | 10.64 | 12.59 | 15.03 | 16.81 | 22.46 | **6** | 4 | .58 | 2.0 |
| **7** | 1.24 | 1.56 | 2.17 | 2.83 | 3.82 | 4.67 | 6.35 | 8.38 | 9.80 | 12.02 | 14.07 | 16.62 | 18.48 | 24.32 | **7** | 5 | .53 | 1.7 |
| **8** | 1.65 | 2.03 | 2.73 | 3.49 | 4.59 | 5.53 | 7.34 | 9.52 | 11.03 | 13.36 | 15.51 | 18.17 | 20.09 | 26.12 | **8** | 6 | .50 | 1.5 |
| **9** | 2.09 | 2.53 | 3.32 | 4.17 | 5.38 | 6.39 | 8.34 | 10.66 | 12.24 | 14.68 | 16.92 | 19.68 | 21.67 | 27.88 | **9** | 7 | .47 | 1.3 |
| **10** | 2.56 | 3.06 | 3.94 | 4.86 | 6.18 | 7.27 | 9.34 | 11.78 | 13.44 | 15.99 | 18.31 | 21.16 | 23.21 | 29.59 | **10** | 8 | .45 | 1.2 |
| **11** | 3.05 | 3.61 | 4.58 | 5.58 | 6.99 | 8.15 | 10.34 | 12.90 | 14.63 | 17.28 | 19.68 | 22.62 | 24.72 | 31.26 | **11** | 9 | .43 | 1.1 |
| **12** | 3.57 | 4.18 | 5.23 | 6.30 | 7.81 | 9.03 | 11.34 | 14.01 | 15.81 | 18.55 | 21.03 | 24.05 | 26.22 | 32.91 | **12** | 10 | .41 | 1.0 |
| **13** | 4.11 | 4.76 | 5.89 | 7.04 | 8.63 | 9.93 | 12.34 | 15.12 | 16.98 | 19.81 | 22.36 | 25.47 | 27.69 | 34.53 | **13** | 11 | .39 | .92 |
| **14** | 4.66 | 5.37 | 6.57 | 7.79 | 9.47 | 10.82 | 13.34 | 16.22 | 18.15 | 21.06 | 23.68 | 26.87 | 29.14 | 36.12 | **14** | 12 | .38 | .86 |
| **15** | 5.23 | 5.98 | 7.26 | 8.55 | 10.31 | 11.72 | 14.34 | 17.32 | 19.31 | 22.31 | 25.00 | 28.26 | 30.58 | 37.70 | **15** | 13 | .37 | .80 |
| **16** | 5.81 | 6.61 | 7.96 | 9.31 | 11.15 | 12.62 | 15.34 | 18.42 | 20.46 | 23.54 | 26.30 | 29.63 | 32.00 | 39.25 | **16** | 14 | .35 | .75 |
| **17** | 6.41 | 7.26 | 8.67 | 10.08 | 12.00 | 13.53 | 16.34 | 19.51 | 21.62 | 24.77 | 27.59 | 31.00 | 33.41 | 40.79 | **17** | 15 | .34 | .71 |
| **18** | 7.02 | 7.91 | 9.39 | 10.86 | 12.86 | 14.44 | 17.34 | 20.60 | 22.76 | 25.99 | 28.87 | 32.35 | 34.80 | 42.31 | **18** | 16 | .33 | .67 |
| **19** | 7.63 | 8.57 | 10.12 | 11.65 | 13.72 | 15.35 | 18.34 | 21.69 | 23.90 | 27.20 | 30.14 | 33.69 | 36.19 | 43.82 | **19** | 17 | .32 | .63 |

**TABLE D** *Continued*

| | | | | | | | | | | $\alpha = .05$ | | $\alpha = .01$ | | | | *Skewness* | *Kurtosis* |
|---|---|---|---|---|---|---|---|---|---|---|---|---|---|---|---|---|---|
| $v$ | $p = .01$ | .02 | .05 | .10 | .20 | .30 | .50 | .70 | .80 | .90 | .95 | .98 | .99 | .999 | $v$ | *Mode* | $\Omega K$ | $\gamma_2$ |
| **20** | 8.26 | 9.24 | 10.85 | 12.44 | 14.58 | 16.27 | 19.34 | 22.78 | 25.04 | 28.41 | 31.41 | 35.02 | 37.57 | 45.32 | **20** | 18 | .32 | .60 |
| **21** | 8.90 | 9.92 | 11.59 | 13.24 | 15.44 | 17.18 | 20.34 | 23.86 | 26.17 | 29.62 | 32.67 | 36.34 | 38.93 | 46.80 | **21** | 19 | .31 | .57 |
| **22** | 9.54 | 10.60 | 12.34 | 14.04 | 16.31 | 18.10 | 21.34 | 24.94 | 27.30 | 30.81 | 33.92 | 37.66 | 40.29 | 48.27 | **22** | 20 | .30 | .55 |
| **23** | 10.20 | 11.29 | 13.09 | 14.85 | 17.19 | 19.02 | 22.34 | 26.02 | 28.43 | 32.01 | 35.17 | 38.97 | 41.64 | 49.73 | **23** | 21 | .29 | .52 |
| **24** | 10.86 | 11.90 | 13.85 | 15.66 | 18.06 | 19.94 | 23.34 | 27.10 | 29.55 | 33.20 | 36.42 | 40.27 | 42.98 | 51.18 | **24** | 22 | .29 | .50 |
| **25** | 11.52 | 12.70 | 14.61 | 16.47 | 18.94 | 20.87 | 24.34 | 28.17 | 30.68 | 34.38 | 37.65 | 41.57 | 44.31 | 52.62 | **25** | 23 | .28 | .48 |
| **26** | 12.20 | 13.41 | 15.38 | 17.29 | 19.82 | 21.79 | 25.34 | 29.25 | 31.80 | 35.56 | 38.88 | 42.86 | 45.64 | 54.05 | **26** | 24 | .28 | .46 |
| **27** | 12.88 | 14.12 | 16.15 | 18.11 | 20.70 | 22.72 | 26.34 | 30.32 | 32.91 | 36.74 | 40.11 | 44.14 | 46.96 | 55.48 | **27** | 25 | .27 | .44 |
| **28** | 13.56 | 14.85 | 16.93 | 18.94 | 21.59 | 23.65 | 27.34 | 31.39 | 34.03 | 37.92 | 41.34 | 45.42 | 48.28 | 56.89 | **28** | 26 | .27 | .43 |
| **29** | 14.26 | 15.57 | 17.71 | 19.77 | 22.48 | 24.58 | 28.34 | 32.46 | 35.14 | 39.09 | 42.56 | 46.69 | 49.59 | 58.30 | **29** | 27 | .26 | .41 |
| **30** | 14.95 | 16.31 | 18.49 | 20.60 | 23.36 | 25.51 | 29.34 | 33.53 | 36.25 | 40.26 | 43.77 | 47.96 | 50.89 | 59.70 | **30** | 28 | .26 | .40 |
| **40** | 22.16 | 23.84 | 26.51 | 29.05 | 32.38 | 34.81 | 39.34 | 44.17 | 47.27 | 51.81 | 55.76 | 60.44 | 63.69 | 73.40 | **40** | 38 | .22 | .30 |
| **50** | 24.71 | 31.66 | 34.76 | 37.69 | 41.45 | 44.31 | 49.33 | 54.72 | 58.16 | 63.17 | 67.51 | 72.61 | 76.15 | 81.66 | **50** | 48 | .20 | .29 |
| **60** | 37.48 | 38.70 | 43.19 | 46.46 | 50.64 | 53.81 | 54.33 | 65.23 | 68.97 | 74.40 | 79.08 | 84.58 | 88.38 | 99.61 | **60** | 58 | .18 | .20 |
| **70** | 45.44 | 47.89 | 51.74 | 55.33 | 59.90 | 63.35 | 69.33 | 75.69 | 79.72 | 85.53 | 90.53 | 96.39 | 100.4 | 112.3 | **70** | 68 | .17 | .17 |
| **80** | 53.54 | 56.21 | 60.34 | 64.28 | 69.2 | 72.9 | 79.33 | 86.1 | 90.4 | 96.58 | 101.9 | 108.1 | 112.3 | 124.8 | **80** | 78 | .16 | .15 |
| **90** | 61.75 | 64.64 | 69.13 | 73.29 | 78.6 | 82.5 | 89.33 | 96.5 | 101.1 | 107.6 | 113.1 | 119.6 | 124.1 | 137.2 | **90** | 88 | .15 | .13 |
| **100** | 70.06 | 73.14 | 77.43 | 82.36 | 87.9 | 92.1 | 99.33 | 106.9 | 111.7 | 118.5 | 124.3 | 131.1 | 135.8 | 149.4 | **100** | 98 | .14 | .12 |

[a]Mode = $v - 2$, $\mu = v$, $\sigma^2_{\chi^2} = 2v$, see Secs. 6.9 and 6.10 for definition of $\Omega$ and $\gamma_2$.

**TABLE E** Fisher's *Z*-transformation[a, b] of $r$: $|z| = \frac{1}{2}\ln\left(\frac{1+|r|}{1-|r|}\right)$.

| $r$ | $Z$ | $r$ | $Z$ | $r$ | $Z$ | $r$ | $Z$ | $r$ | $Z$ |
|---|---|---|---|---|---|---|---|---|---|
| .000 | .000 | .200 | .203 | .400 | .424 | .600 | .693 | .800 | 1.099 |
| .005 | .005 | .205 | .208 | .405 | .430 | .605 | .701 | .805 | 1.113 |
| .010 | .010 | .210 | .213 | .410 | .436 | .610 | .709 | .810 | 1.127 |
| .015 | .015 | .215 | .218 | .415 | .442 | .615 | .717 | .815 | 1.142 |
| .020 | .020 | .220 | .224 | .420 | .448 | .620 | .725 | .820 | 1.157 |
| .025 | .025 | .225 | .229 | .425 | .454 | .625 | .733 | .825 | 1.172 |
| .030 | .030 | .230 | .234 | .430 | .460 | .630 | .741 | .830 | 1.188 |
| .035 | .035 | .235 | .239 | .435 | .466 | .635 | .750 | .835 | 1.204 |
| .040 | .040 | .240 | .245 | .440 | .472 | .640 | .758 | .840 | 1.221 |
| .045 | .045 | .245 | .250 | .445 | .478 | .645 | .767 | .845 | 1.238 |
| .050 | .050 | .250 | .255 | .450 | .485 | .650 | .775 | .850 | 1.256 |
| .055 | .055 | .255 | .261 | .455 | .491 | .655 | .784 | .855 | 1.274 |
| .060 | .060 | .260 | .266 | .460 | .497 | .660 | .793 | .860 | 1.293 |
| .065 | .065 | .265 | .271 | .465 | .504 | .665 | .802 | .865 | 1.313 |
| .070 | .070 | .270 | .277 | .470 | .510 | .670 | .811 | .870 | 1.333 |
| .075 | .075 | .275 | .282 | .475 | .517 | .675 | .820 | .875 | 1.354 |
| .080 | .080 | .280 | .288 | .480 | .523 | .680 | .829 | .880 | 1.376 |
| .085 | .085 | .285 | .293 | .485 | .530 | .685 | .838 | .885 | 1.398 |
| .090 | .090 | .290 | .299 | .490 | .536 | .690 | .848 | .890 | 1.422 |
| .095 | .095 | .295 | .304 | .495 | .543 | .695 | .858 | .895 | 1.447 |
| .100 | .100 | .300 | .310 | .500 | .549 | .700 | .867 | .900 | 1.472 |
| .105 | .105 | .305 | .315 | .505 | .556 | .705 | .877 | .905 | 1.499 |
| .110 | .110 | .310 | .321 | .510 | .563 | .710 | .887 | .910 | 1.528 |
| .115 | .116 | .315 | .326 | .515 | .570 | .715 | .897 | .915 | 1.557 |
| .120 | .121 | .320 | .332 | .520 | .576 | .720 | .908 | .920 | 1.589 |
| .125 | .126 | .325 | .337 | .525 | .583 | .725 | .918 | .925 | 1.623 |
| .130 | .131 | .330 | .343 | .530 | .590 | .730 | .929 | .930 | 1.658 |
| .135 | .136 | .335 | .348 | .535 | .597 | .735 | .940 | .935 | 1.697 |
| .140 | .141 | .340 | .354 | .540 | .604 | .740 | .950 | .940 | 1.738 |
| .145 | .146 | .345 | .360 | .545 | .611 | .745 | .962 | .945 | 1.783 |
| .150 | .151 | .350 | .365 | .550 | .618 | .750 | .973 | .950 | 1.832 |
| .155 | .156 | .355 | .371 | .555 | .626 | .755 | .984 | .955 | 1.886 |
| .160 | .161 | .360 | .377 | .560 | .633 | .760 | .996 | .960 | 1.946 |
| .165 | .167 | .365 | .383 | .565 | .640 | .765 | 1.008 | .965 | 2.014 |
| .170 | .172 | .370 | .388 | .570 | .648 | .770 | 1.020 | .970 | 2.092 |
| .175 | .177 | .375 | .394 | .575 | .655 | .775 | 1.033 | .975 | 2.185 |
| .180 | .182 | .380 | .400 | .580 | .662 | .780 | 1.045 | .980 | 2.298 |
| .185 | .187 | .385 | .406 | .585 | .670 | .785 | 1.058 | .985 | 2.443 |
| .190 | .192 | .390 | .412 | .590 | .678 | .790 | 1.071 | .990 | 2.645 |
| .195 | .198 | .395 | .418 | .595 | .685 | .795 | 1.085 | .995 | 2.994 |

[a]Values reported in this table were calculated by Thomas O. Maguire and are reproduced with his kind permission. For research purposes, use spreadsheet functions such as EXCEL's "FISHER" and "FISHERINV" functions to eliminate the need for interpolation. The transformations can also be obtained via many scientific calculators.

[b]Or $|z| = 1.151 \log\left(\frac{1+|r|}{1-|r|}\right)$

**TABLE F** Critical Values of $F$: ${}_{1-\alpha}F_{\nu_B,\,\nu_e}$ (from EXCEL's FDIST function)

| | | $\nu_B$ (degrees of freedom for numerator) | | | | | | | | | | | |
|---|---|---|---|---|---|---|---|---|---|---|---|---|---|
| $\nu_e$ | $\alpha$ | 1 | 2 | 3 | 4 | 5 | 6 | 7 | 8 | 9 | 10 | 12 | 15 |
| 1 | .25 | 5.828 | 7.500 | 8.200 | 8.581 | 8.820 | 8.983 | 9.102 | 9.192 | 9.263 | 9.320 | 9.406 | 9.493 |
| | .10 | 39.86 | 49.50 | 53.59 | 55.83 | 57.24 | 58.20 | 58.91 | 59.44 | 59.86 | 60.19 | 60.71 | 61.22 |
| | .05 | 161.4 | 199.5 | 215.7 | 224.6 | 230.2 | 234.0 | 236.8 | 238.9 | 240.5 | 241.9 | 243.9 | 245.9 |
| | .025 | 647.8 | 799.5 | 864.2 | 899.6 | 921.8 | 937.1 | 948.2 | 956.6 | 963.3 | 968.6 | 976.7 | 984.9 |
| | .01 | 4052 | 4999 | 5404 | 5624 | 5764 | 5859 | 5928 | 5981 | 6022 | 6056 | 6107 | 6157 |
| 2 | .25 | 2.571 | 3.000 | 3.153 | 3.232 | 3.280 | 3.312 | 3.335 | 3.353 | 3.366 | 3.377 | 3.393 | 3.410 |
| | .10 | 8.526 | 9.000 | 9.162 | 9.243 | 9.293 | 9.326 | 9.349 | 9.367 | 9.381 | 9.392 | 9.408 | 9.425 |
| | .05 | 18.51 | 19.00 | 19.16 | 19.25 | 19.30 | 19.33 | 19.35 | 19.37 | 19.38 | 19.40 | 19.41 | 19.43 |
| | .025 | 38.51 | 39.00 | 39.17 | 39.25 | 39.30 | 39.33 | 39.36 | 39.37 | 39.39 | 39.40 | 39.41 | 39.43 |
| | .010 | 98.50 | 99.00 | 99.16 | 99.25 | 99.30 | 99.33 | 99.36 | 99.38 | 99.39 | 99.40 | 99.42 | 99.43 |
| | .001 | 998.4 | 998.8 | 999.3 | 999.3 | 999.3 | 999.3 | 999.3 | 999.3 | 999.3 | 999.3 | 999.3 | 999.3 |
| 3 | .25 | 2.024 | 2.280 | 2.356 | 2.390 | 2.409 | 2.422 | 2.430 | 2.436 | 2.441 | 2.445 | 2.450 | 2.455 |
| | .10 | 5.538 | 5.462 | 5.391 | 5.343 | 5.309 | 5.285 | 5.266 | 5.252 | 5.240 | 5.230 | 5.216 | 5.200 |
| | .05 | 10.13 | 9.552 | 9.277 | 9.117 | 9.013 | 8.941 | 8.887 | 8.845 | 8.812 | 8.785 | 8.745 | 8.703 |
| | .025 | 17.44 | 16.04 | 15.44 | 15.10 | 14.88 | 14.73 | 14.62 | 14.54 | 14.47 | 14.42 | 14.34 | 14.25 |
| | .010 | 34.12 | 30.82 | 29.46 | 28.71 | 28.24 | 27.91 | 27.67 | 27.49 | 27.34 | 27.23 | 27.05 | 26.87 |
| | .001 | 167.1 | 148.5 | 141.1 | 137.1 | 134.6 | 132.8 | 131.6 | 130.6 | 129.9 | 129.2 | 128.3 | 127.4 |
| 4 | .25 | 1.807 | 2.000 | 2.047 | 2.064 | 2.072 | 2.077 | 2.079 | 2.080 | 2.081 | 2.082 | 2.083 | 2.083 |
| | .10 | 4.545 | 4.325 | 4.191 | 4.107 | 4.051 | 4.010 | 3.979 | 3.955 | 3.936 | 3.920 | 3.896 | 3.870 |
| | .05 | 7.709 | 6.944 | 6.591 | 6.388 | 6.256 | 6.163 | 6.094 | 6.041 | 5.999 | 5.964 | 5.912 | 5.858 |
| | .025 | 12.22 | 10.65 | 9.979 | 9.604 | 9.364 | 9.197 | 9.074 | 8.980 | 8.905 | 8.844 | 8.751 | 8.657 |
| | .010 | 21.20 | 18.00 | 16.69 | 15.98 | 15.52 | 15.21 | 14.98 | 14.80 | 14.66 | 14.55 | 14.37 | 14.20 |
| | .001 | 74.13 | 61.25 | 56.17 | 53.43 | 51.72 | 50.52 | 49.65 | 49.00 | 48.47 | 48.05 | 47.41 | 46.76 |
| 5 | .25 | 1.692 | 1.853 | 1.884 | 1.893 | 1.895 | 1.894 | 1.894 | 1.892 | 1.891 | 1.890 | 1.888 | 1.885 |
| | .10 | 4.060 | 3.780 | 3.619 | 3.520 | 3.453 | 3.405 | 3.368 | 3.339 | 3.316 | 3.297 | 3.268 | 3.238 |
| | .05 | 6.608 | 5.786 | 5.409 | 5.192 | 5.050 | 4.950 | 4.876 | 4.818 | 4.772 | 4.735 | 4.678 | 4.619 |
| | .025 | 10.01 | 8.434 | 7.764 | 7.388 | 7.146 | 6.978 | 6.853 | 6.757 | 6.681 | 6.619 | 6.525 | 6.428 |
| | .010 | 16.26 | 13.27 | 12.06 | 11.39 | 10.97 | 10.67 | 10.46 | 10.29 | 10.16 | 10.05 | 9.888 | 9.722 |
| | .001 | 47.18 | 37.12 | 33.20 | 31.08 | 29.75 | 28.83 | 28.17 | 27.65 | 27.24 | 26.91 | 26.42 | 25.91 |
| 6 | .25 | 1.621 | 1.762 | 1.784 | 1.787 | 1.785 | 1.782 | 1.779 | 1.776 | 1.773 | 1.771 | 1.767 | 1.762 |
| | .10 | 3.776 | 3.463 | 3.289 | 3.181 | 3.108 | 3.055 | 3.014 | 2.983 | 2.958 | 2.937 | 2.905 | 2.871 |
| | .05 | 5.987 | 5.143 | 4.757 | 4.534 | 4.387 | 4.284 | 4.207 | 4.147 | 4.099 | 4.060 | 4.000 | 3.938 |
| | .025 | 8.813 | 7.260 | 6.599 | 6.227 | 5.988 | 5.820 | 5.695 | 5.600 | 5.523 | 5.461 | 5.366 | 5.269 |
| | .010 | 13.75 | 10.92 | 9.780 | 9.148 | 8.746 | 8.466 | 8.260 | 8.102 | 7.976 | 7.874 | 7.718 | 7.559 |
| | .001 | 35.51 | 27.00 | 23.71 | 21.92 | 20.80 | 20.03 | 19.46 | 19.03 | 18.69 | 18.41 | 17.99 | 17.56 |
| 7 | .25 | 1.573 | 1.701 | 1.717 | 1.716 | 1.711 | 1.706 | 1.701 | 1.697 | 1.693 | 1.690 | 1.684 | 1.678 |
| | .10 | 3.589 | 3.257 | 3.074 | 2.961 | 2.883 | 2.827 | 2.785 | 2.752 | 2.725 | 2.703 | 2.668 | 2.632 |
| | .05 | 5.591 | 4.737 | 4.347 | 4.120 | 3.972 | 3.866 | 3.787 | 3.726 | 3.677 | 3.637 | 3.575 | 3.511 |
| | .025 | 8.073 | 6.542 | 5.890 | 5.523 | 5.285 | 5.119 | 4.995 | 4.899 | 4.823 | 4.761 | 4.666 | 4.568 |
| | .010 | 12.25 | 9.547 | 8.451 | 7.847 | 7.460 | 7.191 | 6.993 | 6.840 | 6.719 | 6.620 | 6.469 | 6.314 |
| | .001 | 29.25 | 21.69 | 18.77 | 17.20 | 16.21 | 15.52 | 15.02 | 14.63 | 14.33 | 14.08 | 13.71 | 13.32 |
| 8 | .25 | 1.538 | 1.657 | 1.668 | 1.664 | 1.658 | 1.651 | 1.645 | 1.640 | 1.635 | 1.631 | 1.624 | 1.617 |
| | .10 | 3.458 | 3.113 | 2.924 | 2.806 | 2.726 | 2.668 | 2.624 | 2.589 | 2.561 | 2.538 | 2.502 | 2.464 |
| | .05 | 5.318 | 4.459 | 4.066 | 3.838 | 3.688 | 3.581 | 3.500 | 3.438 | 3.388 | 3.347 | 3.284 | 3.218 |
| | .025 | 7.571 | 6.059 | 5.416 | 5.053 | 4.817 | 4.652 | 4.529 | 4.433 | 4.357 | 4.295 | 4.200 | 4.101 |
| | .010 | 11.26 | 8.649 | 7.591 | 7.006 | 6.632 | 6.371 | 6.178 | 6.029 | 5.911 | 5.814 | 5.667 | 5.515 |
| | .001 | 25.41 | 18.49 | 15.83 | 14.39 | 13.48 | 12.86 | 12.40 | 12.05 | 11.77 | 11.54 | 11.19 | 10.84 |

**TABLE F** *Continued*

| $\nu_B$ (degrees of freedom for numerator) | | | | | | | | | | | | |
|---|---|---|---|---|---|---|---|---|---|---|---|---|
| 20 | 25 | 30 | 40 | 50 | 100 | 120 | 200 | 500 | 1000 | ∞ | $\alpha$ | $\nu_e$ |
| 9.581 | 9.634 | 9.670 | 9.714 | 9.741 | 9.795 | 9.804 | 9.822 | 9.838 | 9.844 | 9.849 | **.25** | 1 |
| 61.74 | 62.05 | 62.26 | 62.53 | 62.69 | 63.01 | 63.06 | 63.17 | 63.26 | 63.30 | 63.33 | **.10** | |
| 248.0 | 249.3 | 250.1 | 251.1 | 251.8 | 253.0 | 253.3 | 253.7 | 254.1 | 254.2 | 254.3 | **.05** | |
| 993.1 | 998.1 | 1001 | 1006 | 1008 | 1013 | 1014 | 1016 | 1017 | 1018 | 1018 | **.025** | |
| 6209 | 6240 | 6260 | 6286 | 6302 | 6334 | 6340 | 6350 | 6360 | 6363 | 6366 | **.01** | |
| 3.426 | 3.436 | 3.443 | 3.451 | 3.46 | 3.47 | 3.47 | 3.47 | 3.47 | 3.48 | 3.48 | **.25** | 2 |
| 9.441 | 9.451 | 9.458 | 9.466 | 9.47 | 9.48 | 9.48 | 9.49 | 9.49 | 9.49 | 9.49 | **.10** | |
| 19.45 | 19.46 | 19.46 | 19.47 | 19.5 | 19.5 | 19.5 | 19.5 | 19.5 | 19.5 | 19.5 | **.05** | |
| 39.45 | 39.46 | 39.46 | 39.47 | 39.5 | 39.5 | 39.5 | 39.5 | 39.5 | 39.5 | 39.5 | **.025** | |
| 99.45 | 99.46 | 99.47 | 99.48 | 99.5 | 99.5 | 99.5 | 99.5 | 99.5 | 99.5 | 99.5 | **.010** | |
| 999.3 | 999.3 | 999.3 | 999.3 | 999.3 | 999.3 | 999.3 | 999.3 | 999.3 | 999.3 | 999.3 | **.001** | |
| 2.460 | 2.463 | 2.465 | 2.467 | 2.469 | 2.471 | 2.472 | 2.473 | 2.474 | 2.474 | 2.474 | **.25** | 3 |
| 5.184 | 5.175 | 5.168 | 5.160 | 5.155 | 5.144 | 5.143 | 5.139 | 5.136 | 5.135 | 5.134 | **.10** | |
| 8.660 | 8.634 | 8.617 | 8.594 | 8.581 | 8.554 | 8.549 | 8.540 | 8.532 | 8.529 | 8.526 | **.05** | |
| 14.17 | 14.12 | 14.08 | 14.04 | 14.01 | 13.96 | 13.95 | 13.93 | 13.91 | 13.91 | 13.90 | **.025** | |
| 26.69 | 26.58 | 26.50 | 26.41 | 26.35 | 26.24 | 26.22 | 26.18 | 26.15 | 26.14 | 26.13 | **.010** | |
| 126.4 | 125.8 | 125.4 | 125.0 | 124.7 | 124.1 | 124.0 | 123.7 | 123.6 | 123.5 | 123.5 | **.001** | |
| 2.083 | 2.083 | 2.082 | 2.082 | 2.082 | 2.081 | 2.081 | 2.081 | 2.081 | 2.081 | 2.081 | **.25** | 4 |
| 3.844 | 3.828 | 3.817 | 3.804 | 3.795 | 3.778 | 3.775 | 3.769 | 3.764 | 3.762 | 3.761 | **.10** | |
| 5.803 | 5.769 | 5.746 | 5.717 | 5.699 | 5.664 | 5.658 | 5.646 | 5.635 | 5.632 | 5.628 | **.05** | |
| 8.560 | 8.501 | 8.461 | 8.411 | 8.381 | 8.319 | 8.309 | 8.288 | 8.270 | 8.264 | 8.257 | **.025** | |
| 14.02 | 13.91 | 13.84 | 13.75 | 13.69 | 13.58 | 13.56 | 13.52 | 13.49 | 13.47 | 13.46 | **.010** | |
| 46.10 | 45.69 | 45.43 | 45.08 | 44.88 | 44.47 | 44.40 | 44.27 | 44.14 | 44.09 | 44.05 | **.001** | |
| 1.882 | 1.880 | 1.878 | 1.876 | 1.875 | 1.872 | 1.872 | 1.871 | 1.870 | 1.870 | 1.869 | **.25** | 5 |
| 3.207 | 3.187 | 3.174 | 3.157 | 3.147 | 3.126 | 3.123 | 3.116 | 3.109 | 3.107 | 3.105 | **.10** | |
| 4.558 | 4.521 | 4.496 | 4.464 | 4.444 | 4.405 | 4.398 | 4.385 | 4.373 | 4.369 | 4.365 | **.05** | |
| 6.329 | 6.288 | 6.227 | 6.175 | 6.144 | 6.080 | 6.069 | 6.048 | 6.028 | 6.022 | 6.015 | **.025** | |
| 9.553 | 9.449 | 9.379 | 9.291 | 9.238 | 9.130 | 9.112 | 9.075 | 9.042 | 9.032 | 9.020 | **.010** | |
| 25.39 | 25.08 | 24.87 | 24.60 | 24.44 | 24.11 | 24.06 | 23.95 | 23.85 | 23.82 | 23.79 | **.001** | |
| 1.757 | 1.753 | 1.751 | 1.748 | 1.746 | 1.741 | 1.741 | 1.739 | 1.738 | 1.737 | 1.737 | **.25** | 6 |
| 2.836 | 2.815 | 2.800 | 2.781 | 2.770 | 2.746 | 2.742 | 2.734 | 2.727 | 2.725 | 2.722 | **.10** | |
| 3.874 | 3.835 | 3.808 | 3.774 | 3.754 | 3.712 | 3.705 | 3.690 | 3.678 | 3.673 | 3.669 | **.05** | |
| 5.168 | 5.107 | 5.065 | 5.012 | 4.980 | 4.915 | 4.904 | 4.882 | 4.862 | 4.856 | 4.849 | **.025** | |
| 7.396 | 7.296 | 7.229 | 7.143 | 7.091 | 6.987 | 6.969 | 6.934 | 6.901 | 6.891 | 6.880 | **.010** | |
| 17.12 | 16.85 | 16.67 | 16.44 | 16.31 | 16.03 | 15.98 | 15.89 | 15.80 | 15.77 | 15.75 | **.001** | |
| 1.671 | 1.667 | 1.663 | 1.659 | 1.657 | 1.651 | 1.650 | 1.648 | 1.646 | 1.646 | 1.645 | **.25** | 7 |
| 2.595 | 2.571 | 2.555 | 2.535 | 2.523 | 2.497 | 2.493 | 2.484 | 2.476 | 2.473 | 2.471 | **.10** | |
| 3.445 | 3.404 | 3.376 | 3.340 | 3.319 | 3.275 | 3.267 | 3.252 | 3.239 | 3.234 | 3.230 | **.05** | |
| 4.467 | 4.405 | 4.362 | 4.309 | 4.276 | 4.210 | 4.199 | 4.176 | 4.156 | 4.149 | 4.142 | **.025** | |
| 6.155 | 6.058 | 5.992 | 5.908 | 5.858 | 5.755 | 5.737 | 5.702 | 5.671 | 5.660 | 5.650 | **.010** | |
| 12.93 | 12.69 | 12.53 | 12.33 | 12.20 | 11.95 | 11.91 | 11.82 | 11.75 | 11.72 | 11.70 | **.001** | |
| 1.609 | 1.603 | 1.600 | 1.595 | 1.591 | 1.585 | 1.584 | 1.581 | 1.579 | 1.578 | 1.578 | **.25** | 8 |
| 2.425 | 2.400 | 2.383 | 2.361 | 2.348 | 2.321 | 2.316 | 2.307 | 2.298 | 2.295 | 2.293 | **.10** | |
| 3.150 | 3.108 | 3.079 | 3.043 | 3.020 | 2.975 | 2.967 | 2.951 | 2.937 | 2.932 | 2.928 | **.05** | |
| 3.999 | 3.937 | 3.894 | 3.840 | 3.807 | 3.739 | 3.728 | 3.705 | 3.684 | 3.677 | 3.670 | **.025** | |
| 5.359 | 5.263 | 5.198 | 5.116 | 5.065 | 4.963 | 4.946 | 4.911 | 4.880 | 4.869 | 4.859 | **.010** | |
| 10.48 | 10.26 | 10.11 | 9.919 | 9.804 | 9.572 | 9.532 | 9.453 | 9.382 | 9.358 | 9.333 | **.001** | |

**TABLE F** *Continued*

| $\nu_e$ | $\alpha$ | $\nu_B$ (degrees of freedom for numerator) 1 | 2 | 3 | 4 | 5 | 6 | 7 | 8 | 9 | 10 | 12 | 15 |
|---|---|---|---|---|---|---|---|---|---|---|---|---|---|
| 9 | .25 | 1.512 | 1.624 | 1.632 | 1.625 | 1.617 | 1.609 | 1.602 | 1.596 | 1.591 | 1.586 | 1.579 | 1.570 |
| | .10 | 3.360 | 3.006 | 2.813 | 2.693 | 2.611 | 2.551 | 2.505 | 2.469 | 2.440 | 2.416 | 2.379 | 2.340 |
| | .05 | 5.117 | 4.256 | 3.863 | 3.633 | 3.482 | 3.374 | 3.293 | 3.230 | 3.179 | 3.137 | 3.073 | 3.006 |
| | .025 | 7.209 | 5.715 | 5.078 | 4.718 | 4.484 | 4.320 | 4.197 | 4.102 | 4.026 | 3.964 | 3.868 | 3.769 |
| | .010 | 10.56 | 8.022 | 6.992 | 6.422 | 6.057 | 5.802 | 5.613 | 5.467 | 5.351 | 5.257 | 5.111 | 4.962 |
| | .001 | 22.86 | 16.39 | 13.90 | 12.56 | 11.71 | 11.13 | 10.70 | 10.37 | 10.11 | 9.894 | 9.570 | 9.239 |
| 10 | .25 | 1.491 | 1.598 | 1.603 | 1.595 | 1.585 | 1.576 | 1.569 | 1.562 | 1.556 | 1.551 | 1.543 | 1.534 |
| | .10 | 3.285 | 2.924 | 2.728 | 2.605 | 2.522 | 2.461 | 2.414 | 2.377 | 2.347 | 2.323 | 2.284 | 2.244 |
| | .05 | 4.965 | 4.103 | 3.708 | 3.478 | 3.326 | 3.217 | 3.135 | 3.072 | 3.020 | 2.978 | 2.913 | 2.845 |
| | .025 | 6.937 | 5.456 | 4.826 | 4.468 | 4.236 | 4.072 | 3.950 | 3.855 | 3.779 | 3.717 | 3.621 | 3.522 |
| | .010 | 10.04 | 7.559 | 6.552 | 5.994 | 5.636 | 5.386 | 5.200 | 5.057 | 4.942 | 4.849 | 4.706 | 4.558 |
| | .001 | 21.04 | 14.90 | 12.55 | 11.28 | 10.48 | 9.926 | 9.517 | 9.204 | 8.956 | 8.754 | 8.446 | 8.129 |
| 11 | .25 | 1.475 | 1.577 | 1.580 | 1.570 | 1.560 | 1.550 | 1.542 | 1.535 | 1.528 | 1.523 | 1.514 | 1.504 |
| | .10 | 3.225 | 2.860 | 2.660 | 2.536 | 2.451 | 2.389 | 2.342 | 2.304 | 2.274 | 2.248 | 2.209 | 2.167 |
| | .05 | 4.844 | 3.982 | 3.587 | 3.357 | 3.204 | 3.095 | 3.012 | 2.948 | 2.896 | 2.854 | 2.788 | 2.719 |
| | .025 | 6.724 | 5.256 | 4.630 | 4.275 | 4.044 | 3.881 | 3.759 | 3.664 | 3.588 | 3.526 | 3.430 | 3.330 |
| | .010 | 9.646 | 7.206 | 6.217 | 5.668 | 5.316 | 5.069 | 4.886 | 4.744 | 4.632 | 4.539 | 4.397 | 4.251 |
| | .001 | 19.69 | 13.81 | 11.56 | 10.35 | 9.579 | 9.047 | 8.655 | 8.355 | 8.116 | 7.923 | 7.625 | 7.321 |
| 12 | .25 | 1.461 | 1.560 | 1.561 | 1.550 | 1.539 | 1.529 | 1.520 | 1.512 | 1.505 | 1.500 | 1.490 | 1.480 |
| | .10 | 3.177 | 2.807 | 2.606 | 2.480 | 2.394 | 2.331 | 2.283 | 2.245 | 2.214 | 2.188 | 2.147 | 2.105 |
| | .05 | 4.747 | 3.885 | 3.490 | 3.259 | 3.106 | 2.996 | 2.913 | 2.849 | 2.796 | 2.753 | 2.687 | 2.617 |
| | .025 | 6.554 | 5.096 | 4.474 | 4.121 | 3.891 | 3.728 | 3.607 | 3.512 | 3.436 | 3.374 | 3.277 | 3.177 |
| | .010 | 9.330 | 6.927 | 5.953 | 5.412 | 5.064 | 4.821 | 4.640 | 4.499 | 4.388 | 4.296 | 4.155 | 4.010 |
| | .001 | 18.64 | 12.97 | 10.80 | 9.633 | 8.892 | 8.378 | 8.001 | 7.711 | 7.480 | 7.292 | 7.005 | 6.709 |
| 13 | .25 | 1.450 | 1.545 | 1.545 | 1.534 | 1.521 | 1.511 | 1.501 | 1.493 | 1.486 | 1.480 | 1.470 | 1.459 |
| | .10 | 3.136 | 2.763 | 2.560 | 2.434 | 2.347 | 2.283 | 2.234 | 2.195 | 2.164 | 2.138 | 2.097 | 2.053 |
| | .05 | 4.667 | 3.806 | 3.411 | 3.179 | 3.025 | 2.915 | 2.832 | 2.767 | 2.714 | 2.671 | 2.604 | 2.533 |
| | .025 | 6.414 | 4.965 | 4.347 | 3.996 | 3.767 | 3.604 | 3.483 | 3.388 | 3.312 | 3.250 | 3.153 | 3.053 |
| | .010 | 9.074 | 6.701 | 5.739 | 5.205 | 4.862 | 4.620 | 4.441 | 4.302 | 4.191 | 4.100 | 3.960 | 3.815 |
| | .001 | 17.82 | 12.31 | 10.21 | 9.073 | 8.355 | 7.856 | 7.489 | 7.206 | 6.982 | 6.799 | 6.519 | 6.231 |
| 14 | .25 | 1.440 | 1.533 | 1.532 | 1.519 | 1.507 | 1.495 | 1.485 | 1.477 | 1.470 | 1.463 | 1.453 | 1.441 |
| | .10 | 3.102 | 2.726 | 2.522 | 2.395 | 2.307 | 2.243 | 2.193 | 2.154 | 2.122 | 2.095 | 2.054 | 2.010 |
| | .05 | 4.600 | 3.739 | 3.344 | 3.112 | 2.958 | 2.848 | 2.764 | 2.699 | 2.646 | 2.602 | 2.534 | 2.463 |
| | .025 | 6.298 | 4.857 | 4.242 | 3.892 | 3.663 | 3.501 | 3.380 | 3.285 | 3.209 | 3.147 | 3.050 | 2.949 |
| | .010 | 8.862 | 6.515 | 5.564 | 5.035 | 4.695 | 4.456 | 4.278 | 4.140 | 4.030 | 3.939 | 3.800 | 3.656 |
| | .001 | 17.14 | 11.78 | 9.730 | 8.622 | 7.922 | 7.436 | 7.078 | 6.802 | 6.583 | 6.404 | 6.130 | 5.848 |
| 15 | .25 | 1.432 | 1.523 | 1.520 | 1.507 | 1.494 | 1.482 | 1.472 | 1.463 | 1.456 | 1.449 | 1.438 | 1.426 |
| | .10 | 3.073 | 2.695 | 2.490 | 2.361 | 2.273 | 2.208 | 2.158 | 2.119 | 2.086 | 2.059 | 2.017 | 1.972 |
| | .05 | 4.543 | 3.682 | 3.287 | 3.056 | 2.901 | 2.790 | 2.707 | 2.641 | 2.588 | 2.544 | 2.475 | 2.403 |
| | .025 | 6.200 | 4.765 | 4.153 | 3.804 | 3.576 | 3.415 | 3.293 | 3.199 | 3.123 | 3.060 | 2.963 | 2.862 |
| | .010 | 8.683 | 6.359 | 5.417 | 4.893 | 4.556 | 4.318 | 4.142 | 4.004 | 3.895 | 3.805 | 3.666 | 3.522 |
| | .001 | 16.59 | 11.34 | 9.335 | 8.253 | 7.567 | 7.091 | 6.741 | 6.471 | 6.256 | 6.081 | 5.812 | 5.535 |
| 16 | .25 | 1.425 | 1.514 | 1.510 | 1.497 | 1.483 | 1.471 | 1.460 | 1.451 | 1.443 | 1.437 | 1.426 | 1.413 |
| | .10 | 3.048 | 2.668 | 2.462 | 2.333 | 2.244 | 2.178 | 2.128 | 2.088 | 2.055 | 2.028 | 1.985 | 1.940 |
| | .05 | 4.494 | 3.634 | 3.239 | 3.007 | 2.852 | 2.741 | 2.657 | 2.591 | 2.538 | 2.494 | 2.425 | 2.352 |
| | .025 | 6.115 | 4.687 | 4.077 | 3.729 | 3.502 | 3.341 | 3.219 | 3.125 | 3.049 | 2.986 | 2.889 | 2.788 |
| | .010 | 8.531 | 6.226 | 5.292 | 4.773 | 4.437 | 4.202 | 4.026 | 3.890 | 3.780 | 3.691 | 3.553 | 3.409 |
| | .001 | 16.12 | 10.97 | 9.006 | 7.944 | 7.272 | 6.805 | 6.460 | 6.195 | 5.984 | 5.812 | 5.547 | 5.275 |

**TABLE F** *Continued*

| $\nu_B$ (degrees of freedom for numerator) | | | | | | | | | | | | |
|---|---|---|---|---|---|---|---|---|---|---|---|---|
| 20 | 25 | 30 | 40 | 50 | 100 | 120 | 200 | 500 | 1000 | $\infty$ | $\alpha$ | $\nu_e$ |
| 1.561 | 1.555 | 1.551 | 1.545 | 1.541 | 1.534 | 1.533 | 1.530 | 1.527 | 1.527 | 1.526 | **.25** | 9 |
| 2.298 | 2.272 | 2.255 | 2.232 | 2.218 | 2.189 | 2.184 | 2.174 | 2.165 | 2.162 | 2.159 | **.10** | |
| 2.936 | 2.893 | 2.864 | 2.826 | 2.803 | 2.756 | 2.748 | 2.731 | 2.717 | 2.712 | 2.707 | **.05** | |
| 3.667 | 3.604 | 3.560 | 3.505 | 3.472 | 3.403 | 3.392 | 3.368 | 3.347 | 3.340 | 3.333 | **.025** | |
| 4.808 | 4.713 | 4.649 | 4.567 | 4.517 | 4.415 | 4.398 | 4.363 | 4.332 | 4.321 | 4.311 | **.010** | |
| 8.898 | 8.689 | 8.547 | 8.368 | 8.260 | 8.038 | 8.002 | 7.926 | 7.858 | 7.836 | 7.813 | **.001** | |
| 1.523 | 1.517 | 1.512 | 1.506 | 1.502 | 1.493 | 1.492 | 1.489 | 1.486 | 1.485 | 1.484 | **.25** | 10 |
| 2.201 | 2.174 | 2.155 | 2.132 | 2.117 | 2.087 | 2.082 | 2.071 | 2.062 | 2.059 | 2.055 | **.10** | |
| 2.774 | 2.730 | 2.700 | 2.661 | 2.637 | 2.588 | 2.580 | 2.563 | 2.548 | 2.543 | 2.538 | **.05** | |
| 3.419 | 3.355 | 3.311 | 3.255 | 3.221 | 3.152 | 3.140 | 3.116 | 3.094 | 3.087 | 3.080 | **.025** | |
| 4.405 | 4.311 | 4.247 | 4.165 | 4.115 | 4.014 | 3.996 | 3.962 | 3.930 | 3.920 | 3.909 | **.010** | |
| 7.803 | 7.604 | 7.469 | 7.297 | 7.192 | 6.980 | 6.944 | 6.872 | 6.807 | 6.785 | 6.762 | **.001** | |
| 1.493 | 1.486 | 1.481 | 1.474 | 1.469 | 1.460 | 1.459 | 1.455 | 1.452 | 1.451 | 1.450 | **.25** | 11 |
| 2.123 | 2.095 | 2.076 | 2.052 | 2.036 | 2.005 | 2.000 | 1.989 | 1.979 | 1.975 | 1.972 | **.10** | |
| 2.646 | 2.601 | 2.570 | 2.531 | 2.507 | 2.457 | 2.448 | 2.431 | 2.415 | 2.410 | 2.404 | **.05** | |
| 3.226 | 3.162 | 3.118 | 3.061 | 3.027 | 2.956 | 2.944 | 2.920 | 2.898 | 2.890 | 2.883 | **.025** | |
| 4.099 | 4.005 | 3.941 | 3.860 | 3.810 | 3.708 | 3.690 | 3.656 | 3.624 | 3.613 | 3.602 | **.010** | |
| 7.008 | 6.815 | 6.884 | 6.517 | 6.416 | 6.210 | 6.175 | 6.105 | 6.041 | 6.020 | 5.998 | **.001** | |
| 1.468 | 1.460 | 1.454 | 1.447 | 1.443 | 1.433 | 1.431 | 1.428 | 1.424 | 1.423 | 1.422 | **.25** | 12 |
| 2.060 | 2.031 | 2.011 | 1.986 | 1.970 | 1.938 | 1.932 | 1.921 | 1.911 | 1.097 | 1.904 | **.10** | |
| 2.544 | 2.498 | 2.466 | 2.426 | 2.401 | 2.350 | 2.341 | 2.323 | 2.307 | 2.302 | 2.296 | **.05** | |
| 3.073 | 3.008 | 2.963 | 2.906 | 2.871 | 2.800 | 2.787 | 2.763 | 2.740 | 2.733 | 2.725 | **.025** | |
| 3.858 | 3.765 | 3.701 | 3.619 | 3.569 | 3.467 | 3.449 | 3.414 | 3.382 | 3.372 | 3.361 | **.010** | |
| 6.405 | 6.217 | 6.090 | 5.928 | 5.829 | 5.627 | 5.593 | 5.524 | 5.462 | 5.441 | 5.420 | **.001** | |
| 1.447 | 1.438 | 1.432 | 1.425 | 1.420 | 1.409 | 1.408 | 1.404 | 1.400 | 1.399 | 1.398 | **.25** | 13 |
| 2.007 | 1.978 | 1.958 | 1.931 | 1.915 | 1.882 | 1.876 | 1.864 | 1.853 | 1.850 | 1.846 | **.10** | |
| 2.459 | 2.412 | 2.380 | 2.339 | 2.314 | 2.261 | 2.252 | 2.234 | 2.218 | 2.212 | 2.206 | **.05** | |
| 2.948 | 2.882 | 2.837 | 2.780 | 2.744 | 2.671 | 2.659 | 2.634 | 2.611 | 2.603 | 2.595 | **.025** | |
| 3.665 | 3.571 | 3.507 | 3.425 | 3.375 | 3.272 | 3.255 | 3.219 | 3.187 | 3.176 | 3.165 | **.010** | |
| 5.934 | 5.751 | 5.626 | 5.467 | 5.370 | 5.172 | 5.138 | 5.070 | 5.009 | 4.988 | 4.967 | **.001** | |
| 1.428 | 1.420 | 1.414 | 1.405 | 1.400 | 1.389 | 1.387 | 1.383 | 1.380 | 1.378 | 1.377 | **.25** | 14 |
| 1.962 | 1.933 | 1.912 | 1.885 | 1.869 | 1.834 | 1.828 | 1.816 | 1.805 | 1.801 | 1.797 | **.10** | |
| 2.388 | 2.341 | 2.308 | 2.266 | 2.241 | 2.187 | 2.178 | 2.159 | 2.142 | 2.136 | 2.131 | **.05** | |
| 2.844 | 2.778 | 2.732 | 2.674 | 2.638 | 2.565 | 2.552 | 2.526 | 2.503 | 2.495 | 2.487 | **.025** | |
| 3.505 | 3.412 | 3.348 | 3.266 | 3.215 | 3.112 | 3.094 | 3.059 | 3.026 | 3.015 | 3.004 | **.010** | |
| 5.557 | 5.377 | 5.254 | 5.098 | 5.002 | 4.807 | 4.773 | 4.707 | 4.645 | 4.625 | 4.604 | **.001** | |
| 1.413 | 1.404 | 1.397 | 1.389 | 1.383 | 1.372 | 1.370 | 1.366 | 1.362 | 1.360 | 1.359 | **.25** | 15 |
| 1.924 | 1.894 | 1.873 | 1.845 | 1.828 | 1.793 | 1.787 | 1.774 | 1.763 | 1.759 | 1.755 | **.10** | |
| 2.328 | 2.280 | 2.247 | 2.204 | 2.178 | 2.123 | 2.114 | 2.095 | 2.078 | 2.072 | 2.066 | **.05** | |
| 2.756 | 2.689 | 2.644 | 2.585 | 2.549 | 2.474 | 2.461 | 2.435 | 2.411 | 2.403 | 2.395 | **.025** | |
| 3.372 | 3.278 | 3.214 | 3.132 | 3.081 | 2.977 | 2.959 | 2.923 | 2.891 | 2.880 | 2.868 | **.010** | |
| 5.249 | 5.071 | 4.950 | 4.796 | 4.702 | 4.508 | 4.475 | 4.408 | 4.348 | 4.327 | 4.307 | **.001** | |
| 1.399 | 1.390 | 1.383 | 1.374 | 1.369 | 1.356 | 1.354 | 1.350 | 1.346 | 1.345 | 1.343 | **.25** | 16 |
| 1.891 | 1.860 | 1.839 | 1.811 | 1.793 | 1.757 | 1.751 | 1.738 | 1.726 | 1.722 | 1.718 | **.10** | |
| 2.276 | 2.227 | 2.194 | 2.151 | 2.124 | 2.068 | 2.059 | 2.039 | 2.022 | 2.016 | 2.010 | **.05** | |
| 2.681 | 2.614 | 2.568 | 2.509 | 2.472 | 2.396 | 2.383 | 2.357 | 2.333 | 2.324 | 2.316 | **.025** | |
| 3.259 | 3.165 | 3.101 | 3.018 | 2.967 | 2.863 | 2.845 | 2.808 | 2.775 | 2.764 | 2.753 | **.010** | |
| 4.992 | 4.817 | 4.697 | 4.545 | 4.451 | 4.259 | 4.226 | 4.160 | 4.100 | 4.080 | 4.059 | **.001** | |

**TABLE F** *Continued*

| $\nu_e$ | $\alpha$ | $\nu_B$ (degrees of freedom for numerator) 1 | 2 | 3 | 4 | 5 | 6 | 7 | 8 | 9 | 10 | 12 | 15 |
|---|---|---|---|---|---|---|---|---|---|---|---|---|---|
| 17 | .25 | 1.419 | 1.506 | 1.502 | 1.487 | 1.473 | 1.460 | 1.450 | 1.441 | 1.433 | 1.426 | 1.414 | 1.401 |
| | .10 | 3.026 | 2.645 | 2.437 | 2.308 | 2.218 | 2.152 | 2.102 | 2.061 | 2.028 | 2.001 | 1.958 | 1.912 |
| | .05 | 4.451 | 3.592 | 3.197 | 2.965 | 2.810 | 2.699 | 2.614 | 2.548 | 2.494 | 2.450 | 2.381 | 2.308 |
| | .025 | 6.042 | 4.619 | 4.011 | 3.665 | 3.438 | 3.277 | 3.156 | 3.061 | 2.985 | 2.922 | 2.825 | 2.723 |
| | .010 | 8.400 | 6.112 | 5.185 | 4.669 | 4.336 | 4.101 | 3.927 | 3.791 | 3.682 | 3.593 | 3.455 | 3.312 |
| | .001 | 15.72 | 10.66 | 8.727 | 7.683 | 7.022 | 6.562 | 6.224 | 5.962 | 5.754 | 5.584 | 5.324 | 5.055 |
| 18 | .25 | 1.413 | 1.499 | 1.494 | 1.479 | 1.464 | 1.452 | 1.441 | 1.431 | 1.423 | 1.416 | 1.404 | 1.391 |
| | .10 | 3.007 | 2.624 | 2.416 | 2.286 | 2.196 | 2.130 | 2.079 | 2.038 | 2.005 | 1.977 | 1.933 | 1.887 |
| | .05 | 4.414 | 3.555 | 3.160 | 2.928 | 2.773 | 2.661 | 2.577 | 2.510 | 2.456 | 2.412 | 2.342 | 2.269 |
| | .025 | 5.978 | 4.560 | 3.954 | 3.608 | 3.382 | 3.221 | 3.100 | 3.005 | 2.929 | 2.866 | 2.769 | 2.667 |
| | .010 | 8.285 | 6.013 | 5.092 | 4.579 | 4.248 | 4.015 | 3.841 | 3.705 | 3.597 | 3.508 | 3.371 | 3.227 |
| | .001 | 15.38 | 10.39 | 8.487 | 7.460 | 6.808 | 6.355 | 6.021 | 5.763 | 5.557 | 5.390 | 5.132 | 4.866 |
| 19 | .25 | 1.408 | 1.493 | 1.487 | 1.472 | 1.457 | 1.444 | 1.432 | 1.423 | 1.414 | 1.407 | 1.395 | 1.382 |
| | .10 | 2.990 | 2.606 | 2.397 | 2.266 | 2.176 | 2.109 | 2.058 | 2.017 | 1.984 | 1.956 | 1.912 | 1.865 |
| | .05 | 4.381 | 3.522 | 3.127 | 2.895 | 2.740 | 2.628 | 2.544 | 2.477 | 2.423 | 2.378 | 2.308 | 2.234 |
| | .025 | 5.922 | 4.508 | 3.903 | 3.559 | 3.333 | 3.172 | 3.051 | 2.956 | 2.880 | 2.817 | 2.720 | 2.617 |
| | .010 | 8.185 | 5.926 | 5.010 | 4.500 | 4.171 | 3.939 | 3.765 | 3.631 | 3.523 | 3.434 | 3.297 | 3.153 |
| | .001 | 15.08 | 10.16 | 8.280 | 7.265 | 6.622 | 6.175 | 5.845 | 5.591 | 5.387 | 5.222 | 4.967 | 4.703 |
| 20 | .25 | 1.404 | 1.487 | 1.481 | 1.465 | 1.450 | 1.437 | 1.425 | 1.415 | 1.407 | 1.399 | 1.387 | 1.374 |
| | .10 | 2.975 | 2.589 | 2.380 | 2.249 | 2.158 | 2.091 | 2.040 | 1.999 | 1.965 | 1.937 | 1.892 | 1.845 |
| | .05 | 4.351 | 3.493 | 3.098 | 2.866 | 2.711 | 2.599 | 2.514 | 2.447 | 2.393 | 2.348 | 2.278 | 2.203 |
| | .025 | 5.871 | 4.461 | 3.859 | 3.515 | 3.289 | 3.128 | 3.007 | 2.913 | 2.837 | 2.774 | 2.676 | 2.573 |
| | .010 | 8.096 | 5.849 | 4.938 | 4.431 | 4.103 | 3.871 | 3.699 | 3.564 | 3.457 | 3.368 | 3.231 | 3.088 |
| | .001 | 14.82 | 9.953 | 8.098 | 7.096 | 6.461 | 6.019 | 5.692 | 5.440 | 5.239 | 5.075 | 4.823 | 4.562 |
| 22 | .25 | 1.396 | 1.477 | 1.470 | 1.454 | 1.438 | 1.424 | 1.413 | 1.402 | 1.394 | 1.386 | 1.374 | 1.359 |
| | .10 | 2.949 | 2.561 | 2.351 | 2.219 | 2.128 | 2.060 | 2.008 | 1.967 | 1.933 | 1.904 | 1.859 | 1.811 |
| | .05 | 4.301 | 3.443 | 3.049 | 2.817 | 2.661 | 2.549 | 2.464 | 2.397 | 2.342 | 2.297 | 2.226 | 2.151 |
| | .025 | 5.786 | 4.383 | 3.783 | 3.440 | 3.215 | 3.055 | 2.934 | 2.839 | 2.763 | 2.700 | 2.602 | 2.498 |
| | .010 | 7.945 | 5.719 | 4.817 | 4.313 | 3.988 | 3.758 | 3.587 | 3.453 | 3.346 | 3.258 | 3.121 | 2.978 |
| | .001 | 14.38 | 9.612 | 7.796 | 6.814 | 6.191 | 5.758 | 5.437 | 5.190 | 4.993 | 4.832 | 4.583 | 4.326 |
| 24 | .25 | 1.390 | 1.470 | 1.462 | 1.445 | 1.428 | 1.414 | 1.402 | 1.392 | 1.383 | 1.375 | 1.362 | 1.347 |
| | .10 | 2.927 | 2.538 | 2.327 | 2.195 | 2.103 | 2.035 | 1.983 | 1.941 | 1.906 | 1.877 | 1.832 | 1.783 |
| | .05 | 4.260 | 3.403 | 3.009 | 2.776 | 2.621 | 2.508 | 2.423 | 2.355 | 2.300 | 2.255 | 2.183 | 2.108 |
| | .025 | 5.717 | 4.319 | 3.721 | 3.379 | 3.155 | 2.995 | 2.874 | 2.779 | 2.703 | 2.640 | 2.541 | 2.437 |
| | .010 | 7.823 | 5.614 | 4.718 | 4.218 | 3.895 | 3.667 | 3.496 | 3.363 | 3.256 | 3.168 | 3.032 | 2.889 |
| | .001 | 14.03 | 9.340 | 7.554 | 6.589 | 5.977 | 5.551 | 5.235 | 4.991 | 4.797 | 4.638 | 4.393 | 4.139 |
| 26 | .25 | 1.384 | 1.463 | 1.454 | 1.437 | 1.420 | 1.406 | 1.393 | 1.383 | 1.374 | 1.366 | 1.352 | 1.337 |
| | .10 | 2.909 | 2.519 | 2.307 | 2.174 | 2.082 | 2.014 | 1.961 | 1.919 | 1.884 | 1.855 | 1.809 | 1.760 |
| | .05 | 4.225 | 3.369 | 2.975 | 2.743 | 2.587 | 2.474 | 2.388 | 2.321 | 2.265 | 2.220 | 2.148 | 2.072 |
| | .025 | 5.659 | 4.265 | 3.670 | 3.329 | 3.105 | 2.945 | 2.824 | 2.729 | 2.653 | 2.590 | 2.491 | 2.387 |
| | .010 | 7.721 | 5.526 | 4.637 | 4.140 | 3.818 | 3.591 | 3.421 | 3.288 | 3.182 | 3.094 | 2.958 | 2.815 |
| | .001 | 13.74 | 9.117 | 7.357 | 6.406 | 5.802 | 5.381 | 5.070 | 4.829 | 4.637 | 4.480 | 4.238 | 3.986 |
| 28 | .25 | 1.380 | 1.457 | 1.448 | 1.430 | 1.413 | 1.399 | 1.386 | 1.375 | 1.366 | 1.358 | 1.344 | 1.329 |
| | .10 | 2.894 | 2.503 | 2.291 | 2.157 | 2.064 | 1.996 | 1.943 | 1.900 | 1.865 | 1.836 | 1.790 | 1.740 |
| | .05 | 4.196 | 3.340 | 2.947 | 2.714 | 2.558 | 2.445 | 2.359 | 2.291 | 2.236 | 2.190 | 2.118 | 2.041 |
| | .025 | 5.610 | 4.221 | 3.626 | 3.286 | 3.063 | 2.903 | 2.782 | 2.687 | 2.611 | 2.547 | 2.448 | 2.344 |
| | .010 | 7.636 | 5.453 | 4.568 | 4.074 | 3.754 | 3.528 | 3.358 | 3.226 | 3.120 | 3.032 | 2.896 | 2.753 |
| | .001 | 13.50 | 8.930 | 7.193 | 6.253 | 5.657 | 5.241 | 4.933 | 4.695 | 4.505 | 4.349 | 4.109 | 3.859 |

**TABLE F** *Continued*

| $\nu_B$ (degrees of freedom for numerator) | | | | | | | | | | | | |
|---|---|---|---|---|---|---|---|---|---|---|---|---|
| 20 | 25 | 30 | 40 | 50 | 100 | 120 | 200 | 500 | 1000 | $\infty$ | $\alpha$ | $\nu_e$ |
| 1.387 | 1.377 | 1.370 | 1.361 | 1.355 | 1.343 | 1.341 | 1.336 | 1.332 | 1.330 | 1.329 | **.25** | 17 |
| 1.862 | 1.831 | 1.809 | 1.781 | 1.763 | 1.726 | 1.719 | 1.706 | 1.694 | 1.690 | 1.686 | **.10** | |
| 2.230 | 2.181 | 2.148 | 2.104 | 2.077 | 2.020 | 2.011 | 1.991 | 1.973 | 1.967 | 1.960 | **.05** | |
| 2.616 | 2.548 | 2.502 | 2.442 | 2.405 | 2.329 | 2.315 | 2.289 | 2.264 | 2.256 | 2.247 | **.025** | |
| 3.162 | 3.068 | 3.003 | 2.920 | 2.869 | 2.764 | 2.746 | 2.709 | 2.676 | 2.664 | 2.653 | **.010** | |
| 4.775 | 4.602 | 4.484 | 4.332 | 4.240 | 4.049 | 4.016 | 3.950 | 3.890 | 3.870 | 3.849 | **.001** | |
| 1.376 | 1.366 | 1.359 | 1.350 | 1.344 | 1.331 | 1.328 | 1.324 | 1.319 | 1.318 | 1.316 | **.25** | 18 |
| 1.837 | 1.805 | 1.783 | 1.754 | 1.736 | 1.698 | 1.691 | 1.678 | 1.665 | 1.661 | 1.657 | **.10** | |
| 2.191 | 2.141 | 2.107 | 2.063 | 2.035 | 1.978 | 1.968 | 1.948 | 1.929 | 1.923 | 1.917 | **.05** | |
| 2.559 | 2.491 | 2.445 | 2.384 | 2.347 | 2.269 | 2.256 | 2.229 | 2.204 | 2.195 | 2.187 | **.025** | |
| 3.077 | 2.983 | 2.919 | 2.835 | 2.784 | 2.678 | 2.660 | 2.623 | 2.589 | 2.577 | 2.566 | **.010** | |
| 4.590 | 4.418 | 4.301 | 4.151 | 4.059 | 3.869 | 3.836 | 3.770 | 3.710 | 3.690 | 3.670 | **.001** | |
| 1.367 | 1.356 | 1.349 | 1.339 | 1.333 | 1.320 | 1.317 | 1.312 | 1.308 | 1.306 | 1.305 | **.25** | 19 |
| 1,814 | 1.782 | 1.759 | 1.730 | 1.711 | 1.673 | 1.666 | 1.652 | 1.639 | 1.635 | 1.631 | **.10** | |
| 2.155 | 2.106 | 2.071 | 2.026 | 1.999 | 1.940 | 1.930 | 1.910 | 1.891 | 1.884 | 1.878 | **.05** | |
| 2.509 | 2.441 | 2.394 | 2.333 | 2.295 | 2.217 | 2.203 | 2.176 | 2.150 | 2.142 | 2.133 | **.025** | |
| 3.003 | 2.909 | 2.844 | 2.761 | 2.709 | 2.602 | 2.584 | 2.547 | 2.512 | 2.501 | 2.489 | **.010** | |
| 4.430 | 4.259 | 4.143 | 3.994 | 3.902 | 3.713 | 3.680 | 3.615 | 3.555 | 3.534 | 3.514 | **.001** | |
| 1.358 | 1.348 | 1.340 | 1.330 | 1.324 | 1.310 | 1.307 | 1.302 | 1.298 | 1.296 | 1.294 | **.25** | 20 |
| 1.794 | 1.761 | 1.738 | 1.708 | 1.690 | 1.650 | 1.643 | 1.629 | 1.616 | 1.612 | 1.607 | **.10** | |
| 2.124 | 2.074 | 2.039 | 1.994 | 1.966 | 1.907 | 1.896 | 1.875 | 1.856 | 1.850 | 1.843 | **.05** | |
| 2.464 | 2.396 | 2.349 | 2.287 | 2.249 | 2.170 | 2.156 | 2.128 | 2.103 | 2.094 | 2.085 | **.025** | |
| 2.938 | 2.843 | 2.778 | 2.695 | 2.643 | 2.535 | 2.517 | 2.479 | 2.445 | 2.433 | 2.421 | **.010** | |
| 4.290 | 4.121 | 4.005 | 3.856 | 3.765 | 3.576 | 3.544 | 3.478 | 3.418 | 3.398 | 3.378 | **.001** | |
| 1.343 | 1.332 | 1.324 | 1.314 | 1.307 | 1.293 | 1.290 | 1.285 | 1.280 | 1.278 | 1.276 | **.25** | 22 |
| 1.759 | 1.726 | 1.702 | 1.671 | 1.652 | 1.611 | 1.604 | 1.590 | 1.576 | 1.571 | 1.567 | **.10** | |
| 2.071 | 2.020 | 1.984 | 1.938 | 1.909 | 1.849 | 1.838 | 1.817 | 1.797 | 1.790 | 1.783 | **.05** | |
| 2.389 | 2.320 | 2.272 | 2.210 | 2.171 | 2.090 | 2.076 | 2.047 | 2.021 | 2.012 | 2.003 | **.025** | |
| 2.827 | 2.733 | 2.667 | 2.583 | 2.531 | 2.422 | 2.403 | 2.365 | 2.329 | 2.317 | 2.305 | **.010** | |
| 4.058 | 3.891 | 3.776 | 3.628 | 3.537 | 3.349 | 3.317 | 3.251 | 3.191 | 3.171 | 3.150 | **.001** | |
| 1.331 | 1.319 | 1.311 | 1.300 | 1.293 | 1.278 | 1.275 | 1.270 | 1.264 | 1.263 | 1.261 | **.25** | 24 |
| 1.730 | 1.696 | 1.672 | 1.641 | 1.621 | 1.579 | 1.571 | 1.556 | 1.542 | 1.538 | 1.533 | **.10** | |
| 2.027 | 1.975 | 1.939 | 1.892 | 1.863 | 1.800 | 1.790 | 1.768 | 1.747 | 1.740 | 1.733 | **.05** | |
| 2.327 | 2.257 | 2.209 | 2.146 | 2.107 | 2.024 | 2.010 | 1.981 | 1.954 | 1.945 | 1.935 | **.025** | |
| 2.738 | 2.643 | 2.577 | 2.492 | 2.440 | 2.329 | 2.310 | 2.271 | 2.235 | 2.223 | 2.211 | **.010** | |
| 3.873 | 3.707 | 3.593 | 3.447 | 3.356 | 3.168 | 3.136 | 3.070 | 3.010 | 2.989 | 2.969 | **.001** | |
| 1.320 | 1.309 | 1.300 | 1.289 | 1.282 | 1.266 | 1.263 | 1.257 | 1.251 | 1.249 | 1.247 | **.25** | 26 |
| 1.706 | 1.671 | 1.647 | 1.615 | 1.594 | 1.551 | 1.544 | 1.528 | 1.514 | 1.509 | 1.504 | **.10** | |
| 1.990 | 1.938 | 1.901 | 1.853 | 1.823 | 1.760 | 1.749 | 1.726 | 1.705 | 1.698 | 1.691 | **.05** | |
| 2.276 | 2.205 | 2.157 | 2.093 | 2.053 | 1.969 | 1.954 | 1.925 | 1.897 | 1.888 | 1.878 | **.025** | |
| 2.664 | 2.569 | 2.503 | 2.417 | 2.364 | 2.252 | 2.333 | 2.193 | 2.156 | 2.144 | 2.131 | **.010** | |
| 3.723 | 3.558 | 3.445 | 3.299 | 3.208 | 3.020 | 2.987 | 2.922 | 2.861 | 2.840 | 2.819 | **.001** | |
| 1.311 | 1.299 | 1.291 | 1.279 | 1.271 | 1.255 | 1.252 | 1.246 | 1.240 | 1.238 | 1.236 | **.25** | 28 |
| 1.685 | 1.650 | 1.625 | 1.592 | 1.572 | 1.528 | 1.520 | 1.504 | 1.489 | 1.484 | 1.478 | **.10** | |
| 1.959 | 1.906 | 1.869 | 1.820 | 1.790 | 1.725 | 1.714 | 1.691 | 1.669 | 1.662 | 1.654 | **.05** | |
| 2.232 | 2.161 | 2.112 | 2.048 | 2.007 | 1.922 | 1.907 | 1.877 | 1.848 | 1.839 | 1.829 | **.025** | |
| 2.602 | 2.506 | 2.440 | 2.354 | 2.300 | 2.187 | 2.167 | 2.127 | 2.090 | 2.077 | 2.064 | **.010** | |
| 3.598 | 3.434 | 3.321 | 3.176 | 3.085 | 2.897 | 2.864 | 2.798 | 2.736 | 2.716 | 2.695 | **.001** | |

**TABLE F** *Continued*

| $\nu_e$ | $\alpha$ | $\nu_B$ (degrees of freedom for numerator) 1 | 2 | 3 | 4 | 5 | 6 | 7 | 8 | 9 | 10 | 12 | 15 |
|---|---|---|---|---|---|---|---|---|---|---|---|---|---|
| **30** | **.25** | 1.376 | 1.452 | 1.443 | 1.424 | 1.407 | 1.392 | 1.380 | 1.369 | 1.359 | 1.351 | 1.337 | 1.321 |
| | **.10** | 2.881 | 2.489 | 2.276 | 2.142 | 2.049 | 1.980 | 1.927 | 1.884 | 1.849 | 1.819 | 1.773 | 1.722 |
| | **.05** | 4.171 | 3.316 | 2.922 | 2.690 | 2.534 | 2.421 | 2.334 | 2.266 | 2.211 | 2.165 | 2.092 | 2.015 |
| | **.025** | 5.568 | 4.182 | 3.589 | 3.250 | 3.026 | 2.867 | 2.746 | 2.651 | 2.575 | 2.511 | 2.412 | 2.307 |
| | **.010** | 7.562 | 5.390 | 4.510 | 4.018 | 3.699 | 3.473 | 3.305 | 3.173 | 3.067 | 2.979 | 2.843 | 2.700 |
| | **.001** | 13.29 | 8.773 | 7.054 | 6.125 | 5.534 | 5.122 | 4.817 | 4.582 | 4.393 | 4.239 | 4.001 | 3.753 |
| **40** | **.25** | 1.363 | 1.435 | 1.424 | 1.404 | 1.386 | 1.371 | 1.357 | 1.345 | 1.335 | 1.327 | 1.312 | 1.295 |
| | **.10** | 2.835 | 2.440 | 2.226 | 2.091 | 1.997 | 1.927 | 1.873 | 1.829 | 1.793 | 1.763 | 1.715 | 1.662 |
| | **.05** | 4.085 | 3.232 | 2.839 | 2.606 | 2.449 | 2.336 | 2.249 | 2.180 | 2.124 | 2.077 | 2.003 | 1.924 |
| | **.025** | 5.424 | 4.051 | 3.463 | 3.126 | 2.904 | 2.744 | 2.624 | 2.529 | 2.452 | 2.388 | 2.288 | 2.182 |
| | **.010** | 7.314 | 5.178 | 4.313 | 3.828 | 3.514 | 3.291 | 3.124 | 2.993 | 2.888 | 2.801 | 2.665 | 2.522 |
| | **.001** | 12.61 | 8.251 | 6.595 | 5.698 | 5.128 | 4.731 | 4.436 | 4.207 | 4.024 | 3.874 | 3.643 | 3.400 |
| **60** | **.25** | 1.349 | 1.419 | 1.405 | 1.385 | 1.366 | 1.349 | 1.335 | 1.323 | 1.312 | 1.303 | 1.287 | 1.269 |
| | **.10** | 2.791 | 2.393 | 2.177 | 2.041 | 1.946 | 1.875 | 1.819 | 1.775 | 1.738 | 1.707 | 1.657 | 1.603 |
| | **.05** | 4.001 | 3.150 | 2.758 | 2.525 | 2.368 | 2.254 | 2.167 | 2.097 | 2.040 | 1.993 | 1.917 | 1.836 |
| | **.025** | 5.286 | 3.925 | 3.343 | 3.008 | 2.786 | 2.627 | 2.507 | 2.412 | 2.334 | 2.270 | 2.169 | 2.061 |
| | **.010** | 7.077 | 4.977 | 4.126 | 3.649 | 3.339 | 3.119 | 2.953 | 2.823 | 2.718 | 2.632 | 2.496 | 2.352 |
| | **.001** | 11.97 | 7.768 | 6.171 | 5.307 | 4.757 | 4.372 | 4.086 | 3.865 | 3.687 | 3.542 | 3.315 | 3.078 |
| **100** | **.25** | 1.339 | 1.406 | 1.391 | 1.369 | 1.349 | 1.332 | 1.317 | 1.304 | 1.293 | 1.283 | 1.267 | 1.248 |
| | **.10** | 2.756 | 2.356 | 2.139 | 2.002 | 1.906 | 1.834 | 1.778 | 1.732 | 1.695 | 1.663 | 1.612 | 1.557 |
| | **.05** | 3.936 | 3.087 | 2.696 | 2.463 | 2.305 | 2.191 | 2.103 | 2.032 | 1.975 | 1.927 | 1.850 | 1.768 |
| | **.025** | 5.179 | 3.828 | 3.250 | 2.917 | 2.696 | 2.537 | 2.417 | 2.321 | 2.244 | 2.179 | 2.077 | 1.968 |
| | **.010** | 6.895 | 4.824 | 3.984 | 3.513 | 3.206 | 2.988 | 2.823 | 2.694 | 2.590 | 2.503 | 2.368 | 2.223 |
| | **.001** | 11.496 | 7.408 | 5.857 | 5.017 | 4.482 | 4.107 | 3.829 | 3.612 | 3.439 | 3.296 | 3.074 | 2.840 |
| **120** | **.25** | 1.336 | 1.402 | 1.387 | 1.365 | 1.345 | 1.328 | 1.313 | 1.300 | 1.289 | 1.279 | 1.262 | 1.243 |
| | **.10** | 2.748 | 2.347 | 2.130 | 1.992 | 1.896 | 1.824 | 1.767 | 1.722 | 1.684 | 1.652 | 1.601 | 1.545 |
| | **.05** | 3.920 | 3.072 | 2.680 | 2.447 | 2.290 | 2.175 | 2.087 | 2.016 | 1.959 | 1.910 | 1.834 | 1.750 |
| | **.025** | 5.152 | 3.805 | 3.227 | 2.894 | 2.674 | 2.515 | 2.395 | 2.299 | 2.222 | 2.157 | 2.055 | 1.945 |
| | **.010** | 6.851 | 4.787 | 3.949 | 3.480 | 3.174 | 2.956 | 2.792 | 2.663 | 2.559 | 2.472 | 2.336 | 2.191 |
| | **.001** | 11.38 | 7.321 | 5.781 | 4.947 | 4.416 | 4.044 | 3.767 | 3.552 | 3.379 | 3.237 | 3.016 | 2.783 |
| **200** | **.25** | 1.331 | 1.396 | 1.380 | 1.358 | 1.337 | 1.319 | 1.304 | 1.291 | 1.279 | 1.269 | 1.252 | 1.232 |
| | **.10** | 2.731 | 2.329 | 2.111 | 1.973 | 1.876 | 1.804 | 1.747 | 1.701 | 1.663 | 1.631 | 1.579 | 1.522 |
| | **.05** | 3.888 | 3.041 | 2.650 | 2.417 | 2.259 | 2.144 | 2.056 | 1.985 | 1.927 | 1.878 | 1.801 | 1.717 |
| | **.025** | 5.100 | 3.758 | 3.182 | 2.850 | 2.630 | 2.472 | 2.351 | 2.256 | 2.178 | 2.113 | 2.010 | 1.900 |
| | **.010** | 6.763 | 4.713 | 3.881 | 3.414 | 3.110 | 2.893 | 2.730 | 2.601 | 2.497 | 2.411 | 2.275 | 2.129 |
| | **.001** | 11.15 | 7.152 | 5.634 | 4.812 | 4.287 | 3.920 | 3.647 | 3.434 | 3.263 | 3.123 | 2.904 | 2.672 |
| **500** | **.25** | 1.326 | 1.390 | 1.374 | 1.351 | 1.330 | 1.312 | 1.296 | 1.283 | 1.271 | 1.261 | 1.243 | 1.223 |
| | **.10** | 2.716 | 2.313 | 2.095 | 1.956 | 1.859 | 1.786 | 1.729 | 1.683 | 1.644 | 1.612 | 1.559 | 1.501 |
| | **.05** | 3.860 | 3.014 | 2.623 | 2.390 | 2.232 | 2.117 | 2.028 | 1.957 | 1.899 | 1.850 | 1.772 | 1.686 |
| | **.025** | 5.054 | 3.716 | 3.142 | 2.811 | 2.592 | 2.434 | 2.313 | 2.217 | 2.139 | 2.074 | 1.971 | 1.859 |
| | **.010** | 6.686 | 4.648 | 3.821 | 3.357 | 3.054 | 2.838 | 2.675 | 2.547 | 2.443 | 2.356 | 2.220 | 2.075 |
| | **.001** | 10.96 | 7.004 | 5.506 | 4.693 | 4.175 | 3.813 | 3.542 | 3.332 | 3.163 | 3.023 | 2.806 | 2.576 |
| **1000** | **.25** | 1.325 | 1.388 | 1.372 | 1.349 | 1.328 | 1.309 | 1.294 | 1.280 | 1.268 | 1.258 | 1.240 | 1.220 |
| | **.10** | 2.711 | 2.308 | 2.089 | 1.950 | 1.853 | 1.780 | 1.723 | 1.676 | 1.638 | 1.605 | 1.552 | 1.494 |
| | **.05** | 3.851 | 3.005 | 2.614 | 2.381 | 2.223 | 2.108 | 2.019 | 1.948 | 1.889 | 1.840 | 1.762 | 1.676 |
| | **.025** | 5.039 | 3.703 | 3.129 | 2.799 | 2.579 | 2.421 | 2.300 | 2.204 | 2.126 | 2.061 | 1.958 | 1.846 |
| | **.010** | 6.660 | 4.626 | 3.801 | 3.338 | 3.036 | 2.820 | 2.657 | 2.529 | 2.425 | 2.339 | 2.203 | 2.056 |
| | **.001** | 10.89 | 6.956 | 5.464 | 4.655 | 4.139 | 3.778 | 3.508 | 3.299 | 3.130 | 2.991 | 2.774 | 2.544 |
| $\infty$ | **.25** | 1.323 | 1.386 | 1.369 | 1.346 | 1.325 | 1.307 | 1.291 | 1.277 | 1.265 | 1.255 | 1.237 | 1.216 |
| | **.10** | 2.706 | 2.303 | 2.084 | 1.945 | 1.847 | 1.774 | 1.717 | 1.670 | 1.632 | 1.599 | 1.546 | 1.487 |
| | **.05** | 3.841 | 2.996 | 2.605 | 2.372 | 2.214 | 2.099 | 2.010 | 1.938 | 1.880 | 1.831 | 1.752 | 1.666 |
| | **.025** | 5.024 | 3.689 | 3.116 | 2.786 | 2.566 | 2.408 | 2.288 | 2.192 | 2.114 | 2.048 | 1.945 | 1.833 |
| | **.010** | 6.635 | 4.605 | 3.782 | 3.319 | 3.017 | 2.802 | 2.639 | 2.511 | 2.407 | 2.321 | 2.185 | 2.039 |
| | **.001** | 10.83 | 6.908 | 5.422 | 4.617 | 4.103 | 3.743 | 3.474 | 3.266 | 3.098 | 2.959 | 2.742 | 2.513 |

**TABLE F** *Continued*

| | | | | | $\nu_B$ (degrees of freedom for numerator) | | | | | | | |
|---|---|---|---|---|---|---|---|---|---|---|---|---|
| 20 | 25 | 30 | 40 | 50 | 100 | 120 | 200 | 500 | 1000 | ∞ | $\alpha$ | $\nu_e$ |
| 1.303 | 1.291 | 1.282 | 1.270 | 1.263 | 1.245 | 1.242 | 1.236 | 1.230 | 1.228 | 1.226 | **.25** | *30* |
| 1.667 | 1.632 | 1.606 | 1.573 | 1.552 | 1.507 | 1.499 | 1.482 | 1.467 | 1.462 | 1.456 | **.10** | |
| 1.932 | 1.878 | 1.841 | 1.792 | 1.761 | 1.695 | 1.683 | 1.660 | 1.637 | 1.630 | 1.622 | **.05** | |
| 2.195 | 2.124 | 2.074 | 2.009 | 1.968 | 1.882 | 1.866 | 1.835 | 1.806 | 1.797 | 1.787 | **.025** | |
| 2.549 | 2.453 | 2.386 | 2.299 | 2.245 | 2.131 | 2.111 | 2.070 | 2.032 | 2.019 | 2.006 | **.010** | |
| 3.493 | 3.330 | 3.217 | 3.072 | 2.981 | 2.792 | 2.760 | 2.693 | 2.631 | 2.610 | 2.589 | **.001** | |
| 1.276 | 1.263 | 1.253 | 1.240 | 1.231 | 1.212 | 1.208 | 1.201 | 1.193 | 1.191 | 1.188 | **.25** | *40* |
| 1.605 | 1.568 | 1.541 | 1.506 | 1.483 | 1.434 | 1.425 | 1.406 | 1.389 | 1.383 | 1.377 | **.10** | |
| 1.839 | 1.783 | 1.744 | 1.693 | 1.660 | 1.589 | 1.577 | 1.551 | 1.526 | 1.517 | 1.509 | **.05** | |
| 2.068 | 1.994 | 1.943 | 1.875 | 1.832 | 1.741 | 1.724 | 1.691 | 1.659 | 1.648 | 1.637 | **.025** | |
| 2.369 | 2.271 | 2.203 | 2.114 | 2.058 | 1.938 | 1.917 | 1.874 | 1.833 | 1.819 | 1.805 | **.010** | |
| 3.145 | 2.984 | 2.872 | 2.727 | 2.636 | 2.444 | 2.410 | 2.341 | 2.277 | 2.255 | 2.233 | **.001** | |
| 1.248 | 1.234 | 1.223 | 1.208 | 1.198 | 1.176 | 1.172 | 1.163 | 1.154 | 1.151 | 1.147 | **.25** | *60* |
| 1.543 | 1.504 | 1.476 | 1.437 | 1.413 | 1.358 | 1.348 | 1.326 | 1.306 | 1.299 | 1.291 | **.10** | |
| 1.748 | 1.690 | 1.649 | 1.594 | 1.559 | 1.481 | 1.467 | 1.438 | 1.409 | 1.399 | 1.389 | **.05** | |
| 1.944 | 1.869 | 1.815 | 1.744 | 1.699 | 1.599 | 1.581 | 1.543 | 1.507 | 1.495 | 1.482 | **.025** | |
| 2.198 | 2.098 | 2.028 | 1.936 | 1.877 | 1.749 | 1.726 | 1.678 | 1.633 | 1.617 | 1.601 | **.010** | |
| 2.826 | 2.667 | 2.555 | 2.409 | 2.316 | 2.118 | 2.082 | 2.009 | 1.939 | 1.915 | 1.890 | **.001** | |
| 1.226 | 1.210 | 1.198 | 1.182 | 1.171 | 1.145 | 1.140 | 1.129 | 1.118 | 1.114 | 1.109 | **.25** | *100* |
| 1.494 | 1.453 | 1.423 | 1.382 | 1.355 | 1.293 | 1.282 | 1.257 | 1.232 | 1.223 | 1.214 | **.10** | |
| 1.676 | 1.616 | 1.573 | 1.515 | 1.477 | 1.392 | 1.376 | 1.342 | 1.308 | 1.296 | 1.283 | **.05** | |
| 1.849 | 1.770 | 1.715 | 1.640 | 1.592 | 1.483 | 1.463 | 1.420 | 1.378 | 1.363 | 1.347 | **.025** | |
| 2.067 | 1.965 | 1.893 | 1.797 | 1.735 | 1.598 | 1.572 | 1.518 | 1.466 | 1.447 | 1.427 | **.010** | |
| 2.591 | 2.431 | 2.319 | 2.170 | 2.076 | 1.867 | 1.829 | 1.749 | 1.671 | 1.644 | 1.615 | **.001** | |
| 1.220 | 1.204 | 1.192 | 1.175 | 1.164 | 1.137 | 1.131 | 1.120 | 1.108 | 1.103 | 1.099 | **.25** | *120* |
| 1.482 | 1.440 | 1.409 | 1.368 | 1.340 | 1.277 | 1.265 | 1.239 | 1.212 | 1.203 | 1.193 | **.10** | |
| 1.659 | 1.598 | 1.554 | 1.495 | 1.457 | 1.369 | 1.352 | 1.316 | 1.280 | 1.267 | 1.254 | **.05** | |
| 1.825 | 1.746 | 1.690 | 1.614 | 1.565 | 1.454 | 1.433 | 1.388 | 1.343 | 1.327 | 1.310 | **.025** | |
| 2.035 | 1.932 | 1.860 | 1.763 | 1.700 | 1.559 | 1.533 | 1.477 | 1.421 | 1.401 | 1.381 | **.010** | |
| 2.534 | 2.375 | 2.262 | 2.113 | 2.017 | 1.806 | 1.767 | 1.684 | 1.603 | 1.574 | 1.543 | **.001** | |
| 1.209 | 1.192 | 1.179 | 1.162 | 1.149 | 1.120 | 1.114 | 1.100 | 1.086 | 1.080 | 1.074 | **.25** | *200* |
| 1.458 | 1.414 | 1.383 | 1.339 | 1.310 | 1.242 | 1.228 | 1.199 | 1.168 | 1.157 | 1.144 | **.10** | |
| 1.623 | 1.561 | 1.516 | 1.455 | 1.415 | 1.321 | 1.302 | 1.263 | 1.221 | 1.205 | 1.189 | **.05** | |
| 1.778 | 1.698 | 1.640 | 1.562 | 1.511 | 1.393 | 1.370 | 1.320 | 1.269 | 1.250 | 1.229 | **.025** | |
| 1.971 | 1.868 | 1.794 | 1.694 | 1.629 | 1.481 | 1.453 | 1.391 | 1.328 | 1.304 | 1.279 | **.010** | |
| 2.424 | 2.264 | 2.151 | 2.000 | 1.902 | 1.682 | 1.641 | 1.552 | 1.460 | 1.427 | 1.390 | **.001** | |
| 1.198 | 1.181 | 1.168 | 1.149 | 1.136 | 1.103 | 1.096 | 1.081 | 1.062 | 1.055 | 1.045 | **.25** | *500* |
| 1.435 | 1.391 | 1.358 | 1.313 | 1.282 | 1.209 | 1.194 | 1.160 | 1.122 | 1.106 | 1.087 | **.10** | |
| 1.592 | 1.528 | 1.482 | 1.419 | 1.376 | 1.275 | 1.255 | 1.210 | 1.159 | 1.138 | 1.113 | **.05** | |
| 1.736 | 1.655 | 1.596 | 1.515 | 1.462 | 1.336 | 1.311 | 1.254 | 1.192 | 1.166 | 1.137 | **.025** | |
| 1.915 | 1.810 | 1.735 | 1.633 | 1.566 | 1.408 | 1.377 | 1.308 | 1.232 | 1.201 | 1.164 | **.010** | |
| 2.328 | 2.168 | 2.054 | 1.900 | 1.800 | 1.571 | 1.526 | 1.427 | 1.319 | 1.276 | 1.226 | **.001** | |
| 1.195 | 1.177 | 1.164 | 1.145 | 1.131 | 1.097 | 1.090 | 1.073 | 1.053 | 1.044 | 1.031 | **.25** | *1000* |
| 1.428 | 1.383 | 1.350 | 1.304 | 1.273 | 1.197 | 1.181 | 1.145 | 1.103 | 1.084 | 1.060 | **.10** | |
| 1.581 | 1.517 | 1.471 | 1.406 | 1.363 | 1.260 | 1.239 | 1.190 | 1.134 | 1.110 | 1.078 | **.05** | |
| 1.722 | 1.640 | 1.581 | 1.499 | 1.445 | 1.316 | 1.290 | 1.230 | 1.162 | 1.132 | 1.094 | **.025** | |
| 1.897 | 1.791 | 1.716 | 1.613 | 1.544 | 1.383 | 1.351 | 1.278 | 1.195 | 1.159 | 1.112 | **.010** | |
| 2.297 | 2.136 | 2.022 | 1.868 | 1.767 | 1.533 | 1.487 | 1.383 | 1.266 | 1.216 | 1.153 | **.001** | |
| 1.191 | 1.174 | 1.160 | 1.140 | 1.127 | 1.091 | 1.066 | 1.066 | 1.042 | 1.030 | 1.0097 | **.25** | ∞ |
| 1.421 | 1.375 | 1.342 | 1.295 | 1.263 | 1.185 | 1.130 | 1.130 | 1.082 | 1.058 | 1.0006 | **.10** | |
| 1.571 | 1.506 | 1.459 | 1.394 | 1.350 | 1.243 | 1.170 | 1.170 | 1.106 | 1.075 | 1.0007 | **.05** | |
| 1.708 | 1.626 | 1.566 | 1.484 | 1.428 | 1.296 | 1.205 | 1.205 | 1.128 | 1.090 | 1.0009 | **.025** | |
| 1.878 | 1.773 | 1.696 | 1.592 | 1.523 | 1.358 | 1.247 | 1.247 | 1.153 | 1.107 | 1.0010 | **.010** | |
| 2.266 | 2.105 | 1.990 | 1.835 | 1.733 | 1.494 | 1.338 | 1.338 | 1.207 | 1.144 | 1.0014 | **.001** | |

**TABLE G** Power $(1-\beta)$ of the $F$-Test Associated with $v_b$ and $v_e$ for $\alpha = .01$.[b]

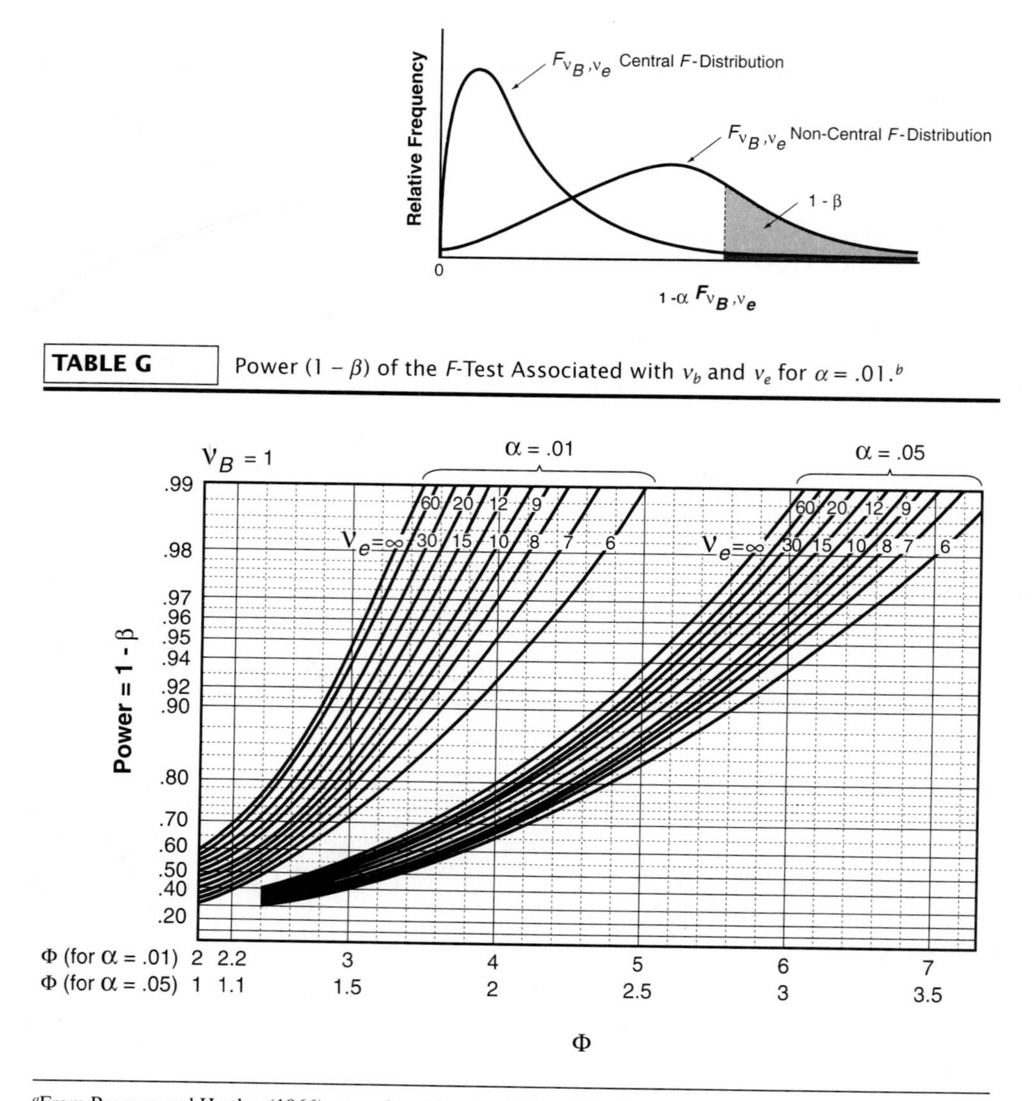


[a]From Pearson and Hartley (1966), reproduced by permission of the *Biometrika* Trustees.

[b]To determine power (Secs. 15.27 to 15.28): (1) locate proper figure by finding the degrees of freedom in the numerator of the $F$-test, $v_b$, in the upper left-hand corner, (2) locate $\phi$ (Eq. 15.23) on the abscissa that corresponds to $\alpha = (.05$ or $.01)$, (3) read up to the intersection of $\phi$ and $v_e$, and (4) read power on the ordinate. For example; if $J = 2$ $(v_b = 1)$, $\alpha = .01$, $v_e = 6$, and $\phi = 3$, then power = .70.

**TABLE G** *Continued*

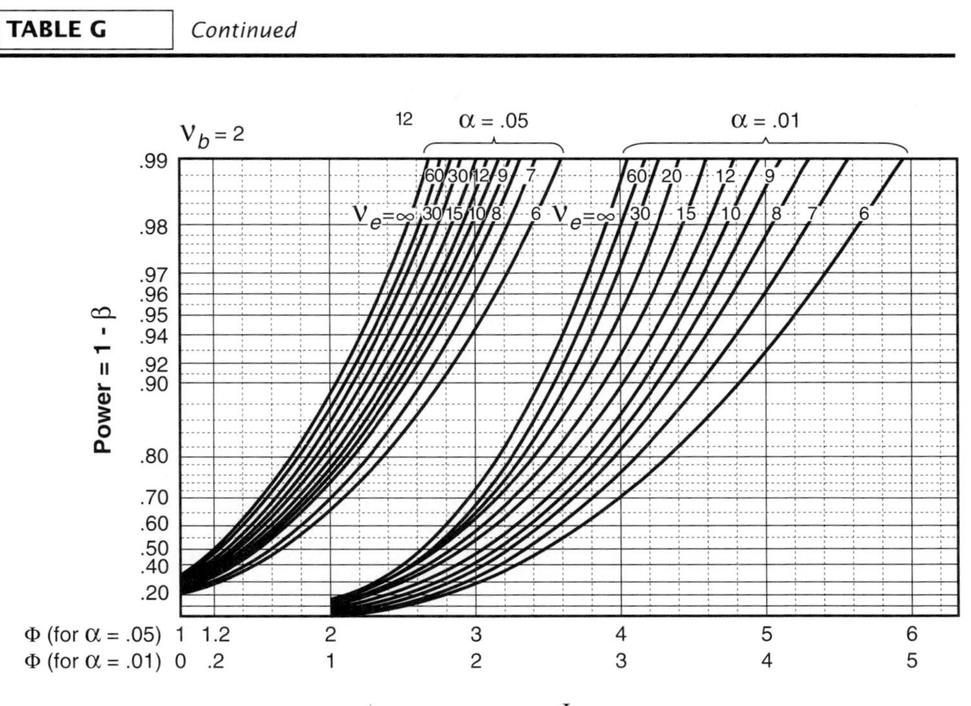


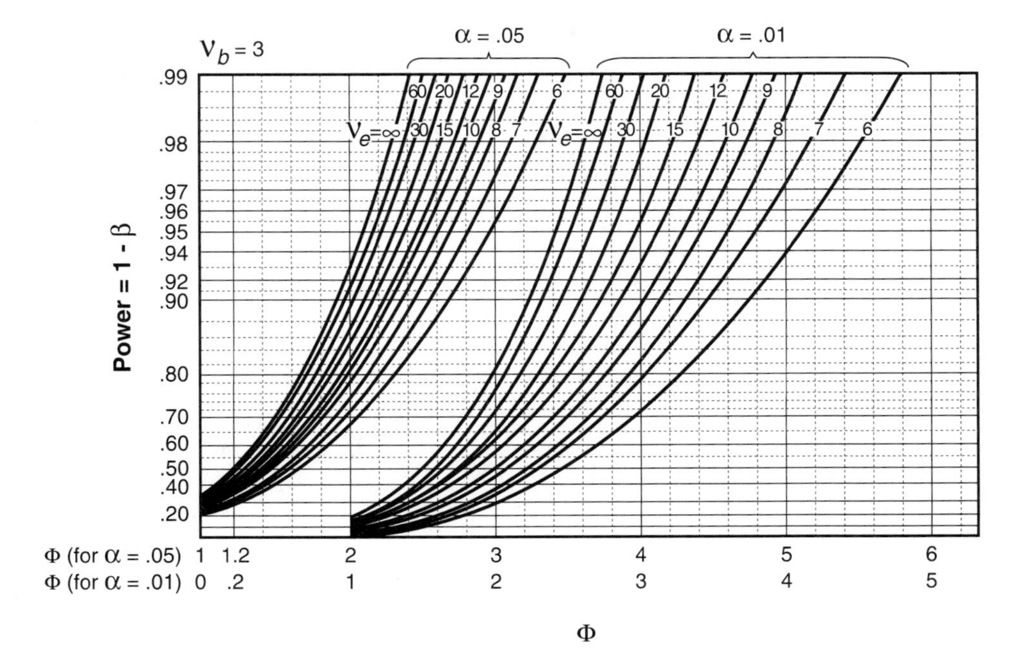

**TABLE G** *Continued*

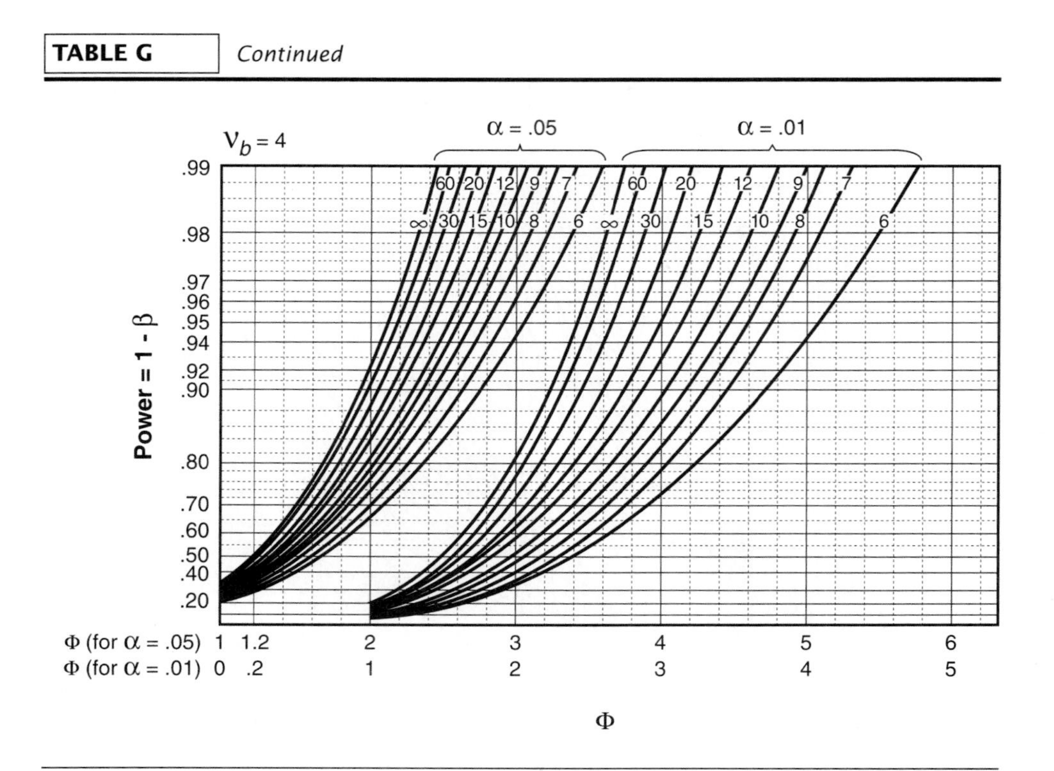

**TABLE H** Distribution of $F_{max} = s^2_{largest}/s^2_{smallest}$ Statistic[a, b]

| $v$ for each $s_j^2$ | $1-\alpha$ | J = Number of Variances: 2 | 3 | 4 | 5 | 6 | 7 | 8 | 9 | 10 | 11 | 12 |
|---|---|---|---|---|---|---|---|---|---|---|---|---|
| 2 | .95 | 39.0 | 87.5 | 142 | 202 | 266 | 333 | 403 | 475 | 550 | 626 | 704 |
| | .99 | 199 | 448 | 729 | 1036 | 1362 | 1705 | 2063 | 2432 | 2813 | 3204 | 3605 |
| 3 | .95 | 15.4 | 27.8 | 39.2 | 50.7 | 62.0 | 72.9 | 83.5 | 93.9 | 104 | 114 | 124 |
| | .99 | 47.5 | 85 | 120 | 151 | 184 | 216 | 249 | 281 | 310 | 337 | 361 |
| 4 | .95 | 9.60 | 15.5 | 20.6 | 25.2 | 29.5 | 33.6 | 37.5 | 41.4 | 44.6 | 48.0 | 51.4 |
| | .99 | 23.2 | 37 | 49 | 59 | 69 | 79 | 89 | 97 | 106 | 113 | 120 |
| 5 | .95 | 7.15 | 10.8 | 13.7 | 16.3 | 18.7 | 20.8 | 22.9 | 24.7 | 26.5 | 28.2 | 29.9 |
| | .99 | 14.9 | 22 | 28 | 33 | 38 | 42 | 46 | 50 | 54 | 57 | 60 |
| 6 | .95 | 5.82 | 8.38 | 10.4 | 12.1 | 13.7 | 15.0 | 16.3 | 17.5 | 18.6 | 19.7 | 20.7 |
| | .99 | 11.1 | 15.5 | 19.1 | 22 | 25 | 27 | 30 | 32 | 34 | 36 | 37 |
| 7 | .95 | 4.99 | 6.94 | 8.44 | 9.70 | 10.8 | 11.8 | 12.7 | 13.5 | 14.3 | 151 | 15.8 |
| | .99 | 8.89 | 12.1 | 14.5 | 16.5 | 18.4 | 20 | 22 | 23 | 24 | 26 | 27 |
| 8 | .95 | 4.43 | 6.00 | 7.18 | 8.12 | 9.03 | 9.78 | 10.5 | 11.1 | 11.7 | 12.2 | 12.7 |
| | .99 | 7.50 | 9.9 | 11.7 | 13.2 | 14.5 | 15.8 | 16.9 | 17.9 | 18.9 | 19.8 | 21 |
| 9 | .95 | 4.03 | 5.34 | 6.31 | 7.11 | 7.80 | 8.41 | 8.95 | 9.45 | 9.91 | 10.3 | 10.7 |
| | .99 | 6.54 | 8.5 | 9.9 | 11.1 | 12.1 | 13.1 | 13.9 | 14.7 | 15.3 | 16.0 | 16.6 |
| 10 | .95 | 3.72 | 4.85 | 5.67 | 6.34 | 6.92 | 7.42 | 7.87 | 8.28 | 8.66 | 9.01 | 9.34 |
| | .99 | 5.85 | 7.4 | 8.6 | 9.6 | 10.4 | 11.1 | 11.8 | 12.4 | 12.9 | 13.4 | 13.9 |
| 12 | .95 | 3.28 | 4.16 | 4.79 | 5.30 | 5.72 | 6.09 | 6.42 | 6.72 | 7.00 | 7.25 | 7.48 |
| | .99 | 4.91 | 6.1 | 6.9 | 7.6 | 8.2 | 8.7 | 9.1 | 9.5 | 9.9 | 10.2 | 10.6 |
| 15 | .95 | 2.86 | 3.54 | 4.01 | 4.37 | 4.68 | 4.95 | 5.19 | 5.40 | 5.59 | 5.77 | 5.93 |
| | .99 | 4.07 | 4.9 | 5.5 | 6.0 | 6.4 | 6.7 | 7.1 | 7.3 | 7.5 | 7.8 | 8.0 |
| 20 | .95 | 2.46 | 2.95 | 3.29 | 3.54 | 3.76 | 3.94 | 4.10 | 4.24 | 4.37 | 4.49 | 4.59 |
| | .99 | 3.32 | 3.8 | 4.3 | 4.6 | 4.9 | 5.1 | 5.3 | 5.5 | 5.6 | 5.8 | 5.9 |
| 30 | .95 | 2.07 | 2.40 | 2.61 | 2.78 | 2.91 | 3.02 | 3.12 | 3.21 | 3.29 | 3.36 | 3.39 |
| | .99 | 2.63 | 3.0 | 3.3 | 3.4 | 3.6 | 3.7 | 3.8 | 3.9 | 4.0 | 4.1 | 4.2 |
| 60 | .95 | 1.67 | 1.85 | 1.96 | 2.04 | 2.11 | 2.17 | 2.22 | 2.26 | 2.30 | 2.33 | 2.36 |
| | .99 | 1.96 | 2.2 | 2.3 | 2.4 | 2.4 | 2.5 | 2.5 | 2.6 | 2.6 | 2.7 | 2.7 |

[a] Reproduced with permission of the trustees of *Biometrika*.

[b] For example, ${}_{1-\alpha}F_{\max_{J,v_j}} = {}_{.95}F_{\max_{4,6}} = 10.4$.

**TABLE I** Critical Values of the Studentized Range Statistic, $q = (\overline{X}_L - \overline{X}_S)/s_{\overline{X}}$[a].

| $v_e$[b] | α | 2 | 3 | 4 | 5 | 6 | 7 | 8 | 9 | 10 | 11 | 12 | 13 | 14 | 15 | 16 | 17 | 18 | 19 | 20 |
|---|---|---|---|---|---|---|---|---|---|---|---|---|---|---|---|---|---|---|---|---|
| | | *r (Number of Means in Set)*[c] | | | | | | | | | | | | | | | | | | |
| 1 | .10 | 8.93 | 13.4 | 16.4 | 18.5 | 20.2 | 21.5 | 22.6 | 23.6 | 24.5 | 25.2 | 25.9 | 26.5 | 27.1 | 27.6 | 28.1 | 28.5 | 29.0 | 29.3 | 29.7 |
| | .05 | 18.0 | 27.0 | 32.8 | 37.1 | 40.4 | 43.1 | 45.4 | 47.4 | 49.1 | 50.6 | 52.0 | 53.2 | 54.3 | 55.4 | 56.3 | 57.2 | 58.0 | 58.8 | 59.6 |
| | .01 | 90.0 | 13.5 | 164 | 186 | 202 | 216 | 227 | 237 | 246 | 253 | 260 | 266 | 272 | 277 | 282 | 286 | 290 | 294 | 298 |
| 2 | .10 | 4.13 | 5.78 | 6.78 | 7.54 | 8.14 | 8.63 | 9.05 | 9.41 | 9.73 | 10.0 | 10.3 | 10.5 | 10.7 | 10.9 | 11.1 | 11.2 | 11.4 | 11.5 | 11.7 |
| | .05 | 6.09 | 8.3 | 9.8 | 10.9 | 11.7 | 12.4 | 13.0 | 13.5 | 14.0 | 14.4 | 14.7 | 15.1 | 15.4 | 15.7 | 15.9 | 16.1 | 16.4 | 16.6 | 16.8 |
| | .01 | 14.0 | 19.0 | 22.3 | 24.7 | 26.6 | 28.2 | 29.5 | 30.7 | 31.7 | 32.6 | 33.4 | 34.1 | 34.8 | 35.4 | 36.0 | 36.5 | 37.0 | 37.5 | 38.0 |
| | .001 | 44.7 | 00.4 | 70.8 | 78.4 | 84.5 | 89.5 | 93.7 | 97.3 | 101. | 103 | 106 | 108 | 110 | 112 | 114 | 116 | 117 | 119 | 120 |
| 3 | .10 | 3.33 | 4.47 | 5.20 | 5.74 | 6.16 | 6.51 | 6.81 | 7.06 | 7.29 | 7.49 | 7.67 | 7.83 | 7.98 | 8.12 | 8.25 | 8.37 | 8.78 | 8.58 | 8.68 |
| | .05 | 4.50 | 5.91 | 6.82 | 7.50 | 8.04 | 8.48 | 8.85 | 9.18 | 9.46 | 9.72 | 9.95 | 10.2 | 10.4 | 10.5 | 10.7 | 10.8 | 11.0 | 11.1 | 11.2 |
| | .01 | 8.26 | 10.6 | 12.2 | 13.3 | 14.2 | 15.0 | 15.6 | 16.2 | 16.7 | 17.1 | 17.5 | 17.9 | 18.2 | 18.5 | 18.8 | 19.1 | 19.3 | 19.6 | 20.0 |
| | .001 | 18.3 | 23.3 | 20.7 | 29.1 | 31.1 | 32.7 | 34.1 | 35.3 | 36.4 | 37.3 | 38.2 | 39.0 | 39.7 | 40.4 | 41.0 | 41.5 | 42.1 | 42.6 | 43.1 |
| 4 | .10 | 3.01 | 3.98 | 4.59 | 5.04 | 5.39 | 5.69 | 5.93 | 6.14 | 6.33 | 6.50 | 6.65 | 6.78 | 6.91 | 7.03 | 7.13 | 7.23 | 7.33 | 7.41 | 7.50 |
| | .05 | 3.93 | 5.04 | 5.76 | 6.29 | 6.71 | 7.05 | 7.35 | 7.60 | 7.83 | 8.03 | 8.21 | 8.37 | 8.52 | 8.66 | 8.79 | 8.91 | 9.03 | 9.13 | 9.23 |
| | .01 | 6.51 | 8.12 | 9.17 | 9.96 | 10.6 | 11.1 | 11.5 | 11.9 | 12.3 | 12.6 | 12.8 | 13.1 | 13.3 | 13.5 | 13.7 | 13.9 | 14.1 | 14.2 | 14.4 |
| | .001 | 12.2 | 15.0 | 16.8 | 18.2 | 19.3 | 20.3 | 21.0 | 21.7 | 22.3 | 22.9 | 23.4 | 23.8 | 24.2 | 24.6 | 24.9 | 25.3 | 25.6 | 25.9 | 26.1 |
| 5 | .10 | 2.85 | 3.72 | 4.26 | 4.66 | 4.98 | 5.24 | 5.44 | 5.65 | 5.82 | 5.97 | 6.10 | 6.22 | 6.34 | 6.44 | 6.54 | 6.63 | 6.71 | 6.79 | 6.86 |
| | .05 | 3.64 | 4.60 | 5.22 | 5.67 | 6.03 | 6.33 | 6.58 | 6.80 | 6.99 | 7.17 | 7.32 | 7.47 | 7.60 | 7.72 | 7.83 | 7.93 | 8.03 | 8.12 | 8.21 |
| | .01 | 5.70 | 6.97 | 7.80 | 8.42 | 8.91 | 9.32 | 9.67 | 9.97 | 10.2 | 10.5 | 10.7 | 10.9 | 11.1 | 11.2 | 11.4 | 11.6 | 11.7 | 11.8 | 11.9 |
| | .001 | 9.71 | 11.7 | 13.0 | 13.9 | 14.7 | 15.4 | 15.9 | 16.4 | 16.8 | 17.2 | 17.5 | 17.9 | 18.1 | 18.4 | 18.7 | 18.9 | 19.1 | 19.3 | 19.5 |
| 6 | .10 | 2.75 | 3.56 | 4.07 | 4.44 | 4.73 | 4.97 | 5.17 | 5.34 | 5.50 | 5.64 | 5.76 | 5.88 | 5.98 | 6.08 | 6.16 | 6.25 | 6.33 | 6.40 | 6.47 |
| | .05 | 3.46 | 4.34 | 4.90 | 5.31 | 5.63 | 5.89 | 6.12 | 6.32 | 6.49 | 6.65 | 6.79 | 6.92 | 7.03 | 7.14 | 7.24 | 7.34 | 7.43 | 7.51 | 7.59 |
| | .01 | 5.24 | 6.33 | 7.03 | 7.56 | 7.97 | 8.32 | 8.61 | 8.87 | 9.10 | 9.30 | 9.49 | 9.65 | 9.81 | 9.95 | 10.1 | 10.2 | 10.3 | 10.4 | 10.5 |
| | .001 | 8.43 | 9.96 | 11.0 | 11.7 | 12.3 | 12.8 | 13.3 | 13.6 | 14.0 | 14.3 | 14.5 | 14.8 | 15.0 | 15.2 | 15.4 | 15.6 | 15.8 | 15.9 | 16.1 |
| 7 | .10 | 2.68 | 3.45 | 3.93 | 4.28 | 4.56 | 4.78 | 4.97 | 5.14 | 5.28 | 5.41 | 5.53 | 5.64 | 5.74 | 5.83 | 5.91 | 5.99 | 6.06 | 6.13 | 6.20 |
| | .05 | 3.34 | 4.16 | 4.69 | 5.06 | 5.36 | 5.61 | 5.82 | 6.00 | 6.16 | 6.30 | 6.43 | 6.55 | 6.66 | 6.76 | 6.85 | 6.94 | 7.02 | 7.10 | 7.17 |
| | .01 | 4.95 | 5.92 | 6.54 | 7.01 | 7.37 | 7.68 | 7.94 | 8.17 | 8.37 | 8.55 | 8.71 | 8.86 | 9.00 | 9.12 | 9.24 | 9.35 | 9.46 | 9.55 | 9.65 |
| | .001 | 7.65 | 8.93 | 9.77 | 10.4 | 10.9 | 11.3 | 11.7 | 12.0 | 12.3 | 12.5 | 12.7 | 13.0 | 13.1 | 13.3 | 13.5 | 13.6 | 13.8 | 13.9 | 14.0 |

[a]Reproduced from H. Leon Harter, "Tables of range and studentized range," *Annals of Mathematical Statistics,* 31 (1960), 1122–47, by permission of the author and editor.

[b]In the one-factor ANOVA with *n* observations in each of *J* groups, $v_e = n_{\bullet} - J_{\bullet}$ $v_e$ is the number of degrees of freedom for the error mean square in the ANOVA.

[c]For the Tukey method $r = J$; for the Newman-Keuls method *r* is the number of means in the set being evaluated.

**TABLE I** *Continued*

| $v_e$[b] | $\alpha$ | r (Number of Means in Set)[c] 2 | 3 | 4 | 5 | 6 | 7 | 8 | 9 | 10 | 11 | 12 | 13 | 14 | 15 | 16 | 17 | 18 | 19 | 20 |
|---|---|---|---|---|---|---|---|---|---|---|---|---|---|---|---|---|---|---|---|---|
| 8 | .10 | 2.63 | 3.37 | 3.83 | 4.17 | 4.43 | 4.65 | 4.83 | 4.99 | 5.13 | 5.25 | 5.36 | 5.46 | 5.56 | 5.64 | 5.74 | 5.83 | 5.87 | 5.94 | 6.00 |
| | .05 | 3.26 | 4.04 | 4.53 | 4.89 | 5.17 | 5.40 | 5.60 | 5.77 | 5.92 | 6.05 | 6.18 | 6.29 | 6.39 | 6.48 | 6.57 | 6.65 | 6.73 | 6.80 | 6.87 |
| | .01 | 4.74 | 5.63 | 6.20 | 6.63 | 6.96 | 7.24 | 7.47 | 7.68 | 7.78 | 8.03 | 8.18 | 8.31 | 8.44 | 8.55 | 8.66 | 8.76 | 8.85 | 8.94 | 9.03 |
| | .001 | 7.13 | 8.25 | 8.98 | 9.52 | 9.96 | 10.3 | 10.6 | 10.9 | 11.2 | 11.4 | 11.6 | 11.7 | 11.9 | 12.1 | 12.2 | 12.3 | 12.5 | 12.6 | 12.7 |
| 9 | .10 | 2.59 | 3.32 | 3.76 | 4.08 | 4.34 | 4.55 | 4.72 | 4.87 | 5.01 | 5.13 | 5.23 | 5.33 | 5.42 | 5.51 | 5.58 | 5.66 | 5.72 | 5.79 | 5.84 |
| | .05 | 3.20 | 3.95 | 4.42 | 4.76 | 5.02 | 5.24 | 5.43 | 5.60 | 5.74 | 5.87 | 5.98 | 6.09 | 6.19 | 6.28 | 6.36 | 6.44 | 6.51 | 6.53 | 6.64 |
| | .01 | 4.60 | 5.43 | 5.96 | 6.35 | 6.66 | 6.91 | 7.13 | 7.32 | 7.49 | 7.65 | 7.78 | 7.91 | 8.03 | 8.13 | 8.23 | 8.33 | 8.41 | 8.50 | 8.57 |
| | .001 | 6.76 | 7.77 | 8.42 | 8.91 | 9.30 | 9.62 | 9.90 | 10.1 | 10.4 | 10.6 | 10.7 | 10.9 | 11.0 | 11.2 | 11.3 | 11.4 | 11.5 | 11.6 | 11.8 |
| 10 | .10 | 2.56 | 3.28 | 3.70 | 4.02 | 4.26 | 4.47 | 4.64 | 4.78 | 4.91 | 5.03 | 5.13 | 5.23 | 5.32 | 5.40 | 5.47 | 5.54 | 5.61 | 5.67 | 5.73 |
| | .05 | 3.15 | 3.88 | 4.33 | 4.65 | 4.91 | 5.12 | 5.30 | 5.46 | 5.60 | 5.72 | 5.83 | 5.93 | 6.03 | 6.11 | 6.19 | 6.27 | 6.34 | 6.41 | 6.49 |
| | .01 | 4.48 | 5.27 | 5.77 | 6.14 | 6.43 | 6.67 | 6.87 | 7.05 | 7.21 | 7.36 | 7.48 | 7.60 | 7.71 | 7.81 | 7.91 | 8.00 | 8.08 | 8.15 | 8.23 |
| | .001 | 6.49 | 7.41 | 8.01 | 8.45 | 8.80 | 9.10 | 9.35 | 9. | 9.77 | 9.95 | 10.1 | 10.3 | 10.4 | 10.5 | 10.6 | 10.8 | 10.9 | 11.0 | 11.0 |
| 11 | .10 | 2.54 | 3.23 | 3.66 | 3.97 | 4.21 | 4.40 | 4.57 | 4.71 | 4.84 | 4.95 | 5.05 | 5.15 | 5.23 | 5.31 | 5.38 | 5.45 | 5.51 | 5.57 | 5.63 |
| | .05 | 3.11 | 3.82 | 4.26 | 4.57 | 4.82 | 5.03 | 5.20 | 5.35 | 5.49 | 5.61 | 5.71 | 5.81 | 5.90 | 5.99 | 6.06 | 6.18 | 6.20 | 6.27 | 6.33 |
| | .01 | 4.39 | 5.14 | 5.62 | 5.97 | 6.25 | 6.48 | 6.67 | 6.84 | 6.99 | 7.13 | 7.26 | 7.36 | 7.46 | 7.56 | 7.75 | 7.73 | 7.81 | 7.88 | 7.95 |
| | .001 | 6.28 | 7. | 7.69 | 8.10 | 8.43 | 8.70 | 8.93 | 9.14 | 9.32 | 9.48 | 9.63 | 9.77 | 9.89 | 10.0 | 10.1 | 10.2 | 10.3 | 10.4 | 10.5 |
| 12 | .10 | 2.52 | 3.20 | 3.62 | 3.92 | 4.16 | 4.35 | 4.51 | 4.65 | 4.78 | 4.89 | 4.99 | 5.08 | 5.16 | 5.24 | 5.31 | 5.37 | 5.44 | 5.50 | 5.55 |
| | .05 | 3.08 | 3.77 | 4.20 | 4.51 | 4.75 | 4.95 | 5.12 | 5.27 | 5.40 | 5.51 | 5.62 | 5.71 | 5.80 | 5.88 | 5.95 | 6.02 | 6.09 | 6.15 | 6.21 |
| | .01 | 4.32 | 5.04 | 5.50 | 5.84 | 6.10 | 6.32 | 6.51 | 6.67 | 6.81 | 6.94 | 7.06 | 7.17 | 7.26 | 7.36 | 7.44 | 7.52 | 7.50 | 7.67 | 7.73 |
| | .001 | 6.11 | 6.92 | 7.44 | 7.82 | 8.13 | 8.38 | 8.60 | 8.79 | 8.96 | 9.12 | 9.25 | 9.38 | 9.50 | 9.61 | 9.71 | 9.80 | 9.89 | 9.98 | 10.1 |
| 13 | .10 | 2.51 | 3.18 | 3.59 | 3.89 | 4.12 | 4.31 | 4.46 | 4.60 | 4.72 | 4.83 | 4.93 | 5.02 | 5.10 | 5.18 | 5.25 | 5.31 | 5.37 | 5.43 | 5.48 |
| | .05 | 3.06 | 3.73 | 4.15 | 4.45 | 4.69 | 4.88 | 5.05 | 5.19 | 5.32 | 5.43 | 5.53 | 5.63 | 5.71 | 5.79 | 5.86 | 5.93 | 6.00 | 6.06 | 6.11 |
| | .01 | 4.26 | 4.96 | 5.40 | 5.73 | 5.98 | 6.19 | 6.37 | 6.53 | 6.67 | 6.79 | 6.90 | 7.01 | 7.10 | 7.19 | 7.27 | 7.37 | 7.42 | 7.49 | 7.55 |
| | .001 | 5.97 | 6.74 | 7.23 | 7.60 | 7.89 | 8.13 | 8.33 | 8.51 | 8.67 | 8.82 | 8.95 | 9.07 | 9.18 | 9.28 | 9.38 | 9.47 | 9.55 | 9.63 | 9.70 |
| 14 | .10 | 2.99 | 3.16 | 3.56 | 3.83 | 4.08 | 4.27 | 4.42 | 4.56 | 4.68 | 4.79 | 4.88 | 4.97 | 5.05 | 5.12 | 5.19 | 5.26 | 5.32 | 5.37 | 5.43 |
| | .05 | 3.03 | 3.70 | 4.11 | 4.41 | 4.64 | 4.83 | 4.99 | 5.13 | 5.25 | 5.36 | 5.46 | 5.55 | 5.64 | 5.72 | 5.79 | 5.85 | 5.92 | 5.97 | 6.03 |
| | .01 | 4.21 | 4.89 | 5.32 | 5.63 | 5.88 | 6.08 | 6.26 | 6.41 | 6.54 | 6.66 | 6.77 | 6.87 | 6.96 | 7.05 | 7.13 | 7.20 | 7.27 | 7.33 | 7.40 |
| | .001 | 5.86 | 6.59 | 7.06 | 7.41 | 7.69 | 7.92 | 8.11 | 8.28 | 8.43 | 8.57 | 8.70 | 8.81 | 8.91 | 9.01 | 9.10 | 9.19 | 9.27 | 9.34 | 9.41 |
| 16 | .10 | 2.47 | 3.12 | 3.52 | 3.80 | 4.03 | 4.21 | 4.36 | 4.49 | 4.61 | 4.71 | 4.81 | 4.89 | 4.97 | 5.04 | 5.11 | 5.17 | 5.23 | 5.28 | 5.33 |
| | .05 | 3.00 | 3.65 | 4.05 | 4.33 | 4.56 | 4.74 | 4.90 | 5.03 | 5.15 | 5.26 | 5.35 | 5.44 | 5.52 | 5.59 | 5.66 | 5.73 | 5.79 | 5.84 | 5.90 |
| | .01 | 4.13 | 4.78 | 5.19 | 5.49 | 5.72 | 5.92 | 6.08 | 6.22 | 6.35 | 6.46 | 6.56 | 6.66 | 6.74 | 6.82 | 6.90 | 6.97 | 7.03 | 7.09 | 7.15 |
| | .001 | 5.68 | 6.37 | 6.80 | 7.12 | 7.37 | 7.59 | 7.77 | 7.92 | 8.06 | 8.19 | 8.30 | 8.41 | 8.50 | 8.59 | 8.68 | 8.76 | 8.83 | 8.90 | 8.96 |

**TABLE I** *Continued*

| $v_e$[b] | $\alpha$ | 2 | 3 | 4 | 5 | 6 | 7 | 8 | 9 | 10 | 11 | 12 | 13 | 14 | 15 | 16 | 17 | 18 | 19 | 20 |
|---|---|---|---|---|---|---|---|---|---|---|---|---|---|---|---|---|---|---|---|---|
| | | *r (Number of Means in Set)*[c] | | | | | | | | | | | | | | | | | | |
| 18 | .10 | 2.45 | 3.10 | 3.49 | 3.77 | 3.98 | 4.16 | 4.31 | 4.44 | 4.55 | 4.66 | 4.75 | 4.83 | 4.91 | 4.98 | 5.04 | 5.10 | 5.16 | 5.21 | 5.26 |
| | .05 | 2.97 | 3.61 | 4.00 | 4.28 | 4.49 | 4.67 | 4.82 | 4.96 | 5.07 | 5.17 | 5.27 | 5.35 | 5.43 | 5.50 | 5.57 | 5.63 | 5.69 | 5.74 | 5.79 |
| | .01 | 4.07 | 4.70 | 5.09 | 5.38 | 5.60 | 5.79 | 5.94 | 6.08 | 6.20 | 6.31 | 6.41 | 6.50 | 6.58 | 6.65 | 6.73 | 6.79 | 6.85 | 6.91 | 6.97 |
| | .001 | 5.55 | 6.20 | 6.60 | 6.91 | 7.14 | 7.34 | 7.51 | 7.66 | 7.79 | 7.91 | 8.01 | 8.11 | 8.20 | 8.28 | 8.36 | 8.43 | 8.50 | 8.57 | 8.63 |
| 20 | .10 | 2.44 | 3.08 | 3.46 | 3.74 | 3.95 | 4.12 | 4.27 | 4.40 | 4.51 | 4.61 | 4.70 | 4.78 | 4.86 | 4.92 | 4.99 | 5.05 | 5.10 | 5.16 | 5.21 |
| | .05 | 2.95 | 3.58 | 3.96 | 4.23 | 4.45 | 4.62 | 4.77 | 4.90 | 5.01 | 5.11 | 5.20 | 5.28 | 5.36 | 5.43 | 5.49 | 5.55 | 5.61 | 5.66 | 5.71 |
| | .01 | 4.02 | 4.64 | 5.02 | 5.29 | 5.51 | 5.69 | 5.84 | 5.97 | 6.09 | 6.19 | 6.29 | 6.37 | 6.45 | 6.52 | 6.59 | 6.65 | 6.71 | 6.77 | 6.82 |
| | .001 | 5.44 | 6.07 | 6.45 | 6.74 | 6.97 | 7.15 | 7.31 | 7.45 | 7.58 | 7.69 | 7.79 | 7.88 | 7.97 | 8.04 | 8.12 | 8.19 | 8.25 | 8.31 | 8.37 |
| 24 | .10 | 2.42 | 3.05 | 3.42 | 3.69 | 3.90 | 4.07 | 4.21 | 4.34 | 4.45 | 4.54 | 4.63 | 4.71 | 4.78 | 4.85 | 4.91 | 4.97 | 5.02 | 5.07 | 5.12 |
| | .05 | 2.92 | 3.53 | 3.90 | 4.17 | 4.37 | 4.54 | 4.68 | 4.81 | 4.92 | 5.01 | 5.10 | 5.18 | 5.25 | 5.32 | 5.38 | 5.44 | 5.49 | 5.55 | 5.59 |
| | .01 | 3.96 | 4.54 | 4.91 | 5.17 | 5.37 | 5.54 | 5.69 | 5.81 | 5.92 | 6.02 | 6.11 | 6.19 | 6.26 | 6.33 | 6.39 | 6.45 | 6.51 | 6.57 | 6.61 |
| | .001 | 5.30 | 5.88 | 6.24 | 6.50 | 6.71 | 6.88 | 7.03 | 7.16 | 7.27 | 7.37 | 7.47 | 7.55 | 7.63 | 7.70 | 7.77 | 7.83 | 7.89 | 7.95 | 8.00 |
| 30 | .10 | 2.40 | 3.02 | 3.39 | 3.65 | 3.85 | 4.02 | 4.16 | 4.28 | 4.38 | 4.47 | 4.56 | 4.64 | 4.71 | 4.77 | 4.83 | 4.89 | 4.94 | 4.99 | 5.03 |
| | .05 | 2.89 | 3.49 | 3.84 | 4.00 | 4.30 | 4.46 | 4.60 | 4.72 | 4.83 | 4.92 | 5.00 | 5.08 | 5.15 | 5.21 | 5.27 | 5.33 | 5.38 | 5.43 | 5.48 |
| | .01 | 3.89 | 4.45 | 4.80 | 5.05 | 5.24 | 5.40 | 5.54 | 5.56 | 5.76 | 5.85 | 5.93 | 6.01 | 6.08 | 6.14 | 6.20 | 6.26 | 6.31 | 6.36 | 6.41 |
| | .001 | 5.16 | 5.70 | 6.03 | 6.28 | 6.47 | 6.63 | 6.76 | 6.88 | 6.98 | 7.08 | 7.16 | 7.24 | 7.31 | 7.38 | 7.44 | 7.48 | 7.55 | 7.60 | 7.65 |
| 40 | .10 | 2.38 | 2.99 | 3.35 | 3.61 | 3.80 | 3.96 | 4.10 | 4.22 | 4.32 | 4.41 | 4.49 | 4.56 | 4.63 | 4.70 | 4.75 | 4.81 | 4.86 | 4.91 | 4.95 |
| | .05 | 2.86 | 3.44 | 3.79 | 4.04 | 4.23 | 4.39 | 4.52 | 4.63 | 4.74 | 4.82 | 4.91 | 4.98 | 5.05 | 5.11 | 5.16 | 5.22 | 5.27 | 5.31 | 5.36 |
| | .01 | 3.82 | 4.37 | 4.70 | 4.93 | 5.11 | 5.27 | 5.39 | 5.50 | 5.60 | 5.69 | 5.77 | 5.84 | 5.90 | 5.96 | 6.02 | 6.07 | 6.11 | 6.17 | 6.21 |
| | .001 | 5.02 | 5.53 | 5.84 | 6.06 | 6.24 | 6.39 | 6.51 | 6.62 | 6.71 | 6.80 | 6.87 | 6.94 | 7.01 | 7.07 | 7.12 | 7.17 | 7.22 | 7.27 | 7.31 |
| 60 | .10 | 2.36 | 2.96 | 3.31 | 3.56 | 3.76 | 3.91 | 4.04 | 4.16 | 4.26 | 4.34 | 4.42 | 4.49 | 4.56 | 4.62 | 4.68 | 4.73 | 4.78 | 4.82 | 4.86 |
| | .05 | 2.83 | 3.40 | 3.74 | 3.98 | 4.16 | 4.31 | 4.44 | 4.55 | 4.65 | 4.73 | 4.81 | 4.88 | 4.94 | 5.00 | 5.06 | 5.11 | 5.15 | 5.20 | 5.24 |
| | .01 | 3.76 | 4.28 | 4.60 | 4.82 | 4.99 | 5.13 | 5.25 | 5.36 | 5.45 | 5.53 | 5.60 | 5.67 | 5.73 | 5.79 | 5.84 | 5.89 | 5.93 | 5.97 | 6.02 |
| | .001 | 4.87 | 5.37 | 5.05 | 5.86 | 6.02 | 6.16 | 6.27 | 6.37 | 6.45 | 6.53 | 6.60 | 6.66 | 6.72 | 6.77 | 6.82 | 6.87 | 6.91 | 6.96 | 7.00 |
| 120 | .10 | 2.34 | 2.93 | 3.28 | 3.52 | 3.71 | 3.86 | 3.99 | 4.10 | 4.19 | 4.28 | 4.35 | 4.42 | 4.49 | 4.59 | 4.60 | 4.65 | 4.69 | 4.74 | 4.78 |
| | .05 | 2.80 | 3.36 | 3.69 | 3.92 | 4.10 | 4.24 | 4.36 | 4.48 | 4.56 | 4.64 | 4.72 | 4.78 | 4.84 | 4.90 | 4.95 | 5.00 | 5.04 | 5.09 | 5.13 |
| | .01 | 3.70 | 4.20 | 4.50 | 4.71 | 4.87 | 5.01 | 5.12 | 5.21 | 5.30 | 5.38 | 5.44 | 5.51 | 5.56 | 5.61 | 5.66 | 5.71 | 5.75 | 5.79 | 5.83 |
| | .001 | 4.77 | 5.21 | 5.48 | 5.67 | 5.82 | 5.94 | 6.04 | 6.13 | 6.21 | 6.28 | 6.34 | 6.40 | 6.45 | 6.50 | 6.54 | 6.58 | 6.62 | 6.66 | 6.70 |
| ∞ | .10 | 2.33 | 2.90 | 3.24 | 3.48 | 3.66 | 3.81 | 3.93 | 4.04 | 4.13 | 4.21 | 4.29 | 4.35 | 4.41 | 4.47 | 4.52 | 4.57 | 4.62 | 4.65 | 4.69 |
| | .05 | 2.77 | 3.31 | 3.63 | 3.86 | 4.03 | 4.17 | 4.29 | 4.39 | 4.47 | 4.55 | 4.62 | 4.68 | 4.74 | 4.80 | 4.85 | 4.89 | 4.93 | 4.97 | 5.01 |
| | .01 | 3.64 | 4.12 | 4.40 | 4.60 | 4.76 | 4.88 | 4.99 | 5.08 | 5.16 | 5.23 | 5.29 | 5.35 | 5.40 | 5.45 | 5.49 | 5.54 | 5.57 | 5.61 | 5.65 |
| | .001 | 4.05 | 5.06 | 5.31 | 5.48 | 5.62 | 5.73 | 5.82 | 5.90 | 5.97 | 6.04 | 6.09 | 6.14 | 6.19 | 6.23 | 6.27 | 6.31 | 6.35 | 6.38 | 6.41 |

| TABLE J | Critical Values of $r$ for $H_o$: $\rho = 0$[a]. |
|---|---|

| $n$[b] | $\alpha_1 = .05$ $\alpha_2 = .10$ | $\alpha_1 = .025$ $\alpha_2 = .05$ | $\alpha_1 = .01$ $\alpha_2 = .02$ | $\alpha_1 = .005$ $\alpha_2 = .01$ | $\alpha_1 = .0005$ $\alpha_2 = .001$ | $\nu$[c] |
|---|---|---|---|---|---|---|
| 3 | .988 | .997 | .9995 | .9999 | .99994 | **1** |
| 4 | .900 | .950 | .980 | .990 | .999 | **2** |
| 5 | .805 | .878 | .934 | .959 | .991 | **3** |
| 6 | .729 | .811 | .882 | .917 | .974 | **4** |
| 7 | .669 | .754 | .833 | .874 | .951 | **5** |
| 8 | .622 | .707 | .789 | .834 | .925 | **6** |
| 9 | .582 | .666 | .750 | .798 | .898 | **7** |
| 10 | .549 | .632 | .716 | .765 | .872 | **8** |
| 11 | .521 | .602 | .685 | .735 | .847 | **9** |
| 12 | .497 | .576 | .658 | .708 | .823 | **10** |
| 13 | .476 | .553 | .634 | .684 | .801 | **11** |
| 14 | .458 | .532 | .612 | .661 | .780 | **12** |
| 15 | .441 | .514 | .592 | .641 | .760 | **13** |
| 16 | .426 | .497 | .574 | .623 | .742 | **14** |
| 17 | .412 | .482 | .558 | .606 | .725 | **15** |
| 18 | .400 | .468 | .542 | .590 | .708 | **16** |
| 19 | .389 | .456 | .528 | .575 | .693 | **17** |
| 20 | .378 | .444 | .516 | .561 | .679 | **18** |
| 21 | .369 | .433 | .503 | .549 | .665 | **19** |
| 22 | .360 | .423 | .492 | .537 | .652 | **20** |
| 23 | .352 | .413 | .482 | .526 | .640 | **21** |
| 24 | .344 | .404 | .472 | .515 | .629 | **22** |
| 25 | .337 | .396 | .462 | .505 | .618 | **23** |
| 26 | .330 | .388 | .453 | .496 | .607 | **24** |
| 27 | .323 | .381 | .445 | .487 | .597 | **25** |
| 28 | .317 | .374 | .437 | .479 | .588 | **26** |
| 29 | .311 | .367 | .430 | .471 | .579 | **27** |
| 30 | .306 | .361 | .423 | .463 | .570 | **28** |
| 35 | .282 | .333 | .391 | .428 | .531 | **33** |
| 40 | .264 | .312 | .366 | .402 | .501 | **38** |
| 45 | .248 | .296 | .349 | .381 | .471 | **43** |
| 50 | .235 | .276 | .328 | .361 | .451 | **48** |
| 60 | .214 | .254 | .300 | .330 | .414 | **58** |
| 70 | .198 | .235 | .277 | .305 | .385 | **68** |
| 80 | .185 | .220 | .260 | .286 | .361 | **78** |
| 90 | .174 | .208 | .245 | .270 | .342 | **88** |
| 100 | .165 | .196 | .232 | .256 | .324 | **98** |
| 150 | .135 | .161 | .190 | .210 | .267 | **148** |
| 200 | .117 | .139 | .164 | .182 | .232 | **198** |
| 250 | .104 | .124 | .147 | .163 | .207 | **248** |
| 300 | .095 | .113 | .134 | .148 | .189 | **298** |
| 400 | .082 | .098 | .115 | .128 | .169 | **398** |
| 500 | .074 | .088 | .104 | .115 | .147 | **498** |
| 1,000 | .052 | .062 | .074 | .081 | .104 | **998** |
| 5,000 | .0233 | .0278 | .0329 | .0364 | .0465 | **4,998** |
| 10,000 | .0164 | .0196 | .0233 | .0258 | .0393 | **9,998** |

[a]Column entries for $\alpha_2 = .10$, .05, .02, and .01 for $n = 3$ to $n = 100$ are taken from Table 13 in E. S. Pearson and H. O. Hartley (Eds.), *Biometrika Tables for Statisticians,* 2nd ed. (1966), by permission of the *Biometrika* Trustees. Other entries were obtained using Equation 14.3.

[b]If the *value* of an $r$ from a sample of size $n$ exceeds the tabled value for $\alpha$ and $n$, the null hypothesis that $\rho = 0$ may be rejected at the $\alpha$-level of significance. For example, a sample of $r$ of .561 or more with $n = 20$ leads to rejection of the hypothesis $\rho = 0$ at $\alpha_2 = .01$. Use $n$ only for testing Pearson $r$'s.

[c]The degrees of freedom $\nu$ for a Pearson $r$ are $n - 2$; for partial correlation coefficients, $\nu = n - 2 - p$, where $p$ is the number of variables partialed out.

**TABLE K** Critical Values of Spearman's Rank Correlation Coefficient,[c] $r_{\text{ranks}}$ for Testing the Null Hypothesis of No Correlation[a].

| $n$ | $\alpha_1 = .05$ $\alpha_2 = .10$ | $\alpha_1 = .025$ $\alpha_2 = .05$ | $\alpha_1 = .01$ $\alpha_2 = .02$ | $\alpha_2 = .005$ $\alpha_2 = .01$ | $n$ |
|---|---|---|---|---|---|
| 5 | 0.900 | — | — | — | 5 |
| 6 | 0.829 | 0.886 | 0.943 | — | 6 |
| 7 | 0.714 | .0786 | 0.893 | — | 7 |
| 8 | 0.643 | 0.738 | 0.833 | 0.881 | 8 |
| 9 | 0.600 | 0.683 | 0.783 | 0.833 | 9 |
| 10 | 0.564 | 0.648 | 0.745 | 0.818 | 10 |
| 11 | 0.523 | 0.623 | 0.736 | 0.794 | 11 |
| 12 | 0.497 | 0.591 | 0.703 | 0.780 | 12 |
| 13 | 0.475 | 0.566 | 0.673 | 0.745 | 13 |
| 14 | 0.457 | 0.545 | 0.646 | 0.716 | 14 |
| 15 | 0.441 | 0.525 | 0.623 | 0.689 | 15 |
| 16 | 0.425 | 0.507 | 0.601 | 0.666 | 16 |
| 17 | 0.412 | 0.490 | 0.582 | 0.645 | 17 |
| 18 | 0.399 | 0.476 | 0.564 | 0.625 | 18 |
| 19 | 0.388 | 0.462 | 0.549 | 0.608 | 19 |
| 20 | 0.377 | 0.450 | 0.534 | 0.591 | 20 |
| 21 | 0.368 | 0.438 | 0.521 | 0.576 | 21 |
| 22 | 0.359 | 0.428 | 0.508 | 0.562 | 22 |
| 23 | 0.351 | 0.418 | 0.496 | 0.549 | 23 |
| 24 | 0.343 | 0.409 | 0.485 | 0.537 | 24 |
| 25 | 0.336 | 0.400 | 0.475 | 0.526 | 25 |
| 26 | 0.329 | 0.392 | 0.465 | 0.515 | 26 |
| 27 | 0.323 | 0.385 | 0.456 | 0.505 | 27 |
| 28 | 0.317 | 0.377 | 0.448 | 0.496 | 28 |
| 29 | 0.311 | 0.370 | 0.440 | 0.487 | 29 |
| 30[b] | 0.305 | 0.364 | 0.432 | 0.478 | 30[b] |

[a]Adapted from E. G. Olds, "Distributions of sums of squares of rank differences for small numbers of individuals," *Annals of Mathematical Statistics,* 9 (1938), 133–48, and "The 5% significance levels for sums of squares of rank differences and a correction," *Annals of Mathematical Statistics,* 20 (1949), 117–18, by permission of The Institute of Mathematical Statistics.

[b]Table J may be used for $n > 30$.

[c]For improved accuracy at the third decimal value, and for $n \leq 100$ see Ramsey (1989).

**TABLE L** Critical $t$-ratios for the Dunn (Bonferonni) Method of Multiple Comparisons[a].

| $\nu_e$ | $\alpha_{\Sigma_2}$[b] | Number of Comparisons (C) | | | | | | | | | | | | | |
|---|---|---|---|---|---|---|---|---|---|---|---|---|---|---|---|
| | | 2 | 3 | 4 | 5 | 6 | 7 | 8 | 9 | 10 | 12 | 15 | 20 | 25 | 30 |
| 2 | .20 | 2.828 | 3.531 | 4.116 | 4.628 | 5.089 | 5.512 | 5.904 | 6.272 | 6.620 | 7.265 | 8.138 | 9.415 | 10.537 | 11.552 |
| | .10 | 4.243 | 5.243 | 6.081 | 6.816 | 7.480 | 8.090 | 8.656 | 9.188 | 9.691 | 10.625 | 11.890 | 13.742 | 15.371 | 16.844 |
| | .05 | 6.164 | 7.582 | 8.774 | 9.823 | 10.769 | 11.639 | 12.449 | 13.208 | 13.927 | 15.263 | 17.071 | 19.721 | 22.054 | 24.163 |
| | .01 | 14.071 | 17.248 | 19.926 | 22.282 | 24.415 | 26.370 | 28.196 | 29.905 | 31.525 | 34.543 | 38.613 | 44.592 | 49.882 | 54.613 |
| 3 | .20 | 2.944 | 2.734 | 3.077 | 3.363 | 3.610 | 3.829 | 4.028 | 4.209 | 4.377 | 4.681 | 5.076 | 5.628 | 6.091 | 6.495 |
| | .10 | 3.149 | 3.690 | 4.115 | 4.471 | 4.780 | 5.055 | 5.304 | 5.532 | 5.744 | 6.127 | 6.627 | 7.326 | 7.914 | 8.427 |
| | .05 | 4.156 | 4.826 | 5.355 | 5.799 | 6.185 | 6.529 | 6.841 | 7.128 | 7.394 | 7.876 | 8.505 | 9.387 | 10.129 | 10.778 |
| | .01 | 7.447 | 8.565 | 9.453 | 10.200 | 10.853 | 11.437 | 11.965 | 12.452 | 12.903 | 13.723 | 14.794 | 16.298 | 17.569 | 18.682 |
| 4 | .20 | 2.084 | 2.434 | 2.697 | 2.911 | 3.092 | 3.250 | 3.391 | 3.518 | 3.635 | 3.842 | 4.107 | 4.468 | 4.763 | 5.015 |
| | .10 | 2.751 | 3.150 | 3.452 | 3.699 | 3.909 | 4.093 | 4.257 | 4.406 | 4.542 | 4.785 | 5.097 | 5.521 | 5.870 | 6.169 |
| | .05 | 3.481 | 3.941 | 4.290 | 4.577 | 4.822 | 5.036 | 5.228 | 5.402 | 5.562 | 5.848 | 6.214 | 6.714 | 7.126 | 7.480 |
| | .01 | 5.594 | 6.248 | 6.752 | 7.165 | 7.520 | 7.832 | 8.112 | 8.367 | 8.601 | 9.019 | 9.555 | 10.293 | 10.901 | 11.423 |
| 5 | .20 | 1.973 | 2.278 | 2.503 | 2.683 | 2.834 | 2.964 | 3.079 | 3.182 | 3.275 | 3.441 | 3.649 | 3.928 | 4.153 | 4.343 |
| | .10 | 2.549 | 2.882 | 3.129 | 3.327 | 3.493 | 3.638 | 3.765 | 3.880 | 3.985 | 4.170 | 4.403 | 4.718 | 4.972 | 5.187 |
| | .05 | 3.152 | 3.518 | 3.791 | 4.012 | 4.197 | 4.358 | 4.501 | 4.630 | 4.747 | 4.955 | 5.219 | 5.573 | 5.861 | 6.105 |
| | .01 | 4.771 | 5.243 | 5.599 | 5.888 | 6.133 | 6.346 | 6.535 | 6.706 | 6.862 | 7.140 | 7.491 | 7.967 | 8.354 | 8.685 |
| 6 | .20 | 1.904 | 2.184 | 2.387 | 2.547 | 2.681 | 2.795 | 2.895 | 2.985 | 3.066 | 3.208 | 3.385 | 3.620 | 3.808 | 3.965 |
| | .10 | 2.428 | 2.723 | 2.939 | 3.110 | 3.253 | 3.376 | 3.484 | 3.580 | 3.668 | 3.822 | 4.015 | 4.272 | 4.477 | 4.649 |
| | .05 | 2.959 | 3.274 | 3.505 | 3.690 | 3.845 | 3.978 | 4.095 | 4.200 | 4.296 | 4.464 | 4.675 | 4.956 | 5.182 | 5.372 |
| | .01 | 4.314 | 4.695 | 4.977 | 5.203 | 5.394 | 5.559 | 5.704 | 5.835 | 5.953 | 6.164 | 6.428 | 6.782 | 7.068 | 7.309 |
| 7 | .20 | 1.858 | 2.120 | 2.309 | 2.457 | 2.579 | 2.684 | 2.775 | 2.856 | 2.929 | 3.056 | 3.214 | 3.423 | 3.588 | 3.725 |
| | .10 | 2.347 | 2.618 | 2.814 | 2.969 | 3.097 | 3.206 | 3.302 | 3.388 | 3.465 | 3.600 | 3.768 | 3.990 | 4.167 | 4.314 |
| | .05 | 2.832 | 3.115 | 3.321 | 3.484 | 3.620 | 3.736 | 3.838 | 3.929 | 4.011 | 4.156 | 4.336 | 4.574 | 4.764 | 4.923 |
| | .01 | 4.027 | 4.352 | 4.591 | 4.782 | 4.941 | 5.078 | 5.198 | 5.306 | 5.403 | 5.576 | 5.790 | 6.077 | 6.305 | 6.498 |
| 8 | .20 | 1.824 | 2.075 | 2.254 | 2.393 | 2.508 | 2.605 | 2.690 | 2.765 | 2.832 | 2.950 | 3.095 | 3.286 | 3.435 | 3.559 |
| | .10 | 2.289 | 2.544 | 2.726 | 2.869 | 2.987 | 3.088 | 3.176 | 3.254 | 3.324 | 3.446 | 3.598 | 3.798 | 3.955 | 4.086 |
| | .05 | 2.743 | 3.005 | 3.193 | 3.342 | 3.464 | 3.569 | 3.661 | 3.743 | 3.816 | 3.945 | 4.105 | 4.316 | 4.482 | 4.621 |
| | .01 | 3.831 | 4.120 | 4.331 | 4.498 | 4.637 | 4.756 | 4.860 | 4.953 | 5.038 | 5.185 | 5.370 | 5.614 | 5.807 | 5.969 |

[a]The critical values in this table are slightly smaller than those based on the Bonferroni inequality; they are based on: $\alpha = 1\ (1 - \alpha_{\Sigma})^{1/C}$ (Sidak, 1967). For example, If C = 12, $\nu_e = 120$, and $\alpha_{\Sigma} = .05$, $\alpha = 1 - (.95)^{1/12} = .04265$, which corresponds to a critical $t$-ratio of 2.971; (use EXCEL's TINV function.)

[b]These critical values are nondirectional; for one-tailed tests, divide the tabled alpha by 2, e.g., for $\alpha_{\Sigma_1} = .10$, use the tabled values for $\alpha_{\Sigma_2} = .20$.

**TABLE L** *Continued*

| $v_e$ | $\alpha_{\Sigma_2}{}^b$ | 2 | 3 | 4 | 5 | 6 | 7 | 8 | 9 | 10 | 12 | 15 | 20 | 25 | 30 |
|---|---|---|---|---|---|---|---|---|---|---|---|---|---|---|---|
| | | *Number of Comparisons (C)* | | | | | | | | | | | | | |
| 9 | .20 | 1.799 | 2.041 | 2.212 | 2.345 | 2.454 | 2.546 | 2.627 | 2.698 | 2.761 | 2.872 | 3.008 | 3.185 | 3.324 | 3.438 |
| | .10 | 2.246 | 2.488 | 2.661 | 2.796 | 2.907 | 3.001 | 3.083 | 3.155 | 3.221 | 3.334 | 3.474 | 3.658 | 3.802 | 3.921 |
| | .05 | 2.677 | 2.923 | 3.099 | 3.237 | 3.351 | 3.448 | 3.532 | 3.607 | 3.675 | 3.793 | 3.938 | 4.130 | 4.280 | 4.405 |
| | .01 | 3.688 | 3.952 | 4.143 | 4.294 | 4.419 | 4.526 | 4.619 | 4.703 | 4.778 | 4.909 | 5.072 | 5.287 | 5.458 | 5.598 |
| 10 | .20 | 1.779 | 2.014 | 2.180 | 2.308 | 2.413 | 2.501 | 2.578 | 2.646 | 2.706 | 2.812 | 2.941 | 3.108 | 3.239 | 3.346 |
| | .10 | 2.213 | 2.446 | 2.611 | 2.739 | 2.845 | 2.934 | 3.012 | 3.080 | 3.142 | 3.249 | 3.380 | 3.552 | 3.686 | 3.796 |
| | .05 | 2.626 | 2.860 | 3.027 | 3.157 | 3.264 | 3.355 | 3.434 | 3.505 | 3.568 | 3.677 | 3.813 | 3.990 | 4.128 | 4.243 |
| | .01 | 3.580 | 3.825 | 4.002 | 4.141 | 4.256 | 4.354 | 4.439 | 4.515 | 4.584 | 4.703 | 4.852 | 5.045 | 5.199 | 5.326 |
| 11 | .20 | 1.763 | 1.993 | 2.154 | 2.279 | 2.380 | 2.465 | 2.539 | 2.605 | 2.663 | 2.764 | 2.888 | 3.048 | 3.172 | 3.274 |
| | .10 | 2.186 | 2.412 | 2.571 | 2.695 | 2.796 | 2.881 | 2.955 | 3.021 | 3.079 | 3.181 | 3.306 | 3.468 | 3.595 | 3.699 |
| | .05 | 2.586 | 2.811 | 2.970 | 3.094 | 3.196 | 3.283 | 3.358 | 3.424 | 3.484 | 3.587 | 3.715 | 3.880 | 4.010 | 4.117 |
| | .01 | 3.495 | 3.726 | 3.892 | 4.022 | 4.130 | 4.221 | 4.300 | 4.371 | 4.434 | 4.545 | 4.682 | 4.860 | 5.001 | 5.118 |
| 12 | .20 | 1.750 | 1.975 | 2.133 | 2.254 | 2.353 | 2.436 | 2.508 | 2.571 | 2.628 | 2.725 | 2.845 | 2.999 | 3.118 | 3.216 |
| | .10 | 2.164 | 2.384 | 2.539 | 2.658 | 2.756 | 2.838 | 2.910 | 2.973 | 3.029 | 3.127 | 3.247 | 3.402 | 3.522 | 3.621 |
| | .05 | 2.553 | 2.770 | 2.924 | 3.044 | 3.141 | 3.224 | 3.296 | 3.359 | 3.416 | 3.515 | 3.636 | 3.793 | 3.916 | 4.017 |
| | .01 | 3.427 | 3.647 | 3.804 | 3.927 | 4.029 | 4.114 | 4.189 | 4.256 | 4.315 | 4.419 | 4.547 | 4.714 | 4.845 | 4.952 |
| 13 | .20 | 1.739 | 1.961 | 2.116 | 2.234 | 2.331 | 2.412 | 2.482 | 2.544 | 2.599 | 2.693 | 2.809 | 2.958 | 3.074 | 3.168 |
| | .10 | 2.146 | 2.361 | 2.512 | 2.628 | 2.723 | 2.803 | 2.872 | 2.933 | 2.988 | 3.082 | 3.198 | 3.347 | 3.463 | 3.558 |
| | .05 | 2.526 | 2.737 | 2.886 | 3.002 | 3.096 | 3.176 | 3.245 | 3.306 | 3.361 | 3.455 | 3.571 | 3.722 | 3.839 | 3.935 |
| | .01 | 3.371 | 3.582 | 3.733 | 3.850 | 3.946 | 4.028 | 4.099 | 4.162 | 4.218 | 4.317 | 4.438 | 4.595 | 4.718 | 4.820 |
| 14 | .20 | 1.730 | 1.949 | 2.101 | 2.217 | 2.312 | 2.392 | 2.460 | 2.520 | 2.574 | 2.667 | 2.779 | 2.924 | 3.036 | 3.128 |
| | .10 | 2.131 | 2.342 | 2.489 | 2.603 | 2.696 | 2.774 | 2.841 | 2.900 | 2.953 | 3.045 | 3.157 | 3.301 | 3.413 | 3.504 |
| | .05 | 2.503 | 2.709 | 2.854 | 2.967 | 3.058 | 3.135 | 3.202 | 3.261 | 3.314 | 3.406 | 3.518 | 3.662 | 3.775 | 3.867 |
| | .01 | 3.324 | 3.528 | 3.673 | 3.785 | 3.878 | 3.956 | 4.024 | 4.084 | 4.138 | 4.232 | 4.347 | 4.497 | 4.614 | 4.710 |
| 15 | .20 | 1.722 | 1.938 | 2.088 | 2.203 | 2.296 | 2.374 | 2.441 | 2.500 | 2.553 | 2.644 | 2.754 | 2.896 | 3.005 | 3.094 |
| | .10 | 2.118 | 2.325 | 2.470 | 2.582 | 2.672 | 2.748 | 2.814 | 2.872 | 2.924 | 3.013 | 3.122 | 3.262 | 3.370 | 3.459 |
| | .05 | 2.483 | 2.685 | 2.827 | 2.937 | 3.026 | 3.101 | 3.166 | 3.224 | 3.275 | 3.364 | 3.472 | 3.612 | 3.721 | 3.810 |
| | .01 | 3.285 | 3.482 | 3.622 | 3.731 | 3.820 | 3.895 | 3.961 | 4.019 | 4.070 | 4.160 | 4.271 | 4.414 | 4.526 | 4.618 |
| 16 | .20 | 1.715 | 1.929 | 2.077 | 2.190 | 2.282 | 2.359 | 2.425 | 2.483 | 2.535 | 2.624 | 2.732 | 2.871 | 2.978 | 3.064 |
| | .10 | 2.106 | 2.311 | 2.453 | 2.563 | 2.652 | 2.726 | 2.791 | 2.848 | 2.898 | 2.985 | 3.092 | 3.228 | 3.334 | 3.420 |
| | .05 | 2.467 | 2.665 | 2.804 | 2.911 | 2.998 | 3.072 | 3.135 | 3.191 | 3.241 | 3.327 | 3.433 | 3.569 | 3.675 | 3.761 |
| | .01 | 3.251 | 3.443 | 3.579 | 3.684 | 3.771 | 3.843 | 3.907 | 3.963 | 4.013 | 4.100 | 4.206 | 4.344 | 4.452 | 4.540 |
| 18 | .20 | 1.704 | 1.914 | 2.059 | 2.170 | 2.259 | 2.334 | 2.399 | 2.455 | 2.505 | 2.592 | 2.696 | 2.830 | 2.933 | 3.017 |
| | .10 | 2.088 | 2.287 | 2.426 | 2.532 | 2.619 | 2.691 | 2.753 | 2.808 | 2.857 | 2.941 | 3.043 | 3.174 | 3.275 | 3.358 |

**TABLE L** *Continued*

| $v_e$ | $\alpha_{\Sigma_2}^{b}$ | Number of Comparisons (C) | | | | | | | | | | | | | |
|---|---|---|---|---|---|---|---|---|---|---|---|---|---|---|---|
| | | 2 | 3 | 4 | 5 | 6 | 7 | 8 | 9 | 10 | 12 | 15 | 20 | 25 | 30 |
| | .05 | 2.439 | 2.631 | 2.766 | 2.869 | 2.953 | 3.024 | 3.085 | 3.138 | 3.186 | 3.269 | 3.370 | 3.499 | 3.599 | 3.681 |
| | .01 | 3.195 | 3.379 | 3.508 | 3.609 | 3.691 | 3.760 | 3.820 | 3.872 | 3.920 | 4.001 | 4.102 | 4.231 | 4.332 | 4.414 |
| 20 | .20 | 1.695 | 1.902 | 2.045 | 2.154 | 2.241 | 2.315 | 2.378 | 2.433 | 2.482 | 2.566 | 2.668 | 2.798 | 2.898 | 2.979 |
| | .10 | 2.073 | 2.269 | 2.405 | 2.508 | 2.592 | 2.663 | 2.724 | 2.777 | 2.824 | 2.906 | 3.005 | 3.132 | 3.229 | 3.309 |
| | .05 | 2.417 | 2.605 | 2.736 | 2.836 | 2.918 | 2.986 | 3.045 | 3.097 | 3.143 | 3.223 | 3.320 | 3.445 | 3.541 | 3.620 |
| | .01 | 3.152 | 3.329 | 3.454 | 3.550 | 3.629 | 3.695 | 3.752 | 3.802 | 3.848 | 3.926 | 4.021 | 4.144 | 4.239 | 4.317 |
| 25 | .20 | 1.679 | 1.881 | 2.020 | 2.125 | 2.210 | 2.280 | 2.341 | 2.394 | 2.441 | 2.522 | 2.619 | 2.743 | 2.838 | 2.914 |
| | .10 | 2.047 | 2.236 | 2.367 | 2.466 | 2.547 | 2.614 | 2.672 | 2.722 | 2.767 | 2.845 | 2.938 | 3.058 | 3.149 | 3.224 |
| | .05 | 2.379 | 2.558 | 2.683 | 2.779 | 2.856 | 2.921 | 2.976 | 3.025 | 3.069 | 3.144 | 3.235 | 3.351 | 3.440 | 3.513 |
| | .01 | 3.077 | 3.243 | 3.359 | 3.449 | 3.521 | 3.583 | 3.635 | 3.682 | 3.723 | 3.795 | 3.882 | 3.995 | 4.082 | 4.152 |
| 30 | .20 | 1.669 | 1.867 | 2.003 | 2.106 | 2.189 | 2.258 | 2.317 | 2.369 | 2.414 | 2.493 | 2.587 | 2.707 | 2.798 | 2.872 |
| | .10 | 2.030 | 2.215 | 2.342 | 2.439 | 2.517 | 2.582 | 2.638 | 2.687 | 2.731 | 2.805 | 2.895 | 3.010 | 3.098 | 3.169 |
| | .05 | 2.354 | 2.528 | 2.649 | 2.742 | 2.816 | 2.878 | 2.932 | 2.979 | 3.021 | 3.093 | 3.180 | 3.291 | 3.376 | 3.445 |
| | .01 | 3.029 | 3.188 | 3.298 | 3.384 | 3.453 | 3.511 | 3.561 | 3.605 | 3.644 | 3.712 | 3.794 | 3.900 | 3.981 | 4.048 |
| 40 | .20 | 1.656 | 1.850 | 1.983 | 2.083 | 2.164 | 2.231 | 2.288 | 2.338 | 2.382 | 2.457 | 2.548 | 2.663 | 2.751 | 2.821 |
| | .10 | 2.009 | 2.189 | 2.312 | 2.406 | 2.481 | 2.544 | 2.597 | 2.644 | 2.686 | 2.757 | 2.843 | 2.953 | 3.036 | 3.103 |
| | .05 | 2.323 | 2.492 | 2.608 | 2.696 | 2.768 | 2.827 | 2.878 | 2.923 | 2.963 | 3.031 | 3.113 | 3.218 | 3.298 | 3.363 |
| | .01 | 2.970 | 3.121 | 3.225 | 3.305 | 3.370 | 3.425 | 3.472 | 3.513 | 3.549 | 3.612 | 3.689 | 3.787 | 3.862 | 3.923 |
| 60 | .20 | 1.643 | 1.834 | 1.963 | 2.061 | 2.139 | 2.204 | 2.259 | 2.308 | 2.350 | 2.423 | 2.511 | 2.621 | 2.705 | 2.772 |
| | .10 | 1.989 | 2.163 | 2.283 | 2.373 | 2.446 | 2.506 | 2.558 | 2.603 | 2.643 | 2.711 | 2.793 | 2.897 | 2.976 | 3.040 |
| | .05 | 2.294 | 2.456 | 2.568 | 2.653 | 2.721 | 2.777 | 2.826 | 2.869 | 2.906 | 2.971 | 3.049 | 3.148 | 3.223 | 3.284 |
| | .01 | 2.914 | 3.056 | 3.155 | 3.230 | 3.291 | 3.342 | 3.386 | 3.425 | 3.459 | 3.517 | 3.589 | 3.679 | 3.749 | 3.805 |
| 120 | .20 | 1.631 | 1.817 | 1.944 | 2.039 | 2.115 | 2.178 | 2.231 | 2.278 | 2.319 | 2.390 | 2.474 | 2.580 | 2.660 | 2.724 |
| | .10 | 1.968 | 2.138 | 2.254 | 2.342 | 2.411 | 2.469 | 2.519 | 2.562 | 2.600 | 2.666 | 2.744 | 2.843 | 2.918 | 2.978 |
| | .05 | 2.265 | 2.422 | 2.529 | 2.610 | 2.675 | 2.729 | 2.776 | 2.816 | 2.852 | 2.913 | 2.987 | 3.081 | 3.152 | 3.209 |
| | .01 | 2.859 | 2.994 | 3.087 | 3.158 | 3.215 | 3.263 | 3.304 | 3.340 | 3.372 | 3.427 | 3.493 | 3.577 | 3.641 | 3.693 |
| $\infty$ | .20 | 1.618 | 1.801 | 1.925 | 2.017 | 2.091 | 2.152 | 2.204 | 2.249 | 2.289 | 2.357 | 2.438 | 2.540 | 2.616 | 2.678 |
| | .10 | 1.949 | 2.114 | 2.226 | 2.311 | 2.378 | 2.434 | 2.481 | 2.523 | 2.560 | 2.622 | 2.697 | 2.791 | 2.862 | 2.920 |
| | .05 | 2.236 | 2.388 | 2.491 | 2.569 | 2.631 | 2.683 | 2.727 | 2.766 | 2.800 | 2.858 | 2.928 | 3.016 | 3.083 | 3.137 |
| | .01 | 2.806 | 2.934 | 3.022 | 3.089 | 3.143 | 3.188 | 3.226 | 3.259 | 3.289 | 3.340 | 3.402 | 3.479 | 3.539 | 3.587 |

**TABLE M** Critical $t$-Values for the Dunnett Statistic for Comparing Treatment Means with a Control[a].

| | *Alpha* | | *J = Number of Means (Including Control)* | | | | | | | | |
|---|---|---|---|---|---|---|---|---|---|---|---|
| $v_e$ | $\alpha_{\Sigma_2}$ | $\alpha_{\Sigma_1}$ | 2 | 3 | 4 | 5 | 6 | 7 | 8 | 9 | 10 |
| 5 | .10 | .05 | 2.02 | 2.44 | 2.68 | 2.85 | 2.98 | 3.08 | 3.16 | 3.24 | 3.03 |
| | .05 | | 2.57 | 3.03 | 3.29 | 3.48 | 3.62 | 3.73 | 3.82 | 3.90 | 3.97 |
| | .02 | .01 | 3.36 | 3.90 | 4.21 | 4.43 | 4.60 | 4.73 | 4.85 | 4.94 | 5.03 |
| | .01 | | 4.03 | 4.63 | 4.98 | 5.22 | 5.41 | 5.56 | 5.69 | 5.80 | 5.89 |
| 6 | .10 | .05 | 1.94 | 2.34 | 2.56 | 2.71 | 2.83 | 2.92 | 3.00 | 3.07 | 3.12 |
| | .05 | | 2.45 | 2.86 | 3.10 | 3.26 | 3.39 | 3.49 | 3.57 | 3.64 | 3.71 |
| | .02 | .01 | 3.14 | 3.61 | 3.88 | 4.07 | 4.21 | 4.33 | 4.43 | 4.51 | 4.59 |
| | .01 | | 3.71 | 4.21 | 4.51 | 4.71 | 3.87 | 5.00 | 5.10 | 5.20 | 5.28 |
| 7 | .10 | .05 | 1.89 | 2.27 | 2.48 | 2.62 | 2.73 | 2.82 | 2.89 | 2.95 | 3.01 |
| | .05 | | 2.36 | 2.75 | 2.97 | 3.12 | 3.24 | 3.33 | 3.41 | 3.47 | 3.53 |
| | .02 | .01 | 3.00 | 3.42 | 3.66 | 3.83 | 3.96 | 4.07 | 4.15 | 4.23 | 4.30 |
| | .01 | | 3.50 | 3.95 | 4.21 | 4.39 | 4.53 | 4.64 | 4.74 | 4.82 | 4.89 |
| 8 | .10 | .05 | 1.86 | 2.22 | 2.42 | 2.55 | 2.66 | 2.74 | 2.81 | 2.87 | 2.92 |
| | .05 | | 2.31 | 2.67 | 2.88 | 3.02 | 3.13 | 3.22 | 3.29 | 3.35 | 3.41 |
| | .02 | .01 | 2.90 | 3.29 | 3.51 | 3.67 | 3.79 | 3.88 | 3.96 | 4.03 | 4.09 |
| | .01 | | 3.36 | 3.77 | 4.00 | 4.17 | 4.29 | 4.40 | 4.48 | 4.56 | 4.62 |
| 9 | .10 | .05 | 1.83 | 2.18 | 2.37 | 2.50 | 2.60 | 2.68 | 2.75 | 2.81 | 2.86 |
| | .05 | | 2.26 | 2.61 | 2.81 | 2.95 | 3.05 | 3.14 | 3.20 | 3.26 | 3.32 |
| | .02 | .01 | 2.28 | 3.19 | 3.40 | 3.55 | 3.66 | 3.75 | 3.82 | 3.89 | 3.94 |
| | .01 | | 3.25 | 3.63 | 3.85 | 4.01 | 4.12 | 4.22 | 4.30 | 4.37 | 4.43 |
| 10 | .10 | .05 | 1.81 | 2.15 | 2.34 | 2.47 | 2.56 | 2.64 | 2.70 | 2.76 | 2.81 |
| | .05 | | 2.23 | 2.57 | 2.76 | 2.89 | 2.99 | 3.07 | 3.14 | 3.19 | 3.24 |
| | .02 | .01 | 2.76 | 3.11 | 3.31 | 3.45 | 3.56 | 3.64 | 3.71 | 3.78 | 3.83 |
| | .01 | | 3.17 | 3.53 | 3.74 | 3.88 | 3.99 | 4.08 | 4.16 | 4.22 | 4.28 |
| 11 | .10 | .05 | 1.80 | 2.13 | 2.31 | 2.44 | 2.53 | 2.60 | 2.67 | 2.72 | 2.77 |
| | .05 | | 2.20 | 2.53 | 2.72 | 2.84 | 2.94 | 3.02 | 3.08 | 3.14 | 3.19 |
| | .02 | .01 | 2.72 | 3.06 | 3.25 | 3.38 | 3.48 | 3.56 | 3.63 | 3.69 | 3.74 |
| | .01 | | 3.11 | 3.45 | 3.65 | 3.79 | 3.89 | 3.98 | 4.05 | 4.11 | 4.16 |
| 12 | .10 | .05 | 1.78 | 2.11 | 2.29 | 2.41 | 2.50 | 2.58 | 2.64 | 2.69 | 2.74 |
| | .05 | | 2.18 | 2.50 | 2.68 | 2.81 | 2.90 | 2.98 | 3.04 | 3.09 | 3.14 |
| | .02 | .01 | 2.68 | 3.01 | 3.19 | 3.32 | 3.42 | 3.50 | 3.56 | 3.62 | 3.67 |
| | .01 | | 3.05 | 3.39 | 3.58 | 3.71 | 3.81 | 3.89 | 3.96 | 4.02 | 4.07 |
| 13 | .10 | .05 | 1.77 | 2.09 | 2.27 | 2.39 | 2.48 | 2.55 | 2.61 | 2.66 | 2.71 |
| | .05 | | 2.16 | 2.48 | 2.65 | 2.78 | 2.87 | 2.94 | 3.00 | 3.06 | 3.10 |
| | .02 | .01 | 2.65 | 2.97 | 3.15 | 3.27 | 3.37 | 3.44 | 3.51 | 3.56 | 3.61 |
| | .01 | | 3.01 | 3.33 | 3.52 | 3.65 | 3.74 | 3.82 | 3.89 | 3.94 | 3.99 |
| 14 | .10 | .05 | 1.76 | 2.08 | 2.25 | 2.37 | 2.46 | 2.53 | 2.59 | 2.64 | 2.69 |
| | .05 | | 2.14 | 2.46 | 2.63 | 2.75 | 2.84 | 2.91 | 2.97 | 3.02 | 3.07 |
| | .02 | .01 | 2.62 | 2.94 | 3.11 | 3.23 | 3.32 | 3.40 | 3.46 | 3.51 | 3.56 |
| | .01 | | 2.98 | 3.29 | 3.47 | 3.59 | 3.69 | 3.76 | 3.83 | 3.88 | 3.93 |

**TABLE M** Critical *t*-Values for the Dunnett Statistic for Comparing Treatment Means with a Control[a].

| | *Alpha* | | *J = Number of Means (Including Control)* | | | | | | | | |
|---|---|---|---|---|---|---|---|---|---|---|---|
| $\nu_e$ | $\alpha_{\Sigma_2}$ | $\alpha_{\Sigma_1}$ | 2 | 3 | 4 | 5 | 6 | 7 | 8 | 9 | 10 |
| 16 | .10 | .05 | 1.75 | 2.06 | 2.23 | 2.34 | 2.43 | 2.50 | 2.56 | 2.61 | 2.65 |
| | .05 | | 2.12 | 2.42 | 2.59 | 2.71 | 2.80 | 2.87 | 2.92 | 2.97 | 3.02 |
| | .02 | .01 | 2.58 | 2.88 | 3.05 | 3.17 | 3.26 | 3.33 | 3.39 | 3.44 | 3.48 |
| | .01 | | 2.92 | 3.22 | 3.39 | 3.51 | 3.60 | 3.67 | 3.73 | 3.78 | 3.83 |
| 18 | .10 | .05 | 1.73 | 2.04 | 2.21 | 2.32 | 2.41 | 2.48 | 2.53 | 2.58 | 2.62 |
| | .05 | | 2.10 | 2.40 | 2.56 | 2.68 | 2.76 | 2.83 | 2.89 | 2.94 | 2.98 |
| | .02 | .01 | 2.55 | 2.84 | 3.01 | 3.12 | 3.21 | 3.27 | 3.33 | 3.38 | 3.42 |
| | .01 | | 2.88 | 3.17 | 3.33 | 3.44 | 3.53 | 3.60 | 3.66 | 3.71 | 3.75 |
| 20 | .10 | .05 | 1.72 | 2.03 | 2.19 | 2.30 | 2.39 | 2.46 | 2.51 | 2.56 | 2.60 |
| | .05 | | 2.09 | 2.38 | 2.54 | 2.65 | 2.73 | 2.80 | 2.86 | 2.90 | 2.95 |
| | .02 | .01 | 2.53 | 2.81 | 2.97 | 3.08 | 3.17 | 3.23 | 3.29 | 3.34 | 3.38 |
| | .01 | | 2.85 | 3.13 | 3.29 | 3.40 | 3.48 | 3.55 | 3.60 | 3.65 | 3.69 |
| 24 | .10 | .05 | 1.71 | 2.01 | 2.17 | 2.28 | 2.36 | 2.43 | 2.48 | 2.53 | 2.57 |
| | .05 | | 2.06 | 2.35 | 2.51 | 2.61 | 2.70 | 2.76 | 2.81 | 2.86 | 2.90 |
| | .02 | .01 | 2.49 | 2.77 | 2.92 | 3.03 | 3.11 | 3.17 | 3.22 | 3.27 | 3.31 |
| | .01 | | 2.80 | 3.07 | 3.22 | 3.32 | 3.40 | 3.47 | 3.52 | 3.57 | 3.61 |
| 30 | .10 | .05 | 1.70 | 1.99 | 2.15 | 2.25 | 2.33 | 2.40 | 2.45 | 2.50 | 2.54 |
| | .05 | | 2.04 | 2.32 | 2.47 | 2.58 | 2.66 | 2.72 | 2.77 | 2.82 | 2.86 |
| | .02 | .01 | 2.46 | 2.72 | 2.87 | 2.97 | 3.05 | 3.11 | 3.16 | 3.21 | 3.24 |
| | .01 | | 2.75 | 3.01 | 3.15 | 3.25 | 3.33 | 3.39 | 3.44 | 3.49 | 3.52 |
| 40 | .10 | .05 | 1.68 | 1.97 | 2.13 | 2.23 | 2.31 | 2.37 | 2.42 | 2.47 | 2.51 |
| | .05 | | 2.02 | 2.29 | 2.44 | 2.54 | 2.62 | 2.68 | 2.73 | 2.77 | 2.81 |
| | .02 | .01 | 2.42 | 2.68 | 2.82 | 2.92 | 2.99 | 3.05 | 3.10 | 3.14 | 3.18 |
| | .01 | | 2.80 | 2.95 | 3.09 | 3.19 | 3.26 | 3.32 | 3.37 | 3.41 | 3.44 |
| 60 | .10 | .05 | 1.67 | 1.95 | 2.10 | 2.21 | 2.28 | 2.35 | 2.39 | 2.44 | 2.48 |
| | .05 | | 2.00 | 2.27 | 2.41 | 2.51 | 2.58 | 2.64 | 2.69 | 2.73 | 2.77 |
| | .02 | .01 | 2.39 | 2.64 | 2.78 | 2.87 | 2.94 | 3.00 | 3.04 | 3.08 | 3.12 |
| | .01 | | 2.66 | 2.90 | 3.03 | 3.12 | 3.19 | 3.25 | 3.29 | 3.33 | 3.37 |
| 120 | .10 | .05 | 1.66 | 1.93 | 2.08 | 2.18 | 2.26 | 2.32 | 2.37 | 2.41 | 2.45 |
| | .05 | | 1.98 | 2.24 | 2.38 | 2.47 | 2.55 | 2.60 | 2.65 | 2.69 | 2.73 |
| | .02 | .01 | 2.36 | 2.60 | 2.73 | 2.82 | 2.89 | 2.94 | 2.99 | 3.03 | 3.06 |
| | .01 | | 2.62 | 2.85 | 2.97 | 3.06 | 3.12 | 3.18 | 3.22 | 3.26 | 3.29 |
| $\infty$ | .10 | .05 | 1.64 | 1.92 | 2.06 | 2.16 | 2.23 | 2.29 | 2.34 | 2.38 | 2.42 |
| | .05 | | 1.96 | 2.21 | 2.35 | 2.44 | 2.51 | 2.57 | 2.61 | 2.65 | 2.69 |
| | .02 | .01 | 2.33 | 2.56 | 2.68 | 2.77 | 2.84 | 2.89 | 2.93 | 2.97 | 3.00 |
| | .01 | | 2.58 | 2.79 | 2.92 | 3.00 | 3.06 | 3.11 | 3.15 | 3.19 | 3.22 |

[a]This table is reproduced from "A multiple comparison procedure for comparing several treatments with a control." *Journal of the American Statistical Association,* 1955, **50,** 1096–1121, and "New tables for multiple comparisons with a control." *Biometrics,* 1964, **20,** 482–491, with the permission of the author, C. W. Dunnett, and the editors.

**TABLE N** Coefficients of Orthogonal Polynomials for Trend Analysis[a].

| *J* | *Trend* | $j = 1$ | 2 | 3 | 4 | 5 | 6 | 7 | 8 | 9 | 10 | 11 | 12 | $\Sigma c_j^2$ |
|---|---|---|---|---|---|---|---|---|---|---|---|---|---|---|
| 3 | Linear | –1 | 0 | 1 | | | | | | | | | | 2 |
| | Quadratic | 1 | –2 | 1 | | | | | | | | | | 6 |
| 4 | Linear | –3 | –1 | 1 | 3 | | | | | | | | | 20 |
| | Quadratic | 1 | –1 | –1 | 1 | | | | | | | | | 4 |
| | Cubic | –1 | 3 | –3 | 1 | | | | | | | | | 20 |
| 5 | Linear | –2 | –1 | 0 | 1 | 2 | | | | | | | | 10 |
| | Quadratic | 2 | –1 | –2 | –1 | 2 | | | | | | | | 14 |
| | Cubic | –1 | 2 | 0 | –2 | 1 | | | | | | | | 10 |
| | Quartic | 1 | –4 | 6 | –4 | 1 | | | | | | | | 70 |
| 6 | Linear | –5 | –3 | –1 | 1 | 3 | 5 | | | | | | | 70 |
| | Quadratic | 5 | –1 | –4 | –4 | –1 | 5 | | | | | | | 84 |
| | Cubic | –5 | 7 | 4 | –4 | –7 | 5 | | | | | | | 180 |
| | Quartic | 1 | –3 | 2 | 2 | –3 | 1 | | | | | | | 28 |
| | Quintic | –1 | 5 | –10 | 10 | –5 | 1 | | | | | | | 252 |
| 7 | Linear | –3 | –2 | –1 | 0 | 1 | 2 | 3 | | | | | | 28 |
| | Quadratic | 5 | 0 | –3 | –4 | –3 | 0 | 5 | | | | | | 84 |
| | Cubic | –1 | 1 | 1 | 0 | –1 | –1 | 1 | | | | | | 6 |
| | Quartic | 3 | –7 | 1 | 6 | 1 | –7 | 3 | | | | | | 154 |
| | Quintic | –1 | 4 | –5 | 0 | 5 | –4 | 1 | | | | | | 84 |
| 8 | Linear | –7 | –5 | –3 | –1 | 1 | 3 | 5 | 7 | | | | | 168 |
| | Quadratic | 7 | 1 | –3 | –5 | –5 | –3 | 1 | 7 | | | | | 168 |
| | Cubic | –7 | 5 | 7 | 3 | –3 | –7 | –5 | 7 | | | | | 264 |
| | Quartic | 7 | –13 | –3 | 9 | 9 | –3 | –13 | 7 | | | | | 616 |
| | Quintic | –7 | 23 | –17 | –15 | 15 | 17 | –23 | 7 | | | | | 2,184 |
| 9 | Linear | –4 | –3 | –2 | –1 | 0 | 1 | 2 | 3 | 4 | | | | 60 |
| | Quadratic | 28 | 7 | –8 | –17 | –20 | –17 | –8 | 7 | 28 | | | | 2,772 |
| | Cubic | –14 | 7 | 13 | 9 | 0 | –9 | –13 | –7 | 14 | | | | 990 |
| | Quartic | 14 | –21 | –11 | 9 | 18 | 9 | –11 | –21 | 14 | | | | 2,002 |
| | Quintic | –4 | 11 | –4 | –9 | 0 | 9 | 4 | –11 | 4 | | | | 468 |
| 10 | Linear | –9 | –7 | –5 | –3 | –1 | 1 | 3 | 5 | 7 | 9 | | | 330 |
| | Quadratic | 6 | 2 | –1 | –3 | –4 | –4 | –3 | –1 | 2 | 6 | | | 132 |
| | Cubic | –42 | 14 | 35 | 31 | 12 | –12 | –31 | –35 | –14 | 42 | | | 8,580 |
| | Quartic | 18 | –22 | –17 | 3 | 18 | 18 | 3 | –17 | –22 | 18 | | | 2,860 |
| | Quintic | –6 | 14 | –1 | –11 | –6 | 6 | 11 | 1 | –14 | 6 | | | 780 |
| 11 | Linear | –5 | –4 | –3 | –2 | –1 | 0 | 1 | 2 | 3 | 4 | 5 | | 110 |
| | Quadratic | 15 | 6 | –1 | –6 | –9 | –10 | –9 | –6 | –1 | 6 | 15 | | 858 |
| | Cubic | –30 | 6 | 22 | 23 | 14 | 0 | –14 | –23 | –22 | –6 | 30 | | 4,290 |
| | Quartic | 6 | –6 | –6 | –1 | 4 | 6 | 4 | –1 | –6 | –6 | 6 | | 286 |
| | Quintic | –3 | 6 | 1 | –4 | –4 | 0 | 4 | 4 | –1 | –6 | 3 | | 156 |
| 12 | Linear | –11 | –9 | –7 | –5 | –3 | –1 | 1 | 3 | 5 | 7 | 9 | 11 | 572 |
| | Quadratic | 55 | 25 | 1 | –17 | –29 | –35 | –35 | –29 | –17 | 1 | 25 | 55 | 12,012 |
| | Cubic | –33 | 3 | 21 | 25 | 19 | 7 | –7 | –19 | –25 | –21 | –3 | 33 | 5,148 |
| | Quartic | 33 | –27 | –33 | –13 | 12 | 28 | 28 | 12 | –13 | –33 | –27 | 33 | 8,008 |
| | Quintic | –33 | 57 | 21 | –29 | –44 | –20 | 20 | 44 | 29 | –21 | –57 | 33 | 15,912 |
| *J* | *Trend* | $j = 1$ | 2 | 3 | 4 | 5 | 6 | 7 | 8 | 9 | 10 | 11 | 12 | $\Sigma c_j^2$ |

[a]Reproduced with permission of the trustees of *Biometrika*.

## TABLE O Binomial Probabilities when $\pi = .5$[1].

| | | Number of B events = N − r = "Misses" | | | | | | | | |
|---|---|---|---|---|---|---|---|---|---|---|
| | | 0 | 1 | 2 | 3 | 4 | 5 | 6 | 7 | 8 |
| *Number of Events N* | *Number of Outcomes* | *Number of A events = r = "Hits"* N | N − 1 | N − 2 | N − 3 | N − 4 | N − 5 | N − 6 | N − 7 | N − 8 |
| **1** | 1 | 1.00 | | | | | | | | |
| **2** | 4 | .2500 | .75 | .100 | | | | | | |
| **3** | 8 | .1250 | .50 | .875 | 1.00 | | | | | |
| **4** | 16 | .0625 | .3125 | .6875 | .9375 | 1.00 | | | | |
| **5** | 32 | .031250 | .1875 | .500 | .8125 | .96875 | 1.00 | | | |
| **6** | 64 | .015625 | .10938 | .34375 | .65625 | .89063 | .98438 | 1.00 | | |
| **7** | 128 | .007813 | .06250 | .22656 | .50000 | .77344 | .93750 | .99219 | 1.00 | |
| **8** | 256 | .003906 | .03516 | .14453 | .36328 | .63672 | .85547 | .96484 | .99609 | 1.00 |
| **9** | 512 | .001953 | .01953 | .08984 | .25391 | .50000 | .74609 | .91016 | .98047 | .99805 |
| **10** | 1,024 | .000977 | .01074 | .05469 | .17188 | .37695 | .62305 | .82813 | .94531 | .98926 |
| **11** | 2,048 | .000488 | .00586 | .03271 | .11328 | .27441 | .50000 | .72559 | .88672 | .96729 |
| **12** | 4,096 | .000244 | .00317 | .01929 | .07300 | .19385 | .38721 | .61279 | .80615 | .92700 |
| **13** | 8,192 | .000122 | .00171 | .01123 | .04614 | .13342 | .29053 | .50000 | .70947 | .86658 |
| **14** | 16,384 | 6.10E-05 | 9.16E-04 | .00647 | .02869 | .08978 | .21198 | .39526 | .60474 | .78802 |
| **15** | 32,768 | 3.05E-05 | 4.88E-04 | .00369 | .01758 | .05923 | .15088 | .30362 | .50000 | .69638 |
| **16** | 65,536 | 1.53E-05 | 2.59E-04 | .00209 | .01064 | .03841 | .10506 | .22725 | .40181 | .59819 |
| **17** | 131,072 | 7.63E-06 | 1.37E-04 | .00117 | .00636 | .02452 | .07173 | .16615 | .31453 | .50000 |
| **18** | 262,144 | 3.81E-06 | 7.25E-05 | 6.56E-04 | .00377 | .01544 | .04813 | .11894 | .24034 | .40726 |
| **19** | 524,288 | 1.91E-06 | 3.81E-05 | 3.64E-04 | .00221 | .00961 | .03178 | .08353 | .17964 | .32380 |
| **20** | 1,048,576 | 9.54E-07 | 2.00E-05 | 2.01E-04 | .00129 | .00591 | .02069 | .05766 | .13159 | .25172 |
| **21** | 2,097,152 | 4.77E-07 | 1.05E-05 | 1.11E-04 | 7.45E-04 | .00360 | .01330 | .03918 | .09462 | .19166 |
| **22** | 4,194,304 | 2.38E-07 | 5.48E-06 | 6.06E-05 | 4.28E-04 | .00217 | .00845 | .02624 | .06690 | .14314 |
| **23** | 8,388,608 | 1.19E-07 | 2.86E-06 | 3.30E-05 | 2.44E-04 | .00130 | .00531 | .01734 | .04657 | .10502 |
| **24** | 16,777,216 | 5.96E-08 | 1.49E-06 | 1.79E-05 | 1.39E-04 | 7.72E-04 | .00331 | .01133 | .03196 | .07579 |
| **25** | 33,554,432 | 2.98E-08 | 7.75E-07 | 9.72E-06 | 7.83E-05 | 4.55E-04 | .00204 | .00732 | .02164 | .05388 |
| **26** | 67,108,864 | 1.49E-08 | 4.02E-07 | 5.25E-06 | 4.40E-05 | 2.67E-04 | .00125 | .00468 | .01448 | .03776 |
| **27** | 134,217,728 | 7.45E-09 | 2.09E-07 | 2.82E-06 | 2.46E-05 | 1.55E-04 | 7.57E-04 | .00296 | .00958 | .02612 |
| **28** | 268,435,456 | 3.73E-09 | 1.08E-07 | 1.52E-06 | 1.37E-05 | 9.00E-05 | 4.56E-04 | .00186 | .00627 | .01785 |
| **29** | 536,870,912 | 1.86E-09 | 5.59E-08 | 8.12E-07 | 7.62E-06 | 5.19E-05 | 2.73E-04 | .00116 | .00407 | .01206 |
| **30** | 1,073,741,824 | 9.31E-10 | 2.89E-08 | 4.34E-07 | 4.22E-06 | 2.97E-05 | 1.62E-04 | 7.15E-04 | .00261 | .00806 |

[1]For example, what is the probability of guessing the incorrect answer on all 10 of the T-F items?

When $N = 10$, $r = 0$; the .000977 indicates that the probability is less than 1 in 1,000 of missing (or correctly answering) all 10 items by chance.

When the cell entries are very small, scientific notation is used. For example, for $N = 14$, the cell entry for $r = N$ is 6.10E-05; this means that the decimal place must be moved five places to the left; thus, 6.10E-05 = .0000610. For other values of $p(A)$, use Equation 9.15.

When $N > 30$, the normal curve approximation can be used. For example, if there are $N = 30$ Bernoulli events ($A$ or $B$), and $p(A) = .5$, ($A$, a "hit" or success), what is the probability that 22 $A$'s will be observed in the 30 events? When $N = 40$, $\mu = (N/2)$ is 20.0, and $\sigma = 2.7386$, ($\sigma_p^2 = N\pi(1 - \pi)$]. A value of 22 has a lower-limit of 21.5, and a $z$-value of 2.373 = [(21.5 – 15.0)/2.7386]. From Table A, find that .0089 or the area in a normal curve falls above a $z$-score of 2.37, whiich agrees closely with the exact value of .00806 found in Table O.

**TABLE O** *Continued*

| *Number of B events = N − r = "Misses"* | | | | | | | |
|---|---|---|---|---|---|---|---|
| 9 | 10 | 11 | 12 | 13 | 14 | 15 | |
| *Number of A events = r = "Hits"* | | | | | | | |
| $N-9$ | $N-10$ | $N-11$ | $N-12$ | $N-13$ | $N-13$ | $N-14$ | $N$ |
| | | | | | | | **1** |
| | | | | | | | **2** |
| | | | | | | | **3** |
| | | | | | | | **4** |
| | | | | | | | **5** |
| | | | | | | | **6** |
| | | | | | | | **7** |
| | | | | | | | **8** |
| 1.00 | | | | | | | **9** |
| .99902 | 1.00 | | | | | | **10** |
| .99414 | .999512 | 1.00 | | | | | **11** |
| .98071 | .99683 | .999756 | 1.00 | | | | **12** |
| .95386 | .98877 | .99829 | .999878 | 1.00 | | | **13** |
| .91022 | .97131 | .99353 | .99908 | .999939 | 1.00 | | **14** |
| .84912 | .94077 | .98242 | .99631 | .99951 | .999969 | 1.00 | **15** |
| .77275 | .89494 | .96159 | .98936 | .99791 | .99974 | .999985 | **16** |
| .68547 | .83385 | .92827 | .97548 | .99364 | .99883 | .99986 | **17** |
| .59274 | .75966 | .88106 | .95187 | .98456 | .99623 | .99934 | **18** |
| .50000 | .67620 | .82036 | .91647 | .96822 | .99039 | .99779 | **19** |
| .41190 | .58810 | .74828 | .86841 | .94234 | .97931 | .99409 | **20** |
| .33181 | .50000 | .66819 | .80834 | .90538 | .96082 | .98670 | **21** |
| .26173 | .41591 | .58409 | .73827 | .85686 | .93310 | .97376 | **22** |
| .20244 | .33882 | .50000 | .66118 | .79756 | .89498 | .95343 | **23** |
| .15373 | .27063 | .41941 | .58059 | .72937 | .84627 | .92421 | **24** |
| .11476 | .21218 | .34502 | .50000 | .65498 | .78782 | .88524 | **25** |
| .08432 | .16347 | .27860 | .42251 | .57749 | .72140 | .83653 | **26** |
| .06104 | .12389 | .22103 | .35055 | .50000 | .64945 | .77897 | **27** |
| .04358 | .09247 | .17246 | .28579 | .42528 | .57472 | .71421 | **28** |
| .03071 | .06802 | .13247 | .22913 | .35554 | .50000 | .64446 | **29** |
| .02139 | .04937 | .10024 | .18080 | .29233 | .42777 | .57223 | **30** |

# BIBLIOGRAPHY

Addelman, S. 1970. "Variability of treatment and experiment units in the design and analysis of experiments," *Journal of the American Statistical Association, 65,* 1095–1108.

Alexander, R. A., M. J. Scozzaro, and L. J. Borodkin. 1990. "Statistical and empirical examination of the chi-square test for homogeneity of correlations in meta-analysis. *Psychological Bulletin, 106,* 329–331.

Allison, D. E. 1970. "Test anxiety, stress, and intelligence performance," *Canadian Journal of Behavioral Science, 2,* 26–37.

Anderson, R., and S. Nida. 1978. "Effect of physical attractiveness on opposite and same-sex evaluations," *Journal of Personality, 46,* 401–413.

Appelbaum, M. I., and E. M. Cramer. 1974. "Some problems in the nonorthogonal analysis of variance," *Psychological Bulletin, 81,* 335–43.

Augustine, N. R. 1978. "Augustine's laws and major system development programs," *Defense Systems Management Review, 1,* 50–76.

Baker, F. B. 1965. "An investigation of the sampling distributions of item discrimination indices," *Psychometrika, 30,* 165–78.

Bancroft, T. A. 1968. *Topics in Intermediate Statistical Methods.* Ames: Iowa State University Press.

Bennet, R. W. 1972. "The magnitude of the teacher effect." Ph.D. thesis, University of Colorado.

Bennett, G. K., H. G. Seashore, and A. G. Wesman. 1974. *Differential Aptitude Tests: Fifth Edition Manual.* New York: Psychological Corporation.

Binder, A. 1959. "Consideration of the place of assumptions in correlational analysis," *American Psychologist, 14,* 504–510.

Bleakley, M. L., V. Westerberg and K. D. Hopkins. 1988. "The experimental effect of character sex on story interest and comprehension in children," *American Educational Research Journal, 25,* 145–155.

Bolch, B. W. 1968. "More on unbiased estimation of the standard deviation," *American Statistician, 20,* 27.

Boneau, C. A. 1960. "The effects of violations of assumptions underlying the *t*-test," *Psychological Bulletin, 57,* 49–64.

Box, G. E. P. 1953. "Non-normality and tests on variances," *Biometrika, 40,* 318–35.

____ 1954. "Some theorems on quadratic forms applied in the study of analysis of variance problems.

II, effects of inequality of variance and of correlation between errors in the two-way classification," *Annals of Mathematical Statistics, 25,* 484–98.

Box, G. E. P., and S. L. Anderson. 1955. "Permutation theory in the derivation of robust criteria and the study of departures from assumptions," *Journal of the Royal Statistical Society, Series B, 17,* 1–26.

Box, G. E. P., W. G. Hunter, and J. S. Hunter. 1978. *Statistics for Experimenters.* New York: John Wiley.

Bracht, G. H., and K. D. Hopkins. 1970. "The communality of essay and objective tests of academic achievement," *Educational and Psychological Measurement, 30,* 359–364.

Bridgeman, B., and C. Lewis. 1994. "The relationship of essay and multiple-choice scores with grades in college courses," *Journal of Educational Measurement, 31,* 37–50.

Brinzer, R. J., and R. L. Sinatra. 1982. "Survey of statistics textbooks used by the top 100 American Educational Research Association contributors." Paper presented to the American Educational Research Association, New York.

Brown, George I. 1964. "The relationship between barometric pressure and relative humidity and classroom behavior," *Journal of Educational Research, 57,* 368–70.

Brown, M. B., and A. B. Forsythe. 1974a. "The ANOVA and multiple comparisons for data with heterogeneous variances," *Biometrics, 30,* 719–24.

Brown, M. B., and A. B. Forsythe. 1974b. "The small sample behavior of some statistics which test the equality of several means," *Technometrics, 16,* 129–32.

Brown, M. B., and A. B. Forsythe. 1974c. "Robust tests for the equality of variances," *Journal of the American Statistical Association, 69,* 264–7.

Burdick, R. K. and F. A. Graybill. 1992. *Confidence Intervals on Variance Components.* New York: Marcel Dekker, Inc.

Burstein, H. 1971. *Attribute Sampling: Tables and Explanations. Tables for Determining Confidence Limits and Sample Sizes Based on Close Approximations of the Binomial Distribution.* New York: McGraw-Hill.

Camilli, G., and K. D. Hopkins. 1978. "Applicability of *chi*-square 2 × 2 contingency tables with small expected frequencies," *Psychological Bulletin, 85,* 163–7.

____ 1979. "Testing for association in 2 × 2 contingency cables with very small sample sizes," *Psychological Bulletin, 86,* 1011–4.

Campbell, D. T. and J. C. Stanley. 1966. *Experimental and Quasi-experimental Designs for Research.* Chicago: Rand McNally.

Carlson, J. E., and N. H. Timm. 1974. "Analysis of nonorthogonal fixed-effects designs," *Psychological Bulletin, 81,* 563–70.

Carrier, C. C., and A. Titus. 1982. "Effects of notetaking pretraining and test mode expectations on learning from lectures," *American Educational Research Journal, 18,* 385–98.

Carroll, J. B. 1961. "The nature of the data, or how to choose a correlation coefficient," *Psychometrika, 26,* 247–72.

Carter, E. S. 1979. "Comparison of different shrinkage formulas in estimating population multiple correlation coefficients," *Educational and Psychological Measurement, 39,* 261–66.

Chambers, A. C., K. D. Hopkins, and B. R. Hopkins. 1972. "Anxiety, physiologically and psychologically measured: Its effects on mental test performance," *Psychology in the Schools, 9,* 198–206.

Church, J. D. and E. L. Wike. 1976. "The robustness of homogeneity of variance tests for asymmetric distributions: A Monte Carlo study," *Bulletin of the Psychometric Society, 7,* 417–20.

Cleary, T. A. and R. L. Linn. 1969. "Error of measurement and the power of a statistical test," *British Journal of Mathematical and Statistical Psychology, 22,* 49–55.

Cochran, W. G. 1957. "Analysis of covariance: Its nature and uses," *Biometrics, 13,* 261–81.

Cochran, W. 1977. *Sampling Techniques* (3rd ed.). New York: John Wiley.

Cohen, J. 1988. *Statistical Power Analysis for the Behavioral Sciences* (3rd ed.). New York: Academic Press.

Cohen, J., and P. Cohen. 1975. *Applied Multiple Regression/Correlation Analysis for the Behavioral Sciences.* Hillsdale, NJ: Lawrence Erlbaum Publishers.

Collier, R. O., Jr., F. B. Baker, G. K. Mandeville, and H. T. Hays. 1967. "Estimates of test size for several test procedures based on conventional variance ratios in the repeated measures design," *Psychometrika, 32,* 339–54.

Collins, J. R. 1970. "Jackknifing generalizability." Ph.D. thesis, University of Colorado.

Conover, W. J. 1974. "Some reasons for not using the Yates' Continuity Correction on 2 × 2 contingency tables," *Journal of the American Statistical Association, 69,* 374–82.

Conover, W. J. 1980. *Practical Nonparametric Statistics* (2nd ed.). New York: John Wiley.

Conover, W. J., and R. L. Iman. 1981. "Rank transformations as a bridge between parametric and nonparametric statistics," *The American Statistician, 35,* 124–9.

Conover, W. J., M. E. Johnson, and M. M. Johnson. 1981. "A comparative study of tests for homogeneity of variances with applications to the outer continental shelf bidding data," *Technometrics, 23,* 357–61.

Cook, T. D., and D. T. Campbell. 1979. *Quasi-Experimentation: Design and Analysis Issues for Field Settings.* Chicago: Rand-McNally.

Cornfield, J., and J. W. Tukey. 1956. "Average values of mean squares in factorials," *Annals of Mathematical Statistics, 27,* 907–49.

Cox, C. P. 1987. *A Handbook of Introductory Statistical Methods.* New York: John Wiley.

Cox, D. R. 1970. *The Analysis of Binary Data.* London: Chapman and Hall.

Cronbach, L. J., and others. 1977. "Analysis of covariance in nonrandomized experiments: Parameters affecting bias." Occasional paper of the Stanford Evaluation Consortium, Stanford, CA: Stanford University.

Cronbach, L. J., and H. Azuma. 1962. "Internal-consistency reliability formulas applied to randomly sampled single-factor tests: An empirical comparison," *Educational and Psychological Measurement, 22,* 45–65.

Darlington, R. B. 1968. "Multiple regression in psychological research and practice," *Psychological Bulletin, 69,* 161–82.

Davidson, M. L. 1972. "Univariate versus multivariate tests in repeated measures experiments," *Psychological Bulletin, 77,* 446–52.

Delucchi, K. L. 1983. "The use and misuse of *chi*-square: Lewis and Burke revisited," *Psychological Bulletin, 94,* 166–76.

DeRosia, P. 1980. "A comparative study of pupil achievement and attitudes and involvement of parents of children enrolled in extended-day and half-day kindergarten programs." Ed.D. thesis, University of Colorado.

Dixon, W. J., and F. J. Massey. 1983. *Introduction to Statistical Analysis* (4th ed.). New York: McGraw-Hill.

Dixon, W. J., M. B. Brown, L. Engelman, M. A. Hill, and R. I. Jennrich. 1988. *BMDP Statistical Software.* Los Angeles: University of California Press.

Dunn, O. J. 1961. "Multiple comparisons among means," *Journal of the American Statistical Association, 56,* 52–64.

Dunn, O. J., and V. A. Clark. 1987. *Applied Statistics: Analysis of Variance and Regression* (2nd ed.). New York: John Wiley.

Dunnett, C. W. 1955. "A multiple comparison procedure for comparing several treatments with a control," *Journal of the American Statistical Association, 50,* 1096–1121.

____ 1964. "New tables for multiple comparisons with a control," *Biometrics, 20,* 482–91.

____ 1980a. "Pairwise multiple comparisons in the homogeneous variance, unequal sample size case," *Journal of the American Statistical Association, 75,* 789–95.

____ 1980b. "Pairwise multiple comparisons in the unequal variance case," *Journal of the American Statistical Association, 75,* 796–800.

Durrand, A. L. 1969. "Comparative power of various tests of homogeneity of variance." M. A. thesis, University of Colorado.

Dyson, E. 1967. "A study of ability grouping and the self-concept," *Journal of Educational Research, 60,* 403–5.

Edgington, E. S. 1974. "A new tabulation of statistical procedures used in APA journals," *American Psychologist, 25,* 25–8.

Edwards, A. L. 1960. *Experimental Design in Psychological Research.* New York: Holt, Rinehart and Winston.

____ 1964. *Expected Values of Discrete Random Variables and Elementary Statistics.* New York: John Wiley.

Efron, B. 1975. "The efficiency of logistic regression compared to normal discriminant analysis," *Journal of the American Statistical Association, 70,* 892–8.

Elmore, P. B., and P. L. Woehlke. 1988. "Statistical methods employed in *American Educational Research Journal, Educational Researcher,* and *Review of Educational Research* from 1978 to 1987," *Educational Researcher, 17,* 19–20.

Erlenmeyer-Kimling, L., and L. F. Jarvik. 1963. "Genetics and intelligence: A review," *Science, 142,* 1477–9.

Everitt, B. S. 1977. *The Analysis of Contingency Tables.* London: Chapman and Hall.

Federighi, E. T. 1959. "Extended tables of the percentage points of Student's $t$-distribution," *Journal of the American Statistical Association, 54,* 683–8.

Feller, W. 1957. *An Introduction to Probability Theory and its Application, Volume I,* (2nd ed.). New York: John Wiley.

Fetler, M. 1990. "A method for the construction of differentiated school norms," *Applied Measurement in Education, 4,* 53–66.

Fisher, R. A. 1958. *Statistical Methods for Research Workers* (eds. 1–13). Edinburgh: Oliver and Boyd.

____ 1959. *Statistical Methods and Scientific Inference* (2nd ed.). New York: Hafner.

____ 1966. *The Design of Experiments* (eds. 1–8). Edinburgh: Oliver and Boyd.

French, J. W. 1962. "Effect of anxiety on verbal and mathematical examination scores," *Educational and Psychological Measurement, 22,* 553–64.

Gabriel, R. M., and K. D. Hopkins. 1974. "Relative merits of MANOVA, repeated measures ANOVA, and univariate ANOVAs for research utilizing multiple criterion measures," *Journal of Special Education, 8,* 377–89.

Games, P. A. 1977. "An improved $t$ table for simultaneous control on g contrasts," *Journal of American Statistical Association, 72,* 531–4.

Games, P. A., H. B. Winkler, and D. A. Probert. 1972. "Robust tests for homogeneity of variance," *Educational and Psychological Measurement, 32,* 887–909.

Gay, L. R., P. Campbell, and P. D. Gallagher. 1978. "SIG: Professors of educational research text analysis survey." Paper presented to the American Educational Research Association, Toronto.

Gehler, T. M. G. 1979. "An analysis of kindergarten achievement including the effects of time-of-day and sex." Ph.D. thesis, University of Colorado.

Ghosh, B. K. 1979. "A comparison of some approximate confidence intervals for the binomial parameter," *Journal of the American Statistical Association, 74,* 894–900.

Gibbons, J. D., and S. Chakraborti. 1991. "Comparisons of the Mann-Whitney, Student's $t$, and alternate $t$-tests for means of normal distributions," *Journal of Experimental Educational, 59,* 258–67.

Glass, G. V. 1966. "Note on rank-biserial correlation," *Educational and Psychological Measurement, 26,* 623–31.

Glass, G. V, and J. R. Collins. 1970. "Geometric proof of the restriction on the possible values of $r_{xy}$ when $r_{xz}$ and $r_{yz}$ are fixed," *Educational and Psychological Measurement, 30,* 37–39.

Glass, G. V, and A. R. Hakstian. 1969. "Measures of association in comparative experiments: Their development and interpretation," *American Educational Research Journal, 6,* 403–14.

Glass, G. V, and K. D. Hopkins. 1984. *Statistical Methods in Education and Psychology* (2nd ed.). Englewood Cliffs, NJ: Prentice-Hall.

Glass, G. V, B. McGaw, and M. L. Smith. 1981. *Meta-analysis in Social Research.* Beverly Hills: Sage Publications.

Glass, G. V, P. D. Peckham, and J. R. Sanders. 1972. "Consequences of failure to meet assumptions underlying the fixed-effects analysis of variance and covariance," *Review of Educational Research, 42,* 237–88.

Glass, G. V, and J. C. Stanley. 1970. *Statistical Methods in Education and Psychology.* Englewood Cliffs, NJ: Prentice-Hall.

Glass, G. V, V. L. Willson, and J. M. Gottman. 1975. *Design and Analysis of Time-Series Experiments.* Boulder: Colorado Associated University Press.

Golladay, M. A. 1976. *The Condition of Education.* U.S. Department of Health, Education, and Welfare, National Center for Educational Statistics. Washington, DC: U. S. Government Printing Office.

Goodman, L. A. 1978. *Analyzing Qualitative/Categorical Data.* Cambridge, MA: Abt Books.

Goodwin, L. D., and W. L. Goodwin. 1985. "Statistical techniques in AERJ articles, 1979–1983: The preparation of graduate students to read the educational research literature," *Educational Researcher, 14,* 5–11.

Grant, D. A. 1962. "Testing the null hypothesis and the strategy and tactics of investigating theoretical models," *Psychological Review, 69,* 54–61.

Graybill, F. A. 1961. *An Introduction to Linear Statistical Models, Volume 1.* New York: McGraw-Hill.

Green, B. F., and J. W. Tukey. 1960. "Complex analysis of variance: General problems," *Psychometrika, 25,* 127–52.

Greenhouse, S. W., and S. Geisser. 1959. "On methods in the analysis of profile data," *Psychometrika, 24,* 95–112.

Guenther, W. C. 1964. *Analysis of Variance.* Englewood Cliffs, NJ: Prentice-Hall.

Gullickson, A., and K. D. Hopkins. 1976. "Interval estimation of correlation coefficients corrected for restriction of range," *Educational and Psychological Measurement, 36,* 9–25.

Gustav, A. 1963. "Response set in objective achievement tests," *Journal of Psychology, 56,* 421–7.

Hakstian, A. R. 1971. "The effect on study methods and test performance of objective and essay examinations," *Journal of Educational Research, 64,* 319–24.

Hakstian, A. R., W. Schroeder, and W. T. Rogers. 1988. "Inferential procedures for correlations corrected for attenuation," *Psychometrika, 53,*

Hald, A. 1952. *Statistical Tables and Formulas.* New York: John Wiley.

Hammond, E. C. 1964. "Smoking in relation to mortality and morbidity," *Journal of the National Cancer Institute, 32,* 1161–87.

Hansford, B. C., and J. A. Hattie. 1982. "The relationship between self and achievement measures," *Review of Educational Research, 52,* 123–42.

Harrington, S. A. 1968. "Sequencing organizers in meaningful verbal learning," Research Paper No. 10. Boulder: University of Colorado, Laboratory of Educational Research.

Harter, H. L. 1960. "Tables of range and studentized range," *Annals of Mathematical Statistics, 31,* 1122–47.

Hartley, H. O. 1950. "The maximum *F* ratio as a short-cut test for heterogeneity of variance," *Biometrika, 37,* 308–12. *Psychological Bulletin, 111,* 352–60.

Hartshorne, H., and M. A. May. 1928. *Studies in the Nature of Character, I: Studies in Deceit.* New York: Macmillan.

Hays, W. L. 1988. *Statistics* (4th ed.). New York: Harcourt, Brace, Jovanovich.

Hedges, L. V. 1981. "Distribution theory for Glass's estimator of effect size and related estimators," *Journal of Educational Statistics, 6,* 21–32.

Hedges, L. V., and I. Olkin. 1985. *Statistical Methods for Meta-analysis.* New York: Academic Press.

Heermann, E. F., and L. A. Braskamp. 1970. *Readings in Statistics for the Behavioral Sciences.* Englewood Cliffs, NJ: Prentice-Hall.

Heffernan, P. M. 1988. "New measures of spread and a simpler formula for the normal distribution," *American Statistician, 42,* 100–2.

Henderson, C. R. 1959. "Design and analysis of animal husbandry experiments," in *Techniques and Procedures of Animal Production Research.* American Society of Animal Production, Beltsville, MD.

Hendrickson, G. F., and J. R. Collins. 1970. "Note correcting the results in Olkin's new formula for the significance of $r_{13}$ vs. $r_{23}$ compared with Hotelling's methods," *American Educational Research Journal, 7,* 639–64.

Herr, D. G. 1986. "On the history of ANOVA in unbalanced, factorial designs: The first 30 years," *The American Statistician, 40,* 265–70.

Herr, D. G., and J. Gaebelein. 1978. "Nonorthogonal two-way analysis of variance," *Psychological Bulletin, 85,* 207–16.

Hochberg, Y. 1970. "A modification of the *T*-method of multiple comparisons for a one-way layout with unequal variances," *Journal of the American Statistical Association, 71,* 200–3.

____ 1975. "An extension of the *T*-method to general unbalanced models of fixed-effects," *Journal of the Royal Statistical Society, Ser. B, 37,* 426–33.

Hochberg, Y., and A. C. Tamhane. 1987. *Multiple Comparison Procedures.* New York: John Wiley.

Hollander, M., and D. A. Wolfe. 1971. *Nonparametric Statistical Inference.* New York: McGraw-Hill.

Hopkins, K. D. 1969. "Regression and the matching fallacy in quasi-experimental research," *Journal of Special Education, 3,* 329–36.

____ 1971. "Confidence intervals in research: The gap between theory and practice," *Journal of Special Education, 5,* 301–2.

____ 1973. "Preventing the number one misinterpretation of behavioral research, or how to increase statistical power," *Journal of Special Education, 7,* 103–7.

____ 1976. "A simplified method for determining expected mean squares and error terms in the analysis of variance," *Journal of Experimental Education, 45,* 13–18.

____ 1979. "Obtaining *chi*-square tests of association and goodness of fit from proportions and percents," *Journal of Experimental Education, 47,* 380–6.

____ 1982. "The unit of analysis: group means vs. individual observations," *American Educational Research Journal, 19,* 5–18.

____ 1983. "A strategy for analyzing ANOVA designs having one or more random factors," *Educational and Psychological Measurement, 43,* 107–13.

Hopkins, K. D., and B. L. Anderson. 1973. "Multiple comparisons guide," *Journal of Special Education, 7,* 319–28.

Hopkins, K. D., and M. Bibelheimer. 1971. "Five-year stability IQ's from language and non-language group tests," *Child Development, 42,* 645–9.

Hopkins, K. D., and G. Bracht. 1975. "Ten-year stability of verbal and nonverbal IQ scores," *American Educational Research Journal, 12,* 469–77.

Hopkins, K. D., and D. Chappell. 1994. "Quick power estimates for comparing proportions," *Educational and Psychological Measurement, 54,* 903–912.

Hopkins, K. D., D. K. Coulter, and B. R. Hopkins. 1981. "Tables for quick power estimates when comparing means," *Journal of Special Education, 15,* 389–94.

Hopkins, K. D., C. George, and D. D. Williams. 1985. "The concurrent validity of standardized achievement tests by content area using teachers' ratings as criteria," *Journal of Educational Measurement, 22,* 177–82.

Hopkins, K. D., G. V Glass, and B. R. Hopkins. 1987. *Basic Statistics for the Behavioral Sciences.* Englewood Cliffs, NJ: Prentice-Hall.

____ 1996. *Basic Statistics for the Behavioral Sciences* (3rd ed.). Needham Heights, MA: Allyn and Bacon.

Hopkins, K. D., and P. R. Hester. 1995. "The non-centrality parameter for the *F*-distribution, mean squares, and effects size: An examination of some mathematical relationships," *Educational and Psychological Measurement,* (in press).

Hopkins, K. D., and B. R. Hopkins. 1979. "The effect of the reliability of the dependent variable on power," *Journal of Special Education, 13,* 463–6.

Hopkins, K. D., and G. L. Kretke. 1976. "*N*/cell considerations: Asking the wrong question for the right reason," *Journal of Special Education, 10,* 321–4.

Hopkins, K. D., G. L. Kretke, N. C. Harms, R. M. Gabriel, D. L. Phillips, C. Rodriquez, and M. Averill. 1974. *A Technical Report on the Colorado Needs-Assessment Program, Spring, 1973.* Boulder, University of Colorado, Laboratory of Educational Research.

Hopkins, K. D., and L. McGuire. 1966. "Mental measurement of the blind: The validity of the Wechsler Intelligence Scale for Children," *International Journal for Education of the Blind, 15,* 65–73.

Hopkins, K. D., and E. G. Sitkie. 1969. "Predicting grade-one reading performance: Intelligence vs. reading readiness tests," *Journal of Experimental Education, 37,* 31–3.

Hopkins, K. D., and J. C. Stanley. 1981. *Educational and Psychological Measurement and Evaluation* (6th ed.). Englewood Cliffs, NJ: Prentice-Hall.

Hopkins, K. D., J. C. Stanley, and B. R. Hopkins. 1990. *Educational and Psychological Measurement and Evaluation* (7th ed.). Needham Heights, MA: Allyn and Bacon.

Hopkins, K. D., C. Vojir, and N. Hester. 1995. "The equivalence of ANOVA and the *chi*-square test of association," *Educational and Psychological Measurement* (in process).

Hopkins, K. D., and D. L. Weeks. 1990. "Tests for normality and measures of skewness and kurtosis: Their place in research reporting," *Educational and Psychological Measurement, 50,* 717–29.

Hoppe, F. M. (Ed.) 1993. *Multiple Comparisons, Selection, and Applications in Biometry.* New York: Marcel Dekker.

Horst, P. 1931. "A proof that the point from which the sum of the absolute deviations is a minimum is the median," *Journal of Educational Psychology, 22,* 463–4.

Hosking, J. D., and R. M. Hamer. 1979. "Nonorthogonal analysis of variance programs: An evaluation," *Journal of Educational Statistics, 4,* 161–85.

Hotelling, H. 1940. "The selection of variates for use in prediction with some comments on the general problem of nuisance parameters," *Annals of Mathematical Statistics, 11,* 271–83.

Houston, S. R., C. E. Crosswhite, and R. S. King. 1974. "The use of judgmental analysis in capturing student policies of rated teacher effectiveness," *Journal of Experimental Education, 43,* 28–34.

Howie, P. M. 1981. "Concordance for stuttering in monozygotic and dizygotic twin pairs," *Journal of Speech and Hearing Research, 24,* 317–21.

Hsu, P. L. 1938. "Contributions of the theory of Student's *t*-test as applied to the problem of two samples," *Statistical Research Memoirs, 2,* 1–24.

Hsu, T. C., and L. S. Feldt. 1969. "The effects of limitations on the number of criterion score values on the significance of the *F*-test," *American Educational Research Journal, 6,* 515–27.

Huberty, C. J., and S. A. Mourad. 1980. "Estimation in multiple correlation/prediction," *Educational and Psychological Measurement, 40,* 101–12.

Huitema, B. E. 1980. *The Analysis of Covariance and Alternatives.* New York: John Wiley.

Humphreys, L. G., and F. Drasgow. 1989. "Some comments on the relation between reliability and statistical power," *Applied Psychological Measurement, 13,* 419–25.

Huynh, H., and L. S. Feldt. 1970. "Conditions under which mean squares ratios in repeated measures designs have exact *F*-distributions," *Journal of the American Statistical Association, 65,* 1582–9.

Huynh, H., and L. S. Feldt. 1976., "Estimation of the Box correction for degrees of freedom in randomized block and split-plot designs," *Journal of Educational Statistics, 1,* 29–82.

Jaeger, R. M. 1984. *Sampling in Education and the Social Sciences.* New York: Longman.

Joiner, B. L. 1985. "The key role of statisticians in the transformation of North American industry," *American Statistician, 39,* 224–5.

Jones, L. V. 1952. "Tests of hypotheses: One-sided vs. two-sided alternatives," *Psychological Bulletin, 49,* 43–6.

____ 1954. "A rejoinder on one-tailed tests," *Psychological Bulletin, 51,* 585–86.

Kaiser, H. F. 1960. "Directional statistical decisions," *Psychological Review, 67,* 160–7.

Kaplan, A. 1964. *The Conduct of Inquiry.* San Francisco: Chandler.

Kelley, T. L. 1939. "The selection of upper and lower groups for the validation of test items," *Journal of Educational Psychology, 30,* 17–24.

Kendall, M. G. 1962. *Rank Correlation Methods* (3rd ed.). London: Griffin.

Keppel, G. 1982. *Design and Analysis: A Researcher's Handbook* (2nd ed.). Englewood Cliffs, NJ: Prentice-Hall.

Kerlinger, F. N., and E. J. Pedhazer. 1973. *Multiple Regression in Behavioral Research.* New York: Holt, Rinehart, and Winston.

Keselman, J. C., H. J. Keselman, and J. P. Shaffer. 1991. "Multiple pairwise comparisons of repeated measures means under violation of multi-sample sphericity," *Psychological Bulletin, 110,* 162–70.

Keselman, J. C., L. M. Lix, H. J. Keselman. 1993. "The analysis of repeated measurements: A quantitative research synthesis." Paper presented at the annual meeting of the American Educational Research Association, Atlanta.

Kirk, R. E., 1982. *Experimental Design: Procedures for the Behavioral Sciences* (2nd ed.). Monterey, CA: Brooks/Cole.

Kish, L. 1965. *Survey Sampling.* New York: John Wiley.

____ 1987. *Statistical Design for Research.* New York: John Wiley.

Knoke, D., and P. J. Burke. 1980. *Log-Linear Models.* Beverly Hills, CA: Sage Publications.

Kotz, S., and N. L. Johnson. (Eds.). 1982. *Encyclopedia of Statistical Sciences* (Vols. 1–9). New York: John Wiley.

Kraemer, H. C., and Thiemann, S. 1987. *How Many Subjects?: Statistical Power Analysis in Research.* London: Sage Publications.

Kramer, C. Y. 1956. "Extension of multiple range test to group means with unequal numbers of replications," *Biometrics, 57,* 649–55.

Kruskal, W., H. 1958. "Ordinal measures of association," *Journal of the American Statistical Association, 53,* 814–61.

____ 1980. "The significance of Fisher: A review of R. A. Fisher: The life of a scientist," *Journal of the American Statistical Association, 75,* 1019–29.

Kruskal, W., and R. Majors. 1989. "Concepts of relative importance in recent scientific literature," *American Statistician, 43,* 2–5.

Kupper, L. L., and K. B. Hafner. 1989. "How appropriate are popular sample size formulas?" *American Statistician, 43,* 101–5.

Lee, W. 1975. *Experimental Design and Analysis.* San Francisco: Freeman and Co.

Leinhardt, S., and S. S. Wasserman. 1970. "Teaching regression: An exploratory approach," *The American Statistician, 33,* 196–203.

Leinhardt, G., and S. Leinhardt. 1980. "Exploratory data analysis: New tools for the analysis of empirical data," in *Review of Research in Education,* D. C. Berliner (Ed.). *American Educational Research Association.*

Levene, H. 1960. "Robust tests for equality of variance," in *Contributions to Probability and Statistics.* I. Olkin (Ed.), Palo Alto: Stanford University Press.

Levy, K. J. 1975. "Large-sample pairwise comparisons involving correlations, proportions, or variances," *Psychological Bulletin, 82,* 174–6.

____ 1977. "Pairwise comparisons involving unequal sample sizes associated with correlations, proportions, or variances," *British Journal of Mathematical and Statistical Psychology, 30,* 137–9.

Lewis, D., and C. J. Burke. 1949. "The use and misuse of the *chi*-square test," *Psychological Bulletin, 46,* 433–89.

Li, J. C. R. 1964. *Statistical Inference II.* Ann Arbor, MI: Edwards Brothers.

Lindquist, E. F. 1940. *Statistical Analysis in Educational Research.* New York: Houghton Mifflin.

Linn, R. L. (Ed.). 1987. *Educational Measurement* (3rd ed.). Washington, DC: American Council on Education.

Lipsey, M. W. 1990. *Design Sensitivity: Statistical Power for Experimental Research.* London: Sage Publications.

Lord, F. M. 1963. "Elementary models for measuring change," in *Problems in Measuring Change,* C. W. Harris (Ed.) Madison, WI: University of Wisconsin Press, 21–38.

____ 1967. "A paradox in the interpretation of group comparisons," *Psychological Bulletin, 68,* 304–5.

Lord, F. M., and M. R. Novick. 1968. *Statistical Theories of Mental Test Scores.* Reading, MA: Addison-Wesley.

Lubin, A. 1962. "The interpretation of significant interaction," *Educational and Psychological Measurement, 21,* 807–17.

Luce, R. D., D. H. Krantz, P. Suppes, and A. Tversky. 1990. *Foundations of Measurement, Volume III.* New York: Academic Press.

Lunney, G. H. 1970. "Using analysis of variance with a dichotomous dependent variable: An empirical study," *Journal of Educational Measurement, 7,* 263–9.

Mainland, M. B. 1960. "The use and misuse of statistics in medical publications," *Clinical Pharmacology and Therapeutics, 1,* 411–22.

Mandell, A. J., and M. P. Mandell. 1967. "Suicide and the menstrual cycle," *Journal of the American Medical Association, 200,* 132–33.

Marascuilo, L. A. 1966. "Large-sample multiple comparisons," *Psychological Bulletin, 65,* 280–90.

Marascuilo, L. A., and J. R. Levin. 1970. "Appropriate post hoc comparisons for interaction and nested hypotheses in analysis of variance designs: The elimination of type IV errors," *American Educational Research Journal, 7,* 397–421.

Marascuilo, L. A., and M. McSweeney. 1978. *Nonparametric and Distribution-Free Methods for the Social Sciences.* Monterey, CA: Brooks/Cole.

Martin, C. G., and P. A. Games. 1977. "ANOVA tests for homogeneity of variance: Nonnormality and unequal samples," *Journal of Educational Statistics, 2,* 187–206.

McGaw, B., and G. V Glass. 1980. "Choice of the metric for effect size in meta-analysis," *American Educational Research Journal, 17,* 325–37.

McNamara, W. J., and J. W. Dunlap. 1934. "A graphical method for computing the standard error of biserial *r*," *Journal of Experimental Education, 2,* 274–77.

McNemar, Q. 1962. *Psychological Statistics* (3rd. ed.). New York: John Wiley.

Meng, X., R. Rosenthal, and D. B. Rubin. 1992. "Comparing correlated correlation coefficients," *Psychological Bulletin, 111,* 172–175.

Metfessel, N. S., and G. Sax. 1957. "Response set patterns in published instructors' manuals in education and psychology," *California Journal of Educational Research, 8,* 195–7.

Michael, W. B. 1970. "Review of statistical methods in education and psychology by G. V Glass and J. C. Stanley," *Educational and Psychological Measurement, 30,* 1015–8.

Miller, D. C. 1991. *Handbook of Research Design and Social Measurement,* (5th ed.). Newbury Park, CA: Sage Publications.

Miller, R. 1985. "Multiple comparisons," in S. Kotz and N. L. Johnson (Eds.), *Encyclopedia of Statistical Sciences, Volume 5,* 679–89. New York: John Wiley.

Miller, R. G. 1966. *Simultaneous Statistical Inference.* New York: McGraw-Hill.

____ 1977. "Developments in multiple comparisons, 1966–1976," *Journal of the American Statistical Association, 72,* 779–88.

Millman, J., and G. V Glass. 1967. "Rules of thumb for writing the ANOVA table," *Journal of Educational Measurement, 4,* 41–51.

Mitchell, J. 1986. "Measurement scales and statistics: A clash of paradigms," *Psychological Bulletin, 100,* 398–407.

Moore, D. S., and G. P. McCabe. 1989. *Introduction to the Practice of Statistics* (2nd ed.). New York: W. H. Freeman.

Morow, J. R., A. S. Jackson, and J. A. Bell. 1978. "The function of age, sex, and body mass on distance running," *Research Quarterly, 49,* 491–7.

Mosteller, F. 1988. "Broadening the scope of statistics and statistical education," *American Statistician, 42,* 93–9.

Munsinger, H. 1975. "Children's resemblance to their biological and to their adopting parents in two ethnic groups," *Behavior Genetics, 5,* 239–54.

Myers, J. L. 1977. *Fundamentals of Experimental Design* (3rd ed.). Boston: Allyn and Bacon.

Myette, B. M., and K. R. White. 1982. "Selecting an appropriate multiple comparison technique: An integration of Monte Carlo studies." Paper presented to the *American Educational Research Association,* New York.

Nair, K. R. 1940. "Table of confidence interval for the median in samples from any continuous population," *Sankhya, 4,* 551-8.

National Center for Health Statistics. 1977. *Vital and Health Statistics: Advance Data.* Series 16, No. 7, U.S. Department of Health, Education, and Welfare.

Newman, H. H., F. N. Freeman, and K. J. Holzinger. 1937. *Twins: A Study of Heredity and Environment.* Chicago: University of Chicago Press.

Nunnally, J. C. 1960. "The place of statistics in psychology," *Educational and Psychological Measurement, 20,* 641–50.

____ 1994. *Psychometric Theory* (3rd ed.). New York: McGraw-Hill.

O'Brien, R. G., and M. K. Kaiser. 1985. "MANOVA method for analyzing repeated measures designs: An extensive primer," *Psychological Bulletin, 97,* 316–33.

Olds, E. G. 1938. "Distributions of sums of squares of rank differences for small numbers of individuals," *Annals of Mathematical Statistics, 9,* 133–48.

____ 1949. "The 5% significance levels for sums of squares of rank differences and a correction," *Annals of Mathematical Statistics, 20,* 117–18.

Olejnik, S. F., and J. Algina. 1987. "Type I error rates and power estimates of selected parametric and nonparametric tests of scale," *Journal of Educational Statistics, 12,* 45–61.

Olkin, I. 1967. "Correlations revisited," in *Improving Experimental Design and Statistical Analysis,* J. C. Stanley. Chicago: Rand McNally.

Olkin, I., and J. Finn. 1990. "Testing correlated correlations," *Psychological Bulletin, 108,* 330–3.

Olkin, I., and J. W. Pratt. 1958. "Unbiased estimation of certain correlation coefficients," *Annals of Mathematical Statistics, 29,* 201–11.

Omey, S. H. 1987. "Conservation in the hearing-impaired child: The relationship between age and consistency of mode of communication on correct performance of Piagetian conservation tasks." Ph.D. thesis, University of Colorado.

O'Neill, R., and G. B. Wetherill. 1971. "The present state of multiple comparison methods," *Journal of the Royal Statistical Society, 33,* 218–50.

Ostle, B., and R. W. Mensing. 1975. *Statistics for Research.* Ames, IA: Iowa State University Press.

Pearson, E. S., and C. J. Clopper. 1934. "The use of confidence intervals or fiducial limits illustrated in the case of the binomial," *Biometrika, 26,* 404–13.

Pearson, E. S., and H. O. Hartley. 1966. *Biometrika Tables for Statisticians.* Cambridge, MA: Cambridge University Press.

Peckham, P. D., G. V Glass, and K. D. Hopkins. "The experimental unit in statistical analysis." *Journal of Special Education, 3,* 337–349, 1969.

Pedhazur, E. J. 1982. *Multiple Regression in Behavioral Research* (2nd ed.). New York: Holt, Rinehart and Winston.

Peters, C. C. 1950. "The misuse of *chi*-square—a reply to Lewis and Burke," *Psychological Bulletin, 47,* 331–7.

Petrinovich, L. F., and C. D. Hardyck. 1969. "Error rates for multiple comparison methods: Some evidence concerning the frequency of erroneous conclusions," *Psychological Bulletin, 71,* 43–54.

Pomerance, H. H., and J. M. Krall. 1981. "Linear regression to approximate longitudinal growth curves: Revised standards for velocity of weight and length in infants," *Pediatric Research, 15,* 1390–5.

Poor, D. S. 1973. "Analysis of variance for repeated measures designs: Two approaches," *Psychological Bulletin, 80,* 204–9.

Porter, T. M. 1986. *The Rise of Statistical Thinking 1820–1900.* Princeton, NJ: Princeton University Press.

Ragosa, D. 1980. "Comparing nonparallel regression lines," *Psychological Bulletin, 88,* 307–21.

Ramsey, P. H. 1981. "Power of univariate pairwise multiple comparison procedures," *Psychological Bulletin, 90,* 352–66.

____ 1989. "Critical values for Spearman's rank order correlation," *Journal of Educational Statistics, 14,* 245–53.

____ 1990. "Critical values for two multiple comparison procedures based on the studentized range distribution," *Journal of Educational Statistics, 15,* 241–52.

Reichardt, C. S. 1979. "The statistical analysis of data from nonequivalent group designs," in Chapter 4 of Cook and Campbell, *Quasi-Experimentation.* New York: Rand McNally.

Reynolds, H. T. 1977. *The Analysis of Cross-Classifications.* New York: Free Press.

Roberts, H. V. 1980. "Statistical bases in the measurement of employment discrimination," in E. R. Livernash (Ed.), *Comparable Worth: Issues and Alternatives.* Washington, DC: Equal Employment Advisory Council.

Rock, D. A., T. L. Hilton, J. Pollack, R. B. Ekstrom, and M. E. Goertz. 1985. *Psychometric Analysis of the NLS and the High School and Beyond Test Batteries.* U.S. Government Printing Office, Washington, DC (NCES 85–218).

Rodgers, J. L., and W. A. Nicewander. 1988. "Thirteen ways to look at the correlation coefficient," *American Statistician, 42,* 59–66.

Rogan, J. D., and H. J. Keselman. 1977. "Is the ANOVA *F*-test robust to variance heterogeneity when sample sizes are equal?: An investigation via a coefficient of variation," *American Educational Research Journal, 14,* 493–8.

Rogers, W. T. 1976. "Jackknifing disattenuated correlations," *Psychometrika, 41,* 121–33.

Rogers, W. T., and K. D. Hopkins. 1988a. "Power estimates in the presence of a covariate and measurement error," *Educational and Psychological Measurement, 48,* 647–56.

Rogers, W. T., and K. D. Hopkins. 1988b. "Quick power estimates incorporating the joint effects of measurement error and a covariate," *Journal of Experimental Education, 57,* 86–94.

Roney, R. C. 1975. "The effects of two promotional teaching techniques on the amount of personal reading and selection of books." Ph.D. thesis, University of Colorado, Boulder.

Roscoe, J. T., and J. A. Byars. 1971. "An investigation of the restraints with respect to sample size commonly imposed on the use of the *chi*-square statistic," *Journal of the American Statistical Association, 66,* 755–9.

Rosenthal, R. 1978. "Combining results of independent studies," *Psychological Bulletin, 85,* 185–93.

Rothkopf, E. Z. 1966. "Learning from written instructive materials: An exploration of the control of inspection behavior by test-like events," *American Educational Research Journal, 3,* 241–9.

Sachs, L. 1982. *Applied Statistics: A Handbook of Techniques* (Translated by Z. Reynarowych). New York: Springer-Verlag.

Salsburg, D. S. 1985. "The religion of statistics as practiced in medical journals," *American Statistician, 39,* 220–3.

Saville, D. J. 1990. "Multiple comparison procedures: The practical solution," *American Statistician, 44,* 174–180.

Sawilowsky, S. S., and R. C. Blair. 1992. "A more realistic look at the robustness and type II error properties of the *t*-test to departures from population normality," *Psychological Bulletin, 111,* 352–60.

Scheffé, H. 1959. *The Analysis of Variance.* New York: John Wiley.

Schmidt, W. 1972. "Review of statistical methods in education and psychology by G. V Glass and J. C. Stanley," *American Educational Research Journal, 9,* 169–73.

Schon, I., K. D. Hopkins, and C. Vojir. 1983. "The effects of special curricular study of Mexican culture on Anglo and Mexican-American students' perceptions of Mexican-Americans," *Journal of Experimental Education, 61,* 215–8.

Seaman, M. A., J. R. Levin, and R. C. Serlin. 1991. "New developments in pairwise multiple comparisons: Some powerful and practicable procedures," *Psychological Bulletin, 110,* 577–586.

Sedlmeier, P., and G. Gigerenzer. 1989. "Do studies of statistical power have an effect on the power of studies?" *Psychological Bulletin, 105,* 309–16.

Shepard, L. A., and K. D. Hopkins. 1977. "Regression and the matching fallacy in quasi-experimental research." *National Association for Business Teachers Education Review, 4,* 11–15.

Shepard, L. A., M. E. Graue, and S. F. Catto. 1989. "Delayed entry into kindergarten and escalation of academic demands," Paper presented to the *American Educational Research Association,* San Francisco.

Shiffler, R. E. 1988. "Maximum *z*-scores and outliers," *American Statistician, 42,* 79–80.

Shlomo, S. S., and R. C. Blair. 1992. "A more realistic look at the robustness and type II error properties of the *t*-test to departures from population normality," *Psychological Bulletin, 111,* 352–60.

Sidak, Z. 1967. "Rectangular confidence regions for the means of multivariate normal distributions," *Journal of the American Statistical Association, 62,* 626–33.

Siegel, S. 1956. *Nonparametric Statistics for the Behavioral Sciences.* New York: McGraw-Hill.

Siegel, S., and J. J. Castellan. 1988. *Nonparametric Statistics for the Behavioral Sciences.* New York: McGraw-Hill.

Siegel, S., and J. W. Tukey. 1960. "A nonparametric sum of ranks procedure for relative spread in unpaired samples," *Journal of the American Statistical Association, 55,* 429–444.

Smith, R. A. 1971. "The effect of unequal group size on Tukey's HSD procedure," *Psychometrika, 36,* 31–4.

Snedecor, G. W., and W. G. Cochran. 1980. *Statistical Methods* (8th ed.). Ames, IA: Iowa State University Press.

Solso, R. L. 1979. "Twenty-five years of recommended readings in psychology," *American Psychologist, 34,* 703–5.

Sparks, J. N. 1963. "Expository notes on the problem of making multiple comparisons on a completely randomized design," *Journal of Experimental Education, 31,* 343–9.

Spinner, B., and R. M. Gabriel. 1981. "Factorial analysis of variance with unequal cell frequencies," *Canadian Psychology, 22,* 975–8.

Spjotvoll, E., and M. R. Stoline. 1973. "An extension of the *T*-method of multiple comparisons to include the cases with unequal sample sizes," *Journal of the American Statistical Association, 68,* 975–8.

SPSS. 1991. *SPSS Statistical Algorithms* (2nd ed.). Chicago: SPSS, Inc.

Stanley, J. C. 1962. "Analysis of a double nested design," *Educational and Psychological Measurement, 21,* 831–7, Errata, *22.*

____ 1966. "The influence of Fisher's 'The Design of Experiments' on educational research thirty years later," *American Educational Research Journal, 3,* 233–9.

Stein, S. L., and J. B. Kuenne. 1979. "Readability and textbook evaluation for textbooks in educational research and statistics." Paper presented to the American Educational Research Association, San Francisco.

Stember, M., S. Lewis, N. Hester, L. Clark, and K. D. Hopkins. 1995. *Infant Growth Study.* Denver, CO: University of Colorado (in process).

Sternberg, R. J. 1982. *Handbook of Human Intelligence.* Cambridge, MA: Cambridge University Press.

Stevens, J. 1986. *Applied Multivariate Statistics for the Social Sciences.* Hillsdale, NJ: Lawrence Erlbaum Publishers.

Stevens, S. S. (Ed.) 1951. *Handbook of Experimental Psychology.* New York: John Wiley.

Stine, W. W. 1989. "Meaningful inference: The role of measurement in statistics," *Psychological Bulletin, 105,* 147–55.

Stone, C. L. 1954. "Church participation and social adjustment of high school and college youth." Rural sociology series on youth, No. 12, bulletin 550. Pullman, WA: Washington State University.

Terman, L. M., and M. A. Merrill. 1937. *Measuring Intelligence.* Boston: Houghton Mifflin.

____ 1973. *Stanford-Binet Intelligence Scale: Manual for the Third Revision.* Boston: Houghton Mifflin.

Thorndike, R. L. 1949. *Personnel Selection.* New York: John Wiley.

____ 1963. *The Concepts of Over-and Under-achievement.* New York: Columbia University Press.

Tomarken, A. J., and R. C. Serlin. 1986. "Comparison of ANOVA alternatives under variance heterogeneity and specific noncentrality structures," *Psychological Bulletin, 99,* 90–9.

Toothaker, L. E. 1991. *Multiple Comparisons for Researchers.* Newbury Park, CA: Sage Publications.

Townsend, J. T., and F. G. Ashby. 1984. "Measurement scales and statistics: The misconception misconceived," *Psychological Bulletin, 96,* 394–401.

Traub, R. E., and G. L. Rowley. 1991. "Understanding reliability." *Educational Measurement: Issues and Practice, 10,* 37–45.

Tufte, E. R. 1983. *The Visual Display of Quantitative Information.* Cheshire, CN: Graphics Press.

Tukey, J. W. 1960. "Conclusions vs. Decisions," *Technometrics, 2,* 423–433.

____ 1977. *Exploratory Data Analysis.* Reading, MA: Addison-Wesley.

Vecchio, R., and F. Costin. 1977. "Predicting teacher effectiveness from graduate admissions predictors," *American Educational Research Journal, 14,* 169–76.

Vellman, P. F., and D. C. Hoaglin. 1981. *Applications, Basics, and Computers of Exploratory Data Analysis.* Boston: Duxburg Press.

Vellman, P. F., and L. Wilkinson. 1993. "Nominal, ordinal, interval, and ratio typologies are misleading," *American Statistician, 47,* 65–72.

Wainer, H. 1992. "Understanding graphs and tables," *Educational Researcher, 21,* 14–23.

Wainer, H., and D. Thissen. 1981. "Graphical data analysis," *Annual Review of Psychology, 32,* 191–241.

Walker, H. M. 1940. "Degrees of freedom," *Journal of Educational Psychology, 31,* 253–69.

Ware, M. E., and C. L. Brewer (Eds.). 1988. *Handbook for Teaching Statistics and Research Methods.* Hillsdale, NJ: Lawrence Erlbaum Publishers.

Wechsler, D. 1967. *Manual for the Wechsler Preschool and Primary Scale of Intelligence.* New York: Psychological Corporation.

____ 1974. *Manual for the Wechsler Intelligence Scale for Children-Revised.* New York: Psychological Corporation.

Weston, T., S. Marion, A. Durrand, and K. D. Hopkins. 1995. "Robustness of Various Tests of Homogeneity of Variance," *Educational and Psychological Measurement,* (in press).

White, K. R. 1976. "The relationship between socioeconomic status and academic achievement." Ph.D. thesis, University of Colorado.

____ 1982. "The relationship between socioeconomic status and academic achievement," *Psychological Bulletin, 91,* 461–81.

White, K. R., and K. D. Hopkins. 1975. "The reliability of a self-report measure of socioeconomic

status, and the relationship of SES and pupil achievement in grades 2–6." Paper presented to the National Council on Measurement in Education, Washington, DC.
Wick, J. W., and C. Dirkes. 1973. "Characteristics of current doctoral dissertations in education," *Educational Researcher, 2,* 20–2.
Wilcox, R. R. 1989. "Adjusting for unequal variances when comparing means in one-way and two-way fixed-effects ANOVA models," *Journal of Educational Statistics, 14,* 269–78.
Wilks, S. S. 1962. *Mathematical Statistics.* New York: John Wiley.
Williams, P. A., and others. 1982. "The impact of leisure-time television on school learning: A research synthesis," *American Educational Research Journal, 19,* 19–50.
Williams, R. H., and D. W. Zimmerman, 1989. "Statistical power analysis and reliability of measurement," *Journal of General Psychology, 116,* 359–69.
Willson, V. L. 1980. "Research techniques in AERJ articles: 1969 to 1978," *Educational Researcher, 9,* 5–10.
Winer, B. J. 1971. *Statistical Principles in Experimental Design* (2nd ed.). New York: McGraw-Hill.
Winer, B. J., D. R. Brown, and K. M. Michels. 1991. *Statistical Principles in Experimental Design* (3rd ed.). New York: McGraw-Hill.
Wingerd, J. 1970. "The relation of growth from birth to 2 years to sex, parental size and other factors," *Human Biology, 42,* 105–31.
Zehna, P. W. 1991. "On proving that $\overline{X}$ and $s^2$ are independent," *American Statistician, 45,* 121–2.
Zimmerman, D. W. 1987. "Comparative power of Student $t$ and the Mann-Whitney $U$ tests for unequal sample size and variances," *Journal of Experimental Education, 55,* 171–4.
____ 1992. "Failure of the Mann-Whitney Test," *Journal of Experimental Education, 60,* 359–64.

# INDEX

## AUTHOR INDEX

## SUBJECT INDEX

# Tables



# Disk Information

The enclosed diskette includes three data sets that are needed for the computer assignments that follow each chapter:

1. The CHAPMAN data set is from a cholesterol study of 200 adults who were measured on several variables and followed for ten years.
2. The HSB data set is from the High School and Beyond Study; achievement and demographic data are given for a national representative sample of 600 high school seniors.
3. The EXERCISE data set contains data on 40 persons that pertain to certain exercise-related effects of smoking.

Each data set appears in four PC formats to facilitate their use with a variety of spreadsheet and statistics software:

(1) ASCII (text) code (*.TXT)
(2) EXCEL format (*.XLS)
(3) SPSS for Windows format (*.SAV)
(4) SPSS portable format (*.POR)

All spreadsheet and statistical packages for the PC can read one or more of the above formats. Experienced Macintosh users will be able to read the files and convert them to MAC format. Additional information is given in the README.TXT file.